American
Jewish
Year Book

The American Jewish Committee acknowledges with appreciation the foresight and wisdom of the founders of the Jewish Publication Society (of America) in the creation of the AMERICAN JEWISH YEAR BOOK in 1899, a work committed to providing a continuous record of developments in the U.S. and world Jewish communities. For over a century JPS has occupied a special place in American Jewish life, publishing and disseminating important, enduring works of scholarship and general interest on Jewish subjects.

The American Jewish Committee assumed responsibility for the compilation and editing of the YEAR BOOK in 1908. The Society served as its publisher until 1949; from 1950 through 1993, the Committee and the Society were co-publishers. In 1994 the Committee became the sole publisher of the YEAR BOOK.

American

Jewish

Year Book 1999

VOLUME 99

Editor
DAVID SINGER

Executive Editor
RUTH R. SELDIN

THE AMERICAN JEWISH COMMITTEE

NEW YORK

Preface

This year's featured article, "Jewish Education in the United States: Recent Trends and Issues," by Jack Wertheimer, is a major contribution to the discussion of Jewish "continuity" that has become a matter of urgency in the organized Jewish communal world. The volume also includes a study of Soviet Jews who immigrated to Israel in the 1990s, by Elazar Leshem and Moshe Sicron. Through extensive data and analysis, the authors examine the successes and the shortcomings in the absorption of this large and important *aliyah.*

Jewish life in the United States is treated in four articles: "National Affairs," by Richard T. Foltin; "The United States, Israel, and the Middle East," by George E. Gruen; "Jewish Communal Affairs," by Lawrence Grossman; and "Jewish Culture," by Berel Lang.

Peter Hirschberg provides detailed coverage of events in Israel. Rochelle Furstenberg reports on cultural life in that country. Reports on Jewish communities around the world include Canada, Mexico, Argentina, Great Britain, France, the Netherlands, Italy, Germany, Austria, East-Central Europe, the former Soviet Union, Australia, and South Africa.

Updated estimates of Jewish population are provided—for the United States, by Jim Schwartz and Jeffrey Scheckner of the United Jewish Communities and North American Jewish Data Bank; and for the world, by Sergio DellaPergola of the Hebrew University of Jerusalem.

Carefully compiled directories of national Jewish organizations, periodicals, and federations and welfare funds, as well as religious calendars and obituaries, round out the 1999 AMERICAN JEWISH YEAR BOOK.

We gratefully acknowledge the assistance of our colleagues Cyma M. Horowitz and Michele Anish of the American Jewish Committee's Blaustein Library.

With the publication of this volume, Ruth R. Seldin, who has been editing the Year Book since 1985, leaves to take on new challenges.

THE EDITORS

Contributors

HENRIETTE BOAS: Journalist; Amsterdam, Holland.

GREG CAPLAN: Doctoral candidate in modern German history, Georgetown University; Federal Chancellor Scholar, Berlin, Germany.

ADINA CIMET: Lecturer, YIVO–Columbia University Yiddish summer program.

SERGIO DELLAPERGOLA: Professor and head, Division of Jewish Demography and Statistics, Avraham Harman Institute of Contemporary Jewry, Hebrew University of Jerusalem, Israel.

RICHARD T. FOLTIN: Legislative director and counsel, Office of Government and International Affairs, American Jewish Committee.

ROCHELLE FURSTENBERG: Contributing editor, *The Jerusalem Report;* columnist, *Hadassah Magazine;* Jerusalem, Israel.

ZVI GITELMAN: Professor, political science, and Preston R. Tisch Professor of Judaic Studies, University of Michigan.

MURRAY GORDON: Adjunct professor, Austrian Diplomatic Academy, Vienna, Austria.

LAWRENCE GROSSMAN: Director of publications, American Jewish Committee.

RUTH ELLEN GRUBER: European-based American journalist and author, specialist in contemporary Jewish affairs; Morre, Italy.

GEORGE E. GRUEN: Adjunct professor, international affairs, Middle East Institute and School of International and Public Affairs, Columbia University.

PETER HIRSCHBERG: Senior writer, *The Jerusalem Report*; Jerusalem, Israel.

IGNACIO KLICH: Lecturer, Latin American history, Faculty of Law, Languages and Communication, University of Westminster, London, England.

LIONEL E. KOCHAN: Historian; Wolfson College, Oxford, England.

MIRIAM L. KOCHAN: Free-lance journalist and translator; Oxford, England.

BEREL LANG: Professor of humanities, Trinity College.

ELAZAR LESHEM: Lecturer, Paul Baerwald School of Social Work, Hebrew University of Jerusalem, Israel.

COLIN L. RUBENSTEIN: Executive director, Australia/Israel and Jewish Affairs Council; honorary associate, Monash University, Melbourne, Australia.

JEFFREY SCHECKNER: Research consultant, United Jewish Communities; administrator, North American Jewish Data Bank, City University of New York.

JIM SCHWARTZ: Research director, United Jewish Communities; director, North American Jewish Data Bank, City University of New York.

MILTON SHAIN: Professor, Hebrew and Jewish studies, and director, Kaplan Centre for Jewish Studies and Research, University of Cape Town, South Africa.

MOSHE SICRON: Professor, population studies, Hebrew University of Jerusalem, and former director, Central Bureau of Statistics, Israel.

MEIR WAINTRATER: Editor in chief, *L'Arche*, the French Jewish monthly, Paris, France.

HAROLD M. WALLER: Professor, political science, McGill University; director, Canadian Centre for Jewish Community Studies, Montreal, Canada.

JACK WERTHEIMER: Provost and Joseph and Martha Mendelson Professor of American Jewish History, Jewish Theological Seminary of America.

Contents

PREFACE   v

CONTRIBUTORS   vii

SPECIAL ARTICLES

Jewish Education in the United States:
  Recent Trends and Issues   *Jack Wertheimer*   3

UNITED STATES

National Affairs   *Richard T. Foltin*   119
The United States, Israel,
  and the Middle East   *George E. Gruen*   149
Jewish Communal Affairs   *Lawrence Grossman*   165
Jewish Culture   *Berel Lang*   199
Jewish Population in the   *Jim Schwartz and*
  United States, 1998   *Jeffrey Scheckner*   209

OTHER COUNTRIES

CANADA   *Harold M. Waller*   235

LATIN AMERICA
Mexico   *Adina Cimet*   254
Argentina   *Ignacio Klich*   263

WESTERN EUROPE
Great Britain   *Miriam and Lionel*
                                    Kochan   276
France   *Meir Waintrater*   289
The Netherlands   *Henriette Boas*   309
Italy   *Ruth Ellen Gruber*   320

CENTRAL AND EASTERN EUROPE
Federal Republic of Germany   *Greg Caplan*   334
Austria   *Murray Gordon*   359
East-Central Europe   *Ruth Ellen Gruber*   369
Former Soviet Union   *Zvi Gitelman*   390

AUSTRALIA   *Colin L. Rubenstein*   399

SOUTH AFRICA   *Milton Shain*   411

ISRAEL
Review of the Year   *Peter Hirschberg*   424
The Absorption of Soviet   *Elazar Leshem and*
    Immigrants in Israel   *Moshe Sicron*   484
Culture in Israel   *Rochelle Furstenberg*   523

WORLD JEWISH POPULATION, 1997   *Sergio DellaPergola*   543

DIRECTORIES, LISTS, AND OBITUARIES

NATIONAL JEWISH ORGANIZATIONS
United States   583
Canada   640

JEWISH FEDERATIONS, WELFARE FUNDS,
COMMUNITY COUNCILS
United States   644
Canada   655

JEWISH PERIODICALS
United States   656
Canada   667

OBITUARIES: UNITED STATES   669

SUMMARY JEWISH CALENDAR,
5759-5763 (Sept. 1998–Aug. 2003)   680

CONDENSED MONTHLY CALENDAR,
5758-5761 (1998–2001)   682

SELECTED ARTICLES OF INTEREST IN RECENT VOLUMES
OF THE AMERICAN JEWISH YEAR BOOK   719

INDEX   722

Special Articles

Jewish Education in the United States: Recent Trends and Issues

BY JACK WERTHEIMER

LONG REGARDED BY EDUCATORS AND THEIR ALLIES as the neglected "step-child"[1] of the American Jewish community, the field of Jewish education finds itself at the close of the 20th century the object of intense scrutiny and great expectations. Writing of the current "plastic moment" in American Jewish education, the historian Jonathan Sarna sees it as one of "abundant innovations, an unlimited number of potential directions, innumerable theories, and vast uncertainty."[2] Perhaps never

Note: I wish to acknowledge with appreciation a number of individuals working in the field of education who gave generously of their time and expertise to answer my questions and steer me toward sources of information. At the William Davidson School of Jewish Education of the Jewish Theological Seminary, I consulted with Aryeh Davidson, Barry Holtz, and Carol Ingall. Mary Boys of Union Theological Seminary and Linda Vogel of Garrett-Evangelical Theological Seminary helped me with the larger context of religious education in America. At the Jewish Education Service of North America, Jonathan Woocher and Leora Isaacs conversed with me at length; Paul Flexner and David Shluker provided valuable data. At other Jewish institutions based in New York I was advised by: Robert Abramson of the Education Department at the United Synagogue of Conservative Judaism and Jan Katzew, his counterpart at the Union of American Hebrew Congregations; Steven Bayme of the Department of Jewish Communal Affairs at the American Jewish Committee; Jerome Chanes of the National Foundation for Jewish Culture; Alisa Kurshan at the Continuity Commission of the UJA-Federation of Jewish Philanthropies of Greater New York; Yossi Prager and Marvin Schick at the Avi Chai Foundation; Nessa Rapaport of the Mandel Foundation; and Elliot Spack of the Coalition for the Advancement of Jewish Education. My key informants outside New York were Adrianne Bank of the Whizin Institute at the University of Judaism in Los Angeles; Shulamith Elster of Hillel in Washington, D.C.; Carolyn Keller of the Combined Jewish Philanthropies in Boston; Sara Lee of the Rhea Hirsch School of Education at the Hebrew Union College in Los Angeles; Daniel Margolis of the Bureau of Jewish Education in Boston; and Susan Shevitz of the Hornstein Program at Brandeis University. David Behrman shared his knowledge of curricular materials. Two students at the Jewish Theological Seminary, Dina Gerber Huebner, a doctoral candidate in education, and Lowell Appelbaum, an undergraduate, served as superb research assistants. The Abbell Faculty Research Fund at the Jewish Theological Seminary helped underwrite some of the costs of my research.

[1]Such was the characterization of the field presented by Joseph Schechtman of the Research Department of the Jewish Agency in an unpublished typescript entitled "Jewish Education in the United States: A Working Paper on Facts and Problems," ca. 1967, p. 31.

[2]Jonathan D. Sarna, "American Jewish Education in Historical Perspective," *Journal of Jewish Education,* Winter/Spring 1998, p. 18. One observer who bemoaned the indifference

3

before has there been so much talk about investing large sums of communal and philanthropic dollars in the enterprise of Jewish education. And perhaps never before has a Jewish community pinned so much of its hopes for "continuity"—for the transmission of a strong Jewish identity to the next generation—on programs of formal and informal education. The challenge of strengthening Jewish education is enormous because the field itself is so vast and complicated. Jonathan Woocher, a leading national spokesman on Jewish education, has taken the measure of its expansive dimensions: "American Jews today spend more than $1.5 billion annually to maintain an educational system that includes 3,000 schools and thousands more educational programs held in a wide variety of institutional settings. The system involves close to 50,000 teachers and more than a million Jews who study regularly—almost half of them young people between the ages of three and eighteen."[3] Since this farflung network of autonomous schools and programs is primarily governed and funded through local initiatives in hundreds of Jewish communities throughout the United States, the field of Jewish education is highly diffuse. From a qualitative perspective, the situation is even more complex, for, as Woocher also notes, American Jews maintain a "love-hate relationship" with Jewish education: on the one hand, a broad consensus that Jewish education stands as the final bulwark against powerful tides of assimilation; on the other, a "perception of failure and mediocrity in the system," prompting some to question the wisdom of "pouring additional dollars into the very enterprise that has brought American Jewry to its current sorry condition."[4]

The upgrading of Jewish education—long a preoccupation of insiders—has taken on particular urgency since the release of the 1990 National Jewish Population Survey, which found that younger American Jews identify less intensely than their elders with fellow Jews, the organizations of the Jewish community, and Israel and, most dramatically, that by the late 1980s, more than half of all Jews were marrying outside the faith. "That figure served as a wake-up call to the American Jewish leadership," observed John Ruskay, a top executive of the New York Jewish community.[5]

---

to Jewish education was Isaac Unterman, who claimed that "American Jewry has given abundantly of its thought and wealth to the care of the sick and the aged, to the relief of visible distress and suffering, but it has done nothing, if we except a few attempts, toward grappling with the problem of Jewish education." (Quoted—with a healthy degree of skepticism—by Sarna, p. 9.)

[3]"Foreword" to Joseph Reimer, *Succeeding at Jewish Education: How One Synagogue Made It Work* (Philadelphia, 1998), p. xi.

[4]Ibid., p. xii.

[5]Quoted by J.J. Goldberg, "U.S. Jewry Pins Its Future on Education," *Jerusalem Report,* Oct. 6, 1994, p. 26.

Many analysts of the 1990 study also arrived at the conclusion that "the only serious antidote the Jewish community can muster to stem the escalating rate of intermarriage and other forms of assimilation" is Jewish education.[6] As noted by the Commission on Jewish Education in North America, "the responsibility for developing Jewish identity and instilling a commitment to Judaism . . . now rests primarily with Jewish education."[7]

In light of this assessment, virtually every major sector of the American Jewish community has directed more sustained attention and new resources to the field during the 1990s. The large umbrella agencies of Jewish philanthropy have created "continuity commissions" to plan new initiatives and fund innovative programs. The religious movements of American Judaism have expanded their efforts to address the educational needs of their members, beginning with preschoolers and encompassing various types of formal and informal education for children, teenagers, college students, and adults of all ages. Jewish community centers have strengthened their capacities and their resolve to deliver a strong educational component. Agencies designed to raise money for Jews abroad now offer study opportunities for American Jews. And a number of richly endowed family foundations have begun to invest in educational programs designed to bring about systemic changes.

Not surprisingly, given the high stakes for the future of the American Jewish community and the potentially large financial resources available to be tapped, educational programs and institutions have taken to making extravagant claims to tout their "successes." Advertisements in the Jewish and general press routinely promote the efficacy of particular solutions. "1,000,000 Jews can now be rescued . . . right here in North America," reads the banner headline of one ad, which then goes on to claim that "the intermarriage rate drops to 7% for students who complete a Jewish day school education."[8] After listing some of the major national agencies of the American Jewish community, another ad asks: "What one cause should you also support to guarantee the survival of all these causes in the next generation? Jewish Day School Ed-

---

[6]Bernard Reisman, "Needed: A Paradigm Shift in Jewish Education," *Journal of Jewish Education,* Summer 1993, p. 30. (Note: hereafter the journal will be identified simply as *Jewish Education.*)

[7]*A Time to Act, The Report of the Commission on Jewish Education in North America* (University Press of America, Lanham, Md., 1990), p. 15. That this report was issued prior to the release of the NJPS is indicative of a long-standing concern among some sectors of the American Jewish leadership with the need to strengthen Jewish identity and education. This process will be traced below.

[8]From an ad placed by Torah Umesorah National Society for Hebrew Day Schools, *Jewish Week* (New York), Nov. 6–12, 1992, p. 25.

ucation."[9] A denominational youth movement promotes itself as "not just a youth movement but an answer."[10] And advocates of trips to Israel for teenagers and college students seem to suggest that such an experience alone will transform young people otherwise alienated from Jewish life.[11] If nothing else, these sweeping claims highlight the yearning of many American Jews to stem rates of assimilation and defection through programs of Jewish education.

The heightened sense of urgency to devise new solutions and shore up existing programs has generated a great deal of ferment in the field of Jewish education. In recent years, new ideas have been promoted, new alliances for change forged, bold new initiatives announced, and new "players" and institutions have joined the undertaking.[12] All of these developments have thrown the field into considerable turmoil. The present essay aims in part to clarify the picture, to serve as a guide to the institutions, programs, key figures, and issues in the Jewish education world.

To place the subject in historical context, the essay opens with a glance backward to the state of affairs in the decades following World War II, a time of massive expansion in the field, when many of the major institutions of and dominant approaches to Jewish education were established. Our historical retrospective will clarify why they eventually came under sustained criticism, and why the field has shifted recently, but will also trace important lines of continuity over the past half century.

The bulk of this essay is devoted to the emerging trends of the past two decades, with a particular emphasis on three critical themes: the changing world of formal Jewish education—the types of schools, student populations, educational personnel, and curricular emphases; the burgeoning field of informal education, with its extensive array of new programs for Jews of all ages; and the creation of new alliances, partnerships, and rivalries with institutions outside the field, which have shifted the balance of power in the struggle for control of Jewish education.

Dynamic conditions in each of these three areas are indicative of great fluidity within Jewish education itself and also of the intensified en-

---

[9]*Jewish Week* (New York), Apr. 17, 1998, p. 9. The ad was placed by the Avi Chai Foundation.

[10]From an ad placed by the National Conference of Synagogue Youth of the Orthodox Union, *Jewish Week* (New York), Nov. 20, 1998, p. 9.

[11]Laurie Goodstein, "To Bind the Faith, Free Trips to Israel for Diaspora Youth," *New York Times,* Nov. 16, 1998, p. A8.

[12]Jonathan Sarna has pointed to a comparable explosion of new energy in the field of Jewish education and American Jewish culture at the close of the last century. See his *A Great Awakening: The Transformation That Shaped Twentieth Century American Judaism and Its Implications for Today* (Council for Initiatives in Jewish Education, New York, n.d., ca. 1996).

gagement of leaders and the rank-and-file of the American Jewish community with the field. Indeed, there is strong evidence that the inattention to Jewish education on the part of Jewish communal leaders in the past may finally be giving way to a deeper appreciation of its overarching importance.

The present essay, then, strives to delineate the changing contours of the field of Jewish education and to analyze how these changes reflect and, in turn, are reshaping the larger American Jewish community.

THE POSTWAR ERA

Exactly 30 years ago, in a now classic essay entitled "Jewish Education—For What?"[13] Walter Ackerman summed up the state of Jewish education in the middle decades of the 20th century:

> The present pattern of Jewish education in the United States had taken shape by 1930. Six of the 12 accredited teacher-training schools currently in operation were already in existence then. Bureaus of Jewish education had been established in every major city, and the idea of community responsibility was accepted in theory, if not in practice. Curriculum patterns in every type of school had achieved a form and balance which was to change little in subsequent years. A corps of professional educators gained some visibility; a body of literature was in the process of development, and several professional societies had come into being. The essential nature of the Jewish school enterprise was established. A system of supplementary education composed of autonomous one-day-a-week Sunday schools, midweek afternoon schools and day schools, was maintained by voluntary efforts of their clientele.[14]

Ackerman's overview serves as a useful point of departure to assess the changing and the constant in the recent history of American Jewish education. Building upon his categories of analysis, we will trace (in reverse order) the major trends during the postwar era until the early 1980s, a period that began with unprecedented expansion and ended in near despair for the future of the field.

A Time of Growth

Like so much else in American Jewish communal life after World War II, the field of Jewish education experienced a massive expansion fueled by the baby boom. The sheer upward spiral of enrollment figures tells the story: it has been estimated that in 1937, approximately 200,000 pupils

---

[13]Walter I. Ackerman, "Jewish Education—For What?" *American Jewish Year Book* (hereafter AJYB), 1969, vol. 70, pp. 3–36.

[14]Ibid., pp. 3–4.

attended Jewish schools; by 1950, that figure had risen to 266,000; it kept rising, reaching an estimated 553,600 pupils in 1958, until it peaked at an estimated 588,955 in 1962.[15] The near trebling of the Jewish student population over a 20-year period necessitated a rapid increase in the number of schools, a growth in the cadre of teachers, and an expansion of the educational infrastructure needed to monitor and shape the field.

THE SCHOOLS

According to a Jewish educational census conducted in 1958, the network of schools in the United States numbered 3,367.[16] These institutions fell into the following categories: schools under congregational auspices that met either once a week — generally on Sundays — or two to three times weekly as afternoon schools; day schools offering a five- or even six-day-a-week course of study that included both Jewish and general subjects; and a small number of schools sponsored by communities or secular organizations that offered a supplementary program during weekday afternoons.

The major development of the immediate postwar period was the ascendance of the congregational school, which offered a supplementary religious education to students attending public schools. As of 1966, roughly 86 percent of all Jewish students were enrolled in a congregational school (almost all the rest were enrolled in day schools).[17] By contrast, American Jewry had maintained a greater diversity of school types earlier in the century: in addition to the synagogue-based programs, there were schools providing a Yiddishist, socialist, or Zionist orientation sponsored by secular institutions; and a network of schools under communal auspices (often known as Talmud Torahs) propagated a pan-Jewish cultural outlook that encouraged identification with the Jewish people *(klal yisrael)*. One observer already noted in the late 1960s the important

---

[15]Judah Pilch, "From the Early Forties to the Mid-Sixties," in *A History of Jewish Education,* ed. Judah Pilch (American Association for Jewish Education, New York, 1969), p. 121. The 1958 figure is based on a comprehensive survey conducted by Alexander Dushkin and Uriah Z. Engelman; see Dushkin and Engelman, *Jewish Education in the United States. Report of the Commission for the Study of Jewish Education in the United States* (AAJE, 1959), p. 40. The peak figure is taken from "Trends in Jewish School Enrollment in the United States, 1974/75" (AAJE, Sept. 1976), p. 12. Throughout this essay, we will cite data collected by various school census projects and demographic surveys. These should be understood as approximations, since they are sometimes based on extrapolations of data and sometimes "best estimates."

[16]Dushkin and Engelman, *Jewish Education in the U.S.,* p. 95.

[17]Ackerman, "Jewish Education—For What?" p. 4. Between 1948 and 1958, the congregational school share of all student enrollment rose from 83 percent to 89 percent. Dushkin and Engelman, *Jewish Education in the U.S.,* p. 47.

change in focus that had transformed Jewish education: "Postwar Jewish education has been decidedly religious (rather than secularist or communal) in support and orientation. It has almost totally become a subsystem of the Jewish religion, designed to transmit 'religious-ethnic' rather than 'secularist-ethnic' Jewish culture."[18]

This shift, then, not only moved the setting of Jewish education from the communal institution to the denominationally affiliated congregation, but also wrought an important ideological transformation, which even found expression in a change in nomenclature: Whereas supplementary programs were conventionally known as "Hebrew schools," because they had been committed to a Zionist ideology stressing the twin aims of Hebraic fluency and Jewish cultural literacy, by the 1960s they self-consciously began to call themselves "religious schools." The significance of this change was explicitly articulated by the leading spokesman for Jewish education in the Conservative movement, as follows: "We are dealing in the afternoon congregational school not with a 'Hebrew school' but, rather, with a 'Jewish religious school.' Fundamentally, therefore, the curriculum should reflect those values, that ideology, and those functional aspects which will enhance and articulate the ideology which the school is supposed to mediate to its children."[19] In short, Jewish education was now defined as religious education, and the transmission of religious tradition was "moved from the home and community to the school."[20]

The triumph of the congregational school as the preferred and dominant vehicle for Jewish education was insured by a confluence of several factors. To begin with, American Jews overwhelmingly adopted what historian Jonathan Sarna has called the "Protestant model" of education. This model "held that morality, universal values, patriotism, civics and critical skills all should be taught in state-funded public schools to a mixed body of religiously diverse students, leaving only the fine points of religious doctrine and practice to be mastered by members of each faith in separate denominationally sponsored supplementary schools." By

---

[18]Norman L. Friedman, "Religious Subsystem: Toward a Sociology of Jewish Education," *Sociology of Education,* Winter 1969, p. 106. The shift toward congregational schooling had already begun during the interwar era: in New York, for example, congregational schools overtook the communal Talmud Torahs by 1928. See David Rudavsky, "Trends in Jewish School Organization and Enrollment in New York City, 1917–1950," *YIVO* Annual, 1955, p. 51.

[19]The writer is Rabbi Morton Siegel, who served as director of the Jewish Education Department of the United Synagogue of America. Quoted in Carol K. Ingall, "The Quest for Continuity: The Hebrew College and the Normal Schools," *Religious Education,* Winter 1995, p. 67.

[20]Ibid.

contrast, the "Catholic model" regarded public schools as instruments for the inculcation of Protestant values, and therefore Catholics created a separate parochial school system of all-day schools that would teach a "minority (dissenting) religious tradition." Moreover, American Jews regarded it as their patriotic duty to support public education, for it best insured the egalitarianism and tolerance necessary to maintain the American way—and protect Jewish rights.[21] As one Jewish leader, cited by Sarna, put it: public schools are a place where "the children of the high and low, rich and poor, Protestants, Catholics, and Jews mingle together, play together and are taught that we are a free people, striving to elevate mankind and to respect one another."[22]

The Jewish "love affair" with public education had begun already in the 19th century and helped insure the spread of Jewish Sunday schools.[23] By the middle of the 20th century, two specifically postwar developments fueled the further growth of congregational schools. One was the religious revival of the time that primarily expressed itself through involvement in congregational life. Like their fellow Americans, particularly their suburban neighbors, Jews in record numbers joined religious congregations. But for a great many Jews, the overriding motive for affiliation was to enroll their children in religious schools.[24] The sociologists Marshall Sklare and Joseph Greenblum found in their exhaustive study of a prototypical suburban community of the 1950s that nearly all Jews affiliated with a synagogue at some point in their lives, but they deferred membership until their children were of the ages to go to religious school (under 20 percent joined when their children were preschoolers, a figure that jumped to 87 percent when children were in their peak years of religious education).[25] In fact, for Jewish parents, the most important consideration in evaluating their congregation was the synagogue school. Several parents interviewed for the "Lakeville Study," as Sklare and Greenblum called it, were remarkably candid about their priorities: One said of his synagogue:

---

[21]Perhaps the most influential champion of the "Protestant Model" was Samson Benderly, the leading Jewish educator of the first half of the 20th century. "Shall we withdraw our children from the public schools and establish schools of our own as the Catholics are doing?" he asked. His answer was resoundingly negative: "A parochial system of education would be fatal to [Jewish] hopes" for integration." Quoted in Nathan H. Winter, *Jewish Education in a Pluralist Society* (New York, 1966), p. 62.

[22]Jonathan Sarna, "American Jewish Education in Historical Perspective," pp. 12–13.

[23]For an interesting contemporaneous analysis of why this romance waned, see Milton Himmelfarb, "Reflections on the Jewish Day School," *Commentary,* July 1960, pp. 29–36.

[24]The classic account of this resurgence of public religion and its impact on Jews is to be found in Will Herberg, *Protestant, Catholic, Jew: An Essay in American Religious Sociology* (Garden City, N.Y., 1955).

[25]Marshall Sklare and Joseph Greenblum, *Jewish Identity on the Suburban Frontier: A Study of Group Survival in an Open Society* (Chicago, 1967), p. 181.

"I like [it]. It gives my boy a good Hebrew education. And they've left me alone—I've never been inside." Another acknowledged: "We joined for the kids. The kids like it, we are satisfied. We feel no need for religion." And a third declared: "It's the only temple that satisfies my need, which is basically a Sunday School for the children." It was quite telling, though hardly surprising, that a significant number dropped their memberships once their children had completed their schooling.[26]

Synagogues, in turn—and here is the second factor—which were established at dizzying pace in the burgeoning suburbs spreading across postwar America, recruited their members almost exclusively from parents seeking a congregational school for their children. The school, therefore, became the sustaining force of the congregation and often its primary *raison d'être.* Many congregations, in fact, did not bill tuition fees separately from general membership dues, while others charged nominal amounts for tuition, even though the schools accounted for a quarter or more of the congregational budget.[27] Synagogues assumed a "pediatric" mission, focusing ever more of their programming on children. This child-centered approach represented a major departure from the orientation of immigrant congregations, which in the first half of the century had focused almost exclusively on the needs of foreign-born, non-native-speaking adults, particularly men. As the actual quality of the postwar synagogue revival became more evident, a prominent rabbi mordantly quipped that the synagogue in America had become "to a large degree, a parent-teacher association of the religious school."[28]

The mission of the supplementary schools inevitably was shaped by the confused, if not contradictory, expectations of the parent body. On the one hand, parents expected schools to assume a far greater role than ever before in the religious formation of their children: As Sklare and Greenblum wrote in their study of "Lakeville":

> Parents who hold to a pattern of minimal ritualism appear to rely primarily, and in some cases, almost exclusively, on the religious school for the Jewish socialization of their children. This dependence on the Jewish school constitutes a radical departure from the traditional approach to the rearing of the Jewish child. In past eras, the effort of the school to transmit the culture

---

[26]Ibid., pp. 190, 192–93. See also Leonard Fein et al., *Reform Is a Verb: Notes on Reform and Reforming Jews* (Union of American Hebrew Congregations, New York, 1972), chap. 5, especially p. 90.

[27]I have discussed the impact of these developments on Conservative synagogues in "The Conservative Synagogue," in my edited volume, *The American Synagogue: A Sanctuary Transformed* (Cambridge and New York, 1987), pp. 125–29. For figures on school budgets, see "Survey of Synagogue Finances," issued by the Department of Synagogue Administration, United Synagogue of America, Nov. 1963, p. 21.

[28]This quip is attributed to Rabbi Arthur Hertzberg in Carolyn L. Wiener, "A Merger of Synagogues in San Francisco," *Jewish Journal of Sociology,* Dec. 1972, p. 189.

(albeit to the male in particular) represented merely a continuation of efforts already initiated by the parents. But among Lakeville residents—so many of whom are at lower levels of observance and who in other ways do not provide a distinctive Jewish environment for their children—the function of socialization into Jewish culture has been separated from its traditional moorings in the family.[29]

On the other hand, essentially secular parents sought to circumscribe the nature of what was learned in school about religion in order to keep it safely confined to the synagogue precinct—and at a far remove from the home. The sociologist Herbert Gans commented upon this phenomenon in his study of still another suburban Jewish community: "The Sunday school is an institution which transmits norms of ethnic culture and symbols of identification, whereas the home and the family are run by secular, middle class behavior patterns. Parents expected that the contradictions between the concept of the traditional Jewish home implicit in the Sunday school curriculum and that of the actual one would result in family tensions. Consequently, the parents were firm in not wanting the youngsters to bring the traditional patterns, plus the pressures of their youthful persuasiveness, into the house."[30]

The primary role of the supplementary school from the perspective of parents was to train boys—and eventually girls—for their rite of passage into adolescence, the bar or bat mitzvah, an event limited to the synagogue precincts. And yet even this mission was not embraced wholeheartedly by all parents. Writing in the mid-1970s, sociologist Harold Himmelfarb identified signs of parental ambivalence:

> They wait until the child is about eight or nine years old to send him to Hebrew school, they enroll the child for the least number of days possible so that he will also have time for music lessons or baseball practice, they encourage absence from Hebrew school at the only time for things like clothes shopping or dental visits, and they pressure the school to decrease the amount of time spent on subjects not directly related to Bar or Bat Mitzvah preparation. In this type of environment, it is easy for the child to assume that Jewish education has very low priority.[31]

These minimalist wishes of the parent body played a critical role in shaping the supplementary schools and imposed severe constraints on what the educators hoped and attempted to accomplish.

---

[29]Sklare and Greenblum, *Jewish Identity,* p. 298.

[30]Herbert Gans, "The Origin and Growth of a Jewish Community in the Suburbs: A Study of the Jews in Park Forest," in *The Jews: Social Patterns of an American Group,* ed. Marshall Sklare (Glencoe, Ill., 1958), pp. 205–48, esp. p. 217.

[31]Harold Himmelfarb, "Jewish Education for Naught: Educating the Culturally Deprived Jewish Child," *Analysis* (Synagogue Council of America, New York, 1975), pp. 257–58.

Yet for all the difficulties posed by parental indifference or ambivalence, the general desire of parents to celebrate their child's bar mitzvah provided a lever for educators to increase supplementary school enrollments and add hours of instruction to the school program. Through a combined campaign of rabbis, school principals, and administrators of local education bureaus, whose efforts were encouraged by denominational and other leaders in the field of Jewish education on the national level, congregations imposed mandatory schooling as a prerequisite for the celebration of a bar mitzvah in the synagogue. Moreover, congregations also required school attendance for a minimum number of years, with the Conservative movement establishing a threshold of three years and the Reform movement two years. The bar (and eventually bat) mitzvah preparations served, as the sociologist Stuart Schoenfeld has observed, as a perfect match between the needs of the folk and the aspirations of the elite.[32]

This arrangement, however, as has been noted astutely by the educator Isa Aron, was significantly flawed in that it did not take into account the dissonance between the parental objective—bar mitzvah preparation—and the educators' goals—the transmission of a Jewish religious and national identity and the nurturing of ritual observance. "Beneath the placid and prosperous image" of the mid-century supplementary school, Aron writes, "lay a problematic fissure." Much to the dismay of educators, the "preoccupation with Bar Mitzvah . . . [and] recitation of some prayers . . . tended to divert attention from the study of subjects which were considered the core of the curriculum—Bible, History and the Hebrew Language."[33]

Simply put, the parent body took a minimalist approach to Jewish education, whereas some educational leaders felt compelled to offer a maximalist curriculum, convinced that their young charges would learn about Jewish life either "now or never."

Two census surveys conducted in 1958 and 1966 provided the first extensive data in the postwar period on how these conflicting goals played out in the schools themselves. For promoters of a more intensive Jewish education, the good news was that the one-day-a-week Sunday school was giving way to an afternoon school education that required attendance two

---

[32]This discussion of the bar mitzvah syndrome is based on Isa Aron's analysis. See her essay "From Congregational School to the Learning Congregation: Are We Ready for a Paradigm Shift?" in Isa Aron, Sara Lee, and Seymour Rossel, *A Congregation of Learners* (UAHC Press, New York, 1995), pp. 60–62. See also Stuart Schoenfeld, "Folk Judaism, Elite Judaism and the Role of Bar Mitzvah in the Development of the Synagogue and Jewish School in America," *Contemporary Jewry 1988,* pp. 67–85.

[33]Ibid., pp. 62–63. The discussion of curricular implications is taken from Pilch, "From the Early Forties," p. 131.

or three times weekly for five to six hours per week. In 1958, 47 percent of pupils were enrolled in afternoon schools, 45 percent in one-day-a-week schools, and 8 percent in day schools. The growth of the afternoon schools resulted, as we have noted, primarily from a push by educators to intensify educational programs—despite the severe opposition of many parents. As early as 1949, Louis Katzoff drew attention to those who were fearful that mandatory attendance for a longer period of time would cause some parents to withdraw their children from the congregational school, a fear that, in turn, motivated the school to follow a policy of "a little education is better than none."[34] Conservative rabbis and educators, nonetheless, promoted mandatory educational programs of five to six hours a week spread out over three days, with one-day-a-week schooling reserved exclusively for children under age eight; the Reform movement's Commission on Jewish Education also pressed to increase the number of school hours, but was not as successful.[35]

These campaigns yielded some fruits: by 1958, 60 percent of children enrolled in Conservative congregational schools attended afternoon programs, and the rest attended one-day-a-week schools. In the New York area, the proportion attending afternoon schools almost reached the three-quarter mark. By contrast, the split in Reform schools was 80-20 in favor of one-day schooling; and in New York, 99 percent of children in Reform supplementary schools attended one-day-a-week programs.[36] Largely as a result of the efforts by educators to foster the afternoon school, matters looked very different three decades later: in greater New York, only 5 percent of all Jewish pupils attended one-day supplementary schools, 56 percent two-to-five-day supplementary schools, and the rest day schools; and in the country at large (excepting New York), almost three times as many children were enrolled in the afternoon schools as in the one-day programs.[37]

This expansion of afternoon schooling also entailed some serious compromises. Although they were designed to offer more intensive schooling, the congregational afternoon schools offered a less demanding program as compared to the communal afternoon schools that they had replaced. The communal Hebrew schools and Talmud Torahs in the 1920s

---

[34]Louis Katzoff, *Issues in Jewish Education: A Study in the Philosophy of the Conservative Congregational School* (New York, 1949), p. 42.

[35]Pilch, "From the Early Forties," p. 137.

[36]Dushkin and Engelman, *Jewish Education in the U.S.,* p. 58.

[37]*Trends: Report on Developments in Jewish Education for Federation Leadership* (JESNA, New York, Spring 1986), p. 2. By 1974, only 7 percent of Conservative children attended a one-day-a-week school, whereas three-quarters of Reform children were enrolled in such schools. "Trends in Jewish School Enrollment in the United States, 1974/75" (AAJE, Sept. 1976), pp. iii, 6–7.

and 1930s had maintained a five-day-a-week schedule, offering eight to ten hours per week, 48 weeks per year, for a total of 400 hours per year. By contrast, the average afternoon school of the 1940s provided half the number of hours (four to five per week) for 36 weeks. (Even more remarkably, the Sunday School entailed no more than 64 hours of instruction per year.)[38]

The direction and content of the afternoon school programs also left much to be desired, from the perspective of educators. The average afternoon school of the 1940s and 1950s allocated school hours as follows: Hebrew was taught 2¼ hours per week; the prayer book 1½ hours; Jewish history for 40–45 minutes; religion and current events for a half hour each; and music for 20 minutes.[39] The upshot, according to one early observer of Conservative programs—the predominant type of afternoon school in the initial postwar years—was a schooling that "require[d] . . . pupils [to] be able to participate in the Junior congregational Service, with particular emphasis upon the ability to recite the Torah and Haftorah blessings, to know the various blessings over food, and to possess the knowledge of the customs and ceremonies connected with religious festivals."[40] Not surprisingly, there were already serious concerns in the immediate postwar years that the expanding system of Jewish schooling was "like a river a mile wide and an inch deep."[41]

Nor were the children themselves universally enthusiastic. In a 1958 study, 93 percent of the children answered positively to a question about the value of exposing every Jewish boy and girl to an education about his or her religion. But about a third of supplementary school pupils did not like their Jewish school; and a third stated they would not attend if they had a choice in the matter. (A somewhat higher percentage of Sunday school children answered this way.) Three-quarters of supplementary school pupils indicated that their religious schooling interfered with other things they "would like to do"—31 percent minded this "very much" and another 46 percent professed to be bothered "some times." Significantly, over 90 percent of the same children claimed to like their public schools and answered affirmatively when asked whether they would still attend if given a choice in the matter.[42]

The responses of parents were even more telling. After surveying over 1,350 parents in communities all over the United States who sent their

---

[38]Pilch, "From the Early Forties," pp. 123–24.
[39]Ibid., p. 126, which cites a report by Rabbi Simon Greenberg, a prominent Conservative congregational rabbi.
[40]Katzoff, *Issues in Jewish Education,* p. 135.
[41]Pilch, "From the Early Forties," p. 126.
[42]Dushkin and Engelman, *Jewish Education in the U.S.,* pp. 71–73.

children to Sunday schools and weekday schools, the census takers found that over one-quarter "could not name *a single subject* which their children were learning" in Jewish schools.[43] And when parents were asked why they sent their children to a particular Jewish school, high percentages cited the key reasons as "convenience" and "social considerations." The authors of the census report conclude that only "a minority of the respondents chose the school for its particular ideological orientation (even if family background and synagogue affiliation is added, the total would be 36.6 percent)."[44]

On the more positive side, it should be acknowledged that the congregational schools played a powerful role in normalizing Jewish education and reaching populations that had previously not recognized the utility of formal religious instruction. Communal schools had never attained the popularity of the congregational programs. The congregational setting, moreover, also provided opportunities to connect formal schooling with both the religious life of the synagogue and with venues for informal education. Many synagogues linked children with denominational or ideologically-based youth movements and summer camps. In these ways, the pivotal location of synagogues within Jewish communities served to connect young people to a range of programs that socialized them as Jews—and that complemented the work of the supplementary school.[45]

ENRICHED SCHOOLING

The small population of ideologically or religiously committed parents who sought to expose their children to an enriched Jewish education insured the growth of two types of schools we have not yet discussed. One of these was the Jewish high school. In the 1930s, high-school enrollments accounted for barely 5 percent of the total Jewish student population. This rose to between 8 and 10 percent by the late 1950s, as students were enrolled in about 100 Hebrew high schools, about half congregationally based and the rest community-oriented. Some 54 day high schools existed by then, too. In addition, 67 Reform temples ran post-confirmation programs lasting through 12th grade.[46] To be sure, the bulk of the Jewish school population remained inordinately concentrated in the pre-bar and bat mitzvah cohort, which in 1966 constituted almost 70 percent of all enrollments; the rest were evenly divided between pupils in the primary grades and those in high school. Put differently, it was estimated that of

---

[43]Ibid., p. 138. Emphasis added.
[44]Ibid., p. 86.
[45]Pilch, "From the Early Forties," p. 127.
[46]Ibid., p. 162.

the total population of Jewish children aged 3–5, roughly 12 percent were enrolled in a Jewish school; among those aged 6–7, the number rose to 21 percent; 70 percent of Jewish children aged 8–12 were enrolled; and then the figure for 13- to 17-year-olds dropped to a mere 16 percent.[47]

The second option for an enriched Jewish education was the day school. Day schools are not a 20th-century phenomenon in American Jewish life: a small network of such schools had existed in the 19th century prior to the emerging popularity and widespread availability of public school education.[48] The day schools of the 20th century are unique, however, in the mission they have been assigned. That mission has been astutely analyzed by historian Haym Soloveitchik, who observes that up to the middle of the 20th century, it was widely assumed by Jews of all stripes that "Jewishness was something almost innate, and no school was needed to inculcate it." Jews also were convinced that "their children's *yiddishkeyt* (Jewishness), as their own, was something deep in the bone, and that schools need not—and in all probability, could not—instill it. . . . Until midcentury, the children of immigrants on the right [of the Orthodox world] imbibed their religiosity primarily from home and ethnic neighborhood, much as children of their far more numerous brethren on the left and center imbibed their Jewishness from much the same sources." The inability of families to play their accustomed roles and the collapse of ethnic neighborhoods, according to Soloveitchik, necessitated the creation of a new type of day school movement predicated upon the assumption that

in contemporary society . . . Jewish identity is not inevitable. It is not a matter of course, but of choice: a conscious preference of the enclave over the host society. For such a choice to be made, a sense of particularity and belonging must be instilled by the intentional enterprise of instruction. Without education there is now no identity, for identity in a multi-culture is ideological. . . . Identity maintenance and consciousness raising are ideological exigencies, needs that can be met only by education.[49]

Twentieth-century day schools were established, therefore, to serve as the critical setting for the transmission—in a highly self-conscious and deliberate fashion—of a Jewish identity that could withstand the corrosive effects of modern society.

---

[47]Ackerman, "Jewish Education—For What?" p. 4. See also Hillel Hochberg and Gerhard Lang, "The Jewish High Schools in 1972–73: Status and Trends," AJYB 1974–75, vol. 75, p. 235.

[48]Alvin I. Schiff, *The Jewish Day School in America* (Jewish Education Committee of New York, 1966), chap. 2.

[49]Haym Soloveitchik, "Rupture and Reconstruction: The Transformation of Contemporary Orthodoxy," *Tradition,* Summer 1994, pp. 89–90, 93.

The growth of day schools began in earnest toward the end of World War II, after a national society called Torah Umesorah was founded in 1944 for the express purpose of establishing yeshivas throughout the United States. At the time, there were roughly 30 day schools in the entire country and only a half dozen of these were outside of New York City. Their total enrollment ranged between 6,000 and 7,000 students.[50] In 1946, according to data compiled by the American Association for Jewish Education, there were already 95 such schools, with an enrollment of roughly 14,000 children; within two years, the figure rose to 128 schools with 18,654 children; and by 1958 it had risen to 241 schools with 42,651 children. Just four years later, the enrollments topped 50,000 students,[51] and by the early 1970s the figure exceeded 67,000 pupils in 330 day schools. In just three decades, the number of day schools outside of New York rose from a half dozen to include every community with a population of more than 7,500 Jews; even in communities with fewer than 5,000 Jews there were some 20 day schools.[52]

In contrast to the afternoon schools, which provided children with Jewish schooling for 150 to 200 hours per year over a four- or five-year period, the day schools educated children in Judaic subjects for 800 or more hours each year over at least an eight-year period.[53] This significant expansion in contact hours made it possible for day schools to develop linguistic skills, inculcate a commitment to Jewish observance, and socialize youngsters into Jewish life in a fashion that was beyond the abilities of the supplementary school. Over the course of the typical school day, running from 8:30 or 9:00 A.M. until sometime in the late afternoon, students were expected to master general studies mandated by city and state requirements. In most schools, the morning hours were devoted exclusively to Judaic studies, the afternoon to secular studies. Each school's ideological orientation determined a whole range of pedagogical and curricular choices: whether the language of instruction was to be English, Hebrew, or Yiddish; the amount of time to be devoted to the study of the Pentateuch and later biblical books, as compared to the study of Talmud; the emphasis to be placed on instruction in modern Hebrew, Jew-

---

[50]The precise numbers of day schools and their enrollments during this period are somewhat murky. Most sources estimate the number of institutions during the war years at roughly 30. See Schiff, *Jewish Day School,* p. 49; Stephen Shoenholz, "The Jewish Day Schools at 30," *The Times of Israel,* Mar. 1974, p. 53; and Soloveitchik, "Rupture and Reconstruction," p. 124, note 71, who bases himself on data compiled by Don Well for the Board of Jewish Education of New York.

[51]Pilch, "From the Early Forties," pp. 141–42.

[52]Alvin I. Schiff, "Jewish Day Schools in the United States," *Encyclopedia Judaica Year Book,* 1973, p. 137.

[53]Pilch, "From the Early Forties," p. 144.

ish history, and current events, including references to modern Israel; and the extent to which the curriculum would strive to "integrate American and Jewish cultures and to achieve a blending of Judaism and Americanism" through the linkage of topics addressed in the general studies curriculum with material covered during the Jewish studies classes.[54]

Initially, the Orthodox sector was the sole driving force behind the growth of day schools, and within this sector, newly arrived immigrants played a decisive role. In the two decades bracketing World War II, a new type of immigrant had appeared on American shores, as Jews who had never considered abandoning their traditional communities in Eastern and Central Europe were now forced to uproot themselves in order to survive. These highly traditional Jews harbored no allegiance to the public school and quickly established hundreds of day schools to transmit their Hassidic or Mitnagdic traditions. Modern Orthodox types also participated in this expansion, but depended heavily on the new immigrants and the "sectarian Orthodox" (traditionalists) to staff and administer their schools.[55] Moreover, the parent bodies of Orthodox day schools were disproportionately drawn from the immigrant population: whereas roughly two-thirds of the parent bodies in the afternoon schools were native-born (a figure that exceeded 80 percent for the parent bodies of Sunday schools), barely more than half the fathers of children in modern Orthodox day schools were native born. The ultra-Orthodox schools drew even more of their students from the children of recent immigrants.[56]

Support for these new day schools extended beyond the world of Orthodoxy, however. Conservative, and to a lesser extent Reform, Jews joined in the new venture, as many day schools drew upon a base of families well beyond Orthodox circles. Comparing his own experience as a student in one of the few yeshivas of the interwar era to that of his daughter in a modern Orthodox school of the 1950s, one parent noted the transformation that so captivated him—and his daughter: In the past, wrote Harold Ribalow,

> if you were a yeshiva student, it meant you were Orthodox, and that was that. Today, the parents of the children are far from Orthodox, and indeed most of their homes can scarcely be differentiated from those of their Christian neighbors. The yeshivas, consequently, are radically different from those of ten or fifteen years ago. Talmud, for example, is not the single overtowering subject it used to be. The arts, dancing, painting, drawing, singing, are taught

---

[54]Ibid., pp. 142–43. On the goal of integration, see Joseph Lookstein, "The Jewish Day School in America," in Israel S. Chipkin, *Jewish Schools in America* (American Association for Jewish Education, New York, 1948), pp. 28–36, and the issue devoted to "Integration in Day School Programs," *Jewish Education,* Winter 1978, pp. 4–38.

[55]Charles S. Liebman, "Orthodoxy in American Jewish Life," AJYB 1965, vol. 66, p.70.

[56]Dushkin and Engelman, *Jewish Education in the U.S.,* pp. 86–87.

freely and joyously. . . . Today it is even recognized that attractive classrooms and sufficient lighting do not necessarily block the yeshiva students' ability to absorb Judaism. . . . The child can obtain in the yeshiva a sense of inner security, "sugar-coated," and with few embarrassing compromises concerning school and home environment.[57]

Inspired by what they saw in Orthodox day schools, some educators and parents were moved to establish communal day schools that would attract a broader swathe of the Jewish population.[58]

Gradually, pressure built within the other major denominations to create their own network of day schools. First came the Conservative movement, whose embrace of the day school was tentative, if not ambivalent, in this period. True, the Commission on Jewish Education of the United Synagogue, the congregational arm of the Conservative movement, affirmed its view as early as 1958 that it was "of utmost importance [for] Conservative congregations, singly or cooperatively, . . . to seek to establish Day schools in addition to afternoon religious schools."[59] And it is also true, as Steven Brown has written, that a small number of Conservative day schools were founded already in the 1950s and early 1960s by "a new generation of professional educators, trained in educational techniques learned as staff in the Ramah camps and enriched by graduate studies in secular education, some possessing advanced degrees in Judaica and education."[60]

But even after an Association of Solomon Schechter Day Schools was established in 1964, support within the Conservative movement remained tepid, at best.[61] The reasons are not difficult to discern: many Conservative rabbis maintained a great faith in the public-school system; many also worried about the potential defection of members who would lose inter-

---

[57]Harold U. Ribalow, "My Child Goes to Parochial School: A Parent's Report Card," *Commentary,* Jan. 1954, pp. 64–67. See also the letter from a "shocked" reader who expresses deep concern that such an education "makes for arrogance and creates a lack of genuine understanding of the differences among people, [since it] . . . fosters a spirit of exclusiveness, snobbishness, and childish arrogance" (*Commentary,* Feb. 1954, p. 191).

[58]Community day schools gradually emerged in this period. On one such school founded in 1953, see Ephraim Frankel, "The Hebrew Academy of Atlanta, 1953–1978: An Assessment," *Pedagogic Reporter,* Fall 1977, pp. 17–19. See also Geraldine Nussbaum Kasoff, "The Community Jewish Day School: A New Experience in Jewish Education: The Origins and Development of the Akiba School in Philadelphia, the Charles E. Smith School in Washington, D.C., and the Gesher School in Arlington, Va." Unpublished diss., Univ. of Maryland–College Park, 1993. Most of the founders of these schools were Conservative Jews (Kassoff, pp. 192–93).

[59]Dushkin and Engelman, *Jewish Education in the U.S.,* p. 34.

[60]Steven M. Brown, "The Choice for Jewish Day Schools," *Educational Horizons,* Fall 1992, pp. 45–52.

[61]Morton Siegel, "The Conservative Day School: The Solomon Schechter Day School Association," *Pedagogic Reporter,* Fall 1977, p. 11.

est in the synagogue if they had no need for its supplementary school; and still others placed their faith in the informal educational programs of the Conservative movement—its Ramah camps and United Synagogue Youth programs. Only in the 1970s, after a critical mass of schools and enrollments were attained did the consensus swing to support of the day school. (By 1977, 50 Solomon Schechter schools enrolled close to 10,000 students.)[62]

The day school was even more controversial in the Reform movement. At the convention of the Reform rabbinate in 1950, a keynote speaker denounced the day schools as an instrument of segregation. "The Jewish All Day School," he thundered, "like Jonah's gourd, has come up in the night of despair. It will wither in the broad daylight of renewed faith in freedom and the democratic process."[63] When, 13 years later, Rabbi Alexander Schindler, then director of the Commission on Jewish Education of the Reform congregational arm, denied that "there is a shred of evidence to show that the graduates of the all-day Jewish school . . . are less willing servants of the general community than are graduates of the public school," he was castigated by rabbinic colleagues.[64] Opposition within the movement focused on four specific issues: (1) Day schools were incompatible with Reform Judaism. (2) Parent education was a preferable response to educational weaknesses. (3) Day schools represented a desertion of a public-school system that Reform Jews were bound to support. (4) Day schools posed a threat to liberty.[65]

It was not until the late 1960s that the question was reopened within the Reform movement, as previous positions were reevaluated in light of the Six Day War and the growing success of Conservative day schools. The first Reform day school was established at Temple Beth Am in Miami, Florida, followed quickly by schools in Los Angeles, New York, and Phoenix. By 1981, nine such schools existed in the United States and Canada.[66] Yet it took until 1985 for the board of the Reform movement's congregational arm to endorse "the concept of autonomous,

---

[62]Ibid., p. 12. The association of Conservative rabbis did urge in 1962 "the establishment of Day Schools in our congregations wherever possible." Cited in Schiff, *Jewish Day School,* p. 63.

[63]Schiff, *Jewish Day School,* p. 216.

[64]Daniel B. Syme, "Reform Judaism and Day Schools: The Great Historical Dilemma," *Religious Education,* Spring 1983, pp. 171–72. See also idem., "The Reform Day School: Its History and Future Prospects," *Pedagogic Reporter,* Fall 1977, pp. 14–16.

[65]Syme, "Reform Judaism and Day Schools," p. 173. See also Sylvan D. Schwartzman, "Who Wants Reform All-Day Schools?" *CCAR Journal,* Apr. 1964, and Samuel Glasner and Elliot D. Rosenstock, "The Case For/Against a Reform Jewish Day School," *Dimensions in American Judaism,* Summer 1969, pp. 36–39.

[66]Syme, "Reform Judaism and Day Schools," p. 179.

self-supporting Reform Jewish day schools as a valid educational option."[67]

The ultimate resolution of this long and bitter controversy encapsulated some of the important trends in Jewish schooling during the postwar years. Most of these Reform day schools were initially based in particular congregations, and all were dependent upon congregational, rather than denominational, support. In this sense they reflected the larger trend toward congregational control over formal Jewish education—and a shift away from communal sponsorship. The first Reform day schools, moreover, came into existence due to the initiative of rabbis and educators operating on the local level; only later, after a few such schools had proven themselves, did the national leadership succeed in mustering broader support for so radical a departure in educational strategy. In this sense, too, the Reform day schools mirrored the larger pattern: Jewish education was a local matter, and Jewish schools developed only through the resources of their own communities. The massive expansion of Jewish schooling in the postwar era was a national phenomenon, but it developed through the actions of thousands of autonomous sponsoring institutions.

RESOURCES

Soaring student enrollments and proliferating educational institutions placed an enormous strain on the resources of the Jewish community. A twofold crisis engulfed the field: financial support was barely sufficient to maintain the system, let alone generous enough to improve it; and there was a critical shortage of teaching personnel to staff the schools. The two issues, of course, were intertwined, because, given the inadequate compensation available, it was impossible to recruit enough high-caliber teachers. "Why would a college graduate," one leading educator asked, "embark on a career which is spiritually uninspiring, socially unacceptable and economically unsatisfactory, when many other opportunities knock at his door?"[68]

Susan R. Shevitz, who has traced the history of the teacher shortage in Jewish schools, describes the recurring pattern of response to this crisis: fitful bursts of teeth-gnashing followed by inaction. In 1956, for example, the president of the American Association for Jewish Education

---

[67]Walter Ruby, "Reform Day School Movement Gains Momentum," *Reform Judaism,* Winter 1994, p. 64.

[68]Judah Pilch, quoted in Benjamin B. Rosenberg and Sidney Z. Vincent, "What Can Federations Do to Strengthen Jewish Education?" *Assembly Papers* (Council of Jewish Federations, Nov. 1966), p. 5.

lamented "the constant shortage of teacher personnel." "Many communities," wrote Philip Lown, "have spent . . . millions of dollars to erect up-to-date school buildings. . . . But what benefits can be derived from these splendid structures if there isn't an adequate supply of qualified teachers to fill these modern classrooms? Nearly every Jewish community . . . is almost stymied in trying to solve the problem. . . . Unfortunately, this aspect has been woefully neglected by our leadership."[69] In the same year, a conference devoted to the teacher shortage identified ten causes for the crisis: "(1) inadequate social and economic status; (2) limited opportunities for satisfying work; (3) poor recruitment procedures; (4) inadequate supply from which to draw new teachers; (5) insufficient correlation between teachers' preparation and subsequent work; (6) improper placement machinery; (7) limited growth opportunities; (8) few chances for advancement; (9) growing enrollment; and (10) unduly large turnover."[70]

Three years later, a census of Jewish schools provided solid data on the cadre of educators: It estimated a teaching staff of 17,483, with some 7,900 working in afternoon schools and 9,500 in Sunday schools. These were some of their characteristics:

Almost two-thirds of the teachers in *Sunday Schools* were women, and nearly 90 percent were native born. Only one-fifth had any teacher training, and over two-thirds had only an elementary level Jewish education; as for general education, most were college graduates. Only 23 percent had a teaching license. Roughly half were members of Conservative synagogues and 37 percent of Reform congregations.

By contrast, two-thirds of *afternoon-school* teachers were men; 61 percent were foreign born. Over 80 percent spoke Hebrew fairly fluently; and over 80 percent had attended college and received a Jewish education on that level. Over half had taken at least some courses in pedagogy — generally, at a teachers' seminary or in college. Under 40 percent had a teacher's license. Half were members of Conservative synagogues, and 44 percent belonged to Orthodox ones. In time, this teaching corps would grow through the recruitment of Israeli-born teachers—especially women seeking part-time employment.[71]

Day-school teachers were most likely to be men (70 percent). Sixty-one percent were born abroad. Ninety-two percent claimed to be fluent in Hebrew; 86 percent received a Jewish education on the college level; and

---

[69]Quoted in Susan L. Rosenblum Shevitz, "Communal Responses to the Teacher Shortage in the North American Supplementary School," *Studies in Jewish Education* 3, 1988, p. 26.

[70]Ibid., p. 39.

[71]Ackerman, "Jewish Education—For What?" p. 12.

about 72 percent either attended or graduated from a college. Sixty-one percent had a teacher's license. Ninety-two percent sent their own children to a day school, and 85 percent claimed to be Orthodox.[72]

The broader finding was that significant percentages of teachers did not regard Jewish education as their main occupation—fewer than half the afternoon school teachers devoted their professional time entirely to Jewish education—and many treated their teaching as a stop-gap or very part-time activity.[73]

Subsequent research revealed the extent of the disparity in salaries paid to Jewish educators as compared to teachers in public schools, and thereby further clarified why the Jewish field could not attract sufficient numbers of full-time personnel. A study conducted by the American Association for Jewish Education in the 1975–76 school year found that "teacher salaries in Jewish day and supplementary schools are too low to afford a head of family a decent, comfortable standard of living as the sole wage earner." Data gathered from 382 schools in 31 metropolitan areas revealed that the median maximum salary of a full-time teacher in a supplementary school was $9,400 and $13,433 per year for day-school teachers. Put in comparative terms, the latter figure was 13.2 percent below what public-school teachers earned.[74] Additional research in the early 1970s revealed that full-time teachers in day schools earned a median salary $2,000 less than their counterparts in public schools in the same 15 cities, and for full-time afternoon-school teachers, the difference was twice as great. Moreover, Jewish educators rarely received "adequate fringe benefits," and supplementary-school teachers generally received no benefits at all.[75] Because Jewish schools offered such uncompetitive wage packages, they could not hope to enforce rigorous standards of certification and other professional requirements.

Research conducted during the mid-1970s identified some 1,300–1,400 full-time administrative positions in Jewish schools, bureaus of Jewish education, and national agencies. Reform congregations employed slightly over 1,000 educational administrators, but only a quarter of these worked full time; the rest were part-time educators, rabbis who performed other duties, or lay administrators. In a number of Reform congregations, a single person was in charge of the entire educational function, expected to run such disparate activities as the preschool program and adult education lectures, as well as the religious school itself. Conservative congre-

---

[72]Dushkin and Engelman, *Jewish Education in the U. S.,* pp. 113–16.

[73]Ibid., p. 117.

[74]Ackerman, "Jewish Education Today," AJYB 1980, vol. 80, p. 143.

[75]Hillel Hochberg, "Trends and Developments in Jewish Education," AJYB 1972, vol. 73, p. 212.

gations employed 350 full-time principals in their supplementary schools. While these personnel were found to be well qualified, the shortage created a bidding competition, leaving many congregational employers feeling they were engaged in a game of "musical chairs." Even though salary scales for full-time administrators were competitive, the field still did not attract enough applicants to meet the dire personnel shortage.[76]

The natural providers of educational personnel—the key training institutions—produced some administrators and teachers, but could not keep up with the seemingly unlimited demand. Throughout the country, there were 11 such programs; they were either divisions of the major rabbinical schools—such as the Teachers Institutes of both the Jewish Theological Seminary and Yeshiva University—or community-based teachers colleges, such as Gratz College in Philadelphia, Baltimore Hebrew College, Spertus College of Judaica in Chicago, the Cleveland College of Jewish Studies, and Hebrew College in Boston. (Eventually, new programs were created at the University of Judaism and the Hebrew Union College, both in Los Angeles, and the Hornstein Program at Brandeis University.) Despite their different institutional structures and even ideological commitments, the early teacher-training institutions shared a common goal of training Hebrew teachers. An examination of the curricula of eight such schools conducted in 1935 by Leo Honor found that all placed a common emphasis on teaching the Hebrew language and Jewish national culture; offered a curriculum focused on the study of classical Jewish texts; and set a mission of training Hebrew teachers. Indeed, they had banded together in an association called Iggud Batei HaMedrash Lemorim (The Association of Hebrew Teachers Colleges).[77]

Despite the booming demand for educators, these institutions fell on progressively harder times in the postwar decades. In part, the problem was ideological: as Hebrew schools became religious schools, and as the intensity of study declined, schools no longer needed teachers proficient in Hebrew and well-versed in Jewish texts. Day schools also did not turn to the training institutions for teachers: most men came directly from rabbinical programs, and a great many women from religious programs or directly from Israeli institutions. Moreover, the demographic and economic realities of the teaching profession were such that ever more educators who had never undergone advanced training in Judaica, Hebrew,

---

[76]Ibid., p. 145.

[77]Aryeh Davidson, "The Preparation of Jewish Educators in North America: A Status Report" (Commission on Jewish Education in North America, June 1990), p. 3. Two early studies of these programs were conducted by Leo Honor, "Comparative Study of Hebrew Teacher Training Schools in the United States," *Jewish Education,* Spring 1935, pp. 71–90, and L. Hurwich, "Survey of Hebrew Teacher Colleges in the United States," *Jewish Education,* Winter/Spring 1949, pp. 73–96.

or pedagogy were hired to meet the insatiable demand. As a result, an effect similar to Gresham's law swept the field: since the training institutions could not staff the schools, ever more unlicensed educators overran the profession, thereby eliminating any possibility of raising requirements for educators. Thus, despite the soaring demand for teachers, enrollments in the training institutions remained static in the postwar period. Walter Ackerman found in the late 1960s that the combined enrollments stood at 2,000 students, a figure that included a high percentage of Israelis. Collectively, the teacher-training institutions graduated roughly 200 students annually; of these, no more than 125–150 actually assumed teaching positions. The rest either viewed teaching as a temporary occupation until they completed their training for a different career or never even bothered to enter the field.[78]

Leading educational spokesmen regularly studied the problem and lamented the shortage of personnel; some even proposed remedies. But given the low status and inadequate remuneration of educational personnel, the problem was addressed in only a cursory or piecemeal fashion. In fact, many came to believe that the dearth of trained personnel was endemic to the field and that Jewish education would never attract a large cadre of full-time personnel. As one insider put it: "I do not know of a single school that closed its doors and ceased to exist during the so-called 'crisis.' The heart of American Jewry continued its normal beat, and there was no serious disruption of Jewish education activity in the past 14 years [since the 1956 AAJE Conference on the Manpower Crisis in Jewish Education]."[79] The message seemed to be, perhaps it is best to shrug and muddle through, since the personnel crisis is intractable.

A similar mood of resignation characterized much of the ongoing discussion about the limited financial resources available to the field. Clearly, the bulk of financing came either from tuition fees paid by parents of dayschoolers or, in the case of the supplementary school, synagogue dues that indirectly taxed all members to shoulder the burden for the congregational schools.[80] The larger policy question of whether Jewish education

---

[78]Ackerman, "Jewish Education—For What?" p. 12.

[79]Quoted by Shevitz, p. 41.

[80]Tuition fees in supplementary schools were pegged at "unrealistically low levels for fear that parents might withdraw their children entirely were tuition fees to bear a realistic relationship with the actual cost of educating a child." According to a survey covering the period 1950–1970, the average tuition at supplementary schools rose from $50 for children of members and $65 for children of nonmembers to $85 and $150, respectively. By 1975 the average tuition in Conservative afternoon schools stood at $115. Such low tuition fees meant that congregational budgets funded the schools. *Jewish Education: Who, What, How,* Background Papers in Jewish Education (American Jewish Committee, New York, May 1983), pp. 8–9.

ought to become central to the mission of the broader community, rather than be left to the discretion and abilities of individual schools and synagogues, was rarely discussed. A survey of the Boston Jewish community conducted in 1975 shed some light on how average members of a community answered this question. Most responded affirmatively to the statement, "It is important that every Jewish child be given a serious, continuing Jewish education." But when asked to rank different types of services in order of importance, Jewish education came in 13th among 16 categories deserving of communal funding. The study concluded that "while of great importance to respondents . . . [the] sponsorship [of Jewish education] may be seen as a synagogal rather than a . . . [federation or communal] function."[81]

In truth, the local umbrella organizations for Jewish philanthropy (generally known as federations) did allocate some funds for Jewish education. The lion's share of such money supported central agencies overseeing education on the local level (see below), but some of this money made its way into the schools as well. There was, for example, a long-standing communal effort to underwrite the education of indigent children, and in earlier years, federations supported communal schools, such as Talmud Torahs. But as Jewish education increasingly moved away from communal schooling to either the congregational or the independent day-school setting, the question of federation involvement became far more complicated. The sheer immensity of the costs and the potential pitfalls of entering an arena rife with contentious ideological and denominational issues had to be confronted. In the view of some community leaders, however, federations could not shirk their responsibility to serve as partners in the enterprise of Jewish education. As Mandell L. Berman, a leading federation volunteer, put it in 1958:

> Acceptance of responsibility for Jewish education by a Federation must parallel its responsibility for other functions which Federations finance and plan. Members of the Jewish community have a right to look to the Federation for high standard services in the community hospital, in camping, recreation, child care services, and family counseling. They have the same right in the field of Jewish education.[82]

The precise nature of this partnership and the extent to which communal leaders would involve themselves in the ideologically fraught area of

---

[81]Quoted from "1975 Community Survey: A Study of the Jewish Population of Greater Boston," in Shevitz, "Communal Responses to the Teacher Shortage," p. 50. The three categories ranked even lower than Jewish education were cultural programs, recreational and athletic programs, and adult education.

[82]Quoted in Dushkin and Engelman, *Jewish Education in the U.S.*, p. 149.

Jewish education would bedevil the federation world for a long time to come.

This did not, however, prevent federations from increasing their investment in Jewish education. Rather, it affected the nature of their allocations. According to data compiled from a large number of reporting federations (though not all), communal expenditures on Jewish education continually rose in the postwar period. In 1937, roughly 5 1/2 percent of all sums budgeted for local community needs was allocated for Jewish education. A decade later, the percentage rose to nearly 9 percent, and by 1957, it exceeded 10 percent. But even these increases could not keep up with the expansion of the field: the portion of the costs of elementary and secondary Jewish education covered by federations in 1958 was only 7 percent.[83]

By the mid-1970s, the costs of Jewish education had skyrocketed. The national budget for Jewish education was estimated at $260 million, almost three times the allocations for all local spending by federations in the United States. The actual dollar contributions of federations to the field rose from seven million to twenty million between 1966 and 1974, and the percentage of federation allocations for education rose from 17 percent to 21 percent of domestic spending.[84] Despite these increases, however, allocations by federations continued to support no more than 7 or 8 percent of the Jewish educational enterprise.

As day schools proliferated, the question of federation support for such institutions became a topic of ongoing debate. Strong opposition to communal support came from leaders who argued that day schools served only a narrow band of the population and the interests of particular denominations, rather than the total community. Many federations also rejected requests for allocations because their bylaws prevented beneficiary agencies from conducting their own fund-raising campaigns; the "Catch-22," of course, was that schools could not survive without such campaigns, since federation funding was inadequate to meet their needs. Over the course of the postwar decades, increasing numbers of federations did decide to allocate resources to day schools, persuaded that such schools met local needs and deserved to be considered a community responsibility.[85]

---

[83]Ibid., p. 148.

[84]These figures are based on reports issued by the Council of Jewish Federations and are cited in Alvin I. Schiff, "Jewish Education in America: Achievement and Challenge," *Jewish Education,* Spring 1977, p. 14.

[85]"Summary and Interpretation of the Study of Financing on Financing Jewish Day Schools and Related Areas," prepared by Uriah Z. Engelman for the American Association for Jewish Education, Nov. 1962, pp. 10–12.

The dimensions of this shift in policy are evident from the following data: In 1970–71, 56 federations and welfare funds granted allocations to 82 day schools, an increase of 26 schools over the previous year. The mean per-pupil subsidy also rose steadily in this period: from $113.78 in 1966–67 to $129.62 in 1969–70, and to $139.03 in 1970–71.[86] The implications of these figures, however, were subject to dispute. Writing in 1974, Charles Zibbell, a longtime communal professional, lauded the progress made by federations in support of day schools. Surveying the decade of the 1960s, Zibbell compared the overall increase in the annual campaign (38 percent) and the increase for local purposes (57 percent) with the increase of spending for Jewish education (100 percent). He also noted the pace of increase in support for day schools, which grew at a rate of 20 to 25 percent each year. "We are at the point now," he observed, "where 30 percent of all of the funds allocated for Jewish education by Federations, go to Jewish Day Schools. As a matter of fact, in some of the smaller communities, Day Schools take close to one-half the funds for Jewish education."[87]

Zibbell's interpretation of the figures was challenged by proponents of increased communal funding of Jewish education. Sociologist Harold Himmelfarb, for example, noted that actual dollar allocations to Jewish education had doubled in the seven-year period from 1966 to 1973, but in relative terms, "the percentage of federation local budget support increased by only 4.3% (from 16.8% in 1966 to 21.1% in 1973). Furthermore, if allocations to day schools are indicative of the impact on all Jewish schools, the picture is more clear. While actual dollar allocations to day schools rose, they hardly kept pace with the increases in the day school budgets." (The overall federation subsidy to day schools remained in the vicinity of 13 percent of school budgets.)[88]

Even proponents of increased communal funding for Jewish education acknowledged the immensity of the task and some of the potential pitfalls for all participants. Insofar as funding for day schools was concerned, it was clear that, even as absolute dollars flowing into day schools kept on increasing, they barely kept pace with rising costs. As one staunch day-school advocate conceded, were federations to make a serious dent in day-school costs by assuming responsibility for half their budgets, the

---

[86]Hochberg, "Trends and Developments in Jewish Education," p. 207.

[87]Charles Zibbell, "Federations, Synagogues and Jewish Education in the United States," *Jewish Education,* Fall 1974, p. 41.

[88]We should note that there was great variation in the proportion received by day schools of funds distributed for education within differing communities. In 1981, for example, day schools in Baltimore received more than a third of all education allocations, as compared to St. Louis, which granted barely a fifth of its educational allocations to day schools. *Jewish Education: Who, What, How,* pp. 8–9.

entire domestic spending of the federated system would have to go solely to fund Jewish education, a completely unrealistic option.[89]

Moreover, the intensified involvement of federations with Jewish education would likely saddle schools with new types of burdens. As Leonard Fein put it at the time: "[I]t is inconceivable that federations would undertake a major expansion of their involvement in educational financing without insisting—as they would have every right to—on substantially increased control over education, either through 'their' agencies (i.e.: the bureaus) or through new mechanisms. But there is no reason to suppose that federations have the competence to administer an educational system. Neither their history nor their present staff capability provides them such competence."[90] The shortage of educational personnel and of financial resources thus remained a perennial lament, and despite some increase in communal funding for Jewish education, the field remained severely constrained by its limited resources.

THE INFRASTRUCTURE OF JEWISH EDUCATION

Throughout this period, the major beneficiary of communal funding was the network of bureaus or agencies of Jewish education. These bureaus had long served as the central coordinating bodies for Jewish education in local communities and were linked to a number of national agencies. Their hold on educational policy, however, was challenged by new institutions created to meet the challenges of the postwar expansion.

The bureaus themselves underwent a significant transformation during this era. Originally developed as agencies providing educational services to all schools in a locality, the bureaus expanded their scope of activities in the postwar era; they set educational standards, encouraged teacher education and offered in-service classes, initiated and coordinated adult education, and worked closely with the community Hebrew or Talmud Torah schools. The largest of the 40 Jewish education agencies across the country, with 600 schools under its supervision, was the New York bureau. It published textbooks and a children's magazine (called *World Over*), served as a liaison with the public schools (particularly regarding the teaching of Hebrew), and ran separate departments specializing in music, dance, and the plastic arts. But even smaller bureaus played a role in providing curricular materials directly to schools and connecting local schools with the larger national efforts in the field of Jewish education.[91]

---

[89]Harold Himmelfarb, "Jewish Education for Naught," p. 259.

[2]Leonard J. Fein, "Suggestions Toward the Reform of Jewish Education in America," *Midstream,* Feb. 1972, p. 48.

[91]Pilch, "From the Early Forties," pp. 144–45, and *Jewish Education: Who, What, How,* p. 6.

With the massive expansion of schools under congregational auspices, denominational organizations took a far more active interest in Jewish schools. The Union of American Hebrew Congregations (Reform) and the United Synagogue of America (Conservative) each established a national Commission on Jewish Education to set policy and a Department of Jewish Education to implement policies within their movements. Orthodox groups also supervised schools within their religious movement through agencies such as the National Commission on Torah Education. With the emergence of these agencies, local bureaus had to find a way to coexist with the national denominational arms. A statement of principles issued by the Conservative movement's commission in 1950 sought to define a fair division of labor:

> In consonance with their philosophy of encouraging, promoting, and extending the program of all educational agencies and segments in the community, the Bureaus should cooperate with the congregational schools or their groupings in carrying out the programs as effectively as possible. The congregational schools should accept the Bureaus as the central community instruments for educational coordination and consultation in terms of improving standards of achievement and progress.[92]

If nothing else, the emergence of far-reaching educational arms within the movements limited the monopoly of the bureaus and forced them to tread carefully.

Within the denominational structures, several organizations developed. Each denomination created a separate organization for its own educational administrators — e.g., the Jewish Educators Assembly in the Conservative movement (founded in 1950), the National Association of Temple Educators (Reform, founded in 1954), and separate associations for Orthodox teachers in day schools and those in afternoon schools.[93] These groups paid attention to questions of professional standards, served as vehicles for sharing curricular information, and recognized excellence in teaching.[94] Through the education departments of the denominations, new curricula and workbooks were designed and marketed.[95] In the Con-

---

[92]Quoted by Pilch in "From the Early Forties," p. 147.

[93]Dushkin and Engelman, *Jewish Education in the U.S.*, p. 158.

[94]See Alan D. Bennett, "The Reform Jewish Educators—Then and Now," *Reform Judaism*, Spring 1988, p. 13.

[95]In the Conservative movement, for example, the Education Department of the United Synagogue issued new curricula for congregational schools in 1948 and 1952, with revised editions appearing in 1959; still another curriculum was disseminated in 1978. See Walter I. Ackerman, "Toward a History of the Curriculum of the Conservative Congregational School," *Jewish Education*, Part I, Spring 1980; Part II, Summer 1980; idem., "The New Curriculum: Some Observations," *Conservative Judaism*, Fall 1978, pp. 43–62; Saul P. Wachs, "The New Curriculum for the Conservative Afternoon School," *Conservative Judaism*, July/August 1981, pp. 64–75.

servative movement, the Melton Research Center for Jewish Education was established at the Jewish Theological Seminary in 1960 to create innovative curricular materials based on scholarly research in Jewish studies. By involving academics in specialized areas with educational administrators, teachers, and students, the Melton Center sought to put sophisticated and thoroughly tested curricula into the classrooms.[96]

Several national agencies also linked educators. The National Council for Jewish Education was founded in 1926 to serve as a meeting ground for key leaders in the field of Jewish education, particularly bureau heads. By 1939, this organization was instrumental in founding the American Association for Jewish Education (AAJE) as the national service agency in the field of Jewish education. These two agencies were key national players in the postwar years: the National Council enrolled some 350 members by 1965, drawn from principals of large schools, bureau professionals, and personnel in national organizations dealing with education and culture.[97] The AAJE assumed several new roles: it linked local bureaus and provided them with important data; it initiated community surveys, completing 100 local community studies and several national ones during its first 40 years; it offered consultation services to local communities, often smoothing over rivalries and competition. In addition, the AAJE concerned itself with the welfare of teachers, the quality of curricula, and the training of educators. In this last area, it assumed responsibility for the National Board of License, the primary agency for awarding certification to teachers and principals.[98]

Rounding out our overview of the educational infrastructure, we conclude with the creation of a major transitional institution, the Coalition for Alternatives in Jewish Education (CAJE), the most important new institution established by and for educators in the immediate postwar decades. It was conceived in 1973 by young members of the North American Jewish Students' Network who were impatient with the perceived ineffectiveness of the Jewish education establishment. To gather support and further its agenda, the group organized its first conference at Brown

---

[96]Jack J. Cohen, "New Trends in Jewish Education," in Pilch, *History of Jewish Education,* p. 205. Among the most successful curricular materials produced by the Melton Center were works on teaching Holidays, Mitzvot and Prayer, and curricular material on Bible and history.

[97]Ibid., pp. 159–60.

[98]Alvin I. Schiff, "A National Jewish Education Agency: Communal Perspectives, A Study of the American Association for Jewish Education," *Jewish Education,* Autumn 1978, pp. 19–20, and Hyman Pomerantz, "The National Board of License," *Jewish Education,* Autumn 1978, pp. 40–41. The board was established in 1941.

University (Providence, Rhode Island) in 1976, attracting some 350 participants.

Three primary goals were set by the planners of the conference: "(1) The conference was to be constructed to meet the needs of teachers . . . (2) The term 'Jewish teacher' was defined to include anyone working in the endeavor of Jewish education whose principal concern was the transmission of Jewish custom, culture and belief. This meant inclusion of all those working in informal Jewish educational settings, lay people, parents and students. (3) The conference was . . . for [all] teachers . . . regardless of ideology or institutional affiliation."[99] Each of these goals was to adumbrate coming policies in the organization.

The conference program structure—which to a large extent remains fixed to the present—was designed to allow as many teachers as possible to teach and also learn from each other: in-depth training modules coexisted with shorter study (or Lehrhaus) sessions; small group sessions for educators with particular interests were matched by plenary sessions. A large number of exhibits permitted participants to peruse teaching materials created by peers. The first conference was such a success that in the following year the number of participants doubled; thereafter, CAJE conferences have been held annually in different localities throughout North America and Israel, drawing 1,200 and more registrants.[100]

CAJE was founded to meet a number of needs. Primarily it sought to help educators break out of their isolation by providing a setting in which to exchange information, share pointers on techniques and curricular ideas, and interact with fellow educators. For administrators, it offered a chance to come into contact with counterparts across the denominational divide; no other organization brought together teachers, not even those of the same denomination. It also aimed to break down the barriers between educators working in formal and informal education, between teachers, principals, cantors, and librarians all working in the field, and between teachers of the very youngest children and teachers of senior adults.[101]

On a deeper level, the educational bias of CAJE participants was toward developing "the affective component of learning as opposed to the

---

[99]Jerry Benjamin, "CAJE: Our History," program book for Rutgers CAJE Conference, 1979, pp. 16–17.

[100]Cherie Koller-Fox, "The Founding of CAJE," unpublished typescript available at the CAJE office. On the founding conference, see also David M. Szony, "Good News from Providence," *Inter Change,* Oct. 1976, p. 2; Gary Rosenblatt, "A New Boost for Jewish Education," *Baltimore Jewish Times,* July 4, 1980, p. 36ff; and Seymour Rossel, "CAJE: From 1976 to 1994," *Jewish Post and Opinion,* Aug. 10, 1994, pp. 4–6.

[101]Jerry Benjamin and Cherie Koller-Fox, "Reflections on a Movement A-Making," *Sh'ma,* Sept. 1, 1978, pp. 158–60.

purely cognitive." Was this approach, one critic wondered, mainly a response to the currently faddish "human potential" movement, the preaching of radical school reformers, and the growing permissiveness of American society? Or was it an innovative response to two endemic problems of Jewish education—"the failure of most Jewish schools to impart basic knowledge and the belief that the emotive is the critical influence in the formation of identity?"[102]

The founders of CAJE also had an explicit political agenda. As articulated in their "Declaration on Jewish Education," CAJE demanded of the Jewish community that Jewish education, long "among the lowest priorities of the North American Jewish community, . . . must now become the highest domestic priority."[103] This confrontational approach quickly brought CAJE organizers into clashes with both federation leaders and the established educational organizations. Conference organizers also put forth other politically charged demands—for an end to "sexism" in curricular materials, "Jewish assertiveness training," greater emphasis on family education, and the relocation of Jewish education "from the classroom into the world."[104] At its founding, then, CAJE was designed as a forum for those seeking "alternatives."[105] In time, its change of name to the Coalition for the Advancement of Jewish Education came to symbolize the extent to which this once radical organization had come to occupy a central place in the educational establishment.

---

[102]Ackerman, "Jewish Education Today," p. 138. Despite his skepticism, Ackerman tended to the second possibility.

[103]Benjamin, "CAJE: Our History," p. 18.

[104]Ibid., p. 19; and the "Special Issue Prepared for the Coalition for Alternatives in Jewish Education," *Sh'ma,* Sept. 1, 1978, pp. 145–60.

[105]We should note in this context that CAJE provided an opportunity for an exchange of information about new curricular fields and the latest trends in educational methods, all of which made their way into Jewish schools to one extent or another. Surveying the scene at the time, Harold Himmelfarb described shifts in curriculum "toward subjects of more contemporary relevance. Holocaust courses and materials abound; there are also new courses and materials dealing with Israel, Soviet Jewry, and the American Jewish community. There are new programs for teaching the old subjects too: Bible, Jewish History, Sabbath and Holidays, Modern Hebrew and even Biblical Hebrew.

"With regard to methods, there is a trend toward individualizing and experiential programs. . . . Thus, for better or worse, we can find practically every new idea that has hit the general field of education at work in some Jewish school: open classrooms, contract learning, programmed lessons, learning modules, mini-courses, socio-dramas, field trips, retreats, volunteer work in Jewish agencies; slides, movies, videotapes, audiotapes, and many more." Himmelfarb, "Jewish Education for Naught," p. 262.

INFORMAL EDUCATION

Several ancillary institutions complemented the work of Jewish teachers and schools. Most prominent among them were youth movements and summer camps, whose agenda was to provide young people with informal education. The B'nai B'rith Youth Organization was founded in 1924 to offer cultural programming to high-school students. In time, each of the denominations established youth auxiliaries: first came the Conservative movement's Young People's League (later United Synagogue Youth-USY), which was started in the late teens of the century; the Reform movement established the North American Federation of Temple Youth (NFTY) in 1939; and the Orthodox Union created the National Conference of Synagogue Youth (NCSY) in 1959. Zionist youth movements such as Beitar, Young Judaea, and B'nai Akiva also were important settings for informal education in the postwar years. Although it is difficult to assess the extent or nature of the learning that actually took place within the youth movements, their impact was significant because they provided tens of thousands of young Jews with a setting for intense Jewish engagement during their teen years—a time when few engaged in formal Jewish schooling.[106]

Some Jewish summer camps played a similar role. Two of the oldest Jewish camps to set themselves such a task, Cejwin (founded in 1919) and Modin (1922), were established by Jewish educators to overcome the problem of "summer forgetting" and to offer an intensive setting for Jewish living.[107] By the 1940s an extensive network of Jewish camps with an educational mission had come into existence, ranging from Yiddishist and socialist camps to JCC and federation camps, to religious and Zionist camps.[108] In 1941, the first Massad camp was established with the express goal of creating a Hebrew-speaking environment.[109] The Conservative movement launched its Ramah camping network in 1947 to socialize young people within a setting that offered religious instruction and He-

---

[106]The critical role of youth movements in the postwar years and their eclipse in more recent decades is a rich subject in search of probing analysis. For a flavor of what such research would yield, see "NFTY After Fifty Years: A Symposium," *CCAR Journal,* Fall 1989, pp. 1–54.

[107]Daniel Isaacman, "The Development of Jewish Camping in the United States," *Gratz College Annual,* 1976, pp. 111–20; and A. P. Schoolman, "Jewish Educational Camping— Its Potentialities and Realities," *Jewish Education,* Winter 1966, pp. 71–86.

[108]Edwin Cole Goldberg, "The Beginning of Educational Camping in the Reform Movement," *CCAR Journal,* Fall 1989, p. 6.

[109]Meir Havatzelet, ed., *Kovetz Massad: Essays in Hebrew Literature and Thought by Friends of Massad Camp* (Massad Camps, New York, 1978), in Hebrew. See especially the section on "Hebrew Camping."

brew speaking.[110] The model of Ramah's denominational camping prompted the Reform movement to open its first camp in 1951.[111] And quite a number of Orthodox camps, largely under private auspices, also opened in these years, offering periods of formal religious instruction as well as informal education.

Although the early pioneers of Jewish camping, particularly Samson Benderly and his circle, believed that "two essential problems in Jewish education—time and environment"[112] could be remedied through camping programs, research on Jewish camps in the postwar decades yielded only mixed results. Surveying the literature on these camps, Harold Himmelfarb concluded: "Despite the general impression of Jewish educators that Jewish overnight camps have a very strong impact on their campers, and despite the fact that the participants and alumni of such camps generally have great praise for their experiences and feel that the camps have had great impact upon them, there is not much empirical proof of enduring behavioral effects."[113] Still, proponents have viewed such camps as valuable ancillaries of formal schooling and as ideal environments in which to cultivate some of the affective aspects of Jewish identification in young people.

One of the potential settings for informal education that only slowly began to assume an educational role in this period was the Jewish community center, the JCC. Many of the staff members of centers at midcentury were, at best, divided over whether their institutions should serve a nonsectarian or "Jewish purpose." Indeed, when a major survey of JCCs was conducted right after World War II, nearly a fifth of the centers reported "not a single project or activity of specific Jewish content." All told, a quarter offered no program for children with Jewish content, and over a third also had no such program for adults; over half provided nothing of the sort for teenagers. Most staff members had little to offer in any event: over 20 percent had never received a Jewish education, and an additional 40 percent had never gone beyond an elementary Jewish education. Not surprisingly, the survey discovered that the vast majority of JCC staff members viewed Jewish education as either irrelevant or only a minimal qualification for work in a JCC.[114]

---

[110]Shuly Rubin Schwartz, "Camp Ramah: The Early Years," *Conservative Judaism,* Fall 1987, pp. 12–41.

[111]Goldberg, "Camping in the Reform Movement," pp. 7–9.

[112]Winter, *Jewish Education in a Pluralistic Society,* p. 186 (see note 21).

[113]Harold S. Himmelfarb, "Evaluating the Effects of Jewish Summer Camping in the United States," in *Papers in Jewish Demography 1985* (Jerusalem, 1989), p. 392, and Sheldon A. Dorph, "A Model of Jewish Education in America: Guidelines for the Restructuring of Conservative Congregational Education," unpublished diss., Columbia Univ., 1976.

[114]Oscar I. Janowsky, "A Landmark in the Evolution of Jewish Community Centers," in *The Jewish Community Center: Two Essays on Basic Purpose* (JWB, New York, 1974), pp. 13–14.

Change came gradually to the JCC field. But in the years after the Six Day War, as the American Jewish community grew more concerned with problems of assimilation, "nonsectarianism" gave way in the JCC world to a new responsiveness to the "needs of American Jewry." By 1970, a commission under the volunteer leadership of Morton Mandel issued a mission statement that opened with a declaration urging JCCs to "strengthen . . . Jewish identity and positively affect . . . Jewish survival, including a concern for definitions, enhancing Jewish knowledge and awareness, and permeating Center activity with Jewish character." Gradually, the JCCs began to expand their role as providers of formal and informal Jewish education, an emphasis that would grow considerably in the last 15 years of the century.[115]

A Field in Crisis

Roughly a quarter century after the onset of its booming expansion at the close of World War II, the field of Jewish education entered into a period of demoralization, bordering on a loss in confidence. Journals of Jewish education spanning the 1970s and early 1980s are replete with references to a "crisis" in the field. In 1972, Leonard Fein, a writer not usually given to pessimism or gloom, set as his point of departure for the reform of Jewish education "an understanding of the sources of its present lamentable condition."[116] "Unfortunately," he went on to observe, "the claim that the present educational system makes for itself as a promoter of Jewish identity does not mean that it in fact promotes such identity. Indeed, there has been a failure of startling proportions to derive appropriate educational conclusions from the interest in identity."

As the 1970s wore on, one writer after the next hammered away at those failings: Jewish schools, it was asserted, produced "culturally deprived" children;[117] "most Jewish schools," another study concluded, "produce graduates who are functionally illiterate in Judaism and not clearly positive in their attitudinal identification. . . . Graduates look back without joy on their educational experiences."[118] Indeed, according to a third study, the clash between parental indifference and the goals of Jewish education constituted an "exercise in self-deception."[119] Even the leading

---

[115]Ibid., pp. 8–9.
[116]Fein, "Suggestions Toward the Reform of Jewish Education," pp. 41, 46.
[117]Himmelfarb, "Jewish Education for Naught," p. 256.
[118]From a report issued by a task force of the American Jewish Committee in 1977, quoted by Isa Aron in "From the Congregational School to the Learning Congregation," p. 64.
[119]Ackerman, "Jewish Education Today," p. 131.

national spokesman for Jewish education implicitly conceded the point when in 1983 he enumerated "present assets and liabilities" of the field, with the latter far outnumbering the former.[120]

What had happened to evoke such despair? The most blatant symptom of crisis was the precipitous decline in enrollments. After peaking in 1962 at nearly 600,000, the Jewish student population declined by 6 percent in the next four years; by 1970, the rolls were down by an additional 13 percent, with total enrollments in Jewish schools estimated at 547,196.[121] The 1970s brought no respite from bad news: a census taken at mid-decade enumerated fewer than 400,000 pupils,[122] and by the early 1980s the figure was approximated as 372,000 students.[123] Thus in a 20-year period, the Jewish student population had declined by some 40 percent.

Much of this drop was attributable to two factors: the Jewish baby boom had come to an end during the 1960s, and by the early 1970s, Jewish women, inspired by the feminist revolution, had begun to defer childbearing in order to pursue career goals. These two "natural" circumstances in themselves would have caused a massive decline in enrollments, forcing schools to merge or sharply curtail their programs. Equally disturbing to educators was the noticeable decrease in the proportion of Jewish children who were receiving any Jewish education. The best estimates in the 1950s and 1960s placed the enrollment figure for elementary-age children at 80 percent.[124] Data from a few large cities indicated that by the mid-1970s, the proportion not receiving any Jewish education had risen to between 25 and 30 percent. In New York alone, according to estimates, over 100,000 Jewish children were not receiving any Jewish education, a figure representing one-quarter of all Jewish youngsters.[125] When all "potential" students were counted, matters looked even worse. A school census conducted in 1983 estimated that only 41 percent of all Jewish school-aged children were enrolled at any given time.[126]

Beyond the numerical decline, educators were battered by a series of studies demonstrating the failings of the dominant type of Jewish schooling—the supplementary school. Based on his observation of Sunday school classes, Walter Ackerman drew a devastating portrait, con-

---

[120]Shimon Frost, "Jewish Education: The State of the Art" (excerpts), *Background Papers in Jewish Education* (American Jewish Committee, New York, May 1983), p. 1.

[121]Himmelfarb, "Jewish Education for Naught," p. 253.

[122]Ackerman, "Jewish Education Today," p. 132.

[123]*Trends: Report on Developments in Jewish Education for Federation Leadership,* Spring 1986, p. 3; this figure was based on a JESNA-Hebrew University Census in 1983.

[124]Ackerman, "Jewish Education Today," p. 132.

[125]Himmelfarb, "Jewish Education for Naught," p. 253.

[126]*Trends,* p. 3.

cluding that "when judged by even the least demanding standard of what it means to be an educated Jew, it is hard to avoid the feeling that the academic aspirations of the one-day-a-week school are either a joke or an act of cynical pretentiousness." As for the more intensive three-day-a-week school, he wrote:

> A recent study shows that even when pupils complete the requirements established by the curriculum, they have no recognizable fluency in Hebrew and cannot understand more than carefully edited texts based on a limited vocabulary. . . . Although 50% of the instructional time is devoted to the study of Hebrew and Bible, the pupil graduates from the school with only the most infantile notions of biblical thought and ideas, and a capability in Hebrew which hardly goes beyond monosyllabic responses to carefully worded questions. The study of history is a pious wish. Understanding and generalization fall prey to the hurried accumulation of disconnected fact.[127]

When a number of scholars began to study the long-term impact of supplementary schooling, they drew even more damning conclusions. Geoffrey E. Bock analyzed the relative impact of Jewish schooling on levels of adult identification and concluded that it had a "greater impact on promoting public expressions of Jewishness — synagogue attendance, support for Israel, participation in Jewish organizations — than on personal expressions, such as home ritual observances, participation in Jewish social networks, and appreciating Jewish culture."[128] Harold Himmelfarb examined the effects of schooling on religious behavior and concluded that "there is a threshold below which hours of Jewish schooling have no effect, unless supported by other influences of adult religiosity."[129] According to his study, the vast majority of students attending supplementary schools did not reach the threshold. Himmelfarb warned that "fewer than 1,000 hours of Jewish schooling might even decrease religious involvement,"[130] thus rendering all one-day-a-week education and some supplementary schooling more harmful for the promotion of future religious observance than no Jewish schooling! Such was the degree of doubt engendered by these studies that a leading Jewish educator partially ascribed "the present crisis in supplementary schooling . . . to the fact that [the] perceptible difference in knowledge and in commitment between the product of the six-hour-a-week and the one-day-a-week school has not been demonstrated beyond doubt."[131]

---

[127]Ackerman, "Jewish Education—For What?" pp. 21–22.

[128]Geoffrey E. Bock, "The Functions of Jewish Schooling in America," *Studies in Jewish Education* 2, 1984, p. 233.

[129]Harold S. Himmelfarb, "The Impact of Religious Schooling: A Synopsis," *Studies in Jewish Education* 2, 1984, p. 276.

[130]Himmelfarb, "Jewish Education for Naught," p. 261.

[131]Shimon Frost, "Crucial Challenges to the Non-Orthodox School," *Jewish Education,* Spring 1983, p. 25.

The most devastating critique came in the form of an ethnographic, rather than a quantitative, study. Based on close observation of a single Jewish afternoon school, David Schoem described the entire supplementary-school system as riddled with internal contradictions, confusion over mission, and self-deception. Schoem portrayed a dysfunctional institution whose rabbinic leadership, administration, and parent body were either blind to or uncomprehending of the yawning gap between the Judaism they were professing and the actual life experiences of the students.

> The goals, the values, and the emotions of . . . parents seemed tied to a system that appeared little different than that of the non-Jews residing about them. Although these Jews did identify with a Jewish people, history, culture and religion, they did not in their own suburban American lives live according to any Jewish way of life. It wasn't that these Jews didn't want to be living a Jewish way of life, but rather they seemed to find the demands of modern life uncompromising. The Jewish way, as they understood it for their own lives, could not serve as a standard for living that suited the modern circumstances of life in America. . . . They have been unable to interpret their Jewish heritage so that it makes sense in their American life.[132]

Although Schoem's study included a number of recommendations for improving supplementary schooling, it was hard for his readers to imagine that this broken system could — or should — ever be repaired.

We should note that a parallel mood of disenchantment with public education was very much in vogue within the larger world of American education at precisely this time. "In the early 1980s," writes one historian of American education, "Americans awoke to discover that their public schools were failing them."[133] A flurry of reports issued by blue-ribbon panels were sharply critical of educational failings that had rendered America *"A Nation at Risk,"* to cite perhaps the most famous of these calls for educational reform (issued in 1983). Another such report warned that "the nation's public schools are in trouble. By almost every measure — the commitment and competency of teachers, student test scores, truancy and drop out rates, crimes of violence — the performance of our schools falls far short of expectations. . . . Too many young people are leaving the schools without acquiring essential learning skills, and without self-discipline or purpose."[134] While the criticism of supplementary Jewish

---

[132]David L. Schoem, *Ethnic Survival in America: An Ethnography of a Jewish Afternoon School* (Scholar's Press, Atlanta, 1989). The quotation is taken from Schoem's doctoral diss. as cited by Ackerman in "Jewish Education Today," p. 131.

[133]Joseph Murphy, "The Educational Reform Movement of the 1980s: A Comprehensive Analysis," in *The Educational Reform Movement of the 1980s: Perspectives and Cases,* ed. J. Murphy (Berkeley, 1990), p. 3.

[134]From *Making the Grade,* a report issued by the Twentieth Century Fund in 1983. Quoted in Murphy, ibid.

programs did not focus on truancy and crimes, it was consistent with the pervasive dissatisfaction with schooling that was so much in the air.

Perhaps the only sector of the Jewish educational world immune to sharp criticism was the day school. Students in such schools scored higher on achievement tests in Hebrew language, Jewish history, current events, and knowledge of Jewish holidays and observances than children in afternoon schools, leading one study to conclude that "the average nine-year-old in Day schools does much better than the average 13-year-old in the Afternoon school."[135] A series of studies on the long-term impact of day-school education all concluded that, while "the Jewish involvement of the home or the parents exerts more influence than the school upon levels of Jewish involvement as an adult, they do show that more Jewish schooling—whether measured in terms of years or total number of hours in Jewish studies—is associated with higher levels of subsequent adult Jewish involvement."[136] Not surprisingly, educators were heartened by the steady increase in the proportion of day-schoolers: by 1983, the majority of children receiving a Jewish education in New York were enrolled in day schools, whereas in the rest of the country, around 20 percent of the Jewish student population was in day schools.[137]

There were few other perceived bright spots in the educational galaxy during this period of introspection and worry. The personnel crisis persisted, despite the declining demand for educators. In addition, by the 1970s, most observers had given up on the teacher-training institutions, which in any event were so short on students that they began to refashion their mission. A study completed in 1981 found that these schools

> have begun to develop courses, and sometimes entire programs, to meet the needs of the general community, and to enroll more and more students . . . non-traditional learners. . . . This, of course, can be seen as a positive development—a guarantee for the continued growth and viability of these institutions—or as a negative development—a sign of decline and change of mission, with the possibility that Hebrew teacher preparation programs may gradually lose importance in the institutions, and may even disappear.[138]

By 1981, moreover, only 20 percent of the courses at these schools were still conducted in the Hebrew language. Indeed, in the early 1980s, the Iggud itself disbanded and was replaced by a new Association of Institutions of Higher Learning for Jewish Education.[139]

---

[135]Dushkin and Engelman, *Jewish Education in the U.S.,* p. 207.
[136]David Shluker, "The Impact of Day Schools: A Briefing Paper on Day School Viability and Vitality" (JESNA, July 1998), p. 3.
[137]*Trends,* 1986, p. 3.
[138]Davidson, "Preparation of Jewish Educators," p. 4.
[139]Ibid., p. 47.

There was also little optimism that the larger infrastructure could solve the problems of the field. Bureaus of Jewish education came under attack in this period for abdicating their responsibilities as educational innovators and becoming instead "heavy-handed licensing boards."[140] And few observers were sanguine that federations would direct significant new sums toward Jewish education. The debate over communal funding for day schools and other forms of Jewish education stood deadlocked, leaving partisans embittered and frustrated.[141]

One important educator agreed with the generally bleak view of the field, but urged a rethinking that would go beyond the obvious shortage of resources. Writing in 1973, Seymour Fox, an American-born professor of Jewish education who had settled in Israel, argued that the personnel and funding shortages and weak curricula were secondary problems that distracted from the more fundamental issue: "If Jewish education is discussed only in terms of time, money, and space," Fox warned, "or embedded in slogans that ignore complexity and diversity, we can only repel the very people we most need to attract."[142] Instead, Fox contended, "the most urgent problem facing Jewish education . . . is its lack of purpose, and, consequently, its blandness. Therefore, until we engage in serious deliberation aimed at rectifying this state of affairs, we cannot even hope to deal with all the other issues that demand solution."[143]

RECENT TRENDS

In the closing years of the century, the field of Jewish education finds itself in a paradoxical situation. The leadership of the American Jewish community is, as never before, wracked by deep worry about the potential disappearance of large numbers of its population through disaffiliation, intermarriage, and alienation from Jewish life. Much of this decline in identification, significantly, is attributed to the past failings of Jewish education. At the same time, Jewish education has became the beneficiary of an infusion of new funding and personnel, both being channeled into existing educational programs and a wide range of new initiatives designed to expand the range of opportunities for Jews of all ages to further their education. The critical assault on Jewish education, in short,

---

[140]Fein, "Suggestions Toward the Reform of Jewish Education," p. 265.
[141]Himmelfarb, "Jewish Education for Naught," p. 47.
[142]Seymour Fox, "Toward a General Theory of Jewish Education," in *The Future of the Jewish Community in America,* ed. David Sidorsky (New York, 1973), p. 268.
[143]Ibid., p. 261.

has been replaced by a new appreciation of its vital role in rebuilding American Jewish life.

Jewish Schooling and the Crisis of Jewish "Continuity"

Although the surge of concern about Jewish "continuity"—the ability of American Jews to transmit to the next generations a strong identification with Jewish culture, religion, and peoplehood—is generally linked to the findings of the 1990 National Jewish Population Survey (NJPS), educators, as we have seen, had agonized over these matters for decades. Studies about the impact of schooling conducted in the 1960s and 1970s, in fact, focused both on the scant knowledge and weak skills young people acquired during their school years, and also on the eventual relationship of Jewish education to adult behavior. Indeed, the term "continuity" itself appeared in the writing of educators worried about the future.[144] NJPS and other demographic studies, then, did not invent the issue of "continuity"; rather, they dramatized the dire nature of the problem and impressed upon the wider Jewish public, including its lay leaders, the need to develop a strategy to confront the serious issues. No sector has been deemed more central to this effort than the field of Jewish education.[145]

The point was driven home by a number of studies measuring the long-term impact of Jewish education. Summarizing these studies, the sociologist Sylvia Barack Fishman concluded:

Extensive Jewish education is definitively associated with every measure of adult Jewish identification. Its impact can be clearly seen in every public and private Jewish life. Younger American Jewish adults (25 to 44) who have received six or more years of Jewish education are the group most likely to join, volunteer time for, and donate money to Jewish causes, to belong to synagogues and attend services at least several times a year, to seek out Jewish neighborhoods and Jewish friends, to perform Jewish rituals in their homes,

---

[144]See, for example, Alvin I. Schiff, "Jewish Continuity Through Jewish Education: A Human Resource Imperative," *Jewish Education,* Summer 1980, pp. 5–12.

[145]In 1985 a Commission on Jewish Continuity was convened by the Cleveland federation to bring together lay and professional leaders for the purpose of "strengthen[ing] Jewish continuity and identity." Three years later a Commission on the Jewish Future was established in Los Angeles to address "deeply troubling statistics as well as our awareness and concern that intermarriage is increasing, that ever fewer Jewish children receive a Jewish education, [that] affiliation with Jewish religious and communal/philanthropic organizations is dropping and that the sense of identification with Jewish history, tradition, religion and community diminishes with each generation." That same year, a Commission on Jewish Education in North America was convened through the efforts of Morton Mandel and the Mandel Associated Foundations, which brought together key leaders from across the denominational and organizational spectrum. See Walter I. Ackerman, "Reforming Jewish Education," *Agenda: Jewish Education,* Spring 1996, p. 6, and *A Time to Act: The Report of the Commission on Jewish Education* (see note 7).

to visit and care deeply about Israel, and to marry another Jew. When they marry persons who are not born Jews, their spouses are very likely to convert into Judaism and become Jews by choice. And they are the group most likely to continue the pattern and to provide many years of Jewish education to their children.[146]

A more detailed analysis of national, as well as local, demographic surveys provides ample evidence of such a strong correlation. The authors of two studies analyzed data from the 1990 NJPS, comparing the current Jewish involvement of adults with the type and duration of Jewish education they received as children. These are the key findings:

Positive Identification. When asked "How important is being a Jew for you?" 75 percent of day-school graduates answered "very important," as compared to 47 percent of afternoon-school alumni, 40 percent of those who had attended Sunday school, and only 22 percent of those who received no Jewish education. Put in terms of years of Jewish education, 70 percent of respondents who had spent 11 or more years in Jewish schools answered "very important," as compared to 41 percent of those who had five or fewer years of Jewish education.[147]

Friendship Patterns. Over half the adults who reported having more than 15 years of Jewish education claimed that most or all of their closest friends were Jews, a proportion that dropped to 27 percent for those who had no Jewish education.[148]

Endogamy. Seventy-eight percent of day-school graduates married a born Jew, as compared to two-thirds of those schooled in an afternoon program and 57 percent of those who attended Sunday school. Half of all Jews who had received no Jewish education were married to Gentiles.[149] Among baby-boomers, whose rates of intermarriage are considerably higher than older cohorts, intensity of Jewish education correlates strongly with a lesser propensity to marry out of the faith: of those between the ages of 25 and 44 in 1990, nearly 80 percent who attended six or more years of day school were married to a Jew, as compared to slightly over half of those who attended six or more years of afternoon school and even smaller percentages of those who attended one-day-a-week school.[150]

---

[146]Sylvia Barack Fishman, *Jewish Education and Jewish Identity Among Contemporary American Jews: Suggestions from Current Research* (Bureau of Jewish Education, Center for Educational Research and Evaluation, Boston, 1995), pp. 5–6.

[147]Seymour Martin Lipset, *The Power of Jewish Education* (Susan and David Wilstein Institute of Jewish Policy Studies, Los Angeles, Spring 1994), p. 17.

[148]Ibid., p. 19.

[149]Ibid., p. 20.

[150]Sylvia Barack Fishman and Alice Goldstein, *When They Are Grown They Will Not Depart: Jewish Education and the Jewish Behavior of American Adults,* Research Report no. 8 (Cohen Center, Brandeis Univ., Mar. 1993), table 7.

Ritual Observance. When asked whether they abstain from eating on Yom Kippur, one of the most central of religious obligations, nearly three-quarters of those who had received no Jewish education reported that they do not fast, as compared to 53 percent of Sunday-school graduates, and 30 percent of afternoon- and day-school alumni. Duration of schooling, again, looms large: two-thirds of those with more than 11 years of day school-education fast, as compared to slightly over half of those with five years or less of Jewish schooling, and slightly over a quarter of those with no schooling.[151]

Attachment to Israel. Fewer than half the population that received no Jewish education felt an attachment to Israel; by contrast, far higher rates of attachment were evident among day-school products (63 percent); afternoon-school alumni were less likely to profess such attachment and Sunday-school graduates were least likely to do so.[152]

Voluntarism. The same general pattern characterizes affiliation with and volunteering service to a Jewish organization: 29 percent of adults who attended Jewish schools for over 15 years report volunteer activities, a figure that declines to 16 percent among those who received fewer than five years of Jewish education, and only 10 percent of those with no formal Jewish schooling.[153]

Philanthropy. An exposure to more intensive Jewish education is associated with a higher likelihood of giving to Jewish causes. Adult Jews with six or more years of supplementary- or day-school education are 20 percent more likely to give to a Jewish cause than those with none at all. And adults with a more intensive Jewish education are more likely to give to a Jewish charity than products of one-day-a-week schools.[154]

Synagogue membership. The type and intensity of Jewish education also relates to the decision to join a synagogue. Among men and women, a day-school education of six and more years is related to higher levels of synagogue affiliation than is supplementary-school education; moreover, the correlation between intensive Jewish education and congregational membership is strongest for younger Jews under the age of 45.[155] Among those adults between the ages of 25 and 44 who had studied for six or more years in afternoon schools, 44 percent were synagogue members, a figure that rises to 60 percent among those who studied in day schools for six or more years, and drops to only 28 percent of adults who

---

[151]Ibid., p.18.
[152]Ibid., p. 22.
[153]Ibid., p. 24.
[154]Ibid., p. 10.
[155]Lipset, *Power of Jewish Education,* p. 9.

were enrolled for that many years in Sunday school. (Significantly, fewer than a third of adults who studied for three to five years in a day school were synagogue members, as compared to 21 percent who had studied for that number of years in an afternoon school.)[156]

Summing up the results of his study, Seymour Martin Lipset concluded that "the iron law of 'the more the more' prevails. The longer Jews have been exposed to Jewish education, the greater their commitment to the community, to some form of the religion, and to Israel. The relationships among type of school attended, attitudes, and behavior reiterate this conclusion again and again."[157]

Since the "continuity" crisis came to public attention specifically over the matter of intermarriage, there has been some debate over claims put forth about the efficacy of specific forms of education in stemming the high rates of intermarriage. In his detailed re-analysis of intermarriage trends, the sociologist Bruce Phillips questions "the widely quoted conclusions that only or even mostly day school education reduces mixed

---

[156]Fishman and Goldstein, *When They Are Grown,* table 6.

[157]Ibid., p. 26. Other researchers have analyzed the impact of educational experiences by tracking graduates of particular kinds of schools. Alvin I. Schiff and Mareleyn Schneider, for example, surveyed a sample of 8,536 graduates of 26 Jewish day schools in the United States located in 19 communities of various sizes. They found that products of day schools ranging across the denominational spectrum exhibited relatively high levels of Jewish identification: "(1)About three-quarters of Conservative and trans-ideological graduates and nine-tenths of Orthodox school graduates observe *kashrut* at home, somewhat less than the level of observance in their parental homes. *Kashrut* observance outside the home is less, both for graduates and their parents. (2)More than three-quarters of the Conservative school graduates light candles and make or hear *kiddush* on Friday evening; approximately 40 percent of them make (or hear) *kiddush* on Saturday, attend synagogue Friday evening, refrain from travel, and study Jewish texts on the Sabbath. The level of *Shabbat* observance of trans-ideological school graduates is somewhat less. Approximately two-thirds of them light candles and make or hear *kiddush* on Friday evenings. Over 40 percent attend synagogue on Saturday morning; more than one-quarter refrain from travel and slightly less than one-quarter study Jewish texts on the Sabbath. . . . (3) Of those who are married, 4.5 percent married non-Jews. Another 2.7 percent chose to marry spouses who were agnostics or atheists. Of those who married gentiles, a little more than half indicated that their spouses converted. The most noticeable difference between Jewish day school graduates and other American Jews of their age is in the matter of intermarriage; actual experience and attitude toward it. Whereas the majority of Jews who married between 1985 and 1990, according to the 1990 NJPS, married non-Jews, 4.5 percent of Jewish day school graduates, who married between 1975 and 1990, are intermarried and over 80 percent object to their progeny intermarrying." Schiff and Schneider, *The Jewishness Quotient of Jewish Day School Graduates: Studying the Effect of Jewish Education on Adult Jewish Behavior,* Research Report no. 1 (Azrieli Graduate Institute of Jewish Education and Administration, Yeshiva Univ., New York, Apr. 1994), pp. 9–12. See also Schiff and Schneider's *Far-Reaching Effects of Extensive Jewish Day School Attendance: The Impact of Jewish Education on Jewish Behavior and Attitudes,* Research Report no. 2 (ibid., July 1994).

marriage."[158] Phillips especially challenges the view that afternoon education has only a slight impact in deterring intermarriage, arguing that when we factor in the variable of generation—i.e., how many generations has the family been in America?—the picture is more complex. Since most day-school graduates in the NJPS data base are first- and second-generation Americans, while most of the afternoon-school graduates are third- and fourth-generation Americans, one can say that the day schools are as yet untested. Furthermore, says Phillips, among third- and fourth-generation Americans in the survey who attended afternoon schools, the rates of intermarriage are lower than for products of other types of schooling. Phillips also argues that the duration of Jewish education plays a major role: attendance in an afternoon school after the age of bar or bat mitzvah correlates strongly with endogamy.[159]

The Phillips study, among others, serves as a corrective to the more exaggerated claims put forth by proponents of various types of educational programs.[160] Upon reflection, it should be apparent that education alone does not guarantee a strong degree of Jewish identification, let alone active participation. It serves as a necessary but usually insufficient motivator of later adult behavior. The role of families in most instances can be even more critical in identity formation. On the most basic level, children will not even have the opportunity to receive a Jewish education if their parents do not themselves have a positive identification: NJPS data indicate that, among those parents who enroll their children in a Jewish school, 78 percent regard being Jewish as "very important" and another 20 percent feel it to be "somewhat important"; no parents in this sample who deemed Jewishness unimportant bothered to enroll their children in a Jewish school. Conversely, almost nine out of ten parents who currently do not enroll their children and also indicate no intention of registering them in the future also contend that being Jewish is "not very important."[161]

Still, even with these important caveats, it has been widely acknowledged by leaders of the American Jewish community that the intensity

---

[158]Bruce Phillips, *Re-Examining Intermarriage—Trends, Textures, Strategies* (Susan and David Wilstein Institute of Jewish Policy Studies and William Petschek National Jewish Family Center of the American Jewish Committee, n.d., ca. 1996), p. 16. For a helpful response to Phillips, see Michael Zeldin, "Overselling the Day Schools? The Controversy Lives On," *In Progress,* Fall 1997, pp. 14–15.

[159]Ibid., pp. 17–18.

[160]For a penetrating analysis of just how problematic it is to determine the relationship between Jewish education in childhood and adult Jewish identification, see Stuart Schoenfeld, "Six Methodological Problems in Forecasting the Impact of Jewish Education on Jewish Identity," *Jewish Education,* Winter/Spring 1998, pp. 87–101.

[161]Lipset, *Power of Jewish Education,* p. 40.

and duration of formal Jewish education are critical factors in the formation of future generations of Jews — and perhaps the factors most amenable to communal influence and direction. Given this assessment, it is not surprising that a community preoccupied with its own "continuity" has made a concerted effort to strengthen Jewish schooling.

ENROLLMENT TRENDS

Although the essential contours of Jewish schooling have remained largely the same over the last quarter of the 20th century, several longstanding trends have become more pronounced. To begin with, enrollments began to rebound in the 1980s from their nadir a decade before. The school population swelled as the children of baby-boomers reached school age (and as older boomers who had deferred child-bearing began to have children.) A school census conducted over the period 1986–88 concluded that some 470,000 children were enrolled in formal Jewish education, an increase of some 100,000 enrollments in less than a decade. Based on projections of the 1990 National Jewish Population Survey about the total population of school-aged children, this suggested that, at any given moment, between 35 and 40 percent of that cohort of children were enrolled, a proportion that has remained fairly constant since the late 1960s.[162]

---

[162]Leora W. Isaacs, "What We Know About Enrollment," in *What We Know About Jewish Education: A Handbook of Today's Research for Tomorrow's Jewish Education*, ed. Stuart Kelman (Torah Aura Productions, Los Angeles, 1992), pp. 63–64. There is considerable variability from one community to the next in patterns of school enrollment. Demographic surveys conducted by Jewish communities in the 1990s have found that in some communities, such as Milwaukee, St. Louis, and Harrisburg, over two-thirds of 6–12-year-olds are enrolled in Jewish schools, as compared to Atlanta, Miami, and Las Vegas, where the figure is closer to 50 percent. Ira Sheskin, *Geographic Variations in the Results of Local Demographic Studies*, Report no. 10 (North American Jewish Data Bank, New York, Feb. 1997), p. 70.

Responses to the 1990 NJPS suggest that there will be a significant rise in the percentage of Jewish children who receive no Jewish education. When parents of children under six were asked whether they intended eventually to enroll their offspring in Jewish schools, 35 percent answered no and another 24 percent were uncertain; only 40 percent answered affirmatively. Lipset, *Power of Jewish Education*, p. 34.

We may note in this connection the growing movement to offer Jewish schooling to children with disabilities, which in part reflects the desire to increase the proportion of young Jews exposed to a Jewish education. The key settings created for Jewish special education are found in Orthodox day schools and in programs created by central agencies (bureaus of Jewish education in local communities). On developments in the latter area, see Leora W. Isaacs and Caren N. Levine, *So That All May Study Torah: Communal Provision of Jewish Education for Students with Special Needs* (JESNA, New York, Dec. 1995). On the forming of P'tach (Parents for Torah for All Children), see Harris C. Faigel, "Jewish Special Education," *Hadassah Magazine,* Nov. 1985, pp. 18–20; Natalie Volstad, "Jewish Education for Very Special Children, *Hadassah Magazine,* Feb. 1979, pp. 14–18; Edward

The distribution of students within the Jewish school system continues to shift in directions that became manifest by the 1960s. Within the supplementary schools, both the one-day-a-week and five-day-a-week schools have experienced a further decline in "market share."[163] The latter, more intensive form of schooling has been replaced by day schools, and enrollment in the former continues to erode. By 1982 slightly under a quarter of Jewish students were still in Sunday schools, almost three-quarters of them enrolled in schools under Reform auspices.[164]

Why do parents choose one form of schooling over another? Based on the 1990 NJPS, new research has focused on the factors that correlate strongly with different Jewish educational choices, "the determinants"[165] of schooling. Some of this research focuses on the current population of adults, identifying several key variables:

The parents' own Jewish educational attainments. The more years of Jewish education parents had received, the more likely those parents were to enroll their children in a Jewish school. Interestingly, the type of schooling parents selected for their children was not necessarily the same as they themselves had attended: 43 percent of current day-school parents had attended such a school, and roughly half of parents sending their children to afternoon school were products of such schools; fewer than a third of Sunday-school children had parents who had attended one-day-a-week school.[166]

Generation in America. The more American-born grandparents a child has, the less likely that child is to receive an intensive Jewish education. Roughly a quarter of all children with four foreign-born grandparents received no Jewish education, as compared to 44 percent of children with four native-born grandparents. Conversely, 84 percent of day-school students do not have a single American-born grandparent.[167]

Gender. Males are more likely to have received a Jewish education and to have attended a more intensive form of schooling: roughly two-thirds

---

Shapiro, "Special Education, Yeshiva Style: How One Brooklyn Rabbi Has Made Intensive Jewish Education Available to the Learning Disabled," *Moment,* May 1981, pp. 50–53; and Betsy S. Jacobs, "Teach Your Children, All Your Children: Can Jewish Education Meet the Needs of Kids with Disabilities?" *Moment,* Feb. 1990, p. 34ff.

[163]Leora W. Isaacs, "Four Decades of Jewish Education: A Look Back and a Look Ahead," *Pedagogic Reporter,* Oct. 1989, p. 5.

[164]Ibid., p. 64. A survey conducted in the mid-1990s of supplementary schools under Reform auspices provides somewhat murky findings about the extent to which schools meet more than one day a week and to what extent recent trends represent a shift from the past. See Samuel K. Joseph, *Portraits of Schooling: A Survey and an Analysis of Supplementary Schooling in Congregations* (UAHC Press, New York, 1997), pp. 13–15.

[165]These are Seymour Martin Lipset's terms. See *Power of Jewish Education,* p. 9.

[166]Ibid., p. 37.

[167]Ibid.

of day-school and afternoon-school alumni are males, whereas 62 percent of Sunday-school alumni are women.[168] Some of this gender gap narrows among younger Jews, but it nonetheless persists: thus, only 14 percent of Jewish men between the ages of 25 and 44 claimed to have received no Jewish education as compared to 34 percent of women; among young adults between 18 and 24, this gap narrowed to 19 percent for men and 28 percent for women. Similar patterns are evident when we compare younger and older populations who had received more intensive forms of Jewish education—that is, the youngest women had far more opportunities, but still not as many as males of their own age.[169]

Region. There are also significant regional variations in patterns of school attendance. Jews in the Northeast are more likely to have attended day school (7 percent) and afternoon school (42 percent), as compared to Jews in the South (3 percent and 25 percent, respectively). Almost half the Jews in Western states and a third of Southern Jews never received any formal Jewish education, as compared to 30 percent of Northeastern and 28 percent of Midwestern Jews.[170]

Denominational identification. In the current adult population, there are significant variations in educational exposure from one religious movement to the next. Among all self-identified Conservative Jews, slightly over one-third claim to have attended either a supplementary or day school for six or more years; this figure rises to 52 percent among self-identified Orthodox Jews, declines to 17 percent among Reform Jews, and rises again to 47 percent for Reconstructionists.[171] Overall, around one-fifth of current Orthodox Jews attended a day school, as compared to 7 percent of Conservative Jews and 3 percent of Reform Jews. By contrast, half of all self-identified Conservative Jews attended afternoon schools, compared to 34 percent of Reform Jews. As for Sunday-school attendance, 41 percent of self-identified Reform Jews claim such an educational experience, compared to 16 percent of Conservative Jews and 9 percent of Orthodox Jews.[172] (It is impossible to judge from these figures precisely how adult identification relates to earlier educational experiences—that is, to what extent have large numbers of individuals switched from one denominational identification to another because of their schooling?)

As for the current generation of youngsters, three additional factors determine the extent and nature of the schooling they receive. The first is

---

[168]Ibid., p. 11.

[169]Fishman and Goldstein, *When They Are Grown,* pp. 4–5.

[170]Ibid., p. 16.

[171]Sidney and Alice Goldstein, *Conservative Jewry in the United States: A Demographic Profile* (Jewish Theological Seminary, New York, 1998), p. 132, table 19.

[172]Lipset, *Power of Jewish Education,* p. 15.

intermarriage: Children raised in homes where both parents are Jewish are far more likely to receive a Jewish education than those raised in an interfaith family. Only 30 percent of the latter have attended Jewish schools, as compared to roughly 80 percent of the former.[173] Among children aged six to twelve being raised as non-Jews, roughly 10 percent had received a Jewish education.[174]

The second factor is *family income:* Jewish families earning more than $80,000 a year are considerably more likely to send their children to a Jewish school than are families earning half that income.[175] Income is even more of a factor among non-Orthodox Jews who send their children to a day school. A study of Conservative synagogue members found that among families with incomes under $75,000, roughly 37 percent had sent their oldest child to a day school; the figure dips to 29 percent for those in the $75,000–99,000 income range, and then continues to rise for families with an income over $100,000, peaking at 46 percent for those families earning over $150,000.[176]

The third factor is the parents' *denominational identification:* Alice Goldstein and Sylvia B. Fishman report that "branch of Judaism makes a significant difference in the extent of education among Jewish children. Almost all of those being raised in Orthodox households have had some Jewish education. The percentage is somewhat lower for those living in Conservative or Reform households, 79 percent and 77 percent, respectively. In households that consider themselves 'just Jewish,' only 46 percent of the children have ever been enrolled in programs of Jewish education. Three-fourths of Conservative 16-to-18-year-olds have had six or more years of Jewish education, while this was true of only half among Reform teenagers. Furthermore, Reform teens are more likely to have had no Jewish education."[177] The overall pattern, then, conforms to the conventional wisdom about the spectrum of Jewish engagement: Orthodox Jews are most likely to expose their children to both an intense and longlasting period of Jewish education, Conservative Jews to somewhat less,

---

[173]Ibid., p. 14.

[174]Alice Goldstein and Sylvia Barack Fishman, *Teach Your Children When They Are Young: Contemporary Jewish Education in the United States,* Research Report no. 10 (Cohen Center, Brandeis Univ., Dec. 1993), p. 4.

[175]Lipset, *Power of Jewish Education,* p. 45.

[176]Steven M. Cohen, "Day School Parents in Conservative Synagogues," in *Jewish Identity and Religious Commitment,* ed. Jack Wertheimer (Jewish Theological Seminary, New York, 1997), pp. 22–23. (The dip among families earning between $75,000 and $100,000 may relate to the fact that they are least likely to qualify for tuition scholarships and yet feel themselves unable to shoulder the tuition burden.)

[177]Goldstein and Fishman, *Teach Your Children,* p. 4.

and Reform parents enroll their children for even fewer years and the least intensive schooling.[178]

As is true of so much else in Jewish life today, these tendencies suggest that the more engaged Jews are also the most likely to invest in a good Jewish education for their offspring. "The most highly educated children," report Alice Goldstein and Sylvia Fishman, "are those whose parents also received substantial levels of Jewish education, are in-married, and perform Jewish rituals in their homes, and whose households belong to synagogues."[179]

THE SURGE IN DAY-SCHOOL ENROLLMENT

In light of this assessment, it is particularly noteworthy that ever increasing numbers of parents who themselves never attended day schools have been enrolling their children in such intensive programs, thereby draining the supplementary schools of population. It was estimated that by the late 1990s, over 180,000 children attended day schools, compared to 260,000 enrolled in supplementary schools. In absolute terms, this means that the day-school population has tripled over the past 35 years; and the day schools' share of all Jewish enrollments has grown from under 10 percent in 1962 to nearly 40 percent.[180] Still, there are great variations from one community to the next. In metropolitan New York, by far the largest Jewish community in North America, roughly twice as many Jewish children attend day schools as supplementary schools (88,000 versus 37,000).[181] By contrast, slightly over one-fifth of Jewish students in cities as diverse as Miami, Milwaukee, Pittsburgh, and Las Vegas attend day schools; in communities such as St. Louis, Richmond, and St. Petersburg, the figure drops to 16 percent; and in some smaller communities, such as Wilmington and the southern part of New Jersey, roughly 5 percent attend day schools.[182]

---

[178]Ibid., p. 9.

[179]Ibid., p. 5.

[180]The most recent figures appear in David Shluker, "The Impact of Jewish Day Schools: A Briefing Paper" (JESNA, July 1998), p. 2. See also Debra Nussbaum Cohen, "Day Schools Face Funding Crisis Even As the Demand Flourishes," *JTA Daily News Bulletin,* Aug. 27, 1997, pp. 1–2; Rachel Blustain, "Why More Parents Are Choosing Jewish Day Schools," *Moment,* Feb. 1997, pp. 58–62. For some important qualifications about the reliability of data on Jewish school enrollment, including figures for day schools, see Marvin Schick and Jeremy Dauber, *The Financing of Jewish Day Schools* (Avi Chai Foundation, New York, Sept. 1997), pp. 2, 5–7.

[181]This is based on a report by the Board of Jewish Education of Greater New York issued in 1993. Stewart Ain, "Growth Spurt," *Jewish Week* (New York), Dec. 10–16, 1993, p. 14.

[182]Sheskin, *Geographic Variations,* p. 70.

A variety of factors account for the continuing growth of day-school enrollments. For one, the most important feeder population for such schools, the Orthodox sector, continues to exhibit rising rates of fertility. Orthodox Jews as a group have a fertility rate twice that of Conservative and Reform Jews, and among the "ultra-Orthodox" or *haredi* population, the figure is perhaps as much as four times as high.[183] These rates represent a significant increase over trends at mid-century and account for growing demand in the Orthodox community for places within day schools. The influx of immigrants from Iran, the former Soviet Union, South Africa, and even Israel has in different ways also brought new populations into these schools. South African Jews, for example, have a long tradition of favoring day-school education. In the case of immigrants from the former Soviet Union, the American Jewish community has taken a special interest in their "resettlement" and "re-Judaization," such that communities and individual schools have offered day-school scholarships to win over the children of Russian immigrants and thereby gradually bring entire families into positive engagement with Jewish life.[184]

The crisis in public-school education, moreover, has encouraged many parents to take a second look at day schools, which offer both superior general studies and an intensive Jewish education. Day schools have benefited from the wavering ardor of the Jewish love affair with public education. Since they generally charge lower tuition fees than other private schools, day schools have become a preferred vehicle among Jewish parents who are abandoning public education in favor of private schooling.[185] Even the longer school hours common in day schools make them more attractive to single-parent families and those in which both parents work outside the home, since they occupy children until late into the day.

We also should not underestimate attitudinal changes toward matters Jewish among baby-boomers. Many who had a less intensive Jewish education are receptive to giving their children opportunities they them-

---

[183]Chaim I. Waxman, "The Haredization of American Orthodox Jewry," *Jerusalem Letter/Viewpoints* (Jerusalem Center for Public Affairs), Feb. 15, 1998, pp. 1–2.

[184]Some communities have even insisted that immigrants place their children in day schools as a *condition* for receiving other forms of family assistance. Private organizations have also tried to encourage immigrants to enroll their youth in day schools. In the mid-1990s, the "ultra-Orthodox" community in New York established an agency called Nechamas Yisrael to subvent the day-school education of over 2,000 youngsters from Bukharia and other regions of the former Soviet Union who had immigrated to Brooklyn and Queens. Nussbaum Cohen, "Day Schools Face Funding Crisis," p. 2.

[185]Sylvia B. Fishman, *Learning About Jewish Learning: Insights on Contemporary Jewish Education from Jewish Population Studies,* Research Report no. 2 (Cohen Center, Brandeis Univ., Dec. 1987), p. 37.

selves did not enjoy. Although difficult to quantify, there is ample anecdotal evidence to support the view expressed by a journalist that "anxiety over the effects of assimilation and a realization that most American
Jews have at best a watered-down understanding of Jewish history have
led many parents to seek a more rigorous Jewish education for their children than they received themselves."[186] Here the general tendencies of
baby-boomers to give their children "more" and "better" than they themselves enjoyed are translating into a desire to give Jewish youngsters a
more intensive and enjoyable Jewish schooling.[187] These tendencies cut
across the denominational spectrum and have benefited all day schools
to one extent or another.

As was true in the immediate postwar decades, the preponderant majority of day-school students continue to be drawn from the Orthodox
sector, where virtually all children attend such intensive schooling at least
through the high-school years. This in itself is a dramatic development
of the past few decades, for until recently, a significant percentage of children reared in Orthodox homes still attended public schools and were educated in afternoon supplementary schools. The school census of 1958
found that 65 percent of Orthodox children attended afternoon or one-
day-a-week supplementary schools;[188] and even as day schools grew in
popularity in the 1960s, there continued to be a significant drop-off by
the high-school years, as evidenced by the fact that there were roughly
three times as many Orthodox elementary schools as there were high
schools.[189] By the last quarter of the century, few Orthodox synagogues
sponsored supplementary-school education any longer, and day school
enrollment became well-nigh universal in the Orthodox world, standing
at an estimated 99 percent.[190]

Despite their small proportion in the total population of American
Jewry—some 7 to 9 percent—Orthodox Jews maintain the preponder-
ance of day schools: of the 203 day schools in New York, for example,
192 (or 95 percent) are under Orthodox auspices; seven are Conservative,

---

[186]Blustain, "Why More Parents," p. 58.

[187]Many of these issues are discussed by Alvin I. Schiff in *Jewish Education in New York:
A Demographic Report, 1970–1990* (N.Y. Board of Jewish Education, 1991), p. 3.

[188]Dushkin and Engelman, *Jewish Education in the U.S.,* table 18, p. 58.

[189]Schiff, *Jewish Day School in America,* table 11, p. 92.

[190]Goldstein and Fishman, *Teach Your Children.* By 1990, for example, there were fewer
than 1,000 children enrolled in some 31 Orthodox supplementary schools in New York; by
comparison, over 79,000 children were enrolled in Orthodox day schools in New York.
Schiff, *Jewish Education in Greater New York,* p. 11. Nationally, according to one estimate,
15,000 youngsters were enrolled in supplementary schools under Orthodox auspices in the
early 1990s. See Alvin I. Schiff, "Worlds in Collision or Collaboration: Synagogues, Schools
and Yeshivot," presentation at the convention of the Rabbinical Council of America, June
1993, p. 3.

one is Reform, and three are community schools.[191] Nationally, roughly 500 of the 636 day schools are Orthodox.[192]

Other sectors of the Jewish community have expanded their day-school movements, too. As of 1994, 63 day schools were affiliated with the Solomon Schechter Day School network of the Conservative movement, a figure that climbed to 70 in 1998 with the opening of several new day high schools. Twenty day schools under Reform auspices are member of PARDeS, the Progressive Association of Reform Day Schools.[193] And a network of over 50 transdenominational, communitywide schools form a separate body called RAVSAK (the Hebrew acronym for the Jewish Community Day School Network).[194] Ten new high schools alone opened in September of 1997 and, with the help of several new foundations, still more day schools were being planned.[195]

As noted above, these schools are growing because non-Orthodox parents are increasingly receptive to sending their children to day schools. According to the data of the 1990 NJPS, nearly one-fifth of Conservative children attend day schools, another 59 percent are in afternoon schools, and another 20 percent attend only Sunday school. Among Reform families, 8 percent enroll their children in day schools, 40 percent in afternoon schools, and 48 percent in Sunday schools. Even in the population of self-identified "just Jews," 20 percent send their children to day schools, and almost all the rest employ tutors or send their children to one-day-a-week school.[196]

---

[191]Ain, "Growth Spurt," p. 14.

[192]Blustain, "Why More Parents," p. 61.

[193]Walter Ruby, "Reform Day School Movement Gains Momentum," Reform Judaism, Winter 1994, pp. 62–64. The amount of time devoted to Judaic studies differs considerably from one type of day school to the next—and even within the schools of a particular movement. Whereas Orthodox and Conservative day schools divide school hours fairly evenly between Jewish and general subjects, day schools in the Reform movement devote one-third of the school day to Hebrew and Jewish studies. See Michael Zeldin, "What Makes the Reform Day School Distinctive? A Question of Practice and Purpose," in Curriculum, Community, Commitment: Views on the American Jewish Day School in Memory of Bennett I. Solomon, ed. Daniel J. Margolis and Elliot S. Schoenberg (New Jersey: Behrman House, 1992), p. 77.

[194]David Shluker and Leora Isaacs, Federation Allocations to Jewish Day Schools: Models, Principles and Funding Levels (Mandell L. Berman Jewish Heritage Center at JESNA, May 1994), p. 2. The most recent figures for all these schools are drawn from Shluker, "Impact of Jewish Day Schools," p. 1.

[195]Nussbaum Cohen, "Day Schools Face Funding Crisis," p. 1.

[196]Goldstein and Fishman, Teach Your Children, p. 28. These figures change somewhat when we take the cumulative enrollment rate into account; thus, 39 percent of members of Conservative synagogues stated that their oldest child had at some point attended a day school between ages 6–17. Cohen, "Day School Parents in Conservative Synagogues," p. 18.

The sheer magnitude of growth and investment of resources in day schools is remarkable. At the beginning of the school year in September 1997, the *New York Times* heralded the booming "resurgence in Jewish education that has seen nearly 40 Jewish private schools open in New York, Atlanta, Baltimore, Boston, New Haven, Minneapolis, and Cleveland in the last six years with many others on the way. At least ten new Jewish schools opened."[197] While some of these "new" schools, in fact, result only from the addition of middle-school and high-school grades to existing institutions, others are quite real and represent major new investments in day-school education outside of the Orthodox community.

Unquestionably, one of the great success stories of the past decades in non-Orthodox day schools has been the explosive growth of the schools housed at the Stephen Wise Temple (Reform) in Los Angeles. Under the dynamic leadership of the temple's spiritual leader, Rabbi Isaiah Zeldin, enrollments have grown exponentially. In 1998, the temple opened a new $32-million complex housing the Milken Community High School. With 650 students drawn from Reform and Conservative families, it is the only such enterprise funded by a single synagogue.[198]

Several day schools in the Conservative Schechter network have also experienced rapid expansion in the past decade: among the largest are the 900-student school located on two campuses in West Orange and Cranford, New Jersey;[199] the 1,100-student Schechter schools in Northbrook and Skokie outside Chicago,[200] and the Epstein School in Atlanta; enrollments have increased so rapidly that these and other schools were forced to open classrooms in trailers or find new facilities in order to accommodate the rapid growth. Community-sponsored schools are expanding rapidly too: the Charles E. Smith Day School outside Washington, D.C. is perhaps the largest non-Orthodox day school in the country.[201] Communities are focusing now on establishing high schools so that youngsters who have attended lower and middle school in an intensive Jewish setting will have the opportunity to continue their studies.

---

[197]Peter Appelbome, "Growth in Jewish Private Schools Celebrates Complex Mix," *N.Y. Times,* Oct. 1, 1997, p. A24; and Diego Ribadeneira, "New Jewish School Touches a Chord," *Boston Globe,* Dec. 8, 1997, p. 1.

[198]Herb Brin, "Milken High: Rabbi Zeldin's Shining Dream on a Hilltop," *Heritage Southwest Press,* May 15, 1998, p. 16. Zeldin's passionate advocacy of day schools is on display in his article, "A Resounding Yes to More Day Schools," *Sh'ma,* Nov. 13, 1981, pp. 12, 16.

[199]Debra Nussbaum Cohen and Lori Silberman Brauner, "Day Schools Face Funding Crisis Even as Demand Flourishes," *New Jersey Jewish News — Metrowest,* Sept. 11, 1997, p. 11.

[200]Juanita Poe, "Jewish Schools — A Show of Faith," *Chicago Tribune,* Sept. 28, 1997, sect. 1, p. 14.

[201]Blustain, "Why More Parents," p. 98.

All of these schools represent an enormous investment of capital and volunteer hours by lay leaders who often had no personal experience with day-school education when they were growing up. The herculean labors of such lay leaders across the denominational spectrum to establish and maintain day schools is one of the epic—and underappreciated—sagas of late 20th-century American Jewry.

RESOURCES

Quite apart from the organizational aspects of this effort—the process of bringing together disparate forces to keep such schools functioning—the pragmatic challenges of insuring their fiscal stability and the quality of educational personnel have been exceedingly taxing. An exhaustive study of day-school funding conducted by Marvin Schick and Jeremy Dauber concludes that Jewish day schools are "severely underfunded":

> This is evident when their expenditures on a per student basis are compared with per student expenditures in public schools and secular private schools. . . . Per capita expense ranges from $5,048 in Reform day schools, which primarily have classes in the lower grades, [to $5, 667 in Torah Umesorah Orthodox schools], to $6,145 at Community schools. In the 1995–96 school year, the mean per capita spending in U.S. public schools was $5,653, while the National Association of Independent Schools (NAIS) reports per capita spending at $10,316 for the 1994–95 school year.
> On the income side, day schools generally have tuition and fee schedules which should generate sufficient income to cover their operating costs. . . . The tuition collected from parents is often considerably below what is indicated in the tuition schedules. Torah Umesorah (Orthodox) schools cover only 57.2% of their budgets from tuition and mandatory fees (such as registration fees or building funds). Community schools cover 68.3% of their budgets from these sources, with the percentage jumping to 87.5% for Reform schools and 89% for Solomon Schechter schools.[202]

The upshot is that many day schools operate on exceedingly tight budgets and cannot offer the diversified programming, special education, enriched arts offerings, technological sophistication, or state-of-the-art physical plant that would attract even more students. Instead, since they generally hire two faculties—one for Jewish studies and the other for general studies—and run a longer school day than public schools, they devote most of their resources to paying the salaries of educators. (We will discuss below the intensifying debate over the funding of day schools.)

Yet even with their heavy investment in wages for teachers, day schools must also contend with personnel shortages. The reasons are not difficult to discern: a study of Jewish educators in three disparate American

---

[202]Schick and Dauber, *Financing of Jewish Day Schools,* pp. iii, 8–13.

cities found that half the day-school teachers expressed dissatisfaction with their salaries, a higher percentage than among supplementary-school teachers.[203] Perhaps this stems from the fact that day-school teachers have almost a full teaching load—nearly half teach for 25 or more hours weekly, as compared with three-quarters of supplementary-school teachers who spend only one to four hours in the classroom weekly.[204] As full-time teachers who view their work as their profession,[205] day-school teachers understandably express greater dissatisfaction over inadequate compensation.

The personnel crisis in day schools stems as well from the perennial shortage of well-trained educators that bedevils the larger enterprise of Jewish education. A report on day-school teachers in schools in the Jewish communities of Atlanta, Milwaukee, and Baltimore found that 35 percent had trained in education and Jewish studies, 24 percent had trained in education only, and another 25 percent in Jewish studies only; 16 percent trained in neither.[206] The report concludes: "Compared to other settings, day school teachers of Judaica are relatively well prepared, both Jewishly and pedagogically, . . . still, fewer than half have undergone the level of professional preparation that is standard among public school teachers, although day schools generally require their teachers of secular subjects to meet the standard requirements. In addition, staff development opportunities for day school Judaica teachers are minimal, and are fewer than the requirements for day school teachers of secular subjects, who typically meet state requirements for ongoing certification to maintain their teaching licenses."[207] Similarly, a report on day school teachers in Los Angeles found that "[a]lthough a higher percentage of qualified teachers are found in day schools than in supplementary schools, the difference is not as large as one might expect; nor is there a large difference between Orthodox, Conservative, Reform, and Community schools. In Los Angeles, for example, at least 30% of day school teachers (in all our types of schools) have taken no college Judaica courses."[208] Thus, despite their impressive gains within the overall sector

---

[203]Adam Gamoran et al., *The Teachers Report: A Portrait of Teachers in Jewish Schools* (Council for Initiatives in Jewish Education, New York, 1998), p. 14.

[204]Ibid., p. 14.

[205]Ibid., p. 18. Teachers in Orthodox schools are most likely to view Jewish education as their career.

[206]Adam Gamoran et al., "Background and Training of Teachers in Jewish Schools: Current Status and Levers for Change," *Religious Education,* Fall 1997, p. 541.

[207]Gamoran et al., *The Teachers Report,* p. 10.

[208]Isa Aron, "What We Know About Jewish Teachers," in Kelman, ed., *What We Know About Jewish Education,* p. 37.

of Jewish schooling, day schools continue to contend with severely limited financial and personnel resources.[209]

ISSUES OF IDEOLOGY

Finally, day schools of all stripes must contend with difficult — often intractable — ideological tensions. In recent decades, modern Orthodox schools have been hard-pressed to maintain their fidelity to their founding principles. Alvin Schiff, a leading Orthodox educator, has plaintively asked: "Does the Judaic curriculum reflect the input of the Centrist Orthodox rabbi(s) in the community?" That point of view includes, according to Schiff, the positive evaluation of general studies in the curriculum and a commitment to "the integration of Judaica and secular studies, the role of Israel and Zionism in the school program," and the offering of special prayers to mark key milestones in the history of modern Israel.[210]

One of the major factors accounting for the abandonment of those principles has been the growing reliance of such schools on ultra-Orthodox or *haredi* educators. Because modern Orthodoxy has been unable to produce enough educators of its own, it has resorted to importing large numbers of its lower-school teachers from Israel and engages rabbis ordained at ultra-Orthodox yeshivas to teach Talmud and more advanced Jewish subjects. Day-school principals are also increasingly products of " 'rightist' training" or have " 'rightist' leanings."[211]

But even where modern Orthodox day schools successfully engage the proper personnel, they generally fail to "integrate" Jewish and general studies. Most take the approach advocated by a former president of Yeshiva University, who declared: "Our job is to give the students the materials; their job is to let the materials interact within their minds."[212]

---

[209]The personnel crisis is especially acute at the top administrative level, particularly in non-Orthodox schools. Rabbi Joshua Elkin, a former Solomon Schechter principal and now the head of a consortium to help found still more day schools, has noted that the field of Jewish day schools in America "has grown so rapidly and has undergone such an increase in sophistication and complexity that it has exceeded the capacity of the Jewish community to recruit and train the needed numbers of people to be able to fill all these positions." In numerical terms, at least 48 executive positions in Jewish educational institutions around the country were vacant as of mid-1998, according to Paul Flexner, director of human resources development for the Jewish Education Service of North America. Elissa Gootman, "Day Schools Start Scrambling Over Educators of Top Quality: Principals Pursued, Seminary Swamped, As Continuity Crisis Ignites a Frenzy," *Forward,* May 8, 1998, p. 1.

[210]Schiff, "Worlds in Collision or Collaboration," p. 3. Significantly, Schiff never answers the question.

[211]Alvin I. Schiff, "The Centrist Torah Educator Faces Critical Ideological and Communal Challenges," *Tradition,* Winter 1981, p. 285.

[212]Samuel Belkin as quoted in Jack Bieler, "Integration of Judaic and General Studies in the Modern Orthodox Day School," *Jewish Education,* Winter 1986, p. 19.

Thus, an "integrated" curriculum remains, at best, a pious wish in most schools, which helps account for the ongoing problems of "compartmentalization" in the modern Orthodox world.[213]

Day schools of all stripes also struggle with the broad range of families that have diverse outlooks on Judaism. According to one estimate, in the early 1990s there were between 30,000 and 40,000 children from "non-observant homes in modern Orthodox day schools." Such schools must find ways to socialize and integrate these children into the religious culture of the institution.[214]

In community day schools, diversity creates other tensions, since these schools tend to draw students from the entire spectrum. Whose version of Judaism should be taught? The answer often is a bland, lowest-common-denominator version, which also leaves many parents disappointed. Yet even in denominationally run day schools, conflicting versions of Judaism must be negotiated. The Conservative movement's Solomon Schechter schools, for example, struggle with a gap between the normative view of Judaism espoused by the leadership and the far less structured understanding of Judaism common among many of the folk. "There are a lot of people in the Schechter community with lots of ideas about their Jewishness and how they want to be, and for me that's a plus," says one parent. But for others, the growing diversity brought by mounting enrollments is "a mixed blessing." "It used to be a like-minded community of parents, but it's turning into a sort of Jewish public school," complains another parent. "Now you have kids planning parties on Shabbat, which excludes half the class. You've got debates over equality for girls in the morning minyan—and the newcomers don't even have an opinion. If you're sending your kid to school just to get 'an exposure to Judaism,' you don't care about the nuances. I do."[215]

After studying one particular Solomon Schechter school, the educator Carol Ingall noted the consequences of trying to bridge a widely disparate parent population. "Rather than appealing to the transcendental, the

---

[213]The ultra-Orthodox schools are beset with variations on the same issues: Are "general studies" taken seriously enough so as to provide students with the skills to find gainful employment? And to what extent are ultra-Orthodox schools intentionally leaving their charges ill-equipped to enter the workforce so as to prevent them from venturing out of the religious enclave? These issues are rarely discussed, let alone studied, except in the context of recent discussions of the impoverization of the *haredi* community.

[214]Schiff, "Worlds in Collision or Collaboration," p. 4.

[215]All the quotations in this paragraph are from J.J. Goldberg, "U.S. Jewry Pins Its Future on Education," p. 31 (see note 5). On this theme, see also Cohen, "Day School Parents in Conservative Synagogues," pp. 18–23.

school keeps its message vague," she observes, "allowing parents . . . to attend religious events with the mind-set of a parent attending a piano recital." Not only parents, however, are treated to bland fare. The school, generally, Ingall contends, is "ambivalent about its religious message . . . [and] is reticent about articulating it. When the message is articulated, why is it garbed in functionalist, folk religion terms?" Rabbi Robert Abramson, director of the Conservative movement's department of Jewish education, acknowledges, "As the schools grow, there's got to be some implications for observing less. . . . In an atmosphere as pluralistic as ours, the principal tends to be much more susceptible to pressure." Thus, the very "success" of day schools in capturing the allegiance of a broader band of Jewish parents in recent years has brought with it some quite serious strains. Even worse, many administrators and board members in such schools seek to avoid dealing with these strains and seem "religiously embarrassed to impose [the school's] view upon its parents." The challenge, then, as Ingall observes, is for the school "to refine its message, to firmly fix it to the supernatural and spiritual, without scaring away significant numbers of its parent body."[216]

Day schools in the Reform movement are beset by similar issues. Such schools of necessity tolerate a wide diversity of behaviors and beliefs since the denomination itself is highly "pluralistic." But the upshot, as one educator has noted, is that the 20 schools in the Association of Reform Day Schools differ widely in approach. "For example, each school approaches the teaching of Bible differently. Some schools teach Tanakh in Hebrew while others teach Bible in English. Some schools use the Biblical text, some teach 'Bible stories.' Some have a daily Bible class, some integrate Biblical studies into the weekly celebration of the Shabbat." The lack of a uniform curriculum appears to be the direct result of such wide diversity of approach within the Reform movement itself.[217]

THE RENEWED INTEREST IN SUPPLEMENTARY SCHOOLS

Perhaps the least anticipated trend of the past decade in the realm of schooling has been a resurgence of serious interest in reviving and even recreating supplementary education. Most observers of the postwar afternoon and Sunday schools, as we have already noted, portrayed such programs in the most dismissive of terms—as an irredeemable Jewish wasteland. Some reports on the long-term impact of such an education

---

[216]Carol K. Ingall, "Soul-Turning: Parent Education in a Conservative Day School," *Conservative Judaism,* Summer 1993, esp. pp. 62–65. Abramson is quoted in J.J. Goldberg (see note 5).

[217]See Zeldin, "What Makes the Reform Day School Distinctive?" p. 69.

even argued that "supplementary education was the same as having received no schooling."[218] And yet the late 1980s saw the emergence of intensive new research focusing on supplementary schools that "succeed" and a popular body of literature on the "best practices" of such schools. Both efforts were designed to identify and describe model programs worthy of emulation.[219] Suddenly, the supplementary-school system—long regarded as the most pedestrian, if not hopeless, setting for Jewish education—became "hot," as Jewish educators rushed to reconceive the entire enterprise in bold, if experimental, terms.

What accounts for this turnabout? On the most practical level, few educators were prepared to scrap the largest school system in the field of Jewish education.[220] "Even in the face of . . . 'hard,' seemingly incontrovertible evidence," Isa Aron comments, "few leaders of the organized Jewish community were willing to advocate the dismantling of the . . . 'system,' which accounts for more than two-thirds of the enrollment in Jewish schools."[221] Although the proportions changed over time as day school enrollments continued to grow, the fact that the majority of Jewish children continue to enroll in supplementary schools—and in all likelihood will continue to do so for the foreseeable future—has made it unrealistic to give up on supplementary education, for it would mean abandoning most Jewish youngsters to no Jewish education.

Beyond this pragmatic consideration, a second look at the entire system prompted a reconsideration of basic issues. For one thing, the contention that "a little Jewish education is worse than none"—a conclusion drawn from studies claiming that children not exposed to a basic threshold of schooling (as defined by hours of instruction) were no more likely in the long term to live as committed Jews than children who had never received any Jewish education—seemed to defy common sense. When the sociologist Steven M. Cohen reanalyzed data on the impact of schooling, his findings supported the commonsense view that "no Jewish education is the *least* effective, that a lot of Jewish education helps

---

[218]Aron, "From the Congregational School to the Learning Congregation," p. 67 (see note 32).

[219]Barry W. Holtz, *Supplementary School Education: The Best Practices Project* (Council for Initiatives in Jewish Education, New York, 1993; rev. ed., 1996).

[220]For an exception, see the powerful critique offered by Yehiel Poupko and his suggestion that the Jewish community needs to invest in the education of current and future parents (adults between the ages of 25 and 40), and only later focus on the needs of children. Yehiel E. Poupko, "Needed: Standards for Jewish Education," *Jewish Journal of Education,* Fall 1991, pp. 29–34.

[221]Aron, "From the Congregational School to the Learning Congregation," p. 67. The most recent figures suggest that the supplementary schools now account for approximately 60 percent of Jewish student enrollments. See above, note 180.

Jewish identity *a lot,* and, of course, a little Jewish education helps Jewish identity a *little."*[222] This prompted Donald Feldstein and Barry Shrage, two leading federation professionals, to warn against "writ[ing] off the great middle group of Jewish children who get a limited Jewish education. While day schools continue to provide optimal Jewish education, we should not despair of improving the quality, time and content of Jewish supplementary schools to where they do a little more good than they are doing now. It is not hopeless, and our reliance on limited data may have led us astray."[223]

The reassessment of the supplementary school also took another direction. Some educators contended that supplementary education was being judged unfairly and on the basis of the wrong criteria. David Resnick, an educator actively involved in the work of JESNA, objected to assessments of supplementary-school education that took as their point of departure the goals of school principals (who often judged their own schools quite harshly). Instead, Resnick argued, such afternoon and Sunday programs "are not schools at all, but settings for Jewish socializing." Ironically, to bolster his case, Resnick invoked all the stock arguments usually hurled at such schools by their detractors: they are characterized by "weak involvement and low expectations by both students and their parents, untrained staff, rudimentary or nonexistent curriculum, unsupportive or hostile organizational environment." But for Resnick, it is precisely these circumstances and the absence of explicit goals articulated by schools that necessitate a very different type of evaluation of supplementary programs, for they are already places of informal education and do not really set an explicit goal to transmit information or deep skills.[224]

One conclusion drawn from this new approach is that much greater attention needs to be directed at the affective, rather than the cognitive, side of schooling in the supplementary setting. Writing from such a perspective, the ethnographer Samuel Heilman concluded his study of one af-

---

[222]Steven M. Cohen, "Outreach to the Marginally Affiliated: Evidence and Implications for Policymakers in Jewish Education," *Journal of Jewish Communal Service,* Winter 1985, pp. 147–57. Cohen found that when older women who had received no Jewish education but were often highly engaged in Jewish life because of the socialization they had experienced in embracing Jewish neighborhoods were removed from the population of those who never received a Jewish education, the latter group scored lower in levels of engagement than those who had received a minimal Jewish education.

[223]Donald Feldstein and Barry Shrage, "Myths and Facts for Campaign Planners," *Journal of Jewish Communal Service,* Winter 1986, pp. 98–99.

[224]David Resnick, "Jewish Supplementary Schooling Misperceived," *Contemporary Jewry* 13, 1992, pp. 14–17. See also an earlier call for reassessment: Norman L. Friedman, "On the 'Non-Effects' of Jewish Education on Most Students: A Critique," *Jewish Education,* Summer 1984, pp. 30–33.

ternoon school as follows: "I am convinced that to know, one first must believe; that feeling and being actively Jewish may be a prerequisite to becoming more so; that the number of volumes of the Talmud we have gone through may be less important than how many of them we have let get through to us."[225] Based on such a perspective, educators now counseled a different set of goals for the supplementary school, goals that would nurture a positive attachment to Judaism and Jewish peoplehood, rather than focus primarily on the transmission of information and the development of skills.[226]

Some educators have gone even further, urging a radical rethinking of the relationship between the supplementary school and the congregation that sponsors it. "What would it look like," asks Isa Aron, "if education were seen as the concern of the entire congregation rather than being relegated to its school(s)? Who would be the learner? Who would be the teacher? In what settings and through what modalities might synagogue members learn about being Jewish? . . . Each and every congregation must answer for itself."[227] Here, then, is a "paradigm shift" in the very conception of congregational schooling that suggests a number of potential new options: First, the goal of Jewish schooling needs to be redirected from "instruction" to "enculturation." In the absence of an embracing environment supportive of Jewish educational goals, the school must offer "a loving induction into the Jewish culture and the Jewish community."[228] Second, the Jewish community must strive to create a norm of "lifelong Jewish learning," a process in which all its members must participate. Schools would then be seen as but one component of a communal agenda. Third, synagogues specifically must reconceive of their mission and transform themselves into "learning communities."[229]

The goal of this paradigm shift undoubtedly is to address some of the deep flaws of congregational schooling, particularly the gap between the message of the school and that of the home. Educators intent on reforming supplementary education now aspire to join the congregation and the school in a highly self-conscious and structured fashion. Minimally, they strive to incorporate a large component of Jewish family education into the life of the congregation and its school—to educate parents and

---

[225]Samuel Heilman, "Inside the Jewish School," in Kelman, ed., *What We Know About Jewish Education,* p. 329. The study was published originally by the American Jewish Committee in 1983 and subtitled "A Study of the Cultural Setting for Jewish Education."

[226]See, for example, Larry Cuban, "Changing Public Schools and Changing Congregational Schools," in Aron, Lee, and Rossel, eds., *A Congregation of Learners* (see note 32), pp. 119–38.

[227]Aron, "From the Congregational School to the Learning Congregation," p. 68.

[228]Ibid.

[229]These last two goals form the backbone of Aron, Lee, and Rossel's *A Congregation of Learners: Transforming the Synagogue into a Learning Community.*

children, both separately and together, so that young people observe their parents engaged in Jewish learning, and parents acquire knowledge and skills to nurture their children. (We will have more to say about Jewish family education in the next section.) To create such programs, however, requires a major institutional commitment by the congregation and especially by its professional and lay leadership. But certainly, since the late 1980s, outspoken advocates have promoted "synagogue change" as the key to the rebuilding of supplementary schooling.[230]

There is no single method employed by congregations to restructure their relationship to Jewish schooling. Most observers, in fact, contend that no such effort at "synagogue change" can succeed unless it takes into account the unique and particular culture of the synagogue. A recent report on one such effort illustrates some of the new thinking and also some of the inherent problems in the venture. A large Conservative synagogue in Baltimore introduced a second educational program to run parallel to the existing supplementary school. In its first year, Project Mishpacha, as it was called, enrolled 113 children (in 80 families); an additional 307 children remained in the mainstream three-day-a-week program. In the second year of the pilot program, Project Mishpacha increased its enrollment to 158 (in 120 families), and the number of children in the mainstream program decreased to 286. The new program offered a mix of formal and informal learning opportunities to children and their parents, with a particular emphasis on informal activities. According to the best estimates, "the total number of hours per week spent by children in Project Mishpacha dealing with Jewish topics at home, in the synagogue and at school exceeded that of children in the conventional three-day-a-week in school program. In addition, parents noted that their children were spending 'quality time' on their Jewish studies." From the perspective of synagogue leaders, Project Mishpacha also encouraged more parents to attend Sabbath services and other events, and generally increased participation in the life of the synagogue.[231]

---

[230]There is no shortage of articles on experimental congregational programs. For more sustained discussions of these issues, see Joseph Reimer's ethnography of one congregation in *Succeeding at Jewish Education* (see note 3); Aron, Lee, and Rossel's *Congregation of Learners,* and Adrianne Bank and Ron Wolfson, *First Fruit: A Whizin Anthology of Jewish Family Education* (Whizin Institute, Los Angeles, 1998). The major initiative toward sustained and coordinated synagogue change is called "Synagogue 2000," a program funded by several major foundations and headed up by Lawrence Hoffman and Ron Wolfson. See Lawrence A. Hoffman, "Imagine: A Synagogue for the 21st Century," *Reform Judaism,* Fall 1996, pp. 21–25, and Ron Wolfson, "The Front Line Is the Bottom Line," *Sh'ma,* Apr. 17, 1998, pp. 3–5.

[231]Mark Loeb et al., "The Politics of Change: Transforming a Congregational School Through Family Education," *Agenda: Jewish Education,* Fall 1997, pp. 18–22. Jewish news-

One of the challenges, however, was to sustain a program that required so much planning and coordination. The program required a highly varied approach that would appeal to the broad "diversity of family life styles; Project Mishpacha is finding that the more options it can provide by which families can fulfill their obligations, the more pleased are the parents." Moreover, as the program evaluator, Adrianne Bank, conceded: "The second challenge is that of repeatability—how to keep the new cohorts of parents, who were not participants in the enthusiastic pilot group, interested and motivated. The third challenge is maintaining the balance between educational change and educational stability so that the professional staff can continue to make steady incremental improvements in the Project Mishpacha program without experiencing burnout and a sense of fatigue."[232] Simply put, ambitious programs for "synagogue change" require an enormous investment of time, personnel, and energy. Many synagogue schools cannot marshal these resources, and those that do may have difficulty sustaining them for long.

There are also two big unknowns when it comes to the new thinking and restructuring of Jewish education in the supplementary school. First, it is too early to ascertain the extent to which an emphasis on feeling Jewish is purchased at the expense of Jewish knowledge and skills, and what the consequences might be for such a trade-off. Will young people with even the most positive Jewish feelings, yet lacking in Hebraic skills and Jewish knowledge, find themselves capable of observing Judaism, a religion that requires an extensive understanding and expertise? Second, no one knows whether the heightened synagogue and school morale evident in "learning congregations" will result in greater Jewish engagement in the long run. Joseph Reimer concedes as much at the conclusion of his positive ethnographic study, *Succeeding at Jewish Education:*

> Will this Judaism, this religion-in-the-making, prove convincing and moving to their members? Will the children and adults whom I observed take this Judaism to heart and make it a living part of their lives? That, after all, is the ultimate educational question. But ethnographies cannot answer ultimate questions. Until the record is more complete, answering that question will remain a matter of faith.[233]

Despite the doubts, many educators concerned with supplementary education are prepared to leap into the unknown with experimental "change" programs, convinced that only a radical new initiative will res-

---

papers have become far more interested in recent years in innovative supplementary schools. See, for example, Michael Shapiro, "Building the Future: Six Hebrew Schools That Break the Mold," *Baltimore Jewish Times,* May 29, 1992, p. 52ff.

[232]Ibid., p. 22.

[233]Reimer, *Succeeding at Jewish Education,* p. 185.

cue the supplementary school from its long-standing flaws and internal contradictions.

Although they are the beneficiaries of these good intentions and a significant infusion of new energy and ideas, supplementary schools continue to struggle with several perennial challenges. One is the resistance of parents to a three-day-a-week format, at least in part because late 20th-century social and living patterns make it difficult to deliver children to the synagogue three times a week. These patterns include the tendency of Jews to reside far from their congregation; the daunting logistics of car-pooling when both parents are likely to be working; and the long-standing interest of Jewish parents in enrolling their children in extra-curricular school activities, sports teams, music lessons.[234]

In response to such pressure, a significant percentage of Conservative and Reform supplementary schools either offer only a twice-a-week school program and/or now schedule school meetings for the Sabbath morning. A wide-ranging study of Reform temples conducted in 1996 found that over 94 percent of member congregations sponsor Sunday schools that meet only once a week. This is true especially of congregations with 165 or fewer memberships (which represent 43 percent of the affiliates in the Union of American Hebrew Congregations). Slightly over 60 percent of member congregations also conduct two-day-a-week afternoon schools, and 8 percent of the religious schools meet on Saturdays.[235]

It is more difficult to come by data on patterns in Conservative supplementary schools, but knowledgeable insiders estimate that no more than 70 percent of congregations still require three-day-a-week attendance.[236] Moreover, among these there is a strong trend toward counting a Sabbath morning program—junior congregation, joint service for parents and children, or a study group—toward the five to six hours of weekly schooling. Describing one such Conservative religious school at a West Coast congregation, Lisa Malik writes: "It is no accident that . . . [the] school meets on *Shabbat;* it reflects the school's emphasis on Jewish ritual and observance. . . . Both the school and the synagogue have an informal participatory culture; both emphasize religious skills."[237]

---

[234]Debbie Slevin, "The 1-2-3 Day-A-Week Hebrew School Dilemma," *Jewish Standard* (New Jersey), Oct. 30, 1998, p. 6.

[235]Samuel K. Joseph, *Portraits of Schooling: A Survey and Analysis of Supplementary Schooling in Congregations* (New York: UAHC Press, 1997), pp. 13–15.

[236]Interview with Dr. Robert Abramson, director, Department of Jewish Education, United Synagogue of Conservative Judaism, Jan. 5, 1999.

[237]Lisa S. Malik, "The Institutionalization of Synagogue Change: Case Studies in Jewish Family Education," *Journal of Jewish Communal Service,* forthcoming (typescript, p. 12).

Indeed, if the primary goal of religious schools is to prepare young people for their bar or bat mitzvah and other forms of participation in synagogue life, mandatory school attendance on the Sabbath is a highly efficient strategy to foster religious socialization: young people whose parents would not otherwise bring them to religious services now are required to attend school and inevitably observe worship in the main sanctuary on a regular basis.[238] The youngsters are generally asked to assume some responsibility for the service, either in the main sanctuary or in a youth service. Thus, Sabbath schooling, a widespread phenomenon in churches, insures congregations of a youthful presence on Saturday mornings, a time when it is difficult to woo more than a minority of members into the synagogue, and it provides an opportunity to integrate youngsters into the religious life of the congregation. Whether the informal learning that takes place on the Sabbath morning is an adequate substitute for formal education remains to be seen.

Personnel and Curriculum

The severe limit on the number of school hours in supplementary schools is matched by another perennial shortage, namely the continuing personnel crisis. As we have seen, this deficiency has a long history, and there is little reason to dispute the bald assessment offered a decade ago by Isa Aron and Adrianne Bank that "the most serious challenge facing Jewish education today is the recruitment and training of supplementary school teachers who combine Judaic knowledge and pedagogic expertise with enduring personal dedication to Jewish teaching and learning."[239] In fact, the weaknesses remain much as they were 50 years ago: a large percentage of educators working in supplementary education lack adequate credentials in Judaica and/or pedagogy. A large proportion do not regard their teaching as a career. Few are assigned enough teaching hours to make a living in Jewish education. Large numbers, of necessity, teach only on a part-time basis, and quite a few are volunteers rather than professional educators. And few teachers receive any in-service or continuing education to further hone their skills and expand their knowledge.

---

[238]It appears that parents of supplementary-school children continue to drop off their youngsters at the curb—whether school meets on a weekday or on the Sabbath. Malik writes of the Sabbath program: "You see some parents and children dressed up to go to *shul* in the sanctuary. At the same time, you see many religious school parents dressed in sweat pants or shorts who never get out of their cars to come to services; they just drop off their children for school and pick them up when it is over." Ibid. (typescript, p. 11).

[239]Isa Aron and Adrianne Bank, "The Shortage of Supplementary School Teachers: Has the Time for Concerted Action Finally Arrived?" *Journal of Jewish Communal Service,* Spring 1988, p. 264.

The preponderant majority of teachers are women, although males are more likely to take positions in high schools, a pattern that exactly matches trends in public education.

All this has been exhaustively documented in a number of recent studies.

A wide-ranging study of the 15,000 teachers working in Reform religious schools found that high percentages are college-educated, and many have a master's degree. A third of the teachers are or have been secular-school teachers. They overwhelmingly tend to identify as Reform Jews; two-thirds are members of the congregation in which they teach; and 72 percent are women.[240] "Avocational teaching," in short, is the norm in all but the largest of congregations.[241] Only 16 percent of the teachers in Reform schools hold a master's degree in Jewish education, and only 30 percent hold credentials as Reform Jewish Educators (RJE), a form of certification within the Reform movement.[242]

A detailed study of supplementary-school Jewish educators in Atlanta, Baltimore, and Milwaukee, cutting across the denominational spectrum, arrived at many similar findings. Eighty percent of the supplementary-school teachers had earned a college degree; but only 18 percent had certification in Jewish education, and 12 percent had earned a degree in Jewish studies. Fewer than a quarter had studied in a day school or in Israel prior to age 13; but 40 percent had themselves attended a supplementary-school meeting two or more days a week.[243] Only 4 percent of these supplementary-school teachers worked in Jewish schools more than 12 hours per week. Unsurprisingly, only a bit more than half (56 percent) indicated they planned to continue working in the same position in the future. Quite remarkably, only 26 percent expressed dissatisfaction with their work—perhaps because they had had only limited expectations in the first place.[244]

The authors of still another local study conclude: "Teachers in Boston area Jewish schools are overwhelmingly female, American-born, 'young middle-aged,' not particularly well-trained academically in Judaic stud-

---

[240]Joseph, *Portraits of Schooling,* pp. 24, 34.

[241]Isa Aron, "From Where Will the Next Generation of Jewish Teachers Come?" *CCAR Journal,* Fall 1988, pp. 51–65, which examines how Reform congregations recruit and train "congregant-teachers." Aron notes that "the deliberate recruitment of avocational teachers seems to be much more common in schools affiliated with the Reform, rather than the Conservative movement." The main reason for this is that "a teacher in the Reform religious school would not have to know Hebrew, could teach only on Sundays, and could therefore more easily be recruited from the congregation" (p. 60).

[242]Joseph, *Portraits of Schooling,* p. 37.

[243]Gamoran et al., *The Teachers Report,* pp. 5–7.

[244]Ibid., pp. 14–19.

ies, though well-educated secularly. . . . Two-thirds of those currently teaching feel that Jewish education is their career, though there is some uncertainty about how firm a commitment this may be. . . . There is a large amount of fluidity in the field, with teachers not remaining in their current jobs very long, nor staying in the field over time, either."[245]

The similarity of these findings confirms the fact that supplementary-school education continues to suffer from many of the same liabilities as were noted half a century ago. If anything has changed, it is the greater inclination of bureaus, religious denominations, and training institutions to develop programs to recruit and nurture avocational teachers and provide in-service training to increase the competence of supplementary-school educators—that is, to work with the existing personnel rather than bemoan the shortage.[246]

Severe financial constraints encourage congregations to seek "avocational teachers" who are either volunteers recruited from within the congregation or teachers paid a minimal salary. School budgets are preponderantly paid out of the annual budgets of congregations, rather than through tuition fees. In Conservative synagogues, for example, in 1995, annual tuition fees for three-day supplementary schooling ranged from $230 to $440 per student. Such fees alone would hardly even cover the salaries of teachers, let alone administrative costs, supplies, textbooks, or special events. As currently structured, congregations are caught on the horns of a dilemma: they need to allocate significant amounts of the congregational budget to underwrite the religious school because the school is vital for the recruitment and retention of members; at the same time, congregations are afraid to ask parents to shoulder tuition fees that would pay for a superior Jewish education, lest those parents balk and abandon both the school and the congregation. The upshot is that religious schools are underfunded, yet their budgets drain congregational resources; this breeds resentment of the schools for their failings, even as those schools must function with inadequate funding.[247]

---

[245]Naava Frank, Daniel J. Margolis, and Alan Weisner, *The Jewish School Teacher: Preliminary Report of a Study* (Bureau of Jewish Education of Greater Boston, Center for Educational Research and Evaluation, 1992), p. 27.

[246]For reports on some of these efforts, see Paul A. Flexner, "The Goals of Staff Development: An Overview," *Pedagogic Reporter*, Mar. 1989, pp. 3–5; Saul B. Troen, "The Teacher Development Institute," *Pedagogic Reporter*, Mar. 1989, pp. 19–21; Carol K. Ingall, "Teaching Teachers: One Community's Experience," *Pedagogic Reporter*, Fall 1991/Winter 1992, pp. 16–17; Barry W. Holtz, Gail Zaiman Dorph, and Ellen B. Goldring, "Educational Leaders as Teacher Educators: The Teacher Educator Institute—A Case from Jewish Education," *Peabody Journal of Education*, Spring 1997, pp. 147–66.

[247]On tuition fees at Conservative synagogues, see Maurice Potosky and Martin S. Kunoff, "The United Synagogue Databank Survey: An Initial Report," *United Synagogue Review*, Spring 1995, p. 21. Tuition in Reform congregations ranges from $233–$533 for nonmem-

In addition to suffering from serious limitations of time and personnel, many supplementary schools also are weakened by unclear curricular goals. In fact, the actual, as compared to the prescribed, curriculum is one of the most obscure aspects of supplementary-school education. What is actually taught in such schools? To be sure, the education departments of the Conservative and Reform movements have developed curricular plans, and bureaus of Jewish education on the local level strive to define curricular goals. But it is acknowledged by most observers that schools are highly autonomous and often must shape their curricula to accommodate the abilities and limitations of their educational personnel.

A detailed survey conducted by the Union of American Hebrew Congregations provides valuable data on the curricular emphases in Reform supplementary schools. Holidays and the Bible are the most frequently taught subjects from kindergarten through grade 5, after which material on Jewish history, liturgy, and the Jewish life cycle is gradually woven in. In the middle-school years, some attention is devoted to rabbinic Judaism through the study of Midrash, rabbinic commentaries, and ethics. In the high-school years, the curriculum includes a potpourri of material ranging from sex ethics to comparative religions to comparative Judaism. The same schools also claim to teach Hebrew for prayer services for an average of 100 minutes per week, and two-thirds of the schools also claim to offer worship as part of the religious school. Since these schools meet only twice a week, it is far from clear when they have time to offer so broad a range of courses.[248]

An additional prism through which to view curriculum is the record of the textbooks that schools actually purchase. In the past 15 years, Behrman House, a trade publisher, has gained firm command of the field, taking orders from an estimated 70 percent of Reform supplementary schools;[249] in all likelihood, Conservative schools do not lag far behind in using materials produced outside their denomination. (Another house, Torah Aura Productions, has also captured some of this market.) Behrman House publications are generally the most handsomely produced on the market. They incorporate many of the newer production techniques, such as sidebars, boxes containing arresting statements, illustrations, and a magazine-like format.

---

bers and averages $343 per student; members presumably pay less. See Joseph, *Portraits of Schooling,* p. 17.

[248]Joseph, *Portraits of Schooling,* pp. 53–60. Only a tiny percentage of congregations claim to teach Hebrew primarily for conversation (table 26.1, p. 60).

[249]Interview with Rabbi Jan Katzew, director, UAHC Department of Jewish Education, Jan. 14, 1998.

According to the publisher, David Behrman, the key curricular emphases have shifted in the 1990s to the "3 H's"—Hebrew, History, Holidays.[250] Hebrew is primarily taught to prepare children to perform within the synagogue setting, especially at the celebration of their bar or bat mitzvah—that is, Hebrew is taught as a language of prayer, not as a language of modern communication or textual study.[251] This approach apparently satisfies parents and many rabbis and cantors charged with the responsibility of preparing young people for their bar or bat mitzvah, but it leaves products of supplementary schools sorely lacking in Hebrew language skills. Those who attempt to take Hebrew on the college level are rudely shocked when it becomes apparent, as the head of one such program has put it, that they "do not demonstrate any knowledge of the language, and consequently are placed in classes for complete beginners."[252]

The focus of teaching about the holidays is again to prepare children to participate in synagogue and home rituals.[253] The teaching of history includes Bible stories and current events, with a focus on great heroes whose lives serve as a "hook" for human-interest stories and "Jewish values."[254] The consequence of this approach to history was made manifest in a study of recent bar and bat mitzvah celebrants who had been educated in a Conservative setting. When asked to name a Jewish hero, they overwhelmingly chose biblical figures or modern Israeli leaders; few identified a Jewish hero of the Middle Ages—or a woman.[255] The coming generation in all likelihood will have fewer positive Israeli role models to call upon, because all the evidence suggests a declining amount of instruction devoted to Israel. Judging by the interest in curricular materials, ethics and Jewish values are replacing Israel as key subjects in the supplementary school.

---

[250]Interview with David Behrman, Dec. 18, 1998.

[251]Hence, Behrman House Hebrew textbooks have titles such as *Hebrew Through Prayer* (Terry Kaye, Karen Trager, and Patrice Goldstein Mason, 1994; revised 1996) and *The New Siddur Program: Hebrew and Heritage* (Pearl and Norman Tarnor, 1990). Most recently published, *The New Hebrew Primer* (Pearl Tarnor and Carol Levy, 1999) focuses almost exclusively on synagogue Hebrew.

[252]Ruth Raphaeli, "The Melton Curriculum and the Melton Hebrew Language Program for Afternoon Hebrew Schools," *Studies in Jewish Education* 4, 1989, p. 127, note 9.

[253]Ruth Lurie Kozodoy, *Jewish Holidays* (revised ed., 1997).

[254]Barry L. Schwartz, *Jewish Heroes, Jewish Values: Living Mitzvot in Today's World* (1996)

[255]Barry A. Kosmin, "My Hero—Insights into Jewish Education," in Wertheimer, ed., *Jewish Identity and Religious Commitment*, pp. 12–14. Kosmin poses the question: "Where have all the female heroes gone?" In fact, there have been ongoing efforts to redesign curricula to take gender into account, ranging from the language of prayer to the choice of classical texts that include women's experiences, to teaching "gender sensitivity." See, for example, Janna Kaplan and Shulamit Reinharz, *Gender Issues in Jewish Day Schools* (Women's Studies Program, Brandeis Univ., 1997).

The limited ability of the denominational arms (the Reform efforts were more successful than Conservative ones) to produce popular textbooks has led to a homogenizing effect, since it is now the publisher and the market that determine the essential goals and worldviews that are to be conveyed in supplementary schools. Educational leaders in both the United Synagogue and the Union of American Hebrew Congregations remain committed to shaping the curricula of schools within each of their denominations and aspire to recapture the market for curricular and text materials.[256] But until they succeed in producing, let alone distributing, their own materials widely, the texts that are used are not likely to include strong normative statements. Thus, workbooks on prayer expose young people not to the liturgical works of their own religious denomination, but rather to a neutral and inoffensive rendering of commonly used prayers. If there is any controversial question facing the nondenominational publisher today it is whether to picture boys and girls both wearing a skullcap—because some consumers require neither to don a yarmulke, others require only boys to do so, and still others require the equal treatment of boys and girls. As for the content of Jewish educational texts, the goal is to downplay what is particular to each movement.

Apart from the issues of time, personnel, and adequate textbooks, there is one additional drain on the resources of supplementary schools that stems, ironically, directly from the increasing success of day schools. As the latter have expanded, they have siphoned off many of the most engaged Jewish families and educators who in the past had invested themselves in supplementary education, thus depriving the schools of the most energetic and committed leadership. Moreover, the decision of leaders in the Conservative movement, especially, and to a lesser extent in the Reform movement, to speak out publicly in favor of day-school education has created a crisis of morale among the parent bodies of many supplementary schools. When the rabbi, educators, and denominational leaders favor day-school education over the congregation's own program, parents who opt for the synagogue school are left with a very ambiguous message. Should they listen to the religious leadership and send their children to a day school? Or should they send their children to their synagogue's school, which after all absorbs so much of the congregation's budget? As day-school education has spread in the Conser-

---

[256]Both Rabbis Abramson and Katzew (who head up the education departments of their organizations) stated their intentions to produce such materials for their movements. On the planned new Conservative curriculum, see Robert Abramson and Steven M. Brown, "Synagogue School Curriculum Initiative for the Conservative Synagogue School," *Melton Gleanings,* Winter 1998, p. 1ff. The Reform movement's department of Jewish education disseminates new curricular ideas and material in a handsomely produced journal called *Torah at the Center.*

vative and Reform movements, the gap within congregations between families who enroll their children in day schools and those who use the supplementary school has grown, thereby fragmenting many congregations at precisely a time when educational reformers seek to revive the supplementary school by winning assent for congregational "change."[257] Thus, even as educators are calling for its regeneration, the supplementary school is faced with a range of troubling dilemmas and ongoing limitations.

THE BRANCHING OUT OF FORMAL JEWISH STUDY

The last decades of the century have also witnessed an important growth in Jewish schooling during the years bracketing bar and bat mitzvah. Early childhood, long understood by psychologists and educators to be a formative period, has received new emphasis. "These are the magic years in which we can lay the foundation for a positive Jewish identity in our kids," says one parent. "At this age, they love learning about the holidays, singing Hebrew songs, and learning some Hebrew words . . . and it carries over into our family, too. They go around the house singing what they learned in school, and we celebrate Shabbat and holidays more because they demand it. . . . We hope that this positive attitude will be a solid foundation when their studies have to be more serious and when other interests and pressures may distract them."[258] Indeed, a limited amount of research has substantiated the claim that family observance of Jewish religious rituals increases when parents enter their children into child-care programs rich in Jewish content.[259] One study found greater observance of home rituals, such as lighting Friday-night candles and reciting the *kiddush,* and even increases in the number of Jewish friendships reported by parents.[260]

Preschool and early school programs have been growing apace both at Jewish community centers and in synagogues. Indeed, many of the latter regard such programs as vital feeders of the congregational schools — and thereby as a vehicle for recruiting new members. It is not unusual for synagogue-based preschool programs to enroll an average of 250 children

---

[257]Cohen, "Day School Parents in Conservative Synagogues," pp. 18–23.

[258]Leora Isaacs, "Jewish Schools of Thought," *Hadassah Magazine,* Mar. 1989, p. 32.

[259]Fishman, *Jewish Education and Jewish Identity,* p. 8, citing a study conducted by Ruth Pinkenson Feldman in Philadelphia. See also the latter's unpublished doctoral diss., "The Impact of the Jewish Day Care Experience on Parental Identity," Temple Univ., 1987.

[260]Ruth Pinkenson Feldman, "What We Know About Early Childhood Education," in Kelman, ed., *What We Know About Jewish Education,* esp. her reference to another study by Ruth Ravid and Marvell Ginsburg that arrived at similar conclusions based on a study conducted in Chicago; pp. 82–83.

in ten or more classrooms. Jewish community centers have also bolstered their programming for preschoolers, viewing it as a "portal" of entry into the organized Jewish community for many unaffiliated families. In short, early-childhood Jewish schools are booming, enrolling an estimated 50,000–70,000 preschoolers by the later 1980s, including some as young as 18 months, but mainly targeted at three-and-four-year-old toddlers.[261]

The major limitation of such schools is one of personnel. Due to the unusually low salaries commanded by early childhood educators, it is difficult to recruit well-trained teachers. A study of educators in three communities, for example, found that more than half of the early childhood teachers had no Jewish education beyond the age of 13, and nearly a quarter had received no Jewish education before age 13 either. Preschool programming, moreover, is a sector of Jewish education that employs large numbers of non-Jews.[262] Until this shortage of suitable personnel is solved, the growth of Jewish preschool programs may amount to a lost opportunity for the field of Jewish education—and the community at large.

Early childhood programs are also experiencing surging enrollments. Until the 1980s, only a small percentage—in the vicinity of 15–20 percent—of six-and-seven-year-olds were receiving a Jewish education, and those who were enrolled in programs either attended brief one-day-a-week sessions or day schools. Most parents were afraid to start their children too young, fearing they would grow bored quickly.[263] Due to the surge in enrollments in day school, a form of Jewish education that begins with kindergarten, and the greater receptivity of parents to Jewish schooling during the early childhood years, by the early 1990s approximately 55 percent of six- and seven-year-olds were enrolled in a Jewish school.[264]

The high-school years also offer the potential for serious study, but once students pass the age of bar and bat mitzvah, their levels of enrollment begin to plummet. Overall, it is estimated that among Jewish teenagers aged 16–18, fewer than one-quarter are involved in Jewish educational programs: 44 percent in day high schools, 29 percent in afternoon schools, and 27 percent in Sunday schools.[265] This stands in marked contrast to

---

[261]For some interesting accounts of model programs and curricula in some schools, see *Early Childhood Jewish Education,* ed. Barry Holtz (Council for Initiatives in Jewish Education, New York, 1996).

[262]Ibid., p. 7.

[263]Isaacs, "Jewish Schools of Thought," p. 32.

[264]Goldstein and Fishman, *Teach Your Children,* table 1, p. 8. Some 38 percent of these children are in day schools, and most of the rest are in Sunday-only programs (p. 11).

[265]Fishman, *Jewish Education and Jewish Identity Among Contemporary American Jews,* p. 6; and Goldstein and Fishman, *Teach Your Children,* p. 28.

the approximately 75 percent of children aged 8–13 who are enrolled in Jewish schools.[266] A comparison of enrollments in different communities reveals the following drop-off from ages 6–12 to 13–17: In Milwaukee the decline is from 83 percent to 28 percent; in St. Louis, by contrast, the decrease, not as sharp, goes from 72 percent to 52 percent; in Atlanta the figure drops from 54 percent to 25 percent; and in St. Petersburg, from 40 percent to 23 percent.[267]

This variability from one community to the next suggests that the two key factors determining whether teenagers will continue their Jewish education are the availability of schools and the expectations of parents and the local culture. The shortage of non-Orthodox day high schools renders it unlikely for teenagers to continue their intensive Jewish education (unless they are prepared to enroll in Orthodox high schools); in fact, the absence of such schools reflects and also encourages a culture of dropping out after the completion of lower- and middle-school education among day-schoolers. But it is also evident that some communities and synagogues are far more effective than others in winning over young people and their parents to sustaining Jewish education well into the teenage years, even if it is through supplementary schooling.[268]

Beyond the high-school years, a significant percentage of college-age Jews continue to enroll in formal Jewish schooling. In the Orthodox community, study at advanced yeshivas in Israel has become *de rigeur,* usually for a year or two before entering college. Most Orthodox day high schools encourage their graduates to pursue such study, viewing it as a kind of "finishing school" experience.[269] It is difficult to come by data on the precise count of such students (some estimates put the figure at 3,000 students annually by the mid-1990s), but certainly a majority of young Orthodox men and women study at Israeli yeshivas for the first year after high school.

Returning students and quite a number of others also study at advanced yeshivas in the United States. Depending on their ideological out-

---

[266]Goldstein and Fishman, *Teach Your Children,* p. 8. Interestingly, only 71 percent of boys and 86 percent of girls enroll during these peak years, possibly suggesting, as Goldstein and Fishman note, the strong peer pressure on boys to engage in team sports.

[267]Sheskin, *Geographic Variations,* table 59, p. 72.

[268]A recent study of education in Reform temples indicates that "nationally, there is an average 21% drop-off in religious school between grades 7 and 10, a 60% drop-off between grades 7 and 11, and a 63% drop-off between grades 7 and 12. It is probable that students leave the school once the bar/bat mitzvah is over (during grades 7 and 8), so that fewer congregations have post-bar/bat mitzvah classes." Indeed, half of all schools in Reform temples do not offer classes for 11th- and 12th-graders. Joseph, *Portraits of Jewish Schooling,* pp. 7, 66.

[269]For a study of students from modern Orthodox high schools who went on to spend a year in a yeshivah in Israel, see Shalom Berger, "A Year of Study in an Israeli Yeshiva Program: Before and After," unpublished diss., Yeshiva Univ., 1997.

look, they may devote the daytime hours to religious study and pursue their college education in the evenings. Numerous advanced yeshivas function in the New York metropolitan area—the Lakewood Yeshivah in New Jersey is one of the oldest—and other such programs can be found in communities as far-flung as Baltimore, Cleveland, and Memphis.[270] To these must be added undergraduate programs at Yeshiva University's colleges for men and women and Touro College, which also offer advanced Jewish studies and studies leading to a bachelor's degree. A novel development of recent years is the opening of advanced yeshivas for women, such as Drisha in New York.[271] Smaller but significant programs of full-time college-level study are offered by the List College of the Jewish Theological Seminary and some of the Jewish teachers' colleges, usually in a joint-program format with a nearby university or college.

To round out our discussion of post-high-school options, we should note the burgeoning of Jewish studies programs at colleges and universities. Since the 1960s, young Jews spanning the denominational spectrum have been able to continue formal Judaica studies while in college. These programs, with their rich offerings in Hebrew language, classical texts, Jewish history, literature, and culture, represent a remarkable efflorescence of Jewish learning. Writing in the *American Jewish Year Book* in 1966, Arnold Band enumerated a total of 60 positions for academics in Jewish studies; by the late 1980s, this figure had multiplied tenfold, and today it is even greater.[272]

It is not clear, however, what percentage of young Jews avail themselves of these courses or whether those who enroll are already among the more committed to Jewish life. A study conducted by the National Association of Professors of Hebrew in 1989 claimed an enrollment of 5,000 students in all Hebrew-language courses out of a Jewish undergraduate population of 240,000.[273] In the early 1980s, Hillel directors at

---

[270]A valuable listing of "Known Yeshivot Providing Intensive, Post-High School Talmudic Study in the United States" is appended to Charles Liebman's trailblazing essay, "Orthodoxy in American Jewish Life," pp. 93–97 (see note 54). See also William Helmreich, *The World of the Yeshiva: An Intimate Portrait of Orthodox Jewry* (New York, 1982). One of the leading advanced yeshivas currently is Ner Israel in Baltimore, which in 1992 enrolled 400 post-secondary-school students. Gary Rosenblatt, "Opening the Yeshiva Doors," *Baltimore Jewish Times,* Nov. 8, 1991, p. 67.

[271]See a description of this college and graduate-level program in a profile of Drisha's founder, David Silber, "Opening Traditional Texts to Women," *Moment,* Aug. 1989, pp. 33–34.

[272]Arnold J. Band, "Jewish Studies in American Liberal-Arts Colleges and Universities," AJYB 1966, vol. 67, pp. 3–30; idem., "Jewish Studies: A Generation Later," *Sh'ma,* Dec. 8, 1989, p. 17.

[273]Gilead Morhag, "Language Is Not Enough," in *Hebrew in America: Perspectives and*

14 campuses polled Jewish students and discovered that 42 percent had taken courses in Judaic studies.[274] It appears, therefore, that such courses supplement the Jewish education of but a minority of Jewish collegians.

Far more difficult to quantify is the correlation between enrollment in such academic courses and later forms of engagement with Jewish life. Certainly, courses do not explicitly prescribe how students ought to behave. University norms of dispassionate scholarship and academic freedom militate against professors' assuming an overt role in socializing young Jews to abide by communal norms.[275] Thus, from the perspective of this overview, Jewish studies on campuses should be regarded as "a parallel or independent entity," outside the structure of Jewish education. "Even though many programs were initiated because of the interest and financial support of a local Jewish community, once established," as Walter Ackerman has observed, "they are part of another world."[276] Even though many Jewish studies programs have local governing boards, they are guided by the requirements of the academic world and do not serve the Jewish community. Therefore, we will merely acknowledge this rich and important ancillary to the field of Jewish education and leave it to others to examine its contours and impact.[277]

Informal Education

By the middle of the century, as we have previously noted, a number of ancillary programs already complemented the extensive network of Jewish schools. These included summer camps, youth movements, campus programs, trips to Israel, and the like. For the most part, however, formal and informal education were viewed as distinct entities: Jewish schooling was "responsible for teaching the basic building blocks of Jewish literacy and knowledge," and informal Jewish education was thought

---

Prospects, ed. Alan Mintz (Detroit, 1992), p. 193. My discussion of Jewish studies programs draws upon a rich, unpublished paper written by Lisa Grant, a doctoral student in education at the Jewish Theological Seminary.

[274]Lawrence Sternberg, "A Profile of Hillel Leaders" (B'nai Brith Hillel Foundation and the Cohen Center, Brandeis Univ., Aug. 1990), cited by Lisa Grant in her essay "Companions in Conflict: Jewish Studies and the American Jewish Community," Spring 1996.

[275]See, for example, the symposium on "Jewish Studies in the Jewish Community," *AJS Newsletter,* Fall 1996.

[276]Walter I. Ackerman, *The Structure of Jewish Education, A Report to the Commission for Jewish Education in North America,* May 1990, p. 8.

[277]In this context we note as well the range of training institutions that prepare professionals for leadership in the Jewish community—rabbis, cantors, educators, communal workers, and academics. The programs of such training institutions also warrant separate treatment.

to focus on "Jewish sociability and identification."[278] By the 1980s, educators began to rethink the relationship between the two. In part, the distance between these two areas of Jewish education narrowed because many educators themselves straddled both: summer camps, for example, were often administered by school principals, and teachers often led trips to Israel. But on a deeper level, a change in thinking had begun to take place in the 1970s that blurred the lines between formal and informal education. As Bernard Riesman, a leading authority on the American Jewish community, put it: "Informal Jewish educators have been increasingly seeking to upgrade the priority given to formal Jewish content in their programs; formal Jewish educators have been increasingly attentive to utilizing informal educational values and methodology as means of better achieving their educational goals."[279]

What, then, is informal Jewish education? Its objective, according to educator Barry Chazan, is "to enable people to participate—usually with others—in a diverse series of Jewish life experiences for the inherent value in them. It is aimed at affecting Jewish attitudes and experiences of a person in the present, with the hope that these patterns will continue in the future." Informal education takes place in a structured and planned setting, but is far more focused on interactivity and student participation than is schooling.[280]

Some have interpreted the new receptivity to informal education as an act of desperation. In the words of one educator, the change in outlook "emerged from the growing sense of frustration with existing models and from a sense of success with some new alternatives."[281] Others, however, have argued for change on the grounds that Jewish education must not be understood as an analogue to public education; instead, as the former head of Jewish education in the Reform movement claimed, "We're simply not in the same business as the public schools. Our business is to teach how lives should be lived."[282] Given such a holistic and encompassing goal, it is argued, Jewish education must embrace Jews, especially young people, in a rich and interconnected network of settings for Jewish living and learning.

---

[278]Barry Chazan, "What Is Informal Jewish Education?" *Journal of Jewish Communal Service,* Summer 1991, p. 304. Chazan takes exception to the use of the terms "schooling" and "formal education" as synonyms, since the former refers to an organizational structure and the latter refers to an educational approach. The point is well taken, but this essay will continue to use the terms interchangeably.

[279]Bernard Riesman, *Informal Jewish Education in North America* (Commission on Jewish Education in North America, Dec. 1990), pp. 5–6.

[280]Chazan, "What Is Informal Jewish Education?" p. 304.

[281]Barry Chazan, as quoted in Riesman, *Informal Jewish Education,* p. 9.

[282]Quoted by Janet Marder in "The Trouble with Jewish Education," *Reform Judaism,* Summer 1993, p. 19.

FAMILY EDUCATION

Given this objective, it is hardly surprising that educators have been paying increasing attention to the family, the most important setting for all learning. The premise of Jewish family education was enunciated already in the late 1970s by Bernard Riesman, who argued that American Jews have adapted so well to the American scene that "Jewish families today have to work at Judaizing their lives just as their parents and grandparents had to work at Americanizing theirs."[283] Such a goal could be attained only through a deliberate educational program that would help narrow the oft-remarked-upon gap between the family and the school. By the late 1970s and early 1980s, demographic changes also created some new opportunities for family educators. For one thing, the baby-boom generation now began to have children. "Many of these parents," Joseph Reimer observes, went "through childbirth classes, read the extensive literature on raising children and [were] in general more ready to be involved in their children's education. They also, on the whole, have weak Jewish educations that need refreshing if they are to keep up with their children's Jewish learning." In addition, a significant population of converts to Judaism and interfaith families clamored for opportunities to educate themselves sufficiently so that they could participate actively in their children's Jewish upbringing. Jewish family education thus arose as a response to a particular *zeitgeist* and the needs of very specific populations.[284]

Jewish family education has developed in a variety of settings—including Jewish community centers,[285] day schools, and retreat centers—but it has been most prominently practiced within congregations and in conjunction with supplementary schooling. The primary goal of Jewish family education is to involve parents in their children's Jewish education. As one pioneer in this field explained, Jewish family education rejects the conventional strategy of Jewish education that asserts: "Send us your children and we'll send you back Jews." Rather it offers a different message: "Please take your child to his/her classroom. After roll-call, the class will join us for a program from the 'Curriculum of Caring.' You and your child will learn about. . . ."[286] Or, as another educator puts it: "Instead of doing the traditional Sunday school child drop-off, the Jewish family

[283]Bernard Riesman, "Jewish Family Education," *Pedagogic Reporter,* Spring 1977, p.

[284]Joseph Reimer, "Jewish Family Education: Evaluating Its Course, Looking to Its Future," *Journal of Jewish Communal Service,* Summer 1991, pp. 269–70.

[285]For a discussion of Jewish family education within the JCC setting, see Harlene W. Appelman, "Mission Mishpacha: A Continental Agenda for Jewish Community Centers," *JCC Circle,* Oct. 1991, pp. 8–9. See also Bernard Riesman's discussion of different venues for family education in *Informal Jewish Education in North America,* pp. 32–42.

[286]Harlene W. Appelman, "Parents and Children Find Judaism Works," *Moment,* Aug. 1993, p. 46.

education specialist wants parents to park their cars once in a while and spend the afternoon learning with their children."[287] Jewish family education, in short, builds upon the investment that parents are already making in their children's education to encourage more intensive parental engagement in the actual process of learning.

Although there is no unanimity on the exact definition of Jewish family education, certain basic elements are commonly accepted. First and foremost, the programs regard the family as the unit receiving an education and, accordingly, seek to involve every member of the family in the process.[288] They strive to give parents the skills and information they will need to live as Jews and thereby serve as Jewish role models for their children. However, the primary goal is neither the transfer of skills nor the acquisition of knowledge, but change in behavior within the family setting. Family education strives to communicate the need for lifelong engagement in Jewish study and other forms of Jewish living; it offers "props" and other materials to enhance the Jewish home; and it seeks to create a "non-judgmental," highly pluralistic setting in which participants will not feel coerced.[289]

In practice, most Jewish family education programs work to link families in joint celebrations and activities so that adults and children develop peer groups that reinforce each other's participation. Practitioners also strive to create settings in which parents interact with their children while learning about Jewish holidays, history, and culture. The most complicated goal, however, is to educate parents seriously on an adult level while simultaneously engaging in family education.[290] Some programs create parallel learning opportunities for parents to develop a sophisticated understanding of the material their children are studying in their formal school settings.[291]

Although it has caught on in congregations around the country, Jewish family education is hardly without serious deficiencies. The absence of a strong curriculum and structure results in an improvisational quality, and provides no means to enable adults or children to engage in

---

[287]Teresa Strasser, "Teaching Judaism Is Family Enterprise, Educators Say," *Jewish Bulletin of Northern California,* Feb. 7, 1997 (from the Web site).

[288]Some programs seek to involve grandparents and other members of the extended family. On these and other issues in Jewish family education, see Leora W. Isaacs and Jeffrey Schein, *Targilon: A Workbook for Charting the Course of Family Education* (Jewish Education Service of North America, New York, Feb. 1996).

[289]Harlene Winnick Appelman and Joan S. Kaye, "Curricularizing Jewish Family Education," *First Fruits,* pp. 491–92.

[290]Reimer, "Jewish Family Education," pp. 271–72.

[291]On an early experiment with such parallel learning for adults, see David Brusin, "The Promise of PEP," *Conservative Judaism,* Fall 1981, pp. 53–55.

graded learning designed to help them progress from one level to the next. Thus, when educators refer to the goal of "lifelong learning," they rarely can point to a defined structure of study that builds upon earlier stages of learning. In addition, while it is well and good to encourage parents and children to learn together, it is an entirely different matter to structure programs that can challenge both simultaneously. Jewish family education programs also attract significant populations of interfaith families, but they do not necessarily address the unique challenges within such family structures. It is also far from clear whether family education is directed at all families, including those with preschoolers or empty nests, or solely at families with school-age children.

The personnel issues that beset other forms of Jewish education bedevil this field too. When teachers of young children are suddenly asked to work with adults too, they may find themselves out of their depth. At a minimum, family educators require very different sets of skills than do teachers of children—although it is not always apparent what kinds of skills and training family educators require. Finally, while there is much excitement about family education, it is not a well-tested field and little is known about its impact.[292]

ADULT EDUCATION

Much of the same weakness and murkiness is evident in adult education programs. Adult study has proliferated helter-skelter in a wide variety of Jewish settings—congregations, JCCs, elderhostels, retreat centers, and the like.[293] Indeed, a great many institutions have invested heavily in adult study opportunity. To name just a few: Hebrew Union College runs a "Kollel" with adult education lectures; the Jewish Theological Seminary sponsors "Havruta" programs all over the country focused on classical texts; CLAL, the National Jewish Center for Learning and Leadership, sends Jewish educators to teach federation leaders about Judaism; Hadassah and other women's organizations promote study within chapters and for leadership groups; Holocaust museums offer public lectures; and the

---

[292]These dilemmas were outlined by Joseph Reimer in the early 1990s ("Jewish Family Education," pp. 275–77). On more recent efforts to address some of these issues, see the useful collection co-edited by Adrianne Bank and Ron Wolfson, *First Fruits*.

For an interesting dissenting view that frets over the "use of children as a lever to change adults" and argues that parental involvement may subvert the goals of the educational institution, see Fishman, *Learning About Learning,* citing the views of Samuel Schafler, p. 43.

[293]Betsy Dolgin Katz, "What We Know About Adult Education," in Kelman, ed., *What We Know About Jewish Education,* p. 99.

Florence Melton Adult Mini-School program has established 34 sites around the country for its two-year, 120-hour course.[294]

Many Reform and Conservative synagogues sponsor not only adult education courses that meet weekly, but also specific courses of study, including classes for potential converts to Judaism. Among the most popular have been special courses for women leading to celebration of an adult bat mitzvah; these programs, which entail intensive study over a year or two, enable women who never had much Jewish education or the opportunity to become a bat mitzvah to acquire key synagogue skills, such as reading Torah and leading the prayer services.[295] Within the Orthodox world, a Daf Yomi ("page a day") project that encourages daily Talmud study has attracted ever larger number of participants all across the country, some of whom meet in corporate and law office suites during the lunch hour.[296]

An entire industry also serves what has come to be called "outreach" — an imprecise term that may refer to bringing moderately engaged Jews into forms of greater participation, or to reaching the unaffiliated, or to reaching interfaith families. In the first category is the National Jewish Outreach Program founded by Rabbi Ephraim Z. Buchwald, which offers crash courses in Hebrew, Judaica, and prayer. The NJOP claims to have reached 100,000 Jews in its first six years. A number of other Orthodox groups, ranging from the Lubavitch Hassidic movement to the Jewish Learning Exchange of Ohr Somayach to Aish ha'Torah, also seek to appeal to non-Orthodox Jews and lead them to become *"baalei teshuvah," "returnees"* to Orthodox Judaism. Generally these programs score their greatest successes with Jews who have had some involvement with Jewish life and a Jewish education, that is, with the already moderately engaged. At the other end of the spectrum are programs to reach interfaith couples and their children. These may meet in JCCs or in synagogues. Stepping Stones to a Jewish Me, for example, offers two years of Jewish education for free to children of intermarried couples. In between are many programs offered by local institutions to attract the unaffiliated but curious.[297]

---

[294]For a good survey of the range of programs available, see Debra Nussbaum Cohen, "In Growing Numbers, Jewish Adults Are Seeking to Fill a Knowledge Gap," *Charlotte Jewish News,* Sept. 1998, p. 31. On the Florence Melton Adult Mini-School, see Betsy Dolgin Katz, "Creating A Learning Community: It Doesn't Just Happen," *Jewish Education News,* Spring 1998, pp. 26–28.

[295]Stuart Schoenfeld, "Ritual and Role Transition: Adult Bat Mitzvah As a Successful Rite of Passage," in *The Uses of Tradition: Jewish Continuity in the Modern Era,* ed. Jack Wertheimer (Jewish Theological Seminary and Harvard Univ. Press, 1992), pp. 349–76. According to one estimate, approximately 70 percent of Reform temples sponsored such programs. See "To Learn and To Teach," *Agenda: Jewish Education,* Fall 1997, pp. 29–30.

[296]Alfred I. Neugut, "Moonlighting as a Daf Yomi Student," *Sh'ma,* Mar. 20, 1998, pp. 3–5.

[297]Rahel Musleah, "The Identity Superhighway," *Hadassah Magazine,* Mar. 1994, pp. 10–13.

In recent years, enterprising Jewish groups have begun to harness the new electronic media to offer Jewish adult education. First came cable television programs with Jewish content in cities such as Boston, New York, Chicago, Miami, and Los Angeles. Often sponsored by local federations of Jewish philanthropy, these cable stations carry programs for youngsters and also adults. At the same time, the VCR revolution provided the opportunity to market educational tapes on Jewish holidays, the Hebrew language, and many historical subjects.[298] Most recently, there has been an explosion of Jewish Web sites on the Internet offering Jewish news and commentary, text study, formal Jewish courses, and even distance learning for college credit.[299]

The range and number of courses and lectures and computer learning opportunities offered across North America clearly attest to the interest of adults in further Jewish study. However, research is needed to assess their efficacy as educational instruments and their long-term effect on learners.[300]

THE JEWISH COMMUNITY CENTER MOVEMENT

Aside from the synagogue, no other Jewish institution in this country attracts as many members and participants as the Jewish community center (JCC). It is estimated that the 265 JCCs and their affiliated camps serve between one and one-and-a-half million Jews in some 120 cities of the United States (and nine in Canada).[301] JCCs offer a range of recreational activities—usually including a gym, work-out room, and pool—and sponsor programs and classes for all ages, especially crafts, drama, and the arts; most JCCs also run preschool programs, teen groups, and camping programs. Given this enormous reach and scope, it was a noteworthy development, indeed, when the JCC movement embraced Jewish education as a central feature of its mission.

---

[298]Moshe Waldoks, "Jewish Television," *Hadassah Magazine,* Feb. 1990, pp. 34–36.

[299]For some assessments by educators of the possibilities and pitfalls of Jewish distance learning, see the essays of Eli Birnbaum, Debbie Findling, and Burton I. Cohen and Judith Z. Abrams in *Jewish Education News,* Spring 1998, pp. 36–43.

[300]A survey conducted by the Syracuse federation found that adults were far more willing to engage in informal than formal Jewish education, particularly as the former is more adaptable to their needs and time constraints. Rae W. Rohfeld and Louis J. Zachary, "Participation in Adult Jewish Learning: Some Implications for Strengthening Jewish Identity and Continuity," *Jewish Journal of Communal Service,* Winter/Spring 1995, pp. 234–41.

[301]Richard Greenberg, "JCCs Soft-Sell Judaism: The Fine Line Between Jewish and 'Too Jewish,' " *Moment,* Apr. 1997, p. 34ff., offers a fine introduction to these issues. See also Steven M. Cohen and Barry W. Holtz, *Jewish Education in JCCs* (Council for Initiatives in Jewish Education, New York, 1996).

As noted above, JCCs came late to the field of Jewish education and had to overcome considerable internal resistance before they could take on a mission to offer serious Jewish education. A number of JCCs began to move in this direction during the 1970s, but the turning point came in 1984 with the publication of a report by the Commission on Maximizing Jewish Educational Effectiveness of Jewish Community Centers (known as COMJEE). The commission adopted a platform that defined

the Jewish Community Center in North America [as] uniquely qualified to function as a Jewish educational instrumentality of the Jewish community by providing a format of experiences, programs and services addressed to: (a) developing and reinforcing Jewish identity; (b) motivating and enabling the acquisition of Jewish knowledge; (c) developing and strengthening Jewish involvement; and (d) enhancing Jewish practices and participation based on Jewish values and pride.[302]

The commission went on to recommend specific goals to help members and their children understand the importance of Jewish schooling, learn more about a range of Jewish topics, identify more strongly with the Jewish people and Israel, and so on. To put some teeth into this new agenda, the commission urged JCCs to direct funding to Jewish education and to hire personnel capable of carrying out the new mandate.[303]

A follow-up task force convened in 1995 assessed the extent of changes after ten years and sharpened the educational mission further. Its "Vision Statement" urged the JCC movement

to maximize the use of the programs and services, the position in the community, and the accessibility of the Jewish Community Center to welcome all Jews, to help each Jew move along a continuum of Jewish growth, and to build Jewish memories. The ultimate goal is to create a community of learning Jews who are consciously Jewish; who are respectful of Jewish differences; who are knowledgeable of and committed to Jewish values and practice; who participate in synagogue life and in Jewish communal and cultural life; who make Israel a central component in their identities as Jews; and who manifest their Jewishness in lifestyle, life choices, and life commitment, thus creating a Jewish community capable of continuing creative renewal.[304]

One can hardly imagine a more dramatic change in direction from the positions of the JCCs just 40 years earlier.

What accounts for this about-face? Certainly, it is possible to read these documents as responses to the altered mood within the American Jewish community at large. Beginning in the late 1960s, a series of events in this

---

[302]*Report: Commission on Maximizing Jewish Educational Effectiveness of Jewish Community Centers* (JWB, New York, Sept. 1984), p. 6.

[303]Ibid.

[304]*COMJEE II: Task Force on Reinforcing the Effectiveness of Jewish Education in JCCs* (JCC Association, New York, May 1995), p. 9.

country and abroad redirected the weight of Jewish concern from its earlier integrationist agenda to a survivalist mission, a change from a primary emphasis on fitting into American society to a new preoccupation with insuring the inner strength of the Jewish community. The leadership of JCCs could not help but take notice of this shift in orientation. Moreover, as the JCCs were dependent upon local federations of Jewish philanthropy for considerable sums of communal money, they had to justify their importance to the Jewish community as more than a place for Jews to engage in recreational and social activities, but also as a setting with the capacity to strengthen Jewish life at home.[305] What better way than to redefine themselves as agencies vitally involved in a Jewish educational mission! Hence, the JCCs' new direction can be read as an astute adaptation to the changing mood of the American Jewish community, on which they have depended for considerable financial support. The second COMJEE vision statement, in fact, makes it dramatically clear that JCCs now project themselves as allies of other Jewish institutions, committing themselves to fostering greater support among their members for synagogues, Israel, and other forms of Jewish participation. Indeed, they portray JCCs as unique "entry points" for minimally affiliated Jews who are gradually encouraged by JCC personnel to deepen their involvement with other sectors of the organized Jewish community.

But there is also considerable evidence suggesting that the JCCs were undergoing an internal revolution, driven by a new type of leadership intent on remaking the centers. The new outlook was captured in 1986 in the following analysis: "The days when JCCs were primarily institutions for recreational activities with relatively incidental Jewish education qua Jewish education is no longer sufficient to meet the changing needs of today's Jewish communities in a world marked by computerization of the human condition and the trivialization of the Jewish ethos. The old type of JCC is obsolete and an albatross around the neck of the Jewish community."[306] This new outlook, moreover, preceded the so-called continuity agenda by six to seven years, suggesting a rethinking of JCC priorities well before the results of the 1990 NJPS created a bandwagon effect. Under the leadership of national leaders such as Morton Mandel and a cadre of local professionals, the JCC movement reinvented itself as an institution committed to a Jewish educational mission.

In the early 1990s, the extent of the changes that had taken place was measured in a survey commissioned by the JCC Association. Among the

---

[305]I have written at some length on this theme in my essay, "Jewish Organizational Life in the United States Since 1945," AJYB 1995, vol. 95, pp. 31–83.

[306]Murray Zuckoff, "JCCs: The Jewish Connection," *JTA Daily News Bulletin:* part 1, May 12, 1986, p. 3; part 2, May 13, 1986, pp. 3–4.

key findings: (1) Virtually all JCCs included adult Jewish learning in their programming, and over half offered classes on Basic Judaism and Basic Jewish Literacy. Half also ran programs for interfaith families. (2) Three quarters ran Jewish family education programs. (3) One-third sponsored trips to Israel with a Jewish educational objective. (4) The vast majority publicly recognized Jewish holidays and decorated their facilities to mark these festivals. (5) Significant percentages displayed the Jewish component of their work in visible ways—by having a Jewish library, Hebrew signs, exhibits of Jewish art, and the like. (6) Over 80 percent sponsored Jewish book fairs and sold Jewish art. (7) Growing numbers of JCCs encouraged their staff members to enhance their own Jewish education and to study in Israel. "The most important change," the survey researchers concluded, "has been the metamorphosis of a culture whereby 'things Jewish' have become more rather than less of a norm in the Center world."[307]

Perhaps the most tangible change has come in the area of staffing. In 1994, 45 percent of JCCs reported that they had hired a Jewish educational specialist.[308] By 1997, JCCs employed 70 full-time specialists in Jewish education, including a growing number of rabbis. As the former director of Jewish educational services put it: "We don't provide Jewish education because it is popular but because that's what we're about. We have to show our customers that we're taking Jewish education as seriously as Nike takes its shoe customers."[309]

This bold assertion also highlights some of the weaknesses of the JCC agenda. To begin with, as a half-billion-dollar a year enterprise, the JCC movement has no choice but to pay attention to its customers—and a growing number of these are not even Jewish. In order to qualify for government funding, all the major JCCs have altered their membership policies to admit members regardless of religion.[310] One can only wonder how a strong Jewish educational push squares with the open-door policy. But even among its Jewish members, educational programming is not a high priority. When JCC directors were asked in 1982 and 1988—that is, before and after the COMJEE initiative was begun—to list the key reasons

---

[307]Barry Chazan and Steven M. Cohen, *Assessing the Jewish Educational Effectiveness of Jewish Community Centers—The 1994 Survey* (JCC Association, New York, Oct. 1994), pp. i-iii. See also the earlier study of Bernard Reisman, *Social Change and Response: Assessing Efforts to Maximize Jewish Educational Effectiveness in Jewish Community Centers in North America* (JCC Association, New York, 1988).

[308]Ibid., p. ii.

[309]Greenberg, "JCCs Soft-Sell Judaism," p. 38.

[310]Gary Rosenblatt, "For the JCCs, A Quiet Change," *Baltimore Jewish Times,* Oct. 16, 1990, pp. 22–24; and Alan Hitsky, "Last Jewish JCC?" *Detroit Jewish News,* Oct. 30, 1992, p. 1.

why members come to centers, programs with Jewish content were listed as a distant third choice.[311]

The nature of such programs is also much in dispute, especially the extent to which they ought to address normative questions. One longtime Jewish professional, Gerald Bubis, flatly declares that "a center can never be prescriptive"; its ideology, he contends, "has been not to *have* an ideology." Instead, centers will always offer "Judaism on demand, rather than demanding Judaism." But the implicit message of JCCs does suggest a normative direction, for when an ever-rising percentage of JCCs remain open on the Jewish Sabbath[312] and run programs that do not serve kosher food, a certain type of Jewish ideology is being communicated — the ideology of secular Jewish culture. This approach is rejected by Rabbi Yehiel Poupko, director of the Pritzker Center for Jewish Education at the Chicago JCCs, and the chief proponent within the JCC movement for a more demanding Jewish content. Poupko has fought for a stronger emphasis on God and Torah within the JCC setting, for without them "there is no Judaism, no effective Jewish civilization, and there is no transmission of Jewishness from generation to generation."[313]

Summing up their findings on "the Jewish educational effectiveness of the centers," Steven M. Cohen and Barry Chazan acknowledge the significant distance JCCs have traveled on their own road to heightened Jewish identification, but they also concede that "Jewish education has [not] conquered the local JCC"— despite the best intentions of the national leadership of the movement. According to Chazan and Cohen:

> Many Centers still engage high proportions of non-Jewish staff. Most Jewish staff remains Jewishly ignorant or modestly knowledgeable at best. The funding of Jewish education remains an ambiguous area.... Boards are still unclear about their role in the process—and in some cases, as to whether the process is their responsibility.... All executives are not ideologically committed to the cause.[314]

Thus, despite its heartfelt embrace of a more positive Jewish mission and its self-conscious agenda of infusing center programming with Jewish learning, the JCC movement continues to struggle with what it means to "have special Jewish educational opportunities and obligations."[315]

---

[311]Reisman, *Social Change and Response,* "Summary of Findings," p. 3.
[312]Chazan and Cohen, *Assessing the Jewish Educational Effectiveness,* p. 16.
[313]Bubis and Poupko are quoted in Greenberg, "JCCs Soft-Sell Judaism," pp. 74–75.
[314]Chazan and Cohen, *Assessing the Jewish Educational Effectiveness,* p. 37.
[315]From *COMJEE II,* p. 8.

YOUTH ACTIVITIES

Jewish organizations have built a sprawling infrastructure of summer camps, youth programs, travel programs, and campus groups to offer young people attractive environments for informal Jewish education. These networks have assumed greater importance in recent decades as alarm over the "continuity" crisis has grown, particularly since their programs seem to produce more engaged Jews. Unfortunately, they reach only small proportions of the populations for which they are intended. Thus, despite their considerable potential to build and strengthen Jewish identity among youth, they exemplify the division of the Jewish community between those who have opportunities to become socialized and educated as Jews and the far larger population that is deprived of such learning experiences.

Perhaps the most powerful vehicle for informal Jewish education is the summer camp, an embracing institution that offers round-the-clock Jewish living. "The ability to impact on a kid in an emotional way can only happen at a camp where you develop personal relationships with the kids and they feel they have role models," says one camp director. "It's not taken out of context, like leaving Little League to go to Hebrew School and sitting and listening to someone teach you about Judaism, and then going home to watch television. Every activity we do relates to Jewish life. Campers experience it. They feel it. It makes the internalization that much more powerful." Not surprisingly, each of the major Jewish religious movements sponsors a network of Jewish summer camps, including day camps and residential ones. So, too, do a number of Zionist organizations and of course the JCC movement and federations.[316]

There is ample anecdotal evidence that camp experiences have shaped the Jewish lives of individuals who went on to become leaders in the American Jewish community. The title of an article in *Moment* magazine says it all — "Making Machers" — and in truth, quite a few rabbis, communal leaders, and other prominent individuals claim that their lives were transformed by intense camp experiences. For many young people, summer camp is their first exposure to a community dedicated to Jewish living, something they never witnessed in their own home communities. A tearful youngster bidding farewell at the end of a camp season is reputed to have remarked that "until next year, I won't see 300 Jews together on Shabbat." At their best, summer camps afford new opportunities for

---

[316]Jessica Davidson, "Summer Time and the Living Is Jewish," *Moment,* Feb. 1993, p. 57ff. The same journal publishes an annual directory listing the various Jewish camps and the locations of specific sites run by major Jewish organizations. See, for example, *Moment,* Feb. 1993, pp. 60–77.

glimpsing Jewish possibilities, especially for young Jews growing up in an environment bereft of a strong Jewish culture.[317] Unfortunately, only a small percentage of Jewish youngsters enjoy the chance to experience Jewish camping—perhaps fewer than 10 percent. A directory published by the Jewish Community Center movement enumerated slightly over 100 summer camps under organizational sponsorship. The Conservative movement's Ramah network of ten camps has enough beds for 4,000 campers; the Reform movement's camping network serves about 2,600 children. Both camping movements, in fact, have grown smartly in the past ten years. Orthodox camps and various Zionist and cultural ones are also burgeoning.[318] Yet even if we add in camps under private ownership that have some Jewish dimensions, there are probably no more than 55,000 young people attending Jewish residential camps annually, out of a potential population of some 600,000 Jewish youngsters between the ages of 8 and 17. One recent estimate put the number of children attending "the 100 overnight camps in North America run by Jewish religious or Zionist movements and communal organizations" at 30,000 annually, which amounted to some "4 percent of the camp-age population."[319] While cost is certainly a factor, many camps sponsored by Jewish agencies, in fact, offer scholarship assistance. And so, as we shall see, with other settings for informal education, the relatively low rate of enrollment results more from parental indifference than anything else.[320]

---

[317]Julie Greenbaum Fax, "Jewish Summer Camps: Making Machers," *Moment,* Feb. 1994, pp. 50–52. Clearly, this field warrants far more sophisticated examination. For an example of such research tracing the impact of the Conservative movement's Ramah camps, see Steven M. Cohen, "Camp Ramah and Jewish Identity: The Long-Term Influence on Conservative Congregants in North America," forthcoming in a volume to be edited by Sheldon Dorph.

[318]E.J. Kessler, " 'It's A-Camping We Will Go' Rings Out From the Woods," *Forward,* May 1, 1998, p. 1.

[319]Julia Goldman, "Bunks and Bug Juice: Boosting the Camp Trail to Jewish Identity," *JTA Daily New Bulletin,* Feb. 12, 1999, p. 1. This figure excludes children who attended privately owned camps that offer Jewish programming. Significantly, the article reports on the formation of a new Foundation for Jewish Camping designed to help camps create partnerships within the Jewish community and train counselors.

[320]Livia Bardin, "Are Jewish Camps Educational Stepchildren?" *Moment,* Feb. 1992, pp. 23–25. The article offers a valuable corrective to some inflated numbers that had appeared in Reisman, *Informal Jewish Education in North America,* pp. 44–46.

One of the more unusual camps catering to young people aged 18–28 is the Brandeis-Bardin Institute in Simi Valley, California. It offers a powerful educational program designed to challenge "disaffected young Jews to discover a Jewish world 'with depth, variety, passion and great meaning.' " Thomas Fields-Meyer, "When Generation X Asks 'Why?' " *Moment,* June 1995, p. 25ff.

Jewish youth movements also dot the landscape of the organized Jewish community. As previously noted, the Reform, Conservative, and Orthodox streams each sponsor youth movements, as do a few non-ideological organizations, such as the B'nai B'rith, and Zionist organizations. Among the latter, Hadassah's Young Judaea and the Orthodox B'nai Akiva are the most successful. According to one count taken around 1990, as many as 75,000 young people actually join, and perhaps another 25,000 occasionally attend programs of these teen-oriented movements, leaving at least two-thirds of Jewish adolescents without any youth movement involvement.[321]

Although data are hard to come by, it appears that rates of membership have plummeted in recent decades, and many youth organizations are mere shadows of their former selves—in both size and vigor. A spokeswoman for the Reform movement recently estimated that by 1998 no more than 15 percent of Reform youth were joining the North American Federation of Temple Youth.[322] An estimated 6,000 youngsters are members of Young Judaea, the youth movement of Hadassah.[323] The National Conference of Synagogue Youth (Orthodox) claims to serve 30,000 preteens and adolescents in 13 regions and several hundred chapters across North America.[324] And the youth programs of the Conservative movement claim a membership of 10,000 preteens in the Kadima program and 15,000 teens in United Synagogue Youth.[325] These figures indicate that only a minority of youngsters affiliated with these denominations join their youth movements. In fact, when a demographic survey of New York Jews conducted in 1991 examined participation in youth movements and summer camps, it found that 56 percent of Jewish children between the ages of 6 and 18 joined neither type of program, and only 12 percent were members of a Jewish youth group.[326] Thus, at precisely the time when young Jews become most keenly susceptible to peer pressure, most are not

---

[321]Reisman, *Informal Jewish Education in North America,* p. 31.

[322]Eric J. Greenberg, "Reform Targets Teens," *Jewish Week* (New York), Dec. 18, 1998, p. 8.

[323]Rahel Musleah, "Jewish Youth: Get with the Program," *Hadassah Magazine,* June/July 1995, p. 32.

[324]Nathalie Friedman, *Faithful Youth: A Study of the National Conference of Synagogue Youth* (NCSY, New York, 1998), p. 19.

[325]Data provided by United Synagogue Youth from its Annual Report, 1998.

[326]Bethamie Horowitz, *1991 New York Jewish Population Study* (UJA-Federation, New York, 1993), p. 125. (The study found that 23 percent had attended a Jewish camp.) A *Jewish Youth* Databook compiled by Amy L. Sales and produced under the auspices of Hadassah, JESNA, Jewish Community Centers Association, and the Combined Jewish Philanthropies of Boston managed to locate virtually no information on the numbers of teenagers in youth programs (Brandeis University, 1996).

involved in a youth movement that could channel them toward positive Jewish experiences in a program specifically geared to Jewish teens.[327]

CAMPUS PROGRAMS

The remarkable revival of Jewish campus programs in the 1990s stands as a dramatic counterpoint to the relatively anemic condition of contemporary Jewish youth movements. After nearly sliding into oblivion during the 1970s and 1980s, campus programs have received a significant infusion of new energy and capital. Impressive new Jewish centers have been rising on campuses across the country; and, even more important, a new generation of professional and lay leaders is transforming the entire field.

Jewish campus life has long been dominated by the Hillel network, which began with an organization founded at the University of Illinois in 1923 and then spread to many more colleges and universities. For much of its history, the B'nai B'rith Hillel system offered programs of disparate quality. On some campuses, Jewish student life was well organized, with a highly visible central address; in other instances, college campuses were in close proximity to strong Jewish communities where students could find services. But large numbers of Jewish students were situated on campuses where they could benefit from neither.[328] As a result, the campus was often seen by Jewish leaders as a place where Jewish identity would attenuate rather than gain strength.

As admission barriers to Jews dropped in the postwar decades, the sheer scope of the challenge to serve Jews on campus grew beyond the capacity of the B'nai B'rith, the parent organization of the Hillel network. It has been estimated that 80 percent of all Jewish college students are located at 109 universities with Jewish student populations greater than

---

[327]Recent research on alumni of the National Conference of Synagogue Youth, an Orthodox youth movement, concludes that the long-term impact of such programs can be quite beneficial in strengthening the Jewish commitments of young people. Although the population that joins NCSY is drawn from a narrow band of the already engaged, and respondents to the survey were self-selected, thereby insuring—as the author concedes—an overly positive set of responses, the findings are sufficiently intriguing to warrant further research on the immediate and the long-term impact of youth groups. See Friedman, *Faithful Youth*. There is an urgent need for programs to train and support youth workers who staff youth movements or work in synagogues or JCCs. A recent study found that most youth workers feel inadequately prepared and burn out quickly. See Gary Tobin and Meryle Weinstein, "Leadership Development and Professional Training of Jewish Youth Professionals," a joint publication of the Institute for Jewish and Communal Research and the Cohen Center for Modern Jewish Studies, Nov. 1998.

[328]See the survey *Campus and Community: Strengthening the Identity of Jewish College Students* (Ukeles Associates, New York, n.d.), p. 7.

1,000;[329] yet hundreds more campuses attract smaller Jewish student bodies. Even at its apogee of strength, B'nai B'rith could not reach all these students. And then, in the 1980s, the parent organization went into a decline and was forced to slash its allocations to Hillel by 50 percent. It is therefore all the more remarkable that during the 1990s Hillel severed its ties to B'nai B'rith—renaming itself Hillel–The Foundation for Jewish Campus Life—and not only rebounded but gained unprecedented vigor. By the late 1990s, it encompassed 120 Hillel foundations and affiliates at an additional 400 campuses.[330]

Under the energetic leadership of Richard Joel, Hillel has won support from major Jewish family foundations and local federations of Jewish philanthropy, both to build impressive new facilities and to underwrite new ventures. In recent years, spanking-new Jewish centers have risen on campuses such as Harvard, Columbia, New York University, the University of Maryland, and in Houston, one for students at Rice and the University of Houston. Its "Campaign for a Jewish Renaissance" raised $37.5 million in 1998 alone.[331] And new programs funded by large Jewish family foundations are expanding the scope of Hillel's work, which includes professional development courses for Hillel staff members, sponsored by the Schusterman Foundation; study trips to Israel for staff members, sponsored by the Gruss Life Monument Funds; the Steinhardt Jewish Campus Service Corps, a program to nurture Jewish student leaders on campuses; the National Jewish Student Service Campaign, funded by the Cummings Foundation for the purpose of encouraging Jewish students to design social action programs on campuses; and the Joseph Meyerhoff Center for Jewish Learning, which aims to establish batei midrash, traditional Torah study centers, albeit for men and women equally, and for the entire range of Jewish students on campuses.[332]

All of these programs are designed to create opportunities for Jewish learning that will complement formal courses of study offered by Jewish studies programs on campus. The distinctive experience Hillel aspires to offer is a form of traditional Jewish learning explicitly aimed at nurturing Jewish identification, an aspiration few Jewish academics would set for their courses and probably could not accomplish in any event. As the director of Princeton's Hillel observed: "There is no substitute for the

---

[329]Ibid.

[330]From a promotional booklet, "Hillel: The Campaign for Jewish Renaissance," n.d., ca. 1998.

[331]*Communities: 1998 Hillel Annual Report,* p. 10.

[332]Ibid., p. 6. *A Week in the Life of Hillel: 1997 Annual Report,* p. 9. And "Hillel Takes Torah to College," *Forward,* Nov. 21, 1997, p. 5, on the Meyerhoff Center for Jewish Learning.

kind of curricular critical analysis that Jewish Studies provides. Rabbis and the Jewish community do not 'own' the study of Jewish tradition and institutions. In the total economy of Jewish life on campus both Jewish Studies and Jewish Learning are requisite; both have their place and their role." Whether these two modes of Jewish study will coexist easily remains to be seen. But Hillel surely is intensifying its capacity to deliver informal Jewish education, and has set for itself a goal of nothing less than "a Jewish Renaissance."[333]

That task, as Hillel leaders would readily concede, is enormous. A survey conducted in 1990 found that only 15 percent of the 400,000 Jewish students on college campuses were affiliated; another 25 percent were thoroughly alienated and probably unreachable; and about 60 percent were inactive but potentially reachable.[334] By 1998 matters had not improved: a survey found that almost three-quarters of Jewish students rated their Jewish campus activity as minimal, and fully one-third did not participate at all; still, 8 percent claimed to be fully satisfied with their Jewish campus life, and another 32 percent said their Jewish campus organization sponsored many interesting activities.[335]

With its renewed energy and important new funding, Hillel is laboring to reverse these trends by reaching the inactive population while continuing to work with its core of affiliated members. Its leaders fervently embrace a mission to overcome the "Jewish illiteracy" of vast numbers of otherwise bright and well-educated young people who never had the chance to acquire a solid Jewish education prior to arriving on college campuses.[336]

ISRAEL TRIPS

Study trips to Israel, the last type of program of informal Jewish education to be discussed, are sponsored by over one hundred agencies within the American Jewish community. These trips have been touted as a "new

---

[333]James Diamond, "Creating a Culture of Jewish Learning on Campus," from a draft of "Toward an Educational Philosophy: Informing Hillel's Joseph Meyerhoff Center for Jewish Learning," Dec. 1997, pp. 24–25.

[334]Sales, *Jewish Youth Databook,* p. 31. We may note in this connection that Hillel often works in conjunction with campus organizations sponsored by the three major Jewish religious movements. But the Hillel foundations and their affiliates carry the major responsibility of reaching Jewish students on campuses.

[335]"It's Greek to Us," *Jewish Week* (New York), Feb. 12, 1999, p. 3. This study confirms that only a narrow band of young Jews participate in campus life, and of those who do, an overwhelming 75 percent had either attended a Jewish summer camp or youth group; some 29 percent also had attended a day school.

[336]Alvin Mars, "A Plurality of Learners," in "Toward an Educational Philosophy," p. 10.

rite of passage" critical for strengthening the Jewish identity of the coming generation.[337] According to one study, between 1992 and 1996, approximately 36,500 Jewish teenagers participated in an "organized educational trip" to Israel. This means that 2 percent of all Jewish youth aged 13–19 visit Israel on such a program in any given year, and that, overall, approximately 14 percent of teens participate.[338]

Most sober observers understand that a two- or four-week trip cannot serve as a substitute for a highly deficient Jewish education. It is not an elixir that will magically transform an alienated young person. For some visitors, however, particularly those who come with proper preparation, such a trip can be deeply moving and even transformative. During such trips, young people, if receptive, are confronted with profound questions of Jewish identity, morality, and peoplehood. They come into contact with a sovereign Jewish state, a Jewish army, and of course *eretz yisrael,* a parcel of land rich in religious and historical meaning to the Jewish people. For some participants, the experience serves as a critical opportunity to enlarge their Jewish self-understanding—but no one can guarantee such an effect.[339]

Research on these programs indicates that they are rated highly by participants. Measuring their long-term impact is a bit more complicated. Some studies suggest a kind of "domino effect," whereby "going to Israel leads to other positive Jewish experiences which . . . eventually leads to a more intense Jewish lifestyle." Others view it as part of a "cluster" of Jewish experiences that collectively shape a positive Jewish identity. And still others suggest that such a trip itself can have an independent positive influence.[340]

Still, such travel programs draw upon a relatively narrow band of the American Jewish community. For example, a study of teen programs found that one-third of participants had already been to Israel at least once before and that virtually all had a Jewish education and were already affiliated with the Jewish community. The most likely participants in teen programs are day-school students or alumni of such schools, members of synagogues and Zionist youth movements, alumni of Jewish summer camps, children of parents who have been to Israel, and products of rit-

---

[337]"The Most Complete Guide to the Israel Experience 1998," a supplement to the *Jerusalem Report;* David Breakstone, "Holy Land or Disneyland? The Israel Experience," *Moment,* Dec. 1995, p. 58ff.

[338]Barry Chazan, *What We Know About the Israel Experience* (The Israel Experience, New York, n.d., ca. 1997), p. 5.

[339]Breakstone discusses these issues quite sensibly in "Holy Land or Disneyland?"

[340]This research is summed up in Barry Chazan with Arianna Koransky, *Does the Teen Israel Experience Make a Difference?* (The Israel Experience, New York, Nov. 1997), pp. 12–14.

ually active families of some financial means.[341] In 1992 more than 6,000 Jewish high-schoolers and more than 1,000 college-age students participated in study programs in Israel, out of a pool of 350,000 potential participants.[342]

In recent years, a number of local federations and synagogues, as well as national Jewish organizations, have made stipends available so that every Jewish college student can undertake the journey. These subventions are predicated on the assumption that financial costs deter many young Jews from traveling to Israel. No doubt this is true in some cases; and even in families of some means, a free trip might tip the balance in deciding to send a child on one of these programs. Still, there is substantial evidence that a great many young Jews simply are not open to the idea. One such program sponsored by the New York Jewish community offers free round-trip airfare annually to as many as 300 Jewish college students who wish to visit Israel for the first time. Finding takers proved to be so much more difficult than expected that the program surveyed students to learn why they had declined the offer. Almost all the students who indicated that they would be traveling to other countries instead of to Israel also pleaded poverty when it came to the Israel trip—despite the fact that they would be given a free ticket. Others expressed fear: "I don't go to Bosnia, and I don't go to Israel," one of them told a recruiter. And still others expressed a different anxiety: a trip to Israel "might be 'transformative' "; it might lead them to become "too Jewish."[343]

Israeli institutions of higher learning also sponsor programs of more sustained study for college-age students. In 1998–99, approximately 1,800 college students from the United States enrolled at Israeli universities for a semester or a year, and, as we have noted earlier, around 3,000 also studied at a yeshivah in Israel. By comparison, it is estimated that in the same academic year, between 20 and 30 percent of the 67,000 American students matriculated at universities abroad were Jews. Clearly, study programs in Israel attract only a fraction of current Jewish undergraduates seeking to broaden their horizons.[344]

And again, those who choose to study in Israel represent the most Jewishly engaged population of young people. A study of students enrolled in 1987–88 found that half had studied in a day school, 31 percent in an

[341]Sales, *Jewish Youth Databook,* p. 27.

[342]Arthur Vernon, "An Educational Context for the Israel Experience," *Agenda: Jewish Education,* Fall 1992, p. 35.

[343]See Leora W. Isaacs, "Evaluations of Programs of the Israel Experience Center of UJA-Federation of New York" (JESNA, New York, Oct. 15, 1996). See also Samuel G. Freedman, "Why Birthright Israel Can't Work," *Jewish Week* (New York), Dec. 25, 1998, p. 22.

[344]Information provided by Moshe Margolin of the Lowy School for Overseas Students, Tel Aviv University.

afternoon school, and 19 percent in a Sunday school. The preponderant population came from Conservative homes, and 51 percent of these had attended a day school. (A high proportion also had attended a Ramah camp.) Moreover, a disproportionately high 20 percent of collegians from the Reform movement had also attended a day school. The researchers concluded that "prior Jewish education . . . turns out to play a dominant role in the students' socio-demographic profile. The year of study becomes in effect part of a wider process of Jewish socialization involving schools, youth groups, and prior visits to Israel. The one-year program is a link in a chain."[345]

This last image is perhaps a fitting one with which to conclude our discussion of informal Jewish education. Most programs draw upon populations that are already linked to formal Jewish schooling—and the more intensive the formal education, the more likely that younger Jews will also participate in informal settings for Jewish learning. For children, the key determinant is the disposition of their family—that is, whether their parents will deliberately decide to immerse their children in a range of Jewish educational settings that will, like links in a chain, reinforce one another. As these youngsters reach the age when they make more independent decisions, those who opt to place themselves in settings of informal Jewish education are generally continuing on a path they had begun to traverse at earlier ages. In turn, those engaged in such programs are most likely to mature into committed Jewish adults.[346] Unfortunately, many of the young people who most need informal educational settings to substitute for a weak Jewish schooling are the least likely to be given such opportunities.

Jewish Education as a Communal Endeavor

The field of Jewish education, as we have noted, has long suffered from insufficient coordination among the numerous autonomous schools, programs of informal education, and various communal agencies. Most in-

---

[345]Dov Friedlander, Penina Morag Talmon, and Daphne Ruth Moshayov, *The One Year Program in Israel: An Evaluation. North American Jewish Students in the Rothberg School for Overseas Students at the Hebrew University* (American Jewish Committee, New York, Feb. 1991), pp. 3–4. Relatively few Orthodox students were in the sample, presumably because they opt to study at a yeshivah rather than a university.

[346]The impact of these various programs on rates of intermarriage is assessed by Bruce Phillips in *Re-Examining Intermarriage*, pp. 14–41. Phillips concludes that "the lowest rates of mixed marriage by far are found among respondents with the most intensive and longest continuing formal Jewish education who also participated in non-formal Jewish educational experiences" (p. 32). He places special emphasis on high-school dating patterns as determinative of future marital choices (pp. 35–40).

stitutions in the field fend for themselves, coping on their own with the challenges of maintaining financial solvency, hiring educational personnel, shaping curricular goals, and defining their roles within the larger Jewish community. There have been some efforts to overcome this, but for the most part, there has been more diffusion than coordination in the field. Moreover, until recently, Jewish education was not able to recruit enough strong advocates to argue its case within the leadership circles of the organized Jewish community—the local federations and the national umbrella organizations. As a result, the needs of Jewish education have never benefited from the kind of financial investment and passionate advocacy that the American Jewish community mustered in behalf of the great campaigns to rescue and defend needy Jews abroad or even the struggle to influence American public policy on matters of Jewish interest.[347]

All that has begun to change in the last 15 years. Precisely as the field reached its lowest point of morale, a number of wealthy and powerful patrons embraced the cause of Jewish education. Quite by design, these benefactors have fostered new partnerships between Jewish foundations and local federations to fund programs of formal and informal Jewish education. The cumulative impact of these communal and philanthropic initiatives has been to infuse the field with a new vitality and optimism—and to draw attention to its needs.

The goal of the new benefactors is not only to remake particular educational programs, but to achieve something much more ambitious—the creation of new partnerships between the field of Jewish education and other sectors of the larger Jewish community. In short, a new kind of thinking seeks to minimize the diffusion and replace it with something approaching a strategic plan. This means, in the first instance, that educators seek to recreate American Jewry as "a community of learners." As one writer has put it:

> There is growing recognition around the country that the total community ought to become the learning environment for Jews (adults as well as children). Yet, there has yet to develop a serious, integrated, systematic approach to education within the Jewish community context. This . . . ought to be the main agenda for Jewish educational and community professionals and lay leaders—dreaming and designing a Jewish community in which all its institutions are educative, in which all the settings in which Jews live and work and play meet to capitalize on their educational potential for enriching Jews and Jewish life.[348]

---

[347]On the evolving agenda of the organized Jewish community and the emergence of new types of organizations to address changing needs, see Wertheimer, "Jewish Organizational Life in the U.S."

[348]Ronald Kronish, "Jewish Education: Schools and Society," *Religious Education,* Winter 1987, pp. 37–38.

Jonathan Woocher, the field's leading communal professional on the national level, has embraced this goal and called for "more Jewish *community,* not just more Jewish *programs,"* for only "a holistic Jewish education, anchored in the life of real Jewish communities and capable of interpreting and communicating the depth and complexity of that life, is . . . likely to have a decisive impact on the development of Jewish identity."[349]

In order to achieve this strategic goal, it is now argued, new alliances have to be forged between institutions, including schools of various types, synagogues, Jewish community centers, the religious denominations, federations of philanthropy, and major foundations. Rather than continue to live with great diffusion of energy, these agencies are now urged to orchestrate "the interplay of various institutional actors so that the whole is indeed greater than the sum of its parts."[350] Given the strong centrifugal forces generated by American voluntarism and individualism, these efforts will in all likelihood fail to achieve widespread coordination, but in the short term, some remarkable new partnerships have been formed that have made it possible to experiment with new approaches and to imagine bold new educational ventures.

THE NEW PARTNERSHIPS WITH FOUNDATIONS AND FEDERATIONS[351]

Much of this new thinking has been promoted by a cadre of professionals working for federations of Jewish philanthropy and grants officers at large family foundations. The latter institutions, in fact, have emerged in the last years of the century as major vehicles for funding Jewish activities and encouraging new endeavors. According to one estimate, some 3,000 Jewish family foundations had been established by 1996, a number that undoubtedly continues to increase.[352] Many of these foundations allocate virtually none of their resources to Jewish causes, and even those that do contribute to Jewish institutions still direct the bulk of their funding to nonsectarian philanthropies. Nonetheless, a sufficient number of foundations offer grants to Jewish institutions and projects so as to make a difference, especially in the field of Jewish education, which has managed for so long on a bare-bones budget.

---

[349]Jonathan Woocher, "Toward a 'Unified Field Theory' of Jewish Continuity," in Aron, Lee, and Rossel, *A Congregation of Learners,* p. 33 (see note 31).

[350]Ibid., p. 47.

[351]For a broader analysis of family foundations and donor-advised funds under federations, see Jack Wertheimer, "Current Trends in American Jewish Philanthropy," AJYB 1997, vol. 97, pp. 15–18, 73–78.

[352]Evan Mendelson, "New Ways of Giving," *Sh'ma,* Sept. 6, 1996, p. 3.

A parallel effort has also been launched by quite a few federations of Jewish philanthropy to channel new money to local educational institutions. Some federations have increased the amounts they allocate for Jewish educational programs from the funds they raise annually. In addition, a number of federations have tried to direct new money to the field from endowment funds and foundations under their purview. The latter include donor-advised funds and supporting foundations, which are incorporated under federations of Jewish philanthropy. Collectively, these endowment and other so-called participatory funds amounted to $6.2 billion by 1998; rising sums of money from these funds are channeled to Jewish agencies in the form of grants, including to educational institutions. With these funds and new allocations from their annual campaigns, local federations have helped underwrite educational projects and have created "continuity commissions" to devise new educational programs and coordinate existing ones.

The various private foundations and those under federation auspices often work closely together with federations and other agencies of the Jewish community. In part, this cooperation is based upon pragmatic needs: family foundations must rely on existing institutions to implement programs, since the federation agencies have the direct contacts with key communal institutions and leaders. Many foundations also prefer to "leverage" their money by offering "matching grants"; they see a benefit in working with partners so as to maximize the impact of their giving. Equally important, a number of wealthy donors wish to foster cooperation between different sectors of the community and various institutions because they are convinced that a more comprehensive strategic plan will best serve the interests of the field.

Given the overlap among funding sources, it is sometimes difficult to disentangle the various funders of programs. A case in point is some of the Hillel and Israel travel programs discussed in the previous section, many of which are funded by local federations, synagogues, and Jewish community centers, as well as foundation sources. All of these institutions are helping to underwrite the costs of programs—and often they do so cooperatively. What follows then is an attempt to identify some of the more interesting new educational ventures and the types of funding they are drawing upon, including foundation money, federation allocations, and a mixture of the two. Our purpose is to illustrate some of the larger trends, rather than to provide a comprehensive survey of every program.

Foundation Initiatives[353]

Wealthy Jewish families have long served as benefactors of Jewish educational institutions by supporting the ongoing work of schools, training programs, seminaries, summer camps, and the like. Much of the infrastructure of Jewish education continues to rely upon such largess. In recent years, however, a number of larger family foundations have attempted to move beyond the funding of an individual school or program to tackle broader issues in a more systematic fashion.

One such challenge that has received perhaps the greatest amount of attention is the funding crisis within day schools. A comprehensive study of this issue by Marvin Schick and Jeremy Dauber found that day schools expended between $5,400 to $5,600 per student in 1995–96.[354] In order to raise these funds, they must rely upon tuition income, fees, and fundraising. Yet, with all this, most day schools remain underfunded and cannot offer the types of facilities, sophisticated technology, "enrichment programs," and extracurricular activities found in many other private and public schools. The funding crisis also creates a dilemma for schools: Should they continue to increase tuition fees in order to offer as enriched a program as possible (thereby attracting only families that can afford to pay steep tuition), or should they work to make it affordable for as many families as possible to send their children to day-school—and do away with frills in favor of scholarship assistance?

Orthodox schools tend to stretch their resources to the limit in order to avoid turning anyone away, and they then pay a price in reduced salaries for their teachers, shabby facilities, and so on. Non-Orthodox day schools offer somewhat less scholarship assistance, with the result that some middle-class families reluctantly decide against day-school education for their children because they cannot afford to pay tuition for several children in addition to other household expenses. Making such hard decisions is often quite painful to schools and families. "This letter is extremely difficult to write, as it marks the end of a dream," wrote one parent to the principal of a Solomon Schechter school, "the dream of our children receiving a Jewish day school education."[355] For ardent proponents of intensive Jewish education, such a letter is heartbreaking—and shameful, if not hypocritical, in a Jewish community preoccupied with

---

[353]My discussion of foundations draws upon a graduate school paper, "Jewish Family Foundations and Their Role in Jewish Day School Policy," written by Dina Huebner Gerber for a course I taught at the Jewish Theological Seminary.

[354]*The Financing of Jewish Day Schools,* p. 9.

[355]Lisa Hostein, "The Cost of Jewish Education," *NCJW Journal,* Fall 1992, p. 4.

insuring its "continuity" but unable to marshal the resources to offer an intensive Jewish education to every child who wants it.[356]

Several foundations have begun to address the tuition crunch. The Samis Foundation in Seattle, for example, determined that high tuition was a serious deterrent to enrollment in the local day high school. It therefore developed a program with the school whereby tuition was capped at $3,000, and the foundation agreed to pick up the tab for the difference.[357] The idea proved so attractive that the Avi Chai Foundation, based in New York, which has a strong interest in promoting day school education, initiated voucher programs in Cleveland and Atlanta entitling families to $3,000 of free tuition a year, provided that children are not currently attending a day school or have not been enrolled in recent years. The goal, clearly, is to attract new families to day schools by helping them with tuition costs.[358]

Similar efforts have now been launched by private donors in a number of local communities. Eight individuals in Northern Virginia founded the Jewish Education Fund to make a day-school education financially accessible. In a number of communities, such as Los Angeles, Baltimore, and Chicago, proponents of day-school education are threatening to organize a campaign to discourage giving to federated campaigns in favor of support for special endowments that will underwrite day-school costs.[359] Indeed, George Hanus, an outspoken leader in Chicago, has challenged the local federation to establish such an endowment and to help him raise $50 million to underwrite scholarships for children.[360] (His

---

[356]For a good overview of these issues, see Marilyn Henry, "Jewish Education at a Price: A Re-Examination of Day Schools Is Under Way," *Manhattan Jewish Sentinel,* Jan. 29–Feb. 4, 1999, pp. 6–7. The funding crisis in day schools and the inability of many middle-class families to afford tuition costs has prompted some rethinking in the American Jewish community about school vouchers and other forms of government aid to parochial schools. For some discussion of these controversial issues, see the contributions by Daniel J. Elazar, Martha Minow, Jacqueline Kates, and Steven Brown to a symposium in *Sh'ma,* Dec. 1998 (vol. 29, no. 557). See also Alan M. Fisher, "Jewish Attitudes Toward Private Schools Vouchers: A Research Note" (Wilstein Institute, Fall 1993).

[357]*Parent/Student Update—Special Edition,* a publication of Northwest Yeshiva High School, Nov. 1997.

[358]"Nurturing Jewish Education," *Cleveland Plain Dealer,* Sept. 12, 1998, p. 1F, and Susan Bernstein, "$1 Million Voucher for Atlanta Jewish Schools," *Baltimore Jewish Times,* Apr. 10, 1998, p. 8. Not accidentally, given its strong interests in day-school education, the Avi Chai Foundation sponsored the Schick/Dauber study.

[359]"Baltimore Federation Is Faulted As Schools Struggle Moves East," *Forward,* Dec. 19, 1997, p. 1; Elissa Gootman, "Tensions Flare Over Day Schools," *Forward,* Apr. 24, 1998, p. 1.

[360]George Hanus, "Tuition's True Costs," *Baltimore Jewish Times,* Apr. 17, 1998, p. 8; Cohen and Brauner, "Day Schools Face Funding Crisis," p. 11 (see note 196).

organization is known as the National Jewish Day School Scholarship Committee.)

Equally noteworthy was the creation in 1997 of an $18-million fund by leading Jewish philanthropists to help underwrite the start-up costs of 25 new day schools around the country. Known as the Partnership for Excellence in Jewish Education, the new fund offers challenge grants to developing day schools of every denomination, and expects to make average grants in the vicinity of $300,000. The partnership has drawn attention because it brings together a number of major Jewish philanthropists in a collaborative effort with the UJA-Federation of New York. As such, it not only represents a new infusion of capital into the day-school sector of Jewish education, but also tangibly furthers the goal of greater coordination among schools, federations, and foundations. Each of the donors to the partnership already has a track record of giving to favorite causes; the decision of major donors to band together also symbolizes the new desire to further Jewish education by bringing together key institutions and leaders to work in concert toward larger ends.[361]

Supplementary-school education has won foundation support of a different sort. Since almost all supplementary schools operate out of congregations, a number of foundations have developed programs aimed at "synagogue change." Among the first of these was the Experiment in Congregational Education sponsored by the Mandel Associated Foundations and the Nathan Cummings Foundation. Based at the Rhea Hirsch School of Education at the Hebrew Union College in Los Angeles, this program worked exclusively with schools in Reform temples.[362] The ongoing efforts of Synagogue 2000, by contrast, cuts across the denominations and receives substantial funding from a number of foundations. Designed to foster a broad-gauged "transformation of synagogue structure and culture" by employing business and management techniques, Synagogue 2000 has, inevitably, also addressed learning within the congregation.[363]

Finally, we may note various programs to develop educators at both

---

[361]Debra Nussbaum Cohen, "Heavy Hitters Pledge $18 Million to Create New Jewish Day Schools," *JTA News Bulletin,* Oct. 22, 1997, p. 1. See also *The North American Jewish Day School Challenge Grant* (Partnership for Excellence in Jewish Education, New York, July 1997). The partnership also provides services and information to help the new day schools with curriculum and staff development. Contributors to the partnership are Leonard Abramson, the Avi Chai Foundation, Charles Bronfman, Edgar Bronfman, Harold Grinspoon, Erika and Michael Jesselson, Morton Mandel, Charles Schusterman, Michael Steinhardt, and Leslie Wexner.

[362]See Aron, Lee, and Rossel, *A Congregation of Learners* (note 31).

[363]The overall goals and mission of Synagogue 2000 are described in "Synagogue 2000 — Facts at a Glance," issued by the organization.

supplementary and day schools, funded by the Mandel Associated Foundations (through the Council for Initiatives in Jewish Education, CIJE), the Avi Chai Foundation (especially in the field of family education), and the Covenant Foundation, which seeks to nurture leadership through its awards program.[364] In most instances, these foundation-funded programs required grant recipients to work cooperatively either with parallel institutions in other Jewish communities or with agencies within their own communities. These efforts demonstrate how an independent foundation "unrelated in any formal way to communal organizations nor constrained by their investment in what is, can mobilize an entire community in the name of Jewish education."[365] Such is the power of the purse.

Several foundations are also investing heavily in leadership development within the field of Jewish education. The pioneer in this area has been the Wexner Foundation, which has run fellowship programs since 1988. With probably the most sharply focused program of any foundation working in this area, the Wexner Foundation annually awards fellowships to graduate-level students entering programs of study for the rabbinate, Jewish communal service, Jewish education, and Jewish academic studies. It has also supported programs at training institutions.[366]

Finally, several foundations have invested heavily in programs of informal Jewish education. Among those that have won the widest attention are study programs in Israel. A consortium of the UJA-Federation of North America, the Jewish Agency, and the Charles R. Bronfman Foundation was established in 1996 to double the number of participants in study programs in Israel. Subsequently, Michael Steinhardt, a leading Jewish philanthropist, announced a program called Birthright Israel; its goal is to make it possible for every Jewish youngster to participate in a study trip to Israel.[367] A different consortium of private foundations, led by the Koret Foundation and several family foundations, has

---

[364]On the CIJE, see Barry Holtz, Gail Dorph, and Ellen Goldring, "Educational Leaders as Teacher Educators: The Teacher Educator Institute—A Case from Jewish Education." On the Avi Chai Foundation, see the report *Avi Chai 1995–97.* And on the Covenant grants, *The Covenant Awards 1997: The Spirit of Jewish Education in North America.*

[365]Ackerman, "Reforming Jewish Education," p. 13. Ackerman was specifically describing the Lead Community Project of the CIJE.

[366]Steven M. Cohen, Sylvia Barack Fishman, Jonathan D. Sarna, and Charles Liebman, *Expectations, Education and Experience of Jewish Professional Leaders: Report of the Wexner Foundation Research Project on Contemporary Jewish Professional Leadership,* Research Report no. 12 (Cohen Center, Brandeis Univ., Apr. 1995) and *The Wexner Foundation: Marking a Decade,* 1997. We may note in this context a $15 million endowment given by William Davidson to establish a school of Jewish education at the Jewish Theological Seminary, the largest single gift to a training institution for Jewish educators.

[367]Julia Goldman, "Israel or Bust: Philanthropists, Educators Join to Make a Trip to the Holy Land Integral for Youth," *Manhattan Jewish Sentinel,* Oct. 9, 1998, p. 13.

teamed with the Jewish Community Federation of San Francisco, the Peninsula, Marin and Sonoma Counties to provide Jewish teenagers with a variety of opportunities to "enhance their Jewish identities through synagogues and organizations serving Jewish youth." The Teen Initiative, as it is called, includes trips to Israel, but focuses primarily on a range of programs sponsored by local groups to embrace teens in Jewish activities.[368]

FEDERATION EFFORTS AND "CONTINUITY COMMISSIONS"

The participation of the federation world in Israel study programs is illustrative of the increasing role such communal agencies are playing in the field of Jewish education. Much of the federation investment in Jewish education is channeled either through the traditional conduit of bureaus or central agencies for Jewish education or through newly created Jewish Continuity Commissions. The latter were established primarily in response to the "continuity crisis" identified by the 1990 NJPS; but in fact several continuity commissions had begun to function in the mid-1980s.

According to a survey conducted in 1993 of 158 Jewish communities, 42 reported that they had established a communitywide planning process on Jewish continuity, identity, or education (sometimes this was directed by a standing agency and in other cases by a newly formed commission). Among the concerns of these commissions were the "ability to identify and reach the unaffiliated; avoiding duplication of efforts by congregations, agencies and institutions [and] reaching consensus regarding priorities and/or special initiatives (e.g., a community in which there was some feeling that there was too much emphasis on the Israel Experience)." After studying quite a number of mission statements issued by these agencies or commissions, Walter Ackerman concluded that "Jewish continuity means different things in different places. In some communities continuity was equated with Jewish education, values and culture; in others it was comprehended as ensuring the vitality of the Jewish community; another group thought of it as promoting the Jewish identity of individuals."[369]

A number of communities have in fact developed ambitious programs to channel federation money into Jewish education. Here is a sampling of some of the diverse programs devised by continuity commissions: In New York, the Jewish Continuity Commission has been awarding grants to a range of institutions since 1994–95. The goal is to fund "institution

---

[368]"The Teen Initiative: Year Two Plan for Comprehensive Teen Programs" (Bureau of Jewish Education, San Francisco, Mar. 5, 1999).

[369]Ackerman, "Reforming Jewish Education," p. 8.

wide initiatives, not programs" falling into four categories—block grants to institutions, target population grants, professional or volunteer leadership development grants, and special initiative grants. During the first five years of the program, some 80 institutions were awarded grants of up to $75,000 each, mainly to reach marginally affiliated Jews. Recipients included synagogues that won grants to hire special personnel, such as artists-in-residence, to fund teen programs, and to create new forms of study, including those harnessing new technology; schools were awarded grants to reach new immigrants and serve populations with special needs; Jewish community centers benefited from grants for creating Jewish museums, family education programs, and centers for immigrants from the former Soviet Union.[370]

The Boston Commission on Jewish Continuity has developed three major initiatives: (1) A two-year adult study program called Me'ah offers 100 hours of learning over a two-year period. The program is cosponsored by the commission and the Boston Hebrew College and is aimed at adults. (2) Sh'arim is a program to provide families with direct access to family educators. (3) A Youth Educator Initiative trains professional youth educators and places them in settings where they work with teenagers. (The latter two programs strive to create full-time positions for teen workers and family educators and then allocate workers to a number of institutions.) All of these programs are designed to work with synagogues, day schools, and JCCs; as of the spring of 1998, 29 such institutions participated in some or all of these efforts.[371]

In Philadelphia, a strong emphasis has been placed on developing early childhood programs and building cooperation between federations and synagogues to strengthen congregational schools.[372] The Jewish Federation of Metropolitan Detroit has proposed a $10-million "Millennium Campaign" to fund "innovative" educational programs in synagogues. "The creative survival of our Jewish community into the 21st century," asserts the Detroit federation's executive director, Robert Aronson, "will depend upon two partners working together: the federation and the synagogue." The goal of the Detroit campaign is to "create a model in how federations and congregations can work together to strengthen the synagogue as a whole and the educational system in particular."[373]

In the San Francisco Bay Area, the federation has established a special

---

[370]*Jewish Continuity: 1995–98 Grants of the UJA-Federation Jewish Continuity Commission* (UJA-Federation, New York, n.d.); and *Jewish Continuity: 1996–99 Grants of the UJA-Federation Jewish Continuity Commission* (n.d., ca. 1998).

[371]*To Be Continued . . . An Update from the Boston Commission on Jewish Continuity,* Spring 1998, p. 1.

[372]*Networking for Planning Information 6, 1994–1995* Update (JESNA, Aug. 1995), p. 69.

[373]Elissa Gootman, "Charities Shifting Focus, Are Starting New Drive for Jewish Renaissance," *Forward,* Feb. 5, 1999, p. 4.

umbrella campaign to help fund educational programs such as the renovation of the Stanford University Hillel and an $11 million development plan for the community day school.[374] The Jewish federation in Chicago has agreed to help manage and supplement a $30-million endowment fund specifically for day schools. One aspect of this program will enable individual schools to organize their own endowment campaigns with staff help from the federation; a second prong will be an effort by the federation itself to encourage individuals to contribute to a federation-run fund through planned gifts or outright gifts.[375] And in Minneapolis the Continuity Commission initiated its efforts by developing programs to reach and educate uninvolved business people and also interfaith families.[376]

The significance of these efforts and many others across the country is twofold: First, federations are managing to channel additional money to Jewish education out of a mix of allocations from annual campaigns and various endowments and philanthropic funds under their auspices. In 1997, for example, the New York UJA-Federation made grants of over $3.3 million to its Jewish Continuity efforts above and beyond its allocation of over $2.7 million to Jewish education. Similarly, Boston's Combined Jewish Philanthropies gave out grants of over $900,000 to its Jewish Continuity programs in addition to over $2 million allocated to ongoing educational programs; in Washington, D.C., over three-quarters of a million dollars went to "continuity" efforts in addition to the nearly $1.3 million allocated to schools. Put in relative terms, this means that in a few communities, special educational funds for Jewish continuity efforts equaled anywhere from 50 to 100 percent of regular allocations for Jewish education, a considerable supplement.[377]

Second, through their new vehicles of support, federations are also connecting institutions that often worked in isolation from one another — and sometimes were sharply at odds. Federations are funding synagogue school programs and informal education for teenagers and families;[378]

---

[374]Ibid.

[375]Sid Singer, "Chicago Leads the Way: Federation Launches Day School Endowments," *JUF News,* Oct. 1998, p. 7; Elissa Gootman, "Continuity Crisis Inspires Chicago," *Forward,* July 24, 1998, p. 1.

[376]*Networking for Planning Information 6,* pp. 84, 86.

[377]"1997 Allocations for Jewish Education Agencies," CJF Research Department, Oct. 20, 1998. I am grateful to Donald Kent for providing me with these data. (We should note that these special funds were allocated by only a select group of the larger and intermediate-size federations; smaller federations gave far smaller amounts in absolute and relative terms.)

[378]The evolution of synagogue-federation relations and an examination of model programs of collaboration for formal and informal education between the two types of institutions are detailed in *Planning for Jewish Continuity: Synagogue-Federation Collaboration,* a joint publication of JESNA, the Union of American Hebrew Congregations, the United Synagogue of Conservative Judaism, and the Council of Jewish Federations. An earlier ex-

joint ventures between synagogues and JCCs are now planned; and educators are offered full-time jobs in which they divide their time between day schools and congregational programs. In brief, a higher level of coordination and cooperation is being built through federation initiatives.

WINNERS AND LOSERS

Not all institutions are benefiting from these new alliances and structural changes. Among the biggest losers have been bureaus or central agencies for Jewish education. In Detroit, the United Hebrew Schools, described by Walter Ackerman as "perhaps the only real communal system of education in the country," was replaced by the Agency for Jewish Education. Chicago's Board of Jewish Education gave way to the Community Federation for Jewish Education. New York's Jewish Continuity Commission works independently of its large Board of Jewish Education. And in communities as diverse as Baltimore, Cleveland, and Atlanta major structural changes have weakened or reorganized the bureaus.[379]

A number of factors account for the hard times that have befallen many central agencies. To begin with, the bureaus invested heavily in supplementary education, playing a far more significant role in Sunday and afternoon schools than in day schools. Now they are paying a price for this investment. As David Shluker has observed:

> There has been especially harsh criticism of the supplementary schools (both elementary and high). . . . The bureaus, which have been extensively involved with these schools, are being held accountable for them, even for the congregational schools where their influence is limited. With day schools, on the other hand, where quality varies and educational, financial, and governance problems also often exist, there is a great deal of satisfaction. They are viewed as highly effective with substantially increased enrollments over the past few years. Yet many bureaus provide only limited services to day schools. . . .[380]

In short, the bureaus bet on the wrong horse: "Having contributed significantly to the demise of the communal school," writes Daniel Elazar, "they are now dying with their creatures because they have little or nothing to offer the day school movement as they are presently constituted."[381]

Second, central agencies have encountered stiff competition in those

---

ploration of these questions was edited by David Resnick, *Communal Support for Congregational Schools: Current Approaches* (JESNA, New York, 1988).

[379]Ackerman, "Reforming Jewish Education," pp. 8–9.

[380]David Shluker, "The Communal Education Restructuring Conundrum," *Journal of Jewish Communal Service,* Spring 1992, p. 245.

[381]Daniel J. Elazar, "The Future of the Central Agencies for Jewish Education," *Jewish Education,* Fall/Winter 1990, p. 9. This entire issue is devoted to the relationship between the central agencies and the federations. On the total dismissal of the agencies by the Orthodox Torah Umesorah day-school movement, see the contribution of Joshua Fishman,

communities that also have teacher-training institutions—in Boston, Baltimore, Chicago, Philadelphia, and others. These schools, as we have seen, suffered serious losses in enrollments in the 1970s and 1980s and, in order to survive, remade themselves as institutions serving the wider Jewish community—by offering adult education courses, opening their libraries to the wider community, and providing other services that placed them at the center of Jewish education in their localities. Leaders of the teachers' colleges also promoted themselves as authorities on Jewish education. When the dust settled, a number of central bureaus were either restructured or shunted to the side because they had lost out in the competition with the local Jewish teachers' colleges.[382]

Most important, bureaus have fallen on hard times because federations have become increasingly involved in the field of Jewish education—and have forced the bureaus to restructure.

As Daniel Elazar puts it:

> Jewish community federations, which rose to their present prominence at the same time that day schools did, have moved from being the framing institutions of the Jewish community, concerned primarily with the fund-raising and community planning, to a more proactive stance in matters of particular concern to them. Jewish education has become one of those matters. Federations . . . are now becoming more centralized in their own operations, less willing to see the bureaus as educational policy-making bodies and more as service agencies designed to carry out educational programs developed within the federations themselves. Thus, bureau directors have increasingly been faced by the dilemma of whether they should be educators or federation planners. More than that, the question of who should decide the future of Jewish education, educators or federation planners, has moved to center stage.[383]

Many bureau executives balked at federation demands that they engage in planning. Yet, as David Shluker has noted, when some bureaus develop an expertise in planning, they are often shunted aside anyway by federations.[384] We may note that, in smaller communities, the agencies have less competition and have fared far better. It is in the larger communities, where competing institutions now vie for a leadership role, that quite a number of the bureaus have lost ground or have been put out of business.[385]

"The Bureaus and the Denominations," which concludes: "Let the Zionists teach Zionism in the schools; let the Orthodox teach orthodoxy; and let the bureaus not compete among the name denominations and passions which distinguish American Jewry" (p. 32).

[382]See Carol K. Ingall, "The Quest for Continuity" (note 19). I have also learned about this subject during conversations with Prof. Ingall.

[383]Elazar, "The Future of the Central Agencies for Jewish Education," p. 8.

[384]Shluker, "The Communal Education Restructuring Conundrum," p. 245.

[385]In a few cities, such as Boston, Hartford, San Francisco, and Washington, D.C., central agencies have managed to maintain or redefine their roles.

By contrast, the Jewish Education Service of North America, the national agency that was to have served as an umbrella for local bureaus, has been highly adept at working with the new communal realities. As the continuity agenda has risen in importance within the federation world, JESNA has seized the opportunity to coordinate national and local continuity initiatives. In addition to playing its historical role as a central address for the exchange of ideas among communities and as a resource for evaluating and planning programs, JESNA quite self-consciously announces its role in "building coalitions with partners in North America and Israel to develop and implement high quality educational programs and to promote broad scale organizational and communal change."[386] JESNA has adroitly become a key instrument in education efforts of the national federation leadership and has made itself an indispensable resource to continuity commissions.[387]

Aside from the central agencies, the other big losers in the new communal arrangements are congregational schools. True, in some communities there is now an effort to provide such schools with communal funds to help pay for special programs.[388] But formal schools now must compete with a wide range of informal educational programs for funding, and they are usually deemed less deserving or efficacious. The continuity grants of the New York UJA-Federation, for example, are far more likely to go to a JCC, a camping program, outreach to the unaffiliated, and the like than to a supplementary-school program. With the elevation of informal education to a high status, Israel trips and campus life are far more likely to garner communal funding than the schools that still educate the majority of Jewish children. More generally, the greater involvement of the community with educational matters has, ironically, pushed educators to the periphery: they often are not even at the table when continuity commissions deliberate. Thus, the new communal engagement with Jewish education has not necessarily been beneficial to many educators or their schools. As strategic thinking unfolds about engaging all sectors of the Jewish community in the process of education, it will have to find

---

[386] *Vibrant Jewish Life Through Jewish Learning,* JESNA brochure, n.d., ca. 1998.

[387] There is, of course, a price to be paid for such a close relationship. JESNA was instrumental in forming a National Commission on Jewish Identity and Continuity convened by the Council of Jewish Federations. After laboring for three years, it produced a "Call for Action" endorsing a wide range of programs. The Council of Jewish Federations then decided not to hearken to "the call" and never responded with any national program. The mission document, called *To Renew and Sanctify: A Call to Action,* was released in Nov. 1995.

[388] For a useful inventory of such programs, see *Planning for Jewish Continuity: Synagogue-Federation Collaboration.*

ways to bring these marginalized groups and institutions into that process.[389]

The shifting fortunes of various institutions in the field of education can be measured in the breakdown of allocations made by federations. In 1997 the largest allocations to educational programs in the big and intermediate-size communities went to day schools, while congregational schools in most cases received no funding or only a small fraction of the amounts given to day schools. The following are examples from the few communities that allocated any sums to congregational or communal supplementary schools: In Atlanta, supplementary schools received 6 percent of the Jewish education budget, the day schools 76 percent. In Baltimore, the split was 7 percent for the former and 33 percent for the latter; in Boston, supplementary schools received 13 percent and day schools 37 percent; and in Philadelphia, the former received about a quarter of the Jewish education budget, whereas the latter received almost 50 percent. Moreover, in virtually every large and intermediate-size community, the day schools received considerably more funding than the central agency for Jewish education: in Atlanta, 76 percent versus 8 percent; in Baltimore, 33 percent versus 26 percent; in Boston, 37 percent versus 25 percent. Indeed, only in a few communities, such as New York, Los Angeles, Metrowest (New Jersey), and St. Louis, did central agencies receive the lion's share of Jewish education allocations.[390]

At present it is not yet possible to tally the sum of new dollars flowing into the field of Jewish education—or to assess the impact this new infusion will have upon institutions. The enterprise of Jewish education is sufficiently mammoth to preclude immediate transformation, even when several tens of millions of dollars of new money is flowing into its institutions from federations and philanthropies. To put matters into some perspective, let us note that in 1994 the day-school sector alone was estimated to require a billion dollars a year—that is, just for the maintenance of regular operations. Federation allocations came to an average of 12.5 percent of day school budgets, a figure that varied greatly from one community to the next.[391] Even with the infusion of new money since 1994, the need for student scholarships and direct grants to schools remains

---

[389]This discussion is based heavily on the insightful analysis offered by Ackerman, "Reforming Jewish Education," p. 10.

[390]"1997 Allocations for Jewish Education Agencies," CJF Research Department, Oct. 20, 1998. In communities as diverse as Los Angeles, New York, St. Louis, Washington, Dallas, and Kansas City, as well as many others, the federations allocated no funds for supplementary schools, except indirectly through their continuity commissions.

[391]Shluker and Isaacs, *Federation Allocations to Jewish Day Schools*, p. 3; and David Shluker, *Day School Finances: A Briefing Paper Prepared for the CJF Task Force on Day School Viability and Vitality* (JESNA, New York, Aug. 1998), pp. 2, 9–10.

enormous. To this must be added the supplementary-school system, itself an enterprise costing several hundreds of millions of dollars, and the various programs for informal Jewish education. It is not evident yet whether the Jewish community is prepared to channel vast new resources to restructure the financing of Jewish education—or from where these sums will be diverted. Still, these are heady times for the field. It now has the support of a new generation of communal leaders and philanthropists intent on creating ambitious new plans to coordinate and fund Jewish education, and it is winning over powerful advocates to argue the merits of its case in the decision-making circles of communal leadership.

Conclusion: Great Expectations

It is instructive to situate our discussion of Jewish education within the larger field of American religious education. To what extent are the concerns of Jewish educators different from those of their Christian counterparts? And how does the system of Jewish education compare to Protestant and Catholic structures?

A recent listing of 19 religious high schools—Protestant, Catholic, and Jewish—in the Seattle area[392] provides an illuminating perspective on the second question. Among the data presented are enumerations of the hours per week students engage in mandatory religious instruction. Only one of those schools reported that it required more than ten hours per week—the Northwest Yeshiva, the only Jewish day school in the sample. Three others offered six to ten hours, and the rest five hours or fewer, of religious instruction. Virtually all Protestant and Catholic religious high schools in this sample thus offered the same or fewer hours of religious instruction as do Jewish supplementary schools that meet two to three times per week—and only a fraction of the hours devoted to such subjects by Jewish day schools. While it is extremely difficult to get national statistics, a few surveys of Protestant and Catholic religious schooling suggest that there is nothing unusual in the Seattle figures. A study of Catholic parochial high schools in different sections of the country found that only one period per day was devoted to religious instruction—the equivalent of under five hours per week.[393]

Jewish supplementary education is also more intensive than its Christian equivalents. Indeed, as the figures on religious day schools make evident, most Jewish students enrolled in such schools receive a more intensive education—five to six hours per week—than do Protestant and

[392]"An In-Depth High School Guide," *Seattle Times,* Nov. 20, 1996, pp. 17–18.
[393]Anthony S. Bryk, Valerie Lee, and Peter B. Holland, *Catholic Schools and the Common Good* (Cambridge, Mass., 1993), p. 110.

Catholic children enrolled in private religious all-day schools. Supplementary religious education in Christian settings tends to be limited to Sunday school. By contrast, one-day-a-week religious education has steadily eroded in the Jewish community in favor of more intensive forms of Jewish education.

The major weaknesses of Jewish education are evident in Christian schools too. A wide-ranging survey of religious education in six mainline Protestant denominations, encompassing a sample of over 560 churches, estimated that only 60 percent of children in churches are involved in religious education.[394] By contrast, the percentage of all Jewish children receiving a Jewish education—not only ones who affiliate—is higher. Moreover, the dropout rate from church schools is exactly parallel to the pattern in Jewish schools: in both there is a steep decline during the junior and especially senior high-school years. In Protestant mainline churches, some 17 percent drop out between grades nine and ten.[395]

Christian religious schools also have reshaped their curricula to strengthen the affective dimension of education at the expense of more rigorous cognitive learning. When asked to describe the greatest strength of Protestant mainline schooling, respondents noted the "warm and positive feelings" engendered by discussions and activities; only a small amount of time is devoted to the acquisition of knowledge. Commenting on this finding, a Protestant educator bemoaned the tendency to engage in "fun and games" at the expense of more challenging and demanding study.[396]

The perennial bane of Jewish education, the crippling shortage of trained religious educators, is even more severe in Christian church schools. Some 91 percent of teachers in Protestant mainline churches are women, mainly engaged in avocational—unpaid—teaching. Only the religious educators—i.e., the principals—are paid, but many churches cannot afford to hire such personnel. The predictable result is that only a third of religious teachers for youth ever studied educational theory, and fewer have received serious training.[397]

Thus, when viewed against the backdrop of American religious education, Jewish schooling is no less intensive and no more troubled than its counterparts in the Christian communities. To a significant extent,

---

[394]Eugene C. Roehlkepartain, *The Teaching Church: Moving Christian Education to Center Stage* (Nashville, 1993), p. 27.

[395]Ibid.

[396]Ibid., p. 74–76. Since 1965, Catholic schools have also replaced textual study and the memorization of the catechism with discussions of ethical issues. Bryk, Lee, and Holland, *Catholic Schools and the Common Good,* pp. 110–13.

[397]Roehlkepartain, *The Teaching Church,* chap. 7.

Jewish children receive a more extensive and demanding religious education. Indeed, Christian educators periodically have cited developments in the Jewish community as worthy of emulation. Over 30 years ago, a Catholic periodical ran an article tellingly entitled "What Can We Learn About the Religious Education of Youth . . . from the Jews?" The author, a rabbi, observed: "At a time when some Catholics would be satisfied to develop merely a limited after-school program for Catholic students, Jews are pressing hard to increase the already substantial number of hours that are devoted to weekday Jewish religious education. Without demur most Jewish leaders consider a one-day-a-week program of after-school religious instruction to be a complete failure."[398]

While such a comparison might reassure some within the Jewish community about the relative health and vitality of the field of Jewish education, it should, in fact help clarify the extent to which the enterprise of Jewish education differs radically from Christian religious schooling. Simply put, Jewish education addresses a multiplicity of goals and therefore must provide students with many more skills, greater know-how, and more wide-ranging understanding than does Christian religious education. In part this results from the complex nature of Jewish identity, a mix of religious and ethnic components—both of which must be integrated into the lives of young people. And in part it results from the nature of Jewish life in the United States, where Jews constitute a minority striving to sustain a distinctive religion and culture.[399]

The multiple goals of Jewish education inevitably create much confusion in the field, as has been aptly noted by Jonathan Woocher: "If Jewish education is vague, unfocused and often over-ambitious in its goals, it is primarily because those concerned—parents, professionals, institutional leaders, religious authorities—can rarely agree on what is important to achieve. What do we want our educational efforts to produce: A Jew who prays? One who can speak Hebrew as well as an Israeli? One who can read a *blatt* [folio] of Gemara [Talmud]? One who will give to UJA, [the United Jewish Appeal]? One who won't intermarry? All of the above, or none of the above? Without consensually validated goals education becomes a medium of mixed messages, and nothing gets accomplished."[400]

Yet, for all these serious shortcomings, the field of Jewish education is currently the object of great expectations. Much energetic effort is now

---

[398] *Ave Maria,* Apr. 22, 1967, p. 30ff. The author was Rabbi Arthur Gilbert of the Anti-Defamation League.

[399] On this theme, see David Resnick, "Jewish Multicultural Education: A Minority View," *Religious Education* 91, no. 2, Spring 1996, pp. 209–21.

[400] Jonathan Woocher, "Jewish Education: Crisis and Vision," in *Imagining the Jewish Future: Essays and Responses,* ed. David Teutsch (Albany, N.Y., 1992), p. 65.

directed toward a mammoth, if somewhat chaotic, effort to revamp and expand the field and integrate it more directly with other sectors of the Jewish community. Although not nearly as popular with the masses of American Jews as previous campaigns to rescue endangered co-religionists abroad, the present drive to revitalize Jewish education is drawing upon a small but well-heeled cadre of philanthropists, passionately engaged lay and professional communal leaders, sophisticated educational thinkers within the field and in the academy, and a newly energized parent body.

To be sure, many observers question the wisdom of current priorities and the very process whereby decisions are made. Others express justifiable skepticism about the ability of new initiatives to reverse long-term trends away from Jewish identification. Undoubtedly, expectations are inordinately great. There is little doubt, however, that over the course of the past 15 years, the mood of demoralization has lifted, giving way to a more hopeful and expansive era. The field of Jewish education today, perhaps as never before, is arguably the most dynamic sector of the American Jewish community.

Review
of
the
Year

UNITED STATES

United States

National Affairs

FOR THE JEWISH COMMUNITY—as for the entire nation—1998 was the year of the Monica Lewinsky scandal, a black hole that swallowed up media attention and the time and energies of countless government officials and commentators. The diversion created by the scandal notwithstanding, the year was filled with issues and events of considerable importance to the Jewish community.

Congressional elections were held in 1998. It was also a year in which the House of Representatives voted down a proposed constitutional amendment that would have had profound implications for religious liberty, as well as a year in which the constitutionality of vouchers was addressed by the highest American court ever to consider the issue. It was a year, too, of profound developments in Catholic-Jewish relations, including the release by the Vatican of its historic statement on the Holocaust, and a year in which the U.S. Supreme Court declined to find that the American Jewish community's leading voice on American-Israeli relations was obligated to register as a "political action committee" (but left the issue open for further consideration). Finally, 1998 was the year when it appeared that John Demjanjuk, at one time sentenced to death as a war criminal and still viewed as such by many in the Jewish community, might well be allowed to live out his remaining years as an American citizen.

THE POLITICAL ARENA

Congressional Elections

As election year 1998 progressed, it was difficult to discern any overriding theme. The common wisdom was that the Republicans would gain seats in Congress, given that the party not occupying the White House virtually always gains in an off-year election, but the strong economy seemed to be a factor in the president's, and therefore the Democratic party's, favor. As the Lewinsky scandal deepened—with President Bill Clinton admitting in August that he had, in fact,

119

had an improper relationship with a White House intern—nobody could say what the impact of the unfolding drama would be.

When the smoke cleared after Election Day 1998, it was evident that the nation's voters had defied pollsters and political commentators, electing a marginally more Democratic House of Representatives, retaining the 55–45 Republican majority in the Senate, and cutting by one statehouse the Republicans' dominance in governorships. The Democrats' gain of five House seats broke the traditional pattern of midterm election losses by the president's party (in midterm contests since World War II, the party in control of the White House has posted an average 27-seat loss).

Although the national vote was, roughly speaking, split evenly, exit polls had Jewish voters favoring Democratic candidates over Republicans by 78 to 21 percent. This was within the norm for the Jewish community, reflecting a traditional commitment to the Democratic Party in the face of Republican efforts to expand the Jewish vote for their candidates. Only one Republican Senate candidate, Peter Fitzgerald, won more than 30 percent of the Jewish vote, doing so in his successful bid to unseat Sen. Carol Moseley-Braun (D., Ill.), and he was largely seen as the beneficiary of an ABM—"anybody but Moseley-Braun"—movement, the result of repeated missteps by the Democratic incumbent.

The Jewish "caucus" in the House—24 members in the 105th Congress (down from 25 at the start of that session because of the death in March 1998 of New Mexico Republican Steve Schiff)—stood at 23 to be inaugurated in January 1999: 21 Democrats, one Republican, and one Independent (Bernard Sanders of Vermont, a nominal Socialist). Two Jewish Democrats did not seek reelection and were replaced in kind: nine-termer Charles Schumer—who gambled his safe seat in Brooklyn and came from behind to win the Senate nomination, defeating three-term Republican Alfonse D'Amato—relinquished his district to Anthony Weiner; Sidney Yates of Chicago, "dean" of the caucus and longtime champion of education and the arts, as well as Israel, stepped down after 24 terms (in his 90th year) and was succeeded by Janice Schakowsky. One Jewish Democrat was succeeded by a non-Jew: three-termer Jane Harman of Los Angeles gambled and lost in a bid for the California gubernatorial nomination; her seat was won by Republican Steven Kuykendall. One Jewish Republican lost and was replaced by a non-Jewish Democrat: two-termer Jon Fox of Philadelphia, who was defeated by Joseph Hoeffel. In the only election of a new Jewish member to a House seat formerly held by a non-Jew, Jewish Democrat Shelley Berkley won in the contest for an open Las Vegas seat.

The lone Jewish House Republican in the 106th Congress, New Yorker Benjamin Gilman, was elected to a 14th term. The most senior member of the "caucus," his reelection meant that he would continue to hold the position of chairman of the International Relations Committee, crucial to a broad range of policy issues of concern to the Jewish community. In the 105th Congress, Gilman, a strong advocate of a close U.S.-Israel relationship, increasingly found his consistent support for the overall foreign aid program putting him in conflict with the more isolationist elements in his party. In an unprecedented development, the committee's ranking Democrat in the 106th Congress was also expected to be Jewish. Sam Gejdenson of Connecticut, a son of Holocaust survivors, was slated to succeed Lee Hamilton, of Indiana, who retired after 17 terms. Gejdenson, who won by razor-thin margins in his last three reelection efforts (including a 21-vote victory in 1994), cruised to his 10th term with a stunning 61 percent of the vote. The senior Jewish Democrat in the coming House session, Henry Waxman of Westside Los Angeles, also won decisively for his 13th term.

Other members of the Jewish "caucus" elected in 1998 were Gary Ackerman (D., N.Y.); Howard Berman (D., Calif.); Benjamin Cardin (D., Md.); Peter Deutsch (D., Fla.); Eliot Engel (D., N.Y.); Bob Filner (D., Calif.); Barney Frank (D., Mass.); Martin Frost (D., Tex.); Tom Lantos (D., Calif.); Sander Levin (D., Mich.); Nita Lowey (D., N.Y.); Jerrold Nadler (D., N.Y.); Steven Rothman (D., N.J.); Brad Sherman (D., Calif.); Norman Sisisky (D., Va.); and Robert Wexler (D., Fla.).

Three of the most closely followed Senate races involved Jewish candidates — the New York race pitting D'Amato against Schumer, and the reelection bids of first-termers Barbara Boxer of California and Russ Feingold of Wisconsin. Feingold conducted his campaign by rules he hoped to see imposed on all Senate candidates by his "campaign finance reform" legislation—cosponsored by Sen. John McCain (R., Ariz.)—with tight restrictions on contributions and no campaign "issue-ads" by supportive interest groups. In the process, Feingold was nearly buried, but he stuck to his plan and finished three points ahead of his opponent.

Schumer defeated D'Amato, a three-term incumbent, by a 55 to 45 margin. New York exit polls showed Jewish voters splitting roughly three to one for Schumer, in comparison to 1992 when D'Amato won some 40 percent of the Jewish vote. Many felt that D'Amato had hurt his standing with Jewish voters by his reference to Schumer as a "putzhead" at a meeting with Jewish supporters. D'Amato's loss was deeply felt by some in the Jewish community, who credited the senator for his persistent attention to the community's calls for justice in matters relating to Holocaust restitution. D'Amato's relentless campaign against Swiss banks, including hearings he led as chairman of the Banking Committee, ultimately yielded a $1.25 billion settlement for Holocaust victims. D'Amato was also a passionate friend and defender of Israel. Nevertheless, Schumer also had a strong pro-Israel record, and his advocacy of tough antiterrorism legislation had resonated with many in the Jewish community. On domestic issues, notably reproductive rights and church-state separation in matters of public education, Schumer's positions were closer than D'Amato's to those held by a majority of American Jews.

With Boxer and Feingold retaining their seats, and the Schumer pick-up, the number of Jews in the Senate had, for the first time, grown beyond the required prayer quorum of ten (*minyan*) (first reached in 1992) to 11. Other Jewish senators up for reelection in 1998—Republican Arlen Specter of Pennsylvania and Democrat Ron Wyden of Oregon—coasted to easy wins. Six Jewish senators, all Democrats, were not on the ballot in this cycle and rounded out the roster of the 106th Congress: Dianne Feinstein, California; Herbert Kohl, Wisconsin; Frank Lautenberg, New Jersey; Carl Levin, Michigan; Joseph Lieberman, Connecticut; and Paul Wellstone, Minnesota.

In the wake of the Republican Party's reversal of expected fortune, Georgia Republican Newt Gingrich, Speaker of the House, was under fire; within days of the election, he announced that he would not seek reelection as Speaker and would soon resign from Congress. In short order, House Appropriations Committee chairman Bob Livingston (R., La.) became the likely successor to Gingrich. Questions were immediately raised within the Jewish community as to what this portended for the U.S.-Israel relationship. Gingrich had been a strong supporter of the Jewish state; Livingstone was a lesser known quantity.

The question of "Who is Bob Livingston?" had barely been asked when the Louisiana legislator announced that he would step down, a decision related to the House's move toward impeachment of President Clinton in late December 1998. The question became, instead, "Who is Dennis Hastert?" as the deputy chief whip emerged as the likely Speaker for the incoming Congress. It was quickly noted that Hastert had a solid record in terms of Israel, but one less acceptable to much of the Jewish community on social issues, such as church-state relations and pro-choice issues. In another by-product of Livingston's announcement that he would resign, David Duke quickly moved to run for the open seat. Republican National Committee chairman Jim Nicholson responded by asserting, "There is no room in the party of Lincoln for a Klansman like David Duke."*

Governors' Races

A notable feature of several of the tight gubernatorial races—and in line with the congressional results—was the trend away from candidates favored by the religious right. Governors David Beasley of North Carolina and Fob James, Jr., of Alabama, both closely aligned with the Christian Coalition, went down to defeat. Each held positions on school prayer and other church-state issues traditionally viewed with disfavor by Jews and other religious minorities and regarded as unconstitutional. James had been widely criticized for, among other things, his claim that the Bill of Rights did not apply to Alabama, as well as his defiance of court orders directing a state judge not to display the Ten Commandments in his courtroom and ordering an end to school-sponsored religious activities.

Even as Governors James and Beasley, not to mention Sen. Lauch Faircloth of North Carolina, anchors of their party's right wing, went down to defeat, the

---

*The preceding section is based in part on a paper written jointly with Jason Isaacson, director, Office of Government and International Affairs, American Jewish Committee.

Bush brothers, George W. and Jeb, were handily reelected and elected, respectively, as the governors of Texas and Florida, both running—explicitly or implicitly—on campaigns premised on "compassionate conservatism." These more conciliatory candidates tended also to do better with Jews and other minorities than their more conservative counterparts. This play in the Jewish vote was demonstrated, as well, by New York's Republican governor, George Pataki, who received 38 percent of the Jewish vote in his reelection effort. The Michigan gubernatorial race drew attention when Geoffrey Fieger, the controversial Democratic candidate and lawyer for Dr. Jack Kevorkian, compared Orthodox rabbis who oppose doctor-assisted suicide to Nazis. To nobody's surprise, Fieger went down to resounding defeat.

With the return of a Republican Congress—albeit one likely to be tempered by a more moderate tone—Jewish groups expected to continue to battle against such unwelcome initiatives as education vouchers, a school prayer constitutional amendment, restrictions on choice in reproductive rights, and problematic proposals to reform the Immigration and Naturalization Service (INS) and naturalization procedures. But, observed Mark Pelavin, associate director of the Religious Action Center of Reform Judaism, "there's still room to make some positive advances," as in, for instance, the battle to strengthen hate-crimes laws and restore eligibility for public benefits to legal immigrants.

The election results notwithstanding, the religious right was expected to remain a crucial constituency of the Republican Party, and especially of its leadership in Congress. But with the ranks of congressional moderates of both parties now increased, the balance of power, at least in terms of the ability to stop extreme initiatives, was shifted toward the center. Thus, the so-called "religious freedom" amendment of the outgoing session—in actuality, an expanded school-prayer constitutional amendment—was even less likely to garner a two-thirds vote in the House, a target from which it fell short in the 105th Congress.

The election results suggested no lessening of support for Israel in the 106th Congress, nor any change in existing patterns of support for U.S. engagement in international affairs (an issue often tangled in partisanship and affected by fiscal decision making).

The Clinton Administration

The scandal that engulfed the administration for virtually all of 1998 had an extra fillip for the Jewish community because of Monica Lewinsky's Jewish background. And the press's first opportunity to question President Clinton about the unfolding story came as he sat with Yasir Arafat at a photo opportunity following a meeting of the two leaders, distracting attention from both the meeting and the peace process. There was even speculation in a number of Arab newspapers that Lewinsky's role in the affair was part of a "Zionist conspiracy" to undo President Clinton because of the pressure he had begun to put on Israel to be more forthcoming in negotiations with the Palestinians. And in the Jewish world, those who strongly objected to presidential pressure on Israel termed Lewinsky a "latter-day Esther," referring to the Purim story heroine who saved the Jewish people from destruction. The Jewish dimension of the story was amplified when Lewinsky's attorney, William Ginsburg, said that he and Lewinsky respected the president because of his policies regarding Israel. And, while rejecting any notion that Lewinsky might flee to Israel, Ginsburg suggested that "after it's all over" it might be good for Lewinsky to go to the Jewish state.

President Clinton's admission in August 1998 that he had misled the American people about the nature of his relationship with Monica Lewinsky at first left even his supporters in the Jewish community uncertain as to how to respond. After an initial silence, some, like erstwhile Clinton supporters Letty Cottin Pogrebin and Leonard Fein, urged him to resign. In contrast, Jack Rosen, president of the American Jewish Congress and a former Democratic party official, issued a statement on AJCongress letterhead, saying, "For too long, the Congress and the American people as a whole have been caught up in the president's troubles. It is time to set aside our preoccupation with foolish things and for the Congress together with the president to deal with those matters that count." Steve Grossman, national chairman of the Democratic National Committee and former head of AIPAC, insisted that the latter was more reflective of attitudes in the broader Jewish community, pointing to a continuation of Jewish community responsiveness to Democratic fund-raising appeals.

In September 1998, with the House of Representatives on the verge of releasing the report of independent prosecutor Kenneth Starr in all its lurid detail, President Clinton turned to a Reform Jewish text for Yom Kippur to make his most explicit expression of atonement for having misled the American people about the Lewinsky affair. At a national prayer breakfast held at the White House on September 11, he read a selection from *Gates of Repentance*, the Reform prayer book, that focuses on the Jewish steps for repentance—acknowledging wrongdoing, apologizing to those who have been wronged, and taking steps to avoid repeating the transgression. The prayer book had been given to the president one week earlier by Miami attorney Ira Leesfield with a note suggesting that the passage was one that the president might "appreciate looking at."

Jewish representatives joined their colleagues in largely voting along party lines on the articles of impeachment presented to the House. The 21 Jewish Democrats unanimously voted against all four articles during the Saturday session. The two Jewish Republicans each voted for at least the two articles that were passed by the House, sending the matter over to the Senate for trial.

With year's end, and a new congressional session and an impeachment trial looming, the question was whether an already distracted Congress and president would be able to focus on issues of concern to the Jewish community. The Jewish Telegraphic Agency quoted one anonymous "Jewish activist" as saying, "There's nothing coming down from the White House anymore. The bureaucrats will continue to grind away, but there are no initiatives on anything but the top-tier issues." Others pointed to the president's famed ability to compartmentalize, as witnessed by the impeachment-eve bombing of Iraq, and suggested that he would press to demonstrate his capacity to govern, the scandal notwithstanding.

In the first appearance of his second term before a Jewish audience, President Clinton addressed the convention of the National Council of Jewish Women in February 1998. He praised the group's historic role in exposing the child-care crisis in America—some 25 years earlier—and called for support for the administration's initiative in this area and various educational programs.

AIPAC AND PACS

In May 1998 the U.S. Supreme Court rendered a decision in a case with substantial potential implications not only for the nature of the involvement of the American Israel Public Affairs Committee (AIPAC) in the political process but for the nature of that process overall. In December 1996 the full U.S. Court of Appeals for the D.C. Circuit had upheld a lower-court ruling that AIPAC should be regulated as a political action committee or "PAC," a status that would compel the organization to file complete public reports on its receipts and expenditures. Notwithstanding its acronym, AIPAC is organized not as a PAC but as a nonprofit membership organization engaged in lobbying that is entitled to share information on politics and elections with its members.

The Supreme Court found that the plaintiffs—longtime adversaries of U.S. support for Israel—had standing to bring the case, a ruling that opened the door to additional lawsuits against the Federal Election Commission (FEC) by voters who believe that campaign regulation laws are not being adequately enforced. But the Court declined to render a determination as to AIPAC's status, ruling instead, 6-3, that the case be sent back to the FEC for further consideration as to whether, in light of recent developments in the law, "AIPAC's expenditures qualify as 'membership communications' and thereby fall outside the scope of 'expenditures' that could qualify it as a political committee." AIPAC declared victory, predicting that the FEC would be compelled to treat AIPAC as a membership organization. But with the FEC's final decision yet to come and appeals sure to follow whichever way its ruling went, American Jewish Congress counsel Marc Stern asserted that "it may not be tomorrow or the next day or even the next month before this matter is out of the way."

While AIPAC continued its fight not to be classified as a PAC, the pro-Israel PACs continued their work of fund-raising on behalf of congressional candidates. An analysis of FEC data released by the Center for Responsive Politics in October 1998 indicated that these pro-Israel groups, as of that point in the election cycle, were giving some two-thirds of their funds to Democrats, as opposed to Republicans. (This was in contrast to the general practice of political action committees to strongly favor Republicans, an unsurprising phenomenon given that Republicans controlled the Congress.) The continued high Democratic affiliation of pro-Israel contributors was undoubtedly a factor in the allocation of funds. Nevertheless, the center's study reflected a proportionate increase in the contributions made to Republicans (prior to the Republican takeover of Congress in 1994, contributions by pro-Israel PACs favored Democrats three to one), as well as the fact that senior Republicans with a strong record of support for Israel received high levels of support from pro-Israel PACs.

Terrorism

In January 1998 Ramzi Yousef, the man earlier convicted by a New York federal court of masterminding the World Trade Center bombing that killed six people was sentenced to life in prison without parole.

A lawsuit was filed in the U.S. District Court of Los Angeles in March 1998 challenging as unconstitutional provisions of the 1996 antiterrorism act that criminalize fund-raising on behalf of foreign groups designated by the State Department as terrorist organizations, even where the moneys being raised are for "lawful and non-violent activities." A number of Jewish organizations had strongly supported enactment of the challenged provisions, and Michael Lieberman, Washington counsel of the Anti-Defamation League (ADL), predicted that his organization would be in court defending the measure. "There is a seamless web," he said, "between the terrorist activities of groups like Hamas and their social welfare initiatives."

In March 1998 the Flatow family, New Jersey residents who had sued Iran for its role in supporting terrorists who murdered their daughter Alisa in an attack in Gaza, obtained a $247.5 million judgment against the Iranian government. Iran had been held in default for failing to respond to a lawsuit brought against it pursuant to provisions of the 1996 antiterrorism act. To the dismay of the Flatow family, the Clinton administration went to court seeking to prevent execution on the default judgment, arguing that foreclosing on Iran's assets would be inconsistent with the nation's national security and foreign policy interests.

Congress responded to the administration's action by including the so-called "Flatow amendment" in legislation enacted as the congressional session ended. The amendment, sponsored by Sen. Frank Lautenberg (D., N.J.) and Rep. Jim Saxton (R., N.J.), required the administration to assist in the identification and location of assets of state sponsors of terrorism against which judgment has been obtained. The amendment also authorized the president to waive these requirements in the interest of national security. Almost as soon as the budget bill was signed, the president invoked the waiver provision. The White House argued that this action not only relieved it of its obligation to cooperate with asset identification, but also blocked the courts from executing a judgment.

In June 1998 the FBI seized $1.4 million in cash and property alleged to have been used by a Chicago-area couple as part of a money-laundering scheme that resulted in funds being channeled to Hamas operatives in Israel and the West Bank. The husband, Mohammad Salah, had returned to the United States in November 1997, following a prison term of nearly five years in Israel arising out of similar charges. Salah, an American citizen, denied the charges, while representatives of Jewish organizations hailed the FBI's action and called for Salah to be prosecuted under American antiterrorism laws.

Soviet Jewry, Refugees, and Immigration

Extension of the Lautenberg amendment, which relaxes refugee admission criteria to the United States for Jews and persecuted Christian minorities from the former Soviet Union, among others, was far from certain in 1998, in part because of questions as to whether changed circumstances in the former Soviet Union necessitated this step. Pro-immigrant groups, spearheaded by the Council of Jewish Federations (CJF) and the Hebrew Immigrant Aid Society (HIAS), were able, however, in October 1998 to secure an extension for one year (through September 30, 1999), thanks to the backing of Senators Arlen Specter and Frank Lautenberg. The Jewish groups applauded this step and hailed as well an understanding between the administration and the Congress that the number of refugee slots allocated to Eastern Europe and the former Soviet Union would be maintained at the same level as in the previous year.

Even as these efforts were under way, HIAS and its affiliated agencies were grappling with the consequences of a dramatic downturn in the number of new refugees arriving in this country and requiring resettlement — some 9,000 in 1997 compared to 40,000 in a typical year during the early 1990s. The reduction in arrivals had led to a concomitant reduction in federal funding of resettlement agencies, which is calculated on a per capita basis and constitutes a major part of the funding of those agencies. In light of the changing circumstances, HIAS executive vice-president Leonard Glickman asserted, "We simply cannot sustain a [resettlement] structure this large in the years ahead." At the same time, Glickman noted, there were tens of thousands of refugees remaining in the system who would need the services of HIAS-affiliated agencies for some time to come, and recent increases in expressions of anti-Semitism in the former Soviet Union had led to an increase in "interest" by Jews there in the possibility of resettlement.

In other immigration-related developments, Congress granted an INS request to reprogram $171 million that had been previously allocated for other Justice Department and INS purposes. The money would be used to speed up the processing of citizenship applications, by reducing the backlog in applications that, as of the end of 1998, numbered approximately two million. The money was not a new appropriation, but rather a reshuffling of previously authorized funds. This reauthorization was also intended to be used to bolster technical and support staff, centralize key record-keeping systems, and make the entire naturalization process more user-friendly.

Rep. Lamar Smith (R.,Tex.), chairman of the House Judiciary subcommittee on immigration, pushed for passage of the Naturalization Reform Act of 1998, an initiative which, in the view of Jewish advocates, would have made the citizenship application process unreasonably onerous by, among other things, requiring immigrants to produce letters of reference from the governments that persecuted them. The bill died in the House Judiciary Committee but was expected to reemerge in the next Congress.

U.S. – Israel Relations

A Maryland murder case with international ramifications continued to receive worldwide attention throughout 1998. One of two suspects in the crime, 17-year-old Samuel Sheinbein, fled to Israel in September 1997, where he claimed that his father's Israeli citizenship made him a citizen as well. Israeli law forbids extradition of its citizens, although a citizen may be tried in an Israeli court for a crime committed abroad. A furor erupted immediately when it appeared that Sheinbein might avoid prosecution in the United States through this "loophole," and efforts were made at the highest levels of government to bring about his return. Concerns were raised that the case presented a palpable danger to U.S.-Israel relations.

By early 1998 Israeli officials had determined that they would, within the limits imposed by the Israeli legal system, seek to comply with the request of American authorities for extradition. In February Israeli government officials took the position in Jerusalem district court that Sheinbein was not an Israeli because his father, a citizen by virtue of having been born in pre-state Palestine, had left the country at an early age. District court judge Moshe Ravid ruled in September that the accused teenager was "extraditable," even though he found that Sheinbein was a citizen, grounding his conclusion on the lack of close ties between Sheinbein and Israel. An appeal to the Israel Supreme Court was still pending at year's end.

On April 6, 1998, in the wake of the March killing of students by other students at a school in Jonesboro, Arkansas, President Clinton announced an executive order closing a loophole in a 1994 assault weapons ban that had enabled manufacturers, including Israel Military Industries, to ship thousands of military-style rifles to the United States. The loophole had received widespread attention the previous year when Sen. Dianne Feinstein (D., Calif.), a gun-control advocate, became aware of the Israeli manufacturer's intention to modify the Uzi American and the Galil Sporter so as to qualify those weapons "for sporting purposes," thereby making them eligible for export to the United States. Even before a temporary action by the president in November 1997, blocking import of many of the weapons later covered by the April 1998 action, the Israeli government (after an initial reluctance to do so) suspended sale of its assault weapons to the United States because of the "special sensitivity" of the issue in that country. The president's actions did, however, prevent import of weapons from other countries, such as Russia, Greece, and Bulgaria, that had geared up to take advantage of the loophole.

Jonathan Pollard

Efforts to free convicted spy Jonathan Pollard were rekindled early in 1998 when the Conference of Presidents of Major Jewish Organizations wrote to President Clinton urging that some "immediate action" be taken. "We believe," stated the letter, signed by conference chairman Melvin Salberg and executive vice-chairman Malcolm Hoenlein, "that Mr. Pollard has paid his debt after more than 13 years of incarceration." The appeal was rejected in fairly short order, when, in March, Charles Ruff, the president's counsel, wrote back indicating that President Clinton was reaffirming his 1996 decision that, "based upon all the information before him, . . . the extraordinary remedy of executive clemency should not be used in this case."

This was far from the end of the Pollard story for the year. In April, Reform, Conservative, and Orthodox leaders joined in a letter urging the president to "grant mercy" to Pollard. And, a month later, Israel admitted for the first time that Pollard had been its agent when he was arrested in front of the Israeli embassy in Washington in 1985. Pollard responded by stating that he was "relieved, thankful and honored by the Israeli government's action." Supporters of an early Pollard release, including Seymour Reich, former chairman of the Conference of Presidents of Major Jewish Organizations, suggested that the Israeli admission could make a difference because it put "the full weight of the . . . government behind the request for his release."

The Pollard matter emerged conspicuously, and unexpectedly, in the waning hours of the peace process negotiations at Wye River in Maryland in October. On Friday morning, October 23, the White House and the State Department announced that an accord had been reached between Israeli prime minister Benjamin Netanyahu and Palestinian Authority chairman Yasir Arafat. The accord nearly fell apart, however, when Netanyahu indicated that it was his understanding that President Clinton had agreed to release Pollard immediately, leading to a five-hour impasse. Ultimately, a compromise was reached, with Clinton agreeing to give further study to the matter and Netanyahu agreeing to go forward with the accord.

Even given the limited nature of his undertaking, President Clinton drew strong criticism from U.S. intelligence officials and some members of Congress for even considering Pollard's release. House Speaker Newt Gingrich asserted, "I think it would be a tremendous mistake for the United States to start putting traitors on the negotiating tables as a pawn, and I hope the Administration will now say they will not, under any circumstances, release Pollard." Some Jewish leaders expressed surprise over the vehemence of the response regarding Pollard. In December President Clinton asked several top administration officials to provide him with a recommendation by January 11, 1999, as to whether Pollard's life sentence should be reduced.

Arab Boycott

Ben & Jerry's, the international ice cream manufacturer with a reputation for social consciousness, found itself caught in the crossfire of the Middle East dispute when it was accused of boycotting certain Israeli products. In the summer of 1998, Ben & Jerry's, which licensed eight stores in Israel, received demands from dovish interfaith and Arab American groups that it cease purchasing water from Mei Eden, an Israeli water company located in the Golan Heights. An international spokesperson for the Ben & Jerry's parent company was thereafter quoted as saying that the Israeli licensees would comply with the demand. This resulted in protests from American Jewish groups, with Avi Zenger, president of Ben & Jerry's Israeli outlets, finally asserting that "the company is not boycotting products from the Golan Heights, nor would it join in such a boycott if one were organized." The Anti-Defamation League asserted that it would only consider the matter closed when Ben & Jerry's, in fact, purchased additional water from the Golan. In a September 25 letter to the company, ADL national director Abraham Foxman noted that, with Arab organizations and countries urging boycotts of Israeli goods, "Ben & Jerry's has given the appearance of acquiescing to this campaign against Israeli products."

Communal Implications of the Budget Process

From the inception of the 1996 welfare reform law, the American Jewish community was at the forefront of a campaign to roll back provisions that stripped away eligibility for federal public benefits from legal immigrants. Following some restoration of disability benefits in 1997, that campaign saw another success when, in June 1998, President Clinton signed into law a bill restoring eligibility for food stamps for children, elderly, and disabled legal immigrants present in the United States at the time the 1996 law was enacted. Overall, the restoration of benefits amounted to $818 million over five years. In addition, the period of time for which refugees remain eligible for food stamps was extended from five years to seven. Noting that 85 to 90 percent of Jewish immigrants and refugees would now continue to be eligible to receive food stamps, Diana Aviv, director of the Council of Jewish Federations' Washington Action Office, stressed that the battle to restore benefits further would nevertheless continue. A future increase in immigrants ineligible for these benefits could leave local federations with a burden that, without government assistance, they would not "be able to handle."

The United Nations and Israel

Congress included language in supporting documentation that accompanied the omnibus appropriations bill, passed in October 1998, expressing that body's concern with UN bias against Israel. For the 50 years since it became a member of the UN, Israel had suffered the unique disability of being ineligible to serve on the Security Council, the Human Rights Commission, and other key bodies because it is not a member of a regional bloc. (Several members of the Asia bloc, to which Israel, in the normal course, should belong, had prevented Israel from taking a seat in that body.) The supporting documentation for the omnibus bill included the sense of Congress that the secretary of state and the U.S. ambassador to the UN should take all steps necessary to insure Israel's acceptance into the Western European and Others Group (WEOG) regional bloc. The secretary of state was also requested to report to Congress in March 1999 on actions taken by representatives of the United States to promote Israel's acceptance into the WEOG and the diplomatic responses by other nations to this effort. Additionally, on May 22, 1998, the Senate adopted by voice vote a resolution, introduced by Senators Daniel Moynihan (D., N.Y.) and Richard Lugar (R.,Ind.), expressing the sense of the Senate that the United States should take steps to promote Israel's acceptance into an appropriate UN regional group. The American Jewish Committee played an active role in pressing European and foreign officials, the administration, and Congress to take steps to end UN discrimination against Israel. In addition to launching a major advertising effort and mobilizing AJC chapters across the country, in April AJC president Robert Rifkind wrote a letter to UN Secretary-General Kofi Annan commending him for his public call to end UN bias against Israel.

ANTI-SEMITISM AND EXTREMISM

Assessing Anti-Semitism

The FBI's annual report on numbers of hate-crimes incidents, issued in January 1998 for calendar year 1996, continued to reflect an overall increase in such offenses, 8,734 as compared to approximately 8,000 for 1995, of which 1,400 were classified as religion-motivated crimes. Thirteen percent of hate crimes overall were committed against Jews; approximately 80 percent of religion-linked incidents were directed at Jews. Analysts were quick to caution that the increased numbers were as likely to be a product of improved compliance by law enforcement authorities in reporting incidents as an actual increase in incidents. Nevertheless, a jurisdiction-by-jurisdiction breakdown included in the report reflected that many areas continued to be lax in providing information. "You have bizarre things that leap off the page," said ADL Washington counsel Michael Lieberman, "like Miami reporting zero [hate crimes], New Orleans one, Detroit five."

In November 1998 the FBI issued its annual report on hate crimes for 1997, with figures that once again showed Jews and Jewish property to be disproportionate targets of religious bias. There were 1,087 such incidents against Jews reported, almost 80 percent of religious hate crimes. Disturbingly to some observers, the statistics were collected by fewer law enforcement agencies than in 1996, the first decline in the number of participating agencies as compared to the prior year since these statistics were first gathered in 1991.

Crown Heights Riots

A number of loose ends were tied up during 1998, left over from the 1991 anti-Jewish riots in the Brooklyn neighborhood of Crown Heights, when crowds of blacks, enraged by the death of a young black boy who was hit accidentally by a car driven by a Lubavitcher Hassid, rampaged in the streets. In January 1998 the City of New York paid $200,000 in settlement of a lawsuit by Isaac Bitton and his son Yechiel, a hassidic father and son who alleged that police officers saw them being attacked during the riots but did not come to their aid. Their story received substantial attention when the *New York Post* ran a front-page picture of Yechiel Bitton crying over his father's bloodied body.

Some two months later, U.S. district judge David Trager sentenced Lemrick Nelson, Jr., to 19 1/2 years in prison, more than one year after a federal jury had convicted Nelson for violating the civil rights of Yankel Rosenbaum, a young talmudic scholar who was killed during the riots. Nelson had earlier been acquitted of state criminal charges stemming from Rosenbaum's death. Judge Trager ruled that Nelson could be prosecuted on the federal charges because the record provided sufficient basis to establish that Rosenbaum had been singled out for attack because he was a Jew. Nelson's sentencing notwithstanding, Jacob Goldstein, a Lubavitcher and chairman of the community board for the area that included Crown Heights, asserted that there was still no "closure." "As far as we're concerned," he told the Jewish Telegraphic Agency, "there were more than 20 other thugs involved in that pack, and the feds seem to be saying that they got us one or two, and that's all they're willing to do."

Within a day of Nelson's sentencing, New York City announced a $1.1 million settlement with 91 members of the Crown Heights Jewish community who had brought a class-action lawsuit claiming that the city had not done enough to protect the community during the riots. Mayor Rudolph Giuliani apologized to the victims on behalf of the city for the "mistakes" that had been made, declaring that "there is no excuse for allowing people to victimize others based on their race, religion, ethnicity for any other reason without a strong and immediate response from city government." Michael Miller, executive vice-president of the New York Jewish Community Relations Council, proclaimed the settlement and apology "warranted and appropriate," while Franklyn Snitow, attorney for the class-action plaintiffs, asserted that the city's action meant, "finally, official recognition for the horrible, anti-Semitic violence to which they were subjected."

Legislative Activity

The organized Jewish community continued its efforts to enact the Hate Crimes Prevention Act, a bill introduced in 1997 that would extend existing hate-crimes law to those victimized because of their gender, sexual orientation, or disability, and would remove judicial impediments that sometimes prevent federal authorities from stepping in when local officials are unable or unwilling to investigate and prosecute. In the aftermath of the murder in Wyoming of Matthew Shepard, a crime apparently committed because of the victim's homosexual orientation, the bill received increased attention during the waning days of the 105th Congress, but failed to pass in either house before the end of 1998.

Other Matters

On February 23, 1998, three men were arrested for plotting to blow up the headquarters of the ADL in New York, the Southern Poverty Law Center in Montgomery, Alabama, and the Simon Wiesenthal Center in Los Angeles, as well for a number of other offenses. The alleged perpetrators were said to be members of a neo-Nazi group, the New Order.

In August 1998 a Los Angeles jury awarded $2.2 million to Jeffrey Graber, a former employee of Litton Guidance and Control Systems, based on his claims that he had been subject to constant anti-Semitic harassment over a period of nine years. Graber charged that the harassment caused him to develop digestive problems as well as depression so severe that he was ultimately placed on permanent disability leave.

INTERGROUP RELATIONS

Black-Jewish Relations

LOUIS FARRAKHAN AND THE NATION OF ISLAM

The Million Youth March led by former Nation of Islam official Khalid Muhammad in New York City on September 5 failed to attract anything close to the advertised number; by one estimate, there were perhaps 6,000 in attendance. However, unlike the much better attended—and more peaceful—Million Man March led by Louis Farrakhan in Washington in October 1995, the Million Youth

March ended with a set-to when police officers moved to end the event because it had gone beyond its court-imposed ending time. This followed a months-long effort by New York mayor Rudolph Giuliani to prevent the march from taking place, in the course of which he was rebuffed by the courts for overstepping the boundaries set by the First Amendment. In the aftermath of the rally, there was talk of bringing criminal charges against Muhammad for what city officials characterized as incitement to riot. Along with barbs directed at Mayor Giuliani and the police, Muhammad let loose from the platform with virulent anti-white and anti-Semitic invective, calling Jews the "blood-suckers of the black nation."

At first it was feared that the Million Youth March would do harm to black-Jewish relations, but the fact that some African American leaders joined their Jewish counterparts to condemn Muhammad and denounce him as an unfit leader for black youth was seen as encouraging.

MAINSTREAM CIVIL-RIGHTS ORGANIZATIONS

A study issued in early 1998 by the Foundation for Ethnic Understanding, an organization headed by Rabbi Marc Schneier of New York, found that cooperation, rather than conflict, was "the dominant theme between African-Americans and Jews." The report asserted that the media prefer to report on conflict, leading to the false perception of a relationship in decline. The second annual conference on black-Jewish relations at Yeshiva University in New York focused on that study, in particular its finding that approximately 43 percent of Jews and 53 percent of blacks believed that black-Jewish relations in the United States had gotten better in the past year. These findings, as well as agreement that public schools should do more to teach children about slavery and the Holocaust and other points of agreement, led Rabbi Schneier to reiterate his point that relations between the two groups should not be regarded as in decline.

Nevertheless, points of tension remained in evidence. Murray Friedman, Philadelphia area director of the American Jewish Committee and author of *Why the Black/Jewish Alliance Failed*, acknowledged that blacks and Jews were "feeling more positive this year than others," but asserted that polls showed as well that "racial preference policies and black leaders such as Nation of Islam leader Louis Farrakhan, who preach anti-Semitic views, are the two issues that continue to splinter blacks and Jews all over the country."

One cooperative effort did not end well when, in February, the Rev. Henry Lyons, president of the National Baptist Convention, was arrested on fraud charges stemming from misuse of $225,000 donated in 1996 by the Anti-Defamation League to help rebuild black churches that had been burned down. It was claimed that only $31,000 of the gift was used by Rev. Lyons as intended; following the disclosure, the missing money was returned to the ADL and redistributed to churches in need.

Julian Bond, chairman of the NAACP, appeared before the annual meeting of the ADL in April 1998, urging that blacks and Jews must work together to "make the American promise real" and toward a day when groups like the NAACP and the ADL were no longer necessary.

Interreligious Relations

CATHOLICS

Pope John Paul II's historic path of reconciliation with the Jewish community continued through 1998, even as specific actions at times led to some tensions between the Jewish and Catholic communities. Perhaps the most visible such occasion was the release in March of "We Remember: A Reflection on the Shoah," in which the Vatican expressed repentance for the failings of individual Catholics, but did not accept institutional responsibility for the Holocaust. The document also defended Pope Pius XII against criticism over his silence during that era.

Many in the Jewish community expressed disappointment following release of the document. Rabbi Mark Winer, president of the National Council of Synagogues, commented that "in ascribing sinfulness to individual Catholics, it sidesteps responsibility on the part of the Church. It never says that Catholic teaching was central to the teaching of contempt about the Jewish people." But, whatever the disappointment, most spokespersons for Jewish groups were quick to look also to the positive side. Rabbi A. James Rudin, director of interrreligious affairs of the American Jewish Committee, pointed out that the Vatican had created a teaching document on the Holocaust that "doesn't give credence to Holocaust deniers," and possibly had opened the door to allowing access to the Vatican archives, a step for which Jewish groups had long called. A series of meetings at the Vatican later in March between Jewish leaders and senior Vatican officials, scheduled long before the Vatican released the document, underscored the strong continuing relationship and resulted in a joint communiqué calling for a range of new cooperative efforts.

This ambivalent attitude toward the Vatican document seemed destined to be the prevailing Jewish verdict on the effort. In September, the International Jewish Committee on Interreligious Consultations (IJCIC), a coalition of Jewish groups that deals with senior Church officials, commended the document's recognition of the Holocaust as a historical fact. This, the IJCIC statement noted, "should render impossible the obscenity of Holocaust Denial among Catholics." At the same time, the IJCIC response pointed to shortcomings in the document, such as its minimization of the connection between church doctrine and anti-Semitism and its praise of Pope Pius XII for saving "hundreds of thousands of Jewish lives" without sufficient supporting evidence. Even with these perceived deficiencies, Jewish leaders expressed their hope that "We Remember" would be used as the basis to educate the world's one billion Catholics about the Holocaust.

Many Jews voiced dismay when, in October, Pope John Paul II canonized Edith Stein, a Jewish-born Catholic convert who died in the Holocaust, praising her as "an eminent daughter of Israel and a faithful daughter of the Church" and announcing that Stein's saint's day would be commemorated as a memorial "of that bestial plan to eliminate a people, which cost millions of Jewish brothers and sisters their lives." Rabbi Daniel Farhi, leader of France's Reform movement, among others, protested that the pope's action could only be understood as sending a message that "it is a Jew converted to Catholicism that is being shown as an example to the Christian people," and warned that the move had created "a new stumbling block in the Judeo-Christian dialogue." Rabbi Rudin, of the American Jewish Committee, took a more cautious approach, saying that while Stein's canonization is filled "with ambiguity, ambivalence and confusion," he believed that the movement toward more positive relations between Jews and Catholics would continue. Jewish objections were also heard when the Vatican beatified Croatian archbishop Alojzije Stepinac, accused of having been a collaborator with Croatia's wartime Nazi puppet regime.

Steven Spielberg's Righteous Persons Foundation funded an American Jewish Committee program in Philadelphia this year, the Catholic/Jewish Educational Enrichment Program, in which rabbis and priests attend each other's religious day schools. This followed similar programs established in New York, Chicago, Los Angeles, and San Francisco.

MUSLIMS

As 1997 ended, American Jewish leaders quickly moved to express solidarity with American Muslims by condemning the defacement with a swastika of a star-and-crescent that had been placed on the White House Ellipse to mark the winter holiday season. But, proving that no good deed goes unpunished, M. T. Mehdi, president of the National Council on Islamic Affairs (the group that had arranged for placement of the Muslim symbol near a Christmas tree and a Hanukkah menorah traditionally placed on the Ellipse at that time of year) was quoted in the *Washington Post* as responding to the incident by calling the Nazis "the real founders of Israel." "We hate the swastika," he said, "because it reflects the Nazis and the hated Hitler, who killed six million Jews and frightened Jews to go to Palestine and create the Jewish state." Mehdi also asserted that "Hitler helped Israel more than Herzl." Jewish leaders were quick to condemn Mehdi's remarks. They were supported by James Zogby of the Arab American Institute, who termed Mehdi's comments "absolutely the wrong response to what happened."

In another incident, several Jewish groups protested when the State Department invited the Council on American Islamic Relations (CAIR) to participate in two events related to the department's work promoting religious freedom abroad. In a letter to the State Department, the Anti-Defamation League described CAIR as an organization that condones terrorism and serves as a propaganda arm for the terrorist group Hamas and urged the State Department "to scrutinize those groups it invites." The Zionist Organization of America objected, as well, to the inclusion of the American Muslim Council and the Muslim Public Affairs Council as "groups that publicly endorse groups on the State Department terror list" and defend regimes that engage in religious persecution abroad. Noting that these were public events, a State Department official said that "attendance by groups in meetings open to the public should not be interpreted to constitute an endorsement by the department of the views of those attending the meeting."

CHURCH-STATE MATTERS

In the most closely watched church-state case of the year, on June 10, 1998, the Wisconsin Supreme Court ruled, 4-2, that Milwaukee's school voucher program was constitutional. The Wisconsin high court—in the first-ever state supreme court determination on this issue—found that the program, which allows disadvantaged children to attend private and parochial schools at taxpayer expense, did not violate the constitutionally mandated separation of church and state. The Wisconsin court found that the program "has a secular purpose" and "will not have the primary effect of advancing religion," overturning an intermediate appellate court's decision that the Milwaukee scheme was unconstitutional.

The decision immediately provoked strong, but divided, reaction from the Jewish community. For the most part, the organized Jewish community condemned the decision as a breach in the wall of separation of church and state and as a blow to public schools. But Orthodox Jewish groups and Jewish conservatives applauded the decision. "This is a break in the dike," said Marshall Breger, law professor at Catholic University's Columbia School of Law. "We're going to have a full-scale voucher program in Wisconsin, and we'll be able to see what it looks like."

An appeal to the U. S. Supreme Court was filed, with supporters and opponents of vouchers alike urging the high court to accept the case for review. However, on November 9, the Supreme Court voted, 8-1, without comment, not to hear the matter. That action set no legal precedent other than leaving vouchers in place in Wisconsin. Voucher advocates were nevertheless quick to claim victory. "At a minimum, this clearly refutes those who would say that voucher programs are unquestionably unconstitutional," noted Nathan Diament, director of the Orthodox Union's Institute for Public Affairs. In contrast, David Feiff, president of the Milwaukee Jewish Council, expressed disappointment, saying, "Wisconsin taxpayers are going to be compelled to support religious schools in a fashion we believe violates the federal Constitution." All sides seemed to agree, however, with the assessment of Agudath Israel general counsel David Zwiebel that "we all would have been better off if the Supreme Court had taken this case." With the resolution of the Wisconsin case, the constitutional issue remained open, with voucher litigation still pending in several other states and new voucher measures bound to crop up again in Congress and state legislatures and as referendum initiatives.

Another major theme of 1998's church-state cases had to do with attempts to stem official sponsorship of religious practice. In January a federal district court judge ruled that a two-part Bible course could go forward with that part of the curriculum dedicated to the Old Testament, because it was "ostensibly designed to teach history and not religion," but not with the New Testament portion of the curriculum. U.S. district judge Elizabeth Kovachevich found it difficult "to conceive how the account of the resurrection or of miracles [in the New Testament] could be taught as secular history." The American Civil Liberties Union (ACLU) and People for the American Way hailed the decision on the New Testament curriculum as an appropriate response to a "stealth curriculum" designed to teach religion while promising to carefully monitor the Old Testament class. A statement by the American Center for Law and Justice, a legal watchdog group affiliated with the Christian Coalition, commended the decision to allow the Old Testament class while promising to review the injunction against the New Testament class.

Groups advocating church-state separation were not pleased with the Alabama Supreme Court's decision at about the same time striking down, on technical grounds, a "religious liberty" lawsuit brought by Gov. Fob James and Attorney General Bill Pryor. Although the court dismissed the lawsuit and did not, as the plaintiffs hoped, uphold as constitutional Judge Roy Moore's practice of displaying the Ten Commandments in his courtroom and opening court with prayers, the effect of the dismissal was to allow those practices to continue. An earlier lawsuit brought by the ACLU had also been dismissed on procedural grounds.

In another chapter of the seemingly never-ending story of Kiryas Joel, a New York State intermediate appellate court upheld a ruling striking down, for the third time, an effort by the state legislature to create a special school district for a suburban village comprised entirely of Satmar Hassidim. The separate district would enable students residing there to receive publicly financed remedial instruction without having to go to area schools outside the village to receive those services.

Legislative Activity

The so-called religious freedom amendment, introduced in 1997 by Rep. Ernest Istook (R., Okla.), was immediately denounced by most Jewish groups, joined by a broad array of civil liberties and other religious organizations, as an invidious threat to religious liberty that would roll back much of the First Amendment's prohibition on government establishment of religion. In the view of its opponents, the measure would amend the U.S. Constitution so as to allow officially sanctioned prayer in school classrooms and at graduations, allow religious symbols to be placed on government property, and permit government officials, public school teachers, and military officers to endorse religious activities or beliefs. Additionally, opponents maintained, the amendment would permit—if not require—the government to use taxpayer dollars to fund religious activities on the same terms that it funds secular activities. Interestingly, supporters of vouchers within the Jewish community, including leading Orthodox groups, saw fit for the most part to take no position on the amendment, even though it would have allowed for state funding of parochial schools. Opposition to the amendment was spearheaded in Congress by a new champion of church-state separation, Rep. Chet Edwards of Texas, a Democrat.

The amendment took a significant step forward when, on March 4, 1998, it was passed by the House Judiciary Committee on a party-line vote. Commentators widely held that the initiative had little or no chance of garnering the two-thirds vote necessary to pass in the full House, but that it was being moved forward in order to enable the Christian Coalition to include votes on this issue in that group's voters' guides. On June 4, the House voted down the measure by a vote of 224-203, falling 61 votes short of the 285 votes required to pass a constitutional amendment. No Jewish representatives, Republican or Democrat, voted for the measure. Even as the votes were counted, it was anticipated that amendment supporters would not give up the fight. "They're going to look for other ways that don't require two-thirds to push their agenda," commented Steve Silverfarb, deputy director of the National Jewish Democratic Council.

It was a different story for a voucher plan for the District of Columbia and an initiative to create "A-plus education accounts," a variant approach to the effort to allow tax dollars to be used to support parochial and other private schools. Opposed by much of the organized Jewish community as inconsistent with church-state separation and as bad public policy, the measures were strongly supported by Orthodox Jewish organizations such as the Union of Orthodox Jewish Congregations and Agudath Israel of America.

The D.C. voucher bill was touted by supporters as an appropriate trial balloon. "Perhaps Washington, D.C., is the place to do it because things can't get any worse [there]," commented Nathan Diament, director of the Orthodox Union's Institute for Public Affairs. But, retorted Richard Foltin, legislative director and counsel of the AJCommittee, Congress was simply allowing itself to be diverted from "what has to be done to provide proper educational opportunities for children in the inner city in order to enact a nostrum that is not going to work." The AJCommittee organized a letter from leaders of 24 faith-based organizations opposing voucher proposals; the letter was sent to President Clinton early in 1998 and to members of Congress in April, in order to make the point that many religious groups were opposed to such initiatives. Nevertheless, on April 30, the

House of Representatives passed the D.C. vouchers bill by a vote of 214-206, following Senate passage of the bill the previous year. On May 20, 1998, President Clinton vetoed the bill, saying that it would undercut public education and prove to be a "disservice to those children."

A proposal by Sen. Paul Coverdell (R., Ga.) for "A-plus education accounts," although not strictly a vouchers measure, was also opposed by most of the organized Jewish community, with other "separationists," on the ground that it was simply another way of using public money to support private schools. In April 1998 the bill was passed in the Senate, following passage in the House in 1997, only to be vetoed by the president in short order.

During the year the Jewish community paid increased attention to "charitable choice" provisions in federal law allowing taxpayer dollars to be directed to sectarian organizations that offer social services, but without the church-state safeguards that many in the Jewish community regard as essential. Opponents of the initiative argued that, in the absence of these safeguards, churches or synagogues could receive federal funds for programs in which they discriminate on the basis of religion in hiring or, in some instances, could require beneficiaries to adhere to the practice of a certain faith as a condition of receiving the service. Supporters, which—in a familiar scenario—included Orthodox and conservative organizations, argued that this approach was simply a nondiscriminatory and beneficial way for religious institutions to be involved in the provision of social services. "Charitable choice" provisions, previously enacted as part of the welfare reform law of 1996, were included in the Community Service block grant of 1998 signed into law late in the year. In addition, on May 7, 1998, Sen. John Ashcroft (R., Mo.), the main proponent of "charitable choice," introduced legislation which, if enacted, would apply "charitable choice" provisions to all social service programs that receive federal funding.

"Free-Exercise" Developments

In early 1998 a decision by a Delaware court dealt with an unusual variation on the long-simmering controversy over how far secular law should bend in the face of a religious free-exercise claim. Alan and Sonye Grossberg of Wyckoff, New Jersey, were compelled to appear in court to testify about private conversations with their daughter, Amy, who was accused of killing her newborn baby. The Grossbergs had sought to quash the subpoenas requiring their testimony on religious grounds. They claimed that such testimony could not be permitted in a Jewish court, and that to force them to testify would violate their beliefs as Conservative Jews and thus infringe on their First Amendment right of free exercise of religion. In denying their claim, superior court president Judge Henry duPont Ridgely wrote that "the Grossbergs' freedom to act must yield to the compelling state interest in hearing everyone's testimony."

Given the prevailing state of the law, there was actually little for Judge Ridgely to consider. In 1993 Congress had attempted to restore the religious liberty protections weakened by a 1990 Supreme Court decision by passing the Religious Freedom Restoration Act (RFRA), a law that required government at all levels—federal, state, and local—to demonstrate a compelling interest if it passed a law or regulation that substantially impinged on an individual's free exercise of religion. But in 1997 the Supreme Court, in the case of *City of Boerne v. Flores,* struck down RFRA—at least insofar as the law was applied to state and local governments—on the ground that the law infringed on states' prerogatives. This decision left in place a regime under which the state can require individuals to violate their religious beliefs so long as there is a reasonable basis for the regulation in question, and the regulation is not enacted or enforced in a discriminatory fashion with respect to religion.

Immediately following the *Boerne* decision, the politically and religiously broad coalition that had come together in the early 1990s to push for passage of RFRA reconvened to draft and promote passage of new legislation that might survive the High Court's scrutiny. As the difficult drafting process stretched out over several months, hearings were held in Congress setting forth the case for (and against) a replacement bill. Rabbi Chaim Rubin, spiritual leader of an Orthodox congregation in Los Angeles, appeared before a February session of the House Judiciary subcommittee on the Constitution to make the case for legislation to protect religious freedom. Rabbi Rubin's congregation had relocated several years earlier to a community in which many aging congregants were located, only to be sued for violating local zoning ordinances that prohibit houses of worship in the vicinity. Other witnesses reported on their experiences with infringements on religious liberty, and several national experts, including Marc Stern, counsel for the American Jewish Congress, presented testimony.

On June 9, 1998, the Religious Liberty Protection Act (RLPA) was introduced in both houses of Congress as a bill drawn more narrowly so as to meet the constitutional concerns raised in the *Boerne* decision and still afford some protection to religious liberty against government action. The Senate Judiciary Committee and the House Judiciary subcommittee on the Constitution held hearings on RLPA in the summer of 1998. In the face of strong opposition to the bill from some groups on the right that objected to its partial reliance on the Constitution's commerce clause as a basis for jurisdiction, the House subcommittee abruptly held a mark-up of the bill in early August—at which time the provisions that relied on the commerce clause were removed. The RFRA coalition, right and left (including Jewish members of that coalition), strongly registered their opposition to the House Judiciary subcommittee's weakening of the bill. Although efforts to move the bill forward in both houses continued through the end of the session, by year's end there was no further progress.

Even as the RFRA coalition worked throughout 1998 to enact a replacement federal bill, it was also working to pass legislation modeled after RFRA at the state level. By year's end a mixed bag had resulted. Efforts to enact RFRAs in

Maryland, Virginia, New York, and New Jersey, among others, had stalled. A RFRA bill was signed into law in Florida and enacted by state referendum in Alabama. In two states, California and Illinois, RFRAs were passed by the state legislatures but ran into rough waters when they were vetoed by the governors of those states. In California, the bill died with the end of the legislative year. In Illinois, however, the governor's veto was overridden in a special session and the bill became law.

The Workplace Religious Freedom Act, a bill with wide support in the Jewish community that is intended to assure religiously observant employees reasonable accommodation of their religious practices, made little progress during 1998 because of concerns raised by business and labor. The bill was sponsored by Senators John Kerry (D., Mass.) and Dan Coats (R., Ind.) and, in the House, by Representatives Bill Goodling (R., Pa.) and Jerrold Nadler (D., N.Y.). With the retirement of Senator Coats, the chief Senate Republican cosponsor of the bill, its backers indicated that the first priority in the 106th Congress would be to seek another senior Republican as his replacement.

A similarly broad coalition of conservative and liberal groups came together in 1998 to push for passage of legislation directed at religious persecution abroad, but on this initiative there was ultimately more success. The Freedom from Religious Persecution Act, sponsored by Rep. Frank Wolf (R., Va.) and Sen. Arlen Specter, was introduced in 1997 with strong support from conservative religious groups; the bill initially faltered, however, when its inflexible, sanction-based approach was opposed by the administration and business interests and failed to attract the support of many religious organizations, including Jewish groups. The concerns raised by those religious groups were, however, consistently tied to praise for the role the bill's sponsors had played in raising awareness as to the degree of religious persecution still occurring around the world. After changes were made modifying some of the bill's provisions, ADL, the Union of American Hebrew Congregations, and the Orthodox Union endorsed the measure, while others still had concerns they wanted to see addressed. The American Jewish Committee, for its part, continued to express reservations serious enough to keep that organization from endorsing the bill, even as it acknowledged the improvement. The modified bill was passed by the House of Representatives in May 1998.

In late March, Senate Majority Whip Don Nickles (R., Okla.) introduced the International Religious Freedom Act, a bill co-sponsored by, among others, Senate Foreign Relations Committee chairman Jesse Helms (R., S.C.) and Senators Joseph Lieberman (D., Conn.) and Connie Mack (R., Fla.). This initiative was presented as a more nuanced approach, designed to adhere to the requirements of U.S. foreign policy and broader human rights advocacy and include a more calibrated system for imposing sanctions. At a June hearing of the Senate Foreign Relations Committee, various groups that had been skeptical about the Wolf-Specter bill signaled their support for the Senate version (including Felice Gaer of the Jacob Blaustein Institute for the Advancement of Human Rights on behalf of the American Jewish Committee). After this encouraging start, however, the bill stalled. The White House and the State Department, along with Senate Democrats and some Republicans, continued to insist that the bill would make for bad foreign policy and harm those religious minorities that it was intended to help.

The effort to move the Senate bill brought together a left-right coalition that saw the Episcopal Church and the Religious Action Center of Reform Judaism working hand in hand with the National Association of Evangelicals and the National Jewish Coalition to convince senators on both sides of the aisle that this was an initiative worth supporting. At the eleventh hour, with Congress winding down, changes were made in the bill that sufficiently satisfied the administration for the threat of a veto to be withdrawn. On October 9, the International Religious Freedom Act was passed by the Senate 98-0 and, one day later, the House of Representatives followed suit, with the president signing the bill into law on October 27.

HOLOCAUST-RELATED MATTERS

Holocaust Reparations

Efforts by Jewish groups to obtain compensation and restitution for Holocaust survivors continued to receive strong support from U.S. officials and the American Jewish community.

In February 1998, 22 Holocaust victims and lawmakers testified at a daylong hearing of the House Banking Committee about the legal status of art objects seized by the Nazis and about the failure of European insurance companies to pay claims on life insurance policies taken out by Holocaust victims. "These companies sought and obtained premiums up front, with no expectation of paying the claims in the end," Sen. Alfonse D'Amato (R., N.Y.) told the House committee. He proposed the creation of an independent committee to investigate the situation. The Italian firm Assicurazioni Generali, a leading underwriter of policies sold to Jews in Eastern Europe, promised to cooperate with the proposed panel, even as directors of some of America's top art museums pledged to research fully the ownership of holdings that might have come to them by way of wartime looting. This year also saw a raft of other legislative proposals, at both the federal and state levels, directed at looted art and insurance claims. Thus, in February legislation on these issues was introduced by Representatives Mark Foley (R., Fla.) and Elliott Engel (D., N.Y.) and Senators Arlen Specter and Robert Torricelli (D., N.J.), among others. And legislation moved through the California legislature designed to put pressure on insurers who failed to make efforts to resolve Holocaust-era claims.

In November 1998, Generali, joined by German-based Allianz and several other insurance companies, announced, following negotiations with the World Jewish Restitution Organization and a special advisory committee of the National Association of Insurance Commissioners, that they would participate in an international commission to be formed to resolve the problem of unpaid Holocaust-era insurance claims. At the same time, the insurance companies agreed to provide an initial escrow fund of $90 million as proof of their intent to settle these claims over a two-year period. With estimates of the number and value of policies varying greatly, the companies would have to undertake a thorough review of all their records and provide a complete accounting of policy holders' names and other available information. Left unresolved was what disposition would be made by participating insurance companies of heirless or unidentified policies.

On Friday, February 13, President Clinton signed the Holocaust Victims Redress Act into law, authorizing the United States to contribute up to $25 million to a new international fund to benefit Holocaust survivors and calling on all governments to adopt measures to return artworks confiscated by the Nazis or by the Soviets to their rightful owners. A further $5 million was authorized to support archival research and translation services necessary to assist in the restitution of looted and extorted assets. Later in the year, on June 23, he signed into law a bill introduced in April 1998 by Senators D'Amato and Moseley-Braun calling for the establishment of the "Presidential Advisory Commission on Holocaust Assets in the United States" to examine the disposition of assets of Holocaust victims, survivors, and heirs located in the United States. The commission was to focus its attention on dormant U.S. bank accounts, brokerage accounts, securities and bonds, artwork and religious and cultural artifacts, insurance policies, and German-looted gold shipped to the United States. Later in the year, President Clinton named Edgar Bronfman, president of the World Jewish Congress, to head the commission.

U.S. officials also continued to press for a full accounting of assets deposited with Swiss banks during the World War II era by Holocaust victims and their heirs. In addition to pressure from administration officials and members of Congress, several states took punitive measures against Swiss banks or threatened such measures, and multibillion dollar lawsuits were pending against the banks in the U.S. courts. In March, Switzerland's three largest banks pledged to negotiate a settlement of these claims, and, by April's end had participated in settlement negotiations in Washington, with the U.S. team headed up by Stuart Eizenstat, undersecretary of state for economic affairs.

As the efforts to resolve claims against the Swiss banks went forward, Switzerland and the United States issued reports relating to other claims against the Swiss. In late May, a report commissioned by the Swiss government and prepared by an independent panel of historians, concluded—much in line with a U.S. report issued in 1997—that during the war, Swiss bank officials had known, but chose to ignore, that gold they were buying from Nazi Germany had been looted from Jews and other subject populations. The new U.S. report, released early in

June, prepared under the leadership of Stuart Eizenstat, found that Switzerland was one of a number of ostensibly neutral nations that, by trading in war materiel with Nazi Germany, had "helped to sustain the Nazi war effort." The pair of new reports led some in the Jewish community to insist that Switzerland should be part of a global settlement of claims arising from Holocaust-era actions. The Swiss government, in turn, asserted—as it had in the past—that, in light of postwar international treaties and a $68 million humanitarian fund set up by the Swiss National Bank in 1997, any further settlement would have to come from the banks and not from "taxpayers' money."

Negotiations with the Swiss banks seemed in danger by the summer of 1998, following a tender by the banks of a $600 million "best offer" that Jewish groups rejected as "insulting" and in "bad faith." Eizenstat warned against moves toward sanctions, asserting that "Swiss opinion has been so hardened by threats of sanctions and other allegations that flexibility to achieve a settlement will be further complicated." New York State comptroller H. Carl McCall argued that threats of sanctions were appropriate because Holocaust survivors were "exhausted, their patience is spent and they are rapidly running out of time." In August, finally, Credit Suisse and Union Bank of Switzerland, Switzerland's two largest banks, agreed to pay $1.25 billion to settle the claims against them, more than double their "best offer." Politicians, lawyers, and other advocates for Holocaust victims and their heirs pronounced satisfaction in the result, with Estelle Sapir, a Holocaust survivor, asserting, "This is not charity from the Swiss. My father deposited money there. It is my money."

Representatives of 44 nations met in Washington in December for an international conference on the disposition of Holocaust-era assets, including looted artworks and claims on life and property insurance claims. The event, convened by the State Department and the U.S. Holocaust Memorial Museum, opened with a speech by U.S. Secretary of State Madeleine Albright in which she included the most explicit public reflections to date on her discovery in 1997 of her own Jewish roots. Although the conference was not designed as a decision-making forum, Edgar Bronfman, president of the World Jewish Congress, urged that it become the occasion for "practical and immediate proposals to secure financial restitution." In the course of the conference, Russia agreed to take steps to return art looted by the Nazis. At the conference's end, the participating nations, joined by 13 nongovernmental organizations, adopted a set of nonbinding principles, to provide a framework for identifying and publicizing looted works of art, and most endorsed the newly created commission to deal with insurance claims. Restitution of communal property was among the other issues discussed, but no consensus was reached on how to deal with it.

The conference also witnessed some soul-searching as Holocaust survivors pondered whether success in obtaining restitution for Holocaust survivors and their heirs might not detract from a more important focus—the memory of the irreplaceable loss for which no amount of money can compensate. At the opening of the conference, Nobel laureate Elie Wiesel commented, "Permit me to express my hope that we have not come here to speak about money. We have come here to speak about conscience, morality and memory." Michael Hausfeld, a lead attorney in the class-action lawsuit against the Swiss banks, asserted that money was not "the objective," but only "the means of illustrating the symbol and the symbol is still justice."

Late in November, amid continuing intense attention to the actions of European countries during the Nazis era, a *Washington Post* report brought to light allegations that Ford Motor Company and the General Motors Corporation had collaborated with Nazi Germany by allowing German affiliates to convert their facilities into military production plants, while resisting President Roosevelt's calls for increased military production at those companies' American plants. Documents said to support these claims were found by researchers working on behalf of former prisoners of war who had brought a class-action lawsuit against Ford in which they asserted that the company's German affiliate had benefited from their forced labor. Ford and General Motors both denied any collaboration with the Nazis or benefit from forced labor. Ford asserted that it lost contact with its German affiliate once the war began.

As the year ended, following his defeat in a bid for reelection, Senator D'Amato was appointed by a New York federal court as "special master" for settlement talks between Holocaust survivors and the German and Austrian banks accused of having been complicit with the Nazis in the latter's looting of gold.

OSI Actions

Throughout the year, the Justice Department's Office of Special Investigations continued its work in seeking to identify, denaturalize, and deport Nazi war criminals who had entered the United States in the years following World War II. In April a U.S. immigration judge directed that Jonas Stelmokas be deported to his native Lithuania for having lied about his role in killing Jews as a member of a Nazi-sponsored auxiliary police unit. Stelmokas died in November 1998, before he could be deported.

Developments abroad in one case showed that even when the OSI successfully obtained a deportation, justice was not complete without some action on the part of the receiving country. Aleksandras Lileikis left the United States for his native Lithuania in 1996 , one month after he had been stripped of U.S. citizenship for his alleged role in handing Jews over to Nazi death squads. It was February 1998 before Lithuanian authorities filed charges of genocide against Lileikis, following months of speculation as to whether the government was willing to prosecute suspected war criminals. Polls of the Lithuanian population revealed overwhelming public sentiment that Lithuanians were not responsible for the Jewish genocide in their country, notwithstanding strong historical evidence that many

Lithuanians had cooperated with the Nazis. Trial was commenced in September, only to collapse immediately because of the defendant's absence. His attorney claimed that Lileikis was too ill to appear in court or otherwise participate in the proceedings. The court directed that an independent medical examination be held to determine Lileikis's condition, a procedure likely to take weeks. A U.S. State Department spokesperson called upon Lithuania "to take whatever steps are necessary to ensure that justice is rendered in this and other important war crime cases from Nazi occupation."

The year ended without conclusion to the lengthy trial of the Ukrainian-born Jakob Reimer, the first proceeding ever brought by the Department of Justice's Office of Special Investigations in Manhattan to strip an alleged ex-Nazi of his citizenship, a necessary precursor to seeking his deportation. Prosecutors asserted that Reimer would have been denied citizenship had he acknowledged in 1952, the year in which he applied to become an American citizen, that he had murdered a Jew in a Nazi camp and that he was one of 2,500 Ukrainian prisoners who served as auxiliary SS troops at the Trawniki training camp in eastern Poland. With no survivors able to identify Reimer as one of the Trawniki guards who carried out numerous atrocities in Jewish communities in eastern Poland, including the killing of tens of thousands of Jews in the Czestochowa ghetto, OSI prosecutors made their case, in part, by relying on the testimony of a historian who demonstrated that it would have been impossible for Reimer to be unaware of the horrors in which the Trawniki guards were involved.

John Demjanjuk

The decades-long effort to deport the retired Cleveland auto worker accused of having been Nazi war criminal Ivan the Terrible seemingly came to its close when, in February 1998, U.S. federal judge Paul Matia restored to John Demjanjuk the American citizenship that had been stripped from him in 1981. Demjanjuk was extradited to Israel in 1986 where he was convicted of crimes against humanity in 1988 and sentenced to death, but his conviction was overturned on appeal when the Israeli Supreme Court ruled in 1993 that he had not been proved beyond a reasonable doubt to be Ivan the Terrible. The Israeli court decided not to allow further proceedings on the basis of other wrongdoing by Demjanjuk.

The 1998 U.S. court ruling followed in the wake of a 1993 decision of the U.S. Court of Appeals for the Sixth Circuit that the Justice Department had knowingly withheld information in 1981 that could have been used by Demjanjuk to battle against the extradition proceeding. The district court found that, whether knowingly or unknowingly, the U.S. Justice Department actions had left open questions as to whether it had "denied Demjanjuk information or material which he was entitled to receive pursuant to court discovery orders, whether such conduct by the government constitutes a fraud upon the court and, if so, what the appropriate sanction should be." In restoring Demjanjuk's citizenship, the district court left the door open for the Justice Department to file new denaturalization and deportation proceedings, a measure urged by Holocaust survivors.

Other Holocaust-Related Matters

The War Crimes Disclosure Act, introduced by Senators Mike DeWine (R., Ohio) and Daniel Moynihan, was passed by the Senate by unanimous consent on June 19, and by the House by voice vote on August 6. It was signed into law by President Clinton on October 8. (A similar bill was introduced in the House by Rep. Carolyn Maloney [D., N.Y.]). The act is intended to assist families and researchers seeking information about Nazi war criminals who may have entered the United States illegally or about transactions involving assets of Holocaust and other Nazi victims. The legislation established a Nazi War Criminal Records Interagency Working Group to locate, identify, declassify, inventory, and make records relating to these matters public. In addition to possibly assisting in tracking down additional Nazi war criminals and recovering assets looted by the Nazis, said Rabbi Abraham Cooper, associate dean of the Simon Wiesenthal Center, "we expect to learn more details about the U.S. government's knowledge of the Final Solution."

RICHARD T. FOLTIN

The United States, Israel, and the Middle East

THE 50TH ANNIVERSARY OF THE establishment of the independent State of Israel, observed throughout 1998, provided an opportunity in both Washington and Jerusalem not only for celebration but also for reflection and re-examination. From its early years of military vulnerability and economic dependency, Israel had in five decades transformed itself into the strongest military force in the region and a high technology-based industrial power with double the per capita national income of oil-rich Saudi Arabia. Given this evolution, one of the questions that needed to be addressed was how to reshape the relationship between the United States and Israel from one of donor and client to a more balanced partnership.

One area of common concern was terrorism. U.S. vulnerability was highlighted in 1998 by devastating attacks against its embassies in Africa by radical Islamic militants, and by such intractable problems as Iraq's continuing refusal to permit United Nations inspectors to find and eliminate Saddam Hussein's remaining arsenals of offensive missiles and his capacity to develop nonconventional weapons of mass destruction. Israelis too remained vulnerable to terrorist attack, as well as the threat of medium- and long-range missiles, which not only the Iraqis, but also the vociferously anti-Israel Islamic Republic of Iran were actively working to acquire with Russian and other foreign help. Efforts to counter these strategic threats were one area in which Washington and Jerusalem would expand and broaden their close cooperation during 1998.

A far more contentious question that gripped the U.S. Congress and public in 1998 was what role the United States should play in trying to restart the frozen Arab-Israel peace process. As the year opened, there was a stalemate in the discussions between Israel and the Palestinians on the extent of a further redeployment of Israeli forces in the West Bank (Judea and Samaria). At the same time, formal talks with the Syrians, which had been broken off in the spring of 1996, had not resumed despite behind-the-scenes American efforts to bring the parties together.

The Clinton administration believed that it was a matter of urgency to break the logjam in the Palestinian-Israeli talks, that unless Washington could demonstrate signs of tangible progress in the peace process to countries such as Morocco and Tunisia in the West and Oman and Qatar in the Gulf, which had established economic and quasi-diplomatic relations with the Israelis, the carefully nurtured ties between Israel and the more moderate Arab states were in danger of totally unraveling. The prevailing atmosphere of acrimony, frustration, and mutual suspicion was in sharp contrast to the hopeful atmosphere of peace and reconciliation between Israel and the Palestinians that had emerged so dramatically when

149

the Declaration of Principles of mutual recognition and commitment to peace was signed in September 1993 on the White House lawn by the late Israeli prime minister Yitzhak Rabin and Yasir Arafat, chairman of the Palestine Liberation Organization.

The Clinton administration was also eager to break the impasse so as to counter charges from the Arab world that the United States was applying a double standard—imposing harsh UN sanctions on Iraq for its defiance of UN resolutions, while seemingly turning a blind eye to new Israeli settlements in the "occupied territories" and other unilateral actions. In an explicit public response to charges of Washington's alleged double standard, Bruce Reidel, President Clinton's special assistant for Near East and South Asian Affairs, insisted that "there is no equivalency between Israel and Iraq." In a response to a question in a March 4 interview with *Worldview Dialogue*, he pointed out that unlike Saddam Hussein, Israel had never used weapons of mass destruction, nor fired ballistic missiles against its neighbors, nor used poison gas against its own citizens. Instead, Israel was engaged in a process of peace negotiations with its neighbors, a process the United States was committed to moving forward. Although many states in the world and in the Middle East had similar weapons, he stressed, "this Iraqi government is really unique," for it had used such weapons "again and again and again." Since it was a "repeat offender," the international community had a responsibility to prevent Iraq from gaining the capacity to do so again.

The Peace Process

Prime Minister Benjamin Netanyahu had been critical of the "Oslo Peace Process"—as the negotiations with the PLO became popularly known—from the start. His official line after his election was that he would work to correct the deficiencies he saw in the Oslo accords and to insist that the PLO and the Palestinian Authority (PA) scrupulously and completely fulfill their commitments to peace, especially those affecting Israel's security. He warned that unless there was reciprocity by the Palestinians in fulfilling all their commitments, Israel would be justified in halting its own implementation and possibly even abrogating the agreements entirely.

Under the Labor Party government, Israel had begun the process of relinquishing territory with an agreement on May 4, 1994, to withdraw from the Gaza Strip and Jericho on the West Bank. Under the subsequent "Oslo II" accords, signed in September 1995, Israel completed its withdrawal from six of the seven major Palestinian cities in the West Bank (Judea and Samaria) and transferred civil administration of virtually all the Palestinian villages in the West Bank to the Palestinian Authority, retaining only overall security control. (By the end of 1998, more than 98 percent of the Palestinians in the territories lived in areas where the PA was responsible for providing the basic services of daily life, including education, commerce, police, and religious institutions to the local Palestinian population. However, they did not have civil authority over the Israelis living in the settlements. There were complicated arrangements for cooperation between the security forces of the PA and the Israel Defense Forces [IDF], which at times led to confrontations and clashes.)

The United States had played a crucial and intimate part in the months of painstaking negotiations over withdrawal from the seventh city, Hebron, leading to an agreement signed on January 15, 1997. A religiously conservative city with a reputation for fanaticism, the city had witnessed frequent violent confrontations between Palestinian militants and the ideologically driven 500 Israeli religious nationalists who were determined to reestablish a Jewish presence in the heart of the city's 120,000 Palestinian residents. The extent of the exceptionally detailed role that the Clinton administration played in bringing about the complicated Hebron deal was illustrated by the fact that Ambassador Dennis Ross, the U.S. special peace coordinator, personally took a tape measure to determine where the line was to be drawn down the middle of the street dividing the 80 percent of the city to be placed under Palestinian authority from the remaining area that was to be an Israeli-administered enclave! During 1998 the United States was drawn ever more closely into the details of the negotiations, and the subsequent monitoring of the minutiae of the implementation of the Palestinian and Israeli commitments to each other continued. The wisdom of this expanded American involvement aroused concern among legislators and political observers in both the United States and Israel.

At the time of the Hebron agreement, the United States had also provided a "Note for the Record" that provided American assurances to both sides and set ground rules for future Israeli-Palestinian negotiations. The Hebron agreement also called for three further Israel army redeployments (FRDs), i.e., withdrawals from the West Bank, by mid-1998. Washington had formally assured Israel that the extent of each withdrawal was a matter of national security for Israel itself to determine, since the interim agreement stated only that the IDF would move to "*specified* military locations" designated by Israel. This language was taken from the 1987 Camp David agreement with Egypt, where Israel had successfully resisted Egyptian demands that the locations be *agreed* to by both parties. Despite these legal fine points, Washington increasingly sided with the Palestinians in urging Israel to enlarge the percentage of additional territory it was prepared to relinquish.

Netanyahu's reluctance was formally couched in terms of Israel's security requirements, which included not only such strategic considerations as commanding the high ground and the border along the Jordan River, but also control of the major aquifers in the West Bank. American observers were convinced, however, that Netanyahu's position also reflected the severe ideological and domestic political constraints that his right-wing coalition partners sought to impose upon him. Unlike the Labor Party and its left-wing allies, who accepted the principle of trading land for peace, Netanyahu's supporters, particularly the Jewish settlers in the territories, maintained that no part of the historic Land of Israel should be given over to foreign sovereignty. With the support of the Labor opposition, the agreement easily passed the Knesset by 87 to 17. However, cabinet approval of significant further withdrawals became increasingly difficult to obtain.

As 1998 opened, because of the stalemate in Palestinian-Israeli negotiations, the timetable for implementing the remaining provisions of their agreements was far behind schedule. Formal negotiations had not even begun on the "final-status" issues, such as Jerusalem, refugees, and borders, including the fate of Israelis living in settlements in areas that might be relinquished by Israel, which were all supposed to be completed by the end of the five-year interim period on May 4, 1999. Arafat repeatedly threatened that he would issue a unilateral declaration of Palestinian independence (UDI) on that day if no agreement was reached by then.

The impending deadline was another reason the United States was determined to make yet another effort to get the talks moving again. In addition to private warnings to the parties not to take unilateral actions, the Clinton administration for the first time explicitly expressed in public its opposition to Arafat's planned declaration of independence. On July 29, Assistant Secretary of State for Near Eastern Affairs Martin Indyk, in his testimony before the House International Relations Committee, declared that the U.S. government "would oppose a unilateral declaration, and make clear that this is an issue for final status negotiations." In a further statement, on October 2, Indyk explained that a UDI "becomes a recipe for almost immediate confrontation, as Palestinians seek to assert their sovereignty, having made their declaration, and Israelis seek to deny that sovereignty." Israelis expressed the view that following a UDI, Israel would be free to act, possibly even to annex parts of the disputed territories.

Joel Singer, who, as an aide to Prime Minister Rabin and then legal adviser to Israel's Foreign Ministry had played a key role in drafting the texts of the Israeli-Palestinian agreements, pointed out in an interview with the *Near East Report* (September 7, 1998) that, although the interim agreement was set to terminate on May 4, 1999, the underlying principles of the Oslo accords—namely the mutual recognition, the commitment to reaching peace through negotiations, and the other elements of reconciliation between the Palestinians and Israelis—set out in the exchange of letters between Arafat and Rabin, and the Declaration of Principles of September 1993, were meant to have a permanent character. Singer therefore suggested that if no final-status agreement had been reached by the May deadline, the interim agreement could be extended either for a specific time period or indefinitely.

While it was natural for the United States to oppose any unilateral actions by either side during the interim period, Singer conceded that because the Oslo process deferred the most difficult issues to the end of the final-status talks, it created "a strong incentive for both of the parties to advance their relative position by creating facts on the ground," so that at the end of the five-year transitional period it would have "more chips with which to conduct the endgame."

Since control over territory was one of the key bargaining chips, Netanyahu wished to relinquish as little territory as possible, while Arafat sought as much as he could possibly get. At one point Netanyahu even suggested that the way out of this quandary was to move immediately to discussion of the final-status issues without any intervening FRDs. Arafat had rejected out of hand as totally inadequate an Israeli proposal to withdraw from an additional 6 percent of the area. Israel for its part pointed out that as a result of earlier withdrawals by the IDF, some 96 percent of the Palestinians were already living under the civilian administration of the Palestinian Authority.

Washington began its renewed efforts to break the stalemate by inviting both Netanyahu and Arafat to "a working visit" in late January. Although the atmosphere was colored by signs of personal animosity between Clinton and Netanyahu, Secretary of State Albright characterized the talks with Netanyahu on January 20 as "good serious meetings" conducted "in a friendly atmosphere." In response to a reporter's question, Netanyahu denied that President Clinton had tried to "pressure" him. He described the meeting as "a wholehearted and serious effort at finding common ground," adding that there was already much common ground between Washington and Jerusalem, "because we both want to see the peace process go forward." In their meetings, in fact, Clinton had urged Netanyahu to increase withdrawal to the "double digit" range as a credible sign of good faith, and to reduce the total time by compressing the three stages of withdrawal into three months. Netanyahu had explained the difficulties he was facing back home; and to the press he pointed out that it was "very, very painful for us" to part with land, each grain of which was viewed as being "saturated with the tears and blood of the Jewish people and the hopes of generations." Nevertheless, his government was "prepared to consider redeploying" from areas that were "less crucial" to Israel's defense as part of the interim agreement and "of a final settlement." The key to further progress in the negotiations, Netanyahu stressed, was the principle of reciprocity.

In a press conference on his arrival in Washington on January 19, Netanyahu explained that when the Israeli cabinet linked its agreement to further redeployment to the Palestinian Authority's fulfillment of its commitments, this was not meant as an "ultimatum," but as a reiteration of a principle that the Clinton administration had endorsed from the beginning of the talks. The U.S. "Note for the Record," drafted by Ambassador Ross to accompany the Hebron withdrawal agreement, explicitly declared that Arafat and Netanyahu had "reaffirmed their commitment to implement the [Oslo] agreement on the basis of reciprocity." Netanyahu would insist throughout the year that further withdrawal of the IDF depended on the Palestinians fully carrying out the terms of the agreement: the security provisions, including steps to combat terrorism and other violence, and complete renunciation by the Palestine National Council of the anti-Israel provisions of the Palestine National Charter.

As Arafat was preparing to come to Washington for his own talks with the administration on January 22, there were encouraging reports of stepped-up security cooperation between the Israeli and Palestinian intelligence and security forces. For example, the Associated Press reported that on January 12, Palestinian police had raided a Hamas bomb factory in Nablus and had also arrested dozens of Hamas operatives. Thus Arafat expected to receive a favorable American reception from reporters when he came to the White House for his meeting with the president. However, before they could get down to serious discussion, the room was filled with reporters insistently pressing Clinton about news reports that he had engaged in an improper affair with a young White House intern named Monica Lewinsky. As the Palestinian chairman watched in amazement, no one thought to ask him or the president anything about the status of the Palestinian-Israeli talks. Arafat was to learn that not only in Israel, but in the United States as well, domestic politics could seriously threaten hopes for swift and decisive action in the peace process.

While Americans were primarily concerned whether the revelations would lead to the president's impeachment, in the media in the Arab world, where conspiracy theories flourish, the affair and the timing of its revelation were given a sinister interpretation. Since Ms. Lewinsky was not only Jewish but had visited Israel and harbored Zionist feelings, she was obviously an agent of Israel's Mossad, planted in the White House either to persuade Clinton or to so embarrass him that he would be crippled politically and unable to pressure Israel into making concessions to the Palestinians. This same calumny was repeated—on the basis of absolutely no evidence—by some pro-Arab publications in the United States.

Conversely, whenever the Clinton administration pressed the Israelis to be more forthcoming in the negotiations, Netanyahu's supporters in Israel and American critics of the Oslo accords would charge that to enable Clinton to achieve a foreign policy success—to divert American public attention from his domestic difficulties—he would impose any agreement, even if it was prejudicial to Israel's security. The Lewinsky scandal also distorted the interpretation given to Clinton's other foreign policy initiatives. When he failed to act forcefully against Iraq earlier in the year, after Saddam Hussein interfered with the UNSCOM inspectors, this was seen as evidence that the president was either too distracted or politically too weak to risk a confrontation overseas. Yet when he did launch four days of heavy missile strikes and bomb attacks, toward the end of the year, he was criticized in Congress and by some of the media of timing his action to delay his impending impeachment in the House of Representatives.

Until the archives of this period and the memoirs of the participants are made available, it will be impossible to assess fully to what degree and in which ways, if any, the Clinton administration's Middle East policies and actions were affected by the president's need to devote attention to his personal problems. It should be noted that in public-opinion polls throughout the year, the president's job approval rating continued to be quite high, with more than two-thirds of the public opposing his removal from office. Moreover, Clinton's efforts to foster Arab-

Israeli peace received even higher percentages of approval from both the general American public and the Jewish community. For example, in a poll commissioned by the Israel Policy Forum in May 1998, 80 percent of American Jews said they "support the Clinton Administration's current efforts to revive the Israeli-Palestinian negotiations" and agreed that "President Bill Clinton would not do anything that would harm Israel's security."

The Issue of Compliance

There was an ongoing debate and much disagreement during the year not only between the Israelis and the Palestinians, but also between the United States and Israel, as to whether the Palestinian Authority was in fact doing all it could to fight terror and prevent violence and hostile incitement, and how seriously one was to regard such matters as the PA's failure to confiscate illegal arms and reduce the size of the Palestinian police force, which reportedly now had 12,000 more men than authorized under Oslo. PA representatives argued to the Americans that the Israelis were making unrealistic and contradictory demands: on the one hand, they complained that Arafat was not doing enough to dismantle the infrastructure of Hamas and crack down on other opponents of the peace process; on the other hand, they wanted to reduce his capacity to do so!

A national poll conducted in mid-April 1998 for the *New York Times* found that two-thirds of Americans (67 percent) believed the PLO had not done enough to prove it was interested in peace. (Only 15 percent thought they had.) Regarding Israel's policies, Americans generally were more closely divided: 43 percent now said Israel had done enough, while 41 percent said it had not. This was a marked improvement over U.S. public opinion at the height of the *intifada*, a decade earlier, when 70 percent of Americans thought Israel was not doing enough to prove it was interested in peace, and only 17 percent thought it had done enough.

When Secretary Albright testified before the House subcommittee on foreign operations in March, she responded to concerns expressed by Rep. Nita Lowey (D., N.Y.) over reports that the PA was failing to carry out its security obligations and that Washington was planning to issue an "ultimatum" on the peace process. She replied that she had made it clear to Arafat that he must make a "100 percent effort" to stop terrorism and violence. She denied that the United States planned to unveil its own peace plan. When asked why she thought it was in the U.S. and Israeli interests to cooperate with the PLO and to vigorously push negotiations forward, she responded that U.S. help was needed because of the deep distrust between the parties. The Clinton administration was focusing on two things: improving security cooperation between the parties, and securing a "time out" by both sides regarding unilateral measures that were perceived to be "unhelpful."

This, she indicated, was also a principle that the U.S. State Department was following. When earlier in the month Sen. Daniel Inouye (D., Hawaii) asked the secretary for a progress report on the administration's plans to move the U.S. embassy from Tel Aviv to Jerusalem, Albright replied that Jerusalem was a final-status issue and the president was keeping his options open. Albright gave a similar response when Inouye asked why the passports of American citizens born in Jerusalem continued to list Jerusalem, without any mention of Israel, as their place of birth. In a House floor speech, Rep. Brad Sherman (D., Calif.) expressed his disappointment with the administration's request for funds to build an embassy in Berlin while continuing to delay implementing the Jerusalem Relocation Act. Sherman raised the same point, on March 10, when Assistant Secretary Indyk testified before the House International Relations Committee. Indyk assured him that the administration had every intention of upholding the law, but reminded Sherman that the law carried a waiver provision, which the president might use to delay implementation of the move.

During Indyk's testimony the following day before the Senate Foreign Relations subcommittee on Near Eastern affairs, he declared that "pressure is not in our lexicon." But expressing Washington's frustration, he indicated that the administration's capacity to bridge the difference between the parties was rapidly coming to an end. Speaking at the same hearing, Robert Satloff, executive director of the Washington Institute for Near East Policy, cited persistent press reports that the Clinton administration was planning to publicly announce its own proposal calling for a combined first and second Israel redeployment amounting to 13.1 percent of the area. This, he said, was contrary to Washington's earlier assurances that it was up to Israel alone to decide on the extent of the FRDs. American acts of omission and inconsistency, he said, had "helped to relieve the political burden on the Palestinians to fulfill their own obligations" and had, inadvertently, "damaged the integrity of the negotiating process."

Senate Letter

In mid-April the Clinton administration received a clear warning from Capitol Hill against changing its tactics in the peace process. Senators Connie Mack (R., Fla.) and Joseph Lieberman (D., Conn.) authored a letter to President Clinton that was endorsed by an overwhelming bipartisan majority of their colleagues. In the letter, 82 senators declared that it "would be a serious mistake for the United States to change from its traditional role as facilitator of the peace process to using public pressure against Israel." On the substance of the issues in dispute, the senators contended that Israel had generally complied with its Oslo commitments, but that the Palestinians "have not provided Israel with adequate security," and "Arafat has refused to conclude negotiations for the interim status issues." Instead of allowing its frustration with the lack of progress to prompt it to try to force more concessions from the Israelis, the senators advised the Clinton administration quietly to urge the Palestinians to accept Israel's latest withdrawal offer and move to final-status negotiations. Reviewing past U.S. efforts, the senators' letter concluded that "American Middle East diplomacy . . . has always worked best when pursued quietly and in concert with Israel" and urged the president to encourage "the direct negotiations of the parties themselves." A similar bipartisan letter was signed by 236 members of the House.

To allay concerns among friends of Israel in Congress and the nation at large, Assistant Secretary Indyk gave a lengthy interview to the *Near East Report*, the unofficial organ of the powerful pro-Israel American Israel Public Affairs Committee (AIPAC). In the interview, published on April 20, the former assistant National Security Council adviser on the Middle East and former U.S. ambassador to Israel (before his current post), once again asserted: "'Pressure' is not a word in our lexicon—and has not been since day one of this administration." He stressed America's "very special relationship with Israel" and said he agreed that "this is the most pro-Israel administration in history," adding that he was very proud of the Clinton administration's role in "further deepening these relations."

Asked why the United States had been pushing Israel to agree to a specific higher percentage withdrawal figure than it had offered, he explained that while the administration had succeeded in lowering Arafat's expectations, as Israel had asked the Americans to do, it believed there was a minimum amount necessary to end the stalemate and bring about an agreement. Moreover, he pointed out, the administration had not sought the deeper role it had been playing in the peace process since 1996. In the past, the American role was merely "to give support as the parties moved forward." But when the process broke down, following Palestinian riots in the wake of the Israeli opening of a new exit to the archeological tunnel in Jerusalem, in September 1997, the Netanyahu government had specifically asked the administration to play a more active role. "It's important to understand," Indyk stressed, "we didn't seek it. The Prime Minister wanted us in."

The assistant secretary of state, who had long experience in dealing with the Arab-Israel conflict, first as a scholar and then as a diplomat, expressed the administration's frustration with the long deadlock in the peace process: "This is not a very complicated issue. We're not talking about final-status negotiations," he said. "We're talking about *getting* to the final-status negotiations." All the administration was trying to do was to put together a package that is "credible, is reasonable, that meets both sides' needs," and provides a more favorable atmosphere for dealing with the difficult final-status issues.

He warned that when there was a prolonged stalemate, "violence and extremism" were likely to erupt. He was optimistic that once serious negotiations were resumed, the normalization process would also progress. In his travels throughout the Arab world, Indyk added, he had learned that while Arab governments were "facing severe questions from their publics about the value of the peace process," they had expressed their readiness "to re-engage"—provided we can get this process started again. Because of the agreements already achieved, he was optimistic that it would not take 50 years, but hopefully only about ten, to reach a comprehensive settlement of the Arab-Israel conflict.

Wye River Agreement

After the Clinton administration heeded the congressional advice not to publicly chastise or pressure Israel, persistent quiet diplomacy began finally to produce results. In late September, following a meeting with President Clinton in the White House, Netanyahu and Arafat announced that they had made progress on key components of an additional Israeli West Bank withdrawal. They were invited back in October to meet in strict seclusion from the press at the Wye River Plantation in Maryland. It took nine days and eight nights of intensive round-the-clock negotiations to hammer out agreement on all the detailed issues. At one point the Israelis packed their bags and threatened to pull out. By all accounts it was President Clinton, who devoted 90 hours of his time to the negotiations, who played the crucial role in keeping the parties from walking out and finally reaching agreement.

Whether an act of desperation or a stroke of genius, Clinton finally called on a gaunt and hairless King Hussein, who was undergoing intensive chemotherapy in the United States for the cancer that was soon to claim his life, to leave his hospital bed to make a final impassioned appeal for peace. Hussein addressed the "descendants of the children of Abraham — Palestinians and Israelis," and told them forcefully that they had no right to jeopardize the future of "our children and their children's children" through "irresponsible action or narrow-mindedness."

But if King Hussein provided the moral suasion and sense of urgency, it was President Clinton who kept Netanyahu and Arafat at the table — and demonstrated to the American public and to all the world that, despite his impending impeachment trial, he was still in full command of his faculties. At the White House signing ceremony on October 23, President Clinton thanked all the members of his administration's negotiating team, but it was clear from the words of the main players that he himself was the ultimate catalyst. Prime Minister Netanyahu called Clinton "a warrior for peace." He went on to elaborate: "I mean, he doesn't stop. He has this ability to maintain a tireless pace and to nudge and prod and suggest and use a nimble and flexible mind to truly explore the possibilities of both sides, and never on just one side. That is a great gift, I think a precious and unique one, and it served us well." King Hussein noted that he had known every American president since Dwight Eisenhower, "but I have never, with all due respect and all the affection that I held for your predecessors, known someone with your dedication, clearheadedness, focus and determination to help resolve this issue."

Clinton, who was frustrated and exasperated by Netanyahu on more than one occasion, also complimented the negotiating ability of the Israeli leader: "I was, once again, extraordinarily impressed by the energy, the drive, the determination, the will, the complete grasp of every detailed aspect of every issue that this Prime Minister brought to these talks." The embattled president recognized the difficulties that Netanyahu himself faced at home and noted, "He showed himself willing to take political risks for peace." The following day, in Los Angeles, Clinton said that Netanyahu "had gotten some unfair criticism in this country for being too tough in negotiations," but noted that in view of the opposition to further territorial concessions, Netanyahu would have an uphill battle to sell the Wye accord "to the people that are part of his coalition."

In what may have been a desperate effort to make the Israeli concessions to the Palestinians — which included the promise to release 750 Palestinian prisoners — more palatable to his right-wing constituency, Netanyahu at the last moment, after all other issues had seemingly been resolved, demanded that President Clinton release convicted spy Jonathan Jay Pollard from prison and allow Netanyahu to take him with him on the plane to Israel. (Pollard, an American Jew, was serving a life sentence for having passed thousands of pages of classified data to the Israelis, while working as a civilian intelligence analyst for the U.S. Navy.) In May 1998 Netanyahu was the first Israeli official to publicly admit that Pollard had been an Israeli agent. But Pollard had apparently been recruited not by the Mossad, Israel's equivalent of the CIA, but by Lekem, a rival intelligence agency that reported to Raphael Eitan, an associate of Gen. Ariel Sharon. Some speculated, therefore, that in addition to Netanyahu's natural desire to placate his increasingly disgruntled right-wing supporters — unhappy over the territorial concessions he had agreed to in the Wye River Memorandum — by championing the Pollard appeal, another factor was the personal interest taken in the Pollard case by now Foreign Minister and Minister of National Infrastructures Sharon.

While there was considerable support within the American Jewish community for commuting Pollard's sentence to time served on humanitarian grounds, an argument that had also been advanced by successive Israeli prime ministers to the Americans, Netanyahu's undiplomatic timing made many American Jews uneasy and provoked nearly universal outrage in the American press. More significantly, George Tenet, the director of the Central Intelligence Agency, had reportedly threatened to resign if Clinton acceded to Netanyahu's request. This was significant, since under the Wye accord, the CIA was to be given a specific role to monitor and report on compliance by both the Palestinians and the Israelis with the security-related provisions of the agreement.

At a joint press conference with Netanyahu in Jerusalem on December 13, Clinton was asked about Pollard. The president responded that he had instituted an "unprecedented" review of the case, asking the Justice Department and all other involved governmental agencies and all other interested parties to present their views on the matter by January 1999, after which he promised to review the sentence and "make a decision in a prompt way." A reporter then asked Prime Minister Netanyahu: "Can you explain to the American people why you think Mr.

Pollard is worthy of a release at this point?" In a lengthy reply, the prime minister acknowledged that Pollard "did something bad and inexcusable." "He should have served his time, and he did," said Netanyahu, but Pollard had been virtually kept in solitary confinement for nearly 13 years, he went on, which was a "very, very heavy sentence." Since Pollard "was sent by us on a mistaken mission, not to work against the United States," but nevertheless broke the laws of the United States, he was making this appeal purely on humanitarian grounds. The prime minister insisted: "It is not political, it is not to exonerate him, it is merely to end a very, very sorry case that has afflicted him and the people of Israel."

The Wye River agreement provided a detailed timetable over a 12-week period for the Israelis and Palestinians to carry out their obligations. It enshrined the principle of reciprocity, and each step in the process was linked to successful completion of the previous step. At the end of the process, 99 percent of the Palestinians would be living under their own rule in 40 percent of the West Bank, with PA control being complete in 18 percent; in the other 22 percent Israel would still retain some security functions. A Palestinian airport in Gaza was to be opened, with a discreet behind-the-scenes Israeli security role. A new joint industrial park would be built straddling the border between Israel and the Gaza Strip, which could conceivably provide employment for 20,000 Palestinians. Two corridors for travel between the West Bank and Gaza were also to be established.

Opponents of the accord noted that the IDF withdrawals would leave some settlements isolated and vulnerable, and that 25 percent of the land over the Yarkon aquifer, a key water resource for Israel, would be in Palestinian-controlled territory. Although the PA was committed to working together with the Israelis on monitoring and developing their shared water resources, critics of the accord pointed out that in the Gaza Strip, Palestinian overpumping and other mismanagement had exacerbated the problem of sea-water intrusion and had contaminated much of the area's fresh-water supply.

On the positive side, from Israel's standpoint, the Palestinian Authority committed itself to apprehend and imprison wanted terrorists, to outlaw and dismantle the infrastructure of terrorist groups, to confiscate unauthorized weapons, and to bring the Palestine police down to the authorized level. As a further move to demonstrate that the Palestinian commitment to peace with Israel was genuine and permanent, Arafat agreed to convene the Palestine National Council to publicly and finally revoke the anti-Israel provisions of the Palestine National Charter. In addition, a trilateral Israeli-Palestinian-American anti-incitement committee was to meet regularly to monitor and prevent incitement to violence and terror in the press, on radio and television, in textbooks, and in other vehicles of information.

In his trip to the area in mid-December, President Clinton placed a stone from the White House lawn on the grave of Prime Minister Rabin, joined Premier Netanyahu in lighting Hanukkah candles at the Hilton in Jerusalem, and reassured the Israelis of the American commitment to their security and peace. However, the most noteworthy event was Clinton's visit to Gaza, where he landed at the new Palestinian airport in his Marine One helicopter, to meet with the Palestine National Council. In his presence, roughly 500 members—out of an estimated total membership of 650—stood and raised their hands before a worldwide television audience to reaffirm Arafat's earlier written declarations that the anti-Israel provisions of the PLO charter had indeed been removed. In Jerusalem, Prime Minister Netanyahu said he accepted the vote as "a real change, a very positive change." Nevertheless, he refused to move further with the redeployment process, beyond the first 2 percent post-Wye withdrawal, until the Palestinians had met all their other commitments. This caused much disappointment not only among the Palestinians but also in the Clinton administration.

Facing right-wing defections from his government over the terms of the Wye agreement and an imminent vote of no-confidence, Netanyahu agreed on December 21 to dissolution of the Knesset and a call for early elections, which, after some debate, were scheduled for May 17, 1999. Although Netanyahu said he was still committed to implementing the Wye accord, in fact the process was again to be frozen as the Israelis geared up for their election campaign.

In contrast to the frustration in Washington over the Israeli failure to move forward, which threatened to put a strain on the much vaunted Israel-U.S. "special relationship," 1998 marked the year in which the Clinton administration moved closer to recognition of a Palestinian state and developed a closer relationship with its leadership. In his speech to the PLO leadership in Gaza, Clinton declared: "I am profoundly honored to be the first American president to address the Palestinian people in a city governed by Palestinians." Congratulating them on their vote to formally renounce their opposition to Israel's right to exist, he said that they were "taking the lead in writing a new story for the future," adding pointedly: "And you have issued a challenge to the Government and leaders of Israel to walk down that path with you."

First Lady Hilary Rodham Clinton was greeted with thunderous applause and hailed as a champion of Palestinian statehood wherever she went in Gaza. Although she walked a careful diplomatic line in her public appearances, praising Palestinian national aspirations while avoiding comments that could be considered a call for sovereignty, the Palestinians remembered the comment she had made some seven months earlier, in response to a televised question from a gathering of Israeli and Palestinian schoolchildren, to the effect that at the end of the peace process a responsible Palestinian state could make a positive contribution to regional peace and security. Although that statement was immediately disavowed by the White House press secretary as not reflecting official U.S. policy, statehood was clearly the direction in which Washington was moving.

Indeed, even in Israel there was a widespread and growing body of opinion that eventually there would be a Palestinian state west of the Jordan River. The task of Israel's negotiators was, as Ariel Sharon put it, to make sure that that Palestinian entity or state's exercise of sovereignty was so limited as to prevent it from constituting a military or political threat to Israel and its neighbors, notably the Hashemite Kingdom of Jordan, which already had a Palestinian majority in its population.

The degree of achievement in the Middle East peace process at the end of 1998 was given a rating of only 3.5 out of a possible 10 from "Peace Pulse," an index prepared each year since 1990 by a team headed by Prof. Steven Spiegel at the UCLA Center for International Relations and cosponsored by the dovish Israel Policy Forum (IPF). Peace Pulse monitors prospects for peace according to 14 indices, ranging from terrorism to the unemployment rate to tourism. On the positive side, the 1998 report noted that a decade-low total of 40 Israelis and Palestinians died in "political violence," and that Israeli-Jordanian relations had improved. Among the negative factors were the decline in the Israeli economy and the assessment that Iranian and Iraqi threats had increased "because of the successful Iranian tests of [missiles that could deliver] weapons of mass destruction and the decline of UNSCOM in Iraq." The report estimated that had the Wye agreement not been signed, the Peace Pulse for the year would have declined to 2.7, "making it the worst year of the decade." (The highest rating was 6.4 in 1994 following the start of Israel-PLO talks and the signing of the Jordanian-Israeli peace treaty.) "The bottom line is that the peace process is still teetering on the brink," the report stated. Assessing the American role, it concluded: "The U.S. was the hero . . . in 1998, preventing disaster through dogged diplomacy. Only the U.S. can make a difference, and if it does not keep constantly at the task, frustration and violence will result."

Economic and Defense Cooperation

The United States was maintaining its high level of current aid to Israel and agreed to increase the amount of military assistance because of the increasing costs of defending Israel against the new threats in the region. In January the Netanyahu government proposed gradually eliminating the $1.2 billion in annual U.S. nonmilitary aid over a 10–12-year period. Welcoming this proposal, Assistant Secretary of State Indyk pointed out that the phasing out of economic aid was occurring in the context of "a growing Israeli economy with a GDP of $90 billion — an economy which really does stand on its own two feet." He also noted that the Israeli-American bilateral relationship was helped "when the dependence is reduced." Indyk added that the administration planned to use the dollars freed up by the cut in economic aid to Israel to enable the Middle East Peace and Stability Fund to help other countries either engaged in the peace process, or who were normalizing relations with Israel. The first immediate beneficiary was to be Jordan, which was undergoing severe economic difficulties.

The appropriations bill passed by Congress for Fiscal Year 1999 (which began on October 1, 1998) was the first to implement the new arrangements worked out between Washington and Jerusalem. It earmarked $1.08 billion in Economic

Support Funds (ESF)—$120 million less than in previous years, and $1.86 billion in Foreign Military Funding (FMF). Of the latter amount, Israel was authorized to spend $490 million in Israel itself to research, develop, and produce sophisticated new defense systems to meet the challenge of the increased missile capacity of its potential Arab adversaries and Iran. Congress also agreed that all the aid would be disbursed 30 days after passage of the bill, rather than being doled out gradually. The bill also provided $70 million for refugee assistance in Israel. Egypt received $1.3 billion for FMF and $775 million for ESF, reflecting a $40 million reduction in economic aid from the previous year. Of the $75 million in U.S. aid to the Palestinians, Congress prohibited any funds going directly to the Palestinian Authority or to the Palestinian Broadcasting Authority because of its continuing inflammatory anti-Israeli broadcasts.

While there was little progress on the diplomatic front in 1998, there was enhanced Israeli-American cooperation in the area of defense and confronting terrorism. Congress was active in its efforts to stop the spread of missile technology to Iran, especially from Russia. Although President Mohammed Khatami made some positive remarks about favoring a cultural dialogue between Iranians and Americans in a lengthy CNN interview in January, he rejected Washington's offers to begin an official dialogue to discuss outstanding issues, and he and other Iranian officials reiterated in the most vitriolic terms the Islamic Republic's opposition to the State of Israel. They also denounced the Palestinians for seeking to reach a peace agreement with Israel. In the face of the evidence that Iran had not really moderated its anti-American and anti-Israel policies, in May the U.S. Senate passed by 90 votes to 4 the Iran Missile Proliferation Sanctions Act (IMPSA), which was designed to impose sanctions on Russian companies supplying missile technology to Iran. In June the House passed IMPSA by an overwhelming 392-22 margin. The president at first vetoed the bill, claiming it would interfere with ongoing negotiations with Moscow on this issue. However, when faced with overwhelming congressional support for overriding his veto, in July Clinton issued an executive order imposing sanctions on nine Russian companies for aiding the Iranian ballistic-missile program.

Congress also took additional steps to bolster Israel's ability to defend itself against the growing missile threat. The United States had been working with Israel for several years to develop the Arrow antimissile rockets to intercept incoming missiles while they were still in the upper atmosphere. In May Congress appropriated an additional $45 million for the program, so that Israel would obtain a third Arrow missile battery, beyond the two originally budgeted. In the FY 1999 defense appropriation bill, Congress approved an additional $47 million for the Arrow program—some $9 million more than the Pentagon had requested. Congress also added funds for some other joint U.S.-Israeli missile-defense programs. This followed the news that Iran had in July test-fired the first prototype of its Shihab-3 rocket, almost a year ahead of Western defense estimates. With a predicted range of 900 miles, and with the planned Shihab-4 reaching even further, Israel was now potentially a target of Iranian nuclear or chemical weapons. The launch on May 31 by North Korea of a missile that landed near Alaska caused additional concern, since North Korea had been a traditional supplier of ballistic missiles to Iran, Syria, and Egypt.

In September the close defense cooperation between Washington and Jerusalem was highlighted by the inauguration of the U.S.-Israeli Interparliamentary Commission on National Security. A joint hearing was held, with a bipartisan group of American members of the House and Senate and a group of Knesset members from across Israel's political spectrum. The first meeting dealt with the danger of missiles in the hands of rogue states. Further institutionalizing their defense cooperation, on October 31 Clinton and Netanyahu signed a new Memorandum of Understanding to enhance cooperation in the defense field. There were also a variety of joint military training exercises during the year.

Symbolic of the broadening strategic cooperation among America's friends in the turbulent Middle East, in January 1998 the U.S. Sixth Fleet joined with units from the Israeli and Turkish navies in their first trilateral military exercise. Significantly, Jordan sent military observers. Although this initial exercise, dubbed operation "Reliant Mermaid," was ostensibly only to demonstrate humanitarian search-and-rescue missions at sea, it served to underscore to potentially unfriendly states in the region that the rapidly developing strategic ties between Jerusalem and Ankara had the blessing of the Clinton administration in Washington.

During the year both the United States and Israel suffered casualties from terrorist attacks, most of them by radical Islamic militants. By far the worst incidents were the August 7 bombings of the U.S. embassies in Nairobi, Kenya, and Dar es-Salaam, Tanzania. Reportedly 257 persons were killed, including 12 Americans, and over 5,000 were wounded. Israel won universal praise from the African states and the United States for the heroic round-the-clock efforts of the Israeli rescue teams that were sent to the sites immediately following the disasters.

Washington was convinced that the mastermind of the attacks was Osama Bin-Laden, a wealthy Saudi exile who had become a militant Islamic extremist, who was suspected of involvement in earlier terrorist attacks, including against U.S. installations in Saudi Arabia. In February 1998, Bin-Laden had issued a "Declaration of the World Islamic Front for Jihad against the Jews and the Crusaders," which urged Muslims around the world to kill Americans, because, among other reasons, the United States had defiled the sacred soil of Saudi Arabia by stationing its troops there. The United States offered a $5 million reward for his capture and also bombed his suspected headquarters in Afghanistan. The bombings at the U.S. embassies, like the World Trade Center bombing several years earlier, once again awakened Americans to the grim realization that they and the Israelis faced a common threat from radical Islamic terrorists.

GEORGE E. GRUEN

Jewish Communal Affairs

THE CELEBRATION OF ISRAEL'S 50th anniversary, a highlight of 1998, was colored by continuing tension between many American Jews and the Israeli government over Israeli-Arab peace-making efforts and the issue of religious pluralism in Israeli society. The year also saw a historic merger of the two major American Jewish fund-raising bodies, a move intended to restructure Jewish philanthropy for the 21st century.

The Peace Process

The year opened with a harsh reminder of the split within the American Jewish community over the direction of Israeli policy under Prime Minister Netanyahu's Likud government. On January 6 the Smithsonian Institution announced that it was canceling a lecture series, "Israel at Fifty: Yesterday's Dreams, Today's Realities," that had been planned for the spring. The series, which was to have been cosponsored with the dovish New Israel Fund (NIF), had come under heavy criticism from Americans for a Safe Israel, a pro-Likud organization, as well as a number of political figures and Jewish newspapers, for allegedly favoring the Palestinian side both in the topics for discussion and the list of speakers. NIF executive director Norman Rosenbaum called the cancellation "Jewish McCarthyism," a charge picked up by *New York Times* columnist Anthony Lewis (January 12), who blamed it on "a small band of American Jews who want to intimidate into silence those in the community whose political views they dislike."

Prime Minister Netanyahu—whose government had refused American calls for further redeployment from the West Bank on the ground that the Palestinians had not fulfilled their pledges under the Oslo accords—was scheduled to arrive on January 19 for talks in Washington, and his champions and detractors in the American Jewish community competed for control of American public opinion. The Israel Policy Forum (IPF), which had released a survey in October 1997 showing that most American Jews backed American policy and favored pressure on both Israel and the Palestinians to move the peace process forward, ran an advertisement in major newspapers supportive of the American administration's peace policy—and implicitly critical of Netanyahu—that called the U.S. government "an honest and effective broker." But the IPF's attempt to convince other organizations to sign on to a letter to President Clinton expressing these sentiments found little support. Meanwhile, the *Middle East Quarterly*, edited by peace-process skeptic Daniel Pipes, published the results of a poll claiming to show that 65.3 percent of American Jews opposed U.S. pressure on Netanyahu, with only 23.7 percent favoring such tactics.

The Conference of Presidents of Major American Jewish Organizations, the umbrella organization whose mission is to articulate a consensus of the Jewish community, was able to agree only on sending a letter to Clinton complaining of the persistence of anti-Jewish propaganda in the Palestinian media, urging the extradition from PLO-controlled areas of terrorists who had killed Americans, and requesting the release, on humanitarian grounds, of convicted spy Jonathan Pollard. Alarmed at the news that Clinton planned to show his displeasure with Netanyahu by limiting their meeting to a session in the Oval Office—with no public dinner or even "working lunch," no joint news conference, and no invitation for the Israeli prime minister to stay at Blair House, the official government guest quarters—leaders of the Presidents Conference met with Clinton and his top Middle East advisers just hours before Netanyahu's arrival and urged him not to foster the perception that U.S. policy was turning hostile toward Israel. Clinton responded, according to the *Forward* (January 23), that while there was no intention to pressure either side, the administration was losing patience. Emerging from the meeting with the president, Presidents Conference executive vice-chairman Malcolm Hoenlein said that "reports about an administration cold shoulder during this trip aren't true."

Upon his arrival, Netanyahu proceeded to exasperate Clinton and the organized Jewish community, first, by breaching protocol and meeting with Newt Gingrich, the Republican Speaker of the House, prior to seeing the president, and, second, by taking his case directly to evangelical Protestant leaders, who were both hostile to the American president and deeply distrusted by mainstream American Jewry. Not only did the prime minister address an enthusiastic rally of the National Unity Coalition for Israel, a politically conservative and predominantly evangelical group, but he also held a private meeting with the Rev. Jerry Falwell and other Southern Baptist leaders, who promised to mobilize "about 200,000 evangelical pastors" to "use their influence in support of the state of Israel and the Prime Minister." A number of Jewish leaders told reporters—though not for attribution—that Netanyahu had blundered, offending President Clinton and insulting the Presidents Conference by his attention to the evangelicals. One of the few leaders willing to comment on the record, David Harris, executive director of the American Jewish Committee, was more judicious: "Israel needs support from a broad range of the American public, this [evangelical] community included, but if it's inordinately focused on this community alone, it's going to raise some questions" (*New York Times*, January 21).

As it turned out, Netanyahu's session with Clinton went unexpectedly well. Apparently encouraged by indications that Israel was serious about further withdrawals if the Palestinians made reciprocal moves toward peace, Clinton publicly acknowledged that "Israel has to make its own decisions about its own security," and in a meeting with Yasir Arafat later that week Clinton stressed the need for the Palestinians to do more to control terrorism.

But when Secretary of State Madeleine Albright followed up these Washington meetings with a visit to the Middle East at the beginning of February and found that the parties were as far apart as ever, she publicly chided both sides, renewing the internal debate in the American Jewish community over Israel's stance. There was a new "battle of the polls." The Jewish Council for Public Affairs (JCPA, previously known as the National Jewish Community Relations Advisory Council, NJCRAC), released a survey at its annual plenum in February indicating that 70 percent of a sample of 6,800 affiliated Jews in 14 American communities wanted pressure on both Netanyahu and Arafat to move toward peace. This poll, however, made no claim to being scientific. In March the American Jewish Committee issued its own annual scientific survey of American Jewish opinion and came up with rather different results: 69 percent said that the United States should pressure Arafat, but only 45 percent favored pressure on Netanyahu. The AJC poll also showed rising pessimism in the American Jewish community about the chances for Middle East peace.

Rumors spread that the U.S. administration, frustrated at the Israeli-Palestinian deadlock, was about to set forth its own detailed plan for the next stage of Israeli withdrawal from the West Bank, an eventuality that many anti-Likud American Jews welcomed, but one that pro-Netanyahu opinion viewed as unacceptable "pressure." One sign of the administration's intentions was the welcome President Clinton extended to Ehud Barak, the leader of Israel's opposition Labor Party, who visited the White House and Capitol Hill in late February. His warm reception by the president was in striking contrast to the way Netanyahu had been treated in January. In fact, sources claimed that Clinton had unveiled to Barak the general outlines of a proposed American plan to break the peace-process deadlock, including the extent of the suggested next Israeli withdrawal from the West Bank. Barak reportedly responded that the Israeli public would welcome such an American initiative so long as it was not put forward as an attempt to "pressure." Speaking to the Presidents Conference after his session with Clinton, Barak asserted that a U.S. proposal to move negotiations along should not be interpreted as pressure.

To counteract Barak's encouragement of administration policy, in early March Netanyahu sent senior adviser David Bar-Illan to lobby the Republican-controlled Congress against the imposition of pressure on Israel. Pro-Netanyahu American Jewish leaders also hoped the growing Monica Lewinsky scandal would weaken the president sufficiently to discourage any new Middle East initiatives.

The Presidents Conference, buffeted by contending American Jewish forces, voiced an ambiguous consensus position on March 2. "We believe strongly," said conference president Melvin Salberg, "that preconditions, or conditions imposed, as in the past, will not find success." He did not indicate whether the public announcement of an American plan constituted the imposition of conditions. But Howard Kohr, executive director of the American Israel Public Affairs Committee (AIPAC), the pro-Israel lobby, publicly accused unnamed State Department officials "of promulgating a so-called American plan and then using pressure tactics to try to coerce Israel into accepting it."

Kohr's outright attack on her department brought Secretary of State Albright's patience to an end. On March 27 she initiated a conference call to the Presidents Conference, speaking to some two dozen Jewish leaders. According to an unofficial transcript of the call obtained by the Jewish Telegraphic Agency (*JTA Daily News Bulletin*, March 31), Albright insisted that the administration was committed to Israel's security and asked these American Jewish leaders to help convince the Israeli government that the American initiative—not a "plan," she said, but merely a "set of ideas"—was in Israel's best interest. "I have to tell you, in all honesty," she went on, "we are coming to the end of the road here. . . . One of the options is to let them deal with each other and for us to walk away."

WAR OF LETTERS

Not bound by the Presidents Conference's need to negotiate an internal Jewish consensus, AIPAC needed only four days to get the signatures of 81 U.S. senators on a letter sponsored by Senators Joseph Lieberman (D., Conn.) and Connie Mack (R., Fla.) highly critical of the administration. The letter opposed publication of any proposed U.S. plan for the Middle East, since such publicity would constitute pressure on Israel, and it would be "a serious mistake for the United States to change from its traditional role as a facilitator of the peace process to using public pressure against Israel." A somewhat milder letter sponsored by Rep. Eliot Engel (D.,N.Y.) attracted the signatures of 150 members of the House. An important element in the AIPAC campaign was a series of three "action alerts" to its members around the country stressing the importance of contacting their legislators and convincing them to sign. So convincing was AIPAC in lobbying for these letters that some legislators signed even after being urged not to by Ambassador Dennis Ross, the chief U.S. negotiator in the Middle East.

AIPAC's rush to criticize administration policy was questioned by some leaders of the Presidents Conference who agreed with AIPAC on the substance of the issue. For one thing, they argued, AIPAC had not consulted with the Presidents Conference until the two letters were already being circulated. For another, where was the hard evidence that the president and secretary of state were planning a strategy of pressure? Was it wise to antagonize an administration that was basically friendly to Israel? Might the administration retaliate against Israel? Was it not damaging to AIPAC's future credibility for it to react so explosively to a danger that was not clear and present? AIPAC's Howard Kohr brushed aside these qualms. "The issue of U.S. pressure is far from imaginary," he said. "People are pushing the President to go off course to a dead end."

Meanwhile, the Israel Policy Forum, which favored a more aggressive American role, initiated its own letter supportive of the administration, sponsored by Rep. Sam Gejdenson (D., Conn.) and signed by 31 House members. Dovish American Jewish leaders were quick to note that, for all of AIPAC's success with non-Jewish legislators, 15 of the 24 Jewish members of the House signed the Gejdenson letter; furthermore, four of the ten Jewish senators refused to sign the Lieberman-Mack letter, and two of them—Carl Levin (D., Mich.) and Dianne Feinstein (D., Cal.)—wrote their own letters of support to the administration.

This undignified "battle of the letters" publicized splits in the Jewish community that had previously been kept from public view. "Jewish Groups Go to Capitol Squabbling Among Themselves," was the headline in the *New York Times* (April 7). Hopelessly divided over whether to applaud or criticize the administration, the Presidents Conference first decided to ignore the Lieberman-Mack letter, but then reversed gears and thanked the 81 senators for speaking up for Israel, while also notifying the administration that its efforts to achieve Middle East peace were appreciated. The administration, meanwhile, impressed by AIPAC's clout and worried that the Republicans might use the issue of "pressure" on Israel to appeal to Jewish voters, held off on unveiling any new plan. The political wisdom of such an approach was underscored by a *New York Times* poll (April 26) showing that 58 percent of Americans sided with Israel in the Middle East conflict—up ten points in one year—while support for the Palestinians remained at 13 percent.

But the easing of American demands for progress toward peace proved temporary. Early in May, after the failure of two days of U.S.-sponsored Israeli-Palestinian talks in London, Secretary Albright suggested passing over interim matters and jump-starting final-status talks—on such crucial issues as permanent borders, Jerusalem, settlements, and Arab refugees—at a Washington summit. Once again, Albright hinted at what might happen if this did not work: Washington would "reexamine" its approach to the Middle East peace process. Since Arafat had quickly assented to a summit, and at least one American precondition for the summit—Israel's commitment to a 13.1 percent withdrawal from West Bank territory—was opposed by Netanyahu, her warning was clearly aimed at Israel.

Nevertheless, at a May 6 meeting of the Presidents Conference, when a motion was put forward to criticize the administration publicly for pressuring Israel, chairman Salberg did not allow it to come to a formal vote. Two days later the *New York Times* quoted an unidentified U.S. government official as suggesting that the administration would give Israel a "reprieve"; the connotation that Israel was guilty of criminal behavior outraged the organized Jewish community. First Lady Hillary Rodham Clinton added to the perception of pressure on Israel by telling a group of Arab and Jewish young people that it was in the long-term interest of the Middle East for the Palestinians to have their own state.

These events had an effect: on May 11, just five days after taking no action on the matter, the Presidents Conference voted 27 to 3 to issue a public statement about its concerns over U.S. policy, to communicate these concerns via a letter to the president, and to seek a meeting with him. While acknowledging that the conference encompassed a variety of views on the substance of the peace process, the public statement announced "full agreement that the Israeli government alone must make the difficult decisions affecting Israel's security." And alluding to Mrs. Clinton's remark, the statement urged President Clinton to make clear that a unilateral Palestinian declaration of independence was unacceptable.

While there was to be no summit, Netanyahu did visit the United States May 13–17 for a round of public appearances marking Israel's 50th anniversary—including the Salute to Israel parade in New York and the AIPAC policy conference and American Jewish Committee annual meeting in Washington—as well as a number of private meetings. Once again, Netanyahu spent much of his time with congressional Republicans, seeing them as a counterweight to the administration. In his speeches, the Israeli prime minister stressed the ongoing friendship between his country and the United States, and reminded his audiences that the administration was on record in support of the proposition that only Israel could make decisions about its security. Coming at a time of American Jewish concern about U.S. "pressure," Netanyahu's visit struck a deep emotional chord. The enthusiasm with which he was greeted gave the impression that American Jewish opinion had turned sharply in a hawkish direction. One AIPAC activist told journalist J. J. Goldberg, "There's been a big sea change. . . . You can see it on people's faces. . . . This administration has been sending out trial balloons to see what the Jewish public will put up with. Finally it struck home and kind of woke Jews up. Bibi had the guts to stand up, and Americans appreciate that" (*New York Jewish Week*, May 22).

It was, indeed, at the AIPAC policy conference that the new American Jewish hard line was most evident. A proposed policy statement opposing a fully sovereign Palestinian state was ultimately rejected because it seemed to leave the door open to a less than fully sovereign state, and a clause denouncing Holocaust denial by Palestinian leaders was overwhelmingly adopted. Hisses greeted Martin Indyk, assistant secretary of state for Near Eastern affairs, when he brought up Palestinian grievances against Israel under the Oslo accords.

Pro-administration Jewish groups, insisting that this tilt to the right did not really reflect bedrock American Jewish sentiment, ascribed it to an understandable but temporary reaction to the clumsy and undiplomatic official statements of the week before. But the president and secretary of state seemed to have gotten the message, and, in the wake of the Netanyahu visit, the administration, for the second time in 1998, backed away from anything resembling "pressure." In a letter to the Presidents Conference, President Clinton wrote: "At no time have I given an ultimatum to either party. Decisions concerning Israel's security, and on the peace process, must be made by Israel."

Months passed with no sign of movement toward peace in the Middle East. Moreover, looming large on the horizon was May 4, 1999, the date set by the Oslo accords for a final peace treaty. What might happen if that day came with no resolution of the stalemate, no one knew. Ironically, each side of the Israeli political spectrum put part of the blame on American Jews. Natan Sharansky, the famous refusenik now serving as Israel's minister of industry and trade, visited the

United States in July and declared that President Clinton tended to pressure Israel because he was surrounded by Jewish advisers sympathetic to Peace Now. The next month brought Israeli Labor Party leader Ehud Barak, who blasted AIPAC at a meeting with its staff for "becoming an extreme right-wing organization." He was especially upset about its role in the letter of the 81 senators to the president, which, he felt, harmed the chances for peace by restricting the administration's room to maneuver.

September 13, 1998, marked the fifth anniversary of the Declaration of Principles signed by Prime Minister Rabin and Chairman Arafat on the While House lawn. The Zionist Organization of America (ZOA) marked the event by publishing a 52-page report on alleged Palestinian violations of the agreement. But over 400 supporters of the peace process gathered in Washington that day to hear Leah Rabin, widow of the assassinated prime minister Yitzhak Rabin, and other speakers. Organizations participating included the Reform, Conservative, and Reconstructionist movements, Americans for Peace Now, the National Council of Jewish Women, and the New Israel Fund. Rabbi David Saperstein, director of Reform Judaism's Religious Action Center, expressed the hope that "somehow, the new spirit all of us felt five years ago this day can be regenerated and dispel the current gloom." Assistant Secretary of State Indyk represented the administration. To the surprise of dovish Jewish leaders who had gathered at the White House for a pre-rally meeting with administration officials, President Clinton walked into the room and spoke to them at length about the status of the peace process. The Jewish leaders, in turn, told him that the great majority of American Jews supported the Oslo accords and a strong U.S. role in bringing peace.

WYE CONFERENCE

After considerable prodding from President Clinton, in October Prime Minister Netanyahu suddenly reversed course. Protecting his right political flank through the appointment of Ariel Sharon as foreign minister, he flew to the United States to confer with Yasir Arafat, King Hussein of Jordan, and President Clinton at the Wye Plantation conference center in Maryland. The key provisions of the agreement they finalized on October 23 called for a phased Israeli withdrawal from 13 percent of the West Bank and agreement by the Palestinian National Council to renounce clauses in its charter calling for the destruction of Israel, to confiscate illegal weapons, and to reduce the Palestinian police force.

While the mainstream Jewish organizations applauded the agreement, some that had previously backed Netanyahu felt he had ceded too much. At the November 1 dinner of the Zionist Organization of America, Dore Gold, Israel's UN ambassador, endured some heckling when he explained why Israel signed the agreement, and one of the honorees charged that Netanyahu "gives strength and credence to a morally bankrupt, lame-duck U.S. president." There was also some criticism — not confined to hawkish circles — of an American pledge to allow the

CIA to be used to monitor Palestinian compliance, a proposal that had reportedly played a crucial role in gaining Netanyahu's assent to the whole package. Might not the CIA wink at Palestinian violations in order not to threaten the success of this Clinton-sponsored agreement, thus allowing the agency to become a tool in pressuring Israel once again? Republican congressional leaders, briefed by the Zionist Organization of America and other Jewish groups suspicious of administration intentions, promised to investigate this proposed new CIA role.

Three Orthodox rabbis, faculty members at Yeshiva University, attacked the Wye agreement on the basis of their interpretation of Jewish law. In a newspaper ad in the November 1 *New York Post*, these rabbis claimed that handing over any land to the Palestinians endangered Jewish lives and was therefore against Torah. While the opinion of these three rabbis would ordinarily have been ignored, the fact that Yitzhak Rabin had been assassinated by an Orthodox Jew imbued with their ideology raised fears of further violence. After attracting considerable publicity, however, their stand was roundly repudiated by mainstream Orthodox leaders.

Whether or not Israel was keeping its pledges under the Wye agreement became the next bone of contention for the American Jewish community. Just two weeks after the agreement was signed, Americans for Peace Now released a list of examples of Israeli noncompliance, while expressing agreement with a State Department report that the Palestinians had largely kept their side of the bargain. Morton Klein, ZOA president, charged that the APN report "whitewashes Arafat."

As agreed at Wye, President Clinton traveled to Gaza on December 14 to witness personally the Palestinian revocation of charter provisions calling for the destruction of Israel. While the revocation went as planned, and Clinton did not pressure Netanyahu to proceed immediately with the next stage of redeployment, the American president's public remarks in Gaza alarmed Israelis and American Jews. Clinton said that he had spoken to Palestinian children whose fathers were in Israeli jails, and Israeli children whose fathers had been killed by Palestinians, and that both brought tears to his eyes—as if there was some moral equivalence between Palestinian terrorists and Israeli victims. Further, the president mentioned the "dispossession and dispersal" of the Palestinian people and talked of their "legitimate rights," which was widely understood to mean a Palestinian state. ZOA president Morton Klein called this "the most pro-Arab speech ever given by an American president," and leaders of AIPAC, the Presidents Conference, and the Anti-Defamation League criticized Clinton's talk. A number of the other mainstream Jewish organizations ignored the president's remarks and focused instead on the positive news of the changes in the Palestinian charter.

The four-day bombing of Iraq, which took place the week after Clinton's return from the Middle East, drew virtually unanimous praise from the Jewish community—including a public statement of support from the Presidents Conference—because Iraq was viewed as an implacable enemy of Israel. If anything,

Jewish opinion, as reflected in editorial comment, would have preferred even stronger measures, including the ouster of Saddam Hussein.

Fifty Years of Israel

Israel's 50th anniversary evoked a flood of American Jewish comment about Israel's role in the lives of American Jews. Some writers stressed the Jewish state's positive contributions to American Jewry. Few went as far as Charles Krauthammer (*Weekly Standard,* May 11), who argued that a still-vulnerable Israel had become so vital for the survival of Diaspora Jewry that Israel's liquidation would mean the end of the Jewish people. More common was the sober expression of satisfaction that the Jewish state, with all its faults, had achieved the Zionist dream of creating a "normal" Jewish society, while simultaneously strengthening Jewish morale, culture, and political clout in the United States.

Others emphasized growing tensions between Israel—perceived as increasingly bellicose toward its neighbors and theocratic and undemocratic in relation to its own citizens—and the overwhelmingly liberal American Jewish community. "Is Israel Still Good for the Jews?" asked a *New York* magazine cover story (April 27). "A Family Feud? Americans Troubled by Shifts in Israel," was the headline in the *International Herald Tribune* (April 29). And the *New York Jewish Week*, in its review of the Jewish year (September 18), called American Jewish-Israeli relations "A Love Affair Gone Stale." At a scholarly conference at the City University of New York in May, only Dore Gold, Israel's ambassador to the UN—the sole nonacademic on the program—expressed optimism about relations between the two Jewish communities, while all the scholars who spoke—Israelis and Americans—agreed that the gap was widening.

In March and April the *Los Angeles Times* and the Israeli newspaper *Yediot Aharonot* conducted an ambitious poll comparing the attitudes of American and Israeli Jews on a wide variety of issues. From the data it was clear that the distancing of American Jews from Israel coexisted, paradoxically, with a striking affinity between the views of the two communities. True enough, only 58 percent of American Jews felt close to Israel, a decline of 17 percent over ten years (the decline was even steeper in the under-40 age bracket). But the two Jewries supported the peace process and objected to the Israeli Orthodox establishment in Israel in roughly similar percentages, and even levels of religious observance of Israelis and American Jews were not all that different.

Israel-Diaspora relations were the overriding theme of the Council of Jewish Federations' General Assembly (GA), held in November. For the first time ever, in recognition of the 50th anniversary, the GA took place in Israel. Some 3,000 delegates attended from the United States and Canada. Many of the public sessions addressed aspects of the Israel-Diaspora relationship, and a variety of practical suggestions were put forward to bridge the divisions, such as philanthropic partnerships between communities, heavily subsidized trips to Israel, and face-to-face connections between members of the same profession in the two countries. At the close of the GA, Israeli and North American participants signed a "covenant" affirming belief in God, "respect for the infinite value of human life," Jewish peoplehood, and the duty to "repair the world." Many who were there suggested that the long-range significance of this GA for American Jews was the suggestion of an equal partnership between Israel and Diaspora, replacing the outmoded model of Israel as primarily an object of Diaspora philanthropy.

Religious Pluralism

The sharpest American Jewish complaints about Israel—surpassing even the criticisms of Netanyahu's peace policy—were over the question of religious pluralism in Israel. Since the very legitimacy of American non-Orthodox movements seemed to be at stake—some 85 percent of affiliated American Jews belonged to them—the issue struck much closer to home than the debate over what percentage of West Bank land should be given to the Palestinians.

January 31, 1998, was the deadline for Israel's Ne'eman Commission to come up with a compromise solution for the performance of conversions in Israel that would be acceptable to all branches of Judaism. If no such arrangement proved possible, looming in the background was, on one side, an Orthodox-sponsored Knesset bill that would codify in law the previously informal Orthodox monopoly on conversions, and, on the other side, pending court cases brought by the non-Orthodox movements that could put a judicial end to the Orthodox monopoly.

Agudath Israel of America intensified its Am Echad (One People) media campaign for the conversion bill and against the Ne'eman Commission, arguing that even the secular founders of the Jewish state had recognized that only Orthodox law, the sole universally accepted criterion, could keep the Jewish people united, and that non-Orthodox American versions of Judaism had proven to be way stations on the road to assimilation. A 75-person American delegation brought this message to Israel in early January. But American Orthodoxy was hardly monolithic. Shvil Hazahav, a group of modern Orthodox rabbis and lay leaders, endorsed compromise in the name of Jewish unity. And a delegation from the trans-denominational New York Board of Rabbis came to Israel to lobby for the Ne'eman Commission and against the conversion bill. Speaking in the name of 800 New York area rabbis—225 of them Orthodox—this group cited its own experience of fruitful interdenominational cooperation as an example of what pluralism might accomplish in Israel.

The Ne'eman Commission presented its recommendations on January 23, a week ahead of schedule. It provided for Reform and Conservative rabbis to participate together with their Orthodox colleagues in conducting classes for conversion candidates, but left the Orthodox in charge of the actual conversion procedure. Israel's chief rabbis pointedly refrained from endorsing this compromise—indeed, they were quoted as heaping abuse on non-Orthodox Judaism—and that seemed to confirm Reform and Conservative suspicions that Orthodox rabbinical courts were unlikely to approve converts prepared by the projected pluralistic conversion classes. A proposed alternative to the Ne'eman recommendations, dubbed a "technical solution," that would split the secular and religious dimensions of Jewish identity and allow non-Orthodox converts the former but not the latter, elicited little enthusiasm.

Finance Minister Yaakov Ne'eman, chairman of the commission, met with the Presidents Conference in New York early in February. Expressing frustration with both sides, he blamed American Jewry for exporting its internecine strife to Israel. The Orthodox, said Ne'eman, must appreciate that the willingness of non-Orthodox members of his commission to leave the actual conversions in Orthodox hands signaled a "new attitude" of respect for Jewish law. And the Reform, he went on, must understand the abhorrence with which traditional Israeli Jews viewed such innovations as patrilineal descent, gay marriage, and rabbinic officiation at intermarriages. Rabbi Ammiel Hirsch, executive director of the Association of Reform Zionists of American (ARZA), noting that the Israeli Reform movement did not endorse any of these practices, accused Ne'eman of Reform bashing.

Adding to the sense of moral outrage in non-Orthodox leadership circles was the partial release, on January 30, of the results of a poll commissioned in Israel by the Orthodox Union. Contrary to OU expectations, attitudes were so surprisingly positive toward Reform and Conservative Judaism—43 percent, for example, were willing to accept more than one conversion standard—that the responses to ten of the 16 questions were suppressed. Commented the Reform movement's Israel Religious Action Center, "A modern-day Balaam, the Orthodox Union, set out to curse the Reform and Conservative movements and wound up blessing them instead."

A few days later the Israeli Chief Rabbinate approved part of the Ne'eman Commission recommendations—that all conversions be performed by Orthodox rabbis—and it promised to set up more conversion courts. But the rabbinate was still silent about the other component of the deal—the joint conversion classes. Asked if an Orthodox court would convert someone trained in such a class, Ashkenazi chief rabbi Yisrael Meir Lau responded diplomatically: "Each person will be judged as an individual." Yet the rabbinate's silence was generally interpreted as rejection, given the fact that the Chief Rabbinate Council simultaneously issued a statement denouncing those "trying to shake the foundations of the Jewish religion," which surely meant the non-Orthodox movements. The two major Orthodox groups in the United States—Agudath Israel and the Orthodox Union—expressed satisfaction. Ammiel Hirsch of ARZA reacted angrily, calling for the total disestablishment of Orthodoxy in Israel and its replacement by complete equality for all forms of Judaism. His Reform colleague Rabbi Eric Yoffie, president of the Union of American Hebrew Congregations (UAHC), announced that his movement would press ahead with its legal challenges to the Orthodox monopoly. Rabbi Jerome Epstein, executive vice-president of the United Synagogue of Conservative Judaism, was more cautious. Calling for "patience and persistence" in what would surely be a long struggle, Epstein expressed the fear that American Jews might distance themselves from Israel over this issue.

But since the Chief Rabbinate had not explicitly rejected the Ne'eman formula, those elements in Israel desperate for a solution to this vexing issue acted as if the commission proposals were still alive, an assessment the *New York Times* (February 15) said could only be reached by dissecting "with a fine Talmudic scalpel." Prime Minister Netanyahu actually congratulated the chief rabbis and joined 71 other Knesset members in a petition supporting implementation of the commission's recommendations. Reassuring Conservative rabbis who were in Israel for their international convention, Netanyahu said, "I am not willing to give it up." President Ezer Weizman explained to another skeptical group of visiting American rabbis why the Ne'eman process was continuing: "It's your problem that it started, and now we have to solve it."

If, in many Israeli minds, the Ne'eman recommendations were going to make the conversion problem disappear even without official endorsement by the Chief Rabbinate, that message did not resonate in the United States. The UAHC's Yoffie, arguing that the absence of chief rabbinical sanction meant the end of the Ne'eman compromise, called the Israeli government's claim to the contrary an outright fraud. Rabbi Joel Meyers, executive director of the Conservative movement's Rabbinical Assembly, agreed that it was a fraud, but suggested that it might become "a fraud for good purposes" if the Israeli government proceeded to set up the joint conversion panels, and the chief rabbis, even without any official acquiescence, simply passed the word to the judges of the religious courts that these conversion candidates should be evaluated leniently.

At the Jewish Council for Public Affairs plenum in February, a seemingly innocuous resolution hailing Israel's 50th anniversary got caught up in the pluralism debate. Sponsored by Hadassah, the women's Zionist organization, it lauded Israel's "guarantee of the social, political, religious, and cultural rights" of all of its people. Bernice Balter, executive director of the Women's League for Conservative Judaism, objected that this was "not true. There is no equality of Judaism in Israel." David Luchins, representing the Orthodox Union, compared her statement to the UN resolution equating Zionism and racism. After considerable debate and negotiation, the wording was changed, praising Israel's "commitment" to "the pursuit of the social, political, religious and cultural rights of all its citizens."

FUNDING ISSUE

In March new fuel was added to the fire. The previous September, the United Jewish Appeal (UJA) and the Council of Jewish Federations (CJF) had responded to complaints by the non-Orthodox movements about the paucity of funding for their operations in Israel by announcing a special fund-raising drive for religious pluralism in Israel. Now, six months later, instead of the $30 million that had been projected, only $6.3 million had been pledged. When officials from the fund-raising agencies explained the difficulties in translating a national commitment onto the level of the individual federation in a system based on local autonomy, Conservative and Reform leaders retorted that the national UJA-CJF had not given the matter sufficient priority. By the end of August the total of pledges had reached $10.5 million, but the religious movements had still not received any of the money.

Through the spring, Reform and Conservative leaders continued to complain that, absent chief rabbinical support, the Ne'eman compromise was insufficient. Bobby Brown, Netanyahu's Diaspora affairs adviser, countered by pointing to what the Ne'eman plan had accomplished, turning Reform and Conservative Judaism in Israel "from small, marginal groups into full-fledged partners," despite the chief rabbis. In fact, Netanyahu had reinforced this shift personally by visiting American Reform and Conservative synagogues for the first time since assuming office. But when the non-Orthodox made it known that they would not wait to see how the joint conversion system would operate, but would press ahead in the courts for legal recognition—the immediate issue was a pending suit by Conservative converts asking for Jewish status—Brown warned, "If they want confrontation, that's what they'll get." Visiting the United States in May, Brown was more specific: a court decision upholding religious pluralism could easily induce the religious parties to revive the conversion bill in the Knesset, codifying in law the Orthodox monopoly on conversions.

Sure enough, plans for the introduction of the conversion bill were begun in early June. All the work of the Ne'eman Commission seemed to have gone for naught, and non-Orthodox American Jews were once again up in arms. The Reform movement resolved to press forward with its court cases despite the threat of a conversion bill. But the Conservative movement was divided. While its Israeli leadership agreed with their Reform counterparts, Jewish Theological Seminary chancellor Ismar Schorsch sought to avoid confrontation by freezing the litigation until the joint conversion system had a chance to get off the ground.

Championing Reform's hard line on equal religious rights in Israel, UAHC president Yoffie lashed out against both organized Orthodoxy and UJA-Federation for blocking the movement toward pluralism. Accusing the Israeli chief rabbis of poisoning relations between the movements in the United States, he claimed that extremist pressures on American Orthodoxy had pushed its more liberal wing to cut ties with the liberal movements and even to support a "ghetto Judaism" that seeks to wall itself off from the outside world (*New York Jewish Week*, July 24). As for the fund-raising establishment, in Yoffie's eyes it had become a tool of the Israeli government, attacking Conservative and Reform leaders who wanted to use the Israeli court system for redress. Yoffie charged that a decision at the June meeting of the Jewish Agency executive to table a resolution opposing a conversion bill and supporting the legal struggle of the non-Orthodox movements had been made under Israeli government pressure. What galled Yoffie the most was that the leading American fund-raisers who, he felt, had succumbed to the pressure, were themselves Reform and Conservative Jews. In July, dissatisfied with UJA-Federation's allocations to Reform and angry about its failure to push for religious pluralism, the Reform movement announced its own fundraising drive earmarked for its Israeli operations. In an open challenge to the establishment fund-raisers, Reform rabbis were urged to make appeals for "this bold, new campaign" on the High Holy Days from their pulpits. UJA-Federation leaders, however, for whom the unity of the campaign came before any other consideration, accused Reform of biting the hand that fed it, since the established fund-raising system, they claimed, had contributed significantly to the growth of all the movements in Israel.

A special task force set up by the nation's largest local Jewish fund-raising body — UJA-Federation of Jewish Philanthropies of New York — to examine how to handle the pluralism question gave Reform little cause for comfort. The task force report, issued in September, advised reversing the pro-pluralism position that the federation had taken in December 1997. Noting that individual members of the task force endorsed an end to the Orthodox monopoly in Israel, the report nevertheless recognized that a pro-pluralism stand was interpreted by the Orthodox as siding against all of Orthodoxy in a debate the Orthodox considered internal to Israeli politics. And in order for UJA-Federation to continue to function in the name of the entire New York Jewish community, it "should not promote a particular ideological position with respect to pluralism." But the disappointed spokespersons for Reform and Conservative Judaism countered that there was no way that the fund-raising establishment could really remain neutral: not taking a position was, in effect, taking a position in favor of the status quo, if not on the theology of conversion, then on continuing to deny civil rights in Israel.

In October detailed plans were announced for the February 1999 opening of the first joint conversion institute in Beersheba. It would be run by a seven-member board, five Orthodox, one Reform, and one Conservative. Representatives of both the latter movements announced that their movements were reluctant participants, hoping for the best even though the lack of endorsement by the chief rabbis meant that the arrangement was far from what had originally been intended by the Ne'eman Commission.

As it happened, the delicate compromise represented by the conversion institutes was soon jeopardized by Israeli courts. In November the Israeli Supreme Court ruled that Reform and Conservative Jews could not be barred from serving on local religious councils. These bodies, which supervise the provision of religious services to their communities, had until then only included the Orthodox. And in late December a Jerusalem district court ruled that individuals converted in Israel by Reform or Conservative rabbis should be registered as Jews in the population registry. These and two other judicial rulings against the religion-state status quo—one freeing kibbutz economic activities from the legal restrictions on Sabbath labor, the other questioning the draft exemptions of yeshivah students— elicited outrage from the Orthodox parties in Israel and their supporters in the United States.

As the year ended, Orthodox forces in the Knesset were seeking to circumvent both the religious councils and conversion decisions through legislation. On December 28, the Knesset passed the first reading of a bill (three readings are needed for passage) requiring members of religious councils to pledge to obey rulings of the Chief Rabbinate. In addition, a bill codifying the Orthodox monopoly on conversions in Israel, which had already passed one reading in 1997, was reintroduced. Since Prime Minister Netanyahu had recently called for new elections in the spring, Reform and Conservative leaders in the United States worried that Israeli politicians desperate for votes might make pledges to the religious parties to back the measures that would undermine the court decisions.

The prospect of having their victories in court nullified by the Israeli legislative branch drove the American Reform and Conservative movements to issue a joint statement at the end of the year warning Knesset members that they were "about to make a terrible personal political mistake" if they voted for the Orthodox-sponsored bills. While the institutions of the Reform and Conservative movements, as nonprofit organizations, could not engage in political activity, this was a clear threat that wealthy non-Orthodox American Jews might withhold their contributions to the political campaign funds of Israeli politicians—a source of money which, in the past, had provided most of the funding for Israeli election campaigns.

Denominational Developments

The bitterness of the Orthodox–non-Orthodox polemics on the Israeli scene continued to poison denominational relations in the United States. Indeed, the palpable anger of the Reform and Conservative movements about the situation in Israel spilled over into unusually harsh anti-Orthodox stereotyping in the United States.

Both Eric Yoffie, UAHC president (Reform), and Ismar Schorsch, JTS chancellor (Conservative), publicly castigated Orthodoxy for its narrow-mindedness. Yoffie called it "ghetto Judaism" because it allegedly obligated its followers "to avoid any but essential contacts with the general society," and this, he wrote— impugning Orthodox patriotism—constituted "nothing less than a betrayal of America" (*New York Jewish Week*, July 24). Schorsch, in one of his widely distributed weekly columns on the Torah portion, attacked Orthodoxy for insisting on an ever more stringent interpretation of Jewish law, the "quantification of piety," propounding the idea that "there are no questions but only answers," and attempting to set up "hermetically sealed ghettos."

In contrast, the sectarian Orthodox Agudath Israel, previously a major source of barbed rhetoric against the non-Orthodox denominations as well as against the modern Orthodox, toned down its criticisms in 1998. The decision to do so reflected sensitivity to the negative reactions that greeted earlier statements that seemed to question the Jewishness of the other denominations and cast aspersions on modern Orthodox leaders. Indeed, intemperate rhetoric could hurt Orthodox fund-raising. The Sapirstein-Stone-Weiss Foundation, administered by the owners of American Greeting Cards—a major source of funding for numerous Orthodox causes—announced in 1998 that it would no longer help institutions that fomented divisiveness in the Jewish community. The statement specifically cited remarks at the 1997 Agudath Israel convention castigating Yeshiva University president Norman Lamm for his support of the Ne'eman Commission recommendations as an example of such divisiveness. Taking the high road, Agudath Israel interpreted its campaign early in the year against religious pluralism in Israel as matching "the non-Orthodox leadership's aggressive outrages with our own aggressive outreaches" (*Jewish Observer,* January). And at its annual convention in November, Agudath Israel resolved to make the improvement of relations with other sectors of the Jewish community a priority.

Moderated rhetoric, however, did not imply any relaxation of the Orthodox opposition to any activity that might even resemble Jewish religious pluralism. Such opposition was especially noticeable, since it was so unexpected, within modern Orthodoxy, and it impelled philanthropist Michael Steinhardt, in a speech at Yeshiva University in October, to charge Orthodoxy as a whole with "moral self-centeredness." Thus the Orthodox Union (OU) refused to participate in "Shabbat Across America," a project to encourage Jews of any or no denomination to observe the Sabbath—even though 148 Orthodox synagogues took part—because it might seem to condone non-Orthodox forms of Sabbath observance. The OU also declined to be part of Jewish Web/Net Week, linking over 600 Jewish Web sites—even though a number of Orthodox and even hassidic institutions participated—since that, too, might appear to associate the OU with non-Orthodox Web sites. The president of the Rabbinical Council of America, the modern Orthodox rabbinic body, turned down an invitation to participate in a joint study session with non-Orthodox rabbis at the Council of Jewish Federations' General Assembly. This attitude extended even to high school basketball in the New York City area, where Conservative Solomon Schechter schools, seeking to play against other Jewish schools, were rebuffed in their attempt to join the league of Orthodox yeshivas. One Orthodox principal explained that he wanted his students to associate only with those "who share our philosophy of Judaism."

There were, to be sure, efforts by nondenominational bodies to counteract the forces of division. The Wexner Foundation, which provided funding for graduate work in the rabbinate, Jewish education, and other Jewish communal fields, sponsored joint Torah study sessions for its fellows and alumni of all the movements. The American Jewish Committee had an ongoing interdenominational women's group that met regularly throughout the year for study and conversation, and in November AJC announced that it would make intermovement dialogue a national program priority.

Upon his inauguration as president of the interdenominational New York Board of Rabbis in late March, Rabbi Marc Schneier (Orthodox) announced an ambitious plan for the creation of a national interdenominational rabbinic organization out of the roughly 30 local boards of rabbis across America. With the religious pluralism issue in Israel driving the denominations apart, Schneier intended this new body to play the mediating role that had been performed by the lay-constituted Synagogue Council of America till its collapse in 1994. The responses from both Orthodox and non-Orthodox were lukewarm: among the Orthodox, the sectarians opposed any cooperation with non-Orthodox rabbis, while the modernists preferred behind-the-scenes cooperation that would not get them into trouble with their Orthodox peers; and the non-Orthodox feared that yet another American rabbinic body could complicate the Reform and Conservative struggle for recognition in Israel. Still, 28 rabbis held a planning meeting with Schneier in May.

Hoping to generate a wave of public enthusiasm for a national rabbinic body by dispelling the prevailing pessimism about the future of interdenominational ties, Schneier's New York Board of Rabbis issued a report, "Unity in Diversity: A Vision of Rabbinic Cooperation," in September. This summary of activities around the country noted such programs as interdenominational study groups, combined community *hakafot* on Simhat Torah, a pluralistic conversion institute in California, and a variety of "unity" proclamations—some initiated by local federations—signed by a cross-section of community rabbis. But just as some observers began to talk of Schneier—not entirely in jest—as a potential chief rabbi of America, doubts were raised about his unity report. Not only, it seems, were some of the descriptions of cooperation exaggerated, but the exclusion of divisive phenomena gave an unrealistically rosy picture of the situation. "The big picture," commented Rabbi Irving Greenberg, a veteran of the interdenominational scene, "is that there's less cooperation and communal activity and willingness to do things together than there's ever been."

As if to prove just how difficult it would likely be for Schneier to navigate the shoals of intermovement cooperation, his own New York Board of Rabbis committed a serious faux pas by scheduling an interfaith service on behalf of the poor for September 9, at St. Patrick's Cathedral. The Reform rabbi heading the board's interfaith committee was simply unaware that Orthodox rabbis would not pray in a church, and an embarrassed Rabbi Schneier, who said he had not been told of the plan in advance, announced that neither he nor any other Orthodox rabbi would attend. None did.

ORTHODOX JUDAISM

Despite criticism from other sectors of the community for its exclusiveness and failure to accept the legitimacy of plural versions of Judaism, American Orthodoxy continued to flourish in 1998. It could seriously claim to be retaining the loyalties of a far higher percentage of its young people than the other movements. Its numerical clout was increasingly respected by American business—as was clear from the proliferation of new products with kosher certification, including, for the first time, some made by Nabisco. And the respectful, almost awed reaction of the media and the public to the measured and anguished denunciation of President Clinton's behavior uttered on the Senate floor on September 3 by Sen. Joseph Lieberman (D., Conn.), which clearly arose out of his Orthodox Jewish values, highlighted the moral credibility of Orthodoxy at its best.

It was the more sectarian Orthodox who felt most secure about their future, buoyed by extrapolations from recent Jewish population surveys purporting to indicate that, within a few generations, the sectarians' high birthrate and low attrition rate would make them the overwhelming majority of American Jewry. Such a perception was reinforced by recognition from the most eminent of the secular media. The *New York Times Magazine* (November 15), in its special issue devoted to forms of "status" in America, included only one specifically "Jewish" form of status. "For Orthodox Jews," it related, status means "studying, studying and more studying" of the sacred texts—even at the sacrifice of career and creature comforts—exactly the sectarian role model.

Agudath Israel, the primary institutional expression of sectarian Orthodoxy, experienced a smooth transition of leadership following the death of Rabbi Moshe Sherer, the president of the organization, in May. Over the course of a half century, Rabbi Sherer had transformed it from a marginal group to a potent religious and political force. In November Agudath Israel announced that the lay presidency and the executive authority—which had been combined in Sherer's hands—would now be divided. A member of the organization's Council of Torah Sages, Rabbi Yaakov Perlow, known as the Novominsker Rebbe, was the new president, and a three-man executive committee would be in charge of day-to-day operations.

Modern Orthodoxy continued to suffer from defensiveness and low morale as its own institutions came increasingly under sectarian influence. A telling example of the trend was Yeshiva University's handling of the award of an honorary degree to Yaakov Ne'eman "for service to the Jewish people" at a convocation for YU's recent rabbinic graduates held in March. Although YU president Norman Lamm had endorsed the Ne'eman Commission proposals for solving the conversion crisis in Israel, the school did no advance publicity about the award to Ne'eman, for fear of antagonizing Orthodox sectarians. Even so, some senior rabbis on the faculty heard about the planned award and boycotted the event.

Another sign of the erosion of modern Orthodoxy was the spread of sectarian tendencies even among Orthodox American Sephardim. A major theme at the national convention of the American Sephardi Federation in May was the loss of the traditional spirit of religious tolerance in the Sephardi community and its replacement by a narrower worldview inculcated in Ashkenazi-controlled schools.

One factor encouraging the movement to the "right" among Orthodox young people was the widespread practice of high-school graduates spending a year or more at Israeli yeshivas, from which they often returned antagonistic to modernity, hostile to religious pluralism, and committed to sectarian Orthodoxy. Gary Rosenblatt, editor of the *New York Jewish Week,* publicized the new term for this phenomenon: "flipping" (August 21). A good number of the "flipped" young people rejected a college education, and some who did not insisted that the secular university accommodate to their Orthodox sensibilities. A lawsuit filed by five (later four) Orthodox students against Yale University for not granting them exemptions from the requirement of living on campus in mixed-sex dormitories— which, they said, conflicted with their religious beliefs—drew widespread attention, including a *New York Times Magazine* article, "Yeshivish at Yale" (May 24). When a U.S. district court ruled in Yale's favor in August, the students appealed.

Despite the movement toward separatism in the Orthodox community, countervailing tendencies survived. A three-day conference in Israel in mid-October, sponsored by, among others, the modern Orthodox Bar-Ilan University, the religious kibbutz movement, and the Israeli alumni of Yeshiva University, featured leading Israeli and American modern Orthodox thinkers addressing the challenges of modernity. The publication of Irving Greenberg's *Living in the Image of God: Jewish Teachings to Perfect the World* provided the general reader with a sharp critique of the rightward trend in Orthodoxy. And two relatively new modern Orthodox organizations continued to function: the Orthodox Caucus sought to counteract what it saw as Orthodoxy's neglect of the ethical component of Jewish tradition, while the more broadly focused Edah, which advertised itself as having "the courage to be modern and Orthodox," ran ads favoring the Ne'eman Commission recommendations.

Unquestionably, the issue with the greatest potential to reinvigorate modern Orthodoxy was the religious role of women. Indeed, so heated was the intra-Orthodox debate over feminism in 1998 that predictions of a denominational split over the issue came from both the sectarian Orthodox camp and from some of the modernists.

The second International Conference on Feminism and Orthodoxy, held February 15–16 in New York City, attracted some 2,000 people, double the attendance of the previous year. The program gave evidence of the strides made by the movement. This time, unlike the inaugural conference, some mainstream modern Orthodox rabbis consented to speak, as did the noted Israeli halakhic authority Rabbi Yehuda Henkin, two heads of women's seminaries in Israel, and a Lubavitch woman. And while in 1997 discussion of the prospects for ordination of women was considered too controversial to be on the program, in 1998, with two women already employed as "rabbinic interns" in New York synagogues, a session was devoted to the subject. Another sign that Orthodox feminism had become less defensive was a panel of non-Orthodox feminists providing their perspectives on trends in Orthodoxy. While Amit, the Orthodox women's Zionist organization that had officially cosponsored the first conference, withdrew its endorsement this time, many Amit members were in attendance.

One topic prominent on the conference agenda—how to help the *agunah*, the "chained woman" whose husband refuses to grant her a Jewish divorce—generated controversy throughout the year. Since Halakhah dictates that only the husband may initiate a divorce, the *agunah* problem, in the eyes of many, epitomized Orthodoxy's male bias. In 1996, 88-year-old Rabbi Emanuel Rackman, who had been a leading modern Orthodox rabbi in the United States and then served as chancellor of Bar-Ilan University in Israel, joined with some other rabbis in initiating a new *bet din*—religious court—to deal with such cases. Using the assumption that cruel or abusive behavior on the husband's part reflected character traits existing already at the time of the marriage, this court annulled the marriages on the grounds that the wife would never have agreed to marry had she known the truth about her husband. She was now free to remarry.

By early 1998 this *bet din* had quietly annulled some 100 marriages, but the generally favorable attention it received at the Conference on Orthodoxy and Feminism in February generated criticism from several quarters. Arguing that annulments can be effected only if there is definite proof that information about the husband had been withheld at the time of the marriage, Agudath Israel declared all acts of the Rackman court invalid; the Young Israel Council of Rabbis called it "heartless and foolish" to "lull unfortunate women into the illusory impression that they are free to remarry"; and even the rabbinical court sponsored by the moderate Rabbinical Council of America and the Orthodox Union called the court's reasoning "incorrect." In June, 31 mainstream Orthodox rabbis, several of whom were prominent supporters of Jewish feminism, signed onto a statement declaring that, since there was no halakhic basis for the court's actions, no Orthodox rabbi would officiate at the remarriage of any woman freed through these "annulments." Even after an extensive *New York Times* article about the controversial court (August 13) triggered a two-page advertisement in the *New York Jewish Week* in which the court provided a point-by-point explanation of its operations (August 28), the solid wall of rabbinic opposition remained.

As if the issues of feminism and the *agunah* problem did not pose enough of a challenge to Orthodoxy, a well-publicized lawsuit in November opened up another contentious issue of concern to women. Chani Lightman of Long Island sued two local rabbis, charging that they had breached confidentiality by telling her estranged husband, in the course of a custody battle, information about her religious behavior that she had revealed to them in private conversation. As the year ended, one of the rabbis had been found guilty and fined but was appealing the verdict, and the other was awaiting trial. As lawyers, other rabbis, and the Orthodox laity debated whether the two rabbis had acted appropriately, many women saw the case as one more example of male rabbinic bias.

CHABAD-LUBAVITCH

The Lubavitch hassidic sect, whose leader, Rabbi Menachem Mendel Schneerson, died in 1994, continued to be wracked by controversy. Although the demise of the childless Rebbe left the group without a leader, Lubavitch centers around the world, which had always operated with considerable autonomy, continued to thrive, enlisting the allegiance of many previously unaffiliated Jews. Yet the exact status of the dead Rabbi Schneerson in the eyes of his followers aroused sharp dispute.

In January, Prof. David Berger—an Orthodox rabbi and the president of the Association for Jewish Studies, who had previously complained that many Lubavitchers believed that the dead Rebbe was the messiah—charged that the Rebbe was now actually being worshiped as a god. All such idolators, he went on, should be cast out of the community. After Berger's pronouncement, the Agudath Israel broke its silence on the issue with a long and heavily footnoted article in the March issue of the *Jewish Observer* that largely confirmed Berger's analysis. On February 19, the Central Committee of Chabad-Lubavitch Rabbis issued a statement condemning as un-Jewish "the deification of any human being" as well as "conjecture as to the possible identity of the Moshiach (messiah)," and stating that the late Rebbe would not have wanted his followers to have a "preoccupation" with identifying him as the messiah. But Lubavitch messianists, seizing on the wording of the statement, noted that only "preoccupation" was criticized, not belief, and beginning on the fourth anniversary of the Rebbe's death, they held a four-day "Moshiach Congress" in Crown Heights, Brooklyn. And a *New York Times* reporter (June 29) discovered that many Lubavitch schools ended daily prayers with the chant, "Long Live the Rebbe, King Moshiach, for ever and ever."

CONSERVATIVE JUDAISM

Through the year, the Conservative movement was subjected to intense analysis. One of the outstanding Jewish publication events of 1998 was the release of *Tradition Renewed,* an erudite two-volume collection of scholarly essays on the history of the Jewish Theological Seminary, edited by its provost, Jack Wertheimer, which demonstrated the central role of the Conservative rabbinical school in shaping American Judaism.

Wertheimer was also responsible for another publication (actually released at the very end of in 1997) that suggested weaknesses in the movement. *Jewish Identity and Religious Commitment* consisted of eight essays analyzing data from a 1995–96 survey of Conservative Jews in North America. Consistent with trends toward "spirituality" in the broader society, belief in God was evidently on the upsurge, with young Conservative Jews far more likely than their parents to consider God an important element of their Jewishness. Yet there were signs of erosion of Jewish group identity: fully 65 percent of adolescents who had recently become bar or bat mitzvah considered it acceptable to marry a non-Jew. And the data called into question the long-term efficacy of conversion as an antidote to intermarriage—at least in the Conservative movement. In families where one spouse had converted to Judaism, while levels of observance resembled those in nonconversionary families, 61 percent of the oldest married children had married non-Jews, as compared to 29 percent of oldest married children of in-married families.

By 1998 the three-year-old institutional rift between the New York-based JTS and the Ziegler School of Rabbinic Studies in Los Angeles had been healed, with JTS now viewing the newer school as a partner rather than a competitor. Ideologically, however, the Conservative movement still struggled over the perennial "hot" issues of gender, homosexuality, and intermarriage.

A new edition of the Conservative *Sim Shalom* prayer book for Sabbath and festivals appeared in 1998. Seven years in the making, it broke radically with tradition by replacing "sexist" language with gender-neutral terms—modifying masculine references to God and including the names of the biblical matriarchs along with the patriarchs. It also removed, rather than just rephrased or reinterpreted, as in earlier prayer books, liturgical mention of the ancient sacrifices. Some of the more traditionalist rabbis in the movement objected that the modifications destroyed the connection between the wording of the prayers and the language of Scripture, but the critics were clearly in the minority. A new *Rabbi's Manual* published by the Rabbinical Assembly, after ten years of deliberation, showed a similar sensitivity to gender equality. In addition, this rabbinic handbook for life-cycle events, heavily influenced by the popular quest for spirituality in everyday life, included prayers for such milestones as "retirement, a special birthday, when a young person goes off to college, and when a child goes to sleepaway camp for the first time" (*New York Jewish Week,* October 23).

The continuing resistance of Conservative institutions to the religious legitimization of homosexuality confronted mounting criticism. Members of the popular B'nai Jeshurun Synagogue in New York City—including such celebrities as Letty Cottin Pogrebin, Bella Abzug, and Debra Winger—petitioned the congregational board to omit from its annual membership form the option of donating money to the JTS scholarship fund, so long as the seminary continued to bar open homosexuals from its rabbinical program. After meeting with JTS officials in April and failing to secure a change in policy, the congregational board agreed to the petition and cut off funding.

Meanwhile, the Conservative hard line against accepting homosexuality showed signs of weakening in California, where two prominent rabbis—Elliot Dorff, rector of the University of Judaism and vice-chairman of the movement's Committee on Law and Standards, and Bradley Artson, a congregational rabbi—argued both the justice and the inevitability of Conservative acceptance of gay relationships. And a Conservative rabbinical court in Northern California went so far as to sanction rabbinic officiation at "covenants of amity" between same-sex partners, a move repudiated by the Rabbinical Assembly of Conservative Judaism. But the RA soon had to confront another aspect of the issue when one of its members, Rabbi Benay Lappe, publicly stated that she was a lesbian. Rabbi Seymour Essrog, RA president, told a reporter, "We don't want to go on any witch hunts" (*Forward,* November 6).

The place of the intermarried in the Conservative movement appeared to pit the official rabbinic authority of the movement against grass-roots sentiment. The Committee on Law and Standards — made up primarily of scholars — ruled overwhelmingly that a Jew married to a non-Jew was disqualified from holding any position in a Conservative synagogue or school in which that person could be viewed as a role model for other Jews. This elicited reactions of dismay from some Conservatives active on the local level (*JTS Magazine*, Fall), who considered the decision narrow-minded and discriminatory. United Synagogue executive vice-president Rabbi Jerome Epstein responded that the actual application of the decision to individual cases remained in the hands of the local rabbi.

JTS chancellor Ismar Schorsch issued several controversial statements during the year. In July he urged elimination of the traditional three-week mourning period (a regimen that few Conservative Jews practiced anyway) prior to the Tishah b'Ab fast that commemorates the destruction of the two holy temples in Jerusalem. His rationale was that excessive emphasis on the tragedies of Jewish history encouraged "an abiding angst over insecurity and a messianic zeal to right past wrongs." In September Schorsch became the only prominent Jewish leader in the country to call for the resignation of President Clinton because of the Monica Lewinsky affair. That same month the annual JTS High Holy Day advertisement in the *New York Times* dealt with gun control, and when critics wondered why the seminary had departed from its tradition of highlighting Jewish themes appropriate to the season, Schorsch said he was "thrilled with the timeliness and punch" of the new ad. Also in September Schorsch publicly singled out for opprobrium Jews who owned sports teams for not supporting Jewish education.

The United Synagogue of Conservative Judaism, the movement's congregational body, sought ways to reinvigorate the Conservative synagogue, which was suffering from falling membership and a perceived apathy among young people. A management-consulting firm was hired to examine the operations of the United Synagogue. Synagogue 2000, a joint program with Reform congregations, experimented with unconventional services to attract adult attendance, and Stephen Wolnek, the new president of the United Synagogue, called for tripling the amount of money spent on informal Jewish education for Conservative youngsters. Whether such measures would be enough to reinvigorate the movement was an open question. In a widely discussed article on the weaknesses of Conservative Judaism (*Commentary*, September), Reform rabbi Clifford Librach suggested that declining numbers and the movement's "continuous tilt and drift to the Left" could bring about an eventual merger with Reform—a scenario that Conservative leaders vehemently denied.

RECONSTRUCTIONIST JUDAISM

True to its history as a pioneer on the frontiers of Jewish life, the Reconstructionist movement issued the 66-page "Boundaries and Opportunities: The Role of Non-Jews in Jewish Reconstructionist Congregations," the first set of recommendations on this topic produced by any of the Jewish denominations. The product of a task force appointed in 1994, it addressed the reality that 30 percent of Reconstructionist congregants under the age of 40 were part of interfaith households, and that about a quarter of Reconstructionist rabbis officiated at intermarriages, a practice that was still officially discouraged by the movement. The guidelines suggested that non-Jews be allowed membership if they were not active participants in another religion, and that children of mixed marriages be admitted to religious school so long as they were not receiving instruction in another religion. The report also recommended that non-Jews not perform Jewish rituals of a public nature—such as being called to the Torah or leading the services—and not serve as synagogue officers.

Like the Conservative movement, Reconstructionism also published a manual for rabbis, but, in keeping with the movement's democratic spirit, it presented the rituals of Jewish life as suggestions rather than laws, and was designed to be used not only by rabbis but also by lay people interested in creating their own rituals. Produced in loose-leaf format so that material for new types of occasions might be added, the manual addresses feminist concerns—including blessings for lesbian marriages—and sacralizes the most up-to-date life-cycle events, with prayers for surrogate mothers and sperm donors.

Although small in absolute terms—fewer than 100 congregations encompassing some 12,000 households—leaders of the movement announced that membership was growing at a rate of 15 percent a year, which made Reconstructionism, they said, the fastest growing denomination. In May the movement held a "Future Search" conference to ponder the direction of Reconstructionism. On the agenda were locating the resources for further expansion, integrating spirituality and social justice, and developing a clear ideological vision.

The galleys of a new Reconstructionist prayer book for the High Holy Days were distributed at the biennial convention of the Jewish Reconstructionist Federation in November. As in the previous prayer books produced by the movement, references to a chosen people and to the ancient sacrifices were eliminated, and language about God was gender-neutral. A notable topic of discussion at the biennial was the establishment of a Reconstructionist presence in Israel, where an office had already been set up and meetings planned with Israelis who might be interested in the nondogmatic form of Judaism offered by the movement.

REFORM JUDAISM

Reform continued to be pulled from the left and from the right, between the forces pressing for accommodation to the norms of American culture and those calling on the movement to reclaim major elements of the Jewish tradition. 1998 was supposed to be the year that the Central Conference of American Rabbis (CCAR) finally decided whether to approve of rabbinic officiation at ceremonies celebrating same-sex unions. The movement had gone on record two years earlier in favor of civil marriage for homosexuals, and an unknown number of Reform rabbis were already performing ceremonies of commitment or actual "marriages." A CCAR Committee on Human Sexuality, convinced that the time had come for Reform to join Reconstructionism in removing discrimination against gays and lesbians as a matter of civil rights and simple justice, was proposing a resolution to the entire organization that, while not mentioning the word marriage, would affirm the "sanctity" of same-sex unions. Some suggested that it was just a matter of time before the Conservatives followed suit.

A vocal opposition countered that what is expressly forbidden by Scripture, while perhaps licit when viewed from a modern perspective, could hardly be sanctified. Furthermore, opponents argued, the proposed policy statement would place intolerable pressure on rabbis who, as a matter of conscience, could not officiate at these ceremonies, and would spill over into similar pressure to perform intermarriages. But the most potent reason against passage was the dire prediction from Reform leaders in Israel that approval of the resolution would provide further ammunition to those Orthodox groups seeking to deny recognition to Reform by charging it with radical rejection of the tradition. The opponents also noted that, since their movement was based on the principle of rabbinic autonomy, any individual Reform rabbi was always free to officiate as he or she saw fit, even without the resolution. By an 8 to 2 vote, the CCAR Responsa Committee ruled against the resolution, which, the majority feared, "would break so sharply with the standards of religious practice maintained by virtually all Jewish communities" that it would push Reform "toward the margins of our people."

Debate grew heated in the months leading up to the June convention of the CCAR. Rabbi Eric Yoffie, president of the UAHC, initially expressed support for the resolution, but soon stopped responding to the media and referred questioners to the CCAR. To head off a nasty floor fight, some rabbis suggested sending the resolution back to committee, while others favored passing both the resolution and the majority decision of the Responsa Committee, even though the two were directly contradictory.

In the end, the issue was removed from the agenda of the June convention. Reform rabbis were urged to study the arguments on both sides of the issue, which would be revisited in 1999. This compromise was generally viewed as a victory for the opponents of homosexual unions. But proponents predicted that approval was just a matter of time, and more than 500 rabbis signed their names to a statement declaring that they had performed, or would be willing to perform, ceremonies for same-sex couples.

The CCAR convention did discuss another controversial matter—patrilineal descent. In 1983 the Reform movement had sought to encourage the Jewish identification of the children of intermarriage by declaring that children of Jewish fathers—not just of Jewish mothers—might be considered Jews if they performed "appropriate and timely public acts of identification" with Judaism. After 15 years, complaints that some Reform rabbis—especially outside the United States—refused to accept the ruling, and confusion about just which "public acts" were required, impelled the movement to study the impact of the decision. A special task force reported that 81 percent of Reform rabbis made use of the patrilineal standard, the bulk of them interpreting "acts of identification" as Jewish life-cycle events or involvement in the synagogue, with about a third of the rabbis insisting that the "acts" had to occur in childhood. The task force recommended replacing the "patrilineal" nomenclature with "equilineal descent" so as to emphasize the gender equality inherent in the policy, and strongly urged the adoption of clear guidelines defining those "acts of identification" required for children and those for adults, with the aim of insuring that no Reform rabbi would question the Jewishness of any Jew affiliated with Reform.

The Reform movement's Jewish Literacy Initiative, announced by UAHC president Eric Yoffie in 1997, moved into high gear in 1998. Each issue of *Reform Judaism* magazine listed, described, and presented excerpts from significant Jewish books, and study guides were available to encourage subscribers to read the books. In addition, classic Jewish texts were made available for group study, as were tapes and cassettes teaching how to chant the Torah and weekly summaries of the Torah portion—provided via Internet—for use by families.

But there were limits to Reform's return to tradition. A draft of a new statement of Reform doctrine, "Ten Principles for Reform Judaism," was circulated in the fall in the expectation that it would be acted upon at the 1999 CCAR convention and become the new guiding program of the movement. The document explicitly renounced the centrality of modernity characteristic of classical Reform and replaced it with a more traditional view of Judaism, specifically the ritual practices ordained in the Torah that had been abandoned by the great majority of Reform Jews. To be sure, these rituals were not presented as binding, but as ways to enhance one's Jewish spirituality. They included observance of the Sabbath and dietary laws, the traditional fasts, and even immersion in the *mikveh* (ritual bath) for women after menstruation. As if this were not radical (or reactionary) enough, the document also endorsed the traditional biblical account of revelation.

The document triggered a massive outcry—the *Forward* dubbed it the "Cheeseburger Rebellion"(November 27)—from rabbis and especially lay people, for whom Reform by definition meant ethics and excluded serious attention to ritual. The winter issue of *Reform Judaism* devoted considerable space to arguments pro and con. Rabbi Richard Levy, CCAR president and the guiding force behind the new principles, explained that they were meant to supply people with "the knowledge and permission to experience more ways of living a holy life." Hunter College professor Robert Seltzer, however, warned that emphasis on ritual could turn Reform into "Conservative Judaism Lite." But the Levy-Seltzer debate in the magazine was overshadowed by the cover photo of the bearded Rabbi Levy wearing a yarmulke and reverently kissing the fringes of his prayer shawl, an image so fraught with premodern associations that one rabbi told the *New York Jewish Week* (December 4) that "people freaked out."

Rabbi Levy agreed to tone down some of the emphasis on ritual in the document and strengthen references to Reform's traditional inclusiveness and its ethical thrust. But as the year ended, most observers doubted that even a more moderately formulated "Ten Principles" would be accepted by the movement.

Jewish Continuity

Most leaders of the Jewish community had been convinced for some time that the major threat to American Jewish life came, not from those who hated Jews, but from a culture so accepting that it eroded Jewish distinctiveness. "It is no longer rape that threatens us," said John Ruskay, chief operating officer of New York UJA-Federation, "but seduction" (*New York Times*, December 12).

The seduction was evident on many levels, politics and popular culture among them. At a September 11 White House prayer breakfast, President Clinton expressed remorse and repentance for the Monica Lewinsky affair by reading aloud from the Jewish High Holy Day prayers. Rabbi David Saperstein, director of the Religious Action Center of the Reform movement, who was sitting next to the teary-eyed First Lady, was touched that the president, "at a moment of crisis," would "turn to the Jewish prayer book for inspiration." A few months earlier, on May 14, millions of television viewers tuned in to the final episode of *Seinfeld*, the vaguely "Jewish" situation comedy that was the most widely watched show in America. "The Jews have arrived," commented Rabbi Harold Schulweis.

The question of what priority to give outreach programs to the intermarried and unaffiliated, a debate that had wracked the community since the 1990 National Jewish Population Survey revealed accelerating intermarriage, receded in 1998, with proponents of outreach seemingly the winners. While arguments for the rival "inreach" approach—calling for primary attention to those already somewhat connected to the Jewish community, and insisting on maintaining the traditional negative evaluation of intermarriage—could still be heard, most federations and a number of the most influential Jewish family foundations were putting hundreds of thousands of dollars into projects aimed at attracting Jews who were either outside the organized community and/or married to non-Jews.

Attention was increasingly focusing on plans for the 2000 Jewish Population Survey, which was expected to cost $3.6 million, one-third of it to come from the federations and the rest from private donations. Several controversial issues surfaced during the year in regard to the survey. Although it was deemed essential to repeat questions from the 1990 survey so as to establish a trend line, many communal leaders called for adding new questions that would probe issues of Jewish identity, and some funders sought the inclusion of questions of particular interest to them. More explosive was the complaint by some demographers that the 1990 survey's 52 percent intermarriage rate was exaggerated, since the percentage was calculated by counting as Jewish many non-Jewish families where one spouse had once been a Jew, or had a Jewish parent.

As plans for the year 2000 proceeded, two new studies gave added credibility to a pessimistic vision of the American Jewish future. In an April survey of American Jewish opinion conducted for the *Los Angeles Times*, only 21 percent of the sample said they would marry only a Jew, 57 percent believed that religion made no difference in choosing a spouse, and 58 percent would not object to their children marrying out of the faith. A report released in October of American Jewish identification, conducted by Prof. Steven M. Cohen for the Jewish Community Centers Association, had equally serious implications. While younger American Jews differed little from their elders when measured by the religious dimensions of Jewish identity, Cohen found that ethnic Jewish attachments were drastically eroding: far fewer young Jews than older Jews believed it important to marry a Jew, felt an attachment to Israel, or had close friends who were Jews.

Interest in Jewish day schools as a potent force for Jewish continuity increased in 1998. In a series of clever full-page ads in Jewish newspapers, the Avi Chai Foundation highlighted graduates of day schools, as knowledgeable in Jewish culture as they were in the arts and sciences, attending Ivy League colleges, and contended that a day-school education was "the one cause" whose support guaranteed the survival of all other worthwhile Jewish causes. It was clear, however, that the expansion of existing day schools and the launching of new ones had created a shortage of qualified personnel. As noted in a front-page story in the *Forward* (May 8), entitled "Day Schools Start Scrambling Over Educators of Top Quality," there were 48 openings for executives of Jewish educational institutions around the country, and some schools, despairing of finding Jewish educators, were hiring non-Jews for administrative positions.

Lack of funds remained a serious problem for the day schools. A study released by the Conservative movement in January gave new evidence of how hard it was becoming for middle-class families to afford day-school tuition and strongly suggested that many more youngsters would attend if greater financial aid were available. At its annual plenum, the Jewish Council for Public Affairs passed a resolution asserting that day schools promote Jewish continuity and that their students should continue to receive constitutionally acceptable government benefits. In fact, the JCPA came within 40 votes of approving "charitable choice," whereby sectarian organizations might receive government funds for nonsectarian activities — Jewish day schools, for example, for their secular programs — despite traditional Jewish qualms over church-state entanglement. The closeness of the vote may have reflected shifting sentiment in the broader society. A poll conducted in June by the Gallup Organization found, for the first time, a bare majority of Americans favoring government aid for tuition in private and sectarian schools. So long as judicial interpretation continued to bar direct government aid, advocates of funding for day schools focused their efforts on the Jewish federations. The efforts of George Hanus in Chicago were particularly noteworthy: the creation of endowment funds in the city's 14 day schools, and the commitment by federation to match 10 percent of those funds. The ultimate aim, said Hanus, was to provide free day-school education in Chicago. A National Jewish Day School Scholarship Committee, organized by Hanus in 1997, sought to have every federation in the country accept the principle that the community was responsible for providing all Jewish children with a day-school education, and urged every American Jew to bequeath 5 percent of his or her estate to a day school. But none of the other major federations emulated the Chicago model, and day-school advocates in several communities charged anti-Orthodox bias: since the schools were popularly associated with the Orthodox, the argument went, resentment against the Orthodox position on religious pluralism in Israel was being translated into inadequate levels of funding for day schools.

Though it drew the most attention, the interest in day schools was just one expression of a broader concern about programs for young Jews, which included informal Jewish education as well. The Jewish Education Service of North America (JESNA), the coordinating body for local boards of Jewish education, published a report charging that the 13–18-year-old population was being neglected by the community. Indeed, two studies appearing in 1998 indicated the positive impact that Jewish youth groups could have on teenagers. A survey of the alumni of Hadassah's Young Judaea programs found that an astounding 95 percent of those who were married had Jewish spouses, and that even among those under age 40, only 9 percent were intermarried. Meanwhile, the Orthodox Union released the findings of a study of alumni of its National Conference of Synagogue Youth, financed by the Lily Endowment. Of those who started out in public schools, 80 percent had found their way to yeshivas and day schools; moreover, only 2 percent of all alumni had intermarried, and 94 percent of those who started out Orthodox remained in the fold, contrasting sharply with the less-than-one-third Orthodox retention rate within American Jewry as a whole. In December, reflecting this same renewed interest in youth groups, the Reform movement authorized the expenditure of over half a million dollars to reinvigorate its North American Federation of Temple Youth (NFTY).

Jewish camping—which, unlike school or youth groups, enabled participants to "live Jewishly" 24 hours a day—was another form of informal Jewish education that had the potential to awaken the Jewish consciousness of teenagers. In fact, many prominent rabbis and Jewish lay leaders could testify that it was their early camp experiences that laid the groundwork for their later Jewish involvement. In 1998, with many of the Jewish summer camps, religious and secular, filled to capacity, the Wexner Foundation launched a study of how philanthropy might best aid Jewish camping, and a New Jersey couple, Robert and Elisa Spungeon Bildner, set up a Foundation for Jewish Camping, to help camps rebuild and expand to accommodate more youngsters.

Trips to Israel, widely considered a potent way to energize the Jewish feelings of young people, received a boost in 1998 from the Birthright Israel project, the brainchild of philanthropists Charles Bronfman and Michael Steinhardt. First unveiled in February, the plan was to give every Jew in the world aged 15–26, as a "birthright," the opportunity to visit Israel for ten days. The total cost was estimated at $300 million. Bronfman and Steinhardt pledged $5 million each, federations were urged to contribute, and by summer the Israeli government had agreed to contribute $1 million out of its own budget. "Our hope," Steinhardt told the *New York Times* (November 16), "is that the trip to Israel will be another rite of passage of Jewish life." But critics pointed out that young Jews were not even taking advantage of heavily subsidized trips to Israel that were already available, and that time spent in Israel, while certainly valuable as part of a serious Jewish educational or cultural program, was no panacea for the problem of weak Jewish identity.

The plethora of strategies to strengthen the Jewishness of young people reflected the community's frustration at its seeming inability to determine an effective policy. That same frustration lay behind the UJA-Federation decision late in the year to elevate its rhetoric: it announced plans to replace the three-year-old North American Commission on Jewish Identity and Continuity with a National Commission on Jewish Renaissance.

Holocaust-Related Developments

Fascination with the Holocaust showed no signs of abating. It was the subject of two successful movies—the tragicomedy *Life Is Beautiful*, and the thriller based on a Stephen King story, *Apt Pupil*—and two remarkable books: *I Will Bear Witness*, the English translation of the first volume of the diary of Victor Klemperer, a Jew who lived through the Nazi years in Germany, and Yaffa Eliach's *Once There Was a World*, a detailed recreation of the author's hometown of Eishyshok, Poland, destroyed by the Nazis. Steven Spielberg's Survivors of the Shoah Visual History Foundation, well on the way toward its goal of videotaping interviews with 50,000 survivors around the world, issued a CD-ROM for use by schools containing 80 minutes of interviews, along with an interactive timeline and map. Even politicians got into the act, with both critics and defenders of President Clinton invoking "lessons" of the Holocaust during the impeachment controversy, and New York senator Alfonse D'Amato, in his unsuccessful bid for reelection against a Jewish opponent, running a TV ad of an elderly Holocaust survivor thanking him for helping her get restitution money.

The United States Holocaust Memorial Museum marked its fifth anniversary in April. In some respects it had surpassed the hopes of its founders. The museum had become a major Washington tourist attraction. Of the 10 million visitors since the opening, more than 7 million were not Jewish, and one million were school-age children. A museum-sponsored survey of public attitudes showed that 77 percent of Americans had heard of the museum and 66 percent wanted to learn more about the Holocaust. In an effort to reach out beyond the capital, the museum arranged traveling exhibits and announced the imminent opening of a Center for Advanced Holocaust Studies for the training of a new generation of Holocaust scholars.

Yet the political entanglements that inevitably come with federal sponsorship involved the museum in a series of controversies. In January, high-level State Department officials who were on the museum council urged museum director Miles Lerman — a presidential appointee — to arrange an official tour for Yasir Arafat. Lerman extended the invitation, but when museum director Walter Reich objected, Lerman — without consulting other council members — withdrew the invitation, only to extend it once again when criticized for snubbing Arafat, who was, after all, Israel's negotiating partner. Arafat declined the invitation. Lerman blamed Reich for giving him bad advice, and Reich resigned. His replacement had still not been named when the year ended.

During early 1998 a coalition of Jewish groups brought together by museum chairman Lerman engaged in talks with the Polish government about the removal of crosses that had been placed at the site of the Auschwitz-Birkenau death camp. In April Rabbi Avi Weiss of New York, a well-known activist, charged Lerman with "selling out Auschwitz" by allegedly negotiating a secret deal that would allow crosses to remain. Weiss went so far as to organize a public demonstration against Lerman on Holocaust Memorial Day outside New York's Temple Emanu-El, where Lerman was participating in the annual Holocaust commemoration. In July the museum announced that its coalition of negotiators had been on the verge of agreement with Poland to remove a 23-foot cross from the site, but that a provocative call by a World Jewish Congress official for the area's "extraterritoriality" had caused the Poles to back out.

Further embarrassment came to the museum in June. Holocaust scholar John K. Roth — a non-Jew — was appointed to head its new Center for Advanced Holocaust Studies when it opened in August. But a *Los Angeles Times* article Roth had written in 1988 came to light in which he compared the platform of Israel's far-right Moledet party to the ideology that led to *Kristallnacht,* and the Palestinians to the German Jews under Hitler. Roth expressed regret for having written the offending piece. Virtually all the noted academics in the field of Holocaust studies followed the lead of Elie Wiesel in defending Roth's record, and the *New York Jewish Week* (June 12) accused ZOA president Morton Klein, who was calling for Roth's resignation, of "Jewish McCarthyism." But just as the museum council was voting overwhelmingly to reaffirm Roth's appointment and denouncing "character assassination" against him, two members of Congress notified Miles Lerman that there was documented proof of additional provocative statements by Roth over the years: that Ronald Reagan's election was comparable to Hitler's assumption of power; that the treatment of America's poor was similar to that of the Jews in Nazi Germany; that the Soviet and American systems were analogous; and that Israeli warfare and PLO terrorism had elements in common. Roth resigned, insisting nevertheless that he had been the victim of "distorted allegations."

The status of Holocaust studies as an academic discipline came under question when Harvard University proved unable or unwilling to fill a $3 million chair in the subject endowed by philanthropist Kenneth Lipper. Some of those involved said that there was no candidate of sufficient stature, while others suggested that the chair was not filled due to controversy between those favoring an expert in Nazi history and those wanting someone familiar with the Jewish sources. Yet a third group questioned whether it was appropriate for Harvard to have an endowed chair dedicated to the story of European Jewry's destruction when there was no chair teaching modern Jewish civilization, the culture that was destroyed.

Questions of restitution continued to occupy the Jewish community. As the year began, Swiss banks were seeking a "global settlement" of all claims by Jews who said that the banks were withholding money they or their families had deposited before the war. The deadline for the agreement was March 26, the day that the financial officers of American states and localities were to meet to decide on sanctions against Switzerland. An American Jewish Committee survey revealed how seriously American Jews viewed the matter: more than two-thirds of the sample believed that the Swiss government was being uncooperative, and 53 percent said they would support sanctions and boycotts. The three largest Swiss banks came up with a proposal in time, and talks were arranged with Jewish organizations and the survivors' lawyers to iron out the details. But the talks deadlocked in June when the Swiss, claiming that the value of the dormant accounts was not as high as previously thought, offered $1.25 billion to settle all claims, far less than had been expected. As the states and municipalities again raised the possibility of sanctions, and the Swiss countered that the World Jewish Restitution Organization had not yet distributed any of the $200 million they had already contributed to a humanitarian fund, the Jewish organizations and the lawyers of the survivors bickered with each other over strategy. "Jewish Groups Fight for Spoils of Swiss Case," was the front-page headline in the *New York Times* (November 29).

Meanwhile, the disposition of artworks stolen by the Nazis became another point of contention. Two such paintings by the Viennese artist Egon Schiele were part of a temporary exhibition at the Museum of Modern Art in New York City. Heirs of the prewar Jewish owners demanded their return, but the museum, arguing that it should not be held responsible for researching the provenance of every painting it showed, sought to send them back to Austria. Manhattan District Attorney Henry Morgenthau prevented the museum from shipping the paintings, pending resolution of the legal issues.

The federal government involved itself in the restitution question. In February Congress passed the Holocaust Victims Redress Act, which called on all governments to make sure that confiscated artworks were returned. And the State Department, in conjunction with the United States Holocaust Memorial Museum, hosted the Washington Conference on Holocaust-Era Assets, November 30–December 3. Forty-seven nations and numerous nongovernmental organizations were represented. Both the State Department, anxious not to strain bilateral relations with other countries, and the Jewish organizations, worried that anti-Semitic stereotypes could be reinforced if the legacy of the Holocaust were identified too closely with money, spoke of restitution only in generalities. Much of the discussion centered on what Elie Wiesel called "moral restitution," the need to educate the world about the lessons of the Holocaust.

The Great Merger •

The desire of American Jewish philanthropists for greater control over where their contributions went remained strong in 1998. According to an investigative report in the *Forward* (March 6), organizations of "American Friends" of specific Israeli cultural, educational, and medical institutions were actually raising more money, in the aggregate, than the UJA. Family foundations were becoming an increasingly popular way of giving money, both domestically and for overseas Jewish causes, outside the UJA-Federation system; the Jewish Funders Network—which brought together such foundations—had 260 members in 1998, up from 222 the year before. (See "Current Trends in American Jewish Philanthropy," by Jack Wertheimer, in the 1997 AJYB.)

The call for more localized control of the philanthropic dollar was heard in the federation world as well. Barry Shrage, president of Combined Jewish Philanthropies of Boston, circulated a memo in January urging that federations be encouraged to choose which Israeli projects to fund, rather than transferring the money to the United Israel Appeal and thence to the Jewish Agency for allocation in Israel. (In fact, the percentage of philanthropic funds going to Israel through the standard route had already declined to the point where the Jewish Agency claimed to be on the verge of bankruptcy.)

Shrage's view had serious implications for the "partnership" that had been devised in 1997 between the Council of Jewish Federations and the United Jewish Appeal. The federation world was eager to turn that partnership into a full merger, in the expectation not only of greater efficiency but also of tighter federation control over funding. Advocates of aid to Israel and other overseas Jewish communities, however, wanted to go slow on the merger, fearing that if Shrage's stance won out, the funding of overseas needs would have to rely on the vagaries of local federations. Their fears were not unfounded: a study commissioned by the Jerusalem Center for Public Affairs found that, while 58 percent of the leaders of American Jewish organizations wanted federations to increase their support of local Jewish causes, only 40 percent favored more money for Israel and other overseas causes.

In June, CJF and UJA (along with the United Israel Appeal) merged their offices, moving into a new joint headquarters in New York City. At a retreat held in a Chicago suburb in July, CJF and UJA leaders agreed in principle on a full merger, but three matters remained unresolved: whether federations should be required to set aside specific percentages of their funds for overseas aid, whether to bring Jewish groups who were outside the federation system — primarily the religious organizations — into the governance structure of the merged body, and who would be its chief executive officer. Another meeting, held in September in Washington, failed to answer any of these questions.

The Pollard Case

Since 1987, Jonathan Pollard had been serving a life sentence for passing classified American documents to Israel, a punishment that many American Jews considered disproportionate. Although President Clinton had already twice refused to commute his sentence, the Conference of Presidents launched a campaign to win Pollard's release. In a letter to Clinton in February, the conference argued that the life sentence was excessive compared to the punishments meted out to other spies, and that both "compassion and justice" were grounds for a commutation. Israeli authorities sought to buttress the campaign for Pollard by publicly admitting, for the first time, that he was not engaged in a rogue operation but had been spying for Israel. Prime Minister Netanyahu, echoing the Conference of Presidents, called on Clinton to release Pollard on humanitarian grounds.

At the Wye talks in October, Prime Minister Netanyahu asked for the release of Pollard as part of the projected agreement, and indeed the final accord was held up for several hours when Netanyahu insisted on bringing Pollard back to Israel with him. In the end, Netanyahu had to be satisfied with a promise that the president would carefully examine the case for clemency. Opinions differed over whether Netanyahu, after being rebuffed, had brought up the issue again at the last minute for domestic political reasons, or whether Clinton had indeed agreed to free Pollard only to switch course on the insistence of his intelligence officials. As the Conference of Presidents prepared yet another letter to the president supporting commutation, Clinton asked for recommendations from the defense and intelligence establishments.

LAWRENCE GROSSMAN

Jewish Culture

Despite dark talk in the American Jewish community about a crisis of Jewish "continuity," American Jewish culture in 1998 continued to flourish. Difficult as it is to identify a Jewish "core" or essence among activities as diverse as music and cooking, literature and politics, humor and science, there can be little doubt of a significant Jewish presence in these and other forms of cultural expression in the United States. Furthermore, although what has emerged has at times reflected the differences between popular and "high" culture, it has also, perhaps more notably, appeared in forms that link the two. Indeed, this interface between levels of culture seems almost as characteristic a feature of American-Jewish cultural achievement as the American-Jewish connection itself.

Among books published during 1998, an important example of the connection between high and popular culture appeared in the unusual assembly of memoirs, autobiographies, and biographies that can be grouped under the common heading of personal history. Coinciding with the 50th anniversary of the founding of Brandeis University (still, as it was originally, the one secular Jewish university in the United States), three biographies appeared of figures both nationally known and prominent in the early history of Brandeis. Thus, the "lives" were told of *Irving Howe* by Edward Alexander, of *Max Lerner* by Sanford Lakoff, and of *Ludwig Lewisohn* by Ralph Melnick (volume one of two). Still another—more recent—Brandeis professor, the sociologist Morrie Schwartz, is the main speaker in the best-selling account of *Tuesdays with Morrie*—a record of conversations which the volume's author, Mitch Albom, recalled from the year of his visits during Morrie's fatal illness. Reaching in a different direction, the first of a two-volume biography of Abraham J. Heschel by Edward Kaplan and Samuel Dresner appeared. Heschel, almost 30 years after his death, has established a claim as the most influential Jewish theologian in the United States during the 20th century.

The proliferation of personal memoirs and autobiographies was still more notable than the more scholarly and distanced writings of biography. These ranged from Stanley Ely's self-described growing up *In Jewish Texas* to David Klinghofer's *The Lord Will Gather Me In*—the account of his journey from secular liberalism to Orthodoxy and an editorial position on the conservative *National Review*—to Susi Bechhofer's autobiographical narrative, which begins with the discovery that secreted behind her Welsh Baptist adoptive parents was a Jewish mother who had died in Auschwitz. Another variation on the theme of identity crisis figures in Stephen Dubner's *Turbulent Souls*—the story of his belated discovery that his ostensibly Catholic parents were converts from Judaism and then of his own return to it. A number of fiction writers also turned their hands to this form of personal history, examples being Grace Paley's *Just as I Thought* and Max Apple's *I Love Gootie: My Grandmother's Story*. The proliferation of autobiographical accounts by groups as well as by individuals has been sufficiently extensive to lead to their collection in anthologies: so, for example, *Growing Up Jewish*, edited by Jay David, and *Daughters of Kings: Growing Up as a Jewish Woman in America*, a series of individual narratives written by members of the Radcliffe Institute and edited by Leslie Brody.

Viewed in social terms, such accounts seem less significant in the writing than in the large readership they have attracted. When the history of the self that is described is so clearly affected by its socially contingent character—in this case, Jewish identity as it emerges in an American context—it is reasonable to conclude that those narratives express deep-seated interests of their readers as well as of their authors.

Other, in some ways even more compelling books could be found on the boundary of these examples of personal narratives. One of the most widely reviewed books of the year was *Kaddish*, in which Leon Wieseltier, the literary editor of the *New Republic,* traces the contours of a year in which he said Kaddish for his father; he here combines the form of a memoir with historical references to the evolving tradition of saying Kaddish.

The historian Vera Schwarcz's *Bridge Across Broken Time* compares the roles of memory in Jewish and Chinese culture through the lens of the author's own history in which those two traditions became interwoven.

It seems more than likely that one effect of Holocaust memoirs, testimonies, and histories (which continued to have substantial additions, as in the Yale historian Peter Gay's *My German Question* and in Yaffa Eliach's *There Was Once a World*) has been to stimulate other similar but non-Holocaust writings. Perhaps spurred on by the "postmodern" emphasis on originality, increasing numbers of authors have come back to the one subject on which they are the exclusive authority—namely, their own views of themselves. But even taken together, these causes would not explain the emphasis on personal or group memory without the additional pressure that a concern about the future adds to the weight of the past—and the question that then arises of how to constitute a "self" in the present. The title of a book by Alan Dershowitz provides an apt formulation of the elements brought together in this tension: *The Vanishing American Jew: In Search of Jewish Identity for the Next Century*.

And of course, as fiction often imitates life (perhaps only more so), there also the turn to personal history was evident. Philip Roth's *I Married a Communist* filled in still another sector of that author's Balzacian map of American Jewish life in the past half century—the 33rd book of Roth's own library, which he began in 1959 with *Goodbye Columbus*. Norman Mailer published a literary analogue to an artist's "retrospective" exhibition in *The Time of Our Time*, an anthology of excerpts from his novels and nonfiction writing over the long career that began explosively with his World War II novel, *The Naked and the Dead*, first published

50 years earlier when Mailer was 25. Among younger writers, the recent visibility and strength of the Orthodox community, reflecting both the Ba'al Teshuvah ("return") movement and the tendency toward more stringent observance within parts of Orthodoxy, seem to have become a significant subject for fiction. So, Allegra Goodman's first novel, *Kaaterskill Falls,* won a place among the finalists for the National Book Award with its depiction of life in an Orthodox community in the Catskills. The principal character in Elizabeth Swados's *Flamboyant* is an Orthodox school teacher who finds herself attracted to, and then entangled with, a drag queen. These follow a sequence of earlier best-selling novels situated on the line between Orthodoxy and the world beyond it by Chaim Potok, as well as the popular series of detective novels by Faye Kellerman, whose detective is led both to Judaism and to the solutions of crimes that come his way by the Orthodox divorcee whom he marries in the course of the series.

Notable in translation from the Hebrew during the year were two novels by the Israeli author, Aharon Appelfeld—*The Conversion*, and *The Iron Tracks*; the latter takes an unusual turn in Appelfeld's continuing journey back to the Holocaust as a subject with its focus on a calculated act of revenge by a survivor. Another outstanding Israeli writer, A. B. Yehoshua, turns much further back in history—foreshadowing the present in the first millennium C.E., with his novel *A Journey to the End of the Millennium.*

A conference on "Writing the Jewish Future," held in California (at Stanford and Berkeley) in February, brought together a number of writers from the United States, including Cynthia Ozick, Chaim Potok, and Grace Paley, but also Appelfeld and Joshua Sobol from Israel, Dan Jacobson from England, and Victor Perera from Guatemala.

A variety of books appeared on aspects of Jewish history and philosophy and culture, again spanning the range from popular to scholarly. Perhaps the most unusual among these was the best-selling *The Gift of the Jews* by Thomas Cahill—the second stop in that author's ecumenical tour of extraordinary cultural contributions after his *How the Irish Saved Civilization.* From the direction of popular therapy and advice books came *The Ten Commandments* by the "conservative" psychologist, Laura Schlesinger (writing together with Stewart Vogel, the rabbi of her congregation); Schlesinger now appears in public as a social and ideological balance to her "liberal" counterpart, Dr. Ruth (Westheimer). "New Age" writing continued to elaborate its Jewish connection in works like Rodger Kamenetz's *Stalking Elijah* and Tirzah Firestone's *With Roots in Heaven.* Toward the scholarly end of this spectrum, a number of important books appeared in the traditional fields of Jewish studies. These include Arnold Eisen's *Rethinking Modern Judaism*, winner of the newly initiated Koret Book Prize in Jewish Philosophy and Thought—an analysis of contemporary Judaism in terms of practice rather than the frameworks of belief more typically regarded as the basis for such analysis; and *Engendering Judaism* by Rachel Adler, which makes a substantial contribution to the growing development of feminist themes in Jewish religious and philosophical thought. (Three $10,000 Koret Institute Book Prizes—in Jewish literature, history and biography, and philosophy and thought—are now to be awarded annually, running parallel to the National Jewish Book Awards.)

The American Jewish presence in academic and scholarly fields of the humanities and the natural and social sciences—in significantly large proportions among faculties of the preeminent private and public universities—has by now come to be taken for granted even more than had its earlier absence. There have as yet been few studies of how this opening of the academy to Jewish students and faculty affected the shape of learning within the academy itself. Susanne Klingenstein's 1998 book on *Enlarging America: The Cultural Work of American Literary Scholars, 1930–1990*, which follows her earlier study of *Jews in the American Academy: 1900–1940*, suggests the lines along which such broader analyses might move. Specific directions followed in several 1998 works provide a concrete view of the evidence and questions that this project would address. Thus, for example, it seems clear that the important subject of slavery for American history has had significant contributions from American Jewish scholars—including Stanley Elkin's early invocation of the Holocaust as a basis for comparing the respective responses of the two groups of victims, extending to the more systematic writings of Herbert Gutman and Herbert Klein, the statistical measurements of Fogel and Engerman's *Time on the Cross*, and David Brion Davis's sweeping studies and comparisons of New World and classical slavery. This body of work, which collectively is quite fundamental to the current study of slavery, was enhanced in 1998 by two significant additions. One of these—Eli Faber's *Jews, Slaves, and the Slave Trade*—is explicitly related to American Jewish history in its description of the (as Faber views it, very limited) role of Jews in the slave trade. The other work is a comprehensive—and, in several reviewers' estimate, "revolutionary"—analysis of stages and varieties in the institution of American slavery, which is more often conceived of as homogeneous; this, in Ira Berlin's *Many Thousands Gone*.

The Cultures of Humor and Cooking

Perhaps more than any other expressive form, humor bridges the divide between popular and high culture, which may account at least in part for the decision of the National Foundation for Jewish Culture to establish a national award in American Jewish Humor. The winner of the first award, celebrated at a December dinner in New York City, was Alan King. The choice of Elie Wiesel to present the award further attests to the convergence, or even confusion, of quite different forms of cultural memory and creativity. The award itself was a useful reminder of both the extent and variety of American Jewish humor—in live performance, in radio and television, in film, on stage, in literature, comic strips, and other venues.

Food and cooking are central markers of cultural expression and examples of the forms that undercut the distinction between popular and "high" culture. Certainly Joan Nathan's 26-part PBS television series on "Jewish Cooking in America" during the year was addressed to an audience of diverse backgrounds and tastes—as had been her best-selling cookbook published under the same title in 1994. That the "genre" of Jewish cookbooks itself has an American history may come as something of a surprise, but the tradition reaches back at least as far as *Jewish Cookery*, by Esther Levy, published in Philadelphia in 1871, followed in Chicago in 1889 by *Aunt Babette's Cookbook*.

The spread of retail food certified as "kosher" has also emerged as a cultural as well as a religious phenomenon. (On this count, 1998 may be recalled as the year of the Oreo—with the largest selling cookie in the United States winning kosher certification.) The growth in kosher food sales is perhaps more notable inasmuch as only about two million of the 7.5 to 10 million regular purchasers of these products are estimated to be Jewish; the other three-quarters of the total—including about three million Muslims—choose them for other religious reasons or because they are lactose-intolerant and want reliably nondairy products, because they are vegetarians who want a guarantee that no meat products are used in the food they buy, or for more general reasons related to quality. However it is explained, the market for kosher foods has grown over the past four years at a rate of 12 percent a year. On the order of 45,000 products are now certified as kosher—up from 1,750 just 20 years ago, with the average supermarket stocking 13,000 of them. "Kosherfest," the kosher-foods trade fair, brought together some 370 different exhibitors in its now annual appearance in New York.

The opening in New York's Shea Stadium during the 1998 baseball season of a *Glatt* kosher food stand selling hot dogs, knishes, and felafel thus reflects both general acculturation (with baseball itself part of this) together with an internal shift in the Orthodox community's observance of religious standards that has raised the bar another rung from the once generally acceptable category of simply "kosher." The 40-odd kosher restaurants in Manhattan alone represent at least a fivefold increase in the past decade. A related development, also with implications for the general question of acculturation in all sectors of the American Jewish community, is the significant expansion in the celebration of Jewish holidays—especially Passover, traditionally a gathering of the family at home—in hotels and resorts and on cruise ships; many of the venues chosen for these are in ever more distant places (Hawaii, Cancun, Banff, the Bahamas), in hotels certified kosher specifically for the occasion.

Holocaust-Related Developments

In the United States, the Holocaust Memorial Museum in Washington, D.C., remained a principal focus of Holocaust-related activities. During the year, it reached the figure of ten million visitors since its opening in 1993 (with the estimate at least constant and perhaps even growing of more than 50 percent non-Jewish visitors). In addition to the research for which the museum provides facilities and fellowships through its Research Institute, it also serves as a forum for regular lectures and for a number of international conferences. Perhaps the most significant in 1998 among the latter was the conference, cosponsored by the State Department and attended by representatives of 44 countries, on "Holocaust Era Assets." Clearly, the moral, legal, and political issues posed by the existence of such assets are both substantive and substantial, but there is also discomfort over the danger that analysis of the Holocaust should be in terms of economic costs and compensation. The museum itself was troubled during the year by turmoil resulting in the forced resignation of its director, Dr. Walter Reich, over a controversial invitation and then dis-invitation to PLO chairman Yasir Arafat to visit the museum; this was followed by the withdrawal—for quite different reasons—of the newly appointed director of the museum's Research Institute, Prof. John K. Roth, primarily related to criticism of statements in Roth's writings about political developments in Israel and the United States. The balancing act forced on the museum by the sometimes conflicting expectations of its several sponsors and constituencies (the U.S. government, the presidentially appointed council of the museum, the Jewish community, individual donors, the public at large) has posed dilemmas since the earliest stages of its planning that, with its present structure, are unlikely to be resolved. The evident accomplishments of the museum seem all the more notable in light of this.

It is of considerable interest that several Americans are playing significant roles in Holocaust institutions in Germany. Probably the single largest cultural issue there during the year concerned the erection of a national Holocaust memorial, with the first round of entries in the design competition set aside as too controversial. In the second round, a design by American Jewish architect Peter Eisenman was selected, but was then challenged during national elections by the Minister of Culture-to-be, Michael Naumann. He proposed that the memorial should be a building housing the survivor video-archives now being assembled on an international scale under the auspices of Steven Spielberg. Spielberg himself, already celebrated for three World War II films—*Schindler's List* in 1993, *Saving Private Ryan* in 1998, and *The Last Days* in 1999—had become enough of an international icon to appear on the front cover of *Stern*, the large-circulation German news weekly.

The new Jewish Museum in Berlin (opened in January 1999) will have a supervisory role over the memorial once it is constructed. The new museum's director, Michael Blumenthal (one-time secretary of the U.S. Treasury), and its chief curator, Tom Freudenheim (formerly an administrative officer of YIVO and before that of the Smithsonian Institution in Washington) are German-born American Jews who escaped the Nazis; the architect for the new and dramatically unusual building is Daniel Libeskind, born in Lodz but also an American citizen. Early on in the planning for the Holocaust memorial, the German government took the unusual step of including in the five-person national commission appointed to judge the competition the American-Jewish scholar and author James Young.

A Holocaust import from Europe made its mark this year. *Life Is Beautiful*, the Italian film written, directed, and acted in by Roberto Benigni, created a considerable stir — evoking both plaudits and negative criticism — through its quasi-comic depiction of a family deported to Auschwitz, where the father attempts to shield his young son from the camp's brutalities by pretending with the boy that the camp's "activities" are part of a game.

I Will Bear Witness, an edited translation of the first section of the diary previously published to acclaim in Germany, by Viktor von Klemperer, was a notable addition to the memoir literature of the Holocaust. The author is a professor of literature who, even as a convert from Judaism to Protestantism and with a non-Jewish wife, escaped deportation only in the confusion of the days after the fire-bombing of Dresden where he lived.

Cultural Cycles and Sites

The spread across the United States of annual cultural events, celebrated at approximately the same time in communities coast to coast, has become an analogue in cultural terms to the expectations and regularity of the religious holidays. National Jewish Book Month (November) has now led to book exhibits and "National Book Weeks" offering lectures and readings in communities across the country, from the major metropolitan areas to much smaller ones, far from urban centers. A similar phenomenon is the Jewish Film Festival, also organized in numerous communities, usually between late January and mid-March. This is not to be confused with the Israel Film Festival, which made its 14th annual appearance in New York City and Los Angeles, with showings there of full-length films, television films, documentaries, and experimental films.

The new building for the Center for Jewish History, which was completed during 1998 and formally opened on January 3, 1999 — located near the lower end of Manhattan's Fifth Avenue — brings under one roof four significant institutions of Jewish culture: YIVO, the American Jewish Historical Society, the Leo Baeck Institute, and the Yeshiva University Museum. The combined collections of these individual agencies represent the single largest Jewish archival site outside of Israel, including more than a half million volumes and 100,000,000 documents. The proximity of the new center to the New York University Skirball Center for Jewish Studies adds to the potential impact of this new entity.

The National Yiddish Book Center, located in handsome quarters (opened in 1997) in Amherst, Massachusetts, continued its work as a collection and distribution center for Yiddish books (in these functions, in fact, it serves as an international center, with both its collections and distributions extending beyond the United States). Beyond this, it has introduced innovative programs for reproducing Yiddish books as well as programs and courses in Yiddish and Yiddish culture. The center's project of "digitalizing" up to half of the 40,000 individual titles estimated to constitute the sum of Yiddish books ever published—a process which would then enable the center to "publish" any individual digitalized title on demand—continues apace; this project received added impetus during the year when the center became the beneficiary of a substantial grant from the Steven Spielberg Foundation.

Continued efforts in the American Jewish theater centered mainly in New York, but spread elsewhere as well (to the Long Wharf in New Haven, the Northlight and the Steppenwolf in Chicago, and the Mark Taper Forum in Los Angeles). *The Diary of Anne Frank*, in its revised version, continued to draw large audiences in its New York venue; there, too, the Folksbiene's *Zise Khaloymes* (with English translation), Mandy Patinkin's *Mamaloshen,* and Avi Hoffman's *Too Jewish Two* were most immediately directed to Jewish audiences. Two other plays with an ostensibly broader reach— *Visiting Mr. Green,* about the relationship between two Jewish men, and *Chaim's Love Song*, about the relationship between a Jewish man and a non-Jewish woman—clearly drew on Jewish themes and idioms.

With the introduction of "cyberspace," the very notion of cultural activity confined to physical structures or centers is undergoing dramatic change; the appearance in the United States of a variety of Web sites and "lists" related to Jewish studies and Jewish culture has increasingly become a phenomenon to reckon with—a new source of communication and potentially of community. The "H-Judaic" list, dedicated to historical, religious, philosophical, and cultural topics in Jewish studies recently entered its tenth year, with about 2,000 members or correspondents and arguably a still larger public reached by its spin-off Web sites.

At least three of these Web sites are related to topics concerning the Holocaust; other sites range in their topics from Kabbalah to the Daf Yomi to Judeo-Maghrebi literature—almost always free and open to anyone who is interested. The National Foundation for Jewish Culture maintains on the Web a continually updated calendar and review of current Jewish cultural events occurring across the country. Such sites, wherever they originate, are international in the novel sense that no more effort (or time) is required to participate in them from 6,000 miles away than locally. The effects of such proximity and of the medium more generally for cultural exchange may still be indeterminate, but there can be little doubt of the long-range potential for encouraging the establishment of communities with quite different structures from the older and more familiar ones.

The 50th anniversary of Israel's Independence in May 1998 was celebrated with relatively little fanfare in the United States. This unexpected development reflected at least in part the muted Jubilee celebration in Israel itself, stemming from organizational disagreements there about how the Jubilee should be celebrated, and from social and political strains that intensified during the year in more general aspects of the relationship between the American Jewish community and Israel.

Notwithstanding such tensions, the relationship between the American Jewish and the Israeli Jewish communities remains a basic and in some ways increasingly important factor in the social and cultural thought and expression of both. Israeli authors—principally, Aharon Appelfeld, David Grossman, Amos Oz, A. B. Yehoshua—continue to draw substantial audiences both for their books in translation and for their personal appearances and lectures. That Israeli authors have more of a presence in the United States than American Jewish authors—and American Jewish culture more generally—have in Israel is undoubtedly related to the larger tradition of Israeli attitudes toward Diaspora communities.

Exhibitions of Israeli art continue to appear in the major venues of Jewish art in the United States; so, for example, "After Rabin: New Art from Israel," shown at the Jewish Museum in New York City. The "Silk Paintings" of Israeli artist Chaim Kirkell were among the eight exhibitions mounted simultaneously by the Yeshiva University Museum. The Israeli singer Chava Alberstein turned to Yiddish rather than Hebrew themes in her CD "The Well," which she recorded with the "American" Klezmatics.

One way of visualizing in a single sweep the diversity and inventiveness of American Jewish culture is by sampling the topics of conferences and other types of gatherings that took place during the year. In addition to those cited above, there were conferences on the History of the Catskills, Babylonian Jewish Research, and "In Search of Ourselves: The Power of Jewish Women" (by the New York City Hadassah). And then there were the (often by now annual) conferences of the Association of Orthodox Jewish Scientists, the Council of American Jewish Museums, and the 8th International Conference on Jewish Medical Ethics; the five-day "KlezKamp," in its 13th annual gathering (featuring both Klezmer performances and scholarly reports on the science of "klezmerology"); the "Kosherfest," also by now an annual exhibition and advertising opportunity for the manufacturers (and retailers) of kosher foods; and the Association for Jewish Studies (with 1,600 members, mostly Jewish studies faculty at American colleges and universities) in its 30th annual meeting in Boston.

The highly touted Hollywood film *The Prince of Egypt* may have led to disappointing box-office receipts, but the fact remains that an animated film (in earlier terms, a feature-length cartoon) based on the biblical life of Moses still had box-office receipts of more than $100,000,000 in the first several months after its release. The historical cogency of the film's focus on the "Hebrews" rather than "Jews" may have reflected an intended distancing effect, and the film had some commercial precedent, as in Cecil B. DeMille's *The Ten Commandments*. Furthermore, it is unclear whether its large audiences were drawn to the film because of traditional associations with the subject, because they knew little about it but wished to know more, or for reasons having nothing to do with the biblical account at all.

In looking back, we find 1998 closing the parentheses of a number of significant obituaries (19??–1998). The year witnessed the deaths of such diverse contributors to American Jewish as well as to American and in some cases international cultural history as Alfred Kazin—a founder of the field of American studies through his path-breaking literary genealogy *On Native Ground*, and author as well of the striking memoir of his own Brownsville youth, *A Walker in the City*; the comedian Henny Youngman (English-born) whose "Take my wife. *Please*," has yielded the distinction of an entry in Bartlett's *Book of Quotations*; the distinctive national political figures of Bella Abzug and Abraham Ribicoff, each of whom shifted the policies of their (Democrat) party at least a measurable length; the world-renowned mathematician Andre Weil of the Institute for Advanced Studies at Princeton (brother of the philosopher Simone Weil, who died in England during World War II), an emigré from their native France; Jeffrey Moss, one of the creative forces in developing and sustaining the television program "Sesame Street," which in English and translated into numerous foreign languages and shown on television screens worldwide has been favored by generations of children and their parents since its inception; Sid Luckman, who went from an undergraduate career at Columbia to an unlikely future as star quarterback for the professional Chicago Bears football team; the popular novelist Jerome Weidman; and a central figure in the development of modern American dance, Jerome Robbins. If there is little likelihood of identifying common themes or meanings among these figures and their accomplishments, it would be no less arbitrary to ignore what was common in their histories and aspirations. As it would also be a failure not to recognize in their works a creative urge and energy that found for itself a fertile ground—fertile in part despite and even perhaps because of the friction their efforts sometimes encountered. Such generalities about the past offer no assurance for the future, but in themselves they say something significant about the present.

BEREL LANG

Jewish Population in the United States, 1998

BASED ON LOCAL COMMUNITY counts—the method for identifying and enumerating Jewish population that serves as the basis of this report—the estimated size of the American Jewish community in 1998 was 6.0 million. This is half a million more than the 5.5 million "core" Jewish population estimated in the Council of Jewish Federations' 1990 National Jewish Population Survey (NJPS).[1]

The difference between the national and aggregated local figures is explained by definitional issues, disparate sample sources (e.g., outdated lists, distinctive Jewish names, and random-digit dialing), and the lapse in time, as well as a lack of uniformity in the methodologies used for research conducted at the local level.

The demographic results of the NJPS suggested that the population was growing slightly due to an excess of Jewish births over Jewish deaths during the late 1980s. However, extrapolation from the age structure suggests that by the mid-1990s the annual numbers of births and deaths have balanced so that zero population growth is being realized. At the same time, some growth in numbers is achieved through Jewish immigration to the United States, particularly by emigres from the former Soviet Union.

The NJPS used a scientifically selected sample to project a total number for the United States, but could not provide accurate information on the state and local levels. Therefore, as in past years, in this article we have based local, state, and regional population figures on reports by local communal leaders.

While the 185 Jewish federations are the chief reporting bodies, their service areas vary in size and may represent several towns, one county, or an aggregate of several counties. In some cases we have subdivided federation areas to reflect the more natural geographic boundaries. Estimates from areas without federations have been provided by local rabbis and other informed Jewish communal leaders. To collect data this year, a form requesting the current population estimates was mailed to 428 relatively small communities, including locales with Jewish populations of less than 100, which are not listed here individually. A total of 228 replies were received. In addition, about 25 requests from very small communities were returned with indications that a synagogue whose leader had previously provided an estimate had closed in recent years. For those communities that did not provide recent estimates, figures have either been retained from

---

[1]See Barry A. Kosmin et al., *Highlights of the CJF 1990 National Jewish Population Survey* (New York, Council of Jewish Federations, 1991).

past years or extrapolations made from older data. The estimates are for the resident Jewish population, including those in private households and in institutional settings. Non-Jewish family members have been excluded from the total.

The state and regional totals shown in Appendix tables 1 and 2 are derived by summing the estimates for individual communities shown in table 3, including communities of less than 100, and then rounding to the nearest hundred or thousand, depending on the size of the estimate.

Because population estimation is not an exact science, the reader should be aware that, in cases where a figure differs from last year's, the increase or decrease did not come about suddenly but occurred over a period of time and has just now been substantiated. The primary sources for changing previously reported Jewish population figures in larger communities are recently completed local sociodemographic studies. The results of such studies should be understood as either updated calculations of gradual demographic changes or corrections of faulty older estimates.

In determining Jewish population, communities count both affiliated and non-affiliated residents who are "core" Jews as defined in NJPS. This definition includes born Jews who report adherence to Judaism, Jews by choice, and born Jews without a current religion ("secular Jews"). In most cases, counts are made by households, with that number multiplied by the average number of self-defined Jewish persons per household. Similarly to NJPS, most communities also include those born and raised as Jews but who at present consider themselves as having no religion. As stated above, non-Jews living in Jewish households, primarily the non-Jewish spouses and non-Jewish children, are not included in the 1998 estimates presented in the Appendix below.

Local Population Changes

The community reporting the largest population gain in 1998 was Phoenix, Arizona, up 10,000 to 60,000. Though no survey has been conducted there since 1983, growth that occurred in the last 15 years is now being acknowledged.

The two other communities reporting the largest Jewish population gains are Tampa, Florida (5,000), and Palm Springs, California (4,150). The latter number was substantiated in a recently completed sociodemographic study, while the Tampa figure reflects continued growth occurring throughout Florida's west-coast communities. Bridgeport, Connecticut; Atlanta, Georgia; and Portland, Oregon, each reported gains of 3,000. Bridgeport's increase reflects a greatly expanded Jewish federation list and the identification of previously unknown households. Atlanta and Portland are experiencing continued Jewish population growth.

Two communities in New Jersey—Ocean County and Passaic County—noted gains of 2,000 each, reflecting growth particularly in their Orthodox populations. Three communities in California—Long Beach, Santa Barbara, and Santa Cruz—and one in Florida, Fort Myers, were the only other locales reporting growth of more than 1,000.

Following the pattern of recent years, most other communities experiencing growth were in the South, the West, and interior New England. These include: Anchorage, Alaska; Cochise County and Flagstaff, Arizona; Eureka, Salinas, and San Luis Obispo, California; Aspen and Pueblo, Colorado; Gainesville, Key West, Pensacola, Tallahassee, and Vero Beach, Florida; Boise, Idaho; Northampton, Massachusetts; Frederick, Maryland; Biloxi-Gulfport, Mississippi; Bethlehem, Nashua, and Portsmouth, New Hampshire; Reno, Nevada; Chapel Hill-Durham and Raleigh, North Carolina; Columbia and Spartanburg, South Carolina; Charlottesville, Virginia; and Bellingham, Olympia, Spokane, and Tacoma, Washington.

The largest percentage increase reported is for Boise, Idaho, reflecting three factors: the small base upon which change is calculated, actual population growth resulting from the development of high-tech industries, and the fact that the estimate had not been updated in many years. Communities reporting gains outside the South and West include Waterbury, Connecticut; Ithaca, New York; State College, Pennsylvania; and Green Bay, Wisconsin.

Several communities are being listed for the first time: Postville, Iowa; Traverse City, Michigan; Joplin, Missouri; and Danville, Virginia. The increase for Traverse City, Michigan, is attributed to an expanding medical facility in this resort community. Postville, Iowa, is an Orthodox community established by the development of a major kosher meat-processing facility.

Mendocino County, California, includes the previously listed Redwood Valley area, which is now combined with growing communities along the Pacific coast to make up the county total.

The community reporting the largest drop was Syracuse, New York, down 1,500 to 7,500. Other declines were primarily in the Northeast and Midwest: Gary–Northwest Indiana; Lafayette and Muncie, Indiana; Topeka, Kansas; Benton Harbor, Michigan; Lincoln, Nebraska; Wildwood, New Jersey; Youngstown, Ohio; Johnstown and Uniontown, Pennsylvania; and Appleton, Wisconsin. Declines in other regions include Fresno and Stockton, California; Shreveport, Louisiana; and Lubbock, Texas. The reduced estimate for the Boston Metro Area—as well as changes in Boston local-area listings—is a correction of information first provided last year. College students and nursing-home residents had not been included in the original figures; non-Jewish members of Jewish households had been included in the prior listing.

Five communities are no longer listed, as their populations have fallen below 100: Dothan, Alabama; Claremont, New Hampshire; Dunkirk, New York; Goldsboro, North Carolina; and Wharton, Texas.

Progress on NJPS 2000

Last year's article on "Jewish Population in the United States" reported plans under way for the National Jewish Population Survey, which will be conducted in the year 2000. This new survey is being developed by the Research Department of the Council of Jewish Federations in close collaboration with its National Technical Advisory Committee (NTAC). The NTAC is a distinguished group of academicians and federation professionals who are experts in demography, research design, methodology, census data, statistics, Judaic studies, Jewish communal organization, sociology, geography, economics, and other disciplines.

The NJPS 2000 questionnaire is being prepared with input from a large number of individuals and groups, including two special subcommittees. One has focused on issues concerning Jewish philanthropy and volunteerism; the other has examined issues regarding Jewish identity, continuity, and education. Federation professionals and lay leaders have also participated in the process.

The 1990 survey questionnaire is being used as the starting point for formulating the new version, which will allow for determining trend lines. The questionnaire draft was to be circulated for review and suggested improvements in mid-1999 to all federations, other major Jewish organizations, scholars of contemporary Jewry, and other communal stakeholders. Revision of the questionnaire and pretesting were scheduled to take place in the second half of 1999.

The process used to select a research firm to conduct NJPS 2000 was thorough and exacting. A comprehensive "Request for Proposal" was prepared and distributed in mid-1998 to all research firms known to have both the necessary intellectual capabilities and a computer-assisted telephone interviewing staff large enough to undertake a study of NJPS's magnitude. After an extensive review process involving evaluation of semifinalist and then finalist firms, Audits and Surveys Worldwide (ASW) was chosen to conduct the next survey.

NJPS 2000 will be administered by telephone, using random-digit dialing techniques; the sample will include approximately 5,000 adults, age 18 and older, residing in the 50 United States. The sample will be stratified by census region, by metropolitan-nonmetropolitan area, and then by zip code within each region. Areas of high incidence and density of Jewish settlement will be sampled at a higher rate than lower-density areas, which will reduce the time needed to carry out the study and result in cost efficiencies. Results will be weighted to insure accurate projectability to the Jewish population at different geographic levels. Interviewing will begin early in January 2000 and be completed by mid-2000. The summary report, with basic findings from the study, will be released by mid-2001.

JIM SCHWARTZ
JEFFREY SCHECKNER

APPENDIX

TABLE 1. JEWISH POPULATION IN THE UNITED STATES, 1998

State	Estimated Jewish Population	Total Population*	Estimated Jewish Percent of Total
Alabama	9,100	4,319,000	0.2
Alaska	3,500	609,000	0.6
Arizona	81,500	4,555,000	1.8
Arkansas	1,600	2,523,000	0.1
California	967,000	32,268,000	3.0
Colorado	68,000	3,893,000	1.8
Connecticut	101,000	3,270,000	3.1
Delaware	13,500	732,000	1.8
Dist. of Columbia	25,500	529,000	4.8
Florida	628,000	14,654,000	4.3
Georgia	87,500	7,486,000	1.1
Hawaii	7,000	1,187,000	0.6
Idaho	1,000	1,210,000	0.1
Illinois	269,000	11,896,000	2.3
Indiana	18,000	5,864,000	0.3
Iowa	6,500	2,852,000	0.2
Kansas	14,500	2,595,000	0.6
Kentucky	11,000	3,908,000	0.3
Louisiana	16,500	4,352,000	0.4
Maine	7,500	1,242,000	0.6
Maryland	214,000	5,094,000	4.2
Massachusetts	274,000	6,118,000	4.5
Michigan	107,000	9,774,000	1.1
Minnesota	42,000	4,686,000	0.9
Mississippi	1,400	2,731,000	(z)
Missouri	62,000	5,402,000	1.2
Montana	800	879,000	0.1
Nebraska	7,000	1,657,000	0.4
Nevada	57,500	1,677,000	3.4
New Hampshire	9,800	1,173,000	0.8
New Jersey	465,000	8,053,000	5.8
New Mexico	10,500	1,730,000	0.6
New York	1,652,000	18,137,000	9.1
North Carolina	25,000	7,425,000	0.3

State	Estimated Jewish Population	Total Population*	Estimated Jewish Percent of Total
North Dakota	700	641,000	0.1
Ohio	145,000	11,186,000	1.3
Oklahoma	5,000	3,317,000	0.2
Oregon	22,500	3,243,000	0.7
Pennsylvania	282,000	12,020,000	2.3
Rhode Island	16,000	987,000	1.6
South Carolina	9,500	3,760,000	0.3
South Dakota	350	738,000	(z)
Tennessee	18,000	5,368,000	0.3
Texas	124,000	19,439,000	0.6
Utah	4,500	2,059,000	0.2
Vermont	5,700	589,000	1.0
Virginia	76,000	6,734,000	1.1
Washington	35,500	5,610,000	0.6
West Virginia	2,400	1,8126,000	0.1
Wisconsin	28,500	5,170,000	0.5
Wyoming	400	480,000	0.1
U.S. TOTAL	**6,041,000	267,636,000	2.3

N.B. Details may not add to totals because of rounding.
* Resident population, July 1, 1997. (Source: U.S. Bureau of the Census, Current Population Reports, series P-25, no. 1106.)
** Exclusive of Puerto Rico and the Virgin Islands, which previously reported Jewish populations of 1,500 and 350, respectively.
(z) Figure is less than 0.1 and rounds to 0.

TABLE 2. DISTRIBUTION OF U.S. JEWISH POPULATION BY REGIONS, 1998

Region	Total Population	Percent Distribution	Estimated Jewish Population	Percent Distribution
Midwest	62,461,000	23.3	700,000	11.6
East North Central ..	43,890,000	16.4	567,000	9.4
West North Central .	18,571,000	6.9	133,000	2.2
Northeast	51,589,000	19.3	2,813,000	46.6
Middle Atlantic	38,210,000	14.3	2,399,000	39.7
New England	13,379,000	5.0	414,000	6.9
South	94,187,000	35.2	1,268,000	21.0
East South Central ..	16,326,000	6.1	40,000	0.7
South Atlantic	48.230,000	18.0	1,081,000	17.9
West South Central ..	29,631,000	11.1	147,000	2.4
West	59,400,000	22.2	1,260,000	20.9
Mountain	16,483,000	6.2	224,000	3.7
Pacific	42,917,000	16.0	1,036,000	17.1
TOTALS	267,636,000	100.0	6,041,000	100.0

N.B. Details may not add to totals because of rounding.

TABLE 3. COMMUNITIES WITH JEWISH POPULATIONS OF 100 OR MORE, 1998
(ESTIMATED)

State and City	Jewish Population	State and City	Jewish Population	State and City	Jewish Population
ALABAMA		**Little Rock	1,100	Oakland (incl. in	
*Birmingham	5,300	Other places	200	Alameda County,	
Decatur (incl. in				under S.F. Bay Area)	
Florence total)		CALIFORNIA		Ontario (incl. in	
Florence	150	***Antelope Valley		Pomona Valley)	
Huntsville	750	. . . .	700	Orange County[N]	
**Mobile	1,100	Aptos (incl. in Santa		. . . .	60,000
**Montgomery . . .	1,300	Cruz total)		Palm Springs[N] . .	14,000
Tuscaloosa	300	Bakersfield-Kern		Palmdale (incl. in	
Tuscumbia (incl. in		County	1,600	Antelope Valley)	
Florence total)		Berkeley (incl. in		Palo Alto (incl. in	
Other places	300	Contra Costa County,		South Peninsula,	
		under S.F. Bay Area)		under S.F. Bay Area)	
ALASKA		Carmel (incl. in		Pasadena (incl. in L.A.	
*Anchorage	2,300	Monterey Peninsula)		area)	
*Fairbanks	540	*Chico	500	Petaluma (incl. in	
Juneau	285	Corona (incl. in		Sonoma County,	
Kenai Peninsula . . .	200	Riverside area total)		under S.F. Bay Area)	
Ketchikan (incl. in		*Eureka	1,000	Pomona Valley[N] .	6,750
Juneau total)		Fairfield	800	*Redding area	150
Other places	200	Fontana (incl. in San		Redwood Valley (incl.	
		Bernardino total)		in Mendocino	
ARIZONA		*Fresno	2,300	County)	
Cochise County . . .	350	Lancaster (incl. in		Riverside area . . .	2,000
*Flagstaff	500	Antelope Valley)		Sacramento[N] . . .	21,300
Lake Havasu City		Long Beach[N] . . .	15,000	Salinas	1,000
. . . .	200	Los Angeles area[N]		San Bernardino area	
*Phoenix	60,000	. . . .	519,000	. . . .	3,000
Prescott	300	*Mendocino County	600	*San Diego	70,000
Sierra Vista (incl. in		*Merced County . . .	190	San Francisco Bay	
Cochise County)		*Modesto	500	Area[N]	210,000
*Tucson	20,000	Monterey Peninsula		Alameda County	
Yuma	125	. . . .	2,300	. . . .	32,500
Other places	200	Moreno Valley (incl. in		Contra Costa County	
		Riverside total)		. . . .	22,000
ARKANSAS		Murrieta Hot Springs		Marin County	
Fayetteville	150	. . . .	600	. . . .	18,500
Hot Springs	150	*Napa County . . .	1,000	N. Peninsula . .	24,500

[N]See Notes below. *Includes entire county. **Includes all of two counties. ***Figure not updated for at least five years.

State and City	Jewish Population	State and City	Jewish Population	State and City	Jewish Population
San Francisco 49,500		Eagle (incl. in Vail total)		New Haven[N] ... 24,300	
San Jose...... 33,000		Evergreen (incl. in Denver total)		New London[N] ... 3,800	
Sonoma County 9,000		*Fort Collins..... 1,000		New Milford (incl. in Waterbury total)	
S. Peninsula ... 21,000		*Grand Junction ... 320		Newtown (incl. in Danbury total)	
*San Jose (listed under S.F. Bay Area)		Greeley (incl. in Fort Collins total)		Norwalk[N] 9,100	
*San Luis Obispo 1,700		Loveland (incl. in Fort Collins total)		Norwich (incl. in New London total)	
*Santa Barbara ... 7,000		Pueblo[N] 425		Rockville (incl. in Hartford total)	
*Santa Cruz 6,000		Steamboat Springs . 160		Shelton (incl. in Bridgeport total)	
Santa Maria...... 700		Telluride........ 125		Southington (incl. in Hartford total)	
Santa Monica (incl. in Los Angeles area)		**Vail........... 650		Stamford....... 9,200	
Santa Rosa (incl. in Sonoma County, under S.F. Bay Area)		Other places...... 200		Storrs (incl. in Willimantic total)	
Sonoma County (listed under S.F. Bay Area)		CONNECTICUT		Torrington area ... 580	
*South Lake Tahoe 150		Bridgeport[N] 13,000		Wallingford (incl. in New Haven total)	
Stockton........ 850		Bristol (incl. in Hartford total)		Waterbury[N] 4,500	
***Sun City....... 200		Cheshire (incl. in Waterbury total)		Westport (incl. in Norwalk total)	
Tulare and Kings counties 300		Colchester 300		Willimantic area... 700	
Ukiah (incl. in Mendocino Co.)		Danbury[N] 3,200		Other places...... 200	
Vallejo area 900		Danielson........ 100		DELAWARE	
*Ventura County[N] 15,000		Darien (incl. in Stamford total)		Dover (incl. in Kent and Sussex counties totals)	
Visalia (incl. in Tulare and Kings counties)		Greenwich...... 3,900		Kent and Sussex counties....... 1,600	
Other places...... 200		Hartford[N] 25,200		Newark area 4,300	
		Hebron (incl. in Colchester total)		Wilmington area . 7,600	
COLORADO		Lebanon (incl. in Colchester total)			
Aspen........... 750		Lower Middlesex County[N]....... 1,600		DISTRICT OF COLUMBIA	
Boulder (incl. in Denver total)		Manchester (incl. in Hartford total)		Washington D.C. 25,500	
Breckenridge (incl. in Vail total)		Meriden (incl. in New Haven total)			
Colorado Springs 1,500		Middletown..... 1,200		FLORIDA	
Denver[N]....... 63,000		New Britain (incl. in Hartford total)		Arcadia (incl. in Port Charlotte-Punta Gorda total)	
		New Canaan (incl. in Stamford total)			

State and City	Jewish Population	State and City	Jewish Population	State and City	Jewish Population
Boca Raton-Delray Beach (listed under Southeast Fla.)		**Sarasota	17,000	IDAHO	
Brevard County.	5,000	Southeast Florida	507,000	**Boise	800
Broward County (listed under Southeast Fla.)		Boca Raton-Delray Beach	86,000	Lewiston (incl. in Moscow total)	
***Crystal River	100	Broward County	220,000	Moscow	100
**Daytona Beach	2,500	Miami-Dade County	134,000	Other places	150
Ft. Lauderdale (incl. in Broward County, under Southeast Fla.)		Palm Beach County (excl. Boca Raton-Delray Beach)	67,000	ILLINOIS	
**Ft. Myers	6,500	***Stuart-Port St. Lucie	3,000	Aurora area	500
Ft. Pierce	1,060			Bloomington-Normal	230
Gainesville	2,200	Tallahassee	2,200	Carbondale (incl. in S. Ill.)	
Hollywood-S. Broward County (incl in Broward County, under Southeast Fla.)		*Tampa	15,000	*Champaign-Urbana	1,400
**Jacksonville	7,300	Venice (incl. in Sarasota total)		Chicago Metro Area[N]	261,000
Key West	650	*Vero Beach	400	**Danville	100
Lakeland	1,000	Winter Haven	300	*Decatur	130
*Miami-Dade County (listed under Southeast Fla.)		Other places	100	DeKalb	180
Naples-Collier County	3,500	GEORGIA		East St. Louis (incl. in S. Ill.)	
New Port Richey (incl. in Pasco County)		Albany	190	Elgin[N]	500
Ocala-Marion County	500	Athens	400	Freeport (incl. in Rockford total)	
Orlando[N]	21,000	Atlanta Metro Area	80,000	*Joliet	450
Palm Beach County (listed under Southeast Fla.)		Augusta[N]	1,300	Kankakee	100
Pasco County	1,000	Brunswick	100	Moline (incl. in Quad Cities)	
**Pensacola	900	**Columbus	1,100	*Peoria	850
Pinellas County	24,200	**Dalton	140	Quad Cities-Ill. portion	550
**Port Charlotte-Punta Gorda	900	Macon	1000	Rock Island (incl. in Quad Cities)	
*St. Petersburg-Clearwater (incl. in Pinellas County)		*Savannah	2,800	Rockford[N]	1,100
		**Valdosta	100	Southern Illinois[N]	600
		Other places	250	*Springfield	1,090
				Waukegan	400
		HAWAII		Other places	250
		Hilo	280		
		Honolulu (incl. all of Oahu)	6,400	INDIANA	
		Kauai	100	Bloomington	1,000
		Maui	210	Elkhart (incl. in S. Bend total)	

State and City	Jewish Population	State and City	Jewish Population	State and City	Jewish Population
Evansville	400	LOUISIANA		Montgomery and Prince Georges	
**Ft. Wayne	950	Alexandria[N]	350	counties	104,500
**Gary-Northwest Indiana	2,000	Baton Rouge[N]	1,500	Ocean City	100
**Indianapolis	10,000	Lafayette (incl. in S. Central La.)		Salisbury	400
**Lafayette	600	Lake Charles area	200	Silver Spring (incl. in Montgomery County)	
*Michigan City	300	Monroe (incl. in Shreveport total)		Other places	250
Muncie	120	**New Orleans	13,000		
South Bend[N]	1,950	**Shreveport	815	MASSACHUSETTS	
*Terre Haute	250	***South Central La.[N]	250	Amherst area	1,300
Other places	200	Other places	150	Andover[N]	2,850
				Athol area (incl. in N. Worcester County)	
IOWA				Attleboro area	200
Ames (incl. in Des Moines total)		MAINE		Beverly (incl. in North Shore, under Boston Metro Region)	
Cedar Rapids	420	Augusta	140		
Council Bluffs	150	Bangor	1,000	Boston Metro Region[N]	227,300
*Davenport (incl. in Quad Cities)		Biddeford-Saco (incl. in S. Maine)		Boston	21,000
*Des Moines	2,800	Brunswick-Bath (incl. in S. Maine)		Brockton-South Central	31,500
*Iowa City	1,300	Lewiston-Auburn	500	Brookline	20,300
Postville	100	Portland (incl. in S. Maine)		Framingham	19,700
Quad Cities-Iowa portion	650	Rockland area	180	Near West	35,800
**Sioux City	500	Southern Maine[N]	5,500	Newton	27,700
*Waterloo	170	*Waterville	200	North Central	22,900
Other places	300	Other places	150	Northeast	7,700
				North Shore	18,600
KANSAS		MARYLAND		Northwest	13,600
Kansas City area-Kansas portion[N]	12,000	Annapolis area	1,800	Southeast	8,500
Lawrence	100	**Baltimore	94,500	Brockton (listed under Boston Metro Region)	
Manhattan	425	Columbia (incl. in Howard County)		Brookline (listed under Boston Metro Region)	
*Topeka	400	Cumberland	275	Cape Cod-Barnstable County	3,250
Wichita[N]	1,300	*Frederick	1,200	Clinton (incl. in Worcester-Central Worcester County)	
Other places	100	*Hagerstown	325		
		*Harford County	1,200	Fall River area	1,100
KENTUCKY		*Howard County	10,000	Falmouth (incl. in Cape Cod)	
Covington-Newport area	500				
Lexington[N]	1,850				
*Louisville	8,700				
Other places	150				

State and City	Jewish Population	State and City	Jewish Population	State and City	Jewish Population

Fitchburg (incl. in N.
Worcester County)
Framingham (listed
under Boston Metro
Region)
Gardner (incl. in N.
Worcester County)
Gloucester (incl. N.
Shore, listed under
Boston Metro
Region)
Great Barrington (incl.
in Pittsfield total)
*Greenfield 1,100
Haverhill 800
Holyoke 600
*Hyannis (incl. in Cape
Cod)
Lawrence (incl. in
Andover total)
Leominster (incl. in N.
Worcester County)
Lowell area 2,000
Lynn (incl. in N. Shore,
listed under Boston
Metro Region)
*Martha's Vineyard
. . . . 300
New Bedford[N] . . . 2,600
Newburyport 280
Newton (listed under
Boston Metro Region)
North Adams (incl. in
N. Berkshire County)
North Berkshire
County 400
North Worcester
County 1,500
Northampton . . . 1,200
Peabody (incl. in N.
Shore, listed under
Boston Metro Region)
Pittsfield-Berkshire
County 3,500
Plymouth area 500

Provincetown (incl. in
Cape Cod)
Salem (incl. in N.
Shore, listed under
Boston Metro Region)
Southbridge (incl. in S.
Worcester County)
South Worcester
County 500
Springfield[N] 10,000
Taunton area 1,300
Webster (incl. in S.
Worcester County)
Worcester-Central
Worcester County
. . . . 11,000
Other places 150

MICHIGAN
*Ann Arbor 5,000
Bay City 150
Benton Harbor area
. . . . 240
**Detroit Metro Area
. . . . 94,000
*Flint 1,800
*Grand Rapids . . . 1,600
**Jackson. 200
*Kalamazoo 1,100
Lansing area 2,100
Midland 120
Mt. Clemens (incl. in
Detroit total)
Mt. Pleasant[N] 130
*Muskegon 210
*Saginaw 115
Traverse City 200
Other places 400

MINNESOTA
**Duluth 485
*Minneapolis . . . 31,500
Rochester 550
**St. Paul 9,200
Other places 150

MISSISSIPPI
Biloxi-Gulfport . . . 250
**Greenville. 120
**Hattiesburg 130
**Jackson. 550
Other places 300

MISSOURI
Columbia 400
Joplin 100
Kansas City area-
Missouri portionN
. . . . 7,100
*St. Joseph. 265
**St. Louis 54,000
Springfield 300
Other places 150

MONTANA
*Billings 300
Butte 100
Helena (incl. in Butte
total)
*Kalispell. 150
Missoula 200
Other places 100

NEBRASKA
Grand Island-Hastings
(incl. in Lincoln total)
Lincoln. 700
**Omaha. 6,350
Other places 50

NEVADA
Carson City (incl. in
Reno total)
*Las Vegas 55,600
**Reno 2,100
Sparks (incl. in Reno
total)

NEW HAMPSHIRE
Bethlehem 200
Concord 500
Dover area 600

State and City	Jewish Population	State and City	Jewish Population	State and City	Jewish Population
Exeter (incl. in Portsmouth total)		Essex County (also incl. in Northeastern		Newark (incl. in Essex County)	
Franconia (incl. in Bethlehem total)		N.J. total)[N]	76,200	New Brunswick (incl. in Middlesex County)	
Hanover-Lebanon	500	East Essex	10,800	Northeastern N.J.N	386,000
*Keene	300	Livingston	12,600		
**Laconia	270	North Essex	15,600	Ocean County (also incl. in Northeastern	
Littleton (incl. in Bethlehem total)		South Essex	20,300	N.J. total)	11,500
Manchester area	4,000	West Orange-Orange	16,900	Passaic County (also incl. in Northeastern	
Nashua area	2,000	*Flemington	1,500	N.J. total)	17,000
Portsmouth area	1,150	Freehold (incl. in Monmouth County)		Passaic-Clifton (incl. in Passaic County)	
Rochester (incl. in Dover total)		Gloucester (incl. in Cherry Hill-S. N.J. total)		Paterson (incl. in Passaic County)	
Salem	150	Hoboken (listed under Hudson County)		Perth Amboy (incl. in Middlesex County)	
Other places	150	Hudson County (also incl. in Northeastern		Phillipsburg (incl. in Warren County)	
NEW JERSEY		N.J. total)	12,200	Plainfield (incl. in Union County)	
Asbury Park (incl. in Monmouth County)		Bayonne	1,600	Princeton area	3,000
**Atlantic City (incl. Atlantic and Cape May counties)	15,800	Hoboken	1,100	Somerset County (also incl. in Northeastern	
		Jersey City	6,000	N.J. total)	11,000
Bayonne (listed under Hudson County)		North Hudson County[N]	3,500	Somerville (incl. in Somerset County)	
Bergen County (also incl. in Northeastern		Jersey City (listed under Hudson County)		Sussex County (also incl. in Northeastern	
N.J. total)	83,700	Lakewood (incl. in Ocean County)		N.J. total)	4,100
Bridgeton	200	Livingston (listed under Essex County)		Toms River (incl. in Ocean County)	
Bridgewater (incl. in Somerset County)		Middlesex County (also incl. in Northeastern		Trenton[N]	6,000
Camden (incl. in Cherry Hill-S. N.J.)		N.J.)[N]	45,000	Union County (also incl. in Northeastern	
Cherry Hill-Southern N.J.[N]	49,000	Monmouth County (also incl. in Northeastern		N.J. total)	30,000
Edison (incl. in Middlesex County)		N.J.)	63,000	Vineland[N]	1,890
Elizabeth (incl. in Union County)		Morris County (also incl. in Northeastern		Warren County	400
Englewood (incl. in Bergen County)		N.J.)	33,500	Wayne (incl. in Passaic County)	
		Morristown (incl. in Morris County)		Wildwood	330
		Mt. Holly (incl. in Cherry Hill-S. N.J.)		Willingboro (incl. in Cherry Hill-S. N.J.)	
				Other places	250

State and City	Jewish Population

NEW MEXICO
*Albuquerque 7,500
Las Cruces 600
Los Alamos 250
Rio Rancho (incl. in
Albuquerque total)
Santa Fe 1,500
Taos 300
Other places 150

NEW YORK
*Albany 12,000
Amenia (incl. in
Poughkeepsie-
Dutchess County)
Amsterdam 150
*Auburn 115
Beacon (incl. in
Poughkeepsie-
Dutchess County)
*Binghamton (incl. all
Broome County)
. . . . 2,600
Brewster (incl. in
Putnam County)
*Buffalo 26,000
Canandaigua (incl. in
Geneva total)
Catskill 200
Corning (incl. in Elmira
total)
*Cortland 150
Ellenville 1,600
Elmira[N] 950
Fleischmanns 100
Geneva area 300
Glens Falls[N] 800
*Gloversville 300
*Herkimer 180
Highland Falls (incl. in
Orange County)
*Hudson 500
*Ithaca area 2,000
Jamestown 100

Kingston[N] 4,300
Kiryas Joel (incl. in
Orange County)
Lake George (incl. in
Glens Falls total)
Liberty (incl. in
Sullivan County)
Middletown (incl. in
Orange County)
Monroe (incl. in
Orange County)
Monticello (incl. in
Sullivan County)
Newark (incl. in
Geneva total)
Newburgh (incl. in
Orange County)
New Paltz (incl. in
Kingston total)
New York Metro Area[N]
. . . . 1,450,000
Bronx 83,700
Brooklyn 379,000
Manhattan . . . 314,500
Queens 238,000
Staten Island
. . . . 33,700
Nassau County
. . . . 207,000
Suffolk County
. . . . 100,000
Westchester County
. . . . 94,000
Niagara Falls 145
Olean 100
**Oneonta 300
Orange County . 15,000
Pawling (incl. in
Poughkeepsie-
Dutchess County)
Plattsburg 250
Port Jervis (incl. in
Orange County)
Potsdam 200

*Poughkeepsie-Dutchess
County 3,600
Putnam County . . 1,000
**Rochester 22,500
Rockland County
. . . . 83,100
Rome 150
Saratoga Springs . . 600
**Schenectady 5,200
Seneca Falls (incl. in
Geneva total)
South Fallsburg (incl.
in Sullivan County)
***Sullivan County . . . .
7,425
Syracuse[N] 7,500
Troy area 800
Utica[N] 1,100
Walden (incl. in Orange
County)
Watertown 100
Woodstock (incl. in
Kingston total)
Other places 450

NORTH CAROLINA
Asheville[N] 1,300
**Chapel Hill-Durham
. . . . 4,000
Charlotte[N] 7,800
Elizabethtown (incl. in
Wilmington total)
*Fayetteville 300
Gastonia 210
*Greensboro 2,500
Greenville 240
*Hendersonville 250
**Hickory 110
High Point (incl. in
Greensboro total)
Jacksonville (incl. in
Wilmington total)
Raleigh-Wake County
. . . . 6,000

State and City	Jewish Population	State and City	Jewish Population	State and City	Jewish Population
Whiteville (incl. in Wilmington total)		Springfield	200	*Butler	250
Wilmington area	1,200	*Steubenville	125	**Chambersburg	150
Winston-Salem	485	Toledo[N]	5,900	Chester (incl. in Delaware County, listed under Phila. area)	
Other places	450	Warren (incl. in Youngstown total)			
		Wooster	135	Chester County (listed under Phila. area)	
NORTH DAKOTA		Youngstown[N]	3,600		
Fargo	500	*Zanesville	100	Coatesville (incl. in Chester County, listed under Phila. area)	
Grand Forks	130	Other places	350		
Other places	100			Easton (incl. in Lehigh Valley)	
		OKLAHOMA			
OHIO		Norman (incl. in Oklahoma City total)		*Erie	850
**Akron	5,500	**Oklahoma City	2,300	Farrell (incl. in Sharon total)	
Athens	100	*Tulsa	2,650	Greensburg (incl. in Pittsburgh total)	
Bowling Green (incl. in Toledo total)		Other places	100		
Butler County	900			**Harrisburg	7,000
**Canton	1,550	OREGON		Hazleton area	300
Cincinnati[N]	22,500	Ashland (incl. in Medford total)		Honesdale (incl. in Wayne County)	
Cleveland[N]	81,000	Bend	175	Jeannette (incl. in Pittsburgh total)	
*Columbus	15,600	Corvallis	175		
**Dayton	5,500	Eugene	3,000	**Johnstown	275
Elyria	175	Grants Pass (incl. in Medford total)		Lancaster area	2,600
Fremont (incl. in Sandusky total)		**Medford	1,000	*Lebanon	350
Hamilton (incl. in Butler County)		Portland[N]	17,500	Lehigh Valley	8,500
Kent (incl. in Akron total)		**Salem	530	Lewisburg (incl. in Sunbury total)	
*Lima	180	Other places	200	Lock Haven (incl. in Williamsport total)	
Lorain	600			McKeesport (incl. in Pittsburgh total)	
Mansfield	150	PENNSYLVANIA		New Castle	200
Marion[N]	125	Allentown (incl. in Lehigh Valley)		Norristown (incl. in Montgomery County, listed under Phila. area)	
Middletown (incl. in Butler County)		*Altoona	570		
New Philadelphia (incl. in Canton total)		Ambridge (incl. in Pittsburgh total)		**Oil City	100
Norwalk (incl. in Sandusky total)		Beaver Falls (incl. in Upper Beaver County)		Oxford-Kennett Square (incl. in Chester County, listed under Phila. area)	
Oberlin (incl. in Elyria total)		Bethlehem (incl. in Lehigh Valley)			
Oxford (incl. in Butler County)		Bucks County (listed Phila. area)			
**Sandusky	105				

State and City	Jewish Population

Philadelphia area[N]
.... 206,000
Bucks County
.... 34,800
Chester County
.... 10,100
Delaware County
.... 15,700
Montgomery County
.... 58,900
Philadelphia . . 86,600
Phoenixville (incl. in
Chester County, listed
under Phila. area)
***Pike County 300
Pittsburgh[N] 40,000
Pottstown........ 650
Pottsville 225
*Reading........ 2,200
*Scranton 3,100
Shamokin (incl. in
Sunbury total)
Sharon 300
State College 700
Stroudsburg 400
Sunbury[N] 200
Tamaqua (incl. in
Hazleton total)
Uniontown area . . . 150
Upper Beaver County
.... 180
Washington (incl. in
Pittsburgh total)
***Wayne County
.... 500
Waynesburg (incl. in
Pittsburgh total)
West Chester (incl. in
Chester County, listed
under Phila. area)
Wilkes-Barre[N] . . . 3,200
**Williamsport 350
York 1,500
Other places...... 800

RHODE ISLAND
Cranston (incl. in
Providence total)
Kingston (incl. in
Washington County)
Newport-Middletown
.... 700
Providence area . 14,200
Washington County
.... 1,200
Westerly (incl. in
Washington County)

SOUTH CAROLINA
*Charleston...... 3,500
**Columbia 2,750
Florence area..... 220
Georgetown (incl. in
Myrtle Beach total)
Greenville 1,200
Kingstree (incl. in
Sumter total)
**Myrtle Beach 425
Rock Hill 100
*Spartanburg..... 500
Sumter[N] 140
York (incl. in Rock Hill
total)
Other places...... 450

SOUTH DAKOTA
Sioux Falls 180
Other places...... 150

TENNESSEE
Chattanooga 1,350
Knoxville....... 1,650
Memphis 8,500
Nashville 6,000
Oak Ridge 250
Other places...... 250

TEXAS
Amarillo[N]........ 200
*Austin 10,000

*** Baytown 300
Beaumont........ 500
*Brownsville 450
***College Station-
Bryan 400
*Corpus Christi . . 1,400
**Dallas 45,000
El Paso 4,900
*Ft. Worth 5,000
Galveston........ 800
Harlingen (incl. in
Brownsville total)
**Houston[N]..... 42,000
Laredo 130
Longview 100
*Lubbock......... 230
*McAllen[N] 500
Midland-Odessa. . . 150
Port Arthur 100
*San Antonio . . . 10,000
South Padre Island
(incl. in Brownsville
total)
Tyler............ 400
Waco[N] 300
Wichita Falls 260
Other places...... 550

UTAH
Ogden........... 150
*Salt Lake City . . . 4,200
Other places...... 100

VERMONT
Bennington area. . . 300
*Brattleboro....... 350
**Burlington..... 3,000
Manchester area. . . 325
Montpelier-Barre . . 550
Newport (incl. in St.
Johnsbury total)
Rutland 550
**St. Johnsbury 140
Stowe 150

State and City	Jewish Population	State and City	Jewish Population	State and City	Jewish Population
Woodstock	270	Portsmouth-Suffolk		Huntington[N]	250
Other places	100	(incl. in Norfolk total)		Morgantown	200
		Radford (incl. in		Parkersburg	110
VIRGINIA		Blacksburg total)		**Wheeling	275
Alexandria (incl. in N.		Richmond[N]	15,000	Other places	300
Virginia)		Roanoke	900		
Arlington (incl. in N.		Staunton[N]	370	WISCONSIN	
Virginia)		Williamsburg (incl. in		Appleton area	300
Blacksburg	175	Newport News total)		Beloit	120
Charlottesville	1,500	Winchester[N]	270	Fond du Lac (incl. in	
Chesapeake (incl. in		Other places	100	Oshkosh total)	
Portsmouth total)				Green Bay	500
Colonial Heights (incl.		WASHINGTON		Janesville (incl. in	
in Petersburg total)		Bellingham	500	Beloit total)	
Danville area	100	Ellensburg (incl. in		*Kenosha	300
Fairfax County (incl. in		Yakima total)		La Crosse	100
N. Virginia)		Longview-Kelso (incl.		*Madison	4,500
Fredericksburg[N]	500	in Vancouver total)		Milwaukee[N]	21,300
Hampton (incl. in		*Olympia	560	Oshkosh area	170
Newport News total)		***Port Angeles	100	*Racine	375
Harrisonburg (incl. in		*Seattle[N]	29,300	Sheboygan	140
Staunton total)		Spokane	1,500	Waukesha (incl. in	
Lexington (incl. in		*Tacoma	2,000	Milwaukee total)	
Staunton total)		Tri Cities[N]	300	Wausau[N]	300
Lynchburg area	275	Vancouver	600	Other places	300
**Martinsville	100	**Yakima	150		
Newport News-		Other places	350	WYOMING	
Hampton[N]	2,400			Casper	100
Norfolk-Virginia Beach		WEST VIRGINIA		Cheyenne	230
	19,000	Bluefield-Princeton		Laramie (incl. in	
Northern Virginia			200	Cheyenne total)	
	35,100	*Charleston	975	Other places	100
Petersburg area	350	Clarksburg	110		

Notes

CALIFORNIA

Long Beach—includes in L.A. County: Long Beach, Signal Hill, Cerritos, Lakewood, Rossmoor, and Hawaiian Gardens. Also includes in Orange County: Los Alamitos, Cypress, Seal Beach, and Huntington Harbor.

Los Angeles—includes most of Los Angeles County, but excludes the eastern portion as well as those places listed above that are part of the Long Beach area. Also includes eastern edge of Ventura County.

Orange County—includes most of Orange County, but excludes towns in northern portion that are included in Long Beach.

Palm Springs—includes Palm Springs, Desert Hot Springs, Cathedral City, Palm Desert, and Rancho Mirage.

Pomona Valley—includes Alta Loma, Chino, Claremont, Cucamonga, La Verne, Montclair, Ontario, Pomona, San Dimas, and Upland.

Sacramento—includes Yolo, Placer, El Dorado, and Sacramento counties.

San Francisco Bay area—North Peninsula includes northern San Mateo County. South Peninsula includes southern San Mateo County and towns of Palo Alto and Los Altos in Santa Clara County. San Jose includes remainder of Santa Clara County.

COLORADO

Denver—includes Adams, Arapahoe, Boulder, Denver, and Jefferson counties.

Pueblo–includes all of Pueblo County east to Lamar, west to Alamosa and south to Trinidad.

CONNECTICUT

Bridgeport—includes Monroe, Easton, Trumbull, Fairfield, Bridgeport, Shelton, and Stratford.

Danbury—includes Danbury, Bethel, New Fairfield, Brookfield, Sherman, Newtown, Redding, and Ridgefield.

Hartford—includes most of Hartford County and Vernon, Rockville, Ellington, and Tolland in Tolland County.

Lower Middlesex County—includes Branford, Guilford, Madison, Clinton, Westbrook, Old Saybrook, Old Lyme, Durham, and Killingworth.

New Haven—includes New Haven, East Haven, Guilford, Branford, Madison, North Haven, Hamden, West Haven, Milford, Orange, Woodbridge, Bethany, Derby, Ansonia, Quinnipiac, Meriden, Seymour, and Wallingford.

New London—includes central and southern New London County. Also includes part of Middlesex County and part of Windham County.

Norwalk—includes Norwalk, Weston, Westport, East Norwalk, Wilton, and Georgetown.

Waterbury—includes Bethlehem, Cheshire, Litchfield, Morris, Middlebury, Southbury, Naugatuck, Prospect, Plymouth, Roxbury, Southbury, Southington, Thomaston, Torrington, Washington, Watertown, Waterbury, Oakville, Woodbury, Wolcott, Oxford, and other towns in Litchfield County and northern New Haven County.

DISTRICT OF COLUMBIA

Washington, D.C.—For a total of the Washington, D.C., metropolitan area, include Montgomery and Prince Georges counties in Maryland, and northern Virginia.

FLORIDA

Orlando—includes all of Orange and Seminole counties, southern Volusia County, and northern Osceola County.

GEORGIA

Augusta—includes Burke, Columbia, and Richmond counties.

ILLINOIS

Chicago—includes all of Cook and DuPage counties and a portion of Lake County.
Elgin—includes northern Kane County and southern McHenry County.
Rockford—includes Winnebago, Boone, and Stephenson counties.
Southern Illinois—includes lower portion of Illinois below Carlinville.

INDIANA

South Bend—includes St. Joseph and Elkhart counties.

KANSAS

Kansas City—includes Johnson and Wyandotte counties. For a total of the Kansas City metropolitan area, include Missouri portion.
Wichita—includes Sedgwick County and towns of Salina, Dodge City, Great Bend, Liberal, Russell, and Hays.

KENTUCKY

Lexington—includes Fayette, Bourbon, Scott, Clark, Woodford, Madison, Pulaski, and Jessamine counties.

LOUISIANA

Alexandria—includes towns in Allen, Grant, Rapides, and Vernon parishes.
Baton Rouge—includes E. Baton Rouge, Ascension, Livingston, St. Landry, Iberville, Pointe Coupee, and W. Baton Rouge parishes.
South Central—includes Abbeville, Lafayette, New Iberia, Crowley, Opelousas, Houma, Morgan City, Thibodaux, and Franklin.

MAINE

Southern Maine—includes York, Cumberland, and Sagadahoc counties.

MASSACHUSETTS

Andover—includes Andover, N. Andover, Boxford, Lawrence, Methuen, Tewksbury, and Dracut.

Boston Metropolitan region—Brockton-South Central includes Avon, Bridgewater, Brockton, Canton, East Bridgewater, Easton, Foxborough, Halifax, Randolph, Sharon, Stoughton, West Bridgewater, Whitman, and Wrentham. Framingham area includes—Acton, Bellingham, Boxborough, Framingham, Franklin, Holliston, Hopkinton, Hudson, Marlborough, Maynard, Medfield, Medway, Milford, Millis, Southborough, and Stow. Northeast includes—Chelsea, Everett, Malden, Medford, Revere, and Winthrop. North Central includes—Arlington, Belmont, Cambridge, Somerville, Waltham, and Watertown. Northwest includes—Bedford, Burlington, Carlisle, Concord, Lexington, Lincoln, Melrose, North Reading, Reading, Stoneham, Wakefield, Wilmington, Winchester, and Woburn. North Shore includes—Lynn, Saugus, Nahant, Swampscott, Lynnfield, Peabody, Salem, Marblehead, Beverly, Danvers, Middleton, Wenham, Topsfield, Hamilton, Manchester, Ipswich, Essex, Gloucester, and Rockport. Near West includes—Ashland, Dedham, Dover, Natick, Needham, Norfolk, Norwood, Sherborn, Sudbury, Walpole, Wayland, Wellesley, Weston, and Westwood. Southeast includes—Abington, Braintree, Cohasset, Duxbury, Hanover, Hanson, Hingham, Holbrook, Hull, Kingston, Marshfield, Milton, Norwell, Pembroke, Quincy, Rockland, Scituate, and Weymouth.

New Bedford—includes New Bedford, Dartmouth, Fairhaven, and Mattapoisett.

Springfield—includes Springfield, Longmeadow, E. Longmeadow, Hampden, Wilbraham, Agawam, and W. Springfield.

MICHIGAN

Mt. Pleasant—includes towns in Isabella, Mecosta, Gladwin, and Gratiot counties.

MISSOURI

Kansas City—For a total of the Kansas City metropolitan area, include the Kansas portion.

NEW HAMPSHIRE

Laconia—includes Laconia, Plymouth, Meredith, Conway, and Franklin.

NEW JERSEY

Cherry Hill-Southern N.J.—includes Camden, Burlington, and Gloucester counties.

Essex County—East Essex includes Belleville, Bloomfield, East Orange, Irvington, Newark, and Nutley in Essex County, and Kearney in Hudson County. North Essex includes Caldwell, Cedar Grove, Essex Fells, Fairfield, Glen Ridge, Montclair, North Caldwell, Roseland, Verona, and West Caldwell. South Essex includes Maplewood, Millburn, Short Hills, and South Orange in Essex County, and Springfield in Union County.

Middlesex County—includes in Somerset County: Kendall Park, Somerset, and Franklin; in Mercer County: Hightstown; and all of Middlesex County.

Northeastern N.J.—includes Bergen, Essex, Hudson, Middlesex, Morris, Passaic, Somerset, Union, Hunterdon, Sussex, Monmouth, and Ocean counties.

North Hudson County—includes Guttenberg, Hudson Heights, North Bergen, North Hudson, Seacaucus, Union City, Weehawken, West New York, and Woodcliff.

Somerset County—includes most of Somerset County and a portion of Hunterdon County.

Trenton—includes most of Mercer County.

Union County—includes all of Union County except Springfield. Also includes a few towns in adjacent areas of Somerset and Middlesex counties.

Vineland—includes most of Cumberland County and towns in neighboring counties adjacent to Vineland.

NEW YORK

Elmira—includes Chemung, Tioga, and Schuyler counties.

Glens Falls—includes Warren and Washington counties, lower Essex County, and upper Saratoga County.

Kingston—includes eastern half of Ulster County.

New York metropolitan area—includes the five boroughs of New York City, Westchester, Nassau, and Suffolk counties. For total Jewish population of the New York metropolitan region, include Fairfield County, Connecticut; Rockland, Putnam, and Orange counties, New York; and Northeastern New Jersey.

Syracuse—includes Onondaga County, western Madison County, and most of Oswego County.

Utica—southeastern third of Oneida County.

NORTH CAROLINA

Asheville—includes Buncombe, Haywood, and Madison counties.

Charlotte—includes Mecklenburg County. For a total of the Charlotte area, include Rock Hill, South Carolina.

OHIO

Cincinnati—includes Hamilton and Butler counties. For a total of the Cincinnati area, include the Covington-Newport area of Kentucky.

Cleveland—includes all of Cuyahoga County and portions of Lake, Geauga, Portage, and Summit counties. For a metropolitan total, include Elyria, Lorain, and Akron.

Marion—includes Marion County and towns of Carey, Delaware, Kenton, Tiffin and Upper Sandusky.

Toledo—includes Fulton, Lucas, and Wood counties.

Youngstown—includes Mahoning and Trumbull counties.

PENNSYLVANIA

Philadelphia—For total Jewish population of the Philadelphia metropolitan region, include the Cherry Hill-Southern N.J., Salem, Princeton, and Trenton areas of New Jersey, and the Wilmington and Newark areas of Delaware.

Pittsburgh—includes all of Allegheny County and adjacent portions of Washington, Westmoreland, and Beaver counties.

Sunbury—includes Shamokin, Lewisburg, Milton, Selinsgrove, and Sunbury.

Wilkes-Barre—includes all of Luzerne County except southern portion, which is included in the Hazleton total.

SOUTH CAROLINA

Sumter—includes towns in Sumter, Lee, Clarendon, and Williamsburg counties.

TEXAS

Amarillo—includes Canyon, Childress, Borger, Dumas, Memphis, Pampa, Vega, and Hereford in Texas, and Portales, New Mexico.

Houston—includes Harris, Montgomery, and Fort Bend counties, and parts of Brazoria and Galveston counties.

McAllen—includes Edinburg, Harlingen, McAllen, Mission, Pharr, Rio Grande City, San Juan, and Weslaco.

Waco—includes McLennan, Coryell, Bell, Falls, Hamilton, and Hill counties.

VIRGINIA

Fredericksburg—includes towns in Spotsylvania, Stafford, King George, and Orange counties.

Newport News—includes Newport News, Hampton, Williamsburg, James City, York County, and Poquoson City.

Richmond—includes Richmond City, Henrico County, and Chesterfield County.

Staunton—includes towns in Augusta, Page, Shenandoah, Rockingham, Bath, and Highland counties.

Winchester—includes towns in Winchester, Frederick, Clarke, and Warren counties.

WASHINGTON

Seattle—includes King County and adjacent portions of Snohomish and Kitsap counties.

Tri Cities—includes Pasco, Richland, and Kennewick.

WISCONSIN

Milwaukee—includes Milwaukee County, Eastern Waukesha County, and Southern Ozaukee County.

Wausau—includes Stevens Point, Marshfield, Antigo, and Rhinelander.

Review
of
the
Year

OTHER COUNTRIES

Canada

National Affairs

THE FEDERAL POLITICAL SCENE in 1998 was stable under the Liberal majority government elected in 1997, with the opposition remaining fragmented. Generally Canada did well economically during the year. GDP growth was moderate but steady, unemployment finally began to trend downward toward 8 percent, and inflation hovered around 1 percent. The main economic problem was the precipitous drop in the dollar, which declined by about 10 percent against its U.S. counterpart during the summer and fall. Canada was elected to a two-year term on the United Nations Security Council, beginning in 1999.

Government policy toward immigrants and refugees continued to be a serious concern of the Jewish community for several reasons — the prospect of Jewish immigration from the former Soviet Union, the problem of refugees from Israel, and general humanitarian issues. Among the recommendations of a federal government report released in March was one that would require new immigrants to speak at least one of the country's two official languages, English and French. Jewish groups, recognizing that most Jews who want to come to Canada speak neither language, expressed great concern. B'nai Brith Canada (BBC) went so far as to claim that the proposals were designed to discourage immigration and were unfair. In contrast, the Quebec offices of Jewish Immigrant Aid Services (JIAS) and Canadian Jewish Congress (CJC) viewed the report with greater balance. Other controversial proposals included separate statutes for immigrants and refugees, eliminating the Immigration and Refugee Board (IRB), and taking appeals out of the hands of the Federal Court and assigning them to civil servants. The proposals had not been enacted by the end of the year.

An ongoing dispute between Canada and Israel over the question of whether an immigrant from Israel can claim refugee status appeared to be cooling off as the number of such applicants diminished. The acceptance rate of claimants from Israel dropped from 50 percent in 1994 to 4 percent in 1997, when only 46 refugee claimants from Israel were accepted. Most were accepted in Montreal, where there is allegedly more sympathy for such claims, despite the vigorous arguments of Israeli officials that there is no persecution in Israel. Since 1989 most such cases have involved former Soviet citizens who immigrated to Israel under the Law of Return and then subsequently claimed that they had suffered persecution and discrimination there, thus qualifying for possible admission to Canada as refugees.

Canadian Jews were generally pleased with an August Supreme Court of Canada ruling that unilateral Quebec secession would be unconstitutional and contrary to international law. The decision, on a reference from the government in the wake of the narrowly defeated 1995 Quebec referendum on independence, was endorsed by most Jewish groups, which enthusiastically support the maintenance of a united Canada. However, the Court went beyond the government's request and held that, should the Quebec separatists obtain a clear majority on a question of secession, the federal government and the other provinces would be obligated to negotiate the terms of such secession. The ruling leaves the future of the country in question so long as the separatist Parti Québécois (PQ) governs Quebec. Prof. Bruce Elman, who teaches law at the University of Alberta, called on Canadian Jews to "take this as a call to action" and reach out to other minority communities with similar federalist views by building on the Court's recognition that the protection of minority rights is central. Elman pointed out that minorities generally fare better in federal states and face serious problems in times of political upheaval, thereby reaffirming a key reason for Jewish opposition to Quebec's secession.

ELECTIONS

Several elections were held during the year, the most important of which was the Quebec provincial election on November 30, in which the Parti Québécois won a new mandate with a comfortable majority in the National Assembly, even though the opposition Liberals won a plurality of the popular vote. The PQ victory created the possibility of yet another referendum on independence within the next few years, even though ardor for a new vote was diminished by the PQ's relatively disappointing showing in the election. B'nai Brith Canada's Quebec regional director Robert Libman contended that the PQ "will not be able to muster the popularity needed for a referendum" and saw the outcome as "a very positive development" because he expects the PQ to face so many difficult challenges during the next four years. Still, the PQ remained committed to what it calls "sovereignty," and Premier Lucien Bouchard reaffirmed his party's intention to proceed when "winning conditions" exist. Among those elected to the National Assembly were Liberals Lawrence Bergman and Russell Copeman, with the former chalking up the largest victory margin of any candidate in the province.

Incumbent Montreal mayor Pierre Bourque defeated challenger Jacques Duchesneau, who had promised that he would be able to obtain investments of $500 million for the city from the "Jewish and anglophone communities." Duchesneau later backtracked, but he did claim to have held meetings with some Jewish developers and business people regarding ways to improve the investment climate. Two key city councillors on the Bourque team, Saulie Zajdel and Gerry Weiner, were appointed to the powerful Executive Committee of the city. Other successful Jewish candidates for the council were Marvin Rotrand and Michael Appelbaum. Irving Adessky was reelected mayor of Hampstead, and Robert Libman won his first term as mayor in Cote St. Luc.

Israel and the Middle East

As a result of the Canada-Israel Free Trade Agreement, which went into effect at the beginning of 1997, trade between the two countries surged, with an increase of about 40 percent from 1996 to 1997 to a level of $440 million (U.S.). Most of the increase involved Israeli importation of goods made in Canada, particularly in the high tech sector. Several Canadian companies also invested in or acquired Israeli firms or won major contracts for work in Israel.

Air Canada inaugurated nonstop flights from Toronto and Montreal to Tel Aviv in May, thereby ending El Al's monopoly and ushering in an era of increased competition.

Ontario premier Mike Harris visited Israel with an entourage of government officials and business people in October. Since most of the bilateral trade between the two countries involved Ontario, the visit had particular economic significance. Harris pointed that out, noting that "the peace process offers substantial business opportunities in the Middle East." In Jerusalem he was met by protesters objecting to the plans for the Trans-Israel Highway, a toll road that is being built by an Ontario company.

The Israeli Foreign Ministry, under pressure from the Ministry of Finance, announced in May the intended closure of several overseas missions, including the Israeli consulate general in Montreal. This sparked an outcry in the local Jewish community, which is sensitive to any symbolic downgrading of Quebec's place in Canada and of its own importance. In response, the Foreign Ministry put the decision on hold for an indefinite period while trying to sort out its budgetary problems. Community leaders promised to maintain the pressure on behalf of the consulate.

Jewish community leaders sharply criticized the government when it voted in July in favor of a United Nations resolution that upgraded the status of the Palestinian delegation. Canada's UN ambassador, Robert Fowler, claimed that the resolution "will permit the Palestinian delegation to better participate in the work of the United Nations." The CIC reacted negatively, questioning whether Canada's traditional evenhandedness still existed.

Canada also came in for sharp criticism for allegedly harboring Middle Eastern terrorists. Yehudit Barsky, an American authority on Arab terrorist groups, asserted during an October visit that Hezballah, Islamic Jihad, and Hamas carried out activities in Canada with relative impunity, mainly through fund raising, recruitment, and public relations activities. She claimed that terrorists regarded Canada as a hospitable place for such operations because of a lack of tight surveillance. Her views corroborated statements made to a Senate committee in June by Ward Elcock, director of the Canadian Security Intelligence Service (CSIS), who pointed out that terrorist groups had found numerous ways to take advantage of Canada's lax procedures in order to build up their infrastructures. CIC research director David Goldberg supported an initiative by Solicitor-General Andy Scott to establish a legal basis for stripping fronts for terrorist groups of their charitable status. However, there was considerable cabinet opposition to the move. Minister of Revenue Herb Dhaliwal, for example, claimed that he saw no evidence of terrorist fronts raising funds under the guise of charitable activities.

In a follow-up to the bungled 1997 Israeli spy caper in Jordan, the Security Intelligence Review Committee found that CSIS was not involved in any way in the use of forged Canadian passports by Israeli agents or the plot to assassinate Hamas leader Khaled Mashaal.

Israel and Canada signed an agreement in June to construct a Regional Rehabilitation Center in Africa for victims of land mines. International Cooperation Minister Diane Marleau also announced that Canada would donate $600 million from its Peacebuilding Fund to several projects and institutions that work to foster understanding and cooperation between Israel and the Palestinians and other Arabs.

In May Israel asked Canada to consider admitting ten men—six Iraqis, two Syrians, and two Iranians—who had been incarcerated in Israel for several years for entering that country illegally. Although Israel did not consider them to be enemies, neither did it want to allow them to stay in Israel. It considered them dissidents, not criminals, and turned to Canada as a country with a reputation for welcoming refugees, contending that the men would face persecution were they to return to their respective homelands.

The Canadian International Development Agency committed $3 million over three years to McGill University to help bring Israeli, Jordanian, and Palestinian students to participate in the Middle East Program in Civil Society and Peace Making. Program director James Torczyner, a social work professor at McGill, expressed the hope that the students would return to their homelands after a year in Canada as "ambassadors for peace," trained in the latest methods of promoting social justice and peaceful cooperation between peoples. In a June statement, Minister for International Cooperation Marleau praised the project for its "potential to make an important contribution to peace in the Middle East." The first cohort of 12 students arrived in the fall of 1998.

Anti-Semitism and Racism

Ernst Zundel, controversial for his active Holocaust-denial activities, was now embroiled in procedures relating to his attempt to gain Canadian citizenship after a lengthy period of residency in the country. The Canadian Security Intelligence Service had already determined that Zundel was a security risk, which would be grounds for denial of his application. When that finding came under consideration by the Security Intelligence Review Committee, Zundel challenged the impartiality of the SIRC. A lower court agreed with him, the Federal Court of Appeal reversed that decision, and in April the Supreme Court of Canada upheld the appeals court. Thus the SIRC was free to proceed, allowing the possibility that he might even be deported at some point. Meanwhile Zundel also faced a tribunal of the Canadian Human Rights Commission, which was assessing whether his "Zundelsite" on the World Wide Web promoted hatred against Jews. His challenge regarding the impartiality of one of the tribunal's members was rejected in June.

Also in June, Zundel announced plans to hold a news conference in the parliamentary press room in Ottawa. An outraged House of Commons quickly passed a unanimous resolution barring him from the premises for the remainder of the session. Government House leader Don Boudria explained that "Ernst Zundel doesn't belong in the temple of understanding and tolerance and democracy." Subsequently Zundel's lawyer, Douglas Christie, who has represented a number of anti-Semites, was also banned. Zundel responded, in November, by filing a lawsuit claiming that his constitutional right to free speech had been abridged; he named Prime Minister Jean Chrétien, all the parliamentary parties and their leaders, several specific MPs, and Canadian Jewish Congress and its president, Moshe Ronen, as defendants, for treating him as "a national pariah who should not be allowed into the precincts of Parliament." Ronen, acknowledging his role in alerting the politicians to Zundel's plan, responded by threatening a counter-suit.

In another legal action, the anti-Semitic former teacher Malcolm Ross won a judgment of $7,500 in April in a New Brunswick defamation suit against cartoonist and illustrator Josh Beutel. At a professional workshop in 1993, Beutel had presented a talk about the Holocaust and anti-Semitism, in which he used an illustration that depicted Ross as a Nazi and compared his views to those of Nazi German leaders. Judge Paul Creaghan of Court of Queen's Bench ruled that although Ross was indeed an anti-Semite and racist, there was no evidence that he was a Nazi. Beutel announced that he would appeal the judgment.

Doug Collins, the Vancouver area journalist who successfully contested a charge of anti-Semitism last year, faced a new human rights complaint filed by a representative of BBC. Harry Abrams charged that Collins had incited hatred against Jews and other minorities through his many columns in the *North Shore News* and the *Daily Victorian*. In his representation to the British Columbia Human Rights Commission, Abrams asserted that Collins had engaged in Holocaust denial and had made allegations about Jewish conspiracies. In its February 1999 decision, the tribunal ruled that Collins's columns were likely to expose Jews to religious hatred or contempt and ordered him to pay Abrams $2,000. He was also told to cease publishing anti-Semitic statements.

There were several incidents of anti-Semitic vandalism during the year. However, one apparent event proved to be misleading. There were two arson attacks on synagogues in London, Ontario, on a single day in February, but the man arrested for the crimes, Jonathan Bishinsky, turned out to be Jewish. Possible motives remained unclear. The fire damage to the two synagogues was minimal. Ecole Maimonides in Ottawa, a French immersion day school, suffered more serious damage, estimated at about $70,000, from an October fire. (A previous arson attack was made on the school in 1994.) Despite the fire's proximity to Yom Kippur, the police were not treating it as a hate crime. Another Yom Kippur incident occurred in suburban Montreal, where a private home was invaded by vandals who caused thousands of dollars in damages and scrawled anti-Semitic slogans on the walls. In Toronto a fire set on Sukkot at the Bloor Jewish Community Center caused about $10,000 in damage. Both incidents were classified by the police as hate crimes.

Jewish cemeteries were also targets of attacks. In August, 43 monuments were knocked over in Montreal's Back River Cemetery, though it was unclear whether the motivation was anti-Semitic. In comparison, vandalism in the Jewish cemetery in St. Catharines, Ontario, clearly reflected racist attitudes. In April, two cousins vandalized the cemetery in separate incidents. The first, Warren Soles, 20, who was charged with toppling or damaging 43 tombstones and other acts, had neo-Nazi affiliations. He pleaded guilty in July to several of the counts against him and later apologized in court. In November he was sentenced to 10 months in jail and fined $4,000. His older cousin, Warren Youmans, desecrated fewer graves and was charged with 11 counts of the same crime.

Nation of Islam speaker Don Muhammad, in a June speech in a Toronto mosque, questioned the historical accuracy of six million Jewish deaths in the Holocaust and asserted that wealthy Jews promote war to enrich themselves. Muhammad was denounced by senior figures in the United Church and the Anglican Church. CJC requested a police investigation of the mosque on the grounds that Muhammad may have acted in violation of the antihate laws.

British Columbia racist Eileen Pressler won a lawsuit in June against an antiracism activist, despite being labeled by the judge as a "missionary for anti-Semitism and pro-white racism." She and her husband had sued a professor and the television station on whose program the professor claimed that a property owned by the Presslers was intended for right-wing military purposes and not as a retirement home. Even though the judge accused the Presslers of promoting hatred and racism, he found that they had been defamed and awarded damages.

In August a Montreal Internet service provider shut down the anti-Semitic Web site of Aryan Nationalist Quebecers as soon as it was informed of its existence by the *Canadian Jewish News*. The Simon Wiesenthal Center's Canadian representative had also focused attention on the French-language hate material.

Nazi War Criminals

Legal proceedings continued against several of the 15 alleged war criminals named by the government. The government sought to strip them of their citizenship (if they had acquired it) on the grounds that they obtained it fraudulently by concealing their past, and then to deport them.

In two cases the government lost. Peteris Vitols was allowed to retain his citizenship after Federal Court judge William McKeown ruled in September that Vitols did not lie about his activities in a Latvian police battalion at the time that he immigrated to Canada. Despite the fact that people with his background were supposed to have been excluded as a matter of policy, many were admitted at the discretion of the immigration officer. Officials of Jewish organizations were shocked by the decision, but Paul Vickery, head of the War Crimes Unit, tried to assure them that the Vitols case was not a precedent. In particular, the judge believed him when he denied personally being involved in atrocities, even though his admitted membership in the suspect organization should have barred his entry automatically.

Another accused man who won in court was Johann Dueck. Judge Marc Noel of Federal Court found in December that he did not gain admission through fraud or misrepresentation. He accepted the accused's contention that he was simply an interpreter in Ukraine and not a member of a police unit.

The Federal Court hearing on Vladimir Katriuk, which culminated in July after several months of sporadic testimony, focused on whether immigration officers had ever asked about his wartime activities, which included participation in a Ukrainian SS battalion notorious for its involvement in mass killings of Jews and other civilians. Unfortunately, his original application for admission to Canada was destroyed decades ago during a general housecleaning by the government, thus making it difficult to answer Katriuk's vehement denials that he had been asked the key questions. A judgment was expected in January 1999.

Mamertas Rolland Maciukas decided to drop efforts to resist the government's citizenship case against him. Thus he was stripped of his citizenship by the cabinet and left the country in April. In February a judge of the Federal Court found that Wasily Bogutin had lied about his wartime activities; his citizenship was removed in July and the government initiated deportation hearings in the fall.

A new accused war criminal was added to the list in July. Ludwig Nebel of St. Catharines, Ontario, was accused of lying about his membership in the Austrian Nazi party when he applied to immigrate to Canada. Since he never obtained citizenship, the proceedings against him were for deportation. The government accused Nebel of belonging to the SA and then the SS and commanding troops that turned Polish Jews over to the Gestapo. In the case against Helmut Oberlander, his lawyer claimed that government policy was to exclude only "major offenders" and that he was not one. His case was still pending as the year ended. A former Nazi collaborator from France, Louis Robin, was found to be living in Vancouver in June. He had been convicted in France after the war but then escaped and came to Canada, where he had not drawn any attention. The government sought information from France before deciding whether to act.

In an article in the *Canadian Jewish News* (January 1998), former war crimes prosecutor Arnold Fradkin analyzed the difficulties in proving such charges, which revolve around alleged lies at the time of application for immigration and/or citizenship. In most cases, the government cannot introduce into evidence the actual immigration forms with the false information written on them, because the forms from 40 or 50 years ago have been destroyed or discarded. Further, testimony by the security officers who administered the forms and verified the information may not be possible if the officers in question are dead or unable to testify. Thus the time factor is a crucial one, because of the advancing age not only of defendants but also of key witnesses.

After allegations in 1997 of anti-Semitic attitudes among officials of the War Crimes Unit of the Justice Department, Osgoode Hall Law School professor John McCamus investigated the situation and issued a report in March. He found no evidence of anti-Semitism in the unit. William Hobson, another former war crimes unit head, and Arnold Fradkin, who worked under him, criticized the report on both substantive and methodological grounds. They were in turn criticized by McCamus for persisting in advancing allegations that he found to be without merit.

In July the government announced a major increase in funding for war crimes prosecutions. The allocation for the unit focusing on the Nazi era would be $12 million over three years, double the previous annual appropriation. For the same period, about $30 million would be spent on cases involving allegations of more recent war crimes violations. The war crimes unit is now expected to mount an additional 14 cases involving alleged Nazi collaborators, doubling the number of cases launched since the intensification of its efforts in 1995. The government also proposed Criminal Code amendments to overcome some of the legal obstacles to criminal prosecution that emerged from the Imre Finta case, which ended in 1994 with Finta's acquittal. Speaking on behalf of BBC, David Matas contended that "the lack of resources was a major cause of serious delay in the commencement of proceedings against suspected war criminals." The increased commitment to pursuing war criminals was lauded by Neal Sher in a Montreal speech in August. The American consultant to the War Crimes Unit said that the group had become more aggressive and had a better staff and improved attitude. In fact, he added, "I wouldn't be on board if the Canadian government was not serious."

The Departments of Justice and Citizenship of the federal government issued a report in July entitled "Canada's War Crimes Program." Since the 1987 Deschenes Report called for action against Nazi war criminals residing in Canada, 1,571 possible suspects had been investigated. Only 15 cases had been launched, with another 14 in the pipeline. Another 75 cases remained active. The rest of the files were either inactive or closed.

Holocaust-Related Matters

Plans to add a Holocaust gallery to the Canadian War Museum in Ottawa were shelved after veterans' groups forcefully objected because they did not want to see the museum's focus diffused. Instead attention shifted to the possibility of constructing a separate Holocaust museum in the nation's capital, even though that would be a more costly option. Jewish community organizations were divided over the preferred solution, especially since the Museum of Civilization, which encompasses the War Museum, had not consulted them when formulating the original plan. Both B'nai Brith Canada and Canadian Jewish Congress supported a free-standing facility, while the Jewish War Veterans wanted a gallery in the War Museum. In February the Museum of Civilization formally decided that the Holocaust Museum would be separate, possibly in an existing building, with funding still uncertain.

The settlement with the Swiss banks in 1997 produced about $2.5 million (U.S.) for needy Canadian Holocaust survivors. In a March announcement, CJC national executive director Jack Silverstone indicated that individual compensation packages would range from $200 to $1,000, according to procedures worked out with survivor groups and local federations. He also expressed dissatisfaction with the amount that was made available. Another agreement, this time with Germany, will bring compensation from Germany to about 1,000 survivors in Canada, most of whom had been confined in various kinds of camps that had not qualified under previous agreements. Others who were previously denied compensation according to income criteria were also included in the July agreement.

There were seven Canadian representatives, including Irving Abella and Rochelle Wilner, at the Washington Conference on Holocaust-Era Assets in December. The purpose of the conference was to establish procedures for the return of looted art works and for the payment of insurance policies.

The Ontario legislature passed a law in December mandating the observance of Holocaust Memorial Day each year on Yom Hashoah.

JEWISH COMMUNITY

Demography

Results from the 1996 mid-decade census created some confusion about the total Jewish population because there was no question on religion, only one on ethnicity. In the 1991 decennial census there were questions about both religion and ethnicity, which allowed for detailed analysis of the country's Jewish population. Normally, there are some Jews who identify themselves as Jewish when asked a religion question but as something other than Jewish in response to an ethnicity question. Hence relying only on ethnicity data understates the Jewish population. McGill University professor James Torczyner, who analyzed the 1991 data in detail, argued that the 1996 data should not be taken too seriously as an indication of a trend because an accurate count requires both ethnicity and religion data. In contrast, Prof. Robert Brym of the University of Toronto contended that the community should be concerned that in 1996 more Jews listed multiple ethnic origins, which he interprets as a weakening of ties to the community.

Moreover, he pointed out, in 1991, as in previous censuses, there were more Jews by ethnicity than by religion. These developments suggest to him that assimilation is growing.

The following table illustrates Brym's concerns:

	Total	Jewish Only	Jewish and Other
1996	351,705	195,810	155,900
1991	369,565	245,840	123,725

The data show a marked shift from people who identify only Jewish ethnicity to those who include Jewish along with one or more other ethnic backgrounds. It should be pointed out that some people who list a Jewish ethnic background may have converted to another religion. Torczyner, who excluded such people from his count, calculated that in 1991 there were 356,315 Jews in the country.

Using the 1996 ethnic data, the major concentrations of Jewish population were Ontario (191,445), Quebec (92,390), British Columbia (30,700), Manitoba (14,955), and Alberta (14,415).

A study by Jay Brodbar, director of research at UJA Federation in Toronto, shows that Toronto, with about 175,000 Jews, is now the 11th largest Diaspora Jewish community. The fast-growing community doubled in size in 25 years, with the most dramatic growth coming in the York region, just north of Metro Toronto. That area, including towns such as Markham, Richmond Hill, and Thornhill, now has over 50,000 Jews. The Toronto community has benefited from an influx of newcomers, some 30,000 between 1981 and 1991, with about half being immigrants and half migrants from other parts of Canada. Most of the latter group simply moved from smaller cities in Ontario to the Toronto area. The immigrants came primarily from the former Soviet Union, Israel, and South Africa. Brodbar also reported that only 9 percent of Toronto Jews were married to someone who was not born Jewish.

Communal Affairs

Historian Irving Abella inaugurated his J. Richard Sheff Chair for the Study of Canadian Jewry at York University with a lecture in September in which he compared the Canadian and American Jewish communities. In his view, things are better than ever for Canadian Jews, who are "arguably the most affluent, integrated community in the country." Canada's policy of cultural diversity has enabled the community to differentiate itself from its American counterpart, making it a more traditional, more unified community. Other differences include a far larger proportion of Holocaust survivors and their children, a lower intermarriage rate, a greater degree of Zionist commitment, a higher proportion of Orthodox identification, more generous charitable giving, more speaking of Hebrew and Yiddish, and higher levels of participation in Jewish day schools.

The place and the prospects of Jews in Quebec continued to be a preoccupation of the Montreal community. Montreal's Federation CJA held a public conference in March, "Directions 2000," another attempt to chart the community's future. McGill University's principal, Bernard Shapiro, told the audience that Montreal's Jews should accept French "not as a language of oppression, but as a language of opportunity." He added that "if our community is to have the vibrant and exciting future that I believe is within our grasp, we cannot just live on the legacy of the past." In various panel discussions, speakers reflected both optimistic and pessimistic scenarios for Montreal Jewry, comparing the increasing vitality of the francophone Jews and the benefits of Montreal life with the despair and frustration that induce young anglophone Jews to depart the city.

On the subject of rapprochement between Jews and Québécois, separatist journalist Josee Legault told the conference that "we have to break down suspicions . . . and show that sovereignists are not bloodthirsty xenophobes and that Jews have deep roots here however they vote." Toward that end a meeting took place at the National Assembly in Quebec City, also in March, between Jewish community leaders and provincial politicians and government officials. The featured event was the screening of a documentary by Ina Fichman about relations between Quebec Jews and the francophone majority entitled *Towards a Promised Land*. In a speech that evening, Premier Lucien Bouchard praised the film for showing the way toward constructive dialogue between the two groups.

The Canadian Jewish Congress held its 25th Plenary Assembly in Winnipeg in May. Incoming president Moshe Ronen, the youngest in the organization's history at age 39, promised "to speak out boldly" on the range of issues confronting Canadian Jewry and to "strengthen Jewish communal cohesion."

In a move parallel to what occurred earlier in the United States, the Council of Jewish Federations and United Israel Appeal merged in July. The new body, known as UIA Federation Canada, will combine governance, coordination, fund raising, and liaison with Israel, functioning on behalf of Canada's ten communities with federations as well as smaller, unfederated communities. It will also have a key role in allocating funds raised in the annual campaigns across the country between local, national, and overseas needs. The proportion of funds sent overseas, primarily to Israel, was a continuing source of debate in the light of increasing demand for local services.

At the February annual meeting of the Communauté Sépharade du Quebec (CSQ) in Montreal, incoming president Moise Amselem outlined his policy priorities, including better relations with Ashkenazi community institutions, promoting Jewish education, increasing Sephardic donations to the Combined Jewish Appeal, meeting the social welfare needs of local Sephardim, firming ties with Israel, attending to the needs of youth, and promoting unity within the community.

The Montreal community's planning for a new campus for various Jewish agencies and institutions picked up steam. By the end of the year the estimated cost had risen to about $30 million, up from the original $23 million, but there were also several new commitments from governments and additional construction plans as well. The governments of Canada, Quebec, and Montreal donated $1.3 million each, with the rest coming from donations by private individuals and corporations. By year end, nearly all the money had been raised, and construction plans for 1999 were at an advanced stage. The project will join the CJA Federation Building, Golden Age Association, YM-YWHA, and Saidye Bronfman Center for the Arts on a campus that will be defined physically by new construction, renovation, and landscaping. Organizations that will relocate to the campus include the Quebec Regions of CJC and CIC, the Communauté Sépharade du Quebec, the Canadian Zionist Federation, and the Israel Aliyah Center. In the words of CJA Federation president Stan Plotnick, the new campus "will be the ultimate reaffirmation by the Montreal Jewish community of its commitment to its future in Montreal and the confidence we have for the stability, and hopefully even growth, of our community."

Ottawa was also in the process of building a campus, which is anchored by the new Soloway Jewish Community Center in the Ages Family Building, which opened in September. The new edifice features health, leisure, and meeting facilities as well as offices. Another addition to the campus is the Ottawa Jewish Archives, which opened a month later. In Toronto the downtown Bloor JCC decided to undertake a major renovation project in order to expand its facilities. The $5 million campaign will cover the cost of the construction, retire existing debt, and provide an endowment for future programming in the facility.

The crash of Swissair 111 off Halifax in September posed challenges to that city's small Jewish community because there were about 20 Jewish victims. Local rabbis were mobilized to counsel the victims' families, a *hevrah kadishah* was set up to handle remains that were recovered, and hospitality was offered to relatives who visited the crash site. The Atlantic Jewish Council (AJC) invited an Israeli forensics expert and rabbi to assist in resolving halakhic issues related to the identification of bodies. Additional rabbis from Israel and the United States were brought in to deal with proper burial procedures. A memorial service was held at Beth Israel Synagogue, and AJC chaplain Rabbi David Ellis and other community leaders participated in an ecumenical service near the crash site.

The government of Quebec gave $820,000 to a Lubavitch group to help establish a $3-million community center for French-speaking Jews, especially youth, in the Montreal suburb of Cote St. Luc. Robert Perreault, the provincial minister responsible for Montreal, said that the new grant was in response "to the ever-growing needs of the members of the Sephardi community of Cote St. Luc." The new Beth Chabad immediately faced opposition from residents of the predominantly Jewish town who felt that its presence would add significantly to traffic and congestion. The required zoning changes were in doubt at the time the project was announced in October.

A sample study of the 6,000 Hassidim in the Montreal suburb of Outremont, carried out by Morton Weinfeld and Randall Schnoor of McGill University and Charles Shahar of Federation CJA, found that over 40 percent of the community were at or below the government poverty line. There was a high level of unemployment, with only 62 percent of men 18-65 years of age being employed full time. Moreover, the younger hassidic men were not being educated adequately for the work force, with over half having a high-school diploma or less.

Israel-Related Matters

Canadian Jews joined enthusiastically in celebrations of Israel's 50th Independence Day. Major events were held in most communities of any size. Thousands of people participated in Toronto and Montreal. In addition, the Canadian National Exhibition, held annually in Toronto in the late summer, featured an "Israel at 50" pavilion, sponsored by 175 Jewish community organizations. It had as its feature attraction a mosaic floor from a fifth-century synagogue in the Galilee that was discovered in 1994.

A "musical extravaganza" to honor Israel's 50th anniversary was held at Montreal's Place des Arts in November. "Journeys Through 5,000 Years," which told the history of the Jewish people through music, featured a symphony orchestra and several choirs. It was directed by Judith Lechter.

There was considerable interest in the work of Israel's Ne'eman Commission and the issue of religious pluralism in the Jewish state. Representatives of the three main streams of Diaspora Judaism in Canada welcomed the attempt by the Ne'eman Commission to resolve the issue of conversions in Israel, while at the same time expressing the concerns of their own movements about possible outcomes. When Israel's Chief Rabbinical Council indicated its unwillingness to accept major recommendations by the commission, the response from the various sectors of the Canadian rabbinate was predictable. Reform and Conservative rabbis expressed disappointment at the lost opportunity to create some unity around the process of conversion and the apparent disregard for the situation of Diaspora Jews. Orthodox rabbis tended to defend their Israeli counterparts for upholding a commitment to traditional Jewish law. However, two Orthodox rabbis, Reuben Poupko of Montreal and Reuven Bulka of Ottawa, voiced concern that divisive issues such as conversion were endangering Jewish unity.

El Al's Canadian manager, Moshe Shamai, said in April that Air Canada's new nonstop service was having an unfavorable impact on his airline and called on Canadian Jews to demonstrate continued loyalty to El Al, which had maintained the route alone for decades. Arguing that the route had not been profitable but had been kept in operation out of a sense of obligation to the community, Shamai suggested that it was time for the community to reciprocate.

Religion

The visit of Israel's Sephardic chief rabbi, Eliyahu Bakshi-Doron, to Canada in January was a major event for Sephardim in the Montreal and Toronto areas. In his remarks to a Montreal audience at an event hosted by the Grand Rabbinat du Quebec, the chief rabbi stressed the values of the centrality of the Land of Israel and the unity of the Jewish people. He spoke out forcefully against internal divisions that threaten Jewish unity. Rabbi Bakshi-Doron also visited the Sephardic Kehilla Center in the Toronto suburb of Thornhill.

A survey of Conservative synagogues across Canada, conducted by Howard Gontovnick of Concordia University, found that they had moved a considerable distance in the direction of the egalitarianism that now characterized most of their American counterparts. For example, over half offered *aliyot* to women and nearly half counted women in a *minyan*. Clearly there was a trend toward greater ritual participation by females, though the extent varied considerably from one synagogue to the next. There was currently one female Conservative rabbi in the country.

In an effort to foster Jewish unity, five Montreal synagogues joined together for *hakafot* on the night of Simhat Torah. Reconstructionist, Conservative, and Orthodox congregations converged on the street in front of Congregation Tifereth Beth David Jerusalem in suburban Cote St. Luc. Rabbi Chaim Steinmetz of that congregation saw the event as an opportunity to demonstrate how love for Torah and for fellow Jews can promote Jewish unity.

Education

Day schools in both Toronto and Montreal faced funding problems. In Toronto, the continued refusal of the provincial government to provide assistance placed a heavy burden of scholarship subsidies on the federation. The scholarships now amounted to over $6 million annually and about half of the federation's budget for local needs was now spent on education. Montreal schools, which had benefited from Quebec government funding for three decades, found the level of support to be declining due to pressures on the provincial budget. Furthermore, a decision by the provincial authorities on income taxes ended the partial deductibility of tuition fees, thereby raising the net cost to families by a significant amount. An increase in immigrant children requiring scholarships also contributed to the pressure on community resources. One school, College Hillel, nearly folded but was bailed out with help from Federation CJA and the CSQ.

Concordia University in Montreal established an Institute for Canadian Jewish Studies, endowed by Charles and Andrea Bronfman and Seagram's. The institute will combine traditional scholarly functions with a community internship program. McGill University received two endowments for Jewish studies, from the family of the late Jack Cummings and from Leanor and Alvin Segal. The funds will be used to staff two new professorships in the field. McGill's Jewish Teacher Training Program was reinvigorated by the renewal of community funding, after a seven-year hiatus. Sen. Jerry and Carole Grafstein established a chair in medieval Jewish studies at the University of Toronto.

Community and Intergroup Relations

A Montreal kosher food importer challenged federal nutritional labeling regulations on the grounds that banning offending products from entry (these were chiefly Passover foods) had the effect of violating constitutional guarantees of religious freedom. In an appeal of the importer's conviction on ten counts of violating the Food and Drug Act, attorney Paul Nadler argued that the unavailability of such Passover products would "make it extremely difficult" for Jews to practice a central aspect of their religion. However, Quebec Superior Court judge Pierre Pinard did not accept the argument and upheld the conviction in October.

In a Montreal case, residents of a condominium development were not allowed to erect *sukkot*—temporary "booths" for the weeklong festival of Tabernacles—on their balconies in 1997 or 1998. A Superior Court judge issued a permanent injunction against the *sukkot* in June after hearing expert testimony from Rabbis B. Barry Levy and Moise Ohana on whether building one's own *sukkah* was a religious obligation. The case was under appeal.

Maccabi Canada won a four-year fight with Revenue Canada to maintain its tax-exempt status as a registered Canadian amateur athletic association. The government had claimed that because it served Jews primarily it did not provide "a public benefit to Canadians in general." A panel of the Federal Court of Appeal found, however, that the statute imposed a geographic and not a demographic requirement.

In a path-breaking report, "Bearing Faithful Witness: United Church-Jewish Relations Today," Canada's largest Protestant denomination calls for a new era in interfaith connections. In particular it urges a new interpretation of the Bible to avoid anti-Jewish stereotyping and recognition that Christian denial of Jesus' Jewishness contributed to pogroms, the Holocaust, the refusal to admit refugees, and "other horrors against the Jewish people." On behalf of CJC, Rabbi Reuven Bulka hailed the report as "a tremendous achievement."

Relations with messianic movements were strained in both Montreal and Toronto. In the former, tensions between Lubavitch students and Christian messianists were high because of a proselytizing campaign aimed at immigrant Russian Jews. The Hassidic students demonstrated and protested in front of the store in a Jewish area that houses the messianic congregation. In June a young Lubavitcher was charged by police with uttering a threat in connection with the protests.

In several Toronto suburbs some 5,000 copies of a publication called *Messianic Times* were distributed to Jewish homes in August. It was designed to look like a Jewish community newspaper and urged Jews to worship Jesus as the messiah. The incident reflected the intensification of messianic activity in the area, which now had two such congregations. In an effort to counter the proselytizers, Jews for Judaism, a counter-missionary group, opened a resource center in a store next to the City of David messianic congregation in a shopping mall in the suburb of Thornhill. Jewish organizations also put pressure on the landlord to cancel the messianists' lease on the grounds that the congregation was masquerading as a synagogue.

Culture

In June Bryna Wasserman, who succeeded her mother Dora as director of Montreal's Yiddish Theater in 1996, took over, in addition, the English theater program of Montreal's Saidye Bronfman Center for the Arts. In November she took a troupe of 36 from the Yiddish Theater to Vienna for a week to perform *On 2nd Avenue* and *The Dybbuk* at the Rabenhof Theater. The tour was sponsored in part by the Canadian government.

A play about the Judenrat in the Lodz Ghetto premiered at the Bathurst Jewish Community Center in Toronto in December. *Suffer the Children* by Maurice Breslow explores some of the ethical dilemmas faced by officials of the Judenrat.

Toronto documentary filmmakers Elliott Halpern and Simcha Jacobovici continued their productive collaboration. Among their new films released during the year was *Quest for the Lost Tribes*, about possible contemporary descendants of the missing tribes of Israel. Ina Fichman's film *Towards a Promised Land* examines the complexities of the evolving relationship between Quebec Jews and the majority French-speaking Quebecois. Fichman contrasts the anti-Semitism that infected Quebec society in the past with much greater opportunities for Jewish integration now. The film was shown on Vision TV in January and in Quebec in March. Eric Scott had completed most of the work on *Je Me Souvien*, a film based on Esther Delisle's controversial book *The Traitor and the Jew*, but was unable to obtain needed funds from either of the two major French-language television networks in Quebec to finish the project. Scott does not shy away from the bitter dispute about the extent to which anti-Semitism and Quebec nationalism were closely intertwined in the 1930s and 1940s. He asserts that "anti-Semites in Quebec were not society's cranks. They were French Canada's leading scholars, church leaders, politicians and professors."

Some 40 films were screened at the Toronto Jewish Film Festival in May. There was also an Israel Film Festival at the Art Gallery of Ontario in October, sponsored by Cinematheque Ontario.

An exhibition from the library of the Jewish Theological Seminary of America was on display during the summer at Quebec's Musée des Religions in Nicolet. Entitled "Kehillat Ha-Kodesh/Creating the Sacred Community," it consisted of rare books, manuscripts, and documents.

The Canadian War Museum in Ottawa presented an exhibition in its temporary Holocaust Gallery from January through September. "Reflections on the Holocaust: The Art of Aba Bayefsky" consisted of about 50 of the artist's works based on his experience as a war artist.

The Quebec government contributed $230,000 toward the renovation of the historic Bagg Street Synagogue in the area of Montreal that was popular with Jewish immigrants during the first half of the 20th century. It is the oldest synagogue in continuous use in the city.

A rare and priceless collection of Yiddish books and manuscripts was displayed for the first time at the McGill University Library during the winter. Described by curator Goldie Sigal as "one of the finest single private libraries of modern Yiddish literature in the world," the exhibit of "A Garment Worker's Legacy: The Joe Fishstein Collection of Yiddish Poetry" displayed works not readily available elsewhere.

CBC Radio ran a five-part series on Israeli authors in February and March entitled "Writing a Nation: Israel at 50." The philosopher Emil Fackenheim was the subject of a five-part documentary on Vision TV in May and June.

Publications

In a departure from his usual fiction writing, Mordecai Richler published *Belling the Cat*, a collection of essays on politics, literature, and other topics. Among his subjects are two of Canada's most prominent Jewish families, the Bronfmans and the Reichmanns.

Noteworthy new works of fiction included *The War to End All Wars* by Morley Torgov, *The Wanderer* by Regine Robin, *Morrow and Other Stories* by Nora Gold, *Love Ruins Everything* by Karen X. Tulchinsky, and *The Tracey Fragments* by Maureen Medved. Two of Yehuda Elberg's Yiddish novels were translated: *Ship of the Hunted* and *The Empire of Kalman the Cripple*. Seymour Mayne published two books of poetry, *Dragon Trees* and *Carbon Filter: Poems in Dedication*.

Esther Delisle continued her exposé of less attractive aspects of Quebec history in *Myths, Memories, and Lies: Quebec's Intelligentsia and the Fascist Temptation 1939-1960*, in which she documents the pro-Nazi sympathies of key members of Quebec's elite during the crucial war period. Other new nonfiction works on Canada included Gerald Tulchinsky's thorough and perceptive history of Canadian Jewry during the last half century, *Branching Out: The Transformation of the Canadian Jewish Community*; Lois Sweet's *Religion in Canada's Schools*; *Who Speaks for Canada? Words That Shape a Country*, edited by Morton Weinfeld and Desmond Morton; Peter C. Newman's study of economic power, including the rise of a Jewish business elite, *Titans: How the New Canadian Establishment Seized Power*; Lesley Marrus Barsky's *From Generation to Generation: A History of Toronto's Mount Sinai Hospital*; and *The Jews of Montreal and Their Judaisms: A Voyage of Discovery* by MacKay Smith.

Other new works of nonfiction included *In Search of Jewish Community: Jewish Identity in Germany and Austria, 1918–1933* by Derek Penslar; *Negotiating Arab-Israeli Peace: Patterns, Problems, Possibilities* by Neil Caplan and Laura Zittrain Eisenberg; Lionel Steiman's *Paths to Genocide: Antisemitism in Western*

History; *Creating the Jewish Future*, edited by Michael Brown and Bernard Lightman; *Tehilla Le-David: Poemes de David Ben Hassine, le chantre du judaisme marocain* by Andre Elbaz and Ephraim Hazan; Kenneth Green's *The Jewish Writings of Leo Strauss*; *The Rhetoric of the Babylonian Talmud: Its Social Meaning and Context* by Jack Lightstone; and *Dawn of the Promised Land* by Ben Wicks. Several works on the Holocaust appeared: *No Time to Die: A Holocaust Survivor's Story* by Karl-Georg Roessler; *L'Abus de Confiance* by Jean-Jacques Fraenkel; *The Fallacy of Race and the Shoah* by Naomi Kramer and Ronald Headlance; *A Nation on Trial: The Goldhagen Thesis and Historical Truth*, edited by Norman Finkelstein and Ruth Bettina Birn; *Carved in Stone* by Manny Drukier; Emery Rodan's *111 Main Street: Life in Hungary During the War*; and Arthur Schaller's *100 Cigarettes and a Bottle of Vodka*.

Religious literature included *Mourning a Baby* by Rabbi Yamin Levy and *Le sens de l'Exil* by Rabbi David Sabbah.

Elaine Kalman Naves won the Canadian Literary Award for *Hair*, a collection of essays about her Hungarian childhood. Toronto Jewish Book Awards went to Naves; Regine Robin; Isabel Vincent; Romer Karsh; Vera Schiff; Alan Davies and Marilyn Nefsky; Carol Matas; Rosalie Sharp, Irving Abella and Edwin Goodman; Elizabeth Greene; Martin Lockshin; Simcha Simchovitch; and Carol Rose.

Personalia

A number of Jews were appointed to the Order of Canada. Companion: Reva Appleby Gerstein; Officers: Charles Dubin, Eva Kushner, Martin Goldfarb, and Henry Mintzberg; Members: Edgar Gold, Sheila Barshay Goldbloom, Rickey Kanee Schachter, and Irving Schwartz. The Order of Ontario was awarded to Bluma Appel, Ydessa Hendeles, and Marvelle Koffler.

Mel Cappe was appointed Clerk of the Privy Council, the highest civil service post in the country. Historian Jack Granatstein assumed the directorship of the Canadian War Museum, while Matthew Teitelbaum took a similar position at the Art Gallery of Ontario. In the music field, Pinchas Zukerman was appointed music director of the National Arts Center Orchestra, and Yoav Talmi became the conductor of the Orchestre Symphonique du Quebec. Mark Wainberg was selected as president-elect of the International AIDS Society. Norman Spector left his post as publisher of the *Jerusalem Post* to become a columnist for the Toronto *Globe and Mail*. Dr. Samuel Freedman won the Prix Armand Frappier, Quebec's highest recognition for lifetime scientific achievement. Mordecai Richler was awarded the Hugh MacLennan Prize for Fiction by the Quebec Society for the Promotion of English Language Literature for *Barney's Version*. Joseph Schwarz won the James H. Stack Award of the American Chemical Society. Yiddish Theater director Dora Wasserman was awarded the Prix Hommage by the Académie québécoise du théâtre in recognition of her lifetime achievements.

Avraham Niznik was appointed chief rabbi of Montreal. Among new presidents of community organizations are Lawrence Hart at B'nai Brith Canada, Joey Steiner at UJA Federation of Greater Toronto, Moshe Ronen at Canadian Jewish Congress, Harvey Wolfe at UIA Federation Canada, David Vineberg at CJA in Vancouver, and Judah Castiel at the Fédération Sépharade du Canada. Brian Morris is the new chairman of the Canada-Israel Committee.

Members of the community who died this year included community leader Joe Ain, in January, aged 85; arts benefactor Arthur Gelber, in January, aged 82; Chief Rabbi of Montreal Pinchas Hirschprung, in January, aged 87; former MP David Orlikow, in January, aged 79; J.B. Salsberg, Yiddishist and former politician, journalist, and community activist, in February, aged 95,; film company executive Harvey Greenberg, in February, aged 61; songwriter Alex Kramer, in February, aged 94; businessman and community activist Morris Goldberg, in March, aged 84; Amnon Ajzensztadt, author, lecturer, and Holocaust survivor, in March, aged 78; Maxwell Cohen, distinguished legal scholar, dean, judge, and public servant, in March, aged 88; congregational rabbi Harold Lerner, in April, aged 72; Antonia Robinson, longtime activist and former president of the National Council of Jewish Women, in April, aged 102; scholar and teacher Rabbi Wolf Gordon, in May, aged 86; government official and community leader Gerald Berger, in July, aged 60; businessman and inventor Frank Roberts, in August, aged 68; organizational leader Bertha Dermer, in August, aged 83; photographer Sylvia Schwartz, in August, aged 83; author and book collector Lawrence Lande, in August, aged 91; Louis Rasminsky, former governor of the Bank of Canada, in September, aged 90; Sheila Freedman, adviser to Jewish students at McMaster University, in October, aged 55; businessman Harold Cummings, in October, aged 80; Yiddish journalist and community leader Max Wolofsky, in October, aged 93; artist Eric Wesselow, in October, aged 87; poet, novelist, and organizational executive Nahum Ravel, in October, aged 75; and journalist and newspaper executive Lou Miller, in December, aged 70.

HAROLD M. WALLER

Latin America

Mexico

National Affairs

Hopes for meaningful change in Mexico were frustrated in 1998, as deep-seated problems continued to plague the country. The death in April of internationally acclaimed poet-politician Octavio Paz highlighted the lack of visionary leadership needed to take the country smoothly into the next millennium. Until his last illness, Paz remained part of the political life of the country, offering a vision of cultural harmony, even while criticizing the political system.

In April Mexico participated in the Second Summit of the Americas in Chile, at which 34 countries in the Western Hemisphere tried to create the world's largest free trade zone. Goals were set for the year 2005. The Mexican polity, however, was still far from solving its own problems. The adoption in 1997 of a new voting system had produced the first signs of national political pluralism, but democracy was still far from being realized.

The dialogue with the indigenous people of Chiapas, in its fifth year, remained at an impasse after the massacre of more than 40 Chiapans in a church in December 1997 by paramilitary groups sympathetic to the government. The proliferation of political voices in that state made negotiations difficult. In March President Ernesto Zedillo sent proposals to Congress designed to give the people of Chiapas greater self-rule and autonomy; however, passage of such measures was contingent on their not infringing on the accepted provisions of the constitution regarding national sovereignty, unity, land ownership, and other provisions.

Economically the country seemed able to stand its ground through the upheavals affecting the ailing Asian economy and other markets. Foreign investment in 1998 was $10.5 billion, 10 percent higher than the previous year, with over half coming from the United States. However, at the end of the year, faced with mounting internal economic problems, the government increased taxes, raised the prices of local oil consumption and electricity, and even lowered the subsidy on corn, which affects the price of tortillas, the staple food of the country. These measures came after three budgetary adjustments: in January, oil prices were revised downward from $15.5 to $13.5 per barrel; in March the oil barrel price went further down to $12.5; and by June a comprehensive oil export reduction was imposed, reducing net production to 200,000 barrels per day. Even with all these measures, the budget deficit of 1.25 percent of GDP for 1998 fiscal year remained unchanged.

The most serious social problem was crime; it affected the whole population regardless of social class and created a pervasive and paralyzing fear everywhere. The causes included both police complicity with the drug cartels, which had infiltrated the northern states and the largest urban centers of the country, and the inability of the police to control the proliferation of pickpockets and armed gangs who carried out theft, kidnapping, rape, and murder in broad daylight. Mexico City was the most embattled area: with its 8.5 million inhabitants in the Federal District plus another ten million outside the district lines, sheer numbers aggravated the problem exponentially. The promise given by Mayor Cuauhtémoc Cárdenas when he took office in 1997, "to control the city in 100 days," evaporated very quickly. The first two weeks in November alone saw an increase of 20 percent in the city's crime rate, to the dismay and fear of the general population.

In foreign relations, Mexico continued to cooperate with the United States to develop cooperative strategies in the hope of stemming the drug traffic.

Israel and the Middle East

President Zedillo designated Juán Antonio Mateos Cicero, former Mexican ambassador to Kenya and Tanzania, as ambassador to Israel, replacing Jorge Alberto Lozoya. Javier Treviño, undersecretary for international cooperation, visited Israel in February to strengthen bilateral relations. Former Israeli prime minister Shimon Peres visited the Mexican Jewish community in the same month.

The renewal of peace negotiations between Israel and the Palestinians was covered in the media, but in general, events in the Middle East received moderate attention in 1998.

In June the Mexico-Israel Institute, celebrating its 50th anniversary in conjunction with the 50th anniversary of the State of Israel, presented the Mexico Israel 1998 Cultural Award to 25 people distinguished in a variety of fields. Recipients included David Amato, columnist for *The News* and *Novedades* and winner of the Order of the Aztec Eagle, Mexico's highest decoration given to foreigners (Amato is an American Sephardic Jew, resident of Mexico for 35 years), who had fostered exchange programs with Israel. Other recipients were former President Miguel de la Madrid; politician Miguel Aleman Velazco; philanthropist Max Shein Heisler; ambassadors Jorge Alberto Lozoya and Rafael Rodriguez Barrera; economist Jesús Rodriguez y Rodriguez; architect Pedro Ramirez Vázquez; television news anchorman Jacobo Zabludovsky; former oil company director Francisco Rojas; philanthropist Alejandro Saltiel Suzette; historian Victoria Cohen; surgeon Jaime P. Constantiner; writer Eduardo Feher; historian Alicia Gojman de Backal; director of Tribuna Israelita Eugenia Hoffs; historian Enrique Krauze; physician Marcos Moshinsky; painter Leonardo Nierman; activist Sergio Nudelstejer; TV director José Maria Perez Gay; sociologist-journalist Esther Shabot; and surgeon Jacobo Zaidenweber. Many of the original founders of the institute, distinguished personalities in the arts, letters, and politics of the country, mostly deceased, were honored posthumously.

In February Mexico hosted the 11th annual forum, "Three Women: Three Expressions," featuring three Israeli academics from the Hebrew University of Jerusalem: Rachel Nechushtai, a botanist who works with pharmaceutical companies; Ronit Nativ, an expert on hydrogeology and water contamination; and Ada Zohar, a psychologist who specializes in genetic behavior. In addition to speaking, the women met with Mexican officials in their fields and lectured at universities. Dr. Leo Joskowics of the Institute of Computer Science at the Hebrew University lectured to 60 second-year students of the Anahuac University. Dr. Carlos Montemayor of the Anahuac University traveled to Israel to teach as part of the recently established (1997) Rosario Castellanos Chair in Literature, named for the former Mexican ambassador, at Tel Aviv University.

Mexican and Israeli medical experts met on several occasions during the year, some of the gatherings arranged by one or more groups of "Friends" of Israeli institutions. A conference on the political situation in the Middle East was held December 1–3, a collaboration between Tel Aviv University, the Colegio de Mexico, and the Ministry of Foreign Relations. The Itzjak Rabin group, a new organization devoted to promoting peace among all peoples, invited Israeli and Palestinian professors, Edy Kaufman from Hebrew University and Manuel Hassasian from Bethlehem University, to speak on issues related to peace. Dr. Adolfo Roitman, Israel Museum curator and expert on the Dead Sea Scrolls, visited Mexico as a guest of the Ministry of Exterior and the Colegio de México.

Israeli ambassador Moshe Melamed was kept busy with celebrations of Israel's 50th anniversary, organized by a committee headed by Lizzet Mussali. Among the many cultural events offered was an exhibit in the Palacio de Bellas Artes on Israel's new Supreme Court building. A widely seen television program about Israel today, presented by now retired television personality Jacobo Zabludovsky, was well received.

Anti-Semitism

Two negative incidents in the national press were surprising: one, in June, was a notorious article by Carlo Coccioli linking President Bill Clinton's personal problems to the Jews. Coccioli argued that the failure of the U.S. Jewish community to dissociate itself from Monica Lewinsky, a Jew, was proof of Jewish involvement in the scandal. Recognized Jewish journalists and private persons protested Coccioli's analysis in the press. Journalist Miguel Angel Granados Chapa denounced two other gratuitous anti-Semitic articles that appeared on August 31, one by Eduardo del Rio and the other by Juan Jose Rodriguez Soto. The latter, who had been promoting himself as a candidate for the year 2000 presidential contest, reiterated his promise to control what he called "Jewish power" and to fight the "exaggerated" stories of Jews under Hitler, their problems in the UN, their sinister intentions toward the Palestinians, and all the self-inflicted problems that Jews attempt to dump on others. Rodriguez Soto even suggested that to solve all of Mexico's problems, one needed to control the international Jewish-Zionist conspiracy rooted in Jewish control of the mass media and the Mexican political system.

In November a swastika was painted on a staircase wall at the Iberoamerican University together with slogans against Jews.

JEWISH COMMUNITY

Demography

Mexico remained home to the third largest Jewish community in Latin America, after Argentina and Brazil, and followed by Uruguay and Venezuela, both with equal numbers of Jews. There are an estimated 40,700 Jews in Mexico, most living in Mexico City, but also in Monterrey, Guadalajara, Tijuana, and a few families in Yucatan and now also Cancun. Although the numbers seem stable, a number of families have left the country, some to the United States, others to Canada. In addition to anecdotal reports of this migration, Jewish schools have reported changes in enrollment as families have left the country. The main reason given for the exodus is the high crime rate that has created a climate of fear.

Communal Affairs

The newly formed Consejo Ashkenazi de México, or Ashkenazi Community Council, continued to organize and promote itself as the legitimate successor to the dismantled Kehillah, the body previously representing Ashkenazi Jews. A new monthly journal, *Tu Mundo*, was established in an effort to clarify the changes that had taken place and to seek needed support. However, the response of the community appeared to be largely apathetic, and critics pointed to a lack of accounting of monies spent (by no means a new issue in the Kehillah) and insufficient explanations of changes to the public. The main justification for the 1997 coup and the changes proposed by the council of 12 members was the desire to unite all Ashkenazi communal organizations and religious congregations under one umbrella. A year later, however, there was no evidence that that had occurred. The Conservative Congregation Bet-El remained independent and showed no interest in deferring to or allying itself with the council. Many small organizations had not been assigned space in the new premises or allotted budgets. Within the

Orthodox camp there were indications of a breakdown in organization, with no clear agreement on the hierarchy of rabbinic positions.

One issue of particular concern to the council was the neglect of the young adult Jewish population, aged 18–30. This cohort includes high-school graduates who enter either the work force (a minority) or the university (the majority). Since neither had a niche within the communal organizations, their needs and interests were not being addressed. Another pressing issue for the council was the community's economic situation, which had worsened under the NAFTA agreements, affecting in particular small business owners, and resulting in larger numbers of people needing psychological and financial support. The council was trying to organize services so as to reach those in need.

To honor the memory of the late Shimshon Feldman, the former president of the Ashkenazi Kehillah, a special ceremony was held at the Nidkhei Israel Community Center, at which his family donated a Torah scroll.

The tightly organized Sephardi communities focused on a variety of social service projects. At their initiative, and with indirect support of the Ashkenazi community as well as other smaller groups, they brought six major hospitals in the capital together to form the Grupo Angeles, offering "integrated health services," such as kosher food and information banks.

The Jewish Community Council, with help from the Jewish Central Committee (the representative political body of Mexican Jewry), Tribuna Israelita, and the Mexican Union of Members of the Resistance and Survivors of the Holocaust, joined the Swiss Fund for Holocaust Victims, in collaboration with the World Jewish Organization for Restitution, seeking compensation for Mexican Holocaust victims.

On October 27, Tribuna Israelita, the human-relations and "defense" arm of the Central Committee, and the American Jewish Committee signed an affiliation agreement that would advance their joint interests in key communal issues without either relinquishing its autonomy. Both institutions base their work on research and analysis and advance their agendas through private diplomacy and public advocacy. The AJCommittee has similar affiliations with London's Institute for Jewish Policy Research (1994) and the Australian/Israel and Jewish Affairs Council (1997).

Israel-Related Activities

As in the past, Yom Ha'atzmaut, Israel Independence Day, was widely celebrated, but this year with greater fanfare to mark the jubilee. On April 29, a multimedia concert was presented in the UNAM's Netzahualcoyotl Theater. Other cultural events in this period included performances by the Anahnu Ve'atem dance group and the Kibbutz dance troupe; the Latinamerican Quartet with violinists Saúl and Aarón Bitrán, cellist Alvaro Bitrán, and violinist Javier Montiel; and several Klezmer groups.

A number of events took place in the fall: a film festival was part of the Jornadas Culturales Judeo Mexicanas; paintings and sculpture by Jewish Mexican artists were exhibited at the Mexico-Israel Cultural Institute; and a festival of dance and music was offered in the Parque México. The Sephardi Zionist Organization and the Sephardi community organized a celebration called Luna Park in the Hebrew-Sephardic school; the Monte Sinai and Maguen David communities, with the Sephardic School and the Jewish National Fund, celebrated the Israeli anniversary with singer Jo Amar and dancers of the Aviv Festival. The Museo del Chopo presented an exhibit of works by Israeli-Canadian artist Dorrit Yacoby, a joint effort with the Israeli and Canadian embassies and the Mexican-Israeli Institute.

The Mexico-Israel Cultural Institute opened its new quarters at República del Salvador #41, in the old center of town, with a photo and document exhibit, "The Jewish Presence in Mexico," and an exhibit on "Jerusalem, Traditions and Festivities, and Festivities of Jews and Israel Today." The work of Ethiopian Israeli artist Tzagaye Barihum was exhibited in Mexico in April, arranged by the Sport Center and ORT.

A special ceremony was held in December to recognize the effort of intellectuals, writers, and politicians who created the Mexican Pro Jewish Palestine Committee in 1945. In Jerusalem, during the Week of the Hebrew Book, the Israeli Association of Writers in the Spanish Language offered a special presentation and workshop on Octavio Paz.

Education

The Universidad Hebraica, which opened in 1989 as the successor to the older Yiddish Teachers Seminary, and whose purpose is to help further the education of teachers within the community, continued to offer courses and degrees. Its faculty, led by rector Asia Levita, includes teachers from abroad who give short-term courses. The school's degrees are recognized by the Ministry of Education in Mexico, UNESCO, and the Ministry of Education in Israel (since March 1997). It offers undergraduate and graduate degrees in fields such as cognitive psychology, philosophy of science, applied mathematics, anthropology, and human development, in addition to specialized education and Jewish studies courses. The school has about 500 part-time students at the diploma level and about 84 full-time BA students.

The Colegio Israelita de México, the first Jewish day school in Mexico to incorporate Yiddish and Hebrew in the curriculum, celebrated 50 years of the founding of its high school. Joined by the Friends of the Hebrew University, in March the school offered a week-long series of symposia, with Howard Dichter, Zeev Mankowitz, Miguel Abruch, and Enrique Krauze among the guest speakers. Students also took part in the programs.

Nearly all Jewish schools reported slight losses in student enrollment due to emigration. The two newest schools, Atid and Gan Montessori, reported increased enrollment. Atid was building a new school; Gan Montessori, which started only last year with 20 students, had 64 for 1998 and was expecting 81 in 1999. These schools used little Hebrew and were not yet connected to the Va'ad Hahinukh, the education committee of the Community Council.

In June the CEJ (Center for Jewish Studies) offered courses at the Bet El Congregation on "The Jewish Communities in Mexico: From the Traditional World to the Postmodern. Challenges for the New Millennium."

Community Relations

Public school No. 15 in Mexico City, known as the Albert Einstein School, celebrated its 50th anniversary this year. It was created by the Jewish community in 1948, after the then president of Mexico requested help in building schools for underprivileged children. To date, some 90,000 children have studied in this middle school. The president of the Central Committee, Isaias (Ishie) Gitlin; the delegate of the Miguel Hidalgo region, Jorge Abraham Fernandez Souza; and the Mexican Council of Jewish Women were all there to mark the occasion. Representatives of the Colegio Hebreo Sefaradi, Colegio Israelita de México, and students of the school performed for the attendees.

The Jewish Journalists and Writers Association organized a commemoration in April of the 60th anniversary of a little-known historical episode: a speech delivered by President Lázaro Cárdenas to the League of Nations, protesting the German invasion of Austria, the *Anschluss*, of March 12, 1938. Prof. Friedrich Katz of the University of Chicago lectured on "Cardenas and Fascism: The Austrian Case" in the University House of the Book, UNAM. Austria had shown its appreciation of the Mexican government's support by naming a square in Vienna Plaza México. The events were coordinated by Dr. Ariel Kleiman, who was also a participant, with Gilda Waldman, both on the faculty at UNAM. Walter Frisch, a member of the Austrian Center in Mexico, offered his own recollections of the episode.

On April 28, WIZO members organized a celebration of Children's Day at the ISSSTESTASNCIA Rosario Castellanos, a day-care facility; they also continued their work with the primary school in Cuajimalpa they support.

A weeklong seminar was held in October to mark the 50th anniversary of the Universal Declaration of Human Rights. It was organized by Tribuna Israelita, the National University UNAM, and the UNESCO Committee for Human Rights.

For the first time, an active member of the Jewish community was elected to a high position in the Red Cross. Noemi Tiktin was elected vice-president of the Women's Committee of the Red Cross for Mexico City. She had been working in the organization for 26 years through the Jewish-Mexican Volunteers.

Culture

Two major exhibitions took place this year. An exhibit of works by painter Tamas Szigeti, who studied in Hungary and in Mexico, opened on May 28 at the Sports Center. The Hungarian ambassador and other dignitaries attended. An event of larger scope, titled "Images of Polish Jews" opened June 24, in the presence of the president of Mexico, Polish and Israeli diplomats, and representatives of the UNAM University, headed by Chancellor Francisco Barnes de Castro. The Central Committee played a key role in coordinating the events, which were held in the old part of the city in the Antiguo Colegio de San Ildefonso. The exhibit presented a photographic record of Jewish life in this century up until World War II, organized by the Shalom Foundation of Warsaw. A program of events held in conjunction with the exhibition included a series of conferences with participants Judith Bokser, Alicia Gojman, Lázaro Azar Boldo, Ludwik Margules, Gilda Waldman, and Raquel Kleinberg; a dialogue among Mexican Jewish writers Margo Glantz, Babina Berman, and Myriam Moscona; and a film festival of six Polish films, with comments by José María Espinasa.

The Habima Theater Festival, a forum for different performing groups, took place early in June at the CDI Sports Center. The jury was made up of well-known Mexican actors: Isaura Espinoza, Muriel Fouilland, Enrique Galván, Luis Miguel Huesca, Veronica Langer, and Carlos Pouliot.

On November 8, the Mexican Association of Friends of the Hebrew University presented a performance of *Brundibar,* an opera for children, by the children's chorus of the Niños Cantores de Chalco, under the direction of Leszek Zawadka. *Brundibar* was written in 1938 by Hans Krasa for a competition organized by the then Czech minister of education and culture; it had its premiere in Terezin concentration camp in 1942, where it was performed 55 times and was extremely popular. In 1944 Krasa was deported to Auschwitz. The CDI Sports Center organized a literary contest open to all members of the community; it received over 100 submissions. Becky Rubinstein received an award from the state of Jalisco for her children's book, illustrated by Santiago Rebolledo.

The Center for Documentation and Research of the Ashkenazi Community, which opened in 1993, had in its short existence developed a library, including photographs, magazines, and an oral history archive in Spanish, Yiddish, Hebrew, Russian, German, and Polish. Under director Alicia Gojman de Backal, the center was carrying out a number of research projects in Mexican Jewish history.

Jewish-Christian Relations

On August 23, the Committee on Jewish-Christian Relations of B'nai Brith hosted a get-together in honor of Norberto Rivera Carrera, archbishop of Mexico, in the Adat Israel Synagogue. B'nai Brith was reciprocating an invitation extended by Rivera Carrera after being appointed a cardinal. The chairman of the committee, José Kably, president of B'nai B'rith Enrique Elías, president of the Central Committee Ishie Gitlin, and Archbishop Rivera Carrera all spoke.

Publications

The first Yiddish book published in Mexico, *Drai Vegn* (Three Roads), in 1928, a collection of works by the poets Glantz, Glikovsky, and Berliner, was published in Spanish, with translations by Becky Rubinstein. *Anita Brenner: A Mind of Her Own*, written by her daughter, Susannah Joel Glusker, is the story of a woman whose archive has been an important source for the study of early Jewish life in Mexico. *Las Genealogías* (The Genealogy), by Margo Glantz, originally published in 1982, was revised by the author to pay homage to her mother who passed away in 1997, 15 years after her husband, poet Jacobo Glantz. Other new nonfiction books were *La Propuesta del Judaismo* (The Proposal of Judaism) by Bernardo Kligsberg; *El Convenio Ilusorio; Refugiados de Guerra en México (1943–1947)* (The Illusory Agreement: War Refugees in Mexico 1943–1947) by Gloria Carreño and Celia Zack; and *Lej Leja, Destino de una Familia* (Go Yourself, Destiny of a Family) by Peter Katz.

New works of fiction include *Muerte Súbita* (Sudden Death) and *La Bobe* (published in English as *Bubbeh*) by Sabina Berman; *Una palabra clave* (A Crucial Word) by Becky Rubinstein; *Las Tierras prometidas* (The Promised Lands) by Rosa Nissan; and *Las Fuerzas Secretas de los Cuarzos* (The Secret Powers of Quartzes) by Sara Maya de Toyber.

Personalia

Recently retired newscaster and media personality Jacobo Zabludovsky, who had received prizes in Spain, the United States, and Mexico, was honored in France by Catherine Trautmann, minister of culture, with the title "Commentator of Arts and Letters." Sara London won an Honorary Mention with her painting "Number of Gold 1.618" in the First Olga Costa Biennial. Architect Carlos Pascal and *Interior Design* magazine received a prize from the International Interior Design Association (IIDA) in Chicago for his work on the Ramat Shalom *mikveh* (ritual bath). The architectural plans were published in *Designing with Spirituality*. The Eishel Old Age Home in Cuernavaca, Morelos, celebrated its 50th anniversary and honored benefactor Max Shein Heisler.

Biologist Simon Brailowsky Klipstein (1948–1998), a distinguished scientist affiliated with the UNAM, died in a car accident in May. He was the author of many books and 79 articles in his field.

ADINA CIMET

Argentina

National Affairs

UNDER PRESIDENT CARLOS MENEM, the country's nearly 35 million inhabitants continued to be ruled by the Justicialist Party (PJ) in 1998. Already preparing for the elections scheduled for October 1999, the Alliance of former president Raúl Alfonsín's Radical party (UCR) and the Solidarity Front (FREPASO) held a primary in 1998, which resulted in Fernando de la Rúa, the UCR head of the city of Buenos Aires's autonomous government, becoming the opposition's presidential candidate. De la Rúa's ample victory over FREPASO's Graciela Fernández Meijide led the latter campaigner for human rights to accept the slot of Alliance candidate for the governorship of the key province of Buenos Aires, with FREPASO's Carlos Alvarez teaming up with De la Rúa as the opposition's aspiring vice-president. Spokespersons for both parties sought to assure investors that the existing one-to-one parity between the Argentine peso and the U.S. dollar would not be compromised by an Alliance victory in October 1999.

Although in principle Menem was barred from seeking a third term—based on the country's 1994 constitution, which he himself had helped craft—like numbers of his supporters, he regarded this as a matter of interpretation. Menem's wish not to leave the Argentine political scene was seen as standing in the way of a PJ decision on who should be the party's presidential candidate, but this did not prevent the Peronist governor of Buenos Aires province, Eduardo Duhalde, from campaigning for the job, with Ramón Ortega, a one-time PJ governor of the northwestern province of Tucumán, temporarily appearing as Menem's favorite for the position.

Israel and the Middle East

The Argentine government, increasingly disappointed with the Netanyahu government's lack of movement on the peace process, postponed a mooted presidential visit to Israel. On the other hand, Argentina's new ambassador in Tel Aviv, Vicente Espeche Gil, was the country's first career diplomat who has achieved a degree of fluency in modern Hebrew. A former head of the foreign ministry's Middle East department during Alfonsín's presidency and a one-time ambassador to Algeria, Espeche also served at the Holy See.

Argentina's support for the Palestine Authority (PA) combined modest contributions for the development of Palestinian infrastructure and occasional political advice. Argentina pledged a total of $1.2 million over three years for the

PA at the international donors' conference organized by the United States at the State Department in Washington in November. Indeed, Argentina was the sole Latin American participant.

Many Argentines did not share Menem's approbation of the U.S.-led military action against Iraq and his interest in pursuing an Argentine role, albeit a non-combative one, in the Persian Gulf. Opposition parties and other Menem critics sought unsuccessfully to challenge in Congress and through the judiciary the right of the president unilaterally to pursue such a policy. The debate was colored largely by the shared conviction that a higher profile in the Middle East than had been historically the case until the early 1990s had turned Argentina into an obvious target for terrorist attacks.

Bearing in mind the attack in February 1992 against the Israeli embassy and the bombing of the Buenos Aires Jewish community headquarters (AMIA) in July 1994, generally believed to have been Middle East-inspired, it was clear that progress on the Palestinian-Israeli and American-Iranian peace fronts—factors well beyond Argentina's control—could still affect the security of the country and the welfare of its inhabitants. Against this background, the importance of goodwill gestures was highlighted during the Argentine president's tour of Lebanon in February 1998, which in part was to reciprocate Lebanese prime minister Rafiq Hariri's 1995 visit to Argentina, and which earned Menem credit among Lebanon's inhabitants, including those suspected, though it was by no means proved, of having had a role in the anti-Israel and anti-Jewish attacks in Buenos Aires that left a toll of some 120 deaths and several hundred wounded.

The view of anti-Menem critics that the visit was prompted by a wish to appease Hezballah and the latter's regional supporters plainly ignored the basics of diplomacy, in this case the need to provide a semblance of equidistance to his country's clear pro-Israel Middle East shift, itself a functional consequence of Argentina's international alignment with the United States during his incumbency. It was also oblivious to the benefits reaped from trade with Lebanon, which had yielded an accumulated surplus of some $100 million in Argentina's favor since 1992. More importantly, the visit provided an opportunity to express Argentine backing for Lebanese territorial integrity: Menem's address to the legislature in Beirut focused on Argentine support for Security Council resolution 425, which calls for Israel's withdrawal from southern Lebanon.

Most importantly for Argentinians of Arab ancestry, whose nonscientific self-estimates include 1.5 million persons of Lebanese descent and 3 million of Syrian descent, was the fact that Argentine journalists, following Menem's visit, described Hezballah as a political party rather than a Shi'ite terrorist organization. However, in Egypt, during the subsequent leg of his trip, Menem clearly condemned "the scourge of international terrorism" and confirmed that Argentina's security controls—including a more thorough screening of non-Israeli Middle Eastern visa applicants, as well as the planned introduction of a new computer link of all the country's border crossings with a central database—had been increased to avoid the possibility of foreign-inspired terrorist attacks.

Menem's tour also helped promote Argentina's exports to its Middle East markets, the foremost being Egypt, Iran, Israel, and Turkey. In Egypt, the Argetine president joined his Egyptian counterpart, Hosni Mubarak, in the opening of a 22-megawatt nuclear reactor, intended for the production of isotopes for medical use and personnel training, built by Invap, an industrial offshoot of Argentina's Bariloche-based Atomic Center. None of this, however, represented a detour from Argentina's Mideast policy since 1991, which remained largely pro-Israel.

With respect to Iran, Argentina's unilateral reduction of diplomatic relations after the AMIA bombing in 1994 was followed in May 1998 by a decision to downgrade diplomatic relations to their minimum expression, limiting the number of Iranian representatives in the country to a single chargé d'affaires. Tehran responded by suspending commodity and other purchases worth more than $658 million in 1997. The decision to downgrade relations followed the visit to Argentina of Louis Freeh, director of the FBI, and an FBI report suggesting the existence of evidence, though not conclusive, of Iranian involvement in the embassy and AMIA bombings. A statement by the Argentine foreign minister that he was awaiting "proof positive [of Iran's role] to cut off diplomatic relations" confirmed why links with Tehran were not severed after all. The decision to avoid such drastic action was also influenced by Iran's acknowledged shift to a more accommodating attitude toward the United States and its allies after the election of Mohamed Khatami as the country's head of state, and Argentina's understandable interest in safeguarding as much as possible its commercial position in Tehran at a time when the world price of commodities has been falling.

The Argentine government took pains to stress that suspicions of an Iranian role in the bombings were not meant to cast aspersions on Islam and its local followers, claiming instead that in Argentina the Muslim faith and Islamic culture enjoy "the utmost respect."

Holocaust-Related Matters

In August the Commission of Inquiry into the Activities of Nazism in Argentina (CEANA)—presented the second of three interim reports at a conference held at American University's Washington School of Law. The commission's charge included determining a reliable estimate of the war criminals who settled in the country and the conditions that made their arrival possible; establishing whether Nazi loot was stashed away in Argentina or shipped elsewhere from Argentine ports; and, at the instigation of the B'nai B'rith, assessing the impact of Nazism in Argentine society, government, and political culture.

CEANA's report referred to the existence of some 150 named war criminals who had struck roots in Argentina, comprising German, Franco-Belgian, and Eastern European war criminals. This number was bound to rise as research in Argentine and foreign archives progressed. Included among the newly detected war criminals were Emile Dewoitine—the father of Argentina's first jet aircraft, the Pulqui I, who was condemned in absentia by the French to a 20-year forced labor term in 1948, when he was already in Argentina—and Radislaw Ostrowsky and Ante Pavelic, the presidents, respectively, of the pro-Nazi regimes of Belorussia and Croatia. Surpassing previous knowledge on the subject, CEANA's report also throws light on Perón's links with collaborationist war criminals who created a society that sponsored the arrival of like-minded Europeans, who lived unmolested long after Perón was deposed.

The CEANA findings were discussed at the commission's plenary session in Buenos Aires in November 1998. The meeting was opened by U.S. undersecretary of state Stuart Eizenstat, who declared CEANA "a world-class effort," an evaluation repeated by Sidney Clearfield, B'nai B'rith's executive vice-president, at the closing press conference. Other favorable comments were made by Sir Sigmund Sternberg, of the International Council of Christians and Jews; David Harris, executive director of the American Jewish Committee; Manuel Tenenbaum, executive director of the Latin American Jewish Congress (CJL); Adolfo Gass, a vice-president of Argentina's Permanent Assembly for Human Rights and former Radical party senator; and Marcos Aguinis, a former CJL assistant deputy director and secretary of culture during the Alfonsín administration. Argentine foreign minister Guido Di Tella, who also addressed the assemblage, urged dissemination of the commission's findings among students of all ages, as well as all Argentinians, since the lessons of the Nazi and other genocides could help prevent their recurrence. The plenary unanimously decided to extend CEANA's mandate for a second year.

NAZI GOLD

In June 1998 the U.S. State Department released the so-called Eizenstat II report, a study of the Nazi-era performance of the various states that remained neutral during World War II, Chile and Ireland excepted. This confirmed the U.S. Treasury's conclusion on Argentina of May 1946, namely, that "Argentina had not become a haven for looted gold or assets." Moreover, Argentine documents scrutinized more recently by the U.S. embassy led to the following clarification: no gold "had come [to Argentina] from Axis sources," a statement in stark contrast to an array of hitherto unsubstantiated claims that wartime transactions in gold between the Portuguese and Argentine central banks were a channel for laundering Nazi gold and that Peronist Argentina had forwarded 25 tons of Nazi gold to Paraguay. The Eizenstat report also declared: "nor were any caches of gems or art treasures looted by Germans officially uncovered in Argentina."

Without ignoring the unique base for operations that Argentina had afforded to Nazi agents in South America, and their smuggling out of the country "small quantities" of strategic materials needed by the Third Reich's war machine, Eizenstat II acknowledged that Argentina, unlike the other neutral states under scrutiny, "did not play a significant role in sustaining the Nazi war effort." Instead, Argentina was described as the Americas' foremost recipient of Jews fleeing Nazi persecution during 1933-45, a period that saw the arrival of some 45,000 Jewish refugees, not all of them legally.

Pursuant to Argentina's pledge at the London conference on Nazi gold to contribute funds to the Eizenstat-proposed compensation fund for Jewish and other victims of Nazism, a bill to that effect was drafted. While the legislature had yet to approve it, Argentina remained the sole Latin American contributor by the time of the Washington Conference on Nazi Era Assets in December 1998, with its proposed contribution of $300,000 exceeding that of some central and Eastern European states.

NAZI WAR CRIMINALS

Argentina's position as the Latin American state with the highest number of extraditions was confirmed in May by the judiciary's expeditious approval of Dinko Sakic's return to Croatia. Sakic was also sought by Yugoslavia because of the countless Serbs murdered at the Jasenovac concentration camp during World War II, run by the pro-Nazi Croatian regime. The case of this former camp commander, active during 1942-44, had already elicited a B'nai B'rith request to Croatian president Franjo Tudjman, in July 1995, to have him brought to justice.

Argentina's evident interest in recent years in erasing the stigma of Nazism also resulted in a headline-grabbing, though unfortunately self-defeating, initiative. Aimed at securing the additional extradition of other former Ustasis in Argentina, the Wiesenthal Center first targeted Juan (Ivo) Rojnica—a Buenos Aires-based industrialist whom Croatian president Tudjman had originally sought to accredit as his country's first ambassador to Argentina, in recognition of his role in promoting South American diplomatic recognition of the newly independent Croatian state. Solid evidence of Rojnica's war criminality amounted to little more than his being the alleged signatory of a 1941 edict banning the free circulation of Serbs, Jews, and others in the region of Dubrovnik. Neither Croatia nor Yugoslavia, nor for that matter other countries with jurisdiction in such cases, sought to bring Rojnica to trial. Not surprisingly, Rojnica's daughter protested her father's innocence in Argentina's largest circulation daily, while the Wiesenthal Center's Buenos Aires representative was left in the unenviable position of having to admit in public that the center was still looking for convicting evidence. The Wiesenthal Center's admission prompted Rojnica to initiate legal action against Magda Drnasin, who had accused him of being a war criminal, in order to clear his name.

The second target was Sakic's wife, Esperanza (Nada) Luburic Sakic, a former commander of the Stara Gradiska concentration camp's female section. Evidence made available to the Argentine Interior Ministry by the Wiesenthal Center in Jerusalem led to her extradition, which had been requested by both Yugoslavia and Croatia and was granted to the latter, where she was flown back in October 1998. Not long after this, though, Mrs. Sakic's case was dismissed, with her release from custody generating no protests on the part of the United States, Israel, and other interested parties. Indeed, an evaluation by the American embassy concluded that Croatian justice had acted fairly in weighing the evidence against her.

The risks posed by claims unsubstantiated by evidence were also on display when Israel's ambassador Yizhak Aviran declared in June 1998 that there were "more war criminals, Nazis, and anti-Semites" in Bariloche, the city from which Erich Priebke had been extradited to Italy three years earlier. While the Israeli envoy's statement was on the mark insofar as Nazis and anti-Semites were concerned, his inability to identify the war criminals he had in mind lent credence to Bariloche mayor César Miguel's riposte: "The passion elicited by the subject of what happened with the persecution of Jews during World War II sometimes results in the loss of perspective, and in generalizations." That official reaction in Bariloche was not limited to Miguel's mild rebuff became evident when city councillors of all political stripes, including the ruling PJ and opposition UCR and FREPASO, supported a resolution directing the Argentine foreign ministry to request Aviran to furnish all the information he had on the subject. This was a polite, though barely concealed, sign of their irritation at the Israeli diplomat's earlier proclaimed inability to name names, and more generally perhaps at his comments over the years on issues that are not part of a foreign representative's bailiwick.

HOLOCAUST MEMORIAL

In November 1998 a replica of the London monument to Raoul Wallenberg was dedicated in a central Buenos Aires square. It commemorated the rescue efforts in wartime Hungary of this Swedish diplomat who had also acted as a sort of Argentine foreign service official, inasmuch as Argentine interests in Berlin, Budapest, and other European capitals were represented by Sweden after Argentina's severance of diplomatic relations with the Axis early in 1944. The initiative for the memorial came from Sir Sigmund Sternberg, who in 1997 approached the Argentine foreign minister, Guido di Tella, and the head of the city of Buenos Aires's autonomous government, Fernando de la Rúa, to secure official funding as well as a site. The unveiling of the monument was presided over by the foreign minister, who took the opportunity to praise Simón Margel, a Jewish clerk of the former Argentine consulate in the wartime Hungarian capital, who was entrusted by the Swedes with the daily running of Argentine affairs and who saved numbers of fellow Jews. Other speakers included Sweden's commerce minister, Leif Pagrotsky; Fernando de la Rúa; and Raoul Wallenberg's half-brother, Guy von Dardel. The ceremony was also attended by an array of Argentine and foreign diplomats and city of Buenos Aires officials, as well as representatives of ethnic and religious groups. Particularly noteworthy was the presence of Arab community representatives, among them religious leaders of Argentina's Orthodox, Muslim, and Druze communities, as well as lay leaders of the Buenos Aires-based Lebanese Club and the Cedars Foundation. In conjunction with the unveiling, the postal authorities issued a Wallenberg commemorative stamp.

Anti-Semitism

According to *Antisemitism World Report*, issued in London by the Institute of Jewish Policy Research and the American Jewish Committee, anti-Jewish manifestations decreased in 1998, after a peak recorded during 1996-97. However, this did not still fears of Judeophobia, especially after the collapse in 1998 of two Jewish-owned banks, Banco Patricios and Banco Mayo. (See below.) Banco Patricios's failure brought with it, among other losses, the evaporation of over $4 million of the monies contributed by the Argentine government toward the rebuilding of the AMIA headquarters. Even more disturbing was the fact that Banco Mayo, DAIA (the representative body of Argentine Jews), and the World Jewish Congress's Latin American constituent (CJL) were presided over by Rubén Beraja, a man who was regarded by many in the Jewish community as having set his bank's interests above his Jewish concerns; indeed, it was felt that for this reason he had failed to support investigations of the AMIA and Israeli embassy bombings as vigorously as some of the victims' relatives and human-rights activists would have expected. All this generated greater media interest in Beraja himself than in the irregularities surrounding Banco Patricios' collapse.

For the first time since antidiscrimination legislation was enacted in 1988, DAIA appeared as the aggrieved party in the trial of suspects accused of anti-Jewish activity. Originally suspected of being responsible for one of the vandalizations of a Buenos Aires Jewish cemetery, the defendants in question were instead prosecuted and convicted as disseminators of literature inciting to anti-Jewish hatred. The chief defendant, Jorge Russo, affiliated with the ruling Justicialist Party, was sentenced to prison for two and a half years; his codefendants—Aparicio Torres, Emilio Cañete, and Juan Núñez—were given shorter sentences. Since the four had been held in custody since 1996, the verdict meant they would all be released. DAIA's legal counsel, Jorge Kirszenbaum, declared himself satisfied with the outcome, an implicit recognition of the possibility that the four could have received lighter sentences. Russo and his codefendants, however, initiated legal action ultimately aimed at a Supreme Court ruling as to whether the entire process had not been vitiated by the trampling of their constitutional rights.

Contrary to the predictions of some doomsayers that Jews would shy away from resorting to the aforementioned legislation, or that the judiciary would not allow such cases to proceed, Kirszenbaum, who for a short while served in 1998 as elected president of the left-of-center Jewish community group Convergencia (Convergence), also acted on behalf of DAIA in the case against Gen. Carlos Suárez Mason, who admitted to a Buenos Aires weekly that he was not free of anti-Jewish prejudice.

JEWISH COMMUNITY

Demography

The size of Argentine Jewry had been estimated in 1994 at 208,000 by the Hebrew University's Institute of Contemporary Jewry, but some Jewish leaders regarded this figure as too low. In November 1998, during a visit to Buenos Aires, Jacob Kovadloff, the American Jewish Committee consultant on Latin America, and the Argentine Ashkenazi Jewish community (AMIA) held talks about the possibility of jointly sponsoring a new demographic study of Argentine Jewry, with Hebrew University demographer Sergio DellaPergola agreeing to undertake such an update once the requisite financing was secured.

Communal Affairs

The year 1998 was dominated by the collapse of two Jewish-owned cooperative banks—Banco Patricios and Banco Mayo—from which various Jewish institutions received a measure of support through overdraft facilities, commercial and soft loans, and/or grants. The failure of Patricios in March 1998, following the discovery of undocumented debts that were reported to the judiciary, and later that of Mayo, took place against the backdrop of banking activities worldwide being increasingly concentrated in the hands of fewer, larger, generally more efficiently run, privately owned credit institutions. (Mayo had been among the early beneficiaries of this trend, having absorbed six other banks in May-December 1995, and bidding successfully for Patricios in June 1998.) Although no depositor lost a single penny, not all the members of the respective work-forces were absorbed by successors after the change in ownership of Patricios and Mayo. Moreover, depositors seeking higher yields with Mayo's offshore operations or through both banks' informal operations in Argentina suffered heavily. Likewise, because some of the grants to institutions were recorded as loans, various Jewish bodies were left saddled with debts, which led several to seek assistance from the World Jewish Congress in New York. For its part, AMIA unsuccessfully sought Israeli and U.S. Jewish support.

Leaving aside the pain endured by numbers of employees and depositors, Patricio's and Mayo's collapse may have signaled the end of an era; without a drastic rethinking of the form and allocation of funds raised locally, the banks' failure was bound to result in the survival of only the economically fittest Jewish institutions. Indeed, this was the alarmist view of some, including Carlos Szraibman, the new DAIA administration's secretary general, for whom both banks' fate was akin to a third terrorist attack.

In fact, rather than being the result of terrorism, Patricios went under due to internal mismanagement and the withdrawal of some $25 million by a big depositor and potential buyer in February 1998. Mayo's problems derived from the proposed sale of its credit-card operations to the Connecticut-based Newbridge fund falling through because of the latter's losses in debt-ridden Russia. In both cases, the chain of developments triggered an unstoppable wave of withdrawals. Seeking to restore investors' confidence, the Central Bank pumped some $326 milion into Banco Mayo, a figure in excess of the latter's assets and the highest level of assistance ever offered to an ailing credit institution since 1991. Some of the monies, the Central Bank later concluded, were "unacceptably" used to benefit firms belonging to Mayo shareholders and associates.

With the closing of Banco Mayo, Rubén Beraja, the high-profile president of both the bank and DAIA, was forced to give up all his communal positions. Briefly mentioned as a candidate for the vacated DAIA presidency was author Marcos Aguinis, a former CJL and Alfonsín administration official, whose bid, had he considered running, would have been supported by, among others, the Israeli ambassador. By year's end, Beraja's former secretary general, Rogelio Cichowolsky, secured the position. Far from being unanimously elected, Cichowolsky's success was due to the support he received from different institutions (whose representatives choose the DAIA president on the basis of one institution-one vote), including the sports and social clubs he hailed from, as well as the Orthodox and Masorti (Conservative) Jewish movements.

The problems created by the loss of a third of government funds for the reconstruction of the destroyed AMIA headquarters, with the AMIA leadership appealing to Israel for aid, prompted the Jewish Agency in Jerusalem to dispatch a delegation to Buenos Aires to report on Argentine Jewry's predicament in the aftermath of the bank debacle. The visit confirmed Israel's traditional perception of Diaspora Jewry as a potential reservoir of immigrants for the Jewish state. Hence, the delegation urged the promotion of a system of Zionist education, rather than recommending that the lion's share of funds raised for Israel be allocated for local use.

Journalist Herman Schiller, the late Masorti rabbi Marshall Meyer's partner as co-founder of the Jewish Movement for Human Rights (MJDH) in the 1980s and more recently involved in the setting up of Memoria Activa, had his four-day-a-week "Memoria y realidad" (Memory and Reality) radio program on FM Chai (spelled Jai in Spanish) cut from two hours daily to single hour and later in the year terminated altogether. Although the management of the Buenos Aires Jewish broadcasting station ascribed both moves to business considerations, political factors were undoubtedly involved as well. Schiller took a consistently anti-Menem government line and was also quite critical toward official Israeli policies. Several hundred listeners and other supporters protested the move. Some of them joined in setting up a Memoria y realidad human-rights organization, and together with a number of city of Buenos Aires lawmakers tried unsuccesfully to intercede on Schiller's behalf with Chai proprietor Miguel Steuermann. A subsequent request to the Buenos Aires legislature that a time slot for a Schiller program be allocated on Radio Ciudad, the local government-supported AM broadcaster, was granted. This gave Schiller the opportunity to reach a potentially wider audience with his one-hour weekly broadcast on Saturdays night.

In September the finances of the Buenos Aires Jewish hospital Ezrah resulted in a drastic reduction in the number of beds, from 400 to 250, and prompted the institution's management to fire over a hundred members of its staff. While the victims of these measures raised questions concerning the ethical probity of what they viewed as Ezrah's self-perpetuating management, many factors contributed to the situation.

Memorials to the Bombing Victims

In September 1998, not long after the fourth anniversary of the attack against AMIA, a sculpture designed and donated by Israeli artist Ya'acov Agam was unveiled in the presence of community leaders, as well as relatives and friends of the victims, at the site where the Jewish community headquarters was being rebuilt. Unlike the competition organized by the sponsors of Project Hatikvah—the planned square to be developed with local and foreign donor support at the former Israel embassy site—the AMIA statue was commissioned from Agam directly. Without calling into question his credentials, some Argentine Jews would have preferred to see the commission go to a local artist, especially in a country that boasts such sculptors as Noemí Gerstein, who in the 1950s was one of the winners of the London-based Institute of Contemporary Arts competition for the design of a monument to the unknown political prisoner, and internationally renowned Marta Minujin, who three decades later created a pyramid of books in central Buenos Aires (to symbolize the freedom of thought that had been recovered after its severe curtailment by the military during 1976-83). In a decision to use local talent, Memoria Activa, an organization dedicated to the memory of those killed in the Israeli embassy and AMIA bombings, commissioned a memorial from Mirta Kuperminc that was erected in July 1996 in Libertad Square, where relatives and supporters of the victims met every Monday morning to demonstrate against the government's apparent unwillingness to investigate the horrors.

Jewish-Christian Relations

In March 1998, Monsignor Justo Laguna, bishop of the greater Buenos Aires town of Morón, opened his cathedral for an ecumenical service for relatives and supporters of the Christian and Jewish victims of the attacks against the Israeli embassy and AMIA, on the occasion of the sixth anniversary of the embassy bombing. Mario Rojzman, a Masorti rabbi of Beth El synagogue, who is also associated with Memoria Activa, participated in the service. He described the commemoration as a truly "historic" occasion.

A month later, Laguna and Rojzman went on a joint pilgrimage to Jerusalem and Rome, described in a volume of their reflections—*Todos los caminos conducen a Jerusalem . . . y tambien a Roma*(All roads lead to Jerusalem . . . and also to Rome)—as the first such sacred journey undertaken ever by a Latin American bishop and a rabbi. During their meeting with Pope John Paul II, they delivered a Memoria Activa letter requesting papal support for the group's efforts to see the cases of both bombings resolved.

In October, Buenos Aires' First Methodist Church organized a dialogue on "Abraham, Faith, and Exile," with presentations based on Jewish, Christian, and Muslim sources, by, respectively, Masorti rabbi Daniel Goldman of Beth El; Catholic priest Hugo Mujica; Methodist bishop Aldo Etchegoyen; and Sheikh Abdul Karim Paz, director of the al-Tawhid Shiite Muslim mosque. All four religious leaders were also the first recipients of the Ecumenical Award for Dialogue and Social Justice, a new honor created by the Ecumenic Press (PE) news agency on its 15th anniversary.

As in previous years, in November B'nai Brith, the Catholic archdiocese of Buenos Aires, and AMIA sponsored a walk in support of the integration of handicapped persons. Later that month, *Kristallnacht* was commemorated at a B'nai Brith-initiated gathering in a Buenos Aires Catholic church, the basilica of Our Lady of Guadeloupe. The program included the reading of a text coauthored by Rabbi Leon Klenicki, a former Buenoes Aires pulpit rabbi currently serving as the Anti-Defamation League's director of interfaith affairs.

In late 1998 the Argentine Episcopal Conference's Commission on Ecumenism and Relations with Judaism and Other Creeds organized a two-day meeting to discuss the concept of spirit in Catholic, Jewish, and Muslim revealed texts. Part of a growing effort to familiarize the country's clergy with Islam and its local leaders, and in the process recover for Argentina's Catholic Church an important role in the construction of a pluralist society, the two-day event included presentations by Imam Mahmud Husain, director of the Buenos Aires-based Center of Islamic Studies; Masorti rabbi Abraham Skorka, rector of the Latin American Rabbinical Seminary; and Monsignor Luis Rivas.

Publications

April 1998 saw the publication of *Proyecto Testimonio* (Memorial Project), a two-volume selection of documents on Nazis and Nazism in Argentina. Arising out of research sponsored by DAIA, the first volume was compiled by Beatriz Gurevich and features documents which reveal that the Perón government had enlisted the support of alleged and convicted war criminals, as well as of other tainted Europeans, as "informal advisers" to the Immigration Directorate. *Tes-*

timonio's second volume was compiled by Paul Warszawski, who also authored an important analysis of Argentina's record on Nazi war criminal extraditions. The two volumes failed to support reports in the *New York Times*, dating back to 1993 and 1997 respectively, about researchers of DAIA having unearthed data on more than 1,000 Nazi war criminal suspects in Argentina. In fact, DAIA executive director Claudio Avruj clarified that his organization subscribes "to no figure that is beyond substantiation in evidence."

Another volume that did not substantiate the claims of the *New York Times* articles was *Perón y los alemanes. La verdad sobre el espionaje nazi y los fugitivos del Reich* (Perón and the Germans: The Truth about Nazi Espionage and the Reich's Fugitives) by Uki Goñi. The volume is noteworthy for its investigative journalism, but it contains a number of factual inaccuracies, such as the suggestion that Joseph Mengele arrived in Buenos Aires with an Argentine passport instead of, as has been proved, a Red Cross travel document (a fact that does not, however, contradict Peronist Argentina's welcoming attitude toward former Nazis).

Another volume on a similar theme was *War Criminals and Nazism in Latin America: Fifty Years Later*, a collection of essays drawn from a conference at the Holocaust Memorial Museum in Washington, by a group of Argentina specialists—Sandra McGee Deutsch, Ignacio Klich, Ronald Newton, Leonardo Senkman, and Paul Warszawski—in addition to contributions by American University legal experts on the subject of Nazi and other war criminal trials, orginally presented at a B'nai B'rith-organized symposium two years earlier.

Alejandro Bertocchi Morán's *El Graf Spee en la trampa de Montevideo* (The Graf Spee in the Montevideo Trap), a book about the German warship scuttled in the Rio de la Plata in 1939, marked the return to Nazi subject matter by one of Argentina's surviving nationalist publishing houses, Ayer y Hoy (earlier responsible for a biography of Martin Bormann and a single issue of a magazine devoted to Eichmann in Argentina).

Memoria activa. 4 años de impunidad (Active Memory: Four Years of Impunity) is a collection of speeches made in 1997–98 by relatives of the victims of the Israeli embassy and AMIA bombings, at weekly gatherings opposite Buenos Aires's foremost court building, as well as statements by local and foreign friends of Memoria Activa and human-rights campaigners.

Arab and Jewish Immigrants in Latin America: Images and Realities, compiled by Ignacio Klich and Jeffrey Lesser, is the first collection of academic essays comparing the experiences of both groups in Argentina and other countries. Raanan Rein's *Peronismo, populismo y politica. Argentina 1943–1955* (Peronism, Populism and Politics: Argentina 1943–1955) is a varied collection of essays, some of which appeared first in Hebrew, highlighting the importance of modern Latin American studies at Tel Aviv University. The American Jewish Joint Distribution Committee-sponsored *En el mundo hay lugar para los dos. Una indagación acerca de la diferencia* (There Is Room for Both in the World: An Exploration of Difference) is a thought-provoking volume about difference and dissent by social psychologist Juan Jorge Nudel, a highly respected Jewish community adviser on group and institutional dynamics.

Financial constraints, in effect the ripple effects of Banco Patricios's failure, led to the shutdown of the weekly newspaper *Masorti*, leaving *Mundo Israelita*, *Comunidades*, and *La Voz Judía* as the sole remaining Jewish weeklies/fortnightlies. The Jewish cable TV channel Alef, partly owned by Rubén Beraja, did not survive the financial turbulence following Banco Mayo's collapse. It was eventually sold to a group led by Fernando Sokolowicz, publisher of the daily *Página/12*.

Personalia

Presidential secretary Alberto Kohan (whose father was Jewish) and Foreign Minister Guido di Tella—who accompanied President Menem to Lebanon—were among the 36 Argentine recipients of Lebanon's National Order of the Cedar.

In November Joseph Domberger was given B'nai B'rith Argentina's Dignity and Justice award for his work in support of Latin American Jewish communities. The Latin American Jewish Congress did not award its Human Rights prize in 1998, but writer Simja Sneh received the organization's Intellectual Merit award.

Alberto Laniado, scion of a prominent Lebanese Jewish family active in Sephardic circles, died, at the age of 94, in June 1998. Felipe Yaryura, president of the Buenos Aires-based Lebanese Club, delivered the eulogy at the ceremony marking the 30th day after burial.

IGNACIO KLICH

Western Europe

Great Britain

National Affairs

IN 1998 THE LABOR GOVERNMENT headed by Tony Blair had to confront the intractable issue of Northern Ireland and to limit the damage arising from dissension within its own ranks, over personalities and policies. On the whole it emerged unscathed, though this good fortune certainly owed much to the weakness of the Tories and their failure to exploit Labor embarrassments.

On the economic front, Chancellor Gordon Brown's second budget in March introduced a tax credit for working families and extended additional help to the poor. This was in line with the government's policy of making work pay. Industry, on the other hand, especially exporters, suffered from the strong pound, which was strengthened even further in June when the Bank of England raised interest rates .25 percent to 7.5 percent, aiming to reduce the risk of inflation induced by wage rises. Not until October did the bank cut base rates, by a quarter of a percent, under growing political pressure, which became especially acute when the chancellor abandoned his relatively optimistic growth forecast in the March budget and in the autumn predicted lower growth than in earlier forecasts.

The unpromising Northern Ireland situation improved markedly with the Good Friday agreement signed in April, which created a new Northern Ireland assembly and extended cooperation between the province and the Irish Republic. A May referendum in favor of the agreement gave a boost to the peace process, but the problem of decommissioning arms remained, a situation that was highlighted in August by one of the worst bombings in 30 years of violence, which killed 29 people in Omagh and wounded 250. This was the work of a splinter group, the "Real IRA," which subsequently announced a ceasefire.

The relative degree of benefit that accrued to the government through its success in the Irish question was offset by the enforced resignation of the Welsh Secretary, Ron Davies, who had to admit to "a very foolish" act on Clapham Common, London. A more serious blow was the enforced resignation in December of Peter Mandelson, minister for Trade and Industry, personal friend of Premier Tony Blair and the man widely credited with organizing Labor's victory in the

1997 general election. Mandelson resigned when it became known that he had accepted a substantial loan of £373,000 from Paymaster General and millionaire businessman Geoffrey Robinson, whose business affairs were being investigated by civil servants from Mandelson's own department. Robinson also had to resign. The Tories were not able to exploit to the full these problems. Not only was their leader, William Hague, unable to reconcile the conflicting pro- and anti-Europe wings within his party but he also became embroiled with the Tory peers, whose leader, Lord Cranbourne, he summarily dismissed in December. This followed the revelation that Cranbourne, unknown to Hague, had entered into a deal with Tony Blair over a proposed change in the structure of the House of Lords. This would have retained 91 hereditary peers in the house, from which Blair was intending to remove the hereditary element entirely.

Israel and the Middle East

"Our policy is neither pro-Israel or pro-Arab, but pro-peace," said Prime Minister Tony Blair in January. Furtherance of the Middle East peace process was Britain's key international priority, not only for her presidency of the European Union (EU) from January to June but for her policy throughout the year, with the proviso that the role envisaged lay solely in supporting the American initiative.

Calls by Britain for the redeployment of Israel troops and for a halt to Jewish settlements on the West Bank punctuated the year up to the Wye accord in October, balanced by demands that the Palestinians make a hundred percent effort in matters of security. In March Alistair Crooke, a British diplomat and expert on security techniques, was appointed to help the Palestinians control terrorism.

Britain's efforts as EU president to unjam the stalled peace process began in January when Foreign Office minister Derek Fatchett visited Israel, where he conveyed British and European concern over the state of the peace negotiations to Prime Minister Benjamin Netanyahu and met with Palestinian Authority president Yasir Arafat in Gaza. Arafat subsequently assured Blair explicitly that the Palestinians' call for Israel's annihilation was annulled, enabling Blair to state, amidst continued Israeli anxiety, that the issue of the Palestine National Covenant "need no longer hamper the peace talks."

Condemnation of Israel's settlement policy caused an upset in March when British foreign secretary Robin Cook, on a six-nation Middle East tour to promote the peace process, visited Israel's controversial Har Homa housing project on the outskirts of Jerusalem. Describing the expansion of settlements "as one of the main difficulties in the peace process," Cook further provoked Israeli wrath by shaking hands with Palestinian official Salah Ta'Amri and placing a wreath at the site of Deir Yassin, where Irgun members killed Arab villagers in 1948. Netanyahu, incensed, canceled a scheduled dinner with Cook, and Labor's opposition leader Ehud Barak said Cook had displayed "great arrogance."

In London, the Board of Deputies of British Jews withdrew an invitation for Cook to address its annual fund-raising dinner. This evoked sharp comments about the board's representative status in the national press from Jewish Labor MP Gerald Kaufman. Notwithstanding, Cook described his talks with Netanyahu as "amicable and productive." Blair, while supporting his foreign secretary's actions, also considered ties with Israel "very good." He worked to cement them when he went to the Middle East in April, winning Israeli favor by visiting Yad Vashem, introducing United Jewish Israel Appeal (UJIA) Blair Fellowships for exchange trips between British and Israeli youth, and initiating London talks between Netanyahu and the Palestinians.

Blair could claim to be "a profound friend of Israel" when he and Cook attended a reception at London's Israeli embassy in May to celebrate Israel's 50th anniversary, marked in synagogues countrywide and at a daylong extravaganza, attended by thousands, in Wembley Stadium in Middlesex. A coalition of groups including the Palestinian Solidarity Campaign, the Council for the Advancement of Arab-British Understanding, and the London Friends of Palestine planned to mark "50 Years of the Palestinian Tragedy" with a service at Westminster Cathedral.

Britain's September decision to raise diplomatic ties with Iran to ambassadorial level alarmed Israeli officials, who cautioned against overlooking Teheran's extremism, noting that Iran still opposed the peace process. Foreign Secretary Cook's address to the Labor Party conference in Blackpool in October, expressing hope for "a new relationship and for wider dialogue between the West and the Islamic world to promote understanding and combat prejudice," was counterbalanced by a speech by Blair at a meeting organized by Labor Friends of Israel in which he described Anglo-Jewry as a source of strength to Britain. The prime minister was presented with an honorary doctorate from the Hebrew University of Jerusalem in recognition of his concern for peace, "illustrated by his pivotal role in Northern Ireland and his furtherance of diplomatic relations between Israel and its neighbors."

Britain welcomed the Wye accord signed by Israel and the Palestinian Authority in October and also Israel's implementation of an initial redeployment from the West Bank under its terms in November. A British-Israeli cooperation pact covering the development of military technology—but not relating to weapons of mass destruction—was signed that month, reflected Whitehall's satisfaction. Both Israeli and British officials described as highly successful a visit by Netanyahu to London in November, when he urged Blair and Cook to express their objection to Arafat's suggestion that he might unilaterally proclaim a Palestinian state in May 1999.

In June a petition was presented at an EU summit meeting in Cardiff, Wales, urging European leaders to help free Israeli servicemen, including airman Ron Arad, missing in action since 1986. The petition was organized by the Campaign for Missing Soldiers and bore 80,000 signatures. In August the government pledged to continue to play a full role in international efforts to discover the servicemen's fate. In November, on the 12th anniversary of Arad's capture, a vigil was held outside the London offices of the Red Cross.

Anti-Semitism and Racism

The number of anti-Semitic incidents increased to 179 in the first nine months of 1998 from 169 in the comparable 1997 period, according to figures issued by the Jewish communal monitoring body, Community Security Trust. The Institute for Jewish Policy Research and the American Jewish Committee, who issued the figures in their annual review of world anti-Semitism, attributed the rise to the tension in the Middle East. The small increase did not, however, interrupt the general downward trend, whihch was ascribed to more effective policing, more criminal prosecutions, and the Jewish community's more determined attitude. Increased incidents were reported in the same 1998 period of the most common offense, abusive behavior (to 104 from 63) and distribution of offensive literature (to 28 from 23); but damage and desecration of communal property decreased (to 21 from 49), with no recurrence of the large-scale desecration of cemeteries and synagogues that occurred in previous years. In general, the review concludes, Jews in Britain do not experience the same levels of discrimination as other, more visible, ethnic groups. Public expressions of anti-Semitic attitudes come mainly from the political fringe, either far right or Islamist.

European cooperation to combat racism was apparent in February when three suspected neo-Nazis were arrested in Essex on extradition warrants by Scotland Yard, acting on behalf of the French authorities. The same month, the British-based Inter-Parliamentary Council Against Racism made plans for a conference to stem proliferating anti-Semitic propaganda on the Internet, following a report by London law firm Denton Hall that it had found 600 anti-Semitic and other racist Web sites. In April a site used by the Muslim extremist group Al Muhajiroun was shut down by its Internet service provider who claimed its contents were offensive and anti-Semitic.

In January charges of incitement to racial hatred against 84-year-old Dowager Lady Birdwood at the Old Bailey were halted on medical grounds. Birdwood had received a suspended jail sentence for distributing racist literature in 1994 but "no longer had the mental capacity" to stand trial, said Attorney-General John Morris, making it clear that he still considered her material a breach of the Public Order Act. Nicholas Griffin, the editor and publisher of a white separatist magazine, *The Rune*, in 1996, was given a nine-month suspended sentence for incitement to racial hatred, while distributor Paul Ballard received a suspended six-month sentence.

Attempts to improve race relations multiplied. The 3 Faiths Forum of Christians, Jews, and Muslims, founded in 1997 by Sir Sigmund Sternberg, announced plans in January to establish affiliated groups in Dublin, Glasgow, Bournemouth,

Brighton, and Barking. Sir Sigmund had started the group because the Council of Christians and Jews (CCJ) failed to include dialogue with Muslims, and he subsequently resigned as CCJ vice-president. In June Lord Janner set up the Maimonides Foundation to improve Muslim-Jewish understanding, which spawned two programs: Alif-Aleph, a forum for business people of both faiths, and the Calimus-Maimonides student forum. (Some 25 members of Al Muhajiroun, an extremist Muslim group, disrupted the opening session of Calimus-Maimonides at London's University College in October.)

In June Home Secretary Jack Straw responded to a campaign by MPs, peers, and Jewish leaders and retained a 12-year-old exclusion order against American black separatist Louis Farrakhan. The order did not apply to leading members of Farrakhan's Nation of Islam, who attended an antiracist meeting in October, organized by the Jewish Council for Racial Equality (JCore) and Westminster's Race Equality Council at Westminster-Marble Arch Synagogue, London. "Sections of the Islamic community clearly would welcome the opportunity to open a dialogue" with the Jewish community, Rabbi Jonathan Sacks told the *Jewish Chronicle*, but a Board of Deputies official said that no meeting could even be considered unless British members of the Nation of Islam repudiated the anti-Semitic statements attributed to their leader.

The board found inadequate the Terrorism and Conspiracy Act passed in September to deal with the Northern Ireland situation, but welcomed new proposals to combat international terrorism in a Home Office White Paper issued in December. Israeli and Jewish officials had warned the government that Middle East groups like Hamas and Islamic Jihad were using London as a conduit for funds. The government's proposals included a crackdown on organizations and individuals suspected of using Britain as a base for funding terror groups abroad, particularly the Middle East, and empowering the police to seize money believed to be earmarked for terrorist purposes.

Holocaust-Related Developments

New efforts were made this year to right the wrongs inflicted on victims of Nazism. In March the government announced that it was making an initial £2 million available for a "practicable scheme" for the return of assets of Holocaust victims deposited in British banks and seized by the Custodian of Enemy Property under the 1939 Trading with the Enemy Act. Trade Secretary Margaret Beckett, launching a Department of Trade report on the treatment of enemy property during and after World War II, expressed the government's "deep regret" at the "insensitive" attitude displayed by some people dealing with claimants after the war. "The general principle must be that confiscated assets placed by victims of Nazi persecution in the United Kingdom should be returned to them where practicable and where claims can be validated." To aid the search, 25,000 names relating to such assets were published on the Internet in April. In June Lord Archer of Sandwell, solicitor-general in the 1974–79 Labor government and former Amnesty International chairman, was appointed to advise the government on compensation claims. By November a 40-point consultative document issued by Archer in July—suggesting the most equitable means of compensating claimants—had been revised to take account of criticisms from the Board of Deputies and others and submitted to Secretary of State Peter Mandelson. In December Mandelson announced a claims program "as a matter of urgency," appointing Archer to head a three-person panel to assess applications. By then 180 persons had submitted claims valued at current rates at £13 million. It was thought that at least £25 million had been allocated to meet anticipated claims.

In July it was announced that British museums and galleries were establishing guidelines for identifying works of art looted from Holocaust victims.

The same month Foreign Secretary Cook released details regarding the £1 million-fund to help victims of Nazi persecution, established by Britain at the Nazi gold conference in December 1997: two-thirds of the sum would go to the American Jewish Joint Distribution Committee for medical aid programs in Eastern Europe; the Board of Deputies would distribute the remaining £300,000 among Britain's estimated 500 Holocaust survivors living on welfare. "I am determined," Cook told the *Jewish Chronicle*, "that those survivors who are left should not have to suffer the double tragedy of surviving the Nazis only to grow old in poverty."

In November, after negotiations in Vienna between the London-based Holocaust Education Trust and the Austrian Post Office Savings Bank, PSK, broke down over repayment of "millions of pounds" in the accounts of Holocaust victims, it was announced that Bank Austria had entered into negotiations with the Trust. Also in November, a first step was taken toward compensating thousands of Holocaust era insurance policy claimants, when six European insurance companies launched a $90 million fund, pledging to complete their work within two years.

NAZI WAR CRIMINALS

In February 1999 Andrzej (Anthony) Sawoniuk, age 77, a retired British Rail worker, would become the second person to face trial under British war crimes legislation. Sawoniuk, who was arrested after investigation by Scotland Yard's war crimes unit, faced charges of killing two Jewish women and two Jewish men between September and December 1942 in his home town, Domachevo, in Nazi-occupied Belarus. A fifth murder charge was withdrawn at the pretrial hearing at Bow Street magistrates court in April after the prosecution offered no evidence. Sawoniuk, who, according to his lawyer, "strenuously denies the allegations against him," was granted bail on condition that he continue to live at his home address and not try to leave the country. Up to 20 witnesses from Belarus and Israel were to be called at his trial, which was expected to last up to eight weeks.

JEWISH COMMUNITY

Demography

Britain's Jewish population continued to decline, according to *A Profile of British Jewry: Patterns and Trends at the Turn of the Century*, by Marlene Schmool and Frances Cohen, published by the Board of Deputies. Total Jewish population in 1995 fell 7 percent to 285,00, from a downwardly revised 1985 figure of 308,000, according to the 40-page booklet, combining research by the Board's Community Research Unit and the Jewish Policy Research Unit's 1995 survey of the community. The numbers of Jews in most major centers had fallen over the decade: in London and the Home Counties from 215,000 to 204,650; in Greater Manchester from 30,000 to 27,800; in Leeds from 12,000 to 10,000; in Glasgow from 7,500 to 5,600; in Brighton from 6,500 to 5,300; in Birmingham from 5,000 to 4,000; in Liverpool from 4,500 to 3,800; and in Southend from 4,500 to 3,400.

Meanwhile, Community Research Unit statistics showed an increase in 1997 in the total number of marriages conducted under synagogue auspices for the second year running, rising 4.1 percent to 986 from 957 in 1996. The number of *gittim* (religious divorces) completed in 1997 fell to 233 from 272 in 1996, while burials and cremations under Jewish religious auspices fell to 4,070 from 4,167 in 1996. The estimated total of births, based on figures for circumcision, was 2,897 in 1996, as compared with 3,013 in 1995.

Communal Affairs

With the approach of the millennium, new communal surveys were initiated and others, completed, published their findings, all aiming to help the community prepare for the 21st century. In February the Jewish Policy Research Unit (JPR) announced the establishment of an independent commission, "Who Speaks for British Jewry?" to examine the role of the Board of Deputies, the Chief Rabbinate, and other key leadership institutions of Anglo-Jewry to evaluate whether existing organizations effectively served the increasingly "pluralistic" community. The commission, coming in the wake of controversies over the representative role of the Chief Rabbinate and debate about the scope and effectiveness of the Board of Deputies, was expected to cost £50,000. It consisted of ten women and nine men, ranging in age between the 20s and 60s, spanning the religious spectrum. In November the commission's first head, former Marks and Spencer deputy chairman Clinton Silver and two commission members resigned. In October JPR launched a four-year survey to investigate the funding, staffing, and leadership structure of Britain's 2000 Jewish voluntary agencies. According to a new JPR publication, *Patterns of Charitable Giving Among British Jews,* by Barry Kosmin and Jacqueline Goldberg, issued in June, 80 percent of charitable donations came from 9 percent of the community. Based on JPR's 1995 survey of over 2,000 Jews, the report's findings showed a link between philanthropy and religious practice, with the strictly Orthodox giving "significantly larger sums" than other sectors.

A study of services for Jewish students, begun in March, issued its findings in December. Commissioned by four organizations supporting Jewish campus life—United Jewish Israel Appeal (IJIA), Hillel, Union of Jewish Students (UJS), and the Community Security Trust—the study was headed by UJIA board member Victor Blank and implemented by UJIA's strategic planning unit. The commission recommended that the Hillel Foundation become the main agency for coordinating student activity, that the Union of Jewish Students establish an "educational curriculum," and that the position of student chaplains be strengthened.

Religion

The major event of the year came in November when leaders of the Orthodox United Synagogue (US), Britain's largest synagogue grouping, and of the Masorti (Conservative), Reform, and Liberal movements signed a declaration pledging themselves "unreservedly to the pursuit of communal peace and cooperation." The declaration, which provides for a permanent "consultative committee" composed of "lay, professional and rabbinic leaders" from each group, followed 18 months of talks aimed at reducing the religious tension sparked by Chief Rabbi Jonathan Sacks's ambivalent response to the funeral of Reform rabbi Hugo Gryn in August 1996. Opposition from London's Bet Din caused US president Elkan Levy to withdraw a clause in the declaration's appendix that left open the possibility of US rabbis attending non-Orthodox synagogues. A Bet Din statement explicitly forbade such attendance and reiterated its long-standing policy of withholding "support of interdenominational committees" because they "ultimately sowed confusion within Anglo-Jewry." According to Joe Lobenstein, vice-president of the right-wing Union of Orthodox Hebrew Congregations, the declaration "marks the beginning of the end of the US as guardian of an Orthodox kehillah (community)."

The year was not without problems for the US. In April it opposed Hendon synagogue's choice of Rabbi Zvi Telsner, head of the Lubavitch universal council, for communal rabbi, but denied it was because of his Lubavitch connections. In September Hendon appointed Rabbi Mordechai Ginsbury to fill the post. In May the US dismissed part-time Bet Din *dayan* Casriel Kaplan for removing valuable documents and books from the Bet Din's library. This, coupled with revelations of "financial irregularities" at Waltham Abbey and Eltham cemeteries, led

US president Levy to announce plans in June to appoint outside accountants to conduct a special inquiry into the protection of US assets. In September the US council voted to sell the valuable collection of rare Hebrew books and manuscripts acquired from Chief Rabbi Solomon Hirschell in 1846, as well as the US's surplus silverware valued at around £80,000.

Although US's annual accounts published in June showed a surplus of £230,000, a cut was planned in the budget for the Chief Rabbinate. Consequently, in July supporters of Chief Rabbi Sacks launched a £900,000 appeal to fund a new phase in his "Decade of Renewal," the action plan for British Jewry he initiated on taking office in 1991. It aimed to strengthen mainstream Orthodoxy and offer "strong and purposeful leadership" for the Jewish people as a whole in an age when "modern and moderate Orthodoxy was in eclipse." Proposed projects included outreach to young people and a Web site to communicate Sack's "vision and teaching." Sacks hoped not only to "internationalize the Chief Rabbi's influence" but also to "cluster" around his office key units of the community involved in youth, day schools, personnel recruitment, and community development. Sacks's image was enhanced in September with his appointment to two visiting professorships: at the Hebrew University of Jerusalem for 1999 and at the department of theology and religious studies, King's College, London University, for three years. In November US co-treasurer Jeremy Jacobs announced an increase in the budget for the Chief Rabbi's Office to £255,000 from £220,000, to insure that "the Chief Rabbi is properly remunerated."

In May, after his book *Kosher Sex* was denounced by the US rabbinical council, maverick American rabbi Shmuel Boteach split with the US in order, he said, to spare the chief rabbi problems with the rabbinate and Beth Din. Although no US member synagogue granted him a pulpit, Boteach came second in a nationwide Preacher of the Year contest sponsored by the *Times* and the College of Preachers.

Synagogues closed and/or merged, reflecting population shifts. In January Liverpool's Pride of Israel synagogue with only 30 members announced closure; in September Elm Park (37 members) and Romford (84 members) in Essex agreed to merge as Romford and District Synagogue. On the other hand, a synagogue donated by the Saatchi brothers (including advertising giants Maurice and Charles) in their parents' honor, housed in a Jewish school in Maida Vale, West London, and under the auspices of the Spanish and Portuguese Jews' Congregation, was dedicated in June. In July American Pini Dunner, former Jewish Spectrum Radio presenter, was appointed rabbi of the Saatchi synagogue, which attracted publicity through its appeal to the under-45s and its full-page ad in the *Jewish Chronicle*: a picture of a piece of gefilte fish with the caption "At our new synagogue, this is the only thing that gets rammed down someone's throat." In September disaffected members of Golders Green, North-West London, synagogue started an alternative minyan at local Jewish Vegetarian Society premises.

Controversy struck the West London Synagogue (Reform) over the selection of American rabbi Mark Winer, and not long-serving associate minister Rabbi

Jacqueline Tabick, as senior minister to replace the late Rabbi Hugo Gryn. A mail ballot in April confirmed Winer's appointment; after a nine-month sabbatical leave, Tabick resigned from the West London in December.

In April, after 18 months of debate, the Assembly of Reform Rabbis voted overwhelmingly for a policy upholding heterosexual marriage as the traditional Jewish ideal, but recognizing "alternative life-styles which are valid and moral." The assembly, a policy paper stated, neither approved commitment ceremonies nor supported rabbis officiating at them but found involvement in them not incompatible with membership in the assembly. Following the vote, Rabbi Elizabeth Sarah resigned from the organization.

In March Sukkat Shalom Reform synagogue in Wanstead, East London, was awarded a £333,000 grant from the Heritage Lottery Fund and English Heritage for refurbishment; in April a grant of £47,000 was provided by the National Lottery, English Heritage, and Canterbury, Kent, city council to fund the restoration of Canterbury's Georgian Jewish cemetery.

Approval was given for revised plans for Britain's first *eruv* (Sabbath boundary marker) in North-West London by Barnet Council's development and protection committee in June and its public works committee in October; however, the approval of the national authority, the Highways Agency, was still required before the plans could be implemented.

Education

Some 27,850 Jewish children or approximately two-thirds of all Jewish children aged 5 to 17 received some form of Jewish education in 1996–97, compared with 23,800 in 1991, according to the Board of Deputies publication *A Profile of British Jewry*. In addition, approximately 2,700 children attended nurseries or kindergartens for the under-fives, while 14,100 Jewish children received no Jewish education at all in 1996–97 (against 19,100 in 1991). In 1996–97 there were 257 Jewish educational establishments, including preschools and kindergartens, over half of them offering part-time classes. In January 1998 the Secretary of State authorized two new Jewish day schools in Hertfordshire and also conferred state-aided status on Mathilda Marks-Kennedy School, Edgware, Middlesex.

In January the United Jewish Israel Appeal (UJIA), formed by the 1997 merger between Jewish Continuity and the Joint Israel Appeal, the community's fundraising programs for education and Israel, respectively, voted to spend £3.8m from its 1998 budget of £14m on Anglo-Jewish education. This included £1.3m on programs for young people, £800,000 on training teachers and educational leaders, and £600,000 on Israel experience schemes. In August UJIA and Limmud, the cross-community educational organization, announced a joint project to provide Jewish literacy for adults in Britain, the Florence Melton Minischool.

Jews' College, founded in 1855 to train rabbis for mainstream Orthodox communities, in July was renamed the London School of Jewish Studies to reflect its standing as an institute of higher education associated with London University.

The name change was part of an overall plan to revitalize the institution, following a six-month review initiated by the college president, Chief Rabbi Sacks. The first change, in February, was the appointment as director of David-Hillel Ruben, American-born philosophy professor at London University. In August Yeshivat Ohr Torah opened quarters on the college's campus, headed by Rabbi Chaim Brovender, head of Yeshivat Hamivtar in Efrat, Israel. Another change was the appointment of two women council members. In the planning were new courses for London University students and new part-time degrees.

The introduction in September of a joint honors degree in Jewish and Islamic studies at the University of Wales was announced in May. In July Stefan Reif, director of the Taylor-Schechter Genizah research unit at Cambridge University library was appointed professor of medieval studies at Cambridge. In October the University of London's School of Oriental and African Studies introduced an MA degree in Yiddish studies. In May seven leading teachers of university Jewish studies formed the Consortium for Higher Jewish Studies in Britain, calling on community leaders to finance an expansion of students, teachers, and scholars and warning that British Jewry was threatened with decline and the loss of collective identity.

Robin and Nitza Spiro, who had launched the Spiro Institute in 1978 to promote Jewish identity through teaching Jewish history and culture, both resigned during the year. In October the couple started the Spiro Ark at Middlesex University's Hendon campus.

Publications

The 1998 *Jewish Quarterly* award for fiction went to Canadian Anne Michaels for her novel *Fugitive Pieces;* the nonfiction prize was given to Claudia Roden for *The Book of Jewish Food.* Writer and publisher Matthew Reisz was appointed editor of the *Jewish Quarterly.*

Works of Jewish local history published during the year included *JFS: The history of the Jews' Free School, London, since 1732* by Gerry Black; *Touching Lives,* a history of the Clapton Jewish youth club, by Celia Rose; *Eight Hundred Years— The Story of Nottingham's Jews* by Nelson Fisher; and *Voices from the Past* by Zoë Josephs, a history of Birmingham's Singers Hill Synagogue.

New works of poetry included *Arcadia, One Mile* by Dannie Abse; *A Whole Olive Tree* by Nomi Zuckerman; *Sugar-Paper Blue* by Ruth Fainlight; and *Scars and Stripes* by Fran Landesman.

Notable works of fiction were *Donna and the Fatman* by Helen Zahavi; *No More Mister Nice Guy* by Howard Jacobson; *The Pink Danube* by Charles Osborne; *The House Gun* by Nadine Gordimer; *Falling Slowly* by Anita Brookner; *Fair Exchange* by Lynne Reid Banks; and *Day of Atonement* by Jay Rayner.

Literary studies included two works edited by Brian Cheyette: *Modernity, Culture and "the Jew"* (with Laura Marcus) and *Contemporary Jewish Writing in Britain and Ireland; Babel Guide to Jewish Fiction,* edited by Ray Keenoy and

Saskia Brown; and *The Experienced Soul: Studies in Amichai,* edited by Glenda Abramson.

Among new biographical and autobiographical works and accounts of personal experiences were *One Hand Alone Cannot Clap* by Greville Janner; *Arthur Koestler: The Homeless Mind* by David Cesarani; *Brief Encounters of a Legal Kind* by Aubrey Rose; *Amélie: The Story of Lady Jakobovits* by Gloria Tessler; *Genesis: A Latvian Childhood* by Chaim Bermant; *Manchester United Ruined My Life* by Colin Shindler; *Heshel's Kingdom* by Dan Jacobson, writing the life of his grandfather; *Wanderer from My Birth* by C.C. Aronsfeld; *A House of Memories* by Hana Raviv, the house being the Israeli ambassador's residence in London's St John's Wood; *Isaiah Berlin: A Life* by Michael Ignatieff; *Providential Accidents* by Geza Vermes; and *Christianity* by Lionel Blue.

Holocaust studies included *From the Wings* by Joseph Harmatz; *Surviving the Holocaust with the Russian Partisans* by Jack Kagan and Dov Cohen; *Holocaust Journey: Travelling in Search of the Past* by Martin Gilbert, who also published *Israel: A History*; *The Way It Was* by Gary Leon; *A Detail of History* by Arek Hersh; *Have You Seen My Little Sister?* by Janina Fischler-Martinho; *Values, Belief and Survival: Dr Elkhanan Elkes and the Kovno Ghetto* by Joel Elkes; *Men of Vision: Anglo-Jewry's Aid to Victims of the Nazi Regime* by Amy Gottlieb (the story of the CBF); *Edith's Book* by Edith Velmans; and *Belsen* by Jo Reilly.

Historical works included *The Illustrated History of the Jewish People,* edited by Nicholas De Lange; *Mandate Days: British Lives in Palestine 1918–1948* by A. J. Sherman; *The Second Republic: Politics in Israel* by Asher Arian; *A History of Palestine, 634–1099* by Moshe Gil; and two books by Ephraim Karsh: *Fabricating Israeli History* and *From Rabin to Netanyahu.*

Israel's 50th anniversary spawned several works, including *The Fifty Years War: Israel and the Arabs* by Ahron Bregman and Jihan el-Tahri and *Israel at Fifty* by Moshe Raviv, Israel's former ambassador in London.

Two tribute volumes were *Noblesse Oblige, Essays in Honour of David Kessler, OBE,* edited by Alan D. Crown, and *Elie Kedourie CBE FBA 1926–1992: History, Philosophy, Politics,* edited by Sylvia Kedourie.

Collective works and anthologies published over the year included *Cultures of Ambivalence and Contempt: Studies in Jewish-non-Jewish relations,* edited by Sian Jones, Tony Kushner, and Sarah Pearce; *Two Cheers for Secularism,* a collection of essays edited by Rabbi Sidney Brichto and Bishop of Oxford Richard Harries; and *A Soap Opera from Hell: Essays on the Facts of Life and the Facts of Death* by Clive Sinclair, who also published his collected stories *For Good or Evil.*

Personalia

The Marxist historian Eric Hobsbawm was created a Companion of Honor; Lord Rothschild received a Knight Grand Cross of the British Empire for services to the arts and heritage; and a life peerage was bestowed on the publisher Paul Hamlyn. Knighthoods went to biochemist Philip Cohen, Royal Society research professor at Dundee University, Scotland; to Nobel Peace Prize winner Joseph Rotblat for his contribution to international understanding;, and to Eli Lauterpacht for services to international law. In October city banker and former senior civil servant Lord Levene was elected the 671st Lord Mayor of London, the eighth Jew to hold the post.

Prominent British Jews who died in 1998 included Leo Sichel, minister, Reading Hebrew Congregation, 1959–88, in January, in London, aged 75; Chaim Bermant, renowned author, journalist, and humorist, in London, in January, aged 68; Ron May, Jewish scholar and Oxford librarian, in February, in Oxford, aged 81; Randolph Jones, writer and historian, in March, in London, aged 84; Rabbi Mordechai Singer, in March, in Gateshead, aged 72; Sir Alexander Stone, merchant banker, solicitor, and philanthropist, in March, in Glasgow, aged 90; Michael Weitzman, Hebraist and Bible scholar, in March, in London, aged 51; Zoë Josephs, historian of Birmingham Jewry, in May, in Birmingham, aged 83; Sam Aaronovitch, economist and activist, in May, in London, aged 78; Carmel Webber, leading British Zionist and communal figure, in May, in London, aged 86; Benny Green, broadcaster, jazzman and raconteur, in June, in London, aged 70; Alfred Rubens, historian of Jewish art, in June, in London, aged 94; Renée Rachel Soskin, leading worker for ORT, in July, in Bedfordshire, aged 81; Frances Rubens, Anglo-Jewish communal figure, in July, in London, aged 88; Cantor Charles Lowy, in London, aged 86; Mark (Monty) Green, instrumental in devising the organization of the Israel Defense Forces, in London, aged 83; Jonathan Fine, Jewish educator, in August, in London, aged 47; Reginald Robinson, *Jewish Chronicle* parliamentary correspondent for 40 years, in September, in London, aged 75; Eva Reichmann, writer, historian, and Jewish civil servant, in September, in London, aged 101; Rabbi Curtis Cassell, in October, in London, aged 85; Douglas Gluckstein, leading caterer, active in Liberal Judaism, in September, in London, aged 89; Fredman Ashe Lincoln, former Recorder and Crown Court deputy judge, author and naval veteran, president of Masorti Association and vice-president AJEX, in September, in London, aged 90; Joseph Sandler, founder and director of the Hebrew University's Sigmund Freud Center, in September, in London, aged 71; Lionel Bloch, lawyer and Zionist, in November, in London, aged 70; Rabbi Eli Cashdan, in November, in London, aged 93; Rabbi Judah Rockman, in December, in London, aged 81.

MIRIAM & LIONEL KOCHAN

France

National Affairs

O N THE POLITICAL LEVEL, 1998 was marked by relatively peaceful coexistence between the president of the Republic, Jacques Chirac, the right-wing leader elected on May 7, 1995, for a seven-year term, and the government headed by the Socialist prime minister, Lionel Jospin, who was supported by the left-wing majority that emerged from the legislative elections of May–June 1997. Real political power was essentially in the hands of Jospin, with Chirac's prerogatives limited to codirecting foreign policy, about which in any case there was no disagreement. Jospin's popularity was sustained by the improved social climate. Unemployment declined to 11.4 percent, and the number of salaried workers reached its highest level since 1990.

Against this background of political stability, debate essentially concerned the redefinition of the boundaries between parties. On the left, and to a greater extent on the right, ideological differences, vested electoral interests, and sometimes feuds between political figureheads led to maneuvering by and within party machines that the general public did not always understand.

The Socialist Party, now led by François Hollande, constituted the major component of the left majority. Joining forces with it was Robert Hue's Communist Party, now espousing democracy; Dominique Voynet's left-ecologist Green Party, whose rolls were bolstered by the arrival of Daniel Cohn-Bendit, a Jew of German-French extraction who helped instigate the 1968 student revolt but who now championed the market economy and the European Union; and Jean-Pierre Chevènement's Citizen's Movement, made up of former Socialists who advocated patriotic values (defined in relation to the specter of European unification) as well as the maintenance of law and order.

The right was divided into three principal components — the Rally for the Republic (RPR), the neo-Gaullist party founded by Jacques Chirac and currently led by Philippe Séguin; the Union for French Democracy (UDF), headed by François Bayrou, a federation of movements of which the principal one, Democratic Force, claimed the heritage of the "Christian-Democratic" movement and affirmed its commitment to European unification; and Liberal Democracy, formerly part of the UDF, whose leader, Alain Madelin, an extreme-right militant in his youth, now supported democratic values and economic liberalism. A hesitant attempt to create an alliance between these parties was met with skepticism both by public opinion and in the political world.

In fact, the right had never recovered from its electoral defeat in 1997. It had trouble assuming its role in the opposition, a difficulty heightened by the continuing popularity of the government and President Chirac's endorsement of certain of its initiatives. Internal discord in the opposition was stronger than ever and primarily concerned two issues. The first was the formation of the European Union. Philippe Séguin rallied to its cause at a very late date, although the then head of his party, Jacques Chirac, had always been favorably disposed to the concept. The second issue was the attitude to be adopted to the far right—not so much the actual National Front of Jean-Marie Le Pen and Bruno Mégret (all the leaders of the right agreed to bar any dialogue with this party) but its ideas— those "national values" whose abandonment, it was said, had been one of the causes of the decline of the right.

In the elections for regional assemblies of March 15, 1998, the parties of the "plural left" received 36.58 percent of the votes; the right, 35.98 percent. But whereas the extreme left of the spectrum—two small Trotskyite parties—brought in 4.32 percent of the vote, the far right of the right, the National Front, won 15.16 percent of the votes (the remaining votes were divided among various small groups). The question of the relationship between what is called the "Republican right" (traditional parties subscribing to the values of the Republic) and the extreme right thus became a central issue of national politics.

The far right was now represented in the assemblies of the 22 "regions" that make up France, in several of which the National Front held the swing votes that could determine the choice of a regional assembly president from either the left or the right. The National Front, prompted by Bruno Mégret, proposed supporting "Republican right" candidates for the presidency of the regions in exchange for a "minimum program." Paris-based party leaders promptly refused such negotiation and announced that any regional assembly presidential candidates who accepted votes coming from the National Front would be immediately expelled. Certain local party officials, however, were tempted to accept such a deal, which had the appeal of its own logic: why leave a regional presidency to the left if it was in a minority position? No "program" was officially signed with the National Front; however, in five regions a president from the right was elected with ballots of the extreme right.

President Chirac reacted to this situation in a television address on March 23, denouncing any compromise with "a party that is racist and xenophobic in nature." Although his intervention was approved, according to public opinion polls, by the great majority of the population irrespective of political orientation, it did not have a decisive influence. One of the five presidents subsequently resigned, and a Socialist was elected to fill the vacated office. The four others remained. One of these, the president of the Picardy region, Charles Baur, is the nephew of André Baur, a Jew, who under the German occupation was named by the Vichy regime to head the General Union of the Jews of France and was subsequently deported to Auschwitz and killed.

THE NATIONAL FRONT CHALLENGE

This episode highlighted the problem that the National Front henceforth posed for the opposition on the right and, more generally, for political life in France. It was out of the question to enter into a compromising agreement with a party animated by an extreme right-wing ideology thoroughly permeated with racism. Yet, could one ignore the vote of 15 percent of the electorate, who probably were not all far-right or racist? Among the leaders of the right, it was the president of Liberal Democracy, Alain Madelin, who most openly acknowledged this concern. In an interview published in *Le Figaro* on September 4, 1998, he defined his approach as follows: "Firmly combat the ideas of the National Front, which we judge to be pernicious, while refusing to ostracize the National Front and its voters." Most of the other leaders on the right adopted much harsher language toward the National Front, but they too wished to leave the door open to those who had voted for it.

In fact, what everyone thought privately but without expressing publicly was that the presence of Jean-Marie Le Pen at the head of the National Front constituted a major obstructive force in political life in France. This fearsome, popular figure had in merely a few years attracted a substantial following to the extreme right, which until then had been practically nonexistent. He accomplished this by playing on the fears of an uncontrolled immigration, escalating unemployment, and feelings of insecurity in the cities. But he also symbolized, in his provocative excesses, all that made the far right intolerable in the eyes of the majority of the French. Thus Le Pen was condemned in April 1998 to a two-year loss of civil rights for acts of violence against a Socialist candidate during the 1997 legislative elections. At the same time, he was prosecuted by the German justice ministry for having declared during a press conference in Munich on December 5, 1997, that the gas chambers were "a detail in the history of the Second World War." (Since Le Pen was at the time a deputy, representing France, in the European Parliament, it was necessary for that body to lift his parliamentary immunity, which was done on October 6, 1998, by a very large majority vote.) All this justified the results of a poll conducted in April 1998 by SOFRES, an opinion research institute, according to which 59 percent of the French considered Le Pen to be "a handicap for the development of the National Front."

Within the National Front, many apparently shared this opinion, but the party sought to maintain at least a façade of internal cohesion. Rumors pertaining to the existence of a conflict between Le Pen, the party's president, and Bruno Mégret, its general delegate, were vigorously denied. Le Pen went so far as to affirm that the relationship between the two was one of "almost perfect agreement."

This façade of unanimity was shattered in December 1998, when formerly faithful friends became unrelenting enemies amid a crossfire of slanderous accusations. Mégret, relying on the majority of party cadres for support, openly defied Le Pen. The crisis resulted in a split in the National Front, with "Mégretists" and "Le Penists" vehemently disputing the use of the organization's name as well as its offices and financial resources. Le Pen hurled such smears at his adversaries as "putschists," "felons," and "racists." Mégret in turn reproached Le Pen for the lack of democracy within the party and for playing into the hands of those who wished to make the National Front appear "diabolic."

In contrast to Le Pen, a longtime militant whose political character was tempered in the battles of the extreme right, Mégret enjoyed a "modernist" image. An engineer educated at one of the most prestigious French universities (the École Polytechnique), he had been a member of Jacques Chirac's RPR who later joined the National Front, where he rapidly rose through the ranks due to his talents as an organizer. Some regarded him as the agent who might integrate the National Front into the "Republican right." Others, on the contrary, saw in him the ideologist of the most hard-line right (hence Le Pen's accusation of "racism"), more dangerous than his fraternal adversary because more intelligent.

Israel and the Middle East

French diplomacy, under the direction of Minister of Foreign Affairs Hubert Védrine, represented the views of both President Chirac and Prime Minister Jospin. This was especially true of Middle East policy where, despite nuances of a personal nature, harmony reigned between the left and the right. As a result, Middle East policy was not the subject of debate and most decisions were made by high-ranking functionaries in the Ministry of Foreign Affairs, with the backing of the foreign minister.

Official expressions of friendship toward the State of Israel were mixed with an evident hostility regarding the policies of the Netanyahu government. On the amicable side of the ledger were such gestures as the issuing of a postage stamp commemorating the 50th anniversary of the establishment of diplomatic relations between France and Israel, as well as the remarks of Prime Minister Jospin at the annual dinner on November 28 of the Representative Council of the Jewish Institutions of France (Conseil Représentatif des Institutions Juives de France, CRIF): "Israel . . . is in the heart of the French people." However, he also took pains to affirm at the same gathering: "The pursuit of colonization [by Israel on the West Bank] is an error that risks having dire consequences."

France had not concealed its support in principle for the creation of a Palestinian state. The Wye agreement between Israel and the Palestinians was hailed as a sign of progress in the direction of peace, but a note of skepticism was also evident in the commentaries on this development. While ostensibly supporting American efforts in the region, France sought to play a particular role with regard to Syria and Lebanon where, for historical reasons, it felt its participation justified. Syrian president Hafez al-Assad's invitation to Paris at the end of July 1998 was a case in point, as was French mediation of the negotiations on an eventual Israeli-Lebanese agreement concerning a future Israeli withdrawal from southern Lebanon—negotiations that were officially denied in Beirut but confirmed by Israeli sources. For the rest, French policy by and large was aligned with European Middle East policy.

On an entirely different level, 1998 was the year of the discovery of Israel by the French general public. During a three-month period, from October through December, France was the scene of the most important series of Israeli cultural events ever to be sent abroad by the Jewish state. There were more than 150 cultural events, including theater, the plastic arts, dance, architecture, literature, and music. These took place in Paris and in a large number of other French cities. The series, called "Israel in the Artists' Mirror," was jointly organized by the respective ministries of culture and foreign affairs of France and Israel and was under the patronage of the presidents of the two countries. A feature of the festival was a 1913 silent film, *The Life of Jews in Palestine*, believed to have been lost for the past 85 years but which was discovered in the Paris Film Archives.

Anti-Semitism and Racism

On January 13, 1998, France commemorated the 100th anniversary of the publication of Emile Zola's famous article, "J'accuse," which marked a decisive turning point in the Dreyfus affair. On this occasion, President Chirac sent a letter to the Zola and Dreyfus families, telling them "how much France is grateful to your ancestors who, with an admirable courage, knew how to give full meaning to the values of liberty, dignity, and justice." In February a memorial plaque was dedicated in the courtyard of the École Militaire in Paris, where Alfred Dreyfus had been publicly degraded in 1895 and later solemnly rehabilitated in 1906. A statue of Captain Dreyfus, conceived by the illustrator Tim and commissioned in 1995 by the then minister of culture, Jack Lang, was, after some delay, finally installed in a small square close to the Paris jail where the wronged Dreyfus had been imprisoned. This official act of contrition on the part of the French state served as an occasion to underscore the connection between the fight against anti-Semitism and the defense of human rights. Happily, during the past year there was no necessity to alert public attention to any anti-Semitic sentiments emanating from political sources. Even Le Pen's egregious remark about the gas chambers was formulated with caution and immediately condemned by public opinion.

In February, 13 persons were simultaneously arrested in several French cities on the charge of belonging to a neo-Nazi organization known as "Charlemagne Hammer Skin." This group was believed to be part of a satanic sect having roughly 1,500 sympathizers in various countries throughout the world.

The summer of 1998 was marked by the desecration of several Jewish cemeteries. In the village of Dieuze in eastern France, four children under the age of 13 who had committed an act of vandalism declared that it was a "game." A few other local incidents were reported involving anti-Semitic graffiti and the vandalizing of several Jewish community centers. These incidents occurred primarily in the Paris suburban area where tensions sometimes arose between the local Jewish and immigrant Muslim communities. They were considered isolated cases of minor significance.

An embarrassing affair concerned one of the country's most prestigious institutions, the Académie Française, whose 40 members are drawn from France's literary and intellectual elites. In 1998 it awarded an important honor, the medal for services to French language and culture (*grande médaille de la francophonie*), to an Egyptian journalist, Mohamad Salmawy, in his capacity as editor-in-chief of *Al Ahram Hebdo*, a French-language newspaper published in Cairo. However, it was discovered shortly thereafter that on February 4, 1998, Salmawy had published an openly anti-Semitic article in his paper, "Seeking Out the Jews." In October the venerable academy was called to task on this matter by the press. While academy members individually declared their profound regret, the institution itself, traditionally slow to act, was not expected to offer an official apology very soon.

Toward the end of 1998, another no less embarrassing affair erupted, this time concerning members of the French judicial system. It began when an examining magistrate (responsible for conducting investigations into felonies and misdemeanors in order to determine whether sufficient evidence exists for arraignment) found himself threatened with prosecution. The magistrate was accused of having transmitted information to the press pertaining to a case he was investigating. Such leaks are a fairly common practice, to which examining magistrates may resort in order to generate public pressure so as to avoid the "squelching" of sensitive cases by their hierarchy, and they are practically never subject to prosecution. However, this incident took place in Toulon, a port city in the south of France run by a National Front mayor, and the magistrate conducting the investigation—considered by a certain number of local politicians as a nuisance because of his persistence in investigating cases of political corruption implicating the mayor's office and other local officials—was named Albert Lévy.

The extreme right press had not missed an opportunity to mention the name of Albert Lévy on every occasion that the question of legal proceedings against the National Front in Toulon came up. At a certain point, a magistrates' union became involved. The Professional Association of Magistrates (APM), a small organization of right-leaning magistrates, published in the October 1998 issue of its official bulletin an article by its former president, Albert Terrail, devoted to the "Lévy affair." The piece concluded with the following remark, which, in French, has the ring of a traditional proverb: "Lévy goes to the oven so often that in the end he will burn." The linking of the words "Lévy" and "oven" caused an uproar. The author, who held the important legal office of assistant public prosecutor to the Supreme Court of Appeals, sought to defend himself by observing that he had wished to give his phrase the appearance of a proverb, that the word "oven" in this context had no sinister intent, and that he had "numerous Jewish friends." Nevertheless, he had to resign from the governing board of the APM; shortly thereafter, APM's president, "still in shock," announced the self-dissolution of the union. Paralleling these developments, legal proceedings were instituted against the bulletin and the article's author, and Minister of Justice Elisabeth Guigou set in motion disciplinary proceedings against Terrail.

The rapidity of the response to this incident testified to the consensus against racism in official circles and also to the existence of a real problem within French society. Jews were far from being the principal victims of this problem. A poll conducted by the CSA Institute, published in July 1998, indicated that 15 percent of the French felt that there were "too many Jews in the country," 27 percent thought that there were "too many blacks," and 56 percent that there were "too many Arabs." In comment on these results it was observed, however, that there had been a decline in anti-minority attitudes as compared with previous findings. An identical survey completed in 1990 showed rates, respectively, of 24 percent, 46 percent, and 76 percent. Resolute opposition to racism appeared to have become a salient feature of national discourse.

A significant case in point was the World Cup Soccer Championship held in France in the summer of 1998, which was won, against all expectations, by the French team. In their origins, the players on the French team represented the broad range of recent immigration to France—from North Africa, Central Africa, the West Indies, South America, southwestern Asia, and the South Pacific. An American might be hard-pressed to grasp the extent of popular enthusiasm triggered by this victory. The team manager, Aimé Jacquet, told *Le Monde* shortly after the victory: "France was able to recognize itself in this multiethnic team. What could be more beautiful? . . . It was said that the Blues [the French team] contributed to the fight against Le Pen. I am very pleased about this and very proud."

For all that, real problems remained. The question of immigration, in particular, divided public opinion. The government's policy aimed at combating clandestine immigration, while at the same time facilitating the integration of legal immigrants, was the target of attacks both by the right, which found the policy too lax, and a part of the left, which found it too restrictive. A law on citizenship that was revised by the left-wing government to be more liberal was adopted in March. It reaffirmed the French principle of *jus soli*, according to which—in contradistinction to laws prevailing in other European countries—citizenship is granted to every person born in the country.

HOLOCAUST DENIAL

The trial of Roger Garaudy concluded in 1998. The 84-year-old philosopher, who had first been a Communist, then a Christian, before converting to Islam, was tried in Paris for "racial defamation" and for "contesting crimes against humanity." In 1995 he published a book entitled *The Founding Myths of Israeli Politics*, in which he questioned the extent of the Holocaust as well as the existence of gas chambers and accused the State of Israel and "the Zionists" of conducting a "Shoah business." On February 27, Garaudy was found guilty of the various offenses with which he had been charged, and was obliged to pay fines totaling 120,000 francs. Although condemned in Paris, Garaudy was soon heralded throughout the Arab-Muslim world as a heroic exponent of freedom of speech unjustly persecuted by the "Zionist lobby." Only a few Arab intellectuals protested the fact that in the name of "anti-Zionism" it was possible to propound notions staunchly advocated by the far right. Garaudy appealed the judgment and, on December 16, was again found guilty, this time receiving fines amounting to 150,000 francs and a suspended sentence of six months in prison. His publisher, Pierre Guillaume — a former ultra-left bookstore owner who had become the ally of the anti-Semitic extreme right — who had been found innocent in the initial proceedings, was given a 30,000- franc fine and a six-month suspended prison sentence.

These guilty verdicts were partially based on legislation passed in 1990, commonly known as the "Gayssot law," which in particular deals with "those who have contested the existence of one or several crimes against humanity as these are defined by article 6 of the statutes of the international military tribunal as appended to the London Agreements of August 8, 1945" — in other words, those who deny the existence of the Holocaust. Such legal provisions are not exceptional, as witnessed by comparable laws in Germany and Switzerland, but they have been misunderstood or opposed, as much in the United States as in certain French intellectual circles. Thus, in an interview published in *Le Monde* (September 1, 1998), the renowned American linguist Noam Chomsky stated, referring expressly to Robert Faurisson, the leading French Holocaust denier: "The state should not be able to determine the truth, even if it happens that it is right. . . . My position on the Holocaust remains in conformity with what I wrote 30 years ago; it is the worst atrocity in human history, and the very fact of debating it is ridiculous. But if people have other positions on this subject, they should be able to have the right to express them." Prof. Chomsky, who as far back as 1979, had taken up the defense of Faurisson in the name of freedom of speech, persisted in presenting him and those close to him as apolitical libertarians, despite the mounting evidence that led to their being considered in France as anti-Semites with close connections to leading circles of the extreme right.

The issue of freedom of speech with respect to Holocaust deniers was the subject of considerable debate in France. At the time of the legislative vote on the Gayssot law, critics on both the right and the left argued that there was a danger of establishing the principle of a "crime of opinion" and creating a precedent that could be extended to other ideas. They also saw the risk of giving Holocaust deniers undue publicity and investing them with an aura of martyrdom.

In actuality, while article 9 of the Gayssot law specifically deals with denial of the Holocaust (it is one of the law's 15 articles that, more generally, are devoted to the repression of "all racist, anti-Semitic, or xenophobic acts"), it has never been invoked against historical researchers, for indeed among all the Holocaust deniers in France there has not been one professional historian. But the nonhistorian deniers of the gas chambers are a different matter. Originally they consisted of individuals with a nostalgia for Nazism along with a fringe group of the extreme left. Within a few years, however, their discourse underwent a transformation: they began to incorporate vehement attacks against the State of Israel, Zionism, and the "Jewish lobbies" that clearly crossed the line between intellectual argument and racist discourse. It is against such propagandists, for whom the "myth of the Holocaust" is an integral part of a wide-ranging offensive against "Jewish power," that the Gayssot law has been used. In a country like France, where every racist declaration, be it written or spoken, is severely punished by law, article 9 effectively closes any legal loophole that would allow the expression of anti-Semitism under the guise of "historical debate." Thus, following Le Pen's statement that the gas chambers were a "detail," for which he was prosecuted in Germany, comparable legal proceedings were instituted against him in France, using the Gayssot law. The Gayssot law similarly permitted the condemnation of Robert Faurisson, who on April 28, 1998, was fined 20,000 francs for a letter addressed to the extreme-right weekly *Rivarol* and published by the latter on July 12, 1996. Faurisson had defended the thesis that "there was no extermination of the Jews by the Germans of the Third Reich."

The capacity to apply the law, however, had become increasingly hampered by a new technological development, the Internet. For instance, Faurisson was again brought to trial in Paris on November 13, 1998, for an article signed with his name, entitled "The Horned Visions of the Holocaust." Its opening words were: "The 'Holocaust' of the Jews is a fiction." This article was published on the Holocaust-denying Internet site "Aaargh," and could still be found in French and English versions in early 1999. The article did not differ, in its essentials, from countless other articles by Faurisson that were reproduced on the same site. Faurisson, however, claimed before the court that he was not the author of the article. As it was materially impossible to prove the contrary, since the "Aaargh" site is located in the United States, Faurisson was acquitted without the court having examined the article's content.

These legal fine points did not affect the French public's condemnation of Holocaust denial. A poll carried out by SOFRES, at the request of CRIF, on October 30-31, 1998, indicated that 79 percent of the French approved (and 18 percent opposed) the Gayssot law, "because no one has the right to say whatever he wishes regarding the extermination of the Jews." In the same poll, 59 percent of the French (versus 37 percent) considered the legal proceedings instituted against Maurice Papon as "necessary," and 74 percent (versus 24 percent) thought that, "in general," the law should "prosecute persons implicated in crimes against humanity even if this occurs a very long time after the facts." This poll also revealed that more than two-thirds of the French approved the "declaration of repentance" made by the bishops of France as well as other professional groups (for instance, the police) for the behavior of their predecessors under the German occupation. The rate of approval rose to 80 percent (versus 16 percent) with respect to President Chirac's 1995 declaration on "France's responsibility in the extermination of the Jews of France during the Second World War." Finally, 90 percent of the French (versus 7 percent) considered "justified" the measures undertaken by Jewish institutions in France "so that property would be restituted that had been stolen from exterminated Jewish families during the Second World War."

Other Holocaust-Related Matters

PAPON TRIAL

The year 1998 began in the shadow of the trial of Maurice Papon. This former high functionary, who from 1942 to 1944 during the German occupation had been secretary-general of the Gironde Prefecture in Bordeaux, was accused of having played a role in the arrest and deportation of more than 1,500 Jews. (See 1998 AJYB, pp. 257-59.) His trial, which began on October 8, 1997, came to end on April 2, 1998. Beyond the trial of one man was the trial of a regime—the Vichy regime—of which Papon had been a faithful civil servant. Did Papon know, or did he not, that the Jews were fated to a certain death? Could he have done anything other than apply the orders of the German occupation authorities and could he, as a functionary, be held personally responsible for his actions? These were the questions before the jury. In the end, Papon was found guilty and sentenced to ten years' imprisonment. He would remain free until the Supreme Court of Appeals pronounced its decision on his appeal, sometime in 1999.

The verdict, overall, was well received. Papon was not given the maximum sentence—life imprisonment—because it was not possible to prove that he had been a knowing accessory to the murder of the Jews he delivered to the Germans. Some deplored the fact that the jury rejected the argument that a high functionary could be guilty of what one of the victims' lawyers, Michel Zaoui, called an "office crime." But the ten-year term, which for an elderly man of 87 had the same significance as a life sentence, demonstrated that, in the words of CRIF president Henri Hajdenberg: "The French people hold the governing officials of Vichy and their functionaries fully responsible for the deportation of France's Jews." The fact that among the deported were elderly persons, as well as women and children, particularly moved public opinion. A cartoon that appeared on the day following the verdict in *La Montagne*, a daily published in central France, showed two small children seated on a cloud. One asks the other: "Ten years, what do you think about it?" The other replies: "I can't really say, I never reached ten."

RESTITUTION

Another matter that held the public's attention was the issue of the plundering of Jewish property during the occupation. Hector Feliciano's recent book, *Le musée disparu* (*The Lost Museum*), had revealed that some 2,000 works of art recovered from the Germans after the war—of which at least a part had been pillaged during the occupation from French Jews—were in French museums, still awaiting claim by their rightful owners. Here was further proof that there were still unknown or concealed aspects of the wartime spoliation of French Jewry. In early 1997, then prime minister Alain Juppé had appointed a commission headed by Jean Mattéoli, president of the Economic and Social Council, to examine the conditions under which Jewish property had been plundered during the German occupation and the manner in which restitution had been carried out after liberation, and finally, to formulate proposals concerning the disposition of possessions that had not yet been returned. The vice-president of the commission was medical professor Adolphe Steg, president of the Alliance Israélite Universelle and a former CRIF president. The other members were mostly Jewish and non-Jewish historians.

The question of confiscated or plundered property proved to be most complex. Approximately 330,000 Jews were living in France between 1940 and 1944, of whom somewhat more than 75,000 were deported and exterminated at Auschwitz. The community consisted of a small minority of wealthy Jews, for the most part long established in the country, and a large majority of poor Jews who had recently immigrated to France. The economic discrimination directed against the Jewish population, initially instigated by the Germans and then pursued by the collaborationist Vichy regime, affected the two groups differently and unequally.

The most visible part of the plundering—the "Aryanization" of major business enterprises, real-estate holdings, and stock portfolios; the imposition on the Jewish community of a fine of 1 billion francs, drawn directly from Jewish bank accounts; the outright theft or forced, disadvantageous sale of artworks—these only involved a few hundred families. It was also this group that contained the most survivors and that benefited the most from restitution procedures following liberation. The legal battles surrounding certain paintings, which continued up to the end of 1998, while impinging on public awareness, seemed to be mostly a matter of curiosity.

In contrast, the majority of French Jews who were victims of plundering during the war (numbering in the tens of thousands) were people with little to lose materially because they possessed almost nothing. In their case, expropriation meant the loss of relatively small sums—the result of the forced closing of artisans' small workshops and the sale of their contents by "provisional administrators" named by the Vichy government; the theft by the Germans of the contents of Jewish apartments, a part of which was transferred to Germany; the confiscation, first by the French and then by the Germans, of money or various precious objects that Jews had with them when deported to the internment camp at Drancy, the way station to Auschwitz. The sums involved here were modest, and if they were not claimed after liberation, it was because there was nothing to recover nor anyone to do so. Even if these small sums were to be added together, the resulting amount was insubstantial. But the objective of the inquiry was of an entirely different nature: it was intended, as was the Papon trial, to reconstruct the mechanisms by which a social system and state administration were put in the service of an enterprise of discrimination culminating in murder.

A paradoxical situation arose from this inquiry: the real interest of the investigation into the plundering of French Jewry was inversely proportionate to the amounts at stake. By placing greater emphasis on the financial consequences of the depredation, the fundamental dimension of human lives broken and sacrificed might receive less consideration, and the unspeakable crimes committed by the Germans and the Vichy regime would appear less in evidence. The choice of the appropriate method to investigate spoliation was as much a question of the basic underlying issues as it was a purely tactical one.

On this point, an obvious tension existed throughout the year between the leaders of France's Jewish community and the World Jewish Congress. The WJC, in the aftermath of the Swiss bank affair, stepped up public pressure on the French state and French financial institutions. Yet such pressure, because it consisted mainly of class-action suits brought before American courts, led to a primary focus on the redress of financial grievances. CRIF president Henri Hajdenberg expressed a viewpoint largely shared in France when he dissociated himself from the WJC's strategy, requesting that it limit its involvement in these matters and leave it to the leaders of the country's Jewish community to settle a "Franco-Jewish dossier."

From the viewpoint of the community, what was at stake was not merely a matter of French Jewish nationalism, or a fear that external intervention would place them in an awkward position with respect to local public opinion. Above all, French Jews were dismayed by what they perceived as a lack of understanding on the part of American Jews. They conceded that pressure from the United States might prod French authorities, and especially banks and insurance companies, to participate more actively in the search for information bearing on this unhappy period of their history, but they feared that such pressures, if excessive, would have the opposite effect of the one intended.

It was underscored in Paris that the money at stake in this instance belonged to French Jews and was not, as in the affair of the Swiss banks, money stolen from Jews throughout Europe. Moreover, in contrast to most other European countries, the majority of France's Jews had managed to survive the war, and this led to the conviction that no other Jewish community was entitled to speak on their behalf. Furthermore, seeking a solution in the form of global financial compensation would deflect attention from a central, crucial issue, namely, that France as a nation should undertake a process of reflection regarding its own past.

It was also felt that French judicial and administrative tradition should be taken into account. Within that framework, the idea that reparation could be made for wrongs committed against individuals by means of collective compensation is not only unheard of but also inadmissible. Even the right of the French Jewish community to represent the interests of individual victims was not self-evident. Significantly, the Mattéoli Commission, in the introduction to its interim report issued at the end of 1998, took pains to specify that the term "Jew" was used in the report in the sense defined by the discriminatory regulations that were in force between 1940 and 1944. In effect, apart from the historical fact that a certain number of victims did not consider themselves "Jews," the very idea of distinguishing citizens in terms of their origins or religious beliefs was deemed shocking. The Mattéoli Commission was obliged to obtain special authorization to constitute lists of the victims of spoliation, as such lists, because they are de facto "lists of Jews," are prohibited by law.

The investigation of the question of plundering was undertaken in this context. To the difficulties indicated above were added further problems of a material nature. The inventorying of confiscated property necessitated examination of an almost infinite quantity of archival documents spread over diverse public agencies and a multitude of private organizations. What is more, a great majority of cases of property appropriation had been resolved and the property restored to owners or heirs shortly after the war. There was no purpose, therefore, in gathering data on the plundering without evaluating the extent of the restitution. However, it turned out to be more difficult to identify and inventory the cases of restitution than the acts of spoliation because the former, in contrast to the latter, were carried out by a postwar regime that prohibited racial discrimination, to the extent of not permitting individuals to be identified by religion or ethnicity in official transactions. As a result, Jews who recovered possessions or property were not identified as such, and there is no record of specifically Jewish restitution cases.

To complicate matters even further, sometimes both public and private archives could not be located. Banks, for example, declared that they no longer retained relevant records dating back so far in the past. Many small banks had long since ceased to exist, others had merged. The current directors of these institutions were little motivated to undertake inquiries into a past that seemed utterly alien to them. Jewish authorities did not hide their impatience and were obliged to acknowledge that under the circumstances a little outside pressure — for example, in the form of legal action before New York courts — would be helpful in convincing banks to participate to a greater extent in the investigation of wartime plunder.

One institution, however, demonstrated an exceptional attitude of cooperation — the Office for Deposits and Consignments (Caisse des Dépôts et Consignations, CDC), a state-run organization whose function is to receive funds for provisional deposit, as required by law, until their subsequent appropriation. Under the Vichy government, the CDC had been given the responsibility of managing a portion of the funds that derived from confiscations. Already in 1992, at the request of Jean Kahn, who was then president of CRIF, the CDC had undertaken to establish a team of investigators who would examine documents in its custody, under the supervisory control of renowned historians. The report resulting from these investigations, submitted by the CDC at the end of 1998, depicted with unfailing honesty the behavior of its own former directors who executed the policies of the Germans and the Vichy authorities without the slightest apparent compunction. In the final analysis, the sums involved both in the plundering as well as the restitution of property were quite small, even when inflation and interest were taken into account, and very far from the billions of francs that some had imagined. The person who headed this internal investigation, Pierre Saragoussi, adviser to the president of the CDC, had himself lived through this somber period of French Jewish history. A young Jewish child at the time of the German occupation, Saragoussi saw his parents deported; he was taken in and saved by French Christians. Having become a high-ranking functionary, he found himself, at the end of his career, in charge of an inquiry that concerned his own past.

In November 1998, at the CRIF annual dinner, Prime Minister Jospin announced the creation of an "agency responsible for examining individual claims made by victims of anti-Semitic legislation or their rightful claimants." This measure was taken without awaiting the completion of the Mattéoli Commission's investigation. The prime minister also authorized the increase of operational funds available to the commission so that its final report would be ready at the appointed date, fixed at the end of 1999.

On one significant point, however, the research into spoliation was completed. It dealt with the manner in which the inhabitants of the Marais, a neighborhood located in central Paris, had been expelled by the French authorities between 1940 and 1944. The journalist Brigitte Vital-Durand maintained, in a book published in 1996, that an "administrative pogrom" had taken place. She contended that, under the guise of an urban renewal and public health project, the City of Paris had been able to seize important real-estate holdings by making use of the anti-Semitic legislation then in force. Following these accusations, the Paris mayor's office had put a halt to the sale of all buildings in its possession. An administrative inquiry was launched under the direction of a high-ranking public official, Noël Chahid-Nouraï, in cooperation with experts and representatives from the Jewish community.

The report, made public on November 17, 1998, following a two-year examination of thousands of files, was immediately hailed by CRIF's president as a "remarkable work." The report revealed that in the present instance no Jewish property owner had been harmed. Almost all the Jews residing in the Marais neighborhood lived in rented, often run-down, apartments. Among those Jews who owned property, almost all received indemnities equivalent to those allotted non-Jewish real-estate owners. In only five cases were the sums paid sufficiently below the real value of the property as to indicate economic exploitation. In all these cases, the City of Paris paid additional compensation shortly after liberation.

Other cities established analogous investigatory procedures concerning Jewish real-estate holdings. Lyon (where municipal officials representing the National

Front attempted in vain to oppose the investigation) and Bordeaux (whose mayor, Alain Juppé, had established the Mattéoli Commission when he was prime minister), are noteworthy examples.

NAZI WAR CRIMINALS

At the request of CRIF, on the occasion of Syrian president Hafez al Assad's visit to Paris in mid-July, President Chirac asked for the extradition of Nazi criminal Alois Brünner, now 86 years old, who had long been rumored to be living in Syria. An investigation of Brünner had been under way since 1987 as a result of legal proceedings brought before French courts by Jewish lawyer and historian Serge Klarsfeld, and a summons was issued in 1988. Among his other nefarious activities, Brünner was the director of the Drancy camp, where most of the French Jews who were deported to Auschwitz were first interned. Assad once again asserted that Brünner was entirely unknown to Syrian authorities.

JEWISH COMMUNITY

Demography

Reliable statistical information regarding French Jewry is difficult to come by, but on the basis of available information it is estimated that Jews number approximately 1 percent of the total French population, that is, between 500,000 and 700,000 persons. Even in the absence of hard data, two contradictory demographic trends could be discerned: an upsurge of small, ultra-Orthodox religious communities, whose growth is due essentially to their high birthrates; and an increase in mixed marriages, for the third consecutive generation.

Communal Affairs

Israel's 50th anniversary was observed with a number of public celebrations throughout the country. The major celebration took place in Paris, under the auspices of CRIF — the umbrella organization of the organized French Jewish community — the Israeli embassy, and the mayor's office. In a large pavilion erected in the Trocadéro gardens, across from the Eiffel Tower, leaders of the Jewish community mingled with major figures from the world of politics — President Chirac, Prime Minister Jospin, and ministers and deputies representing all political parties (with the exception, of course, of the National Front). Outside the pavilion, some 25,000 people gathered to watch a live broadcast of the ceremony on a giant screen.

On May 17, Henri Hajdenberg was elected to a second term as president of CRIF, which is primarily concerned with Jewish political and social issues, such as anti-Semitism and the defense of Israel. Hajdenberg, a 51-year-old lawyer, had succeeded Jean Kahn, who subsequently became president of the Central Consistory, the central religious body of French Jewry and one of the founding institutions of CRIF. At the time of his reelection, Hajdenberg had only one opponent, Arié Bensemhoun (age 35), president of CRIF for the Toulouse region, who reproached the incumbent for being insufficiently supportive of Israeli government policies. Hajdenberg was reelected in the first round of voting, receiving 75 votes against 15 for Bensemhoun.

CRIF's aforementioned annual dinner was, as usual, an impressive affair. These dinners are traditionally attended by the current prime minister, and this year's occasion also boasted the presence of 25 ambassadors (including the ambassador of Israel, Eliyahu Ben Elissar, and the general delegate of the Palestine Authority, Leïla Shahid), leading representatives of the Catholic, Protestant, Muslim, and Jewish religious communities, as well as many prominent political figures, with the exception of the extreme right. Prime Minister Jospin's address reaffirmed the French government's sympathy for the State of Israel, its determination to fight racism and anti-Semitism, its support of the new Jewish Museum in Paris and the Holocaust memorial, as well as its intent to strengthen the activity of the Mattéoli Commission.

The launching of the annual community welfare campaign, at the end of 1998, by the United Jewish Philanthropic Fund (Fonds Social Juif Unifié, FSJU), served as a reminder that 36,000 Jewish families, according to estimates of social-welfare organizations, lived under the poverty line, the consequence of the prolonged economic crisis.

Religion

The synagogue of Balbronn (a small village in Alsace with 600 inhabitants) had long remained unused. Since many Alsatian Jews, often the most religious, had settled in Israel, a suggestion was made to dismantle the synagogue and transfer it to Jerusalem. However, the plans encountered a last-minute obstacle: the French Ministry of Culture decided that the Balbronn synagogue was a historical monument and as such should be preserved. Now this memorial to a once flourishing Jewish community will be maintained by the state.

On June 2, Israeli chief Sephardic rabbi Mordecai Eliahu came to Dijon to inaugurate a Jewish day school.

Controversy arose over the certification of kosher food products, taxes on which were the major source of revenue for religious organizations. The Paris Consistory, whose Orthodox religious court (*bet din*) had jurisdiction over the whole country, created a logo to be put on all products it had certified as kosher. However, it met with competition from other Orthodox communities not affiliated with the consistory, such as the Lubavitch movement. The latter had had an ambivalent relationship with the consistory, marked by temporary alliances and frequent denunciations. Tensions reached crisis proportions when an importer close to Lubavitch had frozen meat shipped to France from Argentina, thereby circumventing the regulatory controls of the consistory. During this time, Chief Rabbi Joseph Sitruk, who is affiliated with the Central Consistory of France and not the Consistory of Paris, made an unsuccessful attempt to unify the certification of kosher food under his authority. This would have constituted a redistribution of regulatory authority and consequently a redistribution of revenues among religious organizations.

Jewish-Christian Relations

The year 1998 marked the 50th anniversary of the Jewish-Christian Friendship Society (L'Amitié Judéo-Chrétienne), which brings together Jews and Christians of all denominations in a climate of mutual respect. The anniversary celebration, held on April 25 at the Rashi Jewish community center in Paris, paid special tribute to two prominent figures who played an important role in the organization's recent history—René-Samuel Sirat, former chief rabbi of France, and Father Bernard Dupuy, former secretary of the episcopal committee on relations with Judaism.

The dialogue between Jews and Catholics was put to the test following the issuance, on March 16, of the Vatican's statement dealing with the Church's role during the Holocaust. Jewish leaders, who had warmly greeted the French bishops' earlier "declaration of repentance," concerning Catholic behavior between 1940 and 1944, this time expressed their disappointment with a document that seemed to minimize the connection between Christian anti-Judaism and the anti-Semitism of the 20th century and that rejected all questions bearing on the "silence" of Pope Pius XII as the Holocaust unfolded. Many Catholics shared this critical assessment.

On the occasion of Rosh Hashanah, as had become the tradition in recent years, posters were affixed to the doors of churches wishing a joyous New Year to "our Jewish brothers." New Year's cards were prepared by Catholic authorities in honor of the year 5759, and Sunday, September 27, which fell between Rosh Hashanah and Yom Kippur, was declared "a day for greater awareness between the Christian and Jewish communities."

Culture

The cultural event of the year was the opening in Paris of the Museum of the Art and History of Judaism (Musée d'Art et d'Histoire du Judaïsme), in the planning since the early 1980s. A museum devoted to Jewish art had existed in Paris since shortly after the war. Located in Montmartre (rue des Saules), it possessed a fine permanent collection of paintings and mounted regular exhibitions. Due to limitations of space and budget, however, it was decided to establish an enlarged museum with a broader financial base, to be located in the Marais neighborhood of Paris and housed in a 17th-century city-owned mansion, distinguished for its architecture, the Hôtel de Saint-Aignan. The project received the joint support of the mayor's office and the Ministry of Culture. The work involved in creating modern exhibition halls while preserving the historic character of the building and its gardens took longer than expected, but the museum was finally inaugurated on November 30 by President Chirac. The new museum, which is subsidized equally by the City of Paris and the Ministry of Culture, houses the collections of its predecessor (closed since February 1998), as well as numerous works from state and private sources. Under the direction of Laurence Sigal and an executive committee representing the major French Jewish institutions, its exhibition philosophy is to present works of art together with historical documents, and its general goal is to carry out a program combining education and research. Already in its first year the new museum demonstrated a policy of openness and dynamism, undertaking numerous initiatives both on the international plane (with a conference on Jewish museums and the preservation of the Jewish heritage) and at the national level (participating in a variety of local projects, Jewish and other).

Attempts to create a Jewish television channel were so far unsuccessful, but Jewish radio stations continued to broadcast in the Paris area and several other French cities. These stations were largely financed by advertising, with some institutional and private grants. They offered to a primarily — but not exclusively — Jewish audience programs featuring current events in Israel and subjects with a Jewish focus. Leading French political figures often went on Jewish radio to express their views on topics of current interest, to such a degree that these broadcasts were regularly cited on national news reports, giving the public the impression of a "Jewish presence" out of all proportion to the actual number of Jews in France. However, for all its apparent success, French Jewish radio recently became embroiled in internal disputes. The principal broadcasting frequency for Jewish radio stations, which is in the Paris area, was shared by four competing groups, each with its own studios and staff. Confronted with the inability of these groups to reach some form of operating agreement, the state regulatory agency in charge of broadcasting was obliged to intervene, designating broadcasting time for each group. Listeners generally did not distinguish among them. However, the lack of coordination had the unfortunate consequence, for example, of providing listeners with the coverage of the same news events from Israel at half-hour intervals.

An adaptation of a classic from the Yiddish theater, S. An-Ski's *Dybbuk*, staged at the Rashi Community Center in Paris, was the highlight of the Jewish theatrical season. The production was directed by Shakespearean specialist Daniel Mesguich, a Jewish actor and director born in Algeria, who said that he lived his Jewishness in the form of "a brotherhood with Freud."

Two French films with explicitly Jewish themes were shown this year. The first,

L'homme est une femme comme les autres (Man Is a Woman Like All the Others), directed by Jean-Jacques Zilbermann, is a comedy about a Jewish homosexual clarinetist who marries a (female) Yiddish singer. The second, *Train de vie* (Life Train), by Radu Maihaileanu, recounts the fictional story of the inhabitants of a Jewish village in Eastern Europe who attempt to escape from the Germans by staging their own deportation.

Publications

As in previous years, 1998 saw the appearance of numerous autobiographical accounts dealing with the period of the German occupation. For obvious reasons of chronology, these works are mainly the narratives of persons who were children at the time. Two such efforts were *Dès les premiers jours de l'automne* (From the First Days of Autumn) by Emile Copferman, and *Un hiver à voix basse* (A Winter of Whispers) by Dominique Laury. The year also saw the republication of two testimonial accounts of experiences at the Drancy detention camp: *Camp de représailles* (Camp of Reprisals) by Noël Calef, and *Les lettres de Louise Jacobson et de ses proches* (The Letters of Louise Jacobson and Those Close to Her). José-Alain Fralon, a *Le Monde* journalist, published *Le juste de Bordeaux* (The Righteous One of Bordeaux), a biography of Aristide de Sousa Mendes, the Portuguese consul in wartime Bordeaux who issued visas to a large number of Jews, thus allowing them to escape from the Nazis. Mendes was severely punished by Salazar's Fascist government and died in poverty.

Israel's 50th anniversary was the occasion for the publication of several pertinent works, among them: *Israël imaginaire* (Israel Imagined), a study by Jean-Christophe Attias and Esther Benbassa, addressing Israel's image in Jewish and Israeli culture; *David Gryn* by Pierre Haski, a biography of the young David Ben-Gurion; and *Géopolitique de Jérusalem* by Frédéric Encel.

The year's notable historical studies accorded pride of place to the Jewish-German experience, with such works as *Philologie allemande et tradition juive* (German Philology and the Jewish Tradition) by Céline Trautmann-Waller; *Portraits de Juifs en temps de crise* (Portraits of Jews in a Time of Crisis) by Anne Lagny, an analysis of Jews in German novels during the Weimar Republic; *Hannah Arendt, une Juive* (Hannah Arendt, a Jewish Woman) by Martine Lebovici; the second volume of Maurice-Ruben Hayoun's study *Les Lumières de Cordoue à Berlin* (The Enlightenment from Cordoba to Berlin); and *La philosophie allemande dans la pensée juive* (German Philosophy in Jewish Thought), under the general editorship of Gérard Bensussan.

Another prominent theme of scholarly publication, generally by Christian authors, was the study of Jewish-Christian relations, which included the following works: *Les chrétiens et l'affaire Dreyfus* (Christians and the Dreyfus Affair) by Pierre Pierrard; *Luther était-il antisémite?* (Was Luther an Anti-Semite?) by Lucie Kannel; *Le judaïsme* by Dominique de la Maisonneuve, a Catholic nun; and *Les chrétiens et la loi juive* (Christians and Jewish Law) by Michel Quesnel, which argues that the teachings of Paul were less opposed to traditional Judaism than is usually believed.

Historical writing on Jewish themes was well represented by such works as *Musiques liturgiques juives* (Jewish Liturgical Music) by Hervé Rotem; *Histoire des Juifs en Afrique du Nord* (History of the Jews in North Africa) by André Chouraqui; *Etre juif en Provence au temps du roi René* (Being a Jew in Provence in the Reign of King René) by Danièle Iancu; *Etre juif en Chine* (Being a Jew in China) by Nadine Perront; as well as two biographies (the first by Pierre Assouline, the second by Nora Seni and Sophie Le Tarnec) of Count Moïse de Camondo, a brilliant and tragic figure in Jewish society at the turn of the century whose son died in combat during World War I (a remarkable museum in Paris, created by his father, bears his name) and whose grandchildren died at Auschwitz.

Noteworthy publications in the field of Jewish thought included *Explorations talmudiques* (Talmudic Explorations) by Georges Hansel; *Célébration prophétique* (Prophetic Celebration) by Elie Wiesel; *La séparation d'amour* (Separation Out of Love) by Shmuel Trigano; *L'économie chabbatique* (The Sabbath Economy) by Raphaël Draï; *Ethique juive et modernité* (Jewish Ethics and Modernity) by Chief Rabbi Alexandre Safran; and *La pensée du Retour chez Emmanuel Lévinas* (The Idea of Return in the Work of Emmanuel Lévinas) by Benny Lévy.

Finally, in the category of fiction there were such titles as *Depuis deux mille ans* (For Two Thousand Years) by the Jewish Romanian writer Mihaïl Sebastian (1907-1945), whose *Diary* (1939-1945) was also published this year; *Deux juifs voyagent dans un train* (Two Jews Travel in a Train) by Adam Biro; *Hammerklavier* by Yasmina Réza; *Insomnie* (Insomnia) by Rosie Delpuech; and *Rouge c'est la vie* (Red, That's Life) by Thierry Jonquet, a well-known author of crime novels.

Personalia

Israeli ambassador Avi Pazner was named a Commander of the Legion of Honor on the eve of his return to Israel, where he assumed the office of president of Keren Hayesod. Rabbi Charles Liché was similarly honored. Claude Hampel, director of *Cahiers Yiddish* (Yiddish Notebooks), was named a Knight of the Order of Arts and Letters, affording an opportunity for the Protestant minister of culture Catherine Trautmann to make a speech in praise of the Yiddish language.

Prominent Jews who died in 1998 included Bernard Picard, an educator who directed the Paris Hebrew schools Lucien de Hirsch and Yavneh, in April, in Jerusalem, aged 73; Jacques Orfus, a Zionist leader, in May, aged 93; and Marc Aron, a physician and community leader, in October, aged 68.

MEIR WAINTRATER

The Netherlands

National Affairs

THE YEAR 1998 was one of relative political stability and economic prosperity. In elections for the municipal councils (March 4) and for the 150 seats of the Second Chamber of Parliament (May 6), the Centrum Left D'66 (Democrats 1966) Party, which had been a partner in the government coalition, lost almost half its seats, while the two main coalition partners, Labour (PvdA) and the Liberals (VVD), gained. The more left-wing parties—the Green Left and the Socialist Party (SP))—gained substantially, the small Calvinist parties remained stable, and the extreme right was almost entirely wiped out. With a majority of the seats in the Second Chamber, Labor (PvdA) and the Liberal VVD could have formed a cabinet alone, but preferred to draw in D'66 and to exclude again, as they had done in the outgoing coalition, the Christian Democrats (CDA). Still, the three prospective coalition partners differed on a number of issues, and negotiations lasted over three months.

The new government was again headed by Willem Kok (Labor) as premier. There were a number of changes in cabinet posts. Foreign Minister Hans van Mierlo, since 1966 the personification of D'66, had wanted to remain in the government, but when it was decided that the post of foreign minister would go to the VVD, he decided to leave political life altogether. One of the new officials was Prof. Job Cohen, the undersecretary of justice, formerly rector of the University of Maastricht. He assumed the unenviable task of overseeing policy toward asylum seekers.

Among the newcomers to Parliament was 54-year-old Judith C. Belinfante (PvdA), who, after more than 25 years as director of the Jewish Historical Museum in Amsterdam, decided she wanted a change. She was placed high on the PvdA list of candidates—number ten—though she had not previously been active politically.

The Netherlands had several successes in foreign affairs in 1998. It was elected (from January 1, 1999) to be a nonpermanent member of the United Nations Security Council, winning out over Greece. Willem Duisenberg, until recently president of the Netherlands State Bank, was appointed president of the European Central Bank in Frankfurt, against the initial opposition of France. The appointment is in principle for a period of four years.

The Hague is the seat of the International Court trying war criminals from the former Yugoslavia. The government agreed to provide a site for the tribunal scheduled to try the two Libyans believed responsible for the crash of a Pan-

American aircraft over Lockerbie, Scotland, in December 1988. By the end of the year, however, Libya had not yet agreed to extradite the two men.

Israel and the Middle East

Yasir Arafat visited Holland on several occasions during the year. Two outgoing cabinet ministers, who were in office until August 3, were particularly sympathetic to the demands of the Palestinian Authority—Minister of Foreign Affairs Hans van Mierlo (D'66) and Minister of Development Aid to Third World Countries Jan Pronk (PvdA).

In a visit to The Hague on February 5, where he was received officially by Premier Kok and Foreign Minister van Mierlo, Arafat held a press conference at which he called attention to delays in the construction of the harbor in Gaza, for which the Netherlands government had promised a contribution of 50 million florins (over $25 million). The Netherlands was in fact one of the largest donors for projects in the areas under Palestinian control. Arafat visited Holland again on March 30-31, to address a symposium at the Erasmus University of Rotterdam on the economic development of the areas under the Palestinian Authority.

In Rotterdam he was received by the mayor; in The Hague he was received by Queen Beatrix and by the Parliamentary Foreign Affairs Commission. The next day he visited Amsterdam where, accompanied by Mayor Schelto Patijn and some Dutch sympathizers, he toured the Amsterdam canals by boat and alighted at the Anne Frank House, where he was received by the director, Hans Westra. The Anne Frank House had been cleared of all other visitors and was heavily guarded, even with a helicopter overhead. Arafat stayed there for about 15 minutes. Asked by a journalist at the door what his impression was he answered "Very moving." The Jewish community had not been informed in advance of the visit.

On June 30, the Foreign Ministry delayed the departure of a delegation of officials to Israel indefinitely, until more progress could be seen in the peace negotiations between Israel and the Palestinians.

THE EL AL BOEING CRASH AGAIN

Nearly six years after the crash of an El Al Boeing 747 cargo plane in Amsterdam—on October 4, 1992—in which 43 people were killed, the incident was still the subject of controversy. In September the Dutch newspaper *NRC Handelsblad* reported that the plane had been carrying 49 gallons of dimethyl methylphosphonate, a key component in the nerve gas Sarin, that had come from a Pennsylvania firm and was being sent to the Israel Institute for Biological Research in Nes Ziona, near Tel Aviv. El Al confirmed the report, saying that the chemical was included in the original cargo list and that Dutch authorities had known about it since the crash. The chemical is also used in construction as a flame retardant; the Israelis reportedly told the manufacturer that it would be used to test absorption filters.

The crash had occurred in the Bijlmer district in the southeasternmost tip of Amsterdam, a largely new immigrant neighborhood. The dead included three crew members, the plane's only passenger, a woman, and 39 residents of the new immigrant neighborhood. Boeing assumed full responsibility and paid compensation to the next-of-kin of the victims and others who lived in the area.

In 1998 the issue was not the responsibility for the crash but the nature of the cargo, specifically, whether the newly discovered chemical was related to a variety of health problems that had been reported by some of the residents as well as some firemen and policemen and KLM employees who worked in a hangar where the remnants of the crashed plane were stored. Until this latest revelation, it was claimed that poisonous substances—possibly fumes from burning "depleted uranium" carried in the tail of the plane as ballast—may have caused delayed health problems. At the insistence of members of the Second Chamber of Parliament, 23 reporting centers were set up in the Bijlmer, and a telephone reporting center at the nearby Academic Medical Center (AMC). The latter eventually reported that of some 700 complaints received, only 300 could be connected with the disaster, and that most of these were psychological, such as sleeplessness and nightmares.

Questions and allegations about the episode were widespread. Some of the cargo freight documents were no longer available. Part of the cargo may have been military materiel for Israel. Some eyewitnesses claimed to have seen men in white fireproof suits, speaking a foreign language, at the site of the crash, picking up certain material. It was recalled that the cockpit voice recorder had never been found. And it was charged that El Al at Schiphol Airport constituted "a state within the state," where non-Israelis were denied access, with the consent of Dutch authorities.

Great concern was caused by the belated discovery that the cargo had contained the DMMP chemical. Although it had been mentioned in the freight documents, nobody had paid attention to it. And even after a Dutch expert stated that DMMP in itself is harmless, the unrest continued, fanned by some of the news media and by Labor parliamentarian Robert van Gijzel, chairman of the Parliamentary Transport Committee. Eventually Parliament decided to hold a high-level official inquiry in which witnesses testify under oath. A commission appointed to organize the inquiry began work in November. Some 50 to 100 witnesses were to be heard, and public hearings were scheduled for early in 1999.

Anti-Semitism and Neo-Nazism

At the end of October some 60 neo-Nazis from Holland, Belgium, Germany, and France held a meeting in a hotel in the countryside, where they had hired a hall under an assumed name. The meeting commemorated the coup by Hitler in 1923.

An article in the anarchist periodical *Ravage*, which is connected with the squatters' movement and has a very limited distribution, charged that B'nai

B'rith, in particular in the United States, had before and during World War II collaborated with the German Nazis and with the Ku Klux Klan. The Dutch B'nai B'rith lodges sued the paper and the author of the article, but the court ruled that their claim was inadmissible, because not they but the American B'nai B'rith was the injured party.

Holocaust-Related Matters

Material claims by Jews or their heirs resulting from the Nazi occupation of the Netherlands continued to be in the news. (See AJYB 1998, pp. 274-77.) Following the decision by the special commission headed by Jos van Kemenade, in consultation with the newly formed Committee of Jewish Organizations on External Matters (CJOEB, usually referred to as CJO), that the sum of Fl. 19 million would be turned over to the Jewish community in the Netherlands (rather than to individuals), the money was transferred by the Ministry of Finance to Joods Maatschappelijk Werk (JMW, the Jewish Social Welfare Board). JMW in turn transferred the funds to the JOKOS Foundation, which had been established in the late 1940s and been inactive since 1971 but had never been formally liquidated. Distribution of the money was overseen by an advisory committee headed by Dick Dolman, a former chairman of the Second Chamber of Parliament and a former chairman of the Netherlands-Israel Society, assisted by four Jewish members.

It was eventually decided that Fl. 1.5 million ($750,000) would be allocated to needy survivors living in the Netherlands. To handle distribution of the funds, a Dutch Commission for Needy Victims (NCNW) was established in June, comprising the CJO and five other organizations: the Society of Caring for the Interests of Victims of Persecution (VBV), the Hidden Child Society (HOK), the Jewish War Children's Society (JOK), the Netherlands Auschwitz Committee (NAC), and the Jewish Postwar Generation Committee (JONAG). It was estimated that a maximum of a thousand Jewish persons or households in Holland fit the definition of "needy"; they would receive an average payment of about Fl. 1,500 or $750.

For individual claims to gold, money, and valuables looted by the Nazis, a Central Reporting Point was opened on March 2, which remained open until October. Some 3,500 claims were submitted. The administrative costs of this office were borne by the Ministry of Finance.

Interest continued in the matter of some 3,000 LiRo (Lippman-Rosenthal) cards discovered in December 1997 in the attic of a building formerly occupied by the Amsterdam branch of the Ministry of Finance. These were records from the former Lippman-Rosenthal bank of assets and valuables that Jews were forced to turn over to the Nazis prior to deportation. Thousands of requests to inspect the cards by survivors or their heirs were received by JMW, but few found the names of their relatives.

In addition to the Van Kemenade Commission, the government established three other commissions to examine official reparation activities in Holland in 1945 and after:

The Kordes Commission, chaired by Frans Kordes, a former state comptroller, sought to establish the value of Jewish property that had been looted in Holland during the Nazi occupation but had not been compensated for. Excluded were art objects, for which a special commission was appointed. In December, in its preliminary report, the commission concluded that the manner in which claims were dealt with after the war was correct, but too legalistic and cold. It estimated that the State of the Netherlands should pay the Jewish community an amount of Fl. 48.4 million (nearly $25 million) to compensate for mistakes made with regard to Jewish claims in 1945 and after. The Jewish community, according to the Kordes Commission, was also entitled to the Fl. 25 million which at the time it was taxed in order to pay for the maintenance of the Jewish concentration camp of Westerbork and the Jewish part of the Vught camp. The sum of nearly Fl. 50 million does not, however, take account of the inflation of the intervening 50 years. Kordes himself expressed hope for a generous compensation of some Fl. 200 million (nearly $100 million).

The Scholten Commission, headed by W. Scholten, the vice-president of the Netherlands Council of State, also published its preliminary report in December. This commission was established to investigate whether Dutch banks and insurance companies had illegally retained money deposited with them by Jews. The commission concluded that not only had this hardly occurred, but also that it had been impossible, since in 1941, at the order of the Nazis, Jews had to transfer all assets held by banks—including mortgages, patent rights, and so forth—to the Lippman-Rosenthal bank, which had been taken over by the Nazis. After the war several dozen accounts, most smaller than Fl. 100 ($50), for which no heirs were reported, reverted to the banks. Some 90 percent of the bank balances were refunded to the owners, their heirs, or to JMW. Jewish critics thought the inquiry was flawed, since only the 11 largest banks were thoroughly examined.

A third commission, the Ekkart Commission, was to examine the legal ownership of some 3,585 of the 20,000 art objects removed by the Nazis during the years 1940-45 from Holland and reclaimed from Germany after the war. Some were returned to their original owners; the remainder were turned over to the State of the Netherlands, which donated or loaned them to Dutch museums or government institutions. The Ekkart Commission was to establish whether any of these works originally belonged to Jews, a complicated matter that could take several years to resolve.

The case involving the collection of the late art dealer Jacques Goudstikker was still in the courts (see AJYB 1998, pp. 276–77). The Dutch government was being sued by Goudstikker's daughter-in-law and granddaughters (supported by the World Jewish Congress) for a large sum, in compensation for the valuable collection, which was largely housed in Dutch museums. The government rejected the claim on the ground that in 1952, Goudstikker's widow had accepted a settlement of Fl. 2 million and waived all rights to the collection. The daughter-in-law, Marel von Saher, and her lawyers argued that she had done so only under duress, and that the agreement was therefore invalid.

The mystery of the "Treasure of Almelo" (see AJYB 1998, p. 276) was solved this year. An investigation revealed that the Jewish ritual objects and other valuables contained in a suitcase discovered by a Canadian soldier in April 1945 had in fact been returned to the legitimate heirs, or to the Jewish community of Arnhem, after the war.

The Anne Frank House in Amsterdam, which belongs to the Anne Frank Foundation and is not a Jewish institution, had a record number of visitors this year, over 812,000, 15 percent more than in the previous year. The increase was linked to a general rise in tourism to Amsterdam and to worldwide publicity about the discovery of five previously unknown pages from Anne's diary. Otto Frank, Anne's father, had withheld the pages and entrusted them to a Dutch non-Jewish friend, Cor Suyk, who subsequently worked for the Anne Frank Foundation in Amsterdam and for the Anne Frank Center in New York. The new pages, which suggest that the Franks' marriage was less than ideal, are mentioned in one of the two biographies of Anne Frank that were published in Holland within a week of each other in September. Melissa Muller of Vienna, one of the biographers, had been shown the new pages by Cor Suyk. The other biography is by Carol Ann Lee of London.

A legal dispute broke out between the Anne Frank Fund in Basel, which holds the copyright on the *Diary of Anne Frank*, and the Dutch daily *Het Parool*, which published the paraphrased text of the missing pages. The center in Basel charged that this was an infringement of copyright, but a judge ruled that *Het Parool* had not acted illegally. Another dispute concerned the announcement by Cor Suyk that he was prepared to hand over the five pages in his possession to the RIOD, the Netherlands State Institute for War Documentation in Amsterdam, which has custody of the original manuscript of the diary, in return for a few million guilders for the Anne Frank Center in New York, which was short of money. He later said he would hand over the five pages to the RIOD without any conditions.

In the town of Weesp, some 15 kilometers east of Amsterdam, the small synagogue that had been closed since 1942 and later served as a storeroom was restored to its original condition and will be used for cultural activities connected with Judaism. The initiative for the restoration was taken by a committee headed by Protestant clergyman Dick Pruiksma, who is also the present chairman of OJEC, the Consultative Council of Jews and Christians. Of the 68 Jews who lived in Weesp in 1940, nine survived the war.

JEWISH COMMUNITY

Demography

No official statistics exist on the number of Jews living in the Netherlands, but it is estimated at about 25,000. Of these only about one-third are affiliated with any of the three main communities—Ashkenazic, Sephardic, and Liberal. According to the Jewish Social Welfare Foundation (JMW), there were also some 10,000 Israelis now living in Holland, many with non-Jewish partners. The Netherlands Ashkenazi Community (NIK) had 5,313 members at the end of 1996, some 200 less than the previous year. Of these some 3,000 were in Amsterdam and the Amsterdam suburb of Amstelveen, 340 in The Hague area, and 332 in the Rotterdam area. In Almere, a new satellite town of Amsterdam, a group of some 40 Jews was formed.

Communal Affairs

On February 18, the Central Council of the Ashkenazi Community (NIK) adopted a motion, by a large majority, enabling women to become members of this body. In actuality, women's participation had already been made possible by the revision of the council's electoral regulations of 1982, but the rabbis had always opposed its implementation. Shortly after the recent vote, at its meeting of March 3, the Central Council elected Mrs. Marcelle Lange (né Swaab) to one of the vacant seats. Fifteen members of the NIK, together with Amsterdam rabbi Frank Lewis, opposed the decision and asked Chief Rabbi of Israel Yisrael Meir Lau to bring the matter to a rabbinic court.

On May 12, Johan Sanders, age 60, officially retired as secretary of the NIK, a position he had held for the past 25 years. To mark the occasion, he was awarded a knighthood in the Order of Orange-Nassau. He was succeeded by 30-year-old Ruben Vis.

The Central Council of the NIK designated the sum of Fl. 350,000 (some $175,000) to be used to stimulate Jewish activity outside of Amsterdam. As part of this effort it appointed a full-time religious services director. The NIK also contributed Fl. 75,000 (some $37,500) to help support the new Jewish Center for Young People in Amsterdam, in particular its kosher restaurant; it increased its subsidy for Jewish education by 10 percent (to Fl. 700,000 or some $350,000), the increase made possible by the growth in revenue from the export of kosher meat.

For the first time since 1940 a new congregation joined the NIK. It is located in Almere, a satellite town of Amsterdam that began development 25 years ago on a drained section of the Zuider Zee and now numbers 140,000 inhabitants. There are enough Jews to hold regular religious services, for the present in a rented room. The religious functionary is Moshe Stiefel, an American affiliated with Chabad. (Other Dutch religious officials connected with U.S. Chabad are Rabbi Isaac Vorst of Amsterdam and his son Yuda and Rabbi Binyomin Jacobs, the NIK rabbi serving the provinces.)

The Sephardi Community of Amsterdam (PIG), following the retirement of Rabbi Barend Drukarch, engaged Dayan Pinchas Toledano of the Spanish and Portuguese Synagogue in London as an advisory rabbi, to come to Amsterdam when necessary and to arbitrate religious issues. On one controversial matter, he ruled that Jews married to non-Jewish partners can remain members of the community. The PIG now numbered some 400 members, most of them children of mixed Sephardi-Ashkenazi origin. Others had come to Holland from Israel, Morocco, Iraq, and other countries.

When efforts failed to raise sufficient funds privately to restore the Portuguese-Jewish cemetery at Ouderkerk near Amsterdam, where many of the ancient tombstones have sunk into the swampy soil, the Dutch government agreed to provide the sum of Fl. 1.2 million (some $600,000) for the project.

The Liberal Jewish Community (LJG), with six local congregations, opened a new synagogue in Tilburg, to serve the entire province of North Brabant. The congregation is housed in the former Ashkenazi synagogue, which was renovated after years of disuse.

On June 28, Peter Halpern resigned as *hazzan* of the LJG, which he had served for nearly ten years, to return to the United States, where he was born, to become the full-time cantor at Temple Adath Elohim congregation near Los Angeles. He was succeeded by Ken Gould, an American who had been studying music in Amsterdam since 1995 and was also connected with Beth Chiddush, a progressive group of mainly American Jews living in Holland, which was founded in 1996. Beth Chiddush held a workshop in Amsterdam with the American rabbi Shefa Gold. During the International Gay Games in Amsterdam in the first week of August, the group organized a service for all Jewish participants, conducted by the American rabbi Nancy Wiener. Shalhomo, the Dutch Jewish gay and lesbian organization, also arranged special activities during the games.

A gratifying cooperative effort was the coming together of the Orthodox Jewish women's group, Deborah, and the Women's Group of the LJG to form the Dutch National Council of Jewish Women (NCJW). Until now, the Liberal women had been the only Jewish group in Holland represented in the International Council of Jewish Women (ICJW). The newly formed council held occasional meetings and issued a modest quarterly.

The Jewish Social Welfare Board (Joods Maatschappelijk Werk, JMW) issued a report in December in which it stated that 75 percent of the Jews living in Holland today had a non-Jewish partner or were children of a mixed marriage. How this figure was obtained is not clear, since for a number of reasons no Jewish demographic survey had been carried out in Holland for over 30 years. The report also discussed the changing mission of JMW, noting that some of its former tasks had been superseded or were greatly reduced, since the material needs of the Jews in Holland were largely cared for by the government. While JMW had played a role for many years in processing claims for payments under the WUV, the Law on Payments to War Victims, which was passed in 1972, this work had now been largely completed. In addition to its remaining tasks, such as providing domestic help for the elderly, JMW saw a new role for itself in providing expert help to Jewish persons suffering from alcohol and drug addiction—who might feel most comfortable being treated in a Jewish setting.

ISRAEL'S 50TH ANNIVERSARY

The official celebration of the 50th anniversary of the State of Israel began on December 23, 1997, the first night of Hanukkah, in the courtyard of The Hague town hall, in the presence of Dutch Premier Willem Kok and the mayor of The Hague, Willem Deetman, who was also the new chairman of the Netherlands Israel Society. Israeli ambassador Yossi Gal kindled the first light in a huge menorah, as a symbolic inauguration of the anniversary year.

The central celebration took place on April 29, 1998, in Amsterdam in the large RAI Center. A special committee representing most Jewish organizations in Holland organized the program, which was varied and took account of all ages. The hall, which could seat 2,000 persons, was sold out well in advance, and many requests for tickets had to be rejected for lack of space.

On April 26, a joint worship service for members of the Sephardi and Ashkenazi communities filled the Sephardi Esnoga in Amsterdam. The service was conducted by chief hazzan Naphtali Herstik of Jerusalem; Israeli chief rabbi Lau delivered the sermon. In the main Ashkenazi synagogue of Amsterdam a special service was held on April 30, conducted by Amsterdam chief cantor Hans Bloemendal. The same night Israeli ambassador Gal sponsored a special Yom Ha'atzmaut concert in The Hague for both non-Jewish and Jewish invited guests.

Many television and radio programs devoted attention to the jubilee, some positive and some negative. The VPRO broadcasting organization presented a series of five radio programs on Dutch Jewish immigrants in Israel in various periods. One TV program had an interview with the former Dutch ambassador to Moscow, Pieter Buwalda. During his tenure there, the Netherlands represented Israel's interests, and he issued thousands of exit visas to Russian Jews on Israel's behalf. Now he visited families in Israel with whom he and his wife had become friendly. On a different program, the former Dutch undersecretary for defense, Bernard Stemerdink, told how he and and the then minister of defense secretly supplied spare parts for Israeli tanks during the Yom Kippur war, without the knowledge of the other members of the cabinet.

Some of the TV and radio programs were critical, or at least probing, dealing with such subjects as the loss of the idealism of the pioneers and kibbutz founders, or with the position of the Palestinians, in particular in the refugee camps. The controversial Israeli TV documentary *Tkumah* (see "Israeli Culture" elsewhere in this volume) was also shown on Dutch television. A documentary on Yitzhak Rabin, produced by Willy Lindwer of Amsterdam for Joop van den Ende Productions, had its gala premiere in Amsterdam, in the presence of Leah Rabin.

The anniversary celebration ended on December 13 with a concert of liturgical music in Amsterdam, featuring the Jerusalem Great Synagogue choir and the Amsterdam Synagogue choir, the latter conducted by Barry Mehler.

Culture

A symposium on the history of Dutch Jewry was held in Jerusalem from November 22 to 25, part of an ongoing program of symposia held every two or three years, alternating between Amsterdam and Jerusalem. In Amsterdam the meetings are organized by the Commission for the History of Dutch Jewry of the Royal Academy of Sciences, in Jerusalem by the Institute for the History of Dutch Jewry at the Hebrew University. Of the 36 lectures this year, 23 were given by scholars who had come to Jerusalem from Holland specifically for this conference. Most of the audience were immigrants from Holland living in Israel.

There were signs of growing interest in Yiddish, which was nearly absent in Holland before 1940. The newly established Jiddisjer Krajz, together with the Bibliotheca Rosenthaliana, organized a study day on the Yiddish poet Itzik Manger (1901-1961), on November 29 in Amsterdam. The Second International Yiddish Festival was held in Amsterdam in September. On December 3, the Menasse ben Israel Institute, established in 1997, organized a study day in Amsterdam on Yiddish in Western Europe with the participation of scholars from Holland and abroad. The institute coordinates Jewish studies at the University of Amsterdam and at the Free University.

The most important Jewish exhibition of the year was at the Jewish Historical Museum in Amsterdam: "Vienna and the Jews Around the Year 1900," organized with the participation of the Jewish Museum in Vienna, the Netherlands-Austria Society, the Goethe Institute in Amsterdam, and the Netherlands-Germany Society. The exhibition was scheduled to travel to the Israel Museum in Jerusalem and the Jewish Museum in Vienna. In Amsterdam, where it was on view from October 14 to January 17, 1999, it was accompanied by lectures and other events related to the history of the Jews in Vienna.

The bronze gates created by Albert Drielsma for the ancient Sephardi burial ground in Middelburg were officially unveiled on May 27. In 1994 Drielsma had restored the small synagogue of Middelburg (the capital of the province of Zealand), where all 95 of the tombstones in the town's Jewish cemetery, unused for centuries, were restored at local initiative.

Publications

As in previous years, a large number of books on Jewish subjects were published, fiction and nonfiction, in the original Dutch or in translation, and appealing to non-Jewish as well as Jewish buyers.

On a Sunday afternoon during the annual Book Week in March, the book department of De Bijenkorf, the large Amsterdam department store, presented some 25 Jewish authors—Dutch, Israeli, and American—who signed their books for purchasers, many of them waiting in long queues. That evening, several of these authors, among them Amos Oz, Meir Shalev, and A.B. Yehoshua, participated in a panel discussion and workshop, also before an avid audience.

Among new books in Dutch may be mentioned three personal accounts of wartime experiences. Auschwitz survivor Joseph Hillel Borensjtajn's *Diary 1940-45* was written in Yiddish and later sent by the author to YIVO in New York where it was found by his son, who translated it into Dutch. Yaakov Ben Dror (Van Gelder)'s *Naar de hel en terug* (To Hell and Back) and Hans Kahn's *Mazzel en lef, Tegen de stroom in* (Against the Stream)are the other two personal accounts.

Translations into Dutch included novels by Pearl Abraham, Giorgio Bassani, Yoram Kaniuk, Amos Oz, A.B. Yehoshua, Bernard Malamud, and Meir Shalev, and nonfiction works by Stephen Beller (*Vienna and the Jews*), Deborah Dworak (*Children with a Yellow Star*), and Arthur Hertzberg (*Jews, Identity and Character*), the latter arousing considerable discussion. The biographies of Anne Frank by Carol Ann Lee and Melissa Muller appeared in Dutch translation before their publication in the original English and German, respectively. The same applied to the history of the Nazi persecution of the Jews in the Netherlands 1940-1945 by Bob Moore, *Slachtoffers en Overlevenden* (Victims and Survivors).

Personalia

Judith C. Belinfante retired as director of the Jewish Historical Museum in Amsterdam, with which she had been connected for over 25 years, in order to become a member of the Second Chamber of Parliament for Labor. She was succeeded by Rivkah Blok Weiss from the Israel Museum in Jerusalem, the daughter of Dutch-Jewish parents who had settled in Israel, where she was educated.

Among leading Jews who died in 1998 were Barend Drukarch, 81, a religious functionary, former Haham of the Portuguese congregation of Amsterdam; Prof. Frits Schwarz, 69, former member of the executive of the NIK and chairman of the Jewish community of Utrecht, a survivor of concentration camps who studied medicine in Utrecht, where eventually he became a professor of endocrinology and dean of the Medical Faculty; Prof. David Simon, 94, an emeritus professor of law in Rotterdam, honorary officer of the Dutch Zionist Organization, and one of the three members of the commission that revised the Dutch constitution after World War II; and Mira Rafalowicz, 59, a champion of Yiddish in Holland, daughter of Polish Jewish immigrants who in the 1920s were the founders of ANSKI, the Yiddish Culture Group in Amsterdam. A former student at the YIVO Institute in New York, where she also studied dramaturgy, she was the main organizer of the 1st and 2nd International Yiddish Festivals in Amsterdam.

HENRIETTE BOAS

Italy

National Affairs

PRIME MINISTER ROMANO PRODI resigned in October 1998. His center-left government lost a parliamentary confidence vote by just one vote after the Marxist Communist Refoundation Party rejected the 1999 draft budget and withdrew its support from Prodi's coalition. Italy's 56th postwar government was sworn in later in the month, with Massimo D'Alema, a former Communist, as prime minister. His cabinet included the first Marxists—two ministers—to serve in an Italian government since 1947, as well as three ministers from the centrist UDR Party, whose leader, former president Francesco Cossiga, and D'Alema were once bitter political enemies. Italy's economy meanwhile slowed, with the 1998 GDP growth rate projected as less than 2 percent.

A constant concern throughout the year was how to deal with the waves of illegal immigrants, mainly from the developing world, that arrived on Italian shores on overcrowded boats and rafts. Many clandestine immigrants were Kurds or refugees from Albania and from Yugoslavia's strife-torn Kosovo province. With the abolition of border controls between Italy and its European Union (EU) neighbors, Italy's long coastline was seen by many as an easy gateway into the larger European Union.

Italian right-wing leader Gianfranco Fini continued his efforts to distance his National Alliance Party (AN) from its neofascist roots. At a convention in Verona at the end of February and beginning of March, which was attended by a delegation from Israel's Likud Party, he made overtures of rapprochement to Israel and the Jewish world. Fini—who had long wanted to visit Israel in order to demonstrate his rejection of the Fascist past—gave a lengthy interview to Israeli television in which he called the anti-Semitic laws enacted by Italy's Fascists in 1938 "a horror" and said Mussolini was "by now a figure who is part of history." In his closing speech in Verona, Fini said that people should not forget "the many Italians who were deported [during World War II] only because they were Jews." Before the conference, AN member Franco Perlasca publicly called on Fini to make an even stronger condemnation of the past. (Perlasca is the son of the late Giorgio Perlasca, an Italian businessman who saved as many as 5,000 Jews in the Budapest ghetto by pretending to be a Spanish diplomat and issuing false Spanish passports.)

March 1998 marked the 150th anniversary of the statute issued in 1848 by King Carlo Alberto of Savoy, emancipating Italian Jews under his rule. The Italian government issued a postage stamp to mark the occasion, a commemorative ceremony was held in Parliament, and numerous exhibitions and other events took place around the country, sponsored by both civic authorities and the Jewish community.

Israel and the Middle East

Italy continued its policy of maintaining good relations with both Israel and the Arab world. Italian leaders supported the peace process and did not hide their disapproval of Israeli prime minister Benjamin Netanyahu's hard-line policies. Yitzhak Rabin remained an emblematic figure. In December Italy's Highway (Autostrada) Administration, whose president was a firm supporter of Israel, organized a Christmas concert in a church to promote peace and to honor Rabin's memory. Leah Rabin was a guest of honor, and the orchestra was conducted by Israeli maestro Daniel Oren. Early in the year, the same agency had published a coffee-table book on Jerusalem.

Numerous events were held in Italy to mark the 50th anniversary of Israel, including concerts, exhibitions, broadcasts, and conferences. In March the Israeli embassy and the Rome municipality sponsored a 12-day festival of films, music, lectures, and other events, including a gala fashion show by Israeli designers, called "Journey Through Israel" and held at the Exposition Palace, a major exhibition hall in downtown Rome.

Italy meanwhile took steps to improve relations with Islamic countries. In June Prime Minister Prodi paid an official visit to Tehran, becoming the most important European leader to visit the Iranian capital since the 1979 revolution. Senior Italian leaders visited other Islamic countries. In July Italy signed an agreement with Libya aimed at helping to ease that country's isolation. In December Italian leaders were openly critical of the U.S. and British bombing of Iraq.

During a visit to Italy in mid-June, during which he also met with Pope John Paul II, Palestinian leader Yasir Arafat held talks with Italian leaders and called on Europe to use economic pressure to force Israel to accelerate the peace process. In Florence, Arafat received the Golden Pegasus Peace Prize granted by the region of Tuscany.

Vatican-Mideast Relations

The Vatican maintained an "evenhanded" approach to political events in the Middle East, repeatedly stressing support for the peace process and decrying moves it considered detrimental to negotiations. Pope John Paul II and other Vatican officials were critical of Israeli policy, particularly regarding Jerusalem. In his Easter message in April, for example, John Paul criticized Jewish building activity in Arab east Jerusalem, asserting that peace in Jerusalem was being put at risk by "dangerous political decisions." In October he praised the Wye memorandum signed in Washington as "the fruit of arduous and courageous negotiations."

During a visit to Jerusalem at the end of October, the Vatican's foreign minister, Archbishop Jean-Louis Tauran, said that east Jerusalem was "illegally occupied" by the Israelis and called for international guarantees for sites considered holy by Christians, Jews, and Muslims. Following a suicide bombing in a Jerusalem market in November, carried out by Arab terrorists, the pope condemned the action, saying it raised fears for the success of the peace process.

At the end of April, a PLO delegation met with Vatican officials and agreed to set up a bilateral working commission with the Holy See to further mutual cooperation. The Vatican had established official diplomatic relations with the PLO in 1994, just four months after establishing full diplomatic relations with Israel. In June Palestinian leader Yasir Arafat had a 13-minute private audience with the pope at the Vatican. It was the sixth time the two men had met. According to a Vatican statement, Arafat told the pontiff about "the tragic situation of the Palestinian people, while the peace process is threatened by all sides." The pope confirmed the Vatican's support for the peace process, "which must continue with goodwill from all sides [and] with respect for the commitments already made and international law."

Efforts continued to induce the pope to visit the Holy Land. In January Israeli deputy prime minister and tourism minister Moshe Katzav met with John Paul and reiterated Israel's long-standing invitation for him to come to Israel. During his June stay in Rome, Yasir Arafat invited the pope to visit Bethlehem, sacred to Christians as the birthplace of Jesus, to mark the millennium, and said the pope had given him a "positive reaction." Also in June, Vatican envoy Roger Cardinal Etchegaray toured the Iraqi town of Ur, revered as the birthplace of Abraham, and reiterated the pope's desire to visit biblical sites throughout the Middle East, including Ur. Earlier, in April, Chief Rabbi Elio Toaff of Rome told an interviewer that he was ready to travel with the pope to Israel. Vatican officials said that, while preparations were being made for a papal visit to the Holy Land, such a trip would depend both on the pope's health and on the status of the peace process.

In August Israel and the Vatican clashed over Israel's attempts to block the nomination of a Palestinian refugee living in Brazil, Bishop Boutros Mouallem — a man Israel considered a supporter of the PLO — as the new archbishop of Galilee. Prime Minister Netanyahu accused the Vatican of having acceded to political pressure from the PLO in appointing Mouallem Galilee bishop of the Greek Catholic Church, an Eastern-rite branch of Catholicism that is loyal to Rome. At the same time, the Holy See's observer mission to the United Nations in New York released a document criticizing Israel's decision to expand the jurisdiction of Jerusalem, saying the move "certainly does not favor a dialogue aimed at a solution of the problem of the Holy City." Mouallem took up his post in October without incident.

The Vatican expressed strong disapproval of the U.S. and British bombing of Iraq in December. In May Iraqi deputy prime minister Tariq Aziz had met with the pope and senior Vatican officials in Rome. A Vatican spokesman at that time expressed sympathy for Iraq, saying that it was suffering "negative consequences" from the UN embargo.

Holocaust-Related Developments

This year marked the 60th anniversary of the imposition of anti-Semitic racial laws by the Fascist goverment of Benito Mussolini. Italy's public authorities, as well as Italy's Jews, marked the anniversary with a wide array of commemorations, conferences, exhibits, concerts, publications, and other activities. These were aimed at memorializing the Jews who were persecuted, condemning the policy of the Fascist state, and also examining the behavior of mainstream Italians, most of whom did little to protest or combat the racist restrictions.

The series of anti-Semitic laws—passed between September 2 and November 17, 1938—barred Jews from public life and subjected them to a wide range of restrictions and persecutions. The racist laws were especially shocking for the highly acculturated Jews of Italy, because, unlike in Nazi Germany, the persecution began with relatively little warning, and it more or less reversed the prior, largely nondiscriminatory policy of the Fascist regime. Only about 40,000-50,000 Jews lived in Italy before World War II. They were well integrated into Italian society, so much so that, before 1938, thousands of them had become members of the Fascist Party. Although most Italians did little to actively oppose or protest the racist laws, it was not until Mussolini was deposed in 1943, and the Germans occupied the northern part of Italy, that Italian Jews were rounded up and deported to death camps. After the German occupation, however, many Italians hid Jews and helped them escape deportation. Israeli ambassador Yehudah Millo acknowledged this fact in a speech in late November in which he thanked the Italians for saving Jews during the Holocaust.

A conference on "Anti-Semitism in Europe in the 1930s: Comparing Legislation," was held in Milan in November, sponsored by the Center for Contemporary Jewish Documentation, Italy's only institution devoted to the study of the Holocaust and anti-Semitism. Another conference examined the experience of Jews under the racist laws in one Rome neighborhood. There were also reunions of classmates who were ousted from their schools in 1938 because of these laws. In Rome, a special course for school teachers on the laws and their effects was offered in November.

In January Carlo Maria Cardinal Martini of Milan joined Chief Rabbi Giuseppe Laras of that city in a ceremony unveiling the first public monument to the more than 1,500 Jews and antifascists deported from Milan to Nazi death camps. The memorial plaque, located at Milan's central train station, indicates that the deported included 1,237 Jews and 343 others who had been detained for political reasons. In April the Italian Parliament held a special ceremony attended by Italian Jewish leaders and senior Italian political figures to commemorate the 55th anniversary of the Warsaw Ghetto uprising.

VATICAN ACTIONS

Pope John Paul II bestowed two church honors this year that were viewed as troubling in the Jewish world. On October 3, during a two-day visit to Croatia, he beatified Zagreb's World War II archbishop, Alojzije Stepinac, a controversial prelate revered by Croatians as an anti-Communist martyr but reviled by some others as a Fascist collaborator. A week later, at the Vatican, he canonized Edith Stein, a German Jew who converted to Catholicism, became a nun, and was killed at Auschwitz. He called Stein both "an eminent daughter of Israel and a faithful daughter of the Church" and used the canonization to appeal for tolerance, dialogue, and reconciliation. He said that Stein's saint's day, August 9, would be celebrated each year as a Holocaust memorial, to remind the world "of that bestial plan to eliminate a people, which cost millions of Jewish brothers and sisters their lives."

For the Vatican, elevating Stein to sainthood was viewed as a way to honor Holocaust victims, but the move offended Jewish sensibilities. Efraim Zuroff, head of the Simon Wiesenthal Center's Jerusalem office, said, "The Pope is sending an extremely negative message to the Jewish community, that in the eyes of the Catholic Church, the best Jews are those that convert to Catholicism."

In November Israel's ambassador to the Vatican called for a half-century "moratorium" on the Holy See's plans to beatify controversial Pope Pius XII, whom critics accuse of remaining silent in the face of the Holocaust.

RESTITUTION

The issue of restitution of Jewish property had its echo in Italy, as in other countries. In June, five sacks containing jewels, watches, coins, gold teeth, and other personal belongings of Jews from the Trieste area killed in the Holocaust were returned by the government to the Trieste Jewish community at a ceremony in Rome. The sacks had been discovered in Treasury vaults in 1997 and turned over to the Union of Italian Jewish Communities (UIJC) later that year. In the 1998 ceremony, the valuables were formally restored to the Jews of Trieste.

Also in June, the Italian insurance company Assicurazioni Generali, one of 16 European insurance companies being sued for allegedly refusing to make good on policies taken out by Holocaust victims and survivors, provided Yad Vashem officials with a computer file containing names of some 300,000 Jews and non-Jews who had taken out policies before the war in Eastern and Central Europe. In August Generali pledged to pay $100 million as part of a settlement of Holocaust-era claims. In September, however, Generali canceled the offer. In

November Generali was one of six European insurers who agreed to deposit a total of $90 million in an escrow account as proof of their intent to settle claims by Holocaust victims and their heirs. The decision to establish the fund came during a ten-hour meeting in London of a new International Commission on Holocaust Era Insurance Claims, headed by former U.S. undersecretary of state Lawrence Eagleburger.

In November Treasury Minister Carlo Azeglio Ciampi announced that Italy would contribute 12 billion lire ($7 million) to an international fund designed to help needy victims of wartime Nazi persecution. The fund was established in December 1997 at the first international conference on Nazi gold. Ciampi said Italy's participation in the fund would be administered by the Union of Italian Jewish Communities.

Nazi War Criminals

In March an appeals court in Rome handed down life sentences on former SS officers Erich Priebke and Karl Hass for involvement in the March 1944 massacre of 335 men and boys at the Ardeatine caves near Rome. Italy's highest appeals court, the Court of Cassation, confirmed these verdicts in November, and Priebke, 85, was moved from an apartment where he had been held under house arrest, pending the final appeal, to a jail cell. The November verdict appeared to have brought to a close a long and dramatic affair.

Priebke had already been tried twice for his involvement in the massacre since he was discovered living in Argentina in 1994 and extradited to Rome 18 months later. Military judges at the first trial, in 1996, found Priebke guilty but set him free, citing a statute of limitations and other extenuating circumstances. This verdict was annulled after public protest, and Priebke was tried a second time in 1997, this time along with fellow ex-Nazi Karl Hass, also in his mid-80s. At the second trial, Priebke was given a 15-year sentence, which was sharply reduced due to extenuating circumstances, leaving him only a few months to serve. Hass was sentenced to ten years and eight months but was set free immediately due to extenuating circumstances. Both men appealed these verdicts in order to clear their names; their appeals were rejected and the sentences made more severe.

In March, Tullia Zevi, president of the Union of Jewish Communities in Italy, applauded the life sentences given to Priebke and Hass but indicated that she would be willing to accept an act of clemency that would allow them to be released from custody. Her view angered a militant faction within the Rome Jewish community whose members had been prominent in earlier protests against Priebke.

In January the Rome newspaper *La Repubblica* reported that 83-year-old Wilheim Schubernig, another former Nazi who may have taken part in the Ardeatine Caves massacre, had been discovered living in Austria. In June the trial began in Turin of former SS captain Theodor Saevecke, 87, who was accused of ordering the murder of 15 Italian partisans in Milan in August 1944. Saevecke, who lived in Germany, was being tried in absentia.

Anti-Semitism and Racism

Fallout continued throughout the year from a controversial book published in 1997, *Letter to a Jewish Friend*, by prominent political commentator and former ambassador Sergio Romano. Among other things, the author implied that anti-Semitism could originate in the "separateness" maintained by Jews themselves. He also called Israel an "imperious, arrogant warrior nation" that was exploiting the Holocaust to gain international legitimacy. Numerous Jewish commentators rebutted Romano in the media and on the lecture circuit. Italian-born Israeli diplomat Sergio Minerbi published a book called, simply, *Reply to Sergio Romano*. Romano raised eyebrows again in 1998 with a book and articles that reexamined Spain's Franco regime with a sympathetic eye.

There were a few isolated incidents of apparent anti-Semitism during 1998. In October a Jewish girl was taunted by a fellow pupil in a Rome public junior high school and as a result transferred to the Rome Jewish day school. In November two street signs denoting a city park in Rome named in honor of Yitzhak Rabin were destroyed by vandals. Graffiti on a nearby wall proclaimed "Death to Zionism." A city council representative called the vandalism "a barbarous act of ignoble violence." In December Italy's soccer federation opened a disciplinary investigation of the Rome and Lazio soccer teams after rival fans unfurled anti-Semitic banners at a match between the two teams in Rome.

JEWISH COMMUNITY

Demography

About 26,000 people were registered as members of Italian Jewish communities. Many others did not formally affiliate, and the total number of Jews was estimated at 30,000 to 40,000.

Three-quarters of Italy's Jews live in two cities: Rome, with about 15,000, and Milan, with about 10,000. The rest reside in a score of other towns and cities, mostly in northern Italy, in communities ranging from a handful to one thousand or so people.

About half of Italy's Jews were born in Italy, and half came as immigrants in the past few decades. One-third to one-half of Rome's Jews are Libyans who fled after bloody anti-Jewish riots in 1967 following the Six Day War. The Milan Jewish community consists of recent arrivals from more than two dozen countries, the largest contingent from Iran, and many from other Middle Eastern locales.

Communal Affairs

Official Judaism in Italy is exclusively Orthodox. There are no Reform or Conservative streams, and Reform or Conservative converts are not permitted to formally join Italian Jewish communities. In general, adult conversions are discouraged by the religious authorities.

The Chabad Lubavitch movement, which this year marked 40 years of activity in Italy, had a growing presence in the country. In Milan, in June, Chabad opened a study center and prayer room inside the famous shopping arcade, the Galleria Vittorio Emanuele, near the cathedral. Some 300 people took part in the inauguration ceremony, which included a joyous procession bringing the Torah, carried under a *huppah*, through the gallery past astonished tourists.

Most Italian Jews are highly acculturated and, while nominally Orthodox, are not strictly observant. The rate of intermarriage is 50 percent or more. A move toward stricter Orthodoxy in several communities, including Rome and Milan, has resulted in friction between increasingly militant religious traditionalists and nonobservant and secular Jews. Rabbis have expressed mounting concern that secular Jews have lost sight of what it means to be Jewish. In recent years, some younger people who adopted Orthodox observance became militant in criticizing Jews who were less stringent; they in turn were branded "fundamentalists" by secular Jews. Tensions in the community over who is a Jew and what is Judaism became so high that some predicted the community could be split apart. In Milan, in particular, the fact that many Jews from Muslim countries maintained their own rites and strictly observant life-style, which differ considerably from those of established Italian Jews, contributed to communal tensions. Some Italian Jews expressed the fear that the historic character of their community, with its tradition of integration into the surrounding society, was under siege.

A flashpoint of tension in 1998 was the ongoing controversy over the conversion of young children of mixed marriages. Many intermarried families in Italy raise their children as Jews, obtaining Orthodox conversions for them as infants or toddlers. In 1997, however, a rabbinical ruling decreed that small children could not be converted unless their mothers also converted, and that children of unconverted mothers would be barred from Jewish schools. The blanket ruling was relaxed to some extent, allowing each community with its rabbis to decide specific cases. But the deeper implications of the issue touched off widespread debate, protests, and specially convened public meetings, including a daylong seminar in Rome on March 15 called "To Be Born Jewish, to Become Jewish," devoted to examining many aspects relating to conversion and Jewish identity.

These frictions provided a troubled backdrop for the three-day congress of the Union of Italian Jewish Communities—the umbrella grouping of Italy's Jews—held in June in Rome. The congress is held every four years to chart policy and elect leaders, and delegates come from all Jewish communities around the country. Italy's president, Oscar Luigi Scalfaro, addressed the opening session, praising Jews and their heritage as a continuing patrimony of "enormous richness" for society at large. "Both for Italians in general and for me personally," he said, "friendship with the Jewish people and with Israel in particular is an absolute link that is not subject to discussion."

During the congress, Milan rabbi Giuseppe Laras, president of Italy's Rabbinical Assembly, warned that Jewish continuity was under threat. "At root is a widespread and advanced loss of Jewish identity, in religious, family and social terms," he said. "That which once seemed anomalous, illicit, dangerous and exceptional, today for many people no longer is so."

The congress marked a turning point for Italian Jews. Tullia Zevi stepped down as president of the UIJC after 16 years in office. During her tenure, Zevi had become one of the most prominent women in Italy, recognized as a national voice of moral authority. She also maintained a wide network of contacts with international Jewish organizations.

In July, at the first meeting of the new board chosen at the congress, Amos Luzzatto, 70, was elected to succeed Zevi as president of the UIJC. A physician by profession, Luzzatto, who lives in Venice, is also a respected scholar in Jewish studies and the editor of Italy's intellectual Jewish journal *La Rassegna Mensile di Israel*. He has also long been an active participant in interreligious dialogue.

The choice of Luzzatto appealed to a broad range of factions within the community, and Jews expressed the hope that he would be able to heal the rifts and enable different religious trends and traditions to coexist under an umbrella of unity. Though a secular intellectual himself, Luzzatto, who is descended from a venerable rabbinic family, has a profound knowledge of Jewish religious traditions. In an article published in a Jewish magazine in April, Luzzatto made clear his view that Italian Jews must learn to coexist in a flexible unity. "There should be a dialogue among everyone," he wrote, "not a standoff between rabbis and non-rabbis. . . . We must insist on the specific Italian situation, where the Rabbinate is not divided into opposing Orthodox and liberal, but is one sole entity, and is, with this, quite flexible." The community, too, he wrote, should be one all-encompassing entity that will welcome "Jews who belong to the 'Orthodox' as well as 'non-Orthodox' currents, as long as halakhic norms are respected."

Jewish-Catholic and Jewish-Muslim Relations

On October 16, Pope John Paul II marked the 20th anniversary of his election as pope. The occasion provided an opportunity to reflect on the changes that had taken place in Jewish-Catholic relations under his leadership. Most observers agreed that the two decades of his papacy had revolutionized relations between Roman Catholics and Jews. Through a variety of actions and statements, he instituted an official Catholic opening to Jews and showed an understanding of their sensitivities and their causes unprecedented in 2,000 years of church history. But there have also been serious gaps, particularly regarding the Vatican's handling of issues stemming from church and Catholic actions during the Holocaust.

Both the positive and problematic aspects of the pope's policy were evident throughout 1998. (See the discussion, above, of the canonization of Edith Stein and beatification of Cardinal Stepinac.)

In January the Anti-Defamation League honored Edward Cardinal Cassidy, president of the Vatican's Commission for Religious Relations with Jews, for his work in promoting Jewish-Catholic understanding. Cassidy was presented with the ADL–Joseph Lichten Interfaith Award during a three-day visit to Rome by a 20-member ADL delegation. The group's agenda included meetings with senior Vatican officials and Italian leaders, including an audience with the pope. They also visited Rome's Grand Mosque, marking the first time that an international Jewish organization was received there.

On March 16, the Vatican's Commission for Religious Relations with the Jews released "We Remember: A Reflection on the Shoah," a long-awaited official document on the Holocaust. The paper was represented as an official "act of repentance—teshuva" for the past sins of Catholics both before and during the Holocaust. But it deeply disappointed many Jews on a number of points, chiefly by playing down the involvement of Catholics in the Holocaust, by defending Pope Pius XII, and by distancing historic religious anti-Semitism from Nazi ideology and the Nazi persecution of Jews.

Among other things, the document prompted renewed calls by Jewish leaders for the Vatican to open its World War II-era archives. One such call came a week after the document was released, during talks at the Vatican between the International Jewish Committee on Interreligious Consultations and the Vatican's Commission for Religious Relations with the Jews. Further calls were made in Washington in December, at an international conference on compensation of Holocaust survivors for art and communal property seized by the Nazis, as well as insurance claims. The Vatican rejected demands for complete access to its World War II archives.

The document on the Holocaust came as part of the Vatican's preparations for the millennium year 2000, a Holy Year for the church. The pope made clear that he wanted the church to begin the new era by owning up to and repenting for past sins, including its treatment of the Jews. Several steps in that direction were taken during the year. In March the Bishops' Conference of the Roman Catholic Church in Italy presented Italian Jewish leaders with a formal letter strongly condemning anti-Semitism and apologizing for the church's past mistreatment of Jews. In April the pope's Easter observances included open Catholic self-criticism of the longtime Christian teaching that the Jews were responsible for the death of Jesus. During a visit to Austria in June, the pope said that seeking reconciliation with Jews "is one of the most fundamental duties of Christians in Europe." At the end of October, several dozen international historians, scholars, and other experts met for three days behind closed doors at the Vatican in the church's first official examination of the Inquisition. The pope indicated to the participants that the Vatican planned to ask forgiveness for the injustices committed by that church body.

In September the pope had his first meeting with a United Jewish Appeal group, a mission from Chicago, granting them a half-hour private audience at his summer residence at Castel Gandolfo, south of Rome. The same month, Milan's Carlo Maria Cardinal Martini issued a pastoral letter condemning anti-Semitism and calling for fraternal relations between Christians and Jews.

Culture

A wide range of concerts, lectures, exhibits, conferences, seminars, festivals, and other Jewish cultural initiatives were programmed by Jewish communities all over Italy. The main Jewish communities, in Rome and Milan, featured several cultural or educational events virtually every week. The Union of Italian Jewish Communities' department of cultural assistance held its fifth annual conference and study retreat, Moked, at the end of April and beginning of May. The main theme was the question of Jewish identity. Speakers from Italy, Israel, and elsewhere addressed topics such as "Jewish Identity and Cultural Pluralism in the Jewish World Today," "The Shoah and Israel: Their Role in Jewish Identity," "Jewish Identity and Italian Identity: Contrasts and Convergences."

In addition, many events with Jewish themes were held outside the sponsorship of Jewish bodies, or were jointly sponsored by Jewish and civic or private organizations. Jewish events and cultural programs drew an increasing audience of non-Jews. There was lively interest in Yiddish and East European Jewish culture, with Yiddish classes offered in Rome, Venice, and Bari. Reflecting the growing popularity of Jewish music, particularly Klezmer music, the Rome-based Klezroym group issued its first CD and toured widely around the country. A television special by performer Moni Ovadia, featuring Jewish jokes and Klezmer music, was broadcast on state-run television in January and drew one million viewers. Italian state radio initiated a regular program on Jewish music in the summer. It was produced by Francesco Spagnolo, the director of the Milan-based Yuval Center for the Study of Jewish Music, who also presented a weekly program on Jewish music and culture on a private Milan radio station.

There were numerous Jewish culture or music festivals and other festivals and exhibitions highlighting Jewish culture, music, film, and the arts. Among them: the third annual Klezmer music festival in Ancona, in July; a series of concerts, exhibitions, tours, theater performances, and other events in Trieste, called "Shalom Trieste," that ran from the end of June to the end of the year; a three-week Jewish theater and performance festival in the neighboring cities of Parma and Reggio Emilia in the fall; a Jewish culture festival in Andria, near Bari, in the summer; a Jewish culture festival in Pitigliano in October; open-air Jewish festivals in Rome at Shavuot and in the summer. There was a festival of Roma (Gypsy) and Jewish music in the Abruzzi region in October, and the prestigious Ravenna music festival in July featured Jewish classical music and performers.

Among many conferences and seminars on Jewish themes were a conference in Rome in April on Fascism and anti-Fascism; a conference during the summer in Trento on Science and Judaism in the Middle Ages; a conference in Rome in

October on "Israelis and Palestinians, Two Cultures as a Bridge for Peace?"; a conference on Yiddish in Rome in November; a conference on transmitting Holocaust memory, also in Rome in November.

In the spring, an enlarged and renovated Jewish museum, funded by municipal authorities and operated by the local branch of the Italy-Israel Friendship Association, opened in the city of Gorizia, on the border with Slovenia. In June civic and religious leaders, including the mayor and the local bishop, took part in the ceremonial opening of a new Jewish museum in the synagogue of Merano, a spa town in northern Italy's Alto Adige region, where only a few dozen Jews live today. During the ceremony, Bishop Wilhelm Egger took the opportunity to apologize for Catholic failings in the past in fighting anti-Semitism. Work on the first phase of the restoration of the historic Old Jewish Cemetery on the Lido of Venice, founded in the 14th century, also began in June, and state-funded restoration of other Jewish sites was under way.

La vita e' bella (Life Is Beautiful), a tragicomic film set partly in a Nazi death camp, which was released at the end of December 1997, became Italy's most popular and honored film in 1998. It also prompted much debate in the media and in Jewish circles about how the Holocaust should be depicted on screen, and whether humor can be used in such presentations. In July the movie swept the David of Donatello awards, the Italian film industry's version of the Oscars. It won the prize for best film, and comedian Roberto Benigni won for best director, best actor in a leading role, and, with his cowriter, best screenplay. In November Italy selected the film as its official nominee for Hollywood's Academy Award for best foreign-language film. The movie also won a number of other prizes and honors, including a major award at the Cannes Film Festival, and was highly praised in Israel. It opened in the United States to generally favorable reviews.

In early 1998, the Milan-based Jewish art historian, essayist, poet, and art collector Arturo Schwarz donated some 700 modern works of art, mainly surrealist and Dada pieces, worth about $25 million, to the Israel Museum in Jerusalem.

In November performer Moni Ovadia premiered a new production centered around the image of the mother, with a heavy emphasis on the "Yiddishe Mameh." The musical show began with a rendition of the Kaddish and included Ovadia's trademark Jewish jokes and Yiddish songs. The same month, *Garbage, the City and Death*, a controversial play by the late German playwright and filmmaker Rainer Werner Fassbinder, opened in Milan. Set in postwar Germany, the play is considered by many to be anti-Semitic because of its negative portrayal of a real estate speculator identified as "the Rich Jew," who exploits his position as a Jewish survivor. It was the play's first public production in Italy and took place just over a month after a theater in Berlin dropped plans to produce it. Written in 1975, the play had been performed in various countries, including the United States, but had never been publicly performed in Germany, because of post-Holocaust sensibilities. A reviewer in Milan's Jewish monthly gave the Milan production a sympathetic review, saying that the production "made one think" about all aspects and effects of prejudice and hatred. In the Milan production, he wrote, it was the anti-Semite who was demonized, not the Jew.

Publications

Massimo Caviglia, a well-known mainstream journalist and cartoonist, became the new editor of *Shalom*, the monthly magazine of Rome's Jewish community. He took over from Lia Levi and Luciano Tas, who had founded the magazine 30 years earlier. The change in editorship came amid charges that the Rome community was coming under the control of Orthodox Jews who excluded the nonobservant. Anna Foa, a prominent Jewish writer and intellectual, wrote a letter to *Shalom* saying she would not write for the magazine because Caviglia's editorial stance rejected pluralism and instead represented a "progressive religious and Orthodox closure" that bordered on fundamentalism. Caviglia rejected Foa's charges and said that he regretted the loss of her involvement.

Scores, if not hundreds, of books by Jewish authors or on Jewish themes were published in Italy, including works written originally in Italian or translated from other languages. A Jewish bookstore, Menorah, operated in Rome and maintained a Web site, and the Claudiana bookstore in Milan also specialized partly in Jewish books. A new bookstore called Tikkun, which specialized in part in Jewish books, opened in Milan. Milan was the scene of the second annual Jewish Book Fair, "Sefer," organized by a Milan Jewish cultural association, May 10-13.

Books on Jewish themes were given broad public exposure, with a number of books and authors receiving prominent write-ups in the mainstream press. When two works by performer Moni Ovadia were published simultaneously in the fall — an autobiography, *Speriamo che tenga* (Let's Hope It Lasts), as well as a book of Jewish humor that was sold along with a video of the author telling Jewish jokes — the books' introduction took place in a leading theater in Rome and was treated as a major cultural event. *Viaggio alla fine del millennio* (*A Journey to the End of the Millennium*), by Israeli author A.B. Yehoshua, was published in Italian translation even before the English version, and Yehoshua visited Italy on a well-publicized book tour to promote it.

The following selected titles show the range of Jewish books on the market: Marco Buticchi's thriller *Menorah*, about a search for the candelabrum looted by the Romans when the Temple was destroyed in 70 C.E.; *Per via invisibile* (Invisible Ways) by Alberto Cavalion, the fictionalized story of a family in Turin during the Holocaust; *Lettere della giovinezza* (Letters from Youth), a collection of letters written from prison between 1935 and 1943 by the Jewish anti-Fascist Vittorio Foa; *Come le cinque dita di una mano: Storia di una famiglia di Ebrei da Firenze a Gerusalemme* (Like the Five Fingers of a Hand: The Story of a Family of Jews from Florence to Jerusalem), the stories of five prominent intellectual members of the Nirenstein family; and journalist and European Parliament member Corrado Augias's biography of the Jewish Italian painter Amedeo Modigliani.

Two—out of many—books on Holocaust themes that were particularly well publicized and also well received were *L'uomo che fermo' Hitler* (The Man Who Stopped Hitler), by Gabriele Nissim, the story of the Bulgarian politician Dimitar Peshev, who prevented the deportation of Bulgaria's Jews; and *Il guardiano* (The Guardian), based on interviews with Warsaw Ghetto uprising leader Marek Edelman, edited by Rudi Assuntino and Wlodek Goldkorn.

In August it was announced that the historic Jewish-run publishing house Fratelli Treves, founded in 1861, would be revived, 60 years after it was forced to fold due to the anti-Semitic laws.

Personalia

Moni Ovadia, Italy's best-known Jewish performer, was honored by the city of Pordenone in northern Italy as the subject of its annual "Dedication" program in January-February. This entailed a series of performances and lectures, as well as publication of a special volume of essays dedicated to Ovadia.

In May Rabbi Mordechai Waxman of Great Neck, New York, received a high papal honor in acknowledgement of his work in Catholic-Jewish dialogue. Waxman became the fifth Jew, and first rabbi, to be named a Knight Commander of Saint Gregory the Great.

Jewish author and director Giorgio Pressburger, who was born in Budapest, survived the Budapest ghetto as a child, and moved to Italy in 1956, took up the post of director of the Italian Culture Institute in Budapest in September. Pressburger's collection of short stories, *La neve e la colpa* (Snow and Guilt), was awarded the Viareggio literary prize for 1998. Venice-based historian Riccardo Calimani was named counselor to the administration of the Venice Biennale exhibition. In August Clemente J. Mimun, director of TV news on the state-run RAI-2 channel, received the Golden Quill award honoring outstanding personalities in the field of "Culture in Journalism."

In the summer of 1998, Tullia Zevi was named a member of the Italian National Commission for UNESCO.

Jewish left-wing political folksinger Dodi Moscato died in February at the age of 55. Journalist Vittorio Orefice, a Jew who covered Italian politics for Italian TV and newspapers for more than 40 years, died in October at the age of 74.

A prominent non-Jewish author, Gregor von Rezzori, died in Florence, in April, at age 83. Among his best-known novels, many of which are about life in Central Europe and the Jewish presence there, is *Memoirs of an Anti-Semite*, first published in 1979.

RUTH ELLEN GRUBER

Central and Eastern Europe

Federal Republic of Germany

National Affairs

$\mathbf{F}$OR THE FIRST TIME IN THE HISTORY of the Federal Republic of Germany, in September 1998 a sitting government was voted out of office. Chancellor Helmut Kohl had been in power for 16 years. Had he won the election, he would have overtaken Bismarck as the longest-serving chancellor in German history. Instead, the German electorate opted to replace him with Social Democrat Gerhard Schröder. At 54, Schröder became the first German head of state to have no memory of life in the Third Reich. Though observers interpreted this shift in power as the beginning of a new era, Schröder made every effort to assure German voters and European allies that his government would represent "anything but a revolution."

After the September 27 election, Chancellor Schröder and his Social Democratic Party (SPD) concluded a coalition agreement with the environmentalist Green Party. The tax plan put forward by the Red-Green coalition provoked strong critiques from representatives of industry who had supported Schröder's candidacy. They questioned the degree to which he would be able to influence the policies of his finance minister, Oscar Lafontaine, who had kept his leftist views to himself during the campaign. In another controversial move, the new government proposed reforms that would make Germany the last state in Western Europe to abandon a legal conception of citizenship based on blood.

On the world stage, Germany assured allies that it would maintain the stable partnerships forged during the Kohl era. At the same time, on several policy fronts, the Red-Green government boldly asserted German interests. Within the European Union, Schröder and Lafontaine strained relations with Britain and France by advocating majority voting procedures, the harmonization of tax policies, and reforms to EU finances that would ease the disproportionate share of the budget traditionally shouldered by Germany.

The Party of Democratic Socialism (PDS), controlled by members of the former East German Communist Party, passed the required 5-percent hurdle in the national elections to secure a place in the Bundestag. The party also maintained its strength in state elections in the new federal states of eastern Germany, even joining together with the SPD in Mecklenburg-Vorpommern to form a governing coalition. It marked the first time since German unification that the former Communists played the role of governing party.

In state elections in Saxony-Anhalt in April, the German People's Union (GPU) won a greater percentage of the vote (12.9) than had any other extreme right-wing party in the postwar period. The momentum did not carry through to the national elections in September, however, as neither the GPU nor any of the other right-wing parties topped the 5-percent hurdle. Nevertheless, echoes of their rhetoric could be heard in the speeches of the mainstream Christian Social Union (CSU) and the Christian Democratic Union (CDU) parties. Politicians aimed their declarations that "Germany is not a country of immigration!" at voters angry about persistent unemployment and eager to hold foreigners responsible for their troubles.

Israel and the Middle East

German policy toward Israel cooled in the year preceding the election in response to the standstill in the Middle East peace process. Prime Minister Benjamin Netanyahu visited Chancellor Kohl in Bonn twice in the first three months of 1999, seeking support from a traditional Israeli ally in the face of European Union policies sympathetic to the Palestinians. In early March, during Netanyahu's second visit, Kohl simultaneously reiterated his commitment to Israeli security and confirmed German plans to offer financial support to the Palestinian territories through the European Union. German president Roman Herzog pursued the same policy during his November trip to the Middle East. Herzog visited the Palestinian Autonomous Territory as well as Israel, calling on both sides to implement the recently signed Wye River agreement.

The implications of the change in government for German-Israeli diplomatic relations remained uncertain. Though some questioned Schröder's appreciation of the historic ties that bind the two countries, the coalition agreement signed by the Greens and the Social Democrats did emphasize the importance of maintaining a friendly and productive bilateral relationship with Israel.

The record of the Greens on issues of importance to Israel was mixed. On the one hand, they consistently championed the Palestinian cause. On the other hand, the Greens have always insisted that Germany offer restitution to as yet uncompensated victims of National Socialist persecution. Such willingness to address outstanding claims without being unduly pressured was in marked contrast to the policy of the previous government (see "Restitution," below).

Throughout the first half of 1998, the 50th anniversary of Israel was the subject of panel discussions and special reports in the German media. Press coverage of the anniversary painted a portrait of an Israeli society in the midst of an identity crisis. Often featuring the views of Israeli or German-Jewish analysts, media reports highlighted the contemporary conflicts between religious and secular Israelis, within the fractious Israeli political landscape, and between supporters and opponents of peace with the Palestinians. Israeli and Palestinian scholars and political figures, including several members of the Knesset, addressed these same themes at the mid-June symposium "50 Years of Israel: Jewish State or State of Jews?" Organizers of the event in Munich, including the Goethe Institute and the Department of Jewish History and Culture of the Ludwig Maximilian University, intended this all-day discussion of internal Israeli affairs to counteract the tendency toward generalization, simplification, and stereotype in German public perceptions of Israel.

In addition to critical reflection on the Israeli past and present, an array of celebrations marked the anniversary across Germany. An Israeli bazaar in Mannheim, a play written by members of the Hagen Jewish community, and receptions in the community centers of Trier and Bayreuth typified the commemorations that each community in Germany organized in the spring. On May 20, 1998, Jerusalem Day festivals in the streets of Berlin and Düsseldorf drew large crowds from the Jewish community and the non-Jewish German public as well. Mikhail Gorbachev joined in the anniversary festivities as the guest of honor at the Keren Hayesod benefit gala held at the German Opera of Berlin. The largest and most high-profile affair, however, was the celebration held in early May at the Berliner Schauspielhaus, which drew the likes of Chancellor Kohl, President Herzog, Israeli ambassador to Germany Avi Primor, president of the Bundestag Rita Süssmuth, Defense Minister Volker Rühe, and many other national figures. On August 27, a musical review entitled "Israel Celebrates Its Anniversary," featuring 40 Israeli singers, dancers, and musicians, opened its tour of Germany at the Staatsoper in Berlin to rave reviews.

In the realm of cultural exchange, Germans and Israelis continued to break new ground in 1998. For the first time, a group of 17 German officer cadets spent three midsummer weeks in Israel touring and training with their counterparts in the Israeli army. The first weekend of November, German and Israeli authors met in Mainz, at the invitation of the North Rhine-Westphalian and German federal bureaus for political education to discuss "Israeli and German Literature: Perspectives and Points of Intersection." Participants included Israeli Ruth Almog and the German-Jewish author Barbara Honigmann. Also in November, Israeli ambassador Primor announced that new ground in German-Israeli relations would be broken—literally—in January of 1999, when work would begin on the first Israeli embassy ever to be built in Berlin.

Anti-Semitism and Extremism

The Federal Agency for the Protection of the Constitution reported for 1998 that, in spite of an 11 percent increase in the number of right-wing extremists, the number of crimes attributed to this group fell below 1997 levels. While crimes of all kinds decreased almost 6 percent from just under 12,000 in 1997 to 10,341 in 1998, the number of violent acts committed by right-wing extremists dropped from 790 in 1997 to 708 in 1998, a drop of more than 11 percent. Of course, the trends varied from region to region: Rhineland-Pfalz reported a 62-percent increase in radical rightist crime in the first half of 1998, in comparison with the same period in 1997.

Police in Lower Saxony, Schleswig-Holstein, Hamburg, and Bavaria cooperated in early February to close a notorious association of neo-Nazis and its "colony" in Hetendorf (Lower Saxony), which had been used for years as a neo-Nazi gathering place and site for demonstrations. The movement continued to rely more heavily on the Internet as a medium for organization and recruitment. Of greater concern to German law-enforcement officials was the stockpiling of weapons in neo-Nazi cells, which created a potential for right-wing radical terrorism. Furthermore, study after study pointed to a large reservoir for potential neo-Nazi recruits among the young in the eastern German states.

In the first weeks of 1998, officials in Brandenburg, the federal state surrounding Berlin, acknowledged the seriousness of security threats posed by skinhead youths known to law enforcement agencies in more than 80 Brandenburg localities. Media reports on the topic discouraged people living in Berlin from visiting the Brandenburg countryside, traditionally a popular vacation destination.

A special police unit created in February to deter neo-Nazi crime was unable to prevent a series of attacks in late spring and early summer on groups of schoolchildren from Berlin on field trips to the countryside. On at least eight separate occasions, all in different locations, skinheads assaulted classes composed of students from various ethnic backgrounds. These attacks aside, in early July Interior Minister Alwin Ziel (SPD) credited the "Mobile Action Troops" with cutting in half the number of criminal offenses committed by right-wing radicals in the first half of 1998 in comparison with the previous year.

Although partisan politics prevented unified action against the skinhead threat, the independent justice minister of Brandenburg, Otto Bräutigam, announced in April the creation of an antidiscrimination commission to offer support to the victims of antiforeigner violence. A number of grassroots initiatives at the local level also sought to combat the rising tide of neo-Nazism.

A series of reports indicating the spread of neo-Nazism among rank-and-file soldiers and a lecture by the infamous Manfred Roeder at the Bundeswehr academy (see AJYB 1998, pp. 312-13) provided the impetus for a January 1998 parliamentary investigation of extremism in the army. The head of the Federal Office for the Protection of the Constitution, Peter Frisch, testified before the commission that extremist groups used the Bundeswehr as a means of getting their members to learn the spirit of camaraderie and how to handle weapons. After months of refusing to acknowledge the gravity of the situation, Defense Minister Volker Rühe announced that the Bundeswehr would attempt to recruit soldiers from the parties of the left to achieve a greater balance in its ranks. He also provoked a minor controversy in February when he suggested that the loyalty of career soldiers to the constitution would be subject to investigation. The fact that record numbers of young Germans chose the path of conscientious objection to military service in 1998 further narrowed the population from which the army could draw soldiers of leftist inclinations.

Soccer fans had also become an important source for the recruitment of right-wing radicals. A central police database contained information on some 2,100 "violent hooligans." These soccer fans did not necessarily hold extremist views, but many of them did ultimately join neo-Nazi ranks. A group of German toughs grabbed the international spotlight during the World Cup matches in June when they beat a French police officer into a coma in Lens, France. Football fans in Berlin were responsible for the desecration of a Jewish cemetery in Brandenburg, and in Dresden fans incorporated anti-Semitic symbols into their rhetoric.

Though the vast majority of neo-Nazi crimes targeted foreigners, extremists also desecrated Jewish memorial sites a number of times in 1998. A monument to the 55,000 Berlin Jews deported from the capital city fell victim to vandals four times in the first four months of 1998. In July the Centrum Judaicum in Berlin discovered a neo-Nazi entry in its visitors' book. It was the museum's first such encounter with anti-Semitism. Vandals planted an explosive in early October at the grave of Heinz Galinski, the longtime chairman of the Berlin Jewish community, causing only minor damage. On the 28th of the same month, unknown perpetrators painted a Star of David and the name of the chairman of the Central Council of Jews in Germany on a pig and chased it through one of the most crowded squares in Berlin. The anniversary of Kristallnacht on November 9 was an occasion for vandalism in Schwerin, Berlin, and Potsdam. On December 19, Galinski's tombstone was again a target; this time it was completely demolished.

RIGHT-WING POLITICAL PARTIES

The electoral success of the German People's Union (GPU) in April 26 state parliamentary elections in Saxony-Anhalt represented but the most troublesome of a series of events and trends that reflected the alienation of many Germans from the democratic institutions of the state. Funded exclusively by Gerhard Frey, the Munich-based owner of various nationalist publishing houses, the GPU joined the campaign just three weeks before the election, boasting no more than 100 party members in the state and no organizational headquarters. With DM 3 million of his own money, more than the SPD and the CDU spent on their entire campaigns combined, Frey proceeded to flood the state with 1.2 million letters and 20,000 posters directed at young male voters and sporting slogans such as "Out with Foreign Bandits" and "Jobs to Germans First." His party's share of the vote translated into 16 seats in the state parliament.

Differing explanations of the GPU success were voiced along the political spectrum. Chancellor Kohl offered the clearest expression of the predominant

CDU and SPD view: "It has to do with protest behavior, not neo-Nazism." CDU representatives in Saxony-Anhalt claimed that the Social Democratic-led state government had driven voters into the hands of the GPU by accepting the former Communist party as a de facto coalition partner. The SPD, meanwhile, interpreted it as an indicator of the electorate's dissatisfaction with the Kohl government. In Bavaria, a state dominated by the conservative Christian Social Union (CSU), leading politicians took the appeal of extremist rhetoric to voters more seriously and left little room on the right to the GPU. Even the PDS, the former proponent of Communist internationalism, began to debate the question of how to integrate a German national identity into its platform.

Scholars and public intellectuals, meanwhile, warned against self-serving claims that GPU votes signaled the protest of democratic citizens who could easily be won back to the mainstream parties. The oft-repeated refrain that such protests came mainly from the unemployed, who simply wanted a government that would address their need for work, was belied by the fact that unemployed voters were a minority within the GPU electorate in Saxony-Anhalt. More compelling than employment status as an explanatory factor was the generational experience of the predominantly young voters (including 30 percent of first-time voters) who gave their support to Frey. Socialized in a dictatorship that allowed no forum for political debate, a generation of Germans in the new states have had little or no political education to foster in them the values of civility and liberalism necessary to sustain a commitment to democratic institutions.

Membership in extreme right political parties rose 12 percent in 1998 to 39,000, and experts estimated their voter potential at 13 percent nationwide. Nevertheless, the GPU proved unable to unify the highly fractionalized movement. The Republikaner, the only extreme right party to endure a loss in membership in 1998, appealed primarily to wealthy conservatives with an ideology of chauvinistic affluence who view the losers in the system, primarily foreigners, as potential threats to the system. The other right-wing parties, the GPU and the National Democratic Party (NDP) of Germany, both championed a nationalistic and racist opposition to international finance, globalization, and the presence of foreigners on German soil.

The embrace by the NDP of the neo-Nazi skinhead scene and its desire for mobilization in the streets inhibited cooperation between it and Frey's strictly political machine. By turning its focus from the older generation of diehard Nazis in western Germany to the younger generation of angry, disenchanted youth in the eastern states, the NDP had grown substantially in the last few years. One-third of its 4,300 members came from the states of the former GDR, and 70 percent of those who joined the party in 1997 were below the age of 30. The party draws its support among the young from its youth organization, the Young National Democrats, which has been able to avoid a government ban because of its affiliation with a legitimate political party.

A tension existed within the NPD between the goals of electoral success and activism in the streets. This tension came to the fore at the NPD "Day of Struggle" demonstration in Leipzig on May 1. The party's appeal to young right-wing radicals was enhanced by its determination to take the struggle to the streets, yet the violence that erupted in clashes with leftists attending counterdemonstrations ultimately undercut its potential to win the support of disaffected voters at the ballot box. At the same time, its demonstrations against a museum exhibit documenting the crimes of the German army during World War II won the support of several politicians from the mainstream parties (see AJYB 1998, pp. 314-15).

Particularly in eastern Germany, the National Democrats gained a foothold in communities through their social activism. They maintained a presence on the streets and sometimes even helped locals with their shopping or babysitting. Certain local chapters established such control over their territories that they referred to them as "nationally liberated zones." In these zones, neo-Nazis determined the norms of dress and behavior, insured that no leftist propaganda was displayed, and allowed no foreigners to show themselves in public at night. Much of what made the NDP scene taboo, if not illegal, in western Germany, was perceived as normal in certain towns in the eastern states: the sale of skinhead CDs in music stores, entire high-school classes sporting shaved heads and combat boots, public officials who closed their eyes to right-wing radical tendencies in a community where foreigners and the disabled were regularly assaulted, and so on.

Holocaust-Related Matters

RESTITUTION

In early January the Kohl government announced an agreement with the Conference on Jewish Material Claims Against Germany (also known as the Jewish Claims Conference, or JCC) for the compensation of Jewish survivors of the Holocaust living in Eastern Europe and the former Soviet Union (FSU). In the aftermath of the cold war, the German state made restitution payments of DM 1.5 billion ($900 million) to the states of Eastern Europe, but the individual survivors never received any of the money. German leaders finally brought months of deadlocked negotiations with the Claims Conference to an end early in the new year in response to a high-profile advocacy campaign sponsored by the American Jewish Committee (see AJYB 1998, p. 316). The agreement stipulated that the Federal Republic would place DM 50 million ($30 million) a year into a fund to be administered by the JCC, beginning in 1999 and ending in 2002. The conference will then divide the money among some 18,000 eligible survivors.

The deal allowed both the German government and the JCC to express satisfaction at having addressed a pressing issue, but survivor groups in Eastern Europe were not united in support of the agreement. Only those Jews who could prove that they had spent at least six months in a concentration camp or 18 months in a ghetto, hidden or living under a false identity, were eligible to receive payments, which amounted to half the monthly pension of Jewish survivors in Western Europe, Israel, and the United States. Non-Jewish victim groups were not included in the negotiations.

Efforts of victim groups to win restitution shifted in focus over the course of 1998 from the German state to private enterprises that profited from the wealth and labor of concentration camp inmates. Scholars estimate that several hundred thousand of the 12 million people forced to work for some 12,000 German firms as slave laborers are still alive. In the decades following the war, banks and corporations argued that, because they had been forced to pay the Nazi state for the slave labor they were allegedly compelled to use, the successor state to the Third Reich, the Federal Republic of Germany, should be held responsible for restitution payments. These arguments, however, lost their validity in the wake of recent controversies surrounding Nazi gold and historical research debunking arguments that Germany industry used forced labor under duress.

On behalf of approximately ten thousand Holocaust survivors and their families, New York attorney Edward Fagan and Munich lawyer Michael Witti filed a class-action suit in June against the Deutsche Bank and the Dresdner Bank. The suit alleged that the banks knowingly profited from the wealth of Jewish victims of National Socialism and sought DM 32 billion ($18 billion) in damages. Later in the summer, on the 50th anniversary of the war crimes judgment at Nuremberg against the heads of the IG Farben chemical combine, several Holocaust survivor groups came together with the "Association of Critical Shareholders" to demand the dissolution of still existent IG Farben financial entities. The protest also called on the chemical companies Bayer, BASF, and Hoechst, the successor firms of IG Farben, to abandon their long-standing tactic of denying legal responsibility for the crimes of their parent firm and to resolve in a timely and equitable manner the claims of former forced laborers.

The changing political and legal climate induced a small minority of companies that had used slave labor during the war, including Volkswagen and Siemens, to set up funds voluntarily for the compensation of victims. Arms manufacturer Karl Diehl decided to institute his own system of compensation in 1997 after controversy surrounded the decision of the Nuremberg city council to make him an honorary citizen (see AJYB 1998, pp. 315-16). The gesture did not bring him the rehabilitation he sought, however, as documents surfaced in 1998 detailing Diehl's involvement in a postwar political movement organized by supporters of the defeated National Socialist regime.

After the Schröder government took power in October, it appeared that the German state would play a pivotal role in resolving pending claims against German industry. Throughout the Kohl era, the government had refused to involve itself in the matter. As late as August 1998, state officials flatly refused to consider the establishment of a joint state-industry fund for the compensation of former slave laborers with valid claims against German companies. As opposition parties, meanwhile, the Social Democrats and the Greens called on German industry to accept responsibility for its actions under the Nazi regime. After an October 21 meeting with industry leaders, Chancellor Schröder announced his intention to form a working group to set up just such a fund, as a means of "protecting" German industry.

HOLOCAUST MEMORIALS

Even as numerous new memorials to the victims of the Holocaust were being unveiled, intellectual debates in the German public sphere suggested that the country had entered a new era in the confrontation with its past. A final decision about a proposed central German memorial to the murdered Jews of Europe seemed imminent as 1998 began, but it was destined to remain a source of controversy for yet another year (see AJYB 1998, pp. 317-18). A series of public discussions in Berlin in January centered on each of the four works selected as finalists by a commission of experts and the three sponsors of the project—the federal government, the city of Berlin, and a private Holocaust memorial advocacy group. Before the participating artists had presented all of their proposals to the public, however, Chancellor Kohl made clear his preference for the design of two American collaborators, artist Richard Serra and architect Peter Eisenman. The design featured tightly packed rows of tall stone columns reminiscent of giant gravestones. In spite of protests against Kohl's de facto unilateral dismissal of the remaining three designs, politicians from all parties insisted in late January that construction of the memorial would begin in January 1999.

The first obstacle to the realization of this plan came from beneath the future site of the monument, south of the Brandenburg Gate in central Berlin. Excavation of the area, which had lain desolate in the no-man's-land separating East and West Berlin during the cold war, led to the discovery of the bunker of Nazi propaganda minister Joseph Goebbels. The momentum behind the campaign for the Holocaust memorial quickly overwhelmed voices raised in support of preserving the bunker, in which were found Nazi military gear and skeletons of German soldiers.

In the months that followed, skeptics filled the vacuum created by the silence of the project's advocates. In the first week of February, a group of 19 prominent intellectuals spoke out against the construction of a central monument. An open letter signed by such public figures as novelists Günter Grass and Peter Schneider and historians Reinhard Kosseleck and Jürgen Kocka urged decision makers to postpone a final resolution of the question. The chief criticisms aired in the letter had been raised repeatedly during the nine-year debate: the numerous objectives envisioned for the memorial could not be achieved by a single artistic representation; the size and scope of the projected monument would not move visitors to a state of critical reflection; authentic Holocaust sites in and around

Berlin had already been preserved and were sufficient to the goals of honoring the dead and learning from the past.

The editor-in-chief of the magazine *du*, Dieter Bachmann, provoked another round of discussion with his suggestion that Potsdamer Platz be renamed Judenplatz (Jews' Square). Bachmann argued that his proposal, which he published on the front page of the March 5th issue of the national weekly *Die Zeit*, would be more effective in forcing Germans to do the work of remembering than a monument of stone. The idea found little support in the German public and angered several Jewish commentators for its lack of sensitivity to the concerns of the contemporary Jewish community.

Nevertheless, the episode contributed to an atmosphere of opposition to the central Holocaust memorial as conceived by its supporters. In mid-March, Berlin mayor Eberhard Diepgen, one of the few figures with a direct hand in the decision-making process, confirmed to the press his own skepticism about the project.

While the winds of public debate were turning against the memorial, Chancellor Kohl worked in private to convince Serra and Eisenman to adjust their design more to his liking. On May 22, he met with the Americans to discuss his ideas of what alterations were necessary. The following week, Serra withdrew himself from the competition. Though he refused to go into detail in explaining his decision, press reports suggested that Eisenman's background as an architect left him better prepared than the artist Serra to work with clients to arrive at an acceptable layout for the memorial. Once Kohl viewed and approved Eisenman's reworked design, the chancellor began to apply pressure on Diepgen, whose opposition to the memorial left him isolated within his own municipal government.

Before the various players in the debate could sort out their differences, the memorial issue became hostage to national politics and the campaign for the chancellery. Publisher Michael Naumann, named by SPD candidate Gerhard Schröder as his future minister of culture, echoed in July oft-expressed criticisms of the memorial, arguing that no work of art could reflect the horror of the Holocaust and that exhibits at authentic sites were the appropriate means of memorializing Nazi crimes. Schröder himself advocated a nonpartisan public discussion of the issue and acknowledged that his views approximated those of Naumann. In the resultant volley of condemnations between political opponents, few observers remarked upon the withdrawal of artist Jochen Gerz, whose design was among the four finalists, from a competition that had clearly been decided long before any of the participants were notified. After weeks of back and forth between the Schröder and Kohl camps, it was agreed in August that the memorial debate should not be held hostage to the campaign for the chancellery. A final decision was therefore postponed once again.

In November the new Red-Green government agreed that the Bundestag should have the final say in the matter of a central Holocaust memorial in Berlin. Still opposed to providing the city with nothing more than a "place to lay wreaths," Naumann urged that the Eisenmann design be dropped in favor of a garden and a memorial museum housing temporary exhibits. The project would be coordinated in cooperation with the Holocaust Memorial Museum in Washington, the Leo Baeck Institute in New York, and Yad Vashem in Jerusalem. Naumann planned to place such a proposal before the Bundestag in early 1999.

On January 27, the anniversary of the liberation of Auschwitz, officials from the German rail company Deutsche Bahn AG, the city government, and the Jewish community attended the dedication of a memorial at the Grunewald train station in Berlin, honoring the thousands of German Jews deported from "Track 17." On the same day, designated the official German Day of Remembrance of the Victims of National Socialism, Israeli historian Yehuda Bauer addressed the German Bundestag.

Months later, Jewish youth organizations in Berlin commemorated Yom Hashoah, Holocaust Memorial Day, by calling on volunteers to recite in turn each of the 55,696 names inscribed in the "Berlin Memorial Book of the Jewish Victims of National Socialism." The event, devoted to the idea that "every person has a name," lasted throughout the night of April 22 and into the following afternoon. On June 9, the Jewish community of Munich commemorated the 60th anniversary of the destruction of its main synagogue. In front of the main train station of Bielefeld, local activists and Jewish leaders unveiled a monument on which were engraved the names of the 1,842 Jews deported from that station by the Nazis. Government officials in Lower Saxony announced plans in December for the construction of a "House of Quiet" on the grounds of the former Bergen-Belsen concentration camp. The nondenominational center for private reflection, which will supplement an already existing exhibit on the site, is expected to be completed by the summer of 2000.

People across Germany, particularly the young, volunteered on projects to maintain local Jewish cemeteries or to memorialize the victims of the Holocaust in some way. Of particular significance was the response of German officials and the public at large to the 60th anniversary of *Kristallnacht* on November 9, which is also the anniversary of the opening of the Berlin Wall in 1989. German president Roman Herzog spoke at a Berlin ceremony organized by the Central Council of Jews in Germany. The SPD called on the German public to view the date as a call to action in the struggle for democracy and respect for minorities. Thousands of people participated in a silent march in Berlin.

This display of humility in the face of German history was all the more urgent in light of the debates of the preceding months. In a discussion largely limited to the academy, historians Ingo Haar and Michael Fahlbusch sparked a controversy with their research into the postwar paragons of their own profession. They alleged that the research institutes at which such prominent postwar scholars as Werner Conze and Theodor Scheider worked during the Third Reich facilitated the "ethnic cleansing" of regions that fell under Nazi occupation. Many of the most prominent contemporary German historians, themselves trained by and loyal to these men, took issue with the claims of Goetz Aly—a vocal defender of Haar and Fahlbusch—that their mentors had been among the "intellectual forebears of destruction."

A far more public controversy erupted at the Frankfurt Book Fair in October, at which the German author Martin Walser was awarded the Frankfurt Peace Prize. In his acceptance speech, Walser spoke out against the construction of a central Holocaust memorial in Berlin. Declaring that "public acts of conscience run the risk of becoming mere symbols," Walser called for an end to the "incessant presentation of our disgrace." In response to these comments, the president of the Central Council of Jews in Germany, Ignatz Bubis, charged Walser with "intellectual arson" and "latent anti-Semitism." Though he later toned down his criticism, Bubis saw Walser's comments as reflective of an intellectual climate in Germany less devoted to remembering German crimes than to building a German future.

JEWISH COMMUNITY

Demography

The pace of immigration from the former Soviet Union (FSU) remained steady in 1998. With the addition of 8,299 new arrivals, the membership of the communities registered with the Central Council of Jews in Germany increased from around 68,000 at the end of 1997 to 74,289 as of December 31, 1998. Between 20,000 and 30,000 Jews living in Germany either chose to remain unaffiliated or were affiliated with communities outside the Central Council.

The numbers of affiliated Jews in the largest communities were as follows for 1998 (with 1997 figures in parentheses for comparison): Berlin, 11,008 (up from 10,742); Frankfurt, 6,618 (up from 6,503); Munich, 6,595 (up from 6,194); Hamburg, 3,993 (up from 3,759); Cologne, 3,408 (up from 3,127).

Communal Affairs

The 1990s have been both the best of times and the worst of times for the Jewish community in Germany. The immigration of Jews from the states of the former Soviet Union has caused a demographic revolution, tripling the Jewish population of the community and lowering its average age substantially. To accommodate the increasing numbers, new synagogues, schools, and community centers have been built all across Germany. Since 1995, work has begun on the construction or reconstruction of 30 synagogues in Germany, to say nothing of such projects as community centers and ritual baths. As welcome as these developments have been, however, they have also been accompanied by internal communal bickering over power and resources, bitter criticism of the spiritual state of the community, and scandals involving community leaders. These trends only intensified in 1998.

Immigrants from the FSU continued to contribute to the revitalization of Jewish life in the federal states of eastern Germany. Of the more than 500 Jews in Mecklenburg-Vorpommern, primarily in the cities of Schwerin and Rostock, only one was born in Germany. Nevertheless, there are more Jews living in Schwerin today than there were in 1933, the year Hitler took power. Andrew Steimann, an American teacher, traveled from Berlin to Schwerin and Rostock on alternate weekends to lead Sabbath services and teach Sunday school. In October the congregation in Rostock celebrated the receipt of a Torah scroll from the Jewish community of Aachen. The community centers in each city offer German-language courses, youth group activities, programs for the elderly, and other social services.

In Brandenburg, 60 members established a new community in Frankfurt on the Oder in June, and the state association of Jewish communities opened the doors to a new community center just outside of Potsdam. In the Saxon city of Dresden, meanwhile, construction work began on a new synagogue for the first time since World War II. City and state officials joined community leaders for the groundbreaking ceremony on November 9, the 60th anniversary of the night on which the Nazis destroyed the hundred-year-old Semper Synagogue. As was the case in many German cities, the growth of the Dresden Jewish community over the last several years made a new house of worship a necessity. The Jewish population there quadrupled in the last ten years and saw its average age drop from over 60 to 35. Both the city and state governments subsidized the project, but private initiatives will have to cover much of the remaining cost.

State support contributed to a wave of infrastructure development in the Jewish communities of western Germany as well. At the end of January, the state government of Schleswig-Holstein became one of the last federal states to codify its financial and legal relationship with the Jewish community. In addition to state recognition of Jewish holidays and the protection of Jewish cemeteries, the contract stipulated the amount of annual state subsidies to be granted the Jewish community. The following September, the Schleswig-Holstein community of Kiel opened a new community center to serve the 350 Jewish immigrants living in and around the city. In April the Jewish community of Dortmund had inaugurated its own community center to cater to its membership of three thousand. As Johannes Rau, the minister president of North Rhine-Westphalia, remarked, "He who builds wants to stay." After years of difficult relations between the municipal government and communal leaders, a cornerstone for a new house of worship was laid in mid-September in the Hessian city of Kassel, where the Jewish population had grown from 70 to 800 in recent years. The German government welcomed these developments and, along with the leading representatives of Jews in Germany, pointed to the growth in population and institutions as evidence of reinvigorated Jewish life inside the communities.

The rights and responsibilities of Russian-speaking immigrants stirred controversy in Jewish communities divided between the "old" and the "new" throughout Germany. The "old" Jews mixed their insistence on the use of German language as the avenue to integration with complaints about the selfishness and lack of Jewish education of the "new" Jews. Conflicts between the two groups manifested themselves in a variety of ways.

A particularly bitter dispute between the leader of the Hannover Jewish community and the State Association of Jewish Communities in Lower Saxony originated in the summer of 1995 when Leo Kohn, a survivor of Auschwitz and president of the Hannover community for more than 30 years, refused to tally the votes cast in communal elections. He claimed that the state association had wrongly recognized some 350 immigrants from the former Soviet Union as Jews and thereby granted them the right to vote. Though the court of arbitration of the Central Council of Jews in Germany (CCJG) ruled that Kohn's refusal to recognize the votes cast in the 1995 election was unjustified, Kohn simply disregarded its decision.

In March Kohn convened an assembly of the communal membership for the purpose of organizing new elections. Kohn invited only 840 of the as many as 2,300 Jews estimated to live in Hannover. To be invited, potential members of the community were asked to show the rabbi personal papers proving themselves born of Jewish mothers. This requirement excluded not only the entire immigrant population, who did not have the necessary paperwork even if they did have Jewish mothers, but also the president of the State Association of Jewish Communities, Michael Fürst. The arbitration court of the CCJG then ruled that Kohn and his supporters should be forced to evacuate the administrative offices of the community on May 28. Kohn challenged the legal standing of the CCJG in a German civil court and proceeded to change the locks at the communal offices and to install an alarm system. On August 3, the court ordered that the CCJG's ruling should be executed; however, an appellate court overturned the decision a week later, asserting that the state had no jurisdiction over the affairs of religious institutions.

In Kiel, though the community center was built for the "new" Jews who make up its entire membership, no immigrants were invited to the opening ceremonies, which were attended by prominent politicians, religious leaders, and officials of the "old" Jewish community of Hamburg. In Rhineland-Pfalz, the communal statute adopted in 1996 granted voting rights to Jews after three years of communal membership but also stipulated circumcision as a prerequisite to membership. On May 23, 1998, the CCJG court found this statute to be inconsistent with the constitutional guarantee of equal treatment and ordered the community to alter its charter and subsequently to hold new elections. Nevertheless, little more than half of the 850 members of the community were invited to cast ballots. Like his counterpart in Hannover, communal president Harry Kindermann refused to recognize the CCJG's demand that immigrants be treated equally, protesting that elections were the only aspect of communal life from which the "new" members were excluded.

In response to what they deemed to be the undemocratic methods of the "old" communal authorities, a group calling itself the "Working Group of Jewish Immigrants in Brandenburg" gathered on April 19 to elect an alternative communal council. The communal leadership, headed by Alexander Kogan, then asked the civil courts to forbid the Working Group from claiming the role of communal representatives or council members. After the court granted this request on July 9, Kogan proceeded to rescind the communal membership of those elected to the alternative council. Alexander Nebrat, one of the alternative councilmen expelled from the community, appealed to the CCJG but received no reply and was forcibly prevented, as were his supporters, from attending a June 21 communal assembly. Albert Meyer, a Berlin lawyer and member of that city's Jewish communal parliament, represented the Working Group in Brandenburg as well as the "Association of Immigrants–The Voice," a Berlin-based interest group struggling against alleged abuses in their own community.

BERLIN

With the transfer of the German capital from Bonn to Berlin, the largest Jewish community in Germany took on an even more prominent leadership role within the Jewish world and in the broader German public sphere. A newly established communal integration department devoted itself full time to the interests of recently arrived immigrants from the FSU. Its early successes included obtaining permission from the authorities for the long-term residence in Berlin of immigrants' family members visiting on temporary visas. Language programs and an employment network were also developed by communal representatives. Despite these efforts, opposition arose among a group of Russian-speaking immigrants. Lawyer Albert Meyer claimed to represent their interests in the representative assembly, while a Russian-language magazine lambasting the communal administration was distributed to all members of the community, with the consent of Andreas Nachama, the communal president.

Inside the synagogues, women were demanding a greater role in Jewish life. A chapel in the Centrum Judaicum was placed at the disposal of an egalitarian *minyan*, which took steps toward becoming an official congregation after meeting informally for years. In two of five Berlin synagogues, meanwhile, women were allowed to stand for election as leaders in their congregations, though they were granted no vote in decisions affecting certain rites of worship, such as which men would be called to the Torah.

One of the former hubs of Jewish life in Berlin received a facelift in 1998. Just down the street from the restored 19th-century New Synagogue of Berlin, the nine-year-old Jewish Cultural Association became the first tenant of the Jewish

Communications Center in the Oranienburgerstrasse. An Israeli restaurant and an Anne Frank Center also moved into the building during the year.

Seeing himself duty-bound as the leader of the Berlin Jewish community to play a visible public role, Andreas Nachama participated in a variety of debates during his first year in office. His most controversial public statements came in a June editorial in a Berlin daily attacking Joerg Schönbohm (CDU), the interior minister of Berlin. Upon visiting neighborhoods in Kreuzberg, a district of Berlin populated primarily by Turkish families, Schönbohm had declared, among other things, that the surroundings made him feel as though he were no longer in Germany and that foreigners who had no command of the German language should be invited to leave. Nachama's editorial had references to the Third Reich and condemnations of Schönbohm's "blood and soil" ideology. He also lamented the silence with which the churches had responded to the Berlin politician's remarks. Church officials and Schönbohm himself angrily rejected Nachama's criticism.

AMERICAN JEWISH ORGANIZATIONS

On February 9, 1998, the American Jewish Committee officially opened the doors to its Berlin office. Leaders of the Jewish community in Germany viewed the new American Jewish presence as an example of the self-confidence and strength they sought to foster within their own community and thus a further step in the renaissance of Jewish life in Germany. German foreign minister Klaus Kinkel gave the keynote address at the gala marking the historic event. He welcomed the American Jewish Committee and expressed his confidence that the German-Jewish dialogue would prosper under the watchful eye of the Berlin office. Newspapers across Germany hailed the arrival of the organization as an emblem of the trust enjoyed by the young Berlin republic.

The office was in the news again weeks later when assistant director Wendy Kloke spearheaded a successful campaign to pressure a mobile-phone company into changing the slogan of its billboard advertisements. The slogan of the international ad campaign ("To each his own") had a unique and disturbing connotation in Germany, where those words had been posted atop the gate to the Buchenwald concentration camp during the Nazi era.

As the "ambassador of American Jewry to Germany," Eugene DuBow, the director of the Berlin office, fostered contacts with officials in German government and participated in a variety of public-affairs programs in Berlin. In December he accompanied AJCommittee president Bruce M. Ramer and executive director David A. Harris to Bonn, where they met with leading officials of the new Red-Green coalition government.

Two other American Jewish organizations made their presence felt in the life of the Jews of Germany. The Ronald S. Lauder Foundation announced plans to open the first Jewish seminary (Lehrhaus) in postwar Germany. Rabbi Chaim

Rozwaski was named founding director of the school, which was scheduled to open in 1999. The primary aim of the school is to train religious teachers so that the Jewish community in Germany will have a pool of educators within the country from which to draw. The Chabad Lubavitch movement had also established a presence in Berlin. In the summer of 1998, Rabbi Yehuda Teichtal led the first summer camp for the children of the Berlin Jewish community.

Religion

After enjoying a banner year in 1997 (see AJYB, pp. 323-24), the growing Progressive Jewish movement in Germany began 1998 on a divisive note. Prof. Micha Brumlik, cofounder and chairman of the Union of Progressive Jews in Germany, Austria and Switzerland (UPJGAS), resigned his post and publicly attacked the most prominent rabbi in the German Progressive movement. It had come to Brumlik's attention that Rabbi Walter Homolka, a convert to Judaism, had preached a sermon steeped in Lutheran theology in a Protestant church in Munich as recently as March 1993. In a January 1998 interview with the *Allgemeine jüdische Wochenzeitung,* the national Jewish newspaper, Brumlik argued that Homolka's past should disqualify him from leadership in the movement for the reform of Judaism in Germany. In his view, the issue threatened to undermine the tremendous gains made by that movement in recent years. Brumlik went on to criticize the rabbis in England responsible for endorsing Homolka's written work and ordaining him as a rabbi. Not only these rabbis themselves, but also the majority of the UPJGAS membership and the congregants of the Munich synagogue at which Homolka served, leaped to the rabbi's defense.

Though the character of Homolka, who also served as the president of Greenpeace Germany, received a great deal of attention in the ensuing controversy, the rabbi served more as a lightning rod for two broader, interrelated conflicts within the Jewish community of Germany. Owing to the historical development of church-state relations in Germany, Jewish communities were always organized as *Einheitsgemeinde*, in which religious, social, and financial services were administered under a single institutional roof. The *Einheitsgemeinde* were thus the sole recipients of financial support from the state. As the example of Berlin demonstrated, this arrangement could accommodate a pluralistic religious community. More often, however, the religious life within the *Einheitsgemeinde* was dominated in the postwar era by Orthodox rabbis. Because those Jews wishing to form a liberal congregation were often refused the financial support of the community, conflicts over the religious identity of the community took on a political dimension. Progressive Jews denounced communal officials for their alleged unwillingness to cede their monopoly of power for the sake of pluralistic harmony within the community. Conservatives, meanwhile, accused the Progressives of seeking to replace the Jewish religion with folklore. Against this background, the decision to defend or attack Rabbi Homolka often had as much to do with one's stance on the prospect of institutionalized religious pluralism in Germany as with personal convictions about the rabbi's conversion. Indeed, on January 17, the conservative Conference of Rabbis in Germany released a statement asserting that Homolka was "neither a rabbi nor a Jew."

Jewish-Christian Relations

Evangelical Christians in several German states recognized in Jewish immigrants from the former Soviet Union a promising target group for proselytization. By mid-1998, a Jewish-Messianic congregation in Berlin counted 75 baptized members, 80 percent of them Russian-speaking immigrants of Jewish descent. Missionaries leading the group targeted Jewish immigrants, distributing literature in their neighborhoods in Potsdam and Berlin. The CCJG and the governing body of the Lutheran church in Germany issued a joint statement at their annual meeting condemning the exploitation by Christian missionaries of the economic difficulties and cultural dislocation of immigrants. However, the decentralized nature of the Lutheran church in Germany enabled local and regional hierarchies to ignore the national council and fund the proselytization of Jews. Berlin Jewish community president Andreas Nachama did not, however, accept the protestations of the national church that it was incapable of controlling the practices of its local congregations. "If same-sex marriages were being performed here, the church would know very well how to put an end to it," he said.

The Society for Christian-Jewish Cooperation (SCJC) continued its efforts to fortify interfaith understanding, even as some in the Jewish community questioned the value of such activity. Jewish supporters of the SCJC, particularly of its annual Brotherhood Week, argued that a ghetto mentality on the part of Jews in Germany had blinded them to the changes in the views of German churches toward Judaism over the decades since the war. Christians active in the SCJC, their argument continued, shared with Jews a desire to confront the German past, to fight neo-Nazism, and to speak out against Christian missions to the Jews. Jewish critics countered that Brotherhood Week had become an empty ritual attended by those who did so out of habit or who viewed the week as nothing more than a once-a-year exercise in reconciliation.

At the opening ceremony of Brotherhood Week in March 1998, Leah Rabin was awarded the Buber-Rosenzweig Medal. The widow of assassinated Israeli prime minister Yitzhak Rabin declared that she shared the honor with her late husband.

Education

A Chair for Hannah Arendt Research was established at the University of Oldenburg in Lower Saxony. Political scientist Antonia Gruneberg accepted the position and began to recruit specialists in literature, politics, and sociology to edit the papers of Arendt, the scholar of totalitarianism and author of *Eichmann in Jerusalem*, among other works.

Twenty German doctoral candidates working in the field of German-Jewish history spent a week in Bad Homburg in March discussing their dissertations with one another and with accomplished scholars in the field. The Academic Working Group of the Leo Baeck Institute sponsored the annual event to offer young researchers the opportunity to build relationships with colleagues from across the country with whom they would otherwise never come into contact.

In May the Moses Mendelssohn Center for European Jewish History and Culture at Potsdam University hosted a conference in Berlin on "Jews in United Germany." Scholars from Israel, the United States, Canada, and Germany discussed a variety of topics, including Jewry in the former East German state, the integration of immigrants from the former Soviet Union, and the changing religious landscape of Jews in Germany. Another conference addressed the theme of "Exile and Nation in German Zionism" in Duisburg, in December. Organized by the Salomon Ludwig Steinheim Institute for German-Jewish History at the Gerhard Mercator University, the symposium featured lectures by several prominent scholars, including Frank Stern, Evyatar Friesel, and Michael Berkowitz.

Culture

The theater provided a forum in 1998 for a public examination of both the German past and the current state of German-Jewish relations. In Berlin, artists Esther and Jochen Gerz brought a postmodern conception to their production of *The Investigation*, a play dealing with the Auschwitz trials that took place in Frankfurt during the mid-1960s. After the trials ended in August of 1965, playwright Peter Weiss used the transcript of the trials of concentration-camp doctors and guards as the basis of a play that was performed in 15 cities across Germany that October. More than 20 years later, Esther and Jochen Gerz transformed the play into an interactive group therapy session in which members of the audience read lines from the script. In the early months of 1998, three Berlin theaters participated in this experiment in redefining "the space of the perpetrators."

An even more controversial play, long dormant, returned to the headlines in August when Bernd Wilms, the director of the Maxim Gorki Theater in Berlin, announced his intention to produce Rainer Werner Fassbinder's *Garbage, the City and Death*. The play, originally published in 1976, featured a money-obsessed and sexually fabled, yet nameless "Rich Jew" as the lead character. Fassbinder created the character as the embodiment of stereotyped conceptions of the Jew and surrounded him with a supporting cast designed to shock audiences with the openness and vulgarity of their expression. Members of the Jewish community occupied the stage of a Frankfurt theater in October 1985 and succeeded in preventing the premiere of Fassbinder's play. In an effort to avoid a similar showdown with the Berlin Jewish community, in August 1998 Wilms wrote to Andreas

Nachama of his intent to produce the play as a means of provoking discussion of anti-Semitism and xenophobia in Germany, soliciting his support and cooperation in the effort. Nachama rejected the invitation, instead writing to both Wilms and to Berlin cultural minister Peter Radunski that the Jewish community would do everything in its power to prevent the public presentation of "this document worthy of Goebbels." Radunski expressed an interest in finding a mutually satisfying resolution to the matter.

The Munich Volkstheater staged the premiere in September of *Old Woman Summer*, written by and starring television personality Ilja Richter. The son of a Jewish mother and communist father, both concentration camp survivors, Richter dramatizes the familial, religious, and societal dimensions of Jewish life in postwar Germany in the play.

For the first time since World War II, Jewish theaters were being established in Germany. In Cologne, director and musician Alex Shnaider and journalist Andy Cremer announced plans to bring together an ensemble of artists from Israel, Russia, the United States, and Germany dedicated to carrying on the tradition of German-language Jewish theater. In Berlin, Minister of Culture Michael Naumann announced, soon after the Schröder government took power in the fall, that he would establish a Jewish theater in the capital. Though the state would provide the building, the theater would be a commercial venture dependent on success at the box office, Naumann said.

The Berlinale Film Festival, which ran from February 11 to February 22 in Berlin, featured a number of films dealing with Jewish and Israeli themes. In her documentary *Letter Without Words*, first-time filmmaker Lisa Lewenz drew on over 50 hours of footage shot by her Jewish grandmother in Berlin during the interwar period to explore her family history and her own identity. The work of filmmaking brothers Curt and Robert Siodmak was the focus of the annual Berlinale retrospective.

The fourth annual Jewish Film Festival took new Israeli film as its theme for 1998. The Jüdische Volkshochschule (School for Continuing Education) of the Jewish community organized the event together with the Friends of German Cinema. Julie Shles's *Afula Express* and Ron Havilo's six-hour documentary *Fragments Jerusalem* were among the films shown.

The German Museum in Munich opened the year with an exhibition of works by Israeli artist Ilana Lilienthal. Two other Israelis, photographer Micha Bar-Am and graphic artist Yossi Lemel, showed their work at venues in Hamburg in 1998. In May the Academy of Art in Berlin reintroduced the German public to the work of photographer Ellen Auerbach, who had left her native country in 1933.

In fall 1998, the Museum for Art and Cultural History of Dortmund offered its visitors a representation of "Jewish Life in Westphalia" that moved beyond the standard introduction to the rituals of the Jewish religion and into the everyday life of Jews in the region. In a winter exhibit entitled "Regarding: 'Action 3'— Germans Sell Out Their Jewish Neighbors," the City Museum of Düsseldorf documented the expropriation and auction of Jewish property during the Third Reich. A traveling exhibit called "Sport Under the Star of David" marked the 100th anniversary of the Bar Kochba Jewish athletic association and highlighted the importance of sports in Jewish life in Germany.

JEWISH MUSEUM

The universally acclaimed appointment in December 1997 of Michael Blumenthal, an American businessman and secretary of the treasury in the Carter administration, as director of the Jewish Museum in Berlin opened a new chapter in the decade-long drama of a museum that has yet to open its doors (see AJYB 1998, pp. 327-28). The confidence, decisiveness, and diplomatic grace that Blumenthal brought to the project fostered a public perception in the winter of 1998 that the long-standing dispute over the future relationship between the Jewish Museum and the Berlin Municipal Museum would be resolved swiftly. Despite a few headline-making detours on the road to a codified agreement, the municipal government finally resolved the issue in early November by providing for the creation on January 1, 1999, of the independent public foundation "Jewish Museum Berlin" under Blumenthal's leadership.

At a conference in April sponsored by the Society for a Jewish Museum and the Friedrich Naumann Foundation, the opinions and proposals offered by scholars, museum curators, and journalists demonstrated the range of expectations being attached to the museum, which is scheduled for an October 2000 opening. Though the original scope of the permanent exhibit was to be limited to Jewish history in Berlin, many participants believed that a Jewish Museum in the new capital of Germany should represent Jewish history in all of Germany, if not Europe as a whole. Some expressed the need to educate visitors in the fundamentals of the Jewish religion, while avoiding a mere duplication of Jewish museums elsewhere; others argued for a much broader conception of Jewish culture that would encompass the variety of contributions to European civilization made by a European Jewish community destroyed during World War II. Still others articulated the desire to turn the museum in Berlin into a hub of contemporary European Jewish life.

The challenge of choosing which of these concerns to address and which to neglect was further complicated by several practical considerations. Berlin already boasted a permanent exhibit devoted exclusively to the history of Jews in Berlin. It remained to be determined how the Jewish museum would avoid duplicating the function of the Centrum Judaicum in the renovated New Synagogue, which enjoyed the patronage of all those interested in being exposed to the history of Jews in Berlin or Judaism in general.

More directly bearing on decisions about the constitution of the new museum is the actual structure that will house it. Designed by architect Daniel Libeskind and evoking the image of a star of David pierced by lightning, the building has been called a memorial unto itself, urging its visitors to reflect upon the rich Jewish civilization lost forever in the Holocaust. Some critics have labeled it "ideological architecture," arguing that it virtually compels the museum to tell a story of persecution rather than one of coexistence marked by triumph and tragedy. Furthermore, the provocative architecture obliged the city government to cede to the Jewish museum the entire building, which had initially been intended to house several departments of the Berlin Municipal Museum. However, the Jewish collection at the disposal of the curators could not fill even one-quarter of the space in the Libeskind structure.

To help him overcome these obstacles and to conceptualize and construct a successful museum, Blumenthal recruited two highly qualified advisors. Jeshajahu Weinberg, the man largely credited with the design of the United States Holocaust Memorial Museum in Washington, D.C., arrived in Berlin at the beginning of May to fill the post of curator. His conviction that a museum should tell a story underlay the permanent exhibits not only at the Holocaust Museum, but also at the Diaspora Museum in Tel Aviv and the Museum of the History of Jerusalem. Though initially skeptical that the Libeskind structure could house an effective museum, he enthusiastically accepted the challenge. As assistant director, Blumenthal hired Tom L. Freudenheim, a scholar of Jewish studies who most recently served as director of the YIVO Institute for the study of East European Jewry in New York. Previously, Freudenheim had been an associate secretary of the Smithsonian Institution, the director of art museums in Baltimore and Worcester, and a curator at the Jewish Museum in New York.

Publications

In recognition of the 50th anniversary of the State of Israel, publishers released a number of books dealing with the past and present of the Jewish state. One of the most popular was Ruth Zucker's *Im Auftrag für Israel* (On Orders from Israel), in which the German-Jewish exile tells of her career as an Israeli spy. Micha Brumlik edited a collection of essays entitled *Mein Israel. 21 ertbetene Interventionen* (My Israel: 21 Solicited Interventions), in which various public figures reflect on the prospects of the peace process. Reactions of young Germans visiting the Middle East are recorded in *Impressionen aus Israel* (Impressions from Israel).

German journalists serving as foreign correspondents in Israel also contributed to this publishing wave. In *Schalom Israel: Nachrichten aus einem friedlosen Land* (Shalom Israel: News from a Land Without Peace), Friedrich Schreiber confirms public perceptions of a conflict-ridden society dominated by the military, war, and terrorism. By letting a variety of Israelis and Palestinians tell their own stories, Gisela Dachs conveys in her book *Getrennte Welten: Israelische Lebensgeschichten* (Divided Worlds: Israeli Life Stories) the diversity of life experiences within the polarized worlds of Jews and Muslims in Israel. Casting aside any claims to journalistic objectivity, German-Jewish writer Henryk Broder marked Israel's anniversary with a biting satire, *Die Irren von Zion* (The Lunatics of Zion), an ironic reference to the "wise Jews" of *The Protocols of the Elders of Zion*. Broder's critique is aimed at fundamentalist Jews, in his view an irrational minority that exercises a disproportionate and regrettable influence on Israeli society. Also in 1998, the Aufbau publishing house released the German edition of Hadassa Ben-Itto's historical study of this seminal anti-Semitic tract, *Die Protokolle der Weisen von Zion. Anatomie einer Fälschung* (The Anatomy of a Lie).

Publications on German-Jewish history spanned the centuries and took on a variety of forms. Hellmut G. Haasis challenges historical myths surrounding the legendary 18th-century court Jew in his *Joseph Süss Oppenheimer, genannt Jud Süss. Finanzier, Freidenker, Justizopfer* (Joseph Süss Oppenheimer, Called Jew Süss: Financier, Freethinker, Victim of Injustice). In *Hermann Struck (1876-1944). Das Leben und das graphische Werk eines jüdischen Künstler* (The Life and Work of a Jewish Artist), Jane Rusel documents the story of a prolific artist and Zionist activist known to many as Herzl's portraitist. Ernst Loewy's *Jugend in Palästina: Briefe an die Eltern 1935-38* (Youth in Palestine: Letters to Parents 1935-38) relates the experiences of the future author on a kibbutz near Jerusalem as part of a Youth Aliyah group. Continuing a decade-long trend, several works on local Jewish communities, including Cologne, Bochum, and the Berlin district of Wedding, were published in 1998.

The reintroduction of German-Jewish literary figures to the contemporary reading public also proceeded apace. The AVIVA publishing house issued a new edition of Alice Berend's *Die Bräutigame der Babette Bomberlin* (The Bridegroom of Babette Bomberlin) and promised to release in the coming years other works by the popular 1920s novelist who fled Berlin in 1935, never to return. The first volume of the collected works of Max Zweig, the cousin of Stefan Zweig, includes several of his 22 plays. With the publication of *Schalet*, the Reclam publishing house in Leipzig revived the work of Sammy Gronemann, the sharp-witted Zionist and keen observer of German-Jewish culture before and after World War I.

For the first time in years, Hitler was the focus of several new publications. Historian Ian Kershaw's monumental *Hitler: 1889-1936*—the subject of a cover story by Rudolf Augstein in *Der Spiegel*—promised to remain the standard academic biography of the dictator. By far the most controversial work about Hitler, however, was a comic book. In Walter Moers's *Adolf*, the dictator emerges from the gutter after 50 years in hiding, walks the streets of contemporary Germany in search of adventure, smokes crack, teams up with transsexual Hermann Göring, and causes the deaths of Princess Diana and Mother Teresa. In the wake of the controversy it spawned, *Adolf* became an instant best-seller.

The Goldhagen debate, which had dominated the field of Holocaust studies and transfixed the German public in previous years (see AJYB 1998, pp. 329-30), was rekindled for a time with the publication of critiques by Norman Finkelstein and Ruth Bettina Birn under the title *Eine Nation auf dem Pruefstand. Die*

Goldhagen These und die historische Wahrheit (A Nation on Trial: The Goldhagen Thesis and the Historical Truth).

The reflections of the late journalist Eike Geisel on German efforts to live with their history were published under the title *Triumph des guten Willens: Die Nationalisierung der Erinnerung* (Triumph of Good Will: The Nationalization of Memory). On a lighter note, a German Jew faces an agonizing choice between his German and Israeli girlfriends in Rafael Seligmann's latest novel, *Schalom, meine Liebe* (Shalom, My Love), based on a screenplay the author wrote for German television.

Jews in the former German Democratic Republic were also the subject of academic research published in 1998. Ulrike Offenber recorded the history of the Jewish community in the Soviet Occupation Zone and the GDR in her *Sei vorsichtig gegen die Machthaber* (Be Careful with Those in Power). In *Jewish Claims Against East Germany: Moral Obligations and Pragmatic Policy*, Angelika Timm analyzes the issue of reparations in the post-cold war era.

Personalia

In May the Bavarian town of Fürth conferred honorary citizenship on former U.S. secretary of state Henry Kissinger. Sixty years after he and his family emigrated to the United States from Nazi Germany, Kissinger called the return to his birthplace the "fulfillment of a promise" made on the day of his departure. Former German chancellor Helmut Schmidt attended the May 20 ceremony to pay homage to the statesman with whom he so passionately disagreed during negotiations over nuclear arms in the 1970s.

Another prominent American received one of Germany's highest honors in 1998. In recognition of the contribution made by the 1993 film *Schindler's List* to the education and historical consciousness of Germans, at a September 10 ceremony, President Roman Herzog awarded director Steven Spielberg the Knight Commander's Cross of the Order of Merit of the Federal Republic of Germany. Spielberg commented in his acceptance speech that the award was the greatest honor he had ever received and reiterated his commitment to the work of the Shoah Foundation that he had established.

President Herzog was among several German public figures decorated in 1998 by Jewish organizations for their commitment to Christian-Jewish and German-Israeli relations. In awarding Herzog the Leo Baeck Prize of the Central Council of Jews in Germany, Ignatz Bubis praised him for emphasizing the importance of remembering past German crimes and for fostering a culture of tolerance in contemporary Germany. The Jewish National Fund honored Johannes Rau, the governor of North Rhine-Westphalia, for his contribution to the transformation of the Negev from desert to fertile landscape and to German-Israeli understanding in general. On November 10, on behalf of the World Union for Progressive Judaism, Henry Kissinger bestowed the International Humanitarian

Award on Frank Woessner, chairman of the board of the Bertelsmann Book Corporation.

Several prominent Jews died in 1998. Heinrich Joshua Scheindling died on April 21, in Augsburg, at the age of 82. A native of Nuremberg who had settled in Israel, he returned to Germany in 1961 to teach Judaism in Augsburg. Scheindling spent the rest of his life spreading knowledge of Hebrew and Judaism throughout the Jewish communities of Bavaria. Philosopher Hermann Levin Goldschmidt, who had devoted his life to salvaging the intellectual legacy of German Jewry, died in Zurich in March, at the age of 85. The film star, dancer, and singer Lotti Huber, born in Kiel in 1912, died in Berlin on May 31, on the eve of the publication of her latest book. In 1990 she had published a best-selling autobiography entitled *There Is a Lot of Juice Left in This Lemon*. Pnina Navé Levinson, the 77-year-old theologian and Berlin native, passed away in Jerusalem on August 3. After the war, Levinson played an active role in the reconstituted Jewish community of Heidelberg and engaged regularly in interfaith dialogue. Over the course of her scholarly career, she taught at several universities and published a number of important feminist analyses of Jewish theology.

GREG CAPLAN

Austria

National Affairs

AUSTRIA IN 1998 CONTINUED to be governed by the long-standing coalition of Social Democrats and the conservative People's Party; heading the coalition was Chancellor Viktor Klima, with Wolfgang Schussel, leader of the People's Party, serving as vice-chancellor and foreign minister. Austria was cast into the diplomatic limelight by virtue of its holding the rotating presidency of the European Union during the second half of the year. Meantime, all parties were gearing up for an active political season in 1999, when six elections were scheduled to be held: the national election, four electoral contests at the provincial level, and the election to the European Parliament.

Israel and the Middle East

Relations between Austria and Israel continued to improve, as attested by the official visit of Chancellor Viktor Klima to Israel in March 1998. During his two-day visit, the chancellor met with President Ezer Weizmann, Prime Minister Benjamin Netanyahu, and other officials. He also met with the president of the Palestinian Authority, Yasir Arafat.

In a speech given at the Hebrew University in Jerusalem, Chancellor Klima noted that 1998 marked the 60th year since the annexation of Austria by Germany, and pledged that his government was committed to dealing with the problems of the past. The chancellor, the first Austrian head of government born after World War II, announced the establishment of a chair in history at the Hebrew University, which will focus on the history of the Jews in Austria and their contributions to science, medicine, literature, and the arts.

Klima, who was accompanied by a group of Austrian business executives, emphasized the importance of increasing trade between his country and Israel. At the time of Prime Minister Netanyahu's visit to Austria the previous year, it was agreed that efforts would be made to promote increased trade, which amounted to $250 million. These efforts appeared to be bearing fruit; in the first six months of 1998, Israeli exports to Austria had increased by 11 percent over the comparable period in 1997. During the chancellor's visit, a bilateral agreement was signed to promote joint business ventures in Eastern European countries. As a follow-up to the agreement, 14 Israeli business leaders attended a seminar in June at the Austrian Kontrolbank devoted to the promotion of joint ventures.

Holocaust-Related Developments

In important respects, 1998 was a watershed in dealing with Holocaust-related matters. It was a year marked by special ceremonies and efforts to come to terms with the still unresolved issues of compensation for Holocaust survivors and their heirs, and the restitution of artworks to their rightful owners. Growing attention was now being given to the role played by financial, commercial, and industrial firms that had benefited from the Holocaust and the compensation they owed to the survivors and their heirs. Compensation was also being demanded from certain of these firms for the profits they derived from the use of slave labor during the period of Nazi rule.

May 5th was observed, as decided in November 1997, as a memorial day to the victims of National Socialism. In memorializing the Holocaust victims, Grigori Frid's solo opera *The Diary of Anne Frank* was performed at the National Parliament, with the orchestra conducted by Asher Fisch, the music director of Vienna's Volksopera and the Tel Aviv Symphony. The Israeli singer Anat Efrati performed the role of Anne Frank.

WASHINGTON CONFERENCE

As agreed at the London Tripartite Gold Commission meeting in December 1997, a follow-up conference was convened in 1998 by the U.S. Department of State in Washington, D.C., from November 30 to December 3, to discuss unresolved issues dealing with the property and other assets of Holocaust victims and their heirs. The 52-nation conference, which was jointly sponsored by the State Department and the U. S. Holocaust Memorial Museum, dealt with the issues of gold, looted art, insurance policies, and communal property. The Austrian delegation reported on the status of each of these, though, as will be seen below, some of the information was disputed by Jewish bodies.

Gold. There remained no outstanding claims against Austria by Holocaust survivors. At the London meeting of the Tripartite Gold Commission, which dealt with monetary gold looted by the Nazis, Austria had agreed to relinquish its rights to the 860 kilograms of gold owed to it and to hand over the monetary value of this gold—approximately $8.5 million—to the Austrian *Nationalfond* created by Parliament in 1996, for distribution to needy Holocaust survivors and to worthwhile causes.

Looted Art. Under a law adopted by the Austrian Parliament on November 5, 1998, artworks of uncertain provenance would be returned to rightful owners or their heirs (see below). Where ownership could not be established, the works of art would be auctioned off, with proceeds of the sales to be given to the *Nationalfond.*

Insurance. The Austrian delegation told the Washington conference that the insurance companies active before or during the war were no longer in existence and, therefore, existing companies could not be held responsible for claims against them. Many insurance claims, the Austrian delegation noted, had been honored in the 1950s and 1960s. Despite this hard-line position of the insurance companies, Austrian foreign minister Wolfgang Schussel requested that they make a good-faith effort to cooperate with international efforts to clear up the matter of unpaid insurance claims.

Communal Property. The delegation reported that, except for one claim involving compensation for a sports facility that had been the property of the Federation of Jewish Communities of Austria (Bundesverband der Israelitischen Kultusgemeinden Osterreichs) before the war, there were no outstanding claims for the restitution of communally owned property.

KULTUSGEMEINDE POSITION DIFFERS

Although the fact was not publicly discussed in the media or elsewhere, it was clear that the position staked out by the Austrian delegation at the conference differed from that of the Kultusgemeinde in several important matters. The official Jewish community was at odds with the insurance companies' claim that they had no further obligations on policies dating back to the World War II period. And on the issue of communally owned property, the Kultusgemeinde was withholding comment until the Commission of Historians, or another competent investigative body, came up with more precise information on the status of such property.

COMMISSION OF HISTORIANS

The Austrian government created the Historiker Kommission in September 1998 to examine the matter of property confiscation during the Nazi period and what had been done in the postwar period to restitute such property to the rightful owners or heirs, or compensate them in the event restitution was not possible. The commission was also charged with the task of investigating the use of slave labor in Austrian factories during the war.

The initiative for the creation of the nine-member body of historians came from the new president of the Israelitische Kultusgemeinde, Ariel Muzicant. Political support for the establishment of such a body had developed because of the changing climate of political opinion in Austria, as well as in other European countries that had shown a greater readiness to deal in a definitive manner with the unresolved issues arising from the Holocaust. Although, in setting up the commission, the government did not impose a time limit for the completion of its investigation and the submission of a final report, it was thought likely that the commission would complete its work in two to three years and that it would, periodically, issue interim reports. Nor was it clear whether the final report would be solely factual or be accompanied by recommendations for action. And, while state archives would be made accessible to the commission's investigative staff, it was yet to be determined whether the archives of private firms, such as banks, insurance companies, or industrial firms, would be made available.

THE NATIONALFOND

The special fund established by the Austrian government in June 1995 "for the victims of national socialism" had by June 1998 contacted all the estimated 29,000 people considered eligible to receive payments. By the end of 1998, payments had been made to 24,000 people in 65 countries, the largest number being in the United States (9,540), followed by Austria (4,226), Israel (3,483), United Kingdom (2,949), and Australia (1,312). Of the recipients, 221 were born between 1891 and 1900. The amount paid to each beneficiary was fixed at 70,000 schillings ($5,800), though in special cases this could be tripled. In 1998 the Ministry of Finance allocated 500 million schillings (approximately $41 million) to the fund. It was generally understood that the payments were a goodwill gesture by the government and were not to be considered reparations to the victims.

The legislation creating the fund set forth the categories for eligibility. These included people who were persecuted because of their political beliefs, religion, nationality, sexual orientation, physical or mental disability, or were considered by the Nazis as asocial; people who were forced to flee Austria in order to escape persecution also qualified for payments. Other conditions included certification of Austrian nationality as of March 13, 1938, and proof of residence in the country. This latter condition was considerably eased by allowing people who left after July 12, 1936 (the date of a new German-Austrian treaty), to become eligible for payment. It was estimated that some 400 to 500 people, heretofore ineligible for payments, would now qualify.

In addition to the payments to eligible individuals, the fund was providing money for special projects, such as assistance to the Schiffschule Congregation in Vienna's second district with construction of a synagogue and a yeshiva dormitory. Another project to be financed by the fund is the identification and collection of the names of the 65,000 Austrian Jews who perished in the Holocaust.

LOOTED JEWISH ARTWORK

As of July 1998, 853 of 1,300 applicants had received the sum of $1,000 each from the so-called Mauerbach Fund, established in 1996 from the proceeds of a sale of artworks plundered from Jews by the Nazis. (See 1998 AJYB, pp. 336–37.) The auction of some 8,000 works yielded $14.5 million, of which 12 percent was set aside for needy non-Jewish Holocaust victims and the balance for needy Jewish victims. It was thought that as many as 5,000 Austrians from all over the world would ultimately be eligible to receive grants from the proceeds of the Mauerbach auction.

The dispute that began in December 1997 over the ownership of two paintings by the famed Austrian Secessionist painter Egon Schiele continued into 1998. The paintings were part of a special exhibition, "Egon Schiele: The Leopold Collection," which was on display at the Museum of Modern Art in New York City. (See 1998 AJYB, 337-38.) Relatives of the original owners of the paintings requested the museum to retain them until ownership could be determined. In response to these claims, early in January District Attorney Robert M. Morgenthau of Manhattan secured a grand jury subpoena restraining the museum from returning the paintings until ownership could be established. The museum decided to fight the court order, claiming that the paintings were protected under a state law governing cultural loans. On May 13, a New York State judge ruled in the museum's favor, but the District Attorney's office appealed, and the paintings remained in New York pending a final ruling.

The Austrian government, in an effort to resolve once and for all the matter of looted art, proposed a far-reaching plan to restore appropriated artworks to their rightful owners. On November 5, 1998, the Parliament unanimously approved legislation allowing works of art seized by the Nazis and later incorporated into state museums to be returned to their rightful owners. Valuable artworks belonging to many hundreds of Austrian Jews were confiscated during the Nazi rule of Austria between 1938 and 1945, and much of this art continues to hang on the walls of Austrian museums until this day. Following World War II, the government imposed what amounted to an "art tax" on the survivors of Nazism when they tried to take their recovered artworks to their new homelands. Austria demanded a share of this art in the name of preserving the national patrimony, and there was no legal protection against this procedure.

One of the more prominent people who was forced to leave behind valuable art treasures was the widow of Alphonse de Rothschild, younger brother of Louis de Rothschild, head of the Austrian branch of the family. Following the war, Mrs. Rothschild had to leave 170 works of art, 5 percent of the family's holdings, in Vienna, including three paintings by Frans Hals that she "donated" to the famed Kunsthistorisches Museum. The Osterreichische Galerie and the Kunstgewerbe Museum also secured paintings and furniture from the Rothschild holdings. Under the recently enacted legislation, Bettina Jemima, née Rothschild, a daughter of Alphonse, was expected to recover the 170 works of art that her mother was forced to give to Austrian museums. If fully implemented, the legislation would restore hundreds, if not thousands, of works of art currently held by Austrian museums and other institutions to their rightful owners.

A far more complicated issue is works of art seized by the Nazis and taken out of the country. One such case, uncovered by Oliver Rathkolb of the Kreisky Archives and Institute for Contemporary History at the University of Vienna, involved art belonging to the Gutmann family of Vienna that wound up in the Soviet Union. Rathkolb said 41 Rembrandt engravings owned by the Gutmanns were seized by Hitler's forces, then taken by Soviet troops. It remained to be seen whether the Russian government would restore the engravings to the Gutmann family. At the Washington conference on Holocaust-era assets, the Russian representative, Valery Kulishov, the director of the restitution department at the Russian Culture Ministry, announced that some World War II booty would be returned to individual claimants.

RECOVERY OF JEWISH BANK ASSETS

Negotiations were in progress in London between the American lawyer Edward Fagan and Credit Anstalt, along with its parent company, Bank Austria, and the Landerbank to settle claims of Holocaust victims arising from the activities of these banks during the war. Fagan, who was acting on behalf of numerous victims, was reported to be close to a settlement with the banks. Bank Austria and Landerbank were also prepared to make their archives available to Fagan's investigators. In doing this, the banks would provide documentation of the wartime activities of Deutsche Bank and the Dresden Bank in despoiling Jewish citizens of their money and other assets. Following the annexation of Austria in March 1938 and until the end of the war, these German banks controlled the Austrian banks.

The Austrian Post Office Savings Bank, PSK, refused to enter into negotiations with Jewish organizations to discuss restitution of monies in accounts owned by Austrian Jews before and during the war. After a specially commissioned study of the PSK archives revealed details regarding thousands of Nazi-looted Jewish accounts, the chairman of PSK, Max Rothbauer, stated that he accepted no responsibility for returning accounts, as they had been taken by the Nazis and not returned to the PSK after the war. However, the PSK said that it would repay the remaining balance of dormant accounts, those not seized by the Nazis, amounting to about 120,000 pounds sterling.

OTHER HOLOCAUST-RELATED MATTERS

In a series of memorial events, the medical school of Vienna University belatedly acknowledged the persecution of its Jewish faculty members and students during the Nazi era. In September, the school unveiled a plaque dedicated to "teachers and students who were persecuted, exiled or murdered during the Nazi regime for racial or political reasons."

Before World War II, Jews made up over half the faculty of the medical school. Following the *Anschluss* in March 1938, more than 170 professors and consultants lost their jobs. Dismissals had started even before Hitler annexed the country. Like most other academic institutions, the university never owned up to having cooperated with the Nazi regime. In 1995, this attitude was challenged from within the medical world when Dr. Leslie Bernstein, chairman of the ethics committee of the American Gastroenterology Association, raised doubts about holding the 1998 international gastroenterology conference in Vienna because the university had failed to acknowledge or atone for its past actions. In response, on the eve of the conference, the medical school faculty held a one-day commemorative symposium, and in March it held two public commemorative meetings. The Austrian weekly medical journal *Wiener Klinische Wochenschrift* devoted an entire issue in February to commemorating the "60th anniversary of the dismissal of Jewish faculty members of the Vienna medical school." The journal observed: "The dismissal caused irreparable damage to the formerly distinguished Vienna School of Medicine."

On November 9, 1998, 60 years after the destruction of the synagogues in Hitler's "Grossdeutschland" on *Kristallnacht*, the foundation for a new synagogue was laid in Graz on the exact site where the old synagogue had stood. The city of Graz (Jewish population 120), which in recent years had become increasingly conscious of its one-time role in promoting anti-Semitism in Austria, regarded the construction of the synagogue as a token of remembrance of Jewish life in prewar Graz. Among the guests present at the groundbreaking ceremony was Dr. Heinz Fischer, president of the Parliament *(Nationalrat)*, who announced that the *Nationalfond* would contribute 7.5 million schillings ($630,000) to the constructions costs, which were estimated at 55 million schillings ($4.3 million).

In October, Cardinal Koenig placed a plaque in Judenplatz which expresses the deep sorrow of the Catholic Church over its role in inciting citizens of Vienna to burn down the Judenplatz synagogue in 1421, a tragedy in which many Jews perished, and for its failure to hold out a helping hand to Jews in World War II.

JEWISH COMMUNITY

Demography

The Jewish community of Austria was undergoing changes in size, age, and composition. It was getting somewhat larger and younger, although its growth was expected to slow, if not stop, due to restrictive immigration and asylum laws. Reflecting a trend found in all European Union countries, immigration to Austria had been virtually halted. About 7,000 Jews were registered with the Israelitisch Kultusgemeinde (IKG), the official communal body, but knowledgeable observers claimed that the actual number of Jews in the country was at least twice that.

Continuing a long-established pattern of Jewish population distribution, the overwhelming majority of Jews were concentrated in Vienna, with only about 300 to 400 making their homes in the large provincial cities of Salzburg, Innsbruck, Graz, and Linz.

With the virtual cessation of immigration from the former republics of the Soviet Union, the small but steady growth was now due to the increased fertility rate, mainly among the Sephardic and Orthodox Jews. It was generally agreed that the Sephardic Jews—most of them from the former Soviet republics of Georgia and Uzbekistan (Bukhara) and a smaller number from Tajikistan—would soon outstrip the Ashkenazic community in size. There was some evidence that a handful of families from the Sephardic community were making their way back to Eastern European countries for economic reasons; many members of this community derived their livelihood from the garment and shoe trades, which were in a severe recession.

Communal Affairs

In a closely contested ballot held in April 1998, Ariel Muzicant, a businessman with a long-standing involvement in Jewish community affairs, was elected president of the IKG. He was chosen for the post by the 24-member Gemeinde council following elections to that body in the previous month. Following is a breakdown of the newly elected council based on party affiliation: Jewish Unity (5); Atid (5); Sefardim (4); K'hal Israel (2); Jewish Alliance (2); Mizrachi (2); Bund (2); Religious Bloc (1); and Georgian Jews (1). Of the 5,138 community members eligible to vote, 3,066, or 60.3 percent, cast ballots.

Among the issues debated in the elections were reform of the community's complex institutional structure; restitution of Jewish property taken during the Nazi period; overhaul of the community's financial structure, which was operating at a deficit; and preparation for the six elections to be held in Austria in 1999.

The Gemeinde was taking an active role in winning the restoration of the Jewish property, bank accounts, and other financial assets to their rightful owners. Along with other organizations and interested people, it brought pressure to bear on the government to have Parliament adopt a law for the restitution of looted Jewish artwork along with such paintings that have remained in the possession of Austrian museums since the end of World War II.

Forty Jewish teenagers and college students from the five republics of the former Yugoslavia met in Vienna in November and spent four days in lectures, discussions, and workshops as part of a program organized by the American Jewish Joint Distribution Committee and Vienna's Jewish Welcome Service. One purpose of the program, which was funded by the Austrian Federal Chancellor's Office, the Foreign Ministry, and the Ministry for Environment, Youth and Family Affairs, was to discuss ways of strengthening Jewish community life in these lands wracked by conflict, severe economic decline, and political instability. The students met with Environment Minister Martin Bartenstein and were hosted by Vienna mayor Michael Haupl at City Hall. They also met with their counterparts from Hungary, Slovakia, and the Czech Republic, as well as with some of Austria's leading journalists.

An agreement was signed between the Kultusgemeinde and the Jewish Liberal Community of Austria giving official recognition to that community. Under the terms of the agreement, the synagogue of the Liberal Community, Or Hadash, with a membership of 60 to 70 families, was eligible to receive financial assistance from the Gemeinde and was permitted to place announcements and news of its activities in *Die Gemeinde*, the official organ of the IKG. The IKG also provided limited facilities to Or Hadash in which to conduct prayer services. In return for these benefits, the rabbi of Or Hadash would not perform conversions and weddings; in addition, the Liberal Community pledged that it would not run candidates for seats on the Kultusgemeinde council. Because of financial constraints, Or Hadash did not at present have the services of a full-time rabbi and was limited to holding prayer services on Friday evenings and holidays. It did, however, provide Sunday school instruction to six children and an educational program for adults, as well as activities for its members, including trips to Jewish communities in neighboring countries and discussion groups; it also conducted an interreligious dialogue with leaders of Christian and Muslim organizations and published a bimonthly newsletter called *Keshet*. The president of Or Hadash was Theodore Much, a physician.

The European regional office of the Anti-Defamation League (ADL), which opened in Vienna in August 1997 and is headed by journalist Marta Halpert, continued its work with government officials and Jewish community leaders in neighboring Eastern and Central European countries to promote the rights of Jews and minorities in the region. In February ADL officials met with ministers of the Czech government to protest skinhead violence against Gypsies and to offer assistance in researching the causes of the violence and ways to reduce it. With financial assistance from the Lauder Foundation, ADL adopted an educational program to combat anti-Semitism in Poland, Hungary, and the Czech Republic. In Austria, it was active in combating hate on the Internet, providing information to schools and public-interest groups on dealing with this growing menace. And for the 60th anniversary of *Kristallnacht*, ADL sponsored a nationwide art contest for schoolchildren, asking them to depict their own visions of the burning of Austria's synagogues and the persecution of Jews.

Culture

Among the several exhibitions mounted by the Jewish Museum of Vienna in 1998, two attracted special attention. One, "Der Scheine Jid" (The Fine Jew), shown September 16, 1998–January 24, 1999, focused on positive and negative self-images of Jews from the Middle Ages to the present. The second exhibition, "Brennende Synagogen" (Burning Synagogues), on view November 10-December 18, marked the 60th anniversary of *Kristallnacht*. The exhibition documented the historical background of the March 1938 pogrom, the gradual marginalization and humiliation of the Jewish population, the destruction of the synagogues and prayer-houses in Vienna and the federal provinces, the dissolution of the community, and the murder of 65,000 Austrian Jews in the concentration camps.

In a change of leadership, Karl Albrecht Weinberger was named director of the Jewish Museum as of January 1998. Weinberger had previously been the curator at the Historical Museum of the City of Vienna.

The Institute for Jewish Studies in St. Polten presented research findings at an academic conference in Vienna, July 5–9, on "The Jewish Family in the Past and the Present" (Die Judische Familie in Vergangenheit und Gegenwart). The conference was sponsored by the Federal Ministry for Youth, Environment and Family. The institute, which was founded in 1988 and is headed by Dr. Klaus Lohrmann, is devoted to the study of Jewish life in the framework of European history.

Personalia

The Federation of Jewish Communities of Austria awarded its gold medal to Prof. Kurt Schubert, former chairman of Vienna University's Department of Judaism, for his academic achievements and his role in furthering Christian-Jewish relations.

The Nobel Prize for chemistry was awarded in 1998 to the American scientist Walter Kohn, a native of Austria, whose family was forced to flee the country in 1939 and made its way to the United States. Invited to Vienna by the Austrian government, Dr. Kohn visited the Zvi Peretz Chayes day school that he attended until his family emigrated. He recalled that his interest in chemistry first developed under the encouragement of Emile Nohel, an assistant to Albert Einstein and the school's last director before it was closed in 1939.

Karl Haber, one-time president of *Ha-Koah,* the famous Jewish sports club, died in October at the age of 76. The club, which had achieved great renown for winning the Austrian national soccer championship in the 1920s, was reestablished after the war.

MURRAY GORDON

East-Central Europe

I N 1998, JEWISH COMMUNAL revival continued throughout East-Central Europe. In most of the emerging new communities, lay leadership was increasingly in the hands of members of the postwar generation. Self-confident communal representatives took part in Europe-wide Jewish discourse and grappled with issues and concerns common to communities across the continent. While these leaders recognized that the post-Communist communal revival still had a long way to go, their attitudes reflected a basic change of mind-set, firmly refusing to be labeled the "last Jews" of the region.

Several major issues, as in past years, dominated. One was the continuing linked saga of property restitution and financial compensation to Holocaust survivors and related revelations about Nazi gold, insurance claims, and other such matters. By the end of the year, Germany began paying Holocaust compensation to survivors in East European countries. The issue of Jewish heritage and what to do with remaining or restituted synagogues, cemeteries, and other sites, which often were in bad condition, was also pressing.

Other cross-border issues that continued to engage Jewish communities throughout the region were, as last year, the question of identity and "who is a Jew"; how to deal with mixed marriages and children of mixed marriages; outreach to the unaffiliated; and how to create a new group of community leaders to guide the communities into the future. Dealing with these issues influenced the focus of local Jewish community structures as well as international Jewish organizations working in the region, such as the American Jewish Joint Distribution Committee (JDC), the Lauder Foundation, Chabad, and World Jewish Relief (WJR), as well as the European Council of Jewish Communities (ECJC). Several conferences were held on aspects of these problems, including a conference in Vienna in October and one in Lisbon in December.

Relations with Israel, meanwhile, deepened on the government to government level throughout the region, particularly in economic relations and tourism.

Bulgaria

In February, the JDC presented an award to Bulgarian president Peter Stoyanov, recognizing Bulgaria's success in saving its Jewish population from deportation during World War II. B'nai B'rith presented Stoyanov with its "Award for Courage." Stoyanov, who was on a visit to the United States, also met with a group U.S. Jewish businessmen, whom he urged to invest in his country. In August the Anti-Defamation League asked Stoyanov to "publicly renounce" anti-Semitic statements made by Rumen Vodenitcharov, a prominent member of the Bulgarian Socialist Party. Vodenitcharov was quoted as accusing the Bulgarian government of "selling the country to Jews and Gypsies" and claiming that Bulgaria "is being ruled by Jews." During an official visit to Israel in June, Bulgarian foreign minister Nadezhda Mihailova met with Israeli prime minister Benjamin Netanyahu, signed cooperation agreements, and discussed the situation in Kosovo and in the Middle East.

JEWISH COMMUNITY

About 6,000 Jews lived in Bulgaria, with estimates ranging between 5,000 and 8,000. Most Jews lived in the capital, Sofia, and in Plovdiv. At Purim, in March, a gala ceremony inaugurated the newly enlarged and restored Beit Ha'am, the Jewish community building in Sofia. Beit Ha'am houses a kosher restaurant as well as a youth club, an auditorium, a clinic, a library and computer room, a daycare center, and other activities as well as offices. The $500,000 renovation was sponsored by Britain's World Jewish Relief and entailed adding an entire new floor to the building. Also at Purim, the imposing, newly restored ark in Sofia's recently reconstructed Great Synagogue was rededicated at a service that attracted about 300 people. The synagogue complex also houses a Jewish museum. The Purim festivities were rounded off with a lively children's Purim party at Beit Ha'am, featuring music, pop singers, a clown, a light show, and other entertainment. During these festivities, Shirley and Norman Casdan, two guests on a WJR delegation from Britain, met with the family of Rossen Gramenov, a seven-year-old boy who has leukemia and for whom an international B'nai B'rith effort had raised $70,000 to allow him to go to Israel for bone marrow treatment.

In the spring, the B'nai B'rith Youth Organization (BBYO) organized an intensive leadership training program in Bulgaria for teens from Bulgaria, the United States, and Israel. The BBYO, which also organized groups of local Bulgarian teens, and the B'nai B'rith Carmel Lodge, were among many Jewish groups and clubs operating in Bulgaria.

In July, as many as 200 participants from Turkey, Bulgaria, Croatia, Bosnia-Herzegovina, and Yugoslavia took part in Esperansa '98, a four-day festival of Ladino and Sephardic culture held near Sofia. The festival was organized by the Joint Distribution Committee, the European Council of Jewish Communities, and World Jewish Relief, in collaboration with Shalom, the organization of Bulgarian Jews. Its aim was to promote regional cooperation among Jewish communities and to spark renewed expression of a shared Sephardic civilization.

In November a new Jewish school, sponsored by the Ronald S. Lauder Foundation, opened in Sofia. The 12th Lauder-sponsored Jewish school in post-Communist East-Central Europe, it had an enrollment of about 350 students in grades 1 through 8. The curriculum included Jewish history and Hebrew in addition to standard secular subjects. The Lauder Foundation provided $300,000 in funding and also renovated the 86-year-old building where the school is located.

Czech Republic

The Czech Republic, once the pride of post-Communist development, suffered deepening economic, political, and social malaise in 1998. The GDP was at a zero or negative growth rate, wages and foreign investment were down, and unemployment was up. The health of President Vaclav Havel was also a concern. In parliamentary elections in June, the left of center Social Democrats won a relative majority and in July formed a coalition headed by Prime Minister Milos Zeman. The new government included an Auschwitz survivor, Egon Lansky, as deputy prime minister for European integration.

The far-right nationalist Republican Party, known for anti-Semitic and anti-Romany (Gypsy) rhetoric, won only 3.9 percent of the vote (below the 5 percent threshold) and thus failed to get any seats in Parliament. In 1996 elections, the Republicans won more than 8 percent and held 18 seats. In the wake of this electoral defeat, one of the main ideologists of the party, Josef Krejsa, who also edits the extreme nationalist newspaper *Republika*, issued an apology "to everyone [he] had offended." Earlier, the Federation of Czech Jewish Communities had brought suit against *Republika*, accusing it of propagating anti-Semitism.

Nonetheless, rising racism and intolerance were a continuing concern throughout the year. In a February public opinion poll, 25 percent of respondents expressed feelings of racial intolerance. On May 8, five skinheads were arrested and charged with beating two Indian men in a Prague subway. The attack took place shortly before an antifascist march was to begin nearby. On the same day, police had to separate about 15 skinheads from antifascist marchers to avert incidents. Numerous other incidents took place during the year. At a meeting in December with Zeman and other members of the cabinet to discuss racism and xenophobia, Havel said the situation was "serious" and warned of "growing apathy toward racist violence here." In May, in a speech at a memorial service in Terezin denouncing anti-Romany racism in the Czech Republic, Chief Rabbi Karol Efraim Sidon said, "We Jews feel sooner than others the jeopardy fueled by hatred, now directed against Romanies just as it was once directed against us by the Nazis. Therefore we are convinced that there is a need to mobilize all our strength to ensure that Romanies quickly receive the protection of law that is their inalienable right as citizens of this country and as human beings." Sidon was speaking not long after plans were revealed to wall off a pair of tenement houses occupied mainly by Romanies in the town of Usti nad Labem, not far from Terezin.

Most racist actions were directed against Romanies, but there were also scattered incidents of apparent anti-Semitism. On November 8, a teenage skinhead stabbed a Jewish soldier. He was charged under the Czech Republic's hate-crimes law with attempting racially motivated murder and promoting fascism. The Jewish community said this was the first anti-Semitic criminal act since the fall of Communism. On November 11, vandals spray-painted anti-Semitic slogans on tombstones at the Jewish cemetery in Trutnov. They also defaced a plaque marking the site of the destroyed synagogue and a Holocaust memorial in the town. Four suspects, including three teenaged skinheads, were arrested. A few days later, skinheads in central Prague threatened Rabbi Sidon and his 12-year-old son, but did not harm them. The Federation of Czech Jewish Communities appealed to the government to crack down on xenophobic and anti-Semitic acts.

Holocaust-related developments: A joint Czech-German fund for victims of Nazism, set up in January 1997, began issuing payments to 6,200 people, including about 2,000 Jews, in May. Those imprisoned during the war for up to 12 months will receive $900 a year, those imprisoned 12 to 30 months will receive about $1,100, and those imprisoned longer than 30 months will receive $1,400. In November the government established a commission to oversee the restitution of Jewish property confiscated by the Nazis. Chaired by a deputy prime minister and including state officials and Jews, the commission was charged with making an inventory of assets claimed by Czech Jews and then arranging restitution to prior owners or monetary compensation for the property from a yet-to-be-created fund. The work was to be completed by March 1999. Tomas Kraus, secretary of the Federation of Czech Jewish Communities, said the federation would not make claim to properties that are currently being used for the public good, such as synagogues used now as churches or property where schools were built. The Czech Jewish community claims some 200 properties, 17 now owned by the government, 64 owned by municipalities, and the others by individuals. One day before the formation of the commission was announced, the Czech National Gallery said its collection included dozens of artworks believed to have been stolen from Jews during World War II.

Activists tried to enlist international Jewish support to have a pig farm removed from the site of a wartime concentration camp at Lety where Gypsies had been imprisoned during World War II. The Jewish community in Prague was considering opening a museum-memorial to the Roma tragedy in the former synagogue in Pisek, near Lety, which was returned to Jewish ownership.

In March, 88-year-old Nicolas Winton, an Englishman, visited Prague as part of a project by a Czech-British production team to make a documentary about his World War II rescue work. Just before the war began, he organized transports that sent 664 mostly Jewish children to foster parents in England. One of the film's producers is Martina Stolbova, of Prague's Jewish Museum, who said the film would be called *Nicholas G. Winton—The British Wallenberg.*

JEWISH COMMUNITY

Some 3,500-6,000 Jews were known to live in the Czech Republic, with possibly thousands of others who were unaffiliated but of Jewish background. About half of the Czech Republic's Jews lived in Prague, with the others scattered in nine other communities. In Prague, in addition to the official Jewish community, which is Orthodox, two non-Orthodox communities functioned: Bejt Praha, which called itself the Open Prague Jewish Community, and Bejt Simcha, which maintained links with Progressive Judaism. In addition, Chabad Lubavitch had a representative in the city. In November, members of UJA-Federations of North America's Young Leadership Division delivered a refurbished Torah scroll to Bejt Praha.

In 1998 the Lauder Gur Aryeh Jewish Day School in Prague completed its first year of operation. The Or Chadash Hebrew high school, funded by the Prague Jewish community, opened in September. About a dozen teenagers attended class four afternoons a week, after attending regular public school in the morning.

Restoration work was carried out or completed on several synagogues, including two of the Czech Republic's most magnificent. On February 11, the Great Synagogue in Pilsen was rededicated after completion of the state-financed $1.7 million first phase of a full-scale renovation. The first phase saw the restoration of the facade and most of the interior. Jewish community leaders said another $1 million was needed to complete the work. Czech chief rabbi Sidon and Israeli ambassador Raphael Gvir took part in the ceremony, along with Pilsen's mayor and other local officials. The synagogue, built in 1892, is consecrated as a house of worship, but is too big for regular use by the fewer than 100 Pilsen Jews; it will be used for concerts and cultural events.

In Prague, the ornate Spanish Synagogue was inaugurated in November, with a gala ceremony after a full-scale renovation. This structure, which forms part of the Prague Jewish Museum, now houses an exhibition on the history of Prague Jews. This restoration was a major milestone in the ambitious effort of expansion and change at the museum, whose director, Leo Pavlat, aims to make the institution a tool in educating the non-Jewish public about Jews and Judaism. The museum's Education Center ran public lectures and teacher-training sessions. Pavlat authored a highly critical report on how Jewish themes were presented in Czech public schools. The report, part of the American Jewish Committee's Curriculum Review project surveying textbooks in several post-Communist countries, showed that little was taught about Jews and Judaism, and that what was taught was sometimes distorted.

Work was under way on construction of a new synagogue in the northern Bohemian town of Liberec, on the spot where the destroyed prewar synagogue stood. The Jewish community regained the site through restitution. The new building will hold a 120-seat synagogue and offices of the Jewish community (there are fewer than 100 Jews in Liberec) plus a research library and lecture hall. Financing for the project came from the Czech and German governments. A number of other synagogues were under restoration in towns scattered around the country. During the summer, an archeological survey of a site in central Prague being developed as a parking lot discovered the remains of Prague's oldest Jewish cemetery, dating to about 1250. This prompted Jewish leaders to ask that the site be classified as a historic landmark.

As every year, there were numerous cultural events, concerts, exhibitions, publications, and the like on Jewish themes. Some were sponsored by the Jewish community and some by non-Jewish public and private bodies. In April a number of VIPs attended a special production of the play *Sweet Theresienstadt*, cosponsored by the Jewish Education Center of the Prague Jewish Museum and the Archa Theater. In May, in honor of the 50th anniversary of the Jewish state, Israel was the central theme of an international book fair called Bookworld 98, which featured 680 publishers from 21 countries. As part of events around the book fair, the Jewish Museum organized a symposium on "Czech Jewish Literature, Jewish Themes and Translation." A noteworthy new book, *Clovek neni cislo* (A Person Is Not a Number), one among a number of books on Jewish themes published during the year, contains creative writing and art by Czech schoolchildren who visited the Terezin (Theresienstadt) concentration camp and took part in a national competition in 1997. The competition attracted more than 400 entries from pupils in 59 schools in 16 cities.

In July the small Moravian town of Boskovice hosted its annual culture festival aimed at raising consciousness of local Jewish history. On Sept. 19, a concert was held to mark the first phase of the restoration of the house in the southern Bohemian village of Kaliste, where Jewish composer Gustav Mahler was born. The building eventually is to house the Gustav Mahler Center. There are already museums dedicated to Mahler in the nearby towns of Jihlava and Humpolec. In October a Czech production of *Fiddler on the Roof* opened at a newly renovated theater in Prague. It starred Jewish actor Tomas Topfer, the son of concentration camp survivors, in the role of Tevye. The seventh annual Musica Judaica festival took place in Prague in October-November.

Hungary

Hungary's economy grew about 5 percent, and the average inflation rate fell to 14.3 percent from 18.3 percent in 1997. In general elections in May, rightists swept to power as the center-right Fidesz Young Democrats-Civic Party won 148 of the 386 parliamentary seats, ousting the Socialists who had governed Hungary since 1994. Fidesz leader Viktor Orban, 35, a former student leader, became prime minister at the head of a coalition with the right-wing Independent Smallholders Party. The far-right Hungarian Truth and Life Party (MIEP), led by Istvan Csurka and known for its anti-Semitic and anti-Romany (Gypsy) rhetoric, won 14 parliamentary seats. MIEP was not part of the government, but this marked the first time an extreme right party — some of whose members are skinheads — had entered Parliament since the end of World War II. This raised alarm among many Hungarians, including, in particular, Jews. "We fear an extremist position may become an acceptable level of political discourse," said Peter Feldmajer, president of the Hungarian Jewish Communities. In September Chief Rabbi Jozsef Schweitzer denounced as anti-Semitic a speech in Parliament by a MIEP MP, the Calvinist priest Lorant Hegedus, who, Schweitzer said, used discriminatory code language to refer to Jews. Critics of MIEP noted that since open anti-Semitic references are not acceptable, coded phrases such as "minority origin" have been employed.

In October Sir Sigmund Sternberg, patron of the International Council of Christians and Jews (ICCJ), met for an hour with Prime Minister Orban during a visit to Budapest and voiced concern about anti-Semitic remarks made by Hungarian MPs. During his visit to Budapest, Sternberg presented the ICCJ's interfaith medal to Ferenc Glatz, a scholar and Hungary's former culture minister.

In February the Supreme Court sentenced neo-Nazi leader Albert Szabo to a one-year suspended prison term for incitement against the Jewish community. He was also put on probation for three years. The charge dated back to a speech he made in October 1996. Also in February, some 600 neo-Nazis in black uniforms demonstrated at Buda Castle in Budapest to mark the 53rd anniversary of the surrender of the Nazis to Soviet troops.

Relations with Israel remained close on the governmental, commercial, and personal levels. Many Israeli firms and individuals carried out businesses and joint ventures in Hungary. It was estimated by Jewish sources that some 50,000 Israelis went to Hungary for the High Holy Days. Israelis in Hungary were not always a positive element, however. British-Israeli businessman Joseph Raynor was held in jail on suspicion of smuggling a quantity of chewing gum without paying customs duty. He was arrested in October 1997, but the reason for his arrest was announced only in May 1998. In June an Israeli was arrested along with a German and two Russian citizens on suspicion of involvement in a series of organized crime-related bomb attacks.

Holocaust-related developments: This year was the "year of compensation." Starting at the end of January, some 7,000 of Hungary's elderly Holocaust survivors began receiving a lump sum payment of $400 as compensation from the Swiss Holocaust fund for needy survivors. About 18,000 survivors were eligible for such compensation. Most expressed gratitude, but some Jews expressed concern either that the payments represented "blood money" and were distasteful, or that the payments to Jews would trigger a form of jealous anti-Semitism among Hungarian extremists. These 18,000 survivors were also eligible for a grant of 1,000 German marks from the Red Cross. Some 8,000 survivors were eligible for monthly pensions of 250 marks paid by Germany through the Conference on Jewish Material Claims Against Germany. In September Minister of Cultural Heritage Jozsef Hamori and chairman of the Federation of Hungarian Jewish Communities Peter Feldmajer signed an agreement mandating collective compensation for 152 schools and other Jewish communal properties confiscated under the Communist regime. The Jewish community will receive $63 million, paid out in annual installments of $2.9 million.

JEWISH COMMUNITY

Estimates of the number of Jews in Hungary ranged from 54,000 to 130,000. Only 6,000 or so were formally registered with the Jewish community, and about 20,000 had some sort of affiliation with Jewish organizations or institutions. Some 90 percent of Hungary's Jews lived in Budapest.

The vast majority of Hungary's Jews were unaffiliated or secular. The dominant religious affiliation was Neolog, similar to America's Conservative Judaism. There was a small Reform congregation in Budapest, and also a small Orthodox community, made up of both Hassidim and "modern Orthodox." In fact, Orthodox Jews had become an increasingly visible presence. In March Budapest's resident Lubavitch rabbi, Baruch Oberlander, celebrated an Orthodox wedding, complete with *huppah*, on the street outside the Balint Jewish Community Center. Several Neolog rabbis also took part in the ceremony, which attracted a large crowd. The groom was a student at Budapest's Neolog Rabbinical Seminary and the bride was a student at the seminary's teacher-training school. They said they wanted an Orthodox wedding so that it would be recognized in Israel.

Several new Jewish institutions opened their doors. In May a small prayer house, Holocaust memorial, and Jewish museum complex was opened in Szentendre, a picturesque town on the Danube near Budapest. In July a newly built synagogue and multipurpose education center was dedicated at the Lauder-JDC International Jewish Youth Summer Camp at Szarvas, in southern Hungary. The red-brick, 500-square-meter complex, which houses a library, study rooms, activities rooms, computer center, and synagogue sanctuary, is called Beit David, in honor of the son of JDC honorary executive vice-president Ralph Goldman, who was killed in the bombing of the Israeli embassy in Buenos Aires. Each summer, some 2,000 Jewish young people from all over Eastern and Central Europe attend two-week sessions at Szarvas, where standard summer camp activities are combined with Jewish education.

In Budapest, the start of the school year saw the opening of a state-of-the art campus for the Jewish community's day school, which also changed its name from the Anna Frank school to the Sandor Scheiber school, in honor of Hungary's respected scholar and chief rabbi who died in the 1980s. The Anna Frank high school had been located in the building of the Budapest Rabbinical Seminary. The new Scheiber school was opened on the grounds of the Jewish hospital. Funds for the new campus came from money paid in compensation in lieu of restitution of a former Jewish school building. It started with a high school curriculum but aimed at expanding into a full kindergarten through high school within eight years. The Scheiber school was one of three Jewish day schools operating in Budapest, with a total enrollment of more than 1,500 pupils. The other two were the secular Ronald S. Lauder Javne School, on its own outlying campus, and the downtown Orthodox school.

Budapest's rabbinical seminary and associated teacher-training institute prepared rabbis and cantors as well as educators for Hungary's schools and institutions, enabling locally trained personnel increasingly to take the place of teachers sent by the Jewish Agency to Hungary from Israel. Plans were announced to merge the seminary and teacher-training institute into an officially accredited Jewish university, to begin operation in September 1999.

In the fall, Budapest's central kosher kitchen, which provided meals on wheels and kosher meals at senior centers and other Jewish institutions, closed its long-time premises at the Pava Street senior center and moved into a modern new space at the Scheiber school complex, where it had the capacity to prepare 3,000 kosher meals a day for homebound survivors, senior centers, schools, and the hospital. Numerous cultural events on Jewish themes took place during the year. During Budapest's annual spring culture festival, Budapest's Jewish Museum displayed holographic images of Jewish life from the Jewish Museum in Vienna. At the end of the summer, Budapest hosted its first tourist-oriented Jewish culture festival. Central Europe University held its second annual Jewish summer study program in July and scheduled public lectures on Jewish themes throughout the academic year. In September the first issue of a new Jewish magazine, *Remeny* (Hope), was published, financed by the Federation of Hungarian Jewish Communities.

Work progressed on several synagogue restoration projects, and in Budapest's main Jewish cemetery the beautiful 1904 art nouveau tomb of the Sandor Schmidl family, designed by leading architects Odon Lechner and Bela Lajta, was unveiled after two years of restoration work.

In July shooting began in Budapest on *A Taste of Sunshine*, a movie in which Ralph Fiennes plays the parts of three Jews in a multigenerational saga centering on a family called Sonnenschein—"sunshine" in German. The film was written and directed by Hungarian Jewish director Istvan Szabo.

Poland

Despite being hit by fallout from the financial crisis in Russia, end-of-year reports indicated that 1998 would mark Poland's fifth year of economic growth at 5 percent or higher—a record unmatched in post-Communist Eastern Europe.

In January Poland marked its first ever "Day of Judaism" sponsored by the Roman Catholic Church. The nationwide initiative, designed to bring Jews and Catholics closer together, used a slogan taken from a quotation by Polish-born Pope John Paul II: "Whoever meets Jesus Christ, meets Judaism." Churches all over Poland held special masses, and hundreds of Poles visited synagogues around the country. In Warsaw, hundreds of visitors, including priests and dozens of nuns, attended a Havdalah service in the city's only synagogue. The ceremony was given wide media coverage and was followed by speeches by Bishop Stanislaw Gadecki, head of the Episcopate's Council for Religious Dialogue, and Stanislaw Krajewski, who spoke in the name of the Union of Jewish Religious Communities in Poland.

This year marked the 30th anniversary of the Communist regime's anti-Semitic campaign in 1968 that forced some 20,000 Jews out of Poland. Official state ceremonies as well as Jewish-organized events were held to commemorate the persecutions, and the government took steps to amend the wrongs committed. Jews who were forced to flee in 1968 were invited to reunions in Poland, Sweden—

where many of the refugees found haven—and Israel. A plaque with an inscription commemorating "those who traveled out of Poland after March 1968 with one-way travel documents" was unveiled at a Warsaw train station from which many refugees departed. And the Polish government announced that it would restore Polish citizenship to individual Jews driven out in 1968 who request it. "We remember and we are ashamed," President Aleksander Kwasniewski, himself an ex-Communist turned Social Democrat, said at a ceremony in March. "It is not they who abandoned Poland. Poland abandoned them. We must put this right. . . . Today one thing must be said clearly: March 1968 was a shameful page in Polish history."

A delegation of Polish Jews, led by Jerzy Kichler, the president of the Union of Jewish Religious Communities, met in March with Prime Minister Jerzy Buzek. Buzek was "very sympathetic and seemingly concerned" with the issues raised by the Jewish representatives, including the restitution of Jewish communal property and the need for official reaction against anti-Semitism.

Poland's government-to-government relations with Israel remained good. Prime Minister Benjamin Netanyahu paid a two-day official visit to Poland in April (see Auschwitz, below). In July Israel honored more than 20 non-Jewish Poles for their work in helping to preserve and protect Jewish cemeteries, synagogues, and other sites of Jewish heritage. Israel's ambassador to Poland, Yigal Antebi, presented framed certificates to the honorees at a ceremony held in Krakow at the conclusion of that city's annual festival of Jewish culture. The honored individuals came from Bialystok, Tykocin, Lublin, Pinczow, Bransk, and other towns and cities around the country. They had spent years on a mainly voluntary basis restoring and documenting abandoned Jewish cemeteries, writing books and pamphlets on local Jewish history, seeing that memorial plaques were placed on former synagogues, and working to establish Jewish museums or Jewish departments in other museums. Recognizing them was the idea of Michael Traison, a Jewish lawyer from Detroit who spent time in Poland doing legal work for his firm and had met the honorees personally during trips around the country. The ceremony received ample coverage in the Polish media.

Also in July, a memorial to Jewish Holocaust victims in the southern city of Rzeszow, which had been dedicated the week before, was defaced by anti-Semitic graffiti. City officials in Rzeszow took immediate steps to clean the monument. There were other scattered instances of vandalism against Jewish sites. In May about 35 tombstones were vandalized in two attacks on the Jewish cemetery in Warsaw. In July Prime Minister Buzek condemned an attack on Jewish graves in Palmiry, near Warsaw.

HOLOCAUST-RELATED DEVELOPMENTS

Auschwitz: The former Nazi death camp at Auschwitz-Birkenau, where more than 1.5 million people, 90 percent of them Jews from all over Europe, were killed, remained the center of emotional and sometimes bitter controversy throughout much of the year. On April 13, Holocaust Memorial Day, Israeli prime minister Netanyahu and Polish prime minister Buzek led the biggest ever "March of the Living." Accompanying thousands of Jewish teenagers from many countries, they walked the two miles from the Auschwitz I camp to Birkenau and in speeches pledged increasing dialogue and cooperation between Poles and Jews. It was the first time the event included the head of the Polish government and other government ministers.

The controversy over crosses erected at Auschwitz was a continuing source of tension. In February government representatives said that the 25-ft. cross that had stood for the past decade just outside the walls of the Auschwitz I camp museum would be relocated. The cross stood at the site where 152 Catholic Poles were killed by the Nazis, near the building that had housed a controversial Carmelite convent, vacated by the nuns in 1993. In early March, the Carmelites formally gave up ownership of the convent building and turned it over to the state, but this takeover agreement did not include jurisdiction over the cross. In the wake of the statements that the cross would be moved, a local "defense of the cross" movement became more openly active, igniting national debate. Apparently attempting to head off a crisis, Bishop Stanislaw Gadecki, head of the Polish Episcopate's commission for dialogue with the Jews, in early March proposed to replace the large cross with a monument on that spot to the Polish Christian victims of mass killings, with the understanding that the monument would include a representation of the cross. Under this plan, the large cross—under which Pope John Paul prayed in 1979—would be erected anew at a church in the town of Oswiecim (in German, Auschwitz). Wooden crosses removed at the end of 1997 from Birkenau already had been placed at this church.

Gadecki's plan fell through. On May 1, about 1,000 Roman Catholics prayed at the cross. Some held banners reading "Let's defend the cross" and "God, Honor and Homeland." Other pray-ins, protests, and vigils took place. In late July, radical Catholics began erecting more, smaller, crosses "in defense of" the large cross. In doing so, they defied both the Polish government and Polish church authorities—as well as protests by local Jews, international Jewish organizations, and Israel. The government and church hierarchy wanted the smaller crosses removed but felt that the original, large "papal" cross should stay. At the end of September, the local bishop suspended a priest for his role in erecting a cross. Some of the militants, who also maintained a vigil at the site, issued anti-Semitic statements in the media. By the end of the year, well over 200 crosses formed a forest around the large cross and the situation remained at a tense impasse.

The cross controversy stalled Jewish-Polish dialogue on other issues, including plans for an international restoration and conservation program for Auschwitz, which had been agreed upon in 1997. In the spring, Rev. Waldemar Chrostowski resigned from his position as co-chairman of the Polish Council of Christians and Jews in the wake of controversy over his statements protesting the removal of religious symbols from Auschwitz. The cross conflict also sparked concern over anti-Semitism. In November the one-year suspension from preaching ordered against Gdansk priest Henryk Jankowski was up, and he immediately let loose with an anti-Semitic attack linked to the cross controversy. He had made other anti-Semitic statements outside of the preaching context earlier in the year.

Other Developments: In April Poland presented its highest award to Marek Edelman, the only surviving leader of the Warsaw Ghetto uprising of 1943. President Kwasniewski presented the Order of the White Eagle to the 76-year-old Edelman, who remained in Poland after the war and became a cardiologist and an activist in dissident movements in the 1970s and the Solidarity movement of the 1980s.

Several new monuments to Jewish Holocaust victims were erected or dedicated. In May a monument commemorating 599 Jews murdered by the Nazis was dedicated in the Rakowski forest near the city of Piotrkow Trybunalski in central Poland. More than 100 survivors and descendants of Jews from the town came from Israel, Canada, the United States, and Great Britain for the ceremony. In July Prime Minister Buzek said in Washington that Polish officials, in association with the U.S. Holocaust Memorial Museum, would erect a new monument at the site of the Belzec death camp, in eastern Poland, where a Communist-era monument was neglected and crumbling. Little is known of wartime conditions in Belzec, as only a handful of Jews survived the camp. Archaeologists this year carried out excavations to find out more about the camp before the new monument was built.

A number of events linked to the restoration of synagogues took place in Poland to mark the 60th anniversary of the so-called *Kristallnacht* pogrom in Germany, November 9-10, 1938, when hundreds of synagogues were destroyed in Germany and German-occupied lands. Prime Minister Buzek and other representatives of the Polish government, the Roman Catholic church and other faiths, as well as Jewish groups unveiled a monument to commemorate the *Kristallnacht* pogrom in Wroclaw, a city that before World War II was the German city of Breslau, home to Germany's second-largest Jewish community. The monument was unveiled at the site of one of the synagogues burned down during the pogrom. Wroclaw's 19th-century Storch Synagogue, left ruined after the war, was currently undergoing a full restoration. Meanwhile, a synagogue in the town of Oswiecim (Auschwitz) was rededicated as a "center of prayer and contemplation and eternal memorial to Jewish victims of the Holocaust" at a ceremony attended by a 50-member Jewish delegation and representatives of the Polish, U.S., and Israeli governments. The synagogue, long used as a carpet warehouse, was restored to Poland's Jewish community in April—the first Jewish property to be restituted in Poland under the provisions of a 1997 law on restitution of communal property. The new prayer and education center was to be built in the synagogue and in an adjoining house over the next two years by the New York-based Auschwitz Jewish Center Foundation, at a cost up to $10 million. In December the site of a synagogue destroyed by the Nazis was returned to the 200-member Jewish community in Gdansk under the 1997 restitution law.

In October leaders of Poland's Jewish community and representatives of the World Jewish Restitution Organization (WJRO) signed an agreement on how to divide the proceeds and ownership of communal properties being restituted under the 1997 law. A joint foundation established by the Polish Jewish community and the WJRO would take ownership of all the inactive Jewish cemeteries and communal Jewish heritage monuments. There are estimated to be as many as 1,400 disused Jewish cemeteries scattered around Poland, most of them in ruined condition. Proceeds from restituted communal property would be divided into thirds: one-third would go to the Jewish communities in Poland, one-third would be administered by the foundation, in theory for preservation and conservation of cemeteries and other properties, and one-third would be administered by the WJRO. No figures were estimated, and, given the complex restitution procedure, much about how the process would be carried out remained uncertain.

In December Israel refused a Polish request to extradite Solomon Morel, a Jew accused of torturing and killing German prisoners during World War II, when he commanded a camp for German prisoners in southern Poland. He is alleged to have been responsible for more than 1,500 deaths. An Israeli Justice Ministry spokeswoman said that the statute of limitations in the case had run out.

JEWISH COMMUNITY

Estimates of the number of Jews in Poland ranged from the 7,000-8,000 officially registered with the community or receiving aid from the Joint Distribution Committee, to 10,000-15,000 people of Jewish ancestry who have shown interest in rediscovering their heritage, to as many as 30,000 to 40,000 people of Jewish ancestry. The Lauder Foundation and the JDC were key supporters of a wide range of educational and social programs in Warsaw and other cities. The Lauder Foundation's longtime director in Poland, Rabbi Michael Schudrich, a charismatic figure who was a leading catalyst in the emergence of the reviving Jewish community, ended his tenure. He was replaced by Jonah Bookstein, a young American who had studied in Jerusalem and earlier worked part time for the foundation, and his wife, Rachel. Sixteen Jewish organizations used the premises of the Lauder Community Center for Jewish Education in Warsaw on a weekly basis. The foundation itself sponsored five youth clubs and education centers around Poland. About five hundred people took part in the foundation's summer and winter camps at Rychwald in southern Poland. The foundation supported the glossy Jewish monthly magazine *Midrasz* as well as the student magazine *Jidele* and a new family magazine, *Szterndlech*.

The Jewish Culture Center in Krakow featured cultural events almost daily, and the Shalom Foundation in Warsaw also sponsored many events.

At the beginning of the year, city officials in the town of Plonsk announced a competition for historical work on modern Polish-Jewish relations. They issued a call for memoirs, diaries, interviews, and other written or audiovisual work related particularly to the relations between Jews and non-Jews in Plonsk and its surrounding district as well as in Poland in general in the 20th century. Prizes were to be awarded in the spring of 1999. Plonsk was the birthplace of David Ben-Gurion, and the $1,000 first prize was to be named in his honor.

In March President Kwasniewski and other dignitaries attended a gala benefit concert at Warsaw Castle, organized by the Jewish Historical Institute to raise funds for a planned Museum of Polish Jewish History to be built in Warsaw near the site of the ghetto memorial. In June Krakow's former Jewish quarter, Kazimierz, was once again the scene of an annual weeklong Jewish culture festival, showcasing concerts, lectures, workshops, performances, and exhibits. Among various conferences on Jewish themes was an international interfaith conference on "Religion and Violence" held at Auschwitz, in May, with the participation of Christians, Muslims, and Jews, including several Orthodox rabbis from the United States and Israel. The conference was organized by Orthodox rabbi Joseph Ehrenkranz, director of the Center for Christian-Jewish Understanding at Sacred Heart University in Connecticut. Other conferences included "Ashkenaz: Theory and Nation," on the East European Jewish experience, cosponsored in May by Ohio State University and Krakow's Jagiellonian University, and "Teaching the Holocaust," held in Krakow in September, organized by the London-based Spiro Institute.

During the year, the American Jewish Committee and the Warsaw-based Jewish Historical Institute released studies decrying the lack of material on Jewish themes taught to Polish students in public schools. The American Jewish Committee report, issued in May in Polish and English, was the first of a series of such education surveys to be carried out in several former Communist countries.

Poland's first postwar Jewish book fair took place in Warsaw in November, sponsored by the Lauder Foundation and the Polish Jewish magazine *Midrasz* and held at the Lauder Community Center. More than 300 books—about 200 in Polish and 100 in English—were displayed at the fair by more than half a dozen Polish publishers and distributors, and the event received extensive publicity in the media. The book fair also included well-attended related events, including lectures, readings, and a concert.

The Tempel Synagogue in Krakow, the only 19th-century synagogue still standing intact in Poland, was opened to the public for tours of the full-scale restoration taking place, a project of the New York-based World Monuments Fund. Scaffolding was removed from the synagogue's interior, revealing the newly cleaned, ornate ceiling decoration.

Romania

Romania continued to struggle with deep economic and political problems. Tensions between the two main coalition partners, the Democratic Convention of Romania and the Democratic Party, triggered the collapse of Prime Minister Victor Ciorbea's government in early 1998, and a new government, led by Prime Minister Radu Vasile, took office in April. Personal and political conflicts among the four-party coalition partners persisted throughout the year, stalling reforms and contributing to a sense of political instability. Meanwhile, the economy continued to perform poorly, although inflation was lower and wages were somewhat higher than in 1997. In the first six months of 1998, however, the GDP dropped by 5.2 percent compared to the same period in 1997, marking the second consecutive year of sharp decline. (End-of-year forecasts for the total 1998 drop in GDP ranged from 3 to 6 percent.) Unemployment was estimated at about 9 percent.

In November a poll by the Open Society Foundation showed that 51 percent of respondents thought life was better before the 1989 collapse of Communism, and nearly 75 percent of them said Romania needed a "single, committed person at the head of the country." Some 16 percent of respondents expressed support for the anti-Semitic Greater Romania Party—four times as many as voted for the party in the 1996 general election.

Prime Minister Vasile made a four-day official visit to Israel in early August. He and Israeli prime minister Netanyahu—who described his meeting with Vasile as "excellent"—signed agreements on agricultural cooperation and the mutual protection of investments and pledged to step up efforts to conclude a free trade agreement. He also visited the Israel Aircraft Industries plant and confirmed that Bucharest was examining the possibility of modernizing Cobra helicopters in Israel. During his visit, he met with Palestinian leader Yasir Arafat and offered Romania's "good services" as a mediator in the dispute with Israel over the withdrawal of Israeli forces from the West Bank. Vasile also met with some of the estimated 30,000 Romanians working in Israel, mostly in construction, who complained to him about working and living conditions, including unpaid wages.

Following a visit to Yad Vashem, Vasile said he would push for restitution legislation that would be "a global solution for Romania to return property to all former owners, not only Jews." According to Vasile, five buildings had been returned to their Jewish owners in 1998 as of August, and three or four more were to be returned soon.

There were some incidents of anti-Semitism. In May a Jewish cemetery in Targu Mures was vandalized. In June vandals ransacked a synagogue in Oradea, stealing ritual objects and candelabra and daubing anti-Semitic slogans on the walls. Two teenagers were arrested. In September the government called for legal action against the publishers of an anti-Semitic weekly, *Atac la persoana*.

In October the Romanian Supreme Court rehabilitated Toma Petre Ghitulescu, who had served for seven weeks as deputy state secretary in the government headed by wartime fascist ruler Marshal Ion Antonescu. The court said the crimes of the Antonescu government had been committed after Ghitulescu quit office.

JEWISH COMMUNITY

There were about 12,000-14,000 mostly elderly Jews in Romania, about half of them in the capital, Bucharest. The rest were grouped in more than 45 communities around the country, some with only a handful of members. Of the 94 synagogues owned by the Jewish community, some 58 still functioned on a regular or semi-regular basis. Of more than 750 cemeteries, some 103 still functioned. Two rabbis served the country: a chief rabbi in Bucharest, who spent part of his time in Israel, and an elderly rabbi in Timisoara. The support of the JDC in partnership with the Federation of Romanian Jewish Communities (FEDROM) remained essential for educational and welfare programs. Among other activities, the Jewish community ran a number of clinics and health services around the country, three old-age homes, 12 Talmud Torah classes with a total enrollment of about 200 children, and 11 choirs. In January a new adult day-care center for needy Jews was opened in Bucharest. More and more emphasis was placed on upgrading facilities and infrastructure (some remodeling was carried out with funds from the Conference on Jewish Material Claims Against Germany) and in sponsoring programs aimed at educating young people, including establishing resource centers at six computer clubs around the country. In 1998 the Lauder Re'ut Kindergarten and Lower School, housed in the renovated Jewish Theater building in Bucharest, completed its first year of operation.

Slovakia

Slovakia underwent major political upheavals this year. After Michal Kovac's term ended in March, the country remained without a president, since Parliament, which elects the president, was unable to agree on a successor. In September opposition forces won a general election, ousting nationalist-populist prime minister Vladimir Meciar—politically, Kovac's arch rival—and opening the door to liberalization and European integration after six years of Meciar's pro-Russia, authoritarian rule. Mikulas Dzurinda, a 43-year-old Christian Democrat and former transportation minister, was sworn in as prime minister on October 30. His program aimed at political and economic reform, including closer ties to the West and increased privatization and other drastic economic restructuring that could result in painful belt-tightening. Slovakia's unemployment rate was about 14 percent. A public opinion survey in November revealed growing support for Dzurinda's coalition, which had 65 percent approval, compared with the 58 percent of the vote it won in the elections. In December Meciar announced that he would quit public life entirely.

JEWISH COMMUNITY

Fewer than 4,000 Jews lived in Slovakia. The two largest communities were in the capital, Bratislava, with about 800 Jews, and in the eastern city of Kosice, with about 700. There was a rabbi in each of those cities, as well as a kosher restaurant serving locally produced kosher meat, plus Jewish classes, clubs, and other activities. There were smaller Jewish communities in about a dozen other towns. All came under the umbrella of the Union of Jewish Religious Communities in Bratislava. There were Jewish museums in Bratislava and Presov, and an Institute of Jewish Studies in Bratislava. Restoration work was under way at several Jewish cemeteries and synagogues around the country.

In Bratislava, American-born Chabad rabbi Baruch Myers published a newsletter, *Keser*, in Slovak and English, ran adult classes ranging from basic prayers to the Kabbalah, a match-making service, weekend seminars, and community holiday celebrations. At Passover, about 70 people attended a community first-night seder in Bratislava's Danube Hotel, and about 40 people attended the second seder at Myers' home.

Young Slovak Jews aged 15-35, in both the Czech and Slovak republics, were members of the Czecho-Slovak Union of Jewish Youth (CSUJY). In the summer they organized camps dedicated to restoring Jewish heritage sites, and throughout the year had a program of joint activities including discussions, debates, dancing, and sports, including winter ski camps, and well as the celebration of Jewish festivals such as Purim and Hanukkah. The CSUJY also organized events for non-Jewish young people, in order to educate them about Jews and fight prejudice. Every summer (since 1992) the CSUJY has cosponsored the Bridges-Gesharim project, in which Jewish and non-Jewish young people work together to restore Jewish and Christian monuments.

FORMER YUGOSLAVIA

Bosnia-Herzegovina

Peace reigned in Bosnia-Herzegovina, under the watchful control of international bodies and peace-keeping troops, and what one observer described as "the buzz of life" returned to Sarajevo. The country remained divided into two ethnic sectors, the Republika Srpska of Bosnian Serbs, and the Bosniak (Muslim)-Croatian Federation. But the country as a whole had an "ethnically neutral" currency, license plates, and passport.

In Bosnia, Jews—as during the war years of the 1990s—continued to enjoy a political importance that far outweighed their numbers. The government named a Jew to the important post of ambassador to Washington. According to correspondents, this was a compromise solution, so that no Serb, Muslim, or Croat would represent Bosnia-Herzegovina in such a high-profile job.

There were a number of instances of Jewish leaders working with leaders of other faiths in fostering reconstruction and reconciliation. In February leaders of the Islamic, Jewish, Serbian Orthodox, and Roman Catholic communities in Bosnia asked the European Union for funding to reconstruct war-damaged or destroyed mosques, synagogues, and churches and pledged to promote religious tolerance and the return of refugees. Also in February, religious leaders of the various faiths issued a joint message pledging tolerance and interethnic understanding. Before issuing the statement, Jakob Finci, head of Sarajevo's Jewish community, Roman Catholic cardinal Vinko Puljic, Metropolitan Nikolaj, of the Serbian Orthodox Church, and Mustafa Ceric, the head of Bosnia's Muslim community, held a roundtable discussion on religious issues and the importance of implementing the Dayton agreement.

JEWISH COMMUNITY

Jewish students from Bosnia-Herzegovina were part of a gathering of Jewish students from the various countries of the former Yugoslavia that took place in November in Vienna. The students took part in workshops on youth activities, visited the Vienna Jewish Museum, and attended lectures as well as social get-togethers with Jewish young people from Vienna. The meeting was organized by the JDC with the support of Vienna-based Jewish organizations. It was funded by the Austrian Chancellor's Office, the Austrian Foreign Ministry, and the Ministry for Environment, Youth and Family Affairs.

Norwegian Peoples Aid, the humanitarian assistance arm of the Norwegian government, carried out the job of removing the hundreds of land mines that studded the ancient Jewish cemetery overlooking Sarajevo. The cemetery had been on the frontlines of fighting during the Bosnian war. In September the de-mined cemetery was returned to the possession of the Jewish community in a gala ceremony. In addition, the Central Sarajevo Municipality—the downtown part of the city—allocated some 100,000 German marks (about $65,000) to repair the wall around the cemetery and the entrance gate. In Mostar, work was under way to create a Holocaust memorial in the Jewish cemetery.

Croatia

The growth of Croatia's GDP slowed in 1998 to about 3.4 percent, compared with 6.5 percent in 1997. Wages were higher, but the unemployment rate remained at about 16 percent.

Foreign Minister Mate Granic made an official visit to Israel in May, becoming the first Croatian government leader to visit Israel since the two countries established diplomatic relations in September 1997. On a tour of Yad Vashem, he condemned on behalf of his government the persecution of Jews in wartime Croatia and "the crime of genocide of 6 million Jews."

Two developments, meanwhile, forced Croatians to face the legacy of their World War II fascist government. One was the arrest in Argentina of World War II fascists Dinko Sakic and his wife, Nada, and their extradition to Zagreb to face war crimes charges. Sakic, 76, was arrested in April after he reminisced on Argentine television about his years as commander of Croatia's notorious wartime concentration camp at Jasenovac, south of Zagreb, where tens of thousands of people were tortured and killed. The great majority were Serbs, but victims also included Jews, Romas, and antifascist Croats. Jasenovac was not run by German Nazis but by homegrown Croatian fascists, called Ustashe, who ruled Croatia as a nominally independent Nazi puppet state from 1941 to 1945. Sakic, who with his wife had lived in Argentina for 50 years, was extradited to Zagreb in June. He was formally indicted in December and charged with responsibility for the deaths of at least 2,000 people while he commanded Jasenovac between April and November 1944. Nada Sakic, 72, alleged to have been a guard at another concentration camp, was extradited to Zagreb in November to face charges in a separate trial. The Sakic case had important repercussions in Croatia, where President Franjo Tudjman has used a calculated ambivalence toward the wartime independent Croatia to foster Croatian nationalism. It opened the door to a reexamination of Croatia's past, both its World War II history and the nationalist passions fanned over the past decade with the bloody breakup of Yugoslavia. Before Sakic's extradition, the Jewish community publicly demanded that he be brought back for a fair trial. Jewish leaders were inundated by phone calls either accusing Jews of engineering Sakic's arrest or expressing support for the process.

The other related development was the beatification in October by Pope John Paul II of Zagreb's World War II-era archbishop Alojzije Stepinac, a Croatian nationalist hailed as a martyr to Communism by many Croatian Catholics but reviled by critics as a fascist collaborator. The Simon Wiesenthal Center called on the Vatican to postpone the beatification pending further study into his actions during the war. Stepinac at first supported Ustashe leader Ante Pavelic, but by 1942, he had denounced the Ustashe regime's genocidal policies. A staunch anticommunist, he was tried by Yugoslavia's Communist government after the war and sentenced to jail for having collaborated with the Pavelic regime. He died in 1962, while under house arrest.

JEWISH COMMUNITY

Croatia was home to about 2,000 Jews, most of them in Zagreb. Most community members were secular and well assimilated into the mainstream community, and most children were from mixed marriages.

Rabbi Kotel Dadon, an Israeli who had been teaching at the Rabbinical Seminary in Budapest, Hungary, was formally inaugurated as chief (and so far only) rabbi in Croatia in November. He became the first permanent rabbi based in Zagreb for more than half a century. Dadon had already officiated at High Holy Day services before he was officially installed. He said his goal was to reintroduce Jewish ritual encompassing the entire life cycle and calendar.

In July B'nai B'rith opened a lodge in Zagreb. Jewish students from Croatia took part in the gathering of 40 Jewish students from the various countries of the former Yugoslavia that took place in November in Vienna (see Bosnia-Herzegovina).

Slovenia

Slovenia maintained good relations with Israel, thanks to various military transactions and tourist trade.

Only about 120 Jews lived in Slovenia, most of them in the capital, Ljubljana, but they were recognized as a national minority by the Slovenian constitution. There was a concerted effort to revive communal activities, sponsored by the Joint Distribution Committee, after a change of leadership that took place in late 1997-early 1998. In this change, Andrej Kozar-Beck became president of the community. The community had no rabbi but began negotiations with the Jewish community in Trieste, Italy, to arrange for a rabbi from there to visit on a regular basis.

Yugoslavia (Serbia and Montenegro)

Political, economic, and social conditions in Yugoslavia remained dire and depressing, as violence flared in Serbia's Kosovo province between Serbian police and ethnic Albanian guerrillas demanding independence, and the authorities in Montenegro inched toward possible secession. Yugoslavia remained a pariah state, headed by president Slobodan Milosevic.

Several anti-Semitic acts were reported, including an assault by skinheads who scrawled swastikas and anti-Semitic slogans on an interior corridor of the Belgrade synagogue. A television program during the summer, focusing on the policies of Madeleine Albright and Richard Holbrooke, declared "The Jews are ruling the world. They are responsible for what is happening in (and to) Serbia." On July 5, in response to these and other incidents, Aca Singer, the president of the Federation of Jewish Communities, complained to Serbia's president that nothing was being done to combat anti-Semitism and no arrests had been made.

JEWISH COMMUNITY

Most of the 2,000-3,000 Jews in Yugoslavia lived in Belgrade, with much smaller communities in several other towns. The communities were linked through the federation. In Subotica, near the Hungarian border, a social service organization was set up in cooperation with the Sarajevo Jewish community's La Benevolencija organization to help provide nonsectarian aid to people in the Subotica region. Jewish young people from Belgrade and other towns took part in the meeting in November in Vienna of some 40 young Jews from the various countries of the former Yugoslavia. (See Bosnia-Herzegovina.)

In Belgrade, the Jewish community underwent a leadership change early in the year that replaced most of the communal leaders who had led the community since the early 1990s. This moved some formerly active members to disassociate themselves from most community activities. Friction also developed between the new leadership and the young, Belgrade-based rabbi. Meanwhile, Jacques Beraha, the former vice-president of the Belgrade community, was held under arrest on charges related to the 1997 collapse of an illegal private bank he had operated. Losses amounted to about $1.2 million, wiping out the savings of many of Belgrade's cultural and intellectual elite, including members of the Jewish community.

About 50 to 60 Jews lived in Kosovo. About 40 of them lived in the capital, Pristina—some 30 of them members of one family—and they were safe from the violence that swept parts of the countryside. Three Jews were known to live in Prizen and four in Djakovica, both towns near the Albanian border. Most Jewish women and children left Kosovo during the summer months to stay with friends and relatives elsewhere. Jews in Kosovo (as most Jews elsewhere in Yugoslavia) attempted to keep a low political profile. They faced no special problems as Jews, but shared in the fears and uncertainties of the population in general. In Kosovo, the Jews resisted attempts by the local authorities to have them express public support for official Serbian policy but suffered no consequences from this. Kosovo's Jews remained in close contact with the Jewish Federation in Belgrade and received some financial assistance from the JDC.

Macedonia

About 100-150 Jews lived in Macedonia, most of them in the capital, Skopje, and enjoyed excellent relations with the government. Local authorities supported Holocaust commemorations in several cities, and the 500-year-old Jewish cemetery in Bitola—home now to just one Jew—was being repaired and restored with public funds, at the initiative of Bitola University.

RUTH ELLEN GRUBER

Former Soviet Union

National Affairs

SIGNS OF AN UPTURN in the economy of the Russian Federation had been clearly discernible in 1997, but by the end of 1998 the economy and polity were in disarray. Nevertheless, in July the International Monetary Fund approved and disbursed the first installment of a $22 million aid and bailout package, contingent on President Boris Yeltsin's promise to implement further fiscal reforms. However, Yeltsin had reduced the political and economic responsibilities of two prominent economic reformers, Anatoly Chubais and Boris Nemtsov, early in 1998, though Nemtsov continued as first deputy prime minister. Both were said to be of at least partly Jewish origin.

In March President Yeltsin suddenly dismissed Prime Minister Viktor Chernomyrdin—a potential successor—and his entire cabinet. The prime minister was replaced by 35-year-old Sergei Kirienko, formerly minister of fuel and energy, who was approved as prime minister by the Communist-dominated Duma only after several weeks of wrangling and three votes in the Parliament. When Duma Speaker Gennadi Seleznev, a Communist, demanded that Kirienko be investigated for holding Israeli citizenship, Kirienko gave a television interview in which he explained that his father was Jewish, his mother Russian, his surname Ukrainian, that he was born in Abkhazia (an area in Georgia), and considered himself Russian culturally.

On August 17, Prime Minister Kirienko and Central Bank chairman Sergei Dubinin announced that Russia would default on government debt and devalue the ruble. The Russian ruble immediately lost half its value against the dollar, and Russia's ability to borrow was put in serious doubt. The economic collapse was explained by several factors. One was the $5 billion cost of the war against Chechnya (which also cost 50,000 lives) and the government's mortgaging of many of its most lucrative assets in 1995 to a few well-connected businessmen who agreed to bail out the government in return for shares in major government-owned enterprises. Another, the collapse of oil prices. Russia was no longer able to pay its debt, let alone pay pensions and wages, and default was declared. Several banks became insolvent. President Yeltsin dismissed Kirienko and other economic reformers. Evgeny Primakov, former head of the security services, a career diplomat and most recently foreign minister, replaced Kirienko. Primakov, who was orphaned at an early age, was also rumored to be of Jewish origin. Not surprisingly, opinion polls taken in the fall showed declining trust in politicians, disillusion with democracy, which was associated with corruption and ineptitude, pessimism regarding the future, and low belief in political efficacy (the ability to affect politics). Real per capita income declined 16 percent from 1997 and nearly a quarter of the population had incomes below subsistence levels.

Despair about politics deepened with the murder of Duma deputy Galina Starovoitova on November 20 in St. Petersburg. She was the seventh Duma deputy to be murdered since 1993. Starovoitova, an ethnographer, Yeltsin's adviser on nationality issues, and a well-known democrat and liberal, had declared her intention of running for governor of the Leningrad region in order to block the nationalist Vladimir Zhirinovsky. She was rumored to be investigating corruption in the Communist Party and had criticized Communist Duma deputy general Albert Makashov for anti-Semitic remarks he had made several times in public. While Starovoitova's killers remained at large, her funeral turned into a major rally for democrats, though rival factions and leaders among them failed to unite. At year's end, Prime Minister Primakov had not taken any significant steps in economic policy, Yeltsin's health was more precarious and his public appearances fewer, and the central government seemed to be losing both authority and power vis-à-vis the regions and the citizenry.

Prime Minister Chernomyrdin issued directives in February regarding the registration of foreign religious associations with the Justice Ministry and its regional branches. This followed from the law on religion passed in September 1997, which prohibited unregistered foreign religious associations from operating in the Russian Federation. Since Judaism was considered a religion with historic roots in Russia, Jewish religious organizations were not generally affected, though some local authorities tried to prevent Jewish religious activity on the grounds that there had been none in the region for several decades. In Uzbekistan, as part of President Islam Karimov's drive against Islamic fundamentalism, foreign clergy were limited to 30-day visas.

In Ukraine, inflation doubled from its 1997 rate to 20 percent. Ukraine's foreign debt, $11.5 billion, was 40 percent of the Gross Domestic Product and 70 percent of annual exports. The Communist Party won a quarter of the seats in the election to the national Rada (parliament) in April. No other party got even half as many seats, though the number of independent deputies was greater than that of any party but the Communists. Between 10 and 20 Jews were elected to the Rada, and two Jews, Dmitry Dvorkis in Vinnitsa, and Eduard Gurvits in Odessa, won mayoral elections.

Israel and the Middle East

Israel and the United States on several occasions protested Russia's assistance to Iran's nuclear industry and its development of missile technology. Primakov and other Russian officials made public assurances that Russia's assistance would not enhance Iranian military capacity. In turn, Russia criticized joint naval exercises between the United States, Israel, and Turkey that were held in June, since

Turkey has long been Russia's rival in the Black Sea and Caucasus Mountain regions.

Minister of Trade and Industry Natan Sharansky of Israel, formerly a Soviet prisoner and prominent "refusenik," visited Russia in March in an attempt to increase trade between the countries, which amounted to $400 million a year. Sharansky also visited Kazakhstan, Turkmenistan, and Uzbekistan. Israel exported significant amounts of agricultural products to Kazakhstan, and Gilat, an Israeli communications firm, planned to provide satellite communications for 250 locations in that very large state. Israel was committed to assisting these Central Asian states with irrigation techniques, greenhouse farming, and the development of solar and wind-powered energy systems. In May, Israeli prime minister Netanyahu stopped in Tashkent, Uzbekistan, on the way home from China and invited Uzbek president Islam Karimov to visit Israel. This he did in September, when he signed several agreements with Israel and also met with Palestinian Authority president Yasir Arafat.

Israel and Russia also cooperated in criminal matters, such as the case of Soviet immigrant Grigori Lerner (Zvi Ben-Ari), who was sentenced to six years in jail in Israel. He was convicted for, among other things, fraudulent acquisition of $14 million from Russian and Israeli banks. Russian Federal Security Service head Nikolai Kovalev was in Israel in July to enhance cooperation between Israel and Russia in the struggle against terrorism. Noting that Israeli officials "constantly returned to" the topic of technology transfer to Iran, Kovalev asserted that the transfers were by commercial firms, not the Russian government. A Moscow military court sentenced to a three-year term and fined Lt. Vladimir Tkachenko of the intelligence service for supplying Israel with high resolution satellite photos. The Federal Security Service announced in August that it had uncovered a network of informants who were passing military secrets to Israel and were operating out of the emigration department of the Israeli embassy.

Anti-Semitism

There were several anti-Semitic acts of vandalism this year in widely scattered parts of the FSU, and, for the first time since the breakup of the USSR, political anti-Semitism emerged prominently in Russia. In May vandals damaged 149 tombstones in a Jewish cemetery in Irkutsk (Siberia), the third such incident since the previous December. The Jewish section of Moscow's Vostryakovo cemetery was vandalized in July, and fire extensively damaged Kharkov's (Ukraine) only synagogue in August. In December some 50 gravestones in Tbilisi's (Georgia) Jewish cemetery were destroyed, causing President Eduard Shevardnadze to declare the action "barbaric and inexplicable." In May a bomb went off soon after people left Moscow's Marina Roshcha Synagogue, a building that had been constructed after the previous synagogue building was burned down in 1993.

The governor of Krasnodar region *(krai)*, Nikolai Kondratenko, made disparaging remarks about Jews on several occasions. He assailed "Zionists" at a meeting of regional officials, and the deputy minister of the region, Nikolai Denisov, called for defending the public against the "cosmopolitans [a Stalinist code word for Jews] around the Kremlin who provide intellectual services to the policy of genocide against [ethnic] Russians and other peoples of Russia." In December leaflets appeared in Krasnodar calling for the elimination of all Jews in the area and urging Governor Kondratenko to run for president in 2000.

In October parliamentary deputy and Communist Party member Gen. Albert Makashov made some clearly anti-Semitic remarks in public. He recommended establishing quotas for the numbers of Jews allowed in governmental positions and criticized the media for being under Jewish/Israeli influence. Makashov called Jews "bloodsuckers" in a television interview. On November 4, the Duma defeated a resolution explicitly condemning both anti-Semitism and General Makashov by 120-107, with 7 abstentions and 220 not voting. Nine days later a milder resolution was passed, with no mention made of Makashov or anti-Semitism. The document stated that "some deputies, officials and mass media outlets do not advance friendly and respectful relationships between persons of different nationalities with their statements." A poll of Muscovites by the All-Russian Center for the Study of Public Opinion found that 51 percent condemned and 15 percent approved General Makashov's portrayal of Jews. However, a third approved the idea of limiting the number of Jews holding senior offices (43 percent were opposed), and nearly two-thirds said they would not want a Jew as president. Yet, over three-quarters said that Jews should have equal access to higher education.

In December, State Duma Security Committee chairman and Communist Party member Viktor Ilyukhin said that the "large-scale genocide" of the Russians would have been less massive if "the president's entourage and the government included representatives of other ethnic groups and did not consist exclusively of Jews, though they are a talented group." The next day the Duma rejected a proposal to condemn Ilyukhin, with only 82 deputies voting for the proposal. Other politicians strongly condemned Ilyukhin, but their motivations are telling. Chief of the Presidential Administration Nikolai Bordyuzha said that Ilyukhin's remarks "undermine not only the reputation of the Duma but Russia's international reputation." Not surprisingly, President Aleksandr Lukashenka of Belarus, suggested that "the problem of anti-Semitism has been created by the Jews themselves, the ones who work for the mass media." Communist Party leader Gennadi Zyuganov joined the chorus of anti-Semitic remarks by politicians when he was quoted in December as saying that "Gorbachev, Yeltsin, and Chernomyrdin are all Russians but the harm they have inflicted on Russia is more than that of the Jews Chubais, Gaidar and Kozyrev" (*Komersant,* December 19). Reacting to criticism of his remarks, Zyuganov issued a four-page statement in December explaining that ethnic Russians are disadvantaged in Russia and are "facing genocide." He claimed that the Communist Party had no quarrel with the Jews but was against the "Zionists" who were "blood relatives to Fascism. The only difference between them is that, where Hitlerite Nazism appeared under the mask of German nationalism attempting to subjugate the world openly, Zionists, appearing under the mask of Jewish nationalism, act in secret and employ the hands of others." Jews should either emigrate from Russia, assimilate, or live in a Jewish community in Russia, which they should regard as their "only motherland."

Boris Yeltsin, who had defeated Zyuganov for the presidency of Russia, appeared on television in late December and announced that he would launch a "powerful offensive" against anti-Semitism and extreme Russian nationalism. Representatives of the main military inspectorate and the Security Council were sent to several Russian regions to check with compliance with Yeltsin's instructions on combating political extremism.

Holocaust-Related Developments

Attitudes toward Nazi collaborators and legal proceedings against them remained an issue in some former Soviet states, especially Latvia and Lithuania, where many consider the Soviet "liberation" from the Nazis in 1944 as an "occupation." In February Lithuanian investigators announced formal charges against 90-year-old Aleksandras Lileikis, head of the Vilnius "security police" in World War II, who had been deported from the United States. Lileikis protested that he was the victim of "international political pressure" and asked for postponement of his trial, which was granted several times, so that by the end of the year he had not yet been brought to court. In March Lithuania indicted another war criminal, Kazys Gimzauskas, deputy chief of the security police in Vilnius in 1941–44. Gimzauskas denied the charges and claimed he was a member of the anti-Nazi underground. In September Lithuanian president Valdas Adamkus established a commission to investigate Soviet and Nazi war crimes in Lithuania, chaired by Emanuelis Zingeris, a parliamentary deputy and Jewish community leader. Earlier, in May, Estonian president Lennart Meri had announced the establishment of a similar commission. Twenty-two Lithuanian citizens who had been convicted of war crimes by Soviet tribunals were stripped of the pardons given them when Lithuania became independent. Israel had submitted a list of over a hundred names of war criminals who, it felt, had been wrongly pardoned. It was not known how many of the 22 were alive.

On the eve of his visit to Israel in February 1998, Latvian president Guntis Ulmanis wrote to the parliamentary commission on foreign affairs, urging lawmakers to admit that Latvians had participated in the murder of Jews in World War II. He said that "The historical truth is that there were Latvians who participated in the Holocaust and there were Latvians who helped Jews and hid them in their houses." In Israel Ulmanis "unofficially" apologized for Latvians' role in the Holocaust. Israeli officials asked that the whereabouts of war criminals living in Latvia be investigated; while Ulmanis was in Israel, however, the Latvian Prosecutor-General's Office said it had no information on people living in Latvia who could be prosecuted for the murder of Jews. In March, some five hundred veterans of a Latvian SS division that had fought with the Nazis gathered in Riga to commemorate the 55th anniversary of the establishment of the unit. They marched through the old part of town, where elderly Russians mounted a counterdemonstration. The SS veterans claimed they had not volunteered but had been drafted; the counterdemonstrators were driven off roughly by police. Russian presidential spokesman Sergei Yastrzhembski said that the Russian government was considering an official protest.

President Ulmanis observed that during the war the situation in Latvia had been "complicated," and that the international community could not be expected to understand it fully. He criticized army commander Juris Dalbins and parliamentary speaker Alfreds Cepanis for attending the rally, and Dalbins resigned. The Russian newspaper *Nezavisimaya gazeta* (March 17) charged that the commander of the Latvian navy, the deputy speaker of Parliament, and other politicians had also participated in the SS march.

On April 2, a bomb went off near the Riga synagogue, which had previously been bombed in May 1995. Some Russian journalists (*Nezavisimaya gazeta*, April 4) asked why there was no American protest over the rough treatment of the elderly Russian protesters against the SS veterans' march, and noted that the FBI had offered its services in investigating the bombing of the synagogue. The Latvian government strongly condemned the bombing of the synagogue and dismissed police chief Aldis Lieljuksis and the state secretary of the Ministry of the Interior for failing to protect the building after a swastika had been painted on it. Lieljuksis was later cleared by a court of charges of neglect of duty and was offered reinstatement, which he refused. In July, in Tallinn, there was a rally of 1,500 veterans of an Estonian SS battalion, but no top political or military officials attended.

JEWISH COMMUNITY

Demography

Israeli demographer Mark Tolts estimated that at the beginning of 1998 there were 325,000 Jews in Russia, where they made up 0.2 percent of the population. This represented a 43-percent decline since 1989, when the last census was taken. Moscow's Jewish population was estimated at 135,000 and St. Petersburg's at 61,000. The rate of emigration from the latter was higher than that from the capital. On the other hand, while in 1989 Russian Jews constituted 39 percent of the total Soviet Jewish population, in 1998 they made up 60 percent, since they had a lower proportion of emigrants and also because some Jews had immigrated to Russia from other former Soviet republics. According to the Institute of Contemporary Jewry of the Hebrew University, Ukraine had 155,000 Jews, the next largest concentration. Belarus was estimated to have 23,000 Jews; Uzbekistan, 14,000; Latvia, 12,800; and no other former Soviet republic more than 11,000. Estimates of the Jewish population by Israeli and other Jewish organizations were considerably higher; however, these relied on reports by local Jews and included those eligible for immigration to Israel, i.e., those who might have one Jewish grandparent but were not registered as Jews or were not Jewish according to Halakhah (Jewish law).

By 1997, 70 percent of all children born to Jewish mothers in Russia had non-Jewish fathers. About one-third of Ashkenazi Jews in Russia were over 65, and the median age of Jews was 56. In 1997, 9,546 Jews died, and 663 were born to Jewish mothers in Russia. This highly unfavorable demographic balance reflected a long-term trend and portended a further rapid diminution of the Jewish population.

Emigration

In 1997, 51,745 FSU Jews immigrated to Israel and only 14,143 to the United States. The small number of immigrants to the United States, about half the number who immigrated annually in the early 1990s, was explained by several factors: the drying up of the reservoir of first-degree relatives of those who had already come to the United States; the expense of traveling to Moscow, where American authorities insisted all interviews of potential emigrants be held; and the skeptical attitudes of U.S. Immigration and Naturalization Service officials toward claims of persecution by potential refugees. Concomitantly, there was a rise in the number of Jews immigrating to Germany, though no precise figures were available. Of those going to Israel, 38 percent were under 25 years old, and 11 percent were over 65. The Israeli Interior Ministry announced in late December that "since 1989" (no terminal date was given), 166,029 non-Jews had come to Israel from the FSU, most of them not declaring any religion. Rabbi Yisrael Rosen, head of the conversion unit of the Chief Rabbinate, estimated that only about 5,000 had converted to Judaism.

The Israeli "Liaison Office" *(Lishkat Hakesher)* estimated that between 1989 and 1998, Israel had resettled from the FSU 13,800 scientists; 82,700 engineers; 53,200 technicians; 17,400 physicians; 19,200 other medical professionals; 39,200 teachers and artists, and 81,500 skilled workers. During the decade, some 768,000 immigrants had come from the FSU, 70 percent of them from Russia, Ukraine, and Belarus, and 20 percent from the Central Asian republics. Two-thirds were under 44 years of age and 13 percent (97,600) were over 65.

Communal Affairs

In September a four-day celebration was held in Tbilisi, capital of Georgia, marking 2,600 years of Jewish presence in that republic. According to local tradition, Jews came to Georgia after the Babylonians conquered Jerusalem in 586 B.C.E. Though the Jewish population had shrunk from between 60,000 and 100,000 in the 1960s to about 14,000 at present, largely through emigration to Israel, an estimated 50,000 people attended the events, sponsored mainly by the government. Israeli prime minister Benjamin Netanyahu could not attend due to illness, but both Israeli chief rabbis and Israeli cabinet minister Moshe Katsav were present. Georgian president Eduard Shevardnadze, the former foreign minister of the USSR, spoke in a Tbilisi synagogue, calling the settlement of Jews in Georgia "a landmark in our history." Shevardnadze had visited Israel in January when he signed a "treaty of friendship."

At the same time, a largely symbolic synagogue was dedicated on Moscow's Poklonnaya Gora war memorial complex. Funded by the Russian Jewish Congress, the synagogue joined a church and a mosque that were to be built as symbols of the major faiths with which those who had fought in World War II were associated. President Yeltsin, Moscow mayor Yuri Luzhkov—widely regarded as a potential successor to Yeltsin—Israeli minister of trade and industry Natan Sharansky, and other local and foreign dignitaries spoke at the event. Luzhkov presented Adolf Shaevich, chief rabbi of Russia, with an 18th-century Torah scroll. The synagogue will be used only on major holidays, but it houses Russia's first major Holocaust exhibit and museum.

Another ceremonial event was the January commemoration of the 1948 murder, arranged by Joseph Stalin, of Yiddish actor and theater director Shlomo Mikhoels. That tragedy was the beginning of the official shutdown of Yiddish culture in the Soviet Union, including the arrest, and later murder, of many of its activists. The commemoration included 17 events, but no Yiddish theater productions, as few people in Moscow could follow a Yiddish play.

It was estimated that 20,000 children in Russia were receiving some form of Jewish education, mostly in Russian with some Hebrew instruction. This was said to be a small fraction of the age-eligible population; however, considering that a decade earlier not a single Jewish school operated in the country, this was a signal achievement. An ORT school opened in Odessa (Ukraine) in May. ORT sponsored five model schools in Russia and Ukraine, along with 22 technology centers. These schools provided chiefly vocational and technological education but offered Hebrew and Jewish history classes in addition. Israel's education ministry was connected to 34 schools in the FSU and placed 75 teachers there. In 1997 the American Hillel organization, serving college-age Jews, had sent 240 students to conduct communal Passover seders, which, it claimed, included 10,000 Jews. In 1998, 600 young people conducted 350 seders for 18,000 Jews in various parts of the FSU. Five cities had regularly functioning Hillel Foundations and 14 more were planned.

The American Jewish Joint Distribution Committee (JDC) continued to play the major foreign role in communal reconstruction and service. The "Joint" operated 15 offices and had 24 "expatriate representatives," nearly 400 local employees, and about 5,000 volunteers. It supported Jewish studies at 54 general universities and five specifically Jewish universities, partly through its support of the Sefer organization, which brings together and assists people studying and teaching Judaica in the FSU at the higher education level. JDC set up 145 Jewish libraries in 75 cities and supplied materials to nearly 300 Jewish schools; trained Jewish communal workers at a center in St. Petersburg; and helped communities reclaim nationalized properties. By 1998, 81 buildings had been returned to Jewish communities and 67 other claims were in process. JDC estimated that it served over 100,000 elderly Jews with food packages, hot meals, care visits, and winter relief assistance.

ZVI GITELMAN

Australia

National Affairs

AT THE BEGINNING OF 1998, the Liberal-National Party coalition government led by Prime Minister John Howard entered its third year in office and a prolonged period of preparation for a fall election. The government's priorities included passage in the Senate of far-reaching legislation on Aboriginal native title—after one earlier failure and months of impassioned debate—and also industrial relations reforms. The government's Native Title Amendment Bill (commonly known as the Wik legislation), which would greatly diminish the rights of Aborigines to claim ownership of ancestral lands, and which drew critical responses from many in the Jewish community, was eventually passed in the Senate midyear.

The national election in early October resulted in the return of the Liberal-National coalition government for a second term, albeit with a greatly reduced majority in the Parliament and the prospect of minority parties and independents holding the balance of power in the Senate. Prime Minister Howard went to the election buttressed by a large parliamentary majority, though hampered by his proposed tax reform package, which included an unpopular and previously rejected goods and services tax. Though skeptical of the government's tax proposals, the electorate was not yet ready to re-embrace the opposition Australian Labor Party, led by Kim Beazley since after the last election, which had governed for five consecutive terms from 1983 to 1996.

The federal election also marked the decline of far-right populist Pauline Hanson, perhaps the most controversial figure in Australian politics since 1996. The divisive independent and her party, Pauline Hanson's One Nation, failed to win a lower house seat, even that of its leader. Its sole victory was one of six Senate seats in Hanson's home state of Queensland. Only four months earlier the party performed spectacularly well in the Queensland state election, winning 23 percent of the vote and picking up 11 seats, which sent shock waves through the nation's major political parties. But in the wake of the federal election disaster, the resignation of 6 of its 11 Queensland parliamentarians and deep-seated internal divisions over the party's undemocratic structure, the future of Hanson and One Nation appeared bleak.

The Jewish community was among the most vocal in denouncing the phenomenon of racially charged debate and divisive politics, especially over Aborigine issues. After the shock of One Nation's electoral success in Queensland, the community—and the Australia/Israel and Jewish Affairs Council (AIJAC), in particular—was in the forefront of a campaign that successfully persuaded the governing coalition parties to change their strategy from the Queensland election and to make One Nation their last preference on the "how-to-vote" cards, instead of their natural opponents, the Labor Party. After some division within coalition ranks on the issue, it was finally agreed that One Nation's electoral defeat was the top priority. Even so, by then some within the Jewish community had already decided that the government's handling of the One Nation preferences issue and Aboriginal reconciliation deserved a rebuke. The most notable of such critics was mining magnate and former Liberal Party supporter Joseph Gutnick, who indicated he would switch his vote to Labor.

In a controversial step, the *Australia/Israel Review*, a publication of AIJAC, published in July a list of 2000 One Nation members and 200 donors, obtained from disgruntled senior party figures concerned at the lack of transparency and democracy in the party. The move prompted a vigorous and often ill-tempered debate as to whether the publication infringed the privacy of those members or whether One Nation's divisive policies and internal structure justified publication of the names in the interest of preserving and protecting democracy.

This debate was taken up within the Jewish community also. Some well-known figures expressed concern that publication of the list could make the Jewish community collectively vulnerable to some form of anti-Semitic retribution. Other community figures argued that a Jewish magazine had as much right as any to expose persons who voluntarily joined a party that fosters racial antagonism, bigotry, and division, and deserved praise for so doing.

Despite the continuing economic crisis in Asia throughout the year and some significant domestic currency devaluations, the Australian economy performed with surprising resilience. Inflation remained at less than 2 percent, while economic growth averaged a steady 4 percent. Unemployment, a long-standing problem, fell slightly but still remained around 8 percent.

Israel and the Middle East

The Australian government continued to have warm relations with Israel and expressed full support for a continuation of the Middle East peace process. Indeed, the government's approach was largely shared by the opposition Australian Labor Party.

The contentious nature of the issues surrounding the peace process occasionally resulted in some counter-productive statements. An official Australian parliamentary delegation of five went to Israel (and the West Bank), Jordan, Lebanon, and Syria in June, led by former National Party leader and House Speaker Ian Sinclair. The report they submitted to Parliament in July contained numerous historical errors of fact and unbalanced assessments reflecting only one side of the Arab-Israeli question. A storm of criticism from the local Jewish community and beyond ensued. Foreign Minister Alexander Downer distanced himself from the report, saying it reflected the views of the parliamentary delegation only and was not a representation of the government's position. Another federal parliamentary delegation, sponsored and led by the PLO, visited the Palestinian-controlled territories and Jordan in April. The weeklong trip was led by the PLO's Australian spokesman, Ali Kazak, and funded by Said Meshal, a Palestinian industrialist who resided for many years in the Gulf state of Qatar before emigrating to Australia. Several of the MPs subsequently voiced criticism of Israel in Parliament.

On a more positive note, there was widespread recognition across the political spectrum of the achievement of Israel's 50th anniversary. A motion was passed by the House of Representatives congratulating Israel, and members from all the major parties spoke in support, though one ALP member, Leo McLeay, severely criticized Jewish settlements in the West Bank. Prime Minister Howard spoke of "our strong commitment to and affection for Israel. . . . The [right of the people of Israel] to exist behind secure, defensible and impregnable boundaries is something that successive Australian governments have always held dear, and that will continue to be our policy. I think it is very important that the aspirations of the Palestinian people . . . also be respected. It will be the intention of my government to see that fairness and justice is done to all parties in the Middle East."

Foreign Minister Downer visited Israel and the Middle East for the first time in June, shortly after the anniversary celebrations, and held productive meetings with Prime Minister Benjamin Netanyahu and other senior ministers and officials. He then announced that Australia's continuing financial aid for peace initiatives in the region would include an additional $3.4 million in assistance for Palestinian refugees. Netanyahu was scheduled to visit Australia in August, but the visit was postponed indefinitely shortly beforehand owing to a resumption of talks with the Palestinians and domestic political exigencies in Israel.

Both major parties supported the efforts of the United Nations and U.S.-led military interventions to secure Iraqi compliance in eliminating its weapons of mass destruction. In February, Australian navy vessels and troops were sent to the Persian Gulf to support U.S. forces during a stand-off with the Iraqi dictator, and both party leaders voiced support for the U.S.-British strikes on Iraq in December. Domestic opposition to these moves came largely from elements in the Arab and Islamic communities, students, and long-time academic apologists for Iraq. Similarly, both major parties warmly applauded the Wye River agreement concluded between Israel and the Palestinian Authority in October.

After years of criticism, the Australian government finally moved to revise its credit arrangements with Iran, including the removal of the previous (U.S.) $750 million line of credit made available to Iran. Instead, requests for credit from the Iranian Central Bank would be considered on a case-by-case basis via consultation between the government and the Export Finance and Insurance Corporation. Although it was never drawn upon, the line of credit was the largest offered by Australia to any nation and by far the largest offered to Iran. For several years, the Australia/Israel and Jewish Affairs Council, among others, had called for the withdrawal of the credit because of Iran's poor credit rating and particularly for its long-standing sponsorship and assistance for international terrorism.

In the United Nations, the Australian government continued its relatively favorable support of Israel in the General Assembly. In an Emergency Session resolution in March condemning Israel for construction at Har Homah and proposing to "determine how to enforce provisions of the Geneva Convention relevant to 'Occupied Palestinian Territory,'" Australia was one of five abstaining countries in a vote of 120-3. Australia's representative expressed concern about the state of the peace process but said that such resolutions—described later by Foreign Minister Downer as "sloganeering against Israel"—would not advance the process.

In July, Australia was one of 124 countries to vote in favor (to 4 against) of a resolution granting the Palestinian delegation to the UN additional rights and privileges as part of its Observer status. Australia's representative said the resolution would clarify Palestine's place in the UN, but had no bearing on the issue of Palestinian statehood, which would be determined through negotiations.

Anti-Semitism and Extremism

In its most recent annual report, the Executive Council of Australian Jewry (ECAJ) reported that anti-Semitic telephone calls, hate mail, and threatening electronic mail had reached record levels in the 12-month period ending September 30, 1998, contributing to a large increase in the volume of overall anti-Semitic incidents over the previous year. The total of 324 reports of anti-Jewish violence, physical harassment, vandalism, and intimidation represented an increase of 22 percent over the previous 12 months and was 16 percent higher than the previous worst year. It was also 43 percent higher than the average since detailed record-keeping commenced in 1989. In presenting the report, ECAJ executive vice-president Jeremy Jones noted that the Internet was the main growth area for anti-Semitic rhetoric and incitement, complementing the traditional activities of anti-Jewish groups such as leafleting, articles in the print media, and talk radio.

On the positive side, the number of violent incidents and serious physical confrontations was well below average. Increased security at synagogues and other Jewish institutions was seen as the most important contributing factor in this area. The report also gave good marks to the Australian media for a decline in the volume of commentary, published letters, and reporting that crossed over from political criticism into racist or anti-Jewish abuse. Another area in which there appeared to be a decrease in anti-Jewish commentary was the ethnic media. Addressing the issue of response to anti-Semitism, the report praised the activities of a number of churches and state and federal antidiscrimination bodies and those politicians who "consistently demonstrated moral leadership" in confronting racism.

Prominent mining magnate and Chabad community leader Rabbi Joseph Gutnick was the subject of a series of anti-Semitic incidents in 1998. Gutnick had a particularly high profile in his home city of Melbourne, where he became a household name after financially rescuing the ailing Melbourne (Australian Rules) Football Club. A series of audiotapes of meetings of senior executives in the JB Were & Son brokerage firm, which came to light during an insider trading case, revealed that Gutnick had been the target of venomous anti-Semitic slurs and jokes. In the furor that followed, the company's executive chairman, Terry Campbell, personally and publicly apologized to Gutnick and the wider Jewish community. Two of the company's employees later resigned.

Mainstream media coverage of issues relevant to the Jewish community was extensive — generally positive on issues relating to the domestic Jewish community, but far less favorable on Israel and the Middle East, occasionally exhibiting a bias with some anti-Semitic overtones. One Middle East correspondent for a major newspaper, Robert Fisk in the *Canberra Times*, drew an analogy between the Holocaust and the historical experience of the Palestinians, claiming that Israel escapes criticism due to "its immensely powerful lobby in the United States" and "the pathetic obeisance of journalists (too frightened to criticize Israel for fear of being accused of anti-Semitism)." In the electronic media there was generally much less anti-Jewish commentary, most of it coming from talk-show callers who had not been properly screened before being allowed to speak on air.

Of particular concern for some years had been the anti-Israel bias of the ethnic SBS (Special Broadcasting Commission) television network in its news and current affairs reporting. The occasion of Israel's 50 anniversary was cause for a series of specials, including a biography of Palestinian author Emile Habiby, *I Stayed in Haifa;* a documentary on the wife of Yasir Arafat, *Souha Arafat*; and the three-part series, *Palestine: Story of a Land.* By way of balance, SBS also broadcast the six-part *Tkuma* series produced by the Israeli Broadcasting Corporation, though the documentary proved to be highly controversial in Israel because of its depiction of Israeli history in relation to the Palestinians and Israel's religious-secular divide.

Through the dramatic growth of electronic communication, Australians now had increasingly easy and cheap access to anti-Semitic and racist material that was previously difficult to obtain. In addition, anti-Semitic and threatening e-mail was reported at a steadily increasing rate as more members of the Jewish community, including Holocaust survivors, established e-mail accounts. Unmoderated newsgroups and Internet newsletters dealing with Australian issues gave individual bigots a new and wider audience. Almost all of the major racist groups in Australia now had an Internet presence. The more sophisticated of these had managed to establish links with less overtly racist sites. The sites of concern to the Jewish community focused on the themes of Holocaust denial, White Supremacy/Neo-Nazism, Christian Identity, and Islamic fundamentalism.

One site of particular concern was the *Adelaide Institute*, a small organization devoted to Holocaust denial, run by Frederick Toben. It was linked to other Holocaust denial sites around the world, continually published material designed to influence media opinion, and sent unsolicited copies to Jewish individuals as a form of hate mail. When the site was launched in 1996, the executive vice-president of the ECAJ, Jeremy Jones, lodged a complaint with the Human Rights and Equal Opportunity Commission alleging that the site breached the Racial Hatred Act. Toben issued a series of media releases attacking the complainants and portraying the legal process as a "Stalinist" attempt to conceal the truth. The hearings took place in November, and a decision was expected in 1999.

Sections of the Arabic media also produced anti-Semitic material. Other local anti-Semitic sites included *Covenant Vision Ministry* (linked to the *America's Promise Ministries* of Pastor Dave Barley) and *The Bible Believers*—both cast Jews as the anti-Christ and "the Great Satan" that will ultimately be destroyed by "The Lord"—and neo-Nazi sites such as *Southern Cross Hammerskins* and *National Action* (the site of the white supremacist activist group that engages in harassment, abuse, and often violent assault).

EXTREMIST GROUPS

While the better-known Australian extremist groups did not always articulate open anti-Semitism, the links they had with foreign extremist groups (notably U.S. militia movements), Identity churches, the Lyndon LaRouche organization, a variety of conspiracy theorist groups, the Australian League of Rights, or others who promote anti-Jewish myths indicated their openness to anti-Semitism.

The Australian League of Rights—described by the Human Rights and Equal Opportunity Commission as "undoubtedly the most influential and effective, as well as the best organized and most substantially financed, racist organization in Australia"—received widespread though largely negative publicity. Though the group did not put forward candidates and claimed to stand apart from party politics, the League's "great white hope" was Graeme Campbell and his Australia First party. With the lion's share of the 1998 far-right vote going to Pauline Hanson's One Nation, Campbell lost his largely rural seat of Kalgoorlie after 18 years of incumbency. No other Australia First candidates came close to winning. The League itself continued to equip "actionists" around Australia with information to combat their Zionist, Fabian, and humanist enemies, as well as material encouraging hatred of Jews.

The Citizens Electoral Councils (CEC), based in a well-staffed office in suburban Melbourne, engaged in mass mailings of literature reflecting the views of their guru, Lyndon LaRouche, containing some of the most bizarre and offensive anti-Semitic conspiracy theories. Politically-oriented Jewish organizations in

Australia (and antiracist groups in general) were among the CEC's favorite targets. Compared with the mid-1990s, the scale and effectiveness of the CEC's operations had been curtailed, and the group's operations were now almost entirely funded from LaRouche headquarters in Leesburg, Virginia.

Despite the rise of far-right populism channeled by Pauline Hanson's One Nation, the CEC was unable to capitalize on this activity, and its electoral vote in 1998 was minuscule, even compared with similar parties. It did, however, continue to produce its newsletters and media releases, some of which attacked Jewish targets, including one prompted by the *Australia/Israel Review*'s exposés of One Nation. Titled "The Dirty Secrets Behind the Australia/Israel Review," this long feature was error-ridden and based on a ridiculous conspiracy theory relating to "Australia's financial oligarchy" and "a London-directed international anti-defamation apparatus."

Small groups of neo-Nazis were present in all the major Australian cities. The largest neo-Nazi group, National Action, was based in Adelaide, with a substantial cell in Melbourne. It distributed a newsletter and maintained a Web site.

Holocaust-Related Matters

NAZI WAR CRIMINALS

The prosecution of suspected Nazi war criminals appeared to have ground to a standstill. After the Special Investigations Unit (SIU) was disbanded in June 1992, no new investigations were mounted, and all continuing investigations were passed for handling to the Australian Federal Police (AFP). Two pending cases were those of Konrad Kalejs and Karlis Ozols. Both men, now in their 80s and living in Melbourne, had been deeply involved with the notorious Arajs Kommando, the Latvian internal police units in World War II responsible for the rounding up and mass slaughter of tens of thousands of Jews and Gypsies. Kalejs was deported from the United States and then Canada for misrepresenting his wartime record to immigration authorities, before resuming the Australian citizenship he obtained in 1957 under a similar misrepresentation. Both men profited from an anomaly in the Citizenship Act, a ten-year limit on the revocation of citizenship, even where it is apparent that false or misleading information was given in obtaining citizenship. While this anomaly was finally changed in 1997, it did not apply retroactively; thus, an entire generation of war criminals from World War II who misrepresented their past in gaining Australian citizenship would not be affected.

Evidentiary requirements under Australia's War Crimes Act posed seemingly insurmountable obstacles to mounting viable war-crimes cases, while the AFP's budgetary constraints and other responsibilities prevented it from effectively pursuing war-crimes investigations. The federal government, after stating that it would instruct the AFP to review both cases, indicated in 1998 that there was insufficient evidence to mount a trial. The Latvian government, which had sought Australia's assistance in the Kalejs case, by year's end appeared to have abandoned any attempt to mount a trial for the wartime atrocities. AIJAC's national policy chairman, Colin Rubenstein, continued to call for war criminals to be stripped of their citizenship and deported, and for retrospective legislation to be enacted, if necessary, to close the legal loopholes.

RESTITUTION

In August the Executive Council of Australian Jewry welcomed the agreement reached between Jewish groups, Holocaust survivors, and Swiss institutions for the return of US$1.25 billion worth of assets belonging to Holocaust victims that was seized by the Nazis or wrongly kept by Swiss banks after account holders had been murdered. ECAJ president Diane Shteinman said, "This is not an act of charity—it is the partial return of stolen property. We must also recognize that there is now a chance that the historical record will be written accurately, after so many decades of denial by the Swiss and other governments that they had profited from the Nazis' evil. It is important that there is now a fair and caring formula for the disbursement of the returned assets so that Holocaust survivors can have their needs catered for." The Australian Jewish community had the highest proportion of Holocaust survivors in any Jewish community outside Israel.

JEWISH COMMUNITY

Demography

The Australian Jewish community continued to grow through immigration, particularly from South Africa and the former Soviet Union. Estimates of the total number of Jews in Australia ranged from 100,000 to 120,000, out of a total population of 18.4 million. More than half the total number of Jews in Australia were born overseas, with South African-born Jews being the largest group, followed by natives of Poland, Russia, Hungary, and Germany. The Jewish community was heavily concentrated in Melbourne and Sydney, with the Brisbane-Gold Coast area showing the fastest growth.

There were between 14,000 and 20,000 Jews from the former Soviet Union in Australia, mostly living in Sydney and Melbourne. Per capita, Australia's Jewish community has received more immigrants from this source than even Israel, at least double the proportion received by the American Jewish community and seven times the number to go to Canada. The communal leadership remained concerned that the group was proving to be more successful in its integration into Australia generally than into the Jewish community.

Communal Affairs

At year's end, Nina Bassat was elected president of the Executive Council of Australian Jewry, taking over after three years of leadership by Diane Shteinman. Bassat was formerly president of the Jewish Community Council of Victoria. Ron Weiser continued as president of the Zionist Federation of Australia, while Mark Leibler remained president of the United Israel Appeal.

The Australia/Israel and Jewish Affairs Council continued under the leadership of Mark Leibler as national chairman and Colin Rubenstein as national policy chairman. In October the editor of the *Australia/Israel Review*, Michael Kapel, resigned after five years at the helm and was succeeded by Middle East analyst Adam Indikt. AIJAC continued its affiliation with the American Jewish Committee. A joint research study by AJC's Pacific Rim Institute and AIJAC on the impact of Islamic fundamentalism in the Asia-Pacific region was well advanced.

Sam Lipski retired as editor-in-chief of the *Australian Jewish News* and was replaced by David Bernstein as acting editor.

MACCABIAH TRAGEDY

Reverberations continued from the disastrous collapse of the bridge over the Yarkon River near Tel Aviv before the opening ceremony of the 15th Maccabiah games in July 1997. Four Jewish Australian athletes were killed and over 70 injured. The subsequent furor over the slow reactions of the Israeli government and Maccabiah World Union and their alleged negligence severely strained the Australian Jewish community's ties with Israel. Maccabi Australia president Tom Goldman said that Australia would not attend the 2001 Maccabiah Games unless Israel could guarantee the competitors' safety.

The first official investigation, in 1997, headed by Brig. Gen. Yishai Dotan, refused to assign specific blame for the collapse, although the bridge was reputedly hopelessly substandard and its builder had been selected on the basis of an astonishingly cheap construction bid. In December 1997 Israeli authorities filed criminal negligence charges against five of those involved in the bridge collapse, including the contractors and the engineer. The case in the Tel Aviv magistrates court continued through 1998 and, because each defense was being mounted separately, was expected to last well into 1999.

During the year, Jewish community representatives and the families of the victims pursued the Israeli government for interim compensation while the negligence trial continued. Zionist Federation of Australia president Ron Weiser attended Israeli parliamentary hearings on the matter, and Australian foreign minister Downer also took up the compensation issue with Prime Minister Netanyahu in June. Amid the legal wrangling, Israeli treasury officials had not yet accepted the compensation proposal.

The only good news was that Australian teenager Sasha Elterman was finally released from the hospital in Sydney after battling the life-threatening effects of pollutants in the Yarkon River for almost a year. Visiting Israeli figures in Australia, including former prime minister Shimon Peres and singer David Broza, made a point of visiting Sasha in the hospital. Her father, Colin Elterman, launched a separate legal action in Israel.

Education

There were 19 Jewish day schools in Australia with more than half of all Jewish children aged 4-18 and close to 70 percent of those aged 4-12 receiving fulltime Jewish education. Spanning the religious spectrum, Jewish schools continued to rank at the highest level for academic achievement. This reflected the community's major investment in the schools as a means of preserving Jewish continuity. Day school enrollments continued to expand, despite ongoing concerns over high costs. Melbourne had over 5,500 children in Jewish day schools, and one of Sydney's schools had a waiting list of over 300 children.

During the election campaign, Prime Minister Howard reassured the Jewish community that day schools had "an absolute guarantee that their right to exist and get a reasonable level of government support will continue," adding that tuition fees would be exempt from the proposed goods and services tax, as would any other activities included as part of the normal curriculum.

There was also an increased emphasis on adult education, with the Melton Program enrolling nearly 500 students in Sydney and Melbourne. Other short-term courses utilizing guest scholars also proved popular. In Sydney, the Jewish Free University attracted record crowds this year, with particular interest in the Russian and Yiddish language sections.

The whole system of Diaspora education through the World Zionist Organization and the Jewish Agency was restructured during 1998, with the creation of a new Department of Education under the Jewish Agency. The Zionist Federation of Australia was the sole representative of the new education department in Australia. A conference of Jewish educators from Australia and New Zealand at Mount Scopus College in Melbourne was attended by over 250 participants. Plans were well under way for another conference in 1999 in Sydney.

There were also moves to expand opportunities for isolated communities to interact with educational institutions in Israel and the United States that offer a range of Jewish education programs via the Internet. In another development, the establishment of the US$100,000 Israel Experience Fund by the Zionist Federation of Australia and the United Israel Appeal would make visits to Israel available for the Zionist youth movements, the Australian Union of Jewish Students, and selected high-school students.

Jewish-Christian Relations

Interfaith and Jewish-Christian dialogue continued on a number of levels during the year in review. Jeremy Jones was reelected to chair the Advisory Group of Faith Communities to the Council for Aboriginal Reconciliation, where representatives from a number of Christian denominations, Muslims, Buddhists, Hindus, and Ba'hais, together with the Jewish representative, meet and coordinate joint efforts for social justice and antiracism activity.

The most significant development in Jewish-Christian relations was the inaugural meeting of an official Catholic Bishops' Conference delegation with the Executive Council of Australian Jewry, directly resulting from the issuance by the Vatican of its call to Holocaust remembrance. The other two largest Christian denominations, the Anglicans and the Uniting Church, had previously established formal dialogue groups, and the prospects were positive for the Orthodox churches to commence a formal relationship in 1999.

Culture

Melbourne artist Esther Erlich won the prestigious and lucrative Moran Prize for portraiture for her widely acclaimed painting of long-distance athlete Steve Monaghetti.

The short film *Intolerance* won Australia's most prestigious short film award, with its writer and star, Sandy Gutman, also winning the award for Best Actor. A play about being a Jewish woman, *Hungry*, written and performed by Deborah Leiser, had its inaugural season in 1998. Adelaide surrealist artist Rimona Kedem exhibited a new series of paintings this year.

Publications

Diane Armstrong published *Mosaic*, a family history, to considerable acclaim; Peter Kohn wrote a well-received children's fictional work on the Jewish experience, *View from a Sand Castle*; Anna Rosner Blay wrote a Holocaust autobiography, *Sister Sister*; and Alan Gold published two thrillers centered around Holocaust restitution issues (the third in the trilogy was due in 1999).

Personalia

Sir David Smith, former secretary to the governor-general, retired Justice Howard Nathan, young Sydney lawyer Julian Leeser, and high-profile lipstick entrepreneur Poppy King—all from different political camps—participated as delegates in the Constitutional Convention, held in February 1998, to consider the options for Australia becoming a republic.

Michael Danby was elected to Federal Parliament as the new Australian Labor Party member for Melbourne Ports, the House of Representatives seat located in Melboure's inner bayside suburbs. The son of a Holocaust survivor, he is the first Federal MP to identify as a Jew since the retirement of Peter Baume as a NSW senator in 1991. Danby had a long association with the *Australia/Israel Review* and the Australia/Israel & Jewish Affairs Council—formerly Australia/Israel Publications—as a researcher from the late 1970s, editor of the *Review* from 1984 to 1992, and a member of the *Review*'s national editorial committee from 1993 to 1998. He also previously worked as an adviser to former Labor government ministers Barry Cohen and Alan Griffiths.

In the national honors for 1998, Richard Pratt AO was made Companion in the general division (AC), for service to the community and philanthropy. Pratt had been instrumental in encouraging business leaders to be more involved in the community, and the Pratt Foundation was one of Australia's largest private philanthropies. The Honorable Justice Marcus Einfeld, a judge in the Federal Court of Australia, was made Officer in the general division (AO), for service to international affairs and the protection of human rights. Justice Einfeld held a number of important positions: chairman of Australian International Legal Resources Inc., a group helping to rebuild the Palestinian legal and justice system; AUSTCARE's ambassador for Refugees; and the founding president of the Human Rights and Equal Opportunity Commission. Mervyn and Sue Doobov were awarded the Order of Australia Medal for their religious and cultural support of the Jewish community in the Australian Capital Territory. Also, Sydney judge Jim Spigelman was appointed chief justice of New South Wales.

Sir Asher Joel, a renowned organizer of major events and public-relations consultant, died in November, aged 86. By turns a journalist, a navy officer, a member of NSW Parliament, and a newspaper and television station owner, Joel organized visits by Queen Elizabeth, Pope Paul VI, and U.S. president Lyndon Johnson, as well as the opening of the Sydney Opera House and dozens of other events. He was also awarded two British knighthoods, a Papal knighthood (the first given to an Australian Jew), a U.S. Bronze Star, and many other awards.

Other leading Australian Jews who died during 1998 included Rachel Holzer, an internationally acclaimed Yiddish theater star; Holocaust survivor and author Arthur Spindler; journalist, stockbroker, and community leader Richard Dreyfus; mathematical physicist Jose Enrique Moyal; Federal WIZO executive director Denny Govendir (murdered by unknown assailants in her home); and Adele Cohen, a Jewish community leader and arts advocate.

COLIN L. RUBENSTEIN

South Africa

National Affairs

T HE YEAR 1998 saw the continuing transformation of South Africa in the post-apartheid era. Health, welfare, and educational reforms were undertaken, and the transformation of the "apartheid" civil service was well under way, as was the administration of justice. The housing backlog had been significantly reduced, and progress was being made in land redistribution and in the protection of people who were dispossessed of land as a result of racial discrimination or whose insecure tenure left them vulnerable to arbitrary and unfair eviction.

With general elections due to be held in 1999, there was substantial reflection on the government's performance. The ruling Government of National Unity, led by Pres. Nelson Mandela and the African National Congress (ANC), could point to substantial gains in safe access to clean water, electricity, telephones, meals for schoolchildren, and primary health care. But criminal violence remained at a shockingly high level, and corruption was an increasing source of concern.

The emerging markets crisis in Asia and Russia severely weakened the economy, which grew by only 0.1 percent. Inflation was about 8 percent, and unemployment was estimated at between 20 and 32 percent. However, a study conducted by the South African Institute of Race Relations in 1997 showed that at least 20 percent of people who said they were unemployed had casual employment in the informal sector.

Affirmative action was most evident in black appointments in large companies, and the 53 black-led companies listed on the Johannesburg stock exchange increased their market capitalization from 58 billion rand at the end of 1996 to 111 billion rand (approximately $20 billion), an increase of 92 percent, at the end of 1998.

For several weeks Chief Rabbi Cyril Harris was privy to the best-kept secret in South Africa—the marriage of President Mandela to Graca Machel, widow of the former Mozambican president, Samora Machel, on July 18, to coincide with the president's 80th birthday. While clerics from the Christian, Muslim, and Hindu faiths gave their blessing during the marriage ceremony in Mandela's home, which took place on a Saturday, the president arranged for Rabbi and Mrs. Harris to be present on Friday afternoon, where they were among the limited number of guests invited to the president's birthday celebration.

TRUTH AND RECONCILIATION COMMISSION

The Truth and Reconciliation Commission (TRC), established in 1995 to investigate gross violations of human rights in South Africa and beyond its borders between 1960 and 1994, completed its work. Over a two-year period, the TRC collected over 22,000 statements from victims and perpetrators and called more than 2,000 witnesses at public hearings. Testifying before the commission in May, Mohammed Iqbal Shaik, a member of the military wing, *Umkhonto weSizwe* (Spear of the Nation), of the ANC, admitted bombing the Temple Israel Synagogue in Hillbrow in 1983 because of the military and economic ties between South Africa and Israel at the time. A limpet mine had been planted the night before then state president Marais Viljoen was due to visit the synagogue (*Star*, May 8, 1998).

The TRCs first published report contained a full section on the role of the "faith communities" under apartheid. Among the findings it was noted that Christianity, as South Africa's dominant religion, abetted apartheid in various ways, including the overt promotion of biblical and theological teaching in support of it, as was the case in the white Afrikaans Reformed Churches. The report stated: "Religious communities in general, as a rule, failed adequately to support dissident ministers, priests, imams, rabbis and lay persons who found themselves in confrontation with the state" (*Truth and Reconciliation Commission of South Africa Report,* volume 4, Cape Town, 1998, p. 91). The report argued that "contrary to their own deepest principles, many faith communities mirrored apartheid society, giving lie to their profession of a loyalty that transcended social divisions" (p. 65). "While members of the Jewish community made their greatest contributions to South African human rights as individuals, some organizations also played a role. During the last years of apartheid, Jews for Justice and Jews for Social Justice were important voices of protest" (p. 64), the report noted.

In October Yasmine Sooker, a commissioner from the TRC, spoke to the Cape Council of the Jewish Board of Deputies on the successes of the TRC and the potential role of the Jewish community in nation building. She noted the cooperation and sense of community displayed by the different religious groups in the past in opposing apartheid and urged them to play a role in dealing with corruption and in developing programs to teach young people a sense of right and wrong. "Given the Jewish community's own history when they came to South Africa, the role it can play in teaching tolerance is a critical part of nation building," she said (*Jewish Chronicle,* November 1998).

Israel and the Middle East

In an article in the *Sunday Times* (January 18, 1998), South African foreign minister Alfred Nzo expressed support for the Middle East peace process and indicated that the government would not remain mute when any of the parties disregarded its commitments. Deputy President Thabo Mbeki, in a meeting with Asaad Abdel-Rahman, a special envoy of Yasir Arafat, in February, said the United States should exert greater pressure on Israeli prime minister Benjamin Netanyahu. He did not anticipate President Mandela getting directly involved in the peace process (*Citizen*, February 11, 1998).

Although Israel's ambassador to South Africa, Uri Oren, told the Cape Council of the Jewish Board of Deputies in February that he was optimistic about Israel–South Africa relations, South Africa's self-proclaimed even-handed policy toward the Middle East was a source of concern to Jewish leaders. Nonetheless, Oren believed that "there were members who were listening to Israel's point of view, despite the government's consistent support of the Palestinian cause." He saw these ties to the Palestinians as an asset rather than a disadvantage (*Jewish Chronicle*, March 1998). Writing at the time of Israel's 50th anniversary, Oren noted that trade between South Africa and Israel had steadily increased. South African exports to Israel, which exceeded R1.5 billion ($2.5 million), were nearly equal to South African exports to all other Middle Eastern countries (*Sunday Times*, May 3, 1998).

Although President Mandela offered congratulations to Israel on its 50th anniversary and took note of the achievements of the Jewish state, there were indications that the government informally boycotted the Israeli embassy celebrations in Cape Town. The ANC national treasurer, Mindi Msimang, told the Jewish Board of Deputies that he would ask Deputy President Mbeki if an official boycott instruction had been issued. Commenting on the government's links to countries hostile to Israel, Msimang said the ANC would "never desert Israel and would not support anybody who attacks the country" (*SA Jewish Report*, May 29, 1998).

In May an invitation to the New National Party mayor of the Cape Metropolitan Council, Rev. William Bantom, to attend an international conference of mayors in Israel led to a fierce debate and heavy pressure on Bantom from Muslim organizations (supported by the ANC caucus) not to accept. The president of the Jewish Board of Deputies, Mervyn Smith, expressed annoyance at the ANC, which, he pointed out, had no objections to visits to Libya and Syria. "Jews have contributed to the City of Cape Town as citizens, as business and professional people and served the city as mayors and councilors for over a 100 years. The city owed it to its Jewish citizens to acknowledge this wonderful occasion of the 50th anniversary of the statehood of Israel" (*SA Jewish Report,* May 15, 1998). Bantom, who did not give in to the pressure, attended the conference and reported back positively.

The jubilee celebrations in Cape Town were marred by Muslim protesters led by the radical Islamist group Qibla. About 70 protesters shouted "One Zionist, one bullet," "Viva Hezballah and Hamas." Placards were displayed outside the celebration venue, the Civic Center, equating Zionism with apartheid and praising Hamas. Tensions ran high as protesters and guests came face to face outside the hall. Condemning the protests, the Jewish Board of Deputies issued a statement: "It is repugnant that any South African calls for the death of other South Africans. Let there be no misunderstanding. South African Jews are Zionists and nothing will deter us from standing with Israel on this joyous occasion" (*Cape Argus*, May 1, 1998).

In a letter to the *Cape Times* (May 5, 1998), the secretary-general of the Muslim Judicial Council, Sheikh Achmat Sedick, claimed that it was appalling for any South African to share in the celebration of the Jews and Zionists on the occasion of the jubilee. Seymour Kopelowitz, national director of the Jewish Board of Deputies, said the letter was offensive, irresponsible, and likely to incite tension. These demonstrations, he noted, "were clearly aimed at South African Jews and not towards people living many thousands of miles away in the Middle East" (*Cape Times*, May 11, 1998).

In May the South African government refused to issue a visa to Sheik Ahmed Yassin, spiritual leader of Hamas. In a telephone interview from Kuwait, broadcast on a Cape Town Muslim radio station, Yassin denounced all Zionists as terrorists. The interview was broadcast live to a public meeting in Gatesville, Cape Town, where those who had invited Yassin reported back to the Muslim community.

According to a government spokeswoman, Vikki Maharaj, Yassin was refused a visa "due to the delicate state of the negotiations in the Middle East," but she said a visit could not be ruled out in the future (*SA Jewish Report,* May 15, 1998). The Jewish Board of Deputies welcomed the decision to deny Yassin a visa, although a prominent Jew and former editor of the *Mail & Guardian*, Anton Harber, condemned the refusal. Harber noted that Jewish leaders were silent when the Netanyahu government undertook provocative acts that undermined the peace process and failed to meet its obligations under the Oslo agreement, but were quick to speak out against the Yassin visit.

The government's refusal to grant a visa to the Hamas leader led to a protest outside the gates of Parliament by Qibla, which supported Hamas. An Israeli flag was burned, other flags were hurled into the street, and protesters were urged to "clean their shoes on them." Marchers chanted slogans such as "death to Israel" and "One Zionist, one bullet." Commenting on the burning of the Israeli flag, Sheikh Ebrahim Gabriels of the Muslim Judicial Council said they "did not recognize the Israeli State which was founded illegally on Palestinian land" (*SA Jewish Report,* May 22, 1998).

A spokesman for President Mandela said he did not think the president wished to comment on the protest. Citizens had the right to express themselves on any issue of public concern as long as they did not break the law. Flag burnings were common practice throughout the world as a means of expressing "revulsion," and it was "acceptable" as long as it did not cause harm to individuals or endanger human life.

The Islamic Students' Society at the University of Cape Town staged a protest outside the University's Isaac and Jessie Kaplan Centre for Jewish Studies and Research. The protest marked the 50th anniversary of what the Palestinians call *Al Nakba* (the "catastrophe"), the creation of Israel in 1948.

A high-level South African government delegation led by Deputy Minister of Foreign Affairs Aziz Pahad visited Israel and other Middle Eastern countries in June. The delegation wished to gain firsthand knowledge of the situation and to foster mutual cooperation. On their return, Pahad warned that Israel would face isolation unless Prime Minister Netanyahu demonstrated less intransigence. He believed that the view of the South African government coincided with that of the vast majority of Israelis and Palestinians.

In September Pahad shared a platform in Cape Town with former Israeli ambassador to South Africa Alon Liel, to discuss the Middle East. Pahad said he appreciated the opportunity to have open discussions with the local Jewish community and the Jewish Board of Deputies. Peace, he contended, should be achieved through a process of negotiation. Pahad was critical of Israel and saw Natanyahu's government as deviating from Oslo. "The guns of war must be silenced. . . . If we fail, extremists on all sides will celebrate" (*Jewish Chronicle*, October 1998). Liel shared Pahad's views and accused Netanyahu of "playing games" and causing Israel to lose her international standing. Liel was speaking in his position as political adviser to Ehud Barak, leader of Israel's Labor Party.

At the Cape Council of the Jewish Board of Deputies conference in August, national president Mervyn Smith spoke of the South African Jewish community being "hostages to the peace process. The government has long ago moved away from even-handedness on the Middle East." He believed both that there was an anti-Israel lobby in the high echelons of the ANC, and that Deputy President Mbeki was influenced in his views by the American lobby.

The visit of Yasir Arafat in August to address Parliament and attend the Non-Aligned Movement Summit in Durban generated substantial controversy for the Jewish community. In his speech thanking Arafat after his address to Parliament, ANC parliamentarian Gora Ebrahim equated Zionism with racism. In an official communication to the Speaker of Parliament, Frene Ginwala, Israeli ambassador Oren expressed outrage, noting that Ebrahim should have known that the United Nations General Assembly had revoked the 1975 resolution declaring Zionism as racism in 1991 (*Citizen*, August 14, 1998).

Discussing the Arafat visit, the *SA Jewish Report* called for "cool heads." "The blood has to leave the head before statements are rushed to the media. . . . What has to be remembered at all times is that while all Jews have an umbilical cord attached to our Homeland, they are nevertheless loyal, productive South Africans. There is definitely no conflict of interest" (*SA Jewish Report*, August 21, 1998).

Further insult was added when Ze'ev Luria, political counselor at the Israeli embassy, discovered that his invitation to attend the 113-nation Non-Aligned Movement Summit as an observer had been withdrawn. Luria was unable to get any form of accreditation, and the South African government was unable to solve the problem due to pressures from Libya, Iran, and Syria. At the summit, President Mandela lashed out at the Netanyahu government, which he accused of blocking progress toward a peaceful solution. Predictably, Israel was the subject of much criticism from those present, and solidarity was expressed with the Palestinian people. Arafat called on the international community to "protect" the Middle East peace process, which he called an "international peace process."

The Jewish Board of Deputies indicated its distress and disappointment at the withdrawal of Luria's invitation, and Israel's Ministry of Foreign Affairs expressed "dissatisfaction" with Mandela's speech. "Mandela's call to establish a Palestinian State was a step to dictate facts before negotiations, thereby making the negotiations void" (*SA Jewish Report*, September 11, 1998). Commenting on the debacle, the *SA Jewish Report* noted that Jews "will have to accept that the South African environment has become extremely Jewish-unfriendly. It seems as if a small band of militant Muslim extremists have managed to occupy the high moral ground, despite horrifying atrocities which they either deny, or blame on ulterior factors" (September 11, 1998).

In a wide-ranging interview with the president of Ben-Gurion University, Prof. Avishai Braverman, which took place in Cape Town before Yom Kippur, Mandela reiterated his wish to visit Israel, despite his criticism of the Israeli government's handling of the peace process. He also expressed his admiration for the South African Jewish community.

The Mercury (September 26, 1998) reported that financial support for the Islamic Propagation Centre in Durban came from the Saudi Arabian based Bin Ladin family.

Anti-Semitism

Although anti-Semitism was of marginal significance in South African public life during the period under review, a number of troubling incidents occurred. These included a Nazi salute and chanting of "Heil Hitler" by pupils of Glenvista High School at the start of a rugby match against King David High School; an inter-house sports meeting between two Afrikaans-speaking teams in Sasolburg where vulgar Holocaust associations were made; occasional swastikas painted on Jewish shops; and anti-Jewish letters to the press and e-mails to Jewish lists. According to the Board of Deputies, false letters about Jews and Israel were flooding the pages of the country's daily newspapers.

Of greater concern was an emergent Islamism in which anti-Israel sentiment very often spilled over into blatant anti-Semitism. This could be seen in the rhetoric associated with Al-Quds Day, during the Muslim holy month of Ramadan, and in the slogans of Pagad (People Against Gangsterism and Drugs) and Mago (Muslims Against Global Oppression). Muslims calling in to radio talk programs and letters written to the press were often undisguised in their antipathy to Jews.

In December a pipe bomb exploded outside the Wynberg Synagogue in Cape Town at approximately 2 A.M. on a Friday morning. No one was injured, but extensive damage was done to the synagogue. It was thought that the pipe bomb was related to the bombing of Iraq by the United States and Britain. A statement issued by the Cape Council of the Jewish Board of Deputies pointed out that "the aim of the perpetrators is no doubt to bring aspects of an international political conflict to South Africa through acts of violence targeted at the local Jewish community (*Cape Times*, December 21, 1998).

Discussing the question of Muslim anti-Semitism in his inaugural lecture at the University of Cape Town in September, Prof. Milton Shain contended that a significant element among the Muslim community shared the conspiratorial ideas of the far right with regard to Jews: their anti-Zionist rhetoric revealed and displayed classic anti-Jewish motifs, and for at least some Muslims, Jews and Zionists had become diabolically evil. Shain nonetheless warned that Muslim hostility had to be put into perspective. Their population, although relatively large in the Western Cape, was only about 1.3 percent of the total South African population, and the vast majority of Muslims wished to share a multifaith and multicultural South Africa. Only a small minority, argued Shain, were intent on dragging the Middle East conflict, with all its hostility, into local politics.

JEWISH COMMUNITY

Demography

According to the preliminary results of the 1996 Census, the total South African population was 39.8 million, 4.2 million fewer than previously estimated. At the same time, the World Population Data Sheet projected a South African population of 45.7 million in 2010 — 21 percent fewer than estimated the previous year. The drop in population — both actual and projected — was related both to a decline in the fertility rate and to the impact of AIDS. It was estimated that one in eight South Africans had the AIDS virus.

According to the 1996 Census, the white Jewish population of South Africa was 55,734; however, an estimate of closer to 70,000 was probably more accurate. Either way, the Jewish population had declined significantly: in the 1991 Census, the estimated Jewish population was between 92,000 and 106,000.

David Saks, research officer at the Jewish Board of Deputies, adjusted the white Jewish population total of the census upward to 69,573, based on several factors. For one thing, the question on "religion" in the census was optional, and "Judaism" was excluded from the options, so that respondents had to write in "Judaism" if they wished to indicate their religion. Also, approximately 17 percent of the total population did not indicate any religion. Allowing for a similar proportion of Jews doing the same, and adjusting the figures accordingly, he arrived at a white Jewish population of 65,023. In addition, Saks noted that census figures were widely considered to be too low, and that a total South African population of 43 million was more realistic. If this were the case, the Jewish population should be further adjusted upward by about 7 percent, resulting in a final total of 69,573.

In addition to the figure for white Jews, the census reported 10,449 black Jews; 1,058 coloured Jews, and 359 Indian Jews. Initially it was thought that the black Jews belonged to the Lemba group in the Northern Province, but this was not entirely certain. There were an estimated 40,000 Lemba in all of southern Africa who claimed their origins from a Jewish tribe in Sana'a, Yemen. The claim was greeted with skepticism by Chief Rabbi Cyril Harris, who said they had failed to substantiate their Jewish origins and connections. Prof. Jocelyn Hellig, of the University of the Witwatersrand's department of religious studies, noted that the Lemba had pressed for affiliation for 15 years but had failed to be accepted by Jewish religious authorities on halakhic grounds. She believed the Jewish Board of Deputies should engage with the Lemba and investigate their claims.

It was estimated that an average of 1,500 Jews had emigrated each year over the past three years. Some of this immigration, according to Seymour Kopelowitz of the Jewish Board of Deputies, had been offset by Jews returning to South Africa. Of those emigrating, 50 percent chose Australia, followed by North America, Israel, the United Kingdom, and New Zealand. Kopelowitz noted that Israel's position on the list was not attributable to *aliyah* by South Africans but to Israelis returning to the Jewish state. Kopelowitz also pointed to internal Jewish migration from Johannesburg to Cape Town, "because of the perceived lower rate of crime and the superior quality of life" (*SA Jewish Report,* May 12, 1998). Marlene Bethlehem, national chairwoman of the board, added that Orthodox marriages were on the decrease and divorces were rising. Despite the declining Jewish population, Bethlehem remained upbeat and believed that the Jewish community "will not fail and will survive" (*SA Jewish Report,* July 28 1998).

The impact of emigration on the community could be seen in the decline of members and donors to such organizations as the Jewish Woman's Benevolent Society and the Durban Jewish Club.

Communal Affairs

Financial rationalization, security, and the need to establish sound relations with the wider population dominated the Jewish communal agenda. Among the priorities of the Jewish Board of Deputies were monitoring acts of anti-Semitism and safeguarding the rights of Jews, as South African citizens, under the new constitution. In pursuit of these objectives, the board maintained contact with government and public officials and informed opinion makers, the press, and politicians on issues relevant to the Jewish community.

In June the board indicated that it planned to reduce its operational budget by

10 percent. According to Marlene Bethlehem, the "old donor base is disappearing. In recent years this historically small community has been losing as many as 250 families—or roughly a 1,000 members per year—and the community is aging. As a result, there has been a falling off of subscription fees to the Board which are decided in proportion to the size of each of the 107 affiliated organizations that make up the Board's membership." Cost cutting, said Bethlehem, was to be combined with efficiency.

In order to streamline costs, in October the South African Zionist Federation, the Jewish Board of Deputies, and the Israel United Appeal/United Communal Fund (IUA/UCF) established a joint commission to create a single administration for the three groups. Under the new plan, each organization would continue to follow its own agenda and maintain its own identity. The SAZF would sell its seven-story building in the Johannesburg central business district, a building that had been unoccupied since August 1994, following the SAZF move to the northern suburbs of Johannesburg.

The progressive Jewish organization Gesher (Bridge), which promotes contacts between Jews and the wider South African society, postponed its vote on whether to affiliate with the Board of Deputies. One faction feared the loss of independence and questioned whether the board was a democratically run organization. Vice-chairman Steven Friedman and chairman Geoff Sifrin were reelected to their positions.

Numerous events were held to celebrate Israel's 50th jubilee. In Cape Town over 6,000 people attended a glittering Yom Ha'atzma'ut production, "A Time to Rejoice." The occasion was marred by Muslim protests (see above).

Community Relations

Jewish communal institutions continued to engage with the wider society. An umbrella body, Tikkun, which brings together Jewish organizations working to help the disadvantaged in South Africa, continued to mobilize Jewish community resources in the areas of health, welfare, education, youth, agriculture, business, and sport. Herby Rosenberg was appointed CEO of Tikkun.

The Jewish community and Judaism were represented by Chief Rabbi Harris at a meeting of the National Religious Leaders' Forum in Johannesburg in April. The forum aimed to create a moral lobby to deal with corruption in society and to enable the various religious communities to speak with one voice on issues of common concern. In October the National Religious Leaders' Forum convened a "Moral Summit" in Johannesburg at the request of President Mandela. The summit brought together all the major religious groups in South Africa as well as political representatives of major political parties. A code of conduct for persons in positions of responsibility, called the Ubuntu Pledge, was agreed upon. (Ubuntu means "humanness," an African concept conveying the sense that "people are people through other people.") Rabbi Harris warned the summit to be aware of the "chasm between principle and practice." Rabbi Hillel Avidan, of the Association of Progressive Rabbis, said that the goals of the summit and the Ubuntu Pledge were compatible and that he would encourage congregations to accept the pledge.

In a wide-ranging interview in the *SA Jewish Report* (May 11, 1998), Nobel Peace Prize winner Archbishop Desmond Tutu praised those Jews who had played a significant role in the struggle against apartheid and who had involved themselves in social betterment programs. At the same time, he contended that since South African Jews (together with all whites) had reaped the benefits of apartheid, they should consider paying reparations to the victims. "They've [Jews] made a wonderful packet in South Africa and, as every white person benefited whether they liked it or not, it would be wonderful for the process of healing," he said.

Cape Town Jews sent a warm "mazel tov" to President Mandela on the occasion of his 80th birthday on July 18. Jack Tworetzky, chairman of the Cape Council of the Board of Deputies, wrote to the president expressing "this community's warm appreciation of the manner in which you have always made yourself available to deal with issues of concern to the Jewish people in the Western Cape in particular and the Republic of South Africa in general. . . . The Jewish community applauds you for your efforts to democratize this country and is grateful that you have been spared to see a successful culmination of your struggle for liberation" (*Jewish Chronicle,* August 1998).

In August the Cape Council conference highlighted the need to restructure the Cape Town Jewish community. Also discussed were security hazards in the wake of increasing militance on the part of the Muslim population. A resolution was passed "to establish a forum for dialogue between members of the Muslim community and Jewish community to educate Jews and Muslims about each other's community and to dispel misconceptions that lead to stereotypes within each community about the other." The conference also created a Communal Involvement Forum (CIF), led by Brenda Stern, to develop and train young leaders.

Religion

Messianic Jews, commonly known as Jews for Jesus, stepped up their drive for new recruits. University campuses and Johannesburg Jewish neighborhoods, Jewish day schools, and even old-age homes were targeted. Commenting on the upsurge in this activity, Rabbi Graeme Finkelstein, head of the countercult Jewish group "Jews for Judaism," which monitored messianic Jewish organizations, said the increased missionary efforts were related to the approaching millennium. In the view of Avi Krawitz, national president of the South African Union of Jewish Students (SAUJS), Jewish communal leaders were underestimating the extent of the threat (*SA Jewish Report,* May 22, 1998). In June Jews for Jesus was banned at the University of the Witwatersrand.

After more than 30 years in Yeoville, Johannesburg, the headquarters of the

Union of Orthodox Synagogues (UOS) announced that, in line with other communal institutions, it was moving to the northern suburbs. The move was not motivated by security concerns. A new ultra-modern, multifaceted Mizrachi/Bnei Akiva Kollel was established in Glenhazel, Johannesburg. It was announced that a new Great Park Synagogue was to be built in Glenhove Road, Johannesburg. The Oxford Synagogue in Johannesburg was experiencing financial pressure due to declining membership. Rabbi Ady Assabi of the Shalom Independent Movement in Johannesburg was moving to Israel. The congregation, which was affiliated with the World Council of Conservative Synagogues, was founded after Assabi broke away from the Reform movement in 1993. The synagogue building was sold to the Lubavitch Association of South Africa, and David Alswang, chairman of the Shalom Independent Movement, said the congregation would be looking for smaller premises.

Rabbi Simon Harris, formerly of the Marble Arch Synagogue in London, was appointed to the Great Synagogue, Gardens, Cape Town; Rabbi Chaim Willis was appointed executive director of Aish Hatorah; and Harold Novick was appointed the new chairman of the United Orthodox Synagogues (UOS).

Geoff Ramokgadi was the first black South African to register with the Johannesburg Beth Din for conversion to Judaism.

The newly passed Divorce Amendment Act (Section 5A) empowered the courts to refuse to grant a decree of civil divorce until a religious divorce (*get*) was obtained. The new legislation would remove the barrier preventing a woman from remarrying because her husband refused to grant her a *get*. Under the new act, a judge could no longer claim that the *get* condition was a religious matter and therefore beyond the jurisdiction of the court.

Education

According to David Saks, research officer at the Jewish Board of Deputies, the collapse of apartheid had resulted in a boost for Jewish education. Fears of falling standards in state schools meant a steady exodus of pupils from these schools to private colleges and the Jewish day schools. Despite emigration, therefore, enrollment in Jewish day schools had remained stable and even showed a slight increase in the last few years. Three out of four Jewish children attended these schools—a total of 7,443 out of the estimated 9,850 Jewish children of school age. The schools were concentrated in Johannesburg and Cape Town. The sole exception, a school in Port Elizabeth, survived only because the majority of its pupils were not Jewish. The schools range from tiny splinter institutions like the Yeshiva Maharasha to large day schools like King David High School in Johannesburg. In ideology they encompass the strictly Orthodox (e.g., Yeshivas Toras Emes), the modern/centrist Orthodox (Yeshivah College), and the national-traditional (King David Schools and the United Herzlia Schools).

A perennial cloud over the Jewish day-school horizon was funding. According to Cyril Linde, financial director of the South African Board of Jewish Education (SABJE), subsidies from the state could no longer be relied upon. This meant that Jewish parents were doubly burdened, having to pay school fees and government taxes and receive diminishing assistance from the government. In April a government White Paper effectively cut off state funding for private schools, beginning in April 1999. Under the new formula, any school that charges more than two and a half times what it costs the government to educate a child will not be eligible for state funding. According to Leon Kawalsky, chairman of the SABJE, King David School will not qualify for government funding. Kawalsky argued that as taxpayers, those choosing Jewish education were justified in expecting that a portion of their tax money be returned in the form of education for their children. At one time the Jewish day schools received 45 percent of costs, but this percentage had steadily decreased. Kawalsky anticipated difficult times ahead, not only for the Jewish day schools but for all Jewish communal institutions. Emigration, which by and large involved the wealthier, best-qualified members of the community, would have a continuing impact in this area.

The Rabbi J. L. Zlotnik-Avida Hebrew Teachers' Seminary in Johannesburg was closed due to financial constraints experienced by the South African Board of Jewish Education. Meish Zimmerman, head of Jewish studies at the board, said that student numbers had dwindled. The closure followed the closure of the Jewish Students University Program in 1996. The seminary was established in 1947 by Rabbi Jehuda Leib Zlotnik, from Poland.

Culture

Building began in March of the Cape Town Holocaust Centre. Myra Osrin, chairwoman of the Holocaust Memorial Council, announced that the center would comprise a 205-square meter exhibition, a large seminar room, a reception lobby, an administrative office, and a library as well as computers and other research and study facilities.

It was also announced that Mendel Kaplan, former chairman of the Jewish Agency, would fund the building of a South African Jewish Museum at the site of the Gardens Synagogue in Cape Town. Vivienne Anstey was appointed director, and international and local specialists are involved with the design. The museum will form part of an existing revamped campus, which will house the Jacob Gitlin Library and the Cape Town Holocaust Centre. It will open in early 2000.

The Kaplan Centre at the University of Cape Town, in association with the Mayibuye Centre at the University of the Western Cape, mounted a major photographic exhibition, "Looking Back: Jews in the Struggle for Human Rights and Democracy in South Africa."

The *SA Jewish Report*, a weekly newspaper, began publication in May, under the editorship of Janine Lazarus. An opening editorial, "SA Jewry has much to offer," noted that the birth of the new publication was a symbol of commitment on the part of a Jewish community, which has "something strong, vibrant and universal to offer" (*SA Jewish Report*, May 15, 1998).

Publications

Some noteworthy new publications of Jewish interest, all nonfiction, were *Antisemitism* by Milton Shain; *A Life at Law: The Memoir of IA Maisels, QC,* by Israel Maisels; *The Fraenkel Saga by* Clara Friedman-Spits; and *Final Postponement: Reminiscences of a Crowded Life* by Cecil Margo.

Personalia

Dayan Gross was appointed executive director of the Cape Council of the Board of Deputies in August. He replaced Ian Sacks, who retired. Gross was educated at Rhodes University in South Africa before completing a master's degree in Jewish communal service at Brandeis University in the United States.

Charles Loeb was elected Grand President of the Hebrew Order of David, which was founded in 1904 to assist immigrants from European countries. Dina Saffer was elected chairwoman of the South African Union of Jewish Students.

Prominent industrialist and philanthropist Robert Kaplan received Keren Hayesod's new Yakir Award at a ceremony in Jerusalem; Michael Katz, tax expert, professor of law, and former president of the Jewish Board of Deputies, received an honorary law degree from the University of the Witwatersrand.

Among prominent South African Jews who died in 1998 were Adele Searll, communal personality and fund-raiser in the fight against drug abuse; Olga Horwitz, well-known journalist; Arthur Markowitz, writer and former editor of the *SA Jewish Times*; Minna Levitas, communal fund-raiser and leader of a team from South Africa that joined the Joint Distribution Committee working in the DP camps in Europe in 1946; Xavier Piat, Holocaust survivor and renowned philatelist; Gerald Gordon, lawyer, soldier, politician, author and champion of civil rights; Rabbi Irma Aloy, doyen of the rabbinical fraternity of South Africa; Clara Friedman-Spits, author and one-time curator of the Cape Town Jewish museum; and Rhona Stern, noted sculptor and writer.

MILTON SHAIN

Israel

Israel — Review of the Year

In the first nine months of 1998, the deadlock in the peace process continued despite repeated attempts by the United States to forge an agreement on Israeli redeployment in the West Bank. In October, however, after much U.S. coaxing, Prime Minister Benjamin Netanyahu agreed to meet with Palestinian Authority (PA) chairman Yasir Arafat at a summit at Wye Plantation in Maryland.

After nine days of negotiation, much of it under the watchful eye of President Bill Clinton, the two sides signed an agreement whereby Israel would hand over a further 13.1 percent of West Bank land to the Palestinians in exchange for a firm Palestinian commitment to fight terror and a detailed plan for doing so. But the Wye agreement proved to be only a brief respite from the deep mistrust and enmity between the two sides; by the end of the year Netanyahu had essentially frozen implementation of the agreement, citing Palestinian noncompliance.

U.S.-Israeli diplomatic ties were rocky in the period under review as American leaders became increasingly frustrated by Netanyahu's refusal to move forward with redeployment. The strained links between the two countries were at times reflected in the cool relationship between Netanyahu and President Bill Clinton.

On the domestic political scene, the governing coalition remained shaky. Both the foreign minister and the finance minister resigned in the course of the year, and Netanyahu had to constantly contend with threats from right-wing members of his coalition who said they would topple him if he moved ahead with the peace process. At the same time, centrist members of his coalition warned that they would bolt if he did not. Netanyahu continued to defy predictions of his imminent political demise, but on December 21, his luck ran out: the first reading of a bill calling for the disbanding of the legislature passed in the Knesset, essentially signaling that early elections were almost inevitable.

Labor leader Ehud Barak had his own troubles. For much of the year—until the December 21 vote—he appeared unable to cash in on Netanyahu's coalition woes and faced strong criticism of his leadership within Labor.

There was also growing talk in 1998 of what commentators referred to as "The Big Bang"—a realignment of the traditional Israeli left-right political divide. This was given impetus by the announcement of Tel Aviv mayor Roni Milo that he planned to run for prime minister at the head of a centrist party. Milo, a former member of the Likud, said he aimed to pull leading political figures from the left and the right.

The economic recession deepened in 1998. Growth continued to decline, and unemployment was up markedly. Inflation, which was running at an annual rate of 4 percent in August, shot up to 8.6 percent by the end of the year due to a sharp devaluation of the shekel. Many continued to criticize Jacob Frenkel, the governor of the Bank of Israel, for his tight monetary policy which, they argued, was depressing growth.

While the conversion issue remained at the forefront of the battle over religious pluralism in Israel between the Orthodox, on the one hand, and the Reform and Conservative, on the other, the issue of subjecting the ultra-Orthodox to the military draft also dominated the headlines.

POLITICAL AND DIPLOMATIC DEVELOPMENTS

The Peace Stalemate Continues

The peace process remained in deep freeze for the first nine months of 1998. It had been stalled since March 1997, when the Netanyahu government had announced that a Jewish housing project would be built at Har Homah, a southern Jerusalem hilltop located in the part of the city that the Palestinians hoped would serve as the capital of their future state. In early 1998 Netanyahu was still refusing to carry out a second West Bank troop redeployment as laid out in the Oslo accords and reaffirmed by him in the Hebron agreement signed in January 1997. (Under the Oslo II agreement signed in 1995, Israel had withdrawn from the seven major West Bank cities and had handed them over to the Palestinian Authority. Netanyahu completed this withdrawal after coming to power, when he pulled the army out of most of Hebron in January 1997. But Oslo II also stipulated three further redeployments in the West Bank. The Netanyahu government had determined in March 1997 that the size of the first of these redeployments would be around 2 percent of West Bank land. The withdrawal never took place, however, because Arafat rejected it on the ground that the amount of territory he was to receive was too little. Under discussion now was the second redeployment.)

A visit to Israel and the Palestinian autonomous areas on January 6-9 by Dennis Ross, the U.S. peace envoy to the Middle East, failed to produce a breakthrough, as Netanyahu refused to commit to handing over more West Bank land. Progress looked further away than ever when the government announced on January 7 that it had approved a plan for the construction of 574 new housing units in the West Bank settlement of Efrat. The decision flew in the face of a 1997 American call for a "time-out" in West Bank settlement building—a major point of contention between Israel and the Palestinians. It was followed on January 9 by a report in the daily *Ha'aretz* that the cabinet had approved a plan for the construction of 30,000 homes in the West Bank and Gaza Strip over the next 20 years. Shortly after Ross departed, the government made clear that it would not agree to any further redeployment until the Palestinians met their commitments as set down in the Hebron agreement of January 1997. The government decision, Netanyahu told reporters, was "a very simple idea—it's called a contract." The cabinet then passed another decision outlining what it considered to be Israel's vital security interests in future negotiations over the West Bank. These included an eastern security buffer zone in the Jordan Valley, a western buffer zone, the retention of the area surrounding Jerusalem, and the maintenance of the settlements under Israeli sovereignty.

Both Netanyahu and Arafat flew to Washington in mid-January for separate talks with U.S. president Bill Clinton. In his meeting with Netanyahu, Clinton tried to persuade the Israeli leader to accept a formula whereby the Palestinians would step up their operations against Islamic militants in exchange for a phased Israeli redeployment. While Clinton reportedly wanted Netanyahu to agree to a double-digit withdrawal, there were reports that the Israeli leader was refusing to pull back from more than 9.5 percent of the West Bank. For his part, Arafat was said to be insisting on an Israeli redeployment of 30 percent.

One of the major stumbling blocks, according to the prime minister, was the Palestinian refusal to revoke those clauses in the PLO Charter that called for Israel's destruction. In his talks with Clinton, Netanyahu emphasized the Israeli demand that the Palestinian National Council (PNC, the PLO's parliament) reconvene to adopt an amended charter as a precondition to any further troop pullbacks in the West Bank.

During his meeting with Clinton, Arafat provided the president with a letter saying that 33 clauses in the PLO Charter had already been "nullified" and another 16 amended. As a result, wrote Arafat, "all of the provisions of the Covenant which are inconsistent" with the PLO's commitment to make peace, were "no longer in effect." Arafat added, in the letter, that "this comprehensive" amendment of the Covenant had been carried out in April 1996 by the PNC.

While State Department spokesman James Rubin described the letter as "an important step toward completing the process of revising the charter," a Netanyahu aide pointed out that the Palestinians had pledged in the Hebron agreement to set up a committee to draft an amended covenant, which would then be brought before the PNC for ratification. The Palestinians, he pointed out, had failed to do this. In response to Israel's firm stance on the charter issue, Arafat's special adviser, Dr. Ahmad Tibi, remarked sarcastically, "Even if the Palestinian National Council members sing the Betar anthem in unison, Benjamin Netanyahu won't fulfill his commitments."

The Netanyahu-Clinton meeting failed to produce a breakthrough. While the Israeli prime minister said he would try to "muster the necessary support across the government . . . for something that would move the peace process forward, and maintain secure and defensible boundaries for Israel," he accused Arafat and the PA of fulfilling "none, none, none" of their obligations in the Hebron agreement. A late January visit to the region by Secretary of State Madeleine Albright also failed to get the process back on track. And matters were not helped by an early February announcement that Israel's Interior Ministry had approved plans for the building of 132 Jewish homes in the Ras al-Amud (Arab) neighborhood of East Jerusalem. While there were reports that Netanyahu opposed the plan, it had the full support of Jerusalem mayor Ehud Olmert, considered by many to be a political rival of the prime minister.

The stalemate in the peace process appeared interminable at the beginning of 1998, and there was reason to doubt that the United States could save it. With Clinton distracted by the Monica Lewinsky sex scandal, most observers believed he would have little inclination for Middle East peacemaking. What is more, they pointed out, the president was desperate not to erode his domestic political support further and so was not keen to take on Netanyahu over the issue of the second withdrawal. After the January visits of Arafat and Netanyahu, though, the White House did begin working on a formula to extract Oslo from its deep paralysis. The central plank of such a deal would require Netanyahu to agree to a second troop redeployment that would be carried out in three or four stages, with the first starting parallel with Arafat launching a full-scale assault on terror.

One of the cardinal points of disagreement was how much territory Israel would hand over to the Palestinians. Netanyahu reportedly had agreed to cede 9.5 percent of West Bank land, while the Americans were insisting on 12 percent. There were reports that Arafat was prepared to settle for something close to the U.S. proposal. Another point of contention was the third and final redeployment which, as stipulated in Oslo II, was to take place before final-status negotiations on issues like the definition of the Palestinian entity and the future of Jerusalem got under way. Netanyahu informed Clinton that he did not have the support in his coalition to carry out the third pullback. For his part, Arafat made it clear he would not forego the final withdrawal. There were meetings between Israeli and Palestinian officials in February, but they failed to break the impasse. In a TV interview on February 23, Netanyahu called on Arafat to meet him at a summit where, he said, they could "shut ourselves off someplace" so as to gauge "where the compromise would come, between the Palestinians' demands and Israel's vital needs." But Arafat said he would only meet Netanyahu once Israel had agreed to carry out the second redeployment.

Threats and Recriminations

With the peace process on the rocks, Israeli and Palestinian leaders engaged in sustained mutual recrimination. "If we need to, we will cross [the peace process] out and begin all over," Arafat declared in February, threatening that there would be another *intifada* (uprising) if the peace process collapsed. Netanyahu was quick to respond, warning, "If he carries out his threats, the Oslo Accord will be canceled, not just broken."

And there was always the threat of terror. In late January, for instance, security forces had been placed on high alert following intelligence warnings that the Islamic fundamentalist Hamas movement might try to carry out an attack in a big city. Tension was also high in the West Bank and Gaza Strip, and it boiled over on March 10 when three Palestinian construction workers were killed and four injured at a roadblock outside Hebron where Israeli soldiers opened fire on the van they were driving. The soldiers said the van had veered toward them and hit one of them. Palestinian eyewitnesses insisted the shooting had been unprovoked. The incident sparked Palestinian street protests, and clashes between demonstrators and Israeli troops quickly spread across the West Bank.

Despite the violence and the peace deadlock, Israeli officials doubted that Arafat would allow the confrontations to escalate into a full-scale *intifada*. His main motivation for keeping a lid on the level of violence, they said, was to insure that he did not lose international support for the state he hoped to declare on May 4, 1999, when the Oslo accords were set to expire. Israeli officials also pointed out that Arafat understood that protracted, heavy clashes might scare off much-needed foreign investment in the autonomous areas.

Israeli commentators were often critical of Netanyahu, saying he had become a hostage of the right-wing elements in his coalition and the Jewish settlers in the West Bank and Gaza Strip. "Benjamin Netanyahu is no longer in control of his government," wrote leading Middle East commentator Ehud Ya'ari. "He still sits behind the wheel, but it's being turned by other people. His intention was to drive toward the center; instead of that, he's made a sharp turn to the right. . . . The prime minister has become a hostage of the settler lobby; amid their cheers, he struts about proclaiming that he's standing up to the Americans, while in private his people brag that they are choking Oslo into a coma. The process is nominally alive, but it's stopped showing any movement. . . ."

Another visit by the seemingly tireless Dennis Ross in late March also failed to end the impasse. After the Mideast envoy departed empty-handed, U.S. State Department spokesman James Rubin issued a statement saying that the peace process was in "dire straits" and that during his visit Ross had "been unable to bridge the gaps on hard questions."

Tension rose again on March 29 when Muhi a-Din a-Sharif, a leading member of the Hamas military wing who was wanted by Israel for having planned several suicide bombings, was found dead in the West Bank city of Ramallah. The site where the body was found was immediately sealed off, and Palestinian and Israeli security officials, along with the agents from the U.S. Central Intelligence Agency (CIA), moved in to examine the scene. News of Sharif's death sparked street protests in the West Bank and Gaza.

Initially it appeared that Sharif had been killed in a "work accident" while preparing a car bomb to be detonated inside Israel, but it later emerged that he had been shot and killed and his body had then been moved to the site of the Ramallah explosion. While the PA asserted that Sharif's death was the result of an internal Hamas dispute, the Islamic fundamentalist movement blamed Israel for the killing and vowed revenge. "The Palestinian Authority's false claims and lies are meant to present the Zionists as innocent and save them, but it won't affect our overall plan for revenge in the slightest," read a statement released by Hamas's military wing. Netanyahu strongly denied any Israeli involvement. "I can tell you with certainty that Israel had no part in this event," he told journalists. Nevertheless, Israel was placed on high alert for possible Hamas revenge attacks.

Yasir Arafat's March 31 visit to the Anne Frank House in Amsterdam also did nothing to reduce the growing animosity between the two sides. Cabinet secretary Danny Naveh dismissed it as nothing more than a publicity stunt. Netanyahu also continued to stick to his hard-line public stance. "In this process, the chances of success are measured by one thing—the level of our stubbornness," he declared during an April visit to the settlement of Ma'aleh Adumim near Jerusalem. Ross was back in the region in late April, but once again failed to broker a compromise on a West Bank redeployment. This was due in no small measure to right-wing pressure on Netanyahu not to bow to a U.S. demand to withdraw from 13.1 percent of the West Bank. "Thirteen percent? It's suicide," warned Michael Kleiner, head of the Land of Israel Front, a hard-line Knesset grouping. "We won't agree to even much less than that, and I suggest that the prime minister take that into account."

But there were also other, more moderate, voices in the coalition. Meir Sheetrit, a Likud Knesset member, repeatedly encouraged Netanyahu to call the right wing's bluff, arguing that he should cut a deal with the Palestinians, and that if coalition hawks brought him down as a result, the prime minister would cruise to victory in an early election. "If we go to an election on the platform that we're making peace but they won't let us, Bibi will clean up," said Sheetrit. His preferred solution was a Likud-Labor national unity government that would be able to move forward on the Palestinian as well as the Syrian track. "This could be our last chance because today Likud and Labor together have a majority in the Knesset, which they could lose in a new election," he cautioned.

Nothing came of the talks that Netanyahu and Arafat held—separately—with Secretary of State Albright and other U.S. officials in London on May 4, where the issue of a 13.1 percent Israeli withdrawal from the West Bank—already accepted publicly by Arafat but not Netanyahu—was the key sticking point. Asked what would happen if the Americans continued to insist that Israel agree to redeploy from 13.1 percent of the West Bank, Netanyahu said there would simply be "no agreement." Netanyahu's views, though, were not shared by Defense Minister Yitzhak Mordechai, one of the most moderate members of the cabinet, who repeatedly expressed the need for forward movement on the peace front. "At the end of the day," Mordechai told a group of French parliamentarians in May, "Israel will have no choice but to reach an agreement with the Palestinians based on a two-digit withdrawal." For their part, the Palestinians feared that Israel would make one more small troop redeployment and then freeze the process, leaving them with territorially disjointed patches of land making up less than a third of the West Bank.

At the end of her early May meetings with Netanyahu and Arafat in London, Albright announced that she had invited the Israelis and Palestinians to talks in Washington, D.C., on May 11—on condition they had made progress on the issue of redeployment. If not, she said, the administration "will have to reexamine our approach to the peace process." Since the Palestinians had already publicly accepted the U.S. proposal of 13.1 percent, her comments were seen as a thinly veiled threat against Netanyahu. But the prime minister remained unbowed, declaring on Army Radio that he would not go to Washington if the Americans "tell me that I have to go and accept certain conditions that are unacceptable to us."

In the end, both Arafat and Netanyahu flew to Washington for separate meetings with Albright. After the talks there were reports that the Israeli leader had intimated to U.S. Mideast peace envoy Dennis Ross that he was ready to accept an interim peace package that would include an Israeli troop withdrawal from a further 13.1 percent of West Bank land, but only on condition that the third and final scheduled troop redeployment would be minimal. But it soon became clear that the formula was unacceptable to Arafat, and Netanyahu was quick to declare that he had never agreed to a 13 percent pullback.

Violence again erupted in the territories on May 14 when tens of thousands of protesters took to the streets in East Jerusalem, Gaza, and the West Bank to commemorate *Al Nakba* ("The Catastrophe")—the term used by Palestinians to describe the creation of the State of Israel and the exodus of hundreds of thousands of Arabs in 1948. Five Palestinians were killed and dozens wounded in clashes with Israeli troops. About a dozen Israelis were injured. Palestinian despair at the deadlocked peace process erupted again when top Palestinian figures joined young demonstrators to protest a move by Jewish far-right settlers who had set up nine temporary structures in the Muslim Quarter of the Old City on May 26. The structures were built by Ateret Cohanim, a group that received funding from U.S. Jewish millionaire Irving Moskowitz and worked to boost the Jewish presence in the Muslim Quarter. The move, they said, was a response to the May 6 fatal stabbing of a yeshivah student, Haim Kerman, in the Old City. The situation was defused after a court injunction was issued against the construction and the settlers agreed to leave. But Palestinian leaders continued to warn that with the impasse in the peace process, violence was inevitable. "The Palestinian people's patience is running out," warned Abu Ala, the Speaker of the Palestinian Legislative Council and one of the chief peace negotiators. "We won't accept a peace that comes at the expense of our land and our rights. Such an agreement can go to hell."

The paralyzed peace process and the rising tension in the territories led to growing fears in Israel's security establishment over the possibility of widespread Palestinian violence. In a closed meeting, General Security Services chief Ami Ayalon reportedly warned Netanyahu that Hamas was planning new terror attacks, and that some of the groups within Arafat's Fatah organization were beginning to show signs of independence from the Palestinian Authority. It was possible that they were preparing themselves for a confrontation with the Israel Defense Forces (IDF) if the peace process collapsed altogether. Ayalon also told the prime minister that these groups were stockpiling small arms and antitank weapons. Labor leader Ehud Barak called a press conference in Tel Aviv at the end of May and warned that the situation was reminiscent of the days before the Yom Kippur War in 1973 (when warnings about an imminent Arab attack went unheeded by Israel's leaders). "Innocent citizens, women and children, soldiers and members of the security forces will die here needlessly," he said.

Netanyahu, however, sharply criticized Palestinian leaders who warned of violence in the absence of any progress on the peace front. He appeared to view these threats as an attempt by the Palestinians to force him into making concessions. Some political observers said Netanyahu's unwillingness to heed intelligence reports about growing Palestinian despair and a possible violent eruption in the territories was the result of his belief that these assessments were being made by intelligence officials with a political bias. Hence, he tended to dismiss the views of officers who warned of a possible showdown with the Palestinians if the peace process remained frozen. Meetings, for instance, between Netanyahu and Chief of Staff Amnon Shahak became rare, and a minor scandal broke out after a sharp interchange between Netanyahu and Shahak at a June 14 intelligence briefing to the cabinet on Palestinian sentiment regarding the stalled peace process. The prime minister objected that the issues the general was discussing were of diplomatic, not security, import. "No problem," Shahak was reported to have said. "If the government doesn't want to hear what I have to say, the government won't hear. I'll report only on what you want to hear."

Opinion was divided on Netanyahu's motivations. Some political analysts argued that the prime minister was convinced he could drag his feet as much as he wanted and the Palestinians would be powerless to do anything about it. Others suggested that Netanyahu believed Arafat would keep the level of violence under control at least until May 1999 when he hoped to declare the establishment of a state, so as not to lose international backing for such a move. A third, more apocalyptic, reading of the prime minister was that he saw a showdown with the Palestinians as inevitable and considered it preferable for the confrontation to take place while most of the West Bank was still in Israeli hands. According to this view, a major clash with the Palestinians would also provide Netanyahu with a pretext to annex part of the West Bank and seal the fate of the Oslo accords once and for all. "The Israeli people," said one former intelligence operative, "look on in awe, not sure whether they're watching a masterly performance or a charlatan heading for disaster."

U.S. Impatience

The U.S. remained reluctant to blame Netanyahu for the deadlock, fearing that public pressure on Israel might create the mistaken impression that America was reducing its commitment to Israeli security—a result that could well destabilize the Middle East. American Jewish leaders' strong public support for Netanyahu and the administration's desire not to alienate the Jewish vote further increased Washington's reluctance to force Netanyahu to make a decision on the troop redeployment. Nevertheless, there were increasing signs of U.S. impatience with the prime minister, especially as it became clear that Yasir Arafat had fully accepted the U.S. peace proposal. First, Madeleine Albright made an impassioned plea to the leaders of the region: You have "reached a crossroads," she declared in May. "Act before it is too late. Decide before the peace process collapses." Then, in a comment made via satellite to a group of Israeli and Palestinian children gathered in Switzerland, Hillary Clinton expressed support for a future Palestinian state. "It will be in the long-term interests of the Middle East for Palestine to be a state," she said in answer to a question. (Netanyahu had consistently expressed his strong opposition to the creation of a Palestinian state.) Finally, in June, Albright told Defense Minister Mordechai that the administration was "getting close to the point where we will decide to leave both sides to themselves."

A U.S. plan aimed at breaking the peace deadlock had been leaked to *Ha'aretz* and appeared in that paper on June 4. According to the proposal, Israel was to hand over 13 percent of the land in the West Bank to the Palestinians over a 12-week period. The plan also included a freeze on Israeli settlement building and the establishment of a U.S.-Israeli-Palestinian committee to monitor security matters. The initial response by Israeli officials was that the American proposal failed to deal with the issue of the third redeployment. But in mid-June Netanyahu announced the possibility of a national referendum on the issue of the second redeployment. He even instructed his communications minister, Limor Livnat, to investigate the matter. Within days, though, it was clear that the prime minister had dropped the idea. Observers suggested it had either been a trial balloon that Netanyahu had floated and abandoned or simply an attempt to win time. When Spanish prime minister Jose Maria Aznar visited in late June, Netanyahu floated another idea: a new Mideast peace conference along the lines of the 1991 Madrid conference. But his proposal was immediately rejected by Arab leaders.

The deadlock looked even more intractable when the cabinet, on June 21, approved a plan to broaden the boundaries of Jerusalem. While Netanyahu insisted that the main motive for the plan was to boost municipal services and make tax collection more efficient, Palestinian and Arab leaders attacked it as an effort to strengthen Israel's hold on the capital and the West Bank ahead of final-status talks. In an expression of U.S. dissatisfaction with the decision, State Department spokesman Rubin issued a statement saying that it was "extremely hard to understand why Israel would even consider taking such a provocative step at this sensitive time in the negotiations."

On the domestic front, Netanyahu's hard-line approach to the peace process was repeatedly criticized by President Ezer Weizman. (Adding to the strained relations between the two men, Netanyahu supported Likud candidate Shaul Maor for the post of president in the March 4 Knesset vote, which the 73-year-old Weizman won by 63 to 49.)

In June the president reportedly told a delegation of the left-wing Peace Now movement that Defense Minister Yitzhak Mordechai was "the only ray of light in the government." Then, on June 29, he openly urged the prime minister to call early elections and criticized his leadership, saying that under Netanyahu the peace process was breaking down and Israel's international standing was eroding. "If he doesn't hold a referendum, in my opinion the solution should be elections," said Weizman, recommending that Netanyahu gauge public opinion on a West Bank troop withdrawal. While some opposition politicians tabled a Knesset motion for early elections, coalition members accused the president of overstepping the authority of his office. An unfazed Netanyahu declared that elections would be held as scheduled in the year 2000, and he repeated a list of conditions Arafat had to comply with if there was to be any progress on the peace front. Before any deal could be struck, he insisted, Arafat had to dismantle the Islamic fundamentalist terror infrastructure in the areas under his control, the Palestinian Authority's police force had to be reduced in size to the level mandated in the Oslo accords, terror suspects had to be extradited to Israel, and the Palestinians had to vote unequivocally to remove those clauses in the PLO Charter calling for Israel's destruction. Until these conditions had been fulfilled, he said, Israel would not budge from another inch of West Bank territory. "We don't point a pistol at our own forehead," Netanyahu said.

Incendiary remarks by some Palestinian leaders added to the tension between the two sides. "There is no peace process between us and Israel," declared Palestinian Authority justice minister Freih Abu Medein. "Israel is our enemy and the enemy of the Palestinian people."

Behind the scenes, frustrated U.S. administration officials commented that Netanyahu seemed more ready to risk a showdown with the Palestinians than with his far-right supporters. In mid-July, State Department spokesman Rubin publicly clarified the U.S. position: "Let me make this very clear," he said. "The Palestinians have said yes in principle to [our] ideas . . . in short, the ball is not in the Palestinian court as I've seen it suggested. The ball is in the court of the Israelis. . . ."

An unbowed Netanyahu, buoyed by right-wing elements of his coalition, refused to accede to Albright's insistence that he accept the 13.1 percent second redeployment. One of the spiritual leaders of the National Religious Party (NRP), former Ashkenazi chief rabbi Avraham Shapira, told the prime minister that he would advise members of the NRP to withdraw from the cabinet if Netanyahu acceded to the U.S. demand. Shapira said his directive was based on Jewish law and insisted that a withdrawal of 13 percent would constitute an existential threat to Israel.

Israeli and Palestinians officials held the first round of high-level talks in months when a delegation headed by Defense Minister Mordechai met with a Palestinian team headed by Mahmoud Abbas (Abu Mazen) in Tel Aviv on July 19-22. At the heart of the discussions was the U.S. peace proposal that included the 13.1 percent West Bank pullback. The meetings ended, however, without any apparent breakthrough. While Israel called on the United States to send Mideast envoy Ross back to the region to mediate, the Palestinians announced there had been no progress.

Palestinian State

With the peace process stalled, Yasir Arafat announced on several occasions that on May 4, 1999—the day the Oslo accords were set to expire—he would unilaterally declare an independent Palestinian state in those parts of Gaza and the West Bank that were under his control. There was speculation over how Netanyahu might respond to such a move. Some suggested that the prime minister would react by annexing those parts of the West Bank still under Israeli control. That was, indeed, what some right-wing MKs said Netanyahu had told them he would do, after they emerged from a meeting with him in early June. But the prime minister himself made no clear public statement on the matter. He did, however, portray Arafat's regular threats of a unilateral declaration of statehood as evidence that the Palestinian leader could not be trusted.

Coalition right-wingers pushed Netanyahu to take an unbending line on the issue of statehood. "If Arafat tells us now that he intends to violate Oslo in a year," said the Likud's Uzi Landau, chairman of the Knesset's powerful Foreign Affairs and Defense Committee, "I don't see what's left to talk about. I'd extend Israeli law to all the remaining territory and leave him holding what he has." Opposition Knesset members adopted a different tack. Yossi Beilin, an architect of the Oslo accords, cautioned against reaching a situation where the Palestinians made good on their threat and unilaterally declared a state. Such a development, he said, was not in the interest of either side. Israel would suffer great international embarrassment, he said, while the Palestinians would be left with far less than they hoped to get. Meretz leader Yossi Sarid played down the significance of such a development: "The Palestinian state is already here, and everybody knows it," he said.

If Arafat did unilaterally declare a state, wrote leading Middle East analyst Ehud Ya'ari, he could be confident he would win broad international support. "Arafat is emulating David Ben-Gurion's 1948 strategy: Gradually building international support for the idea of independence, and then declaring it without securing the agreement of the other side," he wrote in the *Jerusalem Report* (April

16, 1998). "Unlike Ben-Gurion, Arafat knows that there will be no military invasion of his territory. He is not certain that American recognition will come immediately, but he will have taken note of the State Department's new wording—that the Palestinians have 'the right to be free in their land'—almost the same language as [the Israeli national anthem] Hatikvah."

One sign of Israel's growing international isolation as a result of the deadlocked peace process was a July 7 vote by the UN General Assembly to upgrade the PLO's observer status. Thus the PLO's representatives were afforded the right to debate in the General Assembly and participate in various UN conferences and meetings. Israel, the United States, and Micronesia voted against the proposal; 124 nations supported it.

Terrorism

While suicide bombings had subsided, terror had not vanished altogether. A major disaster was averted in downtown Jerusalem on July 19 after a van driven by a Palestinian from a village near Ramallah caught fire, but did not explode, on the busy Jaffa Road. Police announced that the vehicle was filled with 160 gallons of flammable liquid, three cooking gas balloons, and several kilos of nails. Two weeks later, on August 4, two residents of the West Bank settlement of Yitzhar—Harel Bin-Nun and Shlomo Liebman—were shot dead in an ambush while patrolling the settlement's perimeter. Police later found tracks leading to a nearby Arab village.

On August 20, a Hebron resident, Rabbi Shlomo Ra'anan, was stabbed to death in his home by a Palestinian who then escaped back into the section of the city under PA control. A small bomb hidden in a trash can exploded on a busy Tel Aviv street on August 27, wounding 25 people. While there was no claim of responsibility, security sources said Palestinian fundamentalists were behind the bombing. Two weeks later, on September 10, Israeli security forces were placed on high alert after IDF troops killed the head of the Hamas military wing, Adel Awadallah, and his brother. Hamas immediately threatened reprisals. Tension rose again after a settler opened fire on a group of Palestinian high-school students in the West Bank town of Beitunia on September 17, killing one and seriously wounding another. The settler later turned himself over to the police, saying that he had opened fire in self-defense after he was attacked with stones.

Against the backdrop of the murders at Hebron and Yitzhar, there was growing despair on the right-wing fringe, which suspected that the government might cut a deal with Arafat for the handover of more West Bank land, and which charged that the army was becoming soft on the Palestinians. This right-wing sentiment, in turn, sparked fears in the security establishment that extremist Jewish violence might reemerge. There were some disturbing signs: When President Weizman visited Hebron to offer his condolences to Ra'anan's widow, he was confronted by Baruch Marzel, a neighbor of Ra'anan's and a former leader of the banned Kach movement, who berated the president, calling him "a spy. You're a danger to the public," shouted Marzel, "and you should be hospitalized in prison or in a hospital." Jewish extremists also demonstrated outside the home of Yitzhak Mordechai, chanting that the defense minister was a murderer.

The daily *Yediot Aharonot* reported that the Shin Bet secret service, which had failed to protect Yitzhak Rabin when he was gunned down by Yigal Amir in 1995, had beefed up security around Netanyahu, Mordechai, and Weizman. When the prime minister visited Hebron after Ra'anan's murder, photographs revealed a puffed-up torso — a clear indication that he was wearing a bulletproof vest. Some experts played down the possibility of another attack on an Israeli leader, arguing that the atmosphere at the time Rabin was assassinated had been very different. Back then, said Ehud Sprinzak, a Hebrew University expert on the far right, the left was in power and large parts of the right had branded Rabin a traitor; they attended wild demonstrations where placards of Rabin in a keffiyeh were burned. "We're not in a situation similar to the one preceding Rabin's assassination," said Sprinzak. "The majority of settlers, especially the settlement council, felt enormous distress under Rabin. Today, they get all the money they need, there is no restriction on building, the prime minister is weak and there is a strong National Religious Party representation in the government."

While security experts spoke of the possibility of revenge attacks by Jewish extremists against Palestinians, their real fear was an attack on a Muslim holy place. The "ultimate" target, some pointed out, could be the Temple Mount — a focal point for some Jews who believed the final redemption was close, as well as for Muslims who viewed the site as a symbol of Islamic religious and national ties to Jerusalem. A strike at the Temple Mount, warned Likud Knesset member and former deputy head of the Shin Bet Gidon Ezra, "wouldn't just result in a Palestinian response, but a worldwide Muslim reaction. There would be mass demonstrations, attempts to carry out terror attacks." Former Shin Bet chief Carmi Gillon painted an even blacker picture: "An attack on the Temple Mount would be a casus belli for all-out war between Israel and the Arab states," he said.

The car of left-wing Meretz Knesset member Ran Cohen was torched in early October by unknown assailants outside his home in the Jerusalem suburb of Mevasseret Tzion. Cohen had led the fight to have the Kiryat Arba grave of Baruch Goldstein, the murderer of 29 Palestinians in Hebron in 1994 — which had become a site of pilgrimage for extremists — demolished and moved elsewhere. He was now given Shin Bet protection.

The Wye Plantation Agreement

U.S. envoy Dennis Ross, who had been trying to persuade Netanyahu to accept the American proposal of a 13 percent pullback, was back in the region for a mid-September visit. In exchange for the withdrawal, Ross told Netanyahu, the Palestinians would take concrete measures to fight terror, and the two sides would begin final-status talks over highly sensitive and complex issues such as the future of Jerusalem and the settlements, the Palestinian refugees, and the final borders of the Palestinian entity. Netanyahu reportedly signaled his willingness to cede the territory, but needed some way to win over his hard-line coalition partners. One suggestion was that 3 percent of the land would be taken from the Judean Desert and declared a nature reserve where Palestinian construction would be forbidden. That way the prime minister could tell his right wing that he had only given up 10 percent.

Meanwhile, Yasir Arafat, fearing that the stalled peace process was undermining his standing among the Arabs in the territories, made increasingly incendiary statements. "Dennis Ross is an Israeli collaborator and we have no faith in him at all," European sources quoted him as telling Miguel Moratinos, the European Union's special Mideast envoy, at a meeting in Ramallah. And, in a speech to the Arab League in Cairo, Arafat accused Israel of preparing "ways to take over our territories" and said that "the [Israeli] army is training for that now."

Reports emerged that Clinton was pushing for a late September summit between Netanyahu and Arafat in New York. While there was little optimism that the scandal-racked U.S. president could get the two sides together, Clinton was to prove the skeptics wrong. After meeting Netanyahu and Arafat separately in the United States, he announced on September 28 that the Israeli and Palestinian leaders would be back in mid-October for a summit at Wye Plantation in Maryland—the same place where talks had been held between the Israelis and Syrians when Yitzhak Rabin was in power.

In early October, before traveling to Wye Plantation, Netanyahu finally announced a replacement for David Levy, who had resigned as foreign minister 10 months earlier: Minister of Infrastructure and ex-general Ariel Sharon, known for his usually hard-line views. Opinion was divided over what Netanyahu hoped to gain by the appointment of the controversial Sharon. Some said the move was a sign that Netanyahu had no intention of making any real concessions on the peace front, pointing to Sharon's oft-stated view that ceding more than 9 percent in the second redeployment would endanger the existence of Israel. Others, however, suggested that the prime minister actually planned to move ahead with the peace process, and that bringing Sharon aboard was an astute move to nullify opposition on his right flank, a way of reassuring settlers that their interests would be protected if Sharon were involved in brokering a deal. According to an agreement reached between the two, Sharon was to be in charge of final-status negotiations with the Palestinians.

There was much speculation as to why Netanyahu agreed to go to Wye after having resisted an agreement for so long. One explanation was his fear of May 4, 1999—the date on which Arafat was threatening to declare a Palestinian state. Israeli security officials feared that such a declaration could lead to widespread violence—a concern that was shared not only by their American colleagues, but also by some PA officials. Among Netanyahu's major aims, therefore, were de-fusing the threat of a unilateral Palestinian declaration of statehood and extracting a firm commitment from the Palestinians to fight terror.

Although Netanyahu had pledged to continue with the implementation of Oslo during his 1996 election campaign, he always portrayed his role as that of a hard bargainer who would salvage what he could from a bad deal cut by his Labor predecessors. At Wye, his aides said, the prime minister would continue his job of damage control by demanding that the third and final interim withdrawal stipulated by Oslo be no more than 1 percent, and that it would only be implemented once final-status negotiations were under way. The prime minister also said he would demand that Palestinians who murdered Israelis be extradited to Israel by the PA, and that the PNC convene to erase the anti-Israel clauses in the PLO Charter.

On October 13, the eve of Netanyahu's departure, a Palestinian gunman attacked and killed one Israeli man and wounded another while they were swimming in a spring southwest of Jerusalem. But that did not prevent the prime minister from departing for Maryland. Netanyahu, however, did not arrive with his full negotiating team. It was only a few days later that he was joined by two key members of the delegation — Yitzhak Mordechai, the dovish defense minister, and the new foreign minister, Ariel Sharon. The result was that little progress was made in the first few days of the summit, while the two sides spent much of their time trying, often successfully, to circumvent U.S. efforts to impose a media blackout on the proceedings.

Already before the summit there was friction between Netanyahu and his American hosts. The prime minister refused to accept a U.S. request that the leaders come without their wives, and so Sara Netanyahu accompanied her husband to Wye. At the talks, the tension between Netanyahu and the Americans did not dissipate. After U.S. officials turned down his request to allow a group of settler leaders to spend the Sabbath with him at Wye, Israeli officials anonymously attacked the Americans in the press. On more than one occasion the summit seemed on the verge of collapse. At one point Netanyahu ordered his team to pack their bags and ready themselves for the journey back home. The Israelis even placed their suitcases on the grass outside their rooms. But the Americans did not appear overly concerned, viewing the move more as a bargaining tactic than a real threat. A few hours later Netanyahu announced that he and his team were staying. When confronted by Madeleine Albright, the prime minister tried to lay the blame for the departure threat at the feet of his spokesman.

Sharon, who had said he would never shake hands with Arafat, stuck to his pledge. According to reports leaked from the first meeting where the two were present, Sharon nodded to the Palestinian leader as he entered the room, and Arafat responded with something resembling a half-salute.

Terror threw a cloud over the talks on October 19, when a Palestinian hurled two grenades at the Beersheba central bus station, injuring more than 60 people. Right-wing leaders in Israel called on Netanyahu to return home, insisting that there was no way Israel could be expected to make peace when there was terror in its streets. In a symbolic act of protest, Netanyahu halted the talks on certain issues for a day, but he did not bail out.

As the talks dragged on, Clinton increased the pressure on the two leaders by inviting Jordan's King Hussein, who was undergoing cancer treatment in Minnesota, to visit Wye and impress upon the participants the critical need to compromise and reach a deal. Ultimately, though, the success of the summit was due to Clinton's tireless efforts. The president shuttled between Washington and Wye, spending a total of 72 hours cajoling the two sides into reaching agreement. Much of the negotiation, it later emerged, had not taken place with the Israelis and Palestinians sitting face to face, but had been conducted by the Americans, who shuttled between the two parties seeking to narrow the differences and come up with an acceptable plan. "I've been working on this deal for 17 months and I'm not prepared to defer it any longer," Clinton reportedly told Netanyahu and Arafat during the talks.

Finally, after nine days of negotiation, the two sides reached an agreement. But the Wye summit was not to be without some last-minute drama, provided by Netanyahu. With the Americans already organizing the signing ceremony, it emerged that Netanyahu was conditioning his signature on an issue entirely unrelated to the peace talks—the release of Jonathan Pollard, the U.S. naval intelligence officer in jail for spying for Israel. Clinton refused to accede to Netanyahu's demand—although he did say he would review Pollard's case—and Netanyahu backed down. Having failed on the Pollard front, the prime minister then tried to bargain down the number of Palestinian prisoners to be released under Wye, but ultimately gave up on that as well.

At the October 23 White House signing, also attended by King Hussein, Netanyahu declared that the agreement had made Israel and the region "more secure," and Arafat vowed that the Palestinians would "never go back to violence and confrontation." While Clinton said the agreement was aimed at rebuilding "trust and hope," he cautioned that "the enemies of peace could seek to extract a price from both sides." The ceremony was also punctuated by several pointed remarks, further evidence of the personal tension between Clinton and Netanyahu. In his address, for instance, Netanyahu thanked a U.S. official who had been present at Wye Plantation for supplying cigars during the talks. This was interpreted by many as a reference to the cigar episode in the Monica Lewinsky saga.

Clinton, and even more so Netanyahu, came in for criticism for failing to mention Yitzhak Rabin's name. Only the two Arab leaders present, Yasir Arafat and King Hussein, recalled the assassinated prime minister and the fact that it was Rabin who had been instrumental in initiating the peace process.

The main clauses in the Wye agreement included the following:

• 13.1 percent of the West Bank to revert from full Israeli control to joint Israeli-Palestinian control. A further 14 percent under joint control to revert to full Palestinian control. (After the implementation of Wye, the Palestinians would have full control of 18 percent of the West Bank and partial control of another 22 percent.)

• The third IDF redeployment, as stipulated under Oslo II, to be negotiated in tandem with final-status talks. (Netanyahu insisted this would be no more than 1 percent; the Palestinians demanded a much bigger chunk of land.)

• PA to beef up antiterror measures—a process that would be monitored by the U.S. Central Intelligence Agency (CIA).

• Palestinians to arrest 30 individuals suspected of terrorism.

• PA to reduce its police force by 25 percent.

• Israel to release 750 Palestinian prisoners in its jails in the course of the implementation of the agreement.

• The Palestinian National Council—the Palestinian "parliament-in-exile"—to revoke those clauses in the PLO Charter calling for Israel's destruction. President Clinton to attend the meeting of the PNC that did this.

• Gaza International Airport to open, with Israeli security presence.

• Opening of "safe-passage" corridor for Palestinians between the Gaza Strip and the West Bank.

Post-Wye Fallout

Netanyahu vigorously marketed the agreement to his constituency on his return, arguing that he had achieved the best deal possible under the circumstances. Furthermore, he said, unlike his Labor predecessors, he had been tough on Arafat, had insisted on full reciprocity in the implementation of Wye, and had stood firm on Israeli security demands. In a televised press conference at Ben-Gurion Airport on his return, he said that it had been painful to give up on "one centimeter" of land, but that his negotiating team had "fought like lions to reduce as much as possible the amount of land to be handed over." He also tried to placate the settlers—a crucial element of his political base. "You are us, we are you, we love you, we will fight for you and there isn't any government that will fight like us," he declared. In a later interview, he added: "I think the basis of peace in our area is founded on security and Israel's ability to defend itself. But also on the idea of mutuality, namely, that it's not only Israel that gives, but also that Israel receives."

But the settlers, who had worked so hard to get Netanyahu into power in 1996, felt betrayed. The Council of Jewish Settlements in Judea, Samaria, and the Gaza District strongly denounced the agreement. Moreover, they said, Netanyahu had given up on some of his basic demands at Wye, such as the extradition of Palestinians who murdered Jews. And the clauses regarding the rescinding of the PLO Covenant, they pointed out, were unclear. What's more, they added, a visit by the American president to Gaza would boost the Palestinian demand for statehood. "You were and still are the most talented at explaining what the Land of Israel is for us," said Benny Elon, a member of the right-wing Moledet Party. "But when you use that talent to explain why we must now trade territory of the Land of Israel, that is a crime that will not be forgiven." Members of Chabad (the Lubavitch Hassidic sect), who had campaigned energetically for Netanyahu during the run-up to the 1996 elections, announced that they were withdrawing their support for the prime minister. By signing Wye, they said, he had broken a promise to them not to cede any more territory. And they produced a document including such a pledge, which had been signed by Netanyahu.

In an attempt to assuage the settlers, Netanyahu announced on October 26 that he would speed up building at the disputed Har Homah hilltop in East Jerusalem. On the same day, his government survived a no-confidence vote brought by the far-right Moledet Party. This was thanks to the Labor-led opposition, which provided the prime minister with a "safety net," opposing the motion in order to save Wye.

Many questions remained unanswered by Wye. The agreement included, for example, a general statement that both sides undertook to desist from taking unilateral steps. This apparently referred to the Palestinian demand that Israel cease building settlements, and the Israeli demand that Arafat cease threatening to declare a Palestinian state. But these two highly sensitive issues did not receive any direct mention in the text. Some of the solutions offered by Wye, such as the involvement of the Americans as referees in the process and particularly the considerable role of the CIA, threatened to generate new problems and tensions. The job of the CIA, in many ways, was more than that of a referee. The organization's operatives were to be brought in to help shape the Palestinian plan to combat militant groups like Hamas. The CIA was also to monitor the Palestinian antiterror program and report back to Washington on the matter. Some Israeli officials welcomed the enhanced American role, saying it would increase Palestinian compliance. Others, however, predicted there would be disagreement between Israel and the United States over the degree of Palestinian compliance, and that this would lead to increased friction between Washington and Jerusalem. The Palestinians seemed generally pleased with the CIA role, pointing out that Israel would no longer be able to invoke the security pretext automatically as a reason not to move forward with implementation of the agreement. (Some observers noted that ever since Netanyahu took office, and especially after Wye, the American administration and Yasir Arafat had become much closer. Clinton's visit to Gaza, they said, would be another significant boost to the relationship.)

The Wye agreement did not impede the extremists. On October 26, a Palestinian shot and killed Danny Vargas, a resident of the West Bank town of Kiryat Arba. The same day, Muhammad Zalout, a 72-year-old Palestinian, was bludgeoned to death near the settlement of Itamar in the West Bank; a few days later an Israeli, Gur Hamel, turned himself over to the police. The Islamic extremists also made their intentions clear on October 29 when a Hamas man drove a car laden with 80 kilograms of explosives directly at a school bus filled with Israeli children, which was traveling along a Gaza road. An alert soldier, Alexey Neykov, saved the children when he intercepted the booby-trapped car with his army jeep, but he lost his life in the ensuing explosion. None of the children were injured, but had the bomber succeeded, the Wye agreement would most likely have been left in tatters. Arafat, fearing stepped-up efforts by extremists bent on wrecking the deal, moved swiftly. His security forces arrested hundreds of Hamas and Islamic Jihad activists; Hamas spiritual leader Sheikh Ahmad Yassin was placed under house arrest and his telephone was disconnected. Israeli officials welcomed the moves but insisted the Palestinians could still do more—like arresting Muhammad Deif, the leader of Hamas's military wing and the man at the top of Israel's "wanted" list.

In signing Wye, Netanyahu seemed to have made a strategic choice—to abandon the far right, which had helped him to power in 1996 and which was strongly opposed to any territorial compromise, and to hitch his political future to the moderate Israeli center, which supported a deal with the Palestinians. Still, a leading *Ma'ariv* political columnist, Hemi Shalev, commented that it remained to be seen whether the prime minister would fully implement Wye. Netanyahu, he said, had plunged into the Rubicon, but had yet to reach the other side.

The political and historical significance of the prime minister's move could not be ignored. By signing Wye, Netanyahu had become the first right-wing leader to agree to cede large tracts of land in the West Bank to the Palestinians. In the process he had obliterated the dream of a Greater Israel. The fact that it was a right-wing leader making these concessions in the heart of the Land of Israel meant that a significant portion of the population that had originally opposed Oslo now supported the agreement. Polls taken in the wake of the Wye agreement revealed that close to 75 percent of the nation favored the agreement—a degree of support that Rabin had never enjoyed, even in the optimistic aftermath of the signing of Oslo.

While official maps demarcating the areas where the IDF would redeploy were not publicized, the agreement generated growing uncertainty among Jewish settlers in the West Bank who feared that the pullback would transform their settlements into Israeli enclaves surrounded by Palestinian-controlled territory. According to reports in the daily *Yediot Aharonot*, about 20 settlements were to be left isolated once Israel completed the Wye-stipulated withdrawals. Residents of these settlements expressed concern for their personal safety. They feared that the army's presence on the ground would be thin and that they would be subject to terror attacks by Palestinian militants, with the perpetrators able to escape back into the areas controlled by the Palestinian Authority. They wanted to know who would control the roads leading to and from their settlements and whether their children would be safe traveling on the bus to school every day. "My children, that's the real fear," said one settler. "When it comes to your children, you put ideology to the side. But if there are good security arrangements, there's no reason to leave. We came here to stay. Unless, of course, it becomes unbearable."

Some residents of the secular settlements of Ganim and Kadim in the northern West Bank began talking of government compensation for their relocation. They argued that by turning these sites into enclaves in Palestinian-controlled territory, the government had a responsibility not only to insure their safety but also to provide them with the option of leaving and moving back across the Green Line (Israel's 1967 border) into Israel proper. This demand grew in December, after a Kadim resident was shot and wounded in a terror attack while driving home. But the government refused to talk about compensation, knowing that even mentioning it ahead of the start of final-status talks would signal to the Palestinians that Israel intended eventually to vacate these settlements. That was a negotiating card the government did not want to give up so early. Some settlers in Ganim and Kadim angrily charged the government with turning them into hostages of its policy.

Implementation of Wye

Almost immediately, problems cropped up over the implementation of the agreement. In late October, Netanyahu postponed a cabinet vote on Wye on the grounds that the Palestinians had yet to present a detailed antiterror plan. He then called Arafat in early November to request a delay until the cabinet and the Knesset had voted on the agreement. Arafat agreed and the prime minister reassured the Palestinian leader that the three transfers of land—the first scheduled for November 16—would take place.

But Netanyahu postponed the cabinet vote again in the first week of November, insisting that it would not take place until the Palestinians presented a written timetable for the arrest of 30 Palestinian militants on an Israeli "wanted" list. (At Wye the sides had reached a general agreement on the issue, but the details had not been put into writing.) Netanyahu's actions drew criticism from both the Palestinians and the Americans, but after Arafat announced that 12 of the 30 had been arrested, the prime minister convened his cabinet on November 5. After 13 hours of deliberation, the meeting ended without a vote. Scheduled to continue the next day, the meeting was further delayed after Islamic extremists carried out an unsuccessful car-bomb attack in Jerusalem. The bombers' target was the capital's bustling Mahaneh Yehudah fruit and vegetable market, but the force of the blast was weakened by faulty explosive devices. Seventeen people were injured; the two bombers died in the explosion. The cabinet finally ratified the agreement on November 11 by eight to four, with five abstentions. The majority of the ministers had not voted in favor of the agreement.

The vote did little to reduce the mistrust between the two sides, and they were soon arguing over the Palestine Covenant issue. While Netanyahu insisted that Wye required the PNC to convene and vote to remove those clauses calling for Israel's destruction, the Palestinians argued that the agreement made no reference to a vote, and that when the PNC held a scheduled meeting in Gaza in December it would simply reaffirm previous decisions to nullify the covenant's anti-Israel clauses.

Relations deteriorated further on November 12 when the government issued invitations for bids for the building of around 1,000 homes at Har Homah. The Palestinians were furious, and Arafat threatened: "We have a rifle and we are ready to take aim if they prevent us from praying in Jerusalem." Netanyahu responded by threatening to halt the redeployment. Sharon further increased the tension when he urged Jewish settlers to seize as much West Bank land as possible before the final-status talks. "Everyone should take action . . . should run, should grab more hills," he said in a November 16 speech. "We'll expand the areas . . . . Whatever is seized will be ours. Whatever isn't seized will end up in their hands." Abu Ala, the head of the Palestinian legislature, responded by calling on Palestinians to block the bulldozers with their bodies. Sharon later adjusted his remarks slightly, saying that he was encouraging settlers to expand existing settlements, not build new ones. Despite all the wrangling, on November 17, the Knesset ratified the Wye agreement by a massive margin of 75-19.

Three days later Israel began the first of the three Wye-stipulated redeployments, withdrawing from territory in the northern West Bank. Israel also released 250 Palestinian prisoners—many of them common criminals—and signed a protocol for the opening of the Gaza international airport. Amid much fanfare, Arafat officially opened the airport on November 24. "The airport is a step toward a Palestinian state with Jerusalem as its capital," he declared triumphantly.

A major row, however, soon developed over the issue of prisoner releases. While the Palestinians insisted that Israel had to free security prisoners—not criminals—the Israelis argued that Wye included no such stipulation and that they would not agree to release prisoners whom they said had "blood on their hands." The disagreement sparked major demonstrations across the West Bank and in East Jerusalem. At least four Palestinians died in the ensuing clashes with Israeli troops.

Clinton Visit to Gaza

By the time President Clinton was set to make his mid-December visit to Israel and Gaza, Netanyahu was threatening to freeze Wye, and the two sides had once again descended into mutual recrimination. Cabinet ministers began to express apprehension over the arrival of the U.S. president. Belatedly awaking to the political significance of a visit by the leader of the world's only remaining superpower to the Palestinian Authority areas, some ministers suggested that it might be better if Clinton stayed home. Netanyahu did not move to quash these statements, and he reportedly remarked in a December cabinet meeting that if Clinton wanted to come he should come, and if he didn't want to come, he didn't have to. This lukewarm Israeli reaction angered U.S. officials, and Netanyahu quickly dispatched a letter to Clinton in an attempt to limit the damage, telling the president he was a welcome guest.

The president's visit to the PA areas on December 14 was of enormous symbolic significance. It generated huge excitement on the Palestinian street and confirmed, for all the world to see, that the United States was closer than ever before to supporting the Palestinian demand for statehood. "Palestinians must recognize the right of Israel and its people to live safe and secure lives today, tomorrow and forever," Clinton told the Palestinians, and then added that "Israel must recognize the right of Palestinians to aspire to live free lives, today, tomorrow and forever." The administration had come to view the Palestinian demands as equally valid as those made by Israel.

Clinton witnessed the meeting of the Palestine National Council in Gaza's Rashad a-Shawwa hall on December 14, where the delegates fulfilled one of the major Palestinian obligations of the Wye agreement when they raised their hands to reaffirm the annulment of those clauses in the PLO Charter calling for Israel's destruction. Addressing the gathering, Clinton declared his support for the Palestinians to "determine their own destiny in their own land." He also appeared to be drawing a distinction between the Netanyahu government, which the Americans believed was undermining the process, and the Israeli public, when he declared after the vote: "You did a good thing today in raising your hands . . . . It has nothing to do with the government of Israel. You have touched the people of Israel."

The visit was rife with symbolism, and both the Israelis and Palestinians did their best to turn the trip to their advantage in the battle for international support and sympathy. There was already controversy when Clinton arrived at Israel's Ben-Gurion Airport. Prime Minister Netanyahu broke with protocol not only by speaking — normally only the presidents of the two countries would have greeted each other — but also by using the opportunity to launch an all-out attack on the Palestinians and what he said was their failure to live up to the Wye agreement. After that chastening welcome, Netanyahu suddenly became Clinton's protector at a joint press conference when he tried to shield the president from questions about his pending impeachment.

Netanyahu refused to cede anything on the Palestinian front. On one occasion he tried to impress upon the U.S. president that Israeli suffering was deeper than that of the Palestinians, when he asked students he was addressing to raise their hands if they had lost relatives in a terror attack. Arafat also did his best to showcase Palestinian suffering. At one point during Clinton's trip to Gaza, he brought in four sobbing girls whose fathers were in Israeli jails, to meet the president. For his part, Clinton did his best to tread carefully, but he did not always succeed. Israeli cabinet ministers, for instance, were angered by a comment he made that implied an equation between the suffering of the children of Israeli terror victims and that of the children of Palestinian security prisoners.

While Netanyahu declared that he was satisfied with the PNC vote, the Clinton visit did not get Wye back on track. The president departed following a December 15 summit with Arafat and Netanyahu at which he failed to extract a pledge from the Israeli leader to continue with the next phase of redeployment, scheduled for December 18.

At the end of the year the peace process was again stalled, with Netanyahu effectively stopping implementation of the agreement on the grounds that the Palestinians had not fulfilled their obligations. The Palestinians, he charged, had violated "every clause" of the agreement. But there was another explanation for Netanyahu's stance: the Knesset vote for early elections. It was clear that Netanyahu had no intention of moving ahead with the agreement and in the process alienating crucial right-wing support, ahead of a national election. With Israelis and Palestinians bickering over even the technical issues agreed upon at Wye, it seemed highly doubtful that they would begin searching for solutions to the vexing final-status issues—including Jerusalem, final borders, the refugee issue, and settlements—any time soon.

RELATIONS WITH ARAB COUNTRIES

The continuing deadlock in the peace process increased Arab criticism of the Netanyahu government and further chilled relations between Israel and many of the Arab states. Even the brief respite brought about by the signing of the Wye deal failed to ease matters between Israel and its neighbors.

Relations with Egypt

Egypt remained one of Netanyahu's most vocal critics in the Arab world, and its leaders repeatedly attacked the prime minister for not honoring obligations. Egyptian foreign minister Amre Moussa, one of Netanyahu's most strident critics, warned on April 15 that if Israel did not carry out the West Bank redeployment by mid-June, "the peace process is dead." After almost a year of not having met with Hosni Mubarak, Netanyahu flew to Cairo on April 28 for talks with the Egyptian president. According to an Egyptian government statement released after the meeting, Mubarak had advised Netanyahu "to respond positively to the U.S. [peace] initiative, which represents the minimum of what is necessary to revive the peace process."

The meeting failed to improve Israel-Egypt ties, and in July a frustrated Mubarak told Israeli journalists that "with Begin, 'yes' was yes; with Shamir, 'no' was no. With Netanyahu, there's no knowing."

Mubarak also expressed his support for a French proposal to convene an international conference to promote the Mideast peace process. But he made it clear that the Europeans could not serve as an alternative to the Americans when it came to moving the process forward. After meeting Syrian president Hafez al-Assad in late July to discuss the peace stalemate and other regional issues,

Mubarak told reporters, "Increased European involvement could help the U.S. in its peace process role, but it cannot be a substitute for American involvement." In an October 5 interview on Israel's Channel Two television station, Mubarak harshly criticized Netanyahu, saying that there was no comparison between former Likud prime minister Menachem Begin, who had signed the Camp David peace treaty with Egyptian president Anwar Sadat, and the present Likud prime minister. "Begin," he said, "was a strong man who honored his word." Mubarak was incensed by comments made by Netanyahu on the 25th anniversary of the Yom Kippur War, in which the Israeli leader said that "there is no doubt that our enemies, and in particular our enemies from the south, came to the realization during the 1973 war that they would never succeed in beating Israel through military means . . . ." The Egyptian president accused Netanyahu of "deepening the feelings of hatred between the Egyptian and Israeli people . . . ."

Mubarak, however, sounded considerably more militant in an interview in the London-based Arabic paper *Al-Hayyat*, when he said that "Egypt is not presently considering joining the 'club of nuclear nations,' but if the time comes when it needs such weaponry . . . we will not hesitate."

Relations with Jordan

Relations between Israel and Jordan through much of 1998 were still conducted in the shadow of the Khaled Mashaal affair—the botched Mossad assassination attempt on a Hamas leader in Amman in September 1997. Still, Defense Minister Mordechai did visit Jordan on January 26, where he met with King Hussein to discuss ways to end the deadlock in the peace process as well as measures for boosting security cooperation between the two countries. It was also announced in early February that King Hussein had sent one million dollars to President Weizman as compensation for the families of the seven Israeli schoolgirls who had been gunned down by a Jordanian soldier in March 1997.

With the resignation of Mossad chief Danny Yatom on February 24, the official Jordanian tone toward Jerusalem began to soften. Following a series of meetings between high-level Israeli and Jordanian officials on March 8-10, Crown Prince Hassan met with Netanyahu in Tel Aviv. "Prime Minister Netanyahu and I have had our differences, and Jordan and Israel have had their differences . . . . But we are looking for a new spirit of mutual respect," Hassan declared at a joint press conference with the Israeli prime minister. According to a joint statement, the two countries had agreed to expand their cooperation in several areas, including electricity and the utilization of water resources. Following a March 9 meeting between Israeli trade and industry minister Natan Sharansky and his Jordanian counterpart, Hani Mulqi, the two countries signed a series of agreements aimed at improving bilateral trade. Israeli infrastructure minister Ariel Sharon, however, caused some concern in Amman when he announced on Israel TV on March 15 that Israel had not abandoned its efforts to eliminate Mashaal.

The official thaw in relations was not reflected on the popular level, since many

Jordanians felt there had been no tangible peace dividend following the 1995 treaty between the two countries. A survey conducted by the University of Jordan's Center for Strategic Studies found that a full 80 percent of Jordanians regarded Israel as the enemy. This was in stark contrast to a similar poll conducted in 1994 that showed 80 percent eager for peace with Israel. "People accepted the idea of trying peace in the beginning," said Jordanian political analyst Hani Hourani. "Since then, there have been two or three shocks that spoiled their optimism, in addition to their anger at Israel's provocation of the Palestinians and refusal to implement signed agreements."

After meeting with Crown Prince Hassan on May 30, Tel Aviv mayor Roni Milo announced that his city and the Jordanian capital, Amman, were to become sister cities.

Relations with Lebanon

Lebanon remained Israel's only active war front, and it continued to exact a heavy price. An ever-growing list of casualties spurred public debate in Israel over the IDF's presence in south Lebanon, where the army continued to occupy a security zone it had imposed at the end of the Lebanon War in the mid-1980s.

Defense Minister Yitzhak Mordechai rekindled the Lebanon debate when he announced in a January 1 interview in the Paris-based Lebanese weekly *Al-Watan al-Arabi* that Israel was ready to implement the 1978 UN Security Council Resolution 425, which called on Israel to withdraw from Lebanon. He did, however, attach a condition: If Israel withdrew, the Lebanese government would have to uphold its obligations under 425 and establish effective security control in areas that Israel evacuated. "Let's put 425 on the table and talk about new security arrangements," Mordechai said in the interview. "Not peace or normalization, only security arrangements." Later he added: "I am not frightened by the three words 'U.N. Resolution 425.' "

Lebanese president Elias Hrawi termed Mordechai's remarks the "first positive sign in 20 years," but there was no real movement beyond the exchange of statements, and the almost daily skirmishes in the security zone returned to the headlines. On February 26, three Israeli soldiers were killed in south Lebanon when a mortar shell fired by members of the Iranian-backed Shi'ite Hezballah movement slammed into their position.

At a cabinet meeting on March 1, Netanyahu announced that Israel was ready to accept Resolution 425 and withdraw from south Lebanon as long as the Lebanese government was prepared to cooperate by taking responsibility for security arrangements. Some commentators said the prime minister's statements reflected a change in the traditional Israeli insistence on a peace treaty with Lebanon and full normalization as conditions for withdrawal. Syrian and Lebanese officials, however, dismissed Netanyahu's remarks and continued to demand that Israel withdraw unconditionally from south Lebanon. In mid-March,

Sharon added his voice to the growing call for a unilateral withdrawal from the security zone. He suggested that Israel should carry out a limited withdrawal first in order to gauge the response of the Lebanese government and Hezballah. If the response was favorable, then Sharon recommended full withdrawal, with a clear warning that if Hezballah tried to cross into Israel to carry out attacks, retribution would be swift and painful.

The issue of withdrawal was back on the national agenda on April 1 when the security cabinet reversed Israel's traditional rejection of 425 as a basis for withdrawal from Lebanon and passed a unanimous decision adopting it. But few believed that this meant the troops were on the verge of coming home.

A solution that did not include Lebanon's patron, Syria, appeared highly impractical. Plans to circumvent the Syrian leader, some Assad-watchers said, might even encourage him to tighten his control over Beirut for fear Israel was trying to make a deal with Lebanon behind his back. Assad was certainly not about to relinquish his leverage on Israel—in the form of Hezballah attacks on the IDF—without getting back the strategic Golan Heights. "Without a simultaneous Israeli promise of retreat from the Golan Heights," wrote leading Middle East analyst Ehud Ya'ari, "there is absolutely no prospect of any agreement on the orderly transfer of the security zone to the regular Lebanese Army. Damascus is not about to discard its trump card in the Golan Heights game—the ability to spill Israeli blood by using its Hezballah proxy" (*Jerusalem Report,* April 30, 1998).

Actually, Lebanon was more vital for Assad than the Golan. Around one million Syrians were working there, and the Syrian political-military elite was benefiting from drug trafficking and smuggling in Lebanon. The Syrian leader also understood that were Lebanon allowed to make a deal with Israel that entailed an IDF withdrawal from the south, there would inevitably be international calls for a Syrian withdrawal from Lebanon as well.

Even some of Netanyahu's aides did not seem to take the security cabinet decision too seriously, suggesting that the Lebanon gambit was more an attempt to embarrass Assad, by showing him up as impeding the return of Arab territory, than a real effort to extricate Israel from the security zone. It was not surprising, then, that both the Americans and the French showed little enthusiasm for the Israeli decision and confined themselves to monitoring reactions.

Meanwhile, hostilities continued in south Lebanon on a daily basis. On May 12, Israeli jets bombarded guerrilla bases, killing an estimated 10 people. In one week of intense fighting later in the month, at least five Hezballah fighters were killed, while four members of Israel's proxy South Lebanon Army lost their lives. On May 27, two Israeli infantry soldiers were killed by a Hezballah roadside bomb in the security zone, and another two died under similar circumstances in June.

As part of a complex deal that took ten months to negotiate, the body of Israeli naval commando Itamar Ilia, killed during a failed raid in south Lebanon in September 1997, was brought back to Israel on a French military cargo plane on June 25, in exchange for the corpses of 40 Lebanese gunmen and the release of 60 Lebanese from jails in Israel and south Lebanon.

Several weeks later, on July 30, an Israeli soldier was killed and five others injured in the security zone when Hezballah gunmen fired mortar shells at an Israeli outpost there. When, in mid-August, two more soldiers and an Israeli civilian were killed in Hezballah roadside bombings in the security zone, the IDF's Northern Command expressed growing concern that the Shi'ite militants were becoming increasingly adept at predicting Israeli troop movements. Security officials explained that it was very difficult to combat committed guerrilla organizations like the Hezballah. In response to the mid-August deaths, Minister of Internal Security Avigdor Kahalani called for Israel to strike at Lebanese infrastructure every time an Israeli soldier was killed in the security zone.

After a senior member of the Shi'ite Amal organization was killed during an IDF artillery bombardment on August 25, Hezballah fired Katyusha rockets into northern Israel in retaliation, wounding several people in the town of Kiryat Shmona. (It was the first cross-border rocket attack in a year.) Two Israeli paratroopers were killed on September 22 when their armored personnel carrier went over the edge of a 300-meter cliff in the security zone, and another two soldiers died and six others were injured on October 5 when they were hit by a Hezballah roadside bomb near the Hatzbaya outpost in the security zone. In a ten-day period in November, seven soldiers lost their lives in Lebanon, bringing to 22 the number killed since the beginning of the year.

The rising death toll again spurred public demands that the government find a solution to the Lebanon quagmire. The "Four Mothers" protest group, set up to pressure the government into pulling out of Lebanon, stepped up its activity, and opinion polls showed increasing support for a unilateral withdrawal from the security zone, even if it was still only a minority who supported such a move.

Tension flared again in the north after an Israeli fighter jet accidentally bombed a home near the town of Baalbeck on December 22, killing a woman and six of her children. According to an initial air force investigation, the actual target was a Hezballah radio installation, and pilot error was the reason for the mistake. In retaliation, Hezballah fired Katyusha rockets into northern Israel the following day, injuring 16 people and damaging over 100 homes. A woman in the northern border town of Kiryat Shmona lost her unborn twins.

Relations with Syria

There was no tangible progress on the Syrian track throughout 1998. While Netanyahu continued to insist that he was ready to return to the negotiating table if Assad arrived without any preconditions, the Syrians continued to demand that the talks resume from where they had left off with the previous Labor government. (There had been reports that Rabin had given the Americans a guarantee that, in exchange for full peace and adequate security arrangements, Israel would be willing to withdraw from the Golan.) Israeli coalition arithmetic also made any progress on the Syrian track unlikely. Real movement on the Golan Heights, the prime minister knew, would result in the loss of the Third Way Party's four votes—a move that would spell the end of the government.

Syria continued to criticize Israel publicly, and in midyear Damascus called for diplomatic and economic pressure on Jerusalem. There were a few encouraging signs, though, like an informal June meeting between Israeli and Syrian officials who were attending a forum at Rice University in Houston under the auspices of the James Baker Institute, a foreign-policy think tank. Several months after that meeting, reports emerged that Uzi Arad, the prime minister's strategic adviser, who had been in Houston, had intimated that the government would agree to a Golan withdrawal proportionate to the level of security guarantees. On July 22, however, the Knesset voted 65-32 to approve a preliminary bill that would make an Israeli withdrawal from the Golan contingent on a national referendum and an absolute majority in the Knesset. (The bill still required three more readings before becoming law.)

After returning from an early August trip of Labor party leaders to the United States, Knesset member Shlomo Ben-Ami revealed that American officials had told the group that Assad was keen on renewing talks. The reason, according to Ben-Ami, was the Syrian leader's fear of the emerging Israel-Turkey strategic alliance. Confronted with Ben-Ami's assertions, Netanyahu's senior adviser, David Bar-Illan, reiterated his boss's position—that Israel was willing to resume talks, but without any preconditions. "We will take into account—but without any obligation—the negotiations between Syria and the Labor government, which did not result in any written agreement," he said. Addressing Assad's fear of the Israel-Turkey relationship, Bar-Illan commented that the alliance was a defensive one, but that "if it makes Assad want to return to the negotiating table, it has had a salutary consequence."

The resumption of talks seemed to become even less likely when Infrastructure Minister Ariel Sharon approved the expansion of four settlements on the Golan Heights in August, including the construction of 2,300 housing units and 2,500 vacation units. Yitzhak Mordechai did generate some speculation in August when he told the German newspaper *Focus* that the "depth of withdrawal from the Golan would match the depth of security." He seemed to be slightly rephrasing Yitzhak Rabin's line that the depth of withdrawal (from the Golan) would be determined by the depth of peace.

Syria was highly critical of the agreement reached at Wye Plantation, accusing Arafat of having capitulated to Israeli demands. The Syrian media attacked the deal, saying Arafat had failed to extract Israeli commitments to a third withdrawal and to freeze settlement construction. By the end of the year there was still no movement on the Israel-Syria track.

Crisis in the Gulf

Another Saddam Hussein-induced crisis over United Nations' weapons inspections hit the Middle East in early February, sending tens of thousands of concerned Israelis flocking to gas-mask distribution centers to refresh their protective equipment. As speculation grew in the media about Saddam's possible nonconventional capability, the country became increasingly edgy. Israelis were also skeptical of assurances by their political leaders that another Scud barrage was highly unlikely. There was a run on pharmacies as anxious customers snapped up anthrax antibiotics, and shops quickly sold out of plastic sheeting and tape used to seal rooms against poison gas. (According to unofficial estimates, the cost of the crisis to the Israeli economy was in the region of 450 million shekels [$130 million].)

While most Israelis did not panic, some of the fear and uncertainty engendered by Saddam's 1991 blitz of Israel returned. The crisis also sparked questions about the vulnerability of Israel's civilian rear to a long-range missile attack, as well as questions about the possible erosion of the public's stamina to withstand crises.

There were also suggestions that Israelis' self-image had been irrevocably changed by the 1991 crisis, and that the 1998 Gulf showdown was further proof of this. "Previous wars," wrote Yossi Klein Halevi in the *Jerusalem Report* (March 19, 1998), "produced images of solidarity and patriotism, symbolized by Israelis flying home from abroad to join their units at the front. Now, this almost-war has reproduced the newer, unsettling images of 1991: an increase, even if exaggerated by the local media, of Israelis flying out of Ben-Gurion Airport for sudden 'vacations.' A surge in hotel bookings at remote Eilat, 'just in case.' Jostling at army distribution centers for scarce children's gas masks. A rush to purchase plastic sheeting of questionable efficacy for sealing rooms."

Some Israeli leaders lamented what they perceived as an erosion in the traditional Israeli norm of stoicism under stress. But the government also had to shoulder some of the burden for the public disquiet. Having decided to halt gas-mask production in 1997, it suddenly had to rush in planeloads of masks from Holland, Sweden, and Germany. Nevertheless, *Yediot Aharonot* columnist Nahum Barnea suggested that Israelis had responded well to the crisis. "The Israeli public was forced to contend this time not just with the danger of missiles, but with a government that doesn't take responsibility, and with a media, especially television, that takes responsibility only for ratings," he wrote. "In the face of those difficult conditions, most Israelis functioned well: They continued to live normally, updated their gas masks, cleaned the air-raid shelters and hoped for the best. There were, of course, also hysterical Israelis. Each of them got his time, if not on Channel 2 then on Channel 1." (Channel 2 is Israel's commercial TV channel; Channel 1 is state-run.)

On the diplomatic front, the U.S. strongly urged Israel not to retaliate if attacked again by Saddam. "Yes, the United States would prefer—very strongly urge—the Israelis not to get involved, even if attacked," said American defense secretary William Cohen. President Ezer Weizman, however, made it clear that if Israel was attacked, "the missile won't be one-way."

While there was some relief when the crisis was finally averted, the settlement brokered by UN secretary-general Kofi Annan was met with little enthusiasm inside Israel, where many believed it was only a matter of time until the next Gulf crisis. "Even if the crisis is resolved," said Netanyahu, "it is clear to us that we live in a new Middle East, a Middle East with radical regimes that are developing ballistic missiles . . . hostile to Israel."

The crisis, at least in the short term, seemed to bolster the prime minister. Political observers suggested that Netanyahu's view of his neighborhood—a threatened Israel constantly fighting for its survival in a nasty region—was reinforced by the crisis. Indeed, while Barak had led Netanyahu in the polls for months, a mid-February Gallup poll showed Netanyahu trailing the Labor leader by a single point. The survey also revealed that, by 47 percent to 41 percent, a plurality of Israelis preferred Netanyahu to Barak at the helm during the emergency. And there were reports that the prime minister had made it clear to his aides that the immediate conclusion to be drawn from recent events was that the government should proceed even more cautiously in its negotiations with the Palestinians. (As in 1991, some West Bank Palestinians demonstrated in support of Saddam Hussein, burning U.S. and Israeli flags and waving models of Iraqi Scuds.)

OTHER FOREIGN RELATIONS

Israel-Turkey ties continued to strengthen through 1998. One example was the January 7 joint naval maneuver off Haifa—called Reliant Mermaid—in which ships from the U.S. Sixth Fleet, Israel, and Turkey participated. A Jordanian admiral was in attendance as an observer, leading to strong criticism from Iraq, Iran, Syria, and Egypt, all fearing the emergence of a new Israel-Turkey-Jordan strategic alliance. Turkish prime minister Mesut Yilmaz made an early September visit to Israel and held talks on economic and military ties. Yilmaz, who dismissed Syrian criticism of his visit, also toured the Palestinian Authority areas.

UN secretary-general Kofi Annan visited Israel during a late March tour of the Middle East and announced his support for a solution in South Lebanon. He also urged Israel not to put too much pressure on Yasir Arafat.

British foreign minister Robin Cook made a highly controversial trip to Israel in March. Cook originally planned to visit the disputed Har Homah site on March 17 with Palestinian leader Faisal Husseini, but after Israel protested he agreed to meet Husseini elsewhere, and to travel to Har Homah with cabinet secretary Danny Naveh. While touring the site, Cook briefly met and shook hands with a member of the Palestinian Legislative Council who was also visiting. Incensed Israeli officials accused the foreign minister of breaking an agreement not to meet with Palestinian officials at the site. Cook denied he had agreed to any such arrangement, but Netanyahu cut short his meeting with Cook in protest, and canceled a dinner engagement with him. "I've had three four-course meals already since I came to the Middle East. It is something of a mercy to be spared a further meal," was Cook's caustic response.

When British prime minister Tony Blair visited Israel and the PA areas during a mid-April trip to the region, he adopted a much more conciliatory tone with his Israeli hosts. During the visit it was announced that both Arafat and Netanyahu would travel to London on May 4 for separate meetings with U.S. secretary of state Madeleine Albright, in an effort to forge agreement on the second West Bank redeployment.

In late April a Ugandan delegation, seeking to attract foreign investment, visited Israel—the first official Ugandan visit since Idi Amin broke off ties with Israel in the 1970s.

Israel and the European Union were at loggerheads in mid-May when the European Commission called upon the EU to look into barring any imports from settlements in the West Bank and Gaza that benefited from trade privileges afforded to Israel. The commission also insisted that Israeli exporters cease the practice of claiming that goods produced by the Palestinians in the territories were "made in Israel." Netanyahu flatly rejected the warnings and countered that if the EU took such a step, it would "put an end to any attempt of the European Union to have any kind of facilitating role in the peace process."

During a four-day visit to China in late May, Netanyahu met with officials who assured him that they were not supplying, and would not supply, Iran with nuclear weapons technology.

Israel-Kenya ties received a boost when Israel dispatched an IDF Home Front Command rescue team to Nairobi after the August 7 bomb attack aimed at the U.S. embassy in the capital. The 150-person team arrived in Nairobi the day after the huge explosion. Working around the clock, sometimes in highly precarious conditions, the Israeli team succeeded in locating four survivors and 29 bodies as they sifted through the rubble. The tragedy turned into something of a media coup for Israel as TV crews covering the attack focused their cameras on the Israeli team's rescue efforts. It was also an opportunity for Israel to repay a favor to Kenya, which had allowed Israeli planes to land in Nairobi on their way back from the Entebbe rescue operation in 1976.

Relations with the United States

Relations between Washington and Jerusalem became increasingly strained in the course of 1998 as a result of the stalled peace process. During much of the year the president's personal troubles seemed to leave him with little time for the Middle East. Dennis Ross continued his shuttle missions to Jerusalem and Ramallah, but seemed to be making little headway. Personal relations between Netanyahu and Clinton also appeared to be at an all-time low. The president did not offer Netanyahu a formal White House lunch during his January 20 trip, and the Israeli leader chose to preface his session with Clinton by meeting with some of the president's major political foes, including House of Representatives Speaker Newt Gingrich and right-wing Christian leader Jerry Falwell.

Madeleine Albright vented her frustration with the Israeli leadership when she met a group of U.S. Jewish leaders on March 29. The U.S. administration, she told them, was "not interested in a phony process," and so one option "is simply for us to remove ourselves."

During a late May visit to Israel, Newt Gingrich was, initially, outspoken on the issue of Jerusalem, telling the Knesset that "even Arafat doesn't believe it's going to cease to be the capital of Israel." Gingrich, who supported moving the U.S. embassy from Tel Aviv to Jerusalem, had planned to lay a symbolic corner-stone on the plot set aside in the capital for the embassy, but changed his mind after administration officials persuaded him that such a gesture would incense the Palestinians. He adopted a more low-key approach on all Jerusalem-related questions and announced during an interview at his hotel that he wasn't going "any-where near" Har Homah, the disputed hilltop on the southern edge of the capital where infrastructure was being laid for a Jewish housing project. When Jerusalem mayor Ehud Olmert insisted that Gingrich visit the site, a compromise was reached whereby the Speaker agreed to view Har Homah from a distance.

With Clinton facing impeachment hearings in Congress, there were suggestions that a foreign policy success would help to divert attention from the Lewinsky scandal. An Israeli-Palestinian deal on the second redeployment in the West Bank was an attractive target, but Ross's September visit to Israel seemed to go completely unnoticed in Washington. "No one in Washington is even talking about Ross," moaned a frustrated Ran Cohen, a member of the left-wing Meretz Party who was in the United States in mid-September. "It's as if his visit just isn't happening . . . . The paralysis of the president, the administration and the Democratic Party means paralysis in the peace process."

On the Israeli right many viewed the president's distraction as a positive development. Some jokingly pointed to the Lewinsky affair as a sign of "divine intervention." "I have no doubt what Bibi would say if you had to ask him whether he prefers a strong president or a president who is neutralized," said Likud member Reuven Rivlin. "Arafat understands that he will not be getting any help from the Americans now." But the glee on the Israeli right over the president's predicament was to be short-lived. Clinton cajoled both Netanyahu and Arafat into attending the mid-October Wye summit and then forged an agreement between the two sides that included the 13.1 percent West Bank withdrawal that the Israeli right had fought so hard to prevent.

If personal ties between Clinton and Netanyahu remained poor in the period under review, that did not affect the president's popularity among Israelis. A poll conducted by the Dahaf Institute on August 19—after Monica Lewinsky testified before the grand jury in Washington—revealed that 88 percent of Israelis supported the American president.

While 1998 was a year of distinctly chilly Israel-U.S. ties, for the Palestinians it was a year of significant improvement in relations with Washington. The initial sign of a change came in January, when Madeleine Albright pointed to Israel's hard-line approach to the Palestinians as a reason why Washington was finding it difficult to cobble together an anti-Saddam Arab alliance. There were other indications, like arms sales to several Arab states, a lifting of the ban on investments in Lebanon, and the removal of Iran from the list of drug-trading nations. And in late November, the administration engineered a donor conference in the United States, where a total of $3 billion was pledged to the Palestinians.

Officials in the Israeli Foreign Ministry, however, insisted that the American strategy was aimed at limiting attempts by Russia to reassert its influence in the Middle East, and was not the result of worsening ties with Israel. "There is no comparison between Israel's position in the U.S. and that of the Palestinians," argued Zalman Shoval, Israel's ambassador in Washington. "Israel is a strategic ally; the Palestinians are seen as a problem that must be solved because it impacts on wider U.S. Middle East interests."

Shoval's reasoning was supported by the signing of an Israel-U.S. strategic memorandum in October. The focus of Israeli and American attention was Iran's long-range Shihab 3 missile, which was expected to be ready for testing by early 1999. With a range of 1,400 kilometers, the missile, which could be fitted with both conventional and nonconventional warheads, would be able to strike from western Iran at targets anywhere in Israel as well as at U.S. facilities in Turkey.

U.S. civilian and military aid to Israel—which amounted to a total of $3 billion annually—also remained unchanged during the period under review, and a further $1.2 billion was earmarked to assist in the financing of the Wye-negotiated troop pullback. In late January, when Finance Minister Yaakov Ne'eman traveled to Washington, Israeli officials began talking with the U.S. administration and members of Congress about a phased reduction in American economic aid. The plan was to effect a gradual reduction of the $1.2 billion in annual civilian aid that Israel received from Washington, while the $1.8 billion in military aid would not be touched. (Some leading Israeli economists welcomed the move, insisting that with a $100-billion-a-year economy and an annual gross domestic product of $17,000, Israel could absorb the loss without too much discomfort.)

Newt Gingrich's resignation following the Republicans' losses in the November 3 midterm elections was seen as a blow to Netanyahu, who had been able to count on the Republican leader to help deflect administration pressure on Israel.

In late February, the Supreme Court ruled that 18-year-old Samuel Sheinbein, whom the United States wanted extradited for the brutal 1997 murder of a Maryland teenager, could claim protection under a 1978 statute that prevented the extradition of Israeli nationals in criminal cases. In a bid to avoid prosecution, Sheinbein, who had never lived in Israel, had fled there and claimed citizenship on the ground that his father was an Israeli national. Despite considerable criticism in the United States and anger in Maryland, Israel's Justice Ministry and State Attorney's Office began preparing to prosecute Sheinbein, and in March Sheinbein was charged in the Tel Aviv district court. The following month, Israeli legislators closed the loophole in the extradition law by adjusting the statute to allow for Israeli citizens who are not residents of the country to be extradited for crimes perpetrated abroad. The law, however, was not retroactive.

Israel and American Jews

The subject of religious pluralism continued to plague relations between Israel and American Jewry. The conversion issue, which had exploded in 1997 when the Orthodox religious parties introduced a bill that effectively barred non-Orthodox conversion in Israel, continued to fester in 1998. It briefly flared up again in early February when the Chief Rabbinate officially rejected the recommendations of the Ne'eman Commission, which would have given the non-Orthodox denominations a degree of recognition in Israel on matters of personal status.

Reform and Conservative leaders in the United States continued to vent their frustration at the efforts of the Israeli Orthodox authorities to delegitimize them. In a *Jerusalem Report* interview (July 6, 1998), Rabbi Eric Yoffie, president of the Reform movement's Union of American Hebrew Congregations (UAHC), lashed out at Israel's chief rabbis, saying that they had poisoned relations between the various denominations of Judaism in the United States. According to Yoffie, American Orthodox bodies were increasingly reluctant to have contact with Reform and Conservative rabbinical groups, and this was the result of vilification coming out of Israel, specifically from the Chief Rabbinate. "Reasonable Israelis, including modern Orthodox, tell us the chief rabbis are irrelevant. I disagree," said Yoffie. "They are senior government employees. And their behavior, the lack of respect they have shown non-Orthodox rabbis—from refusing to shake our hands to calling us 'clowns'—is frightful. Non-Orthodox, North American Jews—who, as it is, don't understand why their rabbis cannot perform a single life-cycle ritual in Israel—aren't willing to tolerate it anymore."

Secretary of State Madeleine Albright tried to enlist the support of U.S. Jewish leaders on a number of occasions in her efforts to pressure Netanyahu into making concessions, but she had little success. According to media reports, Albright told key Jewish leaders in a mid-May meeting that because of the administration's failure to persuade Israel to move on the Palestinian track, U.S. credibility was being harmed, especially in the Middle East. The leaders, though, reportedly rejected Albright's "linkage," arguing that Israel's behavior was not adversely affecting American policy.

The General Assembly of the Council of Jewish Federations, the biggest annual meeting of North American Jewry, was held for the first time ever in Israel, in mid-November. Five thousand people attended the GA sessions in Jerusalem, during which a group of philanthropists announced that they were backing a new project called "Birthright Israel." This would bring every Jewish youth in the world between 15 and 26 years old on a ten-day expenses-paid tour of the Jewish state.

POLITICAL DEVELOPMENTS

Netanyahu Battles On

The domestic political scene was stormy and riveting in the period under review. On several occasions the Netanyahu government looked to be on the verge of collapse, but the prime minister, as he had done many times in the past, skillfully navigated back from the brink. That was until December 21, when the coalition became so unruly and divided that it self-destructed, and the Knesset voted to pass the first reading of a bill calling for the disbanding of the legislature—a move that almost certainly spelled early elections. (The regularly scheduled elections would not be until late in the year 2000.)

The first political bombshell came in the very first week of 1998. During intense budget wrangling, Foreign Minister and Deputy Prime Minister David Levy announced that he would vote against the budget, and he threatened to resign from the cabinet. Most seasoned political observers dismissed Levy's threats as a negotiating ploy to extract budgetary concessions. But on January 4, Levy convened a press conference, broadcast live on TV, where he lashed out at Netanyahu. Finally, citing the lack of progress on the peace front and what he said was the government's insensitivity toward the poorer classes, he announced he was resigning. Levy accused the prime minister of not honoring an agreement the two had reached six months earlier, in which Netanyahu had handed Levy a signed promise to fund education, scholarships for poor students, and housing for young couples. With regard to the peace process, Levy accused the government of "flying to nowhere."

Levy's Gesher Party, which had five seats, exited the coalition with his resignation, leaving Netanyahu with the narrowest of Knesset majorities, 61–59, and there was wide speculation that the government was on the verge of collapse. Levy's decision undoubtedly turned up the pressure on Netanyahu, making it much more difficult for the prime minister to maneuver between the conflicting demands of his coalition partners. While right-wing members of his coalition threatened to bring him down if he agreed to a West Bank pullback, the four members of the centrist Third Way Party and Defense Minister Yitzhak Mordechai were saying the exact opposite—that they would withdraw if the government did not move forward on redeployment.

Since he hoped to appeal largely to working-class Sephardim, Levy's departure appeared well-timed, coming amid a deepening economic recession marked by growing unemployment and a row over funding for social programs in the heat of the 1998 budget debate. Initial polls showed Gesher getting seven seats. "After 18 months in government with the Likud, Gesher was heading for self-destruction," said Maxim Levy, David's younger brother and himself a Gesher Knesset member. "If we'd stayed with the Likud, with its insensitive social policies and foot-dragging on peace, what would we have been able to offer voters? Politically, we'd have been dead meat." But Gesher had to prove itself, and it faced a formidable opponent in the battle for the Sephardi vote—the ultra-Orthodox Shas Party. Shas leader Arye Deri was quick to criticize Levy's decision, saying that the Gesher leader had "committed [political] suicide."

Maxim Levy, however, was confident Netanyahu would not succeed in navigating the political minefield that faced him in the early part of the year, which included having to deal with the overdue West Bank troop pullback, the highly explosive conversion bill, and growing social unrest. But Levy was proven woefully wrong as Netanyahu managed to weather the resignation of his foreign minister and keep his fractious coalition together. Not that life was easy for the prime minister or Likud coalition whip Meir Sheetrit. "Not in all my years in the Knesset can I recall a period of such extortion," Sheetrit complained during yet another bout of coalition wrangling.

Talk of a national unity government had surfaced in January, ahead of Netanyahu's trip to Washington, where he was expected to discuss the overdue West Bank troop redeployment with President Clinton. With hard-liners threatening to topple the government if the prime minister returned from the United States with a peace package, moderate MKs in Shas, the Third Way, and the immigrant party Yisrael ba-Aliya were all urging Netanyahu to initiate talks with Labor. For his part, Labor leader Ehud Barak did not sound entirely opposed to the idea, declaring in a January speech that it was "up to Netanyahu to make the first move." Talks in early May initiated by Netanyahu did not yield a unity government, and opposition Labor members dismissed the meeting as an effort by Netanyahu to scare his divided coalition.

The fact that the government lost several no-confidence votes in 1998 reflected on Netanyahu's coalition woes. But disgruntled coalition members could afford to absent themselves from these votes, because under the new direct election system, an absolute majority of 61 in the 120-seat Knesset was required to bring down the government.

Despite his unruly coalition, Netanyahu continued to defy his critics and those who foretold his imminent downfall. Through July, political observers predicted that if the prime minister did not reach a deal with Arafat by July 29—the start of the Knesset's three-month summer recess—his government would fall apart. But it did not.

Netanyahu did receive a blow, though, in late July when the Knesset passed the preliminary reading of a bill to disband the legislature and move to early elections. Legislators of both the left and the right supported the bill, seeming to indicate that no one felt able to gauge Netanyahu's true intentions with regard to the peace process. Significantly, three of the four Third Way MKs—a centrist party in the ruling coalition—supported the bill, as did former finance minister and Likud MK Dan Meridor, who had resigned from the government in 1997 after a showdown with Netanyahu. (The final vote was 60-6, as many coalition members, realizing they had no chance of defeating the motion, chose to stay away from the plenum. To be passed, the bill would have to go through three more readings, and would ultimately require the support of 61 of the 120 Knesset members in the final reading.)

As in the first 18 months of his term, Netanyahu continued to face charges from inside and outside his coalition that he was duplicitous and untrustworthy. Yet the polls showed that his public support was holding firm. A late July poll in the daily *Ma'ariv* revealed that Netanyahu still led Barak, 42 percent to 41.

While Netanyahu had survived into the summer, it was clear that sooner or later he would have to make a decision with regard to the peace process. Leading Labor MK Uzi Baram predicted that if the prime minister did actually intend moving forward on the Palestinian track, he would have to convince David Levy and his five-member Gesher faction to rejoin the government, and also persuade members of the far right that it was in their interest to stay put, so as to have a say in the final-status talks with the Palestinians. Then, said Baram, Netanyahu might well survive until elections in 2000. Labor leaders pointed out that Barak would have a hard time resisting a unity offer if Netanyahu made one after concluding a deal with the Palestinians—a move that would help him sweep the centrist vote and so remove early elections as an option for Labor.

If Netanyahu was having a tough time trying to keep his often-errant coalition members in line, he could take solace from the fact that the Labor Party, with Barak at its head, was hardly proving an effective political foe. Barak attacked Netanyahu in a July Knesset debate, saying that the country was "being run by a dishonorable man," that world leaders were no longer prepared to talk to the prime minister, and that the only one remaining on Netanyahu's side was his American political strategist, Arthur Finkelstein. But, in a devastating response, Netanyahu took the podium and launched a withering attack on Labor's competence and integrity, and then pointed out that Barak had his own (alleged) U.S. spin doctor, Stanley Greenberg.

In the absence of a clear opposition voice, President Ezer Weizman emerged as the prime minister's most coherent critic. He publicly blamed the prime minister on more than one occasion for the deadlock in the peace process, and he overstepped the largely ceremonial powers of his office to call for early elections. The move was interpreted by many as an expression by the president that he hoped Netanyahu would be replaced. On one occasion Weizman blamed the prime minister for undermining the credibility of the presidency by sending him to Arab leaders laden with promises which, ultimately, were not fulfilled. While some observers suggested that the attacks by the popular Weizman hurt Netanyahu, the president was ultimately powerless, and his outspoken criticism actually helped Netanyahu by relegating Barak and the rest of the opposition to the sidelines. After returning from Wye Plantation in late October, Netanyahu launched an all-out effort to stabilize his coalition. He tried to mollify the right with promises of construction at Har Homah and by turning a blind eye to settlement activity. He also repeatedly warned the right that if they brought him down then they would get Ehud Barak. In early November the government narrowly prevailed in a preliminary vote on the 1999 national budget, thanks to the abstention of Abd al-Wahab Darawshe's Arab Democratic Party. Darawshe's vote evoked the wrath of the Labor-led opposition as well as large sections of the Arab electorate. According to media reports, Darawshe had abstained at the behest of Yasir Arafat, who did not want the government to fall until it had ratified the Wye agreement. But the prime minister, who had slammed Yitzhak Rabin for relying on Arab votes for a parliamentary majority on the peace process, was attacked by Likud MKs for relying on Darawshe to help pass the budget. Sensing the potential political damage, Netanyahu declared that in future he would not depend on "non-Zionist" support.

Still, the vote was yet another sign that the ruling coalition was crumbling. In another effort to stabilize his government, Netanyahu initiated talks with David Levy, aimed at bringing him and his Gesher faction back into the coalition. Initially it appeared that Levy, having spent almost a year in the political wilderness, was on his way back, this time as infrastructure minister. But the emerging arrangement soon ran into trouble. Netanyahu aides were quoted anonymously in the daily *Ha'aretz* saying that Levy had turned down an offer of the treasury portfolio because he was not cut out for the hard work that the job of finance minister required. Resistance to the deal also began to grow within the Likud because of the proposed inclusion of several hundred Gesher delegates in the Likud Central Committee. Then Levy had a change of heart and announced that he did want to be minister of finance. But Netanyahu, a vociferous advocate of the free market, was not keen to relinquish the post to the welfare-minded Levy. The deal ultimately fell through, and Levy launched a bitter attack on Netanyahu in the Knesset plenum as the prime minister listened from his seat.

In late November there were reports that Ariel Sharon had approached Barak about the possibility of a national unity government, but had come away discouraged. By early December there was growing talk among right-wing politicians about the need to go to early elections, and then to form a broad-based right-wing party with a candidate at its head who would run against Netanyahu. Among those mentioned as potential leaders were Benny (Binyamin) Begin, son of the late Menachem Begin, who had resigned his cabinet post in January 1997 when Netanyahu signed the Hebron agreement. Other suggested names were Education Minister Yitzhak Levy, the head of the National Religious Party (NRP), and Likud hard-liner Uzi Landau. NRP Knesset members, however, were divided. While some warned that an early election was a dangerous adventure that might bring the left to power, others were enthusiastic about the prospects of a Greater Israel party uniting all right-wingers.

The bill for disbanding the Knesset, which had passed a preliminary reading in late July, reached the plenum again in early December. In a day of high drama, the opposition Laborites accused Netanyahu of practicing political opportunism in a desperate bid to survive. Reports emerged that, in an effort to defeat the bill, Netanyahu had tried to enlist the support of some Arab MKs by promising that he would move ahead with the implementation of Wye, while at the same time seeking to secure right-wing support by asserting that he had no such intention. As the vote drew closer, it became clear to the prime minister that he did not have enough backing to defeat the bill, and it was decided that one of his coalition partners, the ultra-Orthodox United Torah Judaism Party, would turn the Knesset debate into a vote of confidence in the government—a ploy that delayed the voting by two weeks, winning for Netanyahu some precious breathing space.

The prime minister clearly did not favor early elections. As the vote drew closer, he worked hard to try and restore right-wing support by accusing the Palestinians of not fulfilling their obligations and by making increasingly stiff demands on Arafat. But that move had the effect of upsetting the moderates in his coalition. Further efforts to convince David Levy to rejoin the government also proved fruitless. And Netanyahu received another blow on December 16, when Finance Minister Yaakov Ne'eman, a close ally, resigned. Ne'eman cited the failure of Knesset members to place the country's broad economic concerns above their own special interests as the reason for his resignation.

Netanyahu, commentators observed, might well have avoided early elections had he invited the Labor Party to join him in a national unity government after returning from Wye. There were reports that he and Barak had even reached a coalition agreement during talks held before he traveled to the peace summit. On his return, however, Netanyahu chose instead to launch an all-out attack on Labor. As a result, despite a last-minute unity plea by the prime minister from the Knesset podium, which was met with laughter by many of the Knesset members, the plenum voted to pass the first reading of the bill to disband the legislature and move to early elections. There was little doubt that the outcome of the second and third readings of the bill—likely to be held in early January 1999—would be any different, and it was clear that a new election was only months away. On December 28, Netanyahu and Barak agreed on a date for elections—May 17, 1999.

Labor Pains

Labor leader Ehud Barak seemed unable to capitalize on Netanyahu's coalition troubles. He faced strong criticism within his own party for not adopting a clear line on key policy issues and for being dictatorial in his running of the party. Many Labor members who had voted for Barak in the internal leadership primaries in mid-1997 had hoped that he would, in some way, fill Yitzhak Rabin's shoes, adopting the mantle of "Mr. Security"—an image that had helped Rabin win over enough centrist and right-wing voters in the 1992 election to unseat the Likud. But party members were soon disappointed. "We expected Barak to be Rabin," said one disillusioned Labor Knesset member in early January, "but he's only Barak."

Many had predicted a bright future for Barak when he entered politics. His credentials, they believed, made him a natural for the post of prime minister: former head of one of the country's elite commando units, Israel's most decorated war hero, an ex-chief of staff and former foreign minister, an advanced degree in systems analysis from Stanford University. Yet, despite the fact that in early 1998 the government's credibility was at an all-time low, Barak seemed unable to make an impact. He was increasingly viewed as noncommittal and vague on cardinal issues, and on television he came across as awkward and uncomfortable.

Party leaders who had supported Barak for the leadership bid and not been rewarded for their loyalty became increasingly bitter. They accused him of not consulting them and of failing to set up a leadership team. "The question for us is whether these are teething troubles, or whether there is some deeper personality problem," said Labor MK Hagai Merom.

Barak loyalists in the party pointed to polls indicating that their candidate had a substantial lead over Netanyahu, but political observers warned that polls had traditionally overestimated Labor's strength. Indeed, Laborites were especially cautious after having watched pollsters consistently predict a Shimon Peres victory right up until the last day of the 1996 election campaign, when Netanyahu snatched victory by the narrowest of margins.

Barak drew fire in March when he said in a television interview: "I imagine that if I were a Palestinian of the right age, I would, at some stage, have joined one of the terror organizations." The right immediately attacked him, and many predicted that his statement would feature prominently in the Likud's campaign when elections came around. Matters got worse for Barak when Iman Kfisha, a member of the Hamas unit on trial for the bombing of the Cafe Apropo in Tel Aviv in March 1997, seized on the Labor leader's statement. "Barak said, 'If I were a Palestinian, I'd belong to Hamas.' We, too, are Hamas soldiers and want to liberate Palestinian land," he said.

Barak defended his style and approach with the argument that disaffection with his leadership was due to his strategy of trying to woo the political center—the only way, he insisted, that Labor could triumph in an election. During a visit to the West Bank settlement of Bet-El in May, for instance, Barak declared that Israel would "remain in Bet-El forever." His comments were criticized strongly by elements on the left. "I told Rabin that he couldn't win an election from his Oslo position," Barak explained. "I said, 'Yitzhak, we must capture the center, otherwise Netanyahu will do it—and he'll destroy Oslo.'"

Tension also continued to simmer between Barak and Shimon Peres, especially over the former prime minister's continued flirting with the idea of a national unity government. After David Levy weakened Netanyahu's position by resigning from the cabinet in early January, Peres tried to persuade Labor politicians that the time had come for a national unity government. There were even media reports that Netanyahu had offered Peres the post vacated by Levy, but that Peres had turned it down on the grounds that the government was undermining the peace process.

While Labor members refrained from publicly attacking Peres, in private they complained that he was not displaying enough support for Barak, and so was hurting Labor's chances of getting back into power. There was also speculation that Peres might break with Labor and set up a party of his own, using a peace movement he had set up in January—with the backing of two dozen mayors—as the basis for the new party. When asked in March whether he was planning such a move, Peres answered ambiguously: "We are not facing elections," he said. "We will need to see the political line-up before making a decision."

The disenchantment with Barak led to speculation over the political plans of Amnon Lipkin-Shahak, whose term as chief of staff was set to end in July. Labor insiders intimated that Shahak would not challenge Barak, his predecessor as chief of staff, for the leadership of the Labor opposition, even though some party activists were eager to see that happen. More likely, they suggested, was that Shahak would join the Labor party in a senior position, possibly as Barak's chief subordinate and potential defense minister were Labor to win the next election. "It is simply not in Shahak's character to get into a slugging match with Barak," said one source close to both men. "The conniving, the self-promotion that would be involved are alien to him."

After Shahak ended his term in early July, Labor Party members expressed confidence that he would ultimately team up with Barak, and they insisted the two would make a formidable team. "Amnon is in many ways the antithesis of Ehud—more ready to delegate, more relaxed," said a close Barak adviser. "He doesn't seem super-ambitious. . . . They complement each other perfectly." But Barak's desire to bring in Shahak did not mean that his ex-army buddy would automatically heed the call. Shahak was also being courted by Tel Aviv mayor Roni Milo, who had set up a centrist party and indicated that he would forego the top spot if Shahak joined him. Netanyahu was also said to be watching Shahak closely. There were reports that the prime minister viewed the recently retired general—who came across as relaxed but assertive in TV interviews—as his most serious rival. Polls taken in July showed Shahak leading Netanyahu by 5 percent, while Barak was only 1 percent ahead of the prime minister. Shahak, though, remained tight-lipped about his future plans, telling those close to him that he needed time to study his options.

There was another bout of squabbling within the Labor Party in late July over a proposal by Peres and other Labor MKs that they provide Netanyahu with a Knesset "safety net" if he agreed to go ahead with the West Bank redeployment and the right-wing elements in his coalition moved to bring him down. An enraged Barak, who had not been part of the initiative, castigated party members at a Knesset caucus meeting. The Labor Party, he shouted, "is turning itself into a political and public joke. It needs political Viagra to get itself up." Some observers suggested that Peres hoped that, in exchange for the offer of a "safety net," Netanyahu would invite Labor to join a national unity government, and Peres would be given the responsibility of managing final-status negotiations with the Palestinians. Peres's plan, wrote seasoned Middle East commentator Ehud Ya'ari, "is just an inch away from an outright attempt to overthrow his successor, Ehud Barak, undermining Barak's future challenge to Netanyahu."

Barak was dealt yet another blow in late July—on a day that should have been his most glorious since becoming party leader. The Knesset voted on July 29 to pass the preliminary reading of a bill to dissolve the legislature, a major coup for Barak and the Labor Party. But the victory was eclipsed by an interview appearing in that day's *Ha'aretz* in which Labor MK Ori Orr, a former deputy defense minister, made derogatory remarks about Sephardi Jews. Orr, a close Barak aide, said that Sephardi Jews were hypersensitive and described Moroccan Jews as a "problematic ethnic group." He questioned their intelligence, saying they were "not curious" to know what was going on around them. Netanyahu immediately seized on Orr's comments and ascended the Knesset podium where he proceeded to rip into the Labor Party as arrogant and exclusive. "There's a God and He's a Likudnik," quipped Likud MK Reuven Rivlin, referring to the timing of Orr's comments.

This was a major blow to Barak's attempts to woo traditionally right-wing Sephardi voters, many of whom held the Ashkenazi establishment—with whom Labor was identified—responsible for the cultural and social dislocation their parents and grandparents had experienced in the early years of the state. Barak made things worse for himself when he hesitated in disciplining Orr; a full 36 hours passed before the ex-general was stripped of his party positions. Some in the party suggested that Barak should have gone further, forcing Orr to resign from the Knesset and leave the party altogether. Haim Ramon, a senior Laborite, declared that he would not remain in the party with someone like Ori Orr.

A Labor delegation headed by Barak flew to Britain toward the end of the year to study Tony Blair's victory strategy. After his return, Barak announced that the party would undergo structural and organizational changes. He also launched "One Israel," part of a plan to widen Labor's appeal by bringing in other parties and extra-parliamentary groups who would run for the Knesset under a broad banner along with Labor.

With early elections almost certain, speculation was rife about Shahak's plans. There were increasing signs that the ex-general planned to mount a challenge to Netanyahu at the head of a centrist party, rather than join Labor. At the end of the year, a Gallup poll showed Barak with a 45-38 lead over Netanyahu; the same poll gave Shahak a 48-33 advantage over the prime minister. But in a four-way first-round race—including Benny Begin, who, many believed, would challenge Netanyahu from the right—it was Barak and Netanayhu, not Shahak, who went through to the second round. (In the direct-election system, if none of the candidates got more than 50 percent in the first round, the top two candidates vied in a run-off.) Still, Shahak had said very little, and it remained to be seen whether there was more to his soaring popularity than the public's disillusionment with both Netanyahu and Barak.

Following Netanyahu's 1996 example, Barak hired American campaign advisers. His team included Clinton campaign strategists James Carville, Stanley Greenberg, and Robert Shrum. Some pundits suggested that the race would actually be between the two groups of American spin-doctors employed by Netanyahu and Barak. It became evident very quickly that Barak's advisers had given him some tips on how to improve his TV manner. He abandoned his often heavy style and long, complicated sentences for a more feisty approach employing constant repetition of short messages. As for substance, Barak sought to focus the campaign on social and economic issues like jobs, education, and health.

The vote to disband the Knesset was a serious blow to Netanyahu. But the prime minister—a consummate campaigner—was by no means out of the running, and it was only the bravest of political pundits who would dismiss his chances of winning a second term. Netanyahu's strategy, it seemed, would focus on peace and security, stressing that he had delivered on his promise to reduce the threat of terror and would be a much tougher negotiator with the Palestinians in final-status talks than Labor. While he would present the far right as too extreme to make peace, Netanyahu's aides said he would present the left as too conciliatory.

With the entire political system in flux as 1998 drew to a close, political commentators were loath to predict who would be the next prime minister.

The "Big Bang"

Speculation was rife in the course of 1998 over what many referred to as the "Big Bang"—a code word for the fundamental reordering of the country's traditional left-right political alignment. The first concrete sign of such a realignment was the May 4 announcement by Tel Aviv mayor and former cabinet minister Roni Milo that he was leaving the Likud to set up a centrist party and run for prime minister in the year 2000. Citing as the catalyst for his decision the opposition of Orthodox politicians to the performance of an avant-garde number by a dance troupe at the Independence Day gala celebration, Milo said his new centrist party would draw from both the left and the right to "neutralize the leverage of religious extremists."

Political analysts speculated over whom Milo would hurt more, Netanyahu or Barak. While some argued that Milo would attract right-wing voters dissatisfied with Netanyahu, others said he would cut more into Barak's constituency, especially since he had carved out a dovish and stridently secular image since becoming mayor of Tel Aviv. The fact that Labor was limping along under Barak, and the Likud-led government was looking increasingly vulnerable, added impetus to the formation of a centrist political force.

Several reasons were offered to support the "Big Bang" theory. First, the new system of direct elections had weakened the two major parties. A vast number of voters had split their ballots in 1996, voting for the Labor or Likud candidate for prime minister, but expressing their more specific ideological tendencies by voting for one of the smaller parties for the Knesset. Second, it was asserted, the signing of the peace treaties with the Palestinians and the Jordanians had begun to erode the centrality of the land-for-peace issue that had traditionally divided left and right.

Nevertheless, many questioned whether the platform of a centrist party would be focused enough to give it an identity distinct from that of Labor or Likud. Aides to Barak and Netanyahu poured cold water on Milo's centrist drive. With both the Labor and the Likud leaders aiming to capture the centrist vote, said one Barak aide, there would be no room left for a third candidate, who would find himself squeezed out of the race.

Milo's plan was to put together a highly attractive leadership team of top public figures. Two major players in his sights were Shahak and former Likud finance minister Dan Meridor, who had quit the post in 1997 after a showdown with Netanyahu and who had vowed never again to run on a ticket headed by the prime minister. Milo also met with some top-ranking Laborites unhappy with Barak's leadership performance, including Haim Ramon, Shlomo Ben-Ami, and Jewish Agency head Avraham Burg. And he was eager to recruit the highly popular defense minister, Yitzhak Mordechai, the most moderate member of the cabinet and the man many believed helped tip the balance in favor of Netanyahu in the 1996 elections. Milo also hoped to corral centrist parties like the Third Way, the moderate religious party Meimad, and David Levy's Gesher. Asked who would ultimately lead such a party, Milo said it would be the person most likely to win an election, to be determined by a public opinion poll. In one poll in early August Milo edged out Netanyahu by 44-43.

Many commentators singled out Shahak as the key figure Milo would have to attract. The articulate and telegenic Shahak regularly outscored Netanyahu and Barak in the polls. A mid-July poll, for instance, showed Shahak with 44 percent of the vote and Netanyahu with only 33 percent. But pollsters pointed out that Shahak's popularity stemmed both from the public's disenchantment with Netanyahu and Barak and from the fact that his public positions remained unknown; he was still on official army vacation and so was barred from making any political statements. "Shahak is a stronger candidate than Barak to run against Netanyahu," said Prof. Avi Degani, managing director of the Geocartography research institute, "but I have no doubt that support for him will drop the moment he takes sides." While the polls showed that a third candidate from a centrist party would most likely force a second round in the prime ministerial race, they also revealed that such a candidate was unlikely to make it into the second round. Ultimately, said Degani, it would come down to a runoff between Netanyahu and Barak.

While Milo was trying to woo Shahak, so was Barak. There were reports that the Labor leader had offered Shahak the Ministry of Defense if Labor came to power. In September a noncommittal Shahak held separate meetings with Barak, Meridor, and Milo. Netanyahu responded by labeling Shahak a leftist—a move aimed at undermining Shahak's popularity even before he hitched up with a political party. "Amnon Shahak's place is definitely on the left . . . Shahak took off his army uniform, put on a suit and went to talk to the Palestinian Nabil Sha'ath with his arm around his shoulders," Netanyahu said, following a meeting between Shahak and Barak. "When I met the Palestinians," Shahak responded, "I was sent by the late prime minister Yitzhak Rabin. Prime Minister Netanyahu has also sent generals, in uniform and civilian dress, to negotiate with the Palestinians."

The future of Milo's ambitious plan appeared to hang largely on Netanyahu's course with regard to the Palestinians. A renewed peace process followed by the formation of a national unity government with Labor would clearly bury the centrist initiative.

Challenge to the New Electoral System

Efforts were made during the course of the year to change Israel's new electoral system. Opponents of direct election, which came into effect in 1996 and allowed citizens to cast one ballot for prime minister and a second for a party, argued that it had fragmented the political system. After the 1996 election Netanyahu had cobbled together a coalition with eight parties, and his own Likud party constituted less than half of the votes in the coalition. Such political fragmentation, critics warned, would worsen in the next election. In addition, remarked Dr. Aryeh Carmon, the head of the Israel Democracy Institute, the system promoted the interests of particular sectors of the population over the national interest: "Under the old system the major parties took opposite views, but they were fighting over the great issues on the national agenda. That was an integrating factor. Now, anyone can get elected to the Knesset on a special-interest ticket. That strengthens the forces tearing Israeli society apart." Jews in the Diaspora who had given financial backing to the movement to change the system had been "fooled," said Carmon. "The supporters of direct election went abroad raising money by saying that the new system would destroy Orthodox power. The opposite happened. The religious parties have never been stronger, and their demands on the conversion law are threatening to create a schism with Diaspora Jews."

But the architects of the new system continued to defend it. If the old electoral system were still in effect, argued David Libai, a former justice minister under

Yitzhak Rabin, "the religious parties would have been just as strong, and they would have used their power to change the prime minister three times by now." Uriel Reichman, a law professor and another shaper of the direct-election system, said that reform should go further, with the next step being the introduction of constituency elections for many of the Knesset seats—a move that would help the big parties.

Netanyahu continued to express strong support for the new system, but members of his party did not necessarily share his enthusiasm. In late May, the Knesset voted 50-45 to send a bill to committee that would cancel the 1992 law instituting direct election for prime minister and revert to the old system of proportional representation. Of the Likud's 22 Knesset members, 12 voted in favor of the bill and five absented themselves from the vote rather than kill the proposed legislation. Members of both big parties were extremely worried, however, by secret polls conducted in June that showed the ultra-Orthodox Shas Party getting between 18 and 20 Knesset seats if elections were held then, and Labor and Likud combined only receiving around 50 seats—far from a majority in the 120-seat Knesset.

Still, the bill had a long way to go before becoming law. Netanyahu, Barak, and the smaller parties opposed any change, and the bill required a 61-vote majority because it was a constitutional measure.

RELIGION

Conversion and the Ultra-Orthodox Draft

The battle between the Orthodox and non-Orthodox denominations over conversion resurfaced when the Orthodox Chief Rabbinate officially rejected the recommendations of the Ne'eman Commission on February 9. The seven-member committee, headed by Finance Minister Yaakov Ne'eman, had reached a compromise: all conversion candidates would attend a joint conversion school, where Orthodox, Reform, and Conservative rabbis would teach them. The final conversion ceremonies, however, would be performed exclusively by Orthodox rabbis. (The commission had been established by Netanyahu in 1997 after the ultra-Orthodox parties sponsored a bill that would codify the Orthodox monopoly on conversions and so formally deny state recognition of Reform and Conservative conversions performed in Israel.)

The Reform and Conservative movements, the Chief Rabbinate charged, were trying to "undermine the fundamentals of the Jewish religion and divide the people." The religious parties took the same tack. Avraham Ravitz of the ultra-Orthodox United Torah Judaism party declared that he would reject any proposal that granted any measure of recognition to the Reform and Conservative movements. "We contend that Judaism is not pluralistic," he said.

But the Chief Rabbinate's refusal to support the compromise generated opposition to the conversion bill among centrist parties in the coalition like the Third Way and the Yisrael ba-Aliya immigrant party. They argued that the rabbinate was failing to seize a historic opportunity to insure Jewish unity and avert a major split between Israel and Diaspora Jewry. In contrast to the ultra-Orthodox, Rabbi Yehuda Amital of the moderate religious movement Meimad came out strongly against the conversion bill. He said it "would be a continuation of Hitler's work and would make the Jews disappear." The Reform and Conservative movements filed a petition in the Supreme Court on February 10, demanding that the Ministry of Interior register as Jews their followers who converted in Israel.

The issue of ultra-Orthodox exemption from the military draft—a major flash point between the majority of the population, who served in the IDF, and the ultra-Orthodox, who did not, on the grounds that Torah study took precedence—was once again on the agenda in the period under review. There had only been several hundred yeshivah students when an agreement on deferments was struck between David Ben-Gurion and the ultra-Orthodox in the early years of the state. Since then the number had ballooned to approximately 29,000. In an effort to avoid the draft, many ultra-Orthodox men studied into their thirties, living off small state stipends.

In late January, Shas MK Shlomo Benizri announced a plan for voluntary enlistment of ultra-Orthodox males by providing men-only bases with food that met the stringent ultra-Orthodox *kashrut* standards. He insisted, however, that the deferment from the draft for those men who chose to study remain intact. Nothing came of Benizri's proposal, but the issue was back in the headlines on May 11 when Ehud Barak submitted a bill that would end the mass exemption of yeshivah students and strictly limit the number of annual deferments. Some members in the ruling coalition attacked Barak for trying to make political capital out of a highly sensitive issue, and asked why he had not called for ultra-Orthodox conscription when he was IDF chief of staff. Ultra-Orthodox politicians also decried the proposed legislation. "Even if this law is enacted, thousands of yeshivah students will prefer to go to jail rather than be drafted," declared Shmuel Halpert, a United Torah Jewry Knesset member. Rabbi Eliezer Schach, the leader of the "Lithuanian" yeshivah world, expressed an even more radical view on the draft proposal: "There is an absolute ban on going to the army, and one must be prepared to die to avoid it," he said.

The irony was that the army was not overly enthusiastic about the idea of absorbing large numbers of ultra-Orthodox men, as it would then have to establish single-sex bases and institute stringent *kashrut* standards. On the other hand, at the ultra-Orthodox grassroots level, some suggested that growing economic pressures in a society where many of the adult men did not work could generate interest in army service. In practical terms, without first fulfilling their obligation of military service, ultra-Orthodox men could not enter the job market.

But in July the Knesset voted down Barak's bill 53-45. One of the main reasons for its failure was the opposition of Arab MKs, who formed an alliance with the ultra-Orthodox to defeat the bill. The Arab politicians feared that if the ultra-Orthodox were drafted, there would be moves to draft 18-year-old Arab Israelis next. The issue was back in the news on December 9 when the Supreme Court ruled that the exemption for yeshivah students was illegal, and gave the Knesset a year to pass legislation on the matter.

Another Supreme Court ruling earlier in the year—on religious councils—had also angered the ultra-Orthodox. On August 13, the court ruled that the minister of religious affairs had to include Reform and Conservative representatives on the Jerusalem religious council. (For years the Orthodox had been battling to keep the Reform and Conservative off the councils, which oversaw local services such as synagogue maintenance, ritual baths, and *kashrut* supervision.)

Another confrontation, this time between ultra-Orthodox and Conservative Jews, took place on the Shavuot holiday when a group of close to 300 Conservative worshipers prayed in a mixed service near the Western Wall, under police protection. They were attacked by hundreds of ultra-Orthodox worshipers who hurled paper, water, and bags of chocolate milk at them. There was another case of ultra-Orthodox violence on November 11, when a crowd of ultra-Orthodox men forced their way into an apartment in the Meah She'arim neighborhood of Jerusalem and ransacked it, smashing furniture and pulling off wall-fittings. The apartment was rented to two Swiss women who were out at the time. The crowd then tried to force its way into an adjacent apartment rented by a third woman, and she alerted the police. Participants in the attack, six of whom were arrested, accused the women of being Christian missionaries, a charge all three denied.

In December ultra-Orthodox men stoned customers at a Jerusalem cafe that was open on the Sabbath. Around the same time there was an outcry from the religious parties after a Jerusalem court ruled that the law barring Jews from operating their shops on the Sabbath did not apply to kibbutz stores.

Independence Day Showdown

Despite the fact that Israel was marking its 50th anniversary, the April 30 celebrations—attended by numerous dignitaries including U.S. vice-president Al Gore—were marred by several disturbing incidents that reflected the deep divisions in the country. The most publicized spat was over opposition by Orthodox leaders to a dance sequence at the main Independence Day gala in Jerusalem. During the number, performed by the Batsheva Dance Company to the Passover seder song "*Ehad Mi Yodea*?" ("Who Knows One?"), the male and female performers removed their outer layer of clothes to reveal undershirts and briefs. The dancers rejected a compromise reached by the Orthodox politicians and the Batsheva management whereby the dancers would wear long underwear, and refused to appear at all.

"We never dreamed it would cause problems; the same dance was performed at the opening of the Jubilee celebrations in Washington two months ago," said a spokeswoman for the gala's organizers, the government-appointed Jubilee Committee. One art critic in the daily *Ha'aretz* suggested that "the religious should see this dance as a breakthrough. Batsheva has taken a totally modern art form, and used a religious text as its basis. It appeals to the widest possible audience that modern dance can reach."

But Orthodox leaders did not see it that way. Jerusalem's three religious coalition parties published a letter stating that they had been "shocked and surprised by the performance that was shameful and lacking in morals, and hurt not just the ultra-Orthodox public but the respectability of the entire nation."

ECONOMIC DEVELOPMENTS

The period under review was not a rosy one for the Israeli economy, with many of the indicators pointing to a deepening recession. Gross Domestic Product growth in 1998 was down to 2 percent, compared with 2.7 percent in 1997. Private consumption dropped to 3.3 percent from 4.1 percent the previous year. Export growth was 6 percent versus 7.6 percent in 1997. Imports were also down, from 2.8 percent in 1997 to 2.1 percent in 1998. Unemployment was up from 7.7 percent in 1997 to 8.8 percent at the end of 1998. Another sign of the deepening recession was the drop in residential housing starts, which declined from 26,630 in the first half of 1997, to 19,580 in the first half of 1998. There was, however, a vast improvement in the current account deficit, which was $1.5 billion in 1998 compared with $3.1 billion in 1997. The number of tourists who visited Israel in 1998 — 2,198,800 — was down by 4 percent compared with the previous year.

Economic experts pointed to several external causes for the recession: the slowdown in the peace process and subsequent drop of enthusiasm among foreign investors; the negative impact on tourism and investment of the Gulf crises and threats of domestic terror; the fact that the boom generated by the mass immigration from the former Soviet Union had tapered off; and the Asian and Russian financial crises.

Economic developments in the period under review were also affected by the Bank of Israel's strict monetary policy and by cuts in government spending. Many of the country's economic leaders blamed the deepening recession on Jacob Frenkel, the governor of the Bank of Israel. His tight-money approach, they argued, was depressing growth and boosting unemployment. On January 26, for instance, Frenkel announced the first interest-rate cut in five months when he reduced rates by half a percentage point, to 12.90 percent.

At the Caesarea Conference in June — an annual economic summit attended by the prime minister and the country's leading financial and business figures — Frenkel stubbornly defended his policies in the face of broad criticism. He rejected claims that he had overcooled the economy, continued to argue that inflation was

Israel's major economic problem, and warned that, since Israel was part of the global economy, it was not immune from international economic developments. The collapse of Asian financial markets, he said, was proof that his tight monetary policies were correct. "There is a good chance that if the Asian crisis had taken place a year ago," he said, "the Israeli economy would not have been strong enough to withstand the shocks."

Some of Frenkel's critics, like Minister of Trade and Industry Natan Sharansky, insisted that the governor had too much influence over the economy through his power to set interest rates. Netanyahu backed Frenkel, despite warnings from Likud politicians that the governor's monetary policies would lead to increased unemployment and so cost them votes. "Jacob, are you still standing?" Netanyahu joked during the closing session. "I hear you are bruised and bleeding, but still on your feet."

Israel was not unaffected by the crisis-hit Pacific Rim as the tumbling stock markets and currencies of Southeast Asia and South Korea also had an impact on the Middle East. In early 1998, economic forecasters estimated that Israeli export losses due to the Asian crisis would be in the region of $300-400 million. Due in part to the situation in Asia, the Ministry of Finance also readjusted its projections for the country's 1998 economic growth, predicting that the economy might expand by a full half a percentage point lower than its earlier projection of 3.1 percent. Nevertheless, most economic forecasters did not describe the situation in crisis terms and insisted that Israeli companies exporting to the Pacific Rim were sturdy enough to weather some temporary losses.

Netanyahu received considerable praise for his economic policies, particularly speeding up privatization and implementing a disciplined budgetary policy. In late September, the government sold 15 percent of Bank Leumi on the London and Zurich stock exchanges for 560 million shekels (about $190 million) to various local and foreign investors. That pushed government revenues from privatization in 1998 to $1.3 billion, already past the $1.2 billion target for the year. But analysts pointed out that while the government was having success in selling off the "easy" items like banks and some of the smaller public companies, its record was much poorer when it came to the large public companies like the Israel Electric Corporation and El Al. The sale of the national air carrier, for instance, was complicated by the ongoing debate over whether El Al should be allowed to fly on the Sabbath, an issue made even more difficult by the fact that an Orthodox politician, Shaul Yahalom, was minister of transport. Also, the tourism slump had a negative impact on El Al, making it a less attractive option for private bidders.

There was also mounting criticism over the price of the government's economic policies, especially the rising unemployment rate, which increased by 7.5 percent in the first half of 1998. By the end of the year unemployment was at 8.8 percent, up from 7.7 percent in 1997. In certain poor towns far from the major population centers joblessness was as high as 14 percent. Growing unemployment was also the result of privatization, as well as the restructuring of the Israeli economy from labor-intensive industries to a more open economy where the main earner of foreign currency was technology. The government also received criticism for cutting the education budget and for plans to implement changes in national health insurance that would hurt the poor.

When the consumer price index dropped by 0.1 percent in July—the first negative July index in 26 years—the annual inflation rate was projected at less than 4 percent. But the inflation bugbear returned in the last quarter of the year due to a sharp devaluation of the currency. In early October the shekel devalued by a dramatic 10 percent against the dollar, raising fears of a dangerous currency collapse. That amounted to an overall plunge of around 20 percent from July, when the shekel had stood at 3.65 to the dollar, to October, when it reached a high of 4.40, before declining to between 4.10 and 4.20. (At the end of the year inflation stood at 8.6 percent, compared to 7 percent in 1997.)

Netanayahu surely exaggerated when he claimed that Israel was an "island of stability" in the midst of the world financial crisis. Jonathan Katz, the chief economist for the Solid financial group in Tel Aviv, assessed the situation in a more balanced way. "Russia lost hundreds of percentage points in its currency, in Southeast Asia the losses were 50-60 percent. We have certainly not escaped unscathed. On the other hand, we have not faced a total loss of faith, and while we are still seen as an emerging market, we are at the top of that group, with countries like Greece and Egypt."

Other Economic Developments

Lehman Brothers won a bid, at $52.1 million, to buy a 2 percent share of Bank Leumi. Leumi had offered the shares to four foreign investment banks—Goldman Sachs, Merrill Lynch, UBS, and Lehman.

Following a two-year investigation, the Jerusalem-based News Datacom Research company owned by Rupert Murdoch had to pay Israeli income tax authorities $4.2-million. The company had been suspected of evading local taxes between 1989 and 1992 by reporting that the revenues belonged to another Murdoch company abroad.

The Big Mac Index, published by the London-based *Economist* magazine, revealed that, along with Finland and Venezuela, Israel was one of the world's most expensive countries to live in. The Index, which compares the price of a McDonald's hamburger in different countries, found that a Big Mac in Israel cost $3.52 as compared with the standard U.S. price of $2.63.

One of the longest and most successful business partnerships in Israel came to an end in December when Aharon Dovrat and Itzhak Shrem parted ways. The two had formed Dovrat Shrem, one of the first all-Israeli investment houses, which had been a major force in the investment boom during the first half of the 1990s.

OTHER DOMESTIC AFFAIRS

Demography

As Independence Day approached, the Central Bureau of Statistics announced that Israel's population had increased sevenfold in 50 years, from 806,000 to six million. Forty-three percent of the population growth (some 2.7 million people) was due to immigration.

Immigration

Immigration was down from 67,190 in 1997 to 57,591 in 1998. Much of the drop was due to a decline in the number of immigrants from the former Soviet Union, which dropped from around 55,000 in 1997 to 46,373 in 1998. Another 3,621 immigrants arrived from Africa and 3,100 from Western Europe. The 2,390 immigrants who came from North America in 1998 marked a 23.2 percent drop from 1997.

Several thousand Falas Mora—Ethiopians of Jewish descent whose families had converted to Christianity—were brought to Israel in 1998, at a rate of about 600 a month. The Falas Mora, who had been excluded from Operation Solomon in 1991, had been living near a Jewish Agency-run compound in Addis Ababa in poor conditions. (In June 1997 the government decided to shut the compound and bring the Falas Mora to Israel.)

A row broke out over the fact that the government was sending some of the Falas Mora to West Bank settlements. The immigrants, charged Labor MK Shlomo Ben-Ami, were being sent to "an area outside the [national] consensus . . . into the heart of the storm." But Aharon Domb, the head of the Council of Jewish Settlements in Judea, Samaria, and the Gaza District, rebuffed the charges, arguing that many towns in Israel proper, "including those headed by Labor, are unwilling to absorb these immigrants. It's contemptible. Let them put their energy into absorption instead of undermining those willing to do so," he railed.

The sense of alienation and exclusion felt by many Russian immigrants—almost a fifth of the country's population—was borne out by the vast numbers who voted for Russian candidates in the November 10 municipal elections. That same sense of rejection was brought into sharp relief only days before the local elections when Jan Shefshovitz, a 21-year-old soldier and immigrant from Moldavia, was stabbed to death by a Moroccan patron in an Ashkelon cafe. The patron had allegedly objected to the fact that Russian was being loudly spoken. It was not the first instance of violence between Moroccans and Russian immigrants, and many expressed fear about the growing tension between the two communities. The general rise in unemployment was even more dramatic among new immigrants. While joblessness was close to 9 percent in the general population, over the first nine months of 1998 it reached 12.1 percent among immigrants.

Third Rabin Commemoration

While more than two years had passed since the assassination of Yitzhak Rabin on November 4, 1995, Israelis continued to struggle to come to terms with the murder and its implications for their society. On June 14, attention turned to the Tel Aviv magistrate's court where Margalit Har-Shefi was convicted for failing to inform police that her friend Yigal Amir was planning to assassinate the prime minister. Judge Nira Lidsky rejected the 22-year-old law student's claims that she had not taken Amir's bragging about his plans to kill Rabin seriously. The judge also noted that Har-Shefi had been aware of several other occasions when Amir tried to murder the prime minister, and that she had consulted a rabbi on whether Rabin's peace-process policies merited the death penalty under Jewish law. Leah Rabin, the late prime minister's widow, described the conviction as "a ray of light in the darkness surrounding us." In October Har-Shefi was sentenced to nine months in prison, plus 15 months suspended.

A huge crowd turned out in Tel Aviv's Rabin Square on October 31 to mark the third anniversary of the assassination. While organizers put the number at 400,000, police estimated the crowd at 150,000. The list of speakers included not only left-wing politicians, but also Defense Minister Mordechai and Gesher leader David Levy. The next day, when Netanyahu attended the official memorial ceremony at Rabin's grave on Jerusalem's Mt. Herzl, five demonstrators loudly accused him of being guilty of incitement against Rabin. They were briefly taken into custody by the police. The only speaker at the graveside ceremony was Amnon Lipkin-Shahak—who had been chosen by the Rabin family—and his comments appeared to be aimed directly at Netanyahu. "Forgive me, Yitzhak," he said, " . . . that even today there are some among us who are not able to ask your forgiveness."

The issue of Avishai Raviv's role in the assassination was back on the agenda in 1998. Right-wing activists continued their campaign to have Raviv—a former Shin Bet agent who was the head of an extremist group—tried for having denied under oath during the trial of Yigal Amir's brother, Haggai, that he worked for the agency. While Shin Bet chief Ami Ayalon said he no longer opposed the indictment of Raviv, the State Attorney's Office remained unconvinced. Those pushing for a trial argued that there were sufficient grounds to justify their demand—including incitement to murder Rabin, not reporting Amir's plans to his Shin Bet handlers, and carrying out acts of anti-Arab violence. (The Shamgar Commission, set up to investigate the assassination, had described Raviv as an agent who had not been properly controlled by his handlers.)

Raviv's role in the assassination was at the heart of some conspiracy theories circulating on the right, but it was also part of the bitter argument between left and right over levels of responsibility for the assassination. Some on the right believed that only if Raviv was tried would the truth emerge—that he was really an agent provocateur whose mission had been to incite violence so as to blacken the reputation of the entire right and promote support for the left. On the left, how-ever, some argued that the right's true aim was to escape any responsibility for the campaign of incitement against Rabin by attributing it largely to Raviv. Fi-nally, on November 4, Attorney General Elyakim Rubinstein announced that Raviv would in fact be indicted for failing to prevent the assassination.

Resignation of Mossad Chief

A government-appointed commission set up to investigate the failed assassi-nation attempt by Mossad agents on Hamas leader Khaled Mashaal in Jordan in September 1997 published its report on February 16. It cleared Netanyahu of responsibility for the operation and stated that Israel had the right to act against those seeking its harm. While the commission criticized Maj.-Gen. Danny Yatom, the Mossad chief, it did not recommend his dismissal.

On February 24, however, Yatom handed in his resignation. There were sug-gestions that Yatom's decision had been prompted by another Mossad fiasco—the capture of five of its agents while they were allegedly trying to bug an Iran-ian mission in Bern, Switzerland, on February 19. The Swiss, who submitted a harsh diplomatic protest to Israel, intimated that the whole affair could have been settled discreetly had it not been leaked to the Israeli media. According to some Israeli sources, the leaks came from the Mossad itself, part of an attempt by top officers to oust Yatom.

Former Mossad deputy chief Ephraim Halevy, who had also served as Israel's ambassador to the European Union and had played an important part in the Israeli-Jordanian peace talks, was named Yatom's successor on March 4. The head of the IDF's Northern Command, Maj.-Gen. Amiram Levine, was appointed deputy Mossad chief.

The Mossad was back in the news in November when two of its agents were arrested in Cyprus on suspicion of spying. Despite diplomatic efforts to win their release, the two were indicted in Larnaca on charges of espionage.

New Chief of Staff

The appointment of a new chief of staff to succeed Amnon Lipkin-Shahak, who was to end his term in July, generated much controversy. The front-runner was deputy chief of staff Matan Vilnai, who had even gone off to the United States to prepare an IDF restructuring plan to be implemented once he took over the top post. But with the time for a decision drawing closer, it emerged that De-fense Minister Yitzhak Mordechai preferred Shaul Mofaz, the man many ex-pected to be Vilnai's deputy.

There were reports that Mordechai held a grudge against Vilnai as a result of a series of confrontations between the two when both were still in uniform. While Mofaz also appeared to have the backing of Shahak, Netanyahu was said to prefer Vilnai. After much media speculation, Mordechai announced in May that the 50-year-old Mofaz, who was born in Teheran, would become the IDF's 16th chief of staff.

Jonathan Pollard

The case of Jonathan Pollard, the U.S. naval intelligence officer serving a life term for spying for Israel, was in the headlines on several occasions in the course of 1998. On May 11, Israel officially reversed its long-held position that Pollard had been part of a rogue operation when the government announced that he had in fact been an Israeli agent. Activists working for Pollard's release welcomed the announcement as an important step in the fight to secure his freedom. Cabinet secretary Danny Naveh visited Pollard in his North Carolina jail on May 15 and presented him with a letter from the prime minister in which Netanyahu promised to "make every effort" to bring him home. After the visit Pollard told reporters: "There is nothing good that came as a result of my actions. I tried to serve two countries at the same time. That does not work."

The Pollard affair was back in the headlines in late October when Netanyahu delayed the signing of the Wye accords on the grounds that President Clinton had reneged on a promise to release Pollard as part of the Wye package. A furious Clinton refused to release the convicted spy but did say he would review the case. U.S. officials accused Netanyahu of exploiting the Pollard case for his own personal political gain and suggested that the prime minister had actually hurt Pollard's prospects for release. According to sources in the Clinton administration, Netanyahu had infuriated the entire U.S. political establishment, including his strongest backers in the Republican Party. The House Speaker and the Senate majority leader, Newt Gingrich and Trent Lott, both Republicans, urged Clinton not to grant clemency to Pollard.

Manbar Affair

International businessman Nahum Manbar was sentenced to 16 years imprisonment in July for illegally selling chemical and biological weapons components and know-how to Iran, to the tune of $16 million. The case generated a scandal when Manbar's attorney, Amnon Zichroni, accused the presiding judge, Amnon Shtrashnov, of having had an affair with a member of the defense team. He also claimed that Prime Minister Netanyahu had contacted Shtrashnov during the trial to push for a conviction, a charge the Prime Minister's Office vehemently denied. A police investigation found no wrongdoing.

Local Elections

While Likud and Labor both claimed victory in the November 10 local government elections, the results actually confirmed the trend of the 1996 Knesset elections—the two big parties were shrinking, and the real victors were the ethnic, religious, and special interest groups. The ultra-Orthodox Sephardi Shas Party, for instance, won a total of nearly 140 seats on about 80 councils. Russian immigrant candidates, many of them backed by Natan Sharansky's Yisrael ba-Aliya Party, won a total of 104 council seats in 46 cities and towns. Dor Shalem Doresh Shalom, a pro-peace group set up in the wake of Yitzhak Rabin's assassination, garnered 19 seats on a total of seven councils.

In Tel Aviv, the Labor-affiliated candidate for mayor, Ron Huldai, won easily, taking 50 percent of the vote. In Jerusalem, incumbent Likud mayor Ehud Olmert captured a huge 61 percent of the vote. But when the results of the elections for the Jerusalem city council emerged, it became clear that Olmert was now even more beholden to the ultra-Orthodox than when he first was elected in 1993, thanks to massive ultra-Orthodox support. In 1998 the religious parties picked up a remarkable 15 of the council's 31 seats. Olmert had included ex-Labor figures on his party list for the council, as well as former national police chief Rafi Peled, in an attempt to present a broad alliance. But this strategy failed dismally, and the mayor's list won a paltry three seats, leaving Olmert with the task of having to cobble together a coalition largely based on the religious parties.

In Haifa, Labor's Amram Mitzna won a second term, while in Beersheba, former air force chief Ya'akov Terner took top honors. In Netanyah, the Likud's Miriam Feirberg became the first woman to win a mayoral race in one of Israel's large cities. Feirberg won 48 percent of the vote, more than twice that of her closest rival. Herzliyah produced the Cinderella story of the elections when Yael German, a candidate of the left-wing Meretz Party, beat out six male contenders and went on to win in the second round with a landslide 66 percent of the vote. German had entered the race a mere three months before the election and, at the time, was given no chance to win.

Overall, the number of women running for mayor in Israel's 250 municipalities increased significantly—from two in 1993 to 28 in 1998. Still, there was an acute absence of women in Israeli politics. A study commissioned by the Israel Women's Network revealed that Israel, with nine women in the 120-member Knesset and one out of 17 cabinet ministers, ranked in the bottom one-fifth in the world with regard to women's political representation.

Student Strikes

Strikes by university students at the start of the academic year have not been rare in Israel. But the country had never witnessed anything like the fiery demonstrations that delayed the start of the 1998-1999 academic year. A total of 175,000 students went on strike to demand a 50-percent cut in the annual $3,000 tuition and a fundamental reform of the country's higher education system. In a series of protests in Tel Aviv, Haifa, and Jerusalem, students blocked roads and clashed with police. Dozens were injured and hundreds arrested.

Initially the government tried to ignore the students, hoping that the strike would lose momentum. But after several weeks of protest—including a hunger strike initiated by a group of students outside the prime minister's residence in Jerusalem—it became clear to Netanyahu that the demonstrations were starting to damage him politically. He announced that he would meet with the students. Ultimately, the protest ended in a whimper. Student leaders, who had promised nothing short of a full-scale social revolution, failed to attain their original goal of a 50-percent cut in tuition and settled for additional scholarships and tuition cuts for students who were prepared to do community service. On December 6, thousands of students who had taken to the streets returned to their campuses dispirited and disillusioned.

Sports

After receiving an offer to play with the New York Knickerbockers in mid-1998, it looked as if Maccabi Tel Aviv star guard Oded Katash was about to become the first-ever Israeli to play in the National Basketball Association. The verbal offer to the 23-year-old Katash, however, had to be put on hold because of the dispute between club owners and the players' union that closed down the league. While the NBA forbade the signing of contracts during the lockout, Katash said he was not worried, that the Knicks organization "can be taken at its word."

But as the lockout dragged on and threatened to wipe out the whole 1998-99 NBA season, Katash rejoined Maccabi Tel Aviv, Israel's premier team, which had been struggling in his absence. When the owners and players finally reached an 11th-hour deal, Katash decided to stay put with Maccabi.

The most remarkable sporting achievement of 1998 was the advancement of the Maccabi Haifa soccer team to the quarter-final stage of one of Europe's leading competitions. In the process it pulled off a sensational victory over top French club Paris St. Germain in October and went on to beat Austrian club Ried to reach the quarter finals—the best-ever result by an Israeli team in Europe. (The quarter-final clash with Locomotive Moscow was scheduled for March 1999.)

Miscellaneous

Tatyana Susskin was sentenced to two years' imprisonment in January after being convicted of distributing incendiary posters in Hebron that depicted the Prophet Mohammed with a pig's head.

In a 5-4 decision on January 11, the Supreme Court denied an appeal by two Palestinian detainees against the Shin Bet's interrogation techniques; the two said they had been subjected to various forms of torture, including sleep deprivation and having their heads covered with sacks.

In a suit filed in the Haifa district court, Australian Lynn Zines, whose husband, Warren, died in the Maccabiah bridge disaster in July 1997, sought damages to the tune of $1.3 million.

In March it was announced that Mordechai Vanunu was being allowed out of solitary confinement and would be given permission to exercise with other prisoners at the Shikmah prison in Ashkelon. The 43-year-old Vanunu had served close to two-thirds of his 18-year sentence for revealing Israeli nuclear secrets to the *Sunday Times* of London when he worked as a technician at Israel's nuclear reactor in Dimonah. Vanunu had been kept in isolation since 1986. On May 4, a parole board rejected his request for early release.

On March 4, the Supreme Court permitted publication of the fact that 10 Lebanese citizens were being held in Israeli prisons as bargaining tools to secure the return of missing Israeli soldiers. Eight of them were reported to be Hezballah militants who had been kidnapped during IDF operations in south Lebanon. The court ruled that Israel could "hold in custody people, citizens of another country, that the state believes may be of use during negotiations over the missing and the captured." While the court agreed that the practice was a violation of human rights, it ruled that Israel's "vital interests" took precedence.

In mid-March Gregory Lerner, an immigrant from the former Soviet Union, pleaded guilty to 13 counts of fraud, attempted bribery, and other offenses. The plea bargain stipulated a six-year jail sentence and a fine of five million shekels ($1.4 million).

Dana International won the Eurovision song contest in England on May 9 with her song "Diva." The victory by International — a transsexual born Yaron Cohen — was cited by Israel's gay community as a sign of the growing recognition of its life-style.

The next month, the first-ever gay pride parade in the country's history took place. On June 26, over 1,500 homosexuals, along with some heterosexual supporters, marched through the streets of Tel Aviv.

Nine foreign workers — seven Romanians, one Indian, and one American — fell to their deaths on May 8 when a platform collapsed close to the top of a 250-meter smokestack under construction at the Ashkelon power station.

It was announced on May 12 that Rahman Zuabi, a Nazareth district court judge, would become the first Arab judge appointed to the Supreme Court; his term was scheduled to begin in 1999.

Israel Broadcasting Authority chief Uri Porat ordered the dismissal of two editors of Israel TV's nightly "Mabat" news show on May 26. Porat said the news show had demonstrated bias in its editing of footage that showed Prime Minister Netanyahu waving to a crowd of Betar Jerusalem soccer fans at a rally celebrating the team's championship victory, while some fans chanted, "Death to Arabs." The dismissals were ultimately reversed.

Two boys in their early teens were killed on June 10 when the roof of a Beersheba high-school gym collapsed. The roof was undergoing renovations at the time, and four separate inquiries were set up to investigate the disaster.

Amir Peretz, the incumbent Histadrut chairman, beat out Gesher Knesset member Maxim Levy to win the labor federation election on June 9. Peretz garnered a huge 77.7 percent of the vote.

Israel's indefatigable president, Ezer Weizman, said he would not attend the annual flight-course graduation flyover in early July, which also marked the country's and the air force's jubilees. This was after Commander Eitan Ben-Eliyahu ruled that the 74-year-old president and former air force commander was too old to pilot a jet trainer in the flyover.

Ma'ariv publisher Ofer Nimrodi was sentenced to eight months in prison in July for illegally tapping the phone of his competitor, *Yediot Aharonot*.

Shimon Sheves, the former director-general of the Prime Minister's Office under Yitzhak Rabin, was indicted in August for accepting bribes from contractors; a district court judge ordered that the trial be held in camera.

Markus Klingberg, the ailing 80-year-old former deputy head of the Nes Tzionah Biological Research Institute, was released from jail and put under house arrest in September, after serving more than 15 years of an 18-year sentence for passing biological warfare information to the Soviet Union.

A survey released in October revealed that 34 percent of Israelis rated David Ben-Gurion Israel's most important prime minister. Second was Yitzhak Rabin with 21 percent, followed by Menachem Begin with 20 percent, and Shimon Peres with 7 percent. Benjamin Netanyahu got 2 percent.

Linor Abargil, an 18-year-old Netanyah resident, won the Miss World beauty pageant in the Seychelle Islands in November.

The Knesset passed a bill in December requiring that at least half the songs played on state radio be Israeli. According to the bill's sponsor, Labor MK Yona Yahav, its intent was to limit the Americanization of Israeli society.

Personalia

Zevulun Hammer, the leader of the National Religious Party and education minister, died on January 20 at the age of 62 after a long battle with cancer. Hammer, who first became a minister in 1975, served in numerous governments.

Among other prominent Israelis who died during the year were Robert Friend, 84, a U.S.-born Hebrew University professor and English-language poet; Haim Bar On, 54, publisher of the successful *Globes* financial daily; Mordechai Olmert, 87, a Knesset member for the right-wing Herut party (1955–61) and father of Jerusalem mayor Ehud Olmert; Yitzhak Modai, 72, who served as Likud finance minister and in 1984 helped bring Israel's economy back from triple-digit inflation; Shimon Samet, 94, the doyen of Israeli journalism who worked for the daily *Ha'aretz* from 1932 until his death; Jacob Katz, 93, historian and winner of the 1980 Israel Prize for Jewish history, and former rector of the Hebrew University; David Ayalon, 84, Hebrew University professor emeritus and pioneer Islamic scholar; Menahem Digly, 61, former commander of the elite Sayeret Matkal commando unit; Brother Daniel Rufeisen, 76, the Haifa Carmelite monk who was born Jewish and who helped save hundreds of Jews from the Mir ghetto during World War II by passing himself off as non-Jewish and working for the German police in Poland; Hava Lazarus-Yafeh, 68, a Hebrew University professor, Islamic scholar, and winner of the 1993 Israel Prize for history; Nehama Hendel, 62, well-known Israeli singer; Menashe Zamro, 93, chief *kes* (spiritual leader) of the country's Ethiopian Jews; Aharon Nahmias, 66, former Labor Knesset member and mayor of Safed; Prof. Ra'anan Weitz, 87, regional planning expert, Jewish Agency settlement department head 1963-84, and 1990 winner of the Israel Prize for his contributions to the state; Brig. Gen. Avner (Walter) Bar-On, 90, Israel's first chief military censor.

PETER HIRSCHBERG

The Absorption of Soviet Immigrants in Israel

THE WAVE OF IMMIGRATION from the former Soviet Union (FSU) in the period 1990–1998 brought over 750,000 new immigrants to Israel; the same period saw the arrival of another 130,000 immigrants from other countries. The influx from the FSU was similar in absolute numbers to the mass wave of immigration that entered the new State of Israel during 1948–1951 (690,000 new immigrants), previously the largest in the nation's history. However, relative to the size of the existing, or receiving, population, the new wave was considerably smaller, since the Israeli population had grown sixfold between the state's establishment and the beginning of the 1990s. (The Israeli population was estimated at the end of 1989 as 4.6 million—of whom 3.7 million were Jews; by the end of 1998 it reached more than 6 million—4.8 million Jews.)

A comparison with worldwide migration activity in the 1990s shows that, in absolute numbers, the size of this particular flow of immigrants to one country in such a short period was among the largest; and relative to the size of the receiving population it far exceeded the flow to all other countries that absorb migrant populations. From 1990 to 1994, Israel took in an annual average of 23.7 immigrants per 1,000 persons in its population, as compared to 7.6 per 1,000 in Canada, 6.8 per 1,000 in Australia, and 2.6 per 1,000 in the United States during the same period.

This article provides a profile of the FSU immigrants who arrived in the 1990s, based on findings from the vast body of research that has accumulated to this point. The article focuses on various facets of the absorption process: employment, housing, mastery of Hebrew, geographic distribution, culture, and the like. The impact of this immigration on the Israeli population, on the national economy and workforce, and on the cultural life of the country is also considered. A discussion of the prospects for future immigration from the FSU countries is presented below.

The data and descriptions presented here are based on many sources: statistical data from the Israel Central Bureau of Statistics; surveys of the Ministry of

Note: This article is based on the book *Profile of an Immigration Wave: The Absorption Process of Immigrants from the Former Soviet Union, 1990–1995,* ed. M. Sicron and E. Leshem (Magnes Press, Hebrew University, Jerusalem, 1998, in Hebrew with an English summary). Some new material and updated data (up to 1998, where available) have been added. The authors wish to thank Prof. Sergio DellaPergola for his suggestions and comments.

Immigration Absorption and the Jewish Agency; a series of surveys carried out by research institutes (mainly the JDC-Brookdale Institute of Gerontology and Human Development), documentation from the files of agencies dealing with immigration and absorption, and numerous studies conducted by academic researchers. Use was also made of some as yet unpublished studies. Most of the sources of information noted here are part of an extensive literature on the recent Soviet immigration that has been recorded in a two-volume bibliography containing nearly 600 items, much of it published in Hebrew.[1]

The footnote references include primarily sources available in English, with selected Hebrew sources as well. A comprehensive listing of sources, in Hebrew, is contained in the work by the authors cited on the first page of this article.

SOCIODEMOGRAPHIC PROFILE

Numbers, Origins, Composition[2]

Between 1959 and 1989 the number of Jews registered in the official Soviet censuses—those identifying themselves officially as Jews, the "core" Jewish population—declined from 2.279 million to 1.480 million. This decline was the result of emigration and also of the negative balance between births and deaths. Estimates of the numbers of non-Jews in Jewish families and of those Jews who were not registered as Jews possibly add an additional million to the "enlarged" Jewish community in the FSU at that time. Thus, on the eve of the mass exodus, the Jewish community numbered some 2.5 million.[3]

From the last quarter of 1989 to the end of 1998, about 750,000 new immigrants arrived in Israel from the FSU. The influx was especially massive in 1990 and 1991 (185,000 and 148,000 arrivals, respectively). In the period 1992–95, about 65,000 new immigrants arrived each year. The numbers continued to drop:

---

[1]E. Leshem and D. Sor, *Immigration and Absorption of Former Soviet Union Jewry, Selected Bibliography and Abstracts 1990–1993* (Henrietta Szold Institute and Hebrew University, Jerusalem, 1994); E. Leshem and D. Sor, *Immigration and Absorption of Former–Soviet Union Jewry, Selected Bibliography and Abstracts 1994–1996* (Henrietta Szold Institute and Hebrew University, Jerusalem, 1997).

[2]The source for most demographic data in this section is the Israel Central Bureau of Statistics. See *Statistical Abstract of Israel*, 1998, and previous issues; *Monthly Bulletin of Statistics*; *Immigration to Israel* (annual publication; last issue–1996); and *Immigrant Population from the Former USSR, 1995, Demographic Trends* (Publication no. 1076, 1998), and previous issues.

[3]See S. DellaPergola, "The Global Context of Migration to Israel," in *Immigration to Israel: Sociological Perspectives*, ed. E. Leshem and J. T. Shuval (New Brunswick, 1998), pp. 51–94. See also note 28.

in 1996 the number of arrivals was 59,000; in 1997, 55,000; in 1998, 46,000. (See table 1.)

Immigration to Israel constituted only a part of the emigration of the Jewish community from the FSU. It is estimated that, in the period 1990–98, 1.1 to 1.2 million persons left the FSU: 750,000 immigrated to Israel, some 300,000 left for the United States, 50,000 went to Canada, and around 90,000 settled in Germany.

The new arrivals came from different areas of the FSU, nearly 80 percent originating in the European republics and about 20 percent in the Asiatic republics. Initially the proportion of newcomers from the European republics was even higher, but it later fell off. The largest proportion of immigrants—over 60 percent—arrived from Russia and Ukraine. Among immigrants from Asia, half came from Uzbekistan. (See table 2.)

Non-Jews among immigrants. The immigration that arrived in the 1990s included a larger proportion of non-Jews (mostly Christians) than in any previous body of new arrivals. Under Israel's Law of Return, which grants automatic citizenship to Jewish immigrants, prospective residents are entitled to this status if they have one Jewish parent, a Jewish spouse, or a Jewish grandparent. It is difficult to know the exact number of non-Jewish arrivals, however. For one thing, the registration of religion in Ministry of Interior records generally occurs some time after the immigrant's arrival (sometimes only after a few years). For another, some of the immigrants define themselves as having "no religion." According to data published by the Israel Central Bureau of Statistics on the religion of all immigrants, the proportion of non-Jews among all immigrants in the period 1990–96 was 13.5 percent. (See table 3.) Among FSU immigrants—who constituted 85 percent of the total—the proportion was higher and could have been around 15 percent. The proportion was much lower at the beginning of the mass immigration (around 4 percent among immigrants arriving in 1990–91), but it increased year after year and in 1996 reached 29 percent. The proportion of non-Jews was even higher among immigrants who arrived in 1997–98. The majority of non-Jewish immigrants are spouses of Jews. It is known that in the FSU the proportion of mixed couples among new marriages was higher than 50 percent.

Demographic Characteristics[4]

The immigration from the FSU has a number of distinctive attributes.

Gender. Soviet Jews have a large proportion of women as compared with the Jewish population in Israel. The surplus of women was found in the 30+ age groups and was remarkable in the elderly population (the 65+ group contained 601 men for every 1,000 women, as compared to 832 men per 1,000 women in the

---

[4]See note 2.

Israeli Jewish population). This is due to the large number of one-parent families with children headed by women, many of them divorcees, in some cases widows.

Age structure. The FSU population has a lower percentage of children and a slightly higher percentage of elderly people as compared with the Israeli population (though the percentage of the elderly among the new immigrants is considerably lower than that of the Jews remaining in the FSU). This reflects the low level of fertility among the FSU immigrant families and is reflected in their age composition. (See table 4.)

Marital status. The FSU immigration has a high percentage of divorced women and men as compared with the population in Israel (8 to 15 percent of the new-immigrant females aged 15 and above were divorced, compared to 3 percent of Israeli Jewish women, while 16 percent were widows, as compared to 12 percent of the Israelis).

Household composition. An average household of Soviet immigrants contains 3.2 persons, which is slightly lower than the average among the Jewish population (though considerably higher than that of immigrants of European and American origin in Israel). These households include far fewer children than other Israeli households, but in many cases grandparents are part of the family. There is also a high proportion—8 percent—of one-parent families (more than 13 percent of households with children) and a small number of households comprising single people (less than 10 percent, as compared with nearly 20 percent among the veteran Israeli population). The composition of households has far-reaching implications for housing needs (e.g., joint residence of three generations in the same apartment) and for welfare services (e.g., the support system for one-parent families).

Sociocultural Characteristics

Educational levels. The FSU immigrants are on the average highly educated as compared with the existing population. Of all immigrants aged 15 and up, 56 percent had 13 or more years of schooling.[5] (The relevant figure for Israelis in 1989, on the eve of the immigration influx, though not fully comparable, was 28 percent.) Immigrants from the Asiatic republics were less highly educated than those from Europe, but even among the former the percentage who had 13 or more years of schooling was higher than that of the population of Israel. (See table 5.)

Occupations of immigrants before immigrating. Both male and female immigrants had high rates of participation in the labor force in the Soviet Union. Two-thirds of the employed worked in scientific and academic or in professional and

---

[5]Figures based on surveys carried out some time after arrival; table figures based on data supplied upon entry into the country.

technical occupations. About 75,000 of the new arrivals listed their professions as engineers or architects, along with 15,000 physicians and dentists and some 15,000 musicians, performing artists, and writers (more than half were musicians). These were far higher rates than for Israelis. The proportion of highly skilled immigrants was even higher among the early arrivals, in 1990–91, but that declined somewhat subsequently. (See table 6.)

"Migrant" population.[6] In comparison to the smaller immigration to Israel from the Soviet Union in the 1970s (some 150,000), the influx of the 1990s was more of a "migration" than an *"aliyah,"* an ideologically motivated "ascent" to the Land of Israel. In other words, the 1990s arrivals were motivated more by push factors (a desire to leave the FSU) than by pull factors (an attraction to Israel). Three main factors spurred this migration: (1) high levels of personal and family distress; (2) a perception of crisis in the basic spheres of existence— social order, political regime, economy; and (3) a pessimistic outlook about the future of the FSU at both the personal-family and the general social level in the basic areas just mentioned.

Most of the new arrivals opted to move to Israel by default; they would have preferred the United States or other major Western countries (Canada, Germany, etc.). The scales were tipped in Israel's favor by both negative and positive factors: entry to those other countries was restricted, Israel had an "open-door" policy, and the recommendations of relatives and friends who had already settled in Israel carried weight.

Weak attachment to the Jewish people.[7] Although the majority of the new arrivals identify themselves more as Jews than as Russians or Israelis, their identity and attachment in this regard are largely formal and external (an "imagined Judaism"), deriving from their almost wholly ethnic definition and identity in their places of origin. It must be borne in mind that meaningful Jewish community life, in terms of both substance and organization, was forbidden in the Soviet Union during the entire period of Communist rule; any external display of Jewish identity, whether in its national or its religious aspect, was denounced and persecuted by the authorities. Similarly, on the informal plane of family tradition, scant Jewish content was handed down. This was in part the result of the

---

[6]See H.T. Margoulis and N. Zinger, *Things You See from There . . . Factors Influencing Immigration Tendencies from the FSU* (Center for Development, Rehovot, 1993), in Hebrew; R. Wisel and E. Leshem, *Trends in Immigration from Russia and Ukraine* (Jewish Agency Department of Immigration and Absorption, Jerusalem, 1996), in Hebrew.

[7]See J. Weber, Introduction, in *Jewish Identities in the New Europe,* ed. J. Weber, (Litman Library of Jewish Civilization, London, 1994), pp. 1–32; Z. Gitelman, *Immigration and Identity: The Resettlement and Impact of Soviet Immigrants on Israeli Politics and Society* (Wilstein Institute of Jewish Policy Studies, Los Angeles, 1995); and L. Gozman, "Is Living in Russia Worthwhile?" in *Russian Jews on Three Continents,* ed. N. Levin-Epstein, Y. Ro'i, and P. Ritterband (London, 1997), pp. 406–15.

modernization and sovietization processes that spanned several generations; however, its chief cause was the physical annihilation of the traditional concentrations of Jews in the western Soviet Union during the Holocaust. Despite the severe losses of people and the near eradication of Jewish religion and culture, starting in 1994, there was a significant surge of interest, especially within the younger generation, in Jewish subject matter. This interest was discernible among both the arrivals in Israel and those Jews who remained in the FSU. It was expressed in growing participation in activities related to Jewish life organized by local Jewish groups and by institutions outside the FSU, including Israeli institutions.

Russian identity and culture.[8] In their social and cultural attitudes and behavior, the Jews from the FSU are the products of Soviet socialization and social control, intertwined with the Russian culture that had evolved since the late 19th century. Apart from a relatively small group of immigrants from the traditionalist communities in the FSU's southeast region (Georgia, Caucasus, Bukhara), the majority of Soviet Jews, including those who did not originate in the Russian Federation, perceive themselves as being within the Russian cultural orbit. Far from disavowing the society and culture of their homeland when they immigrated to Israel, they continued to maintain Russian culture as a positive, meaningful element of their identity and self-image, even though they felt compelled to leave their place of birth. These immigrants, few of whom received a Jewish education, were an integral part of the Russian middle class and served as agents of Russian culture throughout the Soviet empire. Moreover, between 1989 and 1995, the immigration included a relatively large number of Jews—some 80,000—from Moscow and St. Petersburg, the centers of culture, government, and science in the FSU. This group not only stands out from the rest of the immigration in its professional and educational attainments; it also defines itself as the elite, or "intelligentsia," of the FSU community. Its members are disproportionately represented in the community's political, cultural, and scientific leadership and in the Russian-language mass media, which is the cement that unites the Russian community in Israel around this leadership elite.

General values of Soviet immigrants.[9] Studies of the world view of immigrants,

---

[8]See M. Lissak and E. Leshem, "The Russian Intelligentsia in Israel: Between Ghettoization and Integration," *Israel Affairs 1995*, 2, no. 2, pp. 20–36; and E. Ben-Refael, E. Olshtain, and E. Gaist, *Aspects of Identity and Language Acquisition Among Immigrants from the Commonwealth of Independent States* (Research Institute for Innovation in Education, Hebrew University, Jerusalem, Publication no. 137, 1994), in Hebrew.

[9]See A. Ben-David, "Cross-cultural Differences Between Russian Immigrants and Israeli College Students: The Effect of the Family on the Sense of Coherence," *Israel Journal of Psychiatry and Related Sciences* 33, no. 1, 1996, pp. 13–20; J. Mirsky, Y. Ginath, E. Perl, and M. Ritsner, "Psychological Profile of Soviet-Jewish Late Adolescents: A Pre-immigration Study, *Israel Journal of Psychiatry and Related Sciences* 29, no. 3, 1992, pp. 150–58;

conducted shortly after their arrival, reveal that they retain the values, concepts, and behavioral patterns in which they were educated and which were the key to their survival in their homeland. These attitudes and perceptions were forged in a Soviet regime and society that sought to mold "modern" individuals able to cope in an advanced industrial society. However, such individuals possess few of the skills necessary to function in a free, democratic, participatory "civic culture." While the immigrants' political outlook and civil orientation were shaped by the Communist tradition, their socioeconomic views were formed during the period of *perestroika*. Thus, Soviet immigrants tend to show a preference for social-democratic solutions to social problems, intertwined with liberal economic attitudes.

The effects of Soviet socialization are also evident in the newcomers' approach to interpersonal relations, which assumes an inherent tension between the family system and external surroundings, between private life and public life. Loyalty, commitment, and openness are directed toward the inner, intimate, informal circle—the immediate family and a small number of friends and relatives; individuals outside that circle are perceived as power-hungry, exploitative, and manipulative.

In the realm of work, the immigrants' values are based on individualism and materialism—the antitheses of the values of the Communist period. The immigrants view work more as a means to obtain material gratification than as a channel through which to achieve self-fulfillment. These values, reflecting an instrumental, pragmatic, rational orientation, guided the immigrants' decisions in their initial period of assimilation in Israel in the realms of housing, job hunting, language acquisition, and recourse to services.

Another element in the immigrants' world view is their attitude toward religion. Seventy years of Communist rule forged a distinctly secularist orientation, although in the final years of Communism, some immigrants became more open to religious influences. Secularization is greater among the younger age groups, those with higher levels of education, and mixed-married families. A comparison of the immigrants with the general Israeli Jewish population shows large disparities in self-definition along the religious-secular divide—in the observance of religious precepts (keeping kosher, traveling on the Sabbath, attending synagogue services) and in attitudes toward religion-state issues (introduction of civil marriage and divorce, secular burial, opening businesses on the Sabbath, per-

T. Horowitz, *Between Three Political Cultures: Immigrants from the FSU in Israel* (Davis Institute, Hebrew University of Jerusalem, pub. no. 50, 1996), in Hebrew; and E. Leshem, "Judaism, Religious Way of Life and Attitudes Towards Questions of Religion and State Among Immigrants from the FSU," in *Yearbook of Religion and State 1993–1994* (Center for Jewish Pluralism of the Movement for Progressive Judaism in Israel, TelAviv, 1994), pp. 35–54, in Hebrew.

mitting the sale of pork, etc.). On these and other issues the new immigrants show a greater propensity toward secularism in defining themselves, in their way of life, and in urging a reduction in the influence of religion in Israeli public life. While most Israelis also regard themselves as secular, they are familiar with religious practice, many incorporate traditional customs in their lifestyle, and they are somewhat more accepting of the role of religion in the state.

ISRAEL ON THE EVE OF THE IMMIGRATION INFLUX

Economic Situation[10]

The period prior to the onset of the wave of immigration at the end of 1989 was characterized by: (1) Relatively slow economic growth. The gross national product grew by 1 percent in 1989, below the population increase for that year. Investments had declined relative to previous years. (2) Rising unemployment, which reached nearly 9 percent in 1989. The number of employed increased by only 0.5 percent that year. (3) A steep increase of 20 percent in prices in 1989— lower than in the years until 1985, but still quite high.

Social and Cultural Patterns[11]

At the end of the 1980s, Israeli society and culture were undergoing significant change, similar to the situation in the FSU, which was in the incipient stages of the transition to a post-Soviet society, whose contours were still indistinct. Israeli society in this period was characterized by processes of cosmopolitanism, ethnicity, and pluralism; it bore the hallmarks of transition from a compact, homogeneous society to a large, heterogeneous one, from a centralized to a decentralized system of government, and from extensive government involvement in the economy to a modified market economy. Israel was developing its ties with the acknowledged international centers of culture, the cultural barriers with the outside world were breaking down, and collectivist values and the national consensus were rapidly eroding, as various subgroups gained political strength and legitimization even though their values often conflicted with those of the dominant value system. The period before late 1989 was also characterized by slow population growth (about 1.5 percent per annum). In the years before 1989 there were fewer immigrants than emigrants, creating a negative migration balance.

---

[10]See Bank of Israel, *Annual Report, 1989* and *Annual Report, 1990* (Jerusalem, 1990, 1991).

[11]See Ben-Refael, Olshtain, and Gaist, *Aspects of Identity and Language Acquisition.*

The Immigration and Absorption Authorities[12]

The huge wave of immigration found the Israeli government and the Jewish Agency unprepared. No detailed program for housing or employing immigrants existed, nor was the situation different in other domains. There was no coordination or division of responsibilities among the public bodies in charge of absorption. Uncertainty prevailed, and contradictory assessments were adduced about the scale and duration of the immigration influx. No one knew where the vast resources needed to absorb the new immigrants would come from. Most serious was the problem of accommodating the immigrants immediately upon their arrival and during their first year in the country: there was no room in the existing absorption centers, which in the 1970s and 1980s had been the principal venue for the immigrants' initial reception.

The system of direct absorption was adopted in mid-1990. The declared government policy limited its involvement in absorption to the direct and indirect financing of the immigrants' basic needs (without the need for bureaucratic approval for each expenditure). The system formally gave the immigrants responsibility for their initial settlement in the country, with the central government assuring them a modest "basic income" during their first year in Israel (the "absorption basket," which consisted of specified financial allocations in accordance with the family's size and composition). At the same time, the central government and the Jewish Agency put into effect a system of incentives through which some of the services for the new immigrants (such as finding housing and jobs) were provided by local governments and volunteer organizations. These bodies and the informal social networks—including relatives and friends of the immigrants who had settled in Israel earlier—were also encouraged to develop services for new immigrants within the community.

At the beginning of the immigration wave, the veteran Jewish population showed itself ready and willing to facilitate the immigrants' absorption by various means—helping individuals to deal with the bureaucracy, accompanying them to health clinics and banks, and collecting clothes, furniture, and other necessities for the newcomers. In attitude surveys, the veteran population even declared itself willing to pay higher taxes for absorption purposes. At the same time, restrictions that had prevented the private business sector from assisting in absorption were lifted, enabling immigrants to turn to nongovernmental sources for various purposes. By channeling the immigrants into the private market in the

---

[12]See R. Alterman, "Can Planning Help in Time of Crisis? Planners' Responses to Israel's Recent Wave of Mass Immigration, *Journal of the American Planning Association* 61, no. 2, 1995, pp. 156–77; A. Doron and H. J. Karger, "The Politics of Immigration Policy in Israel," *International Migration* 31, no. 4, 1993, pp. 497–512; and Israel State Controller, *Annual Reports*: no. 40, 1990; no. 42, 1992; no. 46, 1996 (Jerusalem), in Hebrew.

initial absorption stage, the central government was able to deploy for direct intervention in the next stage of absorption beyond the first year. The critical area necessitating immediate government intervention was that of housing. Following a ten-year period of disengagement from the housing market, the central government now reinvolved itself directly in that sphere in order to bring about a significant expansion and acceleration of housing construction. However, in the spheres of education, health, and social welfare the government acted to reduce reliance on special facilities and programs and to provide the immigrants with the same services and rights as those of the local population.

THE ABSORPTION PROCESS IN VARIOUS SPHERES

Housing[13]

From the beginning of the influx at the end of 1989, in accordance with the policy of "direct absorption," the immigrants were directed to rent apartments on the free market. Because of the limited housing supply in the center of the country and spiraling rents, several households of immigrants occasionally took up residence together within a single apartment, a situation that made for higher housing density than among the Israeli population. (See table 7.) However, housing density generally decreased as a function of length of stay in the country. Rental payments initially and, later, mortgage payments for dwellings that were purchased placed a heavy financial burden on the budgets of new immigrant families. A significant portion of their available income, which was lower than that of the Israeli population, went to meet housing costs. Immigrants generally began to purchase homes after about two years in the country. An upsurge in housing purchases was discernible beginning in 1993, thanks to the extensive supply of flats available as a result of large-scale public construction completed about that time (the government had guaranteed builders that it would purchase unsold flats) and special terms for eligible prospective buyers.

By the middle of 1996, 55 percent of the immigrants who had arrived between

---

[13]See Ch. Fialkoff, "Israel's Housing Policy During a Period of Massive Immigration," in *Planning and Housing in Israel in the Wake of Rapid Changes*, ed. Y. Golani, S. Eldor, and M. Garon (R. & L. Creative Communication, Tel Aviv, 1992); Central Bureau of Statistics, *Households of Immigrants Who Arrived from the Former USSR in October–December 1993, A Follow-up Survey, One and Two Years After Immigration* (Briefing 26, 1997); J. Rosenbaum-Tamari and N. Damian, *First Five Years in Israel, Immigrants from the FSU Who Arrived in September 1991 Compared to Those Who Arrived in July 1990* (Report no. 11, Ministry of Immigration Absorption, Division for Research and Planning, 1997), in Hebrew.

1990 and 1995 had permanent housing, through either ownership or public rental, with the percentage increasing with length of time in the country. Nevertheless, in 1996, 34 percent of the 1990 arrivals and 46 percent of the 1991 arrivals were still renting on the open, private market. Purchasers of homes were mainly families with two working-age parents, whereas most of the elderly, the one-parent families, and the single people continued to rent on the private market and resorted to public housing subsidies. It is noteworthy that flats purchased by immigrants were as a rule cheaper than the average price in the housing market; in many cases the purchase was made by pooling the resources of the extended family and organizing a joint, multigenerational residence.

Geographical Patterns of Settlement[14]

An examination of the new immigrants' distribution throughout the country, based on their chosen places of residence, shows a greater tendency to gravitate toward the peripheral regions as compared with the general Jewish population in 1989. The Southern district contained, in 1995, the largest over-representation of new immigrants as compared with the overall distribution of the Jewish population, while the Tel Aviv and especially the Jerusalem districts showed a pronounced under-representation. The arrivals from the Asiatic republics tended to be concentrated more in the center of the country (Tel Aviv and Central districts), while most of the 1990–95 arrivals from the European republics resided away from the center.

The major geographic pattern that emerges from a perusal of population data for Jews and new immigrants at the level of subdistricts is a relatively high concentration of new immigrants on the fringes of metropolitan Haifa (Acre, Jezre'el, and Hadera subdistricts); in part of the southern fringes of the urban area in the heart of the country (especially in the Ashkelon subdistrict); and in the fringes of metropolitan Tel Aviv (Ramla subdistrict). In other words, in the metropolitan areas, the new immigrants tend to be concentrated in the remote suburban subdistricts, while in the peripheral regions, a significant concentration of new immigrants could be found primarily in the Be'er Sheva subdistrict. Concomitantly, they tended to settle mainly in the development towns that were founded in the 1950s and 1960s on the fringes of the metropolitan centers of Tel Aviv and Haifa, where housing was cheap and the socioeconomic status of the population lower than in the larger cities. Immigrants settled in moderate numbers in the southern development towns—undeterred by the geographic remoteness and low

---

[14]See Central Bureau of Statistics: *Population in Localities, 1994, Demographic Characteristics, by Geographical Divisions* (Special Publication 1026, 1994); "Immigrant Population from the Former USSR, Selected Data, 1995" (Briefing 9, 1997); *Immigrant Population from the Former USSR, 1995, Demographic Trends* (Special Publication 1076, 1998, and previous publications in the series).

socioeconomic status of the population—lured by a large supply of Ministry of Housing flats selling cheaply and on convenient credit terms. (See table 8.)

The pattern of regional distribution that emerged at the national level was replicated at the intra-urban regional level. Thus, we find concentrations of new immigrants in the old neighborhoods of the cities and towns that were built in the 1950s and 1960s and, in the big cities, in the old core neighborhoods that have deteriorated into slums but offer low rental and purchase prices and access to places of employment, commercial outlets, and service institutions.

In the outer ring of metropolitan Tel Aviv, on the fringes of metropolitan Haifa, and in cities distant from the center, immigrants reside in the new government housing projects of the 1990s. The concentration of FSU immigrants in these new construction areas is especially pronounced in the southern towns, where they account for half or more of the population of the new neighborhoods. In the northern periphery, this pattern is found in Upper Nazareth; in Carmiel, by contrast, the pattern of housing acquisition did not create dense concentrations, and the many immigrants there are scattered throughout the town.

It should be noted that the concentrations of immigrants in the medium-size and small towns on the fringes of the metropolitan areas mentioned and in the Southern district are in large degree the outcome of internal migration, a process that encompassed more than half the new immigrants between 1991 and 1994. In the first stage, immigrants were inclined to opt for the center of the country, but afterward, when they were no longer eligible for the enlarged government rent subsidies that they got during their first year in the country and began to consider buying apartments, they often gravitated toward the fringes, especially the southern fringes of metropolitan Tel Aviv and the Southern district. In the initial absorption stage, the considerations that guided the immigrants were primarily social and psychological: a desire to be close to friends and relatives who could induce a sense of security and support. However, when faced with the need to change location, social-psychological factors diminished in importance, and the decision-making process was guided by economic considerations: a desire to stay close to the major centers of employment while reducing housing costs. Thus, immigrants who left the core city for the metropolitan fringes remain close to the employment centers in the core, but enjoy significantly cheaper housing than could be had in the urban center.

Employment[15]

Of the FSU immigrants aged 15+ who arrived in Israel from 1990 to 1997, 380,000, or more than half, were employed before emigrating. As noted above,

[15]See Central Bureau of Statistics, "Employment of Immigrants Who Arrived from the Former USSR in October–December 1993, A Follow-up Survey Two Years After Immigration" (Briefing 27, 1997); CBS, Labour Force Survey 1996 (Special Publication 1080,

more than half had 13 or more years of education, as compared with 28 percent of the Israeli population in 1989. The newcomers found themselves in a labor market that was not prepared to absorb this type or volume of human capital and was itself suffering from relatively high unemployment (above 8 percent), a situation that was constantly aggravated irrespective of the immigration factor. The policy of the central government left employment absorption to the labor market: no effort was made to steer immigrants to particular jobs or to initiate makeshift work for them. At the same time, employers were offered substantial incentives to absorb immigrants and prepare them for employment by teaching them Hebrew and providing job retraining programs, as well as by assisting small entrepreneurs among the newcomers. Nevertheless, 34 percent of the immigrants who had been employed prior to immigration failed to enter the Israeli labor force after three years in the country.

The process of entering the labor force typically lasted two to three years, longer for women than for men. Average rates of participation in the labor force among immigrants of all ages in Israel were higher than those among the veteran population; the immigrants' participation reached a peak at ages 35–44 and declined sharply after age 55. In the 55+ age group, employment absorption was especially problematic in the postretirement group but also in the years just before retirement. Women had a harder time finding work than men at these ages. The participation of males in the labor force was greater among those with higher education than among the less well educated; this phenomenon was even more pronounced among women. The length of time immigrants spent looking for work

---

1996); M. Beenstock and Y. Ben Menahem, *The Labor Market Absorption of CIS Immigrants to Israel 1989–94* (Discussion Paper no. 95.06, Maurice Falk Institute for Economic Research in Israel, Jerusalem, 1995); D. Czamanski, N. Gomelski, and D. Simmons-Cohen, *The Promotion of Immigrant Entrepreneurship: An Evaluation Case Study in the Haifa Area* (The Technion, Faculty of Architecture and Town Planning, Haifa, 1994); Z. Eckstein and R. Schahar, *On the Transition to Work of New Immigrants: Israel 1990–92* (Discussion Paper no. 95.04, Maurice Falk Institute for Economic Research in Israel, Jerusalem, 1995); K. Flug, N. Kasir, and G. Ofer, *The Absorption of Soviet Immigrants in the Israeli Labor Market, Occupational Substitution and Retention* (Discussion Paper no. 92.13, Bank of Israel, Jerusalem, 1992); also appears in *Immigrants: Liability or Asset?* ed. N. Carmon (The Technion, Haifa, 1993); K. Flug and N. Kasir, *The Absorption in the Labor Market of Immigrants from the CIS, The Short Run* (Discussion Paper no. 93.09, Bank of Israel, Jerusalem, 1993); I. Lithwick and J. Habib, *Absorption of Immigrants from the Former Soviet Union into the Labor Force* (Joint-Brookdale Institute of Gerontology and Human Development, Jerusalem, 1996); G. Naveh, G. Noam, and E. Benita, "The Employment and Economic Situation of Immigrants from the Former Soviet Union: Selected Findings from the National Employment Survey," in *Immigrant Absorption in Israel (Selected Research Papers)*, ed. G. Noam (JDC-Brookdale Institute of Gerontology and Human Development, Jerusalem, 1994); Y. Weiss and M. Gotlibovski, *Immigration, Search and Loss of Skill* (Foerder Institute of Economic Research, Tel Aviv University, Tel Aviv, 1995), pp. 19–40.

was a function of the demand for workers and of the immigrants' personal traits: gender, age, education, profession, fluency in Hebrew, knowledge of English, area of residence, and more.

Still, the high percentage (a third) of those from the labor force who were unemployed in the first year in Israel decreased relatively quickly, and within three to four years reached approximately the same level as for the working population overall. The transition from unemployment was more rapid for men than for women and slower for those above the age of 45 than for younger immigrants. However, among both women and the 45+ population, the move from unemployment into employment was relatively rapid.(See table 9.)

The findings of various surveys on employment show clearly that most new immigrants were unable to find work in their professions even after four years in the country. In 1997, 11 percent of all immigrants who had arrived since 1990 (most of them from the FSU) were employed in scientific and academic occupations and another 12 percent in professional and technical occupations (as compared with 34 percent who had been employed in each category in their home countries). On the other hand, the proportion of new immigrants employed in Israel as skilled or unskilled workers in industry, construction, and agriculture was far higher than was the case abroad. In 1997, 52 percent of the new immigrants were employed in the above-mentioned occupations, as compared with 34 percent of the overall population. In most cases the immigrants found employment in new occupations of lower socioeconomic status. (See figure 2 and table 10.) It was also found that immigrants generally remained in the occupations where they first found employment; the majority did not return to their pre-immigration professions.

About 11,000 of the immigrants who arrived from 1990 to 1995 were classified as "scientists" by the government. Considered a major human resource, this group received substantial assistance in its professional absorption: its employment was subsidized, and its access to Israel's scientific community was facilitated. In their home countries, half of the scientists had been engaged in physics and mathematics, a quarter in the life sciences, and a smaller percentage in the social sciences. Fully 76 percent of these professionals found employment in their fields, in the public and private sectors, the majority with the help of government aid. After three years in Israel, most continued to be employed in their areas of specialization, though more than half were no longer the beneficiaries of government support. In the universities, however, only a small fraction of those absorbed were given tenured positions; the majority were employed on a temporary basis. The scientists' integration in industry was more rapid, although here their scientific skills were utilized to a lesser degree.

The situation of the engineers among the 1990s immigrants was radically different from that of the scientists. Some 65,000 new immigrants of the 1990–95 period declared that they had worked as engineers or architects in their home countries. Since in 1989 only 27,000 Israelis were employed in those professions, the result was a sudden large surplus of engineers in the labor market (even with some increase in the number of job openings). Although the professional certificates of 75 percent of the new-immigrant engineers were recognized by the Registrar of Engineers in the Ministry of Labor, in 1995 only 25 percent of new-immigrant engineers aged 20–54 were working as engineers, and another 9 percent were in ancillary professions. The great majority had found work in occupations not commensurate with their education (44 percent as skilled laborers and about 25 percent as unskilled laborers). Of those employed as engineers, the highest percentage is found in the automation, computer, and electrical occupations (40 percent).

About 14,000 of the FSU immigrants who arrived in Israel between 1990 and 1995 stated that they had worked as physicians or dentists (90 percent as physicians). In Israel, on the eve of the influx, there was an identical number of physicians and dentists, and 1,500 immigrants who arrived in Israel during this period from countries other than the FSU also listed their profession as "physician or dentist." An additional 2,000 Israelis — graduates of local or foreign medical and dentistry schools — would join their ranks between 1990 and 1995.

New immigrants wishing to practice medicine in Israel must submit their professional papers for review and undergo a licensing examination or, for the veteran practitioners among them, professional observation. The examination is preceded in most cases by a preparatory course given in the immigrants' language by the Ministry of Health. Of every 100 physicians who arrived in Israel from 1990 to 1995, 72 requested licenses from the Ministry of Health, and 37 were employed as physicians (though only 9 percent of them have tenure). For the most part, those who found work were given temporary positions that were of lower status than their previous employment and that paid poorly (often by the hour).[16]

The rate of absorption of new-immigrant teachers in their profession was even lower than that of the physicians. Of the FSU teachers who entered Israel from 1990 to 1995, 1,654 had taught in institutions of higher learning or at the high-school and post-high-school level, and another 28,870 were junior high school, elementary school, and kindergarten teachers. Yet in 1993 only 2,583 of these teachers were working in the Israeli elementary and post-elementary school system, and that figure included new immigrants from other occupations (engineers, musicians) who had undergone professional retraining. By 1994, the number had

---

[16]See A. Ponizovsky et al., "The Impact of Professional Adjustment on the Psychological Distress of Immigrant Physicians," *Stress Medicine* 12, no. 4, 1996, pp. 251–274; J. Bernstein and J. Shuval, "Occupational Continuity and Change Among Immigrant Physicians from the Former Soviet Union," *International Migration* 33, 1995, pp. 3–29; M. Ritsner et al., "Psychological Adjustment and Distress Among Soviet Immigrant Physicians: Demographic and Background Variables," *Israel Journal of Psychiatry and Related Sciences* 30, no. 4, 1993, pp. 244–54; and A. Fakturovich et al., "Psychological Adjustment Among Soviet Immigrant Physicians: Distress and Self-assessment of Its Sources," *Israel Journal of Psychiatry and Related Sciences* 33, no. 1, 1996, pp. 32–39.

risen to about 4,700 teachers. Younger teachers were more likely to find work in the educational system than older ones.

A high percentage of the FSU immigrants had formerly worked in the arts: 13,500 of the 1990–95 arrivals listed their occupations as musicians, writers, actors, and performing artists, with 55 percent of them having worked as musicians or as music teachers. This was twice or three times the number of working musicians in Israel at the time. As a result, even after the central government, local governments, and various public bodies created new places of employment for the immigrant musicians (new orchestras, more courses involving music studies, and so forth), more than half of the musicians had to take unskilled jobs. Even most of those who found work in the music profession received part-time, temporary employment that had a lower professional status than what they were accustomed to in the FSU and that was based on budgets provided by the authorities for only brief periods. The majority of the musicians augmented their salaries by teaching music.[17]

Acquiring Hebrew[18]

The overwhelming majority of the new immigrants knew no Hebrew when they arrived in Israel. New-immigrant children and adolescents picked up the language within the framework of the educational system, through special intensive courses and a system of extra classes during their first year in Israel. For adults there was a network of special, free, intensive Hebrew-language courses (*ulpan*), offered at different stages and levels of intensity, arranged by the central government in conjunction with the Jewish Agency and local governments. Initially, receipt of the "subsistence funds" given to immigrants during their first six months in the country was contingent on participation for five months in the first stage of such courses. However, starting in July 1990, attendance at Hebrew courses was no longer a condition for receiving the guaranteed income allowance. One result of this change was that many immigrants did not take advantage of the option to attend intensive Hebrew courses during their first months in the country, though some took formal classes later, in connection with work.

Immigrants are instrumentally motivated to learn Hebrew, believing this will help them find work or improve their work performance. The *ulpan* is also per-

---

[17]See J. Hirshberg and B. Brover, "The Russians Are Coming," in *Music in Time*, ed. M. Smoira-Cohen (Rubin Academy of Music and Dance, Jerusalem, 1993); and J. Hirshberg et al., *Profession: Musician; Absorption Processes of the Immigrant Musicians from the Soviet Union, 1989–1994* (Jerusalem Institute for Israeli Studies, Jerusalem, 1997), in Hebrew. See also Rosenbaum-Tamari and Damian, *First Five Years in Israel . . .* ; and Ben-Refael, Olshtain, and Gaist, *Aspects of Identity and Language Acquisition.*

[18]See L. H. Glinert, "Inside the Language Planner's Head: Tactical Responses to a Mass Immigration," *Journal of Multilingual and Multicultural Development* 16, no. 5, 1995, pp. 351–71.

ceived as a means to become acquainted with Israeli society and culture and as a place of social encounter. However, despite the contribution of the *ulpan*, immigrants feel that their knowledge of Hebrew remains passive and that they lack fluency. In April–May 1996, 58 percent of a representative sample of FSU immigrants who arrived from 1990 to 1995 said they spoke a little Hebrew or could barely speak it, while 23 percent said they spoke it fairly well and 19 percent well. The ability to conduct a conversation in Hebrew stands in inverse relation to age. Most of the immigrants up to age 44 speak Hebrew at least "fairly well," whereas older age groups say they speak the language slightly if at all. The ability to speak Hebrew is also higher among those with an academic education. These trends are apparent in all the surveys conducted on this subject. Although there is a definite connection between length of time in Israel and ability to converse in Hebrew, even after five years in the country, 25–39 percent of the 1990 arrivals were able to converse in Hebrew only with enormous difficulty. The major variable related to the ability to converse in Hebrew is frequency of encounters with veteran Israelis.

After five years, 18 percent of the immigrants were using Hebrew as their main or exclusive day-to-day language, while 38 percent spoke Hebrew and a foreign language in equal measure. Hebrew is used mainly at work (by 63 percent after five years in the country). The immigrants show a poorer ability to read and write Hebrew than to speak the language; adults show virtually no improvement in reading and writing Hebrew after 3.5 years in Israel. After five years in the country, 51 percent of immigrants aged 20 and above could read a simple letter in Hebrew. In practice, Hebrew speaking and reading tend to be exercised only in formal contacts with institutions and with bodies providing services, or on the job. In informal circumstances—within the family, in meetings with friends, or in mass media consumption—Russian is the main language of use, even among immigrants proficient in Hebrew. (See tables 11, 12.)

Social-Cultural Absorption[19]

In their attitudes and behavior, FSU immigrants can be seen to range from a segregationist extreme, one seeking to preserve the culture of origin, to various levels of involvement in the integrative and pluralistic culture of 1990s Israeli society. Immigrants maintain significant continuity of cultural patterns and of social values and norms in various spheres: political, professional, educational, health, and family. At the same time, certain processes of change can be discerned in these realms. Based on the studies surveyed for this article, it appears that most immigrants tend to integrate within Israeli society but do not forgo proximity to their group of origin or abandon its cultural indicators; that is, they adopt an Is-

---

[19]See note 9.

raeli identity based on a sense of Jewish belonging, but it goes along with a commitment to the continuity of Russian culture and the formation of a Russian community in Israel. The growth of the Russian cultural enclave has been accelerated by the immigrants' sociocultural traits described above, the widespread use of Russian language in the mass media—including the high-circulation Israel-based Russian press—the residential concentration of the immigrants, and their economic difficulties, which confine their social networks mainly to others from their home countries and largely to the immigrants who arrived together with them.[20]

Immigrant association activities and the attitudes of the veteran Israeli population toward the new arrivals contributed to the formation of the sociocultural profile of the Russian community. Despite the broad consensus within Israel on the importance of immigration, the majority of the public placed government aid to new immigrants at the bottom of the government's scale of priorities and displayed diminishing readiness to do volunteer work on behalf of new immigrants or to become their neighbors. Israel's Arab population manifested an especially hostile attitude toward the new immigrants. Young Israeli Jews, although in favor of immigration, developed negative stereotypes of the arrivals from the FSU and expected them to adapt themselves to Israeli society and culture. The downturn in the public's attitude toward the immigrants was also apparent in kibbutz society. In Israeli society overall, the older those surveyed and the higher their incomes, the more favorable their attitudes toward the new immigrants.[21]

Sharp complaints were voiced in particular by the former Caucasus community (so-called mountain Jews), who felt that Israelis in general had a highly negative attitude toward them, and that they were exploited, deprived, discriminated against, and treated as social outcasts.

At least three stages can be discerned in the evolution of social and cultural contacts between the immigrants and the veteran population. The first stage was relatively brief, lasting until 1992. In this period the immigrants were still in a state of "absorption shock," interested almost exclusively in providing for their basic material needs. Social networks during this stage were largely informal, comprising a small circle of friends and relatives from their home country. Formal organizing on a local or national basis was minimal, and there was intense rivalry among different groups in the Russian community to obtain the immigrants'

---

[20]See E. Leshem and M. Lissak, "Development and Consolidation of the Russian Community in Israel," in *Roots and Routes: Ethnicity and Migration in Global Perspective*, ed. S. Weil (Jerusalem, forthcoming); and N. Zilberg and E. Leshem, "Russian-language Press and Immigrant Community in Israel," *Revue Européenne des Migrations Internationales* 12, no. 3, 1996, pp. 173–90.

[21]E. Leshem, "The Israeli Public's Attitudes Towards the New Immigrants of the 1990s," *Social Security, Journal of Welfare and Social Security Studies* 3, special English ed., 1994, pp. 164–88.

support. The second stage in the formation of the Russian community in Israel began at the end of 1992, when—beyond the extension and consolidation of the informal ties—a formal, hierarchical system of self-help organizations emerged among the FSU immigrants. These groups enjoyed broad community support, were promoted by the Russian-language mass press, and organized public protests against various governmental agencies.

At this stage, the question of the immigrants' cultural identity became a visible and public issue. The central and local governments, which had followed a clearly assimilative approach, were taken aback by manifestations of a collective desire to preserve a cultural distinctiveness within Israeli society, one that went beyond Jewish and Israeli identity. Based on formal community consolidation and the powerful desire of immigrants to preserve and strengthen their distinctive cultural identity, relations with Israeli society entered their third stage in 1996. The dominant expression of this stage was the immigrants' growing political strength and the establishment of a sectorial party that gained their broad support and won substantial representation in the Knesset elections of May 1996 and subsequently in the government coalition. Thus, from their marginal social status at the beginning of the decade, the new immigrants penetrated the society's political core within a relatively brief period, becoming a swing group between the two large political blocs.[22]

The municipal elections held in November 1998 showed that the success of the three-year-old Russian Immigration Party (Yisrael B'Aliyah) in the Knesset elections was not a one-time phenomenon. Running for the first time in the municipal and local council elections, the party won 88 seats (including 16 deputy mayors, by coalition agreements), mainly in medium-size and small towns that had concentrations of immigrants. In addition, other independent lists of Russian immigrants won significant numbers of seats in some large towns, such as Ashdod and Jerusalem.

Integration of Children and Youth[23]

From 1990 to 1997, about 180,000 children and adolescents below the age of 18 arrived from the FSU. Of these, 136,000 were in the 5–17 age group (33,000 aged 15–17), and most of them were integrated into the educational system. How-

---

[22]See E. Rogovin-Frankel, "The Russian Vote in the 1996 Israeli Elections," *East European Jewish Affairs* 26, no. 1, 1996, pp. 3–24; and T. Horowitz, "Determining Factors of the Vote Among Immigrants from the FSU," in *Elections in Israel–1996*, ed. A. Arian and M. Shamir (NYU Press, New York, 1999), pp. 97–114.

[23]See A. Kozulin and A. Venger, "Psychological and Learning Problems of Immigrant Children from the FSU," *Journal of Jewish Communal Services* 70, Fall 1993, pp. 64–72; A. Lieblich, "Looking at Change: Natasha, 21: New Immigrant from Russia to Israel," in *The Narrative Study of Lives*, ed. R. Joselson and A. Lieblich (Sage, Newbury Park, Calif., 1993);

ever, many of them, especially high-schoolers, developed symptoms of psychological distress, manifested in longing for home, feelings of social isolation, and absence from school, with many finally dropping out. Studies of the dropouts showed them to be strongly deficient in knowledge of Hebrew.

In general, the younger the immigrants, the more rapid the language acquisition and adaptation to school. New-immigrant pupils from higher socioeconomic backgrounds scored better in mathematics and language, had a more positive self-image, displayed a higher inner locus of control, and formed more coherent goals for their future than pupils from lower socioeconomic backgrounds. The pupils from higher socioeconomic backgrounds also adapted better to their social milieu. Those who had had positive experiences in school in the FSU functioned better in Israeli schools. The scholastic achievements of new-immigrant students in special classes, or in classes where there was a high proportion of immigrants, were better than in classes where they constituted the minority. The longer they had been in Israel, the better their achievements in Hebrew and the more positive their subjective feeling about the level of their studies and their social adaptation. The more fluent their Hebrew, the higher their grades. The scholastic gap between new-immigrant students from the FSU and Israeli-born students tended to close after three years, especially at the elementary level. However, at the high-school level, immigrant students still experienced pronounced difficulties in language-dependent subjects even after three years. Immigrant youth from the Caucasus experienced special difficulties, including their families' limited incomes, which hindered their ability to meet school expenses. These youths were very dissatisfied with the Israeli school system and had a high dropout rate.[24]

There was relatively intensive social contact between immigrant and Israeli-born pupils in the elementary schools, but at the high-school level the newcomers tended to be ignored. Immigrants and Israelis participated in separate social networks, and the higher the percentage of new immigrants in the upper grades the greater the mutual insularity. The major confrontation was with students from the Oriental communities, mostly in the development towns and in the

---

D. Roer-Stier, "Coping Strategies of Immigrant Parents: Directions for Family Therapy," *Family Process* 35, 1996, pp. 363–76; V. Slonim-Nevo and Y. Sheraga, "Social and Psychological Adjustment of Soviet-born and Israeli-born Adolescents: The Effect of the Family," *Israel Journal of Psychiatry* 34, no. 2, 1997, pp. 128–38; R. Eisikovitz and R. Beck, "Models Governing the Education of New Immigrant Children in Israel," *Comparative Education Review* 34, no. 2, 1990, pp. 177–95; R. Eisikovitz, "I'll Tell You What School Should Do for Us: How Immigrant Youth from FSU View Their High School Experience in Israel," *Youth and Society* 27, no. 2, 1995, pp. 230–55; and A. Ben-Arye and Y. Zionit, eds., *Children in Israel, Statistical Yearbook 1998* (National Council for Child Welfare, Jerusalem, 1998), in Hebrew.

[24]See S. Ellenbogen-Frankovitz and G. Noam, *The Absorption of Immigrant Children and Youth from the Caucasus: Study Findings* (JDC-Brookdale Institute of Gerontology and Human Development, 1998).

distressed neighborhoods of cities. While immigrant students overall believed their Israeli peers had a highly negative perception of them, the more successful their absorption in school, the more inclined they were to view their situation positively.

Dropping out and adopting patterns of socially deviant behavior may be external manifestations of the distress experienced by new-immigrant pupils in the transition from one culture and one educational system to another. No exact statistics exist on the national scale of the dropout phenomenon among immigrants, but experts estimate that it is twice as high as among other Jewish high-school students. In schools under Ministry of Education supervision that were surveyed in several cities, the average dropout rate among new-immigrant children age 14–17 from the FSU was 13 percent (compared to 6 percent for veteran youth). In some cities the dropout rate of youth from the FSU reached 29 percent. Many of the dropouts participated in alternative programs run by the Ministry of Labor and Social Affairs. However, even among adolescents who stayed in the system, there are indications of "hidden" dropping out, manifested in absence from school of more than four days a month.[25]

Crime committed by new-immigrant youth, who constitute 8–10 percent of the total 12–17 age group, is on the upswing. Crime among Israeli youth in general increased by 3 percent in 1995 as compared with 1994, but among new immigrants the rate of increase was 24 percent in the same period. This trend continued throughout 1996 and 1997. In 1997, the number of immigrant youth involved in criminal activity was double that in 1993. Charges were pressed in 13 percent of the cases involving new-immigrant youth, as contrasted with 10 percent for all youth cases in Israel. An exceptionally steep increase was found in drug-related crimes and in thefts and break-ins.

Populations at Risk

Since Israeli government policy on immigration from the FSU is fundamentally nonselective, offering an open door through which immigrants may enter irrespective of age, family situation, health, or social condition, it is not surprising that among the new arrivals were weak and disadvantaged groups of various sorts. These included elderly persons, one-parent famlies, the disabled and others in need of special medical care, the psychologically distressed, and those below the poverty line.

---

[25]Israel Central Bureau of Statistics and the Ministry of Education, Culture and Sport, *Pupils in Post-Primary Schools (grades 9–12): Staying on vs. Dropping out 1986/87–1995/96 (Current Statistics,* 1/1999, Jerusalem, 1999).

The elderly.[26] From 1990 to 1995, 80,000 FSU immigrants aged 65+ arrived in Israel. As compared with the elderly population in Israel, the percentage of women among the immigrants was higher, the percentage of single persons was far higher, and the percentage of those with more than high-school education was fully three times as high. Many came to Israel with relatives or joined relatives who had arrived earlier. Among new immigrants, there is a heavy concentration of elderly in the big cities, as there is among the veteran population.

The major problems faced by elderly immigrants were housing and making ends meet. Most addressed the problem by setting up joint households with their children (also with sons- and daughters-in-law, and grandchildren). This pattern of habitation duplicates similar conditions in the FSU; 43 percent of the elderly immigrants who live with their children in Israel had also done so in the FSU. Although to begin with, older people got larger housing grants covering a longer period, in surveys, most of the elderly immigrants, including those who bought homes, said that their living conditions in Israel were inferior to those in their home country. Their main complaints were high maintenance costs, the small size of the apartments, and the need to share accommodations with co-tenants.

New-immigrant elderly are more limited in activity by health problems than are their Israeli counterparts. Their feeling of psychological well-being is also significantly lower than that of their peers among the veteran population. Hebrew fluency among elderly immigrants is extremely poor, and does not improve with length of residence in Israel. The vast majority of elderly immigrants described their economic situation as poor or very bad, despite housing and pension grants and other assistance. The ability of the elderly to meet their special needs depends significantly on the social networks they belong to. The vast majority (90 percent) have children in Israel, and many live with them or meet with them at least once a week. Half have friends or neighbors to whom they can turn for help. The proportion of those who complain of loneliness is lower than in the parallel age group among the veteran population (15 percent vs. 22 percent, according to one study). Satisfaction with absorption rises significantly among elderly immigrants with length of residence in the country; 80 percent said they would make the same decision to immigrate to Israel again.

One-parent families.[27] The proportion of one-parent families with children below the age of 18 is significantly higher among new-immigrant families than

---

[26]See H. Litwin, *Uprooted in Old Age: Soviet Jews and Their Social Networks in Israel* (Westport, Conn.: Greenwood Press, 1995); D. Naon, Y. King, and J. Habib, "Resettling Elderly Soviet Immigrants in Israel: Family Ties and the Housing Dilemma," *Journal of Psychology and Judaism* 17, no. 4, 1993, pp. 229–313.

[27]See A. Ben-David and Y. Lavee, "Migration and Marital Distress: The Case of Soviet Immigrants," *Journal of Divorce and Remarriage* 21, no. 3/4, 1994, pp. 133–45.

in the veteran population. The most serious difficulty this group of immigrants encountered was housing, followed by employment. In both areas, the situation improved as a function of length of stay in the country. Yet by 1995 only 31 percent of one-parent immigrant families owned their own homes, as compared to 82 percent of immigrant two-parent families. Income disparities between one-parent families and others were also very great; in 1995, only 16 percent of the heads of one-parent families said their income was adequate for their needs, as against 31 percent of two-parent families. In 1992, twice as many married women as single-parent mothers were employed — though this difference had all but disappeared by 1995. The disparity in knowledge of Hebrew between married women and single-parent women, which was found to be high in 1992, had also decreased considerably three years later.

New immigrants with special medical needs. A significant difference was found between new immigrants and the veteran population in their health condition. In 1995, 20 percent of working-age immigrants (20–64) vs. 15 percent of the comparable veteran population had a health problem that hampered their day-to-day activity, whether illness, restrictions on activity, or chronic incapacity. Only 3 percent of the veteran population assessed their health situation as generally "not good or bad," compared with 12 percent of the new immigrants in the age group specified. The immigrants were found to have a much higher incidence of serious ailments, such as heart disease and high blood pressure, than the veteran population. Overall, the immigrants did not make greater use of health services, including hospitalization, though they were less satisfied with these services than the general population.

Psychological distress.[28] FSU immigrants showed a relatively higher level of psychological distress than the veteran Israeli population. This was especially pronounced among those studying in intensive Hebrew-language courses (*ulpan*), those taking preparatory courses for a medical license, and high-school and uni-

---

[28]See Y. Lerner, J. Mirsky, and M. Barasch, "New Beginnings in an Old Land: Refugee and Immigrant Mental Health in Israel," in *Amidst Peril and Pain: The Mental Health and Wellbeing of the World's Refugees* (American Psychological Association, Washington, DC, 1994), pp. 153–89; A. Ponizovsky et al., "Suicide Ideation Among Recent Immigrants: An Epidemiological Study," *Israel Journal of Psychiatry* 34, no. 2, 1997, pp. 139–48; M. Ritsner et al., *Demoralization Among Soviet Immigrants and the Zionist Forum Support: First Year Experience of Psychological Support Project* (Soviet Jewry Zionist Forum and Talbieh Mental Health Center, Jerusalem), 1993; M. Ritsner et al., "Effects of Immigration on the Mentally Ill: Does It Produce Psychological Distress?" *Comprehensive Psychiatry* 37, no. 1, 1996, pp. 17–22; M. Ritsner, A. Ponizovsky, and Y. Ginath, "Changing Patterns of Distress During the Adjustment of Recent Immigrants: A One-Year Follow-up Study, *Acta Psychiat. Scandinavia* 95, no. 6, 1997, pp. 494–99; and V. Rotenberg et al., "Psychosocial Problems Faced During Absorption of Russian-speaking New Immigrants into Israel: A Systematic Approach, *Israel Journal of Psychiatry and Related Sciences* 33, no. 1, 1996, pp. 40–49.

versity students. New-immigrant women were found to display greater distress than men, and a high level of distress was also apparent in single immigrants, adolescents, the elderly, the unemployed, and those from the Chernobyl region and the former Asiatic republics. There was a higher rate of psychiatric hospitalization among FSU immigrants than among veteran Israelis in 1990–91 (3.5 per 1,000 vs. 2.6 per 1,000). Although the impact of length of time in Israel on the level of psychological distress is complex and not entirely clear, there is some indication that it did not decline quickly, at least not within a time span of five years.

Immigrant families below the poverty line. Poverty was rampant among immigrants in the early 1990s. In 1991, its incidence stood at 34.6 percent of all families after transfer payments and taxes, declining to 20.3 percent in 1993. In 1994, there was another upsurge in poverty, to 24 percent, which decreased to 19 percent in 1995–96. However, these data refer to all new immigrants in Israel, including those who arrived from Ethiopia after 1990. The incidence of poverty in 1996 within the 1990s immigrant families (mostly from the FSU) was somewhat lower, standing at 22 percent, but this was still higher than the rate for the veteran population, which was 16 percent in 1996.

Immigrants from the Caucasus.[29] Between 1989 and 1996 some 50,000 immigrants arrived in Israel from the Caucasus region of the FSU (a large portion of them "mountain Jews," with their own identity and dialect, Judeo-Tat). A study found that these immigrants faced particular difficulties—only half were employed, their employment rate was lower than it had been before immigration (46 percent of those employed in the Caucasus were not currently employed), and half of the employed had unskilled jobs. The high rate of unemployment resulted in widespread poverty, in a lack of basic household equipment, in the inability of nearly half to meet most of their daily needs, and in a pessimistic feeling regarding the chances of improving their economic situation. Hebrew proficiency was poor, and they perceived their lack of Hebrew skills as an impediment to getting good jobs and to participating in vocational training courses.

Satisfaction of New Immigrants

The new immigrants' level of satisfaction with various spheres of life in Israel and their view of life overall, as expressed in surveys, are generally positive. After five years in the country, 75 to 80 percent of immigrants said they were satisfied with their housing situation, 60 to 66 percent with their work, and 60 to 70 percent with their social life, but only 35 to 50 percent were satisfied with their cultural life. However, 80 percent said they felt "at home" in Israel, and 90–95 per-

---

[29]See J. King, *The Absorption of Immigrants from the Caucasus in the 1990s* (JDC-Brookdale Institute of Gerontology and Human Development, 1998).

cent were sure they would remain in Israel. The immigrants' satisfaction with each aspect of life was found to increase with length of stay in the country, though the level of overall satisfaction was lower than that for each separate area.

IMPACT OF IMMIGRATION ON ISRAEL

Population and Demography[30]

As a result of the FSU immigration, Israel's population rose by 15 percent from 1989 to 1996, with an annual rate of increase in those years that was double what it had been before (about 2 percent vs. 1 percent). At the end of 1996, Israel's population stood at the level it would have reached five years later, had the wave of immigration not occurred. Immigration on this scale had a major impact, both short- and long-term, on the population's demographic makeup.

For one thing, the population group originating in the Soviet Union (those born there and their offspring) has become the largest ethnic element in Israel. At the end of 1996, more than 900,000 residents of Israel were of Russian/Soviet origin (more than 20 percent of the Jewish population), of whom 75–80 percent had arrived since 1989. The existence of this large community means that Russian occupies a central place among the languages spoken in Israel (besides Hebrew), which is reflected in the media, in cultural life, in politics, and so on.

A distinctive feature of this wave of immigration is the presence of tens of thousands of Christians (spouses of Jewish immigrants and other family members) as well as some who do not profess allegiance to any religion. Cumulatively, non-Jews account for some 15 percent of the immigration. One result is that the Christian community in Israel has received a significant boost.

Some of the demographic effects are as follows: the higher ratio of females to males among the new immigrants has brought about an increase in the proportion of females overall, especially among adults and the elderly. Similarly, the small percentage of children among the newcomers and relatively high proportion of elderly (as compared to the Israeli population) has brought about a slight decline in the percentage of children overall and a rise in the percentage of elderly. The immigrants' age distribution will continue to have an impact along these lines in the decades to come.

The low fertility level of FSU immigrants is having at least a short-term effect on the fertility level of the Israeli population overall (more strikingly on the groups originating in Europe and the Americas). The fertility level of the FSU immigrants rises gradually in relation to length of residence in Israel, but at a slow rate.

---

[30]See note 2.

The relatively high number of divorcees among immigrants, some of them with children, increased the number, both absolute and relative, of divorcees within the Israeli population (between 1989 and 1994, the number of divorcees in Israel rose by 80 percent, with a large part of this increase accounted for by the new immigrants). Similarly, the number of one-parent families increased by 60 percent. The higher frequency of multigenerational households among immigrants reduces the proportion of nuclear families in the overall Jewish population. These demographic modifications have significant implications for the provision of educational, health, and welfare services, especially for the scope of welfare allowances for the elderly, one-parent families, and so forth.

Population Distribution[31]

The immigrants' decisions about where to settle have had important consequences for national population distribution and for various localities and neighborhoods throughout the country. Proportionately, the population in the Southern district (especially the Ashkelon subdistrict), and to a lesser extent that of the Haifa district, rose significantly, while those of the Tel Aviv district and of the Jerusalem district declined. The populations of a large group of communities (mainly those designated as development towns) increased by dozens of percent, and saw their population structures radically altered by large influxes of FSU immigrants (examples are Ma'alot-Tarshiha, Carmiel, Ashdod, Sderot, Upper Nazareth, Arad, and Or Akiva). Certain city neighborhoods (for the most part neighborhoods with a medium or low economic level, where housing prices are lower) changed radically as large numbers of new immigrants moved in. In some cases the impact is judged to be short-term, in others of longer duration.

Labor Force[32]

The massive influx of immigrants produced a large supply of available labor. An examination of employment data for 1990–1995 shows an increase of nearly 500,000 in the number of people working, of whom more than half were Israelis and about 230,000 were immigrants who arrived in this period. The annual ad-

---

[31]See Central Bureau of Statistics, *Population in Settlements, Demographic Characteristics by Geographic Divisions* (Publication no. 1026, Jerusalem, 1996), in Hebrew.

[32]See R. Friedberg, *You Can't Take It with You? Immigrants' Assimilation and the Portability of Human Capital: Evidence from Israel* (Discussion Paper no. 95.02, Maurice Falk Institute for Economic Research in Israel, Jerusalem), 1995; R. Friedberg, *The Impact of Mass Immigration on the Israeli Labor Market* (Discussion Paper no. 98.01, Maurice Falk Institute for Economic Research in Israel, Jerusalem), 1998.

dition of 40,000 people to the ranks of the employed in this period surpassed the figures for 1985–1990. (It should also be noted that about 100,000 foreign workers entered the labor force in Israel during the early 1990s.)

Immigrants were able to compete with veteran Israelis for jobs, in some cases pushing them out of the labor force and thus increasing unemployment among them, concomitantly bringing about lower wages, especially in occupations filled by the newcomers. Veteran Israelis, especially those who were about to join the labor force, felt they would have a hard time finding employment. However, the rate of participation of veteran Israelis in the labor force, far from decreasing, actually rose somewhat: from 75.7 percent in 1990 to 77.3 percent in 1995. That increase included Israelis with higher education (16 or more years of study).

It is difficult to isolate the specific impact of the influx of immigrants on the general labor force from external influences that occurred in the same period (e.g., the Oslo agreements, the peace treaty with Jordan). However, as might be expected, the very existence of such a large immigration increased the demand for workers and, at least in the initial period, produced demand in excess of the immigrants' numbers in the labor force, given the expanded housing construction, the increase in labor-intensive investments, and so on.

The influx of immigrants contributed to shifts in the structure of the economy as well, with the new arrivals entering specific professions and branches in large numbers and veteran Israelis entering others. Although many immigrant scientists, academics, technicians, and other professionals did not find work in their professions, those who did had a significant impact (some 25,000 in academic and scientific occupations, including 9,000 engineers, 5,000 physicians, and another 25,000 in the professional and technical occupations).

The period of heavy immigration, 1989–95, witnessed a rise in the proportions of workers employed in construction and in financial and business services and a decline in the proportions of workers in public and community services (e.g., education, health, welfare, public administration, community organization). However, the proportions of veteran Israelis in the various branches of the economy were modified by the different scale of entry of immigrants into each branch. Increased employment among veteran Israelis was more pronounced in public and business services than in industry and personal services, with the result that their share rose in the former and declined in the latter. In 1994 the new immigrants constituted 25 percent of those employed in personal services, 20 percent of those working in industry, and 15 percent of the personnel in the public services.

In terms of occupations, the proportion of new immigrants employed in the scientific, academic, professional, and technical occupations continued to increase, as in services and sales, while the share of clerical workers fell. However, the occupational structure of veteran Israelis was altered, showing a decline in service workers and in both skilled and unskilled workers in industry and construction, and an increase in managers, clerical workers, and salespeople. Overall, the new immigrants entered lower-status occupations, and the veteran Israelis increased their proportion among white-collar workers and in prestigious occupations.

In 1990 the unemployment rate among veteran Israelis stood at 9.4 percent of the labor force, rising to 11 percent in 1992 but falling below 6 percent by 1995. From 1996, with Israel experiencing recession, unemployment increased, reaching 8.5 percent of the labor force for the whole population of Israel and close to 12 percent for the 1990s FSU immigrants.

Wage and Income Distribution[33]

The large numbers of new immigrants entering the labor force could be expected to bring about a general decrease of wages throughout the economy. In 1990–92, real wages in Israel did not increase; wages changed less than the growth in per capita production during this period. The result was a fall in the cost of labor per unit of production, while at the same time employee compensation in domestic product fell. Real wages rose again from 1993 to 1995, but slowly. Nor were the changes uniform in all occupations. It was to be expected that the wages paid to veteran Israelis in the scientific, academic, professional, and technical occupations would decrease due to the large supply of incoming labor in these occupations. In fact, from 1990 to 1994 the wages of veteran Israelis in these professions increased substantially: by 16 percent in the scientific and academic occupations, by 8 percent in the professional and technical occupations, and by 23 percent in managerial positions. At the same time, the wages of unskilled workers declined by nearly 20 percent and of those in the services by less than 1 percent. We find, then, that the wage gaps among veteran Israelis in different professions increased. Because new immigrants received lower wages than Israelis, the wage gaps also grew throughout the economy.

The net income of families of veteran Israelis rose by an average of 3.5 percent a year from 1990 to 1994, leading also to a higher rate of savings by households. However, the growing wage gaps meant that distribution of income from work among the veteran families became less egalitarian. Similarly, the proportion of veteran families below the "relative poverty line" (according to net income) increased from 13 to 17 percent. Taxation of veteran Israelis did not rise in this period; indeed, there was a slight decline in tax rates relative to income. The level of public services for veteran Israelis remained stable. In this period the housing conditions of the veteran population also improved.

---

[33]See Central Bureau of Statistics, *Family Expenditure Survey 1992/1993, Part D–Immigrants' Households* (Special Publication 1002, 1995); National Insurance Institute, Jerusalem, *Annual Survey 1996/1997*, and previous issues.

Impact on the Israeli Economy[34]

Economic growth was accelerated in the period of the immigration influx, reaching 6 percent per annum during 1989–95 (2.5 percent per capita). This was due primarily to the increase in labor input, as the added capital did not match the added workforce, resulting in a decline in the amount of capital per hour of work and a very slow rise in product per hour of work. Product per worker increased very slightly, indicating a low utilization of the new immigrants' human capital. The rapid growth in investments in this period was reflected almost entirely by an increase in import surplus. This was underwritten mainly by loans from abroad (utilizing the loan guarantees granted by the United States). The economic recession during 1996–97 brought a sharp decrease in economic growth (1–2 percent in 1998).

Impact on Israeli Society and Culture[35]

While it is extremely difficult in the short term to identify the impact on Israeli society and culture of the FSU immigration, it is already clear that this mass influx has heightened "sectoriality" in Israeli society, contributing to observable fragmentation in the social, cultural, and political spheres.

THE PROSPECTS OF FUTURE EMIGRATION FROM THE FSU

The emigration of more than one million Jews and family members has caused a major depletion of the Jewish community in the FSU, a community whose numbers had been declining for some decades.[36]

At the beginning of 1998, the "core" Jewish community remaining in the FSU

---

[34]See Bank of Israel, Jerusalem, *Annual Report 1997*; M. Bar-Natan, M. Beenstock, and Y. Haitovsky, "An Econometric Model of the Israeli Housing Market" (Working Paper no. 314, Department of Economics, Hebrew University, Jerusalem), 1996.

[35]See Z. Gitelman, *Immigration and Identity: The Resettlement and Impact of Soviet Immigrants on Israeli Politics and Society* (Wilstein Institute of Jewish Policy Studies, Los Angeles), 1995; Lissak and Leshem, "The Russian Intelligentsia in Israel," pp. 20–36.

[36]See E. Andrev, "Jews in the Household in Russia," paper presented at the 12th World Congress of Jewish Studies, Hebrew University, Jerusalem, 1998; S. DellaPergola and M. Tolts, "Demographic Trends and Characteristics of the Jews in Russia (Interim Report)" (Division of Jewish Demography and Statistics, Harman Institute of Contemporary Jewry, Hebrew University, Jerusalem), 1998; V. Konstantinov, "Aliya of the 1990s from the Former Soviet Union: A Socio-Demographic Analysis," *Jews in Eastern Europe* 2, no. 27, 1995, pp. 5–26; M. Tolts, "Recent Jewish Emigration and Population Decline in Russia," *Jews in Eastern Europe* 1, no. 35, 1998, pp. 5–24.

was estimated at 540,000.[37] This reflected both the mass emigration of the preceding years and the ongoing loss of population due to negative natural increase (number of deaths exceeding number of births). Taking into account the non-Jews in Jewish families—who are entitled to immigrate to Israel under the Law of Return—the estimate of the "enlarged" Jewish community was 1.0 to 1.1 million persons. Sixty percent of this population live in the Russian Federation and 40 percent in the other republics. The community has a small proportion of children and a very high proportion of older persons; the median age of Russian core Jews in 1998 was 56. The very low and declining fertility (total fertility rate estimated at 0.8 children per woman in the core population), the high death rate, the age structure of emigrants (higher proportions of children and persons in the 20–40 age group and a much lower percentage of older persons, compared to the proportions of these age groups in the Russian Jewish community)—all have contributed to the age structure of the remaining Jewish community. Moreover, the percentage of mixed marriages is on the increase (currently some 50 percent of couples).

What are the prospects of continuing Jewish emigration in the coming years? the prospects of the remaining Jews immigrating to Israel? A number of factors will influence the extent of this future flow, some serving as "push" factors, others effectively discouraging emigration.

Factors Discouraging Emigration

Demography. (1) The existing trend toward negative natural increase will continue, with population loss estimated at 1 percent per year. Thus the potential pool for immigration will be smaller. (2) It will also be smaller because the proportion of older persons is increasing and that of the 20–49 age group is decreasing, and the propensity of the older age group to migrate is lower than that of the younger age group. (3) The increase in the proportion of mixed marriages causes a further diminution of the Jewish community. Moreover, the propensity to migrate is less for mixed-married than for homogeneous couples. (4) The proportion of FSU Jews residing in the Russian Federation is larger than in the past. Historically, Jews in the Russian Federation were less likely to emigrate than Jews in other republics.

Jewish communal and institutional revival.[38] The breakup of the Soviet Union in 1991 opened the door to a revival of Jewish communal life—social, cultural, educational, and religious—especially in the urban concentrations in Russia and the Ukraine. In 1998 some 1,000 Jewish organizations functioned in the FSU.

---

[37]The estimates provided here are from the Institute of Contemporary Jewry, Hebrew University of Jerusalem.
[38]See B. Gidwitz, *Post-Soviet Jewry: The Critical Issues* (Jerusalem Center for Public Affairs, Jerusalem, 1999).

There were 12 Jewish newspapers; a number of radio and television programs; 45 Jewish day schools; 35 kindergartens; 200 Sunday schools; and six institutions of higher learning. Several national roof organizations serve as focal points for the local bodies, some presided over and influenced by wealthy, politically influential persons. Diaspora and Israeli Jewish organizations provide financial support for various institutions and help to train local leaders and Jewish communal teachers and workers. The Jewish community of the Russian Federation was granted cultural autonomy and the right to receive government aid. All these developments enhance Jewish life in the FSU and lessen the impetus to leave the country.

Other factors. The involvement of Jews in the Russian economy, media, and government—disproportionate to their numbers—encourages close ties with Russian society and decreases the inclination to emigrate. This may be somewhat tempered by the fact that the visible success of many Jews sometimes arouses anti-Semitic reactions.

Economic recession in Israel beginning in 1997, increased unemployment, the difficulty immigrants have finding jobs in their previous occupations, and the resulting downgrading in occupational status are factors that discourage potential immigrants from deciding to immigrate. The continuing security tension in Israel, the daily terrorist acts, and the need to serve in the army are also factors that discourage immigration.

Alternatives to immigration to Israel. The potential emigrant from the FSU has alternative possible destinations. The United States has an entry quota of some 40,000 each year for migrants from the FSU that was not fully exploited in the last two years. As a result of a recent reconsideration of immigration policy, regulations were eased regarding the entry of all immigrants in certain critical technological occupations. Germany and Canada have both been willing to accept Jewish emigrants from the FSU republics.

In the United States a large community of Soviet immigrants, who began arriving in 1970, their number now estimated at some 400,000, constitutes a critical mass for attracting family members. Moreover, through its various organs, the Jewish community provides aid and support to immigrant newcomers, in addition to the informal support provided by families and individuals.[39]

Factors Favoring Emigration

The expectations of 1996–97 for a politically and economically stable Russian Republic did not materialize. On the contrary, in 1998 there were strong signs of a possible collapse of the economy and even the political structure. The situation hurt mostly the urban population, which in the past enjoyed economic prosper-

---

[39]See Steven J. Gold, "Soviet Jews in the United States," AJYB 1994, pp. 3–57.

ity and a relatively higher standard of living. The effects are felt not only in the Russian Federation but also in Ukraine, Moldova, and Kazakhstan. The Jewish community has also been affected, and there have been signs of increased interest in immigration to Israel, such as increased study of Hebrew. An important factor is the concern of parents for the future of their children in the FSU.

The existence of a large Russian community in Israel, one that enjoys the possibility of preserving the cultural and social life-style of its country of origin, is a powerful magnet for attracting close family members, other relatives, and friends from the FSU to migrate to Israel. The fact that absorption authorities assure every *oleh* (immigrant) financial support for the first year in Israel as well as housing subsidies, social security benefits, occupational training, and the like serves as an incentive. The standard of living in Israel is close to that of some Western countries. In addition, Israel has strong cultural and economic ties with the United States and the West European countries.

It is difficult to foresee which factors will weigh most heavily in the decision-making process—whether to stay in the FSU republics or to emigrate from the FSU, and if the latter, whether to immigrate to Israel or to another country. Impending economic collapse, political instability, and anti-Semitic manifestations offer a strong impetus to emigrate, but the effects of the other factors mentioned above should not be overlooked.

Immigration figures for 1998 show a continuing decline in the number of immigrants to Israel. The beginning of 1999 saw some preliminary signs of an increase, largely attributed to the deteriorating economic conditions in the Russian Republic and some other republics of the FSU. It is not yet clear as of this writing if this is a short-term, temporary change, or part of a more lasting trend.

CONCLUSION

A large body of research on the 1990s wave of Soviet Jewish immigration to Israel has been carried out, and a number of findings from that literature are reported in the present paper. It should be emphasized, however, that the absorption process is a long one, one that in many of its aspects can extend for years and even more than a generation. Follow-up research will continue, it is hoped, and will explore areas that have not been researched at all or have not been covered in the same detail and depth as others. Examples of areas that have been insufficiently documented and researched are: the extent of emigration from Israel of Soviet immigrants and their characteristics; comparisons of FSU immigrants to Israel with those migrating to the United States, Canada, and Germany; the long-term effects of this immigration on Israeli culture; the differences in the integration of immigrants arriving from various republics; the problems encountered by the large number of non-Jews.

Based on the available data, we have examined the absorption of these immigrants in housing, employment, education, and other domains, showing its accomplishments within a short period and highlighting the problems encountered in the absorption process. Among these were the downgrading in occupation and status experienced by a large proportion of immigrants, and the difficulty of acquiring the Hebrew language, which created a barrier to entry into some occupations and into Israeli society. Older immigrants (55 and over), one-parent families, and Caucasus Jews had the most difficulty in finding employment and appropriate housing; many youths were frustrated in acquiring some mastery of Hebrew and became school dropouts. Most newcomers struggle to achieve social and cultural integration, even as they seek actively to preserve Russian language, culture, and identity.

From the perspective of Israeli society, this wave of immigration has been absorbed in most domains without producing serious economic or social crises. Moreover, though only a few years have elapsed since the beginning of this wave (immigrants were still arriving in 1998, though at a slower rate), and the process of absorption is not completed, a distinctive and dynamic immigrant Russian community has emerged, one that has already had considerable impact on Israel — on its demographic profile, on its geography, on the makeup of its society, on its cultural institutions, and even on the political sphere. The full scope of its influence can, at this point, not even be guessed at.

ELAZAR LESHEM
MOSHE SICRON

TABLE 1. NUMBER OF ALL IMMIGRANTS AND IMMIGRANTS FROM THE FSU, BY YEAR OF ARRIVAL, 1990–1998

Year	From the FSU	All Immigrants
1990	185,227	190,507
1991	147,839	176,100
1992	65,093	77,058
1993	66,145	76,805
1994	68,079	79,884
1995	64,847	76,361
1996	59,049	70,919
1997	54,591	66,000
1998	46,021	56,693

Source: Israel Central Bureau of Statistics (hereafter "CBS"), *Statistical Abstract of Israel* (annual publication; last issue—1998); *Monthly Bulletin of Statistics; Immigration to Israel* (annual publication; last issue—1996).

TABLE 2. REPUBLIC OF ORIGIN OF IMMIGRANTS FROM THE FSU, 1990–1998

Republic of Origin	Number (thousands)	% of FSU Immigrants
Total FSU	753	100.0
European Republics—Total	*585*	*79.7*
Russian Federation	225	30.6
Ukraine	237	32.2
Belarus	62	8.4
Moldova	43	5.9
Baltic republics	19	2.6
Asian Republics—Total	*149*	*20.2*
Azerbaijan	30	4.1
Uzbekistan	70	9.5
Tajikistan	10	1.4
Georgia	18	2.4
Other Asian republics	21	2.9
Not known	*18*	

Source: CBS, *Immigration to Israel* (annual publication; last issue—1996).

TABLE 3. JEWISH AND NON-JEWISH IMMIGRANTS BY YEAR OF IMMIGRATION, 1990–1996

Year of Immigration	Total (thousands)	Jews (thousands)	Non-Jews (thousands)	Unknown (thousands)	% of Non-Jews
1990	199.5	183.8	7.3	8.3	3.8
1991	176.1	151.1	13.6	11.4	8.2
1992	77.1	60.2	9.9	6.9	13.2
1993	76.8	58.5	11.1	7.2	15.9
1994	79.8	57.6	16.3	5.9	22.1
1995	76.4	49.4	18.3	8.6	27.1
1996	70.9	43.7	18.0	9.2	29.2

Source: CBS, Immigration to Israel (annual publication; last issue—1996).

TABLE 4. AGE STRUCTURE OF IMMIGRANTS FROM THE FSU AND ISRAELI JEWISH POPULATION

Age Group	Immigrants 1990–1996		Jewish Pop. 1989
	Number (thousands)	%	%
Total	656	100	100
0–14	137	21	29
15–29	146	22	24
30–44	152	23	21
45–64	133	20	16
65+	88	13	10
Median Age	34.3		27.9

Source: CBS, Statistical Abstract of Israel (annual publication; last issue—1998); Immigration to Israel (annual publication; last issue—1996).

TABLE 5. EDUCATIONAL LEVEL OF IMMIGRANTS (IN FSU) (AGED 15+) AND ISRAELI JEWISH POPULATION (PERCENTAGES)

Years of Study	Immigrants 1990–1996	Jewish Pop. 1989
Total	100.0	100.0
0–4	2.8	6.8
5–8	9.1	14.7
9–12	38.1	50.6
13–15	39.4	15.8
16+	10.5	12.1

Source: CBS, *Statistical Abstract of Israel* (annual publication, last issue—1998); *Immigration to Israel* (annual publication; last issue—1996).

TABLE 6. OCCUPATIONS OF IMMIGRANTS (IN FSU) AND ISRAELI JEWISH POPULATION (PERCENTAGES)

Occupation	Immigrants 1990–1996	Jewish Pop. 1989
Total	100.0	100.0
Scientific & acad. workers	33.0	8.6
Thereof: Engineers & architects	20.8	1.9
Physicians & dentists	4.3	1.0
Professional & technical workers	33.2	16.0
Skilled & unskilled workers	20.0	26.2
Others	13.0	49.2

Source: CBS, *Statistical Abstract of Israel* (annual publication, last issue—1998); *Immigration to Israel* (annual publication; last issue—1996).

TABLE 7. HOUSING DENSITY OF IMMIGRANTS AND ISRAELI JEWISH POPULATION (PERCENTAGES)

Persons per Room	Immigrants 1990–1997	Jewish Pop. 1997
Total	100.0	100.0
Less than 1	34.2	47.3
1	30.0	22.1
1.1–1.9	28.9	24.9
2	5.4	3.4
2.1+	1.5	2.3

Source: CBS, *Statistical Abstract of Israel* (annual publication; last issue—1998); *Immigration to Israel* (annual publication; last issue—1996).

TABLE 8. RESIDENTIAL DISTRIBUTION OF IMMIGRANTS AND ISRAELI JEWISH POPULATION (PERCENTAGES)

District	Immigrants 1990–1995[a]	Immigrants in 1995[b]	Jewish Pop. 1989
Total	100.0	100.0	100.0
Jerusalem district	5.9	5.2	11.0
Northern district	11.7	13.7	9.8
Haifa district	19.4	17.3	12.9
Central district	21.2	20.0	23.9
Tel Aviv district	24.7	17.6	27.7
Southern district	16.2	24.4	12.7
Judea & Samaria, Gaza	0.9	1.8	2.0

[a]Immigrants' first district of residence
[b]Immigrants' district of residence in 1995
Source: CBS, *Statistical Abstract of Israel* 1998, and previous issues; *Monthly Bulletin of Statistics; Immigration to Israel* (annual publication; last issue–1996); and *Immigrant Population from the Former USSR, 1995, Demographic Trends* (Publication no. 1076, 1998), and previous issues.

TABLE 9. PERCENTAGE OF UNEMPLOYED MEN AND WOMEN IN THE LABOR FORCE, TOTAL POPULATION AND IMMIGRANTS BY PERIOD OF IMMIGRATION (1997)

	Total	Men	Women
Total population	7.7	6.8	8.8
Immigrants: 1990–91	8.0	6.0	9.9
1992–93	8.6	7.5	9.8
1994–97	14.2	12.0	17.1

Source: CBS, *Statistical Abstract of Israel* (annual publication, last issue—1998); *CBS, Labour Force Survey, 1997* (Publication no. 1100, 1999).

TABLE 10. OCCUPATIONS OF EMPLOYED IMMIGRANTS WHO ARRIVED 1990–1994, BEFORE IMMIGRATION AND IN ISRAEL (PERCENTAGES)

Occupation[a]	Before Immigration	In Israel, 1994
Total	100	100
Scientific & academic	34	10
Professional & technical[b]	34	13
Managerial & clerical[b]	5	6
Sales workers	3	5
Service workers	4	22
Agricultural workers	1	2
Skilled workers	15	30
Unskilled workers	5	11

[a]Classification of occupations changed in 1995, so data for 1995 on may not be fully comparable.
[b]Managers are included in the professional and technical occupations.
Source: CBS, *Labour Force Survey, 1994* (Special Publication 1024, 1996); *Immigration to Israel, 1994* (Special Publication 1005, 1995).

TABLE 11. IMMIGRANTS' HEBREW KNOWLEDGE AFTER 5 YEARS IN ISRAEL (PERCENTAGES)

Percent who can . . .	Immigrated July 1990	Immigrated Sept. 1991
Understand a simple Hebrew conversation	67	54
Read a simple letter in Hebrew	51	40
Write a simple letter in Hebrew	46	34
Understand discussion on radio, TV, in Hebrew	51	38

Source: J. Rosenbaum-Tamari and N. Damian, *First Five Years in Israel, Immigrants from the FSU Who Arrived in September 1991 Compared to Those Who Arrived in July 1990* (Report no. 11, Ministry of Immigration Absorption, Division for Research and Planning, 1997), in Hebrew.

TABLE 12. IMMIGRANTS' DAILY USE OF HEBREW BY LENGTH OF RESIDENCE IN ISRAEL (PERCENTAGES)

Use of Hebrew	After 1.5 Years		After 5 Years	
	Immigrated July 1990	Immigrated Sept. 1991	Immigrated July 1990	Immigrated Sept. 1991
Total	100	100	100	100
Hebrew only or mainly	9	6	18	12
Hebrew & other language	39	30	38	28
Other language mainly	32	29	28	33
Other language only	20	35	16	27

Source: Ibid.

Culture in Israel

T HE YEAR 1998 was rich in cultural activities, many of which were supported by the government-appointed special Jubilee Committee, which coordinated the celebrations marking Israel's 50th birthday. The milestone anniversary opened with the sounding of shofars by different ethnic groups, in the spirit of the jubilee year. It was followed by a plethora of events throughout the year and throughout the country. A caravan of entertainers, dance troupes, and musical groups toured the development towns and outlying villages. The music of Israel's varied Sephardic communities was celebrated with a special festival. A gathering of Israeli pop singers took place at the Suzanne Dellal Center in Tel Aviv and a dance festival was presented at Carmiel. The Arad Rock Music Festival was held under the sponsorship of the Jubilee Committee, as was the Beersheba Festival of Humor and Satire. The jubilee also included special performances by the Israel Philharmonic and the Jerusalem Symphony Orchestras.

The anniversary became a means of siphoning money to the arts, affording increased opportunities for artists and performers to appear both in Israel and the Diaspora. But most of all, the anniversary became an occasion for cultural stock-taking. Coming at a time of what has been described as "post-Zionist alienation," the anniversary aroused conflicting emotions in the country. There was a desire to say, "How goodly is this creation," to celebrate Israel's impressive accomplishments; at the same time, there was an awareness of Israel's historical mistakes, particularly in relation to the Arabs. In addition, at this historical juncture, Israelis were still struggling with the issue of their cultural identity. Are they Israeli or Jewish, Middle Eastern or global? The art, music, and literature presented by the jubilee were, to some extent, a measure of where Israeli culture stood at that moment.

Indicative of the national ambivalence was the TV series *Tekumah* (Rebirth), which traced Israel's development and accomplishments over the five decades of statehood. The positive achievements shown on the screen were interspersed with more critical images — the expulsion of Palestinians during the 1948 War of Independence, the imposition of the Ashkenazi establishment's values on Jews from Arab countries. Nothing, it seemed, could be presented in unqualified terms.

Inadvertently, the jubilee also exposed the deep cultural schisms in the country. The religious-secular conflict has been particularly acrimonious in recent years. It exploded at the "Jubilee Bells," a spectacular musical production staged on the eve of Independence Day, which starred many of Israel's prominent actors, singers, dancers, and pop groups. As part of the extravaganza, the Batsheva Dance Company was to have performed a section from a work by choreographer

Ohad Naharin, "Anaphase," in which dancers dressed in black suits strip down to skimpy loincloths, to the accompaniment of the Passover song *Ehad Mi Yodeya* (Who Knows One?), as the closing refrain declares "One is our God in heaven and earth." After seeing a rehearsal, Orthodox politicians insisted that Ohad Naharin, who also serves as artistic director of the Batsheva company, modify the work. He refused and the dancers walked out in protest over the encroachment upon their artistic freedom. This exposure of the deep religious-secular rift in Israeli culture cast a shadow over the festivities.

The Batsheva incident reflects only a small part of the deep cultural changes Israel is experiencing. Another indicator of cultural change was the uproar that ensued when Rabbi Yitzhak Levy of the National Religious Party became minister of education and culture. Levy, who is of Moroccan background, declared that he would allocate money to encourage Sephardi culture and would try to compensate for past discrimination. Micha Yinon, director of the Culture Authority of the Ministry of Education, talked frankly of changing priorities. From the beginnings of Zionist settlement, a secular, left-wing, Ashkenazi elite dominated Israeli culture. But as religious and Sephardi groups gained power, writers, filmmakers, and other culture agents of these new elites began demanding their share of the cultural pie. With limited funds available for culture, it was feared that less money would be allotted to venerable cultural institutions like the Habimah Theater and the Israel Philharmonic. In sum, new sources of support have to be found in order to maintain older institutions at the same time that new cultural forces are allowed to emerge and develop.

Much recent Israeli culture is perceived along the religious-secular divide, and political views have tended to fuse with cultural concerns, a potentially dangerous state of affairs for the arts. Secular Israelis fear censorship and worry that the religious authorities will seek to impose their values on the secular population. This is mirrored in the best-selling volume *The Donkey of the Messiah*, by Seffi Rachlevsky, which presents a picture of traditional Judaism as congruent with the beliefs of extreme right-wing religious groups, those who idealize Baruch Goldstein and regard the Palestinians as the wicked Amalek of the Bible. Rachlevsky claims that the beliefs of Rabbi Avraham Yitzhak Kook, the Zohar, and Maimonides are ethnocentric, and that their views ultimately advocate genocide of non-Jews. Although liberal writers like Rabbi Micha Odenheimer have shown the outright falsehoods, half-truths, and exaggerations in Rachlevsky's book, this avenue of thought feeds into the pre-existing Kulturkampf and thus has a ready audience.

A number of recent novels also portray religious life in a negative way, playing upon sensationalistic sexual aspects of the ultra-Orthodox world. At the same time, there is much ambivalence in relation to Judaism. Israelis are still waging the Zionist rebellion of their forebears against religion and the religious establishment—yet Jewish sources are their cultural lifeblood. Many writers and dramatists have taken to studying Jewish texts. Alma, a secular college of Hebrew culture, is thriving. David Grossman has explained that his personal study of Jewish texts helps him excavate the layers of the Hebrew language in all its subtlety and nuance. Dramatists like Rina Yerushalmi have taken up the challenge of translating the Bible into the terms of contemporary culture in "Va-yomer, Vayelekh" (And He Said, and He Went) and "Vayishtahu, Va-yera" (And They Bowed, and He Appeared), dance dramas.

In contrast to the religious-secular conflict, the Sephardic–Ashkenazic divide is more permeable, and there are more points of contact and cultural crossover. In fact, a new East-West synthesis can be perceived in Israeli music and cultural awareness. An important strand running through the 50th anniversary festivities was the affirmation of Israel as a Middle Eastern country. An example of this was the Israel Museum exhibit "To the East: Orientalism in the Arts in Israel" (see below).

One sign of the increased appreciation for Middle Eastern culture has been the flourishing of Eastern pop music. There had always been Eastern singers in Israel, particularly Yemenites, but their music was not characterized by an authentic Eastern trill or instrumentation. The first generation of Jews from Eastern countries kept their music confined to their own circles, coming together in their homes to sing Arab melodies and to chant prayers. Gradually, young people began integrating their parents' music into their own rock compositions, fusing it with popular songs about the Land of Israel, but playing it with unique combinations of mandolins and electric guitars. Many groups now combine Western and Eastern modes and instrumentation. Classical Sephardic music, as performed by the Andalusian Orchestra, has also gained prominence. Popular bands like Tippex performed with the Andalusian ensemble, combining Western and Eastern instrumentation. And in the spirit of postmodern esthetics, the line separating the spheres of high and low culture has become thinner. This was particularly evident during the summer of 1998 when the Israel Museum reached out to a larger public, presenting concerts of Eastern pop music in conjunction with its exhibit on Orientalism in Israeli art.

Paradoxically, the new emphasis on Middle Eastern culture brought two opposing ideological streams into closer contact. The Ashkenazic left-wing stream, which advocates greater involvement with the Arabs politically and culturally, was enjoying a measure of fusion with the generally right-wing Middle Eastern Jewish stream, particularly in the area of pop music. The latter makes use of traditional Jewish liturgy, rendering Israeli pop music more Jewishly oriented, albeit in a Sephardic mode.

During the last two years, books about Israeli culture have begun to challenge the postmodernist, post-Zionist assumptions of much of Israeli culture. In *Hamered Ha-shafuf* (A Dispirited Rebellion), Gadi Taub, a young Tel Aviv short-story writer, analyzes his generation's reaction to the Zionist establishment and the attempt of the secular, Ashkenazi elite to find a voice for itself. Weary of the self-seriousness of the media and the literature spouting Zionist clichés, his generation developed the sarcastic, smart-alecky tone that now characterizes much of the media, the purpose being to expose the bombast of the old order. But Taub is disappointed that he and his cohorts have been unable to replace the old with a new, more authentic ethos, so that in fact an "ideology of despair" has ensued, whereby young people find it difficult to integrate the personal and the public. He puts much of the blame on his peers, who prefer to cloak themselves in a self-righteous "political correctness," rather than fighting to change the political situation. Other works questioning contemporary norms include novelist A.B. Yehoshua's nonfiction book *Kochah Hanora shel Ashmah Ketanah* (The Terrible Power of a Minor Guilt), an analysis of literature that opposes the postmodernist trend to nihilism, calling instead for the return of morality to Hebrew letters. In *Ha-yisra'elim Ha-aharonim* (The Last Israelis,) David Ohana, a secular, left-wing historian, refutes the fashionable post-Zionist stance and takes issue with those who would adopt a geographical, rather than historical, approach to being Israeli by identifying with the Palestinians over fellow Jews. Ohana, a Sephardic Jew, affirms the Jewishness of Israel and advocates an Israel rooted in Jewish history and the Jewish heritage, believing that Zionism can still offer a unifying ideal that excludes extremism on both sides.

Literature

VETERAN WRITERS

A particularly fascinating expression of the Sephardi-Ashkenazi colloquy is A.B. Yehoshua's latest novel, *Nesiyah Lesof Ha-mileniyum* (Voyage to the End of the Millennium). Yehoshua, one of Israel's most important writers, was born in Jerusalem into a Sephardic family that traces its origins in the country back many generations, but only in the last 15 years did the 62-year-old author begin writing about his Sephardic roots. With an uncanny sense of the large issues as they impinge upon literature, in this historical novel Yehoshua brings his readers back to the beginnings of the schism between Sephardim and Ashkenazim and the crucial points of difference between these two Jewish populations, as influenced by the respective cultures in which they reside. Ben-Atar, a wealthy merchant from Tangiers, makes his way to Paris, with his two wives and a boat full of merchandise from North Africa, to urge his beloved nephew Abulafia to resume acting as his business representative in Europe. Abulafia's Ashkenazi wife, appalled and threatened by the fact that her husband's uncle has two wives, had urged Abulafia to break off commercial and personal relationships with the uncle. Ben-Atar in turn hopes to demonstrate the propriety of bigamy to Abulafia's stern Ashkenazi spouse, so that she will allow her husband contact with his Tangiers family. Yehoshua contrasts the sensuous sensibility of the Sephardic Jews, who hail from a more materially developed Arab civilization, with the harsh, ascetic Ashkenazic Jews in 10th-century Christian Europe. Ben-Atar's pilgrimage is ultimately intended to secure the partnership between the Jews of the north and the south, to fulfill "the latent desire of the whole tribe" for oneness. At the symbolic level is the suggestion that, as the contemporary State of Israel moves into its second millennium, it must overcome the schisms that developed in the Diaspora a thousand years ago.

The 82-year-old S. Yizhar, author of the magisterial 1950s novel *Days of Ziglag*, jolted literary Israel when, after a 30-year silence, he resumed writing fiction in the early 1990s. He recently published *Lovely Malcolmia*, his fifth autobiographical lyric novel since his phoenix-like rebirth. Yizhar resurrects the early love of a shy, dreamy youth as it fuses with the erotic sense of the new, untamed Land of Israel.

Amos Oz's latest novel, published to critical acclaim, is *Oto Ha-Yam* (That Sea), a moving depiction of a Bulgarian widower, Alber Danon, a tax adviser from the seaside town of Bat Yam, his son, Riko Dor, who is traveling in Tibet, and Riko's girlfriend, Dita, to whom Alber is attracted. Also present is the ghost of Alber's wife, Nadia, who hovers over the protagonists. The story has none of the national symbolism that is a hallmark of Oz's previous fiction. It has no other reason for being, according to the narrator, reminiscent of Oz himself, than the fact that there is a reality out there calling for expression: the sympathetic Alber, who loves olives and salty cheese, and his family, with all its hopes and disappointments. In actuality, the novel comments on much of what is happening in Israel today. In contrast to the hippy idealism of the disaffected youth in Oz's earlier *Black Box,* who recreates a commune on his grandfather's land, Riko, the youth in this novel, sinks into apathy in Sri Lanka.

David Grossman, a generation younger than Oz and Yehoshua and at 43 already an established writer, is at his truest writer-self portraying the anxiety-laden inner world of adolescence. He sees the overwrought interpretation of reality, which often characterizes adolescence, as the vocation of writers. In his latest novel, *She'tihyi Li Sakin* (Words into Flesh), the protagonist, Ya'ir Einhorn, is an adult, married with a child, but he carries around within himself an adolescent anxiety about his sexuality as well as a yearning for a more honest, intense spiritual experience. This leads him to propose a correspondence with a woman named Miriam, whom he never actually meets but sees across the room at a high-school reunion. He feels somehow that she is a soul mate to whom he can bare his heart. This echoes Franz Kafka's correspondence with Milena Jesenka. Milena's passion and honesty are present in Grossman's depiction of Miriam, an adventurous woman with a deep curiosity about life, who takes him up on his suggestion that they correspond. Like Kafka's K., Yair feels himself to be repulsive and unlovable. At one point in his letter, Ya'ir, referring to Kafka's story "Metamorphosis," implores Miriam to help him evolve from a cockroach into a man. But as he sinks more and more into what he calls his "masturbation of words," there is emotional regression, and it seems less and less likely that Miriam can help him.

FOREIGN-WORKERS THEME

A recent social development in Israel is the prominence of foreign workers. Just as Israeli literature had raised an awareness of the plight of the country's Arab population, it was now beginning to focus on the issue of foreign workers. Reflecting this fact, Israeli writers Shulamit Lapid and Yehoshua Kenaz wrote novels in which the presence of foreign workers is not peripheral to the plot but actually structures the work. In *Chez Babou*, Lapid leaves behind the idiosyncratic protagonist of her detective novels, Lizi Badichi, a Beersheba journalist seeking social justice, and creates instead the silent, isolated Babou, an Israeli war veteran severely burned and accidentally shot by his own comrades during the *intifada*. After years of rehabilitation, he goes to live in a shack on the beach, where he runs a bar for foreign workers, determined to remain uninvolved in life. He believes that in a romantic relationship, one either hurts or is hurt. But when a Brazilian Indian woman is found near his home slashed by her pimp husband, he is drawn into the life of the foreigners' society from which he had remained aloof. There is a primal quality to Lapid's descriptions of the workers who, in this strange land, are seen simply as beasts of burden, lacking the cultural accoutrements of the countries from which they came. Babou becomes particularly attached to the Indian woman's baby, and this enhances his reentry into society.

Yehoshua Kenaz's latest novel, *Mahzir Ahavot Kodmot* (Restoring Former Loves), revolves around various residents in a Tel Aviv neighborhood, with parallel plots intertwining and climaxing in a tragic end. A beautiful woman regularly meets her married lover in an apartment he has rented for these assignations. Outside the sexual connection, there is no other communication or relationship between them. An emotionally stunted bachelor resides next door and has sexual fantasies about the woman. A forgotten old man lives nearby with a young Filipino woman caretaker, who is the center of his existence and the source of his continuing curiosity about life. With a psychological precision that points up all the grotesqueness, the mediocrity, and mean-spiritedness of which human beings are capable, but also their yearning for beauty and life, Kenaz builds to the murder of the innocent Filipino by the bachelor, driven mad by his fantasies and frustrations. The conclusion would indicate that the stranger and the underdog are often the inadvertent victims of our pathologies.

YOUNG WOMEN WRITERS

Literary energy continued to emanate from Tel Aviv-area writers in their 30s and 40s, particularly women. Their number includes Yael Hadaya, whimsically portraying the desire for relationship; Shoham Smith, echoing Orly Castel-Bloom's absurd language-play to depict the sisterhood of women; Eleanora Lev, delving into the imaginative perceptions of a woman as she walks across Tel Aviv to the hospital to deliver her child as a single mother; and Alona Kimche, whose protagonists' pathological involvement with parents leads them into mental illness but also deep human insight.

SECOND-GENERATION WRITERS

In spite of the "me" emphasis of this literary generation, collective memories infiltrate its fiction. Many of these works are fed by dark Holocaust strains. They tell of "second generation" children of survivors, whose parents live in constant fear of catastrophe. An outstanding example of this are the stories of Esty G. Hayim in the collection *Rakdanit Shehorah Be-lahakat Yahid* (Black Dancer in a Solo Troupe). In the title story, the hypochondriac protagonist, hounded by her parents' constant fear of catastrophe, goes off to Amsterdam, where, for the first time in her life, she lets herself go, teams up with a handsome Swede, and forgets about her mother, who calls all over Amsterdam to find her. In the novella "She Loves You, Yeah, Yeah, Yeah," the effects of displacement are evident. Because of the Holocaust, couples have been thrown together who would never have married each other. Mrs. Stein is infantilized, unable to overcome the loss of nurturing parents, while Devorah, the little girl across the court, watches as her catatonic mother lives a "life-in-death" existence brought alive by random affairs with Arab workers.

Savyon Liebrecht, a second-generation child of survivors, has written about survivor parents and grandparents. Following four collections of short stories, she published her first novel, *Ish Ve-isha Ve-ish* (A Man and a Woman and a Man), which integrates the "second generation" theme into the larger narrative. A married woman has a brief affair with a man whom she meets in the hospital, where she is tending her mother who suffers from Alzheimer's disease. The mother is a survivor who has never been able to express love for the daughter, and the daughter struggles between the memories of a loveless childhood and the pressures of family and career. The love affair offers respite from the realities of her life.

FICTION ABOUT THE RELIGIOUS COMMUNITY

Israelis have long enjoyed reading voyeuristic fiction that offers a peek into the life of the ultra-Orthodox community, especially their sexual practices. The late novelist Yehoshua Bar Yosef, who grew up in the Meah Shearim section of Jerusalem in the 1930s, depicted a community wracked by a seething sexuality. Recently, former religiously observant writers Dov Elbaum and Yohi Brandes published novels describing their traumatic encounters with the ultra-Orthodox life-style. Elbaum's vision of the yeshivah, in his novel *Zeman Elul* (The Month of Elul), is filtered through the eyes of an overwrought adolescent obsessed with his emergent sexuality. During the month of Elul, which immediately precedes the High Holy Day season and is the traditional period of penitence and spiritual preparation, the boy goes to extreme measures to purify himself so he can become a pure channel to God. But Elbaum is not only depicting a neurotic adolescent. He has set himself firmly in the naturalistic tradition of the early Haskalah (Enlightenment) prose writers, placing his specimens under a strong magnifying glass to create a picture of a grotesque, represssive ultra-Orthodoxy.

Yohi Brandes's novel *Gemar Tov* (A Good End) exposes the community's weaknesses through the prism of *shiduhim*, the practice of arranged marriages. Sara insists on marrying her cousin Binyamin over the objections of her family, but Binyamin is unable to consummate the marriage. The couple divorce, and Sara moves on to a more conventional marriage. Brandes has heavily weighted the book against the ultra-Orthodox rather than allowing the characters the fictional prerogative to develop freely. She continues her involvement with the Orthodox community in the best-selling novel *Hagar*, where a yeshivah student falls in love with a woman from a kibbutz.

Mira Magen's first novel, *Al Takeh Ba'kir* (Don't Knock Against the Wall), depicts an observant young woman, Iska, from a religious Zionist moshav, who is also rebellious, trying to walk in the footsteps of the ostensibly free-spirited Alma, who married Elisha, Iska's neighbor, and died in childbirth. The religious life-style provides the background of the story. But there is little of the judgmental aspect regarding religious life that characterizes the other novels discussed here. Rather, the moshav is suffused with a certain wisdom and stability, embodied in particular in the character of Elisha.

Chana Bat Shahar is a novelist writing under a pseudonym and known to come from a rabbinic family. Her recent collection of stories, *Sham Sirot Ha'dayig* (Look, the Fishing Boats), depicts intense, high-strung women yearning to break out of the closed-minded, middle-class religious homes in which they live. But there is nothing sensationalist about Bat Shahar. Her dense literary style echoes the claustrophobic world in which her narrators feel imprisoned. In the title story, Sara longs to go on the fishing boats into the open sea, far from the hotel where the family is spending the weekend. She gets carried away by her younger daughter's romantic fantasies. Many of Bat Shahar's heroines are dreamy to the point of being hallucinatory. Their sense of sexual deadness and their fantasies about the freedom to be found outside their own lives often verge on madness.

POSTMODERNIST FICTION

Postmodernism, signaling the breakdown of the divide between high and low culture and the end of ideologies, continued to be best represented in Israeli literature by Orly Castel-Bloom. Her deceptively playful voice, zany plots, and absurdist prose are often used in the service of profound social satire. Castel-Bloom's most recent novel, *Taking the Trend*, depicts the fashionable trends that the narrator and her friends follow blindly—the ultimate absurdity being their concern for petroleum-eating pigmy giraffes. The novel suggests that tomorrow will bring yet another trend and that all are ultimately meaningless and frivolous.

Etgar Keret is another important postmodernist voice. His works veer between high and low culture. Nothing better reflects this than his comic books, of which his most recent is *Simta'ot Haza'am* (Streets of Rage), illustrated by Assaf Hanuka. Keret's latest collection of stories, *Hakaitana shel Kneller* (Kneller's Day Camp), depicts a gang of rudderless boys who take turns smoking pot, going crazy, and even committing suicide. It is written in a Tel Aviv-ish slang that is both funny and deeply poetic. In the long title story, Keret takes the reader to the other side, the hell of suicides, which turns out to be not that much different from life itself. Here the story's protagonist seeks another chance with his girlfriend, but the Messiah spoils it.

S.Y. AGNON AND HAYYIM HAZAZ

During this period, Israel commemorated the 100th birthdays of two great Hebrew writers, S.Y. Agnon and Hayyim Hazaz, whose influence still echo in contemporary Israeli literature.

S.Y. Agnon, Israel's only Nobel Prize winner in literature, wrote ironic, existentialist tales about the disintegration of the shtetl, on one hand, and the new pioneering Jew, on the other. Combining the style of classical *midrash*, a charming storytelling manner, and a modernist's skeptical eye, he succeeded in bridging the old and new worlds, Europe and Israel. The first biography of Agnon was published this year by Prof. Don Leor of Tel Aviv University—a monumental work, weaving together the man and his fiction with subtlety and tact.

Hayyim Hazaz, born in the Ukraine, captured in his fiction the revolutionary spirit that inspired Jews in the 20th century—associated with both the Russian and Zionist revolutions. He is particularly relevant to the present, having already, half a century ago, raised many of the same questions being debated in this post-ideological period. A writer of great range, he was fascinated by the Yemenite and Sephardic life-force. To Hazaz these Eastern Jews embodied a different version of Zionism, the traditional yearning for Eretz Yisrael, and his works portray their adjustment to the Europeanized, Westernized Israeli reality.

Poetry

Poetry no longer holds the central position it once did in Israeli culture. There were some attempts to bring it to larger audiences by combining it with music and art, such as the work of poet Roni Somekh, who collaborates with musicians to combine music with poetry. Many beautiful albums of poetry, coffee-table books, were recently published. *Meirov Ahavah* (From Too Much Love), for example, comprising 75 love poems of Dalia Rabikovitch, is illustrated by a number of Israel's finest artists. In commemoration of the 50th anniversary, Israel witnessed the publication of albums of poetry by poets particularly identified with the period of Israel's nation building. Natan Alterman (1910-1970), best known for his political-satirical poems expressing the feelings of the Zionist collective, was also an imagist poet striving to return to some primal Eden and an idealized Eve. An album of his love poems recently appeared, illustrated by Avner Katz.

VETERAN POETS

In recent years there has been a reevaluation of Haim Guri, the 1948-generation writer who was originally regarded as the heir to Natan Alterman, who served as a kind of poet laureate, reacting sharply and satirically to contemporary social and political events. "Today we realize," wrote critic Haya Hoffman, "that Guri has a complex voice that deals with the personal as well as the public." The appearance of *The Collected Poems of Haim Guri*, on the occasion of Israel Independence Day, allows a reconsideration of his total body of work. It reveals a personal voice in tension with the public one, depicting the struggle over the Land of Israel and the attempt to find a balance between the public and subjective worlds.

Yehuda Amichai, Israel's most renowned poet, published a new collection, *Patah, Segor, Patah* (Open, Close, Open). Here, as in all his work, he perceives the mythic (particularly Jewish and Israeli myths) with ironic humor; at the same time, the irony serves to highlight the power of the mythic and sacred. In his latest poems, characterized by profound whimsy and word-play, Amichai announces his affinity for the world of women relegated to the other side of the *mehitzah*, the partition separating men and women in the synagogue. In reality, the poet declares, it is he who is imprisoned by his "maleness" on the men's side of the divide, unable to partake of the women's love and generosity. In another poem Amichai sensuously describes women as they ritually prepare his body for burial. As critic Michael Glausman noted, "Amichai is a poet with a marvelous inventive ability, linguistic play, large voice. But most surprising is how young the [new] book is."

Another volume by a veteran poet published this year was Arye Sivan's *Dayar Lo Mugan* (An Unprotected Tenant), which points up human vulnerability and loneliness. Yet Sivan is not altogether given to despair and remains amazed at the ability of the word to create worlds. Amir Oren is a poet of the younger generation who works hard to promote Israeli poetry. In his recent volume *Shir* (Poem), he writes about the art of poetry, attempting to show the construction of the poem and how magical a process it is. Ilan Shenfeld, known for his sensitive homosexual poetry, published *Karet* (Cut Off), whose title refers to the prohibition against homosexuality in the Bible, with its warning that the offender will be cut off from God and the community. Shenfeld's poignant poems, exposing his vulnerability but also calling out for love and intimacy in a harsh world, echo John Donne's 18th-century religious poetry.

WOMEN POETS AND RELIGIOUS POETS

Two newly published books of women's poetry grapple with the memories of childhood. Maya Bejarano's latest collection, *Anaseh La'gaat B'tabor Bitni* (I'll Try to Touch My Belly-Button), contrasts with some of her earlier work, in which she attempted to expand poetic discourse to scientific and technological subjects, and to flora and fauna, with the poet fusing with the objects. In the new volume, the subjects are her family, parents and grandparents, and children, and the language becomes more accessible, less specialized. Agi Mishael's recent work also returns to her childhood. In her case, it is as a child of struggling Holocaust survivors in the town of Gedera, where she yearned to be a sabra-type Israeli. Mishael, influenced by the late Yona Wallach, is a powerful poet who uses original, often sexually bold language, taking on both male and female personas.

Although poetry, as such, had become relatively quiescent of late, there was much poetic activity in the religious community. An anthology of poetry by religious writers, *Shirah Hadashah* (A New Song), edited by Admiel Kosman and Meron Isakson, was published; a group of Religious Zionist yeshivah students created a poetry magazine called *Mashiv Haruach* (Who Makes the Wind Blow); and some of the yeshivas developed poetry workshops. Among the most prominent of the religious poets is Admiel Kosman, whose volume *Higanu L'Elokim* (We Have Reached God) appeared recently. Kosman is a religious poet who expresses himself with power and energy and does not shy away from sexual matters and bodily functions. Critic Haya Hoffman feels that Kosman celebrates the holiness of sexual relationship and approaches women with a sense of religious awe, while critic Jeffrey Green sees him in a continuum with the freedom found in rabbinic literature. Other critics, however, regard some poems in his new book as inauthentic and playing to his audience.

Meron Izakson's new collection of poetry, *Raashim U'klai Bayit* (Noises and Housewares), reveals the mystery in the everyday, subtly interweaving Jewish sources with a sharp eye for human detail. Hava Pinchas-Cohen, the editor of the magazine *Dimui* (Image), also came out with a new book of poems, *Nahar Ve-Shikhekhah* (River and Forgetfulness). The eroticism and sensuousness of her poems emerge from a sense of attachment to nature in the Land of Israel. Her voice is direct—the voice of the Israeli sabra—at the same time, it is rich in metaphor and symbol.

Theater

According to a survey by Dr. Shosh Weitz, published *in Yediot Aharonot*, the proportion of theatergoers attending at least one play annually grew in the last decade from 33 percent in 1990 to 48 percent in 1999. Israel was in fact one of the leading countries in theater attendance. During 1998, Israeli theater manifested greater sophistication, less of the simplistic "journalistic" drama that characterized it in former years. At the same time, there was little evidence of new blood. No young group of directors had arisen in rebellion against the establishment, creating new modes of theater, since the founding of the Russian immigrant theater Gesher at the beginning of the decade. The old modes continued, albeit in a more interesting, professional manner. Various reasons have been suggested for the failure of new dramatists to emerge. It is assumed, for example, that increased theater attendance comes from audiences seeking lighter, more popular fare, who are less interested in experimentation. Theater producers, therefore, are afraid to take risks and choose to recycle old-time favorites like Yitzhak Navon's *Bustan Sefardi* (A Sephardic Garden), which has had record attendance. Once a young director fails, he or she is given few chances to continue experimentation. Tom Levi, head of Tel Aviv University's theater department, also claimed that a small clique rules Israeli theater and that if a young, innovative dramatist lacks the right connections, it is difficult to breach the barrier.

RECENT WORKS

Gevulot (Borders), written and directed by Shmulik Levi, is a work that attempts to bring home to the Israeli public the troubling situation in Lebanon. It depicts four young soldiers caught in a bunker, focusing on their hopes and despairs (already they are preparing their funeral speeches). *The Actor*, written and directed by Hillel Mittelpunkt, is about a Yiddish theater group headed by an actor, Natan Mershlak, which has been banned by the rabbinate in a small prewar town in Poland and must travel from place to place to perform. Confronted by overwhelming difficulties, only Mershlak remains to carry the banner of secular theater. Mittelpunkt's analogy to the restrictive Israeli rabbinate of the present day is clear.

Women have achieved an important position in recent drama. The play *Alma*, written and directed by Yehoshua Sobol, depicts Alma Mahler, one of the most charismatic women of the late 19th and early 20th centuries. A female Don Juan, she cast her spell on the great artists of her time—composer Gustav Mahler, architect Walter Gropius, painter Oskar Kokoschka, and finally Jewish writer Franz Werfel, whom she saved from Hitler and with whom she lived out her life as a refugee in the United States.

Women have also taken center stage as the most interesting dramatists in Israel. Edna Mazya, already known for her *Vienna al Ha-Yam* (Vienna on the Sea), *Sippur Mishpahti* (Family Story), and *Mishakim Be-Hatzer Ha-ahori* (Games in the Backyard), a play about teen rape in Kibbutz Shomrat, recently wrote *Hamordim* (The Rebels). The plot revolves around a daughter's rebellion against her right-wing parents, particularly the daughter's misunderstanding of her mother, a member of the terrorist Stern Gang in prestate Israel, who married the girl's South African- born father to escape arrest by the British. Although it lacks deep characterization, the dialogue is sharp and funny and the action utilizes multimedia effects to create a visual context that is often absent in Israeli theater. Director Omri Nitzan has obviously been influenced by world trends, but it would seem that, closer to home, the staging can be traced to the influence of Gesher Theater's Yevgeny Arye's full-blown, spectacular theater vision.

A new play that is not only written and directed by women but also celebrates the complex relationships developed by women with each other is *Ha-haverot Ha-hi Tovot* (Best Friends), written by Anat Gov and directed by Edna Mazya. It traces 30 years of close friendship between three women, their need for each other, their love and jealousy and unfulfilled expectations. It all comes to an end as the three grow apart and go their separate ways.

Another play about relationships is *Ha-Kontzert* (The Concert), written by Goren Agmon, which presents the complex conflicts revealed in a family when the mother, who is a musician, is given the opportunity to conduct the Philharmonic Orchestra.

RELIGIOUS THEMES

Women were also active in writing and directing plays with religious themes. Yosefa Even-Shoshan created *Virgin from Ludmir*, directed by Ophira Hanig, a drama based on a semihistorical figure, a Hassidic woman whose father taught her Talmud and who became a recognized scholar. As women stream to her for advice, she decides to give up the man she loves and to devote herself to rabbinic scholarship. Later, when she realizes what a detrimental influence she is having on other women—who are abandoning their families to follow her—she attempts to marry and live a conventional life. She fails in her efforts, yet she cannot continue to fight her society.

One of the most extraordinary projects on the contemporary Israeli stage is the Bible-based dance-drama "Va-Yomer, Va-Yelekh" (And He Said, and He Went), adapted and directed by Rina Yerushalmi. This work is an interpretation of biblical texts through declamation and body movement. In the first part, "Vayomer," based primarily on the Book of Genesis, the emergence of humans in relation to God and the world is depicted. The second part portrays the national experience, men and women developing into a tribe, with God pledging to bring the Jewish people to the Promised Land. Some of the interpretations of the Bible are highly iconoclastic in traditional terms. God is often portrayed as a harsh, primal force, a tyrannical persona. But the play is also deeply spiritual, ranging over the experience of the Creation, the Psalms, the sense of people filling the earth, all of which brings the Bible to life.

"Va-Yishtahu, Va-Yera" (And They Bowed, and He Appeared), the second work in Yerushalmi's Bible project, relates to the issue of kingship and prophecy. The Books of Samuel and Kings are central to the dance-drama, which captures the feel of metallic armed battles as Hebrews fight the Philistines. There is the comic relief of David as a buffoonish youth fighting the giant woman warrior Goliath, and the poignancy of Saul's madness and whimpering downfall, as he realizes that God is no longer with him.

The entire project points to a search for spirituality in what might be perceived as the secular theater community.

GESHER

During the last year and a half, the Gesher Theater, under the directorship of Yevgeny Arye, created and directed an eloquent version of Chekhov's *Three Sisters;* a rather grotesque play titled *Eating*, by the late Ya'akov Shabtai, which parodies contemporary vulgarity and materialism; and *Ir* (City), a jewel in Gesher's crown. *Ir* can be perceived as a companion piece to a previous production, *Kfar* (Village). While *Kfar* is an *Our Town* depiction of the pioneering roots of Israeli society, *Ir*, an adaptation of the Odessa stories of Isaac Babel, a Russian Jewish writer murdered by Stalin in the 1930s, reveals the artistic roots of the Russian-Jewish Gesher Theater. Through Babel, Arye conjures up an ironic, urban Jewish vision. In his Odessa, there are Jewish Mafia types, but the head of the gang of thieves is also a loving father who seeks a Jewish match for his daughter. There is the intellectual child studying the violin and his whimsical grandfather, but there are also pogroms to which the grandfather falls victim.

HANOCH LEVIN

Hanoch Levin is one of Israel's most prolific and original playwrights. He began his career writing cabaret-type satires in the 1960s and early 1970s. There were many satire groups at the time, but they were generally good-humored in nature. Levin's art emerged from a dark, deep rage, and he attempted to shock middle-class Israel out of its complacency after the Six Day War. Vestiges of his cabaret satire, with its obsessive vulgarity and shock appeal, can still be found throughout the almost 30 works he has written, many of which he has directed. The theme of suppressor and suppressed dominates. In a recent work, *Retzach* (Murder), an Arab child is killed, and then a couple is murdered after their wedding, possibly by the Arab child's father. One murder leads to another, bringing in its wake the murder of an Arab worker by prostitutes—all this in an era that was supposed to be a harbinger of peace.

But Levin's pessimism about the possibilities of peace is only a small part of his misanthropic world. He has created an Israeli Theater of the Absurd where, according to Hebrew University literary historian Gershon Shaked, the attempt to get close to another human being is useless. Human relationships are at their core veritable hells on earth and accentuate how alone human beings really are. People talk in monologues; there is no communication. But the alternative—bare, stark aloneness—is equally terrible. In a style characterized by expletives, by obsession with anal and oral activities, Levin shows that human activities—sex, eating, bowel movements, as well as suffering and hope, victimizing and victimhood—are simply strategies for coping with a meaningless life. In a book that was just published about Hanoch Levin, critic Haim Nagid suggests that Levin seeks the absolute, and unwilling to accept human frailty, finds little consolation in life.

However, there are also works by Levin that expose the cruelty of the human condition with tenderness and depth. This was evident in a recent revival of *M'lekhet Ha'hayim* (The Labor of Living), originally done ten years ago. In the play, Yona Pupik, an abstractly delineated Everyman, wakes up one night in a panic, wondering how his life has slipped through his fingers. Not long ago he was a small boy experiencing the sweetness of his father's company. According to poet-critic Yitzhak La'or, the sweet moments of childhood remembered in Levin's plays and poems constitute the true inner life that has been lost and that the hero, in vain, attempts to regain. Yona Pupik blames his wife, whom he has come to revile, for the loss of his inner self and resolves to leave her. The audience is witness to her pleading, her own disappointments, her tenderness, and, at the same time, her rage. The lonely, unmarried friend who intrudes upon them points up the abyss of loneliness that is Pupik's alternative. Pupik's death leaves nothing in the end but the writer who will write about these people.

Visual Arts

50TH ANNIVERSARY EXHIBITS

The Israel Museum celebrated Israel's 50th anniversary with an extensive exhibit, "To the East: Orientalism in the Arts in Israel." It presented the works of Israeli artists, worthy in their own right, who have sought to assimilate a Middle East ambience—the culture, climate, topography of the land they so embraced—into their art. To some viewers, however, the exhibit seemed to have a political subtext that negated the very achievements being celebrated. Did the very term "Orientalism" imply, it was asked, that Zionism was colonialist, and that the artists had a patronizing view of Arab culture? In actuality, painters of the 1920s like Nahum Guttman, Pinhas Litvinowsky, and Reuven Rubin viewed the Middle East as being closer to nature than the Europe they left behind, as a more sensual and languorous environment, and they idealized the native Arabs who inhabited these landscapes drenched in strong sun and light. After the Arab riots of 1929, the Arabs were often seen through the prism of the Arab-Israeli conflict, but they were never demonized. Israeli artists, instead, turned to painting Sephardic Jews, or expressing their relation to the landscape by evoking a vision of the ancient Near East, a culture rooted in the larger Mediterranean tradition. Itzhak Danziger's primitive Canaanite statue, a feature of the exhibition, represents this trend.

The last decades have produced political artworks that show clear sympathy with the Arab side of the conflict. One example in the exhibit was Larry Abramson's "Tsooba," which echoes an abstract landscape of the same name by Joseph Zaritsky, the father of Israeli modernist painting. In the 1920s, Zaritsky turned his back on Zionist ideology in art, introducing apolitical abstract art influenced by what was then happening in Paris. Forty years later, Abramson took Joseph Zaritsky's abstract landscape to task. Viewing the scene from the same spot where Zaritsky stood to execute his abstract painting, Abramson shows the remains of the Arab village of Tsooba. He implies that Zaritsky and, concomitantly, all who followed him, were guilty of ignoring the Arab plight, consenting by their silence to the banishment of the Arabs from their villages. The Israel Museum's 50th anniversary exhibit, in sum, could be considered as having made a strong political statement.

Also commemorating Israel's 50th anniversary was the Tel Aviv Museum's exhibition "A Selection from the Joseph Hackmey Collection," the largest private collection in Israel, on permanent display at the Israel Phoenix Company. The collection ranges from the products of the Bezalel School of Arts and Crafts, founded in 1906, to contemporary works. It includes Reuven Rubin's 1920s works, works by the abstract New Horizons group, and Yigal Tumarkin's sculpture, represented by his primitive "Canaanite" work, "Portrait of the Artist as a Young Warrior 1966." Among the more contemporary artists included in the collection are Menashe Kadishman, Moshe Kupferman, Michael Gross, Raffi Lavie Pinchas, and Cohen Gan. Altogether, the exhibit offered a comprehensive overview of contemporary Israeli art.

POLITICALLY ORIENTED ART

The Tel Aviv Museum and Tel Aviv University Gallery also featured a joint exhibit, "Perspectives on Israeli Art in the 1970s." The decade of the 1970s was a creative period for Israeli art, influenced by the conceptual art then sweeping the world. Conceptual art broke away from traditional painting and sculpture, using different types of materials, often everyday objects, to express political views. In the United States the political agendas were primarily feminism and ecology. The Israeli art of the 1970s also produced feminist art, such as Yocheved Weinfeld's "Menstruation"(1976), and ecological works like Avital Geva's "Activity" (1973). For the present exhibit, the museum reconstructed Geva's large pool with fish, an echo of the original work, with smelly dead fish floating on the surface. But during the 1970s, as in the 1990s, the primary political focus of Israel's art was on the occupied territories.

The section "Visual Art in a Country Without Boundaries" indicated that while in the 1970s artists throughout the world were breaking down barriers between ethnic groups, as well as between male and female, Israel's elimination of boundaries in the Six Day War actually involved the physical expansion of its borders—a highly problematic situation that led to the abuse of the Palestinians. A series of paintings by Michael Sgan-Cohen traces the borders of the country, giving a sense of the land breaking out beyond its limits. Another installation was Gabi Klezmer and Sharon Keren's "Foreign Labor," based on their "Arab Labor," a 1975 piece that showed a wall built by Arabs, work that more recently was being done by foreign workers. In the same spirit was "Hebrew Labor," an installation consisting of a dirty mat, opened cans of food, and other objects that evoke an Arab worker's living conditions, while he builds homes for Jews. The ironic title underscores the disappearance of the Zionist ideal of creating a new breed of Jews who happily engage in productive physical labor.

The 1970s were being celebrated because a new wave of political art had surfaced. Sigalit Landau uses shipping containers to show how the homeless and the foreign workers live. She participated in the 1997 Venice Biennale, where she exhibited "Foreign Resident II," a container which the observer must enter and climb through, only to discover the paltry belongings of a foreign worker or an Arab brought from the territories to build Israeli houses. Installation art continued to express political attitudes, but much of the new figurative art was also directed to political subjects, such as David Reeb's works, which include coarse portrayals of Israeli soldiers abusing Arabs.

Dani Karavan

There were several exhibits in 1998 celebrating veteran sculptor Dani Karavan, one of Israel's most internationally acclaimed artists. The Tel Aviv Museum and the Museum of Israeli Art in Ramat Gan mounted exhibits devoted to Karavan's political and environmental works. The Tel Aviv Museum ambitiously transformed museum space into a landscape displaying Karavan's environmental sculpture "Passages — Homage to Walter Benjamin." The installation attempted to duplicate the effect of the original, which was created in 1994 at Port-Bou on the French-Spanish border, where the great critic Walter Benjamin, in flight from the Nazis, committed suicide in 1940. It features pathways leading to dead ends, fences, and borders, with nowhere to escape. The Ramat Gan Museum of Israeli Art exhibited Karavan's political works, including "Har Homah," consisting of an uprooted olive tree turned upside down, which suggests Israel's uprooting of the native Palestinians by overturning nature to create new settlements in the West Bank.

Figurative Art

During the last few years there have been signs of a return to figurative art in Israel, as in much of the rest of the world. Some of this art has also been channeled to political subjects. At the forefront of the figurative movement is Yisrael Hershberg, who seeks to refocus on the artistic object itself. Hershberg, who came to Israel from the United States in 1984, established an art school specializing in figurative art. His students learn to paint by studying the Old Masters. The Israel Museum exhibit of Hershberg's works revealed highly physical, tactile images, presented as "things in themselves," almost without context: sunflowers, pine cones, a cow's tongue, all executed with great attention to the contrast between shadow and light. And yet the very physicality of Hirshberg's works points to their disintegration. Sprats on a tray suggest a pile of corpses, a male nude with blemished skin and bulging veins suggests the rotting of the flesh.

Dance

Dance continued to flourish in Israel. Dance critic Ruth Eshel expressed the view that just as Israeli high tech had achieved international renown, so too was Israeli dance gaining a worldwide reputation. She claimed that a distinctive Israeli dance language could be discerned, and attributed this not only to the highly successful Batsheva and Kibbutz Contemporary Dance Companies, but to the many small groups of young dancers that have emerged. The constant flow of visiting dance groups to Israel, the sustained activity at the Suzanne Dellal Center, the young audiences that attend performances—all these have created an exciting dance milieu.

Some of the interesting young dancers include Ido Tadmor and Noa Adar; Barak Marshall, who represents an Eastern mode; Inbal Pinto, who creates Disney-like fantasies for adults; and Ben Gan whose "Dance of Nothing," about a tribe of nomads, is primal in mood.

The most recent work of Ohad Naharin, Batsheva's artistic director, is "Sabotage, Baby," which is, in many ways, a more contemplative piece than some of his previous efforts. The monklike cloaks and the solemn patterns formed by the dancers create an atmosphere of meditative spirituality. By way of counterpoint, the Orkater Ensemble from Holland is on stage with the dancers, playing what is called a "sound machine" made up of machine parts and electronic elements. The presence of this antiquated-looking apparatus, in conjunction with the dance movements, contributes to the sense of total theater, which is Naharin's aim.

The Kibbutz Contemporary Dance Company, under artistic director Rami Be'er, received much acclaim this year as it performed his work "Aide Memoire" throughout the United States and Europe in commemoration of Israel's 50th anniversary. "Aide Memoire," first performed in 1994, grapples with the images of the Holocaust deeply embedded in second- and third-generation children of survivors. Rami Be'er is such a child, while Yehudit Arnon, who established the Kibbutz Company and was its artistic director until 1996, is an Auschwitz survivor. On a pitch-black stage, white spotlights illuminate figures that emerge from between metal slabs that symbolize walls, doors, and trains. The dancers climb, cross over, hit against, and disappear behind these slabs. Threads of the Holocaust reality that echo in the Jewish psyche are suggested by the dancers marching across the stage and shouting. Anna Kisselgoff, the *New York Times* dance critic, found that "Be'er favors a general modern-dance idiom that makes use of the entire body." Another critic found the dancing "forthright and sturdy" and of "powerful simplicity."

Be'er's works make brilliant use of props and stage settings. In his revised choreography of "Naked City," a work about urban alienation first performed in 1993, the set consists of two levels; on the upper level are figures locked in isolated cells, observing dancers on the lower-level street. The work ends spectacularly with red confetti pouring down on the black-clad dancers. The principal dancer, holding an umbrella, slowly lets his rich-colored cloak fall to reveal his naked body. In his newest work, "The Unanswered Question," based on the music of Charles Ives, Be'er uses wood stumps of different heights on which the soloist dances and which become part of the choreography.

The Inbal Dance Company, which brought Yemenite ethnic dance to the fore in the 1950s, is no longer doing new work, but is now rather an ethnic archive, performing old dance versions of such favorites as a Yemenite wedding or the Song of Songs. However, a new Ethiopian ethnic dance company emerged, called the Eskesta Dance Troupe, which means "shaking of the shoulders," a flirtatious gesture that characterizes Ethiopian dance. Ruth Eshel, an Israeli-born dancer-choreographer and critic, founded the group at Haifa University, where the dancers study. Through dance these young Ethiopian students are being reconnected to their community and its leaders, who teach them Sabbath and holiday prayers, which they translate into dance terms, opening and closing their palms, trembling with feeling. The dance "Maharu" is particularly significant, reenacting the long, difficult trek out of Ethiopia, a trauma etched in the collective memory of the Ethiopians.

Music

The 50th anniversary was the occasion for many musical events. There was the concert "50 Years of Eastern Music," which included important Eastern pop singers and appearances by the classical Eastern Andalusian Orchestra. In line with the recent revitalization of ethnic music, the singer-actor Yehoram Ga'on had opened a school for Eastern music.

There were also many concerts of classical Western music. The Israel Philharmonic Orchestra commissioned *B'reshit* (Genesis) from composer Noam Sheriff for the festive concerts celebrating the anniversary. Based on the Book of Genesis, the work, which includes a children's choir, consists of six parts that evoke the emotions aroused by the six days of Creation: awakening; darkness, expressed through a mystical fanfare; chaos, interpreted as a kind of scherzo; light; "and God saw that it was good;" and "The great sadness at the end of the Creation." In recent years, Sheriff also created *Akedah* (The Binding of Isaac), based on Abraham's sacrifice of Isaac. The composition is dedicated to the memory of the late prime minister Yitzhak Rabin, namesake of the biblical Isaac, who can also be seen as a sacrifice of the peace process. Noam Sheriff's *Gomel Le-Ish Hasid* (A Hasid's Reward) for bass-clarinet and string orchestra is another of his recent works, one that artfully integrates *klezmer* themes.

The 1998 Israel Festival featured the world premiere of *Song of Songs*, composed by 24-year-old Gil Shohat. The work is sensual, and, in the postmodernist spirit, draws on composers such as Puccini, Bizet, Verdi, Ravel, and Stravinsky. Shohat could also boast recent premieres of a violin concertino, a children's opera, and a symphonic poem, *The Dry Bones*.

Composer Michael Wolpe, a member of Kibbutz Sde Boker, who frequently fuses Eastern and Western elements in his works, recently composed a Concerto for Flute, Strings and Oriental Instruments. His *Memorial Songs* is based on his experience of the Lebanon War, and uses an oud (an Arab violin), a string quartet, and percussion instruments. "It is on the borderline between East and West," he explains, "expressing the terrible pain the war caused to both Jew and Arab." Another of his recent works, *Sounds of Light and Darkness*, is an oratorio based on the Dead Sea Scrolls.

Yinam Leef, known for his integration of ancient Middle Eastern elements with Western patterns of composition, was commissioned by the Jerusalem Symphony to compose a work in honor of the 50th anniversary. He created a Concerto for Viola for the violist Tabea Zimmermann. This work develops from a very slow movement, the viola against an almost static orchestra, to a symphonic scream, with great agitation that embraces Eastern and even jazz modes. Leef's *Yizkor*, a haunting work for solo flute, created in memory of Yitzhak Rabin, was recently issued on CD.

A folklore trend has emerged among some of the composers coming from the former Soviet Union, like Josef Bardanashvili, who calls upon his Georgian tradition in his compositions. His recent works include *Elegy for String Orchestra*, based on Psalm 22, and *Farewell Song* for alto flute, harp, string quartet, and percussion. Increasingly, Israeli musical compositions have been based on the Psalms and other classic Jewish texts.

ROCHELLE FURSTENBERG

World Jewish Population, 1997

THE WORLD'S JEWISH POPULATION was estimated at just above 13 million at the end of 1997.[1]

Figures on population size, characteristics, and trends are a primary tool in any assessment of the needs and prospects of Jewish communities worldwide.

The estimates for the various countries reported in this article reflect some of the results of a prolonged and ongoing effort to study scientifically the demography of contemporary world Jewry.[2] Data collection and comparative research have benefited from the collaboration of scholars and institutions in many countries, including replies to direct inquiries regarding current estimates. It should be emphasized, however, that the elaboration of a worldwide set of estimates for the Jewish populations of the various countries is beset with difficulties and uncertainties.[3]

Since the end of the 1980s important geopolitical changes have affected the world scene, particularly in Eastern Europe. The major event was the political breakup of the Soviet Union into 15 independent states. Similarly, the former Czechoslovakia and Yugoslavia broke down into several successor states. East and West Germany reunited after a political split of 45 years. The Jewish population has been sensitive to these changes, with large-scale emigration from the former USSR (FSU) being the most visible effect.

Geographical mobility and the increased fragmentation of the global system of nations notwithstanding, about 95 percent of world Jewry is concentrated in ten countries. The aggregate of these major Jewish population centers virtually determines the assessment of the size of total world Jewry. The country figures for 1997 were updated from those for 1996 in accordance with the known or estimated changes in the interval—migrations, vital events (births and deaths), and identificational changes (accessions and secessions).

---

[1]The previous estimates, as of 1996, were published in AJYB 1998, vol. 98, pp. 477–512.

[2]Many of these activities are carried out by, or in coordination with, the Division of Jewish Demography and Statistics at the A. Harman Institute of Contemporary Jewry, the Hebrew University of Jerusalem. The collaboration of the many institutions and individuals in the different countries who have supplied information for this update is acknowledged with thanks.

[3]For overviews of the subject matter and technical issues, see Paul Ritterband, Barry A. Kosmin, and Jeffrey Scheckner, "Counting Jewish Populations: Methods and Problems," AJYB 1988, vol. 88, pp. 204–21; and Sergio DellaPergola, *The Modern Jewish Experience* (New York, 1993), pp. 275–90.

In recent years, new data and estimates became available for the Jewish populations of several countries through official population censuses and Jewish-sponsored sociodemographic surveys. Several national population censuses yielded results on Jewish populations, such as in the Soviet Union (1989); Switzerland (1990); Canada, Australia, and South Africa (in 1991 and 1996); Brazil and the Czech Republic (1991); Romania and Bulgaria (1992); the Russian Republic (1994); and Israel (1995). Independent large-scale studies include the National Jewish Population Survey (NJPS) in the United States (1990) and the Jewish sociodemographic surveys in South Africa (1991), Mexico (1991), Lithuania (1993), Chile (1995), and Venezuela (1998–99), and the survey of social attitudes of British Jews (1995).

Additional evidence on Jewish population characteristics emerged from the systematic monitoring of membership registers, vital statistics, and immigration records available from Jewish communities and other Jewish organizations in many countries or cities: United Kingdom, Germany, and Buenos Aires. Some of this ongoing research is part of a coordinated effort to update the profile of world Jewry in the late 1990s.[4]

A new round of surveys and official censuses is expected to highlight the demographic profile of large Jewish communities at the turn of the new century, in particular the new U.S. National Jewish Population Survey planned for the year 2000 and censuses of the republics of the FSU due to take place over the years 1999–2001.

The more recent findings basically confirm the estimates we reported in previous AJYB volumes and, perhaps more importantly, our interpretation of the trends now prevailing in the demography of world Jewry.[5] While allowing for improved population estimates for the year 1997 under review here, these new data highlight the increasing complexity of the sociodemographic and identificational processes underlying the definition of Jewish populations, hence the estimates of their sizes—the more so at a time of enhanced international migration. Consequently, as will be clarified below, the analyst has to come to terms with the paradox of *the permanently provisional character of Jewish population estimates*. In-

---

[4]Following the 1987 International Conference on Jewish population problems held in Jerusalem, initiated by the late Dr. Roberto Bachi of the Hebrew University and sponsored by the major Jewish organizations worldwide, an International Scientific Advisory Committee (ISAC) was established. Currently chaired by Dr. Sidney Goldstein of Brown University, ISAC aims to coordinate and monitor Jewish population data collection internationally. See Sergio DellaPergola and Leah Cohen, eds., *World Jewish Population: Trends and Policies* (Jerusalem, 1992).

[5]See Roberto Bachi, *Population Trends of World Jewry* (Jerusalem, 1976); U.O. Schmelz, "Jewish Survival: The Demographic Factors," AJYB 1981, vol. 81, pp. 61–117; U.O. Schmelz, *Aging of World Jewry* (Jerusalem, 1984); Sergio DellaPergola, "Changing Cores and Peripheries: Fifty Years in Socio-demographic Perspective," in *Terms of Survival: The Jewish World Since 1945*, ed. R.S. Wistrich (London, 1995), pp. 13–43.

deed, where appropriate, we revised our previous estimates in the light of newly accrued information on Jewish populations (see tables 1 and 2). Corrections were also applied retrospectively to the 1996 figures for major geographical regions so as to allow adequate comparison with the 1997 estimates. Users of Jewish population estimates should be aware of these difficulties and of the inherent limitations of our estimates.

Presentation of Data

DEFINITIONS

A major problem in Jewish population estimates periodically circulated by various scholarly or Jewish organizations across the world is a general lack of coherence and uniformity in the definition criteria followed. Often, the problem of defining the Jewish population is not even addressed. The following estimates of Jewish population distribution on each continent and in each country (tables 2–9 below) consistently aim at the concept of *core* Jewish population.[6]

We define as the *core* Jewish population all those who, when asked, identify themselves as Jews; or, if the respondent is a different person in the same household, are identified by him/her as Jews. This is an intentionally comprehensive and pragmatic approach. Such definition of a person as a Jew, reflecting *subjective* feelings, broadly overlaps but does not necessarily coincide with *halakhic* (rabbinic) or other normatively binding definitions. It does *not* depend on any measure of that person's Jewish commitment or behavior in terms of religiosity, beliefs, knowledge, communal affiliation, or otherwise. The *core* Jewish population includes all those who converted to Judaism by any procedure or joined the Jewish group informally and declare themselves to be Jewish. It excludes those of Jewish descent who formally adopted another religion, as well as other individuals who did not convert out but currently refuse to acknowledge a Jewish identification.

We adopt the term *extended* for the sum of (a) the *core* Jewish population and (b) all other persons of Jewish parentage who are *not* Jews currently (or at the time of investigation). These non-Jews with Jewish background, as far as they can be ascertained, include: (a) persons who have themselves adopted another religion, even though they may claim still to be Jews ethnically; (b) other persons with Jewish parentage who disclaim to be Jews. It is customary in surveys such as these to consider parentage only and not any more distant ancestry. Some censuses, however, do ask about more distant ancestry.

---

[6]The term *core Jewish population* was initially suggested by Barry A. Kosmin, Sidney Goldstein, Joseph Waksberg, Nava Lerer, Ariella Keysar, and Jeffrey Scheckner in *Highlights of the CJF 1990 National Jewish Population Survey* (New York, 1991).

We designate by the term *enlarged*[7] the sum of (a) the *core* Jewish population, (b) all other persons of Jewish parentage included in the *extended* Jewish population, and (c) all of the respective further non-Jewish household members (spouses, children, etc.). For both conceptual and practical reasons, this definition does not include any other non-Jewish relatives living elsewhere in exclusively non-Jewish households.

Israel's distinctive legal framework for the acceptance and absorption of new immigrants is provided by the Law of Return, first passed in 1950 and amended in 1954 and 1970. The law awards Jewish new immigrants immediate citizenship and other civil rights in Israel. According to the current amended version of the Law of Return, a Jew is any person born to a Jewish mother or converted to Judaism (regardless of denomination—Orthodox, Conservative, or Reform). By decision of Israel's Supreme Court, conversion from Judaism, as in the case of some ethnic Jews who currently identify with another religion, entails loss of eligibility for Law of Return purposes. The law extends its provisions to all current Jews and to their Jewish or non-Jewish spouses, children, and grandchildren, as well as to the spouses of such children and grandchildren. As a result of its three-generation time perspective and lateral extension, the Law of Return applies to a wide population, one of significantly wider scope than *core, extended,* and *enlarged* Jewish populations defined above.[8] It is actually quite difficult to estimate what the total size of the Law of Return population could be. These higher estimates are not discussed below systematically, but some notion of their possible extent is given for the major countries.

ACCURACY RATING

We provide separate figures for each country with approximately 100 or more resident *core* Jews. Residual estimates of Jews living in other, smaller communities supplement some of the continental totals. For each of the reported countries, the four columns in tables 3–7 provide an estimate of midyear 1997 total population,[9] the estimated end-1997 Jewish population, the proportion of Jews per 1,000 of total population, and a rating of the accuracy of the Jewish population estimate.

---

[7]The term *enlarged Jewish population* was initially suggested by S. DellaPergola, "The Italian Jewish Population Study: Demographic Characteristics and Trends" in *Studies in Jewish Demography; Survey for 1969–1971,* ed. U.O. Schmelz, P. Glikson, and S.J. Gould (Jerusalem-London, 1975), pp. 60–97.

[8]For a concise review of the rules of attribution of Jewish personal status in rabbinic and Israeli laws, including reference to Jewish sects, isolated communities, and apostates, see Michael Corinaldi, "Jewish Identity," chap. 2 in his *Jewish Identity: The Case of Ethiopian Jewry* (Jerusalem, 1998).

[9]Data and estimates derived from the United Nations, World Bank, the Population Reference Bureau, and the Institute National d'Etudes Démographiques. See Marguerite Boucher, "Tous les pays du monde (1997)," *Population et Sociétés,* 326 (Paris, 1997).

There is wide variation in the quality of the Jewish population estimates for different countries. For many Diaspora countries it would be best to indicate a range (minimum–maximum) rather than a definite figure for the number of Jews. It would be confusing, however, for the reader to be confronted with a long list of ranges; this would also complicate the regional and world totals. The figures actually indicated for most of the Diaspora communities should be understood as being the central value of the plausible range of the respective core Jewish populations. The relative magnitude of this range varies inversely to the accuracy of the estimate.

The three main elements that affect the accuracy of each estimate are the nature and quality of the base data, the recency of the base data, and the method of updating. A simple code, combining these elements, is used to provide a general evaluation of the reliability of the Jewish population figures reported in the detailed tables below. The code indicates different quality levels of the reported estimates: (A) base figure derived from countrywide census or relatively reliable Jewish population survey; updated on the basis of full or partial information on Jewish population movements in the respective country during the intervening period; (B) base figure derived from less accurate but recent countrywide Jewish population investigation; partial information on population movements in the intervening period; (C) base figure derived from less recent sources, and/or unsatisfactory or partial coverage of Jewish population in the particular country; updating according to demographic information illustrative of regional demographic trends; (D) base figure essentially speculative; no reliable updating procedure. In categories (A), (B), and (C), the year in which the country's base figure or important partial updates were obtained is also stated. For countries whose Jewish population estimate of 1996 was not only updated but also revised in the light of improved information, the sign "X" is appended to the accuracy rating.

One additional tool for updating Jewish population estimates is provided by a new set of demographic projections currently being developed at the Hebrew University of Jerusalem.[10] These extrapolate the most likely observed or expected trends out of a Jewish population baseline assessed by sex and detailed age-groups, as of end-year 1995. Even where detailed information on the dynamics of Jewish population change is not immediately available, the powerful connection that generally exists between the age composition of a population and the respective vital and migration movements helps to provide plausible scenarios of the developments bound to occur in the short term. In the absence of better data, we have used indications from these projections to refine the direction and size of estimate revisions for 1997 as against 1996.

---

[10]See S. DellaPergola, U. Rebhun, and M. Tolts, *A New Look at the Jewish Future: World and Regional Population Projections* (Institute of Contemporary Jewry, Division of Jewish Demography and Statistics, Hebrew University, Jerusalem, 1999).

Global Overview

WORLD JEWISH POPULATION SIZE

Table 1 gives an overall picture of Jewish population for the end of 1997 as compared to 1996. For 1996 the originally published estimates are presented along with somewhat revised figures that take into account, retrospectively, the corrections made in certain country estimates, in the light of improved information. These corrections resulted in a net increase of world Jewry's estimated 1996 size by 38,300. This change resulted from upward corrections for Israel (+48,400) and for the Czech Republic (+200), and downward corrections for the United Kingdom (-8,500) and Latvia (-1,800). Explanations are given below for these corrections.

The size of world Jewry at the end of 1997 is assessed at 13,092,800. World Jewry constituted about 2.24 per 1,000 of the world's total population in 1997. One in about 446 people in the world is a Jew. According to the revised figures, between 1996 and 1997 the Jewish population grew by an estimated 29,500 people, or about +0.2 percent. Despite all the imperfections in the estimates, world Jewry continued to be close to "zero population growth," with the natural increase in Israel barely compensating for demographic decline in the Diaspora.

The number of Jews in Israel rose from a revised figure of 4,616,100 in 1996 to 4,701,600 at the end of 1997, an increase of 85,500 people, or 1.9 percent. In contrast, the estimated Jewish population in the Diaspora declined from 8,447,200 (according to the revised figures) to 8,391,200—a decrease of 56,000 people, or -0.7 percent. These changes primarily reflect the continuing Jewish emigration from the former USSR. In 1997, the estimated Israel-Diaspora net migratory balance amounted to a gain of about 34,300 Jews for Israel.[11] Internal demographic evolution produced a further growth of 51,200 among the Jewish population in Israel and a further loss of 21,700 in the Diaspora. Recently, instances of accession or "return" to Judaism can be observed in connection with the emigration process from Eastern Europe and the comprehensive provisions of the Israeli Law of Return (see above). The return or first-time access to Judaism of some such previously unincluded or unidentified individuals has contributed to slowing down the pace of decline of the relevant Diaspora Jewish populations and some further gains to the Jewish population in Israel.

As noted, it is customary to correct previously published Jewish population estimates in the light of improved information that became available at a later date. Table 2 provides a synopsis of world Jewish population estimates for the period 1945–1997, as first published each year in the *American Jewish Year Book* and as corrected retroactively, incorporating all subsequent revisions. These revised data

---

[11]Israel Central Bureau of Statistics, *Population and Vital Statistics 1997* (Jerusalem, 1998), pp. 2–8.

TABLE 1. ESTIMATED JEWISH POPULATION, BY CONTINENTS AND MAJOR GEO-
GRAPHICAL REGIONS, 1996 AND 1997

Region	1996			1997		% Change 1996–1997
	Original Abs. N.	Revised Abs. N.	Percent[a]	Abs. N.	Percent[a]	
World	13,025,000	13,063,300	100.0	13,092,800	100.0	0.2
Diaspora	8,457,300	8,447,200	64.7	8,391,200	64.1	−0.7
Israel	4,567,700	4,616,100	35.3	4,701,600	35.9	1.9
America, Total	6,493,000	6,493,000	49.7	6,490,400	49.6	−0.0
North[b]	6,062,000	6,062,000	46.4	6,062,000	46.3	0.0
Central	53,100	53,100	0.4	52,900	0.4	−0.4
South	377,900	377,900	2.9	375,500	2.9	−0.6
Europe, Total	1,691,700	1,681,600	12.9	1,637,400	12.5	−2.6
European Union	1,023,500	1,015,000	7.8	1,018,300	7.8	0.3
Other West	19,900	19,900	0.2	19,900	0.2	0.0
Former USSR[c]	546,600	544,800	4.2	499,200	3.8	−8.4
Other East and Balkans[c]	101,700	101,900	0.8	100.000	0.8	−1.9
Asia, Total	4,636,300	4,684,700	35.9	4,762,500	36.4	1.7
Israel	4,567,700	4,616,100	35.3	4,701,600	35.9	1.9
Former USSR[c]	48,400	48,400	0.4	41,100	0.3	−15.1
Other[c]	20,200	20,200	0.2	19,800	0.2	−2.0
Africa, Total	104,400	104,400	0.8	102,400	0.8	−1.9
North[d]	8,100	8,100	0.1	7,800	0.1	−3.7
South[e]	96,300	96,300	0.7	94,600	0.7	−1.8
Oceania	99,600	99,600	0.8	100,100	0.8	0.5

[a]Minor discrepancies due to rounding.
[b]U.S.A. and Canada.
[c]The Asian regions of Russia and Turkey are included in Europe.
[d]Including Ethiopia.
[e]South Africa, Zimbabwe, and other sub-Saharan countries.

correct, sometimes significantly, the figures published until 1980 by other authors, and since 1980 by ourselves. Thanks to the development over the years of an improved data base, these new revisions are not necessarily the same revised estimates that we published year by year in the AJYB, based on the information that was available at each date; nor is it unlikely that further retrospective revisions will become necessary as a product of future research.

The revised figures in table 2 clearly portray the slowing down of Jewish population growth globally since World War II. Based on a post-Holocaust world Jewish population of 11,000,000, an estimated growth of 800,000 occurred between 1945 and 1955, followed by growths of 700,000 between 1955 and 1965, 242,000 between 1965 and 1975, 129,000 between 1975 and 1985, and 119,000 between 1985 and 1995. While it took 13 years to add one million to world Jewry's postwar size, it took 38 years to add another million. The modest recovery of the early 1990s mostly reflects the already noted cases of individuals returning to Judaism, especially from Eastern Europe, as well as a short-lived "echo effect" of the postwar baby boom (see below).

TABLE 2. WORLD JEWISH POPULATION ESTIMATES: ORIGINAL AND CORRECTED 1945–1997

Year	Original Estimate[a]	Corrected Estimate[b]	Yearly % Change
1945	11,000,000	11,000,000	
1950	11,490,700	11,373,000	0.67
1955	11,908,400	11,800,000	0.74
1960	12,792,800	12,160,000	0.60
1965	13,411,300	12,500,000	0.55
1970	13,950,900	12,633,000	0.21
1975	14,144,400	12,742,000	0.17
1980	13,027,900	12,840,000	0.15
1985	12,963,300	12,871,000	0.05
1990	12,806,400	12,871,000[c]	–
1995	13,059,000	13,020,000[c]	0.23
1996	13,025,000	13,063,300[c]	0.33
1997	13,092,800	–	0.23

[a]As published in *American Jewish Year Book,* various years.
[b]Based on updated, revised, or otherwise improved information. Estimates for 1980 and after: The Avraham Harman Institute of Contemporary Jewry, Hebrew University of Jerusalem.
[c]Revised 1999.

DISTRIBUTION BY MAJOR REGIONS

Just about half of the world's Jews reside in the Americas, with over 46 percent in North America. Over 36 percent live in Asia, including the Asian Republics of the former USSR (but not the Asian parts of the Russian Republic and Turkey)—most of them in Israel. Europe, including the Asian territories of the Russian Republic and Turkey, accounts for over 13 percent of the total. Less than 2 percent of the world's Jews live in Africa and Oceania. Among the major geographical regions listed in table 1, the number of Jews in Israel—and, consequently, in total Asia—increased in 1997. Moderate Jewish population gains were also estimated for the European Union (including 15 member countries) and Oceania. The number of Jews in North America was estimated to be stable. Central and South America, Eastern Europe, Asian countries other than Israel, and Africa sustained decreases in Jewish population size.

Individual Countries

THE AMERICAS

In 1997 the total number of Jews on the American continents was estimated at close to 6.5 million. The overwhelming majority (93 percent) resided in the United States and Canada, less than 1 percent lived in Central America including Mexico, and about 6 percent lived in South America—with Argentina and Brazil the largest Jewish communities (see table 3).

United States. The 1989–1990 National Jewish Population Survey (NJPS), sponsored by the Council of Jewish Federations and the North American Jewish Data Bank (NAJDB), provided new benchmark information about the size and characteristics of U.S. Jewry—the largest Jewish population in the world—and the basis for subsequent updates.[12] According to the official report of the results of this important national sample study, the core Jewish population in the United States comprised 5,515,000 persons in the summer of 1990. Of these, 185,000 were not born or raised as Jews but currently identified with Judaism. An estimated 210,000 persons, not included in the previous figures, were born or raised as Jews but in 1990 identified with another religion. A further 1,115,000 people—thereof 415,000 adults and 700,000 children below age 18—were of Jewish parentage but had not themselves been raised as Jews and declared a religion

---

[12]The 1990 National Jewish Population Survey was conducted under the auspices of the Council of Jewish Federations with the supervision of a National Technical Advisory Committee chaired by Dr. Sidney Goldstein of Brown University. Dr. Barry Kosmin, of the North American Jewish Data Bank and City University of New York Graduate School, directed the study. See Kosmin et al., *Highlights,* and Sidney Goldstein, "Profile of American Jewry: Insights from the 1990 National Jewish Population Survey," AJYB 1992, vol. 92, pp. 77–173.

TABLE 3. ESTIMATED JEWISH POPULATION DISTRIBUTION IN THE AMERICAS, END 1997

Country	Total Population	Jewish Population	Jews per 1,000 Population	Accuracy Rating
Canada	30,100,000	362,000	12.0	B 1996
United States	267,700,000	5,700,000	21.3	B 1990
Total North America[a]	297,930,000	6,062,000	20.3	
Bahamas	300,000	300	1.0	D
Costa Rica	3,500,000	2,500	0.7	C 1993
Cuba	11,100,000	600	0.1	C 1990
Dominican Republic	8,200,000	100	0.0	D
El Salvador	5,900,000	100	0.0	C 1993
Guatemala	11,200,000	1,000	0.1	B 1993
Jamaica	2,600,000	300	0.1	A 1995
Mexico	95,700,000	40,600	0.4	A 1991
Netherlands Antilles	270,000	300	1.1	C 1995
Panama	2,700,000	5,000	1.9	C 1990
Puerto Rico	3,796,000	1,500	0.4	C 1990
Virgin Islands	110,000	300	2.7	C 1986
Other	19,940,000	300	0.0	D
Total Central America	165,316,000	52,900	0.3	
Argentina	35,600,000	203,000	5.7	C 1990
Bolivia	7,800,000	700	0.1	B 1990
Brazil	160,300,000	100,000	0.6	B 1991
Chile	14,600,000	21,000	1.4	A 1995
Colombia	37,400,000	3,900	0.1	C 1996
Ecuador	12,000,000	900	0.1	C 1985
Paraguay	5,100,000	900	0.2	B 1997
Peru	24,400,000	2,900	0.1	C 1993
Suriname	400,000	200	0.5	B 1986
Uruguay	3,200,000	23,300	7.2	C 1993
Venezuela	22,600,000	19,000	0.8	B 1997
Total South America[a]	324,400,000	375,500	1.2	
Total	787,646,000	6,490,400	8.2	

[a]Including countries not listed separately.

other than Judaism at the time of survey. All together, these various groups formed an extended Jewish population of 6,840,000. NJPS also covered 1,350,000 non-Jewish-born members of eligible (Jewish or mixed) households. The study's enlarged Jewish population thus consisted of about 8,200,000 persons. The 1990 Jewish population estimates are within the range of a sampling error of plus or minus 3.5 percent.[13] This means a range between 5.3 and 5.7 millions for the core Jewish population in 1990.

Since 1990, the international migration balance of U.S. Jewry should have generated an actual increase of Jewish population size. According to HIAS (Hebrew Immigrant Aid Society), the main agency involved in assisting Jewish migration from the FSU to the United States, the number of assisted migrants was 32,714 in 1990, 35,568 in 1991, 46,083 in 1992, 35,928 in 1993, 32,906 in 1994, 24,765 in 1995, 19,489 in 1996, and 14,519 in 1997.[14] These figures refer to the *enlarged* Jewish population concept, therefore incorporating the non-Jewish members of mixed households. The actual number of FSU Jews resettling in the United States was therefore somewhat smaller, yet quite substantial. It should be noted, however, that since 1992 the number of Jewish immigrants from the FSU to the United States has been steadily declining.

In retrospect, the influence of international migration between 1971 and 1990 was less than might have been expected. The first National Jewish Population Study, conducted in 1970–71, estimated the U.S. Jewish population at 5.4 million; the 1990 NJPS estimated a core Jewish population of 5.5 million, a difference of 100,000. However, since Jewish immigration contributed 200,000–300,000 in this period, it is clear that the balance of other factors of core population change over that whole 20-year period must have been negative. Detailed analyses of the 1990 NJPS data actually provide evidence of a variety of contributing factors: low levels of Jewish fertility and the "effectively Jewish" birthrate, increasing aging of the Jewish population, increasing outmarriage rate, declining rate of conversion to Judaism (or "choosing" Judaism), rather low proportions of children of mixed marriages being identified as Jewish, and a growing tendency to adopt non-Jewish rituals.[15]

A temporary increase in the Jewish birthrate occurred during the late 1980s, because the large cohorts born during the "baby boom" of the 1950s and early 1960s were in the prime procreative ages; however, by the mid-1990s this echo effect had faded away, as the much smaller cohorts born since the late 1960s reached

---

[13]See Kosmin et al., p. 39.
[14]See HIAS, *Annual Report 1997* (New York, 1998). See also Barry R. Chiswick, "Soviet Jews in the United States: An Analysis of Their Linguistic and Economic Adjustment," *Economic Quarterly*, July 1991, no. 148, pp. 188–211 (Hebrew), and *International Migration Review*, 1993 (English).
[15]See Goldstein, AJYB 1992; see also U.O. Schmelz and Sergio DellaPergola, *Basic Trends in U.S. Jewish Demography* (American Jewish Committee, New York, 1988); and Sergio DellaPergola, "New Data on Demography and Identification Among Jews in the U.S.: Trends, Inconsistencies and Disagreements," *Contemporary Jewry* 12, 1991, pp. 67–97.

the stage of parenthood. A surplus of Jewish deaths over Jewish births again prevailed among U.S. Jewry.

Taking this evidence into account, our estimate of U.S. Jewish population size starts from the NJPS benchmark core Jewish population of 5,515,000, and attempts to account for Jewish population changes that occurred since the later part of 1990, after completion of NJPS, through the end of 1997. Assuming a total net migration gain of about 60,000 Jews from the USSR, Israel, and other origins for the whole of 1990, we apportioned 20,000 to the later months of 1990. Further Jewish population growth was estimated at 40,000 for 1991, 45,000 for 1992, 30,000 for 1993, 25,000 for 1994, 15,000 for 1995, and 10,000 for 1996. In 1997, as noted, the number of Jewish immigrants from the FSU to the United States continued to decline. At the same time, Israeli statistics continued to show moderate but steady numbers of immigrants from the United States. Between 1990 and 1997, a total of about 15,000 American Jews emigrated to Israel, and larger numbers of Israelis left the United States after a prolonged stay and returned to Israel, bringing with them their U.S.-born children.[16] Accounting for immigration net of emigration and for some attrition based on current marriage, fertility, and age-composition trends in the U.S. core Jewish population, we conclude that the size of U.S. Jewry remained stable in 1997 and could be assessed at 5,700,000 at end of year.

The research team of the North American Jewish Data Bank (NAJDB), which was responsible for the primary handling of NJPS data files, also continued its yearly compilation of local Jewish population estimates. These are reported elsewhere in this volume.[17] NAJDB estimated the U.S. Jewish population in 1986 at 5,814,000, including "under 2 percent" non-Jewish household members. This closely matched our own pre-NJPS estimate of 5,700,000. The NAJDB estimates were later updated as follows, as against our own (ICJ) estimates (in thousands):

Source	1990	1991	1992	1993	1994	1995	1996	1997
NAJDB	5,981	5,798	5,828	5,840	5,880	5,900	5,900	6,005
ICJ	5,535	5,575	5,620	5,650	5,675	5,690	5,700	5,700

---

[16]*Statistical Abstract of Israel*, vol. 49, 1998, pp. 4–3, 4–5, 5–7; Yinon Cohen and Yitchak Haberfeld, "The Number of Israeli Immigrants in the United States in 1990," *Demography* 34, no. 2, 1997, pp. 199–212.

[17]The first in a new series of yearly compilations of local U.S. Jewish population estimates appeared in Barry A. Kosmin, Paul Ritterband, and Jeffrey Scheckner, "Jewish Population in the United States, 1986," AJYB 1987, vol. 87, pp. 164–91. For 1997 see Jim Schwartz and Jeffrey Scheckner, "Jewish Population in the United States, 1997," AJYB 1998, vol. 98, pp. 162–88. The 1998 update appears elsewhere in the present volume.

Besides the significant downward revision in 1991, following NJPS, changes in NAJDB estimates reflect corrections and adaptations made in the figures for several local communities—some of them in the light of NJPS regional results or new local community studies. Clearly, compilations of local estimates, even if as painstaking as in the case of the NAJDB, are subject to a great many local biases and tend to fall behind the actual pace of national trends. This is especially true in a context of vigorous internal migrations, as in the United States.[18] In our view, the NJPS figure, in spite of sample-survey biases, offered a more reliable baseline for assessing national Jewish population than the sum of local estimates.[19] A corrected baseline will be provided by the new NJPS planned to be undertaken in the course of the year 2000.

Canada. Results of the 1996 Canadian census provided new evidence for the estimate of the local Jewish population. As is customary in Canada, this mid-decade census provided information on ethnic origins, whereas the 1991 census included questions on both religion and ethnic origin, besides information on year of immigration of the foreign-born, and languages. In 1996, 351,705 Canadians reported a Jewish ethnic origin, thereof 195,810 as a single response, and 155,900 as one selection in a multiple response with up to four options.[20] To interpret these data it is necessary to make reference to the previous census and to the special processing by a joint team of researchers from McGill University's Consortium for Ethnicity and Strategic Social Planning, Statistics Canada, and Council of Jewish Federations Canada, under the direction of Prof. Jim Torczyner.[21]

The 1991 census enumerated 318,070 Jews according to religion; of these, 281,680 also reported being Jewish by ethnicity (as one of up to four options to the latter question), while 36,390 reported one or more other ethnic origins. Another 38,245 persons reported no religion and a Jewish ethnic origin, again as one of up to four options.[22] After due allowance is made for the last group, a total

---

[18]See Uzi Rebhun, "Changing Patterns of Internal Migration 1970–1990: A Comparative Analysis of Jews and Whites in the United States," *Demography* 34, no. 2, 1997, pp. 213–23.

[19]The NAJDB estimate for the total U.S. Jewry in 1997 exceeds ours by over 300,000 (a difference of 5.4 percent). Over the years 1991–1997 we have estimated a Jewish population increase of 125,000 as against 207,000 according to NAJDB.

[20]The sum inconsistency appears in the original report: Statistics Canada, *Top 25 Ethnic Origins in Canada, Showing Single and Multiple Responses, for Canada, 1996 Census (20% Sample Data)* (Ottawa, 1998).

[21]Jim L. Torczyner, Shari L. Brotman, Kathy Viragh, and Gustave J. Goldmann, *Demographic Challenges Facing Canadian Jewry; Initial Findings from the 1991 Census* (Montreal, 1993); Jim L. Torczyner and Shari L. Brotman, "The Jews of Canada: A Profile from the Census," AJYB 1995, vol. 95, pp. 227–60.

[22]Statistics Canada, *Religions in Canada—1991 Census* (Ottawa, 1993). See also Leo Davids, "The Jewish Population of Canada, 1991" in *Papers in Jewish Demography 1993 in Memory of U.O. Schmelz*, ed. Sergio DellaPergola and Judith Even (Jerusalem, 1997), pp. 311–23.

core Jewish population of 356,315 was estimated for 1991—an increase of 44,255 (14.2 percent) over the corresponding estimate of 312,060 from the 1981 census. A further 49,640 Canadians, who reported being Jewish by ethnic origin but identified with another religion (such as Catholic, Anglican, etc.) were not included in the 1991 core estimate. Including them would produce an extended Jewish population of 405,955 in 1991.

In comparison with the 1981 census, the 1991 data revealed an increase of 21,645 (7.3 percent) in the number of Jews defined by religion. A more significant increase occurred among those reporting a Jewish ethnicity with no religious preference: 22,610 persons, or more than twice (+144.6 percent) as many as in 1981. The increase was comparatively even larger among those reporting a partially Jewish ethnic ancestry, and among ethnic Jews with another religion. Besides actual demographic and identificational trends, changes in the wording of the relevant questions in the two censuses possibly influenced these variations in the size of both the core and the ethnically (or, in our terminology, extended) Jewish population of Canada.[23]

Most of the 1981–1991 Jewish population increase was due to international migration—out of the total increase of 44,255 core Jews, 25,895 (59 percent) had arrived in Canada since 1981. The principal country of origin was the former USSR (6,230), followed by Israel (4,975), the United States (3,630), and South Africa (2,855).[24] Practically all the rest of the Jewish population growth consists of ethnic Jews who did not report a religion, including many whose reported Jewish ethnicity was only one among several others. The latter are quite certainly children of intermarriages, whose frequency increased in Canada by about one-third over the 1980s.[25] All this implies that the 1981–1991 demographic balance of the Jewish population in Canada was close to zero or slightly negative. Taking into account the increasingly aged Jewish population structure, we suggested that, in the years following the 1991 census, the continuing migratory surplus would have generated a modest surplus over the probably negative balance of internal evolution. For the end of 1996 we updated the 1991 baseline of 356,300 to 362,000.

The 1991 census equivalent of the 1996 census figure of 351,705 ethnic Jews (including those not Jewish by religion, but excluding those Jews who did not report a Jewish ethnic origin) was 349,565. Based on a similar criterion of ethnic origin, Canadian Jewry thus increased by 2,140 over the 1991–1996 period. Though it should be stressed that the ethnic-origin definition is not consistent with our concept of a core Jewish population, the evidence of very slow Jew-

---

[23]The results of preceding censuses can be found in Statistics Canada, *1981 Census of Canada: Population: Ethnic Origin; Religion* (Ottawa, 1983, 1984); Statistics Canada, *Population by Ethnic Origin, 1986 Census: Canada, Provinces and Territories and Census Metropolitan Areas* (Ottawa, 1988).

[24]See Torczyner et al., *Demographic Challenges, Appendices*, p. 22.

[25]Ibid., p. 20.

ish population increase—notwithstanding continuing immigration—suggested keeping our 1996 estimate unchanged for 1997. The resulting figure of 362,000 makes the Canadian Jewish population the world's fourth-largest.

Central America. Results of the 1991 population survey of Jews in the Mexico City metropolitan area[26] pointed to a community definitely less affected than others in the Diaspora by the common trends of low fertility, intermarriage, and aging. Some comparatively more traditional sectors in the Jewish community still contribute a surplus of births over deaths, and overall—thanks also to some immigration—the Jewish population has been quite stable or moderately increasing. The new medium Jewish population estimate for 1991 was put at 37,500 in the Mexico City metropolitan area and at 40,000 nationally. Official Mexican censuses over the years provided rather erratic and unreliable Jewish population figures. This was the case with the 1990 census, which came up with a national total of 57,918 (aged five and over). As in the past, most of the problem derived from unacceptably high figures for peripheral states. The new census figures for the Mexico City metropolitan area (33,932 Jews, aged five and over, in the Federal District and State of Mexico) came quite close—in fact were slightly below—our survey's estimates. Taking into account a modest residual potential for natural increase, as shown by the 1991 survey, but also some emigration, we estimated the Jewish population at 40,600 in 1997.

The Jewish population was estimated at about 5,000 in Panama, 2,500 in Costa Rica, and 1,500 in Puerto Rico.

South America.[27] The Jewish population of Argentina, the largest in Latin America and seventh largest in the world, is marked by a negative balance of internal evolution. Various surveys conducted in some central sections of Buenos Aires at the initiative of the Asociación Mutualista Israelita Argentina (AMIA), as well as in several provincial cities, point to increased aging and intermarriage.[28] Short of a major new survey in the Greater Buenos Aires area, the quality of

---

[26]Sergio DellaPergola and Susana Lerner, *La población judía de México: Perfil demográfico, social y cultural* (Mexico-Jerusalén, 1995). The project, conducted in cooperation between the Centro de Estudios Urbanos y de Desarrollo Urbano (CEDDU), El Colegio de Mexico, and the Division of Jewish Demography and Statistics of the A. Harman Institute of Contemporary Jewry, the Hebrew University, was sponsored by the Asociación Mexicana de Amigos de la Universisad Hebrea de Jerusalén.

[27]For a more detailed discussion of the region's Jewish population trends, see U.O. Schmelz and Sergio DellaPergola, "The Demography of Latin American Jewry," AJYB 1985, vol. 85, pp. 51–102; Sergio DellaPergola, "Demographic Trends of Latin American Jewry," in *The Jewish Presence in Latin America,* ed. J. Laikin Elkin and G.W. Merks (Boston, 1987), pp. 85–133.

[28]Rosa N. Geldstein, *Censo de la Población Judia de la ciudad de Salta, 1986; Informe final* (Buenos Aires, 1988); Yacov Rubel, *Los Judios de Villa Crespo y Almagro: Perfil Sociodemográfico* (Buenos Aires, 1989); Yacov Rubel and Mario Toer, *Censo de la Población Judia de Rosario, 1990* (Buenos Aires, 1992); Centro Union Israelita de Cordoba, *First Sociodemographic Study of Jewish Population; Cordoba 1993* (Cordoba, 1995).

the estimates remains quite inadequate. Since the early 1960s, when the Jewish population was estimated at 310,000, the pace of emigration and return migration has been significantly affected by the variable nature of economic and political trends in the country, generating a negative balance of external migrations. Most Jews lived in the Greater Buenos Aires area, with about 25,000–30,000 left in provincial cities and minor centers. The predominantly middle-class Jewish community confronted serious economic difficulties, to the point that the existence of a "new Jewish poverty" was suggested. This in turn negatively affected the Jewish institutional network.[29] Between 1990 and 1997, over 7,000 persons migrated to Israel, while unknown numbers went to other countries. Steady decline in the number of burials performed by Jewish funeral societies was another sign of population decline, though the high cost of Jewish funerals might induce some families to prefer a non-Jewish ceremony. Accordingly, the estimate for Argentinean Jewry was reduced from 205,000 in 1996 to 203,000 in 1997.

In Brazil, results of the population census of 1991 showed a Jewish population of 86,816, thereof 42,871 in the state of São Paulo, 26,190 in the state of Rio de Janeiro, 8,091 in Rio Grande do Sul, and 9,264 in other states.[30] The previous 1980 census showed a countrywide figure of 91,795 Jews, of which 44,569 in São Paulo, 29,157 in Rio de Janeiro, 8,330 in Rio Grande do Sul, and 9,739 elsewhere. Since some otherwise identifying Jews might have failed to declare themselves as such in that census, we adopted a corrected estimate of 100,000 for 1980, and kept it unchanged through 1991, assuming that the overall balance of Jewish vital events, identificational changes, and external migrations was close to zero. The new census figures apparently pointed to a countrywide decline of approximately 5,000 since 1980, most of it in Rio de Janeiro, where Jewish population estimates were, indeed, decreasing since 1960. On the other hand, regarding Brazil's major Jewish community, São Paulo, all previous census returns since 1940 and various other admittedly rough Jewish survey and register data were consistent with the widely held perception of a growing community, but the 1991 census figure contradicted that assumption.[31] A 1992 study in the state of Rio Grande do Sul and its capital, Porto Alegre, Brazil's third-largest community, unveiled an enlarged Jewish population of about 11,000.[32] Excluding the non-Jewish household mem-

---

[29]See a brief overview of the problems in Laura Golbert, Norma Lew, and Alejandro Rofman, *La nueva pobreza judía* (Buenos Aires, 1997).

[30]IBGE, *Censo demográfico do Brasil* (Rio de Janeiro, 1997); Daniel Sasson, *A comunidade judaica do Rio de Janeiro; Metodologia da pesquisa* (Rio de Janeiro, 1997).

[31]Henrique Rattner, "Recenseamento e pesquisa sociológica da comunidade judaica de São Paulo, 1968," in *Nos caminhos da diáspora*, ed. Henrique Rattner (São Paulo, 1972); Claudia Milnitzky, ed., *Apendice estatistico da comunidade judaica do estado de São Paulo* (São Paulo, 1980); Egon and Frieda Wolff, *Documentos V; Os recenseamentos demográficos oficiais do seculo XX* (Rio de Janeiro, 1993–1994).

[32]Anita Brumer, *Identidade em mudança; Pesquisa sociológica sobre os judeus do Rio Grande do Sul* (Porto Alegre, 1994).

bers, the core Jewish population could be estimated at about 9,000, some 10 percent above the 1991 census figure. In the light of this and other evidence of a substantially stable Jewish population, though one confronting high rates of intermarriage and a definite erosion in the younger age groups, we kept the 100,000 estimate for 1991, extending it to 1997. Brazil's was the ninth-largest Jewish community in the world.

In Chile, a sociodemographic survey conducted in the Santiago metropolitan area in 1995 indicated an enlarged Jewish population of 21,450, of which 19,700 were Jews and 1,750 non-Jewish relatives, including persons not affiliated with any Jewish organization.[33] Assuming another 1,300 Jews living in smaller provincial communities, a new countrywide estimate of 21,000 Jews was obtained. Previous lower estimates reflecting results of the 1970 population census and a 1982–83 community survey possibly overestimated the net effects of Jewish emigration. The new survey portrays a rather stable community, with incipient signs of aging and assimilation.

In Venezuela, a new sociodemographic survey was launched in 1998.[34] Preliminary work devoted to preparing a comprehensive list of households for sampling and compilation of death records, and partial returns from the survey itself, suggest a provisional Jewish population estimate of 19,000.

On the strength of fragmentary information available, our estimates for Uruguay and Colombia were slightly reduced to 23,000 and 3,900, respectively, and that for Peru was not changed.[35]

EUROPE

About 1.6 million Jews lived in Europe at the end of 1997; 63 percent lived in Western Europe and 37 percent in Eastern Europe and the Balkan countries—including the Asian territories of the Russian Republic and Turkey (see table 4). In 1997 Europe lost 2.6 percent of its estimated Jewish population, mainly through continuing emigration from the European republics of the FSU.

European Union. Incorporating 15 countries since the 1995 accession of Austria, Finland, and Sweden, the European Union (EU) had an estimated combined Jewish population of 1,018,300—an increase of 0.3 percent over the previous year. Different trends affected the Jewish populations in each member country.[36]

---

[33]Gabriel Berger et al., *Estudio Socio-Demográfico de la Comunidad Judía de Chile* (Santiago-Buenos Aires, 1995).
[34]Sponsored by the two main Jewish community organizations, the Asociación Israelita de Venezuela and the Union Israelita de Caracas.
[35]Local observers had expected quicker reduction of Jewish population size. See Leon Trahtemberg Siederer, *Demográfia judía del Peru* (Lima, 1988).
[36]See Sergio DellaPergola, "Jews in the European Community: Sociodemographic Trends and Challenges," AJYB 1993, vol. 93, pp. 25–82.

TABLE 4. ESTIMATED JEWISH POPULATION DISTRIBUTION IN EUROPE, END 1997

Country	Total Population	Jewish Population	Jews per 1,000 Population	Accuracy Rating
Austria	8,100,000	9,000	1.1	C 1995
Belgium	10,200,000	31,700	3.1	C 1987
Denmark	5,300,000	6,400	1.2	C 1990
Finland	5,100,000	1,300	0.3	B 1990
France[a]	58,600,000	522,000	8.9	C 1990
Germany	82,000,000	78,000	1.0	B 1997
Greece	10,500,000	4,500	0.4	B 1995
Ireland	3,600,000	1,200	0.3	B 1993
Italy	57,430,000	29,800	0.5	B 1995
Luxembourg	400,000	600	1.5	B 1990
Netherlands	15,600,000	26,500	1.7	C 1995
Portugal	9,900,000	300	0.0	C 1986
Spain	39,330,000	12,000	0.3	D
Sweden	8,900,000	15,000	1.7	C 1990
United Kingdom	59,000,000	280,000	4.7	B 1995 X
Total European Union	373,960,000	1,018,300	2.7	
Gibraltar	28,000	600	21.4	B 1991
Norway	4,400,000	1,200	0.3	B 1995
Switzerland	7,130,000	18,000	2.5	A 1990
Other	815,000	100	0.1	D
Total other West Europe	12,373,000	19,900	1.6	
Belarus	10,300,000	19,000	1.8	C 1997
Estonia	1,500,000	2,400	1.6	B 1997
Latvia	2,500,000	9,400	3.8	B 1997 X
Lithuania	3,700,000	4,900	1.3	B 1997
Moldova	4,300,000	6,500	1.5	C 1997
Russia[b]	147,000,000	325,000	2.2	B 1997
Ukraine	50,700,000	132,000	2.6	C 1997
Total FSU in Europe	220,000,000	499,200	2.3	

TABLE 4.—*(Continued)*

Country	Total Population	Jewish Population	Jews per 1,000 Population	Accuracy Rating
Bosnia-Herzegovina	3,600,000	300	0.1	C 1996
Bulgaria	8,300,000	2,800	0.3	B 1992
Croatia	4,800,000	1,300	0.3	C 1996
Czech Republic	10,300,000	2,600	0.3	C 1998 X
Hungary	10,200,000	53,000	5.2	D
Poland	38,600,000	3,500	0.1	D
Romania	22,500,000	12,000	0.5	B 1997
Slovakia	5,400,000	3,500	0.6	D
Slovenia	2,000,000	100	0.1	C 1996
TFYR Macedonia	2,100,000	100	0.0	C 1996
Turkey[b]	63,700,000	19,000	0.3	C 1996
Yugoslavia[c]	10,600,000	1,800	0.2	C 1996
Total other East Europe and Balkans[d]	185,500,000	100,000	0.5	
Total	791,833,000	1,637,400	2.1	

[a]Including Monaco.
[b]Including Asian regions.
[c]Serbia and Montenegro.
[d]Including Albania.

Since the breakup of the USSR, France has had the third-largest Jewish population in the world, after the United States and Israel. The estimated size of French Jewry has been assessed at 530,000 since the major survey that was taken in the 1970s.[37] Monitoring the plausible trends of both the internal evolution and external migrations of Jews in France suggested little net change in Jewish population size. A study conducted in 1988 at the initiative of the Fonds Social Juif Unifié (FSJU) confirmed the basic demographic stability of French Jewry.[38] The French Jewish community continued to absorb a moderate inflow of Jews from North Africa, and its age composition was younger than in other European coun-

---

[37]Doris Bensimon and Sergio DellaPergola, *La population juive de France: socio-démographie et identité* (Jerusalem-Paris, 1984).
[38]Erik H. Cohen, *L'Etude et l'éducation juive en France ou l'avenir d'une communauté* (Paris, 1991).

tries. However, migration to Israel amounted to 7,500 in 1980–1989 and over 11,000 in 1990–1997. In the 1990s, aging tended to determine a moderate surplus of deaths over births. In view of these trends, our French Jewish population estimate was revised to 525,000 in 1995, and 523,000 at the end of 1997.

A significant revision of the size of Jewish population in the United Kingdom was released in 1998 by the Community Research Unit (CRU) of the Board of Deputies of British Jews.[39] Current evaluation of Jewish birth and death records generated a new estimate of 285,000 for 1995 along with an estimated negative vital balance of 2,500 a year. The new findings confirmed the downward trend that had emerged from previous research. An analysis of Jewish deaths during 1975–1979 had helped to establish a population baseline of 336,000 for 1977. A subsequent evaluation of Jewish death records in 1984–1988 suggested a central estimate of 308,000 for 1986. The vital statistical records regularly compiled by the CRU showed an excess of deaths over births in the range of about 1,000–1,500 a year.[40] A study of Jewish synagogue membership indicated a decline of over 7 percent between 1983 and 1990. An attitudinal survey of British Jews conducted in 1995 indicated a significant rise in intermarriage (38 percent of all married men, and 50 percent among Jewish men less than 30 years old), implying increasing assimilatory losses.[41] Further attrition derived from emigration (over 7,000 emigrants to Israel in 1980–1989, and about 4,500 in 1990–1997). Allowing for a further continuation of these well-established trends, we had adopted an estimate of 291,000 for 1996. The new vital statistics and survey findings suggest the 1996 figure should be corrected to 282,500 (8,500 less than we had originally estimated), and the 1997 estimate should be put at 280,000 (sixth-largest worldwide).

In 1990, Germany was politically reunited. In the former (West) German Federal Republic, the 1987 population census reported 32,319 Jews.[42] Immigration used to compensate for the surplus of deaths over births in this aging Jewish population. Estimates of the small Jewish population in the former (East) German Democratic Republic ranged between 500 and 2,000. While there is a lack of cer-

---

[39]Marlena Schmool and Frances Cohen, *A Profile of British Jewry: Patterns and Trends at the Turn of the Century* (London, 1998).

[40]Steven Haberman, Barry A. Kosmin, and Caren Levy, "Mortality Patterns of British Jews 1975–79: Insights and Applications for the Size and Structure of British Jewry," *Journal of the Royal Statistical Society*, A, 146, pt. 3, 1983, pp. 294–310; Steven Haberman and Marlena Schmool, "Estimates of British Jewish Population 1984–88," *Journal of the Royal Statistical Society*, A, 158, pt. 3, 1995, pp. 547–62; Stanley Waterman and Barry Kosmin, *British Jewry in the Eighties: A Statistical and Geographical Guide* (London, 1986); Marlena Schmool, *Report of Community Statistics* (London, yearly publication).

[41]Marlena Schmool and Frances Cohen, *British Synagogue Membership in 1990* (London, 1991); Stephen Miller, Marlena Schmool, and Antony Lerman, *Social and Political Attitudes of British Jews: Some Key Findings of the JPR Survey* (London, 1996).

[42]Statistisches Bundesamt, *Bevölkerung und Erwerbstätigkeit, Volkszählung vom 25 Mai 1987*, Heft 6 (Stuttgart, 1990).

tainty about the number of recent Jewish immigrants from the FSU, according to available reports, over 70,000 settled in Germany since the end of 1989, including non-Jewish family members.[43] The following estimates for unified Germany include figures, in thousands, of Jews affiliated with the Zentralwohlfahrtstelle der Juden in Deutschland (ZDJ),[44] and our own estimates (ICJ), which (a) allow for some time lag between immigration and registration with the organized Jewish community, (b) take into account a certain amount of permanent nonaffiliation, and (c) assume there are enough incentives for most newcomers to be willing to affiliate with the Jewish community:

Source	1989	1990	1991	1992	1993	1994	1995	1996	1997
ZDJ	27.7	28.5	33.7	37.5	40.8	45.6	53.8	61.2	68.2
ICJ	35.0	40.0	42.5	50.0	52.0	55.0	62.0	70.0	78.0

At the beginning of 1996, the number of applicants for Jewish migration to Germany from the FSU had surpassed 108,000.[45] While most of these applications were already approved, the actual number of immigrants was lower, as some of the applicants preferred to move to Israel or the United States, or to remain in their present places of residence. Nevertheless, the potential for growth of the Jewish population in Germany continues to be significant. Moreover, the comparatively younger age composition of immigrants could have some rejuvenating effects on the long established deficit of the local balance of Jewish births and deaths.

Belgium, Italy, and the Netherlands each had Jewish populations ranging around 30,000. There was a tendency toward internal shrinkage of all these Jewries, but in some instances this was offset by immigration. In Belgium, the size of the Jewish population, estimated at 31,700, was probably quite stable owing to the comparatively strong Orthodox section in that community. In Italy, membership in Jewish communities has been voluntary since 1987, a change from the previous, long-standing system of compulsory affiliation. Although most Jews reaffiliated, the new, looser legal framework facilitated the ongoing attrition of the Jewish population. Recent Jewish community records for Milan indicated an affiliated Jewish population of 6,500, against over 8,000 in the 1960s, despite sub-

---

[43]See Madeleine Tress, "Welfare State Type, Labour Markets and Refugees: A Comparison of Jews from the Former Soviet Union in the United States and the Federal Republic of Germany," *Ethnic and Racial Studies* 21, no. 1, 1998, pp. 116–37.

[44]Zentralwohlfahrtstelle der Juden in Deutschland, *Mitgliederstatistik; Der Einzelnen Judischen Gemeinden und Landesverbände in Deutschland per 1 Januar 1998* (Frankfurt, 1998).

[45]Pavel Polian and Klaus Teschemacher, "Jewish Emigration from the Community of Independent States to Germany" (paper presented at 3rd European Population Conference, Milan, 1995); Jewish Agency, Department of Immigration Absorption, internal report (Jerusalem, 1996).

stantial immigration from other countries in the intervening period. This evidence, and data on declining birthrates in most other cities, prompted a reduction in our national estimate for Italy to 29,800.[46] In the Netherlands, a recent study indicated a growing number of residents of Israeli origin. This may have offset the declining trends among veteran Jews.[47] The Jewish population was estimated at 26,500. Other EU member countries have smaller and, overall, slowly declining Jewish populations. Possible exceptions are Sweden and Spain, whose Jewish populations are tentatively estimated at 15,000 and 12,000, respectively. Austria's permanent Jewish population was estimated at 9,000. While a negative balance of births and deaths has long prevailed, connected with great aging and frequent outmarriage, immigration from the FSU has tended to offset the internal losses. The small Jewish populations in other Scandinavian countries are, on the whole, numerically rather stable.

Other West Europe. Few countries remain in Western Europe that have not joined the EU. In 1997 they accounted for a combined Jewish population of 19,900. The estimate of Switzerland's Jewish population is based on the results of the 1990 census. The official count indicated 17,577 Jews, as against 18,330 in 1980—a decline of 4 percent.[48] Allowing for undeclared Jews, we put the estimate at 18,000.

Former USSR (European parts). Since 1989, the demographic situation of East European Jewry has been radically transformed as a consequence of the dramatic geopolitical changes in the region.[49]

The economic and political crisis that culminated in the disintegration of the Soviet Union as a state in 1991 generated an upsurge in Jewish emigration. After rapidly reaching a peak in 1990, emigration continued at lower but significant levels throughout 1997. While mass emigration was an obvious factor in population decrease, the demography of FSU Jewry has been characterized for years by very low levels of "effectively Jewish" fertility, frequent outmarriage, and heavy aging. As a result, the shrinking of the Jewish population has been comparatively rapid.

Official government sources provide the fundamental basis of information on

---

[46]For an overview see Sergio DellaPergola, "La popolazione ebraica in Italia nel contesto ebraico globale" in *Storia d'Italia, Ebrei in Italia*, ed. Corrado Vivanti (Torino, 1997), vol. 2, pp. 895–936.

[47]C. Kooyman and J. Almagor, *Israelis in Holland: A Sociodemographic Study of Israelis and Former Israelis in Holland* (Amsterdam, 1996); Philip van Praag, "Between Speculation and Reality," *Studia Rosenthaliana*, special issue published together with vol. 23, no. 2, 1989, pp. 175–79.

[48]Bundesamt für Statistik, *Wohnbevölkerung nach Konfession und Geschlecht, 1980 und 1990* (Bern, 1993).

[49]For the historical demographic background, see U.O. Schmelz, "New Evidence on Basic Issues in the Demography of Soviet Jews," *Jewish Journal of Sociology* 16, no. 2, 1974, pp. 209–23; Mordechai Altshuler, *Soviet Jewry Since the Second World War: Population and Social Structure* (Westport, 1987); Mordechai Altshuler, *Soviet Jewry on the Eve of the Holocaust: A Social and Demographic Profile* (Jerusalem, 1998).

the number of Jews in the FSU. The Soviet Union's census and subsequent data distinguish the Jews as one in a recognized list of "nationalities" (ethnic groups). In a societal context that, until recently, did not recognize religious identification, the ethnic definition criterion could be considered comprehensive and valid. Data from the last official population census, carried out in January 1989, revealed a total of 1,450,500 Jews.[50] The figure confirmed the declining trend already apparent since the previous three Soviet censuses: 2,267,800 in 1959, 2,150,700 in 1970, and 1,810,900 in 1979.

Our reservation about USSR Jewish population figures in previous AJYB volumes bears repeating: some underreporting is not impossible, but it cannot be easily quantified and should not be exaggerated. The prolonged existence of a totalitarian regime produced conflicting effects on census declarations: on the one hand, it stimulated a preference for other than Jewish nationalities in the various parts of the FSU, especially in connection with mixed marriages; on the other hand, it preserved a formal Jewish identification by coercion, through the mandatory registration of nationality on official documents such as passports. Viewed conceptually, the census figures represent the core Jewish population in the USSR. They actually constitute a good example of a large and empirically measured core Jewish population in the Diaspora, consisting of the aggregate of self-identifying Jews. The figures of successive censuses were remarkably consistent with one another and with the known patterns of emigration and internal demographic evolution of the Jewish population in recent decades.

Systematic analysis of previously inaccessible data about the demographic characteristics and trends of Jews in the FSU has produced important new insights into recent and current trends.[51] The new data confirm the prevalence of very low fertility and birthrates, high frequencies of outmarriage (up to close to 70 percent of Jewish spouses who married in Russia in 1988, and close to 80 percent in Ukraine and Latvia in 1996), a preference for non-Jewish nationalities among the children of outmarriages, aging, and a clear surplus of Jewish deaths

---

[50]Goskomstat SSSR, *Vestnik Statistiki*, 10 (1990), pp. 69–71. This figure does not include about 30,000 Tats (Mountain Jews).

[51]Mark Tolts, "Some Basic Trends in Soviet Jewish Demography," in *Papers in Jewish Demography 1989*, ed. U.O. Schmelz and S. DellaPergola (Jerusalem, 1993), pp. 237–43; Viacheslav Konstantinov, "Jewish Population of the USSR on the Eve of the Great Exodus," *Jews and Jewish Topics in the Soviet Union and Eastern Europe* 3 (16), 1991, pp. 5–23; Mordechai Altshuler, "Socio-demographic Profile of Moscow Jews," ibid., pp. 24–40; Mark Tolts, "The Balance of Births and Deaths Among Soviet Jewry," *Jews and Jewish Topics in the Soviet Union and Eastern Europe* 2 (18), 1992, pp. 13–26; Leonid E. Darsky, "Fertility in the USSR; Basic Trends" (paper presented at European Population Conference, Paris, 1991); Mark Tolts, "Jewish Marriages in the USSR: A Demographic Analysis," *East European Jewish Affairs* 22 (2) (London, 1992); Sidney and Alice Goldstein, *Lithuanian Jewry 1993: A Demographic and Sociocultural Profile* (Jerusalem, 1997).

over Jewish births. These trends are especially visible in the Slavic republics, which hold a large share of the total Jewish population.[52]

In updating the January 1989 census figure to the end of 1997 for each of the republics of the FSU, Jewish emigration played the major role among the intervening changes.[53] An estimated 71,000, thereof about 62,000 declared Jews, left in 1989, as against 19,300 in 1988, 8,100 in 1987, and only 7,000 during the whole 1982–1986 period. The following revised migration estimates (in thousands), since 1990, are based on Soviet, Israeli, American, and other sources:[54]

Immigrants to: (thousands)	1990	1991	1992	1993	1994	1995	1996	1997
Israel	185.2	147.8	65.1	66.1	68.1	64.8	58.9	54.6
United States	32.7	35.6	46.1	35.9	32.9	24.8	22.0	14.5
Elsewhere	10.0	12.0	20.0	14.0	9.0	20.0	24.0	20.0
Total	227.9	195.4	131.2	116.0	110.0	109.6	104.9	99.1
Of which Jews	200.0	159.0	96.0	80.0	75.0	70.0	60.0	55.0

These apparently declining emigration figures should not be misconstrued: when compared to the similarly declining Jewish population figures for the FSU, they actually demonstrate a remarkably stable desire to emigrate.

At the same time, the heavy deficit of internal population dynamics continued and even intensified, due to the great aging that is known to have prevailed for many decades. In 1993–1994, the balance of recorded vital events in Russia in-

---

[52]Mark Tolts, "Demographic Trends of the Jews in the Three Slavic Republics of the Former USSR: A Comparative Analysis," in *Papers in Jewish Demography 1993*, ed. S. DellaPergola, and J. Even (Jerusalem, 1997), pp. 147–75; Mark Tolts, "The Interrelationship Between Emigration and the Sociodemographic Trends of Russian Jewry," in *Russian Jews on Three Continents*, ed. N. Levin Epstein, Y. Ro'i, and P. Ritterband (London, 1997), pp. 147–76.

[53]Dr. Mark Tolts, of the A. Harman Institute of Contemporary Jewry at the Hebrew University, actively contributed to the preparation of FSU Jewish population estimates throughout the present article.

[54]Estimates based on Israel Central Bureau of Statistics and HIAS yearly reports. See also Mark Tolts, "Demography of the Jews in the Former Soviet Union: Yesterday and Today," in *Jewish Life After the USSR: A Community in Transition* (Cambridge, 1999); Yoel Florsheim, "Emigration of Jews from the Soviet Union in 1989," *Jews and Jewish Topics in the Soviet Union and Eastern Europe* 2, no. 12, 1990, pp. 22–31; Sidney Heitman, "Soviet Emigration in 1990," *Berichte des Bundesinstitut fur Ostwissenschaftliche und internationale studien*, vol. 33, 1991; Tress, "Welfare State Type, Labour Markets and Refugees"; and Zentralwohlfahrtstelle.

cluded 2.8 Jewish births versus 30.0 deaths per 1,000 Jewish population; in Ukraine, the respective figures were 4.2 and 35.9 per 1,000; in Belarus, 5.2 and 32.6 per 1,000; in Latvia, 3.1 and 24.5 per 1,000; in Moldova 5.9 and 34.6 per 1,000.[55] These figures imply yearly losses of many thousands to the respective Jewish populations. Aging in the countries of origin was exacerbated by the significantly younger age composition of Jewish emigrants.[56]

On the strength of these considerations, our estimate of the core Jewish population in the USSR (including the Asian regions) was reduced from the census figure of 1,450,500 at the end of 1988/beginning of 1989 to 1,370,000 at the end of 1989, 1,157,500 at the end of 1990, 990,000 at the end of 1991, and 890,000 at the end of 1992. The 1992 estimate, besides considering the intervening changes, also corrected for the past omission of the Tats, also known as Mountain Jews—a group mostly concentrated in the Caucasus area that enjoys fully Jewish status and the prerogatives granted by Israel's Law of Return.

An important new piece of evidence, basically confirming the known trends, became available with the publication of the results of the national Microcensus of the Russian republic conducted February 14–23, 1994.[57] The data, based on a 5-percent sample, revealed a Jewish population of about 400,000 plus approximately 8,000 Tats. We thus obtained a total of 408,000, with a range of variation between 401,000 and 415,000, allowing for sampling errors. Apportioning in retrospect for Jewish population changes (decline) between December 31, 1993, the date of our estimate, and February 23, 1994, the date of the Microcensus, the central estimate rose to 410,000 at the end of 1993. This figure was only 6 percent higher than the estimate we had independently obtained for the same date

---

[55]Mark Tolts, "Russia's Jewish Population: Emigration, Assimilation and Demographic Collapse," *Jews in Eastern Europe* 3, no. 31, 1996; idem., "Demography of the Jews in the Former Soviet Union: Yesterday and Today."

[56]Age structures of the Jewish population in the Russian Federal Republic were reported in Goskomstat SSSR, *Itogi vsesoiuznoi perepisi naseleniia 1970 goda,* vol. 4, table 33 (Moscow, 1973); Goskomstat SSSR, *Itogi vsesoiuznoi perepisi naseleniia 1979 goda,* vol. 4, part 2, table 2 (Moscow, 1989); Goskomstat SSSR, *Itogi vsesoiuznoi perepisi naseleniia 1989 goda* (Moscow, 1991). Age structures of recent Jewish migrants from the USSR to the United States and to Israel appear, respectively, in HIAS, *Statistical Report* (New York, yearly publication) and unpublished annual data kindly communicated to the author; Israel Central Bureau of Statistics, *Immigration to Israel*, Special Series, (Jerusalem, yearly publication); Yoel Florsheim, "Immigration to Israel and the United States from the Former Soviet Union, 1992," *Jews in Eastern Europe* 3 (22), 1993, pp. 31–39; Mark Tolts, "Trends in Soviet Jewish Demography Since the Second World War," in *Jews and Jewish Life in Russia and the Soviet Union*, ed. Ya'acov Ro'i (London, 1995), pp. 365–82; and Mark Tolts, "Demography of the Jews in the Former Soviet Union: Yesterday and Today."

[57]See V. Aleksandrova, "Mikroperepis' naseleniia Rossiiskoi Federatsii," *Voprosy Statistiki,* 1994 (1), p. 37 (Moscow, 1994). See also Mark Tolts, "The Interrelationship Between Emigration and the Socio-Demographic Profile of Russian Jewry," in *Russian Jews on Three Continents*, ed. Noah Levin-Epstein, Paul Ritterband, and Yaakov Ro'i (London, 1996), pp. 147–76.

(385,000), based on our projection of the 1989 census figure of 551,000. After correcting our Russian estimate upward, we obtained a 1993 estimate of 817,000 for the total of the FSU.

Our subsequent estimates were prepared as usual by taking into account for each republic separately all available data and estimates concerning Jewish emigration, births, deaths, and geographical mobility between republics. The total Jewish population for the FSU was estimated at 729,000 in 1994, 660,000 in 1995, 595,000 in 1996, and 540,300 at the end of 1997. Of this total, 499,200 lived in the European republics and 41,100 in the Asian republics (see below). Within this general trend, there were differences in the pace of change of Jewish population in each republic because of variable propensities to emigrate and different rates of assimilation and natural decrease.

The largest Jewish population in the FSU European parts remained in Russia, currently the fifth-largest in the world. Our end-1997 estimate for Russia was 325,000 (as against census-based estimates of 551,000 for end-1988, and 408,000 for end-1993). Jews in Ukraine, which in recent years experienced large-scale emigration, were estimated at 132,000, currently the eighth-largest community worldwide (487,300 in 1988). A further 19,000 Jews were estimated to remain in Belarus (112,000 in 1988) and 6,500 in the Republic of Moldova (65,800 in 1988). Based on updated figures from the local national population registers, a combined total of 16,700 was estimated for the three Baltic states of Latvia, Lithuania, and Estonia (versus 39,900 in 1988). The figure for Latvia includes a downward correction of 1,800, conforming with updated figures from local official sources.[58]

Inconsistencies between recent estimates of the number of Jews in former USSR republics can be explained by any combination of the following five factors: (a) migration of several thousands of Jews between the various republics of the former USSR since 1991, especially to the Russian republic; (b) the presence of a proportion of non-Jews higher than previously assumed among the "enlarged" pool of Jewish emigrants from the former USSR, resulting in excessively lowered estimates of the number of Jews remaining there; (c) adoption of a Jewish identification in the most recent official sources of data on the part of persons who had declared themselves as belonging to another national (ethnic) group in previous censuses; (d) the counting in the Russian Microcensus and in the population registers of other republics of some persons whose status is not yet that of émigrés, based on the legal criteria of the country of origin, but is such based on the criteria of the State of Israel or other countries of current residence; and (e) some definitive returns to Russia (and other republics) from Israel[59] and

---

[58]Goldstein, *Lithuanian Jewry*; Lithuanian Department of Statistics, *Demographic Yearbook 1993* (Vilnius, 1994); "Par Latvijas Republicas cilvekiem," *Latvijas Vestnesim*, 44 (Riga, 1995); Anna Stroi, "Latvia v chelovecheskom izmerenii: etnicheskii aspekt," *Diena* (Riga, 1997).

[59]Council of Europe, *Recent Demographic Developments in Europe* (Strasbourg, 1996).

other countries of migrants who for various reasons are still registered as residents of the latter. While it is impossible at this stage to establish the respective weight of each of these factors, their impact is quite secondary in the context of overall Jewish population changes. Points (d) and (e) above also indicate the likelihood of some double counts of former-USSR Jews in their country of origin and in the countries they have emigrated to. Consequently, it is entirely possible that our statistical synopsis is overestimated by several thousands.

The respective figures for the enlarged Jewish population, including all current Jews as well as other persons of Jewish parentage and their non-Jewish household members, are substantially higher in a societal context like that of the FSU, which has been characterized by high intermarriage rates for a considerable time. While a definitive estimate for the total USSR cannot be provided for lack of appropriate data, evidence for Russia and other Slavic republics indicates a high ratio of non-Jews to Jews in the enlarged Jewish population. In 1994, 409,000 Jews in Russia lived together with 311,000 non-Jewish household members, forming an enlarged Jewish population of 720,000.[60] Nor can definitive information about the proportion of non-Jews in an enlarged Jewish population in the FSU be derived from the statistics of immigrants to Israel. Due to the highly self-selective character of *aliyah,* non-Jews constitute a relatively smaller minority of all new immigrants from the FSU than their share among the Jewish population in the countries of origin.[61] It is obvious, though, that the wide provisions of Israel's Law of Return (see above) apply to virtually the maximum emigration pool of self-declared Jews and close non-Jewish relatives. Any of the large figures attributed in recent years to the size of Soviet Jewry, insofar as they were based on demographic reasoning, did not relate to the core but to various (unspecified) measures of an enlarged Jewish population. The evidence also suggests that in the FSU core Jews constitute a smaller share of the total enlarged Jewish population than in some Western countries, such as the United States.

Just as the number of declared Jews evolved consistently between censuses, the

---

[60]Mark Tolts, "Jews in the Russian Republic Since the Second World War: The Dynamics of Demographic Erosion," in International Union for the Scientific Study of Population, *International Population Conference* (Montreal, 1993), vol. 3, pp. 99–111; Evgeni Andreev, "Jews in the Households in Russia," forthcoming in *Papers in Jewish Demography 1997,* ed. S. DellaPergola and J. Even (Jerusalem).

[61]Israel's Ministry of Interior records the religion-nationality of each person, including new immigrants. Such attribution is made on the basis of documentary evidence supplied by the immigrants themselves and checked by competent authorities in Israel. According to data available from the Interior Ministry's Central Population Register, 90.3 percent of all new immigrants from the USSR during the period October 1989–August 1992 were recorded as Jewish. In 1994 the percentage had declined to 71.6. See Israel Central Bureau of Statistics, *Immigration to Israel 1995* (Jerusalem, 1996). See also Sergio DellaPergola, "The Demographic Context of the Soviet Aliya," in *Jews and Jewish Topics in the Soviet Union and Eastern Europe* 3, no. 16, 1991, pp. 41–56.

number of persons of Jewish descent who preferred not to identified as Jews was rather consistent too, at least until 1994. However, the recent political developments, and especially the current emigration urge, probably led to greater readiness to declare a Jewish self-identification by persons who did not describe themselves as such in past censuses. In terms of demographic accounting, these "returnees" imply an actual net increment to the core Jewish population of the FSU, as well as to world Jewry.

Other East Europe and Balkans. The Jewish populations in Hungary and Romania and the small remnants in Poland, Bulgaria, the Czech and Slovak republics, and the former Yugoslavia are all reputed to be very overaged and to experience frequent outmarriage. In each of these countries, the recent political transformations have allowed for greater autonomy of the organized Jewish communities and their registered membership. Some Jews or persons of Jewish origin may have come out in the open after years of hiding their identity. But, while the gap between core and enlarged Jewish populations tends to be significant in this region, the general demographic pattern is one of inevitable decline.

The size of Hungarian Jewry—the largest in Eastern Europe outside the FSU—is quite insufficiently known. Overall membership in local Jewish organizations is estimated at about 20,000–25,000. Our core Jewish population estimate of 53,500—as against much higher figures that are periodically circulated—attempts to reflect the declining trend that prevails in Hungary according to the available indications. The January 1992 census of Romania reported a Jewish population of 9,107. Based on the detailed Jewish community records available with the Federatia Comunitatilor Evreiesi, our estimate for the end of 1997 was 12,000. The Czech census of 1991 reported 1,292 Jews, but according to the Federation of Jewish Communities there were 2,600 community members—an increase of 200 over our previous estimate. The number of Jews in Slovakia and Poland was very tentatively estimated at 3,500 each. In Bulgaria, the December 4, 1992 census reported 3,461 Jews;[62] our 1997 estimate, reflecting emigration, was 2,800.

Crisis continued in the former Yugoslavia, accelerating Jewish population decline. The core Jewish population for the total of the five successor republics, reduced through emigration, was assessed at about 3,600 at the end of 1997. Of these, roughly 2,000 lived in the territorially shrunken Yugoslavia (Serbia with Montenegro), and 1,300 in Croatia.[63]

The Jewish population of Turkey, where a significant surplus of deaths over births has been reported for several years, was estimated at about 19,000.

---

[62] *Statistical Yearbook* (Sofia, 1992).

[63] For an overview, see Melita Svob, *Jews in Croatia: Migration and Changes in Jewish Population* (Zagreb, 1997).

ASIA

Israel. At the end of 1997, Israel's Jewish population was 4,701,600. Major revisions in Israel's figure were introduced following the November 4, 1995 population census.[64] On census day, 4,459,696 Jews were enumerated, 69,700 fewer than the 4,549,500 that had been estimated by the Central Bureau of Statistics (CBS) through yearly updates of the previous baseline provided by the census of June 4, 1983. Discrepancies between census and population register figures could be due to undercounts or double counts in either the previous or the latest census, and to errors accumulated over the years in the reporting of vital events, migration, and other personal changes to the registrar's office. A major factor in these differences resulted from CBS's initial attribution (for the purpose of calculating current population estimates) of a Jewish identification to several thousands of immigrants from the FSU who were later identified as non-Jewish by the Ministry of Interior. The CBS provisional Jewish population estimate for end-1966 was 4,637,400, still based on the 1983 census; reducing that figure by 69,700, we obtained our estimate of 4,567,700.[65] Following the census, CBS reduced the current Jewish population estimate by 20,000. After the results were evaluated, the census total was increased as a basis for current estimates by 43,000 persons. This generated a revised end-1996 estimate of 4,616,100, and a 4,701,600 estimate for end-1997.

Israel accounts for nearly 99 percent of all the 4.76 million Jews in Asia, including the Asian republics of the former USSR, but excluding the Asian territories of the Russian Republic and Turkey (see table 5). By the end of 1997, Israeli Jews constituted 35.9 percent of total world Jewry.[66] Israel's Jewish population grew in 1997 by 85,500, or 1.9 percent. The pace of growth was slowing down. After reaching growth rates of 6.2 percent in 1990 and 5 percent in 1991, steady population increases of 2–2.5 percent were recorded between 1992 and 1996. The number of new immigrants in 1997 (66,000) declined by 9.3 percent versus 1996 (70,600). About 40 percent of Jewish population growth in 1997 was due to the net migration balance, against a revised estimate of 45 percent in 1996; most Jewish population growth derived from natural increase. Moreover,

---

[64]Israel Central Bureau of Statistics, *Population and Vital Statistics 1997* (Jerusalem, 1998).

[65]This explains the unusual B (rather than A) accuracy rating for our 1996 Israel estimate as published in the 1998 AJYB.

[66]Israel Central Bureau of Statistics, *Statistical Abstract of Israel 1997* (Jerusalem, 1997). For a comprehensive review of sociodemographic changes in Israel, see U.O. Schmelz, Sergio DellaPergola, and Uri Avner, "Ethnic Differences Among Israeli Jews: A New Look," AJYB 1990, vol. 90, pp. 3–204. See also Sergio DellaPergola, "Demographic Changes in Israel in the Early 1990s," in *Israel's Social Services 1992–93*, ed. Y. Kop (Jerusalem, 1993), pp. 57–115. We thank the staff of Israel's Central Bureau of Statistics for facilitating compilation of published and unpublished data.

TABLE 5.   ESTIMATED JEWISH POPULATION DISTRIBUTION IN ASIA, END 1997

Country	Total Population	Jewish Population	Jews per 1,000 Population	Accuracy Rating
Israel[a]	5,900,000	4,701,600	796.9	A 1997 X
Azerbaijan	7,600,000	8,000	1.1	C 1997
Georgia	5,400,000	7,500	1.4	C 1997
Kazakhstan	16,400,000	10,000	0.6	C 1997
Kyrgyzstan	4,600,000	2,200	0.5	C 1997
Tajikistan	6,000,000	1,400	0.2	C 1997
Turkmenistan	4,600,000	1,000	0.2	C 1997
Uzbekistan	23,700,000	11,000	0.5	C 1997
Total FSU in Asia[b]	72,100,000	41,100	0.6	
China[c]	1,241,700,000	1,000	0.0	D
India	969,700,000	4,000	0.0	C 1991
Iran	67,500,000	12,300	0.2	C 1986
Iraq	21,200,000	100	0.0	C 1997
Japan	126,100,000	1,000	0.0	C 1993
Korea, South	45,900,000	100	0.0	C 1988
Philippines	73,400,000	100	0.0	C 1988
Singapore	3,500,000	300	0.1	B 1990
Syria	15,000,000	200	0.0	C 1995
Thailand	60,100,000	200	0.0	C 1988
Yemen	15,200,000	200	0.0	B 1995
Other	775,300,000	300	0.0	D
Total other Asia	3,414,600,000	19,800	1.0	
Total	3,492,600,000	4,762,500	1.4	

[a]Total population of Israel: end year.
[b]Including Armenia. Not including Asian regions of Russian Republic.
[c]Including Hong Kong.

2,162 persons underwent Orthodox conversion in Israel in 1997, against 1,531 in 1996—many of them immigrants from the former USSR and other countries who were previously listed as non-Jews.[67] Additional conversions initiated in Israel through the Conservative and Reform movements, but formally completed in other countries, also contributed minor increases to Israel's Jewish population size.

Former USSR (Asian parts). The total Jewish population in the Asian republics of the former USSR was estimated at 41,100 at the end of 1997. Ethnic conflicts in the Caucasus area and the fear of Muslim fundamentalism in Central Asia continued to cause concern and stimulated Jewish emigration.[68] Internal identificational and demographic processes were less a factor of attrition among these Jewish populations than was the case in the European republics of the FSU. At the beginning of the 1990s, minimal rates of natural increase still existed among the more traditional sections of these Jewish communities, but conditions were rapidly eroding this residual surplus.[69] Reflecting these trends, the largest community remained in Uzbekistan (11,000 in 1997, versus 94,900 at the end of 1988), followed by Kazakhstan (10,000, vs. 19,900 in 1988), Azerbaijan (8,000 vs. 30,800), Georgia (7,500 vs. 24,800), and the balance of the remaining four republics (4,600 vs. 24,000).

Other countries. It is difficult to estimate the Jewish population of Iran, last counted in the 1986 national census.[70] Based on evidence of continuing decline, the 1997 estimate was reduced to 12,300. In other Asian countries with small veteran communities—such as India, or several Muslim countries—the Jewish population has tended to decline. The recent reduction was more notable in Syria and Yemen, where Jews were officially allowed to emigrate. Very small Jewish communities, partially of a transient character, exist in several countries of Southeast Asia. With the reunion in 1997 of Hong Kong with mainland China, that separate listing ceased and China's permanent Jewish population was estimated at roughly 1,000, the same as Japan.

AFRICA

About 102,000 Jews were estimated to remain in Africa at the end of 1997. The Republic of South Africa accounted for 90 percent of total Jews on that continent (see table 6). In 1980, according to a national census, there were about

---

[67]Data released by Rabbinical Courts and special Conversion Courts. See *Ha'aretz*, Jan. 22, 1999.

[68]Israel Central Bureau of Statistics, *Immigration to Israel 1997* (Jerusalem, 1998).

[69]Tolts, "The Balance of Births and Deaths."

[70]Data kindly provided by Dr. Mehdi Bozorghmehr, Von Grunebaum Center for Near Eastern Studies, University of California, Los Angeles.

TABLE 6. ESTIMATED JEWISH POPULATION DISTRIBUTION IN AFRICA,
END 1997

Country	Total Population	Jewish Population	Jews per 1,000 Population	Accuracy Rating
Egypt	64,800,000	200	0.0	C 1993
Ethiopia	58,700,000	100	0.0	C 1995
Morocco	28,400,000	5,900	0.2	B 1995
Tunisia	9,300,000	1,500	0.2	B 1995
Other	63,300,000	100	0.0	D
Total North Africa	224,500,000	7,800	0.0	
Botswana	1,500,000	100	0.1	B 1993
Kenya	28,800,000	400	0.0	B 1990
Namibia	1,700,000	100	0.1	B 1993
Nigeria	107,100,000	100	0.0	D
South Africa	42,500,000	92,500	2.2	B 1991
Zaire	47,400,000	300	0.0	B 1993
Zimbabwe	11,400,000	800	0.1	B 1993
Other	277,800,000	300	0.0	D
Total other Africa	518,200,000	94,600	0.2	
Total	742,700,000	102,400	0.1	

118,000 Jews among South Africa's white population.[71] Substantial Jewish emigration since then was partially compensated for by Jewish immigration and return migration of former emigrants, but an incipient negative balance of internal changes produced some further attrition. The last official population census, in March 1991, did not provide a reliable new national figure on Jewish population size. The question on religion was not mandatory, and only 65,406 white people declared themselves Jewish. Assuming that the proportion of Jews who had not stated their religion was the same as that of other whites, an inflated census figure of 91,859 Jews was arrived at.[72] The results of a Jewish-sponsored survey

---

[71]Sergio DellaPergola and Allie A. Dubb, "South African Jewry: A Sociodemographic Profile," AJYB 1988, vol. 88, pp. 59–140.

[72]Allie A. Dubb, The Jewish Population of South Africa; The 1991 Sociodemographic Survey (Cape Town, 1994).

of the Jewish population in the five major South African urban centers, completed, like the census, in 1991, confirmed the ongoing demographic decline.[73] Based on the new evidence, the most likely range of Jewish population size was estimated at 92,000 to 106,000 for 1991, with a central value of 100,000.[74] Taking into account the pace of continuing emigration from South Africa to Israel and other Western countries (especially Australia), we projected a decline since 1991 and obtained an estimate of 92,500 for South African Jewry at the end of 1997.

In recent years, the Jewish community of Ethiopia was at the center of an international effort of rescue. In the course of 1991, the overwhelming majority of Ethiopian Jews—about 20,000 people—were brought to Israel, most of them in a one-day dramatic airlift operation. Some of these migrants were non-Jewish members of mixed households. In connection with these events, it was assumed that only a few Jews remained in Ethiopia, but subsequently the small remaining core Jewish population appeared to be larger than previously estimated. Over 3,600 immigrants from Ethiopia arrived in Israel in 1992, 900 in 1993, 1,200 in 1994, 1,300 in 1995, 1,400 in 1996, and 1,700 in 1997—mostly non-Jewish immigrants seeking reunification with their Jewish relatives. Although it is possible that more Jews than we know may appear, wanting to emigrate to Israel, and that more Christian relatives of Jews already in Israel will press for emigration before Israel terminates the family reunification program for such relatives, a conservative estimate of 100 Jews was tentatively suggested for the end of 1997. The Quara community, whose situation was still unsettled at the time of writing, is not included in this estimate. Small Jewish populations remained in various African countries south of Sahara.

The remnant of Moroccan and Tunisian Jewry tended to shrink slowly through emigration, mostly to Israel, France, and Canada. The end-1997 estimate was 5,900 for Morocco and 1,500 for Tunisia.[75] As some Jews had a foothold both in Morocco or Tunisia and also in France or other Western countries, their geographical attribution was therefore uncertain.

OCEANIA

The major country of Jewish residence in Oceania (Australasia) is Australia, where 95 percent of the estimated total of nearly 100,000 Jews live (see table 7). A total of 79,805 people in Australia described their religion as Jewish in 1996,

---

[73]The study was directed by Dr. Allie A. Dubb and supported by the Kaplan Centre for Jewish Studies, University of Cape Town.
[74]Dubb, *The Jewish Population of South Africa.*
[75]See George E. Gruen, "Jews in the Middle East and North Africa," AJYB 1994, vol. 94, pp. 438–64; and confidential information obtained through Jewish organizations.

TABLE 7.   ESTIMATED JEWISH POPULATION DISTRIBUTION IN OCEANIA,
            END 1997

Country	Total Population	Jewish Population	Jews per 1,000 Population	Accuracy Rating
Australia	18,500,000	95,500	5.2	B 1996
New Zealand	3,600,000	4,500	1.3	C 1991
Other	6,820,000	100	0.0	D
Total	28,920,000	100,100	3.5	

according to the latest national census figures.[76] This represented an increase of 5,419 (7.3 percent) over the 1991 census figure of 74,386 declared Jews, which in turn was 5,303 (7.7 percent) more than the figure reported in the 1986 census.[77] In Australia the question on religion is optional. In 1996, over 25 percent (and in 1991, over 23 percent) of the country's whole population either did not specify their religion or stated explicitly that they had none. This large group must be assumed to contain persons who identify in other ways as Jews, although it is not sure whether Jews in Australia state their religion more or less often than others. In a 1991 survey in Melbourne, where roughly one-half of all Australia's Jews live, less than 7 percent of the Jewish respondents stated they had not identified as Jews in the census.[78] The Melbourne survey depicted a very stable community, one that combined growing acculturation with moderate levels of intermarriage. Australian Jewry received migratory reinforcements during the last decade, especially from South Africa, the FSU, and Israel. At the same time, there were demographic patterns with negative effects on Jewish population size, such as declining birth cohorts and strong aging.[79] Taking into account these various factors, we updated our estimate for 1997 to 95,500—substantially more than the official census returns, but less than would obtain by adding the full proportion of those who did not report any religion in the census. The Jewish community in New Zealand was estimated at 4,500.

[76]William D. Rubinstein, "Jews in the 1996 Australian Census," *Australian Jewish Historical Society Journal* 14, no. 3, 1998, pp. 495–507.

[77]Bill Rubinstein, "Census Total for Jews Up by 7.7 Percent; Big Gains in Smaller States," unpublished report (Geelong, Victoria, 1993).

[78]John Goldlust, *The Jews of Melbourne; A Report of the Findings of the Jewish Community Survey, 1991* (Melbourne, 1993).

[79]Sol Encel and Nathan Moss, *Sydney Jewish Community; Demographic Profile* (Sydney, 1995).

TABLE 8. DISTRIBUTION OF THE WORLD'S JEWS, BY NUMBER AND PROPORTION (PER 1,000 POPULATION) IN EACH COUNTRY, END 1997

Number of Jews in Country	Jews per 1,000 Population					
	Total	0.0–0.9	1.0–4.9	5.0–9.9	10.0–24.9	25.0+
Number of Countries						
Total[a]	94	61	24	5	3	1
100–900	32	27	4	—	1	—
1,000–4,900	25	22	3	—	—	—
5,000–9,900	8	1	7	—	—	—
10,000–49,900	16	9	6	1	—	—
50,000–99,900	4	1	1	2	—	—
100,000–999,900	7	1	3	2	1	—
1,000,000 or more	2	—	—	—	1	1
Jewish Population Distribution (Absolute Numbers)						
Total[a]	13,091,600	405,100	1,025,800	896,500	6,062,600	4,701,600
100–900	10,000	7,900	1,500	—	600	—
1,000–4,900	59,400	47,600	11,800	—	—	—
5,000–9,900	57,700	5,900	51,800	—	—	—
10,000–49,900	319,900	165,700	131,200	23,000	—	—
50,000–99,900	319,000	78,000	92,500	148,500	—	—
100,000–999,900	1,924,000	100,000	737,000	725,000	362,000	—
1,000,000 or more	10,401,600	—	—	—	5,700,000	4,701,600
Jewish Population Distribution (Percent of World's Jews)						
Total[a]	100.0	3.1	7.8	6.8	46.3	35.9
100–900	0.1	0.1	0.0	—	0.0	—
1,000–4,900	0.5	0.4	0.1	—	—	—
5,000–9,900	0.4	0.0	0.4	—	—	—
10,000–49,900	2.4	1.3	1.0	0.2	—	—
50,000–99,900	2.4	0.6	0.7	1.1	—	—
100,000–999,900	14.7	0.8	5.6	5.5	2.8	—
1,000,000 or more	79.5	—	—	—	43.5	35.9

[a]Excluding countries with fewer than 100 Jews, with a total of 1,200 Jews. Minor discrepancies due to rounding.

Dispersion and Concentration

COUNTRY PATTERNS

Table 8 demonstrates the magnitude of Jewish dispersion. The 94 individual countries listed above as each having at least 100 Jews are scattered over all the continents. In 1997, 9 countries had a Jewish population of 100,000 or more; another 4 countries had 50,000 or more; another 24 had more than 5,000; and 57 out of 94 countries had fewer than 5,000 Jews each. In relative terms, too, the Jews were thinly scattered nearly everywhere in the Diaspora. There is not a single Diaspora country where they amounted even to 25 per 1,000 (2.5 percent) of the total population. In most countries they constituted a far smaller fraction. Only three Diaspora countries had more than 10 per 1,000 (1 percent) Jews in their total population; and only 8 countries had more than 5 Jews per 1,000 (0.5 percent) of population. The respective 8 countries were, in descending order of the proportion, but regardless of the absolute number of their Jews: Gibraltar (21.4), United States (21.3 per 1,000), Canada (12.0), France (8.9), Uruguay (7.2), Argentina (5.7), Hungary (5.2), and Australia (5.2). Other major Diaspora Jewries having lower proportions of Jews per 1,000 of total population were the United Kingdom (4.7 per 1,000), Russia (2.2 per 1,000), Ukraine (2.6), Brazil (0.6), South Africa (2.2), and Germany (0.95).

TABLE 9.   COUNTRIES WITH LARGEST JEWISH POPULATIONS, END 1997

| | | | % of Total Jewish Population | | | |
| | | | In the World | | In the Diaspora | |
Rank	Country	Jewish Population	%	Cumulative %	%	Cumulative %
1	United States	5,700,000	43.5	43.8	67.9	67.4
2	Israel	4,701,600	35.9	79.7	=	=
3	France	522,000	4.0	83.7	6.2	73.6
4	Canada	362,000	2.8	86.5	4.3	77.9
5	Russia	325,000	2.5	88.9	3.9	81.8
6	United Kingdom	280,000	2.1	91.1	3.3	85.1
7	Argentina	203,000	1.6	92.6	2.4	87.6
8	Ukraine	132,000	1.0	93.6	1.6	89.1
9	Brazil	100,000	0.8	94.4	1.2	90.3
10	Australia	95,500	0.7	95.1	1.1	91.5
11	South Africa	92,500	0.7	95.8	1.1	92.6
12	Germany	78,000	0.6	96.4	0.9	93.5
13	Hungary	53,000	0.4	96.8	0.6	94.1
14	Mexico	40,600	0.3	97.2	0.5	94.6
15	Belgium	31,700	0.2	97.4	0.4	95.0

TABLE 10.   METROPOLITAN AREAS WITH LARGEST JEWISH POPULATIONS, END 1997

Rank	Metro Area[a]	Country	Jewish Population	Share of World's Jews %	Cumulative %
1	Tel Aviv[b,c]	Israel	2,424,000	18.5	18.5
2	New York[d]	U.S.	1,969,000	15.0	33.6
3	Haifa[b]	Israel	650,000	5.0	38.5
4	Los Angeles[e]	U.S.	631,000	4.8	43.3
5	Jerusalem[f]	Israel	550,000	4.2	47.5
6	Miami-Ft. Lauderdale	U.S.	354,000	2.7	50.2
7	Paris[g]	France	310,000	2.4	52.6
8	Chicago	U.S.	265,000	2.0	54.6
9	Boston	U.S.	241,000	1.8	56.5
10	Philadelphia[h]	U.S.	231,000	1.8	58.2
11	San Francisco	U.S.	216,000	1.6	59.9
12	London[i]	United Kingdom	195,000	1.5	61.4
13	Buenos Aires	Argentina	177,000	1.4	62.7
14	Washington[j]	U.S.	166,000	1.3	64.0
15	Toronto	Canada	166,000	1.3	65.3
16	W. Palm Beach-Boca Raton	U.S.	153,000	1.2	66.4
17	Be'er Sheva[k]	Israel	145,000	1.1	67.5
18	Moscow[l]	Russia	118,000	0.9	68.4
19	Baltimore[m]	U.S.	107,000	0.8	69.3
20	Montreal	Canada	100,000	0.8	70.0

[a] Most metropolitan areas include extended inhabited territory and several municipal authorities around central city. Definitions vary by country.
[b] As newly defined in the 1995 Census.
[c] Including Netanya and Ashdod, each with a Jewish population above 100,000.
[d] Including areas in New Jersey and Connecticut.
[e] Including Orange County, Riverside, San Bernardino, Ventura County.
[f] Adapted from data supplied by Jerusalem Municipality, Division of Strategic Planning and Research.
[g] Departments 75, 77, 78, 91, 92, 93, 94, 95.
[h] Including areas in New Jersey and Delaware.
[i] Greater London and contiguous postcode areas.
[j] Including areas in Maryland and Virginia.
[k] Central city only. Our estimate from total population data.
[l] Territory administered by City Council.
[m] Including Howard County.

In the State of Israel, by contrast, the Jewish majority amounted to 797 per 1,000 (79.7 percent) in 1997, compared to 803 per 1,000 (80.3 percent) in 1996—not including the Arab population of the administered areas.

While Jews are widely dispersed throughout the world, they are also concentrated to a large extent (see table 9). In 1997, 97 percent of world Jewry lived in the 15 countries with the largest Jewish populations; and nearly 80 percent lived in the two largest communities—the United States and Israel. Similarly, ten leading Diaspora countries together comprised nearly 80 percent of the Diaspora Jewish population; three countries (United States, France, and Canada) accounted for 78 percent, and the United States alone for over 67 percent of total Diaspora Jewry.

CONCENTRATION IN MAJOR CITIES

Intensive international and internal migrations led to the concentration of an overwhelming majority of the Jews into large urban areas. Table 10 provides a ranking of the cities where the largest Jewish populations were found in 1997.[80] Twenty urban areas worldwide had an estimated population of 100,000 Jews or more. These 20 central places and their suburban and satellite areas altogether comprise 70 percent of the whole world Jewish population. Ten of these cities are in the United States, four in Israel, two in Canada, and one each in France, the United Kingdom, Argentina, and Russia. The ten metropolitan areas in the United States include 76 percent of total U.S. Jewry, and the four Israeli major urban areas include 80 percent of Israel's Jewish population.

The extraordinary urbanization of the Jews is evinced even more by the fact that 50 percent of all world Jewry (6,588,000) live in only six large metropolitan areas: New York (including Northern New Jersey), Los Angeles (including Orange, Riverside, and Ventura counties), and Miami-Ft. Lauderdale in the United States; Tel Aviv, Haifa, and Jerusalem in Israel.

SERGIO DELLAPERGOLA

---

[80]Definitions of metropolitan statistical areas vary across countries. Estimates reported here reflect the criteria adopted in each place. For U.S. estimates see Schwartz and Scheckner, AJYB 1998; for Canadian estimates see Torczyner and Brotman; for other diaspora estimates see A. Harman Institute of Contemporary Jewry; for Israeli estimates see Israel Central Bureau of Statistics, *Population and Vital Statistics 1997* (Jerusalem, 1998). Following the 1995 population census in Israel, major metropolitan urban areas were redefined. The two cities of Netanya and Ashdod, each with a Jewish population exceeding 100,000, were included in the outer ring of the expanded greater Tel Aviv area.

Directories
Lists
Obituaries

National Jewish Organizations*

UNITED STATES

Organizations are listed according to functions as follows:

Community Relations	583
Cultural	588
Israel-Related	595
Overseas Aid	608
Religious, Educational Organizations	610
Schools, Institutions	622
Social, Mutual Benefit	632
Social Welfare	634

Note also cross-references under these headings:

Professional Associations	639
Women's Organizations	639
Youth and Student Organizations	640
Canada	640

COMMUNITY RELATIONS

AMERICAN COUNCIL FOR JUDAISM (1943). PO Box 9009, Alexandria, VA 22304. (703)836-2546. Pres. Alan V. Stone; Exec. Dir. Allan C. Brownfeld. Seeks to advance the universal principles of a Judaism free of nationalism, and the national, civic, cultural, and social integration into American institutions of Americans of Jewish faith. *Issues of the American Council for Judaism; Special Interest Report.* (WWW.ACJNA.ORG)

AMERICAN JEWISH COMMITTEE (1906). The Jacob Blaustein Building, 165 E. 56 St., NYC 10022. (212)751-4000. FAX: (212)750-0326. Pres. Bruce M. Ramer; Exec. Dir. David A. Harris. Protects the rights and freedoms of Jews the world over; combats bigotry and anti-Semitism and promotes democracy and human rights for all; works for the security of Israel and deepened understanding between Americans and Israelis; advocates public-policy positions rooted in American de-

---

*The information in this directory is based on replies to questionnaires circulated by the editors. Web site addresses, where provided, appear at end of entries.

mocratic values and the perspectives of Jewish heritage; and enhances the creative vitality of the Jewish people. Includes Jacob and Hilda Blaustein Center for Human Relations, Project Interchange, William Petschek National Jewish Family Center, Jacob Blaustein Institute for the Advancement of Human Rights, Institute on American Jewish-Israeli Relations. *American Jewish Year Book; Commentary; CommonQuest; AJC Journal; Anti-Semitism World Report.* (WWW.AJC.ORG)

AMERICAN JEWISH CONGRESS (1918). Stephen Wise Congress House, 15 E. 84 St., NYC 10028. (212)879-4500. FAX: (212)249-3672. E-mail: pr@ajcongress. org. Pres. Jack Rosen; Exec. Dir. Phil Baum. Works to foster the creative survival of the Jewish people; to help Israel develop in peace, freedom, and security; to eliminate all forms of racial and religious bigotry; to advance civil rights, protect civil liberties, defend religious freedom, and safeguard the separation of church and state; "The Attorney General for the Jewish Community." *Congress Monthly; Judaism; Inside Israel; Radical Islamic Fundamentalism Update.*

ANTI-DEFAMATION LEAGUE OF B'NAI B'RITH (1913). 823 United Nations Plaza, NYC 10017. (212)885-7700. FAX: (212) 867-0779. Chmn. Howard Berkowitz; Dir. Abraham H. Foxman. Seeks to combat anti-Semitism and to secure justice and fair treatment for all citizens through law, education, and community relations. *ADL on the Frontline; Law Enforcement Bulletin; Dimensions: A Journal of Holocaust Studies; Hidden Child Newsletter; International Reports; Civil Rights Reports.*

ASSOCIATION OF JEWISH COMMUNITY RELATIONS WORKERS (1950). 7800 Northaven Road, Dallas, TX 75230. (214)369-3313. FAX: (214)373-3186. Pres. Marlene Gorin. Aims to stimulate higher standards of professional practice in Jewish community relations; encourages research and training toward that end; conducts educational programs and seminars; aims to encourage cooperation between community-relations workers and those working in other areas of Jewish communal service.

CENTER FOR JEWISH COMMUNITY STUDIES (1970). Temple University, Center City Campus, 1616 Walnut St., Suite 507, Philadelphia, PA 19103. (215)204-1459. FAX: (215)204-7784. E-mail: v2026r @vm.temple.edu. Jerusalem office:Jerusalem Center for Public Affairs. Pres. Daniel J. Elazar; Dir. General Zvi Marom; Chmn. Board of Overseers Michael Rukin. Worldwide policy-studies institute devoted to the study of Jewish community organization, political thought, and public affairs, past and present, in Israel and throughout the world. Publishes original articles, essays, and monographs; maintains library, archives, and reprint series. *Jerusalem Letter/Viewpoints; Jewish Political Studies Review.*

CENTER FOR RUSSIAN JEWRY WITH STUDENT STRUGGLE FOR SOVIET JEWRY/SSSJ (1964). 240 Cabrini Blvd., #5B, NYC 10033. (212)928-7451. FAX: (212)795-8867. Dir.-Founder Jacob Birnbaum; Chmn. Dr. Ernest Bloch; Student Coord. Glenn Richter. Campaigns for the human rights of the Jews of the former USSR, with emphasis on emigration and Jewish identity; supports programs for needy Jews there and for newcomers in Israel and USA, stressing employment and Jewish education. As the originator of the grassroots movement for Soviet Jewry in the early 1960s, possesses unique archives.

COALITION ON THE ENVIRONMENT & JEWISH LIFE (1993). 443 Park Ave. S., 11th fl., NYC 10016-7322. (212)684-6950, ext. 210. FAX: (212)686-1353. E-mail: coejl@aol.com. Dir. Mark X. Jacobs. Promotes environmental education, advocacy, and action in the American Jewish community. Sponsored by a broad coalition of Jewish organizations; member of the National Religious Partnership for the Environment. *Bi-annual newsletter.* (WWW.JTSA.EDU/ORG/COEJL)

COMMISSION ON SOCIAL ACTION OF REFORM JUDAISM (1953, joint instrumentality of the Union of American Hebrew Congregations and the Central Conference of American Rabbis). 633 Third Ave., 7th fl., NYC 10017. (212)650-4160. FAX: (212)650-4199. E-mail: csarj@ uahc.org. 2027 Massachusetts Ave., NW, Washington, DC 20036. Chmn. Judge David Davidson; Dir. Leonard Fein; Dir. Religious Action Center of Reform Judaism, Rabbi David Saperstein. Policymaking body that relates ethical and spiritual principles of Judaism to social-justice issues; implements resolutions through the Religious Action Center in Washington, DC, via advocacy, development of educational materials, and congregational programs. *Tzedek V'Shalom (social action newsletter); Chai Impact (legislative update).*

CONFERENCE OF PRESIDENTS OF MAJOR AMERICAN JEWISH ORGANIZATIONS (1955). 110 E. 59 St., NYC 10022. (212)318-6111. FAX: (212)644-4135. Chmn. Melvin Salberg; Exec. V.-Chmn. Malcolm Hoenlein. Seeks to strengthen the U.S.-Israel alliance and to protect and enhance the security and dignity of Jews abroad. Toward this end, the Conference of Presidents speaks and acts on the basis of consensus of its 55 member agencies on issues of national and international Jewish concern.

CONSULTATIVE COUNCIL OF JEWISH ORGANIZATIONS-CCJO (1946). 420 Lexington Ave., Suite 1733, NYC 10170. (212)808-5437. Chmn. Ady Steg and Clemens N. Nathan; Sec.-Gen. Warren Green. A nongovernmental organization in consultative status with the UN, UNESCO, ILO, UNICEF, and the Council of Europe; cooperates and consults with, advises, and renders assistance to the Economic and Social Council of the UN on all problems relating to human rights and economic, social, cultural, educational, and related matters pertaining to Jews.

COORDINATING BOARD OF JEWISH ORGANIZATIONS (1947). 823 United Nations Plaza, NYC 10017. (212)557-9008. FAX: (212)687-3429. Chmn. David L. Ravich; Exec. Dir. Dr. Harris O. Schoenberg. To promote the purposes and principles for which the UN was created.

COUNCIL OF JEWISH ORGANIZATIONS IN CIVIL SERVICE, INC. (1948). 45 E. 33 St., Rm. 310, NYC 10016. (212)689-2015. FAX: (212)447-1633. Pres. Louis Weiser; 1st V.-Pres. Melvyn Birnbaum. Supports merit system; encourages recruitment of Jewish youth to government service; member of Coalition to Free Soviet Jews, NY Jewish Community Relations Council, NY Metropolitan Coordinating Council on Jewish Poverty, Jewish Labor Committee, America-Israel Friendship League. *Council Digest.*

INSTITUTE FOR PUBLIC AFFAIRS (*see* UNION OF ORTHODOX JEWISH CONGREGATIONS OF AMERICA)

INTERNATIONAL LEAGUE FOR THE REPATRIATION OF RUSSIAN JEWS, INC. (1963). 2 Fountain Lane, Suite 2J, Scarsdale, NY 10583. (914)683-3225. FAX: (914) 683-3221. Pres. Morris Brafman; Chmn. James H. Rapp. Helped to bring the situation of Soviet Jews to world attention; catalyst for advocacy efforts, educational projects, and programs on behalf of Russian Jews in the former USSR, Israel, and U.S. Provides funds to help Russian Jewry in Israel and the former Soviet Union.

JEWISH COUNCIL FOR PUBLIC AFFAIRS (formerly NATIONAL JEWISH COMMUNITY RELATIONS ADVISORY COUNCIL) (1944). 443 Park Ave. S., 11th fl., NYC 10016-7322. (212)684-6950. FAX: (212)686-1353. E-mail: contactus@jcpa.org. Chmn. Steven Schwarz; Sec. Mark Schickman; Exec. V.-Chmn. Lawrence Rubin. National coordinating body for the field of Jewish community relations, comprising 13 national and 122 local Jewish community-relations agencies. Promotes understanding of Israel and the Middle East; supports Jewish communities around the world; advocates for equality and pluralism, and against discrimination, in American society. Through the Council's work, its constituent organizations seek agreement on policies, strategies, and programs for effective utilization of their resources for common ends. *JCPA Agenda for Public Affairs; periodic newsletter; JCPA Journal.* (WWW.JEWISHPUBLICAFFAIRS.ORG)

JEWISH LABOR COMMITTEE (1934). Atran Center for Jewish Culture, 25 E. 21 St., NYC 10010. (212)477-0707. FAX: (212)477-1918. Pres. Morton Bahr; Exec. Dir. Avram B. Lyon. Serves as liaison between the Jewish community and the trade union movement; works with the U.S. and international labor movement to combat anti-Semitism, promote intergroup relations, and engender support for the State of Israel and Jews in and from the former Soviet Union; promotes teaching in public schools about the Holocaust and Jewish resistance; strengthens support within the Jewish community for the social goals and programs of the labor movement; supports Yiddish-language and cultural institutions. *Jewish Labor Committee Review; Issues Alert; Alumni Newsletter.*

———, NATIONAL TRADE UNION COUNCIL FOR HUMAN RIGHTS (1956). Atran Center for Jewish Culture, 25 E. 21 St., NYC 10010. (212)477-0707. FAX: (212)477-1918. Chmn. Sol Hoffman; Exec. Dir. Avram Lyon. Works with the American labor movement in advancing the struggle for social justice and equal opportunity, and assists unions in every issue affecting human rights. Fights discrimination on all levels and helps to promote labor's broad social and economic goals.

JEWISH PEACE FELLOWSHIP (1941). Box 271, Nyack, NY 10960. (914)358-4601. FAX: (914)358-4924. Pres. Rabbi Philip Bentley; Sec. Naomi Goodman; Ed. Murray Polner. Unites those who believe that Jewish ideals and experience provide inspiration for a nonviolent philosophy and way of life; offers draft counseling, especially for conscientious objection based on Jewish "religious training and belief"; encourages Jewish community to become more knowledgeable, concerned, and active in regard to the war/peace problem. *Shalom/Jewish Peace Letter.*

JEWISH WAR VETERANS OF THE UNITED STATES OF AMERICA (1896). 1811 R St., NW, Washington, DC 20009. (202)265-6280. FAX: (202)234-5662. E-mail: jwv@erols.com. Natl. Exec. Dir. Herb Rosenbleeth; Natl. Commander Michael B. Berman. Seeks to foster true allegiance to the United States; to combat bigotry and prevent defamation of Jews; to encourage the doctrine of universal liberty, equal rights, and full justice for all; to cooperate with and support existing educational institutions and establish new ones; to foster the education of ex-servicemen, ex-servicewomen, and members in the ideals and principles of Americanism. *Jewish Veteran.*

———, NATIONAL MUSEUM OF AMERICAN JEWISH MILITARY HISTORY (1958). 1811 R St., NW, Washington, DC 20009. E-mail: jwv@erols.com. (202)265-6280. FAX:(202)462-3192. Pres. Harvey S. Friedman; Asst. Dir./Archivist Sandor B. Cohen. Documents and preserves the contributions of Jewish Americans to the peace and freedom of the United States; educates the public concerning the courage, heroism, and sacrifices made by Jewish Americans who served in the armed forces; and works to combat anti-Semitism. *Museum News (quarterly newsletter).*

NATIONAL ASSOCIATION OF JEWISH LEGISLATORS (1976). 65 Oakwood St., Albany, NY 12208. (518)527-3353. FAX: (518) 458-8512. E-mail: najl01@aol.com. Exec. Dir. Marc Hiller; Pres. Sen. Richard Cohen, Minn. state senator. A nonpartisan Jewish state legislative network focusing on domestic issues and publishing newsletters. Maintains close ties with the Knesset and Israeli leaders.

NATIONAL CONFERENCE ON SOVIET JEWRY (formerly AMERICAN JEWISH CONFERENCE ON SOVIET JEWRY) (1964; reorg. 1971). 1640 Rhode Island Ave., NW, Suite 501, Washington, DC 20036-3278. (202)898-2500. FAX: (202)898-0822. E-mail: ncsj@access.digex.net. N.Y. office: 823 United Nations Plaza, NYC 10017. (212)808-0295. Chmn. Denis C. Braham; Exec. Dir. Mark B. Levin. Coordinating agency for major national Jewish organizations and local community groups in the U.S., acting on behalf of Jews in the former Soviet Union (FSU); provides information about Jews in the FSU through public education and social action; reports and special pamphlets, special programs and projects, public meetings and forums. *Newswatch; annual report; action and program kits; Tekuma.* (WWW.NCSJ.ORG)

———, SOVIET JEWRY RESEARCH BUREAU. Chmn. Rabbi Mark Staitman. Organized by NCSJ to monitor emigration trends. Primary task is the accumulation, evaluation, and processing of information regarding Jews in the FSU, especially those who apply for emigration.

NATIONAL JEWISH COALITION (1985). 415 2nd St., NE, Suite 100, Washington, DC 20002. (202)547-7701. FAX: (202) 544-2434. E-mail: njc@njchq.org. Natl. Chmn. Cheryl Halpern; Hon. Chmn. Max M. Fisher, Richard J. Fox, Sam Fox, George Klein, and Amb. Mel Sembler; Exec. Dir. Matt Brooks. Promotes involvement in Republican politics among its members; sensitizes Republican leaders to the concerns of the American Jewish community; promotes principles of free enterprise, a strong national defense, and an internationalist foreign policy. *NJC Bulletin.* (WWW.NJCHQ.ORG)

NATIONAL JEWISH COMMISSION ON LAW AND PUBLIC AFFAIRS (COLPA) (1965). 135 W. 50 St., 6th fl., NYC 10020.

(212)641-8992. FAX: (212)641-8197. Pres. Allen L. Rothenberg; Exec. Dir. Dennis Rapps. Voluntary association of attorneys whose purpose is to represent the observant Jewish community on legal, legislative, and public-affairs matters.

NATIONAL JEWISH COMMUNITY RELATIONS ADVISORY COUNCIL (see Jewish Council for Public Affairs)

NATIONAL JEWISH DEMOCRATIC COUNCIL (1990). 777 N. Capital St., NE, Suite 305, Washington, DC 20002. (202)216-9060. FAX: (202)216-9061. E-mail: njdconline@aol. com. Chmn. Monte Friedkin; Founding Chmn. Morton Mandel; Exec. Dir. Ira N. Forman. An independent organization committed to strengthening Jewish participation in the Democratic party primarily through grassroots activism. The national voice of Jewish Democrats, NJDC is dedicated to fighting the radical right and promoting Jewish values and interests in the Democratic party. *Capital Communiqué; Extremist Watch.* (WWW.NJDC.ORG)

SHALEM CENTER (1994). 1140 Connecticut Ave., NW, Suite 801, Washington, DC 20036. (202)887-1270. FAX: (202)887-1277. E-mail: ken@shalemcenter.org. Dir. Yoram Hazony; Assoc. Dir. Hillel Fradkin. The purposes and activities of the Shalem Center are to increase public understanding and conduct educational and research activities on the improvement of Jewish national public life, and to develop a community of intellectual leaders to shape the state of Israel into a secure, free, and prosperous society. *Azure.*

SHALOM CENTER (1983). PO Box 380, Accord, NY 12404. (914)626-7272. E-mail: shalomctr@aol.com. (Part of Aleph Alliance for Jewish Renewal.) Exec. Dir. Arthur Waskow. National resource and organizing center for Jewish perspectives on dealing with environmental dangers, unrestrained technology, and corporate irresponsibility. Initiated A.J. Heschel 25th Yahrzeit observance. Trains next generation of *tikkun olam* activists. Holds colloquia on issues like environmental causes of cancer. *New Menorah.*

STUDENT STRUGGLE FOR SOVIET JEWRY (see Center for Russian Jewry)

UNION OF COUNCILS (formerly UNION OF COUNCILS FOR SOVIET JEWS) (1970). 1819 H St., NW, Suite 230, Washington, DC 20005. (202)775-9770. FAX: (202)775-9776. E-mail: ucsj@ucsj.com. Pres. Yosef I. Abramowitz; Natl. Dir. Micah H. Naftalin. Devoted to promoting religious liberty, freedom of emigration, and security for Jews in the FSU (former Soviet Union) through advocacy and monitoring of antisemitism, neo-facism, human rights, rule of law, and democracy. Offers educational, cultural, medical, and humanitarian aid through the Yad L'Yad partnership program pairing Jewish communities in the US and the FSU; advocates for refuseniks and political prisoner. (WWW.FSUMONITOR.COM)

WORLD CONGRESS OF GAY AND LESBIAN JEWISH ORGANIZATIONS (1980). PO Box 23379, Washington, DC 20026-3379. E-mail: info@wcgljo.org. Pres. Jack Gilbert (London, UK); V.-Pres. Lee Walzer (Washington, DC). Supports, strengthens, and represents over 65 Jewish gay and lesbian organizations across the globe and the needs of gay and lesbian Jews generally. Challenges homophobia and sexism within the Jewish community and responds to anti-Semitism at large. Sponsors regional and international conferences. *The W.C. Digest.*

WORLD JEWISH CONGRESS (1936; org. in U.S. 1939). 501 Madison Ave., 17th fl., NYC 10022. (212) 755-5770. FAX: (212) 755-5883. Pres. Edgar M. Bronfman; Cochmn. N. Amer. Branch Prof. Irwin Cotler (Montreal) and Evelyn Sommer; Sec.-Gen. Israel Singer; Exec. Dir. Elan Steinberg. Seeks to intensify bonds of world Jewry with Israel; to strengthen solidarity among Jews everywhere and secure their rights, status, and interests as individuals and communities; to encourage Jewish social, religious, and cultural life throughout the world and coordinate efforts by Jewish communities and organizations to cope with any Jewish problem; to work for human rights generally. Represents its affiliated organizations-most representative bodies of Jewish communities in more than 80 countries and 35 national organizations in American section-at UN, OAS, UNESCO, Council of Europe, ILO, UNICEF, and other governmental, intergovernmental, and international authorities. *WJC Report; Bolet'n Informativo OJI; Christian-Jewish Relations; Dateline: World Jewry; Coloquio; Batfutsot; Gesher.*

———, UN WATCH (1993). 1, rue de Varembé, PO Box 191, 1211 Geneva 20, Switzerland. (41-22)734.14.72/3. FAX: (41-22)734.16.13. E-mail: unwatch@unwatch.org. Chmn. Morris B. Abram; Exec. Dir. Michael D. Colson. An affiliate of the World Jewish Congress, UN Watch measures UN performance by the yardstick of that organization's Charter; advocates the non-discriminatory application of the Charter; opposes the use of UN fora to bash Israel and promote anti-Semitism; and seeks to institutionalize at the UN the fight against worldwide anti-Semitism. (www.unwatch.org)

CULTURAL

AMERICAN ACADEMY FOR JEWISH RESEARCH (1929). 53 Washington Sq., NYC 10012. (212)998-3550. FAX: (212)995-4178. Pres. Robert Chazan. Encourages Jewish learning and research; holds annual or semiannual meeting; awards grants for the publication of scholarly works. *Proceedings of the American Academy for Jewish Research; Texts and Studies; Monograph Series.*

AMERICAN GATHERING OF JEWISH HOLOCAUST SURVIVORS. 122 W. 30 St., #205. NYC 10001. (212)239-4230. FAX: (212) 279-2926. Pres. Benjamin Meed. Dedicated to documenting the past and passing on a legacy of remembrance. Compiles the National Registry of Jewish Holocaust Survivors-to date, the records of more than 100,000 survivors and their families-housed at the U.S. Holocaust Memorial Museum in Washington, DC; holds an annual Yom Hashoah commemoration and occasional international gatherings; sponsors an intensive summer program for U.S. teachers in Poland and Israel to prepare them to teach about the Holocaust. *Together (newspaper).*

AMERICAN GUILD OF JUDAIC ART (1991). 15 Greenspring Valley Rd., Owings Mills, MD 21117. (410)902-0411. FAX: (410)581-0108. E-mail: lbarch@erols. com. Pres. Mark D. Levin; 1st V.-Pres. Richard McBee. A not-for-profit membership organization for those with interests in the Judaic arts, including artists, galleries, collectors & retailers of Judaica, writers, educators, appraisers, museum curators, conservators, lecturers, and others personally or professionally involved in the field. Helps to promote members' art. *Hiddur (quarterly); Update (members' networking newsletter).* (WWW.JEWISHART.ORG)

AMERICAN JEWISH HISTORICAL SOCIETY (1892). 2 Thornton Rd., Waltham, MA 02154. (617)891-8110. FAX: (617)899-9208. E-mail: ajhs@ajhs.org. Pres. Kenneth J. Bialkin; Dir. Dr. Michael Feldberg. Collects, catalogues, publishes, and displays material on the history of the Jews in America; serves as an information center for inquiries on American Jewish history; maintains archives of original source material on American Jewish history; sponsors lectures and exhibitions; makes available audiovisual material. *American Jewish History; Heritage.*

AMERICAN JEWISH PRESS ASSOCIATION (1944). Natl. Admin. Off.: 1828 L St. NW, Suite 402, Washington, DC 20036. (202)785-2282. FAX: (202)785-2307. E-mail: toby@dershowitz.com. Pres. Marc Klein; Exec. Dir. Toby Dershowitz. The central voice of the American Sephardic community Seeks the advancement of Jewish journalism and the maintenance of a strong Jewish press in the U.S. and Canada; encourages the attainment of the highest editorial and business standards; sponsors workshops, services for members; sponsors annual competition for Simon Rockower awards for excellence in Jewish journalism. *Membership bulletin newsletter.*

AMERICAN SEPHARDI FEDERATION (1973). 305 7th Ave., Suite 1101, NYC 10001. (212)366-7223. FAX: (212)366-7263. E-mail: asf@amsephfed.org. Pres. Leon Levy; Exec. Dir. Jayne Rosengarten. The central voice of the American Sephardic community, representing a broad spectrum of Sephardic organizations, congregations, and educational institutions. Seeks to strengthen and unify the community through education, communication, advocacy, and leadership development, creating greater awareness and appreciation of its rich and unique history and culture. *ASF Update Newsletter.*

AMERICAN SOCIETY FOR JEWISH MUSIC (1974). 170 W. 74 St., NYC 10023. (212)874-4456. FAX: (212)874-8605. Pres. Hadassah B. Markson; V.-Pres. Judith Tischler & Martha Novick; Sec. Fortuna Calvo Roth; Bd. Chmn. Rabbi Henry D. Michelman; Treas. Michael Leavitt. Promotes the knowledge, appreciation, and development of Jewish music, past and present, for professional and lay audiences; seeks to raise the standards of composition and performance in Jewish music, to encourage research, and to sponsor performances of new and rarely heard works. *Musica Judaica Journal.*

ASSOCIATION OF JEWISH BOOK PUBLISHERS (1962). c/o Jewish Lights Publishing, PO Box 237, Woodstock, VT 05091. (802)457-4000. FAX: (802)457-4004. Pres. Stuart M. Matlins; Exec. Dir. Ariella O'-Connor. As a nonprofit group, provides a forum for discussion of mutual areas of interest among Jewish publishers, and promotes cooperative exhibits and promotional opportunities for members. Membership fee is $85 annually per publishing house.

ASSOCIATION OF JEWISH LIBRARIES (1965). 15 E. 26 St., Rm. 1034, NYC 10010. (212)725-5359. Pres. David T. Gilner; V.-Pres. Tobey Rossner. Seeks to promote and improve services and professional standards in Jewish libraries; disseminates Jewish library information and guidance; promotes publication of literature in the field; encourages the establishment of Jewish libraries and collections of Judaica and the choice of Judaica librarianship as a profession; cocertifies Jewish libraries (with Jewish Book Council). *AJL Newsletter; Judaica Librarianship.*

B'NAI B'RITH KLUTZNICK NATIONAL JEWISH MUSEUM (1957). 1640 Rhode Island Ave., NW, Washington, DC 20036. (202)857-6583. FAX: (202)857-6609. A center of Jewish art and history in the nation's capital, maintains temporary and permanent exhibition galleries, permanent collection of Jewish ceremonial objects, folk art, and contemporary fine art, outdoor sculpture garden and museum shop, as well as the American Jewish Sports Hall of Fame. Provides exhibitions, tours, educational programs, research assistance, and tourist information. *Quarterly newsletter; permanent collection catalogue; temporary exhibit catalogues.*

CENTRAL YIDDISH CULTURE ORGANIZATION (CYCO), Inc. (1943). 25 E. 21 St., 3rd fl., NYC 10010. (212)505-8305. FAX: (212) 505-8044. Mgr. David Kirszencwejg. Promotes, publishes, and distributes Yiddish books; publishes catalogues.

CONFERENCE ON JEWISH SOCIAL STUDIES, INC. (formerly CONFERENCE ON JEWISH RELATIONS, INC.) (1939). Bldg. 240, Rm. 103. Program in Jewish Studies, Stanford University, Stanford, CA 94305-2190. (650)725-0829. FAX: (650)725-2920. E-mail: jss@leland.stanford.edu. Pres. Steven J. Zipperstein; V-Pres. Aron Rodrigue. *Jewish Social Studies.*

CONGREGATION BINA (1981). 600 W. End Ave., Suite 1-C, NYC 10024. (212)873-4261. Pres. Joseph Moses; Exec. V.-Pres. Moses Samson; Hon. Pres. Samuel M. Daniel; Secy. Gen. Elijah E. Jhirad. Serves the religious, cultural, charitable, and philanthropic needs of the Children of Israel who originated in India and now reside in the U.S. Works to foster and preserve the ancient traditions, customs, liturgy, music, and folklore of Indian Jewry and to maintain needed institutions. *Kol Bina.*

CONGRESS FOR JEWISH CULTURE (1948). 25 E. 21 St., NYC 10010. (212)505-8040. FAX: (212)505-8044. Co-pres.'s Prof. Yonia Fain, Dr. Barnett Zumoff. An umbrella group comprising 16 constituent organizations; perpetuates and enhances Jewish creative expression in the U.S. and abroad; fosters all aspects of Yiddish cultural life through the publication of the journal Zukunft, the conferring of literary awards, commemoration of the Holocaust and the martyrdom of the Soviet Jewish writers under Stalin, and a series of topical readings, scholarly conferences, symposiums, and concerts. *Zukunft.*

ELAINE KAUFMAN CULTURAL CENTER (1952). 129 W. 67 St., NYC 10023. (212)501-3303. FAX: (212)874-7865. Chmn. Leonard Goodman; Pres. Elaine Kaufman; Exec. Dir. Lydia Kontos. Offers instruction in its Lucy Moses School for Music and Dance in music, dance, art, and theater to children and adults, in Western culture and Jewish traditions. Presents frequent performances of Jewish and general music by leading artists and ensembles in its Merkin Concert Hall and Ann Goodman Recital Hall. The Birnbaum Music Library houses Jewish music scores and reference books. *Kaufman Cultural Center News; bimonthly concert calendars; catalogues and brochures.* (WWW.ELAINEKAUFMANCENTER.ORG)

HISTADRUTH IVRITH OF AMERICA (1916; reorg. 1922). 426 W. 58ᵗʰ St., NYC 10019. (212)957-6659. Fax: (212)957-5811. E-mail: general@hist-ivrit.org. Pres. Miriam Ostow; Exec. V.-Pres. Rabbi Abraham Kupchik. Emphasizes the primacy of Hebrew in Jewish life, culture, and education; aims to disseminate knowledge of written and spoken Hebrew in N. America, thus building a cultural bridge between the State of Israel and Jewish communities throughout N. America. *Hadoar; Lamishpaha; Tov Lichtov; Hebrew Week; Ulpan.* (WWW.HIST-IVRIT.ORG)

HOLOCAUST CENTER OF THE UNITED JEWISH FEDERATION OF GREATER PITTSBURGH (1980). 5738 Darlington Rd., Pittsburgh, PA 15217. (412)421-1500. FAX: (412) 422-1996. E-mail: lhurwitz@ujf.net. Pres. Holocaust Comm. Edgar Snyder; Bd. Chmn. David Burstin; Dir. Linda F. Hurwitz. Develops programs and provides resources to further understanding of the Holocaust and its impact on civilization. Maintains a library, archive; provides speakers, educational materials; organizes community programs. Published collection of survivor and liberator stories.

HOLOCAUST MEMORIAL CENTER (1984). 6602 West Maple Rd., West Bloomfield, MI 48322. (248)661-0840. FAX: (248) 661-4204. E-mail: info@holocaustcenter. org. Founder & Exec. V.-Pres. Rabbi Charles Rosenzveig. America's first freestanding Holocaust center comprising a museum, library-archive, oral history collection, garden of the righteous, research institute and academic advisory committee. Provides tours, lecture series, teacher training, Yom Hashoah commemorations, exhibits, educational outreach programs, speakers' bureau, computer database on 1,200 destroyed Jewish communities, guided travel tours to concentration camps and Israel, and museum shop. Published *World Reacts to the Holocaust. Newsletter.*

HOLOCAUST MEMORIAL RESOURCE & EDUCATION CENTER OF CENTRAL FLORIDA (1982). 851 N. Maitland Ave., Maitland, FL 32751. (407)628-0555. FAX: (407)628-1079. E-mail: execdir@holocaustedu.org. Pres. Marilyn Goldman; Bd. Chmn. Tess Wise. An interfaith educational center devoted to teaching the lessons of the Holocaust. Houses permanent multimedia educational exhibit; maintains library of books, videotapes, films, and other visuals to serve the entire educational establishment; offers lectures, teacher training, and other activities. *Newsletter; Bibliography; "Holocaust-Lessons for Tomorrow"; elementary and middle school curriculum.*

HOLOCAUST MUSEUM AND LEARNING CENTER (formerly ST. LOUIS CENTER FOR HOLOCAUST STUDIES) (1977). 12 Millstone Campus Dr., St. Louis, MO 63146. (314)432-0020. Chmn. Michael Litwack; Chmn. Emer. Leo Wolf. Develops programs and provides resources and educational materials to further an understanding of the Holocaust and its impact on civilization; has a 5,000 sq. ft. museum containing photographs, artifacts, and audiovisual displays. *Newsletter for Friends of the Holocaust Museum and Learning Center.*

INTERNATIONAL ASSOCIATION OF JEWISH GENEALOGICAL SOCIETIES (1988). 104 Franklin Ave., Yonkers, NY 10705. (914)963-1059. Fax: (212)988-1305. E-mail: khsmus@aol.com. Pres. Karen S. Franklin. Umbrella organization of more than 70 Jewish Genealogical Societies (JGS) worldwide. Represents organized Jewish genealogy, encourages Jews to research their family history, promotes new JGSs, supports existing societies, implements projects of interest to individuals researching their Jewish family histories. Holds annual conference where members learn and exchange ideas.

INTERNATIONAL JEWISH MEDIA ASSOCIATION (1987). U.S.: c/o St. Louis Jewish Light, 12 Millstone Campus Dr., St. Louis, MO 63146. (314)432-3353. FAX: (314)432-0515. E-mail: stlouislgt@aol.com and ajpamr@aol.com. Israel:PO Box 92, Jerusalem 91920. 02-202-222. FAX: 02-513-642. Pres. Robert A. Cohn (c/o St. Louis Jewish Light); Exec. Dir. Toby Dershowitz. 1828 L St. NW, Suite 402, Washington, DC 20036. (202)785-2282. FAX: (202)785-2307. E-mail: toby@dershowitz.com. Israel Liaison, Jacob Gispan, Lifsha Ben-Shach, WZO Dept. of Info. A worldwide network of Jewish journalists, publications and other media in the Jewish and general media, which seeks to provide a forum for the exchange of materials and ideas and to enhance the status of Jewish media and journalists throughout the world. *IJMA Newsletter;*

Proceedings of the International Conference on Jewish Media.

INTERNATIONAL NETWORK OF CHILDREN OF JEWISH HOLOCAUST SURVIVORS, INC. (1981). 3000 NE 151 St., N. Miami, FL 33181. (305)919-5690. FAX: (305)919-5691. E-mail: xholocau@fiu.edu. Pres. Rositta E. Kenigsberg; V.-Pres. Jean Bloch Rosensaft. Links Second Generation groups and individuals throughout the world. Represents the shared interests of children of Holocaust survivors; aims to perpetuate the authentic memory of the Holocaust and prevent its recurrence, to strengthen and preserve the Jewish spiritual, ideological, and cultural heritage, to fight anti-Semitism and all forms of discrimination, persecution, and oppression anywhere in the world.

JACOB RADER MARCUS CENTER OF THE AMERICAN JEWISH ARCHIVES (1947). 3101 Clifton Ave., Cincinnati, OH 45220. (513)221-1875 ext. 403. FAX: (513)221-7812. Dir. Dr. Gary P. Zola. Promotes the study and preservation of the Western Hemisphere Jewish experience through research, publications, collection of important source materials, and a vigorous public-outreach program. *American Jewish Archives; monographs, publications, and pamphlets.*

JEWISH BOOK COUNCIL (1946; reorg. 1993). 15 E. 26 St., NYC 10010. (212)532-4949, ext. 297. E-mail: jbc@jewishbooks.org. Pres. Moshe Dworkin; Bd. Chmn. Henry Everett; Exec. Dir. Carolyn Starman Hessel. Serves as literary arm of the American Jewish community and clearinghouse for Jewish-content literature; assists readers, writers, publishers, and those who market and sell products. Provides bibliographies, list of publishers, bookstores, book fairs. Sponsors National Jewish Book Awards, Jewish Book Month. *Jewish Book Annual; Jewish Book World.*

JEWISH HERITAGE PROJECT (1981). 150 Franklin St., #1W, NYC 10013. (212)925-9067. Exec. Dir. Alan Adelson. Strives to bring to the broadest possible audience authentic works of literary and historical value relating to Jewish history and culture. Distributor of the film *Lodz Ghetto,* which it developed, as well as its companion volume *Lodz Ghetto: Inside a Community Under Siege; Better Tthan*

Gold: An Immigrant Family's First Years in Brooklyn.

JEWISH MUSEUM (1904, under auspices of Jewish Theological Seminary of America). 1109 Fifth Ave., NYC 10128. (212)423-3200. FAX: (212)423-3232. Dir. Joan H. Rosenbaum; Bd. Chmn. Robert J. Hurst. Expanded museum reopened in June 1993, featuring permanent exhibition on the Jewish experience. Repository of the largest collection of Judaica-paintings, prints, photographs, sculpture, coins, medals, antiquities, textiles, and other decorative arts-in the Western Hemisphere. Includes the National Jewish Archive of Broadcasting. Tours, lectures, film showings, and concerts; special programs for children; cafe; shop. *Special exhibition catalogues; annual report.*

JEWISH PUBLICATION SOCIETY (1888). 1930 Chestnut St., Philadelphia, PA 19103. (215)564-5925. FAX: (215)564-6640. E-mail: jewishbook@aol.com. Pres. Harold Cramer; Ed.-in-Chief Dr. Ellen Frankel; Dir. of Marketing David Goldberg. Publishes and disseminates books of Jewish interest for adults and children; titles include TANAKH, religious studies and practices, life cycle, folklore, classics, art, history, belles-lettres. *The Bookmark; JPS Catalogue.*

JUDAH L. MAGNES MUSEUM-JEWISH MUSEUM OF THE WEST (1962). 2911 Russell St., Berkeley, CA 94705. (510)549-6950. FAX: (510)849-3673. E-mail: magnes-admin@eb.jfed.org. Pres. Fred Weiss; Dir. Susan Morris. Collects, preserves, and makes available Jewish art, culture, history, and literature from throughout the world. Permanent collections of fine and ceremonial art; rare Judaica library, Western Jewish History Center (archives), Jewish-American Hall of Fame. Changing exhibits, traveling exhibits, docent tours, lectures, numismatics series, poetry award, museum shop. *Magnes News; special exhibition catalogues; scholarly books.*

JUDAICA CAPTIONED FILM CENTER, INC. (1983). PO Box 21439, Baltimore, MD 21208-0439. Voice (1-800)735-2258; TDD (410)655-6767. E-mail: lweiner@jhu-cep.org. Pres. Lois Lilienfeld Weiner. Developing a comprehensive library of captioned and subtitled films and tapes on Jewish subjects; distributes them to organizations serving the hearing-impaired, including mainstream classes and senior adult groups, on a freeloan, handling/shipping-charge-only basis. *Newsletter.*

LEAGUE FOR YIDDISH, INC. (1979). 200 W. 72 St., Suite 40, NYC 10023. (212)787-6675. E-mail: mschaecht@aol.com. Pres. Dr. Zuni Zelitch; Exec. Dir. Dr. Mordkhe Schaechter. Encourages the development and use of Yiddish as a living language; promotes its modernization and standardization; publisher of Yiddish textbooks and English-Yiddish dictionaries; most recent book publication: *Yiddish Two: An Intermediate and Advanced Textbook, 1995. Afn Shvel (quarterly).*

LEO BAECK INSTITUTE, INC. (1955). 129 E. 73 St., NYC 10021. (212)744-6400. FAX: (212)988-1305. E-mail: lbi1@lbi.com. Pres. Ismar Schorsch; Exec. Dir. Carol Kahn Strauss. A research, study, and lecture center, museum, library, and archive relating to the history of German-speaking Jewry. Offers lectures, exhibits, faculty seminars; publishes a series of monographs, yearbooks, and journals. *LBI News; LBI Yearbook; LBI Memorial Lecture; LBI Library & Archives News; occasional papers.*

LIVING TRADITIONS (1994). 430 W. 14 St., #409, NYC 10014. (212)691-1272. FAX: (212)691-1657. E-mail: livetrads@aol. com. Pres. Henry Sapoznik; V.-Pres. Lorin Sklamberg. Nonprofit membership organization dedicated to the study, preservation, and innovative continuity of traditional folk and popular culture through workshops, concerts, recordings, radio and film documentaries; clearinghouse for research in klezmer and other traditional music; sponsors yearly weeklong international cultural event, "Yiddish Folk Arts Program/'KlezKamp.'" *Living Traditions (newsletter).* (WWW.LIVINGTRADITIONS.ORG)

LOS ANGELES MUSEUM OF THE HOLOCAUST (MARTYRS MEMORIAL) (opened 1978). 6006 Wilshire Blvd., Los Angeles, CA 90036. (323)761-8170. FAX: (323)761-8174. E-mail: kjosephy@earthlink.net. Chmn. Osias G. Goren; Dir./Curator Marcia Reines Josephy. A photo-narrative museum and resource center dedicated to Holocaust history, issues of genocide and prejudice, curriculum development and exhibition. *Educational guides; Those Who Dared; Rescuers and Rescued; Guide to Schindler's List; Modular Curriculum.*

MEMORIAL FOUNDATION FOR JEWISH CULTURE, INC. (1964). 15 E. 26 St., Suite 1703, NYC 10010. (212)679-4074. Pres. Rabbi Alexander Schindler; Exec. V.-Pres. Jerry Hochbaum. Through the grants that it awards, encourages Jewish scholarship culture and education; supports communities that are struggling to maintain Jewish life; assists professional training for careers in communal service in Jewishly deprived communities; and stimulates the documentation, commemoration, and teaching of the Holocaust.

MUSEUM OF JEWISH HERITAGE—A LIVING MEMORIAL TO THE HOLOCAUST (1984). One Battery Park Plaza, NYC 10004-1484. (212)968-1800. FAX: (212)968-1369. Bd. Chmn. Robert M. Morgenthau; Museum Dir. David Altshuler. New York tri-state's principal institution for educating people of all ages and backgrounds about 20th-century Jewish history and the Holocaust. Repository of Steven Spielberg's Survivors of the Shoah Visual History Foundation videotaped testimonies. Core and changing exhibitions. *18 First Place (newsletter); Holocaust bibliography; educational materials.* (WWW.MJH-NYC.ORG)

MUSEUM OF TOLERANCE OF THE SIMON WIESENTHAL CENTER (1993). 9786 W. Pico Blvd., Los Angeles, CA 90035-4792. (310)553-8403. FAX: (310)553-4521. E-mail: avra@wiesenthal.com. Dean-Founder Rabbi Marvin Hier; Assoc. Dean Rabbi Abraham Cooper; Exec. Dir. Rabbi Meyer May. A unique experiential museum focusing on personal prejudice, group intolerance, struggle for civil rights, and 20th-century genocides, culminating in a major exhibition on the Holocaust. Archives, Multimedia Learning Center designed for individualized research, 6,700-square-foot temporary exhibit space, 324-seat theater, 150-seat auditorium, and outdoor memorial plaza. *Response magazine.*

NATIONAL FOUNDATION FOR JEWISH CULTURE (1960). 330 Seventh Ave., 21st fl., NYC 10001. (212)629-0500. FAX: (212)629-0508. E-mail: nfjc@jewishculture.org. Pres. Lynn Korda Kroll; Exec. Dir. Richard A. Siegel. The leading Jewish organization devoted to promoting

Jewish culture in the U.S. Manages the Jewish Endowment for the Arts and Humanities; administers the Council of American Jewish Museums and Council of Archives and Research Libraries in Jewish Studies; offers doctoral dissertation fellowships and grants for documentary films and new plays; coordinates community cultural residencies, local cultural commissions, and regional cultural consortia; organizes conferences, symposia, and festivals in the arts and humanities. *Jewish Cultural News; Plays of Jewish Interest; Jewish Exhibition Traveling Service; Culture Currents (electronic).*

NATIONAL MUSEUM OF AMERICAN JEWISH MILITARY HISTORY (*see* Jewish War Veterans of the U.S.A.)

NATIONAL YIDDISH BOOK CENTER (1980). 1021 West St., Amherst, MA 01002. (413)256-4900. FAX: (413)256-4700. E-mail: yiddish@bikher.org. Founder & Pres. Aaron Lansky. Since 1980 the center has collected 1.5 million Yiddish books for distribution to libraries and readers worldwide; offers innovative English-language programs and produces a magazine. New permanent home in Amherst, open to the public, features a book repository, exhibits, a bookstore, and a theater. *The Pakn Treger (English-language magazine).*

ORTHODOX JEWISH ARCHIVES (1978). 84 William St., NYC 10038. (212)797-9000, ext. 73. FAX: (212)269-2843 Dir. Rabbi Moshe Kolodny. Founded by Agudath Israel of America; houses historical documents, photographs, periodicals, and other publications relating to the growth of Orthodox Jewry in the U.S. and related communities in Europe, Israel, and elsewhere. Particularly noteworthy are its holdings relating to rescue activities organized during the Holocaust and its traveling exhibits available to schools and other institutions.

RESEARCH FOUNDATION FOR JEWISH IMMIGRATION, INC. (1971). 570 Seventh Ave., NYC 10018. (212)921-3871. FAX: (212)575-1918. Pres. Curt C. Silberman; Sec. and Coord. of Research Herbert A. Strauss; Archivist Dennis E. Rohrbaugh. Studies and records the history of the migration and acculturation of Central European German-speaking Jewish and non-Jewish Nazi persecutees in various resettlement countries worldwide, with special emphasis on the American experience. *International Biographical Dictionary of Central European Emigrés, 1933-1945; Jewish Immigrants of the Nazi Period in the USA.*

RUSSIAN TELEVISION NETWORK (RTN) (1991). PO Box 3589, Stamford, CT 06905. (203)359-1570. FAX: (203)359-1381. Pres. Mark S. Golub; V.-Pres. Michael Pravin. Devoted to producing daily television programming for the immigrant Jewish community from the former Soviet Union; seen 24 hours a day on Cablevision of Brooklyn and nationally on the International Channel and NJT/National Jewish Television.

SEPHARDIC EDUCATIONAL CENTER (1979). 10808 Santa Monica Blvd., Los Angeles, CA 90025. (310)441-9361. FAX: (310)441-9561. E-mail:secforever@aol.com. Founder & Chmn. Jose A. Nessim, M.D. Has chapters in the U.S., North, Central, and South America, Europe, and Asia, a spiritual and educational center in the Old City of Jerusalem, and executive office in Los Angeles. Serves as a meeting ground for Sephardim from many nations; sponsors the first worldwide movement for Sephardic youth and young adults. Disseminates information about Sephardic Jewry in the form of motion pictures, pamphlets, and books, which it produces. *Hamerkaz (quarterly bulletin in English).* (WWW.SECWORLDWIDE.ORG)

SEPHARDIC HOUSE (1978). 2112 Broadway, Suite 200A, NYC 10023. (212)496-2173. FAX: (212)496-2264. E-mail: sephardic@juno.com. Pres. Morrie R. Yohai; Exec. Dir. Dr. Janice E. Ovadiah. A cultural organization dedicated to fostering Sephardic history and culture; sponsors a wide variety of classes and public programs, film festivals, including summer program in France for high-school students; publication program disseminates materials of Sephardic value; outreach program to communities outside of the New York area; program bureau provides program ideas, speakers, and entertainers; International Sephardic Film Festival every two years. *Sephardic House Newsletter; Publication Catalogue.* (WWW.SEPHARDIC.ORG)

SIMON WIESENTHAL CENTER (1977). 9760 W. Pico Blvd., Los Angeles, CA 90035-

4701. (310)553-9036. FAX: (310)553-2709. Dean-Founder Rabbi Marvin Hier; Assoc. Dean Rabbi Abraham Cooper; Exec. Dir. Rabbi Meyer May. Regional offices in New York, Miami, Toronto, Paris, Jerusalem, Buenos Aires. The largest institution of its kind in N. America, dedicated to the study of the Holocaust, its contemporary implications, and related human-rights issues through education and awareness. Incorporates 185,000-sq.-ft. Museum of Tolerance, library, media department, archives, "Testimony to the Truth" oral histories, educational outreach, research department, international social action, "Page One" (syndicated weekly radio news magazine presenting contemporary Jewish issues). *Response Magazine.*

SKIRBALL CULTURAL CENTER (1996), an affiliate of Hebrew Union College. 2701 N. Sepulveda Blvd., Los Angeles, CA 90049. (310)440-4500. FAX: (310)440-4595. Pres. & CEO Uri D. Herscher; Bd. Chmn. Howard Friedman. Seeks to interpret the Jewish experience and to strengthen American society though a range of cultural programs, including museum exhibitions, children's Discovery Center, concerts, lectures, performances, readings, symposia, film, and educational offerings for adults and children of all ages and backgrounds. through interpretive museum exhibits and programming; museum shop and café. *Oasis magazine; catalogues of exhibits and collections.*

SOCIETY FOR THE HISTORY OF CZECHOSLOVAK JEWS, INC. (1961). 760 Pompton Ave., Cedar Grove, NJ 07009. (973)239-2333. FAX: (973)239-7935. Pres. Rabbi Norman Patz; V.-Pres. Prof. Fred Hahn; Sec. Anita Grosz. Studies the history of Czechoslovak Jews; collects material and disseminates information through the publication of books and pamphlets; conducts annual memorial service for Czech Holocaust victims. *The Jews of Czechoslovakia (3 vols.); Review I-VI.*

SOCIETY OF FRIENDS OF TOURO SYNAGOGUE, NATIONAL HISTORIC SITE, INC. (1948). 85 Touro St., Newport, RI 02840. (401)847-4794. FAX: (401)847-8121. Pres. Meira Lisman Max; Exec. Dir. B. Schlessinger Ross. Helps maintain Touro Synagogue as a national historic site, opening and interpreting it for visitors; promotes public awareness of its preemi-

nent role in the tradition of American religious liberty; annually commemorates George Washington's letter of 1790 to the Hebrew Congregation of Newport. *Society Update.*

———, TOURO NATIONAL HERITAGE TRUST (1984). 85 Touro St., Newport, RI 02840. (401)847-0810. FAX (401)847-8121. Pres. Bernard Bell; Chmn. Benjamin D. Holloway. Works to establish national education center within Touro compound; sponsors Touro Fellow through John Carter Brown Library; presents seminars and other educational programs; promotes knowledge of the early Jewish experience in this country.

SPERTUS MUSEUM, SPERTUS INSTITUTE OF JEWISH STUDIES (1968). 618 S. Michigan Ave., Chicago, IL 60605. (312)922-9012. FAX: (312)922-6406. Pres. Spertus Institute of Jewish Studies, Dr. Howard A. Sulkin. The largest, most comprehensive Judaic museum in the Midwest with 12,000 square feet of exhibit space and a permanent collection of some 10,000 works reflecting 5,000 years of Jewish history and culture. Also includes the redesigned Zell Holocaust Memorial, permanent collection, changing visual arts and special exhibits, and the children's ARTIFACT Center for a hands-on archaeological adventure. Plus, traveling exhibits for Jewish educators, life-cycle workshops, ADA accessible. *Exhibition catalogues; educational pamphlets.*

SURVIVORS OF THE SHOAH VISUAL HISTORY FOUNDATION (1994). PO Box 3168, Los Angeles, CA 90078-3168. (818)777-7802. FAX: (818)866-0312. Pres. & CEO Dr. Michael G. Berenbaum; Exec. Dir. Ari C. Zev. A nonprofit organization, founded and chaired by Steven Spielberg, dedicated to videotaping and preserving interviews with Holocaust survivors throughout the world. The archive of testimonies will be used as a tool for global education about the Holocaust and to teach racial, ethnic, and cultural tolerance.

UNITED STATES HOLOCAUST MEMORIAL MUSEUM (1980; opened Apr. 1993). 100 Raoul Wallenberg Place, SW, Washington, DC 20024. (202)488-0400. FAX: (202)488-2690. Chmn. Miles Lerman. Federally chartered and privately built, its mission is to teach about the Nazi persecution and murder of six million Jews and millions of others from 1933 to 1945 and to inspire visitors to contemplate their moral responsibilities as citizens of a democratic nation. Opened in April 1993 near the national Mall in Washington, DC, the museum's permanent exhibition tells the story of the Holocaust through authentic artifacts, videotaped oral testimonies, documentary film, and historical photographs. Offers educational programs for students and adults, an interactive computerized learning center, and special exhibitions and community programs. *United States Holocaust Memorial Museum Update (bimonthly); Directory of Holocaust Institutions; Journal of Holocaust and Genocide Studies (quarterly).* (WWW.USHMM.ORG)

THE WILSTEIN (SUSAN & DAVID) INSTITUTE OF JEWISH POLICY STUDIES (1988). 43 Hawes St., Brookline, MA 02146. (617)278-4974. FAX: (617)264-9264. E-mail: wilstein@hebrewcollege.edu. Dir. Dr. David M. Gordis; Assoc. Dir. Rabbi Zachary I. Heller; Chmn. Howard I. Friedman. The Wilstein Institute's West Coast Center in Los Angeles and East Coast Center at Hebrew College in Boston provide a bridge between academics, community leaders, professionals, and the organizations and institutions of Jewish life. The institute serves as an international research and development resource for American Jewry. *Bulletins, various newsletters, monographs, research reports, and books.*

YESHIVA UNIVERSITY MUSEUM (1973). 2520 Amsterdam Ave., NYC 10033-3201. (212)960-5390. FAX: (212)960-5406. E-mail: glickber@ymail.yu.edu. Dir. Sylvia A. Herskowitz; Chmn. Erica Jesselson. Collects, preserves, and interprets Jewish life and culture through changing exhibitions of ceremonial objects, paintings, rare books and documents, synagogue architecture, textiles, decorative arts, and photographs. Oral history archive. Special events, holiday workshops, live performances, lectures, etc. for adults and children. Guided tours and workshops are offered. *Seasonal calendars; special exhibition catalogues.*

YIDDISHER KULTUR FARBAND-YKUF (1937). 1133 Broadway, Rm. 820, NYC 10010. (212)243-1304. FAX: (212)243-1305. E-mail: mahosu@amc.one. Pres.

and Ed. Itche Goldberg. Publishes a bimonthly magazine and books by contemporary and classical Jewish writers; conducts cultural forums; exhibits works by contemporary Jewish artists and materials of Jewish historical value; organizes reading circles. *Yiddishe Kultur.*

YIVO INSTITUTE FOR JEWISH RESEARCH (1925). 15 W. 16 St., NYC 10011. (212)246-6080. FAX: (212)292-1892. Chmn. Bruce Slovin. Engages in social and cultural research pertaining to East European Jewish life; maintains library and archives which provide a major international, national, and New York resource used by institutions, individual scholars, and the public; trains graduate students in Yiddish, East European, and American Jewish studies; offers continuing education classes in Yiddish language, exhibits, conferences, public programs; publishes books. *Yidishe Shprakh; YIVO Annual; YIVO Bleter; Yedies fun Yivo.*

———, MAX WEINREICH CENTER FOR ADVANCED JEWISH STUDIES (1968). 15 W. 16 St., NYC 10011. (212)246-6080. FAX: (212)292-1892. Provides advanced-level training in Yiddish language and literature, ethnography, folklore, linguistics, and history; offers guidance on dissertation or independent research; postdoctoral fellowships available.

YUGNTRUF-YOUTH FOR YIDDISH (1964). 200 W. 72 St., Suite 40, NYC 10023. (212)787-6675. FAX: (212)799-1517. E-mail: ruvn@aol.com. Chmn. Dr. Paul Glasser; V.-Chmn. Dr. Adina Cimet de Singer; Coord. Brucha Lang. A worldwide, nonpolitical organization for young people with a knowledge of, or interest in, Yiddish; fosters Yiddish as a living language and culture. Sponsors all activities in Yiddish:reading, conversation, and creative writing groups; annual weeklong retreat in Berkshires; non-Hassidic play group; sale of shirts. *Yugntruf Journal.*

ISRAEL-RELATED

THE ABRAHAM FUND (1989). 477 Madison Ave., 4th fl., NYC 10022. (212)303-9421. FAX: (212)935-1834. E-mail: abrahamfun@aol.com. Chmn. & co-founder Alan B. Slifka; Co-founder Dr. Eugene Weiner; V.-Pres. Joan Bronk. Seeks to enhance coexistence between Israel's Jewish and Arab citizens. Since 1993, has granted nearly $4.5 million to grassroots coexistence projects in a wide array of fields, including education, social services, economic development, and arts and culture. Publishes *The Handbook of Interethnic Coexistence. The Abraham Fund Quarterly.* (WWW.COEXISTENCE.ORG)

ALYN-AMERICAN SOCIETY FOR HANDICAPPED CHILDREN IN ISRAEL (1934). 19 W. 44 St., NYC 10036. (212)869-8085. FAX: (212)768-0979. E-mail: alynny@juno.com. Chmn. Simone P. Blum; Hon. Pres. Minette Halpern Brown; Exec. Dir. Joan R. Mendelson. Supports the work of ALYN Hospital, rehabilitation center for severely orthopedically handicapped children, located in Jerusalem, whose aim is to prepare patients for independent living.

AMERICA-ISRAEL CULTURAL FOUNDATION, INC. (1939). 317 Madison Ave., Suite 1605, NYC 10017. (212)557-1600. FAX: (212)557-1600. Bd. Chmn. Emer. Isaac Stern; Pres. Vera Stern. Supports and encourages the growth of cultural excellence in Israel through grants to cultural institutions; scholarships to gifted young artists and musicians.

AMERICA-ISRAEL FRIENDSHIP LEAGUE, INC. (1971). 134 E. 39 St., NYC 10016. (212)213-8630. FAX: (212)683-3475. E-mail: aifl@nyworld.com. Pres. Mortimer B. Zuckerman; Bd. Chmn. Kenneth J. Bialkin; Sr. Exec. V.-Pres. Stanley A. Urman; Exec. V.-Pres. Ilana Artman. A nonsectarian, nonpartisan organization which seeks to broaden the base of support for Israel among Americans of all faiths and backgrounds. Activities include educational exchanges, tours of Israel for American leadership groups, symposia and public-education activities, and the dissemination of printed information. *Newsletter.*

AMERICAN ASSOCIATES, BEN-GURION UNIVERSITY OF THE NEGEV (1973). 342 Madison Ave., Suite 1224, NYC 10173. (212) 687-7721. FAX: (212)370-0686. E-mail: info@aabgu.org. Pres. Jules I. Whitman; Bd. Chmn. Harold L. Oshry. Raises funds for Israel's youngest university, an institution dedicated to providing a world-class higher education and fulfilling David Ben-Gurion's vision to develop the Negev and make Israel a 'light unto the nations' through education, research, and projects that fight hunger, disease, and poverty in nearly 50 countries world-wide. *IMPACT Newsletter; Speaking of Israel radio news service; videos and brochures.*

AMERICAN COMMITTEE FOR SHAARE ZEDEK MEDICAL CENTER IN JERUSALEM, INC. (1949). 49 W. 45 St., Suite 1100, NYC 10036. (212)354-8801. FAX: (212)391-2674. Natl. Pres. & Chmn. Intertnational Board of Governors Menno Ratzker; Chmn. Erica Jesselson; Exec. Dir. Dr. Stuart Tauber. Raises funds for the various needs of the Shaare Zedek Medical Center, Jerusalem, such as equipment and medical supplies, nurses' training, and research; supports exchange program between Shaare Zedek Medical Center and Albert Einstein College of Medicine, NY. *Heartbeat Magazine.*

AMERICAN COMMITTEE FOR SHENKAR COLLEGE IN ISRAEL, INC. (1971). 855 Ave. of the Americas, NYC 10001. (212) 947-1597. FAX: (212)643-9887. E-mail: acfsc@worldnet.att.net. Pres. Nahum G. (Sonny) Shar; Exec. Dir. Charlotte A. Fainblatt. Raises funds for capital improvement, research and development projects, laboratory equipment, scholarships, lectureships, fellowships, and library/archives of fashion and textile design at Shenkar College in Israel, Israel's only fashion and textile technology college. New departments of computer science and jewelry design. Accredited by the Council of Higher Education, the college is the chief source of personnel for Israel's fashion and apparel industry. *Shenkar News.*

AMERICAN COMMITTEE FOR THE BEER-SHEVA FOUNDATION (1988). 25 W. 45 St., Suite 1405, NYC 10036. (212)840-1166. FAX: (212) 840-1514. Pres. Ronald Slevin; Sr. V.-Pres. Joanna Slevin; Bd. Chmn. Sidney Cooperman. U.S. fundraising arm of the Beer-Sheva Foundation, which funds vital projects to improve the quality of life in the city of Beer-Sheva: nursery schools for pre-K toddlers, residential and day centers for needy seniors, educational programs, facilities and scholarships (especially for new olim, the physically and mentally challenged), parks, playgrounds, and other important projects. Also offers special services for immigrants—heaters, blankets, clothing, school supplies, etc. *Brochures.*

AMERICAN COMMITTEE FOR THE WEIZMANN INSTITUTE OF SCIENCE (1944). 51 Madison Ave., NYC 10010. (212)779-2500. FAX: (212)779-3209. E-mail: info@acwis.org. Chmn. Robert Asher; Pres. Albert Willner, M.D.; Exec. V.-Pres. Martin Kraar. Through 15 regional offices in the U.S. raises funds, disseminates information, and does American purchasing for the Weizmann Institute in Rehovot, Israel, a world-renowned center of scientific research and graduate study. The institute conducts research in disease, energy, the environment, and other areas; runs an international summer science program for gifted high-school students. *Interface; Weizmann Now; annual report.* (WWW.WEIZMANN-USA.ORG)

AMERICAN FRIENDS OF ASSAF HAROFEH MEDICAL CENTER (1975). PO Box 21051, NYC 10129. (212)481-5653. FAX: (212)481-5672. Chmn. Kenneth Kroned; Exec. Dir. Rhoda Levental; Treas. Robert Kastin. Support group for Assaf Harofeh, Israel's third-largest government hospital, serving a poor population of over 400,000 in the area between Tel Aviv and Jerusalem. Raises funds for medical equipment, medical training for immigrants, hospital expansion, school of nursing, and school of physiotherapy. *Newsletter.*

AMERICAN FRIENDS OF BAR-ILAN UNIVERSITY (1955). 91 Fifth Ave., Suite 200, NYC 10003. (212)337-1270. FAX: (212)337-1274. Chancellor Rabbi Emanuel Rackman; Chmn. Global Bd. of Trustees Selik Wengrowsky; Pres. Amer. Bd. of Trustees Jane Stern Lebell; Exec. V.-Pres. Gen. Yehuda Halevy. Supports Bar-Ilan University, an institution that integrates the highest standards of contemporary scholarship in liberal arts and sciences with a Judaic studies program as a requirement. Located in Ramat-Gan, Israel, and chartered by the Board of Regents of the State of NY. *Bar-Ilan News; Bar-Ilan University Scholar.*

AMERICAN FRIENDS OF BETH HATEFUTSOTH (1976). 633 3rd Ave., 21st fl., NYC 10017. (212)339-6034. FAX: (212)318-6176. E-mail: afbhusa@aol.com. Pres. Stephen Greenberg; Chmn. Sam E. Bloch; Exec. Dir. Gloria Golan. Supports the maintenance and development of Beth Hatefutsoth, the Nahum Goldmann Museum of the Jewish Diaspora in Tel Aviv, and its cultural and educational programs for youth and adults. Circulates its traveling exhibitions and provides various cultural programs to local Jewish communities. Includes Jewish genealogy center (DOROT), the center for Jewish music, and photodocumentation center. *Beth Hatefutsoth quarterly newsletter.*

AMERICAN FRIENDS OF HAIFA UNIVERSITY (*see* American Society of the University of Haifa)

AMERICAN FRIENDS OF HERZOG HOSPITAL/EZRATH NASHIN-JERUSALEM (1895). 800 Second Ave., 8th fl., NYC 10017. (212)499-9092. FAX:(212)499-9085. E-mail:saraherzog@aol.com. Pres. Rabbi Gilbert Epstein; Exec. Dir. David Cohen. Jerusalem's third-largest hospital (330 beds) and Israel's leading geriatric-psychiatric treatment and research center. Comprehensive in- and out-patient clinics, departments of neuro- and psychogeriatrics, state-of-the-art rehabilitation department, specialized geriatric clinics, and community mental health center treating 16,000 patient visits annually. A teaching hospital affiliated with Hadassah-Hebrew University Medical Center, Bar-Ilan University, Baycrest Center for Geriatric Care (Toronto), and McGill University (Montreal).

AMERICAN FRIENDS OF LIKUD. 218 E. 79 St., NYC 10021-1214. (212) 650-1231. Pres. Jack B. Dweck.

AMERICAN FRIENDS OF NEVE SHALOM/WAHAT AL-SALAM (1988). 121 6th Ave., #507, NYC 10013. (212) 226-9246. FAX: (212) 226-6817. E-mail: sgoldberg7@compuserve.com. Pres. David Matz; V.-Pres. David Hitchcock; Exec. Dir. Stephen Goldberg. Supports this hilltop village, midway between Jerusalem and Tel Aviv, which is home to Jewish Muslim and Christian families who maintain their traditions while respecting and being enriched by those of the others. Democratic, egalitarian, and politically independent, its mission is to exemplify and teach the arts of peace. As a center for conflict resolution, offers unique encounter workshops, university courses, and training for youth and adults. *Biannual newsletters.*

AMERICAN FRIENDS OF RABIN MEDICAL CENTER (1994). 1328 Broadway, Suite 826, NYC 10001-2121. (212) 279-2522. Fax: (212)279-0179. E-mail: afrmcny@

jon.cjfny.org. Pres. Woody Goldberg. Supports the maintenance and development of this medical, research, and teaching institution in central Israel, which unites the Golda and Beilinson hospitals, providing 12% of all hospitalization in Israel. Department of Organ Transplantation performs 80% of all kidney and 60% of all liver transplants in Israel. Affiliated with Tel Aviv University's Sackler School of Medicine. New Directions Quarterly.

AMERICAN FRIENDS OF RAMBAM MEDICAL CENTER (1969). 850 Seventh Ave., Suite 305, NYC 10019. (212)397-1123. FAX: (212)397-1132. E-mail: 102177.647@compuserve.com. Pres. Michael R. Stoler; Exec. Dir. Abraham Unger. Represents and raises funds for Rambam Medical Center (Haifa), an 887-bed hospital serving approx. one-third of Israel's population, incl. the entire population of northern Israel (and south Lebanon), the U.S. Sixth Fleet, and the UN Peacekeeping Forces in the region. Rambam is the teaching hospital for the Technion's medical school. Quarterly newsletter.

AMERICAN FRIENDS OF TEL AVIV UNIVERSITY, INC. (1955). 360 Lexington Ave., NYC 10017. (212)687-5651. FAX: (212) 687-4085. Bd. Chmn. Alan L. Aufzien; Pres. Robert J. Topchik; Exec. V.-Pres. Stephen Lecker. Promotes higher education at Tel Aviv University, Israel's largest and most comprehensive institution of higher learning. Included in its nine faculties are the Sackler School of Medicine with its fully accredited NY State English-language program, the Rubin Academy of Music, and 70 research institutes including the Moshe Dayan Center for Middle East & African Studies and the Jaffe Center for Strategic Studies. Tel Aviv University News; FAX Flash.

AMERICAN FRIENDS OF THE HEBREW UNIVERSITY (1925; inc. 1931). 11 E. 69 St., NYC 10021. (212)472-9800. FAX: (212)744-2324. Pres. Keith L. Sachs; Bd. Chmn. Fred S. Lafer; Exec. V.-Pres. Adam Kahan. Fosters the growth, development, and maintenance of the Hebrew University of Jerusalem; collects funds and conducts informational programs throughout the U.S., highlighting the university's achievements and its significance. Wisdom; Scopus Magazine.

AMERICAN FRIENDS OF THE ISRAEL COMMUNITY DEVELOPMENT FOUNDATION (1990). 119 West 40 St., 14th fl., NYC 10018. (212)944-4884. FAX: (212)840-5206. E-mail: 75222.2142@compuserve.com. Pres. Barry Liben; Exec. Dir. Dina Shalit. Supports the ICDF, whose projects are primarily in Judea, Samaria, and Gaza, areas that have often not been eligible for funding from more established philanthropic agencies. ICDF provides funds for educational programs, community centers, medical clinics and first-aid emergency equipment, synagogues, and colleges, working in direct association with communities that request ICDF's assistance in raising funds, on a project-by-project basis. Eretz Israel Fund Report (quarterly).

AMERICAN FRIENDS OF THE ISRAEL MUSEUM (1972). 500 Fifth Ave., Suite 2540, NYC 10110. (212)997-5611. FAX: (212) 997-5536. Pres. Judy A. Steinhardt; Exec. Dir. Carolyn Cohen. Raises funds for special projects of the Israel Museum in Jerusalem; solicits works of art for permanent collection, exhibitions, and educational purposes. Newsletter.

AMERICAN FRIENDS OF THE ISRAEL PHILHARMONIC ORCHESTRA (AFIPO) (1972). 122 E. 42 St., Suite 4507, NYC 10168. (212)697-2949. FAX: (212)697-2943. Pres. Herman Sandler; Exec. Dir. Suzanne K. Ponsot. Works to secure the financial future of the orchestra so that it may continue to travel throughout the world bringing its message of peace and cultural understanding through music. Supports the orchestra's international touring program, educational projects, and a wide array of musical activities in Israel. Passport to Music (newsletter).

AMERICAN FRIENDS OF THE OPEN UNIVERSITY OF ISRAEL. 180 W. 80 St., NYC 10024. (212)712-1800. FAX: (212)496-3296. E-mail: afoui@aol.com. Natl. Chmn. Irving M. Rosenbaum; Exec. V.-Pres. Eric G. Heffler. Open Letter.

AMERICAN FRIENDS OF THE SHALOM HARTMAN INSTITUTE (1976). 42 E.69 St., Suite 401, NYC 10021. (212)772-9711. FAX: (212)772-9720. E-mail: afshi@banet.net. Pres. Richard F. Kaufman; Exec. V.-Pres. Staci Light; Admin. Dorothy Minchin. Supports the Shalom Hartman Institute, Jerusalem, an institute of higher education and research center devoted to applying the teachings of classical Judaism to the issues of modern life. Founded in 1976 by David Hartman, includes:the Institute for Advanced Judaic Studies with research centers in philosophy, theology, political thought, education, ethics, and Halakhah; the Institute for Judaic Educational Leadership, which focuses on teacher training; and the Institute for Diaspora Education, which offers seminars for rabbis, lay leadership, educators, and communal professionals.

AMERICAN FRIENDS OF THE TEL AVIV MUSEUM OF ART (1974). 133 E. 58 St., Suite 701, NYC 10022-1236. (212)319-0555. FAX: (212)754-2987. Chmn. Uzi Zucker; Exec. Dir. Barbara A. Lax. Raises funds for the Tel Aviv Museum of Art for special projects, art acquisitions, and exhibitions; seeks contributions of art to expand the museum's collection; encourages art loans and traveling exhibitions; creates an awareness of the museum in the USA; makes available exhibition catalogues, monthly calendars, and posters published by the museum.

AMERICAN-ISRAEL ENVIRONMENTAL COUNCIL (formerly COUNCIL FOR A BEAUTIFUL ISRAEL ENVIRONMENTAL EDUCATION FOUNDATION) (1973). c/o Perry Davis Assoc., 25 W. 45 St., Suite 1405, NYC 10036. (212)575-7530. Fax: (212)840-1514. Co-Pres. Mel Atlas, Edythe Roland Grodnick. A support group for the Israeli body, whose activities include education, town planning, lobbying for legislation to protect and enhance the environment, preservation of historical sites, the improvement and beautification of industrial and commercial areas, and sponsoring the CBI Center for Environmental Studies located in Yarkon Park, Tel Aviv. *Yearly newsletter; yearly theme oriented calendars in color.*

AMERICAN ISRAEL PUBLIC AFFAIRS COMMITTEE (AIPAC) (1954). 440 First St., NW, Washington, DC 20001. (202)639-5200. FAX: (202)347-4916. Pres. Lonny Kaplan; Exec. Dir. Howard A. Kohr. Registered to lobby on behalf of legislation affecting U.S.-Israel relations; represents Americans who believe support for a secure Israel is in U.S. interest. Works for a strong U.S.-Israel relationship. *Near East Report.* (WWW.AIPAC.ORG)

AMERICAN-ISRAELI LIGHTHOUSE, INC. (1928; reorg. 1955). 545 Madison Ave., Suite 600, NYC 10022. (212)838-5322. Pres. Mrs. Leonard F. Dank; Sec. Mrs. Ida Rhein. Provides a vast network of programs and services for blind and physically handicapped persons throughout Israel, to effect their social and vocational integration into the mainstream of their communities. Center of Services for the blind; built and maintains Rehabilitation Center for blind and handicapped persons (Migdal Or) in Haifa.

AMERICAN JEWISH LEAGUE FOR ISRAEL (1957). 130 E. 59 St., NYC 10022. (212)371-1583. FAX: (212)371-3265. E-mail: AJLImlk@aol.com. Pres. Dr. Martin L. Kalmanson; Exec. Dir. Judith Struhl. Seeks to unite all those who, notwithstanding differing philosophies of Jewish life, are committed to the historical ideals of Zionism; works independently of class, party, or religious affiliation for the welfare of Israel as a whole. Not identified with any political parties in Israel. Member of World Jewish Congress, World Zionist Organization, American Zionist Movement. *Newsletter.*

AMERICAN PHYSICIANS FELLOWSHIP FOR MEDICINE IN ISRAEL (1950). 2001 Beacon St., Suite 210, Brighton, MA 02135-7771. (617)232-5382. FAX: (617) 739-2616. E-mail: apf@apfmed.org. Pres. Sherwood L. Gorbach, M.D.; Exec. Dir. Donald J. Perlstein. Supports projects that advance medical education, research, and care in Israel and builds links between the medical communities of Israel and N. Amer.; provides fellowships for Israeli physicians training in N. Amer. and arranges lectureships in Israel by prominent N. Amer. physicians; sponsors CME seminars in Israel and N. Amer.; coordinates U.S./Canadian medical emergency volunteers for Israel. *APF News.*

AMERICAN RED MAGEN DAVID FOR ISRAEL, INC. (1940) (a.k.a. ARMDI & Red Magen David). 888 Seventh Ave., Suite 403, NYC 10106. (212)757-1627. FAX: (212)757-4662. E-mail: armdi@juno.com. Natl. Pres. Robert L. Sadoff, M.D.; Exec. V.-Pres. Benjamin Saxe. An authorized tax-exempt organization; the sole support arm in the U.S. of Magen David Adom (MDA), Israel's equivalent to a Red Cross Society; raises funds for the MDA emergency medical, ambulance, blood, and disaster services which help Israel's defense forces and civilian population. Helps to supply and equip ambulances, bloodmobiles, and cardiac rescue ambulances as well as 45 prehospital MDA Emergency Medical Clinics and the MDA National Blood Service Center and MDA Fractionation Institute in Ramat Gan, Israel. *Lifeline.*

AMERICANS FOR A SAFE ISRAEL (AFSI) (1971). 1623 Third Ave., Suite 205, NYC 10128. (212)828-2424. FAX: (212)828-1717. E-mail: afsi@interport.net. Chmn. Herbert Zweibon. Seeks to educate Americans in Congress, the media, and the public about Israel's role as a strategic asset for the West; through meetings with legislators and the media, in press releases and publications AFSI promotes Jewish rights to Judea and Samaria and the concept of "peace for peace" as an alternative to "territory for peace." *Outpost.*

AMERICANS FOR PEACE NOW (1984). 1835 K St., NW, Suite 500, Washington, DC 20006. (212)728-1893. FAX: (212)728-1895. E-mail: apndc@peacenow.org. Pres. & CEO Debra DeLee; Chmn. Pat Barr. Conducts educational programs and raises funds to support the Israeli peace movement, Shalom Achshav (Peace Now), and coordinates U.S. advocacy efforts through APN's Washington-based Center for Israeli Peace and Security. *Jerusalem Watch; Peace Now News; Settlement Watch; Fax Facts; Middle East Update (on-line); Benefits of Peace.* (WWW.PEACENOW.ORG)

AMERICAN SOCIETY FOR TECHNION-ISRAEL INSTITUTE OF TECHNOLOGY (1940). 810 Seventh Ave., 24th fl., NYC 10019. (212)262-6200. FAX: (212)262-6155. Pres. Lawrence Jackier; Chmn. Irving A. Shepard; Exec. V.-Pres. Melvyn H. Bloom. Supports the work of the Technion-Israel Institute of Technology in Haifa, which trains over 13,000 students in 19 faculties and a medical school, and conducts research across a broad spectrum of science and technology. *Technion USA.*

AMERICAN SOCIETY FOR THE PROTECTION OF NATURE IN ISRAEL, INC. (1986). 28 Arrandale Ave., Great Neck, NY 11024. (212) 398-6750. FAX: (212) 398-1665. E-mail: aspni@aol.com. Cochmn. Edward I. Geffner, Russell Rothman. A nonprofit organization supporting the work of SPNI, an Israeli organization devoted to environmental protection and nature education. SPNI runs 26 Field Study Centers and has 45 municipal offices throughout Israel; offers education programs, organized hikes, and other activities; seeks ways to address the needs of an expanding society while preserving precious natural resources. *SPNI News.*

AMERICAN SOCIETY FOR YAD VASHEM (1981). 500 Fifth Ave., Suite 1600, NYC 10110-1699. (212)220-4304. FAX: (212) 220-4308. E-mail: yadvashem@aol.com. Chmn. Eli Zborowski; Exec. Dir. Selma Schiffer. Development arm of Yad Vashem, Jerusalem, the central international authority created by the Knesset in 1953 for the purposes of commemoration and education in connection with the Holocaust. *Martyrdom and Resistance (newsletter).* (WWW.YADVASHEM.ORG)

AMERICAN SOCIETY OF THE UNIVERSITY OF HAIFA (formerly AMERICAN FRIENDS OF HAIFA UNIVERSITY) (1972). c/o Lester Schwab Katz & Dwyer, Att.: Robert J. Benowitz, 120 Broadway, Suite 3800, NYC 10271-0071. (212)964-6611. FAX: (212)267-5916. Pres. Paul Amir; Sec./Treas. Robert Jay Benowitz. Promotes, encourages, and aids higher and secondary education, research, and training in all branches of knowledge in Israel and elsewhere; aids in the maintenance and development of Haifa University; raises and allocates funds for the above purposes; provides scholarships; promotes exchanges of teachers and students.

AMERICAN ZIONIST MOVEMENT (formerly AMERICAN ZIONIST FEDERATION) (1939; reorg. 1949, 1970, 1993). 110 E. 59 St., NYC 10022. (212)318-6100. FAX: (212) 935-3578. E-mail: staff@azm.com. Pres. Melvin Salberg; Exec. Dir. Karen J. Rubinstein. Umbrella organization for 20 American Zionist organizations and the voice of unified Zionism in the U.S. Conducts advocacy for Israel; strengthens Jewish identity; promotes the Israel experience; prepares the next generation of Zionist leadership. Regional offices in Chicago, Los Angeles, Detroit, South Florida. Groups in Atlanta, Philadelphia, Baltimore, Pittsburgh, Washington, DC. *The Zionist Advocate.*

AMIT (1925). 817 Broadway, NYC 10003. (212)477-4720. FAX: (212)353-2312. Pres. Evelyn Blachor; Exec. Dir. Marvin Leff. The State of Israel's official reshet (network) for religious secondary technological education; maintains innovative children's homes and youth villages in Israel in an environment of traditional Judaism; promotes cultural activities for the purpose of disseminating Zionist ideals and strengthening traditional Judaism in America. *AMIT Magazine.*

AMPAL-AMERICAN ISRAEL CORPORATION (1942). 1177 Avenue of the Americas, NYC 10036. (212)782-2100. FAX: (212) 782-2114. E-mail: ampal@aol.com. Bd. Chmn. Daniel Steinmetz; CEO Shuki Gleitman. Acquires interests in businesses located in the State of Israel or that are Israel-related. Interests include leisure-time, real estate, finance, energy distribution, basic industry, high technology, and communications. *Annual report; quarterly reports.*

ARZA/WORLD UNION, NORTH AMERICA (1977). 633 Third Ave., 6th fl., NYC 10017-6778. (212)650-4280. FAX: (212)650-4289. E-mail: arza/wupjna@uahc.org. Pres. Philip Meltzer; Exec. Dir. Rabbi Ammiel Hirsch. Membership organization dedicated to furthering the development of Progressive Judaism in Israel, the FSU, and throughout the world. Encourages Jewish solidarity, promoting religious pluralism and furthering Zionism. Works to strengthen the relationship of N. American Reform Jews with Progressive Jewish communities worldwide and to educate and inform them on relevant issues. *Quarterly newsletter.*

BETAR ZIONIST YOUTH ORGANIZATION (1935). 218 E. 79 St., NYC 10021. (212) 650-1231. FAX: (212) 650-1413. North American Central Shlicha Sharon Tzur. Organizes youth groups across North America to teach Zionism, Jewish identity, and love of Israel; sponsors summer programs in Israel for Jewish youth ages 14-22; sponsors Tagar Zionist Student Activist Movement on college campuses.

BOYS TOWN JERUSALEM FOUNDATION OF AMERICA INC. (1948). 91 Fifth Ave., Suite 601, NYC 10003. (212)242-1118, (800) 469-2697. FAX: (212)242-2190. E-mail: 74230.3450@compuserve.com. Pres. Michael J. Scharf; Chmn. Josh S. Weston;

V.-Chmn. Moshe Linchner; Exec. V.-Pres. Rabbi Ronald L. Gray. Raises funds for Boys Town Jerusalem, which was established in 1948 to offer a comprehensive academic, religious, and technological education to disadvantaged Israeli and immigrant boys from over 45 different countries, including Ethiopia, the former Soviet Union, and Iran. Enrollment:over 1,000 students in jr. high school, academic and technical high school, and a college of applied engineering. *BTJ Newsbriefs; Your Town Magazine.*

CAMERA-COMMITTEE FOR ACCURACY IN MIDDLE EAST REPORTING IN AMERICA (1983). PO Box 428, Boston, MA 02456. (617)789-3672. FAX: (617)787-7853. E-mail: media@camera.org. Pres./Exec. Dir. Andrea Levin; Chmn. Leonard Wisse. Monitors and responds to media distortion in order to promote better understanding of Middle East events; urges members to alert Israel and the media to errors, omissions, and distortions. *CAMERA Media Report (quarterly); CAMERA on Campus; Action Alerts; Media Directories; Monographs.*

COUNCIL FOR A BEAUTIFUL ISRAEL ENVIRONMENTAL EDUCATION FOUNDATION (*see* American-Israel Environmental Council)

EMUNAH OF AMERICA (formerly HAPOEL HAMIZRACHI WOMEN'S ORGANIZATION) (1948). 7 Penn Plaza, NYC 10001. (212)564-9045, (800)368-6440. FAX: (212)643-9731. E-mail: info@emunah. org. Natl. Pres. Dr. Sylvia Schonfeld; Exec. V.-Pres. Shirley Singer. Maintains and supports 200 educational and social-welfare institutions in Israel within a religious framework, including day-care centers, kindergartens, children's residential homes, vocational schools for the underprivileged, senior-citizen centers, a college complex, and Holocaust study center. Also involved in absorption of Soviet and Ethiopian immigrants (recognized by Israeli government as an official absorption agency). *Emunah Magazine; Lest We Forget.*

FEDERATED COUNCIL OF ISRAEL INSTITUTIONS—FCII (1940). 4702 15th Ave., Brooklyn, NY 11219. (718)972-5530. Bd. Chmn. Z. Shapiro; Exec. V.-Pres. Rabbi Julius Novack. Central fund-raising organization for over 100 affiliated institutions; handles and executes estates, wills, and bequests for the traditional institutions in Israel; clearinghouse for information on budget, size, functions, etc. of traditional educational, welfare, and philanthropic institutions in Israel, working cooperatively with the Israeli government and the overseas department of the Council of Jewish Federations. *Annual financial reports and statistics on affiliates.*

FRIENDS OF THE ISRAEL DEFENSE FORCES (1981). 21 W. 38 St., 5th fl., NYC 10018. (212)575-5030. FAX: (212)575-7815. E-mail: fidf@fidf.com. Chmn. Marvin Josephson; Pres. Jay Zises; Natl. Dir. Brig. Gen. Eliezer Hemeli. Supports the Agudah Lema'an Hahayal, Israel's Assoc. for the Well-Being of Soldiers, founded in the early 1940s, which provides social, recreational, and educational programs for soldiers, special services for the sick and wounded, and summer programs for widows and children of fallen soldiers.

GESHER FOUNDATION (1969). 421 Seventh Ave., #611, NYC 10001. (212) 564-0338. FAX: (212)967-2726. Chmn. Philip Schatten; Exec. V.-Pres. Hillel Wiener. Seeks to bridge the gap between Jews of various backgrounds in Israel by stressing the interdependence of all Jews. Runs encounter seminars for Israeli youth; distributes curricular materials in public schools; offers Jewish identity classes for Russian youth, and a video series in Russian and English on famous Jewish personalities.

GIVAT HAVIVA EDUCATIONAL FOUNDATION, INC. (1966). 114 W. 26 St., Suite 1001, NYC 10001. (212)989-9272. FAX: (212) 989-9840. E-mail: mail@givathaviva.org. Chmn. Henry Ostberg. Supports programs at the Givat Haviva Institute, Israel's leading organization dedicated to promoting coexistence between Arabs and Jews, with 40,000 people participating each year in programs teaching conflict resolution, Middle East studies and languages, and Holocaust studies. Publishes research papers on Arab-Jewish relations, Holocaust studies, kibbutz life. In the U.S., GHEF sponsors public-education programs and lectures by Israeli speakers. *Givat Haviva News; special reports.*

HABONIM-DROR NORTH AMERICA (1935). 114 W. 26 St., Suite 1004, NYC 10001-

6812. (212)255-1796. FAX: (212)929-3459. E-mail: mazkir@habonimdror.org. Mazkir Tnua Jared Matas; Shaliach David Lehrer. Fosters identification with progressive, cooperative living in Israel; stimulates study of Jewish and Zionist culture, history, and contemporary society; sponsors summer and year programs in Israel and on kibbutz, 7 summer camps in N. America modeled after kibbutzim, and aliyah frameworks. *Batnua (on-line newsletter).*

HADASSAH, THE WOMEN'S ZIONIST ORGANIZATION OF AMERICA, INC. (1912). 50 W. 58 St., NYC 10019. (212)355-7900. FAX: (212)303-8282. Pres. Marlene E. Post; Exec. Dir. Dr. Laura S. Schor. Largest women's, largest Jewish, and largest Zionist membership organization in U.S. Founded and funds Hadassah Medical Organization in Jerusalem, as well as Hadassah College of Technology, Hadassah Career Counseling Institute, summer and year-course Young Judaea youth movement programs. U.S. programs: Jewish and health education; leadership training; advocacy on Israel; Zionism and women's issues; and Young Judaea, largest Zionist movement in U.S., including six summer camps. *Hadassah Magazine; Heart & Soul; Update; Hadassah International Newsletter; Medical Update; American Scene.*

———, YOUNG JUDAEA (1909; reorg. 1967). 50 W. 58 St., NYC 10019. (212)303-4575. FAX: (212)303-4572. Natl. Dir. Doron Krakow. Religiously pluralist, politically nonpartisan Zionist youth movement sponsored by Hadassah; seeks to educate Jewish youth aged 8-25 toward Jewish and Zionist values, active commitment to and participation in the American and Israeli Jewish communities; maintains six summer camps in the U.S.; runs both summer and year programs in Israel, and a jr. year program in connection with both Hebrew University in Jerusalem and Ben Gurion University of Negev. College-age arm, Hamagshimim, supports Zionist activity on campuses. *Kol Hat'nua; The Young Judaean; Ad Kahn.*

HASHOMER HATZAIR, SOCIALIST ZIONIST YOUTH MOVEMENT (1923). 114 W. 26 St., Suite 1001, NYC 10001. (212)868-0377. FAX: (212)868-0364. E-mail: mail@ hashomerhatzair.org. Pres. Gavri Bar-Gil; Natl. Sec. Edo Navot & Alex Dubin; Dir.

Amnon Ophir. Seeks to educate Jewish youth to an understanding of Zionism as the national liberation movement of the Jewish people. Promotes aliyah to kibbutzim. Affiliated with AZYF and Kibbutz Artzi Federation. Espouses socialist-Zionist ideals of peace, justice, democracy, and intergroup harmony. *Young Guard.*

INTERNS FOR PEACE (NITZANEI SHALOM/ BARA'EM AS'SALAAM/BUDS OF PEACE) (1976). 475 Riverside Dr., 16th fl., NYC 10115. (212)870-2226. FAX: (212)870-2119. Internatl. Dir. Rabbi Bruce M. Cohen; Natl. Dir. Karen Wald Cohen. An independent, nonprofit, nonpolitical educational program training professional community peace workers. In Israel, initiated and operated jointly by Jews and Arabs; over 190 interns trained in 35 cities; over 80,000 Israeli citizens participating in joint programs in education, sports, culture, business, women's affairs, and community development; since the peace accord, Palestinians from West Bank and Gaza training as interns. Martin Luther King Project for Black/Jewish relations. *IFP Reports Quarterly; Guidebooks for Ethnic Conflict Resolution.*

ISRAEL CANCER RESEARCH FUND (1975). 1290 Avenue of the Americas, NYC 10104. (212)969-9800. FAX: (212)969-9822. Pres. Dr. Yashar Hirshaut; Chmn. Leah Susskind; Exec. Dir. Milton Sussman. The largest single source of private funds for cancer research in Israel. Has a threefold mission: to encourage innovative cancer research by Israeli scientists; to harness Israel's vast intellectual and creative resources to establish a world-class center for cancer study; to broaden research opportunities within Israel to stop the exodus of talented Israeli cancer researchers. *Annual Report; Research Awards; Glossary; Newsletter.*

ISRAEL HISTADRUT FOUNDATION (*see* Israel Humanitarian Foundation)

ISRAEL HUMANITARIAN FOUNDATION (formerly ISRAEL HISTADRUT FOUNDATION) (1960). 276 Fifth Ave., Suite 901, NYC 10001. (212)683-5676, (800)443-5699. FAX: (212)213-9233. E-mail: info@ihf. net. Pres. Marvin M. Sirota; Exec. V.-Pres. Stanley J. Abrams. Nonprofit American philanthropic organization that supports humanitarian needs in Is-

rael; strives to improve the standard of living of Israel's population in need through its support of education, general health and neonatal care, medical and cancer research, the elderly, disabled and youth-in-need. *Impact.*

ISRAEL POLICY FORUM (1993). 666 Fifth Ave., 21st fl., NYC 10103. (212)245-4227. FAX: (212)245-0517. E-mail: ipforum@ aol.com. 1030 15 St., NW, Suite 850, Washington, DC 20005. (202)842-1700. FAX:(202)842-1722. E-mail: mail@ipforum.org. Chmn. Michael W. Sonnenfeldt; Pres. Jack Bendheim; Exec. V.-Pres. Jonathan Jacoby. An independent leadership institution whose mission is to create greater awareness of the security and economic benefits of the Middle East peace process and to support an active U.S. role in resolving the Arab-Israeli conflict. IPF generates this support by involving leaders from the business, political, entertainment, academic, and philanthropic communitites in the peace effort, and by fostering a deeper understanding of the peace process among the American public. *Policy Paper; Security Watch.*

THE JERUSALEM FOUNDATION, INC. (1966). 60 E. 42 St., Suite 1936, New York City 10165. (212) 697-4188. FAX: (212) 697-4022. E-mail: bdubin@jfoundation.com. Pres. Michael Neiditch; Chmn. Alvin Einbender; Acting Dir. Sandra Rubin. A nonprofit organization devoted to improving the quality of life for all Jerusalemites, regardless of ethnic, religious, or socioeconomic background; has initiated and implemented more than 1,500 projects that span education, culture, community services, beautification, and preservation of the city's historic heritage and religious sites.

JEWISH INSTITUTE FOR NATIONAL SECURITY AFFAIRS (JINSA) (1976). 1717 K St., NW, Suite 800, Washington, DC 20006. (202)833-0020. FAX: (202)296-6452. E-mail: info@jinsa.org. Pres. Norman Hascoe; Exec. Dir. Tom Neumann. A nonprofit, nonpartisan educational organization working within the American Jewish community to explain the link between American defense policy and the security of the State of Israel; and within the national security establishment to explain the key role Israel plays in bolstering American interests. (WWW.JINSA.ORG)

JEWISH INSTITUTE FOR THE BLIND-JERUSALEM, INC. (1902, Jerusalem). 15 E. 26 St., NYC 10010. (212) 532-4155. FAX: (212) 447-7683. Pres. Rabbi David E. Lapp; Admin. Eric L. Loeb. Supports a dormitory and school for the Israeli blind and handicapped in Jerusalem. *INsight.*

JEWISH NATIONAL FUND OF AMERICA (1901). 42 E. 69 St., NYC 10021. (212)879-9300. (1-800-542-TREE). FAX: (212)517-3293. E-mail: jnfcomm@ aol.com. Pres. Ronald S. Lauder; Exec. V.-Pres. Russell F. Robinson. The American fund-raising arm of Keren Kayemeth Leisrael, the official land agency in Israel; supports KKL in reclamation of land for planting and forestry; environmental concerns; water conservation; recreation and agriculture; employment of new immigrants; tourism; and research and development.

JEWISH PEACE LOBBY (1989). 8604 Second Ave., Suite 317, Silver Spring, MD 20910. (301)589-8764. FAX: (301)589-2722. Pres. Jerome M. Segal. A legally registered lobby promoting changes in U.S. policy vis-a-vis the Israeli-Palestinian conflict. Supports Israel's right to peace within secure borders; a political settlement based on mutual recognition of the right of self-determination of both peoples; a two-state solution as the most likely means to a stable peace. *Washington Action Alerts.*

KEREN OR, INC. JERUSALEM CENTER FOR MULTI-HANDICAPPED BLIND CHILDREN (1956). 350 Seventh Ave., Suite 200, NYC 10001. (212)279-4070. FAX: (212)279-4043. Chmn. Dr. Edward L. Steinberg; Pres. Dr. Albert Hornblass; Exec. Dir. Sheila E. Stein. Funds the Keren-Or Center for Multi-Handicapped Blind Children at 3 Abba Hillel Silver St., Ramot, Jerusalem, housing and caring for over 70 resident and day students who in addition to blindness or very low vision suffer from other severe physical and/or mental disabilities. Students range in age from 1 1/2 through young adulthood. Provides training in daily living skills, as well as therapy, rehabilitation, and education to the optimum level of the individual. *Insights Newsletter.*

LABOR ZIONIST ALLIANCE (formerly FARBAND LABOR ZIONIST ORDER; also incorporating Poale Zion-United Labor Zionist Organization of America and American Habonim Association) (1913). 275 Seventh Ave., NYC 10001. (212)366-1194. FAX: (212)675-7685. E-mail: Lab Zion@aol.com. Pres. Daniel Mann; Admin. Stephane Acel. Seeks to enhance Jewish life, culture, and education in U.S.; aids in building State of Israel as a cooperative commonwealth and its Labor movement organized in the Histadrut; supports efforts toward a more democratic society throughout the world; furthers the democratization of the Jewish community in America and the welfare of Jews everywhere; works with labor and liberal forces in America; sponsors Habonim-Dror labor Zionist youth movement. *Jewish Frontier; Yiddisher Kempfer.*

MACCABI USA/SPORTS FOR ISRAEL (formerly UNITED STATES COMMITTEE SPORTS FOR ISRAEL) (1948). 1926 Arch St., 4R, Philadelphia, PA 19103. (215)561-6900. Fax: (215)561-5470. E-mail: maccabi @maccabiusa.com. Pres. Robert E. Spivak; Exec. Dir. Barbara G. Lissy. Sponsors U.S. team for World Maccabiah Games in Israel every four years; seeks to enrich the lives of Jewish youth in the U.S., Israel, and the Diaspora through athletic, cultural, and educational programs; develops, promotes, and supports international, national, and regional athletic-based activities and facilities. *Sportscene Newsletter; commemorative Maccabiah Games journal; financial report.* (WWW.MACCABIUSA.COM)

MERCAZ USA (1979). 155 Fifth Ave., NYC 10010. (212)533-7800, ext. 2016. FAX: (212)533-2601. E-mail: mercaz@compuserve.com. Pres. Evelyn Seelig; Exec. Dir. Rabbi Robert R. Golub. The U.S. Zionist organization for Conservative/Masorti Judaism; works for religious pluralism in Israel, defending and promoting Conservative/Masorti institutions and individuals; fosters Zionist education and *aliyah* and develops young leadership. *Mercaz News & Views.* (WWW.MERCAZUSA. ORG)

MERETZ USA FOR ISRAELI CIVIL RIGHTS AND PEACE (1991). 114 W. 26 St., Suite 1002, NYC 10001. (212)242-4500. FAX: (212)242-5718. E-mail: meretzusa@aol. com. Pres. Harold M. Shapiro; Chmn. Stefi L. Kirschner; Exec. Dir. Charney V. Bromberg. A forum for addressing the issues of social justice and peace in Israel. Educates about issues related to democracy, human and civil rights, religious pluralism, and equality for women and ethnic minorities; promotes the resolution of Israel's conflict with the Palestinians on the basis of mutual recognition, self-determination, and peaceful coexistence. *Israel Horizons*.

NA'AMAT USA, THE WOMEN'S LABOR ZIONIST ORGANIZATION OF AMERICA, INC. (formerly PIONEER WOMEN/NA'AMAT) (1925). 200 Madison Ave., 21st fl., NYC 10016. (212)725-8010. FAX: (212)447-5187. E-mail: naamat@naamat.org. Natl. Pres.Dina Spector; Exec. Dir. Sheila Guston. Part of the World Movement of Na'amat (movement of working women and volunteers), the largest Jewish women's organization in the world, Na'amat USA helps provide social, educational, and legal services for women, teenagers, and children in Israel. It also advocates legislation for women's rights and child welfare in Israel and the U.S., furthers Jewish education, and supports Habonim Dror, the Labor Zionist youth movement. *Na'amat Woman magazine.* (WWW.NAAMAT.ORG)

NATIONAL COMMITTEE FOR LABOR ISRAEL (1923). 275 Seventh Ave., NYC 10001. (212)647-0300. FAX: (212)647-0308. E-mail: laborisrael@jon.cjfny.org. Pres. Jay Mazur; Exec. Dir. Jerry Goodman; Chmn. Trade Union Council Morton Bahr. Brings together diverse groups-Jews and non-Jews-to build support for Israel and advance closer Arab-Israel ties. Conducts educational and communal activities in the Jewish community and among labor groups to promote better relations with labor Israel. Israel Histadrut Campaign raises funds for youth, educational, health, social, and cultural projects. *Occasional background papers.* (www.LABORISRAEL.ORG)

NEW ISRAEL FUND (1979). 1625 K St., NW, Suite 500, Washington, DC 20006. (202)223-3333. FAX: (202)659-2789. E-mail: info@nif.org; www.nif.org. New York office:165 E. 56 St., NYC 10022. (212)750-2333. FAX: (212)750-8043. Pres. Franklin Fisher; Exec. Dir. Norman S. Rosenberg. A partnership of Israelis and North Americans dedicated to promoting social justice, coexistence, and pluralism in Israel, the New Israel Fund helps strengthen Israeli democracy by providing grants and technical assistance to the public-interest sector, cultivating a new generation of social activists, and educating citizens in Israel and the Diaspora about the challenges to Israeli democracy. *Quarterly newsletter; annual report.* (WWW.NIF.ORG)

PEC ISRAEL ECONOMIC CORPORATION (formerly PALESTINE ECONOMIC CORPORATION) (1926). 511 Fifth Ave., NYC 10017. (212)687-2400. Chmn. O. Recanati; Pres. Frank J. Klein; Exec. V.-Pres. James I. Edelson; Treas. William Gold. Primarily engaged in the business of organizing, acquiring interest in, financing, and participating in the management of companies located in the State of Israel or Israel-related. *Annual and quarterly reports.*

PEF ISRAEL ENDOWMENT FUNDS, INC. (1922). 317 Madison Ave., Suite 607, NYC 10017. (212)599-1260. Chmn. Sidney A. Luria; Pres. B. Harrison Frankel; Sec. Harvey Brecher. A totally volunteer organization that makes grants to educational, scientific, social, religious, health, and other philanthropic institutions in Israel. *Annual report.*

PIONEER WOMEN/NA'AMAT (*see* NA'AMAT USA)

POALE AGUDATH ISRAEL OF AMERICA, INC. (1948). 2920 Avenue J, Brooklyn, NY 11210. (718)258-2228. FAX: (718)258-2288. Pres. Rabbi Fabian Schonfeld. Aims to educate American Jews to the values of Orthodoxy and aliyah; supports kibbutzim, trade schools, yeshivot, moshavim, kollelim, research centers, and children's homes in Israel. *PAI News; She'arim; Hamayan.*

———, WOMEN'S DIVISION OF (1948). Pres. Miriam Lubling; Presidium: Sarah Ivanisky, Tili Stark, Peppi Petzenbaum. Assists Poale Agudath Israel to build and support children's homes, kindergartens, and trade schools in Israel. *Yediot PAI.*

PRO ISRAEL (1990). 17 E. 45 St., Suite 603, NYC 10017. (212)867-0577. FAX: (212)867-0615. E-mail: proisrael@aol. com. Pres. Dr. Ernest Bloch. Educates the public about Israel and the Middle East; provides support for community development throughout the Land of Israel, particularly in Judea, Samaria, Gaza, and the Golan Heights. Projects include the Ariel Center for Policy Research in Samaria, support for various communities, and a research and information center. Umbrella organization for 7 affiliate groups:in Israel-Aliyah for the Land of Israel Movement, Generals of "Gamla Won't Fall a Second Time," Internatl. Rabbinic Coalition for Israel, IDF Officers for National Strength, Professors for a Strong Israel; in U.S.-American Academics for Israel's Future, Operation Chizuk.

PROJECT NISHMA (*see* ISRAEL POLICY FORUM)

RELIGIOUS ZIONISTS OF AMERICA. 25 W. 26 St., NYC 10010. (212)689-1414. FAX: (212)779-3043.

———, BNEI AKIVA OF THE U.S. & CANADA (1934). 25 W. 26 St., NYC 10010. (212)889-5260. FAX: (212)213-3053. Exec. Dir. Judi Srebro. The only religious Zionist youth movement in North America, serving over 10,000 young people from grade school through graduate school in 16 active regions across the United States and Canada, six summer camps, seven established summer, winter, and year programs in Israel. Stresses communal involvement, social activism, leadership training, and substantive programming to educate young people toward a commitment to Judaism and Israel. *Akivon; Pinkas Lamadrich; Daf Rayonot; Me'Ohalai Torah; Zraim.*

———, MIZRACHI-HAPOEL HAMIZRACHI (1909; merged 1957). 25 W. 26 St., NYC 10010. (212)689-1414. FAX: (212)779-3043. Pres. Dr. Morris L. Green; Exec. V.-Pres. Israel Friedman. Disseminates ideals of religious Zionism; conducts cultural work, educational program, public relations; raises funds for religious educational institutions in Israel, including yeshivot hesder and Bnei Akiva. *Newsletters; Kolenu.*

———, NATIONAL COUNCIL FOR TORAH EDUCATION OF MIZRACHI-HAPOEL HAM'IZRACHI (1939). 25 W. 26 St., NYC 10010. Pres. Rabbi Israel Schorr. Organizes and supervises yeshivot and Talmud Torahs; prepares and trains teachers; publishes textbooks and educational materials; organizes summer seminars for Hebrew educators in cooperation with Torah Department of Jewish Agency; conducts ulpan. *Hazarkor; Chemed.*

SCHNEIDER CHILDREN'S MEDICAL CENTER OF ISRAEL (1982). 130 E. 59 St., Suite 1203, NYC 10022. (212)759-3370. FAX: (212)759-0120. E-mail: mdiscmci@aol. com. Bd. Chmn. H. Irwin Levy; Exec. Dir. Shlomit Manson. Its primary goal is to provide the best medical care to children in the Middle East. *UPDATE Newsletter.*

SOCIETY OF ISRAEL PHILATELISTS (1949). 24355 Tunbridge Lane, Beachwood, OH 44122. (216)292-3843. Pres Michael Kaltman; Journal Ed. Dr. Oscar Stadtler. Promotes interest in, and knowledge of, all phases of Israel philately through sponsorship of chapters and research groups, maintenance of a philatelic library, and support of public and private exhibitions. *The Israel Philatelist; monographs; books.*

STATE OF ISRAEL BONDS (1951). 575 Lexington Ave., #600, NYC 10022. (212)644-2663. FAX: (212)644-3887. E-mail: rothsteinr@aol.com. Bd. Chmn. William Belzberg; Pres. Gideon Patt; Internatl. Chmn. David B. Hermelin; Internatl. Campaign Chmn. Susan Welkers-Volchok; N. Amer. Chmn. Michael Siegal; Natl. Campaign Chmn. Burton P. Resnick. An international organization offering securities issued by the government of Israel. Since its inception in 1951 has secured $18 billion in investment capital for the development of every aspect of Israel's economic infrastructure, including agriculture, commerce, and industry, and for absorption of immigrants.

THEODOR HERZL FOUNDATION (1954). 110 E. 59 St., NYC 10022. (212)339-6000. FAX:(212)318-6176. Chmn. Kalman Sultanik; Sec. Sam E. Bloch. Offers cultural activities, lectures, conferences, courses in modern Hebrew and Jewish subjects, Israel, Zionism, and Jewish history. *Midstream.*

———, HERZL PRESS. Chmn. Kalman Sultanik; Dir. of Publications Sam E. Bloch. Serves as "the Zionist Press of record," publishing books that are important for the light they shed on Zionist philosophy, Israeli history, contemporary Israel and the Diaspora and the relationship between them. They are important as contributions to Zionist letters and history. *Midstream.*

TSOMET-TECHIYA USA (1978). 185 Montague St., 3rd fl., Brooklyn, NY 11201. (718)596-2119. FAX: (718)858-4074. E-mail: eliahu@aol.com. Central Committee Members:Honey Rackman, Elliot Jager, Melvin D. Shay, Howard B. Weber. Supports the activities of the Israeli Tsomet party, which advocates Israeli control over the entire Land of Israel.

UNITED CHARITY INSTITUTIONS OF JERUSALEM, INC. (1903). 1467 48 St., Brooklyn, NY 11219. (718)633-8469. FAX: (718)633-8478. Chmn. Rabbi Charlop; Exec. Dir. Rabbi Pollak. Raises funds for the maintenance of schools, kitchens, clinics, and dispensaries in Israel; free loan foundations in Israel.

UNITED ISRAEL APPEAL, INC. (1925). 111 Eighth Ave., Suite 11E, NYC 10011. (212)284-6500. FAX: (212)284-6835. Chmn. Bennett L. Aaron; Exec. V.-Chmn. Daniel R. Allen. Provides funds raised by UJA/Federation campaigns in the U.S. to aid the people of Israel through the programs of the Jewish Agency for Israel, UIA's operating agent. Serves as link between American Jewish community and Jewish Agency for Israel; assists in resettlement and absorption of refugees in Israel, and supervises flow and expenditure of funds for this purpose. *Annual report; newsletters; brochures.*

UNITED STATES COMMITTEE SPORTS FOR IS-REAL (*see* Maccabi USA/Sports for Israel)

US/ISRAEL WOMEN TO WOMEN (1978). 275 Seventh Ave., 8th fl., New York City 10001. (212) 206-8057. FAX: (212) 206-7031. E-mail: usisrw2w@aol.com. Chmn. Jewel Bellush; Exec. Dir. Joan Gordon. Provides critical seed money for grassroots efforts advocating equal status and fair treatment for women in all spheres of Israeli life; targets small, innovative, Israeli-run programs that seek to bring about social change in health, education, civil rights, domestic violence, family planning, and other spheres of Israeli life. *Newsletters.*

VOLUNTEERS FOR ISRAEL (1982). 330 W. 42 St., NYC 10036-6902. (212)643-4848. FAX: (212)643-4855. E-mail: vol4israel@aol.com. Pres. Rickey Cherner. Provides aid to Israel through volunteer work, building lasting relationships between Israelis and Americans. Affords persons aged 18 and over the opportunity to participate in various duties currently performed by overburdened Israelis on IDF bases and in other settings, enabling them to meet and work closely with Is-

raelis and to gain an inside view of Israeli life and culture. *Quarterly newsletter; information documents.*

WOMEN'S LEAGUE FOR ISRAEL, INC. (1928). 160 E. 56 St., NYC 10022. (212)838-1997. FAX: (212)888-5972. Pres. Harriet Lainer; Exec. Dir. Dorothy Leffler. Maintains centers in Haifa, Tel Aviv, Jerusalem, Nathanya. Projects include Family Therapy and Training Center, Centers for the Prevention of Domestic Violence, Meeting Places (supervised centers for noncustodial parents and their children), DROR (supporting families at risk), Yachdav-"Together" (long-term therapy for parents and children), Central School for Training Social Service Counselors, the National Library for Social Work, and the Hebrew University Blind Students' Unit.

WORLD CONFEDERATION OF UNITED ZIONISTS (1946; reorg. 1958). 130 E. 59 St., NYC 10022. (212)371-1452. FAX: (212)371-3265. Copres. Marlene Post, Kalman Sultanik. Promotes Zionist education, sponsors nonparty youth movements in the Diaspora, and strives for an Israel-oriented creative Jewish survival in the Diaspora. *Zionist Information Views (in English and Spanish).*

WORLD ZIONIST ORGANIZATION-AMERICAN SECTION (1971). 110 E. 59 St., NYC 10022. (212)688-3197. Chmn. Kalman Sultanik. As the American section of the overall Zionist body throughout the world, it operates primarily in the field of aliyah from the free countries, education in the Diaspora, youth and Hechalutz, organization and information, cultural institutions, publications; conducts a worldwide Hebrew cultural program including special seminars and pedagogic manuals; disperses information and assists in research projects concerning Israel; promotes, publishes, and distributes books, periodicals, and pamphlets concerning developments in Israel, Zionism, and Jewish history. *Midstream.*

——, DEPARTMENT OF EDUCATION AND CULTURE (1948). 110 E. 59 St., NYC 10022. (212)339-6001. FAX: (212)826-8959. Renders educational services to boards and schools: study programs, books, AV aids, instruction, teacher-intraining service. Judaic and Hebrew subjects. Annual National Bible Contest; Israel summer and winter programs for teachers and students.

———, ISRAEL ALIYAH CENTER (1993). 110 E. 59 St., 3rd fl., NYC 10022. (212)339-6060. FAX: (212)832-2597. Exec. Dir. N. Amer. Aliyah Delegation, Kalman Grossman. Through 26 offices throughout N. Amer., staffed by *shlichim* (emissaries), works with potential immigrants to plan their future in Israel and processes immigration documents. Through Israel Aliyah Program Center provides support, information, and programming for olim and their families; promotes long-term programs and fact-finding trips to Israel. Cooperates with Tnuat Aliyah in Jerusalem and serves as American contact with Association of Americans and Canadians in Israel.

YOUTH RENEWAL FUND. 165 E. 56 St., NYC 10022. (212)207-3195. FAX: (212)207-8379. E-mail: yrfny@aol.com. Pres. Samuel L. Katz; Dir. Karen B. Korn. Provides educational opportunities for underpriveleged youth in 10 programs throughout Israel. Initiates, develops, and implements supplemental education programs in core subjects including Math, Hebrew, English, and Computers in order to provide the skills necessary to pursue academic advancement. Committees in New York and in Israel *YRFlash.*

ZIONIST ORGANIZATION OF AMERICA (1897). ZOA House, 4 E. 34 St., NYC 10016. (212)481-1500. FAX: (212)481-1515. E-mail: email@zoa.com. Natl. Pres. Morton A. Klein; Exec. Dir. Bertram Korn, Jr. Strengthens the relationship between Israel and the U.S. through Zionist educational activities that explain Israel's importance to the U.S. and the dangers that Israel faces. Works on behalf of pro-Israel legislation; combats anti-Israel bias in the media, textbooks, travel guides, and on campuses; promotes *aliyah.* Maintains the ZOA House in Tel Aviv, a cultural center, and the Kfar Silver Agricultural and Technical High School in Ashkelon, which provides vocational training for new immigrants. ZOA *Report; Israel and the Middle East:Behind the Headlines.*

OVERSEAS AID

AMERICAN FRIENDS OF THE ALLIANCE IS-RAÉLITE UNIVERSELLE, INC. (1946). 420 Lexington Ave., Suite 1733, NYC 10170. (212)808-5437. FAX: (212)983-0094. Pres.

Henriette Beilis; Exec. Dir. Warren Green. Participates in educational and human-rights activities of the AIU and supports the Alliance System of Jewish schools, teachers' colleges, and remedial programs in Israel, North Africa, the Middle East, Europe, and Canada. *Alliance Review.*

AMERICAN JEWISH JOINT DISTRIBUTION COMMITTEE, INC.—JDC (1914). 711 Third Ave., NYC 10017-4014. (212)687-6200. FAX: (212)370-5467. E-mail: newyork@jdcny.org. Pres. Jonathan W. Kolker; Exec. V.-Pres. Michael Schneider. Provides assistance to Jewish communities in Europe, Asia, Africa, and the Mideast, including welfare programs for Jews in need. Current concerns include rescuing Jews from areas of distress; helping to meet Israel's social-service needs by developing innovative programs that create new opportunities for the country's most disadvantaged populations. Program expansions emphasize community development in the former Soviet Union and youth activities in Eastern Europe and nonsectarian development and disaster assistance. *Snapshots:JDC's Activities in the Former Soviet Union.*

AMERICAN JEWISH PHILANTHROPIC FUND (1955). 122 E. 42 St., 12th fl., NYC 10168-1289. (212)755-5640. FAX: (212)644-0979. Pres. Charles J. Tanenbaum. Provides resettlement assistance to Jewish refugees primarily through programs administered by the International Rescue Committee at its offices in Western Europe and the U.S.

AMERICAN JEWISH WORLD SERVICE (1985). 989 Avenue of the Americas, 10th Fl., NYC 10018. (212)736-2597. FAX: (212) 736-3463. E-mail:jws@jws.org. Chmn. Don Abramson; Pres. Ruth W. Messinger. Provides nonsectarian, humanitarian assistance and emergency relief to people in need in Africa, Asia, Latin America, Russia, Ukraine, and the Middle East; works in partnership with local non-governmental organizations to support and implement self-sustaining grassroots development projects; serves as a vehicle through which the Jewish community can act as global citizens. *AJWS Reports (newsletter).* (WWW.AJWS.ORG)

AMERICAN ORT, INC. (1922). 817 Broadway, NYC 10003. (212)353-5800. FAX:

(212)353-5888. E-mail: info@aort.org. Pres. Michael R. Stoler; Exec. V.-Pres. Brian J. Strum. Umbrella organization for all ORT operations in the U.S.; promotes and raises funds for ORT, the world's largest nongovernmental education and training organization, with a global network teaching over 262,000 students in more than 60 countries. In Israel, 100,000 students attend 154 schools and training centers; there are 22 ORT schools and centers in the former Soviet Union; and in the U.S., over 10,000 students are served by ORT's Technical Institutes in Chicago, Los Angeles, and New York, and in Jewish day school programs. *American ORT News, American ORT Update, American ORT Annual Report.* (WWW.AORT.ORG)

———, WOMEN'S AMERICAN ORT (1927). 315 Park Ave. S., NYC 10010-3677. (212)505-7700; (800)51-WAORT. FAX: (212)674-3057. E-mail: waort@waort. org. Pres. Pepi Dunay; Exec. Dir. Rosina Abramson. Strengthens the worldwide Jewish community by empowering people to achieve economic self-sufficiency through technological and vocational training; educates 262,000 students in 60 countries including the United States, Israel and the former Soviet Union; supports ORT programs through membership, fund raising and leadership development; domestic agenda promotes quality public education, women's rights and literacy. *Women's American ORT Reporter, Women's American ORT Annual Report.* (WWW.WAORT.ORG)

CONFERENCE ON JEWISH MATERIAL CLAIMS AGAINST GERMANY, INC. (1951). 15 E. 26 St., Rm. 906, NYC 10010. (212)696-4944. FAX: (212)679-2126. Pres. Dr. Israel Miller; Exec. V.-Pres. & Sec. Gideon Taylor. Represents Jewish survivors in negotiations for compensation from the German government and other entities once controlled by the Nazis. Also an operating agency that administers compensation funds, recovers Jewish property and allocates funds to institutions that serve Holocaust survivors. The Claims Conference—made up of the conference on Jewish Material Claims Against Germany and the Committee for Jewish Claims on Austria—is one of the founders of the World Jewish Restitution Organization, Memorial Foundation for Jewish Culture and the United Restitu-

tion Organization. *Newsletter, Annual Report.*

HIAS, INC. (HEBREW IMMIGRANT AID SOCIETY) (1880; reorg. 1954). 333 Seventh Ave., NYC 10001-5004. (212)967-4100. FAX: (212)967-4442. E-mail:info@hias. org. Pres. Neil Greenbaum; Exec. V.-Pres. Leonard Glickman. The oldest international migration and refugee resettlement agency in the United States, dedicated to assisting persecuted and oppressed people worldwide and delivering them to countries of safe haven. As the migration arm of the American Jewish community, it also advocates for fair and just policies affecting refugees and immigrants. Since its founding in 1880, the agency has rescued more than four and a half million people. *Annual report.*

THE JEWISH FOUNDATION FOR THE RIGHTEOUS (1986). 305 7th Ave., 19th fl., NYC 10001. (212)727-9955. FAX: (212)727-9956. E-mail: jfr@jfr.org. Chmn. Harvey Schulweis; Exec. Dir. Stanlee J. Stahl. Provides monthly financial support to 1,500 aged and needy Righteous Gentiles living in 26 countries who risked their lives to save Jews during the Holocaust. The Foundation's education program uses the stories of rescue to teach students about the Holocaust, its relevance for these times, and the significance of altruistic behavior for our society. *Newsletter (3 times a year).* (WWW.JFR.ORG)

NORTH AMERICAN CONFERENCE ON ETHIOPIAN JEWRY (NACOEJ) (1982). 132 Nassau St., Suite 412, NYC 10038. (212)233-5200. FAX: (212)233-5243. E-mail: nacoej@aol.com. Pres. Richard Giesberg; Exec. Dir. Barbara Ribakove Gordon. Provides programming for Ethiopian Jews in Israel in the areas of education (preschool through college), vocational training, and cultural preservation. Assists Ethiopian Jews remaining in Ethiopia. National speakers bureau offers programs to synagogues, schools, Jewish, and non-Jewish organizations. Exhibits of Ethiopian Jewish artifacts, photos, handicrafts, etc. available. *Lifeline (newsletter).* (WWW.CIRCUS.ORG/NACOEJ)

RE'UTH WOMEN'S SOCIAL SERVICE, INC. (1937). 130 E. 59 St., Suite 1200, NYC 10022. (212)836-1570. FAX: (212)836-1114. Chmn. Ursula Merkin; Pres. Rosa

Strygler. Maintains in Israel subsidized housing for self-reliant elderly; old-age homes for more dependent elderly; Lichtenstadter Hospital for chronically ill and young accident victims not accepted by other hospitals; subsidized meals; Golden Age clubs. *Annual dinner journal.*

THANKS TO SCANDINAVIA, INC. (1963). 745 Fifth Ave., Rm. 603, NYC 10151. (212)486-8600. FAX: (212)486-5735. Natl. Chmn. Victor Borge; Pres. Richard Netter. Provides scholarships and fellowships at American universities and medical centers to students and doctors from Denmark, Finland, Norway, and Sweden in appreciation of the rescue of Jews from the Holocaust. Informs Americans and Scandinavians of these singular examples of humanity and bravery. Speakers available on rescue in Scandinavia; also books, videos, and tapes. *Annual report.*

UJA FEDERATION OF NORTH AMERICA. (1939). (*see* UNITED JEWISH COMMUNITIES)

UNITED JEWISH COMMUNITIES (1999). 111 Eighth Ave., 11th fl., NYC 10011-5201. (212)284-6500. FAX: (212)284-6873. Bd. Chmn. Charles R. Bronfman; Chmn. Exec. Com. Joel D. Tauber; Acting Pres. Stephen D. Solender. Formed by a merger of the United Jewish Appeal with the Council of Jewish Federations and United Israel Appeal; represents N. American Jewry's primary fund-raising and service-providing agencies.

RELIGIOUS AND EDUCATIONAL ORGANIZATIONS

AGUDATH ISRAEL OF AMERICA (1922). 84 William St., NYC 10038. (212)797-9000. FAX: (212)269-2843. Exec. V.-Pres. Rabbi Samuel Bloom; Exec. Dir. Rabbi Boruch B. Borchardt. Mobilizes Orthodox Jews to cope with Jewish problems in the spirit of the Torah; speaks out on contemporary issues from an Orthodox viewpoint; sponsors a broad range of projects aimed at enhancing religious living, education, children's welfare, protection of Jewish religious rights, outreach to the assimilated and to arrivals from the former Soviet Union, and social services. *Jewish Observer; Dos Yiddishe Vort; Coalition.*

———, AGUDAH WOMEN OF AMERICA-N'SHEI AGUDATH ISRAEL (1940). 84 William St., NYC 10038. (212)363-8940.

FAX: (212)747-8763. Presidium Aliza Grund, Rose Isbee; Exec. Admin. Gitty Pinter. Organizes Jewish women for philanthropic work in the U.S. and Israel and for intensive Torah education.

———, BOYS' DIVISION-PIRCHEI AGUDATH ISRAEL (1925). 84 William St., NYC 10038 (212)797-9000. Natl. Coord. Rabbi Shimon Grama. Educates Orthodox Jewish children in Torah; encourages sense of communal responsibility. Branches sponsor weekly youth groups and Jewish welfare projects. National Mishnah contests, rallies, and conventions foster unity on a national level. *Leaders Guides.*

———, GIRLS' DIVISION—BNOS AGUDATH ISRAEL (1921). 84 William St., NYC 10038. (212)797-9000. Natl. Dir. Leah Zagelbaum. Sponsors regular weekly programs on the local level and unites girls from throughout the Torah world with extensive regional and national activities. *Kol Bnos.*

———, YOUNG MEN'S DIVISION—ZEIREI AGUDATH ISRAEL (1921). 84 William St., NYC 10038. (212)797-9000, ext. 57. Dir. Rabbi Labish Becker. Educates youth to see Torah as source of guidance for all issues facing Jews as individuals and as a people. Inculcates a spirit of activism through projects in religious, Toraheducational, and community-welfare fields. *Am Hatorah; Daf Chizuk.*

AGUDATH ISRAEL WORLD ORGANIZATION (1912). 84 William St., NYC 10038. (212)797-9000. FAX: (212)269-2843. Chmn. Rabbi Yehudah Meir Abramowitz. Represents the interests of Orthodox Jewry on the national and international scenes. Sponsors projects to strengthen Torah life worldwide.

ALEPH: ALLIANCE FOR JEWISH RENEWAL (1963; reorg. 1993). 7318 Germantown Ave., Philadelphia, PA 19119-1720. (215)247-9700. FAX: (215)247-9703. Bd. Chmn. Dr. Sheldon Isenberg; Exec. Dir. R. Daniel Siegel. A multifaceted international organization serving the movement for Jewish renewal, formed out of a merger of P'nai Or Religious Fellowship and the Shalom Center. Activities include creation and dissemination of publications, liturgy, curricula, audio and video tapes; a country retreat center; lay and professional leadership training; spiritual activism on social and environmental issues; and a network of local Jewish renewal communities. *New Menorah (quarterly journal); Pumbedissa (newsletter forum for rabbis and rabbinical students); Or HaDor (newsletter of congregations and havurot affiliated with ALEPH through the Network of Jewish Renewal Communities).*

AMERICAN ASSOCIATION OF RABBIS (1978). 350 Fifth Ave., Suite 3304, NYC 10118. (212)244-3350, (516)244-7113. FAX: (516)344-0779. E-mail: tefu@aol.com. Pres. Rabbi Jeffrey Wartenberg; Exec. Dir. Rabbi David L. Dunn. An organization of rabbis serving in pulpits, in areas of education, and in social work. *Quarterly bulletin; monthly newsletter.*

AMERICAN STUDENTS TO ACTIVATE PRIDE (ASAP/OU College Affairs) (1993). 333 7th Ave., 18th fl., NYC 10001. (212)563-4000. FAX: (212)564-9058. E-mail: davidfel@ix.netcom.com. Pres. Zelda Goldsmith; Natl. Dir. Rabbi David Felsenthal; Chmn. Bernard Falk. A spiritual fitness movement of Jewish college students promoting Torah learning and discussion. Supports 100 learning groups at over 65 campuses as well as regional and national seminars and *shabbatonim. Good Shabbos (weekly); Rimon Discussion Guide (monthly); Jewish Student College Survival Guide (yearly).*

AM KOLEL JUDAIC RESOURCE CENTER (1990). 15 W. Montgomery Ave., Rockville, MD 20850. (301)309-2310. FAX: (301)309-2328. E-mail: amkolel@aol.com. Pres. David Shneyer. An independent Jewish resource center, providing a progressive Jewish voice in the community. Activities include: religion, educational and cultural programs; classes, workshops and seminars; interfaith workshops and programs; tikkun olam (social action) opportunities. The staff provides training and resources to emerging and independent communities throughout N. America. *Directory of Independent Jewish Communities and Havurot in Maryland, DC and Virginia. Rock Creek Haggadah.*

ASSOCIATION FOR JEWISH STUDIES (1969). MB 0001, Brandeis University, PO Box 9110, Waltham, MA 02454-9110. (781)736-2981. FAX: (781)736-2982. E-mail: ajs@brandeis.edu. Pres. David Berger; Exec. Dir. Aaron L. Katchen.

Seeks to promote, maintain, and improve the teaching of Jewish studies in colleges and universities by sponsoring meetings and conferences, publishing a newsletter and other scholarly materials, aiding in the placement of teachers, coordinating research, and cooperating with other scholarly organizations. *AJS Review; Newsletter.*

ASSOCIATION FOR THE SOCIAL SCIENTIFIC STUDY OF JEWRY (1971). Polisher Research Institute, Philadelphia Geriatric Center, 5301 Old York Rd., Philadelphia, PA 19141-2996. (215)456-2981. FAX: (215)456-2017. E-mail: aglicksm@thunder.ocis.temple.edu. Pres. Allen Glicksman; V.-Pres. Riv-Ellen Prell; Sec.-Treas. Jerome Chanes. Journal Ed. Rela Geffen; Mng. Ed. Egon Mayer; Newsletter Ed. Gail Glicksman. Arranges academic sessions and facilitates communication among social scientists studying Jewry through meetings, newsletter, and related materials and activities. *Contemporary Jewry; ASSJ Newsletter.*

ASSOCIATION OF HILLEL/JEWISH CAMPUS PROFESSIONALS *(see* TEKIAH: ASSOCIATION OF HILLEL/JEWISH CAMPUS PROFESSIONALS)

ASSOCIATION OF ORTHODOX JEWISH SCIENTISTS (1948). 1123 Broadway, Rm. 1010, NYC 10010. (212)229-2340. FAX: (212) 691-0573. Pres. Allen J. Bennett, M.D.; Bd. Chmn. Rabbi Nachman Cohen; Exec. Dir. Joel Schwartz. Seeks to contribute to the development of science within the framework of Orthodox Jewish tradition; to obtain and disseminate information relating to the interaction between the Jewish traditional way of life and scientific developments—on both an ideological and practical level; to assist in the solution of problems pertaining to Orthodox Jews engaged in scientific teaching or research. Two main conventions are held each year. *Intercom; Proceedings; Halacha Bulletin; newsletter.*

B'NAI B'RITH HILLEL FOUNDATIONS *(see* HILLEL)

B'NAI B'RITH YOUTH ORGANIZATION (1924). 1640 Rhode Island Ave., NW, Washington, DC 20036. (202)857-6633. FAX: (212)857-6568. Chmn. Youth Comm. Audrey Y. Brooks; Dir. Sam Fisher. Helps Jewish teenagers achieve self-fulfillment and make a maximum contribution to the

Jewish community and their country's culture; helps members acquire a greater knowledge and appreciation of Jewish religion and culture. *Shofar; Monday Morning; BBYO Parents' Line; Hakol; Kesher; The Connector.*

CANTORS ASSEMBLY (1947). 3080 Broadway, Suite 613, NYC 10027. (212)678-8834. FAX: (212)662-8989. E-mail: caoffice @jtsa.edu. Pres. Henry Rosenblum; Exec. V.Pres. Stephen J. Stein. Seeks to unite all cantors who adhere to traditional Judaism and who serve as full-time cantors in bona fide congregations to conserve and promote the musical traditions of the Jews and to elevate the status of the cantorial profession. *Annual Proceedings; Journal of Synagogue Music.*

CENTER FOR CHRISTIAN-JEWISH UNDERSTANDING OF SACRED HEART UNIVERSITY (1992). 5151 Park Ave., Fairfield, CT 06432. (203)365-7592. FAX: (203)365-4815. Pres. Dr. Anthony J. Cernera; Exec. Dir. Rabbi Joseph H. Ehrenkranz. An educational and research division of Sacred Heart University; brings together clergy, laity, scholars, theologians, and educators with the purpose of promoting interreligious research, education, and dialogue, with particular focus on current religious thinking within Christianity and Judaism. *CCJU Perspective.*

CENTRAL CONFERENCE OF AMERICAN RABBIS (1889). 355 Lexington Ave., NYC 10017. (212)972-3636. FAX: (212)692-0819. E-mail: info@ccarnet.org. Pres. Rabbi Charles A. Kroloff; Exec. V.-Pres. Rabbi Paul J. Menitoff. Seeks to conserve and promote Judaism and to disseminate its teachings in a liberal spirit. The CCAR Press provides liturgy and prayerbooks to the worldwide Reform Jewish community. *CCAR Journal: A Reform Jewish Quarterly; CCAR Yearbook.* (WWW.CCARNET. ORG)

CLAL—NATIONAL JEWISH CENTER FOR LEARNING AND LEADERSHIP (1974). 440 Park Ave. S., 4th fl., NYC 10016-8012. (212)779-3300. FAX: (212)779-1009. E-mail: info@clal.org. Pres. Rabbi Irwin Kula; Chmn. Charles R. Bronfman; Exec.V.-Chmn. Donna M. Rosenthal. Provides leadership training for lay leaders, rabbis, educators, and communal professionals. A faculty of rabbis and scholars representing all the denominations of

Judaism make Judaism come alive, applying the wisdom of the Jewish heritage to help shape tomorrow's Jewish communities. Offers seminars and courses, retreats, symposia and conferences, lecture bureau and the latest on-line information through CLAL Web site. *Sacred Days calenda;, monographs; holiday brochures; CLAL Update.* (WWW.CLAL.ORG)

COALITION FOR THE ADVANCEMENT OF JEWISH EDUCATION (CAJE) (1976). 261 W. 35 St., #12A, NYC 10001. (212)268-4210. FAX: (212)268-4214. E-mail: 500-8447@mcimail.com . . . Chmn. Sylvia Abrams; Exec. Dir. Dr. Eliot G. Spack. Brings together Jews from all ideologies who are involved in every facet of Jewish education and are committed to transmitting the Jewish heritage. Sponsors annual Conference on Alternatives in Jewish Education and Curriculum Bank; publishes a wide variety of publications; organizes shared-interest networks; offers mini grants for special projects; sponsors Mini-CAJEs (one- or two-day in-service programs) around the country; maintains a website for Jewish educators (above). *Bikurim; timely curricular publications; Jewish Education News.* (WWW.CAJE.ORG)

CONGRESS OF SECULAR JEWISH ORGANIZATIONS (1970). 19657 Villa Dr. N., Southfield, MI 48076. (248)569-8127. FAX: (248)569-5222. E-mail: rifke@earthlink.net. Chmn. Jeff Zolitor; V.-Chmn. Julie Gales; Exec. Dir. Roberta E. Feinstein. An umbrella organization of schools and adult clubs; facilitates exchange curricula and educational programs for children and adults stressing the Jewish historical and cultural heritage and the continuity of the Jewish people. *New Yorkish (Yiddish literature translations); Haggadah; The Hanuka Festival; Mame-Loshn.*

CONVERSION TO JUDAISM RESOURCE CENTER (1997). 74 Hauppauge Rd., Rm. 53, Commack, NY 11725. (516) 462-5826. E-mail: inform@convert.org. Pres. Dr. Lawrence J. Epstein; Exec. Dir. Susan Lustig. Provides information and advice for people who wish to convert to Judaism or who have converted. Puts potential converts in touch with rabbis from all branches of Judaism.

COUNCIL FOR JEWISH EDUCATION (1926). 111 Eighth Ave., Suite 11E, NYC 10011-

5201. (212)284-6893/6950. FAX: (212) 284-6951. Pres. Rabbi Arthur Vernon; Exec. Sec. Dr. Solomon Goldman. Fellowship of Jewish education professionals-administrators, supervisors, and teachers in Hebrew high schools and Jewish teachers colleges-of all ideological groupings; conducts national and regional conferences; represents the Jewish education profession before the Jewish community; cosponsors, with the Jewish Education Service of North America, a personnel committee and other projects; cooperates with Jewish Agency Department of Education in promoting Hebrew culture and studies. *Journal of Jewish Education.*

FEDERATION OF JEWISH MEN'S CLUBS (1929). 475 Riverside Dr., Suite 450, NYC 10115. (212)749-8100; (800)288-FJMC. FAX: (212)316-4271. E-mail: fjmc@jtsa.edu. Internatl. Pres. Dr. Stephen H. Davidoff; Exec. Dir. Rabbi Charles E. Simon. Promotes principles of Conservative Judaism; develops family-education and leadership-training programs; offers the Art of Jewish Living series and Yom HaShoah Home Commemoration; sponsors Hebrew literacy adult-education program; presents awards for service to American Jewry. *Torchlight; Hearing Men's Voices.* (WWW.JTSA.EDU/FJMC)

FEDERATION OF RECONSTRUCTIONIST CONGREGATIONS AND HAVUROT (*see* JEWISH RECONSTRUCTIONIST FEDERATION)

HILLEL: THE FOUNDATION FOR JEWISH CAMPUS LIFE (formerly B'NAI B'RITH HILLEL FOUNDATIONS) (1923). 1640 Rhode Island Ave., NW, Washington, DC 20036. (202)857-6576. FAX: (202)857-6693. E-mail: info@hillel.org. Chmn. Internatl. Bd. Govs. Edgar M. Bronfman; Chmn. Foundation for Jewish Campus Life Chuck Newman; Chmn. B'nai B'rith Hillel Comm. Robert B. Spitzer; Pres. & Internatl. Dir. Richard M. Joel. The largest Jewish campus organization in the world, its network of 500 regional centers, campus-based foundations, and affiliates serves as a catalyst for creating a celebratory community and a rich, diverse Jewish life on the campus. *The Hillel Annual Report; On Campus newsletter; Calling Home newsletter; Hillel Now newsletter; The Hillel Guide to Jewish Life on Campus (published with Princeton Review).*

INSTITUTE FOR COMPUTERS IN JEWISH LIFE (1978). 7074 N. Western Ave., Chicago, IL 60645. (773)262-9200. FAX: (773)262-9298. E-mail: rosirv@aol.com. Pres. Thomas Klutznick; Exec. V.-Pres. Dr. Irving J. Rosenbaum. Explores, develops, and disseminates applications of computer technology to appropriate areas of Jewish life, with special emphasis on Jewish education; creates educational software for use in Jewish schools; provides consulting service and assistance for national Jewish organizations, seminaries, and synagogues.

INTERNATIONAL FEDERATION OF SECULAR HUMANISTIC JEWS (1983). 28611 West Twelve Mile Rd., Farmington Hills, MI 48334. (248)476-9532. FAX: (248)476-8509. E-mail: iishj@speedlink.net. Co-Chairs Yair Tzaban (Israel), Sherwin Wine (USA). Consists of national organizations in Israel, the United States, Canada, Britain, France, Belgium, Australia, Mexico, Argentina, Uruguay and the countries of the former Soviet Union, involving some 50,000 Jews. The honorary co-chairs are Albert Memmi, well-known French writer and professor of sociology at the University of Paris, and Yehuda Bauer, noted historian and Holocaust scholar at the Hebrew University in Jerusalem. *Newsletter.*

INTERNATIONAL INSTITUTE FOR SECULAR HUMANISTIC JUDAISM (1985). 28611 West Twelve Mile Rd., Farmington Hills, MI 48334. (248)476-9532. FAX: (248)476-8509. E-mail: iishj@speedlink.net. Chmn. Rabbi Sherwin T. Wine. Established in 1985 in Jerusalem to serve the needs of a growing movement, its two primary purposes are to commission and publish educational materials and to train rabbis, leaders, teachers, and spokespersons for the movement. The Institute has two offices-one in Israel (Jerusalem) and one in N. America and offers educational and training programs in Israel, N. America, and the countries of the former Soviet Union. The N. American office, located in a suburb of Detroit, offers the Rabbinic Program, the Leadership Program, and the Adult Education Program. *Brochure, educational papers, and projects.*

JEWISH CHAUTAUQUA SOCIETY, INC. (sponsored by NORTH AMERICAN FEDERATION OF TEMPLE BROTHERHOODS) (1893). 633 Third Ave., NYC 10017. (212)650-4100 or

(800)765-6200. FAX: (212)650-4189. E-mail: jcs@uahc.org. Pres. Stephen K. Breslauer; Chancellor/lst V.-Pres. Irving B. Shnaider; Exec. Dir. Douglas E. Barden. Works to promote interfaith understanding by sponsoring accredited college courses and one-day lectures on Judaic topics, providing book grants to educational institutions, producing educational videotapes on interfaith topics, and convening interfaith institutes. A founding sponsor of the National Black/Jewish Relations Center at Dillard University. *Brotherhood.*

JEWISH EDUCATION IN MEDIA (1978). PO Box 180, Riverdale Sta., NYC 10471. (212)362-7633. FAX: (203)359-1381. Pres. Ken Asher; Exec. Dir. Rabbi Mark S. Golub. Devoted to producing television, film, and video-cassettes for a popular Jewish audience, in order to inform, entertain, and inspire a greater sense of Jewish identity and Jewish commitment. "L'Chayim," JEM's weekly half-hour program, which is seen nationally on NJT/National Jewish Television, features outstanding figures in the Jewish world addressing issues and events of importance to the Jewish community. (WWW.L'CHAYIM.COM)

JEWISH EDUCATION SERVICE OF NORTH AMERICA (JESNA) (1981). 111 Eighth Ave., 11th fl., NYC 10011. (212)284-6950. FAX: (212)284-6951. E-mail: info@jesna. org. Pres. Mark Lainer; Exec. V.-Pres. Dr. Jonathan S. Woocher. The Jewish Federation system's educational coordinating, planning, and development agency. Promotes excellence in Jewish education by initiating exchange of ideas, programs, and materials; providing information, consultation, educational resources, and policy guidance; and collaborating with partners in N. America and Israel to develop educational programs. *Agenda:Jewish Education; planning guides on Jewish continuity; JESNA Update; research reports and bulletins; Jewish Educators Electronic Toolkit.* (WWW.JESNA.ORG)

JEWISH RECONSTRUCTIONIST FEDERATION (formerly FEDERATION OF RECONSTRUCTIONIST CONGREGATIONS AND HAVUROT) (1954). 7804 Montgomery Ave., Suite 9, Elkins Park, PA 19027-2649. (215)782-8500. Fax: (215)782-8805. E-mail: info@ jrf.org. Pres. Richard Haimowitz; Exec. V.-Pres. Mark Seal. Services affiliated congregations and havurot educationally and administratively; fosters the establishment of new Reconstructionist congregations and fellowship groups. Runs the Reconstructionist Press and provides programmatic materials. Maintains regional offices in New York, Los Angeles, and Chicago. *The Reconstructionist; Reconstructionism TODAY.* (WWW.SHAMASHJCCA.ORG/JRF)

———, RECONSTRUCTIONIST RABBINICAL ASSOCIATION (1974). 1299 Church Rd., Wyncote, PA 19095. (215)576-5210. FAX: (215)576-8051. E-mail: rraassoc@aol. com. Pres. Rabbi Dan Ehrenkrantz; Exec. Dir. Rabbi Richard Hirsh. Professional organization for graduates of the Reconstructionist Rabbinical College and other rabbis who identify with Reconstructionist Judaism; cooperates with Jewish Reconstructionist Federation in furthering Reconstructionism in the world. *Newsletters; position papers.*

———, RECONSTRUCTIONIST RABBINICAL COLLEGE (*see* p. 627)

JEWISH TEACHERS ASSOCIATION—MORIM (1931). 45 E. 33 St., Suite 604, NYC 10016. (212)684-0556. Pres. Phyllis L. Pullman; V.-Pres. Ronni David; Sec. Helen Parnes; Treas. Mildred Safar. Protects teachers from abuse of seniority rights; fights the encroachment of anti-Semitism in education; offers scholarships to qualified students; encourages teachers to assume active roles in Jewish communal and religious affairs. *Morim JTA Newsletter.*

KULANU, INC. (formerly AMISHAV USA) (1993). 11603 Gilsan St., Silver Spring, MD 20902. (301)681-5679. FAX: (301)681-5679. Pres. Jack Zeller; Sec. Karen Primack. Engages in outreach to dispersed Jewish communities around the world who wish to return to their Jewish roots. Current projects include the formal conversion of Shinlung-Menashe tribesmen in India currently practicing Judaism, and supplying materials and rabbis for conversos/marranos in Mexico and Brazil. *Newsletter.*

NATIONAL COMMITTEE FOR FURTHERANCE OF JEWISH EDUCATION (1941). 824 Eastern Pkwy., Brooklyn, NY 11213. (718)735-0200; (800)33-NCFJE. FAX: (718)735-4455. Pres. Charles Kupferman; Bd. Chmn. Rabbi Shea Hecht; Chmn.

Exec. Com. Rabbi Sholem Ber Hecht. Seeks to disseminate the ideals of Torah-true education among the youth of America; provides education and compassionate care for the poor, sick, and needy in U.S. and Israel; provides aid to Iranian Jewish youth; sponsors camps and educational functions, family and vocational counseling services, family and early intervention, after-school and preschool programs, drug and alcohol education and prevention; maintains schools in Brooklyn and Queens. *Panorama; Cultbusters; Intermarriage; Brimstone & Fire; Focus; A Life Full of Giving.*

NATIONAL COUNCIL OF YOUNG ISRAEL (1912). 3 W. 16 St., NYC 10011. (212)929-1525. FAX: (212)727-9526. E-mail: ncyi@youngisrael.org. Pres. Chaim Kaminetzky; Exec. V.-Pres. Rabbi Pesach Lerner. Through its network of member synagogues in N. America and Israel maintains a program of spiritual, cultural, social, and communal activity aimed at the advancement and perpetuation of traditional, Torah-true Judaism; seeks to instill in American youth an understanding and appreciation of the ethical and spiritual values of Judaism. Sponsors rabbinic and lay leadership conferences, kosher dining clubs, and youth programs. *Viewpoint; Divrei Torah Bulletin; NCYI Suggestion Box; The Rabbi's Letter.* (WWW.YOUNGISRAEL.ORG)

———, AMERICAN FRIENDS OF YOUNG ISRAEL IN ISRAEL—YISRAEL HATZA'IR (1926). 3 W. 16 St., NYC 10011. (212)929-1525. FAX: (212)727-9526. E-mail: ncyi@youngisrael.org. Pres. Meir Mishkoff; Exec. Dir. Rabbi David Marcus. Promotes Young Israel synagogues and youth work in Israel; works to help absorb Russian and Ethiopian immigrants.

———, YOUNG ISRAEL DEPARTMENT OF YOUTH AND YOUNG ADULTS ACTIVITIES (reorg. 1981). 3 W. 16 St., NYC 10011. (212)929-1525; (800)617-NCYI. FAX: (212)243-1222. Email:youth@youngisrael.org. Chmn. Kenneth Block; Dir. Richard Stareshefsky. Fosters varied program of activities for the advancement and perpetuation of traditional Torah-true Judaism; instills ethical and spiritual values and appreciation for compatibility of ancient faith of Israel with good Americanism. Runs leadership training programs and youth shabbatonim; annual national conference of youth directors; ski week in Canada's Laurentian Mountains and summer programs for teens; Nachala summer program in Israel for Yeshiva H.S. girls and Natzach summer program for Yeshiva H.S. boys. *Torah Kidbits; Shabbat Youth Manual; Y.I. Can Assist You; Synagogue Youth Director Handbook.*

NATIONAL HAVURAH COMMITTEE (1979). 7318 Germantown Ave., Philadelphia, PA 19119-1720. (215)248-9760. FAX: (215)247-9703. E-mail: lauriekatnhc@compuserve.com. Chmn. Leonard Gordon. A center for Jewish renewal devoted to spreading Jewish ideas, ethics, and religious practices through havurot, participatory and inclusive religious mini-communities. Maintains a directory of N. American havurot and sponsors a week-long summer institute, regional weekend retreats. *Havurah! (newsletter).*

NATIONAL JEWISH CENTER FOR LEARNING AND LEADERSHIP (*see* CLAL)

NATIONAL JEWISH COMMITTEE ON SCOUTING (Boy Scouts of America) (1926). 1325 West Walnut Hill Lane, PO Box 152079, Irving, TX 75015-2079. (972)580-2000. FAX: (972)580-7870. Chmn. Jerrold Lockshin. Assists Jewish institutions in meeting their needs and concerns through use of the resources of scouting. Works through local Jewish committees on scouting to establish Tiger Cub groups (1st grade), Cub Scout packs, Boy Scout troops, and coed Explorer posts in synagogues, Jewish community centers, day schools, and other Jewish organizations wishing to draw Jewish youth. Support materials and resources on request.

NATIONAL JEWISH GIRL SCOUT COMMITTEE (1972). 33 Central Dr., Bronxville, NY 10708. (914)738-3986, (718)252-6072. FAX: (914)738-6752. E-mail: njgsc@aol.com. Chmn. Rabbi Herbert W. Bomzer; Field Chmn. Adele Wasko. Serves to further Jewish education by promoting Jewish award programs, encouraging religious services, promoting cultural exchanges with the Israel Boy and Girl Scouts Federation, and extending membership in the Jewish community by assisting councils in organizing Girl Scout troops and local Jewish Girl Scout committees. *Newsletter.*

NATIONAL JEWISH HOSPITALITY COMMITTEE (1973; reorg. 1993). PO Box 53691, Philadelphia, PA 19105. (800)745-0301. Pres. Rabbi Allen S. Maller; Exec. Dir. Steven S. Jacobs. Assists persons interested in Judaism-for intermarriage, conversion, general information, or to respond to missionaries. *Special reports.*

OZAR HATORAH, INC. (1946). 1350 Ave. of the Americas, 32nd fl., NYC 10019. (212)582-2050. FAX: (212) 307-0044. Pres. Joseph Shalom; Sec. Sam Sutton; Exec. Dir. Rabbi Biniamine Amoyelle. An international educational network which builds Sephardic communities worldwide through Jewish education.

PARDES PROGRESSIVE ASSOCIATION OF REFORM DAY SCHOOLS (1990). 838 Fifth Ave., NYC 10021-7064. (212)249-0100. FAX: (212)734-2857. E-mail: educate@uahc.org. Pres. Zita Gardner; Chmn. Carol Nemo. An affiliate of the Union of American Hebrew Congregations; brings together day schools and professional and lay leaders committed to advancing the cause of full-time Reform Jewish education; advocates for the continuing development of day schools within the Reform movement as a means to foster Jewish identity, literacy, and continuity; promotes cooperation among our member schools and with other Jewish organizations that share similar goals. *Visions of Excellence (manual).*

P'EYLIM-LEV L'ACHIM (1951). 1034 E. 12 St. Brooklyn, NY 11230. (718)258-7760. FAX: (718)258-4672. E-mail: joskarmel @aol.com. Natl. Dir. Rabbi Joseph C. Karmel; Exec. V.-Pres. Rabbi Nachum Barnetsky. Seeks to bring irreligious Jews in Israel back to their heritage. Conducts outreach through 12 major divisions consisting of thousands of volunteers and hundreds of professionals across the country; conducts anti-missionary and assimilation programs; operates shelters for abused women and children; recruits children for Torah schools.

RABBINICAL ALLIANCE OF AMERICA (Igud Harabonim) (1942). 3 W. 16 St., 4th fl., NYC 10011. (212)242-6420. FAX: (212)255-8313. Pres. Rabbi Abraham B. Hecht; Admin. Judge of Beth Din (Rabbinical Court) Rabbi Herschel Kurzrock. Seeks to promulgate the cause of Torah-true Judaism through an organized rabbinate that is consistently Orthodox; seeks to elevate the position of Orthodox rabbis nationally and to defend the welfare of Jews the world over. Also has Beth Din Rabbinical Court for Jewish divorces, litigation, marriage counseling, and family problems. *Perspective; Nahalim; Torah Message of the Week; Registry.*

RABBINICAL ASSEMBLY (1900). 3080 Broadway, NYC 10027. (212)280-6000. FAX: (212)749-9166. Pres. Rabbi Seymour L. Essrog; Exec. V.-Pres. Rabbi Joel H. Meyers. The international association of Conservative rabbis; actively promotes the cause of Conservative Judaism and works to benefit *klal yisrael*; publishes learned texts, prayer books, and works of Jewish interest; administers the work of the Committee on Jewish Law and Standards for the Conservative movement; serves the professional and personal needs of its members through publications, conferences, and benefit programs and administers the movement's Joint Placement Commission. *Conservative Judaism; Proceedings of the Rabbinical Assembly; Rabbinical Assembly Newsletter.*

RABBINICAL COUNCIL OF AMERICA, INC. (1923; reorg. 1935). 305 Seventh Ave., Suite 1200, NYC 10001. (212)807-7888. FAX: (212)727-8452. Pres. Rabbi Jacob S. Rubenstein; Exec. V.-Pres. Rabbi Steven M. Dworken. Promotes Orthodox Judaism in the community; supports institutions for study of Torah; stimulates creation of new traditional agencies. *Hadorom; RCA Record; Sermon Manual; Tradition; Resource Magazine.* (www. RABBIS.ORG)

SHOMREI ADAMAH/TEVA LEARNING CENTER (1988). 307 Seventh Ave., #900, NYC 10001. (212)807-6376. FAX: (212)924-5112. E-mail: tevacenter@aol.com. Exec. Dir. Adam Berman; Mng. Dir. Laurie Hollin. Promotes understanding that love of nature and protection of the environment are values deeply embedded in Jewish tradition and texts. Runs Jewish environmental educational programs for Jewish day schools, synagogues, community centers, camps and other organized groups. *A Garden of Choice Fruit; Let the Earth Teach You Torah.*

SOCIETY FOR HUMANISTIC JUDAISM (1969). 28611 W. Twelve Mile Rd., Farmington Hills, MI 48334. (248)478-7610. FAX:

(248)478-3159. E-mail: info@shj.org. Pres. Rick Naimark; Exec. Dir. M. Bonnie Cousens. Serves as a voice for Jews who value their Jewish identity and who seek an alternative to conventional Judaism, who reject supernatural authority and affirm the right of individuals to be the masters of their own lives. Publishes educational and ceremonial materials; organizes congregations and groups. *Humanistic Judaism (quarterly journal); Humanorah (quarterly newsletter)*.

TEKIAH: ASSOCIATION OF HILLEL/JEWISH CAMPUS PROFESSIOANLS (1949). c/o Greater Miami Hillel Jewish Student Center, 1100 Stanford Dr., Coral Gables, FL 33146. (305)665-6948. FAX: (305)661-8540. E-mail: jfalick@miami.flahillel.org. Pres. Rabbi Jeffrey Falick. Seeks to promote professional relationships and exchanges of experience, develop personnel standards and qualifications, safeguard integrity of Hillel profession; represents and advocates before the Foundation for Jewish Campus Life, Council of Jewish Federations. *Handbook for Hillel Professionals; Guide to Hillel Personnel Practices.*

TORAH SCHOOLS FOR ISRAEL–CHINUCH ATZMAI (1953). 40 Exchange Pl., NYC 10005. (212)248-6200. FAX: (212)248-6202. Pres. Rabbi Abraham Pam; Exec. Dir. Rabbi Henach Cohen. Conducts information programs for the American Jewish community on activities of the independent Torah schools educational network in Israel; coordinates role of American members of international board of governors; funds special programs of Mercaz Hachinuch Ha-Atzmai B'Eretz Yisroel; funds religous education programs in America and abroad.

TORAH UMESORAH–NATIONAL SOCIETY FOR HEBREW DAY SCHOOLS (1944). 160 Broadway, NYC 10038. (212)227-1000. FAX: (212)406-6934. E-mail: umesorah@aol.com. Chmn. David Singer; Pres. Yaakov Rajchenbach; Exec. V.-Pres. Rabbi Joshua Fishman. Establishes Hebrew day schools and Yeshivas in U.S. and Canada and provides a full gamut of services, including placement, curriculum guidance, and teacher training. Parent Enrichment Program provides enhanced educational experience for students from less Jewishly educated and marginally affiliated homes through parent-education

programs and Partners in Torah, a one-on-one learning program. Publishes textbooks; runs shabbatonim, extracurricular activities; national PTA groups; national and regional teacher conventions. *Olomeinu-Our World.*

———, NATIONAL ASSOCIATION OF HEBREW Day School Administrators (1960). 1114 Ave. J, Brooklyn, NY 11230. (718)258-7767. Pres. David H. Schwartz. Coordinates the work of the fiscal directors of Hebrew day schools throughout the country. *NAHDSA Review.*

———, NATIONAL ASSOCIATION OF HEBREW DAY SCHOOL PARENT-TEACHER ASSOCIATIONS (1948). 160 Broadway, NYC 10038. (212)227-1000. FAX: (212)406-6934. Natl. PTA Coord. Bernice Brand. Acts as a clearinghouse and service agency to PTAs of Hebrew day schools; organizes parent education courses and sets up programs for individual PTAs. *Fundraising with a Flair; PTA with a Purpose for the Hebrew Day School.*

———, NATIONAL CONFERENCE OF YESHIVA PRINCIPALS (1956). 160 Broadway, NYC 10038. (212)227-1000. FAX: (212)406-6934. E-mail: umesorah@aol. com. Pres. Rabbi Rephael Skaist; Bd. Chmn. Rabbi Dov Leibenstein; Exec. V.-Pres. Rabbi A. Moshe Possick. Professional organization of elementary and secondary yeshivah/day-school principals providing yeshivah/day schools with school evaluation and guidance, teacher and principal conferences-including a Mid-Winter Conference and a National Educators Convention; offers placement service for principals and teachers in yeshivah day schools. *Directory of Elementary Schools and High Schools.*

———, NATIONAL YESHIVA TEACHERS BOARD OF LICENSE (1953). 160 Broadway, NYC 10038. (212)227-1000. Exec. V.-Pres. & Dir. Rabbi Joshua Fishman. Issues licenses to qualified instructors for all grades of the Hebrew day school and the general field of Torah education.

UNION FOR TRADITIONAL JUDAISM (1984). 811 Palisade Ave., Teaneck, NJ 07666. (201)801-0707. FAX: (201)801-0449. E-mail: utj@aol.com. Pres. Burton G. Greenblatt; Exec. V.-Pres. Rabbi Ronald D. Price. Through innovative outreach programs, seeks to bring the greatest possible number of Jews closer to an open-minded observant Jewish life-style. Activities include Operation Pesah, the Panel of Halakhic Inquiry, Speakers Bureau, adult and youth conferences, congregational services, and UTJ Internet Education Program. Includes, since 1992, the MORASHAH rabbinic educational fellowship and Neshamah teen program. *Hagahelet (quarterly newsletter); Kosher Nexus (bimonthly newsletter); Cornerstone (journal); Tomeikh Kahalakhah (Jewish legal responsa).*

UNION OF AMERICAN HEBREW CONGREGATIONS (1873). 633 Third Ave., NYC 10017-6778. (212)650-4000. FAX: (212) 650-4169. E-mail: uahc@uahc.org. Pres. Rabbi Eric H. Yoffie; V.-Pres. Rabbi Lennard R. Thal; Bd. Chmn. Jerome H. Somers. Serves as the central congregational body of Reform Judaism in the Western Hemisphere; serves its approximately 875 affiliated temples and membership with religious, educational, cultural, and administrative programs. *Reform Judaism.*

———, AMERICAN CONFERENCE OF CANTORS (1953). 140 Central Ave., Lawrence, NY 11559. (516)239-3650. FAX: (516)239-4318. E-mail: accantors@aol. com. Pres. David M. Goldstein; Exec. V.-Pres. Howard M. Stahl; Dir. of Placement Richard Botton; Admin. Asst. Jacqueline A. Maron. Members receive investiture and commissioning as cantors at recognized seminaries, i.e., Hebrew Union College-Jewish Institute of Religion, School of Sacred Music, as well as full certification through HUC-JIR-SSM. Through the Joint Cantorial Placement Commission, the ACC serves Reform congregations seeking cantors. Dedicated to creative Judaism, preserving the best of the past, and encouraging new and vital approaches to religious ritual, music, and ceremonies. *Koleinu.*

———, COMMISSION ON REFORM JEWISH EDUCATION OF THE UNION OF AMERICAN HEBREW CONGREGATIONS, CENTRAL CONFERENCE OF AMERICAN RABBIS, NATIONAL ASSOCIATION OF TEMPLE EDUCATORS IN ASSOCIATION WITH THE HEBREW UNION COLLEGE–JEWISH INSTITUTE OF RELIGION (1923). 633 3rd Ave., NYC 10017. (212)650-4110. FAX: (212)650-4229. E-mail: educate@uahc.org. Chmn. Robin L. Eisenberg; Dir. Rabbi Jan Katzew. Long-range planning and policy development for congregational programs of lifelong education; materials concerning Reform Jewish Outreach, Teacher Development and Reform Day Schools; activities administered by the UAHC Department of Education. V'Shinantam; Torah at the Center.

———, COMMISSION ON SOCIAL ACTION OF REFORM JUDAISM (see p. 584)

———, COMMISSION ON SYNAGOGUE MANAGEMENT (UAHC-CCAR) (1962). 633 3rd Ave., NYC 10017-6778. (212)650-4040. FAX: (212)650-4239. Chmn. James M. Friedman; Dir. Dale A. Glasser. Assists congregations in management, finance, building maintenance, design, construction, and art aspects of synagogues; maintains the Synagogue Architectural Library.

———, NATIONAL ASSOCIATION OF TEMPLE ADMINISTRATORS (NATA) (1941). 6114 La Salle Ave., Box 731, Oakland, CA 94611. (800)966-6282. FAX: (925)283-7713. Pres. Fern M. Kamen. Professional organization for UAHC synagogue administrators. Sponsors graduate training in synagogue management with Hebrew Union College; offers in-service training, workshops, and conferences leading to certification; provides NATA Consulting Service, NATA Placement Service for synagogues seeking advice or professional administrators; establishes professional standards. *NATA Journal; Temple Management Manual.*

———, NATIONAL ASSOCIATION OF TEMPLE EDUCATORS (NATE) (1955). 10425 Old Olive St. Rd., Suite 2, St. Louis, MO 63141-5940. (314)692-2224. FAX: (314)692-2225. E-mail: nateoff@aol.com. Pres. Sharon S. Morton; Exec. Dir. Lori S. Lasday; Placement Dir. Richard M. Morin. 707 Summerly Dr., Nashville, TN 37209-4253. FAX (615)352-7800. E-mail:rmorin @nashville.org. Represents the temple educator within the general body of Reform Judaism; fosters the full-time profession of the temple educator; encourages the growth and development of Jewish religious education consistent with the aims of Reform Judaism; stimulates communal interest in and responsibility for Jewish religious education. *NATE NEWS; Compass.*

———, NORTH AMERICAN FEDERATION OF TEMPLE BROTHERHOODS (1923). 633

Third Ave., NYC 10017. (212)650-4100. FAX: (212)650-4189. E-mail: nftb@uahc. org. Pres. Stephen K. Breslauer; 1st V.-Pres./JCS Chancellor Irving B. Shnaider; Exec. Dir. Douglas Barden. Dedicated to enhancing the world through the ideal of brotherhood, NFTB and its 300 affiliated clubs are actively involved in education, social action, youth activities, and other programs that contribute to temple and community life. Supports the Jewish Chautauqua Society, an interfaith educational project. *Brotherhood magazine*. (RJ.ORG/NFTB)

————, WOMEN OF REFORM JUDAISM—THE FEDERATION OF TEMPLE SISTERHOODS (1913). 633 Third Ave., NYC 10017. (212)650-4050. FAX: (212)650-4059. E-mail: wrj@uahc.org. Pres. Judith Silverman; Exec. Dir. Ellen Y. Rosenberg. Serves more than 600 sisterhoods of Reform Judaism; promotes interreligious understanding and social justice; provides funding for scholarships for rabbinic students; founded the Jewish Braille Institute, which provides braille and large-type Judaic materials for Jewish blind; supports projects for Israel; is the women's agency of Reform Judaism, an affiliate of the UAHC; works in behalf of the Hebrew Union College-Jewish Institute of Religion and the World Union for Progressive Judaism. *Notes for Now; Art Calendar; Windows on WRJ*. (RJ.ORG.WRJ)

————, YOUTH DIVISION AND NORTH AMERICAN FEDERATION OF TEMPLE YOUTH (1939). 633 Third Ave, NYC 10017-6778. (212)6500-4070. E-mail: rjyouth@warwick.net. Dir. UAHC Youth Div. Rabbi Allan L. Smith; Dir. NFTY/Jr. & Sr. High School Programs Rabbi Dennis Eisner. Dedicated to Jewishly enhancing the lives of the young people of North America's Reform congregations through a program of informal education carried out in UAHC Camp-Institutes (11 camps for grades 2 and up), UAHC/NFTY Israel Programs (summer and semester), NFTY/Junior & Senior High School Programs (youth groups), and Kesher/College Education Department (Reform havurot on campuses).

UNION OF ORTHODOX JEWISH CONGREGATIONS OF AMERICA (1898). 333 Seventh Ave., NYC 10001. (212)563-4000. FAX: (212)564-9058. E-mail: ou@ou.org. Pres. Mandell I. Ganchrow, M.D.; Exec. V.-Pres. Rabbi Raphael Butler. Serves as the national central body of Orthodox synagogues; national OU kashrut supervision and certification service; sponsors Institute for Public Affairs; National Conference of Synagogue Youth; National Jewish Council for the Disabled; Israel Center in Jerusalem; Torah Center in the Ukraine; New Young Leadership Division; Pardes; provides educational, religious, and organization programs, events, and guidance to synagogues and groups; represents the Orthodox Jewish community to governmental and civic bodies and the general Jewish community. *Jewish Action magazine; OU Kosher Directory; OU Passover Directory; OU News Reporter; Synagogue Spotlight; Our Way magazine; Yachad magazine; Luach & Limud Personal Torah Study.*

————, INSTITUTE FOR PUBLIC AFFAIRS (1989). 333 Seventh Ave., NYC 10001. (212)613-8123. FAX: (212)564-9058. E-mail: ipa@ou.org. Pres. Mandell I. Ganchrow, M.D.; Chmn. Richard Stone; Dir. Nathan Diament; Dir. Internatl. Affairs & Community Relations Betty Ehrenberg. Serves as the policy analysis, advocacy, mobilization, and programming department responsible for representing Orthodox/traditional American Jewry. *IPA Currents (quarterly newsletter).*

————, NATIONAL CONFERENCE OF SYNAGOGUE YOUTH (1954). 333 Seventh Ave., NYC 10001. (212)563-4000. E-mail: ncsy@ou.org. Dir. Rabbi Pinchas Stolper; Exec. Dir. Paul Glasser. Central body for youth groups of Orthodox congregations; provides educational guidance, Torah study groups, community service, program consultation, Torah library, Torah fund scholarships, Ben Zakkai Honor Society, Friends of NCSY, weeklong seminars, Israel Summer Experience for teens and Camp NCSY East Summer Kollel & Michlelet, Teen Torah Center. Divisions include Senior NCSY, Junior NCSY for preteens, Our Way for the Jewish deaf, Yachad for the developmentally disabled, Israel Center in Jerusalem, and NCSY in Israel. *Keeping Posted with NCSY; Darchei Da'at.*

————, WOMEN'S BRANCH (1923). 156 Fifth Ave., NYC 10010. (212)929-8857. Pres. Marilyn Golomb Selber. Umbrella organization of Orthodox sisterhoods in U.S.

and Canada, educating women in Jewish learning and observance; provides programming, leadership, and organizational guidance, conferences, conventions, Marriage Committee and projects concerning mikvah, Shalom Task Force, and Welcoming Guests. Works with Orthodox Union Commissions and outreach; supports Stern and Touro College scholarships and Jewish braille publications; supplies Shabbat candelabra for hospital patients; NGO representative at UN. *Hachodesh; Hakol.*

UNION OF ORTHODOX RABBIS OF THE UNITED STATES AND CANADA (1902). 235 E. Broadway, NYC 10002. (212)964-6337(8). Dir. Rabbi Hersh M. Ginsberg. Seeks to foster and promote Torah-true Judaism in the U.S. and Canada; assists in the establishment and maintenance of yeshivot in the U.S.; maintains committee on marriage and divorce and aids individuals with marital difficulties; disseminates knowledge of traditional Jewish rites and practices and publishes regulations on synagogal structure; maintains rabbinical court for resolving individual and communal conflicts. *HaPardes.*

UNION OF SEPHARDIC CONGREGATIONS, INC. (1929). 8 W. 70 St., NYC 10023. (212)873-0300. FAX: (212)724-6165. Pres. Rabbi Marc D. Angel; Bd. Chmn. Alvin Deutsch. Promotes the religious interests of Sephardic Jews; prints and distributes Sephardic prayer books. Annual International Directory of Sephardic Congregations.

UNITED LUBAVITCHER YESHIVOTH (1940). 841-853 Ocean Pkwy., Brooklyn, NY 11230. (718)859-7600. FAX: (718)434-1519. Supports and organizes Jewish day schools and rabbinical seminaries in the U.S. and abroad.

UNITED SYNAGOGUE OF CONSERVATIVE JUDAISM (1913). 155 Fifth Ave., NYC 10010-6802. (212)533-7800. FAX: (212) 353-9439. E-mail: info@uscj.org. Pres. Stephen S. Wolnek; Exec. V.-Pres. Rabbi Jerome M. Epstein. International organization of nearly 800 Conservative congregations. Maintains 12 departments and 20 regional offices to assist its affiliates with religious, educational, youth, community, and administrative programming and guidance; aims to enhance the cause of Conservative Judaism, further religious observance, encourage establishment of Jewish religious schools, draw youth closer to Jewish tradition. Extensive Israel programs. *United Synagogue Review; Art/Engagement Calendar; Program Suggestions; Directory & Resource Guide; Book Service Catalogue of Publications.* (WWW.USCJ.ORG)

———, COMMISSION ON JEWISH EDUCATION (1930). 155 Fifth Ave., NYC 10010. (212)533-7800. FAX: (212)353-9439. E-mail: education@uscj.org. Chmn. Temma Kingsley; Dir. Rabbi Robert Abramson. Develops educational policy for the United Synagogue of Conservative Judaism and sets the educational direction for Conservative congregations, their schools, and the Solomon Schechter Day Schools. Seeks to enhance the educational effectiveness of congregations through the publication of materials and in-service programs. *Tov L'Horot; Your Child; Shiboley Schechter; Advisories.*

———, COMMISSION ON SOCIAL ACTION AND PUBLIC POLICY (1958). 155 Fifth Ave., NYC 10010. (212)533-7800. FAX: (212)353-9439. Chmn. J.B. Mazer; Dir. Sarrae G. Crane. Develops and implements positions and programs on issues of social action and public policy for the United Synagogue of Conservative Judaism; represents these positions to other Jewish and civic organizations, the media, and government; and provides guidance, both informational and programmatic, to its affiliated congregations in these areas. *HaMa'aseh.*

———, JEWISH EDUCATORS ASSEMBLY (1951). 106-06 Queens Blvd., Forest Hills, NY 11375-4248. (718)268-9452. FAX: (718)520-4369.E-mail: 76757.34@compuserve.com. Pres. Dr. Mark Silk; Exec. Dir. Dr. Esther M. Schulman. Promotes the vitality of the Conservative movement by encouraging professional growth and development, maintaining professional standards, acting as an advocate for Jewish education, and supporting educators' well-being. Services offered:annual conference, placement service, career services, research grants, and personal benefits. *V'Aleh Ha-Chadashot newsletter.*

———, KADIMA (formerly PRE-USY; reorg. 1968). 155 Fifth Ave., NYC 10010-6802. (212)533-7800. FAX: (212)353-9439. E-mail: kadima@uscj.org. Dir. Karen L.

Stein; Dir. of Youth Activities Jules A Gutin. Involves Jewish preteens in a meaningful religious, educational, and social environment; fosters a sense of identity and commitment to the Jewish community and the Conservative movement; conducts synagogue-based chapter programs and regional Kadima days and weekends. *Mitzvah of the Month; Kadima Kesher; Chagim; Advisors Aid; Games; quarterly Kol Kadima magazine.*

———, NORTH AMERICAN ASSOCIATION OF SYNAGOGUE EXECUTIVES (1948). c/o Marilyn Zirl, Admin. Asst., 7 Scotland Dr., Livingston, NJ 07039. (973)992-7845. FAX: (973)992-2292. Pres. Amir Pilch; Hon. Pres. Jan Baron. Aids congregations affiliated with the United Synagogue of Conservative Judaism to further the aims of Conservative Judaism through more effective administration (Program for Assistance by Liaisons to Synagogues— PALS); advances professional standards and promotes new methods in administration; cooperates in United Synagogue placement services and administrative surveys. *NAASE Connections Newsletter; NAASE Journal, Kadima Kesher (Advisor's Newsletter).*

———, UNITED SYNAGOGUE YOUTH OF (1951). 155 Fifth Ave., NYC 10010. (212)533-7800. FAX: (212)353-9439. E-mail: youth@uscj.org. Pres. Joshua Kaplan; Exec. Dir. Jules A. Gutin. Seeks to strengthen identification with Conservative Judaism, based on the personality development, needs, and interests of the adolescent, in a mitzvah framework. *Achshav; Tikun Olam; A.J. Heschel Honor Society Newsletter; SATO Newsletter; USY Program Bank; Hakesher Newsletter for Advisors.*

VAAD MISHMERETH STAM (1976). 4901 16th Ave., Brooklyn, NY 11204. (718) 438-4963. FAX: (718)438-9343. Pres. Rabbi David L. Greenfeld. A nonprofit consumer-protection agency dedicated to preserving and protecting the halakhic integrity of Torah scrolls, tefillin, phylacteries, and mezuzoth. Publishes material for laymen and scholars in the field of scribal arts; makes presentations and conducts examination campaigns in schools and synagogues; created an optical software system to detect possible textual errors in stam. Teaching and certifying sofrim worldwide. Offices in Israel, Stras-

bourg, Chicago, London, Manchester, Montreal, and Zurich. Publishes *Guide to Mezuzah* and *Encyclopedia of the Secret Aleph Beth. The Jewish Quill.*

WASHINGTON INSTITUTE FOR JEWISH LEADERSHIP & VALUES (1988). 11710 Hunters Lane, Rockville, MD 20852. (301) 770-5070. FAX: (301) 770-6365. E-mail: panin@aol.com. Pres. Rabbi Sidney Schwarz; Bd. Chmn. Norman R. Pozez. An educational foundation advancing Tikkun Olam, activism, and civic engagement by American Jews, grounded in Torah and Jewish values. Its flagship program is Panim el Panim:High School in Washington. Also sponsors the Jewish Civic Initiative for communities and day schools and offers leadership training workshops for college and adult audiences. *Jewish Civics: A Tikkun Olam/World Repair Manual; Jews, Judaism and Civic Responsibility.*

WOMEN'S LEAGUE FOR CONSERVATIVE JUDAISM (1918). 48 E. 74 St., NYC 10021. (212)628-1600. FAX: (212)772-3507. Pres. Janet Tobin; Exec. Dir. Bernice Balter. Parent body of Conservative (Masorti) women's synagogue groups in U.S., Canada, Puerto Rico, Mexico, and Israel; provides programs and resources in Jewish education, social action, Israel affairs, American and Canadian public affairs, leadership training, community service programs for persons with disabilities, conferences on world affairs, study institutes, publicity techniques; publishes books of Jewish interest; contributes to support of Jewish Theological Seminary of America. *Women's League Outlook magazine; Ba'Olam world affairs newsletter.*

WORLD COUNCIL OF CONSERVATIVE/ MASORTI SYNAGOGUE (1957). 155 Fifth Ave., NYC 10010. (212)533-7800, ext. 2014, 2018. FAX: (212)533-9439. Pres. Rabbi Marc Liebhaber; Rabbi of Council, Rabbi Benjamin Z. Kreitman. International representative of Conservative organizations and congregations; promotes the growth and development of the Conservative movement in Israel and throughout the world; supports educational institutions overseas; holds biennial international conventions; represents the world Conservative movement on the Executive of the World Zionist Organization. *World Spectrum.*

WORLD UNION FOR PROGRESSIVE JUDAISM, LTD. (1926). 633 Third Ave., NYC 10017. (212)650-4090. FAX: (212)650-4099. E-mail: 5448032@mcimail.com. Pres. Austin Beutel; Exec. Dir. Rabbi Richard A. Block. International umbrella organization of Liberal Judaism; promotes and coordinates efforts of Liberal congregations throughout the world; starts new congregations, recruits rabbis and rabbinical students for all countries; organizes international conferences of Liberal Jews. *World News.*

SCHOOLS, INSTITUTIONS

ACADEMY FOR JEWISH RELIGION (1955). 15 W. 86 St., NYC 10024. (212)875-0540. FAX: (212)875-0541. E-mail: seminary @erols.com. Pres. Rabbi Shohama Wiener; Dean Rabbi Samuel Barth. The only rabbinic and cantorial seminary in the U.S. at which students explore the full range of Jewish spiritual learning and practice. Graduates serve in Conservative, Reform, Reconstructionist, and Orthodox congregations, chaplaincies, and educational institutions. Programs include rabbinic and cantorial studies in NYC and on/off-campus nonmatriculated studies.

ANNENBERG RESEARCH INSTITUTE (*see* CENTER FOR JUDAIC STUDIES)

BALTIMORE HEBREW UNIVERSITY (1919). 5800 Park Heights Ave., Baltimore, MD 21215. (410)578-6900; (888)248-7420. FAX: (410)578-6940. E-mail: bhu@bhu .edu. Pres. Dr. Robert O. Freedman; Bd. Chmn. George B. Hess, Jr . . . Offers PhD, MA, BA, and AA programs in Jewish studies, Jewish education, biblical and Near Eastern archaeology, philosophy, literature, history, Hebrew language, literature, and contemporary Jewish civilization; School of Continuing Education; Joseph Meyerhoff Library; community lectures, film series, seminars. *The Scribe.*

———, BALTIMORE INSTITUTE FOR JEWISH COMMUNAL SERVICE. (410)578-6932. FAX: (410)578-1803. Dir. Karen S. Bernstein. Trains Jewish communal professionals; offers a joint degree program: an MA from BHU and an MAJE from BHU, an MSW from U. of Maryland School of Social Work, or an MPS in policy sciences from UMBC; MA with Meyerhoff Graduate School and Johns Hopkins U. in nonprofit management.

———, BERNARD MANEKIN SCHOOL OF UNDERGRADUATE STUDIES. Dean Dr. George Berlin. BA program; interinstitutional program with Johns Hopkins University; interdisciplinary concentrations: contemporary Middle East, American Jewish culture, and the humanities; Russian/English program for new Americans; assoc. of arts (AA) degree in Jewish studies.

———, LEONARD AND HELEN R. STULMAN SCHOOL OF CONTINUING EDUCATION. Dean Dr. George Berlin. Noncredit program open to the community, offering a variety of courses, trips, and events covering a range of Jewish subjects.

———, PEGGY MEYERHOFF PEARLSTONE SCHOOL OF GRADUATE STUDIES. Dean Dr. Barry M. Gittlen. PhD and MA programs; MA in Jewish studies; MAJE in Jewish education; PhD in Jewish studies; a double master's degree with an MA from BHU and an MAJE from BHU, an MSW from the University of Maryland School of Social Work, or an MPS in policy sciences from UMBC; MA with Baltimore Institute and Johns Hopkins U. in nonprofit management.

BRAMSON ORT TECHNICAL INSTITUTE (1977). 69-30 Austin St., Forest Hills, NY 11375. (718)261-5800. Dean of Academic Services Barry Glotzer. A two-year Jewish technical college offering certificates and associate degrees in technology and business fields, including accounting, computer, electronics technology, business management, office technology. Extension sites in Manhattan and Brooklyn.

BRANDEIS-BARDIN INSTITUTE (1941). 1101 Peppertree Lane, Brandeis, CA 93064. (805)582-4450. FAX: (805)526-1398. E-mail: bbibci4u@aol.com. Pres. Helen Zukia. A Jewish pluralistic, nondenominational educational institution providing programs for people of all ages:BCI (Brandeis Collegiate Institute), a summer leadership program for college-age adults from around the world; Camp Alonim, a summer Jewish experience for children 8-16; Gan Alonim Day Camp for children in kindergarten to 6th grade; weekend retreats for adults with leading contemporary Jewish scholars-in-residence; Jewish music concerts; Family Days and Weekends, Grandparents Weekends, Elderhostel, Young Adult programs, dance weekends, institute for newly marrieds. *Monthly Updates; BBI Newsletter; BCI Alumni News.*

BRANDEIS UNIVERSITY (1948). 415 South St., Waltham, MA 02254. (781)736-2000. Pres. Jehuda Reinharz; Provost Irving Epstein; Exec. V.-Pres. & CEO Peter B. French; Sr. V.-Pres. of Devel. Nancy Winship. Founded under Jewish sponsorship as a nonsectarian institution offering undergraduate and graduate education. The Lown School is the center for all programs of teaching and research in Judaic studies, ancient Near Eastern studies, and Islamic and modern Middle Eastern studies. The school includes the Department of Near Eastern and Judaic Studies; the Hornstein Program in Jewish Communal Service, a professional training program; the Cohen Center for Modern Jewish Studies, which conducts research and teaching in contemporary Jewish studies, primarily in American Jewish studies; and the Tauber Institute for the study of European Jewry. *Various newsletters, scholarly publications.*

CENTER FOR JUDAIC STUDIES, School of Arts and Sciences, University of Pennsylvania. (Merged with University of Pennsylvania, 1993; formerly Annenberg Research Institute, successor of Dropsie College.) 420 Walnut St., Philadelphia, PA 19106. (215)238-1290. FAX: (215) 238-1540. Dir. David B. Ruderman. *Jewish Quarterly Review.*

CLEVELAND COLLEGE OF JEWISH STUDIES (1964). 26500 Shaker Blvd., Beachwood, OH 44122. (216)464-4050. FAX: (216) 464-5827. Pres. David S. Ariel; Dir. of Student Services Ronald M. Horvat. Provides courses in all areas of Judaic and Hebrew studies to adults and college-age students; offers continuing education for Jewish educators and administrators; serves as a center for Jewish life and culture; expands the availability of courses in Judaic studies by exchanging faculty, students, and credits with neighboring academic institutions; grants bachelor's and master's degrees.

DROPSIE COLLEGE FOR HEBREW AND COGNATE LEARNING (*see* CENTER FOR JUDAIC STUDIES)

FEINBERG GRADUATE SCHOOL OF THE WEIZMANN INSTITUTE OF SCIENCE (1958). 51 Madison Ave., NYC 10010. (212)

779-2500. FAX: (212)779-3209. Chmn. Melvin Schwartz; Pres. Robert Asher; Dean Prof. Shmuel Safran. Situated on the Weizmann campus in Rehovot, Israel, provides the school's faculty and research facilities. Accredited by the Council for Higher Education of Israel and the NY State Board of Regents for the study of natural sciences, leading to MSc and PhD degrees.

GRATZ COLLEGE (1895). 7605 Old York Rd., Melrose Park, PA 19027. (215)635-7300. FAX: (215)635-7320. Bd. Chmn. William L. Landsburg; Interim Pres. Dr. Ernest M. Kahn. Offers a wide variety of undergraduate and graduate degrees and continuing education programs in Judaic, Hebraic, and Middle Eastern studies. Grants BA and MA in Jewish studies, MA in Jewish education (joint program in special needs education with La Salle U.), MA in Jewish music, MA in Jewish liberal studies, MA in Jewish communal studies, certificates in Jewish communal studies (joint program with U. of Penna. School of Social Work), Jewish education, Israel studies, Judaica librarianship (joint program with Drexel U.), and Jewish music. Joint graduate program with Reconstructionist Rabbinical College in Jewish education and Jewish music. Netzky Division of Continuing Education and Jewish Community High School. *Various newsletters, annual academic bulletin, scholarly publications, centennial volume, and occasional papers.*

HEBREW COLLEGE (1921). 43 Hawes St., Brookline, MA 02446. (617)232-8710. FAX: (617)264-9264. Pres. Dr. David M. Gordis; Bd. Chmn. Dr. Norman P. Spack. Through training in Jewish texts, history, literature, ethics, and Hebrew language, prepares students to become literate participants in the global Jewish community. Offers graduate and undergraduate degrees and certificates in all aspects of Jewish education, Jewish studies, and Jewish music; serves students of all ages through its Prozdor High School, Camp Yavneh, Ulpan Center for Adult Jewish Learning, and *Me'ah*–One Hundred Hours of Adult Jewish Learning. *Hebrew College Today; Likut.* (WWW.HEBREWCOLLEGE.EDU)

HEBREW SEMINARY OF THE DEAF (1992). 4435 W. Oakton, Skokie, IL 60076. (847) 677-3330. FAX: (847)677-7945. E-mail: hebrewsemdeaf@juno.com. Pres. Rabbi

Douglas Goldhamer; Bd. Cochmn. Rabbi William Frankel, Alan Crane. Trains deaf and hearing men and women to become rabbis and teachers for Jewish deaf communities across America. All classes in the 5-year program are interpreted in Sign Language. Rabbis teaching in the seminary are Reform, Conservative, and Reconstructionist.

HEBREW THEOLOGICAL COLLEGE (1922). 7135 N. Carpenter Rd., Skokie, IL 60077. (847)982-2500. FAX: (847)674-6381. E-mail: htc@htcnet.edu. Chancellor Rabbi Dr. Jerold Isenberg. An accredited institution of higher Jewish learning which includes a rabbinical school; Fasman Yeshiva High School; Anne M. Blitstein Teachers Institute for Women; Wm. and Lillian Kanter School of Liberal Arts & Sciences; Max Bressler School of Advanced Hebrew Studies. *Or Shmuel; Torah Journal; Likutei P'shatim; Turrets of Silver.*

HEBREW UNION COLLEGE–JEWISH INSTITUTE OF RELIGION (1875). 3101 Clifton Ave., Cincinnati, OH 45220. (513)221-1875. FAX: (513)221-1847. Pres. Sheldon Zimmerman; Chancellor Dr. Alfred Gottschalk; V.-Pres., Admin. & Finance Arthur R. Grant; V.-Pres. Devel. Elliot B. Karp; Chmn. Bd. Govs. Burton Lehman; Provost Dr. Norman J. Cohen. Academic centers: 3101 Clifton Ave., Cincinnati, OH 45220 (1875), Dean Kenneth Ehrlich. 1 W. 4 St., NYC 10012 (1922), Dean Rabbi Aaron Panken. FAX: (212) 388-1720. 3077 University Ave., Los Angeles, CA 90007 (1954), Dean Lewis Barth; FAX: (213)747-6128. 13 King David St., Jerusalem, Israel 94101 (1963), Dean Rabbi Michael Marmur; FAX: (972-2)6251478. Prepares students for Reform rabbinate, cantorate, Jewish education and educational administration, communal service, academic careers; promotes Jewish studies; maintains libraries, archives, and museums; offers master's and doctoral degrees; engages in archaeological excavations; publishes scholarly works through Hebrew Union College Press. *American Jewish Archives; Bibliographica Judaica; HUC-JIR Catalogue; Hebrew Union College Annual; Studies in Bibliography and Booklore; The Chronicle; Kesher.*

———, AMERICAN JEWISH PERIODICAL CENTER (1957). 3101 Clifton Ave.,

Cincinnati, OH 45220. (513)221-1875, ext. 294. Dir. Herbert C. Zafren. Maintains microfilms of all American Jewish periodicals 1823-1925, selected periodicals since 1925. *Jewish Periodicals and Newspapers on Microfilm (1957); First Supplement (1960); Augmented Edition (1984).*

———, EDGAR F. MAGNIN SCHOOL OF GRADUATE STUDIES (1956). 3077 University Ave., Los Angeles, CA 90007. (213)749-3424. FAX: (213)747-6128. Dir. Dr. Reuven Firestone. Supervises programs leading to PhD (education), DHS, DHL, and MA degrees; participates in cooperative PhD programs with U. of S. Calif.

———, GRADUATE STUDIES PROGRAM. 1 West 4 St. NYC 10012. (212)674-5300, ext. 228. FAX: (212)388-1720. Dir. Dr. Carol Ochs. Offers the DHL (doctor of Hebrew letters) degree in a variety of fields; the MAJS (master of arts in Judaic studies), a multidisciplinary degree; and is the only Jewish seminary to offer the DMin (doctor of ministry) degree in pastoral care and counseling.

———, IRWIN DANIELS SCHOOL OF JEWISH COMMUNAL SERVICE (1968). 3077 University Ave., Los Angeles, CA 90007. (213)749-3424. FAX: (213)747-6128. Dir. Dr. Steven J. Windmueller. Offers certificate and master's degree to those employed in Jewish communal services, or preparing for such work; offers joint MA in Jewish education and communal service with Rhea Hirsch School; offers dual degrees with the School of Social Work, the School of Public Administration, the Annenberg School for Communication, Marshall School of Business and the School of Gerontology of the U. of S. Calif. and with other institutions. Single master's degrees can be completed in 15 months and certificates are awarded for the completion of two full-time summer sessions.

———, JACOB RADER MARCUS CENTER OF THE AMERICAN JEWISH ARCHIVES (see p. 591)

———, JEROME H. LOUCHHEIM SCHOOL OF JUDAIC STUDIES (1969). 3077 University Ave., Los Angeles, CA 90007. (213)749-3424. FAX: (213)747-6128. Dir. Dr. Reuven Firestone. Offers programs leading to MA, BS, BA, and AA degrees; offers courses as part of the undergraduate program of the U. of S. Calif.

———, NELSON GLUECK SCHOOL OF BIBLICAL ARCHAEOLOGY (1963). 13 King David St., Jerusalem, Israel 94101. (972)2-6203333. FAX: (972)2-6251478. Dir. Avraham Biran. Offers graduate-level research programs in Bible and archaeology. Summer excavations are carried out by scholars and students. University credit may be earned by participants in excavations. Consortium of colleges, universities, and seminaries is affiliated with the school. Skirball Museum of Biblical Archaeology (artifacts from Tel Dan, Tel Gezer, and Aroer).

———, RHEA HIRSCH SCHOOL OF EDUCATION (1967). 3077 University Ave., Los Angeles, CA 90007. (213)749-3424. FAX: (213)747-6128. Dir. Sara Lee. Offers PhD and MA programs in Jewish and Hebrew education; conducts joint degree programs with U. of S. Calif.; offers courses for Jewish teachers, librarians, and early educators on a nonmatriculating basis; conducts summer institutes for professional Jewish educators.

———, SCHOOL OF EDUCATION (1947). 1 W. 4 St., NYC 10012. (212)674-5300, ext. 228. FAX: (212)388-1720. Interim Dir. Dr. Adina Hamik. Trains teachers and principals for Reform religious schools; offers MA degree with specialization in religious education.

———, SCHOOL OF GRADUATE STUDIES (1949). 3101 Clifton Ave., Cincinnati, OH 45220. (513)221-1875, ext. 230. FAX: (513)221-0321. Dir. Dr. Adam Kamesar. Offers programs leading to MA and PhD degrees; offers program leading to DHL degree for rabbinic graduates of the college.

———, SCHOOL OF JEWISH STUDIES (1963). 13 King David St., Jerusalem, 94101. (972)2-6203333. FAX: (972)2-6251478. Dean Rabbi Michael Marmur; Assoc. Dean Rabbi Shaul R. Feinberg. Offers first year of graduate rabbinic, cantorial, and Jewish education studies (required) for American students; program leading to ordination for Israeli rabbinic students; undergraduate one-year work/study program on a kibbutz and in Jerusalem in cooperation with Union of American Hebrew Congregations; Hebrew Ulpan for Olim; Abramov Library

of Judaica, Hebraica, Ancient Near East and American Jewish Experience; Skirball Museum of Biblical Archaeology; public outreach programs (lectures, courses, concerts, exhibits).

———, SCHOOL OF SACRED MUSIC (1947). 1 W. 4 St., NYC 10012. (212)674-5300, ext. 225. FAX: (212)388-1720. Dir. Cantor Israel Goldstein. Trains cantors for congregations; offers MSM degree. *Sacred Music Press.*

———, SKIRBALL CULTURAL CENTER (see p. 594)

INSTITUTE OF TRADITIONAL JUDAISM (1990). 811 Palisade Ave., Teaneck, NJ 07666. (201)801-0707. FAX: (201)801-0449. Rector (Reish Metivta) Rabbi David Weiss Halivni; Dean Rabbi Ronald D. Price. A nondenominational halakhic rabbinical school dedicated to genuine faith combined with intellectual honesty and the love of Israel. Graduates receive "yoreh yoreh" smikhah.

JEWISH THEOLOGICAL SEMINARY OF AMERICA (1886; reorg. 1902). 3080 Broadway, NYC 10027-4649. (212)678-8000. FAX: (212)678-8947. Chancellor Dr. Ismar Schorsch; Bd. Chmn. Gershon Kekst. Operates undergraduate and graduate programs in Judaic studies; professional schools for training Conservative rabbis, educators and cantors; the JTS Library; the Ratner Center for the Study of Conservative Judaism; Melton Research Center for Jewish Education; the Jewish Museum; Ramah Camps and the Ivry Prozdor high-school honors program. Other outreach activities include the Distance Learning Project, the Lehrhaus Adult Learning Institute, the Finkelstein Institute for Religious and Social Studies, the Havruta Program, and the Wagner Institute lay leadership program. *Academic Bulletin; JTS Magazine; Gleanings; JTS News.* (WWW.JTSA.EDU)

———, ALBERT A. LIST COLLEGE OF JEWISH STUDIES (formerly SEMINARY COLLEGE OF JEWISH STUDIES—TEACHERS INSTITUTE) (1909). 3080 Broadway, NYC 10027. (212)678-8826. Dean Dr. Shuly Rubin Schwartz. Offers complete undergraduate program in Judaica leading to BA degree; conducts joint programs with Columbia University and Barnard College enabling students to receive two BA degrees.

———, DEPARTMENT OF RADIO AND TELEVISION (1944). 3080 Broadway, NYC 10027. (212)870-3180. Produces radio and TV programs expressing the Jewish tradition in its broadest sense, including hour-long documentaries on NBC and ABC. Distributes cassettes of programs at minimum charge.

———, GRADUATE SCHOOL OF JTS (formerly INSTITUTE FOR ADVANCED STUDY IN THE HUMANITIES) (1968). 3080 Broadway, NYC 10027-4649. (212)678-8024. FAX: (212)678-8947. E-mail: gradschool @jtsa.edu. Dean Dr. Stephen P. Garfinkel; Asst. Dean Dr. Bruce E. Nielsen. Programs leading to MA, DHL, and PhD degrees in Judaic studies; specializations include Ancient Judaism, Bible and Ancient Semitic Languages, Interdepartmental Studies, Jewish Art and Material Culture, Jewish education, Jewish history, Jewish literature, Jewish philosophy, Jewish Women's Studies, Liturgy, Medieval Jewish Studies, Midrash, Modern Jewish studies, Talmud and Rabbinics and Dual Degree Program with Columbia University School of Social Work.

———, H.L. MILLER CANTORIAL SCHOOL AND COLLEGE OF JEWISH MUSIC (1952). 3080 Broadway, NYC 10027. (212)678-8036. FAX: (212)678-8947. Dean Cantor Henry Rosenblum. Trains cantors, music teachers, and choral directors for congregations. Offers full-time programs in sacred music leading to degree of MSM, and diploma of *Hazzan*.

———, JEWISH MUSEUM (see p. 591)

———, LIBRARY OF THE JEWISH THEOLOGICAL SEMINARY. 3080 Broadway, NYC 10027. (212)678-8075. FAX: (212)678-8998. E-mail: library@jtsa.edu. Librarian Dr. Mayer E. Rabinowitz. Contains one of the largest collections of Hebraica and Judaica in the world, including manuscripts, incunabula, rare books, and Cairo Geniza material. The 320,000-item collection includes books, manuscripts, periodicals, sound recordings, prints, broadsides, photographs, postcards, microform, videos and CD-ROM. Exhibition of items from the collection are ongoing. Exhibition catalogs are available for sale. The Library is open to the public for on-site use (photo identification required). *Between the Lines.* (WWW.JTSA.EDU/LIBRARY)

———, LOUIS FINKELSTEIN INSTITUTE FOR RELIGIOUS AND SOCIAL STUDIES (1938). 3080 Broadway, NYC 10027. (212)870-3180. FAX: (212)678-8947. E-mail: finkelstein@jtsa.edu. Dir. Rabbi Gerald Wolpe. Since 1938 has maintained an innovative interfaith and intergroup relations program, pioneering new approaches to dialogue across religious lines. Through scholarly and practical fellowship, highlights the relevance of Judaism and other contemporary religions to current theological, ethical, and scientific issues, including the emerging challenge of bioethics.

———, MELTON RESEARCH CENTER FOR JEWISH EDUCATION (1960). 3080 Broadway, NYC 10027. (212)678-8031. E-mail: stbrown@jtsa.edu. Dir. Dr. Steven M. Brown; Admin. Lisa Siberstein-Weber. Develops new curricula and materials for Jewish education; prepares educators through seminars and in-service programs; maintains consultant and supervisory relationships with a limited number of pilot schools; develops and implements research initiatives; sponsors "renewal" etreats. *Gleanings; Courtyard: A Journal of Research and Reflection on Jewish Education.*

———, NATIONAL RAMAH COMMISSION (1947). 3080 Broadway, NYC 10027. (212)678-8881. FAX: (212)749-8251. Pres. Alan H. Silberman; Natl. Dir. Sheldon Dorph. Sponsors an international network of 14 summer camps located in the US, Canada, South America, Russia, and Israel, emphasizing Jewish education, living, and culture; offers opportunities for qualified college students and older to serve as counselors, administrators, specialists, etc., and programs for children with special needs (Tikvah program); offers special programs in U.S. and Israel, including National Ramah Staff Training Institute, Ramah Israel Seminar, Ulpan Ramah Plus, and Tichon Ramah Yerushalayim. Family and synagogue tours to Israel and summer day camp in Israel for Americans.

———, REBECCA AND ISRAEL IVRY PROZDOR (1951). 3080 Broadway, NYC 10027. (212)678-8824. E-mail: prozdor@jtsa.edu. Principal Rabbi Judd Kruger Levingston; Community Advisory Board Chmn. Michael Katz. The Hebrew high school of JTS, offers a program of Jewish studies for day school and congregational school graduates in classical texts, Hebrew, interdisciplinary seminars, training in educational leadership, and classes for college credit. Classes meet one evening a week and on Sundays in Manhattan and at affiliated programs. High School Curricula.

———, RABBINICAL SCHOOL (1886). 3080 Broadway, NYC 10027. (212)678-8817. Dean Rabbi William Lebeau. Offers a program of graduate and professional studies leading to the degree of Master of Arts and ordination; includes one year of study in Jerusalem and an extensive fieldwork program.

———, SAUL LIEBERMAN INSTITUTE FOR TALMUDIC RESEARCH (1985). 3080 Broadway, NYC 10027. (212)678-8994. FAX: (212)678D8947. E-mail: liebinst@jtsa.edu. Dir. Shamma Friedman; Coord. Jonathan Milgram. Engaged in preparing for publication a series of scholarly editions of selected chapters of the Talmud. The following projects support and help disseminate the research:Talmud Text Database; Bibliography of Talmudic Literature; Catalogue of Geniza Fragments.

———, SCHOCKEN INSTITUTE FOR JEWISH RESEARCH (1961). 6 Balfour St., Jerusalem, Israel 92102. (972)2-631288. Dir. Shmuel Glick. Comprises the Schocken collection of rare books and manuscripts and a research institute dedicated to the exploration of Hebrew religious poetry (*piyyut*). *Schocken Institute Yearbook (P'raqim)*.

———, WILLIAM DAVIDSON GRADUATE SCHOOL OF JEWISH EDUCATION (1996). 3080 Broadway, NYC 10027. (212) 678-8030. E-mail: edschool@jtsa.edu. Dean Dr. Aryeh Davidson. Offers master's and doctoral degrees in Jewish education; continuing education courses for Jewish educators and Jewish communal professionals; and programs that take advantage of the latest technology, including distance learning and interactive video classrooms.

MAALOT–A SEMINARY FOR CANTORS AND JUDAISTS (1987). 15 W. Montgomery Ave., Suite 204, Rockville, MD 20850. (301)309-2310. FAX: (301)309-2328. Pres./Exec. Off. David Shneyer. An educational program established to train individuals in Jewish music, the liturgical arts, and the use, design, and application of Jewish customs and ceremonies. Offers classes, seminars, and an independent study program.

MESIVTA YESHIVA RABBI CHAIM BERLIN RABBINICAL ACADEMY (1905). 1605 Coney Island Ave., Brooklyn, NY 11230. (718)377-0777. Exec. Dir. Y. Mayer Lasker. Maintains fully accredited elementary and high schools; collegiate and postgraduate school for advanced Jewish studies, both in America and Israel; Camp Morris, a summer study retreat; Prof. Nathan Isaacs Memorial Library; Gur Aryeh Publications.

NER ISRAEL RABBINICAL COLLEGE (1933). 400 Mt. Wilson Lane, Baltimore, MD 21208. (410)484-7200. FAX: (410)484-3060. Rabbi Yaakov S. Weinberg, Rosh Hayeshiva; Pres. Rabbi Herman N. Neuberger. Trains rabbis and educators for Jewish communities in America and worldwide. Offers bachelor's, master's, and doctoral degrees in talmudic law, as well as teacher's diploma. College has four divisions: Israel Henry Beren High School, Rabbinical College, Teachers Training Institute, Graduate School. Maintains an active community-service division. Operates special programs for Iranian and Russian Jewish students. *Ner Israel Update; Alumni Bulletin; Ohr Hanair Talmudic Journal; Iranian B'nei Torah Bulletin*.

RABBINICAL COLLEGE OF TELSHE, INC. (1941). 28400 Euclid Ave., Wickliffe, OH 44092. (216)943-5300. Pres. Rabbi Mordecai Gifter; V.-Pres. Rabbi Abba Zalka Gewirtz; Rosh Hayeshiva Pres. Rabbi Mordechai Gifter. College for higher Jewish learning specializing in talmudic studies and rabbinics; maintains a preparatory academy including a secular high school, postgraduate department, teacher-training school, and teachers' seminary for women. *Pri Etz Chaim; Peer Mordechai; Alumni Bulletin*.

RECONSTRUCTIONIST RABBINICAL COLLEGE (1968). 1299 Church Rd., Wyncote, PA 19095. (215)576-0800. FAX: (215)576-6143. E-mail: rrcinfo@rrc.edu. Pres. David Teutsch; Bd. Chmn. Jacques G. Pomeranz; Genl. Chmn. Aaron Ziegelman. Coeducational. Trains rabbis and cantors for all areas of Jewish communal life:synagogues, academic and educational positions, Hillel centers, federation agencies, and chaplaincy for hospitals, hospices, and geriatric centers; confers title of rabbi and cantor and grants degrees of Master and Doctor of Hebrew Letters and Master of Arts in Jewish Studies. *RRC Report; Reconstructionist.*

SPERTUS INSTITUTE OF JEWISH STUDIES (1924). 618 S. Michigan Ave., Chicago, IL 60605. (312)922-9012. FAX: (312)922-6406. Pres. Howard A. Sulkin; Bd. Chmn. Barbara Levy Kipper; V.-Pres. for Academic Affairs Byron L. Sherwin. An accredited institution of higher learning offering one doctor of Jewish studies degree; master's degree programs in Jewish studies, Jewish education, Jewish communal service, and human-services administration; plus an extensive program of continuing education. Major resources of the college encompass Spertus Museum, Asher Library, Chicago Jewish Archives, and Spertus College of Judaica Press.

————, SPERTUS MUSEUM (see p. 594)

TOURO COLLEGE (1970). Executive Offices: Empire State Bldg., 350 Fifth Ave., Suite 1700, NYC 10118. (212)643-0700. FAX: (212)643-0759. Pres. Dr. Bernard Lander; Bd. Chmn. Mark Hasten. Chartered by NY State Board of Regents as a nonprofit four-year college with Judaic studies, health sciences, business, and liberal arts programs leading to BA, BS, and MA, MS degrees; emphasizes relevance of Jewish heritage to general culture of Western civilization. Also offers JD degree and a biomedical program leading to the MD degree from Technion-Israel Institute of Technology, Haifa.

————, COLLEGE OF LIBERAL ARTS AND SCIENCES. 27-33 W. 23 St., NYC 10010. (212)463-0400. FAX: (212)627-9144. Exec. Dean Stanley Boylan. Offers comprehensive Jewish studies along with studies in the arts, sciences, humanities, and preprofessional studies in health sciences, law, accounting, business, computer science, education, and finance. Women's Division, 160 Lexington Ave., NYC 10016. (212)213-2230. FAX: (212)683-3281. Dean Sara E. Freifeld.

————, JACOB D. FUCHSBERG LAW CENTER (1980). Long Island Campus, 300 Nassau Rd., Huntington, NY 11743. (516) 421-2244. Dean Howard A. Glickstein. Offers studies leading to JD degree.

————, BARRY Z. LEVINE SCHOOL OF HEALTH SCIENCES AND CENTER FOR BIO-MEDICAL EDUCATION (1970). 135 Common Rd., Bldg. #10, Dix Hills, NY 11746. (516)673-3200. Dean Dr. Joseph Weisberg. Along with the Manhattan campus, offers 5 programs: 5-year program leading to MS from Touro and MD from Faculty of Medicine of Technion-Israel Institute of Technology, Haifa; BS/MS-physical therapy and occupational therapy programs; BS-physician assistant and health-information management programs.

————, SCHOOL OF GENERAL STUDIES. 240 E. 123 St., NYC 10021. (212)722-1575. Dean Stephen Adolphus. Offers educational opportunities to minority groups and older people; courses in the arts, sciences, humanities, and special programs of career studies.

————, TOURO COLLEGE FLATBUSH CENTER (1979). 1277 E. 14 St., Brooklyn, NY 11230. (718)253-7538. Dean Robert Goldschmidt. A division of the College of Liberal Arts and Sciences; options offered in accounting and business, education, mathematics, political science, psychology, and speech. Classes are given on weeknights and during the day on Sunday.

————, GRADUATE SCHOOL OF JEWISH STUDIES (1981). 160 Lexington Ave., NYC 10016. (212)213-2230. FAX: (212)683-3281. Pres. Bernard Lander; Dean Michael A. Shmidman. Offers courses leading to an MA in Jewish studies, with concentrations in Jewish history or Jewish education. Students may complete part of their program in Israel, through MA courses offered by Touro faculty at Touro's Jerusalem center.

————, INSTITUTE OF JEWISH LAW. (516) 421-2244. Based at Fuchsberg Law Center, serves as a center and clearinghouse for study and teaching of Jewish law. Coedits *Dinei Israel* (Jewish Law Journal) with Tel Aviv University Law School.

————, TOURO COLLEGE ISRAEL CENTER. 23 Rehov Shivtei Yisrael, Jerusalem. 2-894-086/088. Assoc. Dean Carmi Horowitz; Resident Dir. Chana Sosevsky. Offers undergraduate courses in business, computer science, and education. Houses the MA degree program in Jewish studies. The Touro Year Abroad Option for American students is coordinated from this center.

———, Moscow Branch. Oztozhenka #38, Moscow, Russia 119837. Offers BS program in business and BA program in Jewish studies.

University of Judaism (1947). 15600 Mulholland Dr., Los Angeles, CA 90077. (310) 440-1210. FAX: (310)471-1278. E-mail: jblumberg@uj.edu. Pres. Dr. Robert D. Wexler; V.-Pres. Academic Affairs Dr. Hanan Alexander. The College of Arts and Sciences is an accredited liberal arts college for undergraduates offering a core curriculum of Jewish, Western, and non-Western studies, with majors including bioethics (a premedical track in partnership with Cedars-Sinai Medical Center), business, English, Jewish studies, journalism, literature & politics, political science, psychology, and U.S. public policy. Accredited graduate programs in nonprofit business administration (MBA), Jewish education, and psychology with an emphasis on developmental disabilities. The Ziegler School of Rabbinic Studies provides an intensive four-year program with Conservative ordination. Home of the Center for Policy Options, conducting public policy research in areas of concern to the Jewish community, and the Whizin Center for the Jewish Future, a research and programming institute. Offers the largest adult Jewish education program in the U.S., cultural-arts programs, and a variety of outreach services for West Coast Jewish communities. *The Vision.*

West Coast Talmudical Seminary (Yeshiva Ohr Elchonon Chabad) (1953). 7215 Waring Ave., Los Angeles, CA 90046. (323)937-3763. FAX: (323)937-9456. Dean Rabbi Ezra Schochet. Provides facilities for intensive Torah education as well as Orthodox rabbinical training on the West Coast; conducts an accredited college preparatory high school combined with a full program of Torah-talmudic training and a graduate talmudical division on the college level. *Torah Quiz; Kovetz Migdal Ohr; Kovetz Ohr HaMigdal.*

Yeshiva Torah Vodaath and Mesivta Torah Vodaath Rabbinical Seminary (1918). 425 E. 9 St., Brooklyn, NY 11218. (718)941-8000. Bd. Chmn. Chaim Leshkowitz. Offers Hebrew and secular education from elementary level through rabbinical ordination and postgraduate work; maintains a teachers institute and community-service bureau; maintains a dormitory and a nonprofit camp program for boys. *Chronicle; Mesivta Vanguard; Thought of the Week; Torah Vodaath News; Ha'Mesifta.*

———, Yeshiva Torah Vodaath Alumni Association (1941). 425 E. 9 St., Brooklyn, NY 11218. (718)941-8000. Pres. George Weinberger. Promotes social and cultural ties between the alumni and the schools through classes and lectures and fund-raising; offers vocational guidance to students; operates Camp Ohr Shraga; sponsors research fellowship program for boys. *Annual Journal; Hamesivta Torah periodical.*

Yeshiva University (1886). Main Campus, 500 W. 185 St., NYC 10033-3201. (212)960-5400. FAX: (212)960-0055. Pres. Dr. Norman Lamm; Chmn. Bd. of Trustees David S. Gottesman. In its second century, the nation's oldest and most comprehensive independent university founded under Jewish auspices, with 18 undergraduate and graduate schools, divisions, and affiliates; widespread programs of research and community outreach; publications; and a museum. A broad range of curricula lead to bachelor's, master's, doctoral, and professional degrees. Undergraduate schools provide general studies curricula supplemented by courses in Jewish learning; graduate schools prepare for careers in medicine, law, social work, Jewish education, psychology, Jewish studies, and other fields. It has seven undergraduate schools, seven graduate and professional schools, and four affiliates. *Yeshiva University Review; Yeshiva University Today.* (www.yu.edu)

Yeshiva University has four campuses in Manhattan and the Bronx: Main Campus, 500 W. 185 St., NYC 10033-3201; Midtown Campus, 245 Lexington Ave., NYC 10016-4699; Brookdale Center, 55 Fifth Ave., NYC 10003-4391; Jack and Pearl Resnick Campus, Eastchester Rd. & Morris Pk. Ave., Bronx, NY 10461-1602.

Undergraduate schools for men at Main Campus (212)960-5400: Yeshiva College (Bd. Chmn. Jay Schottenstein;

Dean Dr. Norman T. Adler) provides liberal arts and sciences curricula; grants BA degree. Isaac Breuer College of Hebraic Studies (Dean Dr. Michael D. Shmidman) awards Hebrew teacher's diploma, AA, BA, and BS. James Striar School of General Jewish Studies (Dean Dr. Michael D. Shmidman) grants AA degree. Yeshiva Program/Mazer School of Talmudic Studies (Dean Rabbi Zevulun Charlop) offers advanced course of study in Talmudic texts and commentaries. Beit Midrash Program (Dean Dr. Michael D. Shmidman) offers diversified curriculum combining Talmud with Jewish studies.

Undergraduate school for women at Midtown Campus (212)340-7700: Stern College for Women (Bd. Chmn. Lea Eisenberg; Dean Dr. Karen Bacon) offers liberal arts and sciences curricula supplemented by Jewish studies programs; awards BA, AA, and Hebrew teacher's diploma.

Sy Syms School of Business at Main Campus and Midtown Campus (Bd. Chmn. Josh S. Weston; Dean Dr. Harold Nierenberg) offers undergraduate business curricula in conjunction with study at Yeshiva College or Stern College; grants BS degree.

———, ALBERT EINSTEIN COLLEGE OF MEDICINE (1955). Eastchester Rd. & Morris Pk. Ave., Bronx, NY 10461-1602. (718)430-2000. Pres. Dr. Norman Lamm; Chpers. Bd. of Overseers Burton P. Resnick; Dean Dr. Dominick P. Purpura. Prepares physicians and conducts research in the health sciences; awards MD degree; includes Sue Golding Graduate Division of Medical Sciences (Dir. Dr. Anne M. Etgen), which grants PhD degree. Einstein's clinical facilities and affiliates encompass Jack D. Weiler Hospital of Albert Einstein College of Medicine, Jacobi Medical Center, Montefiore Medical Center, Long Island Jewish Medical Center, Beth Israel Medical Center, Catholic Medical Center of Brooklyn and Queens, Bronx-Lebanon Hospital Center, and Rose F. Kennedy Center for Research in Mental Retardation and Human Development. *Einstein; Einstein Today; Einstein Quarterly Journal of Biology and Medicine.*

———, ALUMNI OFFICE, 500 W. 185 St., NYC 10033-3201. (212)960-5373. E-mail: alumdesk2ymail.yu.edu. University Dir.

Alumni Affairs Robert R. Saltzman; Dir. Undergraduate Alumni Relations Toby Hilsenrad Weiss. Seeks to foster a close allegiance of alumni to their alma mater by maintaining ties with all alumni and servicing the following associations: Yeshiva College Alumni (Pres. Stuart Verstandig); Stern College for Women Alumnae (Pres. Yonina Langer); Sy Syms School of Business Alumni (Copres. Ofer and Elizabeth Naor); Albert Einstein College of Medicine Alumni (Pres. Dr. Neal Flomenbaum); Ferkauf Graduate School of Psychology Alumni (Contact: Michael S. Gill); Wurzweiler School of Social Work Alumni (Copres. Joel Katz and Annette Praeger); Rabbinic Alumni (Pres. Rabbi Gershon C. Gewirtz); Benjamin N. Cardozo School of Law Alumni (Copres. Jonathan and Pamela Henes). *Yeshiva University Review; AECOM Alumni News; Wurzweiler Update; Jewish Social Work Forum.*

———, AZRIELI GRADUATE SCHOOL OF JEWISH EDUCATION AND ADMINISTRATION (1945). 245 Lexington Ave., NYC 10016-4699. (212)340-7705. Dir. Dr. Yitzchak S. Handel. Offers MS degree in Jewish elementary and secondary education; specialist's certificate and EdD in administration and supervision of Jewish education. Block Education Program, initiated under a grant from the Jewish Agency's L.A. Pincus Fund for the Diaspora, provides summer course work to complement year-round field instruction in local communities.

———, BELFER INSTITUTE FOR ADVANCED BIOMEDICAL STUDIES (1978). Eastchester Rd. & Morris Pk. Ave., Bronx, NY 10461-1602. (718)430-3306. Dir. Dr. Dennis Shields. Integrates and coordinates the Albert Einstein College of Medicine's postdoctoral research and training-grant programs in the basic and clinical biomedical sciences. Awards certificate as research fellow or research associate on completion of training.

———, BENJAMIN N. CARDOZO SCHOOL OF LAW (1976). 55 Fifth Ave., NYC 10003-4391. (212)790-0200. E-mail:lawinfo@ymail.yu.edu. Pres. Dr. Norman Lamm; Chmn. Bd. of Dirs. Earle I. Mack; Dean Paul R. Verkuil. Offers a rigorous and enriched legal education leading to juris doctor (JD) degree and two LLM programs—in intellectual property law and in general studies—for those interested in specialized training and for international students. Programs and services include institute for advanced legal studies; center for ethics in the practice of law; legal services clinic; international institute and Israel program; institute of Jewish law; international law and human-rights programs; and other special programs. *Cardozo Law Review; Cardozo Arts and Entertainment Law Journal; Cardozo Women's Law Journal; Cardozo Journal of International and Comparative Law; Cardozo Studies in Law and Literature; Post-Soviet Media Law and Policy Newsletter; New York Real Estate Reporter.*

———, BERNARD REVEL GRADUATE SCHOOL (1935). 500 W. 185 St., NYC 10033-3201. (212)960-5253. Pres. Dr. Norman Lamm; Chmn. Bd. of Dirs. Mordecai D. Katz; Dean Dr. Arthur Hyman. Offers graduate programs in Bible, Talmudic studies, Jewish history, and Jewish philosophy; confers MA and PhD degrees. Harry Fischel School for Higher Jewish Studies offers the Revel program during the summer.

———, FERKAUF GRADUATE SCHOOL OF PSYCHOLOGY (1957). Eastchester Rd. & Morris Pk. Ave., Bronx, NY 10461-1602. (718)430-3850. Pres. Dr. Norman Lamm; Chmn. Bd. of Govs. Samson Bitensky; Dean Dr. Lawrence J. Siegel. Offers MA in general psychology; PsyD in clinical and school-clinical child psychology; and PhD in developmental and clinical health psychology. Project for the Study of the Disturbed Adolescent; Psychological and Psychoeducational Services Clinic.

———, (affiliate) RABBI ISAAC ELCHANAN THEOLOGICAL SEMINARY (1896). 2540 Amsterdam Ave., NYC 10033-9986. (212)960-5344. Chmn. Bd. of Trustees Judah Feinerman; V.-Pres. for Administration & Professional Education Rabbi Robert S. Hirt; Dean Rabbi Zevulun Charlop. Leading center in the Western Hemisphere for higher learning in the Orthodox tradition of Judaism. RIETS complex encompasses 15 educational entities and a major service and outreach center with some 20 programs. Grants semikhah (ordination) and the degrees of master of religious education, master of Hebrew literature, doctor of religious education, and doctor of Hebrew literature. Includes Center of Rabbinic Studies,

Post-Graduate School for Rabbinic Studies, Rabbinic Training Program, Rabbinic Internship Program.

Kollelim include Marcos and Adina Katz Kollel (Institute for Advanced Research in Rabbinics) (Dir. Rabbi Hershel Schachter); Israel Henry Beren Institute for Higher Talmudic Studies (HaMachon HaGavohah Le'Talmud) (Dir. Rabbi Michael Rosensweig); Bella and Harry Wexner Kollel Elyon and Semikhah Honors Program (Dir. Rabbi Mordechai Willig).

RIETS sponsors one high school for boys (Manhattan) and one for girls (Queens).

The Max Stern Division of Communal Services (Dir. Rabbi Robert S. Hirt), provides personal and professional service to the rabbinate and related fields, as well as educational, consultative, organizational, and placement services to congregations, schools, and communal organizations around the world; coordinates a broad spectrum of outreach programs, including Center for Jewish Education, Department for Rabbinic Services, Kiruv College Outreach Program, and others. Sephardic components are Jacob E. Safra Institute of Sephardic Studies and the Institute of Yemenite Studies; Sephardic Community Program; Dr. Joseph and Rachel Ades Sephardic Outreach Program; Maybaum Sephardic Fellowship Program.

———, PHILIP AND SARAH BELZ SCHOOL OF JEWISH MUSIC (1954). 560 W. 185 St., NYC 10033-3201. (212)960-5353. Dir. Cantor Bernard Beer. Provides professional training of cantors and courses in Jewish liturgical music; conducts outreach; publishes *Journal of Jewish Music and Literature;* awards associate cantor's certificate and cantorial diploma.

———, (affiliate) YESHIVA OF LOS ANGELES (1977). 9760 W. Pico Blvd., Los Angeles, CA 90035-4701. (213)553-4478. Dean Rabbi Marvin Hier; Bd. Chmn. Samuel Belzberg; Dir. Academic Programs Rabbi Sholom Tendler. Provides Jewish studies program for beginners. Affiliates are high schools, Jewish Studies Institute for Adult Education, and Simon Wiesenthal Center.

———, SIMON WIESENTHAL CENTER (see p. 593)

———, WOMEN'S ORGANIZATION (1928). 500 W. 185 St., NYC 10033-3201. (212) 960-0855. Chmn. Natl. Bd. Dinah Pinczower. Supports Yeshiva University's national scholarship program for students training in education, community service, law, medicine, and other professions, and its development program.

———, WURZWEILER SCHOOL OF SOCIAL WORK (1957). 500 W. 185 St., NYC 10033-3201. (212)960-0800. Pres. Norman Lamm; Chmn. Bd. of Govs. David I. Schachne; Dean Dr. Sheldon R. Gelman. Offers graduate programs in social work and Jewish communal service; grants MSW and DSW degrees and certificate in Jewish communal service. MSW programs are: Concurrent Plan, 2-year, full-time track, combining classroom study and supervised field instruction; Plan for Employed Persons (PEP), for people working in social agencies; Block Education Plan (Dir. Dr. Adele Weiner), which combines summer course work with regular-year field placement in local agencies; Clergy Plan, training in counseling for clergy of all denominations; Center for Professional Training in the Care of the Elderly. *Jewish Social Work Forum.*

———, YESHIVA UNIVERSITY MUSEUM (see p. 595)

SOCIAL, MUTUAL BENEFIT

ALPHA EPSILON PI FRATERNITY (1913). 8815 Wesleyan Rd., Indianapolis, IN 46268-1171. (317)876-1913. FAX: (317) 876-1057. E-mail: aepihq@indy.net. Internatl. Pres. Rabbi Stanley M. Davids; Exec. V.-Pres. Sidney N. Dunn. International Jewish fraternity active on over 100 campuses in the U.S. and Canada; encourages Jewish students to remain loyal to their heritage and to assume leadership roles in the community; active in behalf of Soviet Jewry, the State of Israel, the United States Holocaust Memorial Museum, Tay Sachs Disease, Mazon:A Jewish Response to Hunger, and other causes. *The Lion of Alpha Epsilon Pi (quarterly magazine).*

AMERICAN ASSOCIATION OF JEWS FROM THE FORMER USSR, INC. (1989). 45 E. 33 St., Suite 3A, New York, NY 10016. (212) 779-0383, (516)937-3819. FAX: (212) 684-0471. Pres. Leonid Stonov; V.-Pres. Inna Arolovich. National not-for-profit mutual-assistance and refugee-advocacy organization, which unites and represents interests of Russian-speaking Jewish immigrants from the former Soviet Union. Has chapters in 12 states, Chapter of Struggle Against Anti-Semitism and Xenophobia, and Club of Intellectuals (House of Scientists) in NYC. Assists newcomers in their resettlement and cultural adjustment; fosters their Jewish identity and involvement in civic and social affairs; encourages acquiring American citizenship and voter registration; monitors anti-Semitism and violation of human rights in the FSU and the U.S.; provides assistance to elderly and disabled; advocates in cases of political asylum for victims of anti-Semitism in the FSU. *Chronicle of Anti-Semitism and Nationalism in Republics of the Former Soviet Union (in English, annually); Information Bulletin (in Russian, bimonthly).*

AMERICAN FEDERATION OF JEWS FROM CENTRAL EUROPE, INC. (1938). 570 Seventh Ave., NYC 10018. (212)921-3871. FAX: (212) 575-1918. Pres. Fritz Weinschenk; Bd. Chmn. Curt C. Silberman; Exec. Asst. Dennis E. Rohrbaugh. Seeks to safeguard the rights and interests of American Jews of German-speaking Central European descent, especially in reference to restitution and indemnification; through its affiliate Research Foundation for Jewish Immigration sponsors research and publications on the history, immigration, and acculturation of Central European émigrés in the U.S. and worldwide; through its affiliate Jewish Philanthropic Fund of 1933 supports social programs for needy Nazi victims in the U.S.; undertakes cultural activities, annual conferences, publications; member, Council of Jews from Germany, London.

AMERICAN VETERANS OF ISRAEL (1949). 136 E. 39 St., NYC 10016. Pres. Sam Klausner; Sec. Sidney Rabinovich. Maintains contact with American and Canadian volunteers who served in Aliyah Bet and/or Israel's War of Independence; promotes Israel's welfare; holds memorial services at grave of Col. David Marcus; is affiliated with World Mahal. *Newsletter.*

ASSOCIATION OF YUGOSLAV JEWS IN THE UNITED STATES, INC. (1941). 130 E. 59 St., Suite 1202, NYC 10022. (212)371-6891. Pres. Mary Levine; V.-pres. and chmn. Emanuel Salom. Assists all Jews originally from Yugoslavia—Bosnia, Serbia, Croatia—and settlers in Israel. *Bulletin.*

BNAI ZION–THE AMERICAN FRATERNAL ZIONIST ORGANIZATION (1908). 136 E. 39 St., NYC 10016. (212)725-1211. FAX: (212)684-6327. Pres. Alan G. Hevesi; Exec. V.-Pres. Mel Parness. Fosters principles of Americanism, fraternalism, and Zionism. The Bnai Zion Foundation supports various humanitarian projects in Israel and the USA, chiefly the Bnai Zion Medical Center in Haifa and homes for retarded children-Maon Bnai Zion in Rosh Ha'ayin and the Herman Z. Quittman Center in Jerusalem. Also supports building of new central library in Ma'aleh Adumim. In U.S. sponsors program of awards for excellence in Hebrew for high school and college students. Chapters all over U.S. and a new leadership division in Greater N.Y. area. *Bnai Zion Voice; Bnai Zion Foundation Newsletter.*

BRITH ABRAHAM (1859; reorg. 1887). 136 E. 39 St., NYC 10016. (212)725-1211. FAX: (212)684-6327. Grand Master Robert Freeman; Grand Sec. Joseph Levin. Protects Jewish rights and combats anti-Semitism; supports Soviet and Ethiopian emigration and the safety and dignity of Jews worldwide; helps to support Bnai Zion Medical Center in Haifa and other Israeli institutions; aids and supports various programs and projects in the U.S.: Hebrew Excellence Program-Gold Medal presentation in high schools and colleges; Camp Loyaltown; Brith Abraham and Bnai Zion Foundations. *Voice.*

BRITH SHOLOM (1905). 3939 Conshohocken Ave., Philadelphia, PA 19131. (215)878-5696. FAX: (215) 878-5699. Pres. Howard P. Rovner; Exec. Dir. Louis Mason. Fraternal organization devoted to community welfare, protection of rights of Jewish people, and activities that foster Jewish identity and provide support for Israel. Through its philanthropic arm, the Brith Sholom Foundation (1962), sponsors Brith Sholom House in Philadelphia, nonprofit senior-citizen apartments; and Brith Sholom Beit Halochem in Haifa, Israel, rehabilitation, social, and sports center for disabled Israeli veterans, operated by Zahal. Chmn. Bennett Goldstein;

Exec. Dir. Saundra Laub. *Brith Sholom Digest; monthly news bulletin.*

CENTRAL SEPHARDIC JEWISH COMMUNITY OF AMERICA WOMEN'S DIVISION, INC. (1941). 8 W. 70 St., NYC 10023. (212) 787-2850. Pres. Irma Lopes Cardozo; Treas. Laura Capelluto; Rec. Sec. Esther Shear. Promotes Sephardic culture by awarding scholarships to qualified needy students in New York and Israel; raises funds for hospital and religious institutions in U.S. and Israel. *Yearly Journal.*

FREE SONS OF ISRAEL (1849). 250 Fifth Ave., Suite 201, NYC 10001. (212)725-3690. FAX: (212)725-5874. Grand Master Charles Mackoff; Grand Sec. Richard Reiner. Oldest Jewish fraternal-benefit order in U.S. Supports the State of Israel; fights anti-Semitism; helps Soviet Jewry. Maintains scholarship fund for members and children of members; insurance fund and credit union; social functions. *Free Sons Reporter.*

JEWISH LABOR BUND (Directed by WORLD COORDINATING COMMITTEE OF THE BUND) (1897; reorg. 1947). 25 E. 21 St., NYC 10010. (212)475-0059. FAX: (212) 473-5102. Sec. Gen. Benjamin Nadel. Coordinates activities of Bund organizations throughout the world and represents them in the Socialist International; spreads the ideas of socialism as formulated by the Jewish Labor Bund; publishes books and periodicals on world problems, Jewish life, socialist theory and policy, and on the history, activities, and ideology of the Jewish Labor Bund. *Unser Tsait* (U.S.); *Lebns-Fragn* (Israel); *Unser Gedank* (Australia).

SEPHARDIC JEWISH BROTHERHOOD OF AMERICA, INC. (1915). 97-45 Queens Blvd., Rm. 610, Rego Park, NY 11374. (718)459-1600. Pres. Bernard Ouziel; Sec. Michael Cohen. A benevolent fraternal organization seeking to promote the industrial, social, educational, and religious welfare of its members. *Sephardic Brother.*

THE WORKMEN'S CIRCLE/ARBETER RING (1900). 45 E. 33 St., NYC 10016. (212)889-6800. FAX: (212)532-7518. E-mail: wcfriends@aol.com. Pres. Mark Mlotek; Exec. Dir. Robert Kestenbaum. Fosters Jewish identity and participation in Jewish life through Jewish, especially Yiddish, culture and education, friendship, mutual aid, and the pursuit of social and economic justice. Offices are located throughout the U.S. and Canada. Member services include:Jewish cultural seminars, concerts, theater, Jewish schools, children's camp and adult resort, fraternal and singles activities, a Jewish Book Center, public affairs/social action, health insurance plans, medical/dental/legal services, life insurance plans, cemetery/funeral benefits, social services, geriatric homes and centers, and travel services. *The Call.* (WWW.CIRCLE.ORG)

ZETA BETA TAU FRATERNITY (1898). 3905 Vincennes Rd., Suite 101, Indianapolis, IN 46268. (317)334-1898. FAX: (317)334-1899. E-mail: zbt@zbtnational.org. Pres. Ronald J. Taylor, M.D. Oldest and historically largest Jewish fraternity; promotes intellectual awareness, social responsibility, integrity, and brotherhood among over 5,000 undergrads and 110,000 alumni in the U.S. and Canada. Encourages leadership and diversity through mutual respect of all heritages; nonsectarian since 1954. A brotherhood of Kappa Nu, Phi Alpha, Phi Epsilon Pi, Phi Sigma Delta, Zeta Beta Tau. *The Deltan (quarterly magazine).* (WWW.ZBT. ORG)

SOCIAL WELFARE

AMC CANCER RESEARCH CENTER (formerly JEWISH CONSUMPTIVES' RELIEF SOCIETY, 1904; incorporated as American Medical Center at Denver, 1954). 1600 Pierce St., Denver, CO 80214. (303)233-6501. FAX: (303)894-8791. E-mail: arnoldm@amc.org. Pres./CEO Bob R. Baker; Scientific Dir. Dr. Tom Slaga. A nationally recognized leader in the fight against cancer; employs a three-pronged, interdisciplinary approach that combines laboratory, clinical, and community cancer-control research to advance the prevention, early detection, diagnosis, and treatment of the disease. *The Quest for Answers (annual report).*

AMCHA FOR TSEDAKAH (1990). 9800 Cherry Hill Rd., College Park, MD 20740. (301)937-2600. Pres. Rabbi Bruce E. Kahn. Solicits and distributes contributions to Jewish charitable organizations in the U.S. and Israel; accredits organizations which serve an important tsedakah purpose, demonstrate efficiency and fiscal integrity, and also support pluralism. Contributors are encouraged to earmark contributions for specific organizations; all contributions to General Fund are forwarded to the charitable institutions, as operating expenses are covered by a separate fund. *Newspaper supplement.*

AMERICAN JEWISH CORRECTIONAL CHAPLAINS ASSOCIATION, INC. (formerly NATIONAL COUNCIL OF JEWISH PRISON CHAPLAINS) (1937). 10 E. 73 St., NYC 10021-4194. (212)879-8415. FAX: (212) 772-3977. (Cooperates with the New York Board of Rabbis.) Pres. Rabbi Irving Koslowe. Supports spiritual, moral, and social services for Jewish men and women in corrections; stimulates support of correctional chaplaincy; provides spiritual and professional fellowship for Jewish correctional chaplains; promotes sound standards for correctional chaplaincy; schedules workshops and research to aid chaplains in counseling and with religious services for Jewish inmates. Constituent, American Correctional Chaplains Association. *Chaplains Manual.*

AMERICAN JEWISH SOCIETY FOR SERVICE, INC. (1950). 15 E. 26 St., Rm. 1029, NYC 10010. (212)683-6178. Founder/Chmn. Henry Kohn; Pres. Lawrence G. Green; Exec. Dirs. Carl and Audrey Brenner. Conducts voluntary work-service camps each summer to enable high-school juniors and seniors to perform humanitarian service.

ASSOCIATION OF JEWISH AGING SERVICES (formerly NORTH AMERICAN ASSOCIATION OF JEWISH HOMES AND HOUSING FOR THE AGING) (1960). 316 Pennsylvania Ave., SE, Suite 402, Washington, DC 20003. (202) 543-7500. FAX: (202)543-4090. E-mail: ajas@ajas.org. Pres. Lawrence M. Zippin; Chmn. Harvey Finkelstein. Represents nearly all the not-for-profit charitable homes and housing for the Jewish aging; promotes excellence in performance and quality of service through fostering communication and education and encouraging advocacy for the aging; conducts annual conferences and institutes. *Directory; Membership Handbook; The Scribe (quarterly newsletter).*

ASSOCIATION OF JEWISH CENTER PROFESSIONALS (1918). 15 E. 26 St., NYC 10010-1579. (212)532-4949. FAX: (212) 481-4174. E-mail: ajcp@jcca.org. Pres. Jay R. Roth; V.-Pres. Karen Stern; Exec. Dir. Marilyn Altman. Seeks to enhance the standards, techniques, practices, scope, and public understanding of Jewish Community Center and kindred agency work. *Kesher.*

ASSOCIATION OF JEWISH COMMUNITY ORGANIZATION PERSONNEL (AJCOP) (1969). 14619 Horseshoe Trace, Wellington, FL 33414. (561)795-4853. FAX: (561)798-0358. E-mail: marlene@ajcop.org. Pres. Allan Gelfond; Exec. Dir. Louis B. Solomon. An organization of professionals engaged in areas of fund-raising, endowments, budgeting, social planning, financing, administration, and coordination of services. Objectives are to develop and enhance professional practices in Jewish communal work; to maintain and improve standards, practices, scope, and public understanding of the field of community organization, as practiced through local federations, national agencies, other organizations, settings, and private practitioners. *Prolog (quarterly newspaper); Proceedings (annual record of papers and speeches).*

ASSOCIATION OF JEWISH FAMILY AND CHILDREN'S AGENCIES (1972). 3086 State Highway 27, Suite 11, PO Box 248, Kendall Park, NJ 08824-0248. (800) 634-7346. FAX: (732)821-0493. E-mail: ajfca@aol.com. Pres. Richard K. Blankstein; Exec. V.-Pres. Bert J. Goldberg. The national service organization for Jewish family and children's agencies in the U.S. and Canada. Reinforces member agencies in their efforts to sustain and enhance the quality of Jewish family and communal life. Operates the Elder Support Network for the national Jewish community. *Tachlis (quarterly); Professional Opportunities Bulletin; Executive Digest (monthly).* (AJFCA.ORG)

BARON DE HIRSCH FUND (1891). 130 E. 59 St., NYC 10022. (212)836-1358. FAX: (212)755-9183. Pres. Seymour W. Zises; Mng. Dir. Lauren Katzowitz. Aids Jewish immigrants in the U.S. and Israel by giving grants to agencies active in educational and vocational fields; has limited program for study tours in U.S. by Israeli agriculturists.

B'NAI B'RITH (1843). 1640 Rhode Island Ave., NW, Washington, DC 20036. (202)857-6600. FAX: (202)857-1099. Pres. Tommy Baer; Exec. V.-Pres. Dr. Sidney Clearfield. International Jewish organization, with affiliates in 55 countries. Offers programs designed to ensure the preservation of Jewry and Judaism: Jewish education, community volunteer service, expansion of human rights, assistance to Israel, housing for the elderly, leadership training, rights of Jews in all countries to study their heritage. *International Jewish Monthly.*

———, ANTI-DEFEMATION LEAGUE OF (see p. 584)

———, HILLEL (see p. 613)

———, KLUTZNICK MUSEUM (see p. 589)

———, YOUTH ORGANIZATION (see p. 611)

CITY OF HOPE NATIONAL MEDICAL CENTER AND BECKMAN RESEARCH INSTITUTE (1913). 1500 E. Duarte Rd., Duarte, CA 91010. (626)359-8111. FAX: (626) 301-8115. E-mail: dhalper@coh.org. Pres. and CEO Gil N. Schwartzberg. Offers care to those with cancer and other catastrophic diseases, medical consultation service for second opinions, and research programs in genetics, immunology, and the basic life process. *City of Hope Cancer Research Center Report.*

CONFERENCE OF JEWISH COMMUNAL SERVICE (*see* JEWISH COMMUNAL SERVICE ASSOCIATION OF N. AMERICA)

COUNCIL OF JEWISH FEDERATIONS (*see* UNITED JEWISH COMMUNITIES)

INTERNATIONAL ASSOCIATION OF JEWISH VOCATIONAL SERVICES (formerly JEWISH OCCUPATIONAL COUNCIL) (1939). 1845 Walnut St., Suite 640, Philadelphia, PA 19103. (215)854-0233. FAX: (215)854-0212. E-mail: iajvs@jevs.org. Pres. Donald Simons; Exec. Dir. Genie Cohen. Not-for-profit trade association of Jewish-sponsored social service agencies in the U.S., Canada, and Israel. Provides member agencies with technical, informational, and communications support; researches funding opportunities, develops collaborative program models, and represents Jewish vocational network nationally and internationally. Sponsors annual conference for members. Member agencies provide a wide range of educational, vocational, and rehabilitation services to both the Jewish and non-Jewish communities. (WWW.JVSNJ.ORG/IAJVS.HTML)

INTERNATIONAL COUNCIL ON JEWISH SO-
CIAL AND WELFARE SERVICES (1961). c/o
American Jewish Joint Distribution Committee, 711 Third Ave., NYC 10017. (NY
liaison office with UN headquarters.)
(212)687-6200. FAX: (212)370-5467. E-
mail: steve@jdcny.org. Chmn. David
Cope-Thompson; Exec. Sec. Eli Benson.
Provides for exchange of views and information among member agencies on
problems of Jewish social and welfare services, including medical care, old age, welfare, child care, rehabilitation, technical
assistance, vocational training, agricultural and other resettlement, economic
assistance, refugees, migration, integration, and related problems; representation
of views to governments and international organizations. Members:six national and international organizations.

JEWISH BRAILLE INSTITUTE OF AMERICA,
INC. (1931). 110 E. 30 St., NYC 10016.
(212)889-2525. FAX: (212)689-3692. Pres.
Barbara B. Friedman; Exec. V.-Pres. Gerald M. Kass. Provides Judaic materials in
braille, talking books, and large print for
blind, visually impaired, and reading-
disabled; offers counseling for full integration into the life of the Jewish community. International program serves
clients in more than 40 countries; sponsors special programs in Israel and Eastern Europe to assist the elderly as well as
students. *Jewish Braille Review; JBI
Voice; Likutim, Hebrew-language magazine on blindness issues.* (WWW.JEWISH
BRAILLE.ORG)

JEWISH CHILDREN'S ADOPTION NETWORK
(1990). PO Box 16544, Denver CO 80216-
0544. (303)573-8113. FAX: (303) 893-
1447. E-mail: jcan@uswest.net. Pres.
Stephen Krausz; Exec. Dir. Vicki Krausz.
An adoption exchange founded for
the primary purpose of locating adoptive families for Jewish infants and children. Works with some 200 children a
year, throughout N. Amer., 85-90% of
whom have special needs. No fees charged
for services, which include birth-parent
and adoptive-parent counseling. *Quarterly newsletter.* (WWW.USERS.USWEST.NET/
NJCAN)

JEWISH COMMUNAL SERVICE ASSOCIATION
OF N. AMERICA (1899; formerly CONFER-
ENCE OF JEWISH COMMUNAL SERVICE).
3084 State Hwy. 27, Suite 9, Kendall
Park, NJ 08824-1657. (732)821-1871.

FAX: (732)821-5335. E-mail: jcsana@
aol.com. Pres. Max L. Kleinman; Exec.
Dir. Joel Ollander. Serves as forum for all
professional philosophies in community
service, for testing new experiences,
proposing new ideas, and questioning or
reaffirming old concepts; umbrella organization for 7 major Jewish communal
service groups. Concerned with advancement of professional personnel practices
and standards. *Journal of Jewish Communal Service; Concurrents.*

JEWISH COMMUNITY CENTERS ASSOCIATION
OF NORTH AMERICA (formerly JWB)
(1917). 15 E. 26 St., NYC 10010-1579.
(212)532-4949. FAX: (212)481-4174.
E-mail: info@jcca.org. Pres. Jerome Ma-
kowsky; Exec. V.-Pres. Allan Finkelstein.
The leadership network of, and central
agency for, the Jewish Community Center
movement, comprising more than 275
JCCs, YM-YWHAs, and camps in the
U.S. and Canada, serving over one million members and a million nonmember
users. Offers a wide range of services
and resources to help affiliates provide
educational, cultural, social, Jewish
identity-building, and recreational programs. Fosters and strengthens ties between N. American Jews and Israel and
with world Jewry. U.S. government-
accredited agency for serving the religious
and social needs of Jewish military personnel, their families, and patients in VA
hospitals through JWB Chaplains Council. *JCC Circle; Chaplines;* other newslet-
tersforJCCprofessionals.(WWW.JCCA.ORG)

———, JEWISH WELFARE BOARD JEWISH
CHAPLAINS COUNCIL (formerly COMMIS-
SION ON JEWISH CHAPLAINCY) (1940). 15
E. 26 St., NYC 10010-1579. (212)532-
4949. FAX: (212)481-4174. Chmn. Rabbi
Jacob J. Greenberg; Dir. Rabbi David
Lapp; Dep. Dir. Rabbi Nathan M. Land-
man. Recruits, endorses, and serves Jewish military and Veterans Administration
chaplains on behalf of the American Jewish community and the major rabbinic
bodies; trains and assists Jewish lay leaders where there are no chaplains, for service to Jewish military personnel, their
families, and hospitalized veterans.
CHAPLINES newsletter.

JEWISH CONCILIATION BOARD OF AMERICA,
INC. (A division of the JEWISH BOARD OF
FAMILY AND CHILDREN'S SERVICES)
(1920). 120 W. 57 St. NYC 10019.

(212)582-9100. FAX: (212)956-5676. E-mail: admin@jbfcs.org. Pres. Joseph S. Kaplan.; Exec. V.-Pres. Dr. Alan B. Siskind. Offers dispute-resolution services to families, individuals, and organizations. Social-work, rabbinic, and legal expertise is available to individuals and families for conciliation. *Connections.*

JEWISH FAMILY AND CHILDREN'S PROFESSIONALS ASSOCIATION (*see* Jewish Social Services Professionals Association)

JEWISH FUND FOR JUSTICE (1984). 260 Fifth Ave., Suite 701, NYC 10001. (212) 213-2113. FAX: (212)213-2233. E-mail: justiceusa@aol.com. Bd. Chmn. Ronna Stamm; Exec. Dir. Marlene Provizer. A national grant-making foundation supporting efforts to combat the causes and consequences of poverty in the U.S. Provides diverse opportunities for giving, including family and youth endowment funds and the Purim Fund for Women in Poverty; develops educational materials linking Jewish teachings and rituals with contemporary social justice issues; supports Jewish involvement in community-based anti-poverty efforts; and works cooperatively with other denominational and social change philanthropies. *Annual report, newsletter.*

JEWISH FUNDERS NETWORK (1990). 15 E. 26 St., Suite 1038, New York City 10010. (212) 726-0177. FAX: (212) 726-0195. E-mail: jfn@jfunders.org. Exec. Dir. Evan Mendelson. A national membership organization dedicated to advancing the growth and quality of Jewish philanthropy through more effective grant making; brings together individual philanthropists, foundation trustees, and foundation staff to discuss emerging issues, gain expertise in the operational aspects of grant making, explore family dynamics and intergenerational issues of family foundations, and exchange information among peers. *JFN Newsletter.* (WWW.JFUNDERS.ORG)

JEWISH SOCIAL SERVICES PROFESSIONALS ASSOCIATION (1965). c/o AJFCA, PO Box 248, Kendall Park, NJ 08824-0493. (800) 634-7346. FAX: (732)821-0493. E-mail: ajfca@aol.com. Chmn. Linda Kislowicz. Brings together executives, supervisors, managers, caseworkers, and related professionals in Jewish Family Service and related agencies.Seeks to enhance profes-

sional skills, improve personnel standards, further Jewish continuity and identity, and strengthen Jewish family life. Provides a national and regional forum for professional discussion and learning; functions under the auspices of the Association of Jewish Family and Children's Agencies. *Newsletter.*

JEWISH WOMEN INTERNATIONAL (formerly B'NAI B'RITH WOMEN) (1897). 1828 L St., NW, Suite 250, Washington, DC 20036. (202)857-1300. FAX: (202)857-1380. E-mail: jwi@jwi.org. Pres. Randee Lefkow; Exec. Dir. Gail Rubinson. Strengthens the lives of women, children, and families through education, advocacy, and action. Focusing on family violence and the emotional health of children, JWI serves as an agent for change—locally, nationally, and around the world. Offers programs in the United States, Canada, and Israel. *Jewish Woman Magazine (quarterly).*

JWB (*see* Jewish Community Centers Association of North America)

LEVI HOSPITAL (sponsored by B'nai B'rith) (1914). 300 Prospect Ave., Hot Springs, AR 71901. (501)624-1281. FAX: (501) 622-3500. Pres. Dr. Hal Koppel; Admin. Patrick G. McCabe. Offers arthritis treatment, including therapy sessions in large thermal heated pool. Other programs: Levi Life Center, adult inpatient and outpatient psychiatric program, child/adolescent psychiatric clinic, hospice care, home health care, osteoporosis clinic, Levi Rehabilitation Unit, a cooperative effort of Levi and St. Joseph's hospitals (inpatient rehab), and TEAM Rehabilitation Center, a joint venture of Levi and St. Joseph's (outpatient rehab). *The Progress Chart.*

MAZON: A JEWISH RESPONSE TO HUNGER (1985). 12401 Wilshire Blvd., Suite 303, Los Angeles, CA 90025. (310)442-0020. FAX: (310)442-0030. E-mail: mazonmail@aol.com. Bd. Chmn. Daniel Levenson; Sr. Exec. Dir. Irving Cramer. A grant-making and fund-raising organization that raises funds in the Jewish community and provides grants to nonprofit 501(c)(3) organizations which aim to prevent and alleviate hunger in the United States and abroad. Grantees include food pantries, food banks, multi-service organizations, advocacy, education and research projects, and international relief and development organizations. 1998 grants totaled $2.3 million. *Mazon Newsletter.*

NATIONAL ASSOCIATION OF JEWISH CHAP-LAINS (1988). 901 Route 10, Whippany, NJ 07981. (201)884-4800. FAX: (201) 736-9193. Pres. Rabbi Howard Kummer; Natl. Coord. Cecille Asekoff. A professional organization for people functioning as Jewish chaplains in hospitals, nursing homes, geriatric, psychiatric, correctional, and military facilities. Provides collegial support, continuing education, professional certification, and resources for the Jewish community on issues of pastoral and spiritual care. *The Jewish Chaplain.*

NATIONAL COUNCIL OF JEWISH PRISON CHAPLAINS, INC. (*see* American Jewish Correctional Chaplains Association, Inc.)

NATIONAL COUNCIL OF JEWISH WOMEN (1893). 53 W. 23 St., NYC 10010. (212)645-4048. FAX: (212)645-7466. E-mail: ncjwomen@jon.cjfny.org. Pres. Nan Rich; Exec. Dir. Susan Katz. Works to improve the lives of women, children, and families in the United States and Israel; strives to insure individual rights and freedoms for all. NCJW volunteers deliver vital services in 500 U.S. communities and carry out NCJW's advocacy agenda through a powerful grassroots network. *NCJW Journal; Washington Newsletter.*

NATIONAL INSTITUTE FOR JEWISH HOSPICE (1985). PO Box 48025, Los Angeles, CA 90048. (800)446-4448. 330 Broad Ave., Englewood, NJ 07631. (201)816-7324. FAX: (201)816-7321. Pres. Rabbi Maurice Lamm; Exec. Dir. Shirley Lamm. Serves as a national Jewish hospice resource center. Through conferences, research, publications, referrals, and counseling services offers guidance, training, and information to patients, family members, clergy of all faiths, professional caregivers, and volunteers who work with the Jewish terminally ill. *Jewish Hospice Times.*

NATIONAL JEWISH CHILDREN'S LEUKEMIA FOUNDATION (1990). 250 E. 63 St., NYC 10021. (212)644-8822. FAX: (212)644-8826. E-mail: leukemia@erols.com. Pres./Founder Zvi Shor. Dedicated to saving the lives of children. Programs: Stem Cell Banking—freezing cells from babies umbilical cord for long-term storage, in case of need for bone marrow; Make-A-Dream-Come True—granting wishes for terminally ill children; referral service; patient advocacy; bone marrow donor search. (WWW.LEUKEMIAFOUNDA TION.ORG)

NATIONAL JEWISH MEDICAL AND RESEARCH CENTER (formerly NATIONAL JEWISH HOSPITAL/NATIONAL ASTHMA CENTER) (1899). 1400 Jackson St., Denver, CO 80206. (800)222-LUNG. E-mail: lung-line@njc.org. Pres. & CEO Lynn M. Taussig, MD; Bd. Chmn. Meyer Saltzman. The only medical and research center in the United States devoted entirely to respiratory, allergic, and immune system diseases, including asthma, tuberculosis, emphysema, severe allergies, AIDS, and cancer, and autoimmune diseases such as lupus. Dedicated to enhancing prevention, treatment, and cures through research, and to developing and providing innovative clinical programs for treating patients regardless of age, religion, race, or ability to pay. New Directions; *Medical Scientific Update.*

NORTH AMERICAN ASSOCIATION OF JEWISH HOMES AND HOUSING FOR THE AGING (*see* Association of Jewish Aging Services)

UNITED JEWISH COMMUNITIES (1999). 111 Eighth Ave., 11th fl., NYC 10011-5201. (212)284-6500. FAX: (212)284-6873. Bd. Chmn. Charles R. Bronfman; Chmn. Exec. Com. Joel D. Tauber; Acting Pres. Stephen D. Solender. Formed by a merger of the United Jewish Appeal with the Council of Jewish Federations and United Israel Appeal; represents N. American Jewry's primary fund-raising and service-providing agencies.

UNITED ORDER TRUE SISTERS, INC. (UOTS) (1846). 100 State St., Albany, NY 12207. (518)436-1670. Pres. Rita Lipkin; Fin. Sec. Betty Peyser; Treas. Rose Goldberg. Charitable, community service, especially home supplies, etc., for indigent cancer victims; supports camps for children with cancer. *Inside UotS.*

WORLD COUNCIL OF JEWISH COMMUNAL SERVICE (1966; reorg. 1994). 711 Third Ave., 10th fl., NYC 10017. (212)687-6200. FAX: (212)370-5467. Pres. Stephen D. Solender; Assoc. Pres. Zvi Feine; Exec. V.-Pres. Theodore Comet. Seeks to build Jewish community worldwide by enhancing professional-to-professional connections, improving professional practice through interchange of experience and sharing of expertise, fostering professional training programs, and stimulating research. Conducts quadrennial conferences in Jerusalem and periodic regional meetings. *Proceedings of international conferences; newsletters.*

PROFESSIONAL ASSOCIATIONS*

AMERICAN ASSOCIATION OF RABBIS (Religious, Educational)

AMERICAN CONFERENCE OF CANTORS, UNION OF AMERICAN HEBREW CONGREGATIONS (Religious, Educational)

AMERICAN JEWISH CORRECTIONAL CHAPLAINS ASSOCIATION, INC. (Social Welfare)

AMERICAN JEWISH PRESS ASSOCIATION (Cultural)

AMERICAN JEWISH PUBLIC RELATIONS SOCIETY (1957). 575 Lexington Ave., Suite 600, NYC 10022. (212)446-5863. FAX: (212)644-6358. Pres. Henry R. Hecker; Treas. Diane Ehrlich. Advances professional status of public-relations practitioners employed by Jewish organizations and institutions or who represent Jewish-related clients, services, or products; upholds a professional code of ethics and standards; provides continuing education and networking opportunities at monthly meetings; serves as a clearinghouse for employment opportunities. *AJPRS Reporter; AJPRS Membership Directory.*

ASSOCIATION OF HILLEL/JEWISH CAMPUS PROFESSIONALS (Religious, Educational)

ASSOCIATION OF JEWISH CENTER PROFESSIONALS (Social Welfare)

ASSOCIATION OF JEWISH COMMUNITY ORGANIZATION PERSONNEL (Social Welfare)

ASSOCIATION OF JEWISH COMMUNITY RELATIONS WORKERS (Community Relations)

CANTORS ASSEMBLY (Religious, Educational)

CENTRAL CONFERENCE OF AMERICAN RABBIS (Religious, Educational)

COUNCIL OF JEWISH ORGANIZATIONS IN CIVIL SERVICE (Community Relations)

INTERNATIONAL JEWISH MEDIA ASSOCIATION (Cultural)

JEWISH CHAPLAINS COUNCIL, JWB (Social Welfare)

JEWISH COMMUNAL SERVICE ASSOCIATION OF N. AMERICA (Social Welfare)

JEWISH EDUCATORS ASSEMBLY, UNITED SYNAGOGUE OF CONSERVATIVE JUDAISM (Religious, Educational)

JEWISH SOCIAL SERVICES PROFESSIONALS ASSOCIATION (Social Welfare)

JEWISH TEACHERS ASSOCIATION–MORIM (Religious, Educational)

NATIONAL ASSOCIATION OF HEBREW DAY SCHOOL ADMINISTRATORS, TORAH UMESORAH (Religious, Educational)

NATIONAL ASSOCIATION OF JEWISH CHAPLAINS (Social Welfare)

NATIONAL ASSOCIATION OF TEMPLE ADMINISTRATORS, UNION OF AMERICAN HEBREW CONGREGATIONS (Religious, Educational)

NATIONAL ASSOCIATION OF TEMPLE EDUCATORS, UNION OF AMERICAN HEBREW CONGREGATIONS (Religious, Educational)

NATIONAL CONFERENCE OF YESHIVA PRINCIPALS, TORAH UMESORAH (Religious, Educational)

NORTH AMERICAN ASSOCIATION OF SYNAGOGUE EXECUTIVES, UNITED SYNAGOGUE OF CONSERVATIVE JUDAISM (Religious, Educational)

RABBINICAL ALLIANCE OF AMERICA (Religious, Educational)

RABBINICAL ASSEMBLY (Religious, Educational)

RABBINICAL COUNCIL OF AMERICA (Religious, Educational)

RECONSTRUCTIONIST RABBINICAL ASSOCIATION (Religious, Educational)

UNION OF ORTHODOX RABBIS OF THE U.S. AND CANADA (Religious, Educational)

WORLD CONFERENCE OF JEWISH COMMUNAL SERVICE (Community Relations)

WOMEN'S ORGANIZATIONS*

AMIT WOMEN (Israel-Related)

BRANDEIS UNIVERSITY NATIONAL WOMEN'S COMMITTEE (1948). MS 132, Waltham, MA 02454-9110. (781) 736-4160. FAX: (781)736-4183. E-mail: bunwc@brandeis.edu. Pres. Marcia F. Levy; Exec. Dir.

Joan C. Bowen. A friends-of-the-library organization whose mission is to provide financial support for the Brandeis Libraries; works to enhance the image of Brandeis, a Jewish-sponsored, nonsectarian university. Offers its members opportunity for intellectual pursuit, continuing education, community service, social interaction, personal enrichment, and leadership development. Open to all, regardless of race, religion, nationality, or gender. *Imprint.*

EMUNAH WOMEN OF AMERICA (Israel-Related)

HADASSAH, THE WOMEN'S ZIONIST ORGANIZATION OF AMERICA (Israel-Related)

JEWISH WOMEN INTERNATIONAL (Social Welfare)

NA'AMAT USA, THE WOMEN'S LABOR ZIONIST ORGANIZATION OF AMERICA (Israel-Related)

NATIONAL COUNCIL OF JEWISH WOMEN (Social Welfare)

UOTS (Social Welfare)

WOMEN OF REFORM JUDAISM—FEDERATION OF TEMPLE SISTERHOODS, UNION OF AMERICAN HEBREW CONGREGATIONS (Religious, Educational)

WOMEN'S AMERICAN ORT, AMERICAN ORT FEDERATION (Overseas Aid)

WOMEN'S BRANCH OF THE UNION OF ORTHODOX JEWISH CONGREGATIONS OF AMERICA (Religious, Educational)

WOMEN'S DIVISION OF POALE AGUDATH ISRAEL OF AMERICA (Israel-Related)

WOMEN'S LEAGUE FOR CONSERVATIVE JUDAISM (Religious, Educational)

WOMEN'S LEAGUE FOR ISRAEL, INC. (Israel-Related)

WOMEN'S ORGANIZATION, YESHIVA UNIVERSITY (Religious, Educational)

YOUTH AND STUDENT ORGANIZATIONS*

AGUDATH ISRAEL OF AMERICA (Religious, Educational)

B'NAI B'RITH YOUTH ORGANIZATION (Religious, Educational)

BNEI AKIVA OF NORTH AMERICA, RELIGIOUS ZIONISTS OF AMERICA (Israel Related)

HABONIM—DROR NORTH AMERICA (Israel-Related)

HASHOMER HATZAIR, SOCIALIST ZIONIST YOUTH MOVEMENT (Israel-Related)

HILLEL (Religious, Educational)

KADIMA, UNITED SYNAGOGUE OF CONSERVATIVE JUDAISM (Religious, Educational)

NATIONAL CONFERENCE OF SYNAGOGUE YOUTH, UNION OF ORTHODOX JEWISH CONGREGATIONS OF AMERICA (Religious, Educational)

NATIONAL JEWISH COMMITTEE ON SCOUTING (Religious, Educational)

NATIONAL JEWISH GIRL SCOUT COMMITTEE (Religious, Educational) (Israel-Related)

NORTH AMERICAN ALLIANCE FOR JEWISH YOUTH (1996). 50 W. 58 St., NYC 10019. (212)303-4598. FAX: (212)303-4572. E-mail: dkrakow@aol.com. Chmn. Doron Krakow. Serves the cause of informal Jewish and Zionist education in America; provides a forum for the professional leaders of the major N. American youth movements, camps, Israel programs, and university programs to address common issues and concerns, and to represent those issues with a single voice to the wider Jewish and Zionist community. Sponsors annual Conference on Informal Jewish Education for Jewish youth professionals from across the continent.

NORTH AMERICAN FEDERATION OF TEMPLE YOUTH, UNION OF AMERICAN HEBREW CONGREGATIONS (Religious, Educational)

STUDENT STRUGGLE FOR SOVIET JEWRY— *see* Center for Russian Jewry (Community Relations)

YOUNG JUDAEA/HASHACHAR, HADASSAH (Israel-Related)

YUGNTRUF–YOUTH FOR YIDDISH (Cultural)

CANADA

AISH HATORAH (1981). 949 Clark Ave., W., Thornhill, ON L4J8G6. (905)764-1818. FAX: (905)764-1606. E-mail: toronto@ aish.edu. Pres. Harold Nashman; Edu. Dir. Rabbi Ahron Hoch. An educational center, a community center, and a network of synagogues throughout Toronto; seeks to reawaken Jewish values, ignite Jewish pride and promote Jewish unity through education; reaches out to Jews from all backgrounds in a friendly, warm and non-judgmental environment. *Shabbat Shalom Fax.*

B'NAI BRITH CANADA (1875). 15 Hove St., Downsview, ONT M3H 4Y8. (416) 633-6224. FAX: (416)630-2159. E-mail: fdimant@bnaibrith.ca. Pres. Dr. Lawrence Hart; Exec. V.-Pres. Frank Dimant. Canadian Jewry's major advocacy and service organization; maintains an office of Government Relations in Ottawa and cosponsors the Canada Israel Committee; makes representations to all levels of government on matters of Jewish concern; promotes humanitarian causes and educational programs, community projects, adult Jewish education, and leadership development; dedicated to the preservation and unity of the Jewish community in Canada and to human rights. *The Jewish Tribune.*

————, INSTITUTE FOR INTERNATIONAL AFFAIRS (1987). Co-Chmn. Richard Bogoroch & Rochelle Wilner. Identifies and protests the abuse of human rights throughout the world. Monitors the condition of Jewish communities worldwide and advocates on their behalf when they experience serious violations of their human rights. *Institute Report.*

————, LEAGUE FOR HUMAN RIGHTS (1964). Co-Chmn. Marvin Kurz & Dr Harriet Morris. National volunteer association dedicated to combating racism, bigotry, and anti-Semitism. Educational programs include multicultural antiracist workshops, public speakers, Holocaust education, Media Human Rights Awards; legal and legislative activity includes government submissions, court interventions, monitoring hate-group activity, responding to incidents of racism and anti-Semitism; community liaison includes intergroup dialogue and support for aggrieved vulnerable communities and groups. Canadian distributor of ADL material. *Heritage Front Report: 1994; Anti-Semitism on Campus; Skinheads in Canada; Annual Audit of Anti-Semitic Incidents; Holocaust and Hope Educators' Newsletter; Combatting Hate: Guidelines for Community Action.*

————, NATIONAL FIELD SERVICES DEPARTMENT. Natl. Dir. Pearl Gladman. Services community affordable housing projects, sports leagues, food baskets for the needy; coordinates hands-on national volunteer programming, Tel-Aide Distress Line; responsible for lodge membership; direct-mail campaigns, annual convention and foundation dinners.

CANADIAN FRIENDS OF CALI & AMAL (1944). 7005 Kildare Rd., Suite 14, Cote St. Luc, Quebec, H4W 1C1. (514)484-9430. FAX: (514)484-0968. Pres. Harry J.F. Bloomfield, QC; Exec. Dir. Fran Kula. Incorporates Canadian Association for Labour Israel (Histadrut) and Canadian Friends of Amal; supports comprehensive health care and education in Israel. Helps to provide modern medical and surgical facilities and the finest vocational, technical education to the Israeli people of all ages.

CANADIAN FRIENDS OF THE HEBREW UNIVERSITY OF JERUSALEM (1944). 3080 Yonge St., Suite 5024, Toronto, ONT M4N 3N1. (416) 485-8000. FAX: (416)485-8565. E-mail: mgoldman@cfhu.org. Pres. Dr. Charles C. Gold; Exec. Dir. Mark Gryfe. Represents the Hebrew University of Jerusalem in Canada; serves as fund-raising arm for the university in Canada; recruits Canadian students and promotes study programs for foreign students at the university; sponsors social and educational events across Canada. *Dateline Jerusalem.*

CANADIAN JEWISH CONGRESS (1919; reorg. 1934). 1590 Dr. Penfield Ave., Montreal, PQ H3G 1C5. (514)931-7531. FAX: (514)931-0548. E-mail: canadianjewishcongress@cjc.ca. Pres. Goldie Hershon; Natl. Exec. Dir. and Genl. Counsel Jack Silverstone. The official voice of Canadian Jewish communities at home and abroad; acts on all matters affecting the status, rights, concerns, and welfare of Canadian Jewry; internationally active on behalf of world Jewry, Holocaust remembrance and restitution; largest Jewish archives in Canada. *National Small Communities Newsletter; DAIS; National Archives Newsletter; regional newsletters.*

ORT CANADA (1948). 3101 Bathurst St., Suite 604, Toronto, ONT M6A 2A6. (416)787-0339. FAX: (416) 787-9420. E-mail: ortcan@pathcom.com. Pres. Kathleen Crook; Admin. Dir. Robyn Raisin; Dir. of Dev. Edna Levitt. Chapters in 11 Canadian cities raise funds for ORT's nonprofit global network of schools, where Jewish students learn a wide range of marketable skills, including the most advanced high-tech professions. *Focus Magazine.*

CANADIAN YOUNG JUDAEA (1917). 788 Marlee Ave., Suite 205, Toronto, ONT M6B 3K1. (416)781-5156. FAX: (416) 787-3100. Natl. Shaliach Ryan Hass; Eastern Region Shaliah Yoram Abrisor; Natl. Exec. Dir. Risa Epstein. Strives to attract Jewish youth to Zionism, with goal of aliyah; educates youth about Jewish history and Zionism; prepares them to provide leadership in Young Judaea camps in Canada and Israel and to be concerned Jews. *The Judaean.*

CANADIAN ZIONIST FEDERATION (1967). 5151 Cote St. Catherine Rd., #210, Montreal, PQ H3W 1M6. (514)739-7300. FAX: (514)739-9412. Pres. Kurt Rothschild; Natl. Sec. Florence Simon. Umbrella organization of distinct constituent member Zionist organizations in Canada; carries on major activities in all areas of Jewish life through its departments of education and culture, aliyah, youth and students, public affairs, and small Jewish communities, for the purpose of strengthening the State of Israel and the Canadian Jewish community. *Canadian Zionist.*

——, BUREAU OF EDUCATION AND CULTURE (1972). Pres. Kurt Rothschild. Provides counseling by pedagogic experts, in-service teacher-training courses and seminars in Canada and Israel; national pedagogic council and research center; distributes educational material and teaching aids; conducts annual Bible contest and Hebrew-language courses for adults; awards scholarships to Canadian high-school graduates studying for one year in Israel.

FRIENDS OF PIONEERING ISRAEL (1950s). 1111 Finch Ave. W., Suite 456, Downsview, ONT M3J 2E5. (416)736-1339. FAX: (416)736-1405. Pres. Joseph Podemski. Acts as a voice of Socialist-Democratic and Zionist points of view within the Jewish community and a focal point for progressive Zionist elements in Canada; Canadian representative of Meretz; affiliated with Hashomer Hatzair and the Givat Haviva Educational Center.

HADASSAH–WIZO ORGANIZATION OF CANADA (1917). 1310 Greene Ave., Suite 900, Montreal, PQ H3Z 2B8. (514)

937-9431. FAX: (514)933-6483. E-mail: natoff@canadian-hadassah-wizo. org. Pres. Patricia Joy Alpert; Exec. V.-Pres. Lily Frank. Largest women's volunteer Zionist organization in Canada, located in 43 Canadian cities; dedicated to advancing the quality of life of the women and children in Israel through financial assistance and support of its many projects, day-care centers, schools, institutions, and hospitals. In Canada, the organization promotes Canadian ideals of democracy and is a stalwart advocate of women's issues. *Orah Magazine.*

HASHOMER HATZAIR (1913). 1111 Finch Ave. W., #456, Downsview, ONT M3J 2E5. (416)736-1339. FAX: (416)736-1405. E-mail: mail@givathaviva.com. Shaliach Noam Massad; Exec. Off. Mintzy Clement. Zionist youth movement associated with the Kibbutz Artzi Federation in Israel. Educational activities emphasize Jewish culture and identity as well as the kibbutz lifestyle and values; runs winter and summer camps as well as programs in Israel.

INTERNATIONAL JEWISH CORRESPONDENCE (IJC) (1978). c/o Canadian Jewish Congress, 1590 Dr. Penfield Ave., Montreal, PQ H3G 1C5.9 (514)931-7531. FAX: (514)931-0548. E-mail: barrys@cjc.ca. Founder-Dir. Barry Simon. Aims to encourage contact between Jews of all ages and backgrounds, in all countries, through pen-pal correspondence. Send autobiographical data and stamped self-addressed envelope or its equivalent (to cover cost of Canadian postage) to receive addresses.

JEWISH IMMIGRANT AID SERVICES OF MONTREAL (JIAS) (1922). 5151 Cote Ste. Catherine Rd., Suite 220, Montreal, PQ H3W 1M6. (514)342-9351. FAX: (514)342-8452. E-mail: jias@pobox.com. Pres. Barry Silverman; Exec. Dir. Bob Luck. Agency for immigration and immigrant welfare and integration.

JEWISH NATIONAL FUND OF CANADA (Keren Kayemeth Le'Israel, Inc.) (1901). 1980 Sherbrooke St. W., Suite 500, Montreal, PQ H3H 1E8. (514)934-0313. FAX: (514)934-0382. Natl. Pres. Naomi Frankenburg; Exec. V.-Pres. Avner Regev. Fund-raising organization affiliated with the World Zionist Organization; involved in afforestation, soil reclamation, and development of the land of Israel, including the construction of roads and preparation of sites for new settlements; provides educational materials and programs to Jewish schools across Canada.

LABOUR ZIONIST ALLIANCE OF CANADA (1909). 272 Codsell Ave., Downsview, ONT. M3H 3X2. (416)630-9444. FAX: (416)630-9451. Pres. Josef Krystal; City Committee Chmn. Montreal-Harry Froimovitch. Associated with the World Labor Zionist movement and allied with the Israel Labor party. Provides recreational and cultural programs, mutual aid, and fraternal care to enhance the social welfare of its membership; actively promotes Zionist education, cultural projects, and forums on aspects of Jewish and Canadian concern.

MIZRACHI ORGANIZATION OF CANADA (1941). 296 Wilson Ave., North York, ONT M3H 1S8. (416)630-2305. Pres. Jack Kahn. Promotes religious Zionism, aimed at making Israel a state based on Torah; maintains Bnei Akiva, a summer camp, adult education program, and touring department; supports Mizrachi-Hapoel Hamizrachi and other religious Zionist institutions in Israel which strengthen traditional Judaism. *Mizrachi Newsletter*.

NATIONAL COMMUNITY RELATIONS COMMITTEE OF CANADIAN JEWISH CONGRESS (1936). 4600 Bathurst St., Willowdale, ONT M2R 3V2. (416)635-2883. FAX: (416)635-1408. E-mail: ncrccjc@ibm.net. Chmn. Mark S. Weintraub; Pres. Moshe Ronen; Dir. Bernie M. Farber. Seeks to safeguard the status, rights, and welfare of Jews in Canada; to combat anti-Semitism, and promote understanding and goodwill among all ethnic and religious groups.

NATIONAL COUNCIL OF JEWISH WOMEN OF CANADA (1897). 118-1588 Main St., Winnipeg, MAN R2V 1Y3. (204)339-9700. FAX: (204)334-3779. E-mail: info@ncjwc.org. Pres. Hinda Simkin; V.-Pres. Gita Arnold, Sharon Allentuck, & Carol Slater. Dedicated to furthering human welfare in the Jewish and general communities, locally, nationally, and internationally; through an integrated program of education, service, and social action seeks to fulfill unmet needs and to serve the individual and the community. *National ByLines*.

STATE OF ISRAEL BONDS (CANADA-ISRAEL SECURITIES, LTD.) (1953). 970 Lawrence Ave. W., Suite 502, Toronto, ONT M6A 3B6. (416)789-3351. FAX: (416)789-9436. Pres. Norman Spector; Bd. Chmn. George A. Cohon. An international securities organization offering interest-bearing instruments issued by the government of Israel. Invests in every aspect of Israel's economy, including agriculture, commerce, and industry. Israel Bonds are RRSP-approved.

Jewish Federations, Welfare Funds, Community Councils

UNITED STATES

ALABAMA

BIRMINGHAM

THE BIRMINGHAM JEWISH FEDERATION (1936; reorg. 1971); PO Box 130219 (35213); (205)879-0416. FAX: (205)803-1526. Pres. Edward Goldberg; Exec. Dir. Richard Friedman.

MOBILE

MOBILE JEWISH WELFARE FUND, INC. (inc. 1966); One Office Park, Suite 219 (36609); (334)343-7197. Pres. Eileen Susman.

MONTGOMERY

JEWISH FEDERATION OF MONTGOMERY, INC. (1930); PO Box 20058 (36120); (334)277-5820. FAX: (334)277-8383. Pres. Alan Weil; Admin. Dir. Susan Mayer Bruchis.

ARIZONA

PHOENIX

JEWISH FEDERATION OF GREATER PHOENIX (1940); 32 W. Coolidge, Suite 200 (85013); (602)274-1800. FAX: (602)266-7875. Pres. Neil Hiller; Exec. Dir. Arthur Paikowsky.

TUCSON

JEWISH FEDERATION OF SOUTHERN ARIZONA (1946); 3822 East River Rd., Suite 100 (85718); (520)577-9393. FAX: (520)577-0734. Pres. Linda Tumarkin; Exec. Dir. Stuart Mellan.

ARKANSAS

LITTLE ROCK

JEWISH FEDERATION OF ARKANSAS (1911); 425 N. University (72205); (501)663-3571.

FAX: (501)663-7286. Pres. Doris Krain; Exec. Dir. Harvey David Luber.

CALIFORNIA

EAST BAY

JEWISH FEDERATION OF THE GREATER EAST BAY (INCLUDING ALAMEDA & CONTRA COSTA COUNTIES) (1917); 401 Grand Ave., Oakland (94610); (510)839-2900. FAX: (510)839-3996. Pres. Jerry Yanowitz; Exec. V.-Pres. Ami Nahshon.

LONG BEACH

JEWISH FEDERATION OF GREATER LONG BEACH AND W. ORANGE COUNTY (1937; inc. 1946); 3801 E. Willow St. (90815); (562)426-7601. FAX: (562)424-3915. Pres. Richard Lipeles; Exec. Dir. Michael S. Rassler.

LOS ANGELES

JEWISH FEDERATION COUNCIL OF GREATER LOS ANGELES (1912; reorg. 1959); 5700 Wilshire Blvd., 2nd fl. (90036); (323)761-8000. FAX: (323)761-8123. Pres. Lionel Bell; Exec. V.-Pres. John Fishel.

ORANGE COUNTY

JEWISH FEDERATION OF ORANGE COUNTY (1964; inc. 1965); 250 Baker St., Costa Mesa (92626); (714)755-5555. FAX: (714)755-0307. Pres. Joseph Balm; Interim Exec. Dir. Bunnie Mauldin.

PALM SPRINGS

JEWISH FEDERATION OF PALM SPRINGS AND DESERT AREA (1971); 255 N. El Cielo, Suite 430 (92262-6990); (760)325-7281. FAX:

(760)325-2188. Pres. Larry Pitts; Exec. Dir. Mitzi Schafer.

SACRAMENTO

JEWISH FEDERATION OF THE SACRAMENTO REGION (1948); 2351 Wyda Way (95825); (916)486-0906. FAX: (916)486-0816. Pres. Bill Slaton; Exec. Dir. Beryl Michaels.

SAN DIEGO

UNITED JEWISH FEDERATION OF SAN DIEGO COUNTY (1936); 4797 Mercury St. (92111-2102); (619)571-3444. FAX: (619) 571-0701. Pres. Dr. Richard Katz; Exec. V.-Pres. Stephen M. Abramson.

SAN FRANCISCO

JEWISH COMMUNITY FEDERATION OF SAN FRANCISCO, THE PENINSULA, MARIN, AND SONOMA COUNTIES (1910; reorg. 1955); 121 Steuart St. (94105); (415)777-0411. FAX: (415)495-6635. Pres. Harold Zlot; Exec. V.-Pres. Wayne Feinstein.

SAN JOSE

JEWISH FEDERATION OF GREATER SAN JOSE (incl. Santa Clara County except Palo Alto and Los Altos) (1930; reorg. 1950); 14855 Oka Rd., Los Gatos (95032); (408)358-3033. FAX: (408)356-0733. Pres. Judy Levin; Exec. Dir. Jon Friedenberg.

SANTA BARBARA

SANTA BARBARA JEWISH FEDERATION (1974); 524 Chapala St., PO Box 90110 (93190); (805)957-1115. FAX: (805)957-9230. Pres. Jeri Eigner; Exec. Dir. Shelly Katz.

COLORADO

DENVER/BOULDER

ALLIED JEWISH FEDERATION OF COLORADO (1936); 300 S. Dahlia St., Denver (80222); (303)321-3399. FAX: (303)322-8328. Chmn. Edward A. Robinson; Pres. & CEO: Steve Gelfand.

CONNECTICUT

BRIDGEPORT

JEWISH CENTER FOR COMMUNITY SERVICES OF EASTERN FAIRFIELD COUNTY. (1936; reorg. 1981); 4200 Park Ave. (06604-1092); (203)372-6567. FAX: (203)374-0770. Chmn. Stanley Strouch; Pres. & CEO Daniel P. Baker.

DANBURY

THE JEWISH FEDERATION (INCL. N. FAIRFIELD & S. LITCHFIELD COUNTIES IN CON-NECTICUT; PUTNAM & N. WESTCHESTER COUNTIES IN NEW YORK) (1945); 105 Newton Rd. (06810); (203)792-6353. FAX: (203)748-5099. Pres. Daniel Wolinsky; Exec. Dir. Rhonda Cohen.

EASTERN CONNECTICUT

JEWISH FEDERATION OF EASTERN CONNECTICUT, INC. (1950; inc. 1970); 28 Channing St., PO Box 1468, New London (06320); (860)442-8062. FAX: (860)443-4175. Pres. Myron Hendel; Exec. Dir. Jerome E. Fischer.

GREENWICH

UJA/FEDERATION OF GREENWICH (1956); One Holly Hill Lane (06830); (203)622-1434. FAX: (203)622-1237. Pres. Jonathan Nelson; Exec. Dir. Pam Zur.

HARTFORD

JEWISH FEDERATION OF GREATER HARTFORD (1945); 333 Bloomfield Ave., W. Hartford (06117); (860)232-4483. FAX: (860)232-5221. Pres. Henry M. Zachs; Acting Exec. Dir. Steven Bayer.

NEW HAVEN

JEWISH FEDERATION OF GREATER NEW HAVEN (1928); 360 Amity Rd., Woodbridge (06525); (203)387-2424. FAX: (203)387-1818. Pres. David Schaefer; Exec. Dir. Howard Bloom.

NORWALK

(See Westport)

STAMFORD

UNITED JEWISH FEDERATION (inc. 1973); 1035 Newfield Ave., PO Box 3038 (06905); (203)321-1373. FAX: (203)322-3277. Pres. Corrine Lotstein; Dir. of Dev. Edith Samers.

WATERBURY

JEWISH FEDERATION OF GREATER WATERBURY AND NORTHWESTERN CONNECTICUT, INC. (1938); 73 Main St. S., Box F, Woodbury (06798); (203)263-5121. FAX: (203)263-5143. Pres. Linda Herrmann; Exec. Dir. Rob Zwang.

WESTPORT-WESTON-WILTON-NORWALK

UNITED JEWISH APPEAL/FEDERATION OF WESTPORT—WESTON—WILTON—NOR-WALK (inc. 1980); 431 Post Road E., Suite 22, Westport (06880); (203)226-8197. FAX:

(203)226-5051. Pres. Sandra Lefkowitz; Exec. Dir. Robert Kessler.

DELAWARE

WILMINGTON

JEWISH FEDERATION OF DELAWARE, INC. (1934); 100 W. 10th St., Suite 301 (19801-1628); (302)427-2100. FAX: (302)427-2438. Pres. Barbara H. Schoenberg; Exec. V. Pres. Judy Wortman.

DISTRICT OF COLUMBIA

WASHINGTON

THE JEWISH FEDERATION OF GREATER WASHINGTON, INC. (1935); 6101 Montrose Rd., Rockville, MD 20852; (301)230-7200. FAX: (301)230-7265. Pres. Dede Feinberg; Exec. V.-Pres. Ted B. Farber.

FLORIDA

BREVARD COUNTY

JEWISH FEDERATION OF BREVARD (1974); 108-A Barton Ave., Rockledge (32955); (407)636-1824. FAX: (407)636-0614. Pres. Gary Singer; Exec. Dir. Joanne Bishins.

BROWARD COUNTY

JEWISH FEDERATION OF BROWARD COUNTY (1943; 1968); 8358 W. Oakland Park Blvd., #200, Ft. Lauderdale (33351); (954)748-8400. FAX: (954)748-6332. Pres. David B. Schulman; Exec. Dir. Gary N. Rubin.

COLLIER COUNTY

JEWISH FEDERATION OF COLLIER COUNTY (1974); 1250 Tamiami Trail N., Suite 304C, Naples (34102); (941) 263-4205. FAX: (941)263-3813. Pres. Ann Jacobson.

DAYTONA BEACH

(See Volusia & Flagler Counties)

FT. LAUDERDALE

(See Broward County)

JACKSONVILLE

JACKSONVILLE JEWISH FEDERATION, INC. (1935); 8505 San Jose Blvd. (32217); (904)448-5000. FAX: (904)448-5715. Pres. Dr. Kenneth Sekine; Exec. V.-Pres. Alan Margolies.

LEE COUNTY

JEWISH FEDERATION OF LEE AND CHARLOTTE COUNTIES (1974); 6237-E Presidential Court, Ft. Myers (33913-3568); (941)481-4449. FAX: (941)481-0139. Pres. Dr. David Heligman; Exec. Dir. Annette Goodman.

MIAMI

GREATER MIAMI JEWISH FEDERATION, INC. (1938); 4200 Biscayne Blvd. (33137); (305)576-4000. FAX: (305)573-8115. Pres. Michael Scheck; Exec. V.-Pres. Jacob Solomon.

ORLANDO

JEWISH FEDERATION OF GREATER ORLANDO (1949); 851 N. Maitland Ave. (32751); PO Box 941508, Maitland (32794-1508); (407)645-5933. FAX: (407)645-1172. Pres. James S. Grodin; Exec. Dir. Eric Geboff.

PALM BEACH COUNTY

JEWISH FEDERATION OF PALM BEACH COUNTY, INC. (1962); 4601 Community Dr., W. Palm Beach (33417-2760); (561)478-0700. FAX: (561)478-9696. Pres. Helen G. Hoffman; Exec. V.-Pres. Jeffrey L. Klein.

PINELLAS COUNTY

JEWISH FEDERATION OF PINELLAS COUNTY, INC. (incl. Clearwater and St. Petersburg) (1950; reincorp. 1974); 13191 Starkey Rd., #8, Largo (33773-1438); (727) 530-3223. FAX: (727)531-0221. Pres. David Abelson; Interim Exec. Dir. Bonnie Friedman.

SARASOTA-MANATEE

SARASOTA-MANATEE JEWISH FEDERATION (1959); 580 S. McIntosh Rd. (34232-1959); (941)371-4546. FAX: (941)378-2947. Pres. Scott Gordon; Exec. Dir. Jan C. Lederman.

TAMPA

TAMPA JCC/FEDERATION (1941); 13009 Community Campus Dr. (33625); (813)264-9000. FAX: (813)265-8450. Pres. Lili Kaufman; Exec. V.-Pres. Howard Borer.

VOLUSIA & FLAGLER COUNTIES

JEWISH FEDERATION OF VOLUSIA & FLAGLER COUNTIES, INC. (1980); 733 S. Nova Rd., Ormond Beach (32174); (904)672-0294. FAX: (904)673-1316. Pres. Steven I. Unatin; Exec. Dir. Gloria Max.

GEORGIA

ATLANTA

JEWISH FEDERATION OF GREATER ATLANTA, INC. (1905; reorg. 1967); 1440 Spring St., NW (30309-2837); (404)873-1661. FAX: (404)874-7043/881-4027. Pres. Arnold Rubenstein; Exec. Dir. David I. Sarnat.

AUGUSTA

Augusta Jewish Federation (1937); 898 Weinberger Way, Evans (30809); (706)228-3636. FAX: (706)868-1660/823-3960. Pres. Dr. Louis Scharff; Exec. Dir. Michael Pousman.

COLUMBUS

Jewish Federation of Columbus, Inc. (1944); PO Box 6313 (31917); (706)568-6668. Pres. Murray Solomon; Sec. Irene Rainbow.

SAVANNAH

Savannah Jewish Federation (1943); PO Box 23527 (31403); (912)355-8111. FAX: (912)355-8116. Pres. Dr. Paul Kulbersh; Exec. Dir. Sharon Gal.

ILLINOIS

CHAMPAIGN-URBANA

Champaign-Urbana Jewish Federation (1929); 503 E. John St., Champaign (61820); (217)367-9872. FAX: (217)367-0077. Pres. Anthony E. Novak; Exec. Dir. (Ms.) L. Lee Melhado.

CHICAGO

Jewish Federation of Metropolitan Chicago/Jewish United Fund of Metropolitan Chicago (1900); Ben Gurion Way, 1 S. Franklin St. (60606-4694); (312)346-6700. FAX: (312)855-2474. Chmn. Manfred Steinfeld; Pres. Steven B. Nasatir.

ELGIN

Elgin Area Jewish Welfare Chest (1938); 330 Division St. (60120); (847)741-5656. FAX: (847)741-5679. Pres. Robert C. Levine.

PEORIA

Jewish Federation of Peoria (1933; inc. 1947); 2000 Pioneer Pwky., Suite 10B (61615); (309)689-0063. FAX: (309)689-0575. Pres. Jennifer Dolin; Exec. Dir. Eunice Galsky.

QUAD CITIES

Jewish Federation of Quad Cities (1938; comb. 1973); 1705 2nd Ave., Suite 405, Rock Island (61201); (309)793-1300. FAX: (309)793-1345. Pres. Paul Light; Exec. Dir. Ida Kramer.

ROCKFORD

Jewish Federation of Greater Rockford (1937); 1500 Parkview Ave. (61107); (815)399-5497. FAX: (815)399-9835. Pres. Sterne Roufa; Exec. Dir. Marilyn Youman.

SOUTHERN ILLINOIS

Jewish Federation of Southern Illinois, Southeastern Missouri, and Western Kentucky (1941); 6464 W. Main, Suite 7A, Belleville (62223); (618)398-6100. FAX: (618)398-0539. Co-Pres. Harvey Cohen & Carol Rudman; Exec. Dir. Steven C. Low.

SPRINGFIELD

Springfield Jewish Federation (1941); 730 E. Vine St. (62703); (217)528-3446. FAX: (217)528-3409. Pres. Rita Victor; Exec. Dir. Gloria Schwartz.

INDIANA

EVANSVILLE

Evansville Jewish Community Council, Inc. (1936; inc. 1964); PO Box 5026 (47716); (812)477-6722. FAX: (812)477-1577. Pres. Susan Shovers; Exec. Sec. Ernest W. Adler.

FORT WAYNE

Fort Wayne Jewish Federation (1921); 227 E. Washington Blvd. (46802-3121); (219)422-8566. FAX: (219)422-8567. Pres. Scott Salon; Exec. Dir. Jeff Gubitz.

INDIANAPOLIS

Jewish Federation of Greater Indianapolis, Inc. (1905); 6705 Hoover Rd. (46260-4120); (317)726-5450. FAX: (317)205-0307. Pres. Claudette Einhorn; Exec. V.-Pres. Harry Nadler.

LAFAYETTE

Federated Jewish Charities (1924); c/o Hillel, 912 W. State St., W. Lafayette (47906); (765)743-1293. FAX: (765)743-0014. Pres. Earl Prohofsky; Finan. Sec. Laura Starr; Admin. Judy Upton.

MICHIGAN CITY

Michigan City United Jewish Welfare Fund; c/o Temple Sinai, 2800 S. Franklin St. (46360); (219)874-4477. FAX: (219)874-4190. Co-Chmn. Iris Ourach, Bob Baseman.

NORTHWEST INDIANA

The Jewish Federation Northwest Indiana (1941; reorg. 1959); 2939 Jewett St., Highland (46322); (219)972-2250. FAX: (219)972-4779. Pres. Carol Karol; Exec. Dir. David Tein.

ST. JOSEPH VALLEY

Jewish Federation of St. Joseph Valley (1946); 105 Jefferson Centre, Suite 805, South Bend (46601); (219)233-1164. FAX:

(219)288-4103. Pres. Dr. Douglas H. Barton; Exec. V.-Pres. Marilyn Gardner.

IOWA

DES MOINES

JEWISH FEDERATION OF GREATER DES MOINES (1914); 910 Polk Blvd. (50312); (515)277-6321. FAX: (515)277-4069. Pres. Robert M. Pomerantz; Exec. Dir. Elaine Steinger.

SIOUX CITY

JEWISH FEDERATION (1921); 815 38th St. (51104-1417); (712)258-0618. FAX: (712)258-0619. Pres. Michele Ivener; Admin. Dir. Doris Rosenthal.

KANSAS

KANSAS CITY

See listing under Missouri

WICHITA

MID-KANSAS JEWISH FEDERATION, INC. (serving South Central Kansas) (1935); 400 N. Woodlawn, Suite 8 (67208); (316)686-4741. FAX: (316)686-6008. Pres. Marie Levy; Exec. Dir. Judy Press.

KENTUCKY

CENTRAL KENTUCKY

CENTRAL KENTUCKY JEWISH FEDERATION (1976); 340 Romany Rd., Lexington (40502-2400); (606)268-0672. FAX: (606)268-0775. Pres. Evelyn Dantzic Geller; Acting Exec. Dir. Kim Slate.

LOUISVILLE

JEWISH COMMUNITY FEDERATION OF LOUISVILLE, INC. (1934); 3630 Dutchmans Lane (40205); (502)451-8840. FAX: (502)458-0702. Pres. Gerald D. Temes MD; Exec. Dir. Alan S. Engel.

LOUISIANA

BATON ROUGE

JEWISH FEDERATION OF GREATER BATON ROUGE (1971); 3354 Kleinert, (70806); (504) 387-9744. FAX: (504)387-9487. Pres. Harvey Hoffman.

NEW ORLEANS

JEWISH FEDERATION OF GREATER NEW ORLEANS (1913; reorg. 1977); 3500 N. Causeway Blvd., Suite 1240, Metarie (70002); (504)828-2125. FAX: (504)828-2827. Pres. Hugo Kahn; Exec. Dir. Eli Skora.

SHREVEPORT

NORTHERN LOUISIANA JEWISH FEDERATION (1941; inc. 1967); 4700 Line Ave., Suite 117 (71106); (318)868-1200. FAX: (318)868-1272. Pres. Rick Murov; Exec. Dir. Howard L. Ross.

MAINE

LEWISTON-AUBURN

LEWISTON-AUBURN JEWISH FEDERATION (1947); 74 Bradman St., Auburn (04210); (207)786-4201. FAX: (207)786-4202. Pres. Scott Nussinow.

PORTLAND

JEWISH FEDERATION COMMUNITY COUNCIL OF SOUTHERN MAINE (1942); 57 Ashmont St. (04103); (207)773-7254. FAX: (207)773-2234. Pres. Michael Peisner; Exec. Dir. David Unger.

MARYLAND

BALTIMORE

THE ASSOCIATED: JEWISH COMMUNITY FEDERATION OF BALTIMORE (1920; reorg. 1969); 101 W. Mt. Royal Ave. (21201); (410) 727-4828. FAX: (410)783-4795. Chmn. Barbara L. Himmelrich; Pres. Darrell D. Friedman.

MASSACHUSETTS

BERKSHIRE COUNTY

JEWISH FEDERATION OF THE BERKSHIRES (1940); 235 East St., Pittsfield (01201); (413)442-4360. FAX: (413)443-6070. Pres. Ellen Silverstein; Exec. Dir. Robert N. Kerbel.

BOSTON

COMBINED JEWISH PHILANTHROPIES OF GREATER BOSTON, INC. (1895; inc. 1961); 126 High St. (02110); (617)457-8500. FAX: (617)988-6262. Chmn. Cynthia B. Shulman; Pres. Barry Shrage.

CAPE COD

JEWISH FEDERATION OF CAPE COD (1990); 396 Main St., PO Box 2568, Hyannis (02601); (508)778-5588. FAX: (508)778-9727. Pres. Ernest Smily.

LEOMINSTER

LEOMINSTER JEWISH COMMUNITY COUNCIL, INC. (1939); 268 Washington St. (01453); (617)534-6121. Pres. Dr. Milton Kline; Sec.-Treas. Howard J. Rome.

MERRIMACK VALLEY

MERRIMACK VALLEY JEWISH FEDERATION (Serves Andover, Haverhill, Lawrence, Lowell, Newburyport, and 22 surrounding communities) (1988); 805 Turnpike St., N. Andover (01845-6182); (978)688-0466. FAX: (978)688-1097. Pres. James H. Shainker; Exec. Dir. Jan Steven Brodie.

NEW BEDFORD

JEWISH FEDERATION OF GREATER NEW BEDFORD, INC. (1938; inc. 1954); 467 Hawthorn St., N. Dartmouth (02747); (508)997-7471. FAX: (508)997-7730. Co-Pres. Harriet Philips, Patricia Rosenfield; Exec. Dir. Wil Herrup.

NORTH SHORE

JEWISH FEDERATION OF THE NORTH SHORE, INC. (1938); 21 Front St., Salem (01970); (978)745-4222. FAX: (978)741-7507. Pres. Shepard M. Remis; Exec. Dir. Neil A. Cooper.

SPRINGFIELD

JEWISH FEDERATION OF GREATER SPRINGFIELD, INC. (1925); 1160 Dickinson St. (01108); (413)737-4313. FAX: (413)737-4348. Pres. Jeffrey Mandell; Exec. Dir. Joel Weiss.

WORCESTER

WORCESTER JEWISH FEDERATION, INC. (1947; inc. 1957); 633 Salisbury St. (01609); (508)756-1543. FAX: (508)798-0962. Pres. Dr. Robert Honig; Exec. Dir. Meyer L. Bodoff.

MICHIGAN

ANN ARBOR

JEWISH FEDERATION OF WASHTENAW COUNTY/UNITED JEWISH APPEAL (1986); 2939 Birch Hollow Dr. (48108); (734)677-0100. FAX: (734)677-0109. Pres. Morley Witus; Exec. Dir. Nancy N. Margolis.

DETROIT

JEWISH FEDERATION OF METROPOLITAN DETROIT (1899); 6735 Telegraph Rd., Suite 30, PO Box 2030, Bloomfield Hills (48303-2030); (248)642-4260. FAX: (248)642-4985. Pres. Penny Blumenstein; Exec. V.-Pres. Robert P. Aronson.

FLINT

FLINT JEWISH FEDERATION (1936); 619 Wallenberg St. (48502); (810)767-5922. FAX:

(810)767-9024. Pres. Dr. Steve Burton; Exec. Dir. Joel B. Kaplan.

GRAND RAPIDS

JEWISH COMMUNITY FUND OF GRAND RAPIDS (1930); 330 Fuller NE (49503); (616)456-5553. FAX: (616)456-5780. Pres. Richard Stevens; Admin. Dir. Rosalie Stein; V.P. Maxine Shapiro.

MINNESOTA

DULUTH-SUPERIOR

TWIN PORTS JEWISH FEDERATION (1937); 1602 E. Second St., Duluth (55812); (218)724-8857. FAX: (218)724-2560. Pres. Neil Glazman.

MINNEAPOLIS

MINNEAPOLIS JEWISH FEDERATION (1929; inc. 1930); 5901 S. Cedar Lake Rd. (55416); (612)593-2600. FAX: (612)593-2544. Pres. Neil N. Lapidus; Exec. Dir. Joshua Fogelson.

ST. PAUL

UNITED JEWISH FUND AND COUNCIL (1935); 790 S. Cleveland, Suite 201 (55116); (651)690-1707. FAX: (651)690-0228. Pres. James Stein; Exec. Dir. Samuel Asher.

MISSISSIPPI

JACKSON

JACKSON JEWISH WELFARE FUND, INC. (1945); 5315 Old Canton Rd. (39211-4625); (601)956-6215. FAX: (601)956-6260. Pres. Erik Hearon.

MISSOURI

KANSAS CITY

JEWISH FEDERATION OF GREATER KANSAS CITY MO/KS (1933); 5801 W. 115 St., Overland Park, KS (66211-1824); (913)327-8100. FAX: (913)327-8110. Pres. John Wuhlmann; Exec. Dir. A. Robert Gast.

ST. JOSEPH

UNITED JEWISH FUND OF ST. JOSEPH (1915); c/o Ms. Sherri Ott, 1816 Walnut (64503); (816)233-1186. Elliot Zidell; Exec. Sec. Sherri Ott.

ST. LOUIS

JEWISH FEDERATION OF ST. LOUIS (incl. St. Louis County) (1901); 12 Millstone Campus Dr. (63146); (314)432-0020. FAX: (314)432-1277. Pres. Mont S. Levy; Exec. V.-Pres. Barry Rosenberg.

NEBRASKA

LINCOLN

LINCOLN JEWISH WELFARE FEDERATION, INC. (1931; inc. 1961); PO Box 67218 (68506); (402)477-4113. FAX: (402)489-1015. Pres. Herb Friedman; Exec. Dir. Karen Sommer.

OMAHA

JEWISH FEDERATION OF OMAHA (1903); 333 S. 132nd St. (68154-2198); (402)334-8200. FAX: (402)334-1330. Pres. Howard Kooper; Exec. Dir. Jan Perelman.

NEVADA

LAS VEGAS

JEWISH FEDERATION OF LAS VEGAS (1973); 3909 S. Maryland Pkwy. (89119-7520); (702)732-0556. FAX: (702)732-3228. Pres. David Dahan; Exec. Dir. Ronni Epstein.

NEW HAMPSHIRE

MANCHESTER

JEWISH FEDERATION OF GREATER MANCHESTER (1974); 698 Beech St. (03104); (603)627-7679. FAX: (603) 627-7963. Pres. Martin Jacobs; Exec. Dir. Richard Friedman.

NEW JERSEY

ATLANTIC AND CAPE MAY COUNTIES

JEWISH FEDERATION OF ATLANTIC AND CAPE MAY COUNTIES (1924); 3393 Bargaintown Rd., Egg Harbor Township (08232-0617; PO Box 196, Northfield (08225)); (609)653-3030. FAX: (609)653-8881. Pres. Joseph Rodgers; Exec. V.-Pres. Bernard Cohen.

BERGEN COUNTY

UJA FEDERATION OF BERGEN COUNTY AND NORTH HUDSON (inc. 1978); 111 Kinderkamack Rd., PO Box 4176, N. Hackensack Station, River Edge (07661); (201)488-6800. FAX: (201)488-3962. Pres. Eva Lynn Gans; Exec. V.-Pres. Ron B. Meier.

CENTRAL NEW JERSEY

JEWISH FEDERATION OF CENTRAL NEW JERSEY (1940; merged 1973); 1391 Martine Ave., Scotch Plains (07076); (908)889-5335. FAX: (908)889-5370. Pres. Zygmunt Wilf; Exec. V.-Pres. Stanley Stone.

CLIFTON-PASSAIC

JEWISH FEDERATION OF GREATER CLIFTON-PASSAIC (1933); 199 Scoles Ave., Clifton (07012). (973)777-7031. FAX: (973)777-6701. Pres. George Kramer; Exec. V.-Pres. Yosef Y. Muskin.

CUMBERLAND COUNTY

JEWISH FEDERATION OF CUMBERLAND COUNTY (inc. 1971); 629 Wood St., Suite 204, Vineland (08360); (609)696-4445. FAX: (609)696-3428. Pres. James Potter; Exec. Dir. Ann Lynn Lipton.

METROWEST NEW JERSEY

UNITED JEWISH FEDERATION OF METROWEST (1923); 901 Route 10, Whippany (07981-1156); (973)884-4800. FAX: (973)884-7361. Pres. Murray Laulicht; Exec. V.-Pres. Max L. Kleinman.

MIDDLESEX COUNTY

JEWISH FEDERATION OF GREATER MIDDLESEX COUNTY (org. 1948; reorg. 1985); 230 Old Bridge Tpk., S. River (08882-2000); (732)432-7711. FAX: (732)432-0292. Pres. Roy Tanzman; Exec. V.-Pres. Michael Shapiro.

MONMOUTH COUNTY

JEWISH FEDERATION OF GREATER MONMOUTH COUNTY (1971); 100 Grant Ave., PO Box 210, Deal (07723-0210); (732)531-6200-1. FAX: (732)531-9518. Pres. David Portman; Chmn. William A. Schwartz; Exec. Dir. David A. Nussbaum.

MORRIS-SUSSEX COUNTY

(Merged with MetroWest New Jersey)

NORTH JERSEY

JEWISH FEDERATION OF NORTH JERSEY (1933); One Pike Dr., Wayne (07470-2498); (973)595-0555. FAX: (973)595-1532. Branch Office: 17-10 River Rd., Fair Lawn (07410-1250); (973)794-1111. Pres. George Liss; Exec. Dir. Martin Greenberg.

NORTHERN MIDDLESEX COUNTY

(See Middlesex County)

OCEAN COUNTY

OCEAN COUNTY JEWISH FEDERATION (1977); 301 Madison Ave., Lakewood (08701); (732)363-0530. FAX: (732)363-2097. Pres. David Rosen; Exec. Dir. Alan Nydick.

PRINCETON MERCER BUCKS

UNITED JEWISH FEDERATION OF PRINCETON MERCER BUCKS (merged 1996); 3131 Princeton Pike, Bldg. 2A, Lawrenceville (08648); (609)219-0555. FAX: (609)219-9040. Pres. Eliot Freeman; Exec. Dir. Andrew Frank.

SOMERSET COUNTY

JEWISH FEDERATION OF SOMERSET, HUN-TERDON & WARREN COUNTIES (1960); 1011 Rte. 22 West, PO Box 6455, Bridgewater (08807); (908)725-6994. FAX: (908)725-9753. Pres. Martin Siegal; Exec. Dir. Daniel A. Nadelman.

SOUTHERN NEW JERSEY

JEWISH FEDERATION OF SOUTHERN NEW JER-SEY (incl. Camden, Burlington, and Glouces-ter counties) (1922); 1301 Springdale Rd., Suite 200, Cherry Hill (08003); (609)751-9500. FAX: (609)751-1697. Pres. Dr. Robert Belafsky; Exec. V.-Pres. Stuart Alperin.

NEW MEXICO

ALBUQUERQUE

JEWISH FEDERATION OF GREATER ALBU-QUERQUE (1938); 5520 Wyoming Blvd., NE (87109); (505)821-3214. FAX: (505)821-3351. Pres. Dr. Larry Lubar; Exec. Dir. An-drew Lipman.

NEW YORK

ALBANY

(See Northeastern New York)

BUFFALO (INCL. NIAGARA FALLS)

JEWISH FEDERATION OF GREATER BUFFALO, INC. (1903); 787 Delaware Ave. (14209); (716)886-7750. FAX: (716)886-1367. Pres. Irving M. Shuman; Exec. Dir. James M. Lodge.

DUTCHESS COUNTY

JEWISH FEDERATION OF DUTCHESS COUNTY; 110 Grand Ave., Poughkeepsie (12603); (914)471-9811. FAX: (914) 471-0659. Pres. Tomasina Schneider; Exec. Dir. Bonnie Meadow.

ELMIRA-CORNING

JEWISH CENTER AND FEDERATION OF THE TWIN TIERS (1942); PO Box 3087, Elmira (14905-0087); (607)734-8122. FAX: (607)734-8123. Pres. John Spiegler; Admin. Diane Huglies.

NEW YORK

UJA-FEDERATION OF JEWISH PHILAN-THROPIES OF NEW YORK, INC. (incl. Greater NY, Westchester, Nassau, and Suffolk coun-ties) (Fed. org. 1917; UJA 1939; merged 1986); 130 E. 59 St. (10022); (212)980-1000. FAX: (212)836-1778. Pres. James S. Tisch; Chmn. Judith Stern Peck; Exec. V.-Pres. Stephen D. Solender.

NORTHEASTERN NEW YORK

UNITED JEWISH FEDERATION OF NORTH-EASTERN NEW YORK (1986); Latham Circle Mall, 800 New Loudon Rd., Latham (12110); (518)783-7800. FAX: (518)783-1557. Pres. Dr. Lewis Morrison; Exec. Dir. Jerry S. Neimand.

ORANGE COUNTY

JEWISH FEDERATION OF GREATER ORANGE COUNTY (1977); 68 Stewart Ave., Newburgh (12550); (914)562-7860. FAX: (914)562-5114. Pres. Mona Rieger; Admin. Dir. Joyce Waschitz.

ROCHESTER

JEWISH COMMUNITY FEDERATION OF GREATER ROCHESTER, NY, INC. (1939); 441 East Ave. (14607); (716)461-0490. FAX: (716)461-0912. Pres. Eileen Grossman; Exec. Dir. Lawrence W. Fine.

SCHENECTADY

(See Northeastern New York)

SYRACUSE

SYRACUSE JEWISH FEDERATION, INC. (1918); PO Box 510, DeWitt (13214); (315)445-0161 or 2040. FAX: (315)445-1559. Pres. Linda Alexander; Exec. V.-Pres. Mary Ann Op-penheimer.

TROY

(See Northeastern New York)

ULSTER COUNTY

JEWISH FEDERATION OF ULSTER COUNTY (1951); 159 Green St., Kingston (12401); (914)338-8131. FAX: (914)338-8131. Pres. Michelle Tuchman; Exec. Dir. Joan Plotsky.

UTICA

JEWISH COMMUNITY FEDERATION OF MO-HAWK VALLEY, NY, INC. (1950; reorg. 1994); 2310 Oneida St. (13501); (315)733-2343. FAX: (315)733-2346. Pres. Ann Siegel; Exec. Dir. Barbara Ratner-gantshar.

NORTH CAROLINA

ASHEVILLE

WESTERN NORTH CAROLINA JEWISH FED-ERATION (1935); 236 Charlotte St. (28801); (828)253-0701. FAX: (828)254-7666. Pres. Stan Greenberg; Exec. Dir. Marlene Berger-Joyce.

CHARLOTTE

THE JEWISH FEDERATION OF GREATER CHARLOTTE (1938); 5007 Providence Rd.

(28226); (704)366-5007. FAX: (704)365-4507. Pres. William Gorelick; Exec. Dir. Marvin Goldberg.

DURHAM-CHAPEL HILL

DURHAM-CHAPEL HILL JEWISH FEDERATION & COMMUNITY COUNCIL (1979); 3700 Lyckan Pkwy., Suite B, Durham (27707); (919)489-5335. FAX: (919)489-5788. Pres. Elaine Marcus; Exec. Dir. Lew Borman.

GREENSBORO

GREENSBORO JEWISH FEDERATION (1940); 5509C W. Friendly Ave. (27410-4211); (336)852-5433. FAX: (336)852-4346. Pres. Ronald Green; Exec. Dir. Marilyn Forman-Chandler.

RALEIGH

WAKE COUNTY JEWISH FEDERATION (includes Cary, Apex, Garner, Knightdale, Zebulon, Wake Forest and Smithfield) (1987); 8210 Creedmoor Rd., Suite 104 (27613); (919)676-2200. FAX: (919)676-2122. Pres. Jim Maass; Exec. Dir. Judah Segal.

OHIO

AKRON

AKRON JEWISH COMMUNITY FEDERATION (1935); 750 White Pond Dr. (44320); (330)869-CHAI (2424). FAX: (330)867-8498. Pres. David Kock; Exec. Dir. Michael Wise.

CANTON

CANTON JEWISH COMMUNITY FEDERATION (1935; reorg. 1955); 2631 Harvard Ave., NW (44709); (330)452-6444. FAX: (330)452-4487. Pres. Edward Buxbaum; Exec. Dir. Neil Berro.

CINCINNATI

JEWISH FEDERATION OF CINCINNATI (1896; reorg. 1967); 4380 Malsbary Rd., Suite 200 (45242); (513) 985-1500. FAX: (513)985-1503. Pres. Harry B. Davidow; Exec. V.-Pres. Aubrey Herman.

CLEVELAND

JEWISH COMMUNITY FEDERATION OF CLEVELAND (1903); 1750 Euclid Ave. (44115); (216)566-9200. FAX: (216)861-1230. Pres. Robert Goldberg; Exec. V.-Pres. Stephen H. Hoffman.

COLUMBUS

COLUMBUS JEWISH FEDERATION (1926); 1175 College Ave. (43209); (614)237-7686. FAX: (614)237-2221. Pres. Gordon Zacks; Exec. Dir. Mitchel Orlik.

DAYTON

JEWISH FEDERATION OF GREATER DAYTON (1910); 4501 Denlinger Rd. (45426); (937)854-4150. FAX: (937)854-2850. Pres. Joseph Bettman; Exec. V.-Pres. Peter H. Wells.

STEUBENVILLE

JEWISH COMMUNITY COUNCIL (1938); 300 Lovers Lane (43952); (614)264-5514. Pres. Curtis L. Greenberg; Exec. Sec. Jennie Bernstein.

TOLEDO

JEWISH FEDERATION OF GREATER TOLEDO (1907; reorg. 1960); 6505 Sylvania Ave., Sylvania (43560); (419)885-4461. FAX: (419)885-3207. Pres. Joel Beren; Exec. Dir. Alix Greenblatt.

YOUNGSTOWN

Youngstown Area Jewish Federation (1935); 505 Gypsy Lane (44504-1314); (330)746-3251. FAX: (330)746-7926. Pres. Dr. Ronald Roth; Exec. V.-Pres. Sam Kooperman.

OKLAHOMA

OKLAHOMA CITY

JEWISH FEDERATION OF GREATER OKLAHOMA CITY (1941); 710 W. Wilshire, Suite C (73116). (405)848-3132. FAX: (405)848-3180. Pres. Harriet Carson; Exec. Dir. Edie S. Roodman.

TULSA

JEWISH FEDERATION OF TULSA (1938); 2021 E. 71 St. (74136); (918)495-1100. FAX: (918)495-1220. Pres. Andrew M. Wolov; Exec. Dir. David Bernstein.

OREGON

PORTLAND

JEWISH FEDERATION OF PORTLAND (incl. Northwest Oregon and Southwest Washington communities) (1920; reorg. 1956); 6651 SW Capitol Hwy. (97219); (503)245-6219. FAX: (503)245-6603. Pres. Gayle Romain; Exec. Dir. Charles Schiffman.

PENNSYLVANIA

ALTOONA

FEDERATION OF JEWISH PHILANTHROPIES (1920; reorg. inc. 1945); 1308 17 St. (16601); (814)944-4072. FAX: (814)944-9874. Pres. William Wallen; Admin. Dir. Reva Dotan.

BUCKS COUNTY

(See Jewish Federation of Greater Philadelphia)

ERIE

JEWISH COMMUNITY COUNCIL OF ERIE (1946); 1611 Peach St., Suite 405 (16501-2123); (814)455-4474. FAX: (814)455-4475. Pres. Robert Cohen; Admin. Dir. Cynthia Penman; Dir. of Soc. Srvcs. Barbara Singer.

HARRISBURG

UNITED JEWISH COMMUNITY OF GREATER HARRISBURG (1941); 3301 N. Front St. (17110); (717)236-9555. FAX: (717)236-8104. Pres. Raphael Aronson; Exec. Dir. Jordan Harburger.

JOHNSTOWN

UNITED JEWISH FEDERATION OF JOHNSTOWN (1938); c/o Beth Sholom Cong., 700 Indiana St. (15905); (814)536-6440 (office), (814)539-9891 (home). Pres. Isadore Suchman.

LANCASTER

LANCASTER JEWISH FEDERATION; 2120 Oregon Pike (17601); (717)569-7352. FAX: (717)569-1614. Pres. Steve Gordon; Exec. Dir. H. Ted Busch.

PHILADELPHIA

JEWISH FEDERATION OF GREATER PHILADELPHIA (incl. Bucks, Chester, Delaware, Montgomery, and Philadelphia counties) (1901; reorg. 1956); 226 S. 16 St. (19102); (215)893-5600. FAX: (215)546-0349. Pres. Michael R. Belman; Exec. V.-Pres. Howard E. Charish.

PITTSBURGH

UNITED JEWISH FEDERATION OF GREATER PITTSBURGH (1912; reorg. 1955); 234 McKee Pl. (15213); (412)681-8000. FAX: (412) 681-3980. Chmn. David Burstin; Pres. Howard M. Rieger.

READING

JEWISH FEDERATION OF READING, PA., INC. (1935; reorg. 1972); 1700 City Line St. (19604); (610)921-2766. FAX: (610)929-0886. Pres. Sheila Lattin; Exec. Dir. Stanley Ramati.

SCRANTON

SCRANTON-LACKAWANNA JEWISH FEDERATION (1945); 601 Jefferson Ave. (18510); (570)961-2300. FAX: (570)346-6147. Pres. Louis Nivert; Exec. Dir. Seymour Brotman.

WYOMING VALLEY

JEWISH FEDERATION OF WYOMING VALLEY (1950); 60 S. River St., Wilkes-Barre (18702-2493); (717)822-4146. FAX: (717)824-5966. Pres. Murray Ufberg; Exec. Dir. Don Cooper.

RHODE ISLAND

PROVIDENCE

JEWISH FEDERATION OF RHODE ISLAND (1945); 130 Sessions St. (02906); (401)421-4111. FAX: (401)331-7961. Pres. Edward D. Feldstein; Exec. Dir. Steven A. Rakitt.

SOUTH CAROLINA

CHARLESTON

CHARLESTON JEWISH FEDERATION (1949); 1645 Raoul Wallenberg Blvd., PO Box 31298 (29407); (843)571-6565. FAX: (843)556-6206. Pres. Anita Zucker; Exec. Dir. Ellen J. Katzman.

COLUMBIA

COLUMBIA JEWISH FEDERATION (1960); 4540 Trenholm Rd., PO Box 6968 (29206); (803)787-2023. FAX: (803)787-0475. Pres. Stephen Serbin; Exec. Dir. Steven Terner.

GREENVILLE

FEDERATED JEWISH CHARITIES OF GREENVILLE, INC.; PO Box 7016-110 (29606); (864)987-0460. Pres. Herbert Silver; Treas. Richard S. Berger.

SOUTH DAKOTA

SIOUX FALLS

JEWISH WELFARE FUND (1938); 510 S. First Ave. (57104); (605)332-3335. FAX: (605)334-2298. Pres. Laurence Bierman; Exec. Sec. Stephen Rosenthal.

TENNESSEE

CHATTANOOGA

JEWISH COMMUNITY FEDERATION OF GREATER CHATTANOOGA (1931); 3601 Ringgold Rd. (37412); PO Box 8947 (37414); (423)493-0270. FAX: (423)493-9997. Pres. Claire Binder; Exec. Dir. Debra Levine.

KNOXVILLE

KNOXVILLE JEWISH FEDERATION, INC. (1939); 6800 Deane Hill Dr. (37919); (423)693-5837. FAX: (423)694-4861. Pres. Mary Linda Schwartzbart; Exec. Dir. Dr. Bernard Rosenblatt.

MEMPHIS

MEMPHIS JEWISH FEDERATION (incl. Shelby County) (1935); 6560 Poplar Ave. (38138-3614); (901)767-7100. FAX: (901)767-7128. Pres. Louise Sklar; Exec. Dir. Jeffrey Feld.

NASHVILLE

JEWISH FEDERATION OF NASHVILLE & MIDDLE TENNESSEE (1936); 801 Percy Warner Blvd. (37205); (615)356-3242. FAX: (615)352-0056. Pres. Peter Haas.

TEXAS

AUSTIN

JEWISH FEDERATION OF AUSTIN (1939; reorg. 1956); 11713 Jollyville Rd. (78759); (512)331-1144. FAX: (512)331-7059. Pres. Linda Millstone; Exec. Dir. Sandy Sack.

DALLAS

JEWISH FEDERATION OF GREATER DALLAS (1911); 7800 Northaven Rd. (75230); (214)369-3313. FAX: (214)369-8943. Pres. Donald Schaffer; Exec. Dir. Gary Weinstein.

EL PASO

JEWISH FEDERATION OF EL PASO, INC. (1937); 405 Wallenberg Dr. (79912); (915)584-4437. FAX: (915)584-0243. Pres. Gary Weiser; Exec. Dir. Larry Harris.

FORT WORTH

JEWISH FEDERATION OF FORT WORTH AND TARRANT COUNTY (1936); 6795 Dan Danciger Rd. (76133); (817)292-3081. FAX: (817)292-3214. Pres. Harold Gernsbacher; Exec. Dir. Naomi Rosenfield.

GALVESTON

GALVESTON COUNTY JEWISH WELFARE ASSOCIATION (1936); PO Box 146 (77553); (409)763-5241. Pres. Dr. Michael Warren.

HOUSTON

JEWISH FEDERATION OF GREATER HOUSTON (1936); 5603 S. Braeswood Blvd., (77096-3998); (713)729-7000. FAX: (713)721-6232. Pres. Marvin Woskow; Exec. V.-Pres. Lee Wunsch.

SAN ANTONIO

JEWISH FEDERATION OF SAN ANTONIO (incl. Bexar County) (1922); 8434 Ahern Dr. (78216); (210)341-8234. FAX: (210)341-2842. Pres. Meyer Lifschitz; Exec. Dir. Mark Freedman.

WACO

JEWISH FEDERATION OF WACO AND CENTRAL TEXAS (1949); PO Box 8031 (76714-8031); (254)776-3740. Pres. Abbye M. Silver; Exec. Sec. Deborah S. Hersh.

UTAH

SALT LAKE CITY

UNITED JEWISH FEDERATION OF UTAH (1936); 2416 E. 1700 South (84108); (801)581-0102. FAX: (801) 581-1334. Pres. Robert Wolff; Exec. Dir. Donald Gartman.

VIRGINIA

RICHMOND

JEWISH COMMUNITY FEDERATION OF RICHMOND (1935); 5403 Monument Ave., PO Box 17128 (23226); (804)288-0045. FAX: (804)282-7507. Pres. Richard J. November; Exec. Dir. Marsha F. Hurwitz.

TIDEWATER

UNITED JEWISH FEDERATION OF TIDEWATER (incl. Norfolk, Portsmouth, and Virginia Beach) (1937); 5029 Corporate Woods Dr., Suite 335, Virginia Beach (23462-4370); (757)671-1600. FAX: (757)671-7613. Pres. David Brand; Exec. V.-Pres. Mark L. Goldstein.

VIRGINIA PENINSULA

UNITED JEWISH COMMUNITY OF THE VIRGINIA PENINSULA, INC. (1942); 2700 Spring Rd., Newport News (23606); (757)930-1422. FAX: (757)930-3762. Pres. Roy H. Lasris; Exec. Dir. Rodney J. Margolis.

WASHINGTON

SEATTLE

JEWISH FEDERATION OF GREATER SEATTLE (incl. King County, Everett, and Bremerton) (1926); 2031 Third Ave. (98121); (206)443-5400. FAX: (206)443-0306. Pres. Lucy Pruzan; Exec. V.-Pres. Michael Novick.

WEST VIRGINIA

CHARLESTON

FEDERATED JEWISH CHARITIES OF CHARLESTON, INC. (1937); PO Box 1613 (25326); (304)345-2320. FAX: (304)925-0793. Pres. Stuart May; Exec. Sec. Lee Diznoff.

WISCONSIN

KENOSHA

KENOSHA JEWISH WELFARE FUND (1938);
8622 Lake Shore Dr., Pleasant Prairie
(53158-4718); (414)697-0777. FAX:
(414)942-1213. Pres. Ben Hagai Steuerman;
Sec.-Treas. Steven H. Barasch.

MADISON

MADISON JEWISH COMMUNITY COUNCIL,
INC. (1940); 6434 Enterprise Lane (53719-
1117. (608)278-1808. FAX:(608)278-7814.
Pres. Joel Minkoff; Exec. Dir. Steven H.
Morrison.

MILWAUKEE

MILWAUKEE JEWISH FEDERATION, INC.
(1902); 1360 N. Prospect Ave. (53202);
(414)390-5700. FAX: (414)390-5782. Pres.
Stephen L. Chernof; Exec. V.-Pres. Richard
H. Meyer.

CANADA

ALBERTA

CALGARY

CALGARY JEWISH COMMUNITY COUNCIL
(1962); 1607 90th Ave. SW (T2V 4V7);
(403)253-8600. FAX: (403)253-7915. Pres.
Nate Feldman; Exec. Dir. Joel R. Miller.

EDMONTON

JEWISH FEDERATION OF EDMONTON (1954;
reorg. 1982); 7200-156th St. (T5R 1X3);
(780)487-0585. FAX: (780)481-1854. Pres.
Stephen Mandel; Exec. Dir. Lesley A. Jacobson.

BRITISH COLUMBIA

VANCOUVER

JEWISH FEDERATION OF GREATER VANCOU-
VER (1932; reorg. 1987); 950 W. 41st Ave.,
Suite 200 (V5Z 2N7); (604)257-5100. FAX:
(604)257-5110. Pres. Bob Wielmot; Exec.
Dir. Drew Staffenberg.

MANITOBA

WINNIPEG

WINNIPEG JEWISH COMMUNITY COUNCIL
(1938; reorg. 1973); 123 Doncaster St., Suite
C300 (R3N 2B2); (204)477-7400. FAX:
(204)477-7405. Pres. Larry Hurtig; Exec. V.-
Pres. Robert Freedman.

ONTARIO

HAMILTON

UJA/JEWISH FEDERATION OF HAMIL-
TON/WENTWORTH & AREA (1932; merged
1971); PO Box 7258, 1030 Lower Lion Club
Rd., Ancaster (L9G 3N6); (905)648-0605
#305. FAX: (905)648-8350. Pres. Cheryl
Greenbaum; Exec. Dir. Patricia Tolkin
Eppel.

LONDON

LONDON JEWISH FEDERATION (1932); 536
Huron St. (N5Y 4J5); (519)673-3310. FAX:
(519)673-1161. Pres. Ron Wolf; Off. Mgr.
Debra Chatterley.

OTTAWA

JEWISH COMMUNITY COUNCIL OF OTTAWA
(1934); 1780 Kerr Ave. (K2A 1R9);
(613)798-4696. FAX: (613)798-4695. Pres.
Barbara Farber; Exec. Dir. Mitchell Bell-
man.

TORONTO

UJA FEDERATION OF GREATER TORONTO
(1917); 4600 Bathurst St. (M2R 3V2);
(416)635-2883. FAX: (416)635-9565. Pres.
Joseph Steiner; Exec. V.-Pres. Allan Reitzes.

WINDSOR

JEWISH COMMUNITY FEDERATION (1938);
1641 Ouellette Ave. (N8X 1K9); (519)973-
1772. FAX: (519)973-1774. Pres. Dr.
Michael Malowitz; Exec. Dir. Steven
Brownstein.

QUEBEC

MONTREAL

FEDERATION CJA (formerly Allied Jewish
Community Services) (1965); 5151 Cote Ste.
Catherine Rd. (H3W 1M6); (514)735-3541.
FAX: (514)735-8972. Pres. Stanley Plotnick;
Exec. V.-Pres. Danyael Cantor.

Jewish Periodicals*

UNITED STATES

ALABAMA

SOUTHERN SHOFAR (1990). PO Box 130052, Birmingham, 35213. (205) 595-9255. FAX: (205)595-9256. E-mail: soshofar@aol.com. Lawrence M. Brook. Monthly.

ARIZONA

ARIZONA JEWISH POST (1946). 3812 East River Rd., Tucson, 85718. (520)529-1500. FAX: (520)577-0734. E-mail: 6809162@mcimail.com. Sandra R. Heiman. Fortnightly. Jewish Federation of Southern Arizona.

JEWISH NEWS OF GREATER PHOENIX (1948). 1625 E. Northern Ave., Suite 106, Phoenix, 85020. (602)870-9470. FAX: (602)870-0426. E-mail:jngphx@aol.com. Ed./Pub. Florence Eckstein. Weekly.

CALIFORNIA

CENTRAL CALIFORNIA JEWISH HERITAGE (1914). 7334 Topanga Canyon Blvd., Suite 110, Canoga Park, 91303-3345. (818) 999-9921. FAX: (818) 999-6715. E-mail: heritagepub@earthlink.net. Dan Brin. Six times a year. Heritage Group.

HERITAGE-SOUTHWEST JEWISH PRESS (1914). 7334 Topanga Canyon Blvd., Suite 110, Canoga Park, 91303-3345. (818) 999-9921. FAX: (818) 999-6715. E-mail: heritagepub@earthlink.net. Dan Brin. Weekly. Heritage Group.

JEWISH BULLETIN OF NORTHERN CALIFORNIA (1896). 225 Bush St., Suite 1480, San Francisco, 94104-4281. (415)263-7200. FAX: (415)263-7223. E-mail: jbnc@jewishsf.com. Marc S. Klein. Weekly. San Francisco Jewish Community Publications, Inc.

JEWISH COMMUNITY CHRONICLE (1947). 3801 E. Willow St., Long Beach, 90815. (562)595-5543. FAX: (562)595-5543. E-mail: jchron@net999.com. Harriette Ellis. Fortnightly. Jewish Federation of Greater Long Beach & West Orange County.

JEWISH COMMUNITY NEWS (1976). 14855 Oka Rd., Suite 2, Los Gatos, 95030. (408)358-3033, ext. 31. FAX: (408)356-0733. E-mail: jcn@jfgsj.org. Eileen Goss. Monthly. Jewish Federation of Greater San Jose.

JEWISH JOURNAL OF GREATER LOS ANGELES (1986). 3660 Wilshire Blvd., Suite 204, Los Angeles, 90010. (213)368-1661. FAX: (213)368-1684. E-mail: jjlagene@aol.com. Gene Lichtenstein. Weekly.

JEWISH NEWS (1973). 11071 Ventura Blvd., Studio City, 91604. (818)786-4000. FAX: (818)760-4648. Phil Blazer. Monthly.

JEWISH SOCIAL STUDIES: HISTORY, CULTURE, AND SOCIETY (1939). c/o Program in Jewish Studies, Bldg. 240, Rm. 103, Stanford University, Stanford, 94305-2190. (650)725-0829. FAX: (650)725-2920. E-mail: jss@leland.stanford.edu. Steven J. Zipperstein, Aron Rodrigue. Three times a year. Conference on Jewish Social Studies, Inc.

JEWISH SPORTS REVIEW. 1800 S. Robertson Blvd., #174, Los Angeles, 90035. (800)510-9003. E-mail: gwallman@igc.apc.org. Shel Wallman/Ephraim Moxson. Bimonthly.

*The information in this directory is based on replies to questionnaires circulated by the editors. For organization bulletins, see the directory of Jewish organizations.

LOS ANGELES JEWISH TIMES (formerly B'NAI B'RITH MESSENGER) (1897). 5455 Wilshire Blvd., Suite 903, Los Angeles, 90036. (323)933-0131. FAX: (323)933-7928. E-mail: lajtimes@aol.com. Ed.-in-Chief Joe Bobker; Mng. Ed. Jane Fried. Weekly.

ORANGE COUNTY JEWISH HERITAGE. 24331 Muirlands Blvd., Suite D-347, Lake Forest, 92630. Phone/FAX: (949)362-4446. Stan Brin. Bi-weekly.

SAN DIEGO JEWISH PRESS HERITAGE. P.O. Box 19363, San Diego, 92159D0363. (619)265-0808. FAX: (619)265-0850. E-mail: sdheritage@aol.com. Don Harrison. Weekly.

SAN DIEGO JEWISH TIMES (1979). 4731 Palm Ave., La Mesa, 91941. (619)463-5515. FAX: (900) 370-1190. E-mail: jewish times@msn.com. Carol Rosenberg. Biweekly.

SHALOM L.A. 15301 Ventura Blvd., Suite 500, Sherman Oaks, 91403. (818)783-3090. FAX: (818)783-1104. Meir Doron. Weekly. Hebrew.

TIKKUN: A BIMONTHLY JEWISH CRITIQUE OF POLITICS, CULTURE & SOCIETY (1986). 26 Fell St., San Francisco, 94102. (415)575-1200. FAX: (415)575-1434. E-mail: magazine@tikkun.org. Michael Lerner. Bimonthly. Institute for Labor & Mental Health.

WESTERN STATES JEWISH HISTORY (1968). 22711 Cass Ave., Woodland Hills, 91364. (818)225-9631. FAX: (818)225-8354. E-mail: david@inpubco.com. Ed. in Chief Gladys Sturman; Ed. David Epstein. Quarterly. Western States Jewish History Association.

COLORADO

INTERMOUNTAIN JEWISH NEWS (1913). 1275 Sherman St., Suite 214, Denver, 80203-2299. (303)861-2234. FAX: (303)832-6942. E-mail: ijn@rmii.com. Exec. Ed. Rabbi Hillel Goldberg; Pub. Miriam Goldberg. Weekly.

CONNECTICUT

CONNECTICUT JEWISH LEDGER (1929). 740 N. Main St., W. Hartford, 06117. (860) 231-2424. FAX: (860)231-2428. E-mail: ctjledger@aol.com. Lisa Lenkiewitz. Weekly.

JEWISH LEADER. 28 Channing St., PO Box 1468, New London, 06320. (860)442-

7395. FAX: (860)443-4175. E-mail: perlsum4@aol.com. Ed. Mimi Perl; Mngr. Sidney Schiller. Biweekly. Jewish Federation of Eastern Connecticut.

DELAWARE

JEWISH VOICE. 100 W. 10th St., Suite 301, Wilmington, 19801. (302) 427-2100. FAX: (302) 427-2438. E-mail: jewishvoic @aol.com. Lynn Edelman. 22 times per year. Jewish Federation of Delaware.

DISTRICT OF COLUMBIA

AZURE (1996). 1140 Connecticut Ave., NW, Suite 801, Washington, 20036. (202)887-1270. FAX: (202)887-1277. E-mail: ken@shalemcenter.org. Ofir Haivry. Quarterly. Hebrew/English. The Shalem Center.

B'NAI B'RITH INTERNATIONAL JEWISH MONTHLY (1886, under the name Menorah). 1640 Rhode Island Ave., NW, Washington, 20036. (202)857-6645. FAX: (202)296-1092. E-mail: erozenman@ bnaibrith.org. Eric Rozenman. Bimonthly. B'nai B'rith International.

CAPITAL COMMUNIQUÉ (1991). 777 N. Capital St., NE, Suite 305, Washington, 20002. (202)216-9060. FAX: (202)216-9061. Jason Silberberg. Bi-annually. National Jewish Democratic Council.

JEWISH VETERAN (1896). 1811 R St., NW, Washington, 20009-1659. (202)265-6280. FAX: (202)234-5662. E-mail: jwv@erols. com. Kevin Barney. 5 times per year. Jewish War Veterans of the U.S.A.

MOMENT (1975). 4710 41 St., NW, Washington, 20016. (202)364-3300. FAX: (202)364-2636. E-mail: editor@moment-mag.com. Hershel Shanks. Bimonthly. Jewish Educational Ventures, Inc.

MONITOR (1990). 1819 H Street, NW, Suite 230, Washington, 20006. (202)775-9770. FAX: (202)775-9776. E-mail: ucsj@ucsj. com. Lindsay Paige Taxman.Quarterly. Union of Councils for Soviet Jews.

NEAR EAST REPORT (1957). 440 First St., NW, Suite 607, Washington, 20001. (202)639-5254. FAX: (202) 347-4916. Dr. Raphael Danziger. Fortnightly. Near East Research, Inc.

SECURITY AFFAIRS (1976). 1717 K St., NW, Suite 800, Washington, 20006. (202)833-0020. FAX: (202)296-6452. E-mail: info@

jinsa.org. Jim Colbert. Quarterly. Jewish Institute for National Security Affairs.

WASHINGTON JEWISH WEEK. *See under* MARYLAND

FLORIDA

THE CHRONICLE (1971). 580 S. McIntosh Rd., Sarasota, 34232. (941)371-4546. FAX: (941)378-2947. Barry Millman. Fortnightly. Sarasota-Manatee Jewish Federation.

HERITAGE FLORIDA JEWISH NEWS (1976). PO Box 300742, Fern Park, 32730. (407)834-8787. FAX: (407)831-0507. E-mail: heritagefl@aol.com. Pub. Jeffrey Gaeser; Assoc. Ed. Chris Allen. Weekly.

JACKSONVILLE JEWISH NEWS (1988). 8505 San Jose Blvd., Jacksonville, 32217. (904) 448-5000, (904)262-1971. FAX: (904)448-5715. Susan R. Goetz. Monthly. Jacksonville Jewish Federation.

JEWISH JOURNAL (PALM BEACH-BROWARD-DADE) (1977). 601 Fairway Dr., Deerfield Beach, 33441. (954)698-6397. FAX: (954) 429-1207. Alan Gosh. Weekly. South Florida Newspaper Network.

JEWISH PRESS OF PINELLAS COUNTY (Clearwater-St. Petersburg) (1985). PO Box 6970, Clearwater, 33758-6970; 13191 Starkey Rd., Crownpointe #8, Largo, 33773-1438. E-mail: jptb@aol. com. (813)535-4400. FAX:(813)530-3039. Karen Wolfson Dawkins. Biweekly. Jewish Press Group of Tampa Bay (FL), Inc. in cooperation with the Jewish Federation of Pinellas County.

JEWISH PRESS OF TAMPA (1987). PO Box 6970, Clearwater 33758-6970; 13191 Starkey Rd., Crownpointe #8, Largo 33773-1438. (727)535-4400. FAX: (813) 530-3039. E-mail: jptb@aol.com. Karen Wolfson Dawkins. Biweekly. Jewish Press Group of Tampa Bay (FL), Inc.

PALM BEACH JEWISH TIMES (1994). 2240 Woolbright Rd., #424, Boynton Beach, 33426. (561) 374-7900. FAX: (561) 374-7999. E-mail: pbjtimes@aol.com. Herb Levine. Weekly.

SHALOM (1994). 8358 W. Oakland Park Blvd., Suite 305, Ft. Lauderdale, 33351. (954)748-8400. FAX: (954) 748-4509. Ed.-in-Chief Rhonda Roseman-Seriani; Mng. Ed. Elliot Goldenberg. Biweekly. Jewish Federation of Broward County.

GEORGIA

JEWISH CIVIC PRESS (1972). 3500 Piedmont Rd., Suite 612, Atlanta, 30305. (404)231-2194. Abner L. Tritt. Monthly.

ILLINOIS

CHICAGO JEWISH NEWS (1994). 2501 W. Peterson, Chicago, 60659. (773)728-3636. FAX: (773)728-3734. E-mail: chijewnes @aol.com. Joseph Aaron. Weekly.

CHICAGO JEWISH STAR (1991). PO Box 268, Skokie, 60076-0268. (847)674-7827. FAX: (847)674-0014. E-mail: chicago-jewish-star@mcimail.com. Ed. Douglas Wertheimer; Assoc. Ed. Gila Wertheimer. Fortnightly.

JEWISH COMMUNITY NEWS (1941). 6464 W. Main, Suite 7A, Belleville, 62223. (618)398-6100. FAX: (618)398-0539. Steve Low. Quarterly. Jewish Federation of Southern Illinois.

JUF NEWS & GUIDE TO JEWISH LIVING IN CHICAGO (1972). One S. Franklin St., Rm. 701G, Chicago, 60606. (312)357-4848. FAX: (312)855-2470. E-mail: jufnews@ juf.org. Aaron B. Cohen. Monthly (Guide, annually). Jewish United Fund/Jewish Federation of Metropolitan Chicago.

INDIANA

ILLIANA NEWS (1976). 2939 Jewett St., Highland, 46322. (219)972-2250. FAX: (219)972-4779. E-mail: jfedofnwi@aol. com. Monthly (except July/Aug.). Jewish Federation of Northwest Indiana, Inc.

INDIANA JEWISH POST AND OPINION (1935). 238 S. Meridian St., Indianapolis, 46225. (317)927-7800. FAX: (317)927-7807. Ed Stattmann. Weekly.

NATIONAL JEWISH POST AND OPINION (1932). 238 S. Meridian St., Indianapolis, 46225. (317)972-7800. FAX: (317)972-7807. Gabriel Cohen. Weekly.

KANSAS

KANSAS CITY JEWISH CHRONICLE (1920). 7373 W. 107 St., Overland Park, 66212. (913)648-4620. FAX: (913)381-1402. E-mail: chronicle@sunpublications.com. Rick Hellman. Weekly. Sun Publications.

KENTUCKY

COMMUNITY (1975). 3630 Dutchmans Lane, Louisville, 40205-3200. (502) 451-8840. FAX: (502) 458-0702. E-mail: fedlouky @jon.cjfny.org. Shiela Wallace. Biweekly.

Jewish Community Federation of Louisville.

KENTUCKY JEWISH POST AND OPINION (1931). 1701 Bardstown Rd., Louisville, 40205. (502)459-1914. Ed Stattman. Weekly.

LOUISIANA

JEWISH CIVIC PRESS (1965). 924 Valmont St., New Orleans, 70115. (504)895-8784. Claire & Abner Tritt, eds. and pubs. Monthly.

JEWISH NEWS (1995). 3500 N. Causeway Blvd., Suite 1240, Metairie, 70002. (504)828-2125. FAX: (504)828-2827. E-mail: jfedrb@aol.com. Marla Shivers. Fortnightly. Jewish Federation of Greater New Orleans.

MARYLAND

BALTIMORE JEWISH TIMES (1919). 2104 N. Charles St., Baltimore, 21218. (410)752-3504. FAX: (410)752-2375. Phil Jacobs. Weekly.

MODERN JUDAISM (1980). John Hopkins University Press, 2715 N. Charles St., Baltimore, 21218-4363. (410)516-6987. FAX: (410)516-6968. (Editorial address: Center for Judaic Studies, Boston University, 745 Commonwealth Ave., Boston, 02215. (617)353-8096. FAX: (617)353-5441.) Steven T. Katz. Three times a year.

PROOFTEXTS: A JOURNAL OF JEWISH LITERARY HISTORY (1980). Johns Hopkins University Press, 2715 N. Charles St., Baltimore, 21218-4319. (410)516-6987. FAX: (410)516-6968. Editorial address (for contributors): NEJS Dept., Brandeis U., Waltham, MA 02254. Alan Mintz, David G. Roskies. Three times a year.

WASHINGTON JEWISH WEEK (1930, as the National Jewish Ledger). 12300 Twinbrook Pkwy., Suite 250, Rockville, 20852. (301)230-2222. FAX: (301)881-6362. E-mail: wjweek@aol.com. Al Erlick. Weekly.

MASSACHUSETTS

AMERICAN JEWISH HISTORY (1893). Two Thornton Rd., Waltham, 02154. (781)891-8110. FAX: (781)899-9208. E-mail: ajhs@ajhs.org. Marc Lee Raphael. Quarterly. American Jewish Historical Society.

JEWISH ADVOCATE (1902). 15 School St., Boston, 02108. (617)367-9100. FAX:

(617)367-9310. E-mail: thejewadv@aol. com. Mng. Ed. Steven Rosenberg. Weekly.

JEWISH CHRONICLE (1927). 131 Lincoln St., Worcester, 01605. (508)752-2512. Sondra Shapiro. Biweekly.

JEWISH GUIDE TO BOSTON & NEW ENGLAND (1972). 15 School St., Boston, 02108. (617)367-9100. FAX: (617)367-9310. Rosie Rosenzweig. Irregularly. The Jewish Advocate.

THE JEWISH JOURNAL/NORTH OF BOSTON (1976). 201 Washington St., PO Box 555, Salem, 01970. (978)745-4111. FAX: (978) 745-5333. E-mail: editorial@jewishjournal. org. Bette W. Keva. Biweekly. Russian section. North Shore Jewish Press Ltd.

THE JEWISH NEWS OF WESTERN MASSACHUSETTS (see Jewish Advocate)

METROWEST JEWISH REPORTER (1970). 76 Salem End Rd., Framingham, 01702. (508)872-4808. FAX: (508)879-5856. Marcia T. Rivin. Monthly. Combined Jewish Philanthropies of Greater Boston.

THE PAKN-TREGER (1980). 1021 West St., Amherst, 01002. (413)256-4900. FAX: (413)256-4700. E-mail: pt@bikher.org. Quarterly. Yiddish & English. National Yiddish Book Center.

MICHIGAN

DETROIT JEWISH NEWS (1942). 27676 Franklin Rd., Southfield, 48034. (248) 354-6060. FAX: (248)354-6069. E-mail: thedjn@aol.com. Robert Sklar. Weekly.

HUMANISTIC JUDAISM (1968). 28611 W. Twelve Mile Rd., Farmington Hills, 48334. (248)478-7610. FAX: (248)478-3159. E-mail: info@shj.org. M. Bonnie Cousens, Ruth D. Feldman. Quarterly. Society for Humanistic Judaism.

WASHTENAW JEWISH NEWS (1978). 2935 Birch Hollow Dr., Ann Arbor, 48108. (734)971-1800. FAX: (734)971-1801. E-mail: wjna2@aol.com. Susan Kravitz Ayer. Monthly.

MINNESOTA

AMERICAN JEWISH WORLD (1912). 4509 Minnetonka Blvd., Minneapolis, 55416. (612)920-7000. FAX: (612)920-6205. E-mail: amjewish@isd.net. Marshall Hoffman. Weekly.

MISSOURI

KANSAS CITY JEWISH CHRONICLE. *See under* KANSAS

ST. LOUIS JEWISH LIGHT (1947; reorg. 1963). 12 Millstone Campus Dr., St. Louis, 63146. (314)432-3353. FAX: (314)432-0515. E-mail: stlouislgt@aol.com. Robert A. Cohn. Weekly. St. Louis Jewish Light.

NEBRASKA

JEWISH PRESS (1920). 333 S. 132 St., Omaha, 68154. (402)334-6450. FAX: (402)334-5422. E-mail: jshpress@aol.com. Carol Katzman. Weekly. Jewish Federation of Omaha.

NEVADA

JEWISH REPORTER (1996). 3909 S. Maryland Pkwy., Suite 405, Las Vegas, 89119-7520. (702)732-0556. FAX: (702)732-3228. Rebecca Herren. Bimonthly. Jewish Federation of Las Vegas.

LAS VEGAS ISRAELITE (1965). PO Box 14096, Las Vegas, 89114. (702)876-1255. FAX: (702)364-1009. Michael Tell. Bimonthly.

NEW HAMPSHIRE

JEWISH SPECTATOR (1935). P.O. Box 267, New London, 03257. (603)526-2513. FAX: (603)526-2514. E-mail: jsisrael@ netmedia.net.il. Rabbi Mark Bleiweiss. Quarterly. Friends of Jewish Spectator, Inc.

NEW JERSEY

AVOTAYNU (1985). 155 N. Washington Ave., Bergenfield, 07621. (201)387-7200. FAX: (201)387-2855. E-mail: info@avotaynu. com. Sallyann Amdur Sack. Quarterly.

JEWISH CHRONICLE (1982). 629 Wood St., Suite 204, Vineland, 08360. (609)696-4445. FAX: (609)696-3428. Ann Lynn Lipton. Bimonthly. The Jewish Federation of Cumberland County.

JEWISH COMMUNITY NEWS. 1086 Teaneck Rd., Teaneck, 07666. (201) 837-8818. FAX: (201) 833-4959. E-mail: jewishstd2 @aol.com. Rebecca Kaplan Boroson. Fortnightly. Jewish Federation of North Jersey and Jewish Federation of Greater Clifton-Passaic.

JEWISH COMMUNITY VOICE (1941). 1301 Springdale Rd., Suite 250, Cherry Hill, 08003-2762. (609)751-9500, ext. 217.

FAX: (609)489-8253. E-mail: jvcheditor @aol.com. Harriet Kessler. Biweekly. Jewish Federation of Southern NJ.

JEWISH RECORD (Atlantic City area) (1939). 1525 S. Main St., Pleasantville, 08232. (609)383-0999. Martin Korik. Weekly.

JEWISH STANDARD (1931). 1086 Teaneck Rd., Teaneck, 07666. (201)837-8818. FAX: (201)833-4959. Rebecca Kaplan Boroson. Weekly.

JEWISH STAR (1985). 230 Old Bridge Turnpike, South River, 08882-2000. (732)432-7711. FAX: (732)432-0292. E-mail: jfgmc@aol.com. Marlene A. Heller. Fortnightly. Jewish Federation of Greater Middlesex County.

JEWISH STATE (1996). 320 Raritan Ave., Suite 203, Highland Park, 08904. (732) 393-0023. FAX: (732)393-0026. E-mail: jewish@castle.net. Ron Ostroff. Weekly.

JEWISH VOICE OF GREATER MONMOUTH COUNTY (1971). 100 Grant Ave., Deal Park, 07723. (732)531-6200. FAX: (732)531-9518. E-mail: pfdnuss@msn. com. Lauren Silver. Monthly. Jewish Federation of Greater Monmouth County and Ocean County Jewish Federation.

JEWISH VOICE & OPINION (1987). 73 Dana Place, Englewood, 07631. (201) 569-2845. FAX: (201)569-1739. Susan L. Rosenbluth. Monthly.

JOURNAL OF JEWISH COMMUNAL SERVICE (1899). 3084 State Hwy. 27, Suite 9, Kendall Pk., 08824-1657. (908)821-1871. FAX: (908)821-5335. E-mail: jcsana@aol. com. Gail Naron Chalew. Quarterly. Jewish Communal Service Association of North America.

METROWEST JEWISH NEWS (1947). 901 Route 10, Whippany, 07981-1157. (973)887-3900. FAX: (973)887-5999. E-mail: 6853202@mcimail.com. David Twersky. Weekly. United Jewish Federation of MetroWest.

OPTIONS, THE JEWISH RESOURCES NEWSLETTER (1974). Box 311, Wayne, 07474-0311. (973)694-2327. Betty J. Singer. Monthly.

NEW MEXICO

NEW MEXICO JEWISH LINK (1971). 5520 Wyoming NE, Albuquerque, 87109. (505)821-3214. FAX: (505)821-3351. E-mail: nmjlink@aol.com. Tema Milstein.

Monthly. Jewish Federation of Greater Albuquerque.

NEW YORK

AFN SHVEL (1941). 200 W. 72 St., Suite 40, NYC, 10023. (212)787-6675. E-mail: yid league@aol.com. Mordkhe Schaechter. Quarterly. Yiddish. League for Yiddish, Inc.

AGENDA: JEWISH EDUCATION (1949; formerly PEDAGOGIC REPORTER). JESNA, 111 Eighth Ave., Suite 11E, NYC, 10011-5201. (212)284-6950. FAX: (212)284-6951. E-mail: info@jesna.org. Rabbi Arthur Vernon. Twice a year. Jewish Education Service of North America, Inc.

ALGEMEINER JOURNAL (1972). 225 E. Broadway, NYC, 10002. (212)267-5561. FAX: (212)267-5624. Gershon Jacobson. Weekly. Yiddish-English.

AMERICAN JEWISH YEAR BOOK (1899). 165 E. 56 St., NYC, 10022. (212)751-4000. FAX: (212)751-4017. E-mail: research@ ajc.org. David Singer, Ruth R. Seldin. Annually. American Jewish Committee.

AMIT (1925). 817 Broadway, NYC, 10003. (212)477-4720. FAX: (212)353-2312. E-mail: amitmag@aol.com. Rita Schwalb. Quarterly. AMIT (formerly American Mizrachi Women).

AUFBAU (1934). 2121 Broadway, NYC, 10023. (212)873-7400. Voice mail: (212) 579-6578. FAX: (212)496-5736. Mng. Ed. Tekla Szymanski; Sr. Ed. Monika Ziegler. Fortnightly. German. New World Club, Inc.

BUFFALO JEWISH REVIEW (1918). 15 E. Mohawk St., Buffalo, 14203. (716)854-2192. FAX: (716)854-2198. E-mail: buffjew rev@aoc.com. Harlan C. Abbey. Weekly. Kahaal Nahalot Israel.

THE CALL (1933). 45 E. 33 St., NYC, 10016. (212)889-6800, ext. 210. FAX: (212)532-7518. E-mail: jra@circle.org. Janel Alania. Quarterly. The Workmen's Circle/Arbeter Ring.

CCAR JOURNAL: A REFORM JEWISH QUARTERLY (formerly JOURNAL OF REFORM JUDAISM) (1953). 355 Lexington Ave., NYC, 10017. (212)972-3636. FAX: (212)692-0819. Ed. Rifat Sonsino. Mng. Ed. Elliot Stevens. Quarterly. Central Conference of American Rabbis.

CIRCLE (1943). 15 E. 26 St., NYC, 10010-1579. (212)532-4949. FAX: (212)481-

4174. E-mail: jason@jcca.org. Jason Black. Quarterly. Jewish Community Centers Association of North America (formerly JWB).

COMMENTARY (1945). 165 E. 56 St., NYC, 10022. (212)751-4000. FAX: (212)751-1174. E-mail: commentary@compuserve. com. Ed. Neal Kozodoy; Ed.-at-Large Norman Podhoretz. Monthly. American Jewish Committee.

CONGRESS MONTHLY (1933). 15 E. 84 St., NYC, 10028. (212)879-4500. Mng. Ed. Rochelle Mancini. Six times a year. American Jewish Congress.

CONSERVATIVE JUDAISM (1945). 3080 Broadway, NYC, 10027. (212)280-6065. FAX: (212)749-9166. E-mail: rapubs@jtsa.edu. Rabbi Benjamin Edidin Scolnic. Quarterly. Rabbinical Assembly and Jewish Theological Seminary of America.

FORVERTS (Yiddish Forward) (1897). 45 E. 33 St., NYC, 10016. (212)889-8200. FAX: (212)684-3949. Boris Sandler. Weekly. Yiddish. Forward Association, Inc.

FORWARD (1897). 45 E. 33 St., NYC, 10016. (212)889-8200. FAX: (212)447-6406. E-mail: newsdesk@forward.com. Seth Lipsky. Weekly. Forward Newspaper, L.L.C.

HADAROM (1957). 305 Seventh Ave., NYC, 10001. (212)807-7888. FAX: (212)727-8452. Rabbi Gedalia Dov Schwartz. Irregularly. Hebrew. Rabbinical Council of America.

HADASSAH MAGAZINE (1914). 50 W. 58 St., NYC, 10019. (212)688-0227. FAX: (212) 446-9521. Alan M. Tigay. Monthly (except for combined issues of June-July and Aug.-Sept.). Hadassah, the Women's Zionist Organization of America.

HADOAR (1921). 426 W. 58 St., NYC, 10019. (212)957-6659. FAX: (212)957-5811. E-mail: general@hist-ivrit.org. Ed. Shlomo Shamir; Lit. Ed. Dr. Yael Feldman. Biweekly. Hebrew. Hadoar Association, Inc., Organ of the Histadruth of America.

JBI VOICE (1978). 110 E. 30 St., NYC, 10016. (212)889-2525, (800)433-1531. Dr. Jacob Freid. Ten times a year in U.S. (audiocassettes). English. Jewish Braille Institute of America.

JEWISH ACTION MAGAZINE (1950). 333 Seventh Ave., 18th fl., NYC, 10001. (212)613-

8146. FAX: (212)564-9058. E-mail: jaedit
@ou.org. Charlotte Friedland. Quarterly.
Union of Orthodox Jewish Congregations of America.

JEWISH BOOK ANNUAL (1942). 15 E. 26 St.,
10th fl., NYC, 10010. (212)532-4949, ext.
297. E-mail: avi@jewishbooks.org. Ed.
Dr. Avi Bernstein-Nahar. Hebrew & English with bibliography in Yiddish. Jewish
Book Council.

JEWISH BOOK WORLD (1945). 15 E. 26 St.,
NYC, 10010. (212)532-4949, ext. 297. FAX:
(212)481-4174. Esther Nussbaum. Three
times annually. Jewish Book Council.

JEWISH BRAILLE REVIEW (1931). 110 E. 30
St., NYC, 10016. (212)889-2525, (800)
433-1531. Dr. Jacob Freid. 10 times a year
in U.S. (braille). English. Jewish Braille
Institute of America.

JEWISH CURRENTS (1946). 22 E. 17 St.,
Suite 601, NYC, 10003-1919. (212)924-
5740. FAX: (212)924-5740. Morris U.
Schappes. Monthly (July/Aug. com-
bined). Association for Promotion of
Jewish Secularism, Inc.

JEWISH EDUCATION NEWS (1980). 261 W. 35
St., Fl. 12A, NYC 10001. (212) 268-4210.
FAX: (212)268-4214. E-mail: 500-8447
@mcimail.com. Mng. Ed. Roselyn Bell.
Tri-annually. Coalition for the Advance-
ment of Jewish Education.

JEWISH FRONTIER (1934). 275 Seventh Ave.,
17th fl., NYC, 10001. (212)229-2280.
FAX: (212)675-7685. Nahum Guttman.
Bimonthly. Labor Zionist Letters, Inc.

JEWISH HERALD (1984). 1689 46 St., Brooklyn, 11204. (718)972-4000. FAX:
(718)972-9400. E-mail: nyjherald@aol.
com. Leon J. Sternheim. Weekly.

JEWISH JOURNAL (1969). 11 Sunrise Plaza,
Valley Stream, 11580. (516)561-6900.
FAX: (516)561-6971. Ed. Paul Rubens;
Pub. Harold Singer. Weekly.

JEWISH LEDGER (1924). 2535 Brighton-
Henrietta Town Line Rd., Rochester,
14623. (716)427-2434. FAX: (716)427-
8521. Barbara Morgenstern. Weekly.

JEWISH OBSERVER (1963). 84 William St.,
NYC, 10038. (212)797-9000. FAX:
(212)269-2843. E-mail: aiamail@aol.com.
Rabbi Nisson Wolpin. Monthly (except
July and Aug.). Agudath Israel of America.

JEWISH OBSERVER OF CENTRAL NEW YORK
(1978). PO Box 510, DeWitt, 13214.
(315)445-2040. FAX: (315)445-1559. E-
mail: jocny@aol.com. Judith Huober. Biweekly. Syracuse Jewish Federation, Inc.

JEWISH PARENT CONNECTION (1992). 160
Broadway, 4th fl., NYC, 10038. (212)227-
1000, ext. 36. FAX: (212)406-6934. E-
mail: cyberjpc@aol.com. Mng. Ed. Rabbi
Eli Gewirtz; Ed. Joyce Lempel. Quarterly.
Torah Umesorah-National Society for
Hebrew Day Schools.

JEWISH POST OF NY (1993). 130 W. 29 St.,
10th fl., NYC, 10001-5312. (212)967-
7313. FAX: (212)967-8321. E-mail: jpostl
@gramercy.ios.com. Ed. Gad Nahshon;
Pub. & Ed.-in-Chief Henry J. Levy.
Monthly. Link Marketing & Promotion,
Inc.

JEWISH PRESS (1950). 338 Third Ave.,
Brooklyn, 11215. (718)330-1100. FAX:
(718)935-1215. E-mail: jpeditor@aol.
com. Rabbi Sholom Klass. Weekly.

JEWISH TELEGRAPHIC AGENCY COMMUNITY
NEWS REPORTER (1962). 330 Seventh
Ave., 11th fl., NYC, 10001-5010. (212)
643-1890. FAX: (212)643-8498. Lisa
Hostein. Weekly.

JEWISH TELEGRAPHIC AGENCY DAILY NEWS
BULLETIN (1917). 330 Seventh Ave., 11th
fl., NYC, 10001-5010. (212)643-1890.
FAX: (212)643-8498. Exec. Ed. Mark
Joffe; Ed. Lisa Hostein. Daily.

JEWISH TELEGRAPHIC AGENCY WEEKLY
NEWS DIGEST (1933). 330 Seventh Ave.,
11th fl., NYC, 10001-5010. (212)643-
1890. FAX: (212)643-8498. Exec. Ed.
Mark Joffe; Ed. Lisa Hostein. Weekly.

JEWISH TRIBUNE. 106 Ramado Plaza,
Pomona, 10976. (914)352-5151. FAX:
(516)829-4776. E-mail: lijeworld@aol.
com. Jerome W. Lippman. Weekly.

JEWISH WEEK (1876; reorg. 1970). 1501
Broadway, NYC, 10036-5503. (212)921-
7822. FAX: (212)921-8420. E-mail: editor@
jewishweek.org. Gary Rosenblatt. Weekly.

JEWISH WORLD (1965). 1104 Central Ave., Albany, 12205. (518)459-8455. FAX: (518)
459-5289. E-mail: 6859675@mcimail.com.
Laurie J. Clevenson. Weekly.

JOURNAL OF JEWISH EDUCATION (formerly
JEWISH EDUCATION) (1929). 111 Eighth
Ave., NYC, 10011-5201. (212)284-6893.

FAX: (212)284-6951. Dr. Bernard Ducoff. Three times a year. Council for Jewish Education.

JOURNAL OF REFORM JUDAISM. *See* CCAR Journal

JTS MAGAZINE (formerly MASORET) (1991). 3080 Broadway, NYC, 10027. (212) 678-8950. FAX: (212)864-0109. E-mail: joginsberg@jtsa.edu. Johanna R. Ginsberg. Three times a year. Jewish Theological Seminary.

JUDAISM (1952). 15 E. 84 St., NYC, 10028. (212)360-1586. FAX: (212)249-3672. Editor's address: Kresge Col., U. of California, Santa Cruz, CA, 95064. (408)459-2566. FAX: (408)459-4872. Subscription address: 15 E. 84 St., NYC 10028. (212)360-1500. E-mail: judaism@cats.ucsc.edu. Prof. Murray Baumgarten. Quarterly. American Jewish Congress.

KASHRUS FAXLETTER-THE MONTHLY KOSHER UPDATE (1990). PO Box 204, Brooklyn, 11204. (718)336-8544. Rabbi Yosef Wikler. Monthly. Kashrus Institute.

KASHRUS MAGAZINE-THE PERIODICAL FOR THE KOSHER CONSUMER (1980). PO Box 204, Brooklyn, 11204. (718)336-8544. Rabbi Yosef Wikler. Five times per year (February, April, June, September, December). Kashrus Institute.

KOL HAT'NUA (Voice of the Movement) (1975). c/o Young Judaea, 50 W. 58 St., NYC, 10019. (212)303-4576. FAX: (212) 303-4572. E-mail: dkog69@aol.com. David Kogan. Quarterly. Hadassah Zionist Youth Commission-Young Judaea.

KULTUR UN LEBN-CULTURE AND LIFE (1960). 45 E. 33 St., NYC, 10016. (212) 889-6800. FAX: (212)532-7518. E-mail: wcfriends@aol.com. Joseph Mlotek. Quarterly. Yiddish. The Workmen's Circle.

LAMISHPAHA (1963). 426 W. 58 St., NYC, 10019. (212)957-6659. FAX: (212)957-5811. E-mail: general@hist-ivrit.org. Dr. Vered Cohen-Raphaeli. Illustrated. Monthly (except July and Aug.). Hebrew. Histadruth Ivrith of America.

LIKUTIM (1981). 110 E. 30 St., NYC, 10016. (212)889-2525. Joanne Jahr. Two times a year in Israel (print and audiocassettes). Hebrew. Jewish Braille Institute of America.

LILITH-THE INDEPENDENT JEWISH WOMEN'S MAGAZINE (1976). 250 W. 57 St., #2432, NYC, 10107. (212)757-0818. FAX: (212)757-5705. E-mail: lilithmag@aol.com. Susan Weidman Schneider. Quarterly.

LONG ISLAND JEWISH WORLD (1971). 115 Middle Neck Rd., Great Neck, 11021. (516)829-4000. FAX: (516)829-4776. E-mail: lijeworld@aol.com. Jerome W. Lippman. Weekly.

MANHATTAN JEWISH SENTINEL (1993). 115 Middle Neck Rd., Great Neck, 11021. (212)244-4949. FAX: (212)244-2257. E-mail: lijeworld@aol.com. Jerome W. Lippman. Weekly.

MARTYRDOM AND RESISTANCE (1974). 500 Fifth Ave., Suite 1600, NYC, 10110-1699. (212)220-4304. FAX: (212)220-4308. E-mail: yadvashem@aol.com. Ed. Dr. Harvey Rosenfeld; Ed.-in-Chief Eli Zborowski. Bimonthly. International Society for Yad Vashem.

MIDSTREAM (1954). 110 E. 59 St., NYC, 10022. (212)339-6040. FAX: (212)318-6176. Joel Carmichael. Seven times a year. Theodor Herzl Foundation, Inc.

NA'AMAT WOMAN (1926). 200 Madison Ave., Suite 2120, NYC, 10016. (212)725-8010. FAX: (212)447-5187. Judith A. Sokoloff. Quarterly. English-Yiddish-Hebrew. NA'AMAT USA, the women's Labor Zionist Organization of America.

OLOMEINU-OUR WORLD (1945). 5723 18th Ave., Brooklyn, 11204. (718) 259-1223. FAX: (718)259-1795. Rabbi Yaakov Fruchter, Rabbi Nosson Scherman. Monthly. English-Hebrew. Torah Umesorah-National Society for Hebrew Day Schools.

PASSOVER DIRECTORY (1923). 333 Seventh Ave., NYC, 10001. (212)563-4000. FAX: (212)564-9058. Rivka Gershon. Annually. Union of Orthodox Jewish Congregations of America.

PROCEEDINGS OF THE AMERICAN ACADEMY FOR JEWISH RESEARCH (1920). 51 Washington Sq. South, NYC, 10012-1075. (212)998-3550. FAX: (212)995-4178. Dr. Nahum Sarna. Annually. English-Hebrew-French-Arabic-Persian-Greek. American Academy for Jewish Research.

PS: THE INTELLIGENT GUIDE TO JEWISH AFFAIRS. (1993) PO Box 48, Mineola, 11501-

0048. (516)487-3758. FAX: (516)829-1248. E-mail: psreports@compuserve.com. Murray Polner, Adam Simms. Biweekly.

RCA RECORD (1953). 305 Seventh Ave. NYC, 10001. (212)807-7888. FAX: (212)727-8452. Rabbi Mark Dratch. Quarterly. Rabbinical Council of America.

REFORM JUDAISM (1972; formerly DIMENSIONS IN AMERICAN JUDAISM). 633 Third Ave., 6th fl., NYC, 10017. (212)650-4240. Aron Hirt-Manheimer. Quarterly. Union of American Hebrew Congregations.

THE REPORTER (1971). 500 Clubhouse Rd., Vestal, 13850. (607)724-2360. FAX: (607)724-2311. E-mail: TReporter@aol.com. Marc S. Goldberg. Weekly. Jewish Federation of Broome County, Inc.

THE REPORTER (1966). 315 Park Ave. S., NYC, 10010. (212)505-7700. FAX: (212) 674-3057. Aviva Patz. Quarterly. Women's American ORT, Inc.

RESPONSE: A CONTEMPORARY JEWISH REVIEW (1967). 114 W. 26th St., Suite 1004, NYC, 10001-6812. (212)620-0350. FAX: (212)929-3459. E-mail: response@panix.com. David R. Adler, Michael R. Steinberg, Chanita Baumhaft. Quarterly. Response Magazine, Inc.

RUSSIAN FORWARD (1995). 45 E. 33rd St., NYC, 10016. (212)576-0866. FAX: (212)448-9124. E-mail: elenaleikind@sprintmail.com. Vladimir Yedidovick. Weekly.

SH'MA (1970). 1001 Watertown St., Suite 3B, W. Newton, MA, 02465. (617)558-9310. FAX: (617)558-9316. E-mail: jflsusan@aol.com. Susan Berrin. Monthly. Jewish Family & Life.

SYNAGOGUE LIGHT AND KOSHER LIFE (1933). 47 Beekman St., NYC, 10038. (212)227-7800. Rabbi Meyer Hager. Quarterly. The Kosher Food Institute.

TRADITION (1958). 305 Seventh Ave., NYC, 10001. (212)807-7888. FAX: (212)727-8452. Rabbi Emanuel Feldman. Quarterly. Rabbinical Council of America.

UNITED SYNAGOGUE REVIEW (1943). 155 Fifth Ave., NYC, 10010. (212)533-7800. FAX: (212)353-9439. E-mail: info@uscj.org. Lois Goldrich. Semiannually. United Synagogue of Conservative Judaism.

UNSER TSAIT (1941). 25 E. 21 St., 3rd fl., NYC, 10010. (212)475-0055. Bimonthly. Yiddish. Jewish Labor Bund.

VIEWPOINT MAGAZINE (1952). 3 W. 16 St., NYC, 10011. (212)929-1525, ext. 131. E-mail: ncyi@youngisrael.org. Meir Solomon. Quarterly. National Council of Young Israel.

VOICE OF THE DUTCHESS JEWISH COMMUNITY (1989). 110 Grand Ave., Poughkeepsie, 12603. (914)471-9811. FAX: (914)471-0659. E-mail: bj@jon.cjfny.org. Business off.:500 Clubhouse Rd., Vestal, 13850. (607)724-2360. FAX: (607)724-2311. Marc S. Goldberg, Sandy Gardner. Monthly. Jewish Federation of Dutchess County, Inc.

WOMEN'S LEAGUE OUTLOOK MAGAZINE (1930). 48 E. 74 St., New York, 10021. (212)628-1600. FAX: (212)772-3507. E-mail: wleague74@aol.com. Marjorie Saulson. Quarterly. Women's League for Conservative Judaism.

WORKMEN'S CIRCLE CALL. See The Call

WYOMING VALLEY JEWISH REPORTER (formerly WE ARE ONE) (1995). 500 Clubhouse Rd., Vestal, 13850. (607)724-2360. FAX: (607)724-2311. E-mail: TReporter @aol.com. Marc S. Goldberg. Every other week. Wilkes-Barre Jewish Community Board.

YEARBOOK OF THE CENTRAL CONFERENCE OF AMERICAN RABBIS (1890). 355 Lexington Ave., NYC, 10017. (212)972-3636. FAX: (212)692-0819. Rabbi Elliot L. Stevens. Annually. Central Conference of American Rabbis.

YIDDISH (1973). Queens College, NSF 350, 65-30 Kissena Blvd., Flushing, 11367. (718)997-3622. Joseph C. Landis. Quarterly. Queens College Press.

DI YIDDISHE HEIM (1958). 770 Eastern Pkwy., Brooklyn, 11213. (718)735-0458. Rachel Altein, Tema Gurary. Twice a year. English-Yiddish. Neshei Ub'nos Chabad-Lubavitch Women's Organization.

YIDDISHE KULTUR (1938). 1133 Broadway, Rm. 820, NYC, 10010. (212)243-1304. FAX: (212)243-1305. E-mail: mahosu@aol.com. Itche Goldberg. Bimonthly. Yiddish. Yiddisher Kultur Farband, Inc.—YKUF.

YIDDISHER KEMFER (1900). 275 Seventh Ave., NYC, 10001. (212)675-7808. FAX:

(212) 675-7685. Dr. Jacob Weitzney. Bimonthly. Yiddish. Labor Zionist Alliance.

Dos YIDDISHE VORT (1953). 84 William St., NYC, 10038. (212)797-9000. Joseph Friedenson. Bimonthly, (November-December monthly). Yiddish. Agudath Israel of America.

YIDISHE SHPRAKH (1941). 555 W. 57 St., Suite 1100, NYC, 10019. (212)246-6080. FAX: (212) 292-1892. Dr. Mordkhe Schaechter. Irregularly. Yiddish. YIVO Institute for Jewish Research, Inc.

YIVO BLETER (1931). 555 W. 57 St., Suite 1100, NYC, 10019. (212)246-6080. FAX: (212)292-1892. David E. Fishman, Abraham Nowersztern. Biannually. Yiddish. YIVO Institute for Jewish Research, Inc.

YOUNG JUDAEAN (1910). 50 W. 58 St., NYC, 10019. (212)303-4579. FAX: (212)303-4572. Deborah Neufeld. Quarterly. Young Judaea, Hadassah Zionist Youth Commission.

YUGNTRUF: YIDDISH YOUTH MAGAZINE (1964). 200 W. 72 St., Suite 40, NYC, 10023. (212)787-6675. FAX: (212)799-1517. Elinor Robinson. Two to four times a year. Yiddish. Yugntruf Youth for Yiddish.

ZUKUNFT (The Future) (1892). 25 E. 21 St., NYC, 10010. (212)505-8040. FAX: (212)505-8044. Yonia Fain. Quarterly. Yiddish. Congress for Jewish Culture.

NORTH CAROLINA

AMERICAN JEWISH TIMES OUTLOOK (1934; reorg. 1950). PO Box 33218, Charlotte, 28233-3218. (704)372-3296. FAX: (704)377-9237. E-mail: geri@pop.vnet.net. Geri Zhiss. Monthly. The Blumenthal Foundation.

CHARLOTTE JEWISH NEWS (1978). 5007 Providence Rd., Charlotte, 28226. (704) 366-5007. FAX: (704) 365-4507. Amy Krakovitz. Monthly (except July). Jewish Federation of Greater Charlotte.

OHIO

AKRON JEWISH NEWS (1929). 750 White Pond Drive, Akron, 44320. (330)869-2424. FAX: (330)867-8498. E-mail: Toby-Liberman@jewishakron.org. Toby Liberman. Fortnightly. Akron Jewish Community Federation.

AMERICAN ISRAELITE (1854). 906 Main St., Rm. 508, Cincinnati, 45202. (513)621-3145. FAX: (513)621-3744. Phyllis R. Singer. Weekly.

AMERICAN JEWISH ARCHIVES JOURNAL (1948). 3101 Clifton Ave., Cincinnati, 45220-2488. (513)221-1875. FAX: (513) 221-7812. E-mail: aja@cn.huc.edu. Ed. Dr. Gary P. Zola; Mng. Ed. Dr. Frederic Krome. Twice a year. Jacob Rader Marcus Center, American Jewish Archives, HUC-JIR.

CLEVELAND JEWISH NEWS (1964). 3645 Warrensville Center Rd., Suite 230, Cleveland, 44122. (216)991-8300. FAX: (216)991-2088. E-mail: clevejewnew@aol. com. Cynthia Dettelbach. Weekly. Cleveland Jewish News Publication Co.

INDEX TO JEWISH PERIODICALS (1963). PO Box 18570, Cleveland Hts., 44118. (216)381-4846. FAX: (216)381-4321. E-mail: index@jewishperiodicals.com. Lenore Pfeffer Koppel. Annually. Available in book and CD-ROM form.

JEWISH JOURNAL (1987). 505 Gypsy Lane, Youngstown, 44504-1314. (330)744-7902. FAX: (330)746-7926. Sherry Weinblatt. Biweekly (except July/Aug.). Youngstown Area Jewish Federation.

OHIO JEWISH CHRONICLE (1922). 2862 Johnstown Rd., Columbus, 43219. (614) 337-2055. FAX: (614)337-2059. Roberta Keck. Weekly.

STARK JEWISH NEWS (1920). 2631 Harvard Ave. NW, Canton, 44709. (330)452-6444. FAX: (330)452-4487. E-mail: canton jcf @aol.com. Linda Sirak. Monthly. Canton Jewish Community Federation.

STUDIES IN BIBLIOGRAPHY AND BOOKLORE (1953). 3101 Clifton Ave., Cincinnati, 45220. (513)221-1875. FAX: (513)221-0519. E-mail: hzafren@cn.huc.edu. Herbert C. Zafren. Irregularly. English-Hebrew-etc. Library of Hebrew Union College-Jewish Institute of Religion.

TOLEDO JEWISH NEWS (1951). 6505 Sylvania Ave., Sylvania, 43560. (419)885-4461. FAX: (419)885-8627. E-mail: Toljewnew @aol.com. Laurie Cohen. Monthly. Jewish Federation of Greater Toledo.

OKLAHOMA

TULSA JEWISH REVIEW (1930). 2021 E. 71 St., Tulsa, 74136. (918)495-1100. FAX: (918)495-1220. Ed Ulrich. Monthly. Jewish Federation of Tulsa.

OREGON

BRIDGES: A JOURNAL FOR JEWISH FEMINISTS AND OUR FRIENDS (1990). PO Box 24839, Eugene, 97402. (541)343-7617. FAX: (541)343-7617. E-mail: ckinberg@pond.net. Mng. Ed. Clare Kinberg. Semiannually.

JEWISH REVIEW (1959). 506 SW Sixth Ave., Suite 606, Portland, 97204. Edit.:(503) 227-7464. FAX: (503) 227-7438. Adv.: 503) 670-2883. FAX: (503) 620-3433. E-mail: jreview@teleport.com. Paul Haist. Regular column in Russian. Fortnightly. Jewish Federation of Portland.

PENNSYLVANIA

COMMUNITY REVIEW (1925). 3301 N. Front St. Annex, Harrisburg, 17110. (717) 236-9555. FAX: (717)236-2552. E-mail: communityreview@desupernet.net. Carol L. Cohen. Fortnightly. United Jewish Community of Greater Harrisburg.

CONTEMPORARY JEWRY (1974, under the name JEWISH SOCIOLOGY AND SOCIAL RESEARCH). Gratz College, 7605 Old York Rd., Melrose Park, 19027. (215) 635-7300. FAX: (215) 635-7320. E-mail: rgeffen@gratz.edu. Ed. Rela Mintz Geffen; Mng. Ed. Egon Mayer. Annually. Association for the Social Scientific Study of Jewry.

JERUSALEM LETTER/VIEWPOINTS (1978). 1616 Walnut St., Suite 507, Philadelphia, 19103. (215)204-1459. FAX: (215)204-7784. Daniel J. Elazar. Fortnightly. Jerusalem Center for Public Affairs.

JEWISH CHRONICLE OF PITTSBURGH (1962). 5600 Baum Blvd., Pittsburgh, 15206. (412)687-1000. FAX: (412)687-5119. E-mail: pittjewchr@aol.com. Joel Roteman. Weekly. Pittsburgh Jewish Publication and Education Foundation.

JEWISH EXPONENT (1887). 226 S. 16 St., Philadelphia, 19102. (215)893-5700. FAX: (215)546-3957. Jonathan S. Tobin. Weekly. Jewish Federation of Greater Philadelphia.

JEWISH POLITICAL STUDIES REVIEW (1989). 1616 Walnut St., Suite 507, Philadelphia, 19103. (215)204-1459. FAX: (215)204-7784. Daniel J. Elazar. Twice yearly. Jerusalem Center for Public Affairs.

JEWISH QUARTERLY REVIEW (1910). 420 Walnut St., Philadelphia, 19106. (215)238-1290. FAX: (215)238-1540. E-mail: jqr@mail.cjs.upenn.edu. Ed. David M. Goldenberg; Mng. Ed. Bonnie L. Blankenship. Quarterly. Center for Judaic Studies, University of Pennsylvania.

NEW MENORAH (1978). 7318 Germantown Ave., Philadelphia, 19119-1793. (215)247-9700. FAX: (215)247-9703. Dr. Arthur Waskow. Quarterly. Aleph: Alliance for Jewish Renewal.

RECONSTRUCTIONISM TODAY (1993). Beit Devora, 7804 Montgomery Ave., Suite 9, Elkins Park, 19027-2649. (215)782-8500. FAX: (215)782-8805. E-mail: jrfnatl@aol.com. Lawrence Bush. Quarterly. Jewish Reconstructionist Federation.

THE RECONSTRUCTIONIST (1935). 1299 Church Rd., Wyncote, 19095-1898. (215) 576-5210. FAX: (215)576-8051.E-mail: ravhirsh@aol.com. Rabbi Richard Hirsh. Semiannually. Reconstructionist Rabbinical College.

SCRANTON FEDERATION REPORTER (1994). 500 Clubhouse Rd., Vestal, NY, 13850. (607)724-2360. FAX: (607)724-2311. E-mail: TReporter@aol.com. Marc S. Goldberg. Biweekly. Scranton-Lackawanna Jewish Federation.

RHODE ISLAND

JEWISH VOICE OF RHODE ISLAND (1973). 130 Sessions St., Providence, 02906. (401)421-4111. FAX: (401)331-7961. E-mail: jvoice@aol.com. Jane S. Sprague. Monthly. Jewish Federation of Rhode Island.

RHODE ISLAND JEWISH HERALD (1930). 99 Webster St., Pawtucket, 02860. (401)724-0200. FAX: (401)726-5820. Kimberly Ann Orlandi. Weekly. Herald Press Publishing Company.

RHODE ISLAND JEWISH HISTORICAL NOTES (1951). 130 Sessions St., Providence, 02906. (401)331-1360. FAX: (401)272-6729. Leonard Moss. Annually. Rhode Island Jewish Historical Association.

SOUTH CAROLINA

CHARLESTON JEWISH JOURNAL. 1645 Wallenberg Blvd., Charleston, 29407. (803) 571-6565. FAX: (803)556-6206. Ellen Katman. Monthly. Charleston Jewish Federation.

TENNESSEE

HEBREW WATCHMAN (1925). 4646 Poplar Ave., Suite 232, Memphis, 38117.

(901)763-2215. FAX: (901)763-2216. Herman I. Goldberger. Weekly.

OBSERVER (1934). 801 Percy Warner Blvd., Suite 102, Nashville, 37205. (615)356-3242, ext. 237. FAX: (615)352-0056. E-mail: nashobserv@aol.com. Judith A. Saks. Biweekly (except July). Jewish Federation of Nashville.

SHOFAR. PO Box 8947, Chattanooga, 37414. (423)493-0270, Ext. 12. FAX: (423) 493-9997. E-mail: shofar@jcfgc.com. Rachel Schulson. Ten times a year. Jewish Federation of Greater Chattanooga.

TEXAS

JEWISH HERALD-VOICE (1908). PO Box 153, Houston, 77001-0153. (713)630-0391. FAX: (713)630-0404. E-mail: joexhk@aol.com. Jeanne Samuels. Weekly.

JEWISH JOURNAL OF SAN ANTONIO (1973). 8434 Ahern, San Antonio, 78213. (210)828-9511. FAX: (210)342-8098. Barbara Richmond. Monthly (11 issues). Jewish Federation of San Antonio.

TEXAS JEWISH POST (1947). 3120 S. Freeway, Fort Worth, 76110. (817)927-2831. FAX: (817)429-0840. 11333 N. Central Expressway, Suite 213, Dallas, 75243. (214)692-7283. FAX: (214)692-7285. Jimmy Wisch. Weekly.

VIRGINIA

RENEWAL MAGAZINE (1984). 5029 Corporate World Dr., Suite 225, Virginia Beach, 23462. (757)671-1600. FAX: (757)671-7613. E-mail: news@ujft.com. Reba Karp. Quarterly. United Jewish Federation of Tidewater.

SOUTHEASTERN VIRGINIA JEWISH NEWS (1959). 5029 Corporate World Dr., Suite 225, Virginia Beach, 23462. (757)671-1600. FAX: (757)671-7613. E-mail: news@ujft.com. Reba Karp. 22 issues yearly. United Jewish Federation of Tidewater.

WASHINGTON

JEWISH TRANSCRIPT (1924). 2041 Third Ave., Seattle, 98121. (206)441-4553. FAX: (206) 441-2736. E-mail: jewishtran@aol.com. Donna Gordon Blankinship. Fortnightly. Jewish Federation of Greater Seattle.

WISCONSIN

WISCONSIN JEWISH CHRONICLE (1921). 1360 N. Prospect Ave., Milwaukee, 53202.

(414)390-5888. FAX: (414)271-0487. E-mail: milwaukeej@aol.com. Vivian M. Rothschild. Weekly. Milwaukee Jewish Federation.

INDEXES

INDEX TO JEWISH PERIODICALS (1963). PO Box 18570, Cleveland Hts., OH 44118. (216)381-4846. FAX: (216)381-4321. Lenore Pfeffer Koppel. Annually. Available in book and CD form.

NEWS SYNDICATES

JEWISH TELEGRAPHIC AGENCY, INC. (1917). 330 Seventh Ave., 11th fl., NYC., 10001-5010. (212)643-1890. FAX: (212)643-8498. Mark J. Joffe, Lisa Hostein. Daily.

CANADA

CANADIAN JEWISH HERALD (1977). 17 Anselme Lavigne, Dollard des Ormeaux, PQ H9A 1N3. (514)684-7667. FAX: (514) 684-7667. Dan Nimrod. Irregularly. Dawn Publishing Co., Ltd.

CANADIAN JEWISH NEWS (1971). 205-1500 Don Mills Rd., North York, ONT M3B 3K4. (416)391-1836. FAX: (416)391-0829 (Adv.); (416)391-1836. FAX: (416)391-0829. Mordechai Ben-Dat. 50 issues per year. Some French.

CANADIAN JEWISH OUTLOOK (1963). #3-6184 Ash St., Vancouver, BC V5Z 3G9. (604)324-5101. FAX: (604)325-2470. E-mail: hjberson@axionet.com. Carl Rosenberg. Eight times per year. Canadian Jewish Outlook Society.

DAIS (formerly INTERCOM) (1985). 1590 Ave. Dr. Penfield, Montreal, PQ H3G 1C5. (514)931-7531. FAX: (514)931-0548. E-mail: mikec@cjc.ca. Mike Cohen. Three times annually. Canadian Jewish Congress.

DIALOGUE (1988). 1590 Ave. Dr. Penfield, Montreal, PQ H3G 1C5. (514)931-7531. FAX: (514)931-3281. E-mail: rebeccar@cjc.ca. Rebecca Rosenberg. Annually. French-English. Canadian Jewish Congress, Quebec Region.

JEWISH FREE PRESS (1990). 8411 Elbow Dr., SW, Calgary, Alberta T2V 1K8. (403)

252-9423. FAX: (403)255-5640. E-mail: jewishfp@cadvision.com. Judy Shapiro. Fortnightly.

JEWISH POST & NEWS (1987). 113 Hutchings St., Winnipeg, MAN R2X 2V4. (204)694-3332. FAX: (204)694-3916. E-mail: jewishp@pangea.ca. Matt Bellan. Weekly.

JEWISH STANDARD (1928). 77 Mowat Ave., Suite 016, Toronto, ONT M6K 3E3. (416)537-2696. FAX: (416)789-3872. Julius Hayman; Mng. Ed. Michael Hayman. Fortnightly.

JEWISH TRIBUNE (1950). 15 Hove St., North York, ONT M3H 4Y8. (416)633-6224. FAX: (416)633-6299. Daniel Horowitz. Bi-weekly.

JEWISH WESTERN BULLETIN (1930). 873 Beatty St., Suite 203, Vancouver, BC V6B 2M6. (604)689-1520. FAX: (604)689-1525. E-mail: jbeditor@istar.ca. Acting Ed. Baila Lazarus. Weekly. Anglo-Jewish Publishers Ltd.

JOURNAL OF PSYCHOLOGY AND JUDAISM (1976). 1747 Featherston Dr., Ottawa, ONT K1H 6P4. (613)731-9119. Reuven P. Bulka. Quarterly. Center for the Study of Psychology and Judaism.

OTTAWA JEWISH BULLETIN (1954). 1780 Kerr Ave., Ottawa, ONT K2A 1R9. (613)798-4696. FAX: (613)798-4730. Myra Aronson. Nineteen times a year. Ottawa Jewish Bulletin Publishing Co. Ltd.

SHALOM (1975). 5675 Spring Garden Rd., Suite 800, Halifax, NS, B3J 1H1. (902)422-7491. FAX: (902)425-3722. E-mail: ajc.halifax@ns.sympatico.ca. Jon M. Goldberg. Quarterly. Atlantic Jewish Council.

LA VOIX SÉPHARADE (1966). 4735 Chemin de la Cote St. Catherine Rd., Montreal, PQ H3W 1M1. (514)733-4998, (514)733-8696. FAX: (514)733-3158. E-mail: csq@csq.qc.ca James Dahan. Bimonthly (five times a year). French and occasional Spanish and English. Communauté Sépharade du Québec.

WINDSOR JEWISH FEDERATION (1942). 1641 Ouellette Ave., Windsor, ONT N8X 1K9. (519)973-1772. FAX: (519)973-1774. Exec. Dir. Steven Brownstein. Three times a year. Windsor Jewish Federation.

THE WORLD OF LUBAVITCH (1980). 770 Chabad Gate, Thornhill, ONT L4J 3V9. (905)731-7000. FAX: (905)731-7005. Rabbi Moshe Spalter. Bimonthly. English-Hebrew. Chabad Lubavitch of Southern Ont.

Obituaries: United States*

ABZUG, BELLA (SAVITSKY), lawyer, politician; b. NYC (Bronx), July 24, 1920; d. NYC, Mar. 31, 1998. Educ.: Hunter Coll., Columbia U. Law School. In private law practice specialized in labor law, representing union workers as well as civil-rights and civil-liberties litigants and targets of the congressional McCarthy Com. In 1960s organized lobbying against nuclear testing and later against the Vietnam War; helped found the Natl. Women's Political Caucus; in 1968 actively opposed reelection of President Lyndon Johnson and supported the candidacy of Eugene McCarthy. As Democratic congresswoman (1971–73 from Manhattan's 19th Cong. Dist. and 1973–76 from the 20th), became famous for her outspoken liberalism and toughness (regarded as abrasive by her critics and sometimes even by her friends) and for her trademark big hats. Ran unsuccessfully for the Senate in 1976, for NYC mayor in 1977, and in two more congressional races. Continued to practice law, started a women's lobbying group, and founded the Women's Environment and Development Org., working with internatl. agencies. Leading figure at NGO conf. in Beijing in 1995, part of UN 4th World Conf. on Women. A Zionist and staunch Jew from youth, strongly identified with Jewish causes and Jewish feminist activity; founder, Amer. Jewish Cong. Comm. for Women's Equality. Au.: *Bella!*

ARONSON, ARNOLD, communal professional; b. Boston, Mass., Mar. 11, 1911; d. Wheaton, Md., Feb. 17, 1998. Educ.: Harvard Coll., U. Chicago (MSW). Prog. dir., Natl. Jewish Community Relations Adv. Council, 1945–76; sec., Natl. Emergency Civil Rights Mobilization and the Natl. Council for a Permanent Fair Employment Practices Comm., late 1940s; a founder in 1950 (along with A. Philip Randolph and Roy Wilkins) and sec. for 30 yrs. of the Leadership Conf. on Civil Rights, an umbrella org. for more than 185 natl. groups. Helped to coordinate lobbying efforts to pass the Civil Rights Acts of 1957 and 1964, the Voting Rights Act of 1965, and the Fair Housing Act of 1968; was one of the 10 people who planned the 1963 March on Washington for civil rights. After retiring, founded and headed the Leadership Conf. on Civil Rights Educ. Fund, a research body and clearinghouse on civil-rights issues. Recipient: Presidential Medal of Freedom (1998); Disting. Alumni Award, U. Chicago; Hubert H. Humphrey Civil Rights Award; NASA Civil Rights Award; awards from the Amer. J. Com., UAHC, NJCRAC, and others.

---

*Including American Jews who died between January 1 and December 31, 1998.

BREINDEL, ERIC, newspaper columnist, commentator; b. NYC, June 2, 1955; d. NYC, Mar. 7, 1998. Educ.: Harvard Coll., Harvard Law School. Fellow, poli. sci., London School of Econ., 1977–79; legis. asst., Sen. Daniel Patrick Moynihan, 1982–83; rsch. dir., Amer. Interests, Public Broadcasting System, 1983–85; edit. page ed., New York Post, 1986–97; syndicated columnist, 1986–; sr. v.-pres., News Corp. (owner of the Post), 1997–; moderator of weekly media analysis show on Fox News Channel, 1997–. Contrib.: Commentary, New Republic, Weekly Standard, Wall Street Journal, and other publications. Founding mem., Com. for the Free World, 1988; mem.: Council on Foreign Relations; bd. and exec. com., America-Israel Friendship League. A political conservative, a critic of liberals, a firm defender of the police, and a staunch Jew and Zionist, who championed the cause of Jews during the 1991 Crown Heights racial unrest. Recipient: 1st prize for edit. writing, Amer. Soc. Professional Journalists; Defender of Jerusalem Award; Jabotinsky Award; Man of the Year, Police Benevolent Assoc. (three times).

COOK, SAMUEL, rabbi; b. Philadelphia, Pa., June 8, 1907; d. Cincinnati, Ohio, Apr. 12, 1998. Educ.: Haverford Coll.; Hebrew Union Coll. (ord.). Chaplain, U.S. Army, WWII. Dir., B'nai B'rith Hillel Found., U. Alabama, 1934–37; asst. rabbi, Cong. Keneseth Israel, Phila., 1937–40; rabbi, Temple Beth Israel, Altoona, Pa., 1940–43; dir., Natl. (later N. Amer.) Fed. of Temple Youth, 1946–67; dir., UAHC dept. of college educ., 1967–72(?). Under his guidance, NFTY grew to 20,000 members, with a broad program incl. summer camps and trips to Israel and Europe, regional conclaves, and community service, and became a significant force in Reform Judaism. Mem., exec. bd., CCAR. Recipient: hon. doctorate, Hebrew Union Coll.

ELMAN, RICHARD, novelist, poet; b. NYC (Brooklyn), Apr. 23, 1934; d. Stony Brook, N.Y., Dec. 31, 1997. Educ.: Syracuse U., Stanford U. Worked as public affairs dir., WBAI-FM (N.Y.), corresp. in Central Amer., and writer for a poverty program before becoming a novelist. Teacher of writing: Bennington Coll. Summer Writing Workshops, Columbia U., Sarah Lawrence Coll., U. Pa., U.

Mich., Notre Dame U. Au.: more than 20 books—novels, stories, journalism, poetry—many reflecting his Jewish background. Novels incl. A Coat for the Tsar (1958), The 28th Day of Elul (1967), Lilo's Diary (1968), The Reckoning (1969), An Education in Blood (1971), Fredi & Shirl & the Kids (1972), The Breadfruit Lotteries (1980), and Tar Beach (1991), selected as one of the 10 best novels of 1991–92 by USA Today. Works of journalism incl. The Poorhouse State: The American Way of Life on Public Assistance (1966), Uptight with the Rolling Stones: A Novelist's Report (1973), and Cocktails at Somoza's (1981). Also au. of three vols. of poetry; numerous articles, essays, and book reviews in many publications; transls. of the Greek plays The Girl from Samos and The Phoenician Women. Namedropping: Mostly Literary Memoirs, was published posthumously.

FEINBERG, ABRAHAM, business executive, philanthropist; b. NYC (Bronx), (?), 1908; d. NYC, Dec. 5, 1998. Educ.: City Coll. of N.Y.; Fordham U. Law School; NYU Law School. Started out in the clothing industry selling hosiery; rose to become chmn. of the Kayser-Roth Corp., a post he held until 1964; chmn., Amer. Bank and Trust Co., which was bought in 1978 by Israel's Bank Leumi; chmn., Central Bottling Corp., Israel (in 1966, led syndicate of Amer. Jews that acquired Coca-Cola franchise for Israel, thus ending Coca-Cola's long-standing adherence to Arab boycott). Active in Democratic fundraising and a close assoc. of Harry Truman; mem., NYC bd. of higher educ. Founder and 1st pres., Americans for Haganah, 1940s, which helped acquire arms for Israeli military; accompanied Chaim Weizmann, Israel's 1st president, to his first meeting with Pres. Truman in Nov. 1947. Major benefactor, Weizmann Inst. of Science (helped to establish Feinberg Graduate School); mem., bd. dirs., Amer. Com. for Weizmann Inst., from 1949 on (pres. and chmn.); hon. fellow and chmn. emer., internatl. bd. of govs., Weizmann Inst. of Science; major benefactor and chmn., bd. trustees, Brandeis U., 1954–61, and founder, Internatl. Center for Ethics, Justice and Public Life; chmn., Development Corp. for Israel (Israel Bonds), for 17 yrs. Recipient: hon. doctorate, Brandeis U.; Man of the Year, B'nai B'rith, and other honors.

FILMUS, TULLY, artist; b. Ataki, Bessarabia, Aug. 29, 1908; d. Great Barrington, Mass., Feb. 25, 1998; in U.S. since 1915. Educ.: Pa. Acad. Fine Arts and private studies in Europe. Instr.: Amer. Artists' School, Cooper Union. Represented in permanent collections of Metropolitan Museum and Whitney Museum in NYC, Natl. Gallery of Art in Washington; and others. A "humanist realist" and portrait painter whose subjects incl. musicians, dancers, and artists, as well as Jewish men studying the Torah or dancing Hassidic-style.

FINE, HILLEL, rabbi; b. Birmingham, England, Feb. 19, 1921; d. NYC, May 25, 1998; in U.S. since 1939. Educ.: U. Cincinnati; Hebrew Union Coll. (ord. and Ph.D.). Asst. prof., Bible and Semitic langs., HUC, 1951–55; chaplain, U.S. Army, 1955–57; rabbi, Temple Ohev Sholom, Pittsburgh, Pa., 1957–70; dir., New Orleans Hillel Found., 1970–86. Au.: *Studies in Middle Assyrian Chronology and Religion* and many articles on Judaica and Semitic langs.

FRIENDLY, FRED W. (Ferdinand Friendly Wachenheimer), broadcast journalist; b. NYC, Oct. 30, 1915; d. NYC (Riverdale), Mar. 3, 1998. Served US Army, WWII. Educ.: Providence Business Coll. (R.I.) . Began his broadcasting career at radio station WEAN in Providence, R.I., 1937–41 (changed his name legally in 1938); quiz show and documentary producer, NBC radio, 1945–50; joined CBS in 1950. Collaboration with Ed Murrow began in 1948 with album of recordings of world leaders, "I Can Hear It Now"; continued with "Hear It Now" program on radio and its highly successful sequel, "See It Now," on TV (1951–58); and included occasional documentaries on "CBS Reports." Most famous documentaries were a profile of Communist-hunting Sen. Joseph McCarthy (1954) and "Harvest of Shame" (1960), an expose of treatment of migrant workers. Pres., CBS News, 1964–66; prof., Columbia U. School of Journalism, 1967–79, and writer on television affairs; adv., Ford Foundation, 1966–80, on development of Corp. for Public Broadcasting; in 1984 began producing "The Fred Friendly Seminars" for public TV, a forum for discussion of crucial issues of the day. Au.: *Due to Circumstances Beyond Our Con-* trol (1967); *The Good Guys, the Bad Guys and the First Amendment: Free Speech vs. Fairness in Broadcasting* (1976); and other works. Recipient: 10 Peabody Awards and many other honors.

GOLDIN, JUDAH, professor; b. NYC, Sept. 14, 1914; d. Bryn Mawr, Pa., May 30, 1998. Educ.: City Coll. of N.Y., Columbia U., Jewish Theological Sem.(D.H.L.). Visiting assoc. prof., Jewish lit. and hist., Duke U., 1943–45; assoc. prof., religion, U. Iowa, 1946–52; dean and assoc. prof., Aggadah, Seminary Coll., Jewish Theol. Sem., 1952–58; adj. prof., religion, Columbia U., 1955–58; prof., classical Judaica, Yale U., 1958–73; prof., postbiblical Hebrew lit., U. Pa., 1973–85. Au.: *The Fathers According to Rabbi Nathan* (1955, 1974); *The Living Talmud: The Wisdom of the Fathers and Its Classical Commentaries* (1955, 1962); *The Last Trial* (transl., with introd., of Shalom Spiegel's *me-Aggadot ha-Akedah*; 1967, 1979); *The Song at the Sea* (1973); *Studies in Midrash and Related Literature* (1988); introds. to various works, which have become classics in their own right—notably to Israel Abrahams' *Hebrew Ethical Wills* and S. Y. Agnon's *Days of Awe*; "The Period of the Talmud," in *The Jews: Their History, Culture, and Religion*, ed. Louis Finkelstein (1960); and articles in *Encyclopaedia Judaica*, scholarly journals, festschrifts, and compilations. Ed.: *The Jewish Expression* (1976); *The Munich Mekilta* (1980). Recipient: Fellow, Amer. Acad. Arts and Sciences; fellow, Amer. Acad. of Jewish Research; Guggenheim fellowship; fellow, Inst. of Advanced Studies, Hebrew Univ. of Jerusalem, 1981.

GOLDMAN, ROBERT I., business executive, communal worker; b. NYC (Brooklyn), Sept. 24, 1932; d. NYC, Aug. 27, 1998. Educ.: Harvard Coll.; Yale Law School. Sec.-treas., Congress Financial Group, 1957–62; exec. v.-pres., 1962–67; pres., 1967–; chmn. and CEO, Congress Financial Corp. and Congress Talcott Corp. Mem., bd. dirs. and exec. com., and chmn. several coms., Commercial Finance Assoc.; mem., bd. trustees, Amer. Acad. Dramatic Arts. Mem., Amer. Jewish Com.'s Communal Affairs Com., Polish-Amer. Jewish-Amer. Council, and funder of AJC programs with Ukrainian community in U.S.; mem., Banking and Finance Com., N.Y. UJA-Federation;

mem., Founders Soc., Open Univ. of Israel; v.-chmn., Jewish Found. for the Righteous; mem., bd. dirs., HIAS, NYANA. Recipient: Stanley M. Isaacs Human Relations Award (Amer. Jewish Com.)

GOLDSTEIN, SYD ROSSMAN, communal worker; b. NYC, Jan. 29, 1903; d. NYC, Jan. 27, 1998. Educ.: N.Y. Training School for Teachers. Natl. pres., Women's League for Conservative Judaism, 1958–62; natl. treas., Torah Fund campaign; mem. bd. overseers, first woman named to exec. com., and hon. bd. mem., Jewish Theol. Sem. of Amer.; bd. mem., World Council of Synagogues; first woman appointed to bd. of the Synagogue Council of Amer. (1962); bd. mem.: Natl. Council of Amer. Jewish Joint Distribution Com.; United Israel Appeal; N.Y. UJA-Federation (chmn., women's campaign and cabinet mem.); Jewish Braille Inst., NCJW, NCRAC, JWB, and other orgs. Recipient: 1st Centennial Medal, JTSA; Louis Marshall Medal, JTSA; Community Service Award, JTSA; Woman of Vision, UJA, and other honors.

GRUBEL, FRED, communal executive; b. Leipzig, Germany, Oct. 22, 1908; d. NYC, Oct. 4, 1998; in U.S. since 1940. Educ.: U. Leipzig (D. Jur.); NYU (CPA and MBA). Jr. govt. attorney, 1930–33; sec., later dir., Jewish community org. of Leipzig, 1934–38, when he was sent to Buchenwald for six months; on release, emigrated to Gr. Brit., and two years later to the U.S. Asst. budget dir., N.Y. Fed. of Jewish Philanthropies, 1941–44; finan. off., Amer. Jewish Joint Distrib. Com., N.Y. and Paris, 1945–51; hosp. admin., Maimonides and Montefiore hospitals, NYC, 1951–65; exec. dir., Leo Baeck Inst., which he helped shape into a leading center for research and study of German-speaking Jewry, 1966–95.

HINDUS, MILTON, professor; b. NYC, Aug. 26, 1916; d. Waltham, Mass., May 28, 1998. Educ.: City Coll. of N.Y., Columbia U., U. Chicago. Lect., lit., Hunter Coll. and New School for Social Research, 1943–46; asst. prof., humanities, U. Chicago, 1946–48; member of original Brandeis U. faculty of 13: asst. prof., English, 1948–54; assoc. prof., 1954–62; prof. of humanities, 1962–81. Au.: 16 books, incl. *Céline: The Crippled Giant* (1950,

1997); *The Proustian Vision* (1954); *Leaves of Grass: One Hundred Years Later* (1955); A *Reader's Guide to Marcel Proust* (1962); *F. Scott Fitzgerald: An Introduction and Interpretation* (1967); *The Old East* Side (1969); *A World at Twilight: A Portrait of East European Jewry on the Eve of the Holocaust* (1971); *Charles Reznikoff: A Critical Essay* (1977); *Charles Reznikoff: Man and Poet* (1984); *The Jewish East Side: 1881–1924* (1995); *The Selected Letters of Charles Reznikoff* (1998); scores of articles and book reviews and poetry. Ed.: *Walt Whitman*, Critical Heritage Series (1997); *Library of Conservative Thought*; Amer. lit. section, Encyclopedia Judaica. Recipient: Walt Whitman Prize, Poetry Soc. of Amer., 1959; hon. doctorate, Brandeis U.

HOLZMAN, WILLIAM ("RED"), basketball player and coach; b. NYC, Aug. 10, 1920; d. Long Island, N.Y., Nov. 13, 1998. Educ.: City Coll. of N.Y. Served U.S. Navy, WW II. An All-Amer. player (1942) at City Coll.; played for the Rochester Royals, 1945–54; player-coach, Milwaukee Hawks, 1954–58; chief scout, N.Y. Knicks, 1958–67; head coach, Knicks, Dec. 1967–77; rehired Nov. 1978; retired May 1982; consult. thereafter. Described as the "molder, conductor and architect of one of the most unusual, most thrilling and . . . most gratifying teams ever assembled" (Ira Berkow), he coached the Knicks during their Golden Era, 1967–73, leading them to their only two NBA championships, in 1970 and 1973. Recipient: Named NBA Coach of the Year, 1970; voted into Basketball Hall of Fame, 1991.

KAMENY, NAT, public relations executive, communal worker; b. NYC, Nov. 6, 1923; d. Bergenfield, N.J., June 1, 1998. Served U.S. Army, WWII. Prop., Camenard Studios (photographers), 1945; founder and chmn., KSW&G Advertising Inc., 1946–78; pres., Israel Communications, Ltd., 1969–78; pres., Kameny Communications, 1978–. Active on behalf of many Jewish causes: nationally—ADL (natl. v.-chmn., chmn. natl. communications com. and mem. natl. exec. com. and budget com.); chmn., Internatl. Center for Holocaust Studies; Jewish Telegraphic Agency (v.-chmn., chmn. planning and devel. com.); N. Amer. Jewish Students Appeal (sec.); mem. bd. dirs.: Natl. Yiddish Book

Center, Radius Inst., Greater N.Y. Conf. on Soviet Jewry, Amer. Friends of Haifa U., Jewish Found. for Christian Rescuers; v.-chmn., NJCRAC. In Bergen County, N.J.–pres., Jewish Fed. Community Svcs.; trustee, United Jewish Community (Fed./UJA); founder and dir., Hebrew Free Loan Soc.; mem. bd. dirs., Solomon Schechter Day School. Also: pres., League of Advt. Agencies; v.-chmn., Bergenfield Planning Bd.

KATSH, ABRAHAM I., professor, university president; b. Indura, Poland, Aug. 10, 1908; d. NYC, July 21, 1998; in U.S. since 1925. Educ.: NYU, Dropsie Coll.(PhD). Began teaching Hebrew at NYU in 1930s—the first modern Hebrew instruction in a U.S. univ.; became full prof., Hebrew lang. and lit., 1947 (later disting. resch. prof.); chmn., dept. of Hebrew culture and educ. in NYU's School of Educ., 1953–67; founder, Jewish Culture Found. and NYU's library of Judaica and Hebraica. Pres., Dropsie Coll. (later U.), Philadelphia, 1967–76. Dir., Amer. Israel Student and Professorial Workshop, 1949–67. In 1956 gained access to Soviet libraries containing historic Jewish documents; in 7 trips, put thousands of documents on microfilm, most now housed at NYU. Fellow, Middle East Studies Assoc. N. Amer.; mem.: Jewish Acad. Arts and Sciences (pres.); Natl Assoc. Profs. of Hebrew (founding pres.); Amer. Schools Oriental Resch. (trustee, 1969–75); Natl. Council Jewish Educ. (exec. com.); Hadoar Assoc. (exec. bd.); ZOA (natl. chmn. 1949–51); Histadruth Ivrith; World Cong. Jewish Studies (hon. mem. exec. com.); and other orgs. Mem. ed. bd.: Bitzaron; Jewish Apocryphal Lit., Hebrew Abstracts; ed. in chief, Jewish Quarterly Review; asst. ed. for Hebrew, Modern Language Journal. Au.: Judaism in Islam (1954; revised ed., Judaism and the Koran, 1980); transl./ed., Scroll of Agony: The C.A. Kaplan Diary of the Warsaw Ghetto (1965); trans.: Midrash David ha-Nagid (1967); co-ed., Israel Through the Eyes of Its Leaders (1971), and other works, as well as hundreds of articles and essays. Recipient: endowed chair in his name at NYU; hon. doctorates from HUC-JIR, Villanova U., Spertus Coll., and others; festschrifts (Natl. Assoc. Profs. of Hebrew, 1965; NYU, 1969); and many other honors.

KAZIN, ALFRED, author, critic; b. NYC (Brooklyn), June 5, 1915; d. NYC, June 5, 1998. Educ.: City Coll. of N.Y.; Columbia U. Lit. ed., New Republic 1942–43, and contrib. ed., 1943–45; contrib. ed., Fortune Magazine, 1943–44; visiting lect. or prof., 1940s-1960s: Black Mountain Coll., U. Minn., Harvard U., Smith Coll., NYU, CCNY, U. Cal.; prof., Amer. studies, Amherst Coll., 1955–58; disting. prof., English, SUNY at Stony Brook, 1963–73 and Hunter Coll., CUNY, 1973–84. His first work, On Native Grounds: An Interpretation of Modern American Prose Literature (1942), established him as a significant critic who opposed the "New Critics," stressing cultural context over textual analysis. Au.: vols. of essays and criticism, incl. The Inmost Leaf (1955); Contemporaries (1960); An American Procession (1984); A Writer's America (1988); Our New York (1990); and God of the American Writer (1997); three volumes of memoirs: A Walker in the City (1951), a lyrical evocation of his childhood in Brownsville; and Starting Out in the 30s (1965)and New York Jew (1978), which recreate the world of the Jewish liberal intellectual; and A Lifetime Burning in Every Moment (1996), selections from his journals. Au. of introds. to literary works, classic and contemporary, incl. Selected Short Stories of Shalom Aleichem (1956) and, with Ann Birstein Kazin, Collected Works of Anne Frank (1959).

KERN, JANET R., journalist, communal professional; b. Chicago, Ill., (?), 1924; d. Chicago, Ill., Feb. 7, 1998. Educ.: Stephens Coll.; Northwestern U. Advertising copywriter, TV and radio producer; syndicated TV columnist for Hearst newspapers in the 1950s; assoc. dir., communications, Jewish Federation/Jewish United Fund of Metro. Chicago, 1970–92. Au.: Yesterday's Child (1962), a best-selling memoir about a Jewish girl coming of age in 1930s Chicago, and many magazine articles.

LEWIS, SHARI, entertainer; b. NYC, Jan. 17, 1934; d. Los Angeles, Calif., Aug. 2, 1998. Educ.: Studied music with her mother, a pianist, and at the H.S. of Music and Art; dance at the School of Amer. Ballet; and acting at the Neighborhood Playhouse; learned stage magic from her father, a teacher at Yeshiva U. Began career as actress and dancer; had first big break on

Arthur Godfrey's "Talent Scout Show" in 1952, with a puppet act; starting 1953 hosted own local TV show in New York; in 1957 introduced Lamb Chop, her signature puppet, on "Captain Kangaroo," which led to "The Shari Show" on NBC, 1957–63; in London, 1968–76, hosted own BBC show and specials; returned to U.S. TV in 1989 with "Lamb Chop's Play-Along"; for PBS created holiday specials, incl. "Lamb Chop's Special Hanukkah" and "Shari's Passover Surprise." Au.: 60 books for children, incl. the "One Minute Bedtime" series (15 vols.), as well as videos, recordings, and filmstrips. Recipient: 12 Emmy Awards, and many other honors.

LOEB, HENRY A., investment banker, philanthropist; b. NYC, Mar. 30, 1907; d. NYC, Jan. 27, 1998. Educ.: Princeton U.; Harvard Law School. Served U.S. Army, WWII. Practiced law in N.Y., 1932–34, and San Francisco, 1934–38; sr. partner in family's investment firm, Carl M. Loeb, Rhoades & Co., starting 1938, and in successor firm, Loeb Rhoades, Hornblower; v.-chmn., Loeb Partners Corp., investment firm, 1979–. Life trustee and benefactor, the New School; v.-chmn., hon. trustee, and benefactor, Mt. Sinai Medical Center, NYC; bd. mem., Langeloth Found.; campaign chmn., Fed. of Jewish Philanthropies of NY, 1964–65; chmn., Amer. Council for Emigrés in the Professions; dir.: Deafness Resch. Found., Ramapo Anchorage Camp. Recipient: Bronze Star medal for participation in Omaha Beach landing on D-Day; hon. doctorate, New School.

LUCKMAN, SID, football player, business executive; b. NYC (Brooklyn), Nov. 21, 1916; d. Aventura, Fla., July 5, 1998. Educ.: Columbia Coll., where he played both baseball and football; All-American in football, 1938. Served U.S. Merchant Marine, 1944 (off-season). Played for the Chicago Bears, 1939–50. The first modern T-formation quarterback, he is credited with changing the nature of the game. The greatest long-range passer in pro-football all his time, led team to 4 straight NFL and Western Div. championships, 1939–42, and a 5th div. title in 1946. After leaving football in 1950, became exec. and later head of Cellu-Craft Products, Chicago, a packaging co. Recipient: inducted into College Football Hall of Fame; Pro Hall of Fame; Jewish Sports

Hall of Fame (Israel); football field at Erasmus Hall H.S., Brooklyn, named in his honor.

MAASS, RICHARD, business executive, communal worker; b. Baltimore, Md., May 20, 1919; d. Purchase, N.Y., Sept. 10, 1998. Educ.: NYU School of Commerce. Served U.S. Navy, WWII. Underwriter, Amer. Surety, 1937–42; partner, Reredel Assoc., 1943–; pres., Lederer Found., 1948–. Pres., Westchester Urban League, 1953–59; founder, pres., and a volunteer teacher for 13 years in Edu-Cage, an alternative school for troubled youths, 1960s and 1970s; Westchester County historian for 7 years; mem., N.Y. and Westchester Historical Socs.; pres., Manuscript Soc., and a well-known collector of Amer. colonial and Revolutionary documents; active in local Democratic politics; mem., housing adv. council, N.Y. State comm. on human rights; bd. mem. and treas., Internatl. League for Human Rights; benefactor, Purchase Coll.; trustee, Purchase Coll. Found. and chmn., Purchase Coll. Council. Active in Amer. J. Com. since 1950s: pres., Westchester chap; chmn., foreign affairs comm., chmn., bd. govs. and natl. exec. council; natl. v.-pres. 1962–65; natl. pres. 1977–80; hon. natl. pres. Founding pres., Natl. Conf. on Soviet Jewry, 1971–73. Recipient: Disting. Citizen Award, State U. of N.Y., and other honors.

MAZER, WILLIAM, business executive, philanthropist; b. NYC, July 30, 1905; d. NYC, July 7, 1998. Educ.: NYU. Purchasing agt., Hudson Pulp and Paper Co.(founded by his father), 1932–37; v.-pres., 1937–47; exec. v.-pres., 1947–55; pres., 1955–73; chmn., 1973–81. Helped to establish Amer.-Israeli Paper Co.; pres. and treas., William and Helen Mazer Found. Active on behalf of many causes and orgs., incl.: pres., Muscular Dystrophy Assoc. of Amer., 1953–63; pres. and bd. chmn. over many decades, Amer. Israel Cultural Found.; benefactor: Mazer Inst. for Research and Advanced Studies in Judaica, City U. of N.Y.; Brandeis U. (trustee for over 4 decades); Beth Israel Medical Center, NYC; Rockefeller U. (Council mem.); Ackerman Inst. for the Family (founding bd. mem.); Yeshiva U.; Hebrew U. of Jerusalem. Chmn.: Greater N.Y. Com., Israel Bond Org.; pulp and paper div., UJA-Federation. Council.

MILGRAM, ABRAHAM EZRA, rabbi, author; b. (?), Russia, Dec. 28, 1900; d. Jerusalem, Israel, Jan. 29, 1998; in U.S. since 1912. Educ.: City Coll. of N.Y.; Columbia U.(M.A.); Dropsie Coll.(Ph.D.); Jewish Theol. Sem. of Amer. (Teachers' Inst. and Rabbinical School). Following ordination in 1927, served congs. in Wilmington, Del., and Philadelphia, Pa., and was founding dir., B'nai B'rith Hillel Found., U. Minnesota; dir., United Synagogue dept. of educ., 1945–61; upon retirement moved to Israel. Au.: *An Anthology of Medieval Hebrew Literature*; *Sabbath, The Day of Delight*; *A Handbook for the Congregational School Board Member*; *Jerusalem Curiosities*; *Jewish Worship*; and *A Short History of Jerusalem*. Ed.: vol. 5 of the B'nai B'rith Great Books Series: *Great Jewish Ideas*. Recipient: hon. doctorate, JTSA.

PAKULA, ALAN, filmmaker; b. NYC (Bronx), Apr. 7, 1928; d. Long Island, N.Y., Nov. 19, 1998. Educ.: Yale U. Producer of *To Kill a Mockingbird* (1962), *Love with the Proper Stranger* (1963), and other films; directed *The Sterile Cuckoo* (1969), *Klute* (1971), *All the President's Men* (1976), *The Devil's Own* (1997), and others; wrote and directed *Sophie's Choice* (1982), *See You in the Morning* (1989), *Presumed Innocent* (1990), and *The Pelican Brief* (1993).

REINES, FREDERICK, physicist; b. Paterson, N.J., Mar. 16, 1918; d. Orange, Calif., Aug. 26, 1998. Educ.: Stevens Inst. of Technology; NYU (PhD). Staff mem., group leader, theoretical div., Los Alamos Science Lab, 1944–59 (dir. resch. on Eniwetok bomb tests, 1951); prof. and chmn., physics dept., Case Inst. of Technology (later Case Western U.), 1959–66; prof., physics, U. Calif.-Irvine, 1966–88 (founding dean, physical sciences, 1966–74; prof., radiol. sciences, Med. School, 1970–; prof. emer., 1988–). His discovery (with Clyde Cowan) in 1956 of elementary nuclear particles, neutrinos, was described as "a keystone to our understanding of elementary particle physics." A serious voice student, sang with chorus of Cleveland Symph. Orch., 1959–62. Centennial lect., U. Md.; Schiff Mem. lect., Stanford U.; Albert Einstein Mem. lect., Israel Acad. Sciences and Humanities. Fellow: Amer. Physical Soc., Amer. Acad. Arts and Sciences, and other schol-

arly bodies. Recipient: Numerous honors, incl. Nobel Prize in physics, 1995; J. Robert Oppenheimer Mem. Prize, 1981; Natl. Medal of Science, 1985; Rossi Prize (co-winner), Amer. Astron. Soc., 1987; Disting. Alumnus Award, NYU, 1990; Franklin Medal, Franklin Inst., 1992.

RIBICOFF, ABRAHAM A., politician; b. New Britain, Conn., Apr. 9, 1910; d. NYC (Riverdale), Feb. 22, 1998. Educ.: U. Chicago Law School. Private law practice, 1933–38; mem., Conn. state legislature, 1938–42; municipal judge, Hartford, Conn., 1941–43 and 1945–47; U.S. congressman, 1948–52; governor, Conn., 1955–61. A promoter and ally of John F. Kennedy, resigned governorship to serve as sec. of Health, Educ. and Welfare for 16 months (1961–62) in Kennedy cabinet; U.S. senator, 1962–81; special counsel, Kaye, Scholer, Fierman, Hays & Handler, thereafter. As gov., pioneered pathbreaking highway safety measures; at 1968 Dem. natl. convention in Chicago, delivered memorable nomination speech for George McGovern in which he confronted Mayor Richard Daley over treatment of anti-Vietnam protesters by police; initially supported U.S. role in Vietnam, but later changed his position; staunch advocate of school integration; supported sale of fighter planes to Saudi Arabia and Egypt, as well as Israel, for which he was criticized in some Jewish circles. V.-chmn., bd. overseers, Jewish Theol. Sem. of Amer. Recipient: Hon. degrees from Trinity Coll., Wesleyan U., Yeshiva U., Hebrew Union Coll., Amherst Coll., NYU, Jewish Theol. Sem., and others; federal bldg. in Hartford named in his honor.

ROBBINS, JEROME, dancer, choreographer; b. NYC, Oct. 11, 1918; d. NYC, July 29, 1998. Began performing modern dance in late 1930s; assoc. with Ballet Theater (later American Ballet Theater) as dancer and later as choreographer, 1940–48; worked with Communist Party's Theatrical Transient Group, 1943–47 (for which connection he was investigated in the 1950s by congressional com.); assoc. artistic dir., N.Y. City Ballet, 1949–59; returned as ballet master 1969; named co-artistic dir. in 1983, succeeding George Balanchine; resigned in 1990 but continued as choreographer. His first choreographed ballet, *Fancy Free*, in 1944, with music by Leonard Bernstein, was developed into Broadway musical *On the Town*; created many other ballets as well as choreography for Broadway shows: *High Button Shoes, Miss Liberty, Call Me Madam, The King and I*, and others; directed and choreographed *Peter Pan, Gypsy, West Side Story*, and *Fiddler on the Roof*, the last two also conceived by him; also directed and/or choreographed plays, films, and TV shows. Recipient: numerous honors, incl. 4 Antoinette Perry Awards, 2 Academy Awards, Capezio Dance Award, Kennedy Center honors, Brandeis U. Creative Arts Award.

SHEPARD, RICHARD F., reporter, editor; b. NYC (Bronx), Dec. 31, 1922; d. Fresh Meadows, NYC, Mar. 6, 1998. Educ.: City Coll. of N.Y. Served U.S. Merchant Marine, WWII. Joined *New York Times* in 1946 as copy boy, while still in college; reporter, shipping news, 1953–61; cultural news reporter, 1962–69; cultural news ed., 1969–71; contributed "Topics of the Times" essays, occasional "About New York" columns, and theater reviews (many of Yiddish and Jewish plays); retired in 1991. Mem.: Soc. of Silurians. Au.: *Live and Be Well; Broadway: From the Battery to the Bronx;* and *The Paper's Papers: A Reporter's Journey Through the Archives of the Times.*

SHERER, MOSHE, rabbi, communal executive; b. NYC (Brooklyn), June 18, 1921; d. NYC, May 17, 1998. Educ.: Mesifta Torah Vodaath Rabbinical Sem., Ner Israel Rabbinical Coll. Joined staff of Agudath Israel, a right-wing Orthodox group, in 1943 as dir. of its Youth Council; named exec. v.-pres. in 1951 and pres. in early '80s, a post he held until his death. Chmn., Agudath Israel World Org., 1980–; chmn. ed. bd., *Dos Yiddishe Vort*; assoc. ed. and mem. ed. bd., the *Jewish Observer*; mem. exec. bd: Natl. Jewish Comm. on Law and Public Affairs; Citizens for Educ. Freedom; Jewish Restitution Successor Org. Credited with building Agudath Israel from a small org. into a relatively large and influential force with a Washington lobbying office and ties to leading political figures, as well as to other Jewish orgs. Publicly supported govt. aid to religious schools; led stand against efforts by Reform and Conservative movements to gain recognition in Israel.

SKLAR, MURRAY, communal professional; b. NYC, June 17, 1913; d. Miami Beach, Fla., Mar. 20, 1998. Educ.: City Coll. of N.Y.; Columbia U. School of Social Work. Caseworker, NYC dept. of welfare; community relations rep. and welfare consult. to Mayor Fiorello LaGuardia; during WWII worked with Internatl. Red Cross providing services to veterans; served Jewish communal agencies in Boston, Chicago, and Kingston, N.Y.; directed Jewish feds. in NYC, Philadelphia, Atlanta, and Montreal; dir., community org. and fund-raising, first for Amer. Jewish Joint Distrib. Com. and later for World ORT Union, in Geneva, Switz., 1959–78. Helped organize the United Jewish Fund of France and the Standing Conf. of European Jewish Community Svcs., which directed reconstruction of Jewish communities in Europe, Israel, North Africa, and Iran. Recipient: Wm. J. Shroder Memorial Award and a "Scroll of Honor" signed by leaders of 18 European Jewish communities.

STREIT, JACK, matzah manufacturer; b. NYC (Brooklyn), May 16, 1908; d. NYC, Feb. 5, 1998. Began working at his parents' matzah bakery, Aron Streit Inc., at age 15, never finishing high school. After the death of their father in 1937, he and older brother Irving became co-owners; Jack became pres. in 1982, following the death of his brother. Streit's is the last independent matzah company in the U.S.

STRIGLER, MORDECHAI, editor, writer; b. Zamosc, Poland, (?), 1921; d. NYC, May 10, 1998; in U.S. since 1953. Educ.: Kletzker Yeshivah (ord. at age 16). Served as secy. to Rabbi Zvi Yehezkel Michelson, in Warsaw, and taught Talmud, 1937–39; after outbreak of WWII, fought with Polish partisans, was captured and spent 5 years in concentration camps, incl. Maidanek and Buchenwald, in the latter joining the resistance and covertly teaching children. After the war, accompanied a group of Jewish orphans to Paris, where he began work on autobiog. and edited Yiddish newspaper, *Unzer Vort* (Our Word). In U.S. in 1953 on speaking trip on behalf of Labor Zionist movement, decided to stay; served as ed. of the *Yidisher Kemfer* (The Jewish Fighter), a Labor Zionist weekly, until 1995. A prolific writer (often under pseudonyms) for that paper and a man of broad erudition, he also published articles in the Yiddish *Forward (Forverts)*, among other subjects on Jewish Responsa literature, Bible, and Jewish philosophy. Named ed. of the *Forverts* in 1987. Au.: thousands of stories, poems, essays, and political opinion pieces; a six-vol. work about his Holocaust experiences, *Oisgebrente Likht* (Extinguished Candles), published between 1947 and 1952; a historical novel about life in 17th- and 18th-century Poland, *Arm in Arm with the Wind; Dialogues with the Time* (essays), and other works of fiction and nonfiction. Recipient: Itzik Manger Prize for Literature (1978); hon. doctorate (posth.), Jewish Theol. Sem. of Amer.

SUALL, IRWIN J., communal executive; b. NYC, Nov. 25, 1924; d. NYC, Aug. 17, 1998. Served U.S. Merchant Marine, 1945–48. Educ.: Brooklyn Coll. (2 yrs.); Oxford U. (Fulbright Scholar, B.A.). Held various positions 1950–67: educ. dir., org. dir., ILGWU; natl. secy., Socialist Party-Social Democratic Fed.; public relations dir., Jewish Labor Com. From 1967 to 1997 served as dir. of domestic fact-finding for the Anti-Defamation League, heading undercover investigations of neo-Nazis, the KKK, and other extremist groups. Au.: *The American Ultras* (1962). Recipient: ADL's Milton A. Senn Award for Professional Excellence.

SULLER, CHAIM, editor; b. Belorussia, (?), 1902; d. NYC, May 26, 1998; in U.S. since 1919 (?). After working as a teacher, joined staff of the *Morning Freiheit*, a left-wing Yiddish newspaper, in 1958, and served as editor for 30 years, until the demise of the paper in 1988. He openly criticized the Soviet Union for its Jewish policies, beginning in 1957 with an article in the *Daily Worker*.

TORCZYNER, HARRY, attorney, communal worker; b. Antwerp, Belgium, Nov. 8, 1910; d. NYC, Mar. 26, 1998; in U.S. since 1941. Educ.: U. Brussels (LLD); Columbia U. Law School (LLB). Consult., OWI, WWII. Practiced law in Belgium before fleeing the Nazis; opened private law practice in N.Y. in 1946, specializing in internatl., foreign, and copyright law and general practice. Among his clients: Harry Winston Inc., the Diamond Trade and Precious Stone Assoc., and the World Fed. of Diamond Bourses; Amer.-Israel Chamber of Commerce and Industry; govts. of Ivory Coast and Sierra Leone. V.-chmn., NY State Joint Legal Com. on Narcotic Study; special counsel, Jewish Agency for Palestine, at 1947 UN Special Assembly; mem., natl. exec. com., Zionist Org. of Amer., 1949 on, and hon. v.-pres.; mem. exec.: Amer. Zionist Council; Amer.-Israel Com.; founder and supporter, Amer. Friends of the Israel Museum. An art collector, helped introduce to the U.S. the works of Belgian artists, chiefly the surrealist painter René Magritte, whose works he collected and about whom he wrote several books. Co-au.: *Forgery in Art and the Law* (1954); au.: *The Castle of the Pyrenees in Jerusalem* (1990); *Magritte-Torczyner: Letters Between Friends* (1994); other books, law journal articles, and two vols. of poetry. Recipient: Knight of the Royal Order of the Lion (Belgian govt.); hon. doctorate, City U. of Antwerp, and other honors.

WOLLHEIM, NORBERT, accountant, communal worker; b. Berlin, Germany, Apr. 26, 1913; d. Long Island, N.Y, Nov. 1, 1998; in U.S. since 1952. Educ.: NYU. After rise of Nazis interrupted his legal studies, worked for Jewish community organizing transports of children to Britain. A prisoner and slave laborer at Auschwitz during WWII, in 1951 successfully brought suit against I.G. Farben, winning small settlement for himself and opening the way for compensation of countless others. Founding leader, Amer. Gathering of Jewish Holocaust Survivors; active in World Fed. of Bergen-Belsen Survivors; v.-pres., Conf. on Jewish Material Claims Against Germany and negotiator with Germany to obtain compensation for survivors.

YOUNGMAN, HENNY, entertainer; b. London, England, Mar. 16, 1906; d. NYC, Feb. 24, 1998; in U.S. since 1908 (?). Known as "the king of the one-liners" (most famously, "Take my wife—please"); started out as a musician and band leader; turned to comedy, using a badly played violin as part of his act; achieved national recognition on the "Kate Smith Show" on radio in the 1930s; entertained chiefly on the nightclub and banquet circuit; appeared in several movies, incl. *History of the World, Part I* (1981) and *Goodfellas* (1990). Au.: several collections of jokes and an autobiog., *Take My Life, Please* (1991).

Calendars

SUMMARY JEWISH CALENDAR, 5759–5763 (Sept. 1998–Aug. 2003)

HOLIDAY	5759		5760		5761		5762		5763	
	1998		**1999**		**2000**		**2001**		**2002**	
Rosh Ha-shanah, 1st day	M	Sept. 21	Sa	Sept. 11	Sa	Sept. 30	T	Sept. 18	Sa	Sept. 7
Rosh Ha-shanah, 2nd day	T	Sept. 22	S	Sept. 12	S	Oct. 1	W	Sept. 19	S	Sept. 8
Fast of Gedaliah	W	Sept. 23	M	Sept. 13	M	Oct. 2	Th	Sept. 20	M	Sept. 9
Yom Kippur	W	Sept. 30	M	Sept. 20	M	Oct. 9	Th	Sept. 27	M	Sept. 16
Sukkot, 1st day	M	Oct. 5	Sa	Sept. 25	Sa	Oct. 14	T	Oct. 2	Sa	Sept. 21
Sukkot, 2nd day	T	Oct. 6	S	Sept. 26	S	Oct. 15	W	Oct. 3	S	Sept. 22
Hosha'na' Rabbah	S	Oct. 11	F	Oct. 1	F	Oct. 20	M	Oct. 8	F	Sept. 27
Shemini 'Azeret	M	Oct. 12	Sa	Oct. 2	Sa	Oct. 21	T	Oct. 9	Sa	Sept. 28
Simhat Torah	T	Oct. 13	S	Oct. 3	S	Oct. 22	W	Oct. 10	S	Sept. 29
New Moon, Heshwan, 1st day	T	Oct. 20	S	Oct. 10	S	Oct. 29	W	Oct. 17	S	Oct. 6
New Moon, Heshwan, 2nd day	W	Oct. 21	M	Oct. 11	M	Oct. 30	Th	Oct. 18	M	Oct. 7
New Moon, Kislew, 1st day	Th	Nov. 19	T	Nov. 9	T	Nov. 28	F	Nov. 16	T	Nov. 5
New Moon, Kislew, 2nd day	F	Nov. 20	W	Nov. 10					W	Nov. 6
Hanukkah, 1st day	M	Dec. 14	Sa	Dec. 4	F	Dec. 22	M	Dec. 10	Sa	Nov. 30
New Moon, Tevet, 1st day	Sa	Dec. 19	Th	Dec. 9	W	Dec. 27	Sa	Dec. 15	Th	Dec. 5
New Moon, Tevet, 2nd day	S	Dec. 20	F	Dec. 10			S	Dec. 16	F	Dec. 6
						2001				
Fast of 10th of Tevet	T	Dec. 29	S	Dec. 19	F	Jan. 5	T	Dec. 25	S	Dec. 15

Event	1999	2000	2001	2002	2003
New Moon, Shevat	M Jan. 18	Sa Jan. 8	Th Jan. 25	M Jan. 14	Sa Jan. 4
Hamishshah-ʿasar bi-Shevaṭ	M Feb. 1	Sa Jan. 22	Th Feb. 8	M Jan. 28	Sa Jan. 18
New Moon, Adar I, 1st day	T Feb. 16	S Feb. 6	F Feb. 23	T Feb. 12	S Feb. 2
New Moon, Adar I, 2nd day	W Feb. 17	M Feb. 7	Sa Feb. 24	W Feb. 13	M Feb. 3
New Moon, Adar II, 1st day		T Mar. 7			T Mar. 4
New Moon, Adar II, 2nd day		W Mar. 8			W Mar. 5
Fast of Esther	M Mar. 1	M Mar. 20	Th Mar. 8	M Feb. 25	M Mar. 17
Purim	T Mar. 2	T Mar. 21	F Mar. 9	T Feb. 26	T Mar. 18
Shushan Purim	W Mar. 3	W Mar. 22	Sa Mar. 10	W Feb. 27	W Mar. 19
New Moon, Nisan	Th Mar. 18	Th Apr. 6	S Mar. 25	Th Mar. 14	Th Apr. 3
Passover, 1st day	Th Apr. 1	Th Apr. 20	S Apr. 8	Th Mar. 28	Th Apr. 17
Passover, 2nd day	F Apr. 2	F Apr. 21	M Apr. 9	F Mar. 29	F Apr. 18
Passover, 7th day	W Apr. 7	W Apr. 26	Sa Apr. 14	W Apr. 3	W Apr. 23
Passover, 8th day	Th Apr. 8	Th Apr. 27	S Apr. 15	Th Apr. 4	Th Apr. 24
Holocaust Memorial Day	T Apr. 13	T May 2	F Apr. 20*	T Apr. 9	Tu Apr. 29
New Moon, Iyar, 1st day	F Apr. 16	F May 5	M Apr. 23	F Apr. 12	F May 2
New Moon, Iyar, 2nd day	Sa Apr. 17	Sa May 6	T Apr. 24	Sa Apr. 13	Sa May 3
Israel Independence Day	W Apr. 21	W May 10	Sa Apr. 28†	W Apr. 17	W May 7
Lag Ba-ʿomer	T May 4	T May 23	F May 11	T Apr. 30	T May 20
Jerusalem Day	F May 14*	F June 2*	M May 21	F May 10*	F May 30*
Shavuʿot, 1st day	F May 21	F June 9	M May 28	F May 17	F June 6
Shavuʿot, 2nd day	Sa May 22	Sa June 10	T May 29	Sa May 18	Sa June 7
New Moon, Tammuz, 1st day	M June 14	M July 3	Th June 21	M June 10	M June 30
New Moon, Tammuz, 2nd day	T June 15	T July 4	F June 22	T June 11	T July 1
Fast of 17th of Tammuz	Th July 1	Th July 20	S July 8	Th June 27	Th July 17
New Moon, Av	W July 14	W Aug. 2	Sa July 21	W July 10	W July 30
Fast of 9th of Av	Th July 22	Th Aug. 10	S July 29	Th July 18	Th Aug. 7
New Moon, Elul, 1st day	Th Aug. 12	Th Aug. 31	S Aug. 19	Th Aug. 8	F Aug. 29
New Moon, Elul, 2nd day	F Aug. 13	F Sept. 1	M Aug. 20	F Aug. 9	Sa Aug. 30

*Observed Thursday, a day earlier, to avoid conflict with the Sabbath.

†Observed Thursday, two days earlier, to avoid conflict with the Sabbath.

CONDENSED MONTHLY CALENDAR
(1998–2001)

1998, Jan. 28–Feb. 26]   SHEVAṬ (30 DAYS)   [5758

Civil Date	Day of the Week	Jewish Date	SABBATHS, FESTIVALS, FASTS	PENTATEUCHAL READING	PROPHETICAL READING
Jan. 28	W	Shevaṭ 1	New Moon	Num. 28:1–15	
31	Sa	4	Bo'	Exod. 10:1–13:16	Jeremiah 46:13–28
Feb. 7	Sa	11	Be-shallaḥ (Shabbat Shirah)	Exod. 13:17–17:16	Judges 4:4–5:31 *Judges 5:1–31*
11	W	15	Ḥamishah-'asar bi-Shevaṭ		
14	Sa	18	Yitro	Exod. 18:1–20:23	Isaiah 6:1–7:6; 9:5–6 *Isaiah 6:1–13*
21	Sa	25	Mishpatim (Shabbat Sheḳalim)	Exod. 21:1–24:18 Exod. 30:11–16	II Kings 12:1–17 *II Kings 11:17–12:17*
26	Th	30	New Moon, first day	Num. 28:1–15	

Italics are for Sephardi Minhag.

1998, Feb. 27–Mar. 27]   ADAR (29 DAYS)   [5758

Civil Date	Day of the Week	Jewish Date	SABBATHS, FESTIVALS, FASTS	PENTATEUCHAL READING	PROPHETICAL READING
Feb. 27	F	Adar 1	New Moon, second day	Num. 28:1–15	
28	Sa	2	Terumah	Exod. 25:1–27:19	I Kings 5:26–6:13
Mar. 7	Sa	9	Teẓawweh (Shabbat Zakhor)	Exod. 27:20–30:10 Deut. 25:17–19	I Samuel 15:2–34 *I Samuel 15:1–34*
11	W	13	Fast of Esther	Exod. 32:11–14 Exod. 34:1–10 (morning and afternoon)	Isaiah 55:6–56:8 (afternoon only)
12	Th	14	Purim	Exod. 17:8–16	Book of Esther (night before and in the morning)
13	F	15	Shushan Purim		
14	Sa	16	Ki tissa'	Exod. 30:11–34:35	I Kings 18:1–39 *I Kings 18:20–39*
21	Sa	23	Wa-yaḳhel, Peḳude (Shabbat Parah)	Exod. 35:1–40:38 Num. 19:1–22	Ezekiel 36:16–38 *Ezekiel 36:16–36*

Italics are for Sephardi Minhag.

Civil Date	Day of the Week	Jewish Date	SABBATHS, FESTIVALS, FASTS	PENTATEUCHAL READING	PROPHETICAL READING
Mar. 28	S	Nisan 1	Wa-yiḳra'; New Moon (Shabbat Ha-ḥodesh)	Levit. 1:1–5:26 Num. 28:9–15 Exod. 12:1–20	Ezekiel 45:16–46:18 *Ezekiel 45:18–46:15* *Isaiah 66:1, 23*
Apr. 4	Sa	8	Ẓaw (Shabbat Ha-gadol)	Levit. 6:1–8:36	Malachi 3:4–24
10	F	14	Fast of Firstborn		
11	Sa	15	Passover, first day	Exod. 12:21–51 Num. 28:16–25	Joshua 5:2–6:1, 27
12	S	16	Passover, second day	Levit. 22:26–23:44 Num. 28:16–25	II Kings 23:1–9, 21–25
13	M	17	Ḥol Ha-mo'ed, first day	Exod. 13:1–16 Num. 28:19–25	
14	T	18	Ḥol Ha-mo'ed, second day	Exod. 22:24–23:19 Num. 28:19–25	
15	W	19	Ḥol Ha-mo'ed, third day	Exod. 34:1–26 Num. 28:19–25	
16	Th	20	Ḥol Ha-mo'ed, fourth day	Num. 9:1–14 Num. 28:19–25	
17	F	21	Passover, seventh day	Exod. 13:17–15:26 Num. 28:19–25	II Samuel 22:1–51
18	Sa	22	Passover, eighth day	Deut. 15:19–16:17 Num. 28:19–25	Isaiah 10:32–12:6
23	Th	27	Holocaust Memorial Day		
25	Sa	29	Shemini	Levit. 9:1–11:47	I Samuel 20:18–42
26	S	30	New Moon, first day	Num. 28:1–15	

Italics are for Sephardi Minhag.

1998, Apr. 27 – May 25]   IYAR (29 DAYS)   [5758

Civil Date	Day of the Week	Jewish Date	SABBATHS, FESTIVALS, FASTS	PENTATEUCHAL READING	PROPHETICAL READING
Apr. 27	M	Iyar 1	New Moon, second day	Num. 28:1–15	
May 1	F	5	Israel Independence Day*		
2	Sa	6	Tazria', Mezora'	Levit. 12:1–15:33	II Kings 7:3–20
9	Sa	13	Aḥare mot, Kedoshim	Levit. 16:1–20:27	Amos 9:7–15 *Ezekiel 20:2–20*
14	Th	18	Lag Ba-'omer		
16	Sa	20	Emor	Levit. 21:1–24:23	Ezekiel 44:15–31
23	Sa	27	Be-har, Be-ḥuḳḳotai	Levit. 25:1–27:34	Jeremiah 16:19–17:14
24	S	28	Jerusalem Day		

*Observed Apr. 30, to avoid conflict with the Sabbath.

Italics are for Sephardi Minhag.

1998, May 26–June 24]   SIWAN (30 DAYS)   [5758

Civil Date	Day of the Week	Jewish Date	SABBATHS, FESTIVALS, FASTS	PENTATEUCHAL READING	PROPHETICAL READING
May 26	T	Siwan 1	New Moon	Num. 28:1–15	
30	Sa	5	Be-midbar	Num. 1:1–4:20	Hosea 2:1–22
31	S	6	Shavu'ot, first day	Exod. 19:1–20:23 Num. 28:26–31	Ezekiel 1:1–28 Ezekiel 3:12
June 1	M	7	Shavu'ot, second day	Deut. 15:19–16:17 Num. 28:26–31	Habbakuk 3:1–19 *Habbakuk 2:20–3:19*
6	Sa	12	Naso'	Num. 4:21–7:89	Judges 13:2–25
13	Sa	19	Be-ha'alotekha	Num. 8:1–12:16	Zechariah 2:14–4:7
20	Sa	26	Shelaḥ lekha	Num. 13:1–15:41	Joshua 2:1–24
24	W	30	New Moon, first day	Num. 28:1–15	

Italics are for
Sephardi Minhag.

1998, June 25 – July 23]   TAMMUZ (29 DAYS)   [5758

Civil Date	Day of the Week	Jewish Date	SABBATHS, FESTIVALS, FASTS	PENTATEUCHAL READING	PROPHETICAL READING
June 25	Th	Tammuz 1	New Moon, second day	Num. 28:1 – 15	
27	Sa	3	Ḳoraḥ	Num. 16:1 – 18:32	I Samuel 11:14 – 12:22
July 4	Sa	10	Ḥuḳḳat	Num. 19:1 – 22:1	Judges 11:1 – 33
11	Sa	17	Balaḳ	Num. 22:2 – 25:9	Micah 5:6 – 6:8
12	S	18	Fast of 17th of Tammuz	Exod. 32:11 – 14 Exod. 34:1 – 10 (morning and afternoon)	Isaiah 55:6 – 56:8 (afternoon only)
18	Sa	24	Pineḥas	Num. 25:10 – 30:1	Jeremiah 1:1 – 2:3

Italics are for Sephardi Minhag.

1998, July 24–Aug. 22]   AV (30 DAYS)   [5758

Civil Date	Day of the Week	Jewish Date	SABBATHS, FESTIVALS, FASTS	PENTATEUCHAL READING	PROPHETICAL READING
July 24	F	Av 1	New Moon	Num. 28:1–15	
25	Sa	2	Maṭṭot, Mas'e	Num. 30:2–36:13	Jeremiah 2:4–28 Jeremiah 3:4 *Jeremiah 2:4–28* *Jeremiah 4:1–2*
Aug. 1	Sa	9	Devarim (Shabbat Ḥazon)	Deut. 1:1–3:22	Isaiah 1:1–27
2	S	10	Fast of 9th of Av	Morning: Deut. 4:25–40 Afternoon: Exod. 32:11–14 Exod. 34:1–10	(Lamentations is read the night before) Jeremiah 8:13–9:23 (morning) Isaiah 55:6–56:8 (afternoon)
8	Sa	16	Wa-etḥannan (Shabbat Naḥamu)	Deut. 3:23–7:11	Isaiah 40:1–26
15	Sa	23	'Eḳev	Deut. 7:12–11:25	Isaiah 49:14–51:3
22	Sa	30	Re'eh; New Moon, first day	Deut. 11:26–16:17 Num. 28:9–15	Isaiah 66:1–24 *Isaiah 66:1–24* *I Samuel 20:18, 42*

Italics are for Sephardi Minhag.

1998, Aug. 23–Sept. 20]   ELUL (29 DAYS)   [5758

Civil Date	Day of the Week	Jewish Date	SABBATHS, FESTIVALS, FASTS	PENTATEUCHAL READING	PROPHETICAL READING
Aug. 23	S	Elul 1	New Moon, second day	Num. 28:1–15	
29	Sa	7	Shofeṭim	Deut. 16:18–21:9	Isaiah 51:12–52:12
Sept. 5	Sa	14	Ki teẓe'	Deut. 21:10–25:19	Isaiah 54:1–55:5
12	Sa	21	Ki tavo'	Deut. 26:1–29:8	Isaiah 60:1–22
19	Sa	28	Niẓẓavim	Deut. 29:9–30:20	Isaiah 61:10–63:9

Italics are for
Sephardi Minhag.

Civil Date	Day of the Week	Jewish Date	SABBATHS, FESTIVALS, FASTS	PENTATEUCHAL READING	PROPHETICAL READING
Sept. 21	M	Tishri 1	Rosh Ha-shanah, first day	Gen. 21:1–34 Num. 29:1–6	I Samuel 1:1–2:10
22	T	2	Rosh Ha-shanah, second day	Gen. 22:1–24 Num. 29:1–6	Jeremiah 31:2–20
23	W	3	Fast of Gedaliah	Exod. 32:11–14 Exod. 34:1–10 (morning and afternoon)	Isaiah 55:6–56:8 (afternoon only)
26	Sa	6	Wa-yelekh (Shabbat Shuvah)	Deut. 31:1–30	Hosea 14:2–10 Micah 7:18–20 Joel 2:15–27 *Hosea 14:2–10* *Micah 7:18–20*
30	W	10	Yom Kippur	Morning: Levit. 16:1–34 Num. 29:7–11 Afternoon: Levit. 18:1–30	Isaiah 57:14–58:14 Jonah 1:1–4:11 Micah 7:18–20
Oct. 3	Sa	13	Ha'azinu	Deut. 32:1–52	II Samuel 22:1–51
5	M	15	Sukkot, first day	Levit. 22:26–23:44 Num. 29:12–16.	Zechariah 14:1–21
6	T	16	Sukkot, second day	Levit. 22:26–23:44 Num. 29:12–16	I Kings 8:2–21
7–10	W–Sa	17–20	Ḥol Ha-mo'ed	W Num. 29:17–25 Th Num. 29:20–28 F Num. 29:23–31 Sa Exod. 33:12–34:26 Num. 29:26–34	Ezekiel 38:18–39:16
11	S	21	Hosha'na' Rabbah	Num. 29:26–34	
12	M	22	Shemini 'Azeret	Deut. 14:22–16:17 Num. 29:35–30:1	I Kings 8:54–66
13	T	23	Simḥat Torah	Deut. 33:1–34:12 Gen. 1:1–2:3 Num. 29:35–30:1	Joshua 1:1–18 *Joshua 1:1–9*
17	Sa	27	Be-re'shit	Gen. 1:1–6:8	Isaiah 42:5–43:10 *Isaiah 42:5–21*
20	T	30	New Moon, first day	Num. 28:1–15	

Italics are for
Sephardi Minhag.

1998, Oct. 21 – Nov. 19]   ḤESHWAN (30 DAYS)   [5759

Civil Date	Day of the Week	Jewish Date	SABBATHS, FESTIVALS, FASTS	PENTATEUCHAL READING	PROPHETICAL READING
Oct. 21	W	Ḥeshwan 1	New Moon, second day	Num. 28:1–15	
24	Sa	4	Noaḥ	Gen. 6:9–11:32	Isaiah 54:1–55:5 *Isaiah 54:1–10*
31	Sa	11	Lekh lekha	Gen. 12:1–17:27	Isaiah 40:27–41:16
Nov. 7	Sa	18	Wa-yera'	Gen. 18:1–22:24	II Kings 4:1–37 *II Kings 4:1–23*
14	Sa	25	Ḥayye Sarah	Gen. 23:1–25:18	I Kings 1:1–31
19	Th	30	New Moon, first day	Num. 28:1–15	

Italics are for Sephardi Minhag.

1998, Nov. 20–Dec. 19]   KISLEW (30 DAYS)   [5759

Civil Date	Day of the Week	Jewish Date	SABBATHS, FESTIVALS, FASTS	PENTATEUCHAL READING	PROPHETICAL READING
Nov. 20	F	Kislew 1	New Moon, second day	Num. 28:1–15	
21	Sa	2	Toledot	Gen. 25:19–28:9	Malachi 1:1–2:7
28	Sa	9	Wa-yeẓe'	Gen. 28:10–32:3	Hosea 12:13–14:10 *Hosea 11:7–12:12*
Dec. 5	Sa	16	Wa-yishlaḥ	Gen. 32:4–36:43	Hosea 11:7–12:12 *Obadiah 1:1–21*
12	Sa	23	Wa-yeshev	Gen. 37:1–40:23	Amos 2:6–3:8
14–18	M–F	25–29	Ḥanukkah, first to fifth days	M Num. 7:1–17 T Num. 7:18–29 W Num. 7:24–35 Th Num. 7:30–41 F Num. 7:36–47	
19	Sa	30	Mi-keẓ; New Moon, first day; Ḥanukkah, sixth day	Gen. 41:1–44:17 Num. 28:9–15 Num. 7:42–47	Zechariah 2:14–4:7 *Zechariah 2:14–4:7* *Isaiah 66:1, 24* *I Samuel 20:18, 42*

Italics are for Sephardi Minhag.

1998, Dec. 20–Jan. 17, 1999] ṬEVET (29 DAYS)   [5759

Civil Date	Day of the Week	Jewish Date	SABBATHS, FESTIVALS, FASTS	PENTATEUCHAL READING	PROPHETICAL READING
Dec. 20	S	Ṭevet 1	New Moon, second day; Ḥanukkah, seventh day	Num. 28:1–15 Num. 7:48–53	
21	M	2	Ḥanukkah, eighth day	Num. 7:54–8:4	
26	Sa	7	Wa-yiggash	Gen. 44:18–47:27	Ezekiel 37:15–28
29	T	10	Fast of 10th of Ṭevet	Exod. 32:11–14 Exod. 34:1–10 (morning and afternoon)	Isaiah 55:6–56:8 (afternoon only)
Jan. 2	Sa	14	Wa-yeḥi	Gen. 47:28–50:26	I Kings 2:1–12
9	Sa	21	Shemot	Exod. 1:1–6:1	Isaiah 27:6–28:13 Isaiah 29:22–23 *Jeremiah 1:1–2:3*
16	Sa	28	Wa-'era'	Exod. 6:2–9:35	Ezekiel 28:25–29:21

Italics are for
Sephardi Minhag.

1999, Jan. 18 – Feb. 16]   SHEVAṬ (30 DAYS)   [5759

Civil Date	Day of the Week	Jewish Date	SABBATHS, FESTIVALS, FASTS	PENTATEUCHAL READING	PROPHETICAL READING
Jan. 18	M	Shevaṭ 1	New Moon	Num. 28:1–15	
23	Sa	6	Bo'	Exod. 10:1–13:16	Jeremiah 46:13–28
30	Sa	13	Be-shallaḥ (Shabbat Shirah)	Exod. 13:17–17:16	Judges 4:4–5:31 *Judges 5:1–31*
Feb. 1	M	15	Ḥamishah-'asar bi-Shevaṭ		
6	Sa	20	Yitro	Exod. 18:1–20:23	Isaiah 6:1–7:6; 9:5–6 *Isaiah 6:1–13*
13	Sa	27	Mishpaṭim (Shabbat Sheḳalim)	Exod. 21:1–24:18 Exod. 30:11–16	II Kings 12:1–17 *II Kings 11:17–12:17*
16	T	30	New Moon, first day	Num. 28:1–15	

Italics are for Sephardi Minhag.

1999, Feb. 17–Mar. 17]   ADAR (29 DAYS)   [5759

Civil Date	Day of the Week	Jewish Date	SABBATHS, FESTIVALS, FASTS	PENTATEUCHAL READING	PROPHETICAL READING
Feb. 17	W	Adar 1	New Moon, second day	Num. 28:1–15	
20	Sa	4	Terumah	Exod. 25:1–27:19	I Kings 5:26–6:13
27	Sa	11	Teẓawweh (Shabbat Zakhor)	Exod. 27:20–30:10 Deut. 25:17–19	I Samuel 15:2–34 *I Samuel 15:1–34*
Mar. 1	M	13	Fast of Esther	Exod. 32:11–14 Exod. 34:1–10 (morning and afternoon)	Isaiah 55:6–56:8 (afternoon only)
2	T	14	Purim	Exod. 17:8–16	Book of Esther (night before and in the morning)
3	W	15	Shushan Purim		
6	Sa	18	Ki tissa' (Shabbat Parah)	Exod. 30:11–34:35 Num. 19:1–22	Ezekiel 36:16–38 *Ezekiel 36:16–36*
13	Sa	25	Wa-yakhel, Peḳude (Shabbat Ha-ḥodesh)	Exod. 35:1–40:38 Exod. 12:1–20	Ezekiel 45:16–46:18 *Ezekiel 45:18–46:15*

Italics are for Sephardi Minhag.

1999, Mar. 18–April 16]   NISAN (30 DAYS)   [5759

Civil Date	Day of the Week	Jewish Date	SABBATHS, FESTIVALS, FASTS	PENTATEUCHAL READING	PROPHETICAL READING
Mar. 18	Th	Nisan 1	New Moon	Num. 28:1–15	
20	Sa	3	Wa-yiḳra'	Levit. 1:1–5:26	Isaiah 43:21–44:24
27	Sa	10	Ẓaw (Shabbat Ha-gadol)	Levit. 6:1–8:36	Malachi 3:4–24
31	W	14	Fast of Firstborn		
Apr. 1	Th	15	Passover, first day	Exod. 12:21–51 Num. 28:16–25	Joshua 5:2–6:1, 27
2	F	16	Passover, second day	Levit. 22:26–23:44 Num. 28:16–25	II Kings 23:1–9, 21–25
3	Sa	17	Ḥol Ha-mo'ed, first day	Exod. 33:12–34:26 Num. 28:19–25	Ezekiel 37:1–14
4	S	18	Ḥol Ha-mo'ed, second day	Exod. 13:1–16 Num. 28:19–25	Ezekiel 45:16–46:18
5	M	19	Ḥol Ha-mo'ed, third day	Exod. 22:24–23:19 Num. 28:19–25	
6	T	20	Ḥol Ha-mo'ed, fourth day	Num. 9:1–14 Num. 28:19–25	
7	W	21	Passover, seventh day	Exod. 13:17–15:26 Num. 28:19–25	II Samuel 22:1–51
8	Th	22	Passover, eighth day	Deut. 15:19–16:17 Num. 28:19–25	Isaiah 10:32–12:6
10	Sa	24	Shemini	Levit. 9:1–11:47 Num. 28:19–25	II Samuel 6:1–7:17 *II Samuel 6:1–19*
13	T	27	Holocaust Memorial Day		
16	F	30	New Moon	Num. 28:1–15	

Italics are for Sephardi Minhag.

1999, Apr. 17–May 15]   IYAR (29 DAYS)   [5759

Civil Date	Day of the Week	Jewish Date	SABBATHS, FESTIVALS, FASTS	PENTATEUCHAL READING	PROPHETICAL READING
Apr. 17	Sa	Iyar 1	Tazria', Mezora'; New Moon, second day	Levit. 12:1–15:33 Num. 28:9–15	Isaiah 66:1–24
21	W	5	Israel Independence Day		
24	Sa	8	Aḥare mot, Kedoshim	Levit. 16:1–20:27	Amos 9:7–15 *Ezekiel 20:2–20*
May 1	Sa	15	Emor	Levit. 21:1–24:23	Ezekiel 44:15–31
4	T	18	Lag Ba-'omer		
8	Sa	22	Be-har, Be-ḥukkotai	Levit. 25:1–27:34	Jeremiah 16:19–17:14
14	F	28	Jerusalem Day*		
15	Sa	29	Be-midbar	Num. 1:1–4:20	I Samuel 20:18–42

*Observed May 13, to avoid conflict with the Sabbath.

Italics are for Sephardi Minhag.

Civil Date	Day of the Week	Jewish Date	SABBATHS, FESTIVALS, FASTS	PENTATEUCHAL READING	PROPHETICAL READING
May 16	S	Siwan 1	New Moon	Num. 28:1–15	
21	F	6	Shavu'ot, first day	Exod. 19:1–20:23 Num. 28:26–31	Ezekiel 1:1–28 Ezekiel 3:12
22	Sa	7	Shavu'ot, second day	Deut. 15:19–16:17 Num. 28:26–31	Habbakuk 3:1–19 *Habbakuk 2:20–3:19*
29	Sa	14	Naso'	Num. 4:21–7:89	Judges 13:2–25
June 5	Sa	21	Be-ha'alotekha	Num. 8:1–12:16	Zechariah 2:14–4:7
12	Sa	28	Shelaḥ lekha	Num. 13:1–15:41	Joshua 2:1–24
14	M	30	New Moon, first day	Num. 28:1–15	

*Italics are for
Sephardi Minhag.*

1999, June 15–July 13]   TAMMUZ (29 DAYS)   [5759

Civil Date	Day of the Week	Jewish Date	SABBATHS, FESTIVALS, FASTS	PENTATEUCHAL READING	PROPHETICAL READING
June 15	T	Tammuz 1	New Moon, second day	Num. 28:1–15	
19	Sa	5	Ḳoraḥ	Num. 16:1–18:32	I Samuel 11:14–12:22
26	Sa	12	Ḥukkat, Balak	Num. 19:1–25:9	Micah 5:6–6:8
July 1	Th	17	Fast of 17th of Tammuz	Exod. 32:11–14 Exod. 34:1–10 (morning and afternoon)	Isaiah 55:6–56:8 (afternoon only)
3	Sa	19	Pineḥas	Num. 25:10–30:1	Jeremiah 1:1–2:3
10	Sa	26	Maṭṭot, Masʿe	Num. 30:2–36:13	Jeremiah 2:4–28 Jeremiah 3:4 *Jeremiah 2:4–28* *Jeremiah 4:1–2*

Italics are for
Sephardi Minhag.

Civil Date	Day of the Week	Jewish Date	SABBATHS, FESTIVALS, FASTS	PENTATEUCHAL READING	PROPHETICAL READING
July 14	W	Av 1	New Moon	Num. 28:1–15	
17	Sa	4	Devarim (Shabbat Ḥazon)	Deut. 1:1–3:22	Isaiah 1:1–27
22	Th	9	Fast of 9th of Av	Morning: Deut. 4:25–40 Afternoon: Exod. 32:11–14 Exod. 34:1–10	(Lamentations is read the night before) Jeremiah 8:13–9:23 (morning) Isaiah 55:6–56:8 (afternoon)
24	Sa	11	Wa-ethannan (Shabbat Naḥamu)	Deut. 3:23–7:11	Isaiah 40:1–26
31	Sa	18	'Eḳev	Deut. 7:12–11:25	Isaiah 49:14–51:3
Aug. 7	Sa	25	Re'eh	Deut. 11:26–16:17	Isaiah 54:11–55:5
12	Th	30	New Moon, first day	Num. 28:1–15	

Italics are for
Sephardi Minhag.

1999, Aug. 13–Sept. 10]   ELUL (29 DAYS)   [5759

Civil Date	Day of the Week	Jewish Date	SABBATHS, FESTIVALS, FASTS	PENTATEUCHAL READING	PROPHETICAL READING
Aug. 13	F	Elul 1	New Moon, second day	Num. 28:1–15	
14	Sa	2	Shofeṭim (Shabbat Ḥazon)	Deut. 16:18–21:9	Isaiah 51:12–52:12
21	Sa	9	Ki teẓe'	Deut. 21:10–25:19	Isaiah 54:1–10
28	Sa	16	Ki tavo'	Deut. 26:1–29:8	Isaiah 60:1–22
Sept. 4	Sa	23	Niẓẓavim, Wa-yelekh	Deut. 29:9–30:20	Isaiah 61:10–63:9

Italics are for
Sephardi Minhag.

1999, Sept. 11–Oct. 10]   TISHRI (30 DAYS)   [5760

Civil Date	Day of the Week	Jewish Date	SABBATHS, FESTIVALS, FASTS	PENTATEUCHAL READING	PROPHETICAL READING
Sept. 11	Sa	Tishri 1	Rosh Ha-shanah, first day	Gen. 21:1–34 Num. 29:1–6	I Samuel 1:1–2:10
12	S	2	Rosh Ha-shanah, second day	Gen. 22:1–24 Num. 29:1–6	Jeremiah 31:2–20
13	M	3	Fast of Gedaliah	Exod. 32:11–14 Exod. 34:1–10 (morning and afternoon)	Isaiah 55:6–56:8 (afternoon only)
18	Sa	8	Ha'azinu (Shabbat Shuvah)	Deut. 32:1–52	Hosea 14:2–10 Micah 7:18–20 Joel 2:15–27 *Hosea 14:2–10* *Micah 7:18–20*
20	M	10	Yom Kippur	Morning: Levit. 16:1–34 Num. 29:7–11 Afternoon: Levit. 18:1–30	Isaiah 57:14–58:14 Jonah 1:1–4:11 Micah 7:18–20
25	Sa	15	Sukkot, first day	Levit. 22:26–23:44 Num. 29:12–16	Zechariah 14:1–21
26	S	16	Sukkot, second day	Levit. 22:26–23:44 Num. 29:12–16	I Kings 8:2–21
27-30	M-Th	17–20	Ḥol Ha-mo'ed	M Num. 29:17–25 T Num. 29:20–28 W Num. 29:23–31 Th Num. 29:26–34	
Oct. 1	F	21	Hosha'na' Rabbah	Num. 29:26–34	
2	Sa	22	Shemini 'Aẓeret	Deut. 14:22–16:17 Num. 29:35–30:1	I Kings 8:54–66
3	S	23	Simḥat Torah	Deut. 33:1–34:12 Gen. 1:1–2:3 Num. 29:35–30:1	Joshua 1:1–18 *Joshua 1:1–9*
9	Sa	29	Be-re'shit	Gen. 1:1–6:8	I Samuel 20:18–42
10	S	30	New Moon, first day	Num. 28:1–15	

Italics are for
Sephardi Minhag.

1999, Oct. 11 – Nov. 9]   ḤESHWAN (30 DAYS)   [5760

Civil Date	Day of the Week	Jewish Date	SABBATHS, FESTIVALS, FASTS	PENTATEUCHAL READING	PROPHETICAL READING
Oct. 11	M	Ḥeshwan 1	New Moon, second day	Num. 28:1–15	
16	Sa	6	Noaḥ	Gen. 6:9–11:32	Isaiah 54:1–55:5 *Isaiah 54:1–10*
23	Sa	13	Lekh lekha	Gen. 12:1–17:27	Isaiah 40:27–41:16
30	Sa	20	Wa-yera'	Gen. 18:1–22:24	II Kings 4:1–37 *II Kings 4:1–23*
Nov. 6	Sa	27	Ḥayye Sarah	Gen. 23:1–25:18	I Kings 1:1–31
9	T	30	New Moon, first day	Num. 28:1–15	

Italics are for
Sephardi Minhag.

1999, Nov. 10–Dec. 9]   KISLEW (30 DAYS)   [5760

Civil Date	Day of the Week	Jewish Date	SABBATHS, FESTIVALS, FASTS	PENTATEUCHAL READING	PROPHETICAL READING
Nov. 10	W	Kislew 1	New Moon, second day	Num. 28:1–15	
13	Sa	4	Toledot	Gen. 25:19–28:9	Malachi 1:1–2:7
20	Sa	11	Wa-yeze'	Gen. 28:10–32:3	Hosea 12:13–14:10 *Hosea 11:7–12:12*
27	Sa	18	Wa-yishlah	Gen. 32:4–36:43	Hosea 11:7–12:12 *Obadiah 1:1–21*
Dec. 4	Sa	25	Wa-yeshev; Hanukkah, first day	Gen. 37:1–40:23 Num. 7:1–17	Zechariah 2:14–4:7
5–8	S–W	26–29	Hanukkah, second to fifth days	S Num. 7:18–29 M Num. 7:24–35 T Num. 7:30–41 W Num. 7:36–47	
9	Th	30	New Moon, first day; Hanukkah, sixth day	Num. 28:1–15 Num. 7:42–47	

Italics are for Sephardi Minhag.

1999, Dec. 10–Jan. 7, 2000]   ṬEVET (29 DAYS)   [5760

Civil Date	Day of the Week	Jewish Date	SABBATHS, FESTIVALS, FASTS	PENTATEUCHAL READING	PROPHETICAL READING
Dec. 10	F	Ṭevet 1	New Moon, second day; Ḥanukkah, seventh day	Num. 28:1–15 Num. 7:48–53	
11	Sa	2	Miḳeẓ; Ḥanukkah, eighth day	Gen. 41:1–44:17 Num. 7:54–8.4	I Kings 7:40–50
18	Sa	9	Wa-yiggash	Gen. 44:18–47:27	Ezekiel 37:15–28
19	S	10	Fast of 10th of Ṭevet	Exod. 32:11–14 Exod. 34:1–10 (morning and afternoon)	Isaiah 55:6–56:8 (afternoon only)
25	Sa	16	Wa-yeḥi	Gen. 47:28–50:26	I Kings 2:1–12
Jan. 1	Sa	23	Shemot	Exod. 1:1–6:1	Isaiah 27:6–28:13 Isaiah 29:22–23 *Jeremiah 1:1–2:3*

*Italics are for
Sephardi Minhag.*

Civil Date	Day of the Week	Jewish Date	SABBATHS, FESTIVALS, FASTS	PENTATEUCHAL READING	PROPHETICAL READING
Jan. 8	Sa	Shevaṭ 1	Wa-'era'; New Moon	Exod. 6:2–9:35 Num. 28:9–15	Isaiah 66:1–24
15	Sa	8	Bo'	Exod. 10:1–13:16	Jeremiah 46:13–28
22	Sa	15	Be-shallah (Shabbat Shirah); Ḥamishah 'asar bi-Shevaṭ	Exod. 13:17–17:16	Judges 4:4–5:31 *Judges 5:1–31*
29	Sa	22	Yitro	Exod. 18:1–20:23	Isaiah 6:1–7:6; 9:5–6 *Isaiah 6:1–13*
Feb. 5	Sa	29	Mishpaṭim	Exod. 21:1–24:18	I Samuel 20:18–42
6	S	30	New Moon, first day	Num. 28:1–15	

Italics are for Sephardi Minhag.

2000, Feb. 7 – Mar. 7]   ADAR I (30 DAYS)   [5760

Civil Date	Day of the Week	Jewish Date	SABBATHS, FESTIVALS, FASTS	PENTATEUCHAL READING	PROPHETICAL READING
Feb. 7	M	Adar I 1	New Moon, second day	Num. 28:1–15	
12	Sa	6	Terumah	Exod. 25:1–27:19	I Kings 5:26–6:13
19	Sa	13	Teẓawweh	Exod. 27:20–30:10	Ezekiel 43:10–27
26	Sa	20	Ki tissa'	Exod. 30:11–34:35	I Kings 18:1–39 *I Kings 18:20–39*
Mar. 4	Sa	27	Wa-yakhel (Shabbat Sheḳalim)	Exod. 35:1–38:20 Exod. 30:11–16	II Kings 12:1–17 *II Kings 11:17–12:17*
7	T	30	New Moon, first day	Num. 28:1–15	

Italics are for Sephardi Minhag.

2000, Mar. 8–Apr. 5]   ADAR II (29 DAYS)   [5760

Civil Date	Day of the Week	Jewish Date	SABBATHS, FESTIVALS, FASTS	PENTATEUCHAL READING	PROPHETICAL READING
Mar. 8	W	Adar II 1	New Moon, second day	Num. 28:1–15	
11	Sa	4	Peḳude	Exod. 38:21–40:38	I Kings 7:51–8:21 *I Kings 7:40–50*
18	Sa	11	Wa-yiḳra' (Shabbat Zakhor)	Levit. 1:1–5:26 Deut. 25:17–19	I Samuel 15:2–34 *I Samuel 15:1–34*
20	M	13	Fast of Esther	Exod. 32:11–14 Exod. 34:1–10 (morning and afternoon)	Isaiah 55:6–56:8 (afternoon only)
21	T	14	Purim	Exod. 17:8–16	Book of Esther (night before and in the morning)
22	W	15	Shushan Purim		
25	Sa	18	Ẓaw (Shabbat Parah)	Levit. 6:1–8:36 Num. 19:1–22	Ezekiel 36:16–38 *Ezekiel 36:16–36*
Apr. 1	Sa	25	Shemini (Shabbat Ha-ḥodesh)	Levit. 9:1–11:47 Exod. 12:1–20	Ezekiel 45:16–46:18 *Ezekiel 45:18–46:15*

Italics are for Sephardi Minhag.

2000, Apr. 6 – May 5] **NISAN (30 DAYS)** [5760

Civil Date	Day of the Week	Jewish Date	SABBATHS, FESTIVALS, FASTS	PENTATEUCHAL READING	PROPHETICAL READING
Apr. 6	Th	Nisan 1	New Moon	Num. 28:1–15	
8	Sa	3	Tazria'	Levit. 12:1–13:59	II Kings 4:42–5:19
15	Sa	10	Mezora' (Shabbat Ha-gadol)	Levit. 14:1–15:33	Malachi 3:4–24
19	W	14	Fast of Firstborn		
20	Th	15	Passover, first day	Exod. 12:21–51 Num. 28:16–25	Joshua 5:2–6:1, 27
21	F	16	Passover, second day	Levit. 22:26–23:44 Num. 28:16–25	II Kings 23:1–9, 21–25
22	Sa	17	Hol Ha-mo'ed, first day	Exod. 33:12–34:26 Num. 28:19–25	Ezekiel 37:1–14
23	S	18	Hol Ha-mo'ed, second day	Exod. 13:1–16 Num. 28:19–25	
24	M	19	Hol Ha-mo'ed, third day	Exod. 22:24–23:19 Num. 28:19–25	
25	T	20	Hol Ha-mo'ed, fourth day	Num. 9:1–14 Num. 28:19–25	
26	W	21	Passover, seventh day	Exod. 13:17–15:26 Num. 28:19–25	II Samuel 22:1–51
27	Th	22	Passover, eighth day	Deut. 15:19–16:17 Num. 28:19–25	Isaiah 10:32–12:6
29	Sa	24	Aḥare mot	Levit 16:1–18:30	Amos 9:7–15 *Ezekiel 22:1–16*
May 2	T	27	Holocaust Memorial Day		
5	F	30	New Moon, first day	Num. 28:1–15	

Italics are for Sephardi Minhag.

2000, May 6–June 3]　　　IYAR (29 DAYS)　　　[5760

Civil Date	Day of the Week	Jewish Date	SABBATHS, FESTIVALS, FASTS	PENTATEUCHAL READING	PROPHETICAL READING
May 6	Sa	Iyar 1	Kedoshim; New Moon, second day	Levit. 19:1–20:27 Num. 28:9–15	Isaiah 66:1–24
10	W	5	Israel Independence Day		
13	Sa	8	Emor	Levit. 21:1–24:23	Ezekiel 44:15–31
20	Sa	15	Be-har	Levit 25:1–26:2	Jeremiah 32:6–27
23	T	18	Lag Ba-'omer		
27	Sa	22	Be-ḥuḳḳotai	Levit. 26:3–27:34	Jeremiah 16:19–17:14
June 2	F	28	Jerusalem Day*		
3	Sa	29	Be-midbar	Num. 1:1–4:20	I Samuel 20:18–42

*Observed June 1, to avoid conflict with the Sabbath.

Italics are for Sephardi Minhag.

2000, June 4 – July 3]　　　SIWAN (30 DAYS)　　　[5760

Civil Date	Day of the Week	Jewish Date	SABBATHS, FESTIVALS, FASTS	PENTATEUCHAL READING	PROPHETICAL READING
June 4	S	Siwan 1	New Moon	Num. 28:1–15	
9	F	6	Shavu'ot, first day	Exod. 19:1–20:23 Num. 28:26–31	Ezekiel 1:1–28, 3:12
10	Sa	7	Shavu'ot, second day	Deut. 15:19–16:17 Num. 28:26–31	Habbakuk 3:1–19 *Habbakuk 2:20–3:19*
17	Sa	14	Naso'	Num. 4:21–7:89	Judges 13:2–25
24	Sa	21	Be-ha'alotekha	Num. 8:1–12:16	Zechariah 2:14–4:7
July 1	Sa	28	Shelaḥ lekha	Num. 13:1–15:41	Joshua 2:1–24
3	M	30	New Moon, first day	Num. 28:1–15	

Italics are for Sephardi Minhag.

2000, July 4 – Aug. 1] TAMMUZ (29 DAYS) [5760

Civil Date	Day of the Week	Jewish Date	SABBATHS, FESTIVALS, FASTS	PENTATEUCHAL READING	PROPHETICAL READING
July 4	T	Tammuz 1	New Moon, second day	Num. 28:1–15	
8	Sa	5	Ḳoraḥ	Num. 16:1–18:32	I Samuel 11:14–12:22
15	Sa	12	Ḥuḳḳat, Balaḳ	Num. 19:1–25:9	Micah 5:6–6:8
20	Th	17	Fast of 17th of Tammuz	Exod. 32:11–14 Exod. 34:1–10 (morning and afternoon)	Isaiah 55:6–56:8 (afternoon only)
22	Sa	19	Pineḥas	Num. 25:10–30:1	Jeremiah 1:1–2:3
29	Sa	26	Maṭṭot, Masʻe	Num. 30:2–36:13	Jeremiah 2:4–28 Jeremiah 3:4 *Jeremiah 2:4–28* *Jeremiah 4:1–2*

Italics are for
Sephardi Minhag.

2000, Aug. 2–Aug. 31]   AV (30 DAYS)   [5760

Civil Date	Day of the Week	Jewish Date	SABBATHS, FESTIVALS, FASTS	PENTATEUCHAL READING	PROPHETICAL READING
Aug. 2	W	Av 1	New Moon	Num. 28:1–15	
5	Sa	4	Devarim (Shabbat Ḥazon)	Deut. 1:1–3:22	Isaiah 1:1–27
10	Th	9	Fast of 9th of Av	Morning: Deut. 4:25–40 Afternoon: Exod. 32:11–14 Exod. 34:1–10	(Lamentations is read the night before) Jeremiah 8:13–9:23 (morning) Isaiah 55:6–56:8 (afternoon)
12	Sa	11	Wa-etḥannan (Shabbat Naḥamu)	Deut. 3:23–7:11	Isaiah 40:1–26
19	Sa	18	'Eḳev	Deut. 7:12–11:25	Isaiah 49:14–51:3
26	Sa	25	Re'eh	Deut. 11:26–16:17	Isaiah 54:11–55:5
31	Th	30	New Moon, first day	Num. 28:1–15	

Italics are for
Sephardi Minhag.

2000, Sept. 1 – Sept. 29]   ELUL (29 DAYS)   [5760

Civil Date	Day of the Week	Jewish Date	SABBATHS, FESTIVALS, FASTS	PENTATEUCHAL READING	PROPHETICAL READING
Sept. 1	F	Elul 1	New Moon, second day	Num. 28:1–15	
2	Sa	2	Shofeṭim	Deut. 16:18–21:9	Isaiah 51:12–52:12
9	Sa	9	Ki teẓe'	Deut. 21:10–25:19	Isaiah 54:1–10
16	Sa	16	Ki tavo'	Deut. 26:1–29:8	Isaiah 60:1–22
23	Sa	23	Niẓẓavim, Wa-yelekh	Deut. 29:9–30:20	Isaiah 61:10–63:9

Italics are for
Sephardi Minhag.

2000, Sept. 30–Oct. 29]   TISHRI (30 DAYS)   [5761

Civil Date	Day of the Week	Jewish Date	SABBATHS, FESTIVALS, FASTS	PENTATEUCHAL READING	PROPHETICAL READING
Sept. 30	Sa	Tishri 1	Rosh Ha-shanah, first day	Gen. 21:1–34 Num. 29:1–6	I Samuel 1:1–2:10
Oct. 1	S	2	Rosh Ha-shanah, second day	Gen. 22:1–24 Num. 29:1–6	Jeremiah 31:2–20
2	M	3	Fast of Gedaliah	Exod. 32:11–14 Exod. 34:1–10 (morning and afternoon)	Isaiah 55:6–56:8 (afternoon only)
7	Sa	8	Ha'azinu (Shabbat Shuvah)	Deut. 32:1–52	Hosea 14:2–10 Micah 7:18–20 Joel 2:15–27 *Hosea 14:2–10* *Micah 7:18–20*
9	M	10	Yom Kippur	Morning: Levit. 16:1–34 Num. 29:7–11 Afternoon: Levit. 18:1–30	Isaiah 57:14–58:14 Jonah: 1:1–4:11 Micah 7:18–20
14	Sa	15	Sukkot, first day	Levit. 22:26–23:44 Num. 29:12–16	Zechariah 14:1–21
15	S	16	Sukkot, second day	Levit. 22:26–23:44 Num. 29:12–16	I Kings 8:2–21
16–19	M–Th	17–20	Ḥol Ha-mo'ed	M: Num. 29:17–25 T: Num. 29:20–28 W: Num. 29:23–31 Th: Num. 29:26–34	
20	F	21	Hosha'na' Rabbah	Num. 29:26–34	
21	Sa	22	Shemini 'Aẓeret	Deut. 14:22–16:17 Num. 29:35–30:1	I Kings 8:54–66
22	S	23	Simḥat Torah	Deut. 33:1–34:12 Gen. 1:1–2:3 Num. 29:35–30:1	Joshua 1:1–18 *Joshua 1:1–9*
28	Sa	29	Be-re'shit	Gen. 1:1–6:8	I Samuel 20:18–42
29	S	30	New Moon, first day	Num. 28:1–15	

Italics are for Sephardi Minhag.

2000, Oct. 30 – Nov. 27]   ḤESHWAN (29 DAYS)   [5761

Civil Date	Day of the Week	Jewish Date	SABBATHS, FESTIVALS, FASTS	PENTATEUCHAL READING	PROPHETICAL READING
Oct. 30	M	Ḥeshwan 1	New Moon, second day	Num. 28:1–15	
Nov. 4	Sa	6	Noaḥ	Gen. 6:9–11:32	Isaiah 54:1–55:5 *Isaiah 54:1–10*
11	Sa	13	Lekh lekha	Gen. 12:1–17:27	Isaiah 40:27–41:16
18	Sa	20	Wa-yera'	Gen. 18:1–22:24	II Kings 4:1–37 *II Kings 4:1–23*
25	Sa	27	Ḥayye Sarah	Gen. 23:1–25:18	I Kings 1:1–31

Italics are for
Sephardi Minhag.

2000, Nov. 28 – Dec. 26]   KISLEW (29 DAYS)   [5761

Civil Date	Day of the Week	Jewish Date	SABBATHS, FESTIVALS, FASTS	PENTATEUCHAL READING	PROPHETICAL READING
Nov. 28	T	Kislew 1	New Moon	Num. 28:1–15	
Dec. 2	Sa	5	Toledot	Gen. 25:19–28:9	Malachi 1:1–2:7
9	Sa	12	Wa-yeẓe'	Gen. 28:10–32:3	Hosea 12:13–14:10 *Hosea 11:7–12:12*
16	Sa	19	Wa-yishlaḥ	Gen. 32:4–36:43	Hosea 11:7–12:12 *Obadiah 1:1–21*
22	F	25	Ḥanukkah, first day	Num. 7:1–17	
23	Sa	26	Wa-yeshev; Ḥanukkah, second day	Gen. 37:1–40:23 Num. 7:18–23	Zechariah 2:14–4:7
24–26	S–T	27–29	Ḥanukkah, third to fifth days	S Num. 7:24–35 M Num. 7:30–41 T Num. 7:36–47	

Italics are for Sephardi Minhag.

2000, Dec. 27–Jan. 24, 2001] ṬEVET (29 DAYS) [5761

Civil Date	Day of the Week	Jewish Date	SABBATHS, FESTIVALS, FASTS	PENTATEUCHAL READING	PROPHETICAL READING
Dec. 27	W	Ṭevet 1	New Moon; Ḥanukkah, sixth day	Num. 28:1–15 Num. 7:42–47	
28	Th	2	Ḥanukkah, seventh day	Num. 7:48–53	
29	F	3	Ḥanukkah, eighth day	Num. 7:54–8:4	
30	Sa	4	Mi-ḳeẓ	Gen. 41:1–44:17	I Kings 3:15–4:1
2001 Jan. 5	F	10	Fast of 10th of Ṭevet	Exod. 32:11–14 Exod. 34:1–10 (morning and afternoon)	Isaiah 55:6–56:8 (afternoon only)
6	Sa	11	Wa-yiggash	Gen. 44:18–47:27	Ezekiel 37:15–28
13	Sa	18	Wa-yeḥi	Gen. 47:28–50:26	I Kings 2:1–12
20	Sa	25	Shemot	Exod. 1:1–6:1	Isaiah 27:6–28:13 Isaiah 29:22–23 *Jeremiah 1:1–2:3*

Italics are for Sephardi Minhag.

SELECTED ARTICLES OF INTEREST IN RECENT VOLUMES OF THE AMERICAN JEWISH YEAR BOOK

American Jewish Fiction Turns Inward, 1960–1990 — Sylvia Barack Fishman 91:35–69

American Jewish Museums: Trends and Issues — Ruth R. Seldin 91:71–113

Anti-Semitism in Europe Since the Holocaust — Robert S. Wistrich 93:3–23

Counting Jewish Populations: Methods and Problems — Paul Ritterband, Barry A. Kosmin, and Jeffrey Scheckner 88:204–221

Current Trends in American Jewish Philanthropy — Jack Wertheimer 97:3–92

Ethiopian Jews in Israel — Steven Kaplan and Chaim Rosen 94:59–109

Ethnic Differences Among Israeli Jews: A New Look — U.O. Schmelz, Sergio DellaPergola, and Uri Avner 90:3–204

Herzl's Road to Zionism — Shlomo Avineri 98:3–15

The Impact of Feminism on American Jewish Life — Sylvia B. Fishman 89:3–62

Israel at 50: An American Perspective — Arnold M. Eisen 98:47–71

Israel at 50: An Israeli Perspective — Yossi Klein Halevi 98:25–46

Israeli Literature and the American Reader — Alan Mintz 97:93–114

Israelis in the United States — Steven J. Gold and Bruce A. Phillips 96:51–101

Jewish Experience on Film—An American Overview — Joel Rosenberg 96:3–50

Jewish Identity in Conversionary and Mixed Marriages — Peter Y. Medding, Gary A. Tobin, Sylvia Barack Fishman, and Mordechai Rimor 92:3–76

719

Jewish Organizational Life in the United States Since 1945   Jack Wertheimer 95:3–98

Jewish Theology in North America: Notes on Two Decades   Arnold Eisen 91:3–33

Jews in the European Community: Sociodemographic Trends and Challenges   Sergio DellaPergola 93:25–82

New Perspectives in American Jewish Sociology   Nathan Glazer 87:3–19

The Population of Reunited Jerusalem, 1967–1985   U.O. Schmelz 87:39–113

Profile of American Jewry: Insights from the 1990 National Jewish Population Survey   Sidney Goldstein 92:77–173

The Rebirth of Jewish Scholarship in Russia   David E. Fishman 97:391–400

Recent Trends in American Judaism   Jack Wertheimer 89:63–162

South African Jewry: A Sociodemographic Profile   Sergio DellaPergola and Allie A. Dubb 88:59–140

South African Jews and the Apartheid Crisis   Gideon Shimoni 88:3–58

Soviet Jews in the United States   Steven J. Gold 94:3–57

A Study of Jewish Denominational Preferences: Summary Findings   Bernard Lazerwitz, J. Alan Winter, Arnold Dashefsky, and Ephraim Tabory 97:115–37

Zionism and the Upheavals of the 20th Century   Anita Shapira 98:17–24

OBITUARIES

Leo Baeck	By Max Gruenwald 59:478–82
Salo W. Baron	By Lloyd P. Gartner 91:544–54
Jacob Blaustein	By John Slawson 72:547–57
Martin Buber	By Seymour Siegel 67:37–43
Abraham Cahan	By Mendel Osherowitch 53:527–29
Albert Einstein	By Jacob Bronowski 58:480–85
Louis Finkelstein	By Abraham J. Karp 93:527–34
Felix Frankfurter	By Paul A. Freund 67:31–36
Louis Ginzberg	By Louis Finkelstein 56:573–79
Jacob Glatstein	By Shmuel Lapin 73:611–17
Sidney Goldmann	By Milton R. Konvitz 85:401–03
Hayim Greenberg	By Marie Syrkin 56:589–94
Abraham Joshua Heschel	By Fritz A. Rothschild 74:533–44
Horace Meyer Kallen	By Milton R. Konvitz 75:55–80
Mordecai Kaplan	By Ludwig Nadelmann 85:404–11
Herbert H. Lehman	By Louis Finkelstein 66:3–20
Judah L. Magnes	By James Marshall 51:512–15
Jacob Rader Marcus	By Jonathan D. Sarna 97:633–40
Alexander Marx	By Abraham S. Halkin 56:580–88
Reinhold Niebuhr	By Seymour Siegel 73:605–10
Joseph Proskauer	By David Sher 73:618–28
Maurice Samuel	By Milton H. Hindus 74:545–53
Isaac Bashevis Singer	By Hillel Halkin 93:535–38
John Slawson	By Murray Friedman 91:555–58
Joseph B. Soloveitchik	By Moshe Sokol 95:575–84
Leo Strauss	By Ralph Lerner 76:91–97
Max Weinreich	By Lucy S. Dawidowicz 70:59–68
Chaim Weizmann	By Harry Sacher 55:462–69
Stephen S. Wise	By Philip S. Bernstein 51:515–18
Harry Austryn Wolfson	By Isadore Twersky 76:99–111

Index

Aaronovitch, Sam, 288
Abargil, Linor, 482
Abbas, Mahmoud(Abu Mazen), 434
Abdel-Rahman, Asaad, 413
Abella, Irving, 243, 244, 252
Abraham, Pearl, 319
Abraham Fund, 595
Abrams, Harry, 239
Abrams, Judith Z., 84n
Abramson, Glenda, 287
Abramson, Larry, 538
Abramson, Leonard, 103n
Abramson, Robert, 3n, 61, 67n, 73n
Abruch, Miguel, 259
Abu Ala, 430, 444
Abu Medein, Freih, 433
Abzug, Bella, 186, 208, 669
Academy for Jewish Religion, 622
Ackerman, Walter, 7, 7n, 8n, 17n, 23n, 26,
    26n, 31n, 34n, 37n, 38, 38n, 39n, 43n,
    78n, 104n, 105, 105n, 108, 108n, 111n
Adamkus, Valdas, 394
Adar, Noa, 540
Adler, Rachel, 201
Afn Shvel, 661
Agam, Ya'acov, 272
Agenda: Jewish Education, 661
Agmon, Goren, 535
Agnon, S.Y., 531
Agudah Women of America-N'Shei Agu-
    dath Israel, 610
Agudath Israel, 138, 139, 174, 175, 179, 180,
    182, 184, 185
Agudath Israel of America, 610
Agudath Israel World Organization, 610
Aguinis, Marcos, 266, 271
Ain, Stewart, 52n, 55n
Aish ha'Torah, 83
Ajzensztadt, Amnon, 253
Akron Jewish News, 665

Alberstein, Chava, 207
Albert Einstein College of Medicine, 630
Albom, Mitch, 199
Albright, Madeleine, 145, 153, 155, 156,
    166, 167, 169, 388, 427, 429, 430, 432,
    433, 438, 454, 455, 456, 457
Aleksandrova, V., 567n
Aleman Velazco, Miguel, 255
ALEPH: Alliance for Jewish Renewal,
    610
Alexander, Edward, 199
Alfonsín, Raúl, 263
Algemeiner Journal, 661
Almagor, J., 564n
Almog, Ruth, 336
Aloy, Irma, 423
Alpha Epsilon Pi Fraternity, 632
Alswang, David, 421
Alterman, Natan, 532
Alterman, R., 492n
Altshuler, Mordechai, 564n, 565n
Alvarez, Carlos, 263
Aly, Goetz, 345
ALYN-American Society for Handicapped
    Children in Israel, 596
Amar, Jo, 259
Amato, David, 255
AMC Cancer Research Center, 634
Amcha for Tsedakah, 634
America-Israel Cultural Foundation, 596
America-Israel Friendship League,596
American Academy for Jewish Research,
    588
American Associates, Ben-Gurion Univer-
    sity of the Negev, 596
American Association for Jewish Educa-
    tion, 18, 32
American Association of Jews from the For-
    mer USSR, 632
American Association of Rabbis, 611

American Committee for Shaare Zedek Medical Center in Jerusalem, 596
American Committee for Shenkar College in Israel, 596
American Committee for the Beer-Sheva Foundation, 596
American Committee for the Weizmann Institute of Science, 597
American Conference of Cantors, 618
American Council for Judaism, 583
American Federation of Jews from Central Europe,632
Americans for Peace Now, 171
American Friends of Assaf Harofeh Medical Center, 597
American Friends of Bar-Ilan University, 597
American Friends of Beth Hatefutsoth, 597
American Friends of Likud, 597
American Friends of Neve Shalom/Wahat al-Salam, 597
American Friends of Rabin Medical Center, 597
American Friends of Rambam Medical Center, 598
American Friends of Tel Aviv University, 598
American Friends of the Alliance Israélite Universelle, 608
American Friends of the Hebrew University, 598
American Friends of the Israel Community Development Foundation, 598
American Friends of the Israel Museum, 598
American Friends of the Israel Philharmonic Orchestra, 598
American Friends of the Open University of Israel, 598
American Friends of the Shalom Hartman Institute, 598
American Friends of the Tel Aviv Museum of Art, 599
American Friends of Young Israel in Israel-Yisrael Hatza'ir, 615
American Gathering of Jewish Holocaust Survivors, 588
American Guild of Judaic Art, 588

American-Israel Environmental Council, 599
American-Israeli Lighthouse, 599
American Israelite, 665
American Israel Public Affairs Committee (AIPAC), 124, 125, 157, 167, 168, 170, 171, 172, 599
American Jewish Archives, Jacob Rader Marcus Center, 624
American Jewish Archives Journal, 665
American Jewish Committee, 131, 134, 135, 136, 139, 142, 143, 166, 180, 196, 258, 269, 279, 340, 349, 373, 382, 407, 583
American Jewish Congress, 124, 125, 141, 584
American Jewish Correctional Chaplains Association, 634
American Jewish Historical Society, 205, 588
American Jewish History, 659
American Jewish Joint Distribution Committee (JDC), 281, 366, 369, 381, 384, 386, 388, 397, 398, 608
American Jewish League for Israel, 599
American Jewish Periodical Center, 624
American Jewish Philanthropic Fund, 608
American Jewish Press Association, 588
American Jewish Public Relations Society, 639
American Jewish Society for Service, 634
American Jewish Times Outlook, 665
American Jewish World, 659
American Jewish World Service, 608
American Jewish Year Book, 661
American ORT, 608
American Physicians Fellowship for Medicine in Israel, 599
American Red Magen David for Israel, 599
American Sephardi Federation, 182, 588
Americans for a Safe Israel, 165, 600
Americans for Peace Now, 172, 600
American Society for Jewish Music, 588
American Society for Technion-Israel Institute of Technology, 600
American Society for the Protection of Nature in Israel, 600
American Society for Yad Vashem, 600
American Society of the University of Haifa, 600

American Students to Activate Pride, 611
American Veterans of Israel, 632
American Zionist Movement, 600
AMIA, 269, 273
Amichai, Yehuda, 532
Amin, Idi, 454
Amir, Haggai, 476
Amir, Yigal, 476
Amit, 184, 601
Amit, 661
Amital, Yehuda, 470
Ampal-American Israel Corporation, 601
Amselem, Moise, 245
Andreev, Evgeni, 569n
Andrev, E., 512n
Annan, Kofi, 131, 453
An-Ski, S., 306
Anstey, Vivienne, 422
Antebi, Yigal, 378
Anti-Defamation League (ADL), 126, 130,
    132, 133, 134, 135,136, 142, 172, 273,
    329, 367, 369, 584
Antonescu, Marshal Ion, 383
Appel, Bluma, 252
Appelbaum, Lowell, 3n
Appelbaum, Michael, 237
Appelbome, Peter, 56n
Appelfeld, Aharon, 201, 207
Appelman, Harlene W., 80n, 81n
Apple, Max, 200
Apt Pupil, 194
Arad, Ron, 278, 279
Arad, Uzi, 451
Arafat, Souha, 403
Arafat, Yasir, 123, 129, 150, 152, 153, 155,
    157, 158, 160, 161, 166, 167, 169, 171,
    195, 204, 277, 310, 321, 322, 359, 383,
    392, 403, 413, 415, 424, 426–435,
    437–441, 443, 445, 446, 451, 453, 454,
    455, 459
Archer, Lord, 281
Arendt, Hannah, 307, 351
Arian, Asher, 287
Arizona Jewish Post, 656
Armstrong, Diane, 409
Arnon, Yehudit, 540
Aron, Isa, 13, 13n, 37n, 58n, 62, 62n, 64,
    64n, 65n, 68, 68n, 69n, 103n
Aron, Marc, 308

Aronsfeld, C.C., 287
Aronson, Arnold, 667
Aronson, Robert, 106
Artson, Bradley, 186
Arye, Yevgeny, 535, 536
ARZA/World Union, North America, 601
Ashcroft, John, 140
Assabi, Ady, 421
Assad, Hafez-al, 292, 303, 446, 449, 450,
    451
Assaf Harofeh Medical Center, American
    Friends of, 597
Association for Jewish Studies, 185, 611
Association for the Social Scientific Study
    of Jewry, 611
Association of Jewish Aging Services, 634
Association of Jewish Book Publishers, 589
Association of Jewish Center Professionals,
    634
Association of Jewish Community Organi-
    zation Personnel, 635
Association of Jewish Community Rela-
    tions Workers, 584
Association of Jewish Family and Children's
    Agencies, 635
Association of Jewish Libraries, 589
Association of Orthodox Jewish Scientists,
    611
Association of Reform Zionists of America
    (ARZA), 175
Association of Yugoslav Jews in the United
    States, 632
Assouline, Pierre, 308
Assuntino, Rudi, 333
Ateret Cohanim, 430
Attias, Christophe, 307
Auerbach, Ellen, 353
Aufbau, 661
Augias, Corrado, 332
Augstein, Rudolf, 356
Auschwitz, 378, 380
Australian/Israel and Jewish Affairs Coun-
    cil, 258
Avi Chai Foundation, 6n, 102, 102n, 103n,
    104, 104n, 192
Avidan, Hillel, 420
Aviran, Yizhak, 268
Aviv, Diana, 130
Avner, Uri, 571n

Avotaynu, 660
Avruj, Claudio, 274
Awadallah, Adel, 435
Ayalon, Ami, 431, 476
Ayalon, David, 482
Azar Boldo, Lázaro, 261
Aziz, Tariq, 323
Aznar, Jose Maria, 432
Azrieli Graduate School of Jewish Education and Administration, 630
Azure, 657

Babel, Isaac, 536
Bachi, Roberto, 544*n*
Bachmann, Dieter, 343
Bakshi-Doron, Eliyahu, 247, 248
Ballard, Paul, 279
Balter, Bernice, 176
Baltimore Hebrew University, 622
Baltimore Jewish Times, 659
Band, Arnold J., 77, 77*n*
Bank, Adrianne, 3*n*, 65*n*, 66, 68, 68*n*, 82*n*
Banks, Lynne Reid, 286
Bantom, William, 413
Barak, Ehud, 167, 171, 277, 415, 424, 431, 453, 459, 461–470
Bar-Am, Micha, 353
Barasch, M., 506*n*
Bardanashvili, Josef, 542
Bardin, Livia, 90*n*
Barihum, Tzagaye, 259
Bar-Ilan University, 183, 184
Bar-Ilan University, American Friends of, 597
Bar-Illan, David, 167, 451
Barley, Dave, 404
Bar-Natan, M., 512*n*
Barnea, Nahum, 452
Bar-On, Avner (Walter), 483
Bar On, Haim, 482
Baron de Hirsch Fund, 635
Barsky, Lesley Marrus, 251
Barsky, Yehudit, 237
Bartenstein, Martin, 366
Bar Yosef, Yehoshua, 529
Bassani, Giorgio, 319
Bassat, Nina, 407
Bauer, Yehuda, 344
Baume, Peter, 410

Baur, André, 290
Bayefsky, Aba, 250
Bayme, Steven, 3*n*
Bayrou, Francois, 289
Beasley, David, 122
Beatrix, Queen, 310
Beazley, Kim, 399
Bechhofer, Susi, 199
Beck, R., 503*n*
Beckett, Margaret, 280
Beenstock, M., 496*n*, 512*n*
Be'er, Rami, 540, 541
Begin, Benny (Binyamin), 461, 466
Begin, Menachem, 447, 461, 482
Behrman, David, 3*n*, 72, 72*n*
Behrman House, 71, 72*n*
Beilin, Yossi, 434
Beitar, 35
Bejarano, Maya, 533
Belfer Institute for Advanced Biomedical Studies, 630
Belinfante, Judith C. 309, 319
Belkin, Samuel, 59*n*
Beller, Stephen, 319
Ben-Ami, Shlomo, 451, 467
Ben & Jerry's, 130
Ben-Arye, A., 503*n*
Benbassa, Esther, 307
Ben-David, A., 489*n*, 505*n*
Benderly, Samson, 10*n*
Ben-Elissar, Eliahu, 304
Ben-Eliyahu, Eitan, 482
Ben-Gurion, David, 307, 382, 434, 435, 470, 482
Ben-Gurion University of the Negev, American Associates, 596
Benigni, Roberto, 205, 331
Benita, E., 496*n*
Ben-Itto, Hadassa, 356
Benjamin N. Cardozo School of Law, 630
Benjamin, Jerry, 33*n*, 34*n*
Benjamin, Walter, 539
Ben Menahem, Y., 496*n*
Bennett, Alan D., 31*n*
Ben-Refael, E., 489*n*, 491*n*, 499*n*
Bensemhoun, Arié, 304
Bensimon, Doris, 561*n*
Bensussan, Gérard, 307
Beraha, Jacques, 389

Beraja, Rubén, 269, 271, 274
Berend, Alice, 356
Berger, David, 185
Berger, Gabriel, 559n
Berger, Gerald, 253
Berger, Shalom, 76n
Bergman, Ahron, 287
Bergman, Lawrence, 236
Berkley, Shelley, 120
Berkowitz, Michael, 352
Berlin, Ira, 202
Berman, Babina, 261
Berman, Howard, 121
Berman, Mandell L., 27
Berman, Sabina, 262
Bermant, Chaim, 287, 288
Bernard Revel Graduate School, 631
Bernstein, David, 407
Bernstein, J., 498n
Bernstein, Leslie, 364
Bernstein, Susan, 102n
Betar Zionist Youth Organization, 601
Beth Hatefutsoth, American Friends of, 597
Bethlehem, Marlene, 418, 419
Beutel, Josh, 239
Bieler, Jack, 59n
Bildner, Elisa Spungeon, 194
Bildner, Robert Spungeon, 194
Bin-Laden, Osama, 164
Bin-Nun, Harel, 435
Birdwood, Lady, 279
Birn, Ruth Bettina, 252, 356
Birnbaum, Eli, 84n
Biro, Adam, 308
Birthright Israel, 104
Bishinsky, Jonathan, 240
Bitrán, Aarón, 258
Bitrán, Saúl, 258
Bitton, Isaac, 132
Bitton, Yechiel, 132
Black, Gerry, 286
Blair, Tony, 276, 277, 278, 454, 465
Blay, Anna Rosner, 409
Block, Lionel, 288
Bloemendal, Hans, 317
Blue, Lionel, 287
Blumenthal, Michael, 204, 354, 355
Blustain, Rachel, 52n, 54n, 55n, 56n
B'nai Akiva, 35, 91

B'nai B'rith, 91, 267, 273, 275, 311, 312, 387, 635
B'nai B'rith Canada, 641
B'nai B'rith Hillel Foundations (see Hillel)
B'nai B'rith International Jewish Monthly, 657
B'nai B'rith Klutznick National Jewish Museum, 589
B'nai B'rith Youth Organization, 35, 370, 611
Bnai Zion-The American Fraternal Zionist Organization, 633
Bock, Geoffrey E., 39, 39n
Bogutin, Wasily, 241
Bokser, Judith, 261
Bond, Julian, 134
Bookstein, Jonah, 381
Bookstein, Rachel, 381
Bordyuzha, Nikolai, 393
Borensjtajn, Joseph Hillel, 319
Bormann, Martin, 274
Boteach, Shmuel, 284
Bouchard, Lucien, 236, 245
Boucher, Marguerite, 546n
Boudria, Don, 239
Bourque, Pierre, 236
Boxer, Barbara, 121
Boys Town Jerusalem Foundation of America, 601
Boys, Mary, 3n
Bozorghmehr, Mehdi, 573n
Bramson ORT Technical Institute, 622
Brandeis-Bardin Institute, 90n, 622
Brandeis University, 199, 623
Brandeis University National Women's Committee, 639
Brandes, Yohi, 529, 530
Brauner, Lori Silberman, 56n, 102n
Bräutigam, Otto, 337
Braverman, Avishai, 416
Breakstone, David, 95n
Breger, Marshall, 137
Breindel, Eric, 670
Brenner, Anita, 262
Breslow, Maurice, 250
Brichto, Sidney, 287
Bridges: A Journal for Jewish Feminists & Our Friends, 666
Brin, Herb, 56n

Brith Abraham, 633
Brith Sholom, 633
Brodbar, Jay, 244
Broder, Henryk, 356
Brody, Leslie, 200
Bronfman, Andrea, 248
Bronfman, Charles, 194, 248
Bronfman, Edgar, 103n, 144, 145
Brookner, Anita, 286
Brotman, Shari L., 555n
Brovender, Chaim, 286
Brover, B., 499n
Brown, Bobby, 177
Brown, Gordon, 276
Brown, Michael, 252
Brown, Saski, 287
Brown, Steven, 20, 20n, 73n, 102n
Broza, David, 408
Brumer, Anita, 558n
Brumlik, Micha, 350, 355
Brünner, Alois, 303
Brusin, David, 81n
Brym, Robert, 243, 244
Bubis, Gerald, 88, 88n
Bubis, Ignatz, 345, 357
Buchwald, Ephraim Z., 83
Buffalo Jewish Review, 661
Bulka, Reuven, 247, 249
Burg, Avraham, 467
Bush, George W., 123
Bush, Jeb, 123
Buticchi, Marco, 332
Buwalda, Pieter, 317
Buzek, Jerzy, 378, 379, 380
Bryk, Anthony S., 112n

Cahill, Thomas, 201
Calef, Noël, 307
Calimani, Riccardo, 333
Call, 661
CAMERA-Committee for Accuracy in
    Middle East Reporting in America, 601
Campbell, Graeme, 404
Campbell, Terry, 403
Canadian Friends of CALI & AMAL, 641
Canadian Jewish Congress, 641
Canadian Jewish Herald, 667
Canadian Jewish News, 667
Canadian Jewish Outlook, 667

Canadian Young Judaea, 642
Canadian Zionist Organization, 642
Cañete, Emilio, 269
Cantors Assembly, 612
Capital Communiqué, 657
Caplan, Neil, 251
Cappe, Mel, 252
Cárdenas, Cuauhtémoc, 255
Cárdenas, Lázaro, 260
Cardin, Benjamin, 121
Carlo Alberto, King, 320
Carmon, Aryeh, 468
Carreño, Gloria, 262
Carville, James, 466
Casdan, Norman, 370
Casdan, Shirley, 370
Cashdan, Eli, 288
Castel-Bloom, Orly, 528, 530
Castellanos, Rosario, 256
Castiel, Judah, 253
Caur, Charles, 290
Cavalion, Alberto, 332
Caviglia, Massimo, 332
CCAR Journal, 661
Cejwin, 35
Center for Christian-Jewish Understanding,
    612
Center for Jewish Community Studies, 584
Center for Jewish History, 205
Center for Judaic Studies, 623
Center for Russian Jewry with Student
    Struggle for Soviet Jewry/SSSJ, 584
Central California Jewish Heritage, 656
Central Conference of American Rabbis
    (CCAR), 189, 191, 612
Central Sephardic Jewish Community of
    America Women's Division, 633
Central Yiddish Culture Organization
    (CYCO), 589
Cepanis, Alfreds, 395
Ceric, Mustafa, 386
Cesarani, David, 287
Chabad-Lubavitch, 185, 327, 350, 369, 373,
    403, 441
Chahid-Nouraï, Noël, 302
Chanes, Jerome, 3n
Charles R. Bronfman Foundation, 104
Charleston Jewish Journal, 666
Charlotte Jewish News, 665

Chazan, Barry, 79, 79n, 87n, 88, 88n, 95n
Chernomyrdin, Viktor, 390, 391
Chevènement, Jean-Pierre, 289
Cheyette, Brian, 286
Chicago Jewish News, 658
Chicago Jewish Star, 658
Chirac, Jacques, 289, 290, 292, 298, 303, 306
Chiswick, Barry R., 553n
Chomsky, Noam, 296
Chouraqui, André, 308
Chrétien, Jean, 239
Christie, Douglas, 239
Chronicle, 658
Chrostowski, Waldemar, 379
Chubais, Anatoly, 390
Ciampi, Carlo Azeglio, 325
Cichowolsky, Rogelio, 271
Ciorbea, Victor, 383
Circle, 661
City of Hope National Medical Center and Beckman Research Institute, 635
CLAL-National Jewish Center for Learning and Leadership, 82, 612
Clearfield, Sidney, 266
Cleveland College of Jewish Studies, 623
Cleveland Jewish News, 665
Clinton, Bill, 119, 122–126, 128, 129, 130, 139, 140, 144, 148, 149, 150, 153–156, 158–161, 163–166, 170, 171, 172, 182, 187, 191, 194, 198, 256, 424, 426, 427, 437, 439, 441, 444, 445, 455, 459, 466, 478
Clinton, Hilary Rodham, 161, 169, 170, 432
Coalition for Alternatives in Jewish Education, 32
Coalition for the Advancement of Jewish Education, 34, 612
Coalition on the Environment & Jewish Life, 584
Coats, Dan, 142
Coccioli, Carlo, 256
Cohen, Adele, 410
Cohen, Barry, 410
Cohen, Burton I., 84n
Cohen, Debra Nussbaum, 52n, 53n, 55n, 56n, 60n, 74n, 83n, 103n
Cohen, Dov, 287
Cohen, Erik H., 561n
Cohen, Frances, 562n

Cohen, Jack J., 32n
Cohen, Job, 309
Cohen, Leah, 544n
Cohen, Maxwell, 253
Cohen, Philip, 287
Cohen, Ran, 436, 455
Cohen, Steven M., 51n, 62, 63n, 84n, 87n, 88, 88n, 102n, 104n, 192
Cohen, Victor, 255
Cohen, William, 453
Cohen, Yinon, 554n
Cohn-Bendit, Daniel, 289
Collins, Doug, 239
Commentary, 661
Commission on Jewish Education (United Synagogue), 620
Commission on Reform Jewish Education, 618
Commission on Social Action and Public Policy (United Synagogue), 620
Commission on Social Action of Reform Judaism, 584
Commission on Synagogue Management, 618
Community, 658
Community Review, 666
Conference of Presidents of Major American Jewish Organizations, 129, 166–170, 172, 175, 198, 585
Conference on Jewish Material Claims Against Germany, 340, 375, 384
Conference on Jewish Social Studies, 589
Congregation Bina, 589
Congress for Jewish Culture, 589
Congress Monthly, 661
Congress of Secular Jewish Organizations, 612
Connecticut Jewish Ledger, 657
Conservative Judaism, 661
Constantiner, Jaime P., 255
Consultative Council of Jewish Organizations-CCJO, 585
Contemporary Jewry, 666
Conversion to Judaism Resource Center, 612
Conze, Werner, 344
Cook, Robin, 277, 278, 281, 453, 454
Cook, Samuel, 670
Cooper, Abraham, 148

Coordinating Board of Jewish Organizations, 585
Copeman, Russell, 236
Copferman, Emile, 307
Corinaldi, Michael, 546n
Cossiga, Francesco, 320
Council for Initiatives in Jewish Education, 104
Council for Jewish Education, 612
Council of Jewish Federations (CJF), 127, 130, 173, 176, 180, 197, 198, 245, 457 (see also United Jewish Communities)
Council of Jewish Organizations in Civil Service, 585
Covenant Foundation, 104, 104n
Coverdell, Paul, 140
Cranbourne, Lord, 277
Creaghan, Paul, 239
Cremer, Andy, 353
Crooke, Alistair, 277
Crown, Alan D., 287
Crown Heights Riots, 132
Cuban, Larry, 64n
Cummings, Harold, 253
Cummings, Jack, 248
Cummings Foundation, 93
Czamanski, D., 496n

Dachs, Gisela, 355
Dadon, Kotel, 387
Dais, 667
Dalbins, Juris, 395
D'Alema, Massimo, 320
D'Amato, Alfonse, 120, 121, 143, 144, 146, 194
Damian, N., 493n
Dana International (Yaron Cohen), 481
Danby, Michael, 410
Danziger, Itzhak, 537
Darawshe, Abd al-Wahab, 461
Darsky, Leonid E., 565n
Dauber, Jeremy, 52n, 57, 57n, 101
David, Jay, 200
Davids, Leo, 555n
Davidson, Aryeh, 3n, 25n, 41n
Davidson, Jessica, 89n
Davidson, William, 104n
Davies, Alan, 252
Davies, Ron, 276

Davis, David Brion, 202
De Backal, Alicia Gojman, 256, 261
De Camondo, Moïse, 308
De Castro, Francisco Barnes, 261
Deetman, Willem, 317
Degani, Avi, 467
Deif, Muhammad, 442
De la Madrid, Miguel, 255
De la Maisonneuve, Dominique, 307
De Lange, Nicholas, 287
De la Rúa, Fernando, 263, 268, 269
Delisle, Esther, 250, 251
DellaPergola, S., 484n, 485n, 270 512n, 543n, 544n, 546n, 547n, 553n, 557n, 559n, 561n, 564n, 569n, 571n, 574n
Delpuech, Rosie, 308
Del Rio, Eduardo, 257
Demjanjuk, John, 119, 147
Denisov, Nikolai, 393
Deri, Arye, 459
Dermer, Bertha, 253
De Rothschild, Alphonse, 363
Dershowitz, Alan, 200
De Sousa Mendes, Aristide, 307
De Toyber, Sara Maya, 262
Detroit Jewish News, 659
Deutsch, Peter, 121
Deutsch, Sandra McGee, 274
DeWine, Mike, 148
Dewoitine, Emile, 266
Dhaliwal, Herb, 238
Dialogue, 667
Diament, Nathan, 137, 139
Diamond, James, 94n
Dichter, Howard, 259
Diehl, Karl, 341
Diepgen, Eberhard, 343
Digly, Menahem, 482
Di Tella, Guido, 266, 268, 274
Dolman, Dick, 312
Domberger, Joseph, 275
Doobov, Mervyn, 410
Doobov, Sue, 410
Dorff, Elliott, 186
Doron, A., 492n
Dorph, Gail Zaiman, 70n, 104n
Dorph, Sheldon A., 36n, 90n
Dotan, Yishai, 407
Dovrat, Aharon, 474

Downer, Alexander, 401, 402, 407
Draï, Raphaël, 308
Dresner, Samuel, 199
Dreyfus, Alfred, 293
Dreyfus, Richard, 410
Drielsma, Albert, 318
Drisha, 77
Drnasin, Magda, 267
Dror, Yaakov Ben, 319
Drukarch, Barend, 315, 319
Drukier, Manny, 252
Dubb, Allie A., 574n, 575n
Dubin, Charles, 252
Dubner, Stephen, 199
DuBow, Eugene, 349
Duchesneau, Jacques, 236
Dueck, Johann, 241
Duhalde, Eduardo, 263
Duisenberg, Willem, 309
Duke, David, 122
Dunner, Pini, 284
Dupuy, Bernard, 305
Dushkin, Alexander, 8n, 14n, 15n, 19n, 20n, 24n, 27n, 31n, 41n, 54n
Dvorkis, Dmitry, 391
Dworak, Deborah, 319
Dzurinda, Mikulas, 384

Eagleburger, Lawrence, 325
Ebrahim, Gora, 415
Eckstein, Z., 496n
Edah, 183
Edelman, Marek, 333, 380
Edwards, Chet, 139
Efrati, Anat, 360
Egger, Wilhelm, 331
Ehrenkranz, Joseph, 382
Einfeld, Marcus, 410
Eisen, Arnold, 201
Eisenberg, Laura Zittrain, 251
Eisenman, Peter, 204, 342, 343, 344
Eisikovitz, R., 503n
Eitan, Raphael, 159
Eizenstat, Stuart, 144, 145, 266, 267
Elaine Kaufman Cultural Center, 589
Elazar, Daniel J., 102n, 108, 108n, 109, 109n
Elbaum, Dov, 529, 530
Elbaz, Andre, 252
Elberg, Yehuda, 251

Elcock, Ward, 238
Eliach, Yaffa, 194, 200
Eliahu, Mordecai, 304
Elías, Enrique, 262
Elkes, Joel, 287
Elkin, Joshua, 59n
Elkin, Stanley, 202
Ellenbogen-Frankovitz, S., 503n
Ellis, David, 246
Elman, Bruce, 236
Elman, Richard, 670
Elon, Benny, 440
Elster, Shulamith, 3n
El-Tahri, Jihan, 287
Elterman, Colin, 408
Elterman, Sasha, 408
Ely, Stanley, 199
Emunah of America, 601
Encel, Frédéric, 307
Encel, Sol, 576n
Engel, Eliot, 121, 143, 168
Engelman, Uriah Z., 8n, 14n, 15n, 19n, 20n, 24n, 27n, 28n, 31n, 41n, 54n
Epstein, Jerome, 176, 187
Erlich, Esther, 409
Eshel, Ruth, 540, 541
Espeche Gil, Vicente, 263
Espinasa, José María, 261
Espinoza, Isaura, 261
Essrog, Seymour, 187
Etchegaray, Roger Cardinal, 322
Etchegoyen, Aldo, 273
Even-Shoshan, Yosefa, 535
Ezra, Gidon, 436

Faber, Eli, 202
Fackenheim, Emil, 251
Fagan, Edward, 341, 364
Fahlbusch, Michael, 344, 345
Faigel, Harris C., 48n
Fainlight, Ruth, 286
Faircloth, Lauch, 122
Fakturovich, A., 498n
Falwell, Jerry, 166, 455
Farhi, Daniel, 136
Farrakhan, Louis, 133, 134, 280
Fassbinder, Rainer Werner, 331, 352
Fatchett, Derek, 277
Faurisson, Robert, 296, 297

Federated Council of Israel Institutions-FCII, 601
Federation of Jewish Men's Clubs, 613
Federation of Reconstructionist Congregations and Havurot (see Jewish Reconstructionist Federation), 613
Feher, Eduardo, 255
Feiff, David, 137
Fein, Leonard, 11n, 30, 30n, 37n, 42n, 124
Feinberg, Abraham, 670
Feinberg Graduate School, Weizmann Institute of Science, 623
Feingold, Russ, 121
Feinstein, Dianne, 122, 128, 169
Feirberg, Miriam, 479
Feldmajer, Peter, 374, 375
Feldman, Ruth Pinkenson, 74n
Feldman, Shimshon, 258
Feldstein, Donald, 63, 63n
Feliciano, Hector, 298
Ferkauf Graduate School of Psychology, 631
Fernández Meijide, Graciela, 263
Fernandez Souza, Jorge Abraham, 260
Fialkoff, Ch., 493n
Fichman, Ina, 245, 250
Fieger, Geoffrey, 123
Fields-Meyer, Thomas, 90n
Fiennes, Ralph, 377
Filmus, Tully, 671
Filner, Bob, 121
Finci, Jakob, 386
Fine, Hillel, 671
Fine, Jonathan, 288
Fini, Gianfranco, 320
Finkelstein, Arthur, 460
Finkelstein, Graeme, 420
Finkelstein, Norman, 252, 356
Finta, Imre, 242
Firestone, Tirzah, 201
Fisch, Asher, 360
Fischer, Heinz, 365
Fischler-Martinho, Janina, 287
Fisher, Alan M., 102n
Fisher, Nelson, 286
Fishman, Joshua, 108n
Fishman, Sylvia Barack, 43, 44n, 46n, 50n, 51, 51n, 52, 53n, 54n, 55n, 74n, 75n, 76n, 82n, 104n

Fisk, Robert, 403
Fitzgerald, Peter, 120
Flatow, Alisa, 126
Flexner, Paul, 3n, 59n, 70n
Florsheim, Yoel, 566n
Flug, K., 496n
Foa, Anna, 332
Foa, Vittorio, 332
Foley, Mark, 143
Foltin, Richard, 139
Forverts, 661
Forward, 661
Fouilland, Muriel, 261
Foundation for Ethnic Understanding, 134
Foundation for Jewish Camping, 194
Fowler, Robert, 237
Fox, Jon, 120
Fox, Seymour, 42, 42n
Foxman, Abraham, 130
Fradkin, Arnold, 242
Fraenkel, Jean-Jacques, 252
Fralon, José-Alain, 307
Frank, Anne, 314, 319, 360
Frank, Barney, 121
Frank, Naava, 70n
Frank, Otto, 314
Frankel, Ephraim, 20n
Freedman, Samuel G., 96n, 252
Freedman, Sheila, 253
Freeh, Louis, 265
Free Sons of Israel, 633
Frenkel, Jacob, 425, 472, 473
Freudenheim, Tom L., 204, 355
Frey, Gerhard, 338, 339
Frid, Grigori, 360
Friedberg, R., 509n
Friedlander, Dov, 97n
Friedman, Murray, 134
Friedman, Nathalie, 91n, 92n
Friedman, Norman L., 9n, 63n
Friedman, Steven, 419
Friedman-Spits, Clara, 423
Friend, Robert, 482
Friendly, Fred W., 671
Friends of Pioneering Israel, 642
Friends of the Israel Defense Forces, 602
Friesel, Evyatar, 352
Frisch, Peter, 337
Frost, Martin, 121

Frost, Shimon, 38n, 39n
Fürst, Michael, 347

Gabriels, Ebrahim, 414
Gadecki, Stanislaw, 377, 379
Gaer, Felice, 142
Gaist, E., 489n, 491n, 499n
Gal, Yossi, 317
Galinski, Heinz, 338
Galván, Enrique, 261
Gamoran, Adam, 58n, 69n
Gan, Ben, 540
Gan, Cohen, 538
Ga'on, Yehoram, 541
Garaudy, Roger, 295, 296
Gass, Adolfo, 266
Gay, Peter, 200
Geisel, Eike, 357
Gejdenson, Sam, 121, 168
Gelber, Arthur, 253
Geldstein, Rosa N., 557n
Gerber, Dina Huebner, 101n
German, Yael, 479
Gerstein, Noemí, 272
Gerstein, Reva Appleby, 252
Gerz, Esther, 352
Gerz, Jochen, 343, 352
Gesher Foundation, 602
Geva, Avital, 538
Ghitulescu, Toma Petre, 383
Gidwitz, B., 513n
Gil, Moshe, 287
Gilbert, Arthur, 114n
Gilbert, Martin, 287
Gillon, Carmi, 436
Gilman, Benjamin, 120
Gimzauskas, Kazys, 394
Ginath, Y., 489n, 506n
Gingrich, Newt, 122, 129, 166, 455, 456, 478
Ginsburg, Marvell, 74n
Ginsburg, William, 124
Ginsbury, Mordechai, 283
Ginwala, Frene, 415
Gitelman, Z., 488n, 512n
Gitlin, Isaias (Ishie), 260, 262
Giuliani, Rudolph, 132, 134
Givat Haviva Educational Foundation, 602
Glantz, Jacobo, 262
Glantz, Margo, 261, 262

Glasner, Samuel, 21n
Glatz, Ferenc, 375
Glausman, Michael, 532
Glickman, Leonard, 127
Glinert, L.H., 499n
Gluckstein, Douglas, 288
Glusker, Susannah Joel, 262
Goebbels, Joseph, 342
Gojman, Alicia, 261
Golbert, Laura, 558n
Gold, Alan, 409
Gold, Dore, 171, 173
Gold, Shefa, 316
Gold, Steven J., 514n
Goldberg, David, 238
Goldberg, Edwin Cole, 35n, 36n
Goldberg, Jacqueline, 283
Goldberg, J.J., 4n, 60n, 170
Goldberg, Morris, 253
Goldfarb, Martin, 252
Goldhagen, Daniel, 356
Goldin, Judah, 671
Goldkorn, Wlodek, 333
Goldlust, John, 576n
Goldman, Daniel, 273
Goldman, Julia, 90n, 104n
Goldman, Ralph, 376
Goldman, Robert I., 671
Goldman, Tom, 407
Goldmann, Gustave J., 555n
Goldring, Ellen B., 70n, 104n
Goldschmidt, Hermann Levin, 358
Goldstein, Alice, 44n, 46n, 50n, 51, 51n, 52, 54n, 55n, 75n, 76n, 565n
Goldstein, Baruch, 436, 524
Goldstein, Jacob, 132
Goldstein, Sidney, 50n, 544n, 545n, 551n, 553n, 565n, 568n
Goldstein, Syd Rossman, 672
Gomelski, N., 496n
Goñi, Uki, 274
Gontovnick, Howard, 248
Goodling, Bill, 142
Goodman, Allegra, 201
Goodman, Edwin, 252
Gootman, Elissa, 59n, 102n, 106n, 107n
Gorbachev, Mikhail, 336
Gordimer, Nadine, 286
Gordon, Gerald, 423

Gordon, Wolf, 253
Gotlibovski, M., 496*n*
Gottlieb, Amy, 287
Goudstikker, Jacques, 313
Gould, Ken, 316
Gov, Anat, 535
Govendir, Denny, 410
Gozman, L., 488*n*
Graber, Jeffrey, 133
Grafstein, Carole, 248
Grafstein, Jerry, 248
Gramenov, Rossen, 370
Granados Chapa, Miguel Angel, 256
Granatstein, Jack, 252
Granic, Mate, 386
Grant, Lisa, 78*n*
Grass, Günter, 342
Gratz College, 623
Green, Benny, 288
Green, Jeffrey, 533
Green, Kenneth, 252
Green, Mark (Monty), 288
Greenbaum, Julie, 90*n*
Greenberg, Eric J., 91*n*
Greenberg, Harvey, 253
Greenberg, Irving, 181, 183
Greenberg, Richard, 84*n*, 87*n*
Greenberg, Stanley, 460, 466
Greenblum, Joseph, 10, 10*n*, 12*n*
Greene, Elizabeth, 252
Griffin, Nicholas, 279
Griffiths, Alan, 410
Grinspoon, Harold, 103*n*
Gronemann, Sammy, 356
Gross, Dayan, 423
Gross, Michael, 538
Grossberg, Alan, 140
Grossberg, Amy, 140
Grossberg, Sonye, 140
Grossman, David, 207, 525, 527
Grossman, Steve, 124
Grubel, Fred, 672
Gruen, George E., 575*n*
Gruneberg, Antonia, 351
Gruss Life Monument Funds, 93
Gryn, Hugo, 283, 285
Guigou, Elisabeth, 295
Gurevich, Beatriz, 273
Guri, Haim, 532

Gurvits, Eduard, 391
Gutman, Herbert, 202
Gutman, Sandy, 409
Gutnick, Joseph, 400, 403
Guttman, Nahum, 537
Gvir, Raphael, 373

Haar, Ingo, 344, 345
Haasis, Hellmut G., 356
Haber, Karl, 368
Haberfeld, Yitchak, 554*n*
Haberman, Steven, 562*n*
Habib, J., 496*n*, 505*n*
Habiby, Emile, 403
Habonim-Dror North America, 602
Hackmey, Joseph, 538
Hadarom, 661
Hadassah, the Women's Zionist Organization of America, 176, 602
Hadassah Magazine, 661
Hadassah-WIZO Organization of Canada, 642
Hadaya, Yael, 528
Hadoar, 661
Hague, William, 277
Haitovsky, Y., 512*n*
Hajdenberg, Henri, 298, 300, 303, 304
Halpern, Elliott, 250
Halpern, Peter, 316
Halpert, Marta, 367
Halpert, Shmuel, 470
Hamel, Gur, 441
Hamilton, Lee, 121
Hamlyn, Paul, 287
Hammer, Zevulun, 482
Hamori, Jozsef, 375
Hampel, Claude, 308
Hanig, Ophira, 535
Hansel, Georges, 308
Hanson, Pauline, 399, 404, 405
Hanuka, Assaf, 531
Hanus, George, 102, 102*n*, 193
Harber, Anton, 414
Hariri, Rafiq, 264
Harman, Jane, 120
Harmatz, Joseph, 287
Harries, Richard, 287
Harris, Cyril, 411, 418, 419
Harris, David A., 166, 266, 349

Harris, Mike, 237
Harris, Simon, 421
Har-Shefi, Margalit, 476
Hart, Lawrence, 253
Harvard University, 196
Hashomer Hatzair, 602, 642
Haski, Pierre, 307
Hass, Karl, 325
Hassan, Prince, 447, 448
Hassasian, Manuel, 256
Hastert, Dennis, 122
Haupl, Michael, 366
Hausfeld, Michael, 146
Havatzelet, Meir, 35n
Havel, Vaclav, 371
Havilo, Ron, 353
Hayim, Esty G., 529
Hayoun, Maurice-Ruben, 307
Hazan, Ephraim, 252
Hazaz, Hayyim, 531
Headlance, Ronald, 252
Hebrew College, 623
Hebrew Seminary of the Deaf, 623
Hebrew Theological College, 624
Hebrew Union College-Jewish Institute of
    Religion, 624
Hebrew University, 270
Hebrew University, American Friends
    of, 598
Hebrew University of Jerusalem, Canadian
    Friends of, 641
Hebrew Watchman, 666
Hegedus, Lorant, 374
Heilman, Samuel, 63, 64n
Heisler, Max Shein, 255, 262
Heitman, Sidney, 566n
Hellig, Jocelyn, 418
Helmreich, William, 77n
Helms, Jesse, 142
Hendel, Nehama, 483
Hendeles, Ydessa, 252
Henkin, Yehuda, 183
Henry, Marilyn, 102n
Herberg, Will, 10n
Heritage Florida Jewish News, 658
Heritage-Southwest Jewish Press, 656
Hersh, Arek, 287
Hershberg, Yisrael, 539, 540
Herstik, Naphtali, 317
Hertzberg, Arthur, 11n, 319

Herzog, Roman, 335, 336, 344, 357
Heschel, Abraham J., 199
HIAS (Hebrew Immigrant Aid Society),
    127, 609
Hillel-The Foundation for Jewish Campus
    Life, 92, 93, 283, 397, 613
Himmelfarb, Harold, 12n, 29, 30n, 34n, 36n,
    37n, 38n, 39, 39n, 42n
Himmelfarb, Milton, 10n
Hindus, Milton, 672
Hirsch, Ammiel, 175
Hirschell, Solomon, 284
Hirschprung, Pinchas, 253
Hirshberg, J., 499n
Histadruth Ivrith of America, 590
Hitler, 356
Hitsky, Alan, 87n
Hobsbawn, Eric, 287
Hobson, William, 242
Hochberg, Hillel, 17n, 24n, 29n
Hoeffel, Joseph, 120
Hoenlein, Malcolm, 129, 166
Hoffman, Avi, 206
Hoffman, Haya, 532, 533
Hoffman, Lawrence, 65n
Hoffs, Eugenia, 256
Holbrooke, Richard, 388
Holland, Peter B., 112n
Hollande, François, 289
Holocaust Center of the United Jewish Fed-
    eration of Greater Pittsburgh, 590
Holocaust Memorial Center, 590
Holocaust Memorial Museum, 203, 344
Holocaust Memorial Resource & Education
    Center of Central Florida, 590
Holocaust Museum and Learning Center,
    590
Holtz, Barry W., 3n, 62n, 70n, 75n, 84n, 104n
Holzer, Rachel, 410
Holzman, William, 672
Homolka, Walter, 350, 351
Honigmann, Barbara, 336
Honor, Leo, 25, 25n
Horowitz, Bethamie, 91n
Horowitz, T., 490n, 502n
Horwitz, Olga, 423
Hostein, Lisa, 101n
Howard, John, 399, 408
Howe, Irving, 199
Hrawi, Elias, 448

Huber, Lotti, 358
Hue, Robert, 289
Huebner, Dina Gerber, 3n
Huesca, Luis Miguel, 261
Huldai, Ron, 479
Humanistic Judaism, 659
Hurwich, L., 25n
Husain, Mahmud, 273
Hussein, King, 158, 171, 439, 447
Hussein, Saddam, 149, 150, 154, 173, 452, 453
Husseini, Faisal, 453

Iancu, Danièle, 308
Ignatieff, Michael, 287
Ilia, Itamar, 449
Illiana News, 658
Ilyukhin, Viktor, 393
Index to Jewish Periodicals, 665
Indiana Jewish Post & Opinion, 658
Indikt, Adam, 407
Indyk, Martin, 152, 156, 157, 162, 170, 171
Ingall, Carol, 3n, 9n, 61n, 70n, 109n
Inouye, Daniel, 156
Institute for Computers in Jewish Life, 613
Institute for Jewish Policy Research, 258, 269, 279
Institute for Public Affairs (UOJC), 137, 619
Institute of Traditional Judaism, 625
Intermountain Jewish News, 657
International Association of Jewish Genealogical Societies, 590
International Association of Jewish Vocational Services, 635
International Council of Christians and Jews (ICCJ), 375
International Council on Jewish Social and Welfare Services, 636
International Federation of Secular Humanistic Jews, 613
International Institute for Secular Humanistic Judaism, 613
International Jewish Committee on Interreligious Consultations (IJCIC), 135
International Jewish Correspondence, 642
International Jewish Media Association, 590
International League for the Repatriation of Russian Jews, 585

International Network of Children of Jewish Holocaust Survivors, 591
Interns for Peace, 603
Irwin Daniels School of Jewish Communal Service, 624
Isaacman, Daniel, 35n
Isaacs, Leora, 3n, 48n, 49n, 55n, 74n, 75n, 81n, 96n, 111n
Isakson, Meron, 533
Israel Cancer Research Fund, 603
Israel Histadrut Foundation (see Israel Humanitarian Foundation), 603
Israel Humanitarian Foundation, 603
Israel Policy Forum, 155, 162, 165, 168, 603
Istook, Ernest, 138
Ives, Charles, 541
Izakson, Meron, 533

Jacksonville Jewish News, 658
Jacob Blaustein Institute for the Advancement of Human Rights, 142
Jacob D. Fuchsberg Law Center, 628
Jacob Rader Marcus Center of the American Jewish Archives, 624
Jacobovici, Simcha, 250
Jacobs, Betsy S., 49n
Jacobs, Binyomin, 315
Jacobs, Jeremy, 284
Jacobson, Dan, 201, 287
Jacobson, Howard, 286
Jacobson, Louise, 307
Jacquet, Aimé, 295
James, Fob, Jr., 122, 138
Jankowski, Henryk, 380
Janner, Greville, 287
Janner, Lord, 280
Janowksy, Oscar I., 36n
Jasenovac, 387
JBI Voice, 661
JDC (*see* American Jewish Joint Distribution Committee)
Jemima, Bettina, 363
Jerome H. Louchheim School of Judaic Studies, 624
Jerusalem Center for Public Affairs, 198
Jerusalem Foundation, 603
Jerusalem Letter/Viewpoints, 666
Jerusalem Relocation Act, 156
Jesselson, Erica, 103n
Jesselson, Michael, 103n

Jewish Action Magazine, 661
Jewish Advocate, 659
Jewish Book Annual, 662
Jewish Book Council, 591
Jewish Book World, 662
Jewish Braille Institute of America,636
Jewish Braille Review, 662
Jewish Bulletin of Northern California, 656
Jewish Chautauqua Society, 613
Jewish Children's Adoption Network, 636
Jewish Chronicle of Pittsburgh, 666
Jewish Chronicle (Mass.), 659
Jewish Chronicle (N.J.), 660
Jewish Civic Press, 658, 659
Jewish Communal Service Association of N. America, 636
Jewish Community Center movement, 84
Jewish Community Centers Association of N. America, 192, 636
Jewish Community Chronicle, 656
Jewish Community Federation of San Francisco, 105
Jewish Community News (Calif.) 656, 658, 660
Jewish Community News (Ill.), 658
Jewish Community News (N.J.), 660
Jewish Community Voice, 660
Jewish Conciliation Board of America, 636
Jewish Council for Public Affairs, 167, 176, 192, 585
Jewish Currents, 662
Jewish Education Fund, 102
Jewish Education in Media, 614
Jewish Education News, 662
Jewish Education Service of North America (JESNA), 110,193, 614
Jewish Educators Assembly, 620
Jewish Exponent, 666
Jewish Family and Children's Professionals Association (*see* Jewish Social Services Professional Association), 637
Jewish Foundation for the Righteous, 609
Jewish Free Press, 667
Jewish Frontier, 662
Jewish Fund for Justice, 637
Jewish Funders Network, 197, 637
Jewish Guide to Boston & New England, 659
Jewish Herald, 662

Jewish Herald-Voice, 667
Jewish Heritage Project, 591
Jewish Immigrant Aid Services of Montreal, 642
Jewish Institute for National Security Affairs, 603
Jewish Institute for the Blind-Jerusalem, 604
Jewish Journal (Fla.), 658
Jewish Journal(Long Island),662
Jewish Journal(Ohio),665
Jewish Journal/North of Boston, 659
Jewish Journal of Greater Los Angeles, 656
Jewish Journal of San Antonio, 667
Jewish Labor Bund, 633
Jewish Labor Committee, 585
Jewish Leader, 657, 662
Jewish Museum, 207, 591, 626
Jewish National Fund, 357
Jewish National Fund of America, 604
Jewish National Fund of Canada, 642
Jewish News, 656 (Calif.)
Jewish News(La.),659
Jewish News of Greater Phoenix, 656
Jewish News of Western Massachusetts, 659
Jewish Observer, 662
Jewish Observer of Central New York, 662
Jewish Parent Connection, 662
Jewish Peace Fellowship, 586
Jewish Peace Lobby, 604
Jewish Political Studies Review, 666
Jewish Post & News, 668
Jewish Post of NY, 662
Jewish Press (Brooklyn), 662
Jewish Press (Neb.),660
Jewish Press of Pinellas County, 658
Jewish Press of Tampa, 658
Jewish Publication Society, 591
Jewish Quarterly Review, 666
Jewish Reconstructionist Federation, 614
Jewish Record, 660
Jewish Reporter, 660
Jewish Review, 666
Jewish Social Services Professionals Association, 637
Jewish Social Studies, 656
Jewish Spectator, 660
Jewish Sports Review, 656
Jewish Standard (N.J.), 660

Jewish Standard (Toronto), 668
Jewish Star, 660
Jewish State, 660
Jewish Teachers Association-Morim, 614
Jewish Telegraphic Agency, 124, 132, 168
Jewish Telegraphic Agency Community News Reporter, 662
Jewish Telegraphic Agency Daily News Bulletin, 662
Jewish Telegraphic Agency Weekly News Digest, 662
Jewish Theological Seminary of America, 186, 187, 625
Jewish Transcript, 667
Jewish Tribune, 668
Jewish Veteran, 657
Jewish Voice, 657
Jewish Voice & Opinion, 660
Jewish Voice of Greater Monmouth County, 660
Jewish Voice of Rhode Island, 666
Jewish War Veterans of the USA, 586
Jewish Week, 662
Jewish Welfare Board Jewish Chaplains Council, 636
Jewish Western Bulletin, 668
Jewish Women International, 637
Jewish World, 662
Joel, Asher, 410
Joel, Richard, 93
Johnson, Lyndon, 410
Jones, Jeremy, 404, 409
Jones, Randolph, 288
Jones, Sian, 287
Jonquet, Thierry, 308
Joseph Meyerhoff Center for Jewish Learning, 93
Joseph, Samuel K., 49n, 67n, 69n, 71n, 76n
Josephs, Zoë, 286, 288
Joskowics, Leo, 256
Jospin, Lionel, 289, 302, 303, 304
Journal of Jewish Communal Service, 660
Journal of Jewish Education, 662
Journal of Psychology and Judaism, 668
JTS Magazine, 663
Judah L. Magnes Museum-Jewish Museum of the West, 591
Judaica Captioned Film Center, 591
Judaism, 663

JUF News & Guide to Jewish Living in Chicago, 658
Juppé, Alain, 299, 303

Kably, José, 262
Kadima, 91, 620
Kadishman, Menashe, 538
Kagan, Jack, 287
Kahalani, Avigdor, 450
Kahn, Hans, 319
Kahn, Jean, 301, 304
Kalejs, Konrad, 405, 406
Kamenetz, Rodger, 201
Kameny, Nat, 672
Kaniuk, Yoram, 319
Kannel, Lucie, 307
Kansas City Jewish Chronicle, 658, 660
Kapel, Michael, 407
Kaplan, Casriel, 283
Kaplan, Edward, 199
Kaplan, Janna, 72n
Kaplan, Mendel, 422
Kaplan, Robert, 423
Karavan, Dani, 539
Karger, H.J., 492n
Karimov, Islam, 391, 392
Karsh, Ephraim, 287
Karsh, Romer, 252
Kashrus Faxletter, 663
Kashrus Magazine, 663
Kasir, N., 496n
Kasoff, Geraldine Nussbaum, 20n
Katash, Oded, 480
Kates, Jacqueline, 102n
Katriuk, Vladimir, 241
Katsav, Moshe, 397
Katsh, Abraham, 673
Katz, Avner, 532
Katz, Betsy Dolgin, 82n, 83n
Katz, Friedrich, 260
Katz, Jacob, 482
Katz, Jonathan, 474
Katz, Michael, 423
Katz, Peter, 262
Katzav, Moshe, 322
Katzew, Jan, 3n, 71n, 73n
Katzoff, Louis, 14, 14n, 15n
Kaufman, Edy, 256
Kaufman, Gerald, 278

Kawalsky, Leon, 422
Kaye, Joan S., 81n
Kaye, Terry, 72n
Kazak, Ali, 401
Kazin, Alfred, 208, 673
Kedem, Rimona, 409
Kedourie, Sylvia, 287
Keenoy, Ray, 286
Keller, Carolyn, 3n
Kellerman, Faye, 201
Kelman, Stuart, 48n, 58n, 64n, 74n, 82n
Kenaz, Yehoshua, 528
Kent, Donald, 107n
Kentucky Jewish Post & Opinion, 659
Keren Or, 604
Keren, Sharon, 539
Keret, Etgar, 531
Kerman, Haim, 430
Kern, Janet R., 673
Kerry, John, 142
Kershaw, Ian, 356
Kessler, E.J., 90n
Kevorkian, Jack, 123
Keysar, Ariella, 545n
Kfisha, Iman, 463
Khatami, Mohammed, 163, 265
Kichler, Jerzy, 378
Kimche, Alona, 528
Kindermann, Harry, 347
King, Alan, 202
King, J., 507n
King, Poppy, 409
King, Y., 505n
Kinkel, Klaus, 349
Kirienko, Sergei, 390
Kirszenbaum, Jorge, 269, 270
Kiryas Joel, 138
Kisselgoff, Anna, 540
Kissinger, Henry, 357
Klarsfeld, Serge, 303
Kleiman, Ariel, 260
Klein, Herbert, 202
Klein, Morton, 172, 195
Kleinberg, Raquel, 261
Kleiner, Michael, 429
Klein Halevi, Yossi, 452
Klemperer, Victor, 194
Klenicki, Leon, 273
Klezmer, Gabi, 539

Klich, Ignacio, 274
Kligsberg, Bernardo, 262
Klima, Viktor, 359
Klingberg, Markus, 482
Klingenstein, Susanne, 202
Klinghofer, David, 199
Klipstein, Simon Brailowsky, 262
Kloke, Wendy, 349
Klutznick Museum, 589
Kocka, Jürgen, 342
Koenig, Cardinal, 365
Koffler, Marvelle, 252
Kogan, Alexander, 348
Kohan, Alberto, 274
Kohl, Helmut, 334, 335, 336, 338, 339, 340,
    342, 343
Kohl, Herbert, 122
Kohn, Leo, 347
Kohn, Peter, 409
Kohn, Walter, 368
Kohr, Howard, 167, 168
Kok, Willem, 309, 310, 317
Kol Hat'nua, 663
Koller-Fox, Cherie, 33n
Kondratenko, Nikolai, 393
Konstantinov, Viacheslav, 512n, 565n
Kook, Avraham Yitzhak, 524
Kooyman, C., 564n
Kopelowitz, Seymour, 414, 418
Koransky, Arianna, 95n
Kordes, Frans, 312
Koret Foundation, 104
Koret Institute Book Prizes, 202
Kosman, Admiel, 533
Kosmin, Barry A., 72n, 209n, 283, 543n,
    545n, 551n, 553n, 554n, 561n
Kosseleck, Reinhard, 342
Kovac, Michal, 384
Kovachevich, Elizabeth, 138
Kovadloff, Jacob, 270
Kovalev, Nikolai, 392
Kozar-Beck, Andrej, 388
Kozodoy, Ruth Lurie, 72n
Kozulin, A., 502n
Krajewski, Stanislaw, 377
Kramer, Alex, 253
Kramer, Naomi, 252
Krasa, Hans, 261
Kraus, Tomas, 372

Krauthammer, Charles, 173
Krauze, Enrique, 256, 259
Krawitz, Avi, 420
Krejsa, Josef, 371
Kronish, Ronald, 98n
Kulanu, 614
Kulishov, Valery, 364
Kultur un Lebn-Culture & Life, 663
Kunoff, Martin S., 70n
Kupferman, Moshe, 538
Kupferminic, Mirta, 272
Kurshan, Alisa, 3n
Kushner, Eva, 252
Kushner, Tony, 287
Kuykendall, Steven, 120
Kwasniewski, Aleksander, 378, 380, 382

Labor Zionist Alliance, 604
Labour Zionist Alliance of Canada, 643
Lafontaine, Oscar, 334
Lagny, Anne, 307
Laguna, Justo, 272, 273
Lajta, Bela, 377
Lakewood Yeshivah, 77
Lakoff, Sanford, 199
Lamishpaha, 663
Lamm, Norman, 180, 182
Landau, Sigalit, 539
Landau, Uzi, 434, 461
Lande, Lawrence, 253
Landesman, Fran, 286
Lang, Gerhard, 17n
Lang, Jack, 293
Lange, Marcelle, 315
Langer, Veronica, 261
Laniado, Alberto, 275
Lansky, Egon, 371
Lantos, Tom, 121
La'or, Yitzhak, 537
Lapid, Shulamit, 528
Lappe, Benay, 187
Laras, Giuseppe, 323, 328
LaRouche, Lyndon, 404
Las Vegas Israelite, 660
Lau, Yisrael Meir, 175, 317
Lauder, Ronald S., Foundation, 349, 367,
    369, 370, 381, 382
Laury, Dominique, 307
Lautenberg, Frank, 122, 126

Lautenberg amendment, 127
Lauterpacht, Eli, 288
Lavee, Y., 505n
La Voix Sepharade, 668
Lazarus, Janine, 422
Lazarus-Yafeh, Hava, 482
League for Human Rights (Canada), 641
League for Yiddish, 592
Lebovici, Martine, 307
Lechner, Odon, 377
Lee, Carol Ann, 314, 319
Lee, Sara, 3n, 13n, 64n, 65n, 103n
Lee, Valerie, 112n
Leef, Yinam, 542
Leeser, Julian, 409
Leesfield, Ira, 124
Legault, Josee, 245
Leibler, Mark, 407
Leiser, Deborah, 409
Lemel, Yossi, 353
Leo Baeck Institute, 205, 344, 592
Leon, Gary, 287
Leor, Don, 531
Le Pen, Jean-Marie, 290, 291, 292, 293,
    297
Lerer, Nava, 545n
Lerman, Antony, 562n
Lerman, Miles, 195, 196
Lerner, Gregory, 481
Lerner, Grigori, 392
Lerner, Harold, 253
Lerner, Max, 199
Lerner, Susana, 557n
Lerner, Y., 506n
Leshem, E., 484n, 485n, 488n, 489n, 490n,
    501n, 512n
Lesser, Jeffrey, 274
Le Tarnec, Sophie, 308
Lev, Eleanora, 528
Levene, Lord, 288
Levi, Lia, 332
Levi, Shmulik, 534
Levi, Tom, 534
Levi Hospital, 637
Levin, Carl, 122, 169
Levin, Hanoch, 536, 537
Levin, Sander, 121
Lévinas, Emmanuel, 308
Levine, Caren N., 48n

Levinson, Pnina Navé, 358
Levita, Asia, 259
Levitas, Minna, 423
Lévy, Albert, 294
Levy, B. Barry, 249
Lévy, Benny, 308
Levy, Caren, 562n
Levy, Carol, 72n
Levy, David, 437, 458, 461, 462, 464, 467, 476
Levy, Elkan, 283, 284
Levy, Esther, 203
Levy, Maxim, 459, 481
Levy, Richard, 191
Levy, Yamin, 252
Levy, Yitzhak, 461, 524
Lew, Norma, 558n
Lewenz, Lisa, 353
Lewinsky, Monica, 119, 123, 124, 154, 167, 187, 191, 256, 427, 439
Lewis, Anthony, 165
Lewis, Frank, 315
Lewis, Shari, 673
Lewisohn, Ludwig, 199
Libai, David, 468
Libeskind, Daniel, 204, 354
Libman, Robert, 236, 237
Librach, Clifford, 187
Liché, Charles, 308
Lidsky, Nira, 476
Lieberman, Joseph, 122, 142, 156, 168, 182
Lieberman, Michael, 126, 132
Lieblich, A., 502n
Liebman, Charles S., 19n, 77n, 104n
Liebman, Shlomo, 435
Liebrecht, Savyon, 529
Liel, Alon, 415
Lieljuksis, Aldis, 395
Life Is Beautiful, 194, 205
Lightman, Bernard, 252
Lightman, Chani, 184
Likutim, 663
Lileikis, Aleksandras, 146, 394
Lilienthal, Ilana, 353
Lilith, 663
Lincoln, Fredman Ashe, 288
Linde, Cyril, 422
Lindwer, Willy, 317
Lipkin-Shahak, Amnon, 464, 476, 477

Lipper, Kenneth, 196
Lipset, Seymour Martin, 44n, 45n, 46, 47n, 48n, 49n, 50n, 51n
Lipski, Sam, 407
Lissak, M., 489n, 501n, 512n
Lithwick, I., 496n
Litvinowsky, Pinhas, 537
Litwin, H., 505n
Living Traditions, 592
Livingston, Bob, 122
Livnat, Limor, 432
Lobenstein, Joe, 283
Lockshin, Martin, 252
Loeb, Charles, 423
Loeb, Henry, 674
Loeb, Mark, 65n
Loevy, Ernst, 356
Lohrmann, Klaus, 368
London, Sara, 262
Long Island Jewish World, 663
Lookstein, Joseph, 19n
Los Angeles Jewish Times, 657
Los Angeles Museum of the Holocaust (Martyrs Memorial), 592
Lott, Trent, 478
Lowey, Nita, 121, 155
Lown, Philip, 23
Lowy, Charles, 288
Lozoya, Jorge Alberto, 255
Luchins, David, 176
Luckman, Sid, 208, 674
Lugar, Richard, 131
Lukashenka, Aleksandr, 393
Luria, Ze'ev, 415, 416
Luzhkov, Yuri, 397
Luzzatto, Amos, 328
Lyons, Henry, 134

Maalot-A Seminary for Cantors and Judaists, 627
Maass, Richard, 674
Maccabi Canada, 249
Maccabi USA/Sports for Israel, 604
Maccabiah World Union, 407
Machel, Graca, 411
Machel, Samora, 411
Maciukas, Mamertas Rolland, 241
Mack, Connie, 142, 156, 168
Madelin, Alain, 289, 291

Magen, Mira, 530
Maharaj, Vikki, 414
Mahler, Alma, 534
Mahler, Gustav, 374
Maihaileanu, Radu, 307
Mailer, Norman, 200, 201
Maisels, Israel, 423
Makashov, Albert, 391, 393
Malamud, Bernard, 319
Malik, Lisa, 67, 67*n*, 68*n*
Maloney, Carolyn, 148
Manbar, Nahum, 478
Mandel, Morton, 43*n*, 103*n*
Mandel Associated Foundations, 103, 104
Mandela, Nelson, 411, 413, 414, 416, 419, 420
Mandelson, Peter, 276, 277, 281
Manger, Itzik, 318
Manhattan Jewish Sentinel, 663
Mankowitz, Zeev, 259
Maor, Shaul, 433
Marcus, Laura, 286
Marder, Janet, 79*n*
Margel, Simón, 268
Margolin, Moshe, 96*n*
Margolis, Daniel, 3*n*, 55*n*, 70*n*
Margoulis, H.T., 488*n*
Margules, Ludwik, 261
Markowitz, Arthur, 423
Marleau, Diane, 238
Mars, Alvin, 94*n*
Marshall, Barak, 540
Martini, Carlo Maria, 323, 330
Martyrdom and Resistance, 663
Marzel, Baruch, 435, 436
Mashaal, Khaled, 238, 447, 477
Mason, Patrice Goldstein, 72*n*
Massad, 35
Matas, Carol, 252
Matas, David, 242
Mateos Cicero, Juán Antonio, 255
Matia, Paul, 147
Mattéoli, Jean, 299
Max Weinreich Center for Advanced Jewish Studies, 595
May, Ron, 288
Mayne, Seymour, 251
Mazer, William, 674
Mazon: A Jewish Response to Hunger, 637

Mazya, Edna, 534, 535
Mbeki, Thabo, 413, 415
McCain, John, 121
McCall, Carl H., 145
McCamus, John, 242
McKeown, William, 241
Meciar, Vladimir, 384
Medved, Maureen, 251
Mégret, Bruno, 290, 291, 292
Mehdi, M.T., 136
Mehler, Barry, 317
Meir, Yisrael, 315
Melamed, Moshe, 256
Melnick, Ralph, 199
Melton Research Center for Jewish Education, 32, 626
Memorial Foundation for Jewish Culture, 592
Mendelson, Evan, 99*n*
Menem, Carlos, 263, 264, 265, 274
Mengele, Joseph, 274
Mercaz USA, 604
Meretz USA for Israeli Civil Rights and Peace, 604
Meri, Lennart, 394
Meridor, Dan, 467, 468
Merom, Hagai, 463
Mesguich, Daniel, 306
Meshal, Leo, 401
Mesivta Yeshiva Rabbi Chaim Berlin Rabbinical Academy, 627
MetroWest Jewish News, 660
MetroWest Jewish Reporter, 659
Meyer, Albert, 348
Meyer, Marshall, 271
Meyers, Joel, 176
Michaels, Anne, 286
Midstream, 663
Miguel, César, 268
Mihailova, Nadezhda, 370
Mikhoels, Shlomo, 397
Milgram, Abraham Ezra, 675
Miller, Lou, 253
Miller, Michael, 132
Miller, Stephen, 562*n*
Miller Cantorial School and College of Jewish Music, 626
Millo, Yehudah, 323
Milnitzky, Claudia, 558*n*

Milo, Roni, 424, 425, 448, 464, 466, 467, 468
Mimun, Clemente J., 333
Minerbi, Sergio, 326
Minow, Martha, 102n
Mintz, Alan, 78n
Minujin, Marta, 272
Mirsky, J., 489n, 506n
Mishael, Agi, 533
Mittelpunkt, Hillel, 534
Mitzna, Amram, 479
Mizrachi Organization of Canada, 643
Modai, Yitzhak, 482
Modern Judaism, 659
Modigliani, Amedeo, 332
Modin, 35
Moers, Walter, 356
Mofaz, Shaul, 477
Moment, 657
Monaghetti, Steve, 409
Monitor, 657
Montemayor, Carlos, 256
Montiel, Javier, 258
Moore, Bob, 319
Moore, Roy, 138
Moratinos, Miguel, 437
Mordechai, Yitzhak, 429, 432, 433, 434, 436, 438, 447, 448, 451, 458, 467, 476, 477, 478
Morel, Solomon, 381
Morgenthau, Henry, 197
Morgenthau, Robert M., 363
Morhag, Gilead, 77n
Morris, Brian, 253
Morris, John, 279
Morton, Desmond, 251
Moscato, Dodi, 333
Moscona, Myriam, 261
Moseley-Braun, Carol, 120, 144
Moshayov, Daphne Ruth, 97n
Moshinsky, Marcos, 256
Moskowitz, Irving, 430
Moss, Jeffrey, 208
Moss, Nathan, 576n
Mouallem, Boutros, 322
Moussa, Amre, 446
Moyal, Jose Enrique, 410
Moynihan, Daniel, 131, 148
Msimang, Mindi, 413

Mubarak, Hosni, 265, 446, 447
Much, Theodore, 367
Muhammad, Don, 240
Muhammad, Khalid, 133, 134
Mujica, Hugo, 273
Muller, Melissa, 314, 319
Mulqi, Hani, 447
Murphy, Joseph, 40n
Museum of Jewish Heritage-A Living Memorial to the Holocaust, 592
Museum of Modern Art, 196
Museum of Tolerance of the Simon Wiesenthal Center, 592
Musleah, Rahel, 83n, 91n
Mussali, Lizzet, 256
Mussolini, Benito, 323
Muzicant, Ariel, 361, 366
Myers, Baruch, 385

Na'amat USA, 605
Na'amat Woman, 663
Nachama, Andreas, 348, 349, 351, 352, 353
Nadler, Jerrold, 121, 142
Nadler, Paul, 249
Nagid, Haim, 537
Naharin, Ohad, 524, 540
Nahmias, Aharon, 483
Naon, D., 505n
Nathan, Howard, 409
Nathan, Joan, 203
Nathan Cummings Foundation, 103
National Association of Hebrew Day School Administrators, 617
National Association of Hebrew Day School Parent-Teacher Associations, 617
National Association of Jewish Chaplains, 638
National Association of Jewish Legislators, 586
National Association of Temple Administrators, 618
National Association of Temple Educators, 618
National Children's Leukemia Foundation, 638
National Committee for Furtherance of Jewish Education, 614

National Committee for Labor Israel, 605
National Community Relations Committee, Canadian Jewish Congress, 643
National Conference of Synagogue Youth (NCSY), 6n, 35, 91, 92n, 193, 619
National Conference of Yeshiva Principals, 617
National Conference on Soviet Jewry, 586
National Council for Jewish Education, 32
National Council of Jewish Women, 125, 171, 638
National Council of Jewish Women of Canada, 643
National Council of Synagogues, 135
National Council of Young Israel, 615
National Foundation for Jewish Culture, 202, 206, 592
National Havurah Committee, 615
National Institute for Jewish Hospice, 638
National Jewish Book Awards, 202
National Jewish Coalition, 586
National Jewish Commission on Law and Public Affairs, 586
National Jewish Committee on Scouting, 615
National Jewish Community Relations Advisory Council (*see* Jewish Council for Public Affairs), 587
National Jewish Democratic Council, 139, 587
National Jewish Girl Scout Committee, 615
National Jewish Hospitality Committee, 616
National Jewish Medical and Research Center, 638
National Jewish Outreach Program, 83
National Jewish Post & Opinion, 658
National Museum of American Jewish Military History, 586, 593
National Ramah Commission, 626
National Trade Union Council for Human Rights, 585
National Unity Coalition for Israel, 166
National Yeshiva Teachers Board of License, 617
National Yiddish Book Center, 205, 593
Nativ, Ronit, 256

Naumann, Michael, 204, 343, 344, 353
Naveh, Danny, 429, 453, 478
Naveh, G., 496n
Naves, Elaine Kalman, 252
Navon, Yitzhak, 534
Near East Report, 657
Nebel, Ludwig, 241
Nebrat, Alexander, 348
Nechushtai, Rachel, 256
Ne'eman, Yaakov, 175, 182, 456, 462, 469
Ne'eman Commission, 174, 175, 177, 178, 180, 247, 457, 469
Nefsky, Marilyn, 252
Nelson Glueck School of Biblical Archaeology, 625
Nelson, Lemrick, Jr., 132
Nemtsov, Boris, 390
Ner Israel Rabbinical College, 77n, 627
Netanyahu, Benjamin, 129, 150, 151, 153, 154, 157–161, 164–167, 169, 170, 171, 172, 176, 177, 179, 198, 263, 277, 278, 292, 321, 322, 335, 359, 370, 378, 379, 383, 392, 397, 401, 407, 413, 415, 416, 424–434, 436–450, 453–469, 473, 476, 477, 480, 481, 482
Netanyahu, Sara, 438
Neugut, Alfred I., 83n
New Israel Fund, 165, 171, 605
New Menorah, 666
New Mexico Jewish Link, 660
New York Board of Rabbis, 181
New York Jewish Community Relations Council, 132
Newman, Peter C., 251
Newton, Ronald, 274
Neykov, Alexey, 441
Nicholson, Jim, 122
Nickles, Don, 142
Nierman, Leonardo, 256
Nikolaj, Metropolitan, 386
Nimrodi, Ofer, 482
Nirenstein family (Italy), 332
Nissan, Rosa, 262
Nissim, Gabriele, 333
Nitzan, Omri, 535
Niznik, Avraham, 252
Noam, G., 496n, 503n
Noel, Marc, 241

Nohel, Emile, 368
North American Alliance for Jewish Youth, 640
North American Association of Synagogue Executives, 621
North American Conference on Ethiopian Jewry (NACOEJ), 609
North American Federation of Temple Brotherhoods, 618
North American Federation of Temple Youth (NFTY), 35, 91, 193, 619
North American Jewish Students' Network, 32
Novick, Harold, 421
Nudelstejer, Sergio, 256
Núñez, Juan, 269
Nzo, Alfred, 412

Oberlander, Baruch, 376
Oberlander, Helmut, 241
Observer, 667
Odenheimer, Micha, 524
Ofer, G., 496*n*
Offenber, Ulrike, 357
Ohana, David, 526
Ohana, Moise, 249
Ohio Jewish Chronicle, 665
Ohr Somayach, 83
Olmert, Ehud, 427, 455, 479, 482
Olmert, Mordechai, 482
Olomeinu-Our World, 663
Olshtain, E., 489*n*, 491*n*, 499*n*
Options, The Jewish Resources Newsletter, 660
Orange County Jewish Heritage, 657
Orban, Viktor, 374, 375
Orefice, Vittorio, 333
Oren, Amir, 532
Oren, Daniel, 321
Oren, Uri, 413
Orfus, Jacques, 308
Orlikow, David, 253
Orr, Ori, 465
ORT, 397
ORT Canada, 641
Ortega, Ramón, 263
Orthodox Caucus, 183
Orthodox Jewish Archives, 593

Orthodox Union's Institute for Public Affairs, 137
Osborne, Charles, 286
Osrin, Myra, 422
Ostrowsky, Radislaw, 266
Ottawa Jewish Bulletin, 668
Ovadia, Moni, 330, 331, 332, 333
Oz, Amos, 207, 319, 527
Ozar Hatorah, 616
Ozick, Cynthia, 201
Ozols, Karlis, 405

Pagrotsky, Leif, 269
Pahad, Aziz, 415
Pakn-Treger, 659
Pakula, Alan, 675
Paley, Grace, 200, 201
Palm Beach Jewish Times, 658
Papon, Maurice, 298, 300
Pardes Progressive Association of Reform Day Schools, 616
Partnership for Excellence in Jewish Education, 103
Pascal, Carlos, 262
Passover Directory, 663
Pataki, George, 123
Patinkin, Mandy, 206
Pavelic, Ante, 266, 387
Pavlat, Leo, 373
Paz, Abdul Karim, 273
Paz, Octavio, 254, 259
Pazner, Avi, 308
Peace Now, 171
Pearce, Sarah, 287
PEC Israel Economic Corporation, 605
PEF Israel Endowment Funds, 605
Pelavin, Mark, 123
Peled, Rafi, 479
Penslar, Derek, 251
Perera, Victor, 201
Peres, Shimon, 255, 408, 463, 464, 465
Peretz, Amir, 481
Perez Gay, José Maria, 256
Perl, E., 489*n*
Perlasca, Franco, 320
Perlasca, Giorgio, 320
Perlow, Yaakov, 182
Perón (Juan), 266

Perreault, Robert, 246
Perront, Nadine, 308
Peshev, Dimitar, 333
Petijn, Schelto, 310
P'eylim-Lev L'achim, 616
Phillips, Bruce, 46, 47, 47*n*, 97*n*
Piat, Xavier, 423
Picard, Bernard, 308
Pierrard, Pierre, 307
Pilch, Judah, 8*n*, 13*n*, 14*n*, 15*n*, 16*n*, 18*n*, 22*n*, 30*n*, 31*n*, 32*n*
Pinard, Pierre, 249
Pinchas, Raffi Lavie, 538
Pinchas-Cohen, Hava, 533
Pinto, Inbal, 540
Pipes, Daniel, 165
Plotnick, Stan, 246
Poale Agudath Israel of America, 605
Poe, Juanita, 56*n*
Pogrebin, Letty Cottin, 124, 186
Polian, Pavel, 563*n*
Pollard, Jonathan, 129, 130, 159, 160, 166, 198, 439, 478
Pomerantz, Hyman, 32*n*
Ponizovsky, A., 498*n*, 506*n*
Pope John Paul II, 135, 136, 273, 321–324, 328, 329, 387
Pope Paul VI, 410
Pope Pius XII, 135, 305, 324, 329
Porat, Uri, 481
Potok, Chaim, 201
Potosky, Maurice, 70*n*
Pouliot, Carlos, 261
Poupko, Reuben, 247
Poupko, Yehiel, 62*n*, 88, 88*n*
Prager, Yossi, 3*n*
Pratt, Richard, 410
Pressburger, Giorgio, 333
Pressler, Eileen, 240
Priebke, Erich, 268, 325
Primakov, Evgeny, 390, 391
Primor, Avi, 336
Pro Israel, 605
Proceedings of the American Academy for Jewish Research, 663
Prodi, Romano, 320, 321
Project Nishma, 606
Pronk, Jan, 310

Prooftexts, 659
Pruiksma, Dick, 314
Pryor, Bill, 138
PS: The Intelligent Guide to Jewish Affairs, 663
P'tach, 48*n*
Puljic, Vinko, 386

Queen Elizabeth, 410
Quesnel, Michel, 308

Ra'anan, Shlomo, 435, 436
Rabbi Isaac Elchanan Theological Seminary, 631
Rabbinical Alliance of America, 616
Rabbinical Assembly, 176, 186, 187, 616
Rabbinical College of Telshe, 627
Rabbinical Council of America, 180, 184, 616
Rabikovitch, Dalia, 531
Rabin, Leah, 171, 317, 321, 351, 476
Rabin, Yitzhak, 150, 152, 160, 171, 172, 317, 321, 326, 351, 436, 437, 439, 442, 450, 451, 461, 463, 468, 469, 476, 477, 482, 541, 542
Rachlevsky, Seffi, 524
Rackman, Emanuel, 184
Radunski, Peter, 353
Rafalowicz, Mira, 319
Ramah, 35
Ramer, Bruce M., 349
Ramirez Vázquez, Pedro, 255
Ramokgadi, Geoff, 421
Ramon, Haim, 465, 467
Rapaport, Nessa, 3*n*
Raphaeli, Ruth, 72*n*
Rasminsky, Louis, 253
Rattner, Henrique, 558*n*
Rau, Johannes, 346, 357
Ravel, Nahum, 253
Ravid, Moshe, 128
Ravid, Ruth, 74*n*
Ravitz, Avraham, 469
Raviv, Avishai, 476, 477
Raviv, Hana, 287
Raviv, Moshe, 287
Rayner, Jay, 286
Raynor, Joseph, 375

RCA Record, 664
Reagan, Ronald, 196
Rebhun, Uzi, 555*n*, 547*n*
Rebolledo, Santiago, 261
Reconstructionism Today, 666
Reconstructionist, 666
Reconstructionist Rabbinical Association, 614
Reconstructionist Rabbinical College, 614, 627
Reeb, David, 539
Reform Judaism, 664
Reform Judaism's Religious Action Center, 171
Reich, Seymour, 129
Reich, Walter, 195, 204
Reichman, Uriel, 469
Reichmann, Eva, 288
Reidel, Bruce, 150
Reif, Stefan, 286
Reimer, Jakob, 147
Reimer, Joseph, 4*n*, 65*n*, 66, 66*n*, 80, 80*n*, 81*n*, 82*n*
Reines, Frederick, 675
Reinharz, Shulamit, 72*n*
Reisman, Bernard, 5*n*, 87*n*, 88*n*, 91*n*
Reisz, Matthew, 286
Religious Action Center for Reform Judaism, 123, 143
Religious Zionists of America, 606
Renewal Magazine, 667
Reporter, 664
Research Foundation for Jewish Immigration, 593
Resnick, David, 63, 63*n*, 108*n*, 114*n*
Response: A Contemporary Jewish Review, 664
RE'UTH Women's Social Service, 609
Réza, Yasmina, 308
Rhea Hirsch School of Education, 625
Rhode Island Jewish Herald, 666
Rhode Island Jewish Historical Notes, 666
Ribadeneira, Diego, 56*n*
Ribalow, Harold, 19, 20*n*
Ribicoff, Abraham A., 208, 675
Richler, Mordecai, 251, 252
Richter, Ilja, 353
Ridgely, Henry duPont, 140
Riesman, Bernard, 79, 79*n*, 80, 80*n*

Rifkind, Robert, 131
Ritsner, M., 489*n*, 506*n*
Ritterband, Paul, 543*n*, 554*n*
Rivas, Luis, 273
Rivera Carrera, Norberto, 261, 262
Rivlin, Reuven, 455, 465
Robbins, Jerome, 208, 675
Roberts, Frank, 253
Robin, Louis, 241
Robin, Regine, 251, 252
Robinson, Antonia, 253
Robinson, Geoffrey, 277
Robinson, Reginald, 288
Rockman, Judah, 288
Rodan, Emery, 252
Rodriguez, Jesús, 255
Rodriguez Barrera, Rafael, 255
Rodriguez Soto, Juan Jose, 257
Roeder, Manfred, 337
Roehlkepartain, Eugene C., 113*n*
Roer-Stier, D., 503*n*
Roessler, Karl-Georg, 252
Rofman, Alejandro, 558*n*
Rogovin-Frankel, E., 502*n*
Rohfeld, Rae W., 84*n*
Roitman, Adolfo, 256
Rojas, Francisco, 255
Rojnica, Juan (Ivo), 267
Rojzman, Mario, 273
Romano, Sergio, 326
Ronen, Moshe, 239, 245, 253
Rose, Aubrey, 287
Rose, Carol, 252
Rose, Celia, 286
Rosen, Yisrael, 396
Rosenbaum, Norman, 165
Rosenbaum, Yankel, 132
Rosenbaum-Tamari, J., 493*n*
Rosenberg, Benjamin B., 22*n*
Rosenberg, Herby, 419
Rosenblatt, Gary, 33*n*, 77*n*, 87*n*, 183
Rosenstock, Elliot D., 21*n*
Ross, Dennis, 151, 153, 168, 425, 426, 428, 429, 430, 434, 436, 437, 454, 455
Ross, Malcolm, 239
Rossel, Seymour, 13*n*, 33*n*, 64*n*, 65*n*, 103*n*
Rotblat, Joseph, 288
Rotem, Hervé, 308
Rotenberg, V., 506*n*

Roth, John K., 195, 204
Roth, Philip, 200
Rothbauer, Max, 364
Rothman, Steven, 121
Rothschild, Lord, 287
Rotrand, Marvin, 237
Rozwaski, Chaim, 350
Rubel, Yacov, 557n
Ruben, David-Hillel, 286
Rubens, Alfred, 288
Rubens, Frances, 288
Rubenstein, Colin, 406, 407
Rubin, Chaim, 141
Rubin, James, 426, 428, 432, 433
Rubin, Reuven, 537, 538
Rubinstein, Becky, 261, 262
Rubinstein, Elyakim, 477
Rubinstein, William D., 576n
Ruby, Walter, 22n, 55n
Rudavsky, David, 9n
Rudin, James A., 135, 136
Rufeisen, Daniel, 482
Ruff, Charles, 129
Rühe, Volker, 336, 337
Rusel, Jane, 356
Ruskay, John, 4, 191
Russian Forward, 664
Russian Television Network, 593
Russo, Jorge, 269

Sabbah, David, 252
Sacks, Ian, 423
Sacks, Jonathan, 280, 283, 284, 286
Sadat, Anwar, 447
Saevecke, Theodor, 325, 326
Saffer, Dina, 423
Safran, Alexandre, 308
Sakic, Dinko, 267, 386, 387
Sakic, Esperanza (Nada)Luburic, 267, 386, 387
Saks, David, 417, 418, 421
Salah, Mohammad, 127
Salberg, Melvin, 129, 167, 169
Sales, Amy L., 91n, 94n, 96n
Salmawy, Mohamad, 294
Salsberg, J.B., 253
Samet, Shimon, 482
Sanders, Bernard, 120
Sanders, Johan, 315

San Diego Jewish Press Heritage, 657
San Diego Jewish Times, 657
Sandler, Joseph, 288
Saperstein, David Rabbi, 171, 191
Sapir, Estelle, 145
Sapirstein-Stone-Weiss Foundation, 180
Saragoussi, Pierre, 302
Sarah, Elizabeth, 285
Sarid, Yossi, 434
Sarna, Jonathan D., 3n, 6n, 9, 10n, 104n
Sassell, Curtis, 288
Sasson, Daniel, 558n
Satloff, Robert, 156
Sawoniuk, Andrzej (Anthony), 281
Saxton, Jim, 126
Scalfaro, Oscar Luigi, 327
Schach, Eliezer, 470
Schachter, Kanee, 252
Schafler, Samuel, 82n
Schahar, R., 496n
Schakowsky, Janice, 120
Schaller, Arthur, 252
Schechtman, Joseph, 3n
Scheckner, Jeffrey, 543n, 545n, 554n
Scheiber, Sandor, 376
Scheider, Theodor, 344
Schein, Jeffrey, 81n
Scheindling, Heinrich Joshua, 358
Schick, Marvin, 3n, 52n, 57, 57n, 101
Schiele, Egon, 196, 363
Schiff, Alvin I., 17n, 18n, 21n, 28n, 32n, 43n, 46n, 54n, 59, 59n, 60n
Schiff, Steve, 120
Schiff, Vera, 252
Schiller, Herman, 271, 272
Schindler's List, 357
Schlesinger, Laura, 201
Schmelz, U.O., 544n, 553n, 557n, 564n
Schmidl, Sandor, 377
Schmidt, Helmut, 357
Schmool, Marlena, 562n
Schneerson, Menachem Mendel, 185
Schneider, Mareleyn, 46n
Schneider, Peter, 342
Schneider Children's Medical Center of Israel, 606
Schneier, Marc, 134, 181
Schnoor, Randall, 246
Schocken Institute for Jewish Research, 627

Schoem, David L., 40, 40n
Schoenberg, Elliott S., 55n
Schoenfeld, Stuart, 13, 13n, 47n, 83n
Scholten, W., 313
Schönbohm, Joerg, 349
Schoolman, A.P., 35n
Schorsch, Ismar, 177, 179, 187
Schreiber, Friedrich, 355
Schröder, Gerhard, 334, 335, 342, 343
Schubernig, Wilheim, 325
Schubert, Kurt, 368
Schudrich, Michael, 381
Schulweis, Harold, 191
Schumer, Charles, 120, 121
Schussel, Wolfgang, 359, 361
Schusterman, Charles, 103n
Schusterman Foundation, 93
Schwarcz, Vera, 200
Schwartz, Barry L., 72n
Schwartz, Irving, 252
Schwartz, Jim, 554n
Schwartz, Morrie, 199
Schwartz, Shuly Rubin, 36n
Schwartz, Sylvia, 253
Schwartzman, Sylvan D., 21n
Schwarz, Arturo, 331
Schwarz, Frits, 319
Schwarz, Joseph, 252
Schweitzer, Jozsef, 374
Scott, Andy, 238
Scott, Eric, 250
Scranton Federation Reporter, 666
Searll, Adele, 423
Sebastian, Mihaïl, 308
Security Affairs, 657
Sedick, Sheikh Achmat, 414
Segal, Alvin, 248
Segal, Leanor, 248
Séguin, Philippe, 289, 290
Seleznev, Gennadi, 390
Seligmann, Rafael, 357
Seltzer, Robert, 191
Seni, Nora, 308
Senkman, Leonardo, 274
Sephardic Educational Center, 593
Sephardic House, 593
Sephardic Jewish Brotherhood of America, Inc., 633
Serra, Richard, 342, 343

Sgan-Cohen, Michael, 539
Shaare Zedek Medical Center in Jerusalem, American Committee for, 596
Shabot, Esther, 256
Shabtai, Ya'akov, 536
Shaevich, Adolf, 397
Shahak, Amnon, 431, 465, 467, 468
Shahar, Chana Bat, 530
Shahar, Charles, 246
Shahid, Leïla, 304
Shaik, Mohammed Iqbal, 412
Shain, Milton, 417, 423
Shaked, Gershon, 536
Shalev, Hemi, 442
Shalom (Fla.),658
Shalom (Halifax),668
Shalom Center, 587
Shalom L.A., 657
Shamai, Moshe, 247
Shapira, Avraham, 433, 434
Shapiro, Bernard, 245
Shapiro, Edward, 48n
Shapiro, Michael, 66n
Sharansky, Natan, 170, 392, 397, 447
Sharif, Muhi a-Din, 428, 429
Sharon, Ariel, 159, 161, 171, 437, 438, 444, 449, 451, 461
Sharp, Rosalie, 252
Sheinbein, Samuel, 128, 456
Shenfeld, Ilan, 532
Shenkar College in Israel, American Committee for, 596
Shepard, Matthew, 133
Shepard, Richard F., 676
Sher, Neal, 242
Sheraga, Y., 503n
Sherer, Moshe, 182, 676
Sheriff, Noam, 541, 542
Sherman, A.J., 287
Sherman, Brad, 121, 156
Sheskin, Ira, 48n, 52n, 76n
Shevardnadze, Eduard, 397
Sheves, Shimon, 482
Shevitz, Susan R., 3n, 22, 23n, 26n, 27n
Shindler, Colin, 287
Shles, Julie, 353
Shluker, David, 3n, 41n, 52n, 55n, 108, 108n, 109, 109n, 111n
Sh'ma, 664

Shnaider, Alex, 353
Shoenholz, Stephen, 18*n*
Shofar, 667
Shohat, Gil, 542
Shomrei Adamah/Teva Learning Center, 616
Shoval, Zalman, 456
Shrage, Barry, 63, 63*n*, 197
Shrem, Itzhak, 474
Shteinman, Diane, 406, 407
Shtrashnov, Amnon, 478
Shuval, J., 498*n*
Shvil Hazahav, 174
Sichel, Leo, 288
Sicron, M., 484*n*
Sidon, Karol Efraim, 371, 372, 373
Siederer, Leon Trahtemberg, 559*n*
Siegel, Morton, 9*n*, 20*n*
Sifrin, Geoff, 419
Sigal, Goldie, 251
Sigal, Laurence, 306
Silber, David, 77*n*
Silver, Clinton, 282
Silverfarb, Steve, 139
Silverstone, Jack, 243
Simchovitch, Simcha, 252
Simmons-Cohen, D., 496*n*
Simon, David, 319
Simon Wiesenthal Center, 133, 148, 240, 267, 387, 593, 631
Sinclair, Clive, 287
Sinclair, Ian, 400
Singer, Aca, 388
Singer, Joel, 152
Singer, Mordechai, 288
Singer, Sid, 107*n*
Siodmak, Curt, 353
Siodmak, Robert, 353
Sirat, René-Samuel, 305
Sisisky, Norman, 121
Sitruk, Joseph, 305
Sivan, Arye, 532
Skirball Center for Jewish Studies, 205
Skirball Cultural Center, 594
Sklar, Murray, 676
Sklare, Marshall, 10, 10*n*, 12*n*
Skorka, Abraham, 273
Slevin, Debbie, 67*n*
Slonim-Nevo, V., 503*n*

Smith, Charles E., 56
Smith, David, 409
Smith, Lamar, 128
Smith, MacKay, 251
Smith, Mervyn, 413, 415
Smith, Shoham, 528
Sneh, Simja, 275
Snitow, Franklyn, 133
Sobol, Joshua (Yehoshua), 201, 534
Society for Humanistic Judaism, 616
Society for the History of Czechoslovak Jews, 594
Society of Friends of Touro Synagogue, 594
Society of Israel Philatelists, 606
Sokolowicz, Fernando, 274
Soles, Warren, 240
Soloveitchik, Haym, 17, 17*n*, 18*n*
Somekh, Roni, 531
Sooker, Yasmine, 412
Sor, D., 485*n*
Soskin, Renée Rachel, 288
Southeastern Virginia Jewish News, 667
Southern Shofar, 656
Spack, Elliot, 3*n*
Spagnolo, Francesco, 330
Specter, Arlen, 122, 127, 142, 143
Spector, Norman, 252
Spertus Institute of Jewish Studies, 628
Spertus Museum, 594
Spiegel, Steven, 162
Spiegelman, Jim, 410
Spielberg, Steven, 136, 194, 204, 357
Spielberg, Steven, Foundation, 206
Spindler, Arthur, 410
Spiro, Nitza, 286
Spiro, Robin, 286
Sprinzak, Ehud, 436
St. Louis Jewish Light, 660
Stalin, Joseph, 397
Stark Jewish News, 665
Starovoitova, Galina, 391
Starr, Kenneth, 124
State of Israel Bonds (Canada), 643
State of Israel Bonds, 606
Steg, Adolphe, 299
Steiman, Lionel, 251
Stein, Edith, 136, 324, 329
Steiner, Joey, 253
Steinhardt, Michael, 103*n*, 104, 180, 194

Steinhardt Jewish Campus Service Corps, 93

Steinmann, Andrew, 346

Steinmetz, Chaim, 248

Stelmokas, Jonas, 146

Stemerdink, Bernard, 317

Stepinac, Alojzije, Cardinal, 136, 324, 329, 387

Stern, Brenda, 420

Stern, Frank, 352

Stern, Marc, 125, 141

Stern, Rhona, 423

Sternberg, Lawrence, 78*n*

Sternberg, Sigmund, 266, 268, 279, 280, 375

Steuermann, Miguel, 272

Stiefel, Moshe, 315

Stolbova, Martina, 372

Stone, Alexander, 288

Stoyanov, Peter, 369

Strasser, Teresa, 81*n*

Straw, Jack, 280

Streit, Jack, 676

Strigler, Mordechai, 676

Stroi, Anna, 568*n*

Studies in Bibliography & Booklore, 665

Suall, Irwin J., 677

Suárez Mason, Carlos, 270

Suller, Chaim, 677

Survivors of the Shoah Visual History Foundation, 194, 594

Susskin, Tatyana, 480

Süssmuth, Rita, 336

Suyk, Cor, 314

Suzette, Alejandro Saltiel, 255

Svob, Melita, 570*n*

Swados, Elizabeth, 201

Sweet, Lois, 251

Syme, Daniel B., 21*n*

Synagogue Council of America, 181

Synagogue Light & Kosher Life, 664

Synagogue 2000, 103, 103*n*, 187

Szabo, Albert, 375

Szabo, Istvan, 377

Szigeti, Tamas, 261

Szony, David M., 33*n*

Szraibman, Carlos, 271

Ta'Amri, Salah, 277

Tabick, Jacqueline, 285

Tadmor, Ido, 540

Talmi, Yoav, 252

Talmon, Penina Morag, 97*n*

Tarnor, Pearl and Norman, 72*n*

Tas, Luciano, 332

Taub, Gadi, 525

Tauran, Jean-Louis, Archbishop, 322

Technion-Israel Institute of Technology, American Society for, 600

Teichtal, Yehuda, 350

Teitelbaum, Matthew, 252

Tekiah: Association of Hillel/Jewish Campus Professionals, 611

Tel Aviv University, American Friends of, 598

Telsner, Zvi, 283

Tenenbaum, Manuel, 266

Tenet, George, 159

Terner, Ya'akov, 479

Terrail, Albert, 294

Teschemacher, Klaus, 563*n*

Tessler, Gloria, 287

Teutsch, David, 114*n*

Texas Jewish Post, 667

Thanks to Scandinavia, 610

Theodor Herzl Foundation, 606

Tibi, Ahmad, 426

Tikkun, 657

Tiktin, Noemi, 260

Tim, 293

Timm, Angelika, 357

Tkachenko, Vladimir, 392

Toaff, Elio, 322

Toben, Frederick, 404

Tobin, Gary, 92*n*

Toer, Mario, 557*n*

Toledano, Pinchas, 315

Toledo Jewish News, 665

Tolts, Mark, 395, 512*n*, 547*n*, 565*n*, 566*n*, 567*n*, 569*n*, 573*n*

Topfer, Tomas, 374

Torah Aura Productions, 71

Torah Schools for Israel-Chinuch Atzmai, 617

Torah Umesorah-National Society for Hebrew Day Schools, 18, 617

Torczyner, Harry, 677

Torczyner, James (Jim), 238, 243, 244, 555*n*

Torgov, Morley, 251

Torres, Aparicio, 269

Torricelli, Robert, 143
Touro College, 77, 628
Touro National Heritage Trust, 594
Tradition, 664
Trager, David, 132
Trager, Karen, 72*n*
Traison, Michael, 378
Trautmann, Catherine, 262, 308
Trautmann-Waller, Céline, 307
Tress, Madeleine, 563*n*, 566*n*
Treviño, Javier, 255
Tribuna Israelita, 258
Trigano, Shmuel, 308
Troen, Saul B., 70*n*
Tsomet-Techiya USA, 606
Tudjman, Franjo, 267, 387
Tulchinsky, Gerald, 251
Tulchinsky, Karen X., 251
Tulsa Jewish Review, 665
Tumarkin, Yigal, 538
Tutu, Desmond, 420
Tworetzky, Jack, 420

UIA Federation Canada, 245
Ulmanis, Guntis, 394, 395
Union for Traditional Judaism, 617
Union of American Hebrew Congregations (UAHC), 142, 175, 189, 618
Union of Councils, 587
Union of Orthodox Jewish Congregations of America, 139, 142, 175, 176, 180, 184, 193, 619
Union of Orthodox Rabbis of the U.S. and Canada, 620
Union of Sephardic Congregations, 620
United Charity Institutions of Jerusalem, 607
United Israel Appeal, 198, 245, 607
United Jewish Appeal (UJA), 104, 176, 178, 194, 197, 198, 329 (*see also* United Jewish Communities)
United Jewish Communities, 610
United Lubavitcher Yeshivoth, 620
United Order True Sisters, 638
United States Committee Sports for Israel (*see* Maccabi USA/Sports for Israel)
United States Holocaust Memorial Museum, 145, 195, 197, 355, 360, 594
United Synagogue of Conservative Judaism, 176, 187, 620

United Synagogue Review, 664
United Synagogue Youth-USY, 35, 91, 91*n*, 621
University of Judaism, 629
Unser Tsait, 664
UN Watch, 588
US/Israel Women to Women, 607

Vaad Mishmereth Stam, 621
Van Gijzel, Robert, 311
Van Kemenade, Jos, 312
Van Mierlo, Hans, 309, 310
Van Praag, Philip, 564*n*
Vanunu, Mordechai, 480, 481
Vargas, Danny, 441
Vasile, Radu, 383
Védrine, Hubert, 292
Velmans, Edith, 287
Venger, A., 502*n*
Vermes, Geza, 287
Vernon, Arthur, 96*n*
Vickery, Paul, 241
Viewpoint Magazine, 664
Viljoen, Marais, 412
Vilnai, Matan, 477, 478
Vincent, Isabel, 252
Vincent, Sidney Z., 22*n*
Vineberg, David, 253
Viragh, Kathy, 555*n*
Vis, Ruben, 315
Vital-Durand, Brigitte, 302
Vitols, Peteris, 241
Vodenitcharow, Rumen, 369, 370
Vogel, Linda, 3*n*
Vogel, Stewart, 201
Voice of the Dutchess Jewish Community, 664
Volstad, Natalie, 48*n*
Volunteers for Israel, 607
Von Klemperer, Viktor, 205
Von Rezzori, Gregor, 333
Von Saher, Marel, 314
Vorst, Isaac, 315
Vorst, Yuda, 315
Voynet, Dominique, 289

Wachs, Saul P., 31*n*
Wainberg, Mark, 252
Waksberg, Joseph, 545*n*

Waldman, Gilda, 260, 261
Waldoks, Moshe, 84n
Wallach, Yona, 533
Wallenberg, Raoul, 268, 269
Walser, Martin, 345
Warszawski, Paul, 274
Washington Institute for Jewish Leadership & Values, 621
Washington Institute for Near East Policy, 156
Washington Jewish Week, 659
Washtenaw Jewish News, 659
Wasserman, Bryna, 250
Wasserman, Dora, 250, 252
Waterman, Stanley, 562n
Waxman, Chaim I., 53n
Waxman, Henry, 121
Waxman, Mordechai, 333
Webber, Carmel, 288
Weber, J., 488n
Weidman, Jerome, 208
Weil, Andre, 208
Weil, Simone, 208
Weinberg, Jeshajahu, 355
Weinberger, Karl Albrecht, 368
Weiner, Anthony, 120
Weiner, Gerry, 236
Weinfeld, Morton, 246, 251
Weinfeld, Yocheved, 538
Weinstein, Meryle, 92n
Weiser, Ron, 407
Weisner, Alan, 70n
Weiss, Avi, 195
Weiss, Rivkah Blok, 319
Weiss, Y., 496n
Weitz, Ra'anan, 483
Weitz, Shosh, 533
Weitzman, Michael, 288
Weizman, Ezer, 176, 359, 433, 435, 436, 447, 453, 460, 481
Weizmann Institute of Science, American Committee for, 597
Well, Don, 18n
Wellstone, Paul, 122
Wertheimer, Jack, 51n, 72n, 83n, 98n, 99n, 197
Wesselow, Eric, 253
West Coast Talmudical Seminary, 629
Western States Jewish History, 657

Westheimer, Ruth, 201
Westra, Hans, 310
Wexler, Robert, 121
Wexner, Leslie, 103n
Wexner Foundation, 104, 180, 194
Wicks, Ben, 252
Wiener, Carolyn L., 11n
Wiener, Nancy, 316
Wiesel, Elie, 146, 195, 197, 202, 308
Wieseltier, Leon, 200
Wiesenthal Center (*see* Simon Wiesenthal Center)
William Davidson Graduate School of Jewish Education, 627
Willis, Chaim, 421
Wilms, Bernd, 352
Wilner, Rochelle, 243
Wilstein (Susan & David) Institute of Jewish Policy Studies, 595
Windsor Jewish Federation, 668
Winer, Mark, 135, 284, 285
Winger, Debra, 186
Winter, Nathan H., 10n, 36, 36n
Winton, Nicolas, 372
Wisconsin Jewish Chronicle, 667
Wisel, R., 488n
Witti, Michael, 341
Woessner, Frank, 358
Wolf, Frank, 142
Wolfe, Harvey, 253
Wolff, Egon, 558n
Wolff, Frieda, 558n
Wolfson, Ron, 65n, 82n
Wollheim, Norbert, 677
Wolnek, Stephen, 187
Wolofsky, Max, 253
Wolpe, Michael, 542
Women of Reform Judaism, 619
Women's American ORT, 609
Women's League for Conservative Judaism, 621
Women's League for Israel, 607
Women's League Outlook Magazine, 664
Woocher, Jonathan, 3n, 4, 99, 99n, 114n
Workmen's Circle/Arbeter Ring, 633
World Confederation of United Zionists, 607
World Congress of Gay and Lesbian Jewish Organizations, 587

World Council of Conservative/Masorti Synagogues, 621
World Council of Jewish Communal Service, 638
World Jewish Congress, 144, 195, 270, 300, 587
World Jewish Relief, 370
World Jewish Restitution Organization (WJRO), 196, 381
World Monuments Fund, 382
World of Lubavitch, 668
World Union for Progressive Judaism, 357, 622
World Zionist Organization, 408
World Zionist Organization-American Section, 607
Wurzweiler School of Social Work, 632
Wyden, Ron, 122
Wye River agreement/conference, 17, 158, 172
Wyoming Valley Jewish Reporter, 664

Ya'ari, Ehud, 428, 434, 449, 465
Yacoby, Dorrit, 259
Yad Vashem, 344, 383, 386
Yahalom, Shaul, 473
Yahav, Yona, 482
Yale University, 183
Yaryura, Felipe, 275
Yassin, Ahmad, 442
Yassin, Sheik Ahmed, 414
Yastrzhembski, Sergei, 395
Yates, Sidney, 120
Yatom, Danny, 477
Yearbook of the Central Conference of American Rabbis, 664
Yehoshua, A.B., 201, 207, 319, 332, 526, 527
Yeltsin, Boris, 390, 391, 394, 397
Yerushalmi, Rina, 525, 535
Yeshiva of Los Angeles, 631
Yeshiva Torah Vodaath and Mesivta Torah Vodaath Rabbinical Seminary, 629
Yeshiva University Museum, 205, 595
Yeshiva University, 134, 172, 180, 182, 183, 207, 629
Yiddish, 664
Yiddishe Heim, 664
Yiddishe Kultur, 664

Yiddishe Vort, 665
Yiddisher Kemfer, 664
Yiddisher Kultur Farband-YKUF, 595
Yidishe Shprakh, 665
Yilmaz, Mesut, 453
Yinon, Micha, 524
YIVO Bleter, 665
YIVO Institute for Jewish Research, 205, 595
Yizhar, S., 527
Yoffie, Eric, 175, 176, 177, 178, 179, 189, 190, 457
Youmans, Warren, 240
Young, James, 205
Young Israel, 184
Young Judaea, 35, 91, 193, 602
Young Judaean, 665
Youngman, Henny, 208, 677
Yousef, Ramzi, 126
Youth Renewal Fund, 608
Yugntruf: Yiddish Youth Magazine, 665
Yugntruf-Youth for Yiddish, 595

Zabludovsky, Jacobo, 255, 256, 262
Zachary, Louis J., 84n
Zack, Celia, 262
Zahavi, Helen, 286
Zaidenweber, Jacobo, 256
Zajdel, Saulie, 236
Zalout, Muhammad, 441
Zamro, Menashe, 483
Zaoui, Michel, 298
Zaritsky, Joseph, 538
Zawadka, Leszek, 261
Zedillo, Ernesto, 254, 255
Zeldin, Michael, 55n, 56, 61n
Zeman, Milos, 371
Zenger, Avi, 130
Zeta Beta Tau Fraternity, 634
Zevi, Tullia, 325, 328, 333
Zhirinovsky, Vladimir, 391
Zibbell, Charles, 29, 29n
Zichroni, Amnon, 478
Ziegler School of Rabbinic Studies, 186
Ziel, Alwin, 337
Zilberg, N., 501n
Zilbermann, Jean-Jacques, 307
Zimmerman, Meish, 422
Zimmermann, Tabea, 542

Zines, Lynn, 480
Zines, Warren, 480
Zinger, N., 488*n*
Zingeris, Emanuelis, 394
Zionist Organization of America, 171, 172, 608
Zionit, Y., 503*n*
Zlotnik, Jehuda Leib, 422
Zogby, James, 136
Zola, Emile, 293
Zuabi, Rahman, 481

Zucker, Ruth, 355
Zuckerman, Nomi, 286
Zuckoff, Murray, 86*n*
Zukerman, Pinchas, 252
Zukunft, 665
Zundel, Ernst, 238, 239
Zuroff, Efraim, 324
Zweig, Max, 356
Zweig, Stefan, 356
Zwiebel, David, 138
Zyuganov, Gennadi, 393, 394